ACTIVATE **REGISTRATION!**

Norton Online Listening Lab

www.wwnorton.com/musichistory

Activate the registration code printed on the back of this card today. This code grants full access to Norton's Online Listening Lab where you can access:

- **Music Library:** over ten hours of music from the Middle Ages through the turn of the twentieth century to broaden the repertory of *A History of Western Music,* 7th edition
- **Composer Biographies**
- **Additional Resources and Special Offers**

You can access this web site from www.wwnorton.com/web/listenonline or direct your browser to Norton's Music History hub for more information about:

- **Electronic Listening Guides:** keyed to every work in the Recorded Anthology
- **The History of Western Music Online Tutor:** outlines, flashcards, and listening quizzes

Look on the other side of this coupon for your registration code.

ISBN 0-393-10726-4

REGISTERING FOR THE WEB SITE:

1 Go to wwnorton.com/musichistory and select Norton Online Listening Lab.

2 Select "Access Premium Content."

3 Click "Register" and enter the registration code printed below. You will be asked to provide an e-mail address. We will send you an initial password. You will be able to change both the e-mail address and the password later.

Please visit our technical support Web site at
wwnorton.com/web/helpdesk
if you have any difficulties or need assistance.

For additional Music History Resources, visit www.wwnorton.com/musichistory

Phormia

HTYE-XLNA

www.wwnorton.com/web/listenonline

A HISTORY OF WESTERN MUSIC

SEVENTH EDITION

A
HISTORY
OF
WESTERN
MUSIC

J. PETER BURKHOLDER
Indiana University

DONALD JAY GROUT
Late of Cornell University

CLAUDE V. PALISCA
Late of Yale University

SEVENTH EDITION

W·W·Norton & Company
New York · London

W. W. Norton & Company has been independent since its founding in 1923, when William Warder Norton and Margaret D. Herter Norton first published lectures delivered at the People's Institute, the adult education division of New York City's Cooper Union. The Nortons soon expanded their program beyond the Institute, publishing books by celebrated academics from America and abroad. By mid-century, the two major pillars of Norton's publishing program—trade books and college texts— were firmly established. In the 1950s, the Norton family transferred control of the company to its employees, and today—with a staff of 400 and a comparable number of trade, college, and professional titles published each year—W. W. Norton & Company stands as the largest and oldest publishing house owned wholly by its employees.

Editor: Maribeth Payne
Development/Copyediting: Kathryn Talalay and Michael Ochs
Project Editor: Kathryn Talalay
Managing Editor: Marian Johnson
Electronic Media Editor: Steve Hoge
Photograph Editor: Neil Ryder Hoos
Assistant Editors: Allison Benter and Allison Courtney Fitch
Design Director: Antonina Krass
Senior Production Manager: JoAnn Simony
Music Typesetter: David Budmen
Page Layout: Alice Bennett
Indexer: Marilyn Bliss
Composition by GGS Information Services, Inc.
Manufacturing by RR Donnelley, Willard, OH

Library of Congress Cataloging-in-Publication Data
Grout, Donald Jay.
    A history of western music / J. Peter Burkholder, Donald Jay Grout, Claude V. Palisca.—
7th ed.
        p. cm.
    Includes bibliographical references and index.
    ISBN 0-393-97991-1
    1. Music—History and criticism. I. Burkholder, J. Peter (James Peter) II. Palisca,
Claude V. III. Title.

    ML160.G872 2005
    780′.9—dc22

                                                                    2005048797

ISBN-0-393-97991-1
W. W. Norton & Company, Inc., 500 Fifth Avenue, New York, N.Y. 10110
        www.wwnorton.com

W. W. Norton & Company, Ltd., Castle House, 75/76 Wells Street, London W1T3QT

5 6 7 8 9 0

Contents

1. Music in Antiquity · 4

2. The Christian Church in the First Millennium · 24

3. Roman Liturgy and Chant · 50

PART THREE   THE SEVENTEENTH CENTURY   287

PART FIVE   THE NINETEENTH CENTURY   567

Maps

Guide to Recordings

Preface to the Seventh Edition

The science fiction writer Ursula K. LeGuin once wrote, "The story—from *Rumplestiltskin* to *War and Peace*—is one of the basic tools invented by the human mind, for the purpose of gaining understanding. There have been great societies that did not use the wheel, but there have been no societies that did not tell stories."

A History of Western Music is a story about where music in the Western tradition came from and how it has changed over the centuries from ancient times to the present. This new edition remains an account of musical styles and genres, as Donald Jay Grout and Claude V. Palisca envisioned the book through the first six editions. But in retelling the tale, I have tried to bring several other themes to the fore:

> the people who created, performed, heard, and paid for this music;
> the choices they made and why they made them;
> what they valued most in the music; and
> how these choices reflected both tradition and innovation.

I have also broadened the story to encompass more music from the Americas, including jazz and popular music, while preserving an emphasis on art music.

We study music history in part because it gives greater understanding to all music, past and present. It may be surprising to discover that composers from the Renaissance to Wagner drew inspiration from ancient Greek music. Or that Bach, Mozart, Beethoven, Brahms, and Schoenberg all borrowed ideas from music written long before they were born. It may be even more surprising to learn that jazz arrangers used harmonies they heard in music by Debussy and Ravel. Or that the multiple simultaneous melodic and textual layers found in recent rap music were first tried out in the thirteenth-century motet. It is not that there is nothing new under the sun, but that almost anything new is a fresh twist on what has become traditional. Sometimes what seems newest is actually borrowed in part from music of the distant past.

We may also be surprised to learn that things we take for granted about music have not always been around. Pop music aimed at teenagers first emerged after World War II. Most wind and brass instruments assumed their current form in the mid-nineteenth century or later. Concerts of music from the past, which are standard features of today's musical life, first appeared in the eighteenth century and were rare before the nineteenth. Tonality, our common musical language of major and minor keys, is not even as old as New York City. Knowing the origins of these and other aspects of musical life increases our understanding.

Many questions about music can only be answered historically. Why do we use a seven-note diatonic scale? Why do we have a notation system with lines, staffs, clefs, and noteheads? Why do Bach and Schumann often use the same rhythmic figure in measure after measure, while Mozart and Schoenberg rarely do? How did jazz change from being a popular form of dance music to a kind of art music? None of these has a common-sense answer, but all can be answered by tracing their history. As a rule, if something does not make sense, there is a historical reason for it, and only knowing its history can explain it.

It is with these themes in mind that I have written the new Seventh Edition of *A History of Western Music.* I have also redesigned the book to make it easier to read and to use. The new text is restructured into generally shorter chapters, each of which can be read in a single sitting, and arranged in six parts corresponding to broad historical periods—*The Ancient and Medieval Worlds, The Renaissance, The Seventeenth Century, The Eighteenth Century, The Nineteenth Century*, and *The Twentieth Century and After.* The parts are further divided into subperiods, each treated in one to three chapters. The first chapter in each chronological segment begins with a summary of the times in order to orient the reader to some of the most important themes of the era. In addition, each chapter starts with an overview of the music that will be discussed and ends with a sketch of its reception and ongoing impact. By restructuring the narrative of music history in this fashion, I have attempted to establish a social and historical context for each repertoire and to suggest its legacy and its significance today. The heart of each chapter explores changing musical styles, the primary composers, genres, and works, and the tension between tradition and innovation, always trying to make clear what is important, where it fits, why it matters, and who cares. Each part, each chapter, and each section tells a story that is in some ways complete in itself, but that connects to all the others like pearls on a string to form a single narrative thread rooted in human choices and values.

FEATURES

The following features are designed to assist the reader throughout:

- **Brief part introductions** highlight some of the most important themes in each period.
- **Chapter overviews and summaries** establish social and historical context at the outset and reception history and musical legacy at the

end to facilitate an understanding of each period and musical repertoire.

- **Key terms** are highlighted in ***boldface italics*** throughout and are defined, for easy reference, in the **Glossary** at the back of the book.
- **Composer biographies** highlight composers' lives and works.
- **Sidebars on Music in Context** emphasize the importance of music in the daily life of people at every level of society, showing what they valued in it, and how they produced and consumed it.
- **Sidebars on Musical Innovation**—one for each part—focus on a key technological or social innovation that significantly changed the dissemination, performance, or consumption of music.
- **Source Readings** offer pithy and colorful excerpts from writings by the people at the center of the story, illuminating their choices and their values for music.
- **Timelines** in every chapter set the music in a social and historical context and facilitate a clearer view of what happened when.
- **Detailed maps** establish a location and context for musical events and works.
- **Vivid artworks and photographs** throughout provide essential cultural context and highlight important ideas, architecture, people, and events, including portraits of many of the composers and performers discussed.
- **Color diagrams** clarify forms of musical works and genres to help the reader grasp some of the essential structures of music.
- **Cross-references to the accompanying scores and recordings** are found throughout the text. The scores are identified by their numbers in the **Norton Anthology of Western Music (NAWM)**. Symbols in the margins refer to the corresponding CD and track numbers on the **Norton Recorded Anthology of Western Music**, using a notched rectangle for the complete set (12 CDs) or a plain rectangle for the Concise set (6 CDs).
- **For Further Reading**, now collected at the back of the book, provides an up-to-date bibliography corresponding to each part, chapter, and section.

ACCOMPANYING TEXTS AND RECORDINGS

Although this book stands on its own as a narrative history, the reader's understanding will be enriched by using it in tandem with the accompanying anthology, recordings, and study guide:

- The two-volume **Norton Anthology of Western Music (NAWM)**, Fifth Edition by J. Peter Burkholder and Claude V. Palisca (Volume 1: Ancient to Baroque; Volume 2: Classic to Twentieth Century), provides a comprehensive collection of 172 scores illustrating the most significant musical trends, genres, and national schools in the Western world from antiquity to the present. I have added over 75 important pieces throughout both volumes. Among these new selections are early works from Spain and Latin America, more compositions by women and by twentieth-century composers, and examples of popular music and jazz through the mid-twentieth century. Each piece is followed by commentary that relates the piece's origins; describes its form, contents, and important stylistic traits; and addresses issues of performance. In addition, all foreign-language texts are accompanied by English translations.

· The **Norton Recorded Anthology of Western Music** includes outstanding recordings of the entire NAWM repertoire by some of the best performers and ensembles working today. It comes in a complete set (12 CDs) and in a Concise set (6 CDs).

· The **Study and Listening Guide** by J. Peter Burkholder and Jennifer L. King offers chapter outlines and objectives, study questions, review questions, key terms and names, and valuable guides to help the student listen more productively and retain the essential material from the main text.

ANCILLARY MATERIALS

Like its predecessors, this new edition comes with a host of ancillary materials to help both student and teacher.

Electronic media are available to assist students in learning about the music and its history. (Details about the Electronic Media to accompany this edition can be found at www.wwnorton.com/musichistory.)

· The **Electronic Listening Guide CD-ROMs** provide electronic Listening Guides for all of the selections in the Norton Recorded Anthology of Western Music, Fifth Edition. These guides offer information and analysis synchronized with the music included in the Recorded Anthology, including historical overviews, commentary, and analysis. The entire glossary is hyperlinked to key terms for easy reference.

· The registration code found in this book grants access to the **Online Listening Lab**, which includes historically significant works in near CD-quality streaming, as well as listening and factual quizzes to test key concepts and listening skills (available at www.wwnorton.com/musichistory).

· The **Online Tutor** offers listening quizzes, chapter outlines, flashcards, and a music glossary (available at www.wwnorton.com/musichistory).

There are also two aides for the instructor:

· The **Instructor's Manual** by Amy Edmonds and Roger Hickman provides instructors with lecture outlines, test questions, and suggestions for further reading as well as listening and other activities.

· The **Norton Resource Library**, available at www.wwnorton.com/nrl, includes a computerized version of the Test-Item file in the Instructor's Manual and PowerPoint chapter outlines. These are also available in Blackboard and WebCT course management format.

ACKNOWLEDGMENTS

No work of this size and magnitude can be written without an army of help. It has truly been a collaborative effort, from the initial proposal to the final product. My profound thanks to all who have contributed.

First of all, I am indebted to my coauthors, Donald Jay Grout and Claude V. Palisca. It is humbling to be walking in the footsteps of two giants. In this edition, most of the words are my own. But many sentences and paragraphs are adapted from previous editions, and I have tried to weave the contributions of all three authors into a unified voice. I am especially grateful to Claude Palisca for agreeing, before his untimely death, that I should undertake the next edition.

I have been assisted at every stage by the members of the Editorial Advisory Board—Rebecca A. Baltzer, Jonathan Bellman, Jane A. Bernstein, Geoffrey Block, Michael Broyles, Richard Crawford, Stephen A. Crist, Andrew Dell'Antonio, Matthew Dirst, Kristine Forney, Jonathan Glixon, Bruce Gustafson, Jan Herlinger, Steven Huebner, Steven Johnson, Jeffrey Kallberg, William Kinderman, Melanie Lowe, Claudia Macdonald, Roberta Montemorra Marvin, Kevin N. Moll, Margaret Murata, Edward Nowacki, Jessie Ann Owens, William F. Prizer, Larry Starr, Pamela F. Starr, and Neal Zaslaw. Various members of the Board commented on the initial proposals for this book; reviewed the proposed contents of NAWM; read and commented on the individual chapters and the commentaries in NAWM; provided assistance on translations; offered advice and suggestions; and answered individual queries. Their help has made this a much better book, and I am deeply grateful.

Several people assisted directly with research and writing. Barbara Russano Hanning drafted many of the sidebars (identified with her initials). Felicia Miyakawa served as a special consultant and researcher for and outlined initial drafts of the material on jazz and popular music in chapters 32, 34, and 35. Patrick Warfield provided materials on band music. Felix O. Cox and Alison Trego offered research support. Russell Murray advised and assisted at every stage in developing NAWM. James Franklin, Robert Green, Donald Fader, Luis Dávila, Rex Sprouse, Karina Avanesian, and Tony Weinstein advised on translations. Alison Trego, Jonathan Shull, Randy Goldberg, Tong Cheng, Ann Shaffer, Travis Yeager, and Felicia Miyakawa assisted with the bibliography. Kathy Talalay cowrote the glossary. Marilyn Bliss prepared the index. John Anderies, David Baker, Angela Mariani, and Edward Roesner answered individual queries. Many thanks for their contributions.

Several others also read and commented on the initial proposal or parts of the draft, including Peter M. Lefferts and Luiz Fernando Lopes; my collaborators Amy Edmonds, Barbara Russano Hanning, Jennifer L. King, and Felicia Miyakawa; my colleagues at Indiana University, Austin B. Caswell, Halina Goldberg, Jeffrey Magee, Thomas J. Mathiesen, Daniel Melamed, and Massimo Ossi; my teaching assistants Jir Shin Boey, Randy Goldberg, Christopher Holmes, Bethany Kissell, Peter Schimpf, and Jennifer Smull; and my undergraduate students Rachel Brook, Mario Carlasare, Carmen Espinosa, Daniel Healy, Jason Hooper, Danielle McShine, Jenny Petkus, Andrew Rehrig, and Ruth Ann Ritchie. Mary Paquette Abt, Judith Barger, Mark J. Butler, David

Griffioen, Luiz Fernando Lopes, and Felicia Miyakawa offered writing advice and support. I am grateful to all of them for their suggestions and guidance.

It has been a pleasure and an inspiration to work with the staff at W. W. Norton. Maribeth Anderson Payne, music editor, has been a constant source of ideas, support, and enthusiasm, helping to refine my approach and offering insightful editorial suggestions. Former editor Michael Ochs brought me into the Norton family to write the *Study and Listening Guide* for previous editions, oversaw the initial planning for this edition, and edited numerous chapters. Kathy Talalay meticulously edited the remaining chapters, copyedited the entire manuscript, and tried to keep me on schedule, with unfailing good humor and good sense. Allison Benter served as the careful editor and copyeditor for NAWM. Neil Ryder Hoos helped to choose the images, including the lovely picture on the cover, and secured permissions for them. Courtney Fitch painstakingly researched and secured other permissions for this book and NAWM. JoAnn Simony oversaw production and found creative ways to make the schedule work when I fell behind. Antonina Krass contributed the beautiful design, David Budmen the elegant music typesetting, and Alice Bennett the attractive layout. Steve Hoge has worked tirelessly on all the electronic media accompanying the book. I cannot thank them all enough for their skill, dedication, and counsel.

Thanks finally but most of all to my family, especially my parents Donald and Jean Burkholder, who introduced me to the love of music, and P. Douglas McKinney, whose unending patience, encouragement, and support made this book possible.

— J. Peter Burkholder
May 2005

ABBREVIATIONS

B.C.E.	Before Common Era (equivalent to B.C.)
C.E.	Common Era (equivalent to A.D.)
SR	*Source Readings in Music History* (see "For Further Reading," p. A22, for citation code).

PITCH DESIGNATIONS

In this book, a note referred to without regard to its octave register is designated by a capital letter (A). A note in a particular octave is designated in italics, using the following system:

C to *B*

c to *b*

c′ to *b′*

c″ to *b″*

A
HISTORY
OF
WESTERN
MUSIC

SEVENTH EDITION

PART OUTLINE

PART ONE

THE ANCIENT AND MEDIEVAL WORLDS

 Many fundamental elements of today's music can be
traced back thousands of years. Prehistoric societies
developed instruments, pitches, melody, and rhythm.
Early civilizations used music in religious ceremonies, to
accompany dance, for recreation, and in education—
much as we do today. Ancient writers directly influenced our ways of
thinking about music, from concepts such as notes, intervals, and scales,
to notions of how music affects our feelings and character. Medieval
musicians contributed further innovations, devising notation systems
that led to our own; creating pedagogical methods and sacred chants
still in use today; developing styles of melody that have influenced the
music of all later periods; inventing polyphony and harmony; and
developing techniques of composition, form, and musical structure that
laid the foundation for music in all subsequent eras.

The music and musical practices of antiquity and the Middle Ages
echo in our own music, and we know ourselves better if we understand
our heritage. Yet only fragments survive from the musical cultures of
the past, especially the distant past. So our first task is to consider how
we can assemble those fragments to learn about a musical world of
long ago.

Music in Antiquity

European culture has deep roots in the civilizations of antiquity. Its agriculture, writing, cities, and systems of trade derive from the ancient Near East. Its mathematics, calendar, astronomy, and medicine grew from Mesopotamian, Egyptian, Greek, and Roman sources. Its philosophy is founded on Plato and Aristotle. Its primary religions, Christianity and Judaism, arose in the ancient Near East and were influenced by Greek thought. Its literature grew out of Greek and Latin traditions and drew on ancient myth and scripture. Its artists imitated ancient sculpture and architecture. From medieval empires to modern democracies, governments have looked to Greece and Rome for examples.

Western music also has roots in antiquity, from concepts such as notes, intervals, and scales to ideas about how music affects emotions and character. The strongest direct influence comes through Greek writings, which became the foundation for European views of music. The influence of ancient music itself is more difficult to trace. Little notated music survived, and few if any European musicians before the sixteenth century could read the ancient notation. Yet some musical practices continued, passed down through oral tradition.

These echoes of ancient music in the European tradition are reason enough to begin our survey by examining the roles of music in ancient cultures, the links between ancient practices and those of later centuries, and the debt Western music owes to ancient Greece. Starting with ancient music also lets us consider how we can learn about music of the past.

Music is sound, and sound is by its nature impermanent. What remains of the music from past eras are its historical traces, which we can divide into four main types: (1) *musical instruments* and other physical remains; (2) *visual images* of musicians and instruments; (3) *writings* about music and musicians; and (4) *music itself*, preserved in notation, through oral tradition, or (since the 1890s) in recordings. Using these traces, we can try to reconstruct what music of a past culture was like, recognizing that our understanding will always be partial and will be influenced by our own values and concerns.

We are most confident of success when we have all four types of evidence in abundance. But for ancient music, relatively little remains. Even for Greece, by far the best-documented ancient musical tradition, we have only a small portion of the instruments, images, writings, and music that once existed. For other cultures we have no music at all. By examining what traces survive and what we can conclude from them, we can explore how each type of evidence contributes to our understanding of music of the past.

THE EARLIEST MUSIC

The earliest evidence of music-making lies in surviving instruments and representations. In the Stone Age, people bored finger holes in animal bones to make whistles and flutes. Figure 1.1 shows one of the oldest bone-flutes found in Europe, dating from before 36,000 B.C.E. Paleolithic cave paintings appear to show musical instruments being played. Pottery flutes, rattles, and drums were common in the Neolithic era, and wall paintings in Turkey from the sixth millennium B.C.E. show drummers playing for dancers and for the hunt, to drive out game. Such images provide our only evidence for the roles music played in these cultures. Once people learned to work with metal, in the Bronze Age (beginning in the fourth millennium B.C.E.), they made metal instruments, including bells, jingles, cymbals, rattles, and horns. Plucked string instruments appeared around the same time, as shown on stone carvings; the instruments themselves were made of perishable materials, and few have survived.

Although we can learn about some facets of prehistoric musical cultures from images and archaeological remains, our understanding is severely limited by the lack of any written record. The invention of writing, which marked the end of the prehistoric period, added a new type of evidence, and it is with these accounts that the history of music properly begins.

Figure 1.1: Front view of a bone flute (made from the radius of a swan) unearthed at Geißenklösterle in Germany and estimated to date from ca. 36,800 ± 1,000 B.C.E.

MUSIC IN ANCIENT MESOPOTAMIA

Mesopotamia, the land between the Tigris and Euphrates rivers (now part of Iraq and Syria), was home to a number of peoples in ancient times. The map in Figure 1.2 shows several of the most important civilizations that developed there and in nearby regions over a span of more than two thousand years. Here in the fourth millennium B.C.E., the Sumerians developed the first true cities and civilization and one of the first known forms of writing, using impressions on flat clay tablets. This system, cuneiform, was adopted by later civilizations including the Akkadians and the Babylonians. Many tablets have been deciphered, and some mention music.

Instruments and images   Archaeological remains and images are still crucial for understanding the music of this time. Pictures show how instruments were held and played and in what circumstances music was used, while surviving instruments reveal details of their construction. For example, archaeologists exploring the royal tombs at Ur, a Sumerian city on the Euphrates, found several **lyres** and **harps,** two kinds of plucked string instruments, as well as pictures of them being played, all from ca. 2500 B.C.E. In a lyre, the strings run parallel to the resonating soundboard and attach to a crossbar supported by two arms; in a harp, the strings are perpendicular to the soundboard, and the neck that supports them is attached directly to the soundbox. Figure 1.3 is a reconstruction of one of the instruments from Ur: a **bull lyre,** a distinctively Sumerian lyre whose soundbox features a bull's head, which had religious significance. Figure 1.4 is part of an inlaid panel depicting a musician playing a bull lyre at a victory banquet. The player holds the lyre, apparently supported by a strap, perpendicular in front of him and plays it with both hands. Together image and instrument reveal that the lyre had a variable number of strings running from a bridge on the soundbox to the crossbar, where they were knotted around sticks that could be turned to change the tension and thus the tuning of each string. Other instruments of the period included lutes, pipes, drums, cymbals, clappers, rattles, and bells.

Combining written records with images of music-making allows a much *Written records* fuller understanding of how Mesopotamian cultures used music, showing that their repertories included wedding songs, funeral laments, military music, work songs, nursery songs, dance music, tavern music, music for entertaining at feasts, music to address the gods or accompany ceremonies and processions, and epics sung with instrumental accompaniment—all except the last uses that continue today. As is true for every era until the nineteenth century, we find the best evidence for music of the elite classes, primarily rulers and priests, who had the resources to induce instrument makers and musicians to make music, artists to depict it, and scribes to write about it.

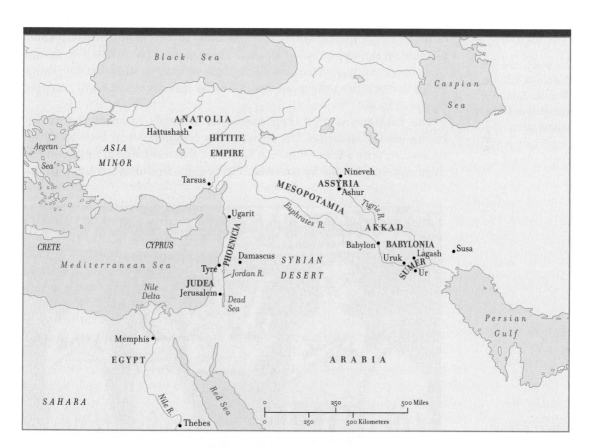

Figure 1.2: The ancient Near East, showing the location of the main cities and civilizations of Mesopotamia and Egypt.

*Figure 1.3:
Reconstruction of a
Sumerian bull lyre
from the Royal
Cemetery at Ur, ca.
2500 B.C.E.*

Written sources also provide a vocabulary for music and some information on musicians. Sumerian and Akkadian word lists from ca. 2500 B.C.E. on include terms for instruments, tuning procedures, performers, performing techniques, and **genres** or types of musical composition. The earliest composer known to us by name is Enheduanna (fl. ca. 2300 B.C.E.), an Akkadian high priestess at Ur, who composed **hymns** (songs to a god) to the moon god Nanna and moon goddess Inanna; their texts, but not their music, survive on cuneiform tablets.

Around 1800 B.C.E., Babylonian musicians began to write down what they knew instead of passing it on by word of mouth only. Their writings describe tuning, intervals, improvisation, performing techniques, and genres, including love songs, laments, and hymns. Here again we find many aspects of music that continued into later times.

Among the writings are instructions for tuning a string instrument that seem to indicate that the Babylonians (and probably their predecessors in Mesopotamia) used seven-note **diatonic** scales. They recognized seven scales of this type, roughly corresponding to the seven diatonic scales playable on the white keys of a piano. These scales have parallels in the ancient Greek musical system as well as in our own, suggesting that Babylonian theory and practice influenced that of Greece, directly or indirectly, and thus European music.

The Babylonians used their names for intervals to create the earliest known musical **notation**. The oldest nearly complete piece, from ca. 1400–1250 B.C.E., is on a tablet shown in Figure 1.5 that was found at Ugarit, a merchant city-state on the Syrian coast. The poem is in Hurrian, a language that

*Figure 1.4: Inlaid
panel from Ur, ca.
2600 B.C.E., showing a
bull lyre being played
at a victory banquet.*

TIMELINE: MUSIC IN ANTIQUITY

3500 BCE	2500	1500	500	400	300	200	100 BCE	1 CE	100 CE	200	300	400

- ca. 3500–3000 B.C.E. Rise of Sumerian cities in Mesopotamia
- ca. 3100 Cuneiform writing established
- ca. 2500 Royal tombs at Ur built
- **ca. 2300 Enheduanna composes her hymns**
- **ca. 1800 Babylonian writings about music**
- ca. 1400–1250 Oldest nearly complete composition in Babylonian notation
- ca. 800 Rise of Greek city-states
- ca. 800 Homer, *Iliad* and *Odyssey*
- 753 Rome founded
- **ca. 500 Pythagoras dies**
- ca. 500 Roman Republic begins
- 458 Aeschylus, *Agamemnon*
- **408 Euripides, *Orestes***
- ca. 380 Plato, *Republic*
- ca. 330 Aristotle, *Politics*
- **ca. 330 Aristoxenus, *Harmonic Elements***
- 146 Greece becomes province of Rome •
- **128–127 Second Delphic Hymn to Apollo composed** •
- 29–19 Virgil, *Aeneid* •
- 27 B.C.E. Rome becomes empire under Augustus •
- **1st cent. C.E. *Epitaph of Seikilos*** •
- 98–117 Roman Empire reaches its peak •
- **ca. 127–148 Ptolemy, *Harmonics*** •
- **2nd cent. Cleonides, *Harmonic Introduction*** •
- **4th cent. Aristides Quintilianus, *On Music*** •

cannot be translated entirely, but the text appears to be a hymn to Nikkal, wife of the moon god. Scholars have proposed possible transcriptions for the music, but the notation is too poorly understood to be read with confidence. Despite the invention of notation, most music was either played from memory or improvised. Musicians most likely did not play or sing from notation, as modern performers do, but used it as a written record from which a melody could be reconstructed, as cooks use a recipe.

OTHER CIVILIZATIONS

For other ancient civilizations we also have instruments, images, and writings that testify to their musical practices. India and China developed independently from Mesopotamia and were probably too distant to affect Greek or European music. Surviving sources that shed light on Egyptian musical traditions are especially rich, including many artifacts, paintings, and

Figure 1.5: Clay tablet from Ugarit, ca. 1400–1250 B.C.E., with text and musical notation for a hymn to Nikkal. The words are written above the double line, the music below.

hieroglyphic writings preserved in tombs. Archaeological remains and images that relate to music are relatively scant for ancient Israel, but music in religious observances as described in the Bible had some influence on later Christian practices in Europe, as we will see in chapter 2. Although some scholars have tried to discover and decipher musical indications in Egyptian hieroglyphics and wall paintings and in ancient copies of the Bible, no consensus has been reached that musical notation is even present. Through physical remains, images, and writings about music we can gain a sense of a vibrant musical life in the ancient Near East, but without actual music to perform, it remains almost entirely silent.

MUSIC IN ANCIENT GREEK LIFE AND THOUGHT

Ancient Greece is the earliest civilization that offers us enough evidence to construct a well-rounded view of musical culture. But there are still many gaps. We will begin with the instruments they used; turn next to writings about music's roles and effects; continue with theoretical writings; and conclude with the music itself. As shown in Figure 1.6, Greek civilization encompassed not only the Greek peninsula but islands in the Aegean, much of Asia Minor, southern Italy, and Sicily, and colonies ringing the Mediterranean and Black Seas.

INSTRUMENTS AND THEIR USES

We know about ancient Greek instruments from writings, archaeological remains, and hundreds of images on pots. The most important instruments were the **aulos** (pl. *auloi*), **lyre,** and **kithara.** The Greeks also used harps, other plucked string instruments, panpipes, horns, an early form of organ, and a variety of percussion instruments such as drums, cymbals, and clappers.

Aulos   The aulos was a pipe typically played in pairs, as pictured in Figure 1.7. Each pipe had fingerholes and a mouthpiece fitted with a reed. No reeds survive, but written descriptions suggest that they were long tubes with a beating tongue. Pitch could be changed by the position of the reed in the mouth, by air pressure, and by fingering. Images of auloi being played show both hands in the same finger position, leading most scholars to conclude that the two pipes were played in unison, with slight differences in pitch between them creating a plangent sound. But modern reconstructions based on surviving auloi can also be played to produce parallel octaves, fifths, or fourths, or a drone or separate line in one pipe against a melody in the other, so that these methods cannot be ruled out.

The aulos was used in the worship of Dionysus, god of fertility and wine. Links to fertility and wine explain its presence in the drinking scene in Figure 1.7; the instrument is played by a woman who was likely a prostitute as well as musician. The great tragedies by Aeschylus, Sophocles, and Euripides, created for the Dionysian festivals in Athens, have choruses and other musical portions that were accompanied by or alternated with the aulos.

Lyres usually had seven strings and were strummed with a plectrum, or pick. There were several forms of lyre, the most characteristic of which used as a soundbox a tortoise shell over which oxhide was stretched. As shown in Figure 1.8, the player held the lyre in front, resting the instrument on the hip and supporting it by a strap around the left wrist. The right hand strummed with the plectrum while the fingers of the left hand touched the strings,

Lyre

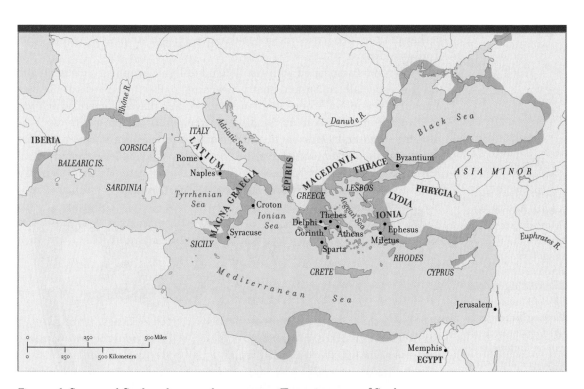

Figure 1.6: Greece and Greek settlements about 550 B.C.E. The main centers of Greek population and culture were the Greek peninsula, the Aegean Islands, the west coast of Asia Minor (modern Turkey), and southern Italy and Sicily, known to the Romans as Magna Graecia (Greater Greece).

Figure 1.7: Greek red-figure drinking cup showing a scene at a symposium, or drinking party, where a woman plays the double aulos. A drinking cup, like the one on which this painting appears, is seen on the right. On the left is the player's aulos bag, with a smaller bag attached to it that held the reeds for the aulos.

perhaps to produce harmonics or to dampen certain strings to prevent them from sounding.

The lyre was associated with Apollo, god of light, prophecy, learning, and the arts, especially music and poetry. Learning to play the lyre was a core element of education in Athens. Both men and women played the lyre, which was used to accompany dancing, singing, or recitation of epic poetry such as Homer's *Iliad* and *Odyssey*; to provide music for weddings; or to play for recreation.

Figure 1.8: Greek red-figure vase showing a lyre lesson. The student (middle) has just strummed the strings using the plectrum in his right hand. Viewing the teacher's lyre from the back, we can see the tortoise-shell sound box, the strap around the left wrist, and the fingers of the left hand touching the strings.

Figure 1.9: Kitharode singing to his own accompaniment on the kithara, with his head tilted back, the fingers of his left hand touching some of the strings, apparently to damp them, and the right hand holding the plectrum, which he has just strummed across the strings. Greek red-figure amphora from the fourth century B.C.E., attributed to the Berlin Painter.

The kithara was a large lyre, used especially for processions and sacred ceremonies and in the theater, and normally played while the musician was standing up. Figure 1.9 shows a picture of a kitharode, a singer accompanying himself on the kithara.

Kithara

Images from ancient Greece rarely show performers reading from a scroll or tablet while playing. It is clear from this and from the written record that the Greeks, despite having a well-developed form of notation by the fourth century B.C.E. (see below), primarily learned music by ear; they played and sang from memory or improvised using conventions and formulas.

Memory and improvisation

From the sixth century B.C.E. or earlier, the aulos and kithara were played as solo instruments. An account of a musical competition in 582 B.C.E. describes a performance of the Nomos Pythicos, a composition for aulos portraying the combat between Apollo and the serpent Python. Contests of kithara and aulos players, as well as festivals of instrumental and vocal music, became increasingly popular after the fifth century B.C.E. Indeed, the image in Figure 1.9 is from an amphora (a jar for wine or oil) awarded as a prize to the winner of a competition. As instrumental music grew more independent, the number of virtuosos rose and the music became more complex and showy. When famous artists appeared, thousands gathered to listen. Some performers accumulated great wealth through concert tours or fees from rich patrons, particularly after they garnered fame by winning competitions. Among the musicians acclaimed for their recitals were a number of women, who were excluded from competitions. Most professional performers, however, were of low status, often slaves or servants.

Competitions and professional musicians

GREEK MUSICAL THOUGHT

Thanks to their writings, we know a great deal about Greek thought concerning music. There were two principal kinds of writings on music: (1) philosophical doctrines on the nature of music, its place in the cosmos, its effects, and its proper uses in society; and (2) systematic descriptions of the materials of musical composition, what we now call music theory. In both realms, the Greeks achieved insights and formulated principles that have survived to this day. The most influential writings on the uses and effects of music are passages by Plato (ca. 429–347 B.C.E.) in his *Republic* and *Timaeus* and by Aristotle (384–322 B.C.E.) in his *Politics*. Greek music theory evolved continually from the time of its founder, Pythagoras (d. ca. 500 B.C.E.), to Aristides Quintilianus (fourth century C.E.), its last important writer. As we might expect in a tradition lasting nearly a millennium, writers expressed differing views, and the meanings of many terms changed. The following emphasizes the features that were most characteristic of Greek music and most important for the later history of Western music.

Music, religion, and society

In Greek mythology, music's inventors and earliest practitioners were gods and demigods, such as Apollo, Hermes, Amphion, and Orpheus. The word *music* (Greek *mousikē*) derives from the word for the Muses and originally denoted any of the arts associated with them, from history to dance. For the Greeks, music was both an art for enjoyment and a science closely related to arithmetic and astronomy. It pervaded all of Greek life, from work, the military, schooling, and recreation to religious ceremonies, poetry, and the theater.

Music, poetry, and dance

Music as a performing art was called *melos*, from which the word **melody** derives. It was primarily **monophonic,** consisting of a single melodic line. There was no concept of what we call harmony or counterpoint, although instruments often embellished the melody while a soloist or chorus sang an unembellished version, creating **heterophony.** Melos could denote an instrumental melody alone or a song with text, and "perfect melos" was melody, text, and stylized dance movement conceived as a whole. For the Greeks, music and poetry were nearly synonymous. In his *Republic*, Plato defined melos as a blend of text, rhythm, and *harmonia* (here meaning relationships among pitches). In his *Poetics*, Aristotle enumerated the elements of poetry as melody, rhythm, and language, and noted that there was no name for artful speech, whether prose or verse, that did not include music. "Lyric" poetry meant poetry sung to the lyre; "tragedy" incorporates the noun *ōdē*, "the art of singing." Many other Greek words for different kinds of poetry, such as *hymn*, were musical terms.

Music and number

For Pythagoras and his followers, numbers were the key to the universe, and music was inseparable from numbers. Rhythms were ordered by numbers, because each note was some multiple of a primary duration. Pythagoras was credited with discovering that the octave, fifth, and fourth, long recognized as consonances, are also related to numbers. These intervals are generated by the simplest possible ratios: for example, when a string is divided, segments whose lengths are in the ratio 2:1 sound an octave, 3:2 a fifth, and 4:3 a fourth.

Because musical sounds and rhythms were ordered by numbers, they were thought to exemplify the general concept of **harmonia,** the unification of parts in an orderly whole. Through this flexible concept—which could encompass mathematical proportions, philosophical ideas, or the structure of society as well as a particular musical interval, scale type, or style of melody—Greek writers perceived music as a reflection of the order of the universe.

Harmonia

Music was closely connected to astronomy through this notion of *harmonia.* Indeed, Claudius Ptolemy (fl. 127–48 C.E.), the leading astronomer of antiquity, was also an important writer on music. Mathematical laws and proportions were considered the underpinnings of both musical intervals and the heavenly bodies, and certain planets, their distances from each other, and their movements were believed to correspond to particular notes, intervals, and scales in music. Plato gave this idea poetic form in his myth of the "harmony of the spheres," the unheard music produced by the revolutions of the planets. This notion was invoked by writers throughout the Middle Ages and later, including Shakespeare in *The Tempest* and Milton in *Paradise Lost,* and underlay the work of Johannes Kepler (1571–1630), the founder of modern astronomy.

Music and astronomy

MUSIC AND *ETHOS*

Greek writers believed that music could affect **ethos,** one's ethical character or way of being and behaving. This idea was built on the Pythagorean view of music as a system of pitch and rhythm governed by the same mathematical laws that operated in the visible and invisible world. *Harmonia* in music reflected, and could therefore influence, *harmonia* (usually translated "harmony") in other realms. The human soul was seen as a composite whose parts were kept in harmony by numerical relationships. Because it reflected this orderly system, music could penetrate the soul and restore its inner harmony.

Through the doctrine of imitation outlined in his *Politics,* Aristotle described how music affected behavior: music that imitated a certain ethos aroused that same ethos in the listener (see Source Reading, p. 16). The imitation of a particular ethos was accomplished partly through the choice of *harmonia,* in the sense of a scale type or style of melody. While later centuries would interpret him as attributing such effects to a mode or scale alone, Aristotle probably also had in mind the melodic turns and general style characteristic of a *harmonia* and the particular rhythms and poetic genres most associated with it.

The doctrine of imitation

Plato and Aristotle both argued that education should stress gymnastics to discipline the body and music to discipline the mind. In his *Republic,* Plato insisted that the two must be balanced, because too much music made one weak and irritable while too much gymnastics made one uncivilized, violent, and ignorant. In addition, only certain music was suitable, since habitual listening to music that roused ignoble states of mind distorted a person's character. Those being trained to govern should avoid melodies expressing softness and indolence. Plato endorsed two *harmoniai*—the Dorian and Phrygian, because they fostered the virtues of temperance and courage—and

Music in education

SOURCE READING

ARISTOTLE ON THE DOCTRINE OF IMITATION, ETHOS, AND MUSIC IN EDUCATION

Music's importance in ancient Greek culture is shown by its appearance as a topic in books about society, such as Aristotle's Politics. *Aristotle believed that music could imitate and thus directly affect character and behavior, and therefore should play a role in education.*

———— • ————

[Melodies] contain in themselves imitations of ethoses; and this is manifest, for even in the nature of the harmoniai there are differences, so that people when hearing them are affected differently and have not the same feelings in regard to each of them, but listen to some in a more mournful and restrained state, for instance the so-called Mixolydian, and to others in a softer state of mind, for instance the relaxed harmoniai, but in a midway state and with the greatest composure to another, as the Dorian alone of the harmoniai seems to act, while the Phrygian makes men divinely suffused; for these things are well stated by those who have studied this form of education, as they derive the evidence for their theories from the actual facts of experience. And the same holds good about the rhythms also, for some have a more stable and others a more emotional ethos, and of the latter some are more vulgar in their emotional effects and others more liberal. From these considerations therefore it is plain that music has the power of producing a certain effect on the ethos of the soul, and if it has the power to do this, it is clear that the young must be directed to music and must be educated in it. Also education in music is well adapted to the youthful nature; for the young owing to their youth cannot endure anything not sweetened by pleasure, and music is by nature a thing that has a pleasant sweetness.

Aristotle, *Politics* 8.5, trans. Harris Rackham, in SR 3, p. 29.

excluded others. He deplored music that used complex scales or mixed incompatible genres, rhythms, and instruments. In both his *Republic* and *Laws*, Plato asserted that musical conventions must not be changed, since lawlessness in art and education led to license in manners and anarchy in society. Similar ideas have been articulated by guardians of morality in the twenty-four centuries since then, and ragtime, jazz, rock, punk, and rap have all been condemned for these very reasons.

Aristotle, in his *Politics*, was less restrictive than Plato. He held that music could be used for enjoyment as well as education and that negative emotions such as pity and fear could be purged by inducing them through music and drama. However, he felt that sons of free citizens should not seek professional training on instruments or aspire to the virtuosity shown by performers in competitions since it was menial and vulgar to play solely for the pleasure of others rather than for one's own improvement.

GREEK MUSIC THEORY

No writings by Pythagoras survive, and those of his followers exist only in fragments quoted by later authors. The earliest theoretical works we have are *Harmonic Elements* and *Rhythmic Elements* (ca. 330 B.C.E.) by Aristoxenus, a pupil of Aristotle. Important later writers include Cleonides (ca. second or third century C.E.), Ptolemy, and Aristides Quintilianus. These theorists defined concepts still used today, as well as ones specific to ancient Greek music. Their writings show how much the Greeks valued abstract thought, logic, and systematic definition and classification, which has influenced all later writing on music. They also show the Greek appreciation for variety, given the abundance of notes, intervals, and scales available in the system they described.

Rhythm

Only part of Aristoxenus' *Rhythmic Elements* survives, but enough remains to show us that rhythm in music was closely aligned with poetic rhythm. Aristoxenus defines durations as multiples of a basic unit of time. This scheme parallels Greek poetry, which features patterns of longer and shorter syllables, not stressed and unstressed syllables as in English.

Note and interval

In *Harmonic Elements*, Aristoxenus distinguishes between *continuous* movement of the voice, gliding up and down as in speech, and **diastematic** (or *intervallic*) movement, in which the voice moves between sustained pitches separated by discrete intervals. A melody consists of a series of **notes,** each on a single pitch; an **interval** is formed between two notes of different pitch; and a **scale** is a series of three or more different pitches in ascending or descending order. Such seemingly simple definitions established a firm basis for Greek music and all later music theory. By contrast, Babylonian musicians apparently had no name for intervals in general, but had names only for intervals formed between particular pairs of strings on the lyre or harp. The greater abstraction of the Greek system marked a significant advance.

Tetrachord and genus

Unique to the Greek system were the concepts of **tetrachord** and **genus** (pl. *genera*). A tetrachord (literally, "four strings") comprised four notes spanning a perfect fourth. There were three genera (classes) of tetrachord, shown in Example 1.1: **diatonic, chromatic,** and **enharmonic.** The outer notes of the tetrachord were considered stationary in pitch, while the inner two notes could move to form different intervals within the tetrachord and create the different genera. Normally the smallest intervals were at the bottom, the largest at the top. The diatonic tetrachord included two whole tones and a semitone. In the chromatic, the top interval was a tone and a half (equal to a minor third) and the others semitones. In the enharmonic, the top interval was the size of two tones (equal to a major third) and the lower ones approximately quarter tones. All these intervals could vary slightly in size, giving rise to "shades" within each genus.

Example 1.1: Tetrachords

The system of genera was not an arbitrary set of rules, but an attempt to explain musical practice. Aristoxenus remarked that the diatonic genus was the oldest and most natural, the chromatic more recent, and the enharmonic the most refined and difficult to hear. Indeed, we have seen that the Babylonian system, which predated the Greek by more than a millennium, was diatonic.

The Greater
Perfect System

Since most melodies exceeded a fourth, theorists combined tetrachords to cover a larger range. Two successive tetrachords were **conjunct** if they shared a note, as do the first two tetrachords in Example 1.2, or **disjunct** if they were separated by a whole tone, as are the second and third tetrachords. The system shown in the example, with four tetrachords plus an added lowest note to complete a two-octave span, was called the **Greater Perfect System.** The outer, fixed tones of each tetrachord are shown in open notes, the movable inner tones in black notes.

Example 1.2: The Greater Perfect System

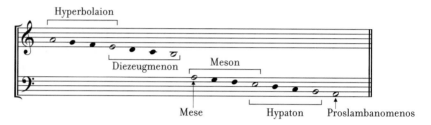

Each note and tetrachord had a name to indicate its place in the system. As we see in the example, the middle note was called "mese" (middle), the tetrachord spanning a fourth below it "meson," the lowest tetrachord "hypaton" (first), and those above the mese "diezeugmenon" (disjunct) and "hyperbolaion" (of the extremes). There was also a Lesser Perfect System, spanning an octave plus a fourth, with only one conjunct tetrachord ("synemmenon," conjunct) above the mese. The system was not based on absolute fixed pitch but on the intervallic relationships of notes and tetrachords to each other. The transcription here in the range $A–a'$ is purely conventional, although we will see that it closely matches the range used in medieval chant.

Species of
consonances

Cleonides noted that in the diatonic genus the three main consonances of perfect fourth, fifth, and octave were subdivided into tones (T) and semitones (S) in only a limited number of ways, which he called **species.** This concept has proven useful in understanding Greek melody, medieval chant, Renaissance polyphonic music, and even twentieth-century music, so it is worthy of special attention. Cleonides identified three species of fourth, shown in Example 1.3a, the first ascending S–T–T (as in $B–c–d–e$), the second T–T–S (as in $c–d–e–f$), the third T–S–T (as in $d–e–f–g$). Only these three arrangements of two tones and one semitone are possible. Example 1.3b shows the four species of fifth.

The seven species of octave, shown in Example 1.3c, are combinations of the species of fourth and fifth, a division of the octave that became important in medieval and Renaissance theory. Cleonides identified the species by what "the ancients" supposedly called them. The first octave species, represented by the span from B to b, was Mixolydian, followed by Lydian ($c–c'$), Phrygian ($d–d'$), Dorian ($e–e'$), Hypolydian ($f–f'$), Hypophrygian ($g–g'$), and Hypodorian ($a–a'$). These seven octave species parallel the seven diatonic tunings recognized by the Babylonians, suggesting a continuity of practice and perhaps of theory. As we will see in chapter 2, some medieval theorists later

Example 1.3: Cleonides' species of consonances

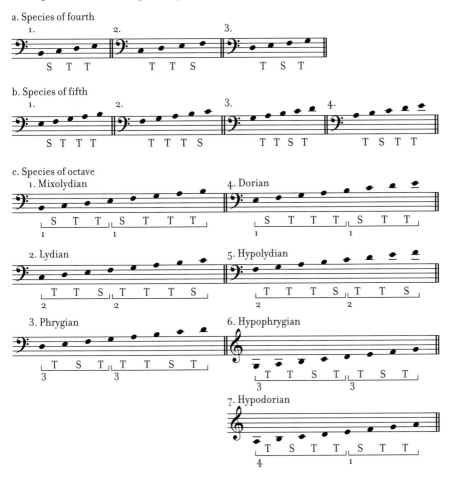

a. Species of fourth

1. S T T
2. T T S
3. T S T

b. Species of fifth

1. S T T T
2. T T T S
3. T T S T
4. T S T T

c. Species of octave

1. Mixolydian
S T T | S T T T
1   1

4. Dorian
S T T T | S T T
1   1

2. Lydian
T T S | T T T S
2   2

5. Hypolydian
T T T S | T T S
2   2

3. Phrygian
T S T | T T S T
3   3

6. Hypophrygian
T T S T | T S T
3   3

7. Hypodorian
T S T T | S T T
4   1

adopted these names for their modes, but the latter do not match Cleonides' octave species, and the octave species lack one defining aspect of mode: a principal note on which a melody is expected to end.

The names Cleonides used for the octave species also had other associa- *Tonoi* tions. Dorian, Phrygian, and Lydian were ethnic names originally associated with styles of music practiced in different regions of the Greek world (see map in Figure 1.6). Plato and Aristotle used these names for *harmoniai*, in the sense of scale types or melodic styles. The addition of prefixes (such as hypo-) multiplied the number of names in use. Later writers, including Aristoxenus, Cleonides, and Aristides Quintilianus, used the same names for up to fifteen different **tonoi**, defining a *tonos* as a scale or set of pitches within a specific range or region of the voice. These essentially involve transposing the system of tones up or down by some number of semitones. Like *harmoniai*, tonoi were associated with character and mood, the higher tonoi being energetic and the lower tonoi sedate.

We should not presume that all music from the Dorian region (southern Greece) used the Dorian octave species, Dorian *harmonia*, and Dorian tonos, or that these three concepts were equivalent or even closely related. Rather, it appears that writers over a span of a thousand years were applying familiar terms to new uses. This tendency for musicians to use old terms in new ways is common to all eras, and we will see it many times in forthcoming chapters. It can be frustrating when learning the history of music, since definitions seem always to be changing. What is most important here is to recognize that not all uses of words such as "harmonia" and "tonos" or of names such as "Dorian" mean the same thing, and to seek to understand how each is used in context.

ANCIENT GREEK MUSIC

About forty-five pieces or fragments of ancient Greek music survive, ranging from the fifth century B.C.E. to the fourth century C.E. Most are from relatively late periods, composed to Greek texts when Greece was dominated by Rome, and most were recovered only in the twentieth century. All employ a musical notation in which letters and other signs are placed above the text to indicate notes and their durations. The earliest examples are two fragmentary choruses from plays by Euripides (ca. 485–406 B.C.E.) with music that is probably by Euripides himself. Later pieces are more complete, including two Delphic hymns to Apollo, the second from 128–127 B.C.E.; a short verse or epigram by Seikilos inscribed as an epitaph on a tombstone from around the first century C.E.; and four hymns by Mesomedes of Crete from the second century C.E. Consistencies among these surviving pieces of music and the theoretical writings reveal a close correspondence between theory and practice.

Epitaph of Seikilos

CD 1|1   CD1|1

The *Epitaph of Seikilos* (NAWM 1), inscribed on the tombstone in Figure 1.10, is shown in Example 1.4 in original notation and modern transcription. Over the modern notation appear alphabetical signs for the notes, and above those are marks indicating when the basic rhythmic unit should be doubled or tripled. The melody is diatonic, covers an octave in range, and uses the Phrygian octave species. The notation indicates the tonos called Iastian by the theorists, in which the system shown in Example 1.2 is transposed up a whole step (resulting in F♯ and C♯). The text balances extremes, counseling us to be lighthearted even while acknowledging death. This is consistent with the Iastian tonos, which is near the middle of the fifteen tonoi in terms of range and thus suggests moderation. The melody seems similarly moderate in ethos, neither excited nor depressed, but balancing the rising fifth and thirds that begin most lines of the poem with falling gestures at the end of each line.

Euripides' Orestes

CD 1|2

The fragment from Euripides' *Orestes* (NAWM 2) survives on a scrap of papyrus from about 200 B.C.E., shown in Figure 1.11. There are seven lines of text with musical notation above them, but only the middle portion of each line survives. The notation calls for either the chromatic or enharmonic genus along with the diatonic and for instrumental notes interspersed with the vocal. Both traits are noted in descriptions of Euripides' music, suggesting that this music is indeed by him.

In this choral ode, the women of Argos implore the gods to have mercy for Orestes, who has murdered his mother Clytemnestra for her infidelity to his father, Agamemnon. The poetry, and thus the music, is dominated by a

Example 1.4: Seikilos song in original notation (above the staff) and transcription

1. "Ο – σον ζῆς φαί – νου
2. μη – δὲν ὅλ – ως σὺ λυ – ποῦ·
3. πρὸς ὀ – λί – γον ἐσ – τὶ τὸ ζῆν,
4. τὸ τέ – λος ὁ χρό – νος ἀ – παι – τεῖ.

Figure 1.10: Tomb stele from Tralles, near Aydin in southern Turkey, probably first century C.E. It is inscribed with an epitaph by Seikilos with pitch and rhythm notation, transcribed in Example 1.4 and NAWM 1.

As long as you live, be lighthearted.
Let nothing trouble you. Life is only too short,
and time takes its toll.

rhythmic pattern (the dochmaic foot) used in Greek tragedy for passages of intense agitation and grief. The music reinforces this ethos through small chromatic or enharmonic intervals, stark changes of register, and truncated lines filled in by instrumental notes.

These examples conform to the descriptions we have of Greek music and show (1) the role of instruments in supporting vocal music; (2) the idea that

Figure 1.11: Papyrus fragment, ca. 200 B.C.E., with part of a chorus from Euripides' Orestes, transcribed in NAWM 2.

music imitates ethos; (3) the importance of poetic rhythm and structure in shaping melody; and (4) the use of diatonic, chromatic, and enharmonic genera as well as notation, tonoi, and octave species. While many questions remain, we can understand the musical culture of ancient Greece through the four types of evidence we have examined in this chapter.

MUSIC IN ANCIENT ROME

We know less about music in ancient Rome. There are plenty of images, some instruments, and thousands of written descriptions, but no settings of Latin texts survive from the Roman period.

The Romans took much of their musical culture from Greece, especially after the Greek islands became a Roman province in 146 B.C.E. As in Greece, lyric poetry was often sung. The *tibia* (Roman version of the aulos) played important roles in religious rites, military music, and theatrical performances, which included musical preludes and interludes, songs, and dances. The *tuba*, a long straight trumpet derived from the Etruscans (earlier residents of the Italian peninsula), was used in religious, state, and military ceremonies. The most characteristic instruments were a large G-shaped circular horn called the *cornu* and a smaller version, the *buccina*. Figure 1.12 shows tibias and cornus being played in a funeral procession. Music was part of most public ceremonies and was featured in private entertainment and education. Cicero, Quintilian, and other writers state that cultivated people should be educated in music.

During the great days of the Roman Empire in the first and second centuries C.E., art, architecture, music, philosophy, and other aspects of Greek culture were imported into Rome and other cities. Ancient writers tell of

Figure 1.12: Roman funeral procession on a sarcophagus relief from Amiternum, end of first century B.C.E. At the bottom right we see four men playing the tibia, which was similar to the Greek aulos. Above them are two men playing the cornu and one on the lituus, both Etruscan-Roman brass instruments.

famous virtuosos, large choruses and orchestras, and grandiose musical festivals and competitions. Many of the emperors supported and cultivated music; Nero even aspired to personal fame as a musician and competed in contests. But with the economic decline of the empire in the third and fourth centuries, production of music on the large and expensive scale of earlier days ceased. Whatever direct influence Roman music may have had on later European developments seems to have left almost no traces.

THE GREEK HERITAGE

Although many details remain uncertain, we know that in the ancient world (1) music consisted essentially of melody; (2) melody was intimately linked with the rhythm and meter of words; (3) musicians relied on their memories and on knowledge of conventions and formulas, rather than reading from notation; and (4) philosophers conceived of music as an orderly system interlocked with the system of nature and as a force in human thought and conduct. To these elements the Greeks contributed two more: (5) an acoustical theory founded on science, and (6) a well-developed music theory.

Many of these characteristics continued in later Western music. Music remained essentially melodic until the rise of polyphony in the eleventh century. Much vocal melody is shaped by the rhythm and meter of the words, if not always as strictly as in Greek music. Many musical traditions, from synagogue cantillation to the blues, still depend on memory and conventions, even as notation became increasingly important in Western music from the ninth century on. Notions of music as an orderly system and an influence on human behavior continue to this day. Plato's concern that changes in musical conventions threaten anarchy in society has been voiced repeatedly by those who resist change, and it echoes today among those lamenting current tastes in popular music.

Despite the virtual disappearance of ancient Greek music until its recovery in the Renaissance, aspects of Greek musical thought influenced medieval church music and music theory. Renaissance and Baroque musicians revived Greek concepts and joined them to modern ones to create new methods and genres, including expression of mood, rhetorical devices, chromaticism, monody, and opera, while citing Plato and Aristotle in defense of their innovations. Opera composers such as Gluck in the eighteenth century and Wagner in the nineteenth looked back to Greek tragedies for models of how to use music to convey drama. Twentieth-century composers such as Olivier Messiaen and Harry Partch have revived Greek rhythms and tuning systems. And although ancient music is still little known, current musical concepts continue those addressed by ancient Greek writers, from the diatonic scales on the piano to the use of music in educating the young and debates about the ethical and moral effects of music. The Greeks are still very much with us, and we will encounter them again and again as we explore the Western musical tradition.

Chapter 2

The Christian Church in the First Millennium

CHAPTER OUTLINE

The history of music in medieval Europe is intertwined with the history of the Christian church, which was the dominant social institution for most of the Middle Ages. Religious services were mostly sung or intoned rather than spoken. Many aspects of Western music, from notation to polyphony, first developed within church music. Most schools were part of the church, and most composers and writers on music were trained there. Moreover, because notation was invented for church music, that type of medieval music is the best preserved today.

This chapter traces the development of the church in the West and of its music, including the traditions and values that shaped how music was used and regarded, the standardization of liturgy and music as a unifying force, and the development of notation as a tool for specifying and teaching melody. The church drew on Greek philosophy and music theory, but also fostered practical theory for training musicians.

THE DIFFUSION OF CHRISTIANITY

Jesus of Nazareth, whose life and teachings gave rise to Christianity, was both a Jew and a subject of the Roman Empire. His teachings drew from Jewish Scripture, yet his charge to "make disciples of all nations" (Matthew 28:19) sparked a movement that spread throughout the Roman world. St. Paul (ca. 10–ca. 67 C.E.) and other apostles traveled the Near East, Greece, and Italy proclaiming Christianity as a religion open to all. The promise of salvation in the afterlife, as well as a strong sense of community and of equality between social classes, drew many converts. Women were attracted to Christianity and played major roles in its growth.

Roman subjects were allowed to practice their own religions as long as they also worshiped the Roman gods and emperors. But any group that worshiped a single god, denying all others, and sought to convert people of all nationalities was a threat to the state religion and thus to the state. Christians were at times persecuted; they had to gather in secret, and some were martyred. Yet Christianity gained adherents, even among leading Roman families.

In 313, the year after his own conversion, Emperor Constantine I (r. 310–37) issued the Edict of Milan, which legalized Christianity and allowed the church to own property. By then, Christianity was firmly established in most cities of the empire. In 392, Emperor Theodosius I (r. 374–95) made Christianity the official religion and suppressed others, except for Judaism. The church organized itself on the model of the empire, with territories called dioceses and a hierarchy of local churches, bishops, and archbishops headed by patriarchs in Rome, Antioch, Alexandria, Constantinople, and Jerusalem. By 600, virtually the entire area once controlled by Rome was Christian, as we see in Figure 2.1.

Legalization and establishment

THE JUDAIC HERITAGE

Christianity sprang from Jewish roots, and some elements of Christian observances derive from Jewish traditions, chiefly the chanting of Scripture and the singing of **psalms,** poems of praise from the Hebrew Book of Psalms.

The second Temple of Jerusalem, built in the late sixth century B.C.E. on the site of the original Temple of Solomon, was a place for public worship

Temple sacrifice

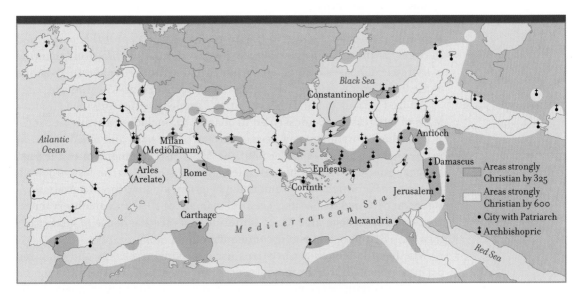

Figure 2.1: The diffusion of Christianity.

Figure 2.2: Interior view of the basilica Emperor Constantine built as a throne room and audience hall in Treveris (now Trier in Germany), then western capital of the Roman Empire, where he resided between 306 and 316. As Christians grew in number, they met for worship in basilicas like this one, where sung words carried better and more clearly through the large, resonant space than did spoken words.

until its destruction by the Romans in 70 C.E. Observances centered around a sacrifice—usually of a lamb—performed by priests, assisted by Levites (members of the priestly class, including musicians), and witnessed by lay worshipers. Depending on the occasion, priests and sometimes worshipers ate some of the offering. Sacrifices were celebrated twice daily, with additional services on festivals and the Sabbath. During the ritual, a choir of Levites sang psalms assigned to that day, accompanied by harp and psaltery. Trumpets and cymbals were also used.

Synagogues   In ancient times, synagogues were centers for readings and homilies rather than worship. Public reading from Scripture was probably performed in chant, as in later centuries, employing a system of ***cantillation*** (chanting of sacred texts) based on melodic formulas that reflected the phrase divisions of the text. Certain readings were assigned to particular days or festivals.

Christian parallels   We find various parallels between the Temple sacrifice and the Christian Mass of later centuries (described in chapter 3), including a symbolic sacrifice in which worshipers and priests partake of the body and blood of Christ in the form of bread and wine. But the Mass also commemorates the Last Supper Jesus shared with his disciples, and thus imitates the festive Jewish Passover meal, which was accompanied by psalm singing. Singing psalms assigned to certain days became a central element of all Christian observances. So did the synagogue practice of gathering in a meeting house to hear readings from Scripture and public commentary upon them.

Whether the melodies Christians used for singing psalms and chanting Scripture were drawn from those used in Jewish observances cannot be known for certain, since none were written down until many centuries later. But similarities between Jewish melodies passed down through oral tradition and medieval melodic formulas for singing psalms in Christian churches suggest that there was some borrowing or intermingling.

MUSIC IN THE EARLY CHURCH

The earliest recorded musical activity of Jesus and his followers was singing hymns (Matthew 26:30, Mark 14:26). The apostle Paul exorted Christian communities to sing "psalms and hymns and spiritual songs" (Ephesians 5:19, Colossians 3:16). In about 112, Pliny the Younger, governor of a Roman province in Asia Minor, reported the Christian custom of singing "a song to Christ as if to a god." Christians often met for communal evening meals at which they sang psalms and hymns.

As the number of converts increased in the fourth century and official recognition grew, small informal gatherings gave way to public meetings in large rectangular buildings called basilicas, such as the one in Figure 2.2. Here the chanting of prayers and Scripture helped carry the text clearly throughout the large space. The most devout believers sought a life of

SOURCE READING

A CHRISTIAN OBSERVANCE IN JERUSALEM, CA. 400

In ca. 400 C.E., a Spanish nun named Egeria on pilgrimage to Jerusalem described the services there, noting the psalms and hymns sung between prayers and Bible readings. Her eyewitness report is a crucial document of early Christian practices. The excerpt below describes the Sunday morning Vigil, which became the service called Matins.

——— • ———

As soon as the first cock crows, straightway the bishop comes down and enters the cave in [the church of] the Anastasis. All the gates are opened, and the entire throng enters the Anastasis, where already countless lamps are burning, and when the people are within, one of the priests sings a psalm and all respond, after which there is a prayer. Then one of the deacons sings a psalm, similarly followed by a prayer, and a third psalm is sung by some cleric, followed by a third prayer and the commemoration of all. When these three psalms

have been sung and the three prayers said, behold censers are brought into the cave of the Anastasis, so that the entire Anastasis basilica is filled with the smell. And then as the bishop stands behind the railings, he takes the Gospel book and goes to the gate and the bishop himself reads the Resurrection of the Lord. When the reading of it has begun, there is such moaning and groaning among everybody and such crying, that even the hardest of hearts could be moved to tears because the Lord has suffered so much for us. When the Gospel has been read, the bishop leaves and is led with hymns to the Cross, accompanied by all the people. There, again, one psalm is sung and a prayer said. Then he blesses the people, and the dismissal takes place. And as the bishop goes out, all approach to kiss his hand.

From *Itinerarium Egeriae* xxiv, 9–11, in *Music in Early Christian Literature*, ed. James W. McKinnon (Cambridge: Cambridge University Press, 1987), 115.

constant prayer. Living in isolation as hermits or together in monasteries, they chanted or recited psalms many times each day as a form of prayer or meditation. By the late fourth century, Christian observances began to reflect a standardized format, and singing became a regular feature, drawing texts both from the Book of Psalms and from nonbiblical hymns (see Source Reading, p. 27). This practice of singing psalms and hymns was codified in the rites of the medieval church (described in chapter 3) and has continued to this day, in modified forms, among Christians worldwide.

Rejection of music for pleasure

While songs of praise were encouraged, some early church leaders rejected other aspects of ancient practice. Influential Christian writers such as St. Basil (ca. 330–379), St. John Chrysostom (ca. 345–407), St. Jerome (ca. 340–420), and St. Augustine (354–430), known today as "the church fathers," interpreted the Bible and set down principles to guide the church. Like the ancient Greeks, they believed the value of music lay in its power to influence the ethos of listeners, for good or for ill; St. Augustine was so deeply moved by the singing of psalms that he feared the pleasure it gave him, while approving its ability to stimulate devout thoughts (see Source Reading). Most church fathers rejected the idea of cultivating music simply for enjoyment and held to Plato's principle that beautiful things exist to remind us of divine beauty. This view underlay many pronouncements about music by church leaders and by later theologians of the Protestant Reformation.

Exclusion of instruments and pagan associations

For early church leaders, music was the servant of religion, and only music that opened the mind to Christian teachings and holy thoughts was worthy of hearing in church. Believing that music without words cannot do this, most church fathers condemned instrumental music. The many references to harp, trumpet, and other instruments in the Book of Psalms and other Hebrew Scriptures were explained away as allegories. Although Christians may have used lyres to accompany hymns and psalms in their homes, instruments were not

SOURCE READING

ST. AUGUSTINE ON THE USEFULNESS AND DANGERS OF MUSIC

Augustine is one of the most significant thinkers in the history of Christianity and of Western philosophy. His Confessions are often considered the first modern autobiography. In the passage below, he expresses the tension between music's abilities to heighten devotion and to seduce with mere pleasure.

———•———

When I recall the tears that I shed at the song of the Church in the first days of my recovered faith, and even now as I am moved not by the song but by the things which are sung—when chanted with fluent voice and completely appro-priate melody—I acknowledge the great benefit of this practice. Thus I waver between the peril of pleasure and the benefit of my experience; but I am inclined, while not maintaining an ir-revocable position, to endorse the custom of singing in church so that weaker souls might rise to a state of devotion by indulging their ears. Yet when it happens that I am moved more by the song than by what is sung, I confess sin-ning grievously, and I would prefer not to hear the singer at such times. See now my condition!

Saint Augustine, *Confessions* 10:33, trans. James W. McKinnon, in SR 13 (2:5), p. 133.

used in church. For this reason, the entire tradition of Christian music for over a thousand years was one of unaccompanied singing. Moreover, early converts associated elaborate singing, large choruses, instruments, and dancing with pagan spectacles. Avoiding such music helped to set off the Christian community from the surrounding pagan society and to proclaim the urgency of subordinating the pleasures of this world to the eternal welfare of the soul.

DIVISIONS IN THE CHURCH AND DIALECTS OF CHANT

Disputes about theology and governance led to several divisions among Christians during the first millennium. The most significant division occurred in 395 with the partition of the Roman Empire into two parts. The Western Empire, ruled from Rome or Milan, suffered invasion by Germanic tribes until it collapsed in 476. The Eastern Empire was centered at Constantinople (formerly Byzantium, now Istanbul), which Constantine had rebuilt as his capital. Later known as the Byzantine Empire, it lasted over a thousand years, until Constantinople fell to the Turks in 1453.

In the Eastern Empire, the church was under the control of the emperor. But as the Western Empire declined and collapsed, the bishop of Rome gradually asserted control of the church in the West. The eastern church continued to use Greek, the language of the early Christian apostles, but after the third century, Latin, the language of the Roman Empire, was used in Rome and the West. Growing theological differences intensified the division until 1054, when it became permanent. The western church became the Roman Catholic Church, and the bishop of Rome was known as the pope (from *papa*, "father" or "bishop"). The Byzantine Church is the ancestor of the present-day Orthodox churches.

Early services were not rigidly determined but followed patterns common among Christian churches as a whole. As Christianity diversified, each branch or region evolved its own ***rite***, consisting of a ***church calendar***, or schedule of days commemorating special events, individuals, or times of year; a ***liturgy***, or body of texts and ritual actions, assigned to each service; and a repertory of ***plainchant***, or ***chant***, unison song with melodies for the prescribed texts. The different regional repertories are called ***chant dialects*** by analogy to language. We will focus on the chant dialect most important for the history of Western music, ***Gregorian chant***, with brief discussions of ***Byzantine***, ***Ambrosian***, and ***Old Roman chant*** and mention of other dialects.

Rite, calendar, liturgy, and music

BYZANTINE CHANT

Byzantine services included Scriptural readings—which were chanted using formulas that reflected the phrasing of the text—and psalms and hymns sung to fully developed melodies. Melodies were classed into eight modes or ***echoi*** (sing. *echos*), which served as a model for the eight modes of the western church (see below).

The most characteristic Byzantine chants were hymns, which became more prominent in the liturgy and more highly developed in eastern churches than in the West, with many different types. Hymn melodies were notated in books from the tenth century on, and many are still sung in Greek Orthodox services. Byzantine missionaries took their rite north to the Slavs starting in the ninth century, resulting in the establishment of the Russian and other Slavic Orthodox churches; the Greek texts were translated into local languages and the melodies adopted faithfully, but over time the traditions diverged.

Centonization   Many Byzantine chant melodies were created through ***centonization*** (from Latin *cento*, "patchwork"), combining standard formulas to make a new melody. Some motives were used for a particular type of chant or melodic style; some suited the beginning, some the middle, and some the end of a melody, while others made good connecting links; some were associated with

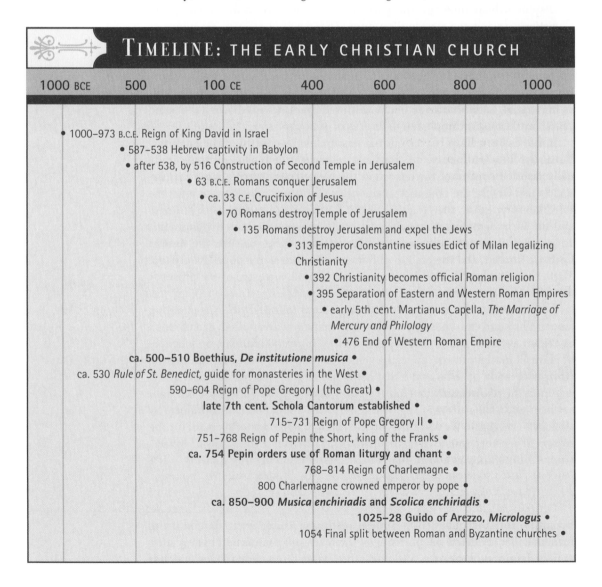

TIMELINE: THE EARLY CHRISTIAN CHURCH

1000 BCE	500	100 CE	400	600	800	1000

- 1000–973 B.C.E. Reign of King David in Israel
  - 587–538 Hebrew captivity in Babylon
  - after 538, by 516 Construction of Second Temple in Jerusalem
    - 63 B.C.E. Romans conquer Jerusalem
    - ca. 33 C.E. Crucifixion of Jesus
      - 70 Romans destroy Temple of Jerusalem
      - 135 Romans destroy Jerusalem and expel the Jews
        - 313 Emperor Constantine issues Edict of Milan legalizing Christianity
          - 392 Christianity becomes official Roman religion
          - 395 Separation of Eastern and Western Roman Empires
            - early 5th cent. Martianus Capella, *The Marriage of Mercury and Philology*
            - 476 End of Western Roman Empire
    - ca. 500–510 Boethius, *De institutione musica* •
- ca. 530 *Rule of St. Benedict*, guide for monasteries in the West •
- 590–604 Reign of Pope Gregory I (the Great) •
- **late 7th cent. Schola Cantorum established** •
  - 715–731 Reign of Pope Gregory II •
- 751–768 Reign of Pepin the Short, king of the Franks •
- **ca. 754 Pepin orders use of Roman liturgy and chant** •
  - 768–814 Reign of Charlemagne •
  - 800 Charlemagne crowned emperor by pope •
- ca. 850–900 *Musica enchiriadis* and *Scolica enchiriadis* •
  - **1025–28 Guido of Arezzo, *Micrologus*** •
  - 1054 Final split between Roman and Byzantine churches •

certain modes, pitches, or accentuation patterns; and some were ornamental figures.

WESTERN DIALECTS

After the Western Empire disintegrated, control of western Europe was distributed among several peoples, including Celts, Angles, and Saxons in the British Isles; Franks in Gaul (approximately modern-day France); Visigoths in Spain; and Ostrogoths and Lombards in northern Italy. All eventually converted to Christianity and adopted the doctrines of the western church. A number of local and regional rites emerged, each with its own liturgy and body of chant. Besides the tradition of Rome itself, these included a variety of usages in Gaul, collectively known as Gallican chant; Celtic chant in Ireland and parts of Britain; Mozarabic in Spain; Beneventan in southern Italy; and Ambrosian in Milan.

The most important center for the western church outside Rome was Milan, a thriving city with close cultural ties to Byzantium and the East. It was the chief residence for the Western emperors and later the capital for the Lombard kingdom in northern Italy, which flourished between 568 and 744. The songs of the Milanese rite became known as **Ambrosian chant**, after St. Ambrose, bishop of Milan from 374 to 397, although we do not know whether any of the music dates from his time. Ambrosian liturgy and chant have survived in Milan to the present day despite attempts to suppress them. Many of these chants are similar to those of Rome, indicating either an interchange or a common source.

Ambrosian chant

From the eighth century on, the liturgy of the western church became increasingly Romanized, as popes and the secular rulers allied with them tried to consolidate their authority by standardizing what was said and sung in church services. In this process liturgy and music were valued not only for their religious functions but also as means of asserting centralized control. Eventually, most of the local dialects disappeared or were absorbed into a single uniform practice with authority emanating from Rome.

The dominance of Rome

THE CREATION OF GREGORIAN CHANT

The codification of liturgy and music under Roman leaders, helped by the Frankish kings, led to the repertory known as **Gregorian chant.** The Schola Cantorum (School of Singers), the choir that sang when the pope officiated at observances, was apparently founded in the late seventh century and probably played a role in standardizing chant melodies in the early eighth century. By midcentury, particular liturgical texts and the melodies to perform them were assigned to services throughout the year in an order that was added to but not essentially changed until the sixteenth century.

Between 752 and 754, Pope Stephen II sojourned in the Frankish kingdom with a retinue that must have included the Schola Cantorum. As a result of this visit, Pepin the Short (r. 751–68), who had become king of the Franks with the support of the previous pope, ordered the Roman liturgy and chant to

Dissemination of Roman chant to the Franks

be performed throughout his domain and suppressed the native Gallican rite. The alliance between pope and king strengthened both, and the imposition of a uniform liturgy and body of music helped Pepin consolidate his diverse kingdom, serving as much a political as a religious function. His son Charlemagne (Charles the Great, r. 768–814), whose conquests expanded his territory throughout modern-day France, the Lowlands, western Germany, Switzerland, and northern Italy, continued this policy, sending for singers from Rome to teach the chant in the north. Ties between Rome and the Franks were strengthened when Pope Leo III crowned Charlemagne emperor in Rome on Christmas 800, initiating what became known as the Holy Roman Empire. Figure 2.3 shows Charlemagne with the pope, and Figure 2.4 a map of his empire.

Frankish contributions   Gregorian chant as we know it drew from an original fund of Roman melodies with many additions and changes by the Franks. We cannot be certain what melodies were brought from Rome to the Frankish lands, since they were not yet written down. Simple chants and melodies later preserved in almost identical form over a wide area may be very ancient. Other chants were probably altered by the Franks, either to suit northern tastes or to fit them into the system of eight modes (see below) imported from the Byzantine Church. Some melodies were drawn from Gallican chant. Furthermore, many new melodies were developed in the north after the eighth century.

The legend of St. Gregory   Books of liturgical texts from this time, which still lacked musical notation, attributed the chant to Pope Gregory I (St. Gregory the Great, r. 590–604), leading to the name Gregorian chant. This may be a case of mistaken identity—as we have seen, the chant was probably codified in the early eighth century by the Schola Cantorum, perhaps during the reign of Pope Gregory II

Figure 2.3: Charlemagne wearing his crown as Holy Roman Emperor, with Pope Leo III on the right. Gold funerary sculpture (ca. 1215) from the Palatine Chapel in the cathedral in Aachen, Charlemagne's capital.

Figure 2.4: Holy Roman Empire under Charlemagne around 800.

(r. 715–31). The misattribution may have arisen among the English, who adopted the Roman rite shortly before the Franks. They revered Gregory I as the founder of their church and consequently attributed their liturgy and its music to him. The legend arose that the chants were dictated to Gregory by the Holy Spirit in the form of a dove, as depicted in Figure 2.5. Both the ascription to a revered pope and this legend enhanced the perception of the chant as old, authentic, and divinely inspired, and thus facilitated its adoption. This is a fascinating development: it shows not only the desire to establish as traditional a repertory that was relatively new in this form but also the use of propaganda to do so. After Charlemagne and his successors promulgated Gregorian chant throughout their lands, it spread across western Europe, until it was in use almost everywhere, serving as the common music of a more unified church.

Ironically, another body of chant survived for some time in Rome itself and is preserved in manuscripts dating from the eleventh and twelfth centuries. Now called **Old Roman chant**, it uses essentially the same texts as Gregorian chant and thus represents the same liturgical tradition, stemming from eighth-century Rome. The melodies resemble those of Gregorian chant but are often more ornate, suggesting that both chant dialects derive from a common source. Whether the Old Roman melodies represent the original stock from which the Gregorian melodies were adapted, or are a variant of that

Old Roman chant

Figure 2.5: Pope Gregory the Great (r. 590–604) alternately listens to the dove (symbolizing the Holy Spirit) reveal the chants to him and dictates them to a scribe. The scribe, puzzled by the pauses in the pope's dictation, has lowered his slate and is peeking from behind the screen. Such manuscript illustrations arose from the legend that Gregory codified the chant that has been named for him and disseminated it in writing. So far as we know, chant was first notated about two centuries later.

eighth-century repertory reflecting centuries of oral transmission and continuing embellishment before they were written down, is still a matter for dispute.

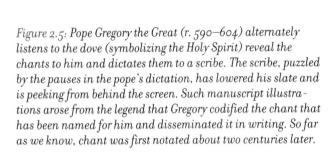

THE DEVELOPMENT OF NOTATION

ORAL TRANSMISSION

We know that the Roman liturgy was determined by the early eighth century because the words were written down by then. Yet the melodies were learned by hearing others sing them, a process called oral transmission, leaving no written traces. We have only one fragment of Christian music before Charlemagne—a hymn to the Trinity from the late third century found on a papyrus at Oxyrhynchos in Egypt and written in ancient Greek notation. But this notation had been forgotten by the seventh century, when Isidore of Seville (ca. 560–636) wrote that "Unless sounds are remembered by man, they perish, for they cannot be written down."

How chant melodies were created and transmitted without writing has been a subject of much study and controversy. Some of the simplest and most frequently sung melodies may have been passed down verbatim. But the corpus of Gregorian chant contains hundreds of elaborate melodies, many sung only once a year. Some scholars suggest that many chants were improvised within strict conventions, following a given melodic contour and using opening, closing, and ornamental formulas appropriate to a particular text or place in the liturgy. This parallels Jewish cantillation and Byzantine centonization, both of which were oral traditions before they were fixed in writing. It also re-

Example 2.1: The second phrases of the first four verses of the Tract Deus, Deus meus

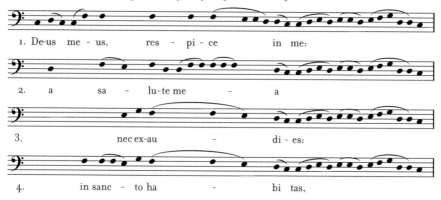

1. De-us me - us, res - pi - ce in me:

2. a sa - lu-te me - a

3. nec ex-au - di - es:

4. in sanc - to ha - bi tas,

sembles other oral traditions; for example, epic singers from the Balkans re-cited long poems seemingly by rote but actually using formulas associating themes, syntax, meters, line endings, and other elements.

We can find evidence for such oral composition in the chants themselves. Example 2.1 compares parallel phrases from the first four verses of *Deus, Deus meus,* a Tract (for the categories of chant, see chapter 3). Each phrase hovers around F, then descends to close with the same cadential figure at the midpoint of the verse. No two verses are exactly the same, but each features the same fund of formulas, which also appear in many other Tracts. Since Tracts were originally performed by a soloist, it seems likely that over the centuries singers developed a standard pattern, consisting of a general melodic contour and a set of formulas to delineate the phrases in each verse, and varied it to fit the syllables and accentuation of the particular text for each verse or chant. When the melodies were written down, these variations were preserved.

STAGES OF NOTATION

Individual variation was not suitable if the chants were to be performed in the same way each time in churches across a wide territory, as the pope and Frankish kings intended. During the eighth century, attempts were made in Rome to standardize the melodies and to train Frankish singers how to repro-duce them exactly. But as long as this process depended on memory and on learning by ear, melodies were subject to change, and accounts from both Roman and Frankish perspectives tell of melodies being corrupted as they were transmitted to the north. What was needed to stabilize the chants was **notation,** a way to write down the music. The earliest surviving books of chant with music notation date from the late ninth century, but their substantial agreement has suggested to several scholars that the notation may already have been in use in Charlemagne's time or soon thereafter. We have some written testimony to support this view, though scholars differ in interpreting the evidence. Whenever notation was invented, writing down the melodies was an attempt to assure that from then on each melody would be sung in es-sentially the same way everywhere. Thus notation was both a result of striving for uniformity and a means of perpetuating that uniformity.

Notation developed through a series of innovations, each designed to make the melodic outline more precise. The significant historical steps are shown in Figures 2.6–2.8, with modern equivalents in Examples 2.2–2.3. All show the Gradual *Viderunt omnes* from the Mass for Christmas Day (NAWM 3d).

CD 1|13

Neumes

In the earliest notations, signs called **neumes** (Latin *neuma*, meaning "gesture") were placed above the words, as in Figure 2.6, to indicate the number of notes for each syllable and whether the melody ascended, descended, or repeated a pitch. Neumes may have derived from signs for inflection and accent, akin to accent marks in modern French. Because neumes did not denote specific pitches or intervals, they served as reminders of the correct melodic shape but could not be read at sight by someone who did not already know the melody. Melodies still had to be learned by ear.

Diastematic notation

In the tenth and eleventh centuries, scribes placed neumes at varying heights above the text to indicate the relative size as well as direction of intervals, as in Figure 2.7. These are called **heighted** or **diastematic neumes** (from the Greek word for "interval").

Lines, clefs, staff

The scribe of this manuscript scratched a horizontal line in the parchment corresponding to a particular note and oriented the neumes around that line. This was a revolutionary idea: a musical sign that did not represent a sound, but clarified the meaning of other signs. In other manuscripts, the line was labeled with a letter for the note it represented, most often F or C because of their position just above the semitones in the diatonic scale; these letters evolved into our clef signs, and with them each pitch in the melody was clear. The eleventh-century monk Guido of Arezzo (ca. 991–after 1033) suggested an arrangement of lines and spaces, using a line of red ink for F and of yellow ink for C, with letters in the left margin identifying each line and one note within each space. This scheme was widely adopted, and the neumes were reshaped to fit the arrangement, as shown in Figure 2.8. From this system evolved a staff of four lines a third apart, the ancestor of our modern five-line staff.

Reading music

The use of lines and letters, culminating in the staff and clefs, enabled scribes to notate pitches and intervals precisely. In practice, pitch was still relative, as it had been for the Greeks; a notated chant could be sung higher or lower to suit the singers, but the notes relative to each other would form the same intervals. The new notation also freed music from its dependence on oral transmission. With his notation, Guido demonstrated that a singer could "learn a verse himself without having heard it beforehand" simply by reading the notes. This achievement was as crucial for the history of Western music as the invention of writing was for the history of language and literature.

Rhythm

Staff notation with neumes conveyed pitch but not durations. Some manuscripts contain signs for rhythm, but scholars have not agreed on their meaning. One modern practice is to sing chants as if all notes had the same basic value; notes are grouped in twos or threes, and these groups are flexibly combined into larger units. This interpretation, worked out in the early twentieth century by the Benedictine monks of the Abbey of Solesmes in France under Dom André Mocquereau, was approved by the Catholic Church as conforming with the spirit of the liturgy. Whatever differences in duration there may have been in early practice, chant was almost certainly relatively free rather than metered in rhythm. Its movement has been compared to the flow of sand

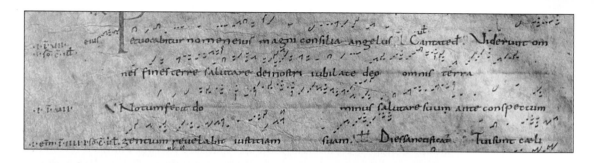

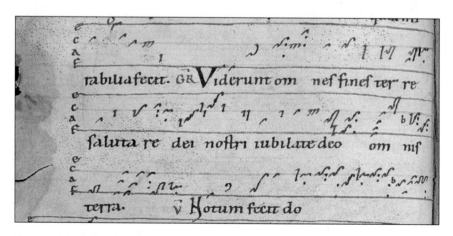

Figure 2.6 (top): The Gradual Viderunt omnes *in neumatic notation, from one of the earliest notated Graduals (books of chants for the Mass), copied in Brittany around 900. The neumes indicate melodic direction, but not precise notes or intervals.*

Figure 2.7 (middle): The Gradual Viderunt omnes *in heighted neumes, from the Gradual of St. Yrieix, near Limoges in southern France, copied in the second half of the eleventh century. The relative height of the neumes over the text indicates the relative pitch. A line scratched in the manuscript identifies the note a.*

Figure 2.8 (bottom): The Gradual Viderunt omnes *in Guidonian notation, from a Gradual from Klosterneuberg, copied ca. 1150. In accordance with Guido's recommendations, the note f (low or high) is indicated with a red line, c with a yellow line, and lines and spaces are identified with letters in the left margin (f, a, c, and e).*

through an hourglass, the medieval standard for timekeeping, as opposed to the ticking of a clock.

SOLESMES CHANT NOTATION

The Solesmes monks prepared modern editions of chant, which Pope Pius X proclaimed in 1903 as the official Vatican editions. Intended for use in church rather than historical study, they use a modernized form of chant notation. Examples 2.2 and 2.3 show the Gradual *Viderunt omnes* in Solesmes notation and in transcription, to facilitate comparison. The staff in chant notation has four lines, one of which is designated by a clef as either middle C (𝄐) or the F below it (𝄐), like our modern C clefs and bass clef. Pitch is relative rather than absolute; singers may perform the chants in any comfortable range.

The notes and notegroups are called neumes. A neume may carry only one syllable of text. *Composite neumes*, representing two or more pitches, are

Example 2.2: The Gradual Viderunt omnes *in Solesmes chant notation*

All the ends of the earth have seen the salvation of our God: sing, joyfully to God, all the earth.

Verse: *The Lord has made known His salvation; He has revealed His justice in the sight of the Gentiles.*

read left to right, except that when one note is below another the lower note is sung first; thus the melody on "fines" in Example 2.2 is *c′–d′–c′–a.* An *oblique neume* () indicates three notes, so that "terrae" begins *c′–a–c′.* Two or more notes in succession on the same line or space, if on the same syllable (as on "-te" of "jubilate"), are sung as though tied (or, in some interpretations, slightly pulsed). Diamond-shaped notes appear in descending patterns, as on "omnes," as a way to save space, but receive the same values as square ones. The small notes indicate partially closing the mouth on a voiced consonant at the end of a syllable, as in "Viderunt" in the first staff. The wavy line in ascending figures (∿, called *quilisma*), as on "omnis" in the third staff, may have indicated a vocal ornament. The only accidentals used are flat and natural signs, which may appear only on B. Except in a signature at the

Example 2.3: The Gradual Viderunt omnes *transcribed in modern notation*

MUSIC IN CONTEXT

IN THE MONASTIC *SCRIPTORIUM*

During the first millennium of Christianity, the growing repertory used in liturgical worship required some kind of written format so that these texts and melodies could be remembered and passed down from one generation to the next. The preservation of this repertory in manuscripts—books laboriously written and copied by hand—became one of the great accomplishments of the monastic communities of the Middle Ages.

Manuscript production became a routine part of monastic life, and special places within the monastery were set aside as writing workshops, or *scriptoria*. The word *scriptorium* also refers to the entire group of monks who were engaged in producing a manuscript, from the novices who prepared the ink and parchment or drew the lines on which the music was then notated, to the skilled workers who put the finishing touches on the book's covers. The bookmaking process extended beyond the *scriptorium* to the monks who toiled outside the monastery. An entire flock of sheep was needed to provide the parchment for a single book; and wild game such as deer and boar were hunted in order to furnish the leather used for binding the volumes.

But the copyist's job was central and involved both manual dexterity and intellectual fortitude. Trainees first had to learn how to make the letters and notes conform exactly to the style of writing that was in use at the time; there was no room for individuality. As a result, the scribes throughout northwestern Europe produced works of incredible regularity and perfect legibility.

Straightforward copying of text and music was only one stage of the manuscript's production. Another was the exacting job of decorating the more important books with elaborate initials and capital letters in gold leaf or colored paints, and illustrating them with miniature scenes or brightening up the text's margins

Figure 2.9: St. Gregory writing with scribes, Franco-German School, ca. 850–75 (ivory).

with illuminated designs. Finally came the binding, which could be more or less elaborate. The most important books were encased in ornamental covers made by specialized craftsmen and enriched with metals and gems.

All this labor helped to keep alive a widespread appreciation for music manuscripts, the creation of which represented so much effort and expense. And for the monks themselves, copying a book was regarded like prayer and fasting, as a way to keep one's unruly passions in check. But the monks also saw in their tedious work a means of spreading the word of God. The abbot of one important Benedictine monastery in the twelfth century has this to say about the solitary monk who devotes his life to the *scriptorium* (as opposed to the garden or vineyards):

> He cannot take to the plow? Then let him take up the pen; it is much more useful. In the furrows he traces on the parchment, he will sow the seeds of the divine words. . . . He will preach without opening his mouth; . . . and without leaving his cloister, he will journey far over land and sea.*—BRH

*Peter the Venerable, Abbot of Cluny in France, quoted by Jean LeClercq, The Love of Learning and the Desire for God (New York: Fordham University Press, 1961), 128.

beginning of a line, a flat is valid only until the beginning of the next word or vertical division line; thus in "omnis terra" in the third staff, the first word features B♭ and the second B♮.

The Solesmes editions include interpretive signs that are not in the manuscripts. A dot doubles the value of a note, used here at the ends of most phrases. A horizontal dash (present in some medieval sources) indicates a slight lengthening, as on "fines." Vertical lines of varied lengths show the division of a melody into periods (double or full barline), phrases (half-barline), and smaller units (a stroke through the uppermost staff-line). An asterisk in the text shows where the chorus takes over from the soloist, and the signs *ij* and *iij* indicate that the preceding phrase is to be sung twice or three times (see Example 3.5).

MUSIC THEORY AND PRACTICE

THE TRANSMISSION OF GREEK MUSIC THEORY

The chant repertory drew on sources in ancient Israel and in Christian communities from Syria and Byzantium in the East to Milan, Rome, and Gaul in the West. But for their understanding of this music, church musicians also drew on the music theory and philosophy of ancient Greece. During the early Christian era, this legacy was gathered, summarized, modified, and transmitted to the West, most notably by Martianus Capella and Boethius.

In his widely read treatise *The Marriage of Mercury and Philology* (early fifth century), Martianus described the seven liberal arts: grammar, dialectic, rhetoric, geometry, arithmetic, astronomy, and harmonics (music). The first three, the verbal arts, came to be called the *trivium* (three paths), while the last four, the mathematical disciplines, were called the *quadrivium* (four paths) by Boethius. The section on music is a modified translation of *On Music* by Aristides Quintilianus. Such heavy borrowing from earlier authorities was typical of scholarly writing and remained so throughout the Middle Ages.

Martianus Capella

Boethius (ca. 480–ca. 524), depicted in Figure 2.10, was the most revered authority on music in the Middle Ages. Born into a patrician family in Rome, he became consul and minister to Theodoric, Ostrogoth ruler of Italy, and wrote on philosophy, logic, theology, and the mathematical arts. His *De institutione musica* (The Fundamentals of Music), written when Boethius was a young man and widely copied and cited for the next thousand years, treats music as part of the quadrivium. Music for Boethius is a science of numbers, and numerical ratios and proportions determine intervals, consonances, scales, and tuning. Boethius compiled the book from Greek sources, mainly a lost treatise by Nicomachus and the first book of Ptolemy's *Harmonics*. Although medieval readers may not have realized how much Boethius depended on other authors, they understood that his statements rested on Greek mathematics and music theory.

Boethius

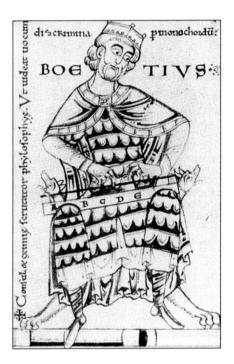

Figure 2.10: Twelfth-century manuscript illumination showing Boethius measuring out notes on a monochord, a string stretched over a long wooden resonator with a movable bridge to vary the sounding length of the string.

The most original part of his book is the opening chapters, where Boethius divides music into three types. The first type he calls ***musica mundana*** (the music of the universe), the numerical relations controlling the movement of stars and planets, the changing of the seasons, and the elements. Second is ***musica humana*** (human music), which harmonizes and unifies the body and soul and their parts. Last is ***musica instrumentalis*** (instrumental music), audible music produced by instruments or voices, which exemplifies the same principles of order, especially in the numerical ratios of musical intervals.

Boethius emphasized the influence of music on character. As a consequence, he believed music was important in educating the young, both in its own right and as an introduction to more advanced philosophical studies. He valued music primarily as an object of knowledge, not a practical pursuit. For him music was the study of high and low sounds by means of reason and the senses; the philosopher who used reason to make judgments about music was the true musician, not the singer or someone who made up songs by instinct.

PRACTICAL THEORY

Treatises from the ninth century through the later Middle Ages were more oriented toward practical concerns than were earlier writings. Boethius was mentioned with reverence, and the mathematical fundamentals of music that he transmitted still undergirded the treatment of intervals, consonances, and scales. But discussions of music as a liberal art did not help church musicians notate, read, classify, and sing plainchant or improvise or compose polyphony. These latter topics now dominated the treatises.

Figure 2.11: Guido of Arezzo (left) with his sponsor Theodaldus, bishop of Arezzo, calculating the string lengths of the steps of the scale. Guido dedicated to the bishop his Micrologus, *in which he proposed a simpler way to produce the diatonic scale on a monochord than Boethius had described. Twelfth-century manuscript of German origin.*

Among the most important treatises were the anonymous ninth-century *Musica enchiriadis* (Music Handbook) and an accompanying dialogue, *Scolica enchiriadis* (Excerpts from Handbooks). Directed at students who aspired to enter clerical orders, both emphasize practical matters over theoretical speculation. *Musica enchiriadis* introduces a system for notating chant, describes eight modes (see below), provides exercises for locating semitones in chant, and explains the consonances and how they are used to sing in polyphony (see chapter 5). The most widely read treatise after Boethius was Guido of Arezzo's *Micrologus* (ca. 1025–28), a practical guide for singers that covers notes, intervals, scales, the modes, melodic composition, and improvised polyphony. It was commissioned by the bishop of Arezzo, shown with Guido in Figure 2.11.

Musica enchiriadis and Micrologus

THE CHURCH MODES

An essential component of the curriculum for church musicians was the system of **modes.** The system evolved gradually, and writers differed in their approaches. In its complete form, achieved by the eleventh century, the system encompassed eight modes identified by number. Example 2.4a shows the important characteristics of each mode, especially its **final, range,** and **tenor.**

The modes are differentiated by the arrangement of whole and half steps in relation to the *final,* the main note in the mode and usually the last note in the melody. Each mode is paired with another that shares the same final. There are four finals, each with a unique combination of tones and semitones surrounding it, as shown in Example 2.4 and outlined below:

Final

Modes	Final	Interval below final	Intervals above final
1 and 2	D	tone	tone, semitone
3 and 4	E	tone	semitone, tone
5 and 6	F	semitone	tone, tone
7 and 8	G	tone	tone, tone

Authentic and plagal modes

Modes that have the same final differ in range. The odd-numbered modes are called **authentic** and typically cover a range from a step below the final to an octave above it, as shown in Example 2.4a. Each authentic mode is paired with a **plagal** mode that has the same final but is deeper in range, moving from a fourth (or sometimes a fifth) below the final to a fifth or sixth above it.

Example 2.4: The church modes

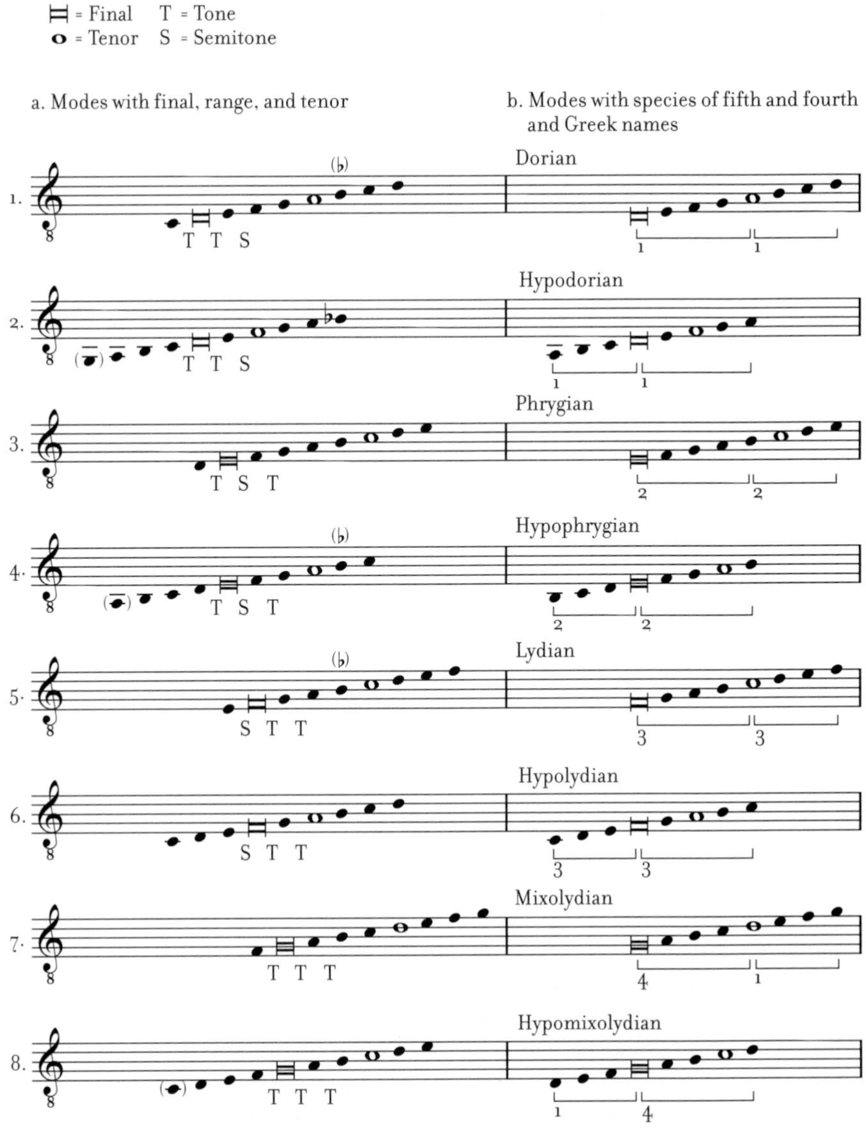

⊨ = Final   T = Tone
o = Tenor   S = Semitone

a. Modes with final, range, and tenor

b. Modes with species of fifth and fourth and Greek names

1. T T S — Dorian
2. T T S — Hypodorian
3. T S T — Phrygian
4. T S T — Hypophrygian
5. S T T — Lydian
6. S T T — Hypolydian
7. T T T — Mixolydian
8. T T T — Hypomixolydian

Since Gregorian chants are unaccompanied melodies that typically use a range of about an octave, the effect of cadencing around the middle of that octave in the plagal modes was heard in the Middle Ages as quite distinct from closing at or near the bottom of the range in the authentic modes. Modern listeners may find this difference hard to understand, since we consider both *Joy to the World* and *Happy Birthday* to be in the major mode, despite the different ranges of their melodies in respect to the tonic. But to medieval church musicians, the combination of different intervals around each final with different ranges relative to the final for authentic and plagal modes gave each of the eight modes an individual sound.

Only one chromatic alteration was normally allowed: B♭ often appears in place of B in chants that give prominence to F, as chants in modes 1, 2, 4, 5, and 6 commonly do.

Use of B♭

Some theorists applied to the modes the species of fifth and fourth described by Cleonides (see chapter 1 and Example 1.3), as diagrammed in Example 2.4b. They divided each mode into two spans, marked by brackets in the example: a fifth rising from the final, and a fourth that is above the fifth in the authentic modes and below the final in the plagal modes. The arrangement of whole tones and semitones above each of the four finals is unique, corresponding to Cleonides' four species of fifth, although in a different order; each scale is then completed with one of the three species of fourth. This way of looking at the modes clarifies the relationship between plagal and authentic modes, helps in analyzing some chants, and is very useful for understanding Renaissance music. In practice, however, the modes as used in the Middle Ages were not really octave species, as the diagrams in Example 2.4b might suggest, but extended to a ninth or tenth and often allowed B♭, as shown in Example 2.4a.

Species of fifth and fourth

In addition to the final, each mode has a second characteristic note, called the **tenor** or **reciting tone.** The finals of corresponding plagal and authentic modes are the same, but the tenors differ (see Example 2.4). The general rule is that in the authentic modes the tenor is a fifth above the final, and in the plagal modes the tenor is a third below the tenor of the corresponding authentic mode, except that whenever a tenor would fall on the note B, then it is moved up to C. The final, range, and tenor all contribute to characterizing a mode. The tenor is often the most frequent or prominent note in a chant, or a center of gravity around which a phrase is oriented, and phrases rarely begin or end above the tenor. In each mode, certain notes appear more often than others as initial or final notes of phrases, further lending each mode a distinctive sound.

Tenor or reciting tone

The modes became a means for classifying chants and arranging them in books for liturgical use. Many chants fit the theory well, moving within the indicated range, lingering on the tenor, and closing on the final. *Viderunt omnes* in Example 2.3 on page 39 is a good example. In mode 5, it begins on the final F; rises to circle around the tenor C, which predominates in most phrases; touches high F an octave above the final three times and E below the final once, using the whole range of the mode; uses both B and B♭, as allowed in this mode; and closes on the final. Most phrases begin and end on F, A, or C, as is typical of the mode. But not all chant melodies conform to modal

Modal theory and chant

theory. Many existed before the theory was developed, and some of these do not fit gracefully in any mode.

Application of Greek names

In the tenth century, some writers applied the names of the Greek scales to the church modes, as shown in Example 2.4b. Misreading Boethius, they mixed up the names, calling the lowest mode in the medieval system (*A–a*) Hypodorian, the highest in Cleonides' arrangement of the octave species (*a–a'*), and moving through the other names in rising rather than descending order (compare Example 2.4b with Example 1.3c). In the resulting nomenclature, plagal modes had the prefix Hypo- (Greek for "below") added to the name of the related authentic mode. Although medieval treatises and liturgical books usually refer to the modes by number, the Greek names have become the nomenclature of choice in modern textbooks.

The attempts by medieval theorists to link their music to ancient Greek theory, despite the poor fit between the modes (which were based on final, tenor, and ranges exceeding an octave) and the Greek system (which was based on tetrachords, octave species, and tonoi), show how important it was for medieval scholars to ground their work in the authoritative and prestigious Greek tradition.

SOLMIZATION

To facilitate sight-singing, Guido of Arezzo introduced a set of syllables corresponding to the pattern of tones and semitones in the succession C–D–E–F–G–A. He noted that the first six phrases of the hymn *Ut queant laxis* began on those notes in ascending order and used their initial syllables for the names of the steps: *ut, re, mi, fa, sol, la* (see Example 2.5). These **solmization** syllables (so called from *sol-mi*) are still used, although the most common version of the set substitutes *do* for *ut* and adds *ti* above *la*. Guido's syllables helped to locate the semitones in chant: only the step between *mi* and *fa* was a semitone, and all others were whole tones. Moreover, C–D–E–F–G–A includes all four finals of the modes plus a tone on each end, so Guido's syllables could be used to teach the pattern of whole and half steps around the final of each mode.

THE HEXACHORD SYSTEM

Guido's followers developed the six-step solmization pattern into a system of **hexachords.** Only three semitones occur in chant: E–F, B–C, and A–B♭. Thus

Example 2.5: Hymn, Ut queant laxis

That thy servants may freely sing forth the wonders of thy deeds, remove all stain of guilt from their unclean lips, O Saint John.

the hexachord, the interval pattern of six notes from *ut* to *la,* could be found in three positions: beginning on C, called the "natural" hexachord; on G, the "hard" hexachord; and on F, the "soft" hexachord. The hexachord on G used B-natural, for which the sign was ♮ ("square b"); the F hexachord used B-flat, which had the sign ♭ ("round b"). These signs evolved into our ♮, ♯, and ♭, but their original purpose was to indicate whether B took the syllable *mi* (as in the G hexachord) or *fa* (as in the F hexachord).

The basic scale described by medieval theorists extended from G (written as Γ, the Greek letter *gamma*) to *e″,* as shown in Example 2.6. Within this range, each note was named by its letter and the position it occupied within the hexachord(s) to which it belonged. Thus *gamma,* the first note of its hexachord, was called *gamma ut,* from which comes our word *gamut.* Middle C, which belonged to three different hexachords, was *C sol fa ut.*

Example 2.6: The system of hexachords

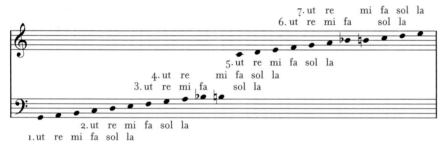

Using the syllables to learn a melody that exceeded a six-note range required changing from one hexachord to another. For example, in the passage from *Viderunt omnes* in Example 2.7, no single hexachord can be found that contains all the notes: the G or hard hexachord accounts for the first ten notes, including B♮, but the F or soft hexachord is needed for the B♭, the C hexachord for the low E, and the F hexachord for the C and B♭ in the cadential phrase. Changing hexachords was done by a process called **mutation,** whereby a note that was shared by both hexachords was begun as if in one hexachord and left as if in another, as shown in the example.

Mutation

Example 2.7: End of Gradual Viderunt omnes *in solmization syllables*

Followers of Guido developed a pedagogical aid called the "Guidonian hand," shown in Figure 2.12. Pupils were taught to sing intervals as the teacher pointed with the index finger of the right hand to the different joints of the open left hand. Each joint stood for one of the twenty notes of the system; any other note, such as F♯ or E♭, was considered to be "outside the hand."

Guidonian hand

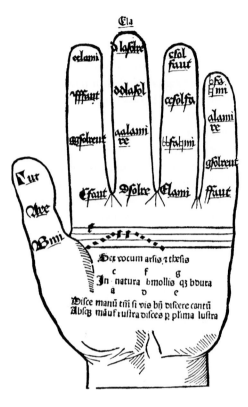

Figure 2.12: The "Guidonian hand," a mnemonic device used for locating the pitches of the system of hexachords (shown in Example 2.6) by pointing to the joints of the left hand. Although credited to Guido, the hand was probably a later application of his solmization syllables. The notes are laid out in a counter-clockwise spiral, beginning with the lowest note (gamma ut) at the tip of the thumb, moving down the thumb, across the base of each finger, up the little finger, across the tips, down the index finger, and around the middle joints. This places the semitones between mi and fa, the most important intervals to locate, near the corners of the hand: between the base of the thumb and index finger, the base of the third and fourth fingers, and the tips and top joints of the outer fingers.

No late medieval or Renaissance music textbook was complete without a drawing of this hand.

Using solmization and staff notation, Guido boasted that he could "produce a perfect singer in the space of one year, or at the most in two," instead of the ten or more it usually took teaching melodies by rote. No statement more pointedly shows the change from three centuries earlier, when all music was learned by ear and the Frankish kings struggled to make the chant consistent across their lands, or more clearly illustrates how innovations in church music sprang from the desire to carry on tradition.

ECHOES OF HISTORY

The stories in this chapter bear witness to astounding continuities and to the transformation of traditions by new circumstances. Although we do not have any music from the ancient Jews or early Christians, their musical customs resonated through the Middle Ages and beyond to the present. From the Temple and synagogue came the practices of singing psalms and chanting Scripture. Early church leaders, drawing on Greek views of music while rejecting pagan customs, elevated worship over entertainment and singing over instrumental music, attitudes that held sway for centuries and persist today. Attempts by popes and secular rulers to consolidate control and unify their realms led to standardized liturgies and fixed melodies that were assigned to certain texts and days. The adoption by the western church of the eight church modes, based on the Byzantine *echoi*, shows both a link to the eastern church and a desire to systematize and classify the vast repertory of chant. Promoting and preserving that repertory in turn led to notation and solmization, which developed over time and are still part of musical life. Many particular features of Western notation have been around for a millennium, including staff lines, clefs, and notes placed above the text and arranged so that higher notes indicate higher pitches. The invention of a notation that could record pitches and intervals precisely and could be read at sight was decisive in the later evolution of Western music, which more than other musical traditions is not just played and heard, but written and read. Indeed, notation is the very reason why we have a thousand years of music we can still perform and hear, and why books like this can be written.

Almost as important, the codification of Gregorian chant and its diffusion in notation made it the basis for much of the music from the ninth through the sixteenth centuries. That these events took place under the Franks was significant, since Charlemagne's empire was the political and cultural center of western Europe. From his day through the fourteenth century, the most important developments in European music took place in the area he once ruled.

Chapter

3

Roman Liturgy and Chant

Gregorian chant is one of the great treasures of Western civilization. Like Romanesque architecture, it stands as a memorial to religious faith in the Middle Ages, embodying the community spirit and artistic sensibility of the time. This body of chant includes some of the oldest and most beautiful melodies, and it served as the basis for much later music.

As beautiful as the chants are, they cannot be separated from their ceremonial context. We saw in chapter 2 how Gregorian chant was codified and notated after centuries of development as an oral tradition and how it played a unifying role in the western church. In this chapter, we will relate chant to liturgy and see how each chant is shaped by its role, text, and manner of performance. We will also see how new chants and types of chant were added to the authorized liturgical chant during a wave of creativity around the margins of the repertory.

THE ROMAN LITURGY

Gregorian chant is music for religious observances. Tunes vary from simple recitation to elaborate melodies, depending on their role in the liturgy. Thus understanding chant requires some knowledge of the services in which it is used. The Roman liturgy is complex, resulting from a long history of addition and codification that was largely unknown to those who participated in services. This historical framework can help us comprehend both the shape of the liturgy and the diversity of chant.

PURPOSE OF THE LITURGY

The role of the church was to teach Christianity and to save souls. Over the centuries, as missionaries spread the faith across Europe from Spain to Sweden, they taught the basic precepts of Roman church doctrine: the immortality of each person's soul; the Trinity of the Father, Son, and Holy Spirit; Jesus' crucifixion, resurrection, and ascension into heaven; salvation and eternal heavenly life for those whom Jesus judges worthy; and damnation in hell for the rest. This external mission to those not part of the church went hand in hand with an internal mission to those who were. The purpose of religious services was to reinforce these same lessons for worshipers, making clear the path to salvation through the church's teachings. This purpose was served chiefly by the liturgy, the texts that were spoken or sung and the rituals that were performed during each service. The role of the music was to carry those words, accompany those rituals, and inspire the faithful.

CHURCH CALENDAR

Part of teaching Christianity was repeating the stories of Jesus and of the saints, exemplary Christians whom the church raised up as models of faith or action. Every year, the church commemorated each event or saint with a feast day, in a cycle known as the **church calendar.** The most important feasts are Christmas (December 25), marking Jesus' birth, and Easter, celebrating his resurrection and observed on the Sunday after the first full moon of spring. Both are preceded by periods of preparation and penitence: Advent begins four Sundays before Christmas, and Lent starts on Ash Wednesday, forty-six days before Easter.

The church calendar is important for understanding the liturgy. Although much of each religious service is the same at every observance, other aspects change with the day or season.

Figure 3.1: A priest consecrates the wine and bread for communion, the central ritual of the Mass, in an eleventh-century German ivory carving.

MASS

The most important service in the Roman church is the **Mass,** which evolved from commemorations of the Last Supper of Jesus with his disciples (Luke 22:14–20). The central act, shown in Figure 3.1, is a symbolic reenactment of the Last Supper in which a priest consecrates bread and wine, designated as the body and blood of Christ, and offers them to the worshipers in communion. This ritual fulfills Jesus' commandment to "do this in remembrance of me" (1 Corinthians 11:23–26) and reminds all present of his sacrifice for the atonement of sin. Over time, other ritual actions and words were added, including prayers, Bible readings, and psalm-singing, since such gatherings gave priests their principal opportunity to teach the Bible and church doctrine to their largely illiterate congregants. The Mass is performed every day in monasteries, convents, and major churches, on Sundays in all churches, and more than once on the most important feast days.

Figure 3.2 outlines the form of the Mass as it stood by the eleventh century. (For the complete Mass for Christmas Day, see NAWM 3.) The most important musical items, each sung to an independent melody by the choir and its

CD 1|4–23

soloists, are shown in blue. The other items were either intoned (recited to a simple melodic formula) or spoken by the priest or an assistant.

Proper and Ordinary　　The texts for certain parts of the Mass vary from day to day and are collectively called the **Proper of the Mass.** The texts of other parts, called the **Ordinary of the Mass,** do not change, although the melodies may vary. The Proper chants are called by their function, the Ordinary chants by their initial words. The sung portions of the Ordinary were originally performed by the

MUSIC IN CONTEXT

The Experience of the Mass

The Mass was the focal point of medieval religious life. For the illiterate populace, it was their main source of instruction, where they were told what to believe and how to live. It was up to the church to present those fundamental truths in a way that would engage and inspire, gripping not only the mind but also the heart.

The building where Mass was celebrated was designed to evoke awe. Whether a simple rural church or a grand cathedral, it was likely to be the tallest structure most people would ever enter. The high ceiling and windows drew the eye heavenward. Pillars and walls were adorned with sculptures, tapestries, or paintings depicting pious saints, the sufferings of Jesus, or the torments of hell, each image a visual sermon. In these resonant spaces, the spoken word was easily lost, but singing carried words clearly to all corners.

European Christians, especially in central and northern Europe, were not long removed from old pagan customs of propitiating the gods to ensure good crops or prevent misfortune, and they looked to Christian observances to serve the same role. Life for most was hard, and with the constant threat of disease, famine, and war, average life expectancy was under thirty years. Worship in a well-appointed church, conducted by clergy arrayed in colorful vestments, using chalices, crosses, and books bedecked with gold, and singing heavenly chants, offered not only an interlude of beauty, but a way to please God and secure blessings in this life and the next.

In such a space, the Mass begins with the entrance procession of the celebrant (the priest) and his assistants to the altar, incense wafting through the air. The choir sings a psalm, the **Introit** (from Latin for "entrance"). After all are in place, the choir continues with the **Kyrie,** whose threefold invocations of *Kyrie eleison* (Lord have mercy), *Christe eleison* (Christ have mercy), and *Kyrie eleison* capture the hopes of the worshipers and symbolize the Trinity of Father, Son, and Holy Spirit. The Greek words and text repetitions reflect the Kyrie's origins in a Byzantine processional litany, a form in which participants repeat a short prayer in response to a leader. On Sundays and feast days (except in Advent and Lent), there follows the **Gloria,** or **Greater Doxology,** a formula of praise to God that encapsulates the doctrine of the Trinity and again asks for mercy. The priest then intones the Collect, a collective prayer on behalf of all those present.

After these introductory items, the Liturgy of the Word focuses on Bible readings, florid chants, and church teachings. Here the service offers instruction, familiarizing worshipers (at least, those who understand Latin) with the Scriptures and central tenets of the faith. First the subdeacon intones the Epistle for the day, a passage from the letters of the apostles. Next come two elaborate chants sung by a soloist or soloists with responses from the choir: the **Gradual** (from Latin *gradus,* "stairstep," from which it was sung) and the **Alleluia** (from the

Hebrew *Hallelujah*, "praise God"), both based on psalm texts. These chants are the musical high points of the Gregorian Mass, performed when no ritual is taking place and text and music are the center of attention. On some days in the Easter season, the Gradual is replaced by another Alleluia as a sign of celebration; during Lent, the joyful Alleluia is omitted or replaced by the more solemn **Tract**, a florid setting of several verses from a psalm. On some occasions the choir sings a **sequence** after the Alleluia. The deacon then intones the Gospel, a reading from one of the four books of the New Testament that relate the life of Jesus. The priest may offer a sermon, seeking now through words alone to increase the understanding and deepen the commitment of those gathered before him. On Sundays and important feast days, this section of the Mass concludes with the **Credo**, a statement of faith summarizing church doctrine and telling the story of Jesus' crucifixion and resurrection.

In the Liturgy of the Eucharist, the priest turns from words to actions. As he prepares the bread and wine for communion, the choir sings the **Offertory**, a florid chant on a psalm. There follow spoken prayers and the Secret, read in silence by the priest. The Preface, a dialogue between priest and choir leads into the **Sanctus** (Holy, holy, holy), whose text begins with the angelic chorus of praise from the vision of Isaiah (Isaiah 6:3). The priest speaks the Canon, the core of the Mass that includes the consecration of bread and wine. He sings the Lord's Prayer, and the choir sings the **Agnus Dei** (Lamb of God), which like the Kyrie was adapted from a litany. In the medieval Mass, the priest then takes communion, consuming the bread and wine on behalf of all those assembled, rather than sharing it with everyone as was the custom earlier (and again today). After communion, the choir sings the **Communion**, based on a psalm. The priest intones the Postcommunion prayer, and the priest or deacon concludes the service by singing *Ite, missa est* (Go, you are dismissed), with a response by the choir; from this phrase came the Latin name for the entire service, *Missa*, which became the English "Mass." When the Gloria is omitted, *Ite, missa est* is replaced by *Benedicamus Domino* (Let us bless the Lord).

Throughout the Mass, the music serves both to convey the words and engage the worshipers. As St. Basil (ca. 330–379) observed,

> when the Holy Spirit saw that mankind was ill-inclined toward virtue and that we were heedless of the righteous life because of our inclination to pleasure, what did he do? He blended the delight of melody with doctrine in order that through the pleasantness and softness of the sound we might unawares receive what was useful in the words.

	Proper	Ordinary
Introductory Section	1. Introit	
		2. Kyrie
		3. Gloria
	4. Collect	
Liturgy of the Word	5. Epistle	
	6. Gradual	
	7. Alleluia (or Tract)	
	8. Sequence (on major feasts)	
	9. Gospel	
	10. Sermon (optional)	
		11. Credo
Liturgy of the Eucharist	12. Offertory	
		13. Prayers
	14. Secret	
	15. Preface	
		16. Sanctus
		17. Canon
		18. Pater noster (Lord's Prayer)
		19. Agnus Dei
	20. Communion	
	21. Postcommunion	
		22. Ite, missa est

Blue: Sung by choir   Burgundy: Intoned   Green: Spoken

Figure 3.2: The Mass.

congregation, but were later taken over by the choir, which was all male (or, in convents, all female).

Evolution of the Mass

Early forms of the ceremony that became the Mass fell into two parts. The community heard prayers, readings from the Bible, and psalms, often followed by a sermon. Then the catechumens, those receiving instruction in Christian beliefs but not confirmed in the church and thus unable to receive communion, were dismissed, ending the first part. The faithful offered gifts to the church, including bread and wine for the communion. The priest said prayers of thanksgiving, consecrated the bread and wine, and gave communion, accompanied by a psalm. After a final prayer, he dismissed the faithful.

From this outline, the Mass as shown in Figure 3.2 and described in the box on pages 52–53 gradually emerged. The opening greeting was expanded into an introductory section. The first part of the early Mass became the Liturgy of the Word, focused on Bible readings and psalms; the second part became the Liturgy of the Eucharist (from Greek *eucharistein*, "to give thanks"), with offerings and prayers leading to communion. The main musical items of the Ordinary—the Kyrie, Gloria, Credo, Sanctus, and Agnus Dei—were relatively late additions. Ironically, these are now the most familiar portions, because their texts do not change and because almost all compositions called "mass" from the fourteenth century on are settings of these portions only.

THE OFFICE

Early Christians often prayed and sang psalms at regular times throughout the day, in private or public gatherings. These observances were codified in the **Office,** a series of eight services that since the early Middle Ages have been celebrated daily at specified times, as shown in Figure 3.3. The Office was particularly important in monasteries and convents, where Mass and Office observances occupied several hours every day and night. All members of the community sang in the services, taking the roles assigned to the choir or congregation in other churches. Figure 3.4 depicts this central focus of monastic life.

Monasteries and convents in the Roman church followed the liturgy for the Office codified in the *Rule of St. Benedict* (ca. 530), a set of instructions on

Figure 3.3: The Office.

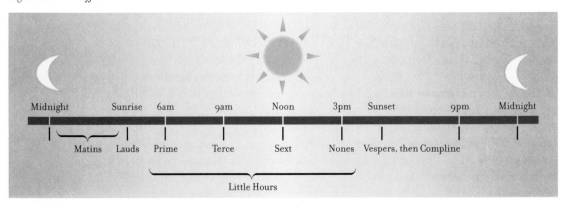

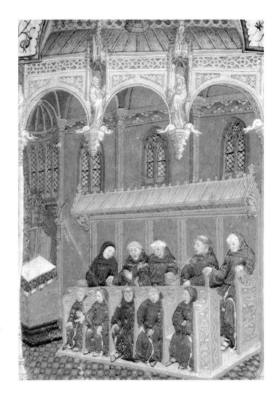

Figure 3.4: Monks and choirboys singing in the choir, celebrating one of the many services that took up most of each day in a monastery. Late-medieval manuscript illumination.

running a monastery. The Office liturgy for churches outside monasteries differed in some respects. Office observances include several psalms, each with an **antiphon,** a chant sung before and after the psalm; lessons (Bible readings) with musical responses called **responsories;** hymns; **canticles,** poetic passages from parts of the Bible other than the Book of Psalms; and prayers. Over the course of a normal week, all 150 psalms are sung at least once. The most important Office services, liturgically and musically, are Matins, Lauds, and Vespers.

LITURGICAL BOOKS

Texts and music for services were gathered in books, copied by scribes in the Middle Ages and later printed under church authority. Texts for the Mass are in a book called the *Missal,* and its chants are in the *Gradual.* Texts for the Office are collected in the *Breviary,* the music in the *Antiphoner* (from "antiphon").

In the late nineteenth and early twentieth centuries, monks of the Bene-dictine Abbey of Solesmes prepared modern editions of the *Gradual* and *Antiphoner* and issued the *Liber usualis* (Book of Common Use), which contains the most frequently used texts and chants for the Mass and Office. The Solesmes editions were adopted as the official books for use in services and are used in most recordings of Gregorian chant. Although these editions re-flect a modern standardization of a repertory that varied over time and from place to place, they provide a good introduction to Gregorian chant and will

Solesmes editions

serve as the basis for the discussion below and in NAWM 3 (Mass) and 4 (Vespers).

CHARACTERISTICS OF CHANT

Gregorian chants are very diverse in style, with varying approaches to performance, treatment of the text, and melodic character. These stylistic differences reflect the disparate functions and histories of the items in the liturgy, and will help guide us through the genres of chant.

Manner of performance

Singers use three manners of performance for chant: **responsorial** (from "response"), in which a soloist alternates with the choir or congregation; **antiphonal** (from Greek for "sound-returning"), in which two groups or halves of the choir alternate; and **direct**, without alternation. Certain genres of chant are traditionally associated with each manner of performance, although the way some chants are sung has changed over time. For example, the Introit and Communion were originally antiphonal psalms, the Gradual and Alleluia responsorial, but by the late Middle Ages all four were performed responsorially.

Text setting

There are also three styles of setting texts. Chants in which almost every syllable has a single note are called **syllabic.** Chants in which syllables carry one to six notes or so are **neumatic** (from "neume"). Long melodic passages on a single syllable are **melismas,** and chants that feature them are **melis-**

TIMELINE: ROMAN LITURGY AND CHANT

500	600	700	800	900	1000	1100	1200

- ca. 530 *Rule of St. Benedict*

884 Notker Balbulus completes *Liber*
Liber hymnorum, book of sequence texts •

late tenth century *Quem queritis in presepe,* trope & liturgical drama •

1000–1300 European population triples •

1014 Credo added to Roman Mass, last major item added •

ca. 1020–50 Wipo?, *Victimae paschali laudes* •

1054 Split between Roman and Byzantine churches •

1066–1200 Taking of monastic orders increases tenfold •

1066 Battle of Hastings: England falls to the Normans •

1095–99 First Crusade •

1146 Adam of St. Victor dies •

ca. 1151 Hildegard of Bingen, *Ordo virtutum* •

1215 Magna Carta signed •

matic. Not every chant can be neatly classified, since chants that are mainly in one style may use another at various points.

Some parts of the Mass and Office are chanted to **recitation formulas,** simple melodic outlines that can be used with many different texts. Other parts of the liturgy are sung to fully formed melodies. The two are not entirely separate, as even complex melodies may be elaborations of an underlying formula.

Recitation formulas and independent melodies

MELODY AND DECLAMATION

Simple or ornate, chant melodies are vehicles for declaiming the words. In the large, reverberant spaces of medieval churches, worshipers could more easily understand words that were sung rather than spoken. The creators of chant made no attempt to express emotions or depict images, as in later opera or song, but their melodies reflect the shape and rhythm of the text. Every chant melody is articulated into phrases and periods corresponding to those of the text. Most phrases resemble an arch, beginning low, rising into a higher range, lingering there, then descending. This parallels the way Latin was spoken. Accented syllables are often set to higher notes. Some syllables are given more notes, lending emphasis through length. But sometimes the reverse is true; melismatic chants may include long melismas on weak sylla- bles and emphasize important words and accents with syllabic settings that stand out in contrast.

GENRES AND FORMS OF CHANT

Given the varied styles and histories of the chants for the Mass and Office, it will be helpful to treat them in broad categories, beginning with syllabic types, proceeding to neumatic and melismatic ones, and considering the Mass Ordinary chants separately at the end. Each type of chant has a distinc- tive form in both text and music, and a particular way to perform it. While ex- amining the chants, we should not lose sight of who sings them and in what places in the liturgy, for these factors explain the differences in musical style.

RECITATION FORMULAS

The simplest chants are the formulas for intoning prayers and Bible readings, such as the Collect, Epistle, and Gospel. Here the music's sole purpose is to project the words clearly, without embellishment, so the formulas are spare and almost entirely syllabic. The text is chanted on a reciting note, usually A or C, with brief motives marking the ends of phrases, sentences, and the entire reading; some formulas also begin phrases with a rise to the reciting note. These recitation formulas are quite old, predating the system of modes, and are not assigned to any mode. They are sung by the priest or an assistant, with occasional responses from the choir or congregation. Priests were not usually trained singers, and they had a lot of text to recite, so it makes sense that their melodies were simple and in a very limited range.

PSALM TONES

Slightly more complex are the **psalm tones,** formulas for singing psalms in the Office. These are designed so they can be adapted to fit any psalm. There is one tone for each of the eight modes, using the mode's tenor as a reciting note; a ninth, very ancient formula has two reciting notes, earning it the name *Tonus peregrinus* ("wandering tone"). These psalm tones are still used today in Catholic, Anglican, and other churches, continuing a practice that is well over twelve hundred years old.

CD 1|24   CD 1|7

Example 3.1 shows the first psalm for Vespers on Christmas Day, *Dixit Dominus* (Psalm 109), using the tone for mode 1 (NAWM 4a). Each psalm tone consists of an **intonation,** a rising motive used only for the first verse; recitation on the tenor; the **mediant,** a cadence for the middle of each verse; further recitation; and a **termination,** a final cadence for each verse. The structure of the music exactly reflects that of the text. Each psalm verse is composed of two statements, the second echoing or completing the first. The mediant cadence marks the end of the first statement, and the termination signals the end of the verse. The last verse of the psalm is followed by the **Lesser Doxology**, a formula of praise to the Trinity (Father, Son, and Holy Spirit), sung to the same psalm tone and shown here as verses 9–10. The addition of this brief text puts the psalm, from the Hebrew Scriptures, firmly into a Christian framework. More elaborate variants of the psalm tones are used for canticles in the Office

CD 1|4

and for the psalm verse in the Introit at Mass (NAWM 3a).

OFFICE ANTIPHONS

An Office psalm or canticle is not complete in itself, but is preceded and followed by an antiphon, resulting in the musical form ABB . . . BBA. Since the

Example 3.1: Office psalm, Dixit Dominus, *Psalm 109 (110)*

Intonation	Tenor	Mediant	Tenor	Termination
1. Di-xit	Dominus	Do-mi-no me - o:	sede a	dex-tris me - is.
2.	Donec ponam ini -	mi - cos tu - os,	scabellum pe -	dum tu - o - rum.
3.	Virgam virtutis tuae emittet Domi-nus	ex Si - on:	dominare in medio inimico -rum tu - o - rum.
. . .				
9.	Gloria	Pa-tri, et Fi - li - o,	et Spiri -	tu - i Sanc - to.
10.	Sicut erat in principio, et	nunc et sem - per,	et in saecula saecu -	lo - rum. A - men.

1. *The Lord says to my Lord: Sit at my right hand.*

2. *Until I make Thy enemies Thy footstool.*

3. *The Lord sends the rod of Thy strength forth from Zion: rule in the midst of Thy enemies.*

. . .

9. *Glory be to the father, and to the Son, and to the Holy Spirit.*

10. *As it was in the beginning, is now, and ever shall be, world without end. Amen.*

cycle of the 150 psalms is sung every week while the antiphon varies with each day in the church calendar, each psalm is framed by many different antiphons during the year. The text of the antiphon, whether from the Bible or newly written, often refers to the event or person being commemorated that day, placing the words of the psalm in a specific ceremonial context.

The mode of the antiphon determines the mode for the psalm tone. On Christmas Day, the first psalm at Vespers is paired with the antiphon *Tecum principium*, shown in Example 3.2 (NAWM 4a). The antiphon is in mode 1, so the psalm tone for mode 1 must be used for the psalm, as in Example 3.1. Because antiphons begin in various ways, medieval singers developed several terminations for each psalm tone, to lead appropriately to different opening notes or gestures. The termination to be used with a particular antiphon is shown at the end of the antiphon, using the vowels for the last six syllables of the Doxology, *E u o u a e* (for *saEcUlOrUm AmEn*), as in Example 3.2. Here the medieval musicians chose G as the most suitable ending note to lead back to the antiphon's opening notes, E–C–D. Thus the psalm tone need not close on the final of the mode, but the antiphon does.

CD 1|24   CD 1|7

Example 3.2: Office antiphon, Tecum principium

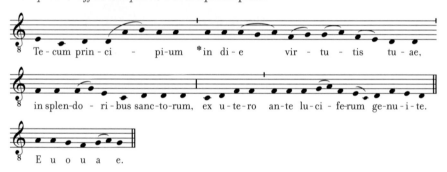

Te - cum prin - ci - pi-um *in di - e vir - tu - tis tu - ae,

in splen-do - ri-bus sanc-to-rum, ex u - te-ro an-te lu-ci - fe-rum ge-nu - i-te.

E u o u a e.

Thine shall be the dominion in the day of Thy strength in the brightness of the Saints:
from the womb before the day star I begot Thee. (Psalm 109:4 [110:3])

The manner of performing psalms and canticles with antiphons has varied over time. Early descriptions include direct performance by soloists, responsorial alternation between a soloist and choir or congregation, and antiphonal alternation between two singers or groups. In medieval monastic practice, the entire community of monks or nuns was divided into two choirs singing the psalm antiphonally, alternating verses or half-verses; the antiphon could be sung by soloists, reading from the *Antiphoner*, or by all, singing from memory. Antiphonal performance was suggested by the division of each psalm verse into two parts, as described above, and encouraged by the layout of medieval churches, with the choir arranged in two sets of stalls flanking the altar, as shown in Figure 3.5.

In most modern performances, the **cantor,** the leader of the choir, sings the opening words of the antiphon to set the pitch (up to the asterisk in modern editions), and the full choir completes the antiphon; the cantor sings the

Performance

Figure 3.5: A mid-fifteenth-century manuscript illumination showing monks singing a memorial service. The choir is seated in two sets of stalls that face each other across the chancel, the area of the church around the altar. Two monks—presumably the cantor, or choir leader, and an assistant—stand in front, leading the singing and probably performing the antiphons.

first half of the first psalm or canticle verse, and half the choir completes it; the two half-choirs alternate verses or half-verses; and the full choir joins together for the reprise of the antiphon.

Style   Office antiphons are simple and mostly syllabic, reflecting their historical association with group singing and the practical fact that over thirty are sung each day, making great length burdensome. Yet they are fully independent melodies. *Tecum principium* (Example 3.2) illustrates the elegance of even simple Gregorian chants. Text phrases and accents are clearly delineated. Each phrase centers around and cadences on important notes of the mode while tracing a unique arch. The opening phrase circles around the final D, rises dramatically to the tenor A, then meanders down to D; the last two phrases both hover around F, then sink to encircle and close on D. Antiphon and psalm tone combine to create a piece with two contrasting styles, free melody and recitation, in which the outer sections emphasize the final, the longer central section the tenor.

OFFICE HYMNS

Hymns are the most familiar type of sacred song, practiced in almost all branches of Christianity from ancient times to the present. The choir sings a hymn in every Office service. Hymns are **strophic,** consisting of several stanzas that are all sung to the same melody. Stanzas may be four to seven lines long, and some include rhymes. Melodies often repeat one or more phrases, producing a variety of patterns.

Like most Gregorian hymns, *Christe Redemptor omnium,* sung at Vespers on Christmas Day (NAWM 4b) and shown in Example 3.3, has one note on most syllables with two or three notes on others. It is in mode 1, and each phrase and the melody as a whole have a shapely rise and fall. The first phrase ascends from C to G and falls to the final D; the second climbs to high C and cadences on the tenor A; the third phrase steps down to E; and the final phrase repeats the first, to close on D. This kind of contour, moving mostly by seconds and thirds to a peak and descending to a cadence, has been typical of western European melodies ever since.

CD 1|8   CD 1|2

Example 3.3: Hymn, Christe Redemptor omnium

Christ, redeemer of all,
One with the Father,
[who] alone, before the beginning,
was born of the Father, [in a way] that cannot be expressed.

ANTIPHONAL PSALMODY IN THE MASS

Psalmody, the singing of psalms, was part of the Mass as well as the Office. In the early Mass, psalms with antiphons were used to accompany actions: the entrance procession and giving communion. Later, these chants—the Introit and Communion—were shifted to come after the rituals rather than accompany them and therefore did not have to be as long as they were originally. Both chants were abbreviated, the Communion to the antiphon alone, the Introit to the antiphon, one psalm verse, Lesser Doxology, and the reprise of the antiphon, for the musical form ABB'A (see NAWM 3a).

CD 1|4

By the later Middle Ages, both the Introit and Communion were performed responsorially, as they typically are today: the cantor begins the antiphon, the choir completes it, and in the Introit soloists and choir alternate for the verse and Doxology, and the whole choir sings the reprise of the antiphon.

Because the greater solemnity of the Mass called for greater musical splendor, Mass antiphons are musically more elaborate than Office antiphons, typically neumatic with occasional melismas. We can see this in Example 3.4, the Communion from Mass for Christmas Day, *Viderunt omnes* (NAWM 3j). In this more ornate style, the characteristics of previous examples are still apparent: articulated phrases; motion mostly by steps and thirds; and arching lines that rise to a peak and sink to the cadence, circling around and closing

CD 1|22

Example 3.4: Communion, Viderunt omnes

Vi - de - runt om - nes * fi - nes ter - rae

Sa-lu - ta - re De - i nos - tri.

All the ends of the earth have seen the salvation of our God.

on important notes in the mode (again mode 1). Here higher notes and longer notegroups emphasize the most important accents and words.

RESPONSORIAL PSALMODY IN OFFICE AND MASS

Early Christians often sang psalms responsorially, with a soloist performing each verse and the congregation or choir responding with a brief refrain. The responsorial psalms of Gregorian chant—the Office responsories and the Gradual, Alleluia, and Offertory in the Mass—stem from this practice. As we will see in later centuries, singers and instrumental virtuosos, given the opportunity, would often add embellishments and display their skill through elaborate passage work. So it should come as no surprise that over the centuries of oral transmission these chants assigned to soloists became the most melismatic. They are the musical peaks of the service, moments when the words for once seem secondary to the expansive melody filling the church.

The different genres of responsorial psalm assumed different configurations. The text was usually shortened to a single psalm verse with a choral **respond** preceding and sometimes following the verse.

Office responsories   Office responsories take several forms, but all include a respond, a verse, and a full or partial repetition of the respond. Matins, celebrated between midnight and sunrise, includes nine Bible readings, each followed by a Great Responsory that ranges from neumatic to melismatic. Several other Office services include a brief Bible reading followed by a Short Responsory that is neumatic rather than melismatic.

Gradual   Graduals are considerably more melismatic than responsories. *Viderunt omnes,* the Gradual for Christmas Day (Example 2.3 and NAWM 3d), contains

CD 1|13   a fifty-two-note melisma on "Dominus" and three other melismas ten to twenty notes long. In some Graduals, the end of the verse repeats or varies the end of the respond. In performance, the cantor begins the respond and the choir completes it; then one or more soloists sing the verse, and the choir joins in on the last phrase. Typically, the respond is not repeated.

Alleluia   Alleluias include a respond on the word "alleluia," a psalm verse, and a repetition of the respond. The final syllable of "alleluia" is extended by an effusive melisma called a **jubilus.** Example 3.5 shows *Alleluia Dies sanctifica-*

CD 1|15   *tus,* from the Mass for Christmas Day (NAWM 3e). The soloist sings the first part of the respond on "alleluia" (to the asterisk), then the choir repeats it (as indicated by *ij*) and continues with the jubilus. The soloist sings the verse, with the choir joining on the last phrase (at the asterisk), then the soloist repeats the first part of the respond, and the choir joins at the jubilus. Often the end of the verse repeats all or part of the respond melody; here, there is instead a varied repetition of the opening of the verse (at "quia hodie descendit lux magna").

Example 3.5: Alleluia Dies sanctificatus

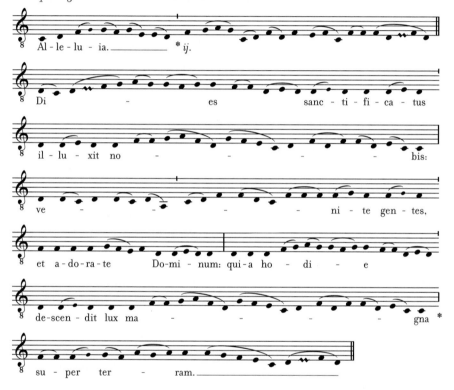

Alleluia. Alleluia.
A sanctified day has shone upon us; come Gentiles, and adore the Lord; for this day a
*   great light has descended upon the earth.*

Despite the longer and more effusive melody, the characteristics seen in other chants are evident, including articulated phrases, motion primarily by steps and thirds, and gently arching contours. This chant is in mode 2, the plagal mode on D. It ranges an octave from low A to high A, centers on the tenor F in several places, cadences most often on D or the C below it, and ends both respond and verse on D. There are several long melismas, most focused around F and D, and some passages that resemble recitation. But underneath the intricacies is the same sense of a melodic curve as in syllabic and neumatic chants.

Offertory

CD 1|19

Offertories are as melismatic as Graduals but include the respond only (see NAWM 3g). In the Middle Ages, they were performed during the offering of bread and wine, with a choral respond and two or three very ornate verses sung by a soloist, each followed by the second half of the respond. When the ceremony was curtailed, the verses were dropped.

Tract

Tracts (from Latin *tractus*, "drawn out") are the longest chants in the liturgy, with several psalm verses set in very florid style. Though now often performed like Graduals, they were originally direct solo psalmody, with no responses and thus no respond. Instead, each verse combines recitation with florid melismas. The sequence of cadences, the melodic outline, and many of the melismas are shared between verses and between different Tracts in the same mode, indicating that the written melodies resulted from a tradition of oral composition based on formulas (see chapter 2 and Example 2.1).

In all these chants derived from responsorial or direct psalmody, we see the hallmarks of solo performance: long, virtuosic melismas that show off the voice, and passages that resemble improvised embellishment of a simple melodic outline. All but the Offertory are attached to Bible readings, ornamenting and thereby honoring that most holy text in a musical parallel to the colorful illuminations that decorate medieval Bible manuscripts.

CHANTS OF THE MASS ORDINARY

The sung portions of the Mass Ordinary were originally performed by the congregation to simple syllabic melodies. As church leaders changed the Mass and reduced the congregation's participation, the choir took over singing these chants. From the ninth century on, church musicians composed many new, more ornate melodies for the Ordinary, suitable for performance by trained singers. These chants tend to be in a later style than most Proper chants, with clearer pitch centers and more melodic repetition. The musical forms used in Ordinary chants vary, but often reflect the shape of their texts. We will consider these types of chant in order, from syllabic to melismatic.

Gloria and Credo

CD 1|18

CD 1|12

The Credo (see NAWM 3f) was always set in syllabic style because it has the longest text and because, as the statement of faith, it was the last to be reassigned to the choir. The Gloria also has a long text, but most settings are neumatic (see NAWM 3c). Gloria and Credo melodies often feature recurring motives but have no set form. In both cases, the priest intones the opening words and the choir completes the chant.

Sanctus and Agnus Dei

CD 1|20

CD 1|21   CD 1|6

Most melodies for the Sanctus and Agnus Dei are neumatic. Their texts include repetition, so melodies composed for them often have musical repetition as well. The Sanctus (see NAWM 3h) begins with the word "Sanctus" (Holy) stated three times, and the third statement often echoes the music for the first. The second and third sections of the text both end with the phrase "Hosanna in excelsis" (Hosanna in the highest) and often are set to variants of the same music (producing the form ABB′) or use the same melody for the Hosanna (creating the form A BC DC). The Agnus Dei (see NAWM 3i) states a prayer three times, altering the final words the last time. Some settings use the same music for all three statements (AAA); others are in ABA form or close all three sections with the same music (AB CB DB).

The Kyrie is even more repetitive, with three statements each of "Kyrie eleison," "Christe eleison," and "Kyrie eleison." The brief text invites a florid setting, and most settings have melismas on the last syllables of "Kyrie" and "Christe" and the first syllable of "eleison." The text repetition is reflected in a variety of musical forms, such as AAA BBB AAA', AAA BBB CCC' (as in NAWM 3b), or ABA CDC EFE'. The Kyrie is usually performed antiphonally, with half-choirs alternating statements. The final "Kyrie" is often extended by a phrase, allowing each half-choir to sing a phrase before both join on the final "eleison."

Kyrie

CD 1|8   CD 1|2

Starting in the thirteenth century, scribes often grouped Ordinary chants in **cycles,** with one setting of each text except the Credo. Similar cycles appear in the *Liber usualis.* Although there were many melodies for *Ite, missa est* in the Middle Ages, in the *Liber usualis* cycles this is set to the melody of the first Kyrie.

Cycles of Ordinary chants

STYLE, USE, AND HISTORY

Each type of chant is unique, reflecting its role and history. Recitation formulas were valued for their ability to project the words clearly in large spaces and for being easy to memorize and apply to many texts. Antiphons and hymns added melodic interest, and during Mass the neumatic chants of the choir adorned the service. Melismatic chants were valued for their decorative beauty and became the jewels of the liturgy, sung by soloists and choir when no ritual actions competed for attention. When revisions in the liturgy changed the function of a chant or who performed it, musicians responded by changing its form or style, as when the Introit and Communion were shortened, or when more ornate melodies were written for the Ordinary chants after they were reassigned to the choir.

But all these chants also shared a common history with ancient roots. Their creators drew on psalm texts, continuing Jewish practice as adapted by early Christians; used modes and melodic formulas, as in the Jewish, Near Eastern, and Byzantine traditions; and emphasized correct phrasing and declamation of the text, borrowing from classical Latin rhetoric. Both the diversity of the chant repertory and the melodic and structural features most chants share become more apparent when we know the histories of plainchant as a whole and of the many individual types of chant.

ADDITIONS TO THE AUTHORIZED CHANTS

Even after the chant repertory was standardized in the eighth and ninth centuries, church musicians continued to add to it. Besides composing new melodies for the Mass Ordinary, they supplied music whenever a new Saint's day or other feast was added to the calendar, creating new chants or adapting existing ones for the day's Mass Proper and Office antiphons. Moreover, they developed three new types of chant, all additions to the liturgy authorized by Rome: tropes, sequences, and liturgical dramas.

TROPE

A **trope** expanded an existing chant in one of three ways: by adding (1) new words and music before the chant and often between phrases; (2) melody only, extending melismas or adding new ones; or (3) text only (usually called *prosula*, or "prose"), set to existing melismas. The first type was by far the most common, used especially with Introits and Glorias. All three types increased the solemnity of a chant by enlarging it, and all offered musicians an outlet for creativity in the margins of the authorized repertory, paralleling the way medieval scribes embellished books with marginal decorations. Moreover, the added words provided a gloss, interpreting the chant text and usually linking it more closely to the occasion. For example, the Introit antiphon for Christmas Day (NAWM 3a) used a text from the Old Testament, a passage Christians view as a prophecy of Jesus' birth (Isaiah 9:6). Prefacing it with a trope text (here in italics) made this interpretation explicit:

> *God the Father today sent his Son into the world, for which we say, rejoicing with the prophet:* A child is born to us, and a Son is given to us: . . .

CD 1|30

Two other tropes to this same Introit appear in NAWM 6: a brief dialogue, *Quem queritis in presepe* (discussed below), and a textless melisma that embellishes the end of the antiphon.

Tropes were typically sung by soloists and set neumatically to fit with the chant to which they were attached, sometimes borrowing melodic figures from the chant. Musicians in France, Germany, Italy, and England composed hundreds of tropes, some adopted widely but most sung only in certain locales.

Trope composition flourished especially in monasteries during the tenth and eleventh centuries. The use of tropes declined during the twelfth century, and all were banned by the Council of Trent (1545–63; see chapter 10) in the interest of simplifying and standardizing the liturgy. Tropes testify to the desire among medieval church musicians to embellish the authorized chant by adding music and words. This is of crucial importance for the development of polyphony, which embodies the same impulse.

SEQUENCE

The **sequence** was a genre popular from the late ninth through the twelfth centuries. Sequences are set syllabically to a text that is mostly in couplets and are sung after the Alleluia at Mass. The origin of the sequence is uncertain, but it derives its name and place in the liturgy from an earlier practice called *sequentia* (Latin for "something that follows"), a melisma that replaced the jubilus at the end of an Alleluia. Composers of sequences sometimes drew melodic material from an Alleluia, but most melodies were newly composed. Manuscript collections of sequences customarily present them in two forms, with text and as extended melismas on "Alleluia." These connections to the Alleluia convinced some historians that sequences originated when scribes

SOURCE READING

NOTKER BALBULUS ON WRITING SEQUENCES

The most famous early writer of sequence texts, Notker Balbulus ("the stammerer," ca. 840–912), a Frankish monk at the monastery of St. Gall in Switzerland, explained how he learned to write words syllabically under long melismas. He appears to be describing the practice of writing new texts for existing sequence melodies. Though historians once interpreted this as a description of the invention of the sequence, it is clear that Notker is refining a practice that developed elsewhere.

——— • ———

When I was still young, and very long melodies—repeatedly entrusted to memory—escaped from my poor little head, I began to reason with myself how I could bind them fast.

In the meantime it happened that a certain priest from Jumièges (recently laid waste by the Normans) came to us, bringing with him his antiphonary, in which some verses had been set to sequences; but they were in a very corrupt state. Upon closer inspection I was as bitterly disappointed in them as I had been delighted at first glance.

Nevertheless, in imitation of them I began to write *Laudes Deo concinat orbis universus, qui gratis est redemptus,* and further on *Colu-* *ber adae deceptor.* When I took these lines to my teacher Iso, he, commending my industry while taking pity on my lack of experience, praised what was pleasing, and what was not he set about to improve, saying, "The individual motions of the melody should receive separate syllables." Hearing that, I immediately corrected those which fell under *ia;* those under *le* or *lu,* however, I left as too difficult; but later, with practice, I managed it easily—for example in "Dominus in Sina" and "Mater." Instructed in this manner, I soon composed my second piece, *Psallat ecclesia mater illibata.*

When I showed these little verses to my teacher Marcellus, he, filled with joy, had them copied as a group on a roll; and he gave out different pieces to different boys to be sung. And when he told me that I should collect them in a book and offer them as a gift to some eminent person, I shrank back in shame, thinking I would never be able to do that.

Notker Balbulus, Preface to *Liber hymnorum* (Book of Hymns), trans. in Richard Crocker, *The Early Medieval Sequence* (Berkeley and Los Angeles: University of California Press, 1977), 1.

set new, syllabic texts to Alleluia melodies, but this is not the case. However, new texts were often written for existing sequence melodies (see Source Reading).

Most sequences consist of an initial single sentence; a series of paired sentences or phrases; and a final unpaired sentence. Within each pair, the two sentences or phrases generally have the same number of syllables and are set to the same music. Both syllable count and music change for each new pair, creating the form A BB CC . . . N. The length of the paired phrases tends to rise or fall in a simple pattern. The tonal focus is usually clear, with most phrases ending on the modal final. These characteristics are evident in the Easter sequence *Victimae paschali laudes* (NAWM 5), attributed to Wipo (ca. 995–ca. 1050), chaplain to the Holy Roman Emperor. In the twelfth century, rhymed poetry in lines of even length became more common for sequences, as in those by Adam of St. Victor in Paris (d. 1146), and many sequences lacked the unpaired phrases at beginning and end.

Form

CD 1|29   CD 1|11

Like tropes, sequences embellished the liturgy and provided an outlet for creativity. Some were widely used, but local practice varied. Seeking greater uniformity, the Council of Trent banned most sequences, retaining only four of the best known, including *Victimae paschali laudes* and the sequence from the Requiem (Mass for the Dead), *Dies irae.*

LITURGICAL DRAMA

Some tropes took the form of dialogues. Among the earliest was the tenth-century *Quem queritis in sepulchro*, preceding the Introit for Easter. In the dialogue, the three Marys come to Jesus' tomb, and the angel asks them, "Whom do you seek in the sepulcher?" They reply, "Jesus of Nazareth," to which the angel answers, "He is not here, He is risen as He said; go and proclaim that He has risen from the grave" (Mark 16:5–7). Accounts from the period show that this dialogue was sung responsively and accompanied by appropriate dramatic action. *Quem queritis in presepe* (NAWM 6), a late-tenth-century trope to the Introit for Mass on Christmas Day, functions in a similar way. The midwives at Christ's birth ask the shepherds who come to admire the child whom they seek. The shepherds answer that they are looking for the Savior, the infant Christ.

CD 1|30

Such dialogues and more elaborate plays in Latin have become known as **liturgical dramas.** Although not strictly part of the liturgy, they were linked to it, recorded in liturgical books, and performed in church, with processions and stylized actions. The Easter and Christmas plays were the most common and were performed all over Europe. Several other plays survive from the twelfth century and later, including the early-thirteenth-century *Play of Daniel* from Beauvais (north of Paris) and *The Slaughter of the Innocents*, from the Benedictine monastery of Fleury in central France. The music for these plays consists of a number of chants strung together, sometimes joined by songs in more secular styles. All parts, even women's roles, were usually sung by the male clergy and choir, except in a few locales where nuns participated.

HILDEGARD OF BINGEN

Women were excluded from the priesthood, and as the choir took over the singing in services, women were silenced in church. But in convents—separate communities of officiating at religious women—they could hold positions of leadership, except for officiating at Mass, and participate fully in singing and composing music. As in monasteries, convent life revolved around singing the eight daily Office services and Mass. Here women learned to read Latin and music and had access to an intellectual life available to few outside convent walls.

In this context, Hildegard of Bingen (1098–1179) achieved great success as prioress and abbess of her own convent and as a writer and composer (see Figure 3.6 and biography). Most of her songs praise the Virgin Mary, the

HILDEGARD OF BINGEN (1098–1179)

Born to a noble family in Bermersheim in the Rhine region of Germany, Hildegard at age eight was consecrated to the church by her parents. Six years later she took vows at the Benedictine monastery of Disiboden-berg, becoming prioress of the attached convent in 1136. Led by a vision, she founded her own convent around 1150 at Rupertsberg near Bingen, where she was abbess.

Famous for her prophecies, Hildegard corresponded with emperors, kings, popes, and bishops and preached throughout Germany. Her many prose works include *Scivias* (Know the Ways, 1141–51), an acount of twenty-six visions, and books on science and healing.

Hildegard wrote religious poems as well as prose, and by the 1140s she began setting them to music. Her songs are preserved in two manuscripts organized in a liturgical cycle, with indications that many were sung in her convents and nearby monasteries and churches. Her *Ordo virtutum* (The Vir-

Figure 3.6: Hildegard of Bingen with Volmar, a monk who assisted her in recording her visions, in an illustration from Scivias.

tues, ca. 1151) is the earliest surviving music drama *not* attached to the liturgy. In a male-dominated church with a prescribed liturgy and repertory of chant, Hildegard had to make a place in the margins, for herself and for her compositions.

MAJOR WORKS: Ordo virtutum, *43 antiphons, 18 responsories, 7 sequences, 4 hymns, 5 other chants*

Trinity, or local saints. Her works vary from syllabic hymns and sequences to highly melismatic responsories. The sequences are unusual in that the paired lines often differ in syllable count and accent, and Hildegard varies the music accordingly. Most striking is the great individuality of Hildegard's melodies. Many exceed the range of an octave by a fourth or fifth. She repeatedly uses a small repertoire of melodic figures in constant variation. Some patterns derive from chant, such as a rising fifth and stepwise descent, or circling around a cadential note; others are extraordinary, such as successive leaps and other patterns that quickly span an octave or more. The music serves to prolong the words, encouraging contemplation of their meaning through sung prayer.

Hildegard's most extended musical work is *Ordo virtutum* (The Virtues, ca. 1151), a sacred music drama in verse with eighty-two songs. It is a morality play with allegorical characters such as the Prophets, the Virtues, the Happy Soul, the Unhappy Soul, and the Penitent Soul. All sing in plainchant except the Devil, who can only speak; the absence of music symbolizes his separation

Ordo virtutum

CD 1|33   CD 1|12

Reputation

from God. The final chorus of the Virtues (NAWM 7) is typical of Hildegard's expansive and individual melodies.

Hildegard claimed that her songs, like her prose writings, were divinely inspired. At a time when women were forbidden to instruct or supervise men, having a reputation for direct communication from God was the only way she could be heard outside the convent. She was renowned as a visionary, but her music, like that of countless other composers, was apparently known only locally. Her writings were edited and published in the nineteenth century, her music only in the late twentieth when she was rediscovered in the search to reclaim the history of music by women. She quickly became the most recorded and best-known composer of sacred monophony, and one of very few known to have written both the music and the words.

THE CONTINUING PRESENCE OF CHANT

Gregorian chant was important in itself and for its influence on other music. It was used in Christian services throughout central and western Europe until the Reformation and in Catholic areas after that. Almost everyone in these areas heard it at least weekly. Chant was reformed in the late sixteenth and early seventeenth centuries and again in the late nineteenth and early twentieth centuries. But the Second Vatican Council of 1962–65, in an effort to engage congregations more directly in worship, permitted holding Catholic services in local languages rather than in Latin. Chant was no longer prescribed, and it has virtually disappeared from regular Catholic services, replaced by new tunes with vernacular texts. In the late twentieth century, chant was practiced mostly in monasteries and convents or performed in concerts, and was known mainly through recordings. One recording by the Benedictine monks of Santo Domingo de Silos in Spain, titled simply *Chant*, was the best-selling CD in Europe for over six months in 1993 and was a bestseller in the United States as well.

From the ninth through the thirteenth centuries, chant formed the foundation for most polyphonic music, and it continued to play a leading role in polyphonic sacred music well into the sixteenth century. The diversity already inherent in chant, from the contrast between syllabic and melismatic styles to the various modes, was reflected in similar diversity in later service music. From the beginning of the Reformation, composers adapted many chants for use as chorale or hymn tunes in the Protestant churches. During the nineteenth and twentieth centuries, composers frequently used chant melodies, in secular as well as sacred music.

Yet the importance of Gregorian chant for later music goes beyond its presence in pieces directly based on it. Chant was part of the musical world of most Europeans for over a thousand years, and it deeply influenced their sense of how melodies should be shaped and how music should go. All later music in the Western tradition wears its imprint.

Chapter

4

Song and Dance Music
in the Middle Ages

Gregorian chant was a revered tradition, preserved in notation, taught in church schools, and discussed in treatises. Outside the church, few in the Middle Ages could read music, and except among the aristocratic and educated elites, secular music was seldom written down or written about. For most people, music was purely aural, and most of the secular and nonliturgical music they heard, sang, and played has vanished. What survives are several hundred monophonic songs, many poems sung to melodies now lost, a few dance tunes, descriptions of music-making, pictures of musicians playing various instruments, and a few actual instruments. From these we can learn how music was used and can identify several important repertories, including the songs of the troubadours and trouvères in France and the Minnesinger in Germany; the Italian lauda and Spanish cantiga; and dance music. In these songs and dances we can see reflections of medieval society and discover traits common in European music ever since.

EUROPEAN SOCIETY, 800–1300

Medieval music was shaped by currents in the wider society: political developments, the emergence of nations and linguistic regions, economic growth, social class, and support for learning and the arts.

By the ninth century, three principal successors to the Roman Empire emerged. The most direct successor was the Byzantine Empire in Asia Minor and southeastern Europe. The strongest and most vibrant was the Arab world, which from the founding of the Islamic religion around 610

Figure 4.1: Europe in 1050.

by Muhammad (ca. 570–632) rapidly expanded to conquer a vast territory from modern-day Pakistan through the Middle East, North Africa, and Spain. The weakest, poorest, and most fragmented of the three was western Europe. In this context, Charlemagne's coronation in 800 as emperor in Rome marked an assertion of continuity with the Roman past, independence from the Byzantine East, and confidence in the future of civilization in western Europe.

European culture owes much to all three empires. The Byzantines preserved Greek and Roman science, architecture, and culture. Most writings that survive from ancient Greece exist only because Byzantine scribes recopied them. The Arabs extended Greek philosophy and science, fostered trade and industry, and contributed to medicine, chemistry, technology, and mathematics. Arab rulers were patrons of literature, architecture, and other arts. Charlemagne also promoted learning and artistic achievement. He improved education, encouraging primary schools in monasteries and cathedral towns throughout his realm. By sponsoring scholarship and the arts, Charlemagne and his son Louis the Pious (r. 814–43) made their courts into centers for intellectual and cultural life, setting a pattern for Western rulers that endured for a thousand years.

After Louis's death, his empire was divided. Over the next few centuries the modern European nations began to emerge, although their boundaries changed frequently. Figure 4.1 shows the situation around 1050. The western part of the empire became France. Until about 1200, the French king was relatively weak, directly ruling only the area around Paris, while other regions were governed by nobles who owed nominal allegiance to the king but often acted independently. Their courts provided opportunities for poets and musicians, nurturing the troubadours and trouvères (see below). In the eastern part of the empire, German kings claimed the title of emperor as Charlemagne's successors. Their realm, eventually known as the Holy Roman Empire, included non-German lands as well, from the Netherlands to northern Italy. The regional nobility and cities in the Empire had considerable autonomy, and by 1250 real power lay in the hands of hundreds of local princes, dukes, bishops, and administrators. They competed for prestige by hiring the best singers, instrumentalists, and composers, which fueled the development of music until the nineteenth century. Outside the former Frankish lands, a centralized kingdom emerged in England in the late ninth century and continued after the Norman Conquest of England in 1066. Italy remained fragmented among several rulers including the pope, and Spain was divided between Christian kingdoms in the north and Muslim lands in the south. The Crusades, a series of campaigns between 1095 and 1270 to retake Jerusalem from the Turks, ultimately failed but showed the growing confidence and military power of western Europe.

Amid these political developments, western Europe saw remarkable economic progress. Technological advances in agriculture and an expansion of lands under cultivation led to great growth in production. Increasing the food supply raised the standard of living and allowed the population to triple between 1000 and 1300. From about 1050 on, water-powered mills and windmills provided mechanical power for milling grain, manufacturing goods, and other uses, further boosting productivity. By 1300, western Europe had surpassed the Byzantine Empire and the Islamic world in economic strength.

The medieval economy was largely agricultural, and the population mostly rural. Society was organized into three broad classes, as shown in Figure 4.2: the nobility and knights, who controlled the land and fought the wars; priests, monks, and nuns, who prayed; and peasants, the vast majority of the population, who worked the land and served the nobles. But by the twelfth century, trade in food and other products promoted the growth of markets, towns, and cities, although the largest cities were still small in modern terms: in 1300, Paris had about 200,000 residents, London about 70,000, Venice, Milan, and Florence about 100,000 each. In every city, independent artisans made products from shoes to paintings, organizing themselves into groups called "guilds" to protect their interests by regulating production, pricing, apprenticeship,

The changing map of Europe

Figure 4.2: The three "estates," or classes, of medieval society: the nobility, who governed and waged war; the clergy, who prayed; and the peasants, who worked the land controlled by the nobles. Fourteenth-century French manuscript illumination from a Latin translation of Aristotle's Politics.

and competition. Together with doctors, lawyers, and merchants, these artisans constituted a new middle class, between nobles and peasants.

Learning and the arts

Prosperity provided resources for learning and the arts. From 1050 to 1300, cathedral schools were established throughout western and central Europe, teaching future church officials Latin grammar, rhetoric, and music. After 1200, independent schools for laymen spread rapidly as well, fostering a more secular culture and a tremendous rise in literacy. Women were excluded from most schools, but many were taught to read at home. From the twelfth century on, universities were founded in Bologna, Paris, Oxford, and other cities, teaching liberal arts, theology, law, and medicine. Works of Aristotle and other important writers were translated from Greek and Arabic into Latin. Western scholars such as Roger Bacon and St. Thomas Aquinas made new contributions to science and philosophy. Writers in Latin and vernacular languages wrote epic, lyric, and narrative poems that grew increasingly independent from ancient models. Much of this poetry was sung, forming the repertories of medieval song.

LATIN AND VERNACULAR SONG

Versus and conductus

One type of Latin song, called **versus** (singular and plural), was normally sacred and sometimes attached to the liturgy. The poetry was rhymed and usually followed a regular pattern of accents. Monophonic versus appeared in the eleventh century, particularly in Aquitaine in southwestern France, and they influenced two other repertories from the same region, troubadour songs (see below) and Aquitanian polyphony (see chapter 5). A related type, **conductus** (singular and plural), originated in the twelfth century as a song that was performed while a liturgical book was carried into place for a reading or a celebrant was "conducted" from one place to another. Later, the term was used for any serious Latin song with a rhymed, rhythmical text on any subject, sacred or secular (other than a hymn or sequence). Both versus and conductus used newly composed melodies not based on chant.

Latin secular songs

Latin was no longer anyone's native tongue, but educated people spoke and understood it. Many Latin songs were composed for performance outside religious contexts, including settings of ancient poetry, laments for Charlemagne and other notables, and satirical, moralizing, or amorous songs. The music, when preserved at all, is usually in staffless neumes that cannot be transcribed unless the melody appears elsewhere in more precise notation.

Goliard songs

Among medieval Latin songs are the so-called **goliard songs** from the late tenth through thirteenth centuries, associated with wandering students and clerics known as goliards. Topics vary from religious and moral themes to satire and celebrations of love, spring, eating, drinking, and other earthly pleasures. The poems show breadth of learning and address an educated audience, and poets who can be identified include respected teachers and courtiers; this suggests that the dissolute way of life celebrated by some songs may be more pose than reality.

VERNACULAR SONG

Many songs were composed in medieval French, English, German, Italian, Spanish, and other vernacular languages. Most pieces are lost; the common people were illiterate, and their work songs, dance songs, lullabies, laments, and other songs have disappeared. There are almost no descriptions of musical life in rural areas, where nine-tenths of the population lived. A few street cries and folk songs are preserved, like flies in amber, only because they were quoted in polyphonic music written for educated audiences.

One type of vernacular poem that survived is the epic, a long heroic narrative. Many were transmitted orally before being written down. The **chanson de geste** ("song of deeds") was an epic in the northern French vernacular recounting the deeds of national heroes and sung to simple melodic formulas. The most famous chanson de geste is the *Song of Roland* (ca. 1100), about a battle of Charlemagne's army against the Muslims in Spain. About one hundred other chansons de geste exist, most from the twelfth century, but little of the music was preserved. Epics in other lands, like the Old English *Beowulf* (eighth century), the Norse eddas (ca. 800–1200), and the German *Song of the Nibelungs* (thirteenth century), were likely also sung, but the music was never written down.

Epics

TIMELINE: EUROPEAN SOCIETY: 800–1300

800	900	1000	1100	1200	1300

• 843 Death of Louis the Pious, Charlemagne's empire divided

• ca. 1050 Windmills and water-powered mills provide mechanical power

• 1066 Normans conquer England

• 1095–99 First Crusade

• ca. 1100 *Song of Roland*

12th cent. Cult of Virgin Mary begins •

12th cent. Universities of Bologna, Paris, and Oxford established •

ca. 1151 Hildegard of Bingen, *Ordo virtutum* •

ca. 1170s Bernart de Ventadorn, *Can vei la lauzeta mover* •

ca. 1200 Comtessa de Dia, *A chantar* •

1208 Pope Innocent III declares crusade against Albigensians •

1215 Magna Carta signed by King John of England •

1225–1274 St. Thomas Aquinas •

ca. 1228 Walther von der Vogelweide, *Palästinalied* •

1270 Seventh Crusade •

ca. 1270–90 *Cantigas de Santa Maria* •

ca. 1284 Adam de la Halle, *Jeu de Robin et de Marion* •

Figure 4.3: Jongleur playing a fiddle while accompanying a dancing bear. French painting on glass, ca. 1350, from the abbey of Jumièges.

MINSTRELS AND OTHER PROFESSIONAL MUSICIANS

As in any age, many people in the Middle Ages must have sung and played music for their own enjoyment or for their friends. Yet there were also professional musicians of various kinds, whose history remains partly obscured by scarce records. Poet-singers, called **bards** in Celtic lands, sang epics at banquets and other occasions, accompanying themselves on harp, fiddle, or similar instrument. **Jongleurs** (from the same root as English "jugglers") traveled alone or in groups, earning a precarious living by performing tricks, telling stories, and singing or playing instruments. Figure 4.3 shows a dancing bear accompanied by a jongleur playing a fiddle. By the thirteenth century, the term **minstrel** (from Latin *minister*, "servant") was used for more specialized musicians, many of whom were employed at a court or city for at least part of the year, although they also traveled. Unlike jongleurs, minstrels came from varied backgrounds, ranging from former clerics to sons of merchants, craftsmen, or knights.

TROUBADOUR AND TROUVÈRE SONG

The most significant body of vernacular song in the Middle Ages was the lyric tradition cultivated in courts and cities under aristocratic sponsorship. The tradition began in the twelfth century with the **troubadours** (from Occitan *trobador*, feminine **trobairitz**), poet-composers in southern France whose language was Occitan, and spread north to the **trouvères,** whose language was Old French. The two languages, whose ranges are shown in Figure 4.4, were also called *langue d'oc* and *langue d'oïl* after their respective words for "yes" (*oïl* = *oui*, yes); *trobar* and *trover* were their words for "to compose a song," which later came to mean "to invent" or "to find."

The many castles and courts throughout France supported the troubadours and trouvères. Their lives are recounted in somewhat fanciful biographies called *vidas* (lives), often our only source of information about them. Some were nobles themselves, such as the first troubadour whose songs we have, Guillaume IX, duke of Aquitaine (1071–1126), and the trobairitz Comtessa de Dia (Countess of Dia, fl. late twelfth and early thirteenth centuries). Some were born to servants at court, as was Bernart de Ventadorn (?ca. 1130–ca. 1200), one of the best-known and most influential troubadours, shown in Figure 4.5. Others came from families of merchants, craftsmen, or even jongleurs, accepted into aristocratic circles because of their accomplishments in poetry and music and their adoption of the value system and behavior practiced at court.

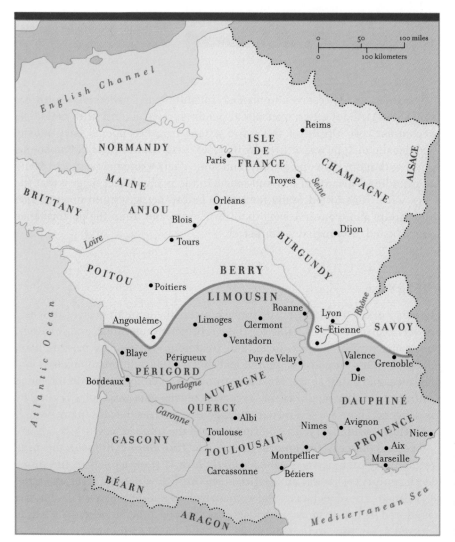

Figure 4.4: Linguistic boundary between Occitan (langue d'oc) in the south of France and Medieval French (langue d'oïl) in the north.

Figure 4.5: Bernart de Ventadorn, as depicted in a thirteenth-century manuscript of troubadour songs.

The songs were preserved in manuscript anthologies called **chansonniers** (songbooks). About 2,600 troubadour poems survive, a tenth with melodies; by contrast, two-thirds of the 2,100 extant trouvère poems have music. Whether the melody was written by the poet is not always clear. Some poems appear with more than one melody, and some poets wrote new words to existing melodies. Variants of text and music in the manuscripts suggest that the songs were transmitted orally for a time before being written down. Some troubadours and trouvères sang their own songs, but often the performance was entrusted to a jongleur or minstrel.

POETRY

The songs of the troubadours and trouvères were the fountainhead of all Western vernacular poetry. Notable for their refinement, elegance, and intricacy, the poems vary in subject, form, and treatment. Love songs predominate, joined by songs on political, moral, and literary topics, dramatic ballads and dialogues, and dance songs. Most are strophic, and dance songs often include a **refrain**—a recurring phrase or verse with music—that was typically sung by the dancers. There are several particular genres, such as the *alba* (dawn-song), *canso* (love-song), and *tenso* (debate-song) of the troubadours.

Fin' amors and fine amour   A central theme is **fin' amors** (Occitan), or **fine amour** (French), meaning "refined love" (sometimes called **courtly love**, a term coined in the nineteenth century). This was an idealized love through which the lover was himself refined. The object was a real woman, usually another man's wife, but she was adored from a distance, with discretion, respect, and humility. The lady is depicted as so lofty and unattainable that she would step out of character if she condescended to reward her faithful lover. Thus Bernart de Ventadorn writes in *Can vei la lauzeta mover* (NAWM 8) the classic lover's complaint:

CD 1|36   CD 1|15

> Alas! I thought I knew so much
> of love, and I know so little;
> for I cannot help loving a lady
> from whom I shall never obtain any favor.
> She has taken away my heart and myself,
> and herself and the whole world;
> and when she left me, I had nothing left
> but desire and a yearning heart.

Such poetry evokes the longing and fluctuating moods familiar from later portrayals of unfulfilled romantic love, but it also serves another purpose: by playing on common themes in fresh ways through artfully constructed lyrics, the poet demonstrates his refinement and eloquence. Since these were the two principal requirements for success in aristocratic circles, the entire genre of poetry and song was more fiction than fact, addressed as much to other men as to women, and rewarded not by love but by social status.

Women poets adopted similar language, yet their poems often seem more direct and realistic. *A chantar* (NAWM 9), shown in Example 4.1, is the only song by a trobairitz to survive with music. In it, the Countess of Dia laments her lover's deception while defending her own virtue, intelligence, courtesy, and beauty.

CD 1|37

MELODIES

Troubadour and trouvère songs are strophic, setting each stanza to the same melody. Text-setting is mostly syllabic with occasional groups of notes, especially on the penultimate syllable of a line. The melodic range is narrow, seldom over a ninth. Secular musicians did not conceive their melodies in terms of the church modes, and some do not fit within any mode; yet most do, with modes 1 and 7 especially common. Many songs make their mode clear throughout, while in others it may remain ambiguous until the end. Most troubadour melodies have new music for each phrase in the stanza, but Bernart de Ventadorn often repeats one or more phrases, and AAB form occurs in some troubadour melodies and most trouvère songs.

A chantar illustrates these characteristics. Its seven-line stanzas are set to phrases in the pattern ab ab cdb, for an AAB form in which A and B share a musical rhyme. Melodic motion is primarily stepwise within an octave range, with frequent high points on the note A and cadences on D clearly indicating mode 1.

Usually the notation does not indicate rhythm, except in some late manuscripts. Some scholars maintain that the melodies were sung in a free, unmeasured style; others that each note or each syllable should have a roughly equal duration; and still others that the songs were sung metrically, with long and short notes corresponding to the accented and unaccented syllables, although there is disagreement on how to apply meter to syllables with more

Rhythm

Example 4.1: Comtessa de Dia, A chanter

1. A chan - tar m'er de so qu'ieu non vol - ri - a
2. tant me ran - cur de lui cui sui a - mi - a,
3. car ieu l'am mais que nui - lla ren que si - a;
4. vas lui no.m val mer - ces ni cor - te - si - a,
5. ni ma bel - tatz ni mos pretz ni mon sens;
6. c'a - tres - si.m sui en - ga nad' e tra - hi - a
7. com de - gr'es - ser, s'ieu fos de - sa - vi - nens.

I must sing of that which I would rather not,
so bitter I am towards him who is my love:
for I love him more than anyone;
my kindness and courtesy make no impression on him,
nor my beauty, my virtue or my intelligence;
so I am deceived and betrayed,
as I should be if I were unattractive.

than one note or to the frequent cases where accentuation differs between stanzas. Thus the treatment of rhythm varies considerably between editions, and performers can choose from a range of approaches. Most likely the dance songs were sung metrically, while the elevated love songs may have been sung more freely.

MUSICAL PLAYS

Musical plays were built around narrative pastoral songs (songs in idealized rural settings). The most famous was *Jeu de Robin et de Marion* (The Play of Robin and Marion, ca. 1284) by the trouvère Adam de la Halle (ca. 1240–?1288), shown in Figure 4.6. Marion's song *Robins m'aime* (NAWM 10) is a **rondeau,** a dance song with a refrain in two phrases whose music is also used for the verse, here in the pattern ABaabAB (where capital letters indicate the refrain). We know the lively rhythm because the song also appears

CD 1|38

Figure 4.6: Adam de la Halle as depicted in a miniature from the Chansonnier d'Arras, *which contains six of his chansons. The text says "Adam the hunchback made these songs."*

in a polyphonic setting notated in precise durations. Adam was the first vernacular poet-composer whose complete works were collected in a manuscript, showing the great esteem in which he was held.

DISSEMINATION

The origins of the troubadour tradition are unclear; possible sources or influences include Arabic songs, the versus (see above), and secular Latin songs. From southern France the tradition spread to the trouvères of northern France by the late twelfth century, and on to England, Germany, Italy, and Spain. In 1208, Pope Innocent III declared a crusade against the Albigensians, a heretical Christian sect centered in southern France, and the northern French joined the crusade as a way to pursue political goals of dominating the south. Soon the aristocracy, courts, and wealth that supported the troubadours collapsed, and the troubadours dispersed, spreading their influence into neighboring lands. The trouvères continued through the thirteenth century. They admired the troubadours and preserved their art; indeed, most extant manuscripts of troubadour song were copied in northern France in the mid- to late-thirteenth century.

SONG IN OTHER LANDS

The troubadour and trouvère tradition inspired types of lyric song in other tongues, spanning subjects from love to religion.

ENGLISH SONG

After the Norman Conquest of 1066, French was the language of the kings and nobility in England. The English king, as duke of Normandy and later also of Aquitaine, held lands in France, and he participated in French politics and culture. The royal house sponsored troubadours and trouvères, including Bernart de Ventadorn. King Richard I (the Lionheart, 1157–1199) was himself a trouvère, writing songs in French.

Few melodies survive for songs in Middle English, the language of the lower and middle classes. Indeed, we have little secular music for these social strata from anywhere in Europe, showing how much our view of medieval music depends on the interest the religious, economic, and intellectual elites had in preserving their own music. But most surviving poems in Middle English, from narrative ballads to secular and religious lyrics, were no doubt meant to be sung, and they suggest a rich musical life.

Figure 4.7: Walther von der Vogelweide as depicted in a fourteenth-century Swiss manuscript. Vogelweide means "bird-meadow," and his shield, shown in the upper left, includes a caged bird.

MINNESINGER

The troubadours were the model for the German **Minnesinger**, knightly poet-musicians who flourished between the twelfth and fourteenth centuries and wrote in Middle High German. The love (*Minne*) of which they sang in their **Minnelieder** (love songs) was even more spiritual than *fin' amors*, with an emphasis on faithfulness, duty, and service that reflected the loyalty that knights and nobles owed to their king and that Christians owed to the church. Most songs are strophic, and the most common melodic form is AAB, called **bar form** by scholars since the nineteenth century. Each A section, or **Stollen,** uses the same poetic meter, rhyme scheme, and melody. The B section, or **Abgesang,** is usually longer and may end with all or the latter part of the melody for the *Stollen*. The rhythm is seldom clear in the notation, raising the same issues as in troubadour song. Genres parallel those of the troubadours. A new genre is the crusade song, recounting the experiences of those who renounced worldly comfort to travel on the Crusades. A famous example is the

CD 1|39

Palästinalied (Palestine Song, NAWM 11) by Walther von der Vogelweide (?ca. 1170–?ca. 1230), perhaps the best-known Minnesinger, shown in Figure 4.7.

LAUDE

Few secular songs in Italian from before 1300 survive with music, but we do have melodies for several dozen **laude** (sing. *lauda*), sacred Italian monophonic songs. Composed in cities rather than at court, laude were sung in processions of religious penitents and in confraternities, associations of citizens who gathered for prayer and mutual support. The lauda tradition continued for several centuries. From the late fourteenth century on, most laude were polyphonic.

CANTIGAS

One of the treasures of medieval song is the *Cantigas de Santa Maria*, a collection of over four hundred **cantigas** (songs) in Galician-Portuguese in honor of the Virgin Mary. The collection was prepared about 1270–90 under the direction of King Alfonso el Sabio (the Wise) of Castile and León (northwest Spain) and preserved in four beautifully illuminated manuscripts. Whether Alfonso wrote some of the poems and melodies is uncertain. Most songs in the collection relate stories of miracles performed by the Virgin, the object of increasing veneration from the twelfth century on. Cantiga 159, *Non sofre Santa María* (NAWM 12), tells of a cut of meat, stolen from some pilgrims, that Mary caused to jump about, revealing where it was hidden. The songs all have refrains, perhaps sung by a group alternating with a soloist singing the verses. Songs with refrains were often associated with dancing, a possibility reinforced by illustrations of dancers in the *Cantigas* manuscripts and by the dancelike rhythm of many of the songs.

CD 1|40   CD 1|16

MEDIEVAL INSTRUMENTS

The songs described above were notated as single melodic lines, but may sometimes have been accompanied by instruments playing in unison or improvising accompaniments. Illustrated manuscripts depict the wide variety of medieval instruments.

A miniature from a thirteenth-century French Bible, in Figure 4.8, shows four musicians playing at a feast. On the left is a ***vielle*** or fiddle, the principal medieval bowed instrument and predecessor of the Renaissance viol and modern violin. Although vielles varied in shape and size, the typical thirteenth-century vielle had five strings tuned in fourths and fifths so the melody could

String instruments

Figure 4.8: Illustration from a French Bible from about 1250 showing a feast with musicians playing a vielle, hurdy-gurdy, harp, and psaltery.

be supported by one or more drones on open strings. Next is a **hurdy-gurdy**, a three-stringed vielle sounded by a rotating wheel inside the instrument turned by a crank at one end; the player presses levers to change pitches on the melody string while the other strings sound drones. The third musician plays a harp of a type that apparently originated in the British Isles. On the right is a **psaltery**, played by plucking strings attached to a frame over a wooden sounding board; it is a remote ancestor of the harpsichord and piano.

Miniatures from the *Cantigas de Santa María* in Figure 4.9 show musicians playing wind and percussion instruments of the time. The **transverse flute** was similar to the modern flute, but made of wood or ivory and without keys. The **shawm** was a double-reed instrument, similar to the oboe. The medieval trumpet was straight and lacked valves, so it could play only the harmonic series. The **pipe and tabor** featured a high whistle fingered with the left hand while the right hand beat a small drum with a stick.

Figure 4.9: Illustrations from the Cantigas de Santa Maria *(ca. 1250–80) showing musicians playing (clockwise from upper left) transverse flutes, shawms, pipes and tabors, and trumpets.*

Other instruments familiar to us today were already in use. The universal folk instrument was the bagpipe, whose player inflated a bag (often made from an animal skin or bladder) that in turn forced an unbroken stream of air through the chanter and one or more drone pipes, all sounded by reeds. Bells were played in church and used as signals. By 1100, monastic churches began to have early forms of the organ, and by 1300, they were common in cathedrals as well. Besides church organs, there were two smaller types. The **portative organ** was small enough to be carried (*portatum*) or suspended by a strap around the neck. It had a single set of pipes, and the right hand played the keys while the left worked the bellows. The **positive organ** had to be placed (*positum*) on a table to be played, and required an assistant to pump the bellows.

Most of these instruments came into Europe from Asia, through either the Byzantine Empire or the Arabs in North Africa and Spain. Their early history is obscure and their nomenclature inconsistent. But in them we can recognize the variety of bowed and plucked strings, winds, brass, percussion, and organs familiar from later eras, and understand that medieval musicians already had a rich palette of instrumental color in their hands.

SOURCE READING

DANCING AS DESCRIBED IN THE *ROMANCE OF THE ROSE*

The Romance of the Rose (ca. 1235) is the best known of the medieval romances, long narrative poems on heroic subjects. It includes a valuable description of the carole, danced to the accompaniment of a retrouenge, a song with a refrain, and of jongleurs and minstrels playing instruments.

———— • ————

Now see the carol go! Each man and maid
Most daintily steps out with many a turn
And arabesque upon the tender grass.
See there the flutists and the minstrel men,
Performers on the fiddle! Now they sing
A retrouenge, a tune from old Lorraine;
For it has better songs than other lands.
A troop of skillful jongleurs thereabout
Well played their parts, and girls with tambourines
Danced jollily, and, finishing each tune,
Threw high their instruments, and as these fell
Caught each on finger tip, and never failed.

Guillaume de Lorris, *Roman de la rose*, trans. Harry W. Robbins (New York: Dutton, 1962), 16 (lines 753–64).

DANCE MUSIC

Dancing in the Middle Ages was accompanied by songs or instrumental music, usually not written down but performed from memory, so that few melodies survive. To judge from written accounts and pictures, the most popular social dance in France from the twelfth through the fourteenth centuries was the **carole**, a circle dance that was usually accompanied by a song sung by one or more of the dancers. The dancers were sometimes also joined by instrumentalists (see Source Reading). Despite the carole's popularity, only about two dozen melodies are extant.

About fifty instrumental dance tunes survive from the thirteenth and fourteenth centuries, most monophonic, some set in polyphony for a keyboard instrument. These dances are the earliest notated instrumental music and must have been preserved because they were particularly admired. Like European dance music ever since, they are marked by a steady beat, clear meter,

Instrumental dances

repeated sections, and predictable phrasing. Although in most cases only the melody was written down, these dances could be performed by several players, including drum and other improvised accompaniments.

Estampie

Of the surviving medieval instrumental dances, the most common form is the **estampie.** It has several sections, each played twice with two different endings, the first with an **open** (*ouvert*) or incomplete cadence and the second with a **closed** (*clos*) or full cadence. The same open and closed endings are usually employed throughout. A late-thirteenth-century chansonnier called *Le manuscrit du roi* (The Manuscript of the King) includes eight "royal estampies" (the fourth is NAWM 13). All French estampies are in triple meter and consist of relatively short sections. A fourteenth-century Italian relative, the *istampita,* uses the same form but is in duple or compound meter, with longer sections and more repetition between sections.

THE LOVER'S COMPLAINT

The lyric songs of the troubadours and their successors share traits typical of European songs ever since. These medieval songs are strophic, diatonic, and primarily syllabic, moving mostly stepwise in a range of around an octave, usually with a clear pitch center. They have short musical phrases, roughly equal in size, each typically rising to a high point and falling to a cadence. Often one or more phrases of music are repeated to different words within each stanza, and some songs have a refrain after every verse. The most common subject, a pure, usually unattainable love, also has many echoes in later music, including popular songs. Equally enduring are the images of the minstrel—the itinerant musician—and the troubadour—the poet-composer.

The songs themselves continued to be sung for a few years or even decades, and many were preserved in writing. Some melodies were borrowed for new songs, sometimes in other languages. Eventually, most of the songs passed from the scene along with the society that gave them birth, replaced by new styles. Dance melodies met a similar fate. In the nineteenth century, a renewed interest in the Middle Ages and in each nation's cultural heritage led to the collection and publication of medieval poetry. Editions of the music followed in the twentieth century, and recent decades have brought a revival of medieval secular and nonliturgical song and instrumental dances in concert and recordings.

Chapter

5

Polyphony through the Thirteenth Century

During Europe's economic growth between 1050 and 1300, the church prospered. Pious donors funded hundreds of new monasteries and convents, filled by rising numbers of men, women, and children seeking a religious life. St. Francis, St. Dominic, St. Clare, and others founded new religious orders. In the eleventh and early twelfth centuries, builders erected large Romanesque churches that used the principles of the Roman basilica and the round arch, and artists decorated these buildings with frescoes and sculptures. Craftsmen in the mid-twelfth century created a new style of church architecture, later called Gothic, which emphasized height and spaciousness with soaring vaults, pointed arches, slender columns, large stained-glass windows, and intricate tracery. As scholars revived ancient learning, St. Anselm, St. Thomas Aquinas, and others associated with the intellectual movement called Scholasticism sought to reconcile the classical philosophy of Aristotle and others with Christian doctrine through commentary on authoritative texts.

These developments found parallels in the art of ***polyphony,*** music in which voices sing together in independent parts. At first, polyphony was a style of performance, a manner of accompanying chant with one or more added voices. Those who sang and heard polyphony valued it as decoration, a concept central to medieval art. Polyphonic performance heightened the grandeur of chant and thus of the liturgy itself, just like art and architectural decoration ornamented the church and thus the service. The added voices elaborated the authorized chants through a musical gloss, resembling both the monophonic trope (see chapter 3) and Scholastic commentary on Scripture, and indeed polyphony was developed in the same regions and contexts as troping. Advances in theory and notation during the eleventh, twelfth, and thirteenth centuries allowed musicians to write down polyphony and develop progressively more elaborate varieties, in genres such as *organum, conductus,* and *motet.*

The rise of written polyphony is of particular interest because it inaugurated four precepts that have distinguished Western music ever since: (1) *counterpoint,* the combination of multiple independent lines; (2) *harmony,* the regulation of simultaneous sounds; (3) the centrality of *notation*; and (4) the idea of *composition* as distinct from performance. These concepts changed over time, but their presence in this music links it to all that followed.

EARLY ORGANUM

Europeans probably performed music in multiple parts long before it was described. The simplest type, singing or playing a melody against a *drone*, is found in most European folk traditions and many Asian cultures, suggesting it dates from antiquity. Drones typically sustain the modal final, sometimes joined by the fifth above. For a listener, drones ground the melody in its tonal center and heighten the sense of closure when the melody cadences on the final.

Another way to enrich a melody, doubling it in parallel consonant intervals, was apparently already an old practice when first explained and illustrated in the ninth-century anonymous treatises *Musica enchiriadis* and *Scolica enchiriadis.* Examples from the former are transcribed in Example 5.1 (NAWM 14a-b).

CD 1|48–49

Organum

The treatises use the term *organum* for two or more voices singing different notes in agreeable combinations. This term was used for several styles of polyphony from the ninth through thirteenth centuries. The resulting piece is always called "an organum" (pl. *organa*), but in referring to the style it is best to add a modifier.

Parallel organum

The type shown in Example 5.1 is known today as *parallel organum.* The original chant melody is the *principal voice,* the other the *organal voice,* moving in exact parallel motion a fifth below. Fifths were consonances, considered both perfect and beautiful. Although parallel fifths would later be forbidden in Renaissance counterpoint, to medieval ears they added resonance and magnificence to an otherwise bare unison.

In early organum, the organal voice is normally sung below the principal voice. Either or both voices may be doubled at the octave, as in Example 5.1b, to create an even richer sound.

Mixed parallel and oblique organum

We might expect parallel organum at the fourth below to be as straightforward as parallel fifths, and it may once have been so in practice. But the scale system described in *Musica enchiriadis* contained augmented fourths (or tritones), such as B♭–e and f–b, and the adjustments necessary to avoid

Example 5.1: Parallel organum at the fifth, from Musica enchiriadis

a. Parallel organum at the fifth below

Principal voice
Organal voice

Tu pa - tris sem - pi - ter - nus es fi - li - us.

You of the father are the everlasting son (from Te Deum laudamus*).*

b. Parallel organum at the fifth below, with octave doublings

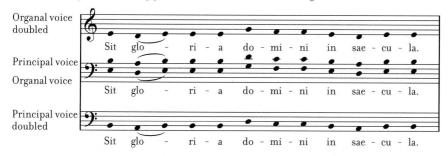

Organal voice doubled

Sit glo - ri - a do - mi - ni in sae - cu - la.

Principal voice
Organal voice

Sit glo - ri - a do - mi - ni in sae - cu - la.

Principal voice doubled

Sit glo - ri - a do - mi - ni in sae - cu - la.

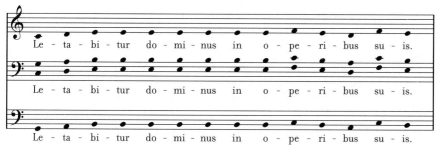

Le - ta - bi - tur do - mi - nus in o - pe - ri - bus su - is.

Le - ta - bi - tur do - mi - nus in o - pe - ri - bus su - is.

Le - ta - bi - tur do - mi - nus in o - pe - ri - bus su - is.

May the glory of the Lord be forever; the Lord will rejoice in his works.

them produced organum that was not strictly parallel. To prevent these tritones from occurring, the writer of the treatise prohibits the organal voice
from moving below *c* when a segment of chant includes *e* or below *g* when
it includes *b*. The singers performing the organal voice must remain on one
note until they can proceed in parallel fourths without sounding a tritone. The
result, illustrated in Example 5.2 (NAWM 14c), combines oblique motion, [CD 1|50]
like a melody moving over a drone, with parallel motion, and thus this style is
called ***mixed parallel and oblique organum.*** Figure 5.1 shows how this example appears in one manuscript copy of the treatise.

Avoiding tritones in this manner had significant effects. When the organal
voice is stationary, harmonic major seconds and thirds may result, but they
were not considered consonant; if either would occur on the last note of a
phrase, the organal voice must move to a unison with the principal voice.
Converging on the unison emphasizes the cadences and phrasing of the

Example 5.2: Mixed parallel and oblique organum, from Musica enchiriadis

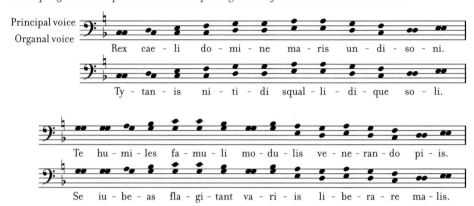

King of Heaven, Lord of the roaring sea,
Of the shining Titan (Sun) and the squalid earth,
Your humble servants, worshipping you with pious melodies,
Beseech you, as you command, to free them from diverse ills.

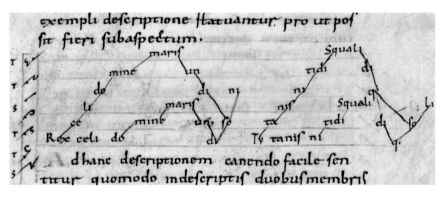

Figure 5.1: Excerpt from a manuscript of Musica enchiriadis, *showing the first two phrases of* Rex caeli domine *(Example 5.2) in mixed parallel and oblique organum. The shapes on the left are signs for pitches, with "T" and "S" in the margin indicating which steps are tones and which are semitones. The height of each syllable indicates its pitch, and the motions in each voice are shown by lines linking the syllables, until the two voices unite on the last two syllables in each phrase. The scribe has not worried about aligning the parts vertically, assuming the reader will understand that the voices will declaim the words together.*

original chant. This break away from simple drones and parallel motion raised the possibility of polyphony as a combination of independent voices.

From performance to composition
The styles of organum described in *Musica enchiriadis* were ways for singers to adorn chant, not methods of composition, and could be performed extemporaneously, deriving the added voices from the chant without having to notate them. But the next theorist to describe organum, Guido of Arezzo in his *Micrologus* (ca. 1025–28), allowed a range of choices that could result in a variety of organal voices combining oblique and parallel motion. These voices

could be improvised by a soloist or worked out in rehearsal, but some were written down. The Winchester Troper (early eleventh century) from Winchester Cathedral in England contains 174 organa, apparently by Wulfstan of Winchester (fl. 992–996), the cantor there, showing that organum could become a form of composition as well as a manner of performing chant.

FREE ORGANUM

As possible ways to add an organal voice multiplied, musicians must have sensed an opportunity to decorate the chants of the service, in the same way that sculptors, painters, and tapestry makers decorated the walls of the churches. By the late eleventh century, singers were improvising and scribes were recording a new style of organum, known today as **free organum** or *note-against-note organum* in which the organal voice has greater independence and prominence.

Rules for improvising or composing in the new style are preserved in *Ad organum faciendum* (On Making Organum, ca. 1100), which gives as an example the solo sections of *Alleluia Justus ut palma* (NAWM 15). As shown in Example 5.3, the added voice now usually lies above the chant rather than below (though the parts may cross), perhaps because that allows a wider range of motion. The organal voice moves against the chant, mostly note for note, in a free mixture of contrary, oblique, parallel, and similar motion while forming consonant harmonic intervals with it. The consonances remain the unison, fourth, fifth, and octave, with cadences on the unison or octave, sometimes preceded by a third or sixth to allow stepwise motion. The organal voice is more disjunct than the chant because of the limited number of harmonic intervals from which the singer may choose. Yet this style of organum offers much more freedom than its predecessors, allowing singers and composers to show their artistry while embellishing the liturgical chant.

During the next several centuries, polyphony was primarily the responsibility of soloists, not the choir. This arrangement makes sense in several ways. By long tradition the most ornate chants, the responsorial psalms, were mainly sung by soloists, and it was appropriate for them to take the lead in any further musical elaboration of the service. Soloists sang the tropes, and

CD 1|51   CD 1|17

Example 5.3: Free Organum from Ad organum faciendum *(ca. 1100)*

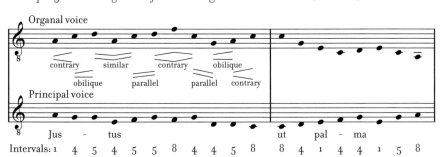

The righteous [shall flourish] like a palm tree.

polyphony was analogous to troping as an addition to the authorized chants. Most important, only a soloist could improvise a free organal line against a given chant, so that when free organum came to be written down it was already associated with solo performance. Thus, although older styles of organum could be sung by choirs and used for any chant, free organum and later styles were used only where soloists sang, primarily in the solo portions of Graduals, Alleluias, and Office responsories, and in troped sections of the Mass Ordinary. Polyphony did not stand alone; rather, soloists singing polyphonic sections alternated with monophonic chant sung by the choir.

AQUITANIAN POLYPHONY

Early in the twelfth century, singers and composers in France developed a new, more ornate type of polyphony. It is known today as **Aquitanian polyphony** because the main sources are three manuscripts once held in the Abbey of St. Martial at Limoges in the duchy of Aquitaine (southwestern France) and copied in Aquitanian notation. A manuscript with similar works, the Codex Calixtinus, was prepared in central France and brought by 1173 to the Cathedral of Santiago de Compostela in northwest Spain.

Polyphonic versus

Aquitanian polyphony includes settings of chant, such as sequences, Benedicamus Domino melodies, and solo portions of responsorial chants. But most of the repertory comprises settings of *versus,* rhyming, scanning, accentual Latin poems, which were also set monophonically (see chapter 4). These versus are the earliest known polyphony *not* based on chant.

Discant and organum

Theorists of the time described two main polyphonic styles, both evident in Aquitanian polyphony. **Discant** occurs when both parts move at about the same rate, with one to three notes in the upper part for each note of the lower voice. Organum now refers to a texture in which the lower voice moves much more slowly than the upper, sustaining each note while the upper voice sings notegroups of varying lengths above it; this style is known today as **florid organum** because of the florid upper part. In both styles, the lower voice holds the principal melody and is called the **tenor** (from Latin *tenere,* "to hold").

 CD 1|53

These styles are illustrated in two passages from *Jubilemus, exultemus* (NAWM 16), a versus whose tenor was apparently newly composed. The section in Example 5.4a uses the style of florid organum, with melismas of three to fifteen notes in the upper part for most notes in the tenor. Example 5.4b shows a passage in discant style, with one to three notes in the upper part for each tenor note until the penultimate syllable, which typically has a longer melisma. In both excerpts, contrary motion is more common than parallel, and most notegroups in the upper voice begin on a perfect consonance with the tenor. As in free organum, phrases end on octaves or unisons, heightening the sense of closure.

Both florid organum and discant exemplify their medieval creators' love of decoration, ornamenting the syllabic tenor line with various melodic gestures in the upper voice and changing harmonies between the parts. By alternating these two styles between or within sections, musicians provided variety and

Example 5.4: Florid organum and discant in Jubilemus, exultemus

Verse 2

To the redeemer, creator, savior of all.

Verse 4

Praise God and eternally applaud.

gave their pieces shape. The use of florid organum style and the length of the text make such works longer than earlier polyphonic pieces. Singers no doubt improvised such music, but the range of choice in the upper voice and the complex coordination of parts lend themselves to written composition.

Jubilemus, exultemus appears in the manuscript in **score notation,** as shown in Figure 5.2. The voices are written above the text, the top voice above

Score notation and rhythm

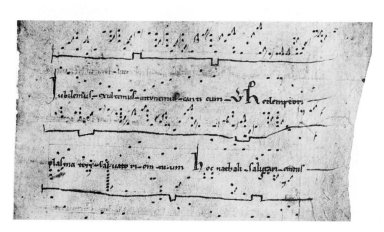

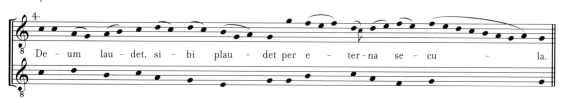

Figure 5.2: Jubilemus, exultemus, *a two-voice versus, in Aquitanian notation. The two voices are written above the words and separated from each other by a line. The coordination between the parts is not always clear.*

the tenor, separated by a line. We presume both voices sang the words. Both are in heighted neumes, so the pitches are reasonably clear but not always certain. The vertical alignment of parts indicates approximately which notes are sung together, yet there are ambiguities. Durations are not indicated, leaving many questions: Should the tenor proceed at a steady pace while the upper voice moves more or less quickly to fit? Or the reverse, in which case the tenor in most florid passages loses its character as a tune and becomes a series of drones? Or were both coordinated through a meter or rhythmic convention understood at the time but not apparent in the notation? These uncertainties may worry historians, but they open opportunities for interpretation by modern editors and performers, who vary considerably in the solutions they offer.

NOTRE DAME POLYPHONY

Musicians in Paris developed a still more ornate style of polyphony in the late twelfth and early thirteenth centuries. The creators of this style were associated with the new Cathedral of Paris, Notre Dame ("Our Lady," the Virgin Mary), shown in Figure 5.3. One of the grandest Gothic cathedrals, Notre Dame took almost a century to build: the foundations were begun around 1160, the apse and choir completed in 1182, the first Mass celebrated in 1183, the transept and nave finished around 1200, and the façade completed about 1250. During this time, musicians at or connected to Notre Dame created a new repertory of unprecedented grandeur and complexity. This new repertory was perhaps the first polyphony to be primarily composed and read from notation rather than improvised, and included the first body of music for more than two independent voices. Such elaborate music was valued for its artistry in decorating the authorized chant, making important services more impressive, and paralleling in sound the stunning size and beautiful decoration of the building itself.

Figure 5.3: Cathedral of Notre Dame in Paris, built ca. 1160–1258. Its great height, elaborate decoration, and innovative architecture have parallels in the unprecedented length, intricacy, and carefully worked-out structure of the music that composers wrote to sing in the cathedral.

THE RHYTHMIC MODES

The Notre Dame composers developed the first notation since ancient Greece to indicate duration, a step of great importance for later music. They devised the notation in the late twelfth century, and it was described in a thirteenth-century treatise attributed to Johannes de Garlandia. Instead of using note shapes to show relative durations, as in modern notation, they used combinations of notegroups, or *ligatures,* to indicate different patterns of *longs* (long notes) and *breves* (short notes). There were six basic patterns, called "modes" by Garlandia and known today as the *rhythmic modes.* These were identified by number and are shown here both as patterns of longs (L) and breves (B) and in modern transcription:

1. LB
2. BL
3. LBB
4. BBL
5. LL
6. BBB

The basic time unit (*tempus,* pl. *tempora*), here transcribed as an eighth note, was always grouped in threes. This grouping resulted naturally from the alternation in modes 1 and 2 of a long (two tempora) and a breve (one tempus). To preserve the groups of three in modes 3, 4, and 5, the long was lengthened to three tempora, and the second breve in modes 3 and 4 was doubled in length. Modes 1 and 5 were most common and apparently the oldest. Mode 4 was rarely employed and may have been included primarily to round out the system.

Variety

In theory, a mode 1 melody would consist of repetitions of the pattern, each phrase ending with a rest:

But such a melody could be monotonous, and in practice the rhythm was more flexible. Notes could be broken into shorter units, or the two notes of the pattern could be combined into one. In some pieces, the mode changes from one phrase to the next, and many pieces combine mode 5 in the tenor with another mode in the upper voice.

Notation

To indicate which rhythmic mode was in force, scribes used ligatures, signs derived from the compound neumes of plainchant notation that denoted groups of notes. When a melody was written as in Example 5.5a, with a single three-note ligature followed by a series of two-note ligatures, it signaled the singer to use mode 1, as shown in the transcription in Example 5.5b. Because the ligatures are the key features of the rhythmic notation, they are represented in modern editions by horizontal brackets over the notes, as here. In this mode, each ligature ends with a long, and all but the first have

Example 5.5: Use of ligatures to indicate a rhythmic mode
a.   b.

the same rhythmic pattern, making the notation easy to read once it becomes familiar. The other rhythmic modes were shown in similar ways, with a different combination of ligatures for each mode. Departures from the prevailing pattern, changes of mode, or repeated tones (which could not be included in ligatures) required modifications.

LÉONIN AND THE *MAGNUS LIBER ORGANI*

Thanks to a treatise from about 1275 by an Englishman known to us only as Anonymous IV, we know the names of two composers of polyphony associated with Notre Dame, Léonin and Pérotin, and something about their compositions (see biographies). Both composers studied at the University of Paris, which was becoming a center of intellectual innovation; a typical classroom situation is shown in Figure 5.4.

Magnus liber organi   Anonymous IV credits Léonin (fl. 1150s–ca. 1201) with compiling a *Magnus liber organi* ("great book of polyphony"). This collection contained two-voice settings of the solo portions of the responsorial chants (Graduals, Alleluias, and Office Responsories) for the major feasts of the church year. For Léonin to undertake such a cycle, elaborating the chants that were the central musical focus of the year's most important services, shows a vision as grand as that of those building Notre Dame Cathedral. The "great book" no longer exists in its original form, but its contents survive in later manuscripts, primarily two in Wolfenbüttel, Germany, and one in Florence, Italy.

Layers of adaptation   We do not know how much of the surviving music is by Léonin himself. What is certain is that Pérotin and other composers freely altered and added to the collection. The manuscripts offer different settings for the same passages of chant, often presenting several alternatives, and include organa for two, three, or four voices as well as pieces in the newer genres of conductus and motet (see below). Clearly the "great book" was not a fixed canon, but a fluid repertory from which material could be chosen for each year's services.

By comparing different settings of a single chant, we can see this process of revision and substitution in action and can trace changes in style. An ideal example is *Viderunt omnes*, the Gradual for Christmas Day, already familiar from our discussion of chant in chapters 2 and 3 (see NAWM 3d and Examples 2.2 and 2.3) and elaborated polyphonically by Léonin, Pérotin, and their colleagues (NAWM 17–19).

LÉONIN ORGANUM

CD 1|57   The setting of *Viderunt omnes* in the earlier Wolfenbüttel manuscript (NAWM 17) may represent the closest we have to Léonin's version. It features two different styles of polyphony, organum and discant, paralleling the contrast we observed in Aquitanian polyphony. Only the solo portions of the chant, the intonation of the respond and most of the verse, were set polyphonically. The choir sang the remaining portions in unison, so that three styles—plainchant, organum, and discant—were heard side by side.

Organum style   The opening intonation on "Viderunt," shown in Example 5.6, exemplifies Léonin's organum style. The chant melody appears in the tenor in unmeasured long notes, like a series of drones. Over these sustained tones the upper voice

sings expansive melismas, moving mostly stepwise, often lingering on dissonances with the tenor, and cadencing at irregular intervals on an octave,
fifth, or unison followed by a rest. Such long, fluid melodies, playing with
dissonance and resolving in consonance, make clear why Anonymous IV called
Léonin "the best composer of organum." The notation does not clearly
indicate any rhythmic mode, suggesting that the upper voice should be sung in

LÉONIN [LEONINUS] (FL. 1150S–CA. 1201)
PÉROTIN [PEROTINUS] (FL. LATE 12TH & EARLY 13TH CENTURIES)

Léonin served at the Cathedral of Paris in many capacities, beginning in the 1150s, before the current Notre Dame was built. He earned a Master of Arts degree, presumably at the University of Paris, and eventually became a priest. He was a canon at Notre Dame and was affiliated with the monastery of St. Victor. As a poet, he wrote a paraphrase of the first eight books of the Bible in verse and several shorter works.

About Pérotin less is known. He also had a Master of Arts and must have held an important position at Notre Dame.

Virtually all we know about the musical activities of Léonin and Pérotin is contained in a treatise from about 1275, known as

Figure 5.4: We have no images of Léonin or Pérotin. But we know from Anonymous IV that both earned masters degrees, presumably at the University of Paris. This illumination from an early-fourteenth-century French manuscript shows a class at the University from their era, taught by Amaury de Bène (d. 1206).

"Anonymous IV" because it was the fourth anonymous treatise in C.-E.-H. de Coussemaker's collection of medieval treatises (Paris, 1864–76). The writer makes a pointed comparison between the two composers:

Note that Master Léonin, according to what was said, was the best composer of organa, who made the great book of organum [*magnus liber organi*] from the gradual and antiphonary to elaborate the divine service. And it was in use up to the time of Pérotin the Great, who edited it and made very many better clausulae or puncta, since he was the best composer of discant, and better than Léonin. But this is not to be said about the subtlety of the organum, etc.

But Master Pérotin himself made excellent quadrupla [four-voice organa], like "Viderunt" and "Sederunt," with an abundance of colors of the harmonic art; and also several very noble tripla [three-voice organa], like "Alleluia posui adiutorium," "Nativitas," etc. He also composed three-part conductus, like "Salvatoris hodie," and two-part conductus, like "Dum sigillum summi patris," and even monophonic conductus with several others, like "Beata viscera," etc.

Jeremy Yudkin, The Music Treatise of Anonymous IV: A New Translation, *MSD 41 (Neuhausen-Stuttgart: AIM/Hänssler-Verlag, 1985),* 39.

free rhythm, although some scholars and performers have applied modal rhythms.

Discant style   Most of Léonin's setting is in organum style, but it is punctuated by passages in discant style where both voices move in modal rhythm, the tenor usually in mode 5 and the upper part primarily in mode 1. The longest discant passage in *Viderunt omnes* is on the syllable "Do-" of "Dominus," shown in Example 5.7. In the original chant, this was by far the longest melisma. Scholars have suggested that Léonin set the long melismas in discant style because organum, with its elongated tenor notes, would have made the music too long. Thus changes of style in the polyphony, from organum to discant and back, occur precisely where, in the chant, the style changes from neumatic text-setting to melismatic and back. In this section, the phrases are relatively short, usually four or six longs in the tenor. As in organum, phrases end on a unison, fifth, or octave, but here consonance is more pervasive, with a perfect consonance on almost every long.

Léonin's organa were in his day by far the longest and most elaborate settings of chant ever created. In weaving intricate strands of melody around the

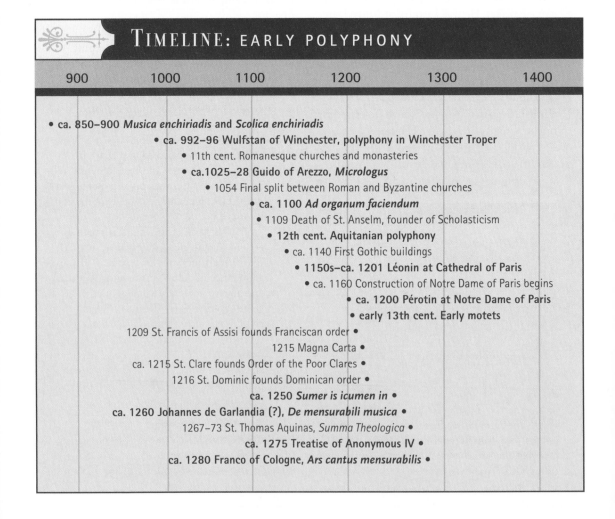

TIMELINE: EARLY POLYPHONY

900	1000	1100	1200	1300	1400

- ca. 850–900 *Musica enchiriadis* and *Scolica enchiriadis*
  - ca. 992–96 Wulfstan of Winchester, polyphony in Winchester Troper
    - 11th cent. Romanesque churches and monasteries
  - ca.1025–28 Guido of Arezzo, *Micrologus*
    - 1054 Final split between Roman and Byzantine churches
    - ca. 1100 *Ad organum faciendum*
    - 1109 Death of St. Anselm, founder of Scholasticism
    - 12th cent. Aquitanian polyphony
    - ca. 1140 First Gothic buildings
    - 1150s–ca. 1201 Léonin at Cathedral of Paris
    - ca. 1160 Construction of Notre Dame of Paris begins
    - ca. 1200 Pérotin at Notre Dame of Paris
    - early 13th cent. Early motets
- 1209 St. Francis of Assisi founds Franciscan order •
- 1215 Magna Carta •
- ca. 1215 St. Clare founds Order of the Poor Clares •
- 1216 St. Dominic founds Dominican order •
- ca. 1250 *Sumer is icumen in* •
- ca. 1260 Johannes de Garlandia (?), *De mensurabili musica* •
- 1267–73 St. Thomas Aquinas, *Summa Theologica* •
- ca. 1275 Treatise of Anonymous IV •
- ca. 1280 Franco of Cologne, *Ars cantus mensurabilis* •

Example 5.6: Léonin, first section of Viderunt omnes, *in organum duplum*

Example 5.7: Léonin, discant section on "Do-" of Viderunt omnes

liturgical chant, they were worthy musical analogues to the sculptures and figuration that adorned Notre Dame Cathedral, then still under construction, or the Scholastic theologians' detailed commentary on Scripture. They must have filled the cathedral with mesmerizing sound, overpowering the sense of hearing just like the tall columns, stained-glass windows, and delicate stonework overwhelmed the sense of sight, and moving worshipers to deeper devotion. But Léonin's organa would not be the last word.

SUBSTITUTE CLAUSULAE

Anonymous IV writes that Pérotin edited the *Magnus liber* and "made very many better clausulae." By **clausula**, the Latin word for a clause or phrase in a sentence, he meant a self-contained section of an organum, setting a word or syllable from the chant and closing with a cadence. Since Léonin's organa consisted of a series of such sections, it was possible for Pérotin and others to write new clausulae designed to replace the original setting of a particular segment of chant. Typically, these new clausulae, known today as **substitute clausulae**, are in discant style, reflecting a growing preference for discant. Hundreds appear in the same manuscripts as the organa themselves; all are unattributed, so we cannot know which are by Pérotin. The Florence manuscript includes ten clausulae on the word "Dominus" from *Viderunt omnes*, any of which could be used at Christmas Mass. The openings of two of them are shown in Example 5.8 (NAWM 18).

CD 1|66

Example 5.8: Two substitute clausulae on "Dominus" from Viderunt omnes

a.

b.

Repetition and structure

Both clausulae exhibit a common trait of discant in Pérotin's generation: the tenor is not just a series of longs, as in Léonin's setting, but repeats a rhythmic motive based on a rhythmic mode, here mode 5 in the first clausula and mode 2 in the second. Some clausulae tenors also repeat the melody (over a much longer span than the rhythmic figure). In both forms of repetition, the composer uses musical means to create a sense of coherence for an extended passage. Anonymous IV's opinion that such clausulae are "better" than Léonin's may reflect the value he placed on this attention to structure. These two kinds of repetition in the tenor, of rhythm and of melody, became very significant in the motet of the thirteenth and fourteenth centuries (see below and chapter 6).

PÉROTIN ORGANUM

Pérotin and his contemporaries also wrote organa for three or even four voices. A two-voice organum was called an **organum duplum** ("double"); a three-voice organum an *organum triplum*, or simply **triplum** ("triple"); and a four-voice organum a **quadruplum** ("quadruple"). The voices above the tenor were likewise named in ascending order **duplum, triplum,** and **quadruplum.** The upper voices all use the rhythmic modes, allowing exact coordination among them, and move in similar ranges, crossing repeatedly.

Anonymous IV tells us Pérotin wrote tripla and quadrupla and names two of each, including a four-voice setting of *Viderunt omnes* (NAWM 19). Like other tripla and quadrupla, it begins in a style of organum with measured phrases in modal rhythm in the upper voices above very long notes in the tenor, as shown in Figure 5.5 and Example 5.9. As in Léonin's setting, such passages alternate with sections of discant, of which the longest is again on "Dominus" (not shown here).

To give long sections in organum style both coherence and variety, Pérotin uses several repetitive and harmonic devices in constantly changing ways. He may repeat a phrase in one voice (quadruplum, phrases a and c) while the

Organum duplum, triplum, and quadruplum

Pérotin's Viderunt

CD 2|1   CD 1|19

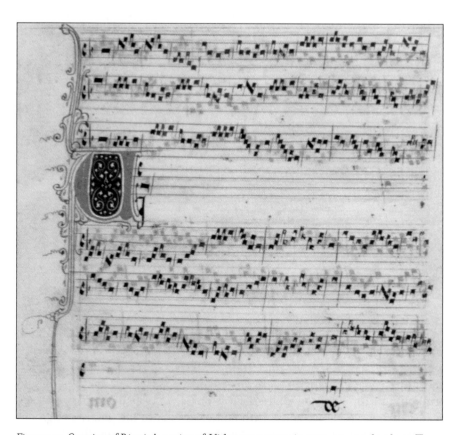

Figure 5.5: Opening of Pérotin's setting of Viderunt omnes *in organum quadruplum. The upper three voices are in modal rhythm over a sustained tenor note. For a transcription, see Example 5.9 and NAWM 19.*

Example 5.9: Pérotin, Viderunt omnes, *opening, with repeating elements indicated by letter*

other voices change, or restate a phrase at a new pitch level (quadruplum, phrases a and a′; duplum, phrases d and d′). Especially characteristic is repetition of a phrase in another voice (phrases b and c throughout the example), including **voice exchange,** where voices trade phrases (as the duplum and triplum do with phrases b and c). Each phrase emphasizes striking dissonances before resolving to the fifth and octave above the tenor, using harmonic tension to reinforce the consonance while sustaining the listener's interest. In the passage shown here, phrases are short and all voices stop together. In the next section (not shown), voices rest at different times, producing longer spans. Each new section introduces and varies new motives in seemingly endless decoration.

Through such means Pérotin created polyphonic works of unprecedented length, even more grandiose than Léonin's, though they served the same liturgical roles. Just as the vastness of Notre Dame Cathedral depended upon a carefully designed structure of pillars, arches, and flying buttresses, Pérotin's organa were the most intricately structured music yet composed, using techniques of musical elaboration to sustain great spans of time. His music sounds glorious, evoking the awe appropriate to its religious setting, but his skill as an architect in tones is just as impressive.

POLYPHONIC CONDUCTUS

The Notre Dame composers and others in France, England, and elsewhere also wrote polyphonic **conductus**. These were settings for two to four voices of the same types of text used in the closely related genres of monophonic conductus (see chapter 4) and Aquitanian versus (see above): rhymed, rhythmic, strophic Latin poems, rarely taken from the liturgy though usually on a sacred or serious topic. Typical is *Ave virgo virginum* (NAWM 20), shown in Example 5.10. It addresses the Virgin Mary and was perhaps used in special devotions and processions.

CD 2|13

Example 5.10: Ave virgo virginum, *early-thirteenth-century conductus*

A - ve vir - go vir - gi - num   Ver - bi car - nis cel - la.

Hail, virgin of virgins, shrine of the word made flesh.

The conductus differs from other Notre Dame polyphony in musical features as well as text. First, the tenor was newly composed rather than taken from chant. Second, all voices sing the text together in essentially the same rhythm. The nearly homorhythmic writing of the conductus has been called "conductus style" when used for other genres. Third, the words are set syllabically for the most part. Some conductus are largely syllabic throughout, but most feature melismatic passages, called **caudae** (sing. *cauda*, "tail"), at the beginning, end, and before important cadences. Conductus with caudae are generally through-composed, although caudae often feature phrase repetitions and voice exchange as in Pérotin's organum. Conductus without caudae, such as *Ave virgo virginum*, tend to be simpler in style and strophic in form.

1. New melody for each stanza

MOTET

Composers at Notre Dame created a new genre in the early thirteenth century by adding newly written Latin words to the upper voices of discant clausulae, like texts added to chant melismas. The resulting piece was called a **motet** (Latin *motetus*, from French *mot*, "word"; the duplum of a motet could also be called *motetus*). Over the course of the century, poets and composers developed new forms of the motet, including some with French words, secular topics, three or more voices, or rhythmic patterns increasingly free of the rhythmic modes. As conductus and organum gradually fell out of fashion in the middle of the century, the motet became the leading polyphonic genre for both sacred and secular music, evolving from a textual trope of a clausula to a newly composed piece valued for its complex patterns and multiple layers of meaning.

EARLY MOTETS

A typical early motet is *Factum est salutare/Dominus* (NAWM 21a), shown in Example 5.11 and based on the discant clausula in Example 5.8a. (Since motets usually have a different text in each voice, they are identified by a compound title comprising the first words of each voice from highest to lowest.) Since the poet fit words to the existing duplum melody, the varying number of notes in each short phrase required him to write a poem with irregular line lengths, accentuation, and rhyme scheme. Like many early Latin motets based on clausulae, this text is a kind of trope on the original chant text, elaborating its meaning and drawing on its words or sounds. The poem ends with the word "Dominus" (Lord), on which the tenor melody was originally sung, and incorporates several other words from the chant (underlined in the example), some of which are echoed in subsequent rhymes. The discant clausula, a musical decoration of a word, is here in turn embellished by the addition of words, like a gloss upon a gloss, both referring back to the original chant and its words, drawn from a psalm. The resulting motet is an ingenious composite artwork with multiple layers of borrowing and of meaning. In an ecclesiastical culture that treasured commentary, allegory, and new ways of reworking traditional themes, such pieces must have been highly esteemed for their many allusions.

Example 5.11: Factum est salutare/Dominus

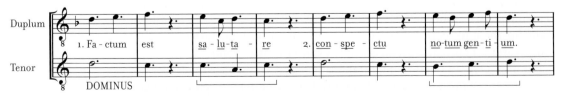

Salvation was made known in the sight of the Gentiles.

This motet would be appropriate for performance at Christmas Mass as part of the Gradual *Viderunt omnes*, like the original clausula. But it could also be sung on other occasions, even for entertainment. Musicians soon regarded the motet as a genre independent of church performance. The tenor lost its liturgical function and became raw material for composition, a supporting framework for the upper voice or voices.

Motet as independent genre

This change in the role of motets raised new possibilities. Composers reworked existing motets in several ways: (1) writing a different text for the duplum, in Latin or French, no longer necessarily linked to the chant text and often on a secular topic; (2) adding a third or fourth voice to those already present; (3) giving the additional parts texts of their own, to create a **double motet** (with two texts above the tenor) or **triple motet** (with three); or (4) deleting the original duplum and writing one or more new voices, each with its own text, to go with the existing tenor. Composers also wrote motets from scratch, by laying out one of the tenor melodies from the Notre Dame clausula repertoire in a new rhythmic pattern and writing new voices to fit it.

The two motets in Examples 5.12 and 5.13 illustrate some of these possibilities. *Fole acostumance/Dominus* (NAWM 21b) features the same tenor as *Factum est salutare/Dominus* (Example 5.11), in both melody and rhythm, but states it twice and substitutes a new, more quickly moving duplum melody for the original one. The doubled length and faster motion accommodate a much longer text, a secular French poem complaining that envy, hypocrisy, and deception have ruined France. Such a motet, with its bitter but amusing text in the vernacular, can only have been intended for entertainment.

CD 2|15   CD 1|23

Example 5.12: Fole acostumance/Dominus

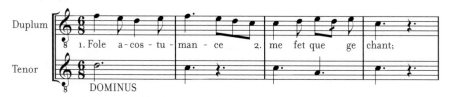

It is only a crazy habit that makes me sing.

The composer of *Super te Ierusalem/Sed fulsit virginitas/Dominus*, on the other hand, did not take a tenor unchanged from a clausula, but used the first half of the same chant melisma on "Dominus" (minus its first two notes) with a different rhythmic pattern. The top two voices set the first and second halves respectively of a Latin poem on the birth of Jesus to the Virgin Mary, appropriate to the feast of Christmas on which the tenor melody was originally sung; such a motet could have been sung in private devotions in that season, or as an addition to the service. The poem was apparently written before the music, to judge from its regular line lengths. As in most motets with more than two voices, the upper parts rarely rest together or with the tenor, so that the music moves forward in an unbroken stream. This motet exists in two

Example 5.13: Super te Ierusalem/Sed fulsit virginitas/Dominus

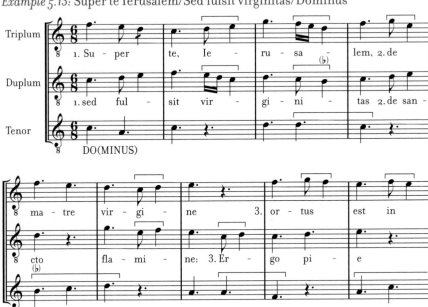

Triplum: *For you, Jerusalem, from a virgin mother, was born in [Bethlehem] . . .*
Duplum: *but her virginity glowed with the Spirit's breath. Therefore, pious . . .*

variants: the Montpellier Codex (late thirteenth century), a major French motet manuscript, has a version for three voices, shown in the example, and one of the English manuscripts known as the Worcester fragments includes an untexted fourth voice (see NAWM 21c). Such alternate versions show that motets, like the clausulae and organa that spawned them, were regarded not as immutable works but as common property open to reworking.

CD 2|17

Performance   When, where, and how motets were performed are interesting questions. Sacred motets might have been performed in services, but secular ones were not. They were almost certainly music for the elite, including clerics, teachers, poets, musicians, and their patrons. Since the words in the tenor no longer needed to be sung, the tenor part may have been played on an instrument, but there is no clear evidence to indicate that this was customary.

Reception   The elite audience must have enjoyed motets for their complex interweaving of familiar borrowed material and new elements, in both music and words. Although it is difficult for modern listeners to imagine how two texts were heard at once in a double motet, the clever interrelationships between topically related poems were part of the appeal, building on the early motet tradition of writing words for the duplum that amplify the meaning and echo the sounds of the tenor's text. Often certain vowels or syllables appear in all voices, so that similarities of sound reinforce the interplay of ideas. This was music for refined and discerning listeners who treasured witty texts, skillful composition, and intriguing juxtapositions.

MOTETS IN THE LATER THIRTEENTH CENTURY

By about 1250, three-voice motets were the rule, with two texts on related topics in Latin or French, or occasionally one in each language. After mid-century, composers drew motet tenor melodies from sources other than Notre Dame clausulae, including other chants and secular music. The tenor became simply a **cantus firmus**, a term introduced around 1270 by the theorist Hieronymus de Moravia to designate an existing melody, usually a plainchant, on which a new polyphonic work is based.

The further motet composers moved away from adding text to a clausula, the more they needed a new rhythmic notation. The rhythmic modes were notated through patterns of ligatures. Except for the tenor, motets were pre-dominantly syllabic; each syllable required a separate note, so ligatures could no longer be used to indicate rhythm. Scribes notated early motets in two versions, with words and without (that is, as clausulae), and only the latter showed the rhythm. Later motets followed the rhythmic modes less closely, in part by subdividing many notes, and their increasing rhythmic variety and complexity called for a new notational system.

Composer and theorist Franco of Cologne codified the new system, called **Franconian notation**, in his *Ars cantus mensurabilis* (The Art of Measurable Music), written around 1280. For the first time, relative durations were signified by note shapes, a characteristic of Western notation ever since. This is such an important innovation, and it had such an impact on what musicians could notate, that we should pause to examine how Franco's system worked.

There were four signs for single notes:

double long	▜
long	▜
breve	■
semibreve	◆

Like the rhythmic modes, Franconian notation is based on ternary groupings of the basic unit, the tempus (now normally transcribed as a quarter note rather than an eighth). Three tempora constitute a **perfection**, akin to a measure of three beats. As in the rhythmic modes, a long may last two or three tempora, and a breve is normally one tempus but can last two tempora (as in modes 3 and 4) if needed to fill a perfection. A double long has the value of two longs, and a tempus may contain two or three semibreves. Signs for rests and for ligatures indicate durations in a similar manner. What we would transcribe as ties across the barline were not possible to notate, except for double longs.

Changes in motet style and notation led to a new way of laying out the music. Scribes wrote the earliest motets in score, like the clausulae from which they were derived. But the upper voices, with each syllable needing a separate note, took up much more room on the page than the tenor, which had fewer notes and could be written in ligatures. In a score, there would be long vacant stretches in the tenor staff, a waste of space and parchment. And since the upper voices sang different texts, it seemed natural to separate them.

Franconian notation

Format

Figure 5.6: Page from the Montpellier Codex in performance format, showing the beginning of Adam de la Halle's De ma dame vient/Dieus, comment porroie/Omnes *and the end of the previous motet. The triplum is in the left column, the motetus (duplum) on the right, and the tenor is written across the bottom. Compare the transcription in Example 5.14.*

Example 5.14: Adam de la Halle, De ma dame vient/Dieus, comment porroie/Omnes

Triplum: *From my lady comes the grievous pain which I bear and of which I will die,*
   if hope does not keep me alive . . .
Duplum: *God, how can I find a way to go to him, whose [lover I am?]*

So, in a three-voice motet, the triplum and motetus came to be written either on facing pages or in separate columns on the same page, with the tenor extending across the bottom, as in Figure 5.6. This format, which allowed all the singers to read their parts from the same opening, remained the customary way of notating polyphony from 1280 until the sixteenth century.

Franconian notation allowed composers to achieve more rhythmic freedom and variety, both between and within voices. This new type of motet, in which each upper voice has a distinctive rhythmic shape, is sometimes called a Franconian motet, after Franco of Cologne. Whereas upper voices in early motets tend to conform closely to the rhythmic modes and repeat the same patterns frequently, this is no longer as true in a motet like Adam de la Halle's *De ma dame vient/Dieus, comment porroie/Omnes* (NAWM 22), shown in Example 5.14 and in Figure 5.6. Here the upper voices tend to differ in rhythm, and the same pattern rarely repeats from one measure to the next in either voice. Differences between the voices reinforce the contrast of texts, the triplum voicing the complaint of a man separated from his lady and the duplum the woman's thoughts of him. The tenor reiterates the melody for "omnes" from the Gradual *Viderunt omnes* twelve times, using three different rhythmic patterns four times each. The first rhythmic mode underlies the rhythm in each voice, transcribed here as alternating half and quarter notes, but is now more like a shared meter than a strict pattern. The tempo is slower

Franconian motet

CD 2|18

than in earlier motets, to accommodate the many semibreves in the upper parts. Phrases may last any number of perfections, and the voices rarely cadence together. The resulting motet is a highly individual composition, no longer part of a common stock of clausulae and motets available for reworking.

Petrus de Cruce   The rhythmic variety of the Franconian motet was extended one step further by Petrus de Cruce (Pierre de la Croix, fl. ca. 1270–1300). The motet in Example 5.15 is a good illustration of this. Here the tenor moves in longs (dotted half notes in transcription) and the duplum has no more than three semibreves per tempus, as in Franco's system, but the triplum may have as many as seven semibreves in a tempus. To accommodate the smallest notes, the tempo must be even slower than in a Franconian motet. The three voices move at quite different paces, producing a highly stratified texture with the tenor as harmonic foundation and the slow duplum as accompaniment to the voluble triplum.

Example 5.15: Petrus de Cruce, Aucun ont trouvé/Lonctans/Annuntiantes

Triplum: *Some compose their songs out of habit, but Love gives me a reason to sing,*
　he who so fills my heart with joy that I have to make a song; . . .
Duplum: *I have long refrained from singing, . . .*

Harmonic vocabulary   The harmonic vocabulary of the motet changed less during the thirteenth century than did the rhythmic structure. By the time of Adam and Petrus, the fifth, octave, or both together were expected at the beginning of each perfection, although thirds were allowed and dissonances appeared occasionally. A fourth above the lowest note, still used as a consonance early in the century (see Example 5.11), was now treated more often as a dissonance. The typical cadence featured the tenor descending by step and the upper voices rising by step to form a 1–5–8 sonority, as shown in Example 5.16. This type of cadence remained standard for the next two centuries.

Example 5.16: Cadence forms

The motet had an astonishing career in its first century. What began as a work of poetry more than composition, fitting a new text to an existing piece of music, was developed by generations of creative composers into the leading polyphonic genre, home to the most complex interplay of simultaneous different rhythms and texts yet conceived. The approach of Adam, Petrus, and other late-thirteenth-century composers reflects a new value placed on the distinctiveness of each piece, heralding an increased interest in the individual that became characteristic of the fourteenth century.

Tradition and innovation

ENGLISH POLYPHONY

After the Norman Conquest of England in 1066, English culture and music were closely allied to those of France. We saw these links in secular song, with English trouvères such as Richard the Lionheart, and it is true as well for organum, conductus, and motet. One of the three main sources for the *Magnus liber*, the earlier Wolfenbüttel manuscript, was made for a monastery in St. Andrews, Scotland, and probably copied there or in England; it was no doubt one of many copies in Britain. English composers wrote in all the Notre Dame genres, as well as discant settings of sequences and of troped chants for the Mass Ordinary. They focused on sacred Latin texts and tended to prefer the relatively homorhythmic style and regular phrasing of the conductus.

A distinctive musical dialect emerged when English composers began to extend certain aspects of Continental practice. Most significant was their use of imperfect consonances, often in parallel motion. Harmonic thirds and sixths were allowed in the Notre Dame repertory, as we have seen, but were much more common in English music. This apparently reflects the influence of folk polyphony. Writing about 1200, Gerald of Wales described improvised part-singing in close harmony in Wales and northern Britain, and a twelfth-century *Hymn to St. Magnus*, patron saint of the Orkney Islands, features parallel thirds. The version of *Super te Ierusalem/Sed fulsit virginitas/Dominus* from England (NAWM 21c), mentioned above, shows this influence, since the fourth voice produces many harmonic thirds and triads; even the final sonority has a third, unheard of in French music at this time. This version also reflects the English preference for four-voice textures and for the long-short rhythms of the first rhythmic mode, as opposed to the short-long rhythms of mode 3 in the French version.

Distinctive features

CD 2|17

Rondellus   One element of Notre Dame style that particularly intrigued English composers was voice exchange, the technique we observed in Pérotin's organum
in which voices trade segments of melody. An elaborate form of this was the
rondellus, in which two or three phrases, first heard simultaneously, are
each taken up in turn by each of the voices:

Triplum	a b c
Duplum	c a b
Tenor	b c a

Since the three voices are in the same range, the listener hears a threefold
repetition of the polyphonic phrase, but with voice parts traded. Rondellus

Figure 5.7: Sumer is
icumen in (ca. 1250)
in its original
notation. The upper
parts have a secondary
Latin text. The pes is
shown at the bottom of
the page.

sections appear frequently in English conductus from the later thirteenth century. There are also independent rondellus and rondellus-motets, such as *Fulget coelestis curia/O Petre flos/Roma gaudet* from the Worcester fragments, which has two three-voice rondellus sections framed by an introduction and coda.

Closely related to the rondellus is the **rota**, a perpetual canon or round at the unison. The most famous is *Sumer is icumen in* (NAWM 23) from about 1250, shown in Figure 5.7 and Example 5.17. Two voices sing a *pes* (Latin for "foot," or "ground"), a repeating melody that serves as a tenor; since the second half of each *pes* is the first half of the other, they form a two-voice

Rota

CD 2|21   CD 1|25

Example 5.17: Sumer is icumen in

Summer is come, sing loud, cuckoo! The seed grows and the meadow blooms,
  and now the wood turns green. Sing, cuckoo!
Pes: *Sing, cuckoo, now; sing, cuckoo!*

rondellus. Above this, two, three, or four voices enter in canon, singing in praise of summer. All the voices have similar rhythms in the first or fifth rhythmic modes, producing an effect of alternating F–A–C–F and G–B♭–D sonorities.

The distinctive qualities of English polyphony, particularly the preference for imperfect consonances and for relatively simple, syllabic, and periodic melodies, exercised an important influence on fifteenth-century Continental composers and contributed to the development of the international Renaissance style (see chapter 8).

A POLYPHONIC TRADITION

Before 1000, virtually all composition consisted of inventing a single melody line. By 1300, composition increasingly meant creating polyphony, although monophonic melodies continued to be composed. The emergence of written polyphony was a major turning point in Western music, as the coordination of multiple parts, interest in vertical sonorities, and use of counterpoint and harmony to create a sense of direction, tension, and resolution became characteristics of the Western tradition that set it apart from almost all others. In this sense, medieval polyphony was of enormous historical importance. Moreover, the notation that composers developed for polyphony introduced two features that became fundamental to later Western notation: vertical placement to coordinate multiple parts, as in Aquitanian and Notre Dame organum and modern scores, and different noteshapes to indicate relative duration, pioneered in Franconian notation and continued in our whole, half, quarter, and eighth notes and rests.

For all the contributions made by composers and theorists of medieval polyphony, their music seldom outlived them by more than a generation or two. As new styles of polyphony were created, older styles fell out of fashion, sometimes persisting for a time in local practice or in distant regions but eventually replaced by newer styles. We saw this in the rewriting of Léonin's *Magnus liber* by later generations, and will see it in the next chapter when fourteenth-century composers and theorists embrace a "new art." When rediscovered and transcribed in the eighteenth and nineteenth centuries, polyphony of the eleventh, twelfth, and thirteenth centuries was regarded as crude and harsh, its open harmonies, casual dissonance, and parallel fifths and octaves lacking the full, sweet, controlled sound of Renaissance music. Although historians recognized its significance, the music itself at first found few listeners.

In the late nineteenth and early twentieth centuries, composers began to draw on medieval music as an exotic element, distant in time rather than geography. Parallel organum found an echo in the parallel chord-streams of Debussy and others. As composers explored sonorities based on fourths, fifths, and seconds, partly inspired by medieval harmony, listeners grew accustomed to such sounds, and polyphony before 1300 began to seem less crude and more appealing. In the late twentieth century, medieval polyphony experienced a revival in concert and recording. What were once seen as defects—its differences from common-practice harmony and counterpoint, lack of instruments, uncertain rhythmic notation, and unfamiliarity—became strengths, offering new sounds, pure vocal beauty, performer freedom, and freshness. Music once employed to add solemnity to religious services or to entertain clerics and intellectuals has now found a small but apparently permanent niche in modern musical life.

Chapter

6

French and Italian Music in the Fourteenth Century

After the comparative stability of the thirteenth century, the fourteenth saw disruption and turmoil. The economy and population of western Europe declined, ravaged by famine, war, and plague. Conflicts and scandals tarnished the Church, and revolts challenged secular authorities. Yet the fourteenth century was also a period of remarkable creativity. The desire to understand and control nature spurred advances in science and technology, and an increasing interest in the world, the individual, and human nature led to art and literature that was more true to life and more eager to please its audience. The elite music of the time is characterized by an interplay between structure and pleasure, the former evident in the rhythmic and melodic patterning known as *isorhythm* and in standardized forms for secular song, and the latter in engaging melodies, chromatic inflections, more frequent imperfect consonances, and new possibilities in rhythm and meter.

EUROPEAN SOCIETY IN THE FOURTEENTH CENTURY

The emphasis on structure and pleasure in fourteenth-century music was in part a response to the forces of disorder and discontent in society at large. The rising economic tide of the previous three centuries reversed in the 1300s. Cooler weather reduced agricultural production, leading to a prolonged economic slump. Floods in northwestern Europe

116

brought famine in 1315–22, and about one person in ten perished. In 1347–50 the Black Death, a terrible combination of bubonic and pneumonic plagues, marched across Europe, wiping out a third of the population; almost everyone infected died in agony within days, and many of those left alive fled the cities and towns. The resulting disruptions in agriculture, manufacturing, and trade deepened the economic problems. So did frequent wars, especially the Hundred Years' War (1337–1453) between France and England. Poverty, war, taxes, and political grievances combined to spark peasant and urban rebellions in France, England, Flanders (modern-day Belgium), Germany, Italy, and Spain.

The Church was also in crisis. In the thirteenth century, Europeans viewed the Church as the supreme authority not only in matters of faith but to a large extent in intellectual and political affairs; now its authority, especially the supremacy of the pope, was widely questioned. In 1305, King Philip IV (the Fair)

The Church in crisis

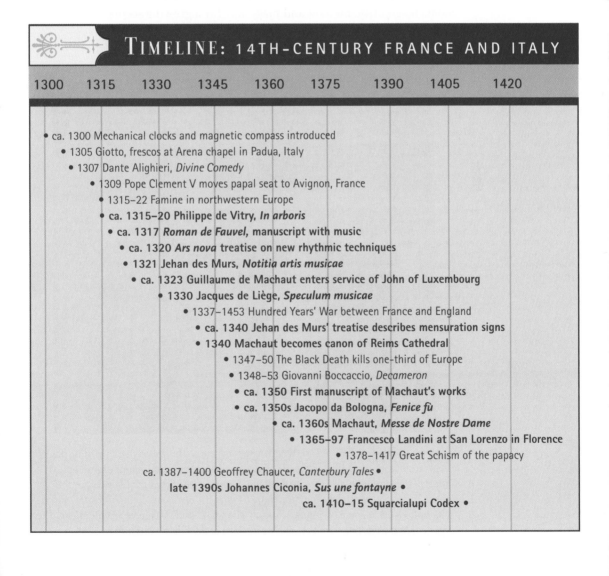

TIMELINE: 14TH-CENTURY FRANCE AND ITALY

1300	1315	1330	1345	1360	1375	1390	1405	1420

- ca. 1300 Mechanical clocks and magnetic compass introduced
- 1305 Giotto, frescos at Arena chapel in Padua, Italy
- 1307 Dante Alighieri, *Divine Comedy*
- 1309 Pope Clement V moves papal seat to Avignon, France
- 1315–22 Famine in northwestern Europe
- ca. 1315–20 Philippe de Vitry, *In arboris*
- ca. 1317 *Roman de Fauvel*, manuscript with music
- ca. 1320 *Ars nova* treatise on new rhythmic techniques
- 1321 Jehan des Murs, *Notitia artis musicae*
- ca. 1323 Guillaume de Machaut enters service of John of Luxembourg
- 1330 Jacques de Liège, *Speculum musicae*
- 1337–1453 Hundred Years' War between France and England
- ca. 1340 Jehan des Murs' treatise describes mensuration signs
- 1340 Machaut becomes canon of Reims Cathedral
- 1347–50 The Black Death kills one-third of Europe
- 1348–53 Giovanni Boccaccio, *Decameron*
- ca. 1350 First manuscript of Machaut's works
- ca. 1350s Jacopo da Bologna, *Fenice fù*
- ca. 1360s Machaut, *Messe de Nostre Dame*
- 1365–97 Francesco Landini at San Lorenzo in Florence
- 1378–1417 Great Schism of the papacy
- ca. 1387–1400 Geoffrey Chaucer, *Canterbury Tales* •
- late 1390s Johannes Ciconia, *Sus une fontayne* •
- ca. 1410–15 Squarcialupi Codex •

of France engineered the election of a French pope, Clement V, who never went to Rome because of hostility there to foreigners. From 1309 until 1377, the popes resided at Avignon in southeastern France, under the virtual control of the French king. This period, known as the Babylonian Captivity of the papacy, was succeeded by the Great Schism: from 1378 to 1417, there were rival claimants to the papacy in Rome, Avignon, and later in Pisa. This state of affairs, compounded by the often corrupt life of the clergy, drew sharp criticism, expressed both in writings and in the rise of popular heretical movements.

Science and secularism

Thirteenth-century Europeans could generally reconcile revelation and reason, the divine and human realms, and religion and politics. But in the fourteenth century, people began to separate science from religion and to see different roles for the church and the state, notions still held today. William of Ockham (ca. 1285–1349) and his followers argued that knowledge of nature and of humanity should rest on the experience of the senses rather than on reason alone and should seek natural rather than supernatural explanations. Without denying the claims of religion, this view laid the foundations for the modern scientific method and made way for a growing secular culture. New

Figure 6.1: Giotto (ca. 1266–1337), Wedding procession. This fresco (wall painting done in wet plaster) is one of a series on the life of the Virgin Mary painted around 1305 in the Chapel of the Madonna della Carità de Arena, known as the Scrovegni Chapel after the banker Enrico Scrovegni, who built the chapel on the site of a Roman amphitheater. Mary (with halo) leads a group of virgins, while a vielle player and two pipers provide music. The large-leaf branch jutting from the window is a sign of the Virgin's pregnancy.

technologies brought social change: eyeglasses enabled the aging to read, the magnetic compass allowed ships to venture farther from land, and mechanical clocks began to change the way people experienced time, from a constant flow, like sand through an hourglass or the movement of the sun across the sky, to a measured rhythm of hours and minutes.

Scientists' reliance on the senses had parallels among artists and writers, in their pursuit of realism and their focus on pleasing their audience. The Florentine painter Giotto (ca. 1266–1337) broke away from the formalized Byzantine style and achieved more naturalistic representation, as seen in the facial expressions, posture, and garments of the wedding participants in the painting shown in Figure 6.1. He created a sense of depth by placing figures and objects on different planes of the pictorial space, and the beauty of the faces and the symmetry of the composition show an interest in pleasing the eye. The growth of literacy among the public encouraged authors in Italy and England to write in the vernacular, including Dante Alighieri's *Divine Comedy* (1307), Giovanni Boccaccio's *Decameron* (1348–53), and Geoffrey Chaucer's *Canterbury Tales* (ca. 1387–1400). The latter two, written to entertain rather than elevate the reader, reflect daily life and portray people of all social classes more realistically than earlier literature had done.

Figure 6.2: In this miniature from the Roman de Fauvel, *a poem by Gervès du Bus , a charivari, or noisy serenade, awakens Fauvel and Vain Glory after their wedding. This manuscript from about 1317, probably prepared at the royal court, includes many interpolated pieces of music.*

The secular interests of the fourteenth century are well represented in music. The best-known composers of the time, Guillaume de Machaut and Francesco Landini, focused on secular music, and even the papal court at Avignon is known today for its cultivation of secular song. But composition of sacred music, including both monophonic chants and polyphony, remained strong, and the most famous piece of the century is Machaut's setting of the Mass Ordinary (discussed below).

Sacred and secular in music

The flavor of the times is captured in the *Roman de Fauvel*, an allegorical narrative poem satirizing corruption in politics and the Church, apparently written as a warning to the king of France and enjoyed in high political circles at court. Fauvel, a horse who rises from the stable to a powerful position, symbolizes a world turned upside down, in which the king outranks the pope and France is defiled. Fauvel embodies the sins represented by the letters of his name: Flattery, Avarice, Villainy ("U" and "V" were interchangeable), Variété (fickleness), Envy, and Lâcheté (cowardice). He ultimately marries and produces little Fauvels who destroy the world. A beautifully decorated manuscript from around 1317, shown in Figure 6.2, has 169 pieces of music interpolated within the poem. These constitute a veritable anthology of works from the thirteenth and early fourteenth centuries, some written for this collection, others chosen for their relevance to the poem's message. Most are monophonic, from Latin chants to secular songs. But thirty-four are motets,

Roman de Fauvel

many with texts that denounce the lax morals of the clergy or refer to political events. Among these motets in the *Roman de Fauvel* are the first examples of a new style, known today as the Ars Nova.

THE ARS NOVA IN FRANCE

Philippe de Vitry (1291–1361), French composer, poet, church canon, administrator for the duke of Bourbon and the king of France, and later bishop of Meaux, is named by one writer as the "inventor of a new art"—in Latin, *ars nova*. Several versions of a treatise from ca. 1320 representing Vitry's teaching, though perhaps not written by him, end with the words "this completes the *Ars nova* of Magister Philippe de Vitry," implying that *Ars nova* is the title of the treatise and Vitry its author. The term **Ars Nova** has come to denote the new French musical style inaugurated by Vitry in the 1310s and continued through the 1370s.

ARS NOVA NOTATION

The "new art" proceeded from two innovations in rhythmic notation, described in the *Ars nova* treatise and in treatises by Jehan des Murs, a mathematician and astronomer as well as music theorist. The first innovation allowed duple ("imperfect") division of note values along with the traditional triple ("perfect") division; the second provided for division of the semibreve, formerly the smallest possible note value, into **minims.** The resulting system offered new meters and allowed much greater rhythmic flexibility, including, for the first time, syncopation. Around 1340, des Murs discussed another innovation, **mensuration signs,** symbols that are the ancestors of modern time signatures. Understanding the new rhythmic profile of fourteenth-century French music requires some knowledge of the notation itself, described in a sidebar (see Innovations: Writing Rhythm).

Arguments against the Ars nova — Opponents as well as supporters acknowledged the new art. The Flemish theorist Jacques de Liège vigorously defended the "ancient art" (*ars antiqua*) of the late thirteenth century against the new innovations (see Source Reading). This marks the first well-documented dispute since ancient times between advocates of newer and older musical styles, a type of argument that has recurred often and always reflects differences in what is valued in music. When Jacques de Liège complained that in the new music "perfection is brought low, [and] imperfection is exalted," he was objecting that the "imperfect" duple division was now equally as valid as the "perfect" three-fold division, which carried associations with the Trinity.

ISORHYTHM

The earliest musical works to exemplify the Ars Nova are the motets of Philippe de Vitry, several of which appear in the *Roman de Fauvel* or are cited in the *Ars nova* treatises. Most are in three voices with Latin texts probably written by Vitry himself. His motets use a device modern scholars have called *isorhythm* ("equal rhythm"), in which the tenor is laid out in segments of identical rhythm. This extends the practice we observed in Notre Dame clausulae and thirteenth-century motets, where the tenor often repeats a rhythmic pattern and may also repeat a segment of melody (see chapter 5 and Examples 5.8 and 5.11–14). In the isorhythmic motet of the fourteenth century, the rhythmic patterns are longer and more complex, and the tenor moves so slowly in comparison to the upper voices that it is heard less as a melody than as a foundation for the entire polyphonic structure.

Theorists of the time recognized two recurring elements in motet tenors, rhythmic and melodic. They called the repeating rhythmic unit the ***talea*** and the recurring segment of melody the ***color.*** The color and talea could be the same length, always beginning and ending together, but most often the color extended over two, three, or more taleae. In some motets, the endings of the color and talea do not coincide, so that repetitions of the color begin in the middle of a talea. Upper voices may also be organized isorhythmically, in whole or part, to emphasize the recurring rhythmic patterns in the tenor.

Talea and color

The motet *In arboris/Tuba sacre fidei/Virgo sum* (NAWM 24), attributed to Vitry, illustrates isorhythm. The tenor, shown in Example 6.1, includes two statements of the color, a segment of chant on "Virgo sum." Each color is divided into three equal parts to fit three statements of the talea. The second color uses the same rhythmic scheme as the first, but the note values are

CD 2|22

SOURCE READING

Innovations: Writing Rhythm

What made the new musical style of the Ars Nova possible was a set of innovations in notating rhythm, innovations that underlie our modern system of whole, half, quarter, and eighth notes and rests.

The new notation required a rethinking of musical time. Remember that a century or so earlier, composers of the Notre Dame school had conceived of musical rhythm in terms of certain repeating patterns of long and short notes—the rhythmic modes (see chapter 5). All six modes fit a framework in which the basic time unit, or tempus, was always grouped in threes, like a measure of triple time. Franconian notation, introduced in the late thirteenth century, made it possible to escape the rigid mold of the rhythmic modes by using the shapes of notes to indicate their durations, yet still relied on the same three-fold groupings, called perfections. As long as theorists insisted on seeing musical time as a succession of perfections, each of which could only be divided in certain ways, many rhythms simply could not be written down, including anything in duple meter.

In Ars Nova notation, units of time could be grouped in either twos or threes, at several different levels of duration, allowing a much wider variety of rhythms to be written. The long (◣), breve (■), and semibreve (♦) could each be divided into either two or three notes of the next smaller value, as shown in Figure 6.3. The division of the long was called **mode** (*modus*), that of the breve **time** (*tempus*), and that of the semibreve **prolation** (*prolatio*). Division was **perfect** or **major** ("greater") if triple, **imperfect** or **minor** ("lesser") if duple. The terms "mode," "tempus," "perfect," and

"imperfect" are all derived from Notre Dame and Franconian notation and applied here to new but closely related uses (see chapter 5). A new note-form was introduced to indicate one-half or one-third of a semibreve: the **minim** (♦), meaning "least" in Latin.

The addition of smaller values was associated with a slowing of the tempo, so that for fourteenth-century music the breve rather than the long is typically transcribed as a measure in modern notation. The four possible combinations of time and prolation, shown in Figure 6.4, produce in effect four different meters, comparable to four in use today. Later in the century, time and prolation were indicated with **mensuration signs** that are the ancestors of modern time signatures: a circle for perfect time or incomplete circle for imperfect, with a dot for major prolation or no dot for minor. The incomplete circle C without a dot has come down to us as a sign for ¼ time (equivalent to imperfect time, minor prolation), showing the link between these four "prolations" and modern conceptions of meter.

In Ars Nova notation, noteshapes could indicate particular durations that remained unchanged by the notes around them. Such specificity made it possible for the first time to notate syncopation, a prominent feature in melodies of composers from the fourteenth century on. Indeed, Jehan des Murs wrote of the new system, "whatever can be sung can be written down." That was certainly not true of rhythmic notation in the thirteenth century, when what could be written down greatly limited what could be composed.

Our modern notation system is the direct descendant of Ars Nova notation, as shown in Figure 6.5. The noteshapes of Ars Nova notation are the

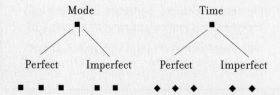

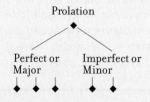

Mode	Time	Prolation
Perfect Imperfect	Perfect Imperfect	Perfect or Major Imperfect or Minor

Figure 6.3: Divisions of the long, breve, and semibreve in Ars Nova notation.

same as those of Franconian notation, with the addition of the minim. In both systems, ligatures continued to be used for certain combinations of longs and breves, as had been true since Notre Dame notation. About 1425, scribes began to write all these forms with open noteheads (sometimes called "white notation") rather than filling each in with ink ("black notation"). This change may have occurred at that time because scribes shifted from writing on parchment (scraped sheepskin or goatskin) to paper; filling in black notes on rough-surfaced paper increased the chance of spattered ink or bleed-through and thus a ruined page. Renaissance composers added still shorter note values, each half the duration of the next higher value, by filling in the notehead of a minim to create a *semiminim* and adding one or two flags to the semiminim to produce a *fusa* and a *semifusa*. Toward the end of the sixteenth century, the diamond-shaped notes of Renaissance notation changed to the round noteheads we use now, and ligatures fell out of use. With the addition of barlines in the seventeenth century, rhythmic notation had evolved from its first manifestations to its modern form in a little over four hundred years.

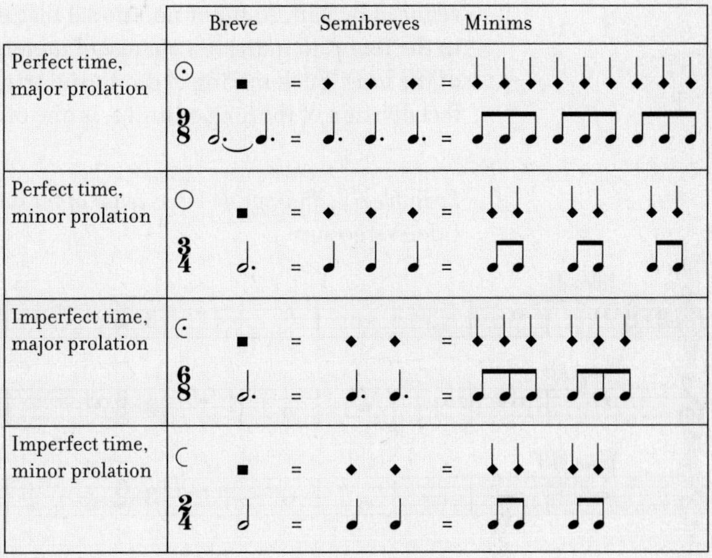

	Breve	Semibreves	Minims
Perfect time, major prolation			
Perfect time, minor prolation			
Imperfect time, major prolation			
Imperfect time, minor prolation			

Figure 6.4: The four combinations of time and prolation, with modern equivalents.

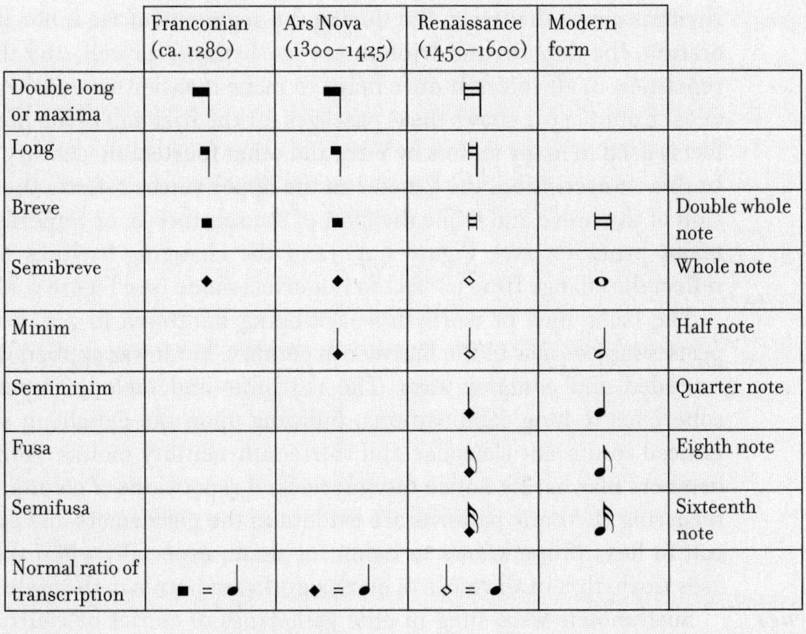

	Franconian (ca. 1280)	Ars Nova (1300–1425)	Renaissance (1450–1600)	Modern form	
Double long or maxima					
Long					
Breve					Double whole note
Semibreve					Whole note
Minim					Half note
Semiminim					Quarter note
Fusa					Eighth note
Semifusa					Sixteenth note
Normal ratio of transcription					

Figure 6.5: Comparison of notation systems.

reduced by half. Another notational feature is the use of "coloration," red ink in the tenor, to indicate a change of meter—here, from duple to triple division of the long. Such mixing of duple and triple groupings, or imperfect and perfect division of the long or breve, is one of the new techniques of the Ars Nova.

Example 6.1: Philippe de Vitry, tenor of the motet In arboris/Tuba sacre fidei/Virgo sum

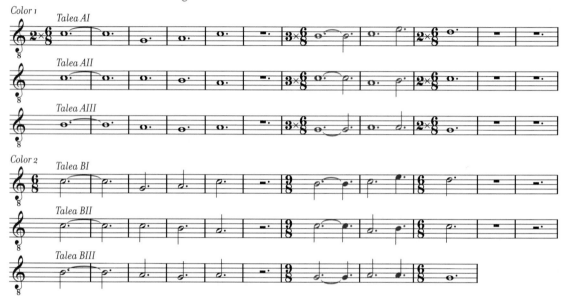

Isorhythm in upper voices For the most part, the upper voices in Vitry's motet move in ever-changing rhythms above the tenor. But during the segments of the tenor that use coloration, the duplum and triplum are isorhythmic as well, and the rhythmic repetition in all voices at once helps to make it easier to hear the end of each talea. Example 6.2 shows these passages for the first half of the piece. This effect is used in many motets by Vitry and other fourteenth-century composers. In this transcription, the $\frac{6}{8}$ meter in the upper voices reflects the duple division of the breve and triple division of the semibreve, or imperfect time and major prolation (see Figure 6.4), and the changing barlines in the tenor reflect the change from perfect to imperfect mode (see Figure 6.3).

The basic idea of isorhythm—arranging durations in a pattern that repeats—was not new in the fourteenth century, but it was applied in ever more extended and complex ways. The rhythmic and melodic repetitions gave coherence to long compositions, building upon the delight in structure we noticed in discant clausulae and thirteenth-century motets. Although some listeners may hardly notice the interlocked repetitions of color and talea, the recurring rhythmic patterns are evident to the performers and are not difficult to hear if one knows to listen for them, especially when the composer uses isorhythm in all voices to mark significant points in the cycle of the talea.

Audience   Such motets were sung in elite gatherings of clerics or courtiers, and no doubt many in the audience understood and appreciated the structure. As in earlier motets, intricate webs of meaning and sound link the texts, here all

Example 6.2: Passages of isorhythm in all voices

focused on the Virgin Mary and the primacy of faith over reason. The complex interrelationships in both text and music were aimed at educated listeners who treasured the search for meaning, whether in motets, in allegories such as the *Roman de Fauvel*, or in interpretations of the Bible itself.

HOCKET

The passages in Example 6.2 illustrate a technique called **hocket** (French *hoquet*, "hiccup"), in which two voices alternate in rapid succession, each resting while the other sings. Passages in hocket appear in some thirteenth-century conductus and motets and are frequently used in fourteenth-century isorhythmic works in coordination with recurrences of the talea, as in this Vitry motet. Pieces that use hocket extensively were themselves called hockets. Most were untexted and could be performed either by voices or by instruments.

HARMONIC PRACTICE

Example 6.2 also illustrates the greater prominence of imperfect consonances in the Ars Nova style, in comparison to earlier polyphony. Although thirds and sixths still needed resolution to a perfect consonance, they could be sustained and their resolution could be delayed (as in Example 6.2a, measures 25–28). The more frequent use of imperfect consonances in fourteenth-century French and Italian music can give it a sweeter sound to modern ears than earlier polyphony from the Continent. Yet open and parallel octaves and fifths were still common, distinguishing this music from the Renaissance practice of the fifteenth and sixteenth centuries.

GUILLAUME DE MACHAUT

The leading composer and poet of the French Ars Nova period was Guillaume de Machaut (ca. 1300–1377; see biography and Figure 6.6). His support by royal and aristocratic patrons allowed Machaut time to produce over 140 musical works, mostly settings of his own poetry, along with almost three hundred other poems. From about 1350 on, he gathered all his works in manuscripts prepared for his patrons. These collections show Machaut's awareness of himself as an individual creator, in stark contrast to the anonymity of most thirteenth-century composers, and his desire to preserve his creations for posterity. He composed in most of the genres then current, from motets to secular songs, and a survey of his music also serves to introduce us to the main types of Ars Nova composition.

MOTETS

Most of Machaut's twenty-three motets date from relatively early in his career. Twenty are isorhythmic, based on tenors from chant, and three use secular songs as tenors. Like other motets of the time, Machaut's are longer and more rhythmically complex than earlier examples and often include hocket and isorhythmic passages in the upper voices. The four four-voice motets show a knowledge of Vitry's motets and an apparent attempt to outdo the older composer in structural complexity.

MASS

Machaut's *Messe de Nostre Dame* (Mass of Our Lady) was one of the earliest polyphonic settings of the Mass Ordinary, probably the first polyphonic mass to be written by a single composer and conceived as a unit. Machaut intended it to be performed with one singer on each part, like most polyphony at the time. He apparently composed the work in the early 1360s for performance at a Mass for the Virgin Mary celebrated every Saturday at an altar of the cathedral in Reims. After his death, an oration for Machaut's soul was added to the service, and his mass continued to be performed there well into the fifteenth century.

Polyphonic settings of the Ordinary　　As we saw in chapter 5, through the thirteenth century chants from the Mass Proper were set polyphonically much more often than Ordinary chants. But in the fourteenth century, there are numerous settings of Ordinary texts by French, English, and Italian composers. Most were set as individual

GUILLAUME DE MACHAUT (CA. 1300–1377)

Machaut was the most important composer and poet in fourteenth-century France. He exercised a profound influence on his contemporaries and later artists, and his music has come to typify the French Ars Nova.

Much of what we know of Machaut's life and career comes from his own narrative poems, many of which describe events in the lives of himself and his patrons. He was born in the province of Champagne in northeastern France, probably to a middle-class family, educated as a cleric, probably in Reims, and later took Holy Orders. Around 1323, he entered the service of John of Luxembourg, king of Bohemia, as a clerk, eventually becoming the king's secretary. In that role, he accompanied John on his travels and military campaigns across Europe, describing these exploits in his poetry. From 1340 until his death in 1377, Machaut resided in Reims as canon of the cathedral, an office whose liturgical duties left ample time for poetry and composition. Machaut had close ties to royalty all his life, always moving in elite circles. Other patrons included John of Luxembourg's daughter Bonne; the kings of Navarre and France; and the dukes of Berry and Burgundy.

Machaut was the first composer to compile his complete works and to discuss his working methods, both signs of his self-awareness as a creator. He addressed *Le livre du voir dit* (The Book of the True Poem, 1363–65) to Peronne, a young admirer with whom he had fallen in love in his sixties. In it he says he typically writes his poems before setting them to music and is happiest when the music is sweet and pleasing.

The strong support of his patrons gave him the resources to supervise the prepa-

Figure 6.6: In this miniature from the last manuscript of Guillaume de Machaut's works prepared during his lifetime (ca. 1372), the elderly Machaut is visited in his study by Love, who introduces his three children, Sweet Thoughts, Pleasure, and Hope.

ration of several illuminated manuscripts containing his works, but the choice to do so seems to have been his own, inspired by a sense of his own worth as an artist and a desire to preserve his music and poetry for future generations. Such attitudes, commonplace today, remained rare among composers before the nineteenth century.

MAJOR MUSICAL WORKS: Messe de Nostre Dame *(Mass of Our Lady)*, Hoquetus David *(hocket)*, 23 motets *(19 isorhythmic)*, 42 ballades *(1 monophonic)*, 22 rondeaux, 33 virelais *(25 monophonic)*, 19 lais *(15 monophonic)*, 1 complainte, and 1 chanson royale *(both monophonic)*

POETICAL WORKS: Remede de Fortune *(Remedy of Fortune)*, Le livre du voir dit, *numerous other narrative poems, over 280 lyric poems*

movements that could be freely combined with others in a service, and a few were gathered into anonymous cycles. Machaut's mass builds on this tradition, but treats the six movements as one composition rather than separate pieces. The movements are linked together by similarities of style and approach, some recurring motives, and a tonal focus on D in the first three movements

Example 6.3: Guillaume de Machaut, Messe de Nostre Dame, *beginning of Christe*

and on F in the last three. All six movements are for four voices, with the duplum and triplum above the tenor and a second supporting voice, called the **contratenor** ("against the tenor"), in the same range as the tenor, sometimes below it and sometimes above.

The Kyrie, Sanctus, Agnus Dei, and Ite, missa est are isorhythmic (see NAWM 25). In each of these movements, the tenor carries a cantus firmus, the melody to a chant on the same Ordinary text, divided into two or more taleae. The contratenor is also isorhythmic, coordinated with the tenor, and together they form the harmonic foundation. Example 6.3 shows the opening of the Christe, including the first two statements of the seven-measure talea, marked by roman numerals. The upper two voices move more rapidly, with syncopation typical of Machaut. They are also partly isorhythmic; during the second statement of the talea, the rhythms in the upper voices closely parallel those in the first, and are virtually identical in all but the second and sixth measures of each talea. The rhythmic repetition in the upper voices makes the recurring talea more evident, as does the alternation of sustained notes on the first and fifth measure of each talea with lively rhythms in the other measures. Such contrast of rhythmic rest and activity is characteristic of Machaut's blocklike construction, and it suggests an architectural parallel, like the alternation of filigreed stained-glass windows and solid pillars along the wall of a Gothic cathedral. To generate rhythmic activity, Machaut often relies on repeating figuration; for example, the descending figure in the second measure of the triplum, echoed later in both duplum and triplum, recurs frequently throughout the mass, serving less as a unifying motive than as a way to create movement.

The Gloria and Credo, with their much longer texts, are set in the style of discant or conductus: essentially syllabic and largely homorhythmic, rapidly declaiming the words in all voices, as illustrated in Example 6.4. The words "Jesu Christe" (Jesus Christ) in the Gloria and "ex Maria Virgine" (of the Virgin Mary) in the Credo are set in relief with long-sustained chords, a musical

Isorhythmic movements

CD 2|28   CD 1|26

Discant-style movements

Example 6.4: Machaut, Messe de Nostre Dame, *excerpt from Gloria*

⌐‾‾¬ = ligature in original notation

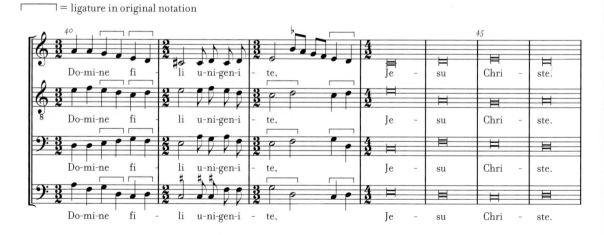

Lord, the only begotten Son, Jesus Christ.

equivalent to the tradition in medieval paintings of depicting Mary and Jesus as much larger than the figures around them, to emphasize their importance. Neither movement is based on chant. Both movements end with elaborate, partially isorhythmic passages on the word "Amen."

MONOPHONIC SONGS

Machaut's monophonic French songs continued the trouvère tradition, and most are on the subject of love. They were performed as entertainment in the courts and elite circles around Machaut. Of his nineteen *lais,* a twelfth-century form akin to the sequence, fifteen are monophonic and four include polyphony.

Virelais   A more popular genre was the **virelai,** one of the three **formes fixes** (fixed forms), in which text and music have particular patterns of repetition including a refrain. The typical virelai has three stanzas, with the refrain at the beginning and after each stanza, in the pattern A bba A bba A bba A. A stands for the refrain, b for a musical phrase used twice at the beginning of each stanza, and a for the last part of the stanza, which uses the music of the refrain but with new words. The b phrases often have open and closed endings, as in an estampie (see chapter 4). The number of lines of poetry for each section of music may vary; the chart in Figure 6.7c shows one disposition Machaut used. Most of Machaut's virelais are monophonic, but eight are polyphonic. (For an example of the form, see the Ciconia virelai discussed below.)

POLYPHONIC SONGS

A major innovation of the Ars Nova period was the development of polyphonic songs, or **chansons** (French for "songs"), in **treble-dominated style.**

Capital letters indicate refrains, lowercase letters repetition of music with new text.

a. Ballade (three stanzas: aab aab aab)

	Stanza					(Refrain)
Sections of music:	a		a		b	
Lines of poetry:	1 2		3 4		5 6 7	8

b. Rondeau (one stanza: ABaAabAB)

	Refrain			Half-refrain			Refrain	
Sections of music:	A B		a	A	a	b	A	B
Lines of poetry:	1 2		3	4 (=1)	5	6	7 (=1)	8 (=2)

c. Virelai (three stanzas, plus final refrain: A bba A bba A bba A)

	Refrain		Stanza			
Sections of music:	A		b	b		a
Lines of poetry:	1 2		3 4	5 6	7 8	

Figure 6.7: The formes fixes *(fixed forms) of fourteenth-century French songs.*

Figure 6.8: Miniature from the earliest manuscript of Machaut's collected works (ca. 1350), showing five couples dancing in a circle. The dancer farthest to the right is singing to accompany the dance. The singer resembles Machaut as pictured in the later manuscript in Figure 6.6, at a younger age. The music under the picture is a monophonic virelai by Machaut, which we may assume is the song being performed in the picture.

In this style the upper voice carrying the text, called the ***treble*** or ***cantus,*** is the principal line, supported by a slower-moving tenor without text. To this essential two-voice framework may be added one or two other untexted voices: a contratenor in the same range as the tenor or, less often, a fast-moving triplum in the treble range. Recent scholarship suggests that Machaut intended all the parts to be sung, with the lack of words in the supporting voices making the cantus stand out as if in relief. Some modern performances sing the text in all voices or use instruments on the untexted lines. That Machaut wrote the cantus before the tenor, reversing the normal order of composition in earlier polyphony, is indicated by the appearance of one of his virelais, *Mors sui se je ne vous voy,* as a monophonic song in an early manuscript and joined with a tenor in later ones.

As is true of Machaut's monophonic songs, his polyphonic chansons set his own poems. Most are in the form of a ***ballade*** or ***rondeau*** (pl. *rondeaux*), the other two *formes fixes* along with the virelai (see Figure 6.7). The three genres tended to differ somewhat in subject matter as well as in form: ballades were the most serious, appropriate for philosophical or historical themes or for celebrating an event or person; rondeaux centered on themes of love; and virelais often related descriptions of nature to feelings of love.

Formes fixes

All the *formes fixes* were derived from genres associated with dancing, as evident by their use of refrains (see chapter 4). Machaut's monophonic virelais could still be danced to; Figure 6.8 shows an illumination from a manuscript of his compositions, in which a singer (perhaps Machaut himself) performs a monophonic virelai while he and several companions dance in a circle. But Machaut's polyphonic chansons were highly stylized and not used

Ballades

for dancing. Often the repetitions of the refrain lines were invested with fresh meanings or contexts by the preceding words.

A ballade consists of three stanzas, each sung to the same music and each ending with the same line of poetry, which serves as a refrain. The musical form of the stanza is aab; it resembles bar form, with two couplets sung to the same music (often with open and closed endings) followed by contrasting music for the remainder of the stanza and culminating in the refrain. The refrain may repeat the ending of the a section. Machaut wrote ballades with two, three, and four parts, but his typical settings were for high male voice with lower voices (or instruments) on the untexted tenor and contratenor. (For an example of the form, see the ballade by Du Fay discussed in chapter 8.)

Rondeaux

The rondeau resembles the ballade and virelai in having a refrain, but differs in two significant ways: it has only one stanza, rather than three, and the refrain is in two sections and includes all the music. The form can be diagrammed ABaAabAB, in which capital letters signify the refrain text and lowercase letters indicate new text set to music from the corresponding section of the refrain. Typically, the A section cadences without finality, akin to an open ending. The B section may echo the final passage of the A section, as

CD 2|35   CD 1|33

in Machaut's *Rose, liz, printemps, verdure* (NAWM 26), but closes conclusively on the tonal center. Most rondeaux are for two or three voices. *Rose, liz* is exceptional in having four voices; its triplum, lacking in one early manuscript, was probably added later. But it is typical of Machaut's style in the varied rhythms, supple syncopations, and mostly stepwise flow of its melody, all designed to make it appealing to the listener. Also characteristic are long melismas near the beginnings and sometimes in the middle of poetic lines. Since these melismas often fall on unimportant words or unaccented syllables, their function is formal and decorative rather than serving to emphasize the text.

REPUTATION

Machaut was widely esteemed in his own time and for several decades after his death, exercising an influence on poets (including Chaucer) and composers alike. His works loom large because they survive, which Machaut ensured they would by having them copied into numerous manuscripts. Too much music by Vitry and other contemporaries has been lost, so we cannot evaluate Machaut's true place. His modern reputation as the most important composer of his time may rest at least in part on his desire that his body of work be preserved as a whole rather than left to the vicissitudes of fortune.

THE ARS SUBTILIOR

Composers in the later fourteenth century continued and extended the genres and traditions of the Ars Nova. In a paradox typical of the century, the papal court at Avignon was one of the main patrons of secular music. There and at other courts across southern France and northern Italy, a brilliant chivalric society allowed composers to flourish. Their music consisted chiefly of polyphonic ballades, rondeaux, and virelais, continuing the *formes fixes*. These chansons, mostly love songs, were intended for an elite audience—aristocrats and connoisseurs who esteemed this music because it developed every possibility of melody, rhythm, counterpoint, and notation. The composers' fascination with technique and their willingness to take a given procedure to new extremes have led music historians to term this repertory **Ars Subtilior** (the more subtle manner). The refined and elevated style of these songs is matched by their sumptuous appearance, including fanciful decorations, intermingled red and black notes, ingenious notation, and occasional caprices that include a love song written in the shape of a heart, shown in Figure 6.9, or a canon in the shape of a circle.

Some songs from this period feature remarkable rhythmic complexities, reaching a level not seen again until the twentieth century. Voices move in contrasting meters and conflicting groupings; beats are subdivided in many different ways; phrases are broken by rests or held in suspense through chains of syncopations; and harmonies are purposely blurred through rhythmic disjunction. Whatever the notation allowed, someone would try.

Rhythmic complexity

Figure 6.9: The rondeau Belle, bonne, sage *by Baude Cordier in a manuscript from ca. 1400. The texted cantus across the top is accompanied by textless tenor and contratenor lines. The red notation indicates changes of mensuration. The heart shape of the notation is a pun on the composer's name (cor is Latin for heart), and the word "heart" in the text is replaced with a red heart.*

CD 2|39

Example 6.5 shows the opening of a virelai, *Sus une fontayne* (NAWM 27), by Johannes Ciconia (ca. 1370–1412), that exemplifies the Ars Subtilior. Born and trained in Flanders, Ciconia spent most of his career in northern Italy, writing music in a variety of genres and styles. He apparently composed this piece while serving at the court of Gian Galeazzo Visconti in Pavia in the late 1390s; it is unlike anything else Ciconia wrote, reflecting the vogue for the Ars Subtilior at Visconti's court. At the beginning of the piece, each voice has a different mensuration sign, creating a metrical conflict between the equivalent of $\frac{6}{8}$ in the tenor, $\frac{2}{4}$ in the cantus (with each eighth note equal to an eighth note of the tenor), and $\frac{2}{4}$ in the contratenor (with the quarter note equal to a dotted quarter note in the other two voices, a proportion indicated by the backwards C mensuration sign). The top two voices feature syncopations, adding further rhythmic complexity. Notes in different voices most often do not coincide, resulting in many passing dissonances. After a few measures, the contratenor and cantus shift to the equivalent of $\frac{3}{4}$, the counterpoint smooths out, and consonance predominates, bringing a point of relative calm in older Ars Nova style. As the music continues, mensuration signs change frequently and new rhythmic arrangements are continually introduced, so that each phrase has a distinctive profile, which helps to articulate the form of the piece. Despite the elaborate compositional techniques and the virtuosic demands this song makes on its performers, the aural effect is quite attractive, with interesting melodies and many sweet consonances.

A limited and brief fashion

Ars Subtilior music was intended for professional performers and cultivated listeners. Its formidable rhythmic and notational complexities were in

Example 6.5: Johannes Ciconia, beginning of Sus une fontayne

By a fountain . . . / Not knowing my chances . . .

fashion for only about a generation. At the same time, guilds of musicians from northern France created a simpler type of secular polyphony. Their poems and music had a popular character: instead of polished courtly sentiments, the texts offered realistic scenes of the hunt and the marketplace, and the music imitated the straightforward rhythms of folk song. Although few examples are preserved, this simpler art must have flourished widely and may ultimately have proven more influential on later musicians.

ITALIAN TRECENTO MUSIC

Unlike France, which had a monarchy, Italy in the late Middle Ages was a collection of city-states, each with its own political, cultural, and linguistic traditions. Italians refer to the fourteenth century as the **Trecento** (from "mille trecento," Italian for 1300), and Italian music of the period has a distinctive character.

Social roles for Italian music

From writings of the time, we learn how music accompanied nearly every aspect of Italian social life. In Boccaccio's *Decameron*, for example, a group of friends who have retreated to the country from plague-ridden Florence pass the time by telling stories, dancing, singing, and playing instruments (see Source Reading). But most Italian music from the times was never written down. Secular music for many levels of society was purely aural. The only music of the people to have come down to us in manuscripts is the lauda repertory (see chapter 4). Church polyphony was mostly improvised, either by a soloist singing in discant style over the written notes of a chant, or by an organist adding a line of counterpoint above the chant while alternating phrases of the Mass Ordinary with a choir singing plainchant. What Italian church polyphony survives in notation, mostly from late in the century, includes primarily settings of Mass Ordinary chants for two to four voices or for keyboard, along with some other liturgical settings and motets.

The largest surviving body of Italian music from the time is the repertory of secular polyphonic songs, written as a refined entertainment for elite circles. The principal centers of Trecento polyphony were cities in central and northern Italy, notably Bologna, Padua, Modena, Milan, Perugia, and above all Florence, a

SOURCE READING

MUSIC-MAKING IN THE DECAMERON

Giovanni Boccaccio (1313–1375) was one of the great fourteenth-century writers whose use of the local dialect of Tuscany, around Florence, made that dialect into the national literary language of Italy. His masterpiece is the Decameron (1348–53), a collection of one hundred witty and sometimes ribald stories, told over a ten-day period by ten friends who have fled to the country to avoid the Black Death ravaging Florence. The evening before the first day of storytelling, they enjoy dinner, dancing, and music.

———— • ————

The tables having been cleared away, the queen commanded that instruments be brought in, for all the ladies knew how to dance the carole [round dance], and the young men too, and some of them could play and sing very well. Upon her request, Dioneo took a lute and Fiammetta a viol, and they began sweetly to play a dance. Then the queen, having sent the servants out to eat, formed a circle with the other ladies and the two young men and struck up a round dance with a slow pace. When this was finished, they began to sing charming and merry songs. They continued in this way for a long time, until the queen thought it was time to go to sleep.

From Giovanni Boccaccio, *Decameron*, Day One, Introduction.

particularly important cultural center from the fourteenth through the sixteenth centuries, and the home of both Dante and Boccaccio.

Italian notation

The Italian notational system differed from that of the French Ars Nova. The most significant differences are that the breve can be broken into two, three, four, six, eight, nine, or twelve equal semibreves or various patterns of unequal ones, and that groupings of semibreves are marked off by dots, akin to the modern barline. This kind of notation, particularly convenient for florid melodic lines, served Italian music well until the later part of the century. By then it was supplemented and eventually replaced by the French system, which had proved itself better adapted to the musical style of the time.

Squarcialupi Codex

Very few examples of Italian secular polyphony from before 1330 have survived, but after that date there are several manuscripts. The most copious source, unfortunately late and not altogether reliable, is the richly decorated *Squarcialupi Codex*, named for its former owner, the Florentine organist Antonio Squarcialupi (1416–1480). This collection, probably copied about 1410–15, contains 354 pieces, mostly for two or three voices, by twelve composers of the Trecento and early Quattrocento (1400s). A miniature portrait of each composer appears at the beginning of the section containing his works, as shown in Figure 6.10. Three types of secular Italian pieces appear in this and other manuscripts: *madrigal, caccia,* and *ballata.*

THE FOURTEENTH-CENTURY MADRIGAL

The fourteenth-century **madrigal** (not to be confused with the better-known sixteenth-century madrigal) is a song for two or three voices without instrumental accompaniment. All the voices sing the same text, usually an idyllic, pastoral, satirical, or love poem. Madrigals consist of two or more three-line stanzas, each set to the same music, followed by a closing pair of lines, called the **ritornello** (Italian for "refrain"), set to different music with a different meter. The form is charted in Figure 6.11 on page 138. Jacopo da Bologna's madrigal *Fenice fù* (NAWM 28) is typical of the earlier Trecento style, exhibiting the characteristic rhythmic variety and fluidity. One difference from the French Ars Nova is that here the two voices are relatively equal, occasionally echoing each other or engaging in hocketlike alternation. In the stanzas, the last accented syllable of each line of poetry is set with a long melisma, somewhat more florid in the upper voice. Such melismas on the last accent are characteristic of the Italian style.

CD 2|42

THE CACCIA

The **caccia** parallels the French *chace*, in which a popular-style melody is set in strict canon to lively, graphically descriptive words. The Italian caccia, in fashion chiefly from 1345 to 1370, features two voices in canon at the unison; unlike its French and Spanish counterparts, it usually has a free untexted tenor in slower motion below. Cacce are irregular in poetic form, although, like madrigals, many have ritornellos, which are not always canonic. *Caccia* and *chace* both mean "hunt," referring to the pursuit of one voice after the other. In some cases it also applies to the subject matter of the text. For

Figure 6.10: A page from the richly illustrated Squarcialupi Codex, an early-fifteenth-century manuscript named for its fifteenth-century owner Antonio Squarcialupi, showing Francesco Landini playing a portative organ. The portrait is set inside the initial letter M of Landini's madrigal Musica son *(I am music). The decorative border features pictures of other instruments, including (counter-clockwise from upper left) lute, vielle, cittern or citole, harp, psaltery, three recorders, portative organ, and three shawms.*

a. Madrigal

	Stanza			Stanza			Ritornello	
Sections of music:	a			a			b	
Lines of poetry:	1	2	3	4	5	6	7	8

b. Ballata

	Ripresa			Stanza (2 piedi)				Volta			Ripresa		
Sections of music:	A			b		b		a			A		
Lines of poetry:	1	2	3	4	5	6	7	8	9	10	1	2	3

Figure 6.11:
Fourteenth-century
Italian song forms.

example, Ghirardello da Firenze's caccia *Tosto che l'alba* (NAWM 29) describes a hunt, and the musical imitations of calling the dogs and sounding the hunting horn are both high-spirited and comic, especially when treated in canon. Besides hunting, cacce may describe other animated scenes, such as a fishing party, a bustling marketplace, a party of girls gathering flowers, a fire, or a battle. The music adds vivid details such as bird songs, shouts, or dialogue, often with the aid of hocket or echo effects between the voices.

THE BALLATA

The polyphonic **ballata** became popular later than the madrigal and caccia and showed some influence from the treble-dominated French chanson style. The word "ballata" (from *ballare*, "to dance") originally meant a song to accompany dancing. Thirteenth-century ballate (of which no musical examples are known today) were monophonic dance songs with choral refrains, and in Boccaccio's *Decameron* the ballata was still associated with dancing. Although a few early fourteenth-century monophonic examples have survived, most ballate in the manuscripts are for two or three voices and date from after 1365.

As shown in Figure 6.11, polyphonic ballate have the form AbbaA, like a single stanza of a French virelai. A *ripresa*, or refrain, is sung before and after a stanza consisting of two *piedi* (feet), couplets sung to the same musical phrase, and the *volta*, the closing lines of text, sung to the same music as the ripresa.

FRANCESCO LANDINI

The leading composer of ballate and the foremost Italian musician of the Trecento was Francesco Landini (ca. 1325–1397; see biography and Figure 6.12). Of his 140 ballate, 89 are for two voices, 42 for three, and nine survive in both two- and three-part versions. Those for two voices, evidently somewhat earlier works, resemble madrigals in texture, with two texted parts. Many of the three-part ballate are in a treble-dominated style, featuring solo voice with two untexted accompanying parts that were most likely sung, as in Machaut's chansons. Example 6.6 shows the opening of a ballata in this later style, Landini's *Non avrà ma' pietà* (NAWM 30).

FRANCESCO LANDINI (CA. 1325–1397)

Landini was born in northern Italy, probably in Florence or nearby Fiesole. The son of a painter, he was blinded by smallpox during childhood and turned to music, becoming an esteemed performer, composer, and poet. A master of many instruments, he was especially known for his skill at the organetto, a small portative organ. According to a fourteenth-century Florentine chronicler, Filippo Villani, Landini played the organetto "as readily as though he had the use of his eyes, with a touch of such rapidity (yet always observing the measure), with such skill and sweetness, that beyond all doubt he excelled all organists within memory."

Landini was organist at the monastery of Santa Trinità in 1361–65, then became a chaplain at the church of San Lorenzo, where he remained until his death. He apparently wrote no sacred music, and is best known for his ballate. Landini is a principal character in Giovanni da Prato's *Paradiso degli Alberti*, a narrative poem from around 1425 that records scenes and conversations in Florence from the year 1389. Prato includes a legendary incident that testifies to Landini's skill as a performer:

Now the sun rose higher and the heat of the day increased. The whole company remained in the pleasant shade, as a thousand birds sang among the verdant branches. Someone asked Francesco [Landini] to play the organ a little, to see whether the sound would make the birds increase or diminish their song. He did so at once, and a great wonder followed. When the sound began many of the birds fell silent and gathered around as if in amazement, listening for a long time. Then they resumed their song and redoubled it,

Figure 6.12: The tombstone of Francesco Landini. The blind composer plays a portative organ, accompanied by two angel musicians.

showing inconceivable delight, and especially one nightingale, who came and perched above the organ on a branch over Francesco's head.

MAJOR WORKS: *140 ballate, 12 madrigals, 1 caccia, 1 virelai*

From Filippo Villani, *Le Vite d'uomini illustri fiorentini*, ed. G. Mazzuchelli (Florence, 1847), 46: Giovanni da Prato, *Il Paradiso degli Alberti*, ed. A. Wesselofsky (Bologna, 1867), 111–13.

Example 6.6: Francesco Landini, beginning of Non avrà ma' pietà

She will never have pity, this lady of mine . . . / Perhaps by her will be extinguished
[the flames] . . .

One of the charms of Landini's music is the sweetness of the harmonies. Sonorities containing thirds and sixths are plentiful, though they never begin or end a section or piece. Equally charming are his graceful vocal melodies, arranged in arching phrases and moving most often by step, decorated with varied and often syncopated rhythms but ultimately smoother in both pitch contour and rhythm than most melodies by Machaut. Melismas on the first and penultimate syllables of a poetic line are characteristic of the Italian style, as is the clear, almost syllabic declamation between melismas. The end of every line, and often the first word and the midpoint, or caesura, of a line, is marked by a cadence. Most are of the type known as an "under-third cadence," in which, as the tenor descends by step, the upper voice decorates its ascent by first descending to the lower neighbor and then skipping up a third (see Example 6.6, measures 3–4, 5–6, and 10–11). Though often called the "Landini cadence," it is ubiquitous in both French and Italian music of the time.

FRENCH INFLUENCE

Toward the end of the fourteenth century, the music of Italian composers began losing its specific national characteristics and absorbing the contemporary French style. Italians wrote songs to French texts and in French genres, and their works recorded in late-fourteenth-century manuscripts often appear in French notation. The blending of national traditions became prominent in the fifteenth century, when northern musicians took up positions in Italy, and traits of French, Italian, Flemish, Netherlandish, and English music were integrated into an international musical style (see chapter 8).

FOURTEENTH-CENTURY MUSIC IN PERFORMANCE

VOICES AND INSTRUMENTS

We know from pictorial and literary sources of the fourteenth and early fifteenth centuries that polyphonic music was usually performed by a small vocal or instrumental ensemble or a combination of the two, with only one voice or instrument to a part. But there was no uniform way of performing any particular piece. Manuscripts did not specify instruments, leaving the choice of forces to the performers, guided by habit and tradition. Purely vocal performance of a piece for two, three, or four parts was most common, but some or all parts could also be played on instruments. Figure 6.13 shows a singer accompanied by an organist, perhaps playing one or two accompanying lines from a polyphonic setting. The presence of a text does not mean the part was always sung, nor does the absence of words mean the part is instrumental. We can say only that performances probably varied according to circumstances, depending on tastes and preferences and on the singers or players who happened to be at hand.

Figure 6.13: Tapestry from the Low Countries (ca. 1420), showing a man in courtly dress singing from a manuscript. He is accompanied by a woman playing a positive organ, the type that is portable but must be placed on a table to be played, rather than resting on a lap like the portative organ played by Landini in Figure 6.10. A boy stands behind the organ, pumping the bellows to force air through the pipes and produce the sounds.

INSTRUMENTS

Musicians in the fourteenth through sixteenth centuries distinguished between instruments based on their relative loudness, using **haut** (French for "high") and **bas** ("low") for volume rather than pitch. The most common low instruments were harps, vielles, lutes, psalteries, portative organs, transverse flutes, and recorders. Among the high instruments were shawms, **cornetts** (hollowed-out wood, with finger holes and a brass-type mouthpiece), and trumpets. Percussion instruments, including kettledrums, small bells, and cymbals, were common in ensembles of all kinds. To judge from representations in the art of the time, instruments of contrasting timbres were often grouped together. Out-of-doors music, dancing, and especially festive or solemn ceremonies called for relatively larger ensembles and louder instruments.

Keyboard instruments

Keyboard instruments became more practical and widely used in the fourteenth and fifteenth centuries. In addition to the portative organ, shown in Figure 6.10, positive organs like that in Figure 6.13 were frequently employed in secular music, and large, unmovable organs were installed in many churches. Pedal keyboards were added to church organs in Germany during the late 1300s. A mechanism of **stops** enabling the player to select different ranks of pipes and the addition of a second keyboard were both achievements of the early fifteenth century. Although the earliest keyboard instruments of the harpsichord and clavichord type were invented in the fourteenth century, they were not commonly used until the fifteenth.

INSTRUMENTAL MUSIC

Little purely instrumental music survives from the fourteenth century. Vocal pieces were sometimes played instrumentally throughout, with added embellishments in the melodic line. Instrumental arrangements were largely improvised, but some for keyboard were written down. The Robertsbridge Codex from about 1325 includes organ arrangements of three motets, and the Faenza Codex from the first quarter of the fifteenth century contains keyboard versions of ballades by Machaut and madrigals and ballate by Landini and others, as well as keyboard pieces based on chants for Mass. We can assume that there was also a large repertory of instrumental dance melodies, but as these pieces were generally either improvised or played from memory, few written examples have been preserved. There are about fifteen surviving instrumental dances from fourteenth-century Italy, most in the Italian form of the estampie, the *istampita*.

MUSICA FICTA

Just as the choice of instruments was normally left to the performers, so was the use of certain chromatic alterations known as **musica ficta.** Musicians from the fourteenth through sixteenth centuries often raised or lowered notes by a semitone to avoid the tritone F–B in a melody, to make a smoother melodic line, to avoid sounding an augmented fourth or diminished fifth above the lowest note, or to provide "a sweeter-sounding harmony" at cadences, as the theorist Prosdocimo de' Beldomandi observed (see Source Reading). This practice was called *musica ficta* ("feigned music"), because most altered notes lay outside the standard gamut. The system of hard, soft, and natural hexachords (see chapter 2) permitted semitones, pronounced *mi-fa* in solmization syllables, between B and C, E and F, and A and B♭. This was the realm of *musica recta* (correct music), the gamut of notes located in the Guidonian hand. A note outside this realm was considered "outside the hand," "false," or "feigned" (*ficta*), as it involved putting the syllables *mi* and *fa* on notes where they would not normally go.

SOURCE READING

PROSDOCIMO DE' BELDOMANDI ON *MUSICA FICTA*

Fourteenth-century musicians avoided tritones and smoothed the harmony and melody by raising or lowering notes a semitone according to a set of rules, a practice called musica ficta. *One of the best explanations of these rules is by Prosdocimo de' Beldomandi (d. 1428), a doctor and professor at the University of Padua. Since musicians of the time were trained to distinguish whole from half steps through solmization syllables and the natural, hard, and soft hexachords (see chapter 2), he used these concepts to explain musica ficta.*

———— • ————

Musica ficta is the feigning of [solmization] syllables or the placement of syllables in a location where they do not seem to be—to apply *mi* where there is no *mi* and *fa* where there is no *fa*, and so forth. Concerning musica ficta, it is necessary to know first of all that it is never to be applied except where necessary, because in art nothing is to be applied without necessity. . . .

3. It must be known, too, that the signs of musica ficta are two, round or soft ♭ [which became the modern ♭] and square or hard ♮ [modern ♮ or ♯]. These two signs show us the feigning of syllables in a location where such syllables cannot be. . . .

6. Last, for understanding the placement of these two signs, round ♭ and square ♮, it must be known that these signs are to be applied to octaves, fifths, and similar intervals as it is necessary to enlarge or diminish them in order to make them good consonances if they earlier were dissonant, because such intervals ought always to be major or consonant in counterpoint. But these signs are to be applied to imperfectly consonant intervals—the third, the sixth, the tenth, and the like—as is necessary to enlarge or diminish them to give them major or minor inflections as appropriate, because such intervals ought sometimes to be major and sometimes minor in counterpoint; . . . for you should always choose that form, whether major or minor, that is less distant from that location which you intend immediately to reach. . . . There is no other reason for this than a sweeter-sounding harmony. . . . This is because the closer the imperfect consonance approaches the perfect one it intends to reach, the more perfect it becomes, and the sweeter the resulting harmony.

From *Contrapunctus* [Counterpoint, 1412], Book 5, Chapters 1–6, trans. Jan Herlinger (Lincoln: University of Nebraska Press, 1984), 71–85.

Cadences   Musica ficta was often used at cadences. Theorists, composers, and singers agreed that a sixth expanding to an octave should be major rather than minor, and a third contracting to a unison should be minor rather than major, because, in Prosdocimo's words, "the closer the imperfect consonance approaches the perfect one it intends to reach, the more perfect it becomes, and the sweeter the resulting harmony." Thus the strictly modal cadences in Example 6.7a were typically altered as shown in Example 6.7b; the last of these, in which both upper notes are raised, is known as a **double leading-tone cadence** and is a characteristic sound in fourteenth- and fifteenth-century music. Cadences on G and C were altered in similar fashion. In cadences on E, however, the penultimate intervals were already the right size, as shown in Example 6.7c, so no alteration was required. Cadences like these, in which the lower voice descends by a semitone and the upper voice rises a whole tone, are called **Phrygian cadences,** since they occur naturally in the Phrygian mode; they may also occur on B or A.

Example 6.7: Alterations at cadences

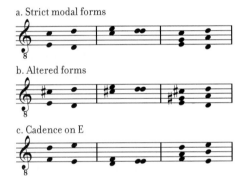

a. Strict modal forms

b. Altered forms

c. Cadence on E

Omission of   Such alterations would present no difficulty to modern performers if com-
accidentals   posers and scribes had consistently entered the appropriate signs in the
in notation   manuscripts: what we think of as accidentals (which they used to indicate the unexpected appearance of *mi* or *fa,* as Prosdocimo explains). Unfortunately for us, they often did not, and when they did they were inconsistent, as the same passage may appear in different manuscripts with different written accidentals. This was no mere carelessness, for it accorded with the theoretical framework of the time. Composers and scribes may sometimes have been reluctant to commit notes "outside the hand" to paper. Singers, meanwhile, were trained to recognize situations in which a note should be altered to produce a smoother melody or progression of intervals, and it was unnecessary, perhaps almost insulting, to specify an accidental where a skilled musician would have known to make an alteration. Modern editions of this music generally place only those accidentals found in the original sources in front of the notes to which they apply and indicate above the staff the additional alterations the editor believes the performers should supply (see Examples 6.2–6.4). The term musica ficta is now often used for any such alterations that are suggested by context rather than notation, even when notes outside the Guidonian gamut are not involved.

ECHOES OF THE NEW ART

Fourteenth-century approaches to music had a profound and continuing impact on music and musical life in later centuries. The increased interest in the individual and in satisfying the human senses that was characteristic of the age grew stronger in the Renaissance and has remained important ever since. Future composers would claim credit for their work more readily and would remain anonymous much less often than was true before 1300. Apparently a piece by Machaut or Landini was esteemed more highly, simply because it was by such a famous composer. This is of course still true today, for composers as disparate as Beethoven, Irving Berlin, Count Basie, or the Beatles.

The interplay between structure and pleasure so typical of fourteenth-century music has also had a continuing resonance. Specific structural devices of the time, such as isorhythm and the *formes fixes*, lasted only to the late fifteenth century, but ideas of musical structure continued and diversified. French structure, Italian smoothness of melody and clarity of declamation, and the growing use in both traditions of prominent harmonic thirds and sixths all contributed to the international Renaissance style of the fifteenth century. The meters and rhythmic combinations made possible by Ars Nova notation, from common time to syncopation, are still part of music today. The creation of a polyphonic style centered on a melodious topmost voice rather than built around the tenor, exemplified in Machaut's chansons, undergirded many later developments.

The music itself did not fare as well. Fourteenth-century styles fell out of use, and figures like Machaut became best known as poets, while their music came to be considered old-fashioned in comparison to the new fifteenth-century style. When first rediscovered in the nineteenth century, fourteenth-century polyphony seemed harsh in its harmonies and crude in allowing parallel fifths and octaves, forbidden in counterpoint since the Renaissance. But twentieth-century music has used a wider range of sounds and techniques and has helped to make fourteenth-century music sound fresh in comparison to common-practice harmony. Now pieces by Machaut, Landini, and others from the fourteenth century are again regularly performed, heard by more people than they were in their own lifetimes.

PART OUTLINE

PART TWO

THE

RENAISSANCE

Europeans in the fifteenth and sixteenth centuries combined a rediscovery of ancient learning with new discoveries and innovations to produce a flowering of culture and the arts that became known as the Renaissance. The changes in music were far-reaching. Responding to a growing interest in pleasing the senses, musicians developed a new kind of counterpoint, featuring strict control of dissonances and pervasive use of sweet-sounding sonorities. They devised new methods for writing polyphonic music that included greater equality between the voices, more varied textures featuring imitation or homophony, and new ways of reworking borrowed material. Reading Ancient Greek texts that extolled music as part of education, that expected every citizen to sing and play music, and described the power of music to evoke emotions and instill character, writers and musicians in the sixteenth century sought the same roles and effects for the music of their times. Building on Greek ideals, composers of vocal music endeavored to reflect in their melodies the accents, inflections, rhythms, and meanings of the words. The invention of music printing made written music more widely accessible and created a market for music that amateurs could sing or play for their own entertainment, alone or as a social activity. The demand stimulated new kinds of secular song and a great increase in instrumental music. Not least important, the Renaissance interest in the invidivual artist brought a new prominence to composers.

All of these developments have affected music ever since. From the very language of music to our belief that music expresses feelings, we are the heirs of the Renaissance.

Chapter

7

The Age of the Renaissance

The fifteenth and sixteenth centuries were a period of great change for European culture, literature, art, and music. To some at the time, it seemed that the arts had been reborn after a period of stagnation. In his 1855 *Histoire de France,* Jules Michelet crystalized this notion in the term **Renaissance** (French for "rebirth"), now widely used to designate the historical period after the Middle Ages. The idea of rebirth captures the aims of scholars and artists to restore the learning, ideals, and values of ancient Greece and Rome. But scholarship, literature, art, and music did far more than revive the old. Currents already strong in the late Middle Ages continued, and the introduction of new technologies, from oil painting to the printing press, brought radical changes. In many cases, classical antiquity provided the inspiration for something really new, including new ways to read and understand the Bible, literature in vernacular languages, and realism and perspective in painting.

In music, this period saw numerous developments. They did not all occur at once, so that the Renaissance is best understood as a time of continual and overlapping changes rather than as a unified style or movement. From the early fifteenth century on, musicians frequently held positions outside their native regions, especially in Italy. This led to the creation of a new international style drawing on elements of French, Italian, and English traditions and new rules for polyphony based on strict control of dissonance. The greater use of thirds and sixths required new tuning systems. The late fifteenth century saw the emergence of two principal textures that would predominate in sixteenth-century music— **imitative counterpoint** and **homophony**. In the later fifteenth and sixteenth centuries, the revival of classical learning had many parallels in music, including a renewed interest in ancient Greek theory and ideals for music and a new focus on setting words with correct declamation while reflecting the meanings and emotions of the text. The development of music printing in the early sixteenth century made notated music available to a wider public. Amateurs bought music to perform for their own entertainment, encouraging composers to produce new and more popular kinds of music, especially songs in vernacular languages and music for instruments. The Reformation brought new forms of religious music for Protestant churches and, in reaction, new styles for Catholic music. All of these changes have affected music in fundamental ways ever since.

These developments will be taken up individually in the next five chapters. Here we will set the stage by placing the changes in music in the wider context of the Renaissance, showing some parallels with the other arts.

The Renaissance in Culture and Art

When the Renaissance began has been debated ever since the term was introduced. No single event or generation inaugurated the Renaissance, and in political and economic terms there is continuity with the late Middle Ages rather than a decisive break. Considering the Renaissance primarily as a movement in scholarship and the arts, some aspects are apparent already in the 1300s, while others emerged only in the 1500s, and many continued into the 1600s. In letters and the visual arts, the Renaissance began in Italy and spread north, emerging at different times in different places; in music, as we will see, northern composers played the leading role in the fifteenth century, not equalled by Italians until the mid-sixteenth century. For our purposes, we will define the span of the Renaissance as the fifteenth and sixteenth centuries, while recognizing that its characteristics developed over time.

EUROPE IN THE RENAISSANCE

Several important political events occurred in the fifteenth and sixteenth centuries, including the end of the Great Schism in the Church in 1417 and the return to a single pope; the end of the Hundred Years' War between the French and English in 1453; the fall of Constantinople to the Ottoman Turks that same year, ending the Byzantine Empire; and the conquest of the Balkans and Hungary by the Turks over the next century.

Most significant in the long run was the rise of Europe as a world power. Larger ships, better navigational aids, and more powerful artillery helped Europeans expand their influence beyond the Mediterranean and northern Atlantic. During the fifteenth century, the Portuguese established colonies and trade routes extending around Africa to India and the East Indies. Columbus's encounter with the New World in 1492 led to Spanish and Portuguese colonies in the Americas, to be followed in the early seventeenth century by the French, English, and Dutch. These events would ultimately lead to the expansion of European culture, including its music, throughout the Americas and in colonies across Africa and Asia.

Economy and society   After the economic turmoil of the fourteenth century, the European economy stabilized around 1400 and began to grow. Regions specialized in different

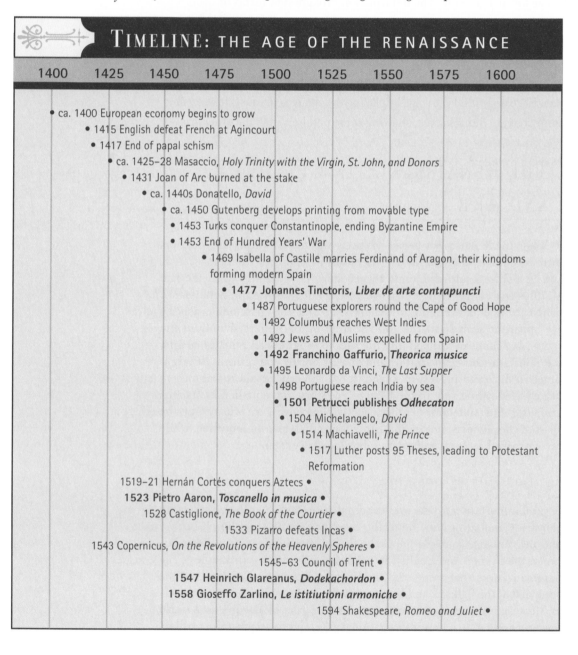

TIMELINE: THE AGE OF THE RENAISSANCE

1400	1425	1450	1475	1500	1525	1550	1575	1600

- ca. 1400 European economy begins to grow
- 1415 English defeat French at Agincourt
- 1417 End of papal schism
- ca. 1425–28 Masaccio, *Holy Trinity with the Virgin, St. John, and Donors*
- 1431 Joan of Arc burned at the stake
- ca. 1440s Donatello, *David*
- ca. 1450 Gutenberg develops printing from movable type
- 1453 Turks conquer Constantinople, ending Byzantine Empire
- 1453 End of Hundred Years' War
- 1469 Isabella of Castille marries Ferdinand of Aragon, their kingdoms forming modern Spain
- **1477 Johannes Tinctoris, *Liber de arte contrapuncti***
- 1487 Portuguese explorers round the Cape of Good Hope
- 1492 Columbus reaches West Indies
- 1492 Jews and Muslims expelled from Spain
- **1492 Franchino Gaffurio, *Theorica musice***
- 1495 Leonardo da Vinci, *The Last Supper*
- 1498 Portuguese reach India by sea
- **1501 Petrucci publishes *Odhecaton***
- 1504 Michelangelo, *David*
- 1514 Machiavelli, *The Prince*
- 1517 Luther posts 95 Theses, leading to Protestant Reformation
- 1519–21 Hernán Cortés conquers Aztecs
- **1523 Pietro Aaron, *Toscanello in musica***
- 1528 Castiglione, *The Book of the Courtier*
- 1533 Pizarro defeats Incas
- 1543 Copernicus, *On the Revolutions of the Heavenly Spheres*
- 1545–63 Council of Trent
- **1547 Heinrich Glareanus, *Dodekachordon***
- **1558 Gioseffo Zarlino, *Le istitiutioni armoniche***
- 1594 Shakespeare, *Romeo and Juliet*

agricultural and manufactured products and traded with each other across great distances. Towns and cities prospered from trade, and many city-dwellers accumulated wealth through commerce, banking, and crafts. The middle class of merchants, artisans, doctors, lawyers, and other independent entrepreneurs continued to increase in numbers, influence, and economic importance, seeking prosperity for their families, property and beautiful objects for themselves, and education for their children. Rulers, especially in the small principalities and city-states of Italy, sought to glorify themselves and their cities' reputations by erecting impressive palaces and country houses decorated with new artworks and newly unearthed artifacts from ancient civilizations; by lavishly entertaining neighboring potentates; and by maintaining chapels of talented singers and ensembles of gifted instrumentalists. These conditions, strongest in Italy but increasing throughout western Europe during the fifteenth and sixteenth centuries, laid the economic and social foundations for the Renaissance.

HUMANISM

Renaissance thinkers had broader access to the classics of Greek and Roman literature and philosophy than their medieval predecessors. Ottoman attacks on Constantinople beginning in 1396 led many Byzantine scholars to flee to Italy, taking with them numerous ancient Greek writings. They taught the Greek language to Italian scholars, some of whom traveled to the east to collect manuscripts of works unknown to the West. Soon the Greek classics were translated into Latin, making most of Plato and the Greek plays and histories accessible to western Europeans for the first time. In the early fifteenth century, scholars rediscovered complete copies of works on rhetoric by Cicero and Quintilian. Later that century, other texts from Roman antiquity also came into circulation, including works by Livy, Tacitus, and Lucretius.

The increasing availability of ancient writings was complemented by new ways of using them. The strongest intellectual movement of the Renaissance was **humanism,** from the Latin phrase "studia humanitatis," the study of the humanities, things pertaining to human knowledge. Humanists sought to revive ancient learning, emphasizing the study of grammar, rhetoric, poetry, history, and moral philosophy, centering on classical Latin and Greek writings. They believed these subjects developed the individual's mind, spirit, and ethics, and prepared students for lives of virtue and service. Alongside their belief in Christian doctrine, humanists had faith in the dignity and nobility of humans and in our capacity to improve our condition through our own efforts. Gradually, humanistic studies replaced Scholasticism, with its emphasis on logic and metaphysics and its reliance on authority, as the center of intellectual life and of the university curriculum. The role of the Church was not diminished; rather, the Church borrowed from classical sources, sponsored classical studies, and supported thinkers, artists, and musicians.

RENAISSANCE ART AND ARCHITECTURE

Renaissance art shows striking contrasts with medieval art and several parallels with the new developments in scholarship and music.

Figure 7.1: David, *by Donatello. David, clad in helmet and leggings but otherwise nude, stands astride the head of the slain Goliath. This bronze statue was commissioned in the mid-fifteenth century by Cosimo de' Medici, the most powerful citizen and de facto ruler of Florence, for the Palazzo Medici.*

The revival of classical antiquity in new guise is embodied in the bronze statue of *David* by Donatello (ca. 1386–1466), shown in Figure 7.1, the first freestanding nude since Roman times. Nakedness in the Middle Ages was used to show shame, as in pictures of the expulsion of Adam and Eve from the Garden of Eden. Here nudity shows the beauty of the human figure, as in the Greek and Roman sculptures Donatello used as models, and proclaims the nobility of the biblical hero. Thus classical means are used to convey a religious theme, paralleling the Church's use of classical and humanistic studies. The work's naturalism—its attempt to reproduce nature realistically—is also in tune with humanists' endeavor to see and understand the world as it really is.

The imitation of classical models, ideal of beauty, and naturalism Donatello exhibits here are typical of Renaissance art. These traits have parallels in music, as composers sought to please the ear with beautiful sonorities and seemingly natural rather than contorted melodies and rhythms. Yet the lack of actual Greek and Roman music made the relationship to classical models different from that in sculpture, focusing primarily on what was *said* about music in Greek writings.

Italian painters had been pursuing greater realism since Giotto in the early fourteenth century (see chapter 6 and Figure 6.1). But far more naturalistic representations were made possible in the early 1400s through two innovations: *perspective*, a method for representing three-dimensional space on a flat surface, creating a sense of depth, and *chiaroscuro*, the naturalistic treatment of light and shade. A contrast between two paintings will illustrate both concepts. Figure 7.2 shows a fourteenth-century fresco of a city scene. Individual parts of the painting look realistic, but the whole does not look real. This is especially true of the use of light, for some buildings are better lit to the right side, others to the left, which cannot happen with natural sunlight. The buildings seem piled on top of one another, their distance from the viewer unclear. The late-fifteenth-century painting of an ideal city in Figure 7.3, by contrast, uses perspective, in which all parallel lines converge to a single vanishing point, and objects of the same size appear smaller in exact proportion as they grow more distant. This reflects how we actually see, creating the illusion of depth. In addition, the light falls on all surfaces as if coming from a single source. The overall effect is much more natural and realistic.

Clarity and classical models in architecture

The later picture is also more orderly, with clean lines, symmetry, and little clutter. The decorative elements on the buildings make their structure clear, highlighting the floors, pillars, and arches. This preference for clarity, typical of Renaissance architecture, contrasts markedly with Gothic decoration, such as the ornate and whimsical filigree on Notre Dame Cathedral in Figure 5.3. The use of columns with capitals on the center and leftmost buildings shows the Renaissance interest in imitating ancient architecture.

Figure 7.2: A panel from The Effects of Good and Bad Government in the Town and in the Country *(1337–39), a fresco by Ambrogio Lorenzetti painted in the Palazzo Pubblico (public palace) in Siena, a city in Tuscany in northern Italy. The subject of the painting illustrates the new humanist concern with government and civic virtues. Yet the technique is still medieval in many respects. While objects further away are depicted as behind and some- what smaller than those closer to the viewer, there is no true perspective.*

The fresco by Masaccio (Tommaso Cassai, 1401–1428) in Figure 7.4 illus- trates all these characteristics and adds another, an interest in individuals. One of the first paintings to use perspective, it creates an impressive sense of depth, as if an actual chapel stood there instead of a flat wall. Faces, bodies, drapery, and poses are natural; contrasting colors and shadings reinforce the impression of space while creating a clear and pleasing composition; and classical influence is reflected in the Greek columns with Ionic and

Interest in individuals

Figure 7.3: Idealized View of the City *(ca. 1480) by a painter from the school of Piero della Francesca, in the ducal palace in Urbino, northern Italy. The scene looks realistic because of the use of perspective and attention to lighting. All the lines that in three-dimensional reality would be parallel to each other, like the lines in the pavement or on the sides of buildings, converge toward a single vanishing point, just under the top of the doorway of the central building. The light is coming from the left and somewhat behind the viewer, since left-facing surfaces are brightest, surfaces facing the viewer somewhat darker, and right- facing surfaces darker still.*

Figure 7.4: Masaccio, Holy Trinity with the Virgin, St. John, and Donors *(ca. 1425–28), fresco in the church of Santa Maria Novella in Florence. The artist used perspective to create a sense of depth and of height, placing the vanishing point at eye level as one faces the painting, below the foot of the cross. The three members of the Trinity are shown: Jesus the Son on the cross in the center, God the Father above him, and the Holy Spirit as a dove flying between them. The colors create a subtle, almost symmetrical pattern of red, gray, and cream, leading the eye from one figure to the next.*

Corinthian capitals, the arches, and the ceiling modeled after that of the Roman Pantheon. Kneeling on either side are the painting's donors, identified as Lorenzo Leni and his wife. Their presence and Masaccio's lifelike portrayal of them reflect the heightened interest in individuals during the Renaissance: not for this well-to-do couple the anonymity of the donors, masons, and artisans that contributed to Notre Dame in Paris two centuries earlier. The many portraits painted in the Renaissance testify to the desire of patrons to be memorialized in art and the ability of artists to capture the personality of each subject.

Musical parallels   Like the ideals of beauty and naturalism discussed above, chiaroscuro, clarity, and interest in individuals also have parallels in music. Renaissance composers expanded the range of their pieces to include lower and higher pitches than before, and employed contrasts between high and low registers and between thin and full textures that recall the contrasts of light and dark in contemporary painting. Many composers sought to make the musical structure clear through such contrasts, through frequent cadences, and by other means, akin to the clarity of line and function in Renaissance architecture. We will encounter a few pieces that, like Masaccio's fresco, memorialize individuals, but even more important is the rising significance of composers as individual artists, celebrated in their sphere as were Donatello and Masaccio in theirs. The notion of a unique personal style in music is rare before the fifteenth century, but becomes typical of the Renaissance and later periods.

THE MUSICAL RENAISSANCE

The broad intellectual and artistic currents of the Renaissance affected music deeply, yet in many respects music followed its own path. Without ancient music to draw on, and without the ability of literature or art to depict reality naturalistically, musicians reflected humanism in other ways.

PATRONAGE AND COSMOPOLITAN MUSICIANS

One key to developments in music in the Renaissance is in the careers of musicians: their training, employment, and travels. New musical institutions and enhanced support for musicians led to an unprecedented flowering of music.

Court **chapels,** groups of salaried musicians and clerics that were associated with a ruler rather than with a particular building, sprang up all over Europe in the late fourteenth and early fifteenth centuries. The first chapels were established by King Louis IX of France and King Edward I of England in the thirteenth century. After the mid-fourteenth century, the fashion spread to other aristocrats and church leaders. Members of the chapel served as performers, composers, and scribes, furnishing music for church services. Figure 7.5 shows the chapel of Philip the Good, duke of Burgundy, at Mass. These musicians probably contributed to the secular entertainment of the court as well and accompanied their ruler on journeys.

Court chapels

Figure 7.5: Philip the Good, duke of Burgundy, at Mass. Philip is in the center of the picture. The celebrant (the priest officiating at Mass) and deacon are at lower left, the singers in the chapel at lower right, and members of the court at the rear. Miniature by Jean le Tavernier (ca. 1457–67).

Training
musicians

Most fifteenth- and sixteenth-century composers whose names are re-membered were trained as choir boys and hired as singers for churches or court chapels, though their reputations rested primarily on their composi-tions. In some cathedrals and chapels, choir schools taught not only singing but also music theory, grammar, mathematics, and other subjects. Cities such as Cambrai, Bruges, Antwerp, Paris, and Lyons, shown on the map in Figure 7.6, were the centers most renowned for their musical training in the fifteenth century; later they were joined by Rome, Venice, and other Italian cities. This helps to explain why the most prominent composers of the fifteenth and early sixteenth centuries, such as Du Fay, Ockeghem, and Josquin, came from Flan-ders, the Netherlands, and northern France, while Italians became more prominent from the mid-sixteenth century on. Because only male children were admitted into choirs, women did not have this educational opportunity or the chance to make careers in public churches and princely courts. Nuns and novices in convents did receive musical instruction, and a few distinguished themselves as composers. Courts also employed instrumentalists, who typi-cally were minstrels or came from families of musicians and were trained in the apprentice system. Few singers, composers, or performers served only as musicians; as in the Middle Ages, most had other duties as servants, adminis-trators, clerics, or church officials.

Patronage
for music

Many rulers avidly supported music and competed with each other for the best composers and performers. Like fine clothes and impressive pageantry, excellent music was both enjoyable in itself and valuable as a way to display wealth and power. The kings of France and England and the dukes of Burgundy

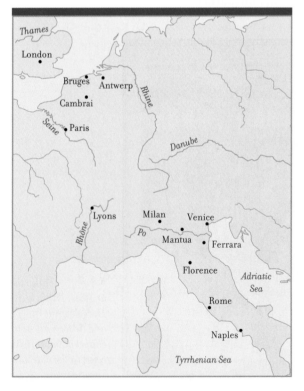

Figure 7.6: Major centers for training musicians or for musical patronage in the Renaissance.

and Savoy were especially notable patrons in the fifteenth century, but most striking is the breadth and depth of patronage in Italy for music alongside the other arts. Since the major centers for training musicians were in the north, this meant that Italian rulers regularly brought to their cities the most talented musicians from France, Flanders, and the Netherlands. The Medici, the leading family in Florence during most of this period, sponsored Franco-Flemish musicians such as Heinrich Isaac (ca. 1450–1517) and Jacques Arcadelt (ca. 1507–1568) as well as native Italian painters and sculptors like Donatello, Botticelli, and Michelangelo. The Sforzas, who ruled Milan from the 1450s, employed eighteen chamber singers and twenty-two chapel singers in 1474; in the 1480s both Josquin des Prez (ca. 1450–1521), the leading composer of his generation, and Leonardo da Vinci, the leading artist, worked for members of the Sforza family. The court of Ferrara under the Este family hosted Josquin and the Netherlandish composers Jacob Obrecht (1457/8–1505), Adrian Willaert (ca. 1490–1562), and Cipriano de Rore (1515/16–1565). Mantua, ruled by the Gonzaga family, was another center of patronage, thanks to the presence of Isabella d'Este (wife of Marchese Francesco II Gonzaga), who had studied music seriously. Popes and cardinals were as committed as secular princes to a high standard of cultural activity and patronage. Some of the best musicians, artists, and scholars of the Renaissance, including Josquin, Leonardo, and Michelangelo, were sponsored by the pope and by cardinals from the Medici, Este, Sforza, and Gonzaga families.

The presence at courts of musicians from many lands allowed composers and performers to learn styles and genres current in other regions. Many composers changed their place of service, exposing them to numerous types of music. Guillaume Du Fay (ca. 1397–1474), for example, served at the Cathedral of Cambrai in the Burgundian lands, at courts in Pesaro (northern Italy) and Savoy (southeastern France), and in the pope's chapel in Rome, Florence, and Bologna (see chapter 8). *Cosmopolitan musicians*

The exchange of national traditions, genres, and ideas fostered the development of an international style in the fifteenth century, synthesizing elements from English, French, and Italian traditions (the theme of chapter 8). As new national styles of vernacular song emerged in the sixteenth century (see chapter 11), the cosmopolitan careers of many composers prepared them to work in more than one style. Franco-Flemish composer Orlando di Lasso (ca. 1532–1594), for example, wrote Italian madrigals, German Lieder, and French chansons with equal flair. *International style, new national styles*

THE NEW COUNTERPOINT

The core of the fifteenth-century international style was a new counterpoint, based on a preference for consonance, including thirds and sixths as well as perfect fifths and octaves, and on strict control of dissonance. This new approach to counterpoint reflects the high value musicians placed on beauty, order, and pleasing the senses, attitudes that closely parallel contemporary trends in art.

The distinction between new and older practice is starkly expressed in *Liber de arte contrapuncti* (A Book on the Art of Counterpoint, 1477) by Johannes Tinctoris (ca. 1435–1511), one of the leading counterpoint treatises of *Johannes Tinctoris*

SOURCE READING

JOHANNES TINCTORIS ON THE MUSIC
OF HIS TIME

*Johannes Tinctoris was a Flemish composer who
settled in Naples at the court of King Ferrante I in
the early 1470s. There he wrote a dozen treatises on
musical topics. He was an enthusiastic supporter of
the northern composers from his own generation and
the previous one, and observed a sharp break between their music and that of previous eras.*

———— • ————

It is a matter of great surprise that there is no
composition written over forty years ago which
is thought by the learned as worthy of performance. At this very time, whether it be due to
the virtue of some heavenly influence or to a
zeal of constant application I do not know,
there flourish, in addition to many singers
who perform most beautifully, an infinite number of composers such as Johannes Okeghem,
Johannes Regis, Anthonius Busnois, Firminus

Caron, and Guillermus Faugues, who glory that
they had as teachers in this divine art Johannes
Dunstable, Egidius Binchois, and Guillermus
Dufay, recently passed from life. Almost all
these men's works exhale such sweetness that,
in my opinion, they should be considered most
worthy, not only for people and heroes, but
even for the immortal gods. Certainly I never
listen to them or study them without coming
away more refreshed and wiser. Just as Virgil
took Homer as his model in his divine work, the
Aeneid, so by Hercules, do I use these as models
for my own small productions; particularly
have I plainly imitated their admirable style of
composition insofar as the arranging of con-
cords is concerned.

Johannes Tinctoris, *The Art of Counterpoint (Liber de
arte contrapuncti),* trans. and ed. Albert Seay (American Institute of Musicology, 1961), 14–15.

the fifteenth century. Tinctoris deplored "the compositions of older musicians, in which there were more dissonances than consonances" and proclaimed that nothing written before the 1430s was worth hearing (see Source
Reading). His sympathy with humanism is shown by his references to numerous Greek and Roman writers, but lacking examples of ancient music, he
claims only the composers of the last two generations as models worth imitating. Nothing could more vividly show the difference between music on the
one hand and literature, art, and architecture on the other in their relation to
the arts of antiquity. Drawing on the practice of the composers he names,
Tinctoris devised strict rules for introducing dissonances, limiting them to
passing and neighbor tones on unstressed beats and to syncopated passages
(what we call suspensions) at cadences. Parallel fifths and octaves, common
even in fourteenth-century styles, were now forbidden. These rules were further refined in later treatises and synthesized by Gioseffo Zarlino
(1517–1590) in *Le istitutioni harmoniche* (The Harmonic Foundations, 1558).

NEW COMPOSITIONAL METHODS AND TEXTURES

While the rules for consonance and dissonance treatment remained fairly consistent throughout the Renaissance and distinguish the music of this period
from that of the preceding and following epochs, styles and textures changed
from each generation to the next, as we will see in subsequent chapters.

A striking change occurred during the second half of the fifteenth century, *Equality of voices* when composers moved away from counterpoint structured around the cantus (top line) and tenor and toward greater equality between voices. Since its origins, polyphony had been conceived as the addition of voices to an existing melody: in eleventh- and twelfth-century organum, adding an organal voice above a chant; in thirteenth-century motets, adding one or more voices above a tenor; in fourteenth-century chansons, composing a tenor to fit with the cantus, then adding a third and sometimes a fourth voice around this two-voice framework. Through the mid-fifteenth century, composers apparently worked as their predecessors had, devising the essential counterpoint between tenor and cantus and then adding the other voices around that framework. Most likely they proceeded phrase by phrase, at times even sonority by sonority, but always attended first to the cantus and tenor and then fit the other voices around them. As a result, it was hard to avoid dissonances or frequent awkward leaps in the other voices (see the contratenors in Examples 8.5 and 8.6). As composers in the later fifteenth century sought to make each part smooth and grateful to sing, they increasingly worked out all the parts at the same time in relation to each other. The cantus-tenor framework was replaced by a more equal relationship in which all voices were essential to the counterpoint. This change in approach was noted by the theorist Pietro Aaron (see Source Reading).

SOURCE READING

A NEW HARMONIC CONCEPTION

Pietro Aaron (ca. 1480–ca. 1550) was a priest, composer, and theorist who wrote some of the first musical treatises in Italian. His writings are particularly revealing about the practices of his time. Here he describes a change from the old linear approach to composition, in which the top line and tenor formed the structural framework, to a new harmonic conception, in which each voice had a more equal role.

———— • ————

Many composers contended that first the cantus should be devised, then the tenor, and after the tenor the contrabass. They practiced this method, because they lacked the order and knowledge of what was required for creating the contralto. Thus they made many awkward passages in their compositions, and because of them had to have unisons, rests, and ascending and descending skips difficult for the singer or performer. Such compositions were bereft of sweetness and harmony, because when you write the cantus or soprano first and then the tenor, once this tenor is done, there is no place for the contrabass, and once the contrabass is done, there is often no note for the contralto. If you consider only one part at a time, that is, when you write the tenor and take care only to make this tenor consonant [with the cantus], and similarly the contrabass, the consonance of every other part will suffer.

Therefore the moderns have considered this matter better, as is evident in their compositions for four, five, six, and more parts. Every one of the parts occupies a comfortable, easy, and acceptable place, because composers consider them all together and not according to what is described above.

From Pietro Aaron, *Toscanello in musica* (Venice, 1524), Book II, Chapter 16.

Imitation and homophony

Associated with this new approach was the emergence of two kinds of musical texture that came to predominate in the sixteenth century. In **imitative counterpoint**, voices **imitate** or echo a motive or phrase in another voice, usually at a different pitch level, such as a fifth, fourth, or octave away. In **homophony**, all the voices move together in essentially the same rhythm, the lower parts accompanying the cantus with consonant sonorities. Both textures allowed composers considerably more freedom than the older approach of layering voices.

TUNING AND TEMPERAMENT

The new emphasis on thirds and sixths posed a challenge to music theory and systems of tuning, both of which had to yield to changing practice.

Pythagorean intonation

Medieval theorists defined only the octave, fifth, and fourth as consonant, because these were generated by the simple ratios Pythagoras had discovered, respectively 2:1, 3:2, and 4:3. In **Pythagorean intonation**, used throughout the Middle Ages, all fourths and fifths were perfectly tuned. In this system, thirds and sixths had complex ratios that made them dissonant by definition and out of tune to the ear; for example, the major third had the ratio 81:64, sounding rough in comparison with the pure major third (5:4 or 80:64). This tuning works very well for medieval music, in which only fourths, fifths, and octaves need to sound consonant. The relatively large major thirds and sixths only increase the power of the late medieval cadence, in which a major third and sixth expand to a fifth and octave.

Just intonation

Around 1300, the English theorist Walter Odington observed that the major and minor third could be considered consonances, since they approach the simple ratios 5:4 and 6:5 and were often tuned to those ratios in performance. This laid the foundation for recognizing thirds and sixths as consonances, in theory and in practice. But not until 1482 did Bartolomé Ramis de Pareia, a Spanish mathematician and music theorist residing in Italy, propose a tuning system that produced perfectly tuned thirds and sixths. Systems like Ramis's became known as **just intonation**. Performers had probably been using forms of just intonation for many years, as Odington testifies to the use of justly tuned thirds in England by 1300.

Temperaments

There are at least two problems with just intonation. First, in order to bring most thirds in the diatonic scale into tune, one fourth, one fifth, and one third must be out of tune, making some sonorities unusable unless the performers adjust the pitch. Second, as musicians increasingly used notes outside the diatonic scale, keeping the fifths and thirds pure meant that notes such as G♯ and A♭ were different in pitch, causing difficulties for keyboard players and for instruments with frets, such as lutes. Some sought to preserve the pure intervals by developing organs and harpsichords with separate keys for such pairs of tones. More common were compromise tuning systems called **temperaments**, in which pitches were adjusted to make most or all intervals usable without adding keys. Most keyboard players in the sixteenth century used what later was called **mean-tone temperament**, in which the fifths were tuned small so that the major thirds could sound well, and the black keys were tuned to C♯, E♭, F♯, G♯, and B♭, making available most of the notes then in use. The temperament best known today is **equal temperament,** in which each semitone is exactly the same; first described by theorists in the late 1500s, it may have been approximated before then by performers on fretted string instruments such as lutes and viols, for whom any nonequal tuning is likely to result in out-of-tune octaves. In equal temperament, all intervals are usable, because all approximate their mathematically pure ratios, but only the octave is exactly in tune, showing that no tuning system is flawless. Indeed, equal temperament is ill-suited to most Renaissance vocal music, where the sound of perfectly tuned fifths and thirds is part of its glory.

The new tuning systems reflect musicians' reliance on what pleased the ear rather than on received theory. This parallels the focus of humanists on human concerns, rather than on deference to past authority.

REAWAKENED INTEREST IN GREEK THEORY

Yet the Renaissance also brought a rebirth of interest in music theory's Greek past. Indeed, the most direct impact of humanism on music lay in the rediscovery of ancient writings on music and in new approaches to studying and interpreting them. During the fifteenth century, Greeks emigrating from Byzantium and Italian manuscript hunters brought the principal Greek writings on music to the West, including the treatises of Aristides Quintilianus, Claudius Ptolemy, and Cleonides, the eighth book of Aristotle's *Politics*, and passages on music in Plato's *Republic* and *Laws* (all discussed in chapter 1). By the end of the fifteenth century, all of these were translated into Latin.

Franchino Gaffurio (1451–1522) read the Greek theorists in Latin translations and incorporated much of their thinking into his writings. Gaffurio's treatises were the most influential of his time, reviving Greek ideas and stimulating new thought on matters such as the modes, consonance and dissonance, the elements and scope of the tonal system, tuning, the relations of music and words, and the harmony of music, of the human body and mind, and of the cosmos.

Franchino Gaffurio

The Swiss theorist Heinrich Glareanus (1488–1563) in his book *Dodeka-chordon* (The Twelve-String Lyre, 1547) added four new modes to the traditional eight, using names of ancient Greek tonoi: Aeolian and Hypoaeolian with the final on A, and Ionian and Hypoionian with the final on C. With these additions, he made the theory of the modes more consistent with the current practice of composers, who frequently employed tonal centers on A and C. In using something borrowed from ancient culture to modify his medieval heritage, Glareanus was typical of his age.

Heinrich Glareanus

NEW APPLICATIONS OF GREEK IDEAS

People in the Renaissance could not experience ancient music itself, as they could ancient architecture, sculptures, and poems. But they could read the writings of classical philosophers, poets, and theorists that were being newly translated and could reexamine current music in the light of what they learned about ancient practice. In the late fifteenth and sixteenth centuries, many ideas came into circulation that were inspired by reading ancient Greek descriptions of music. Among these were music as a social accomplishment, music as servant of the words, conveying emotion through music, the role of the modes, and chromaticism.

Music as social accomplishment

Ancient writers from Plato to Quintilian maintained that music should be part of every citizen's education, and Renaissance writers echoed their call. Gentlemen and ladies were expected to read music, to sing from notation at sight, and to play well enough to join in music-making as a form of entertainment, as others might play cards or tell stories.

Words and music

The ancient Greek view of music and poetry as virtually inseparable, and the image of the ancient poet and musician united in a single person, inspired both poets and composers to seek common artistic aims. Writers became more concerned with the sound of their verses, and composers with imitating that sound. The organization and syntax of a text guided the composer in shaping the structure of the musical setting and in marking punctuation in the text with cadences that express different degrees of finality. By the early sixteenth century, it became the rule to follow the rhythm of speech and not violate the natural accentuation of syllables. The new textures of imitative counterpoint and homophony were useful here, since in both cases all the voices in a polyphonic work could declaim the text in the same rhythm. Where previously singers often had leeway in matching syllables to the notated pitches and rhythms, composers now took charge, seeing the purpose of their music as serving the words.

Emotion and expression

Ancient writings were filled with descriptions of the emotional effects of music, and they inspired composers to try expressing through music the feelings suggested by the texts they set. Whether medieval or early-fifteenth-century music was considered to convey specific emotions or simply support and decorate the text is unclear, since the issue was little discussed, and connections between particular emotions and particular musical elements seem impossible to draw. By the late fifteenth century and throughout the sixteenth, however, composers often used specific intervals, sonorities, melodic contours, contrapuntal motions, and other devices to dramatize the content and convey the feelings of the text.

Power of the modes

One device used was the choice of mode. Both Plato and Aristotle insisted that each of the Greek harmoniai, or scale types, conveyed a different ethos and that musicians could influence a listener's emotions by their choice of harmonia (see chapter 1). The stories that Pythagoras calmed a violent youth by having the piper change from one harmonia to another, and that Alexander the Great suddenly rose from the banquet table and armed himself for battle when he heard a Phrygian tune, were told countless times. Theorists and composers assumed that the Greek harmoniai and tonoi were identical to the similarly named church modes (for the confusion, see chapter 2) and that the latter could have the same emotional effects. Composers sometimes chose to set a text in a certain mode based on the emotions that ancient writers associated with the harmonia or tonos of the same name. Even when this was not the case, the mode of a polyphonic work assumed much greater importance in the Renaissance than in the Middle Ages, and most composers took care to make the mode clear through frequent cadences on the final and tenor of the mode.

Although some accidentals were notated, and other alterations were called *Chromaticism*
for by musica ficta (see chapter 6), European music from Gregorian chant
through the early sixteenth century was essentially diatonic. Only in the mid-
sixteenth century did composers begin to use direct chromatic motion, such
as from B to B♭, inspired by the chromatic genus of ancient Greek music (see
chapters 1 and 11).

Each of these ideas—music as an accomplishment every genteel person
should have, music as servant of the words and conveyor of feelings, and the
expressive power of modes and of chromaticism—is a distinctive new element
in the late fifteenth or sixteenth century, and each originated in imitation of
ancient practice as described in classical writings. While less direct than imitations of Greek and Roman literature, architecture, or sculpture, these concepts show music's participation in the Renaissance movement.

MUSIC PRINTING AND DISTRIBUTION

Alongside the revival of ancient ideas, the Renaissance also saw the influence
of new technologies. Oil paint, apparently first used in Flanders, provided
fresher, more lifelike, longer-lasting colors than tempera and water-based
paints. It also dried more slowly, allowing painters to make corrections and
lavish more attention on details. The introduction of music printing from
movable type had even more far-reaching effects. By making possible much
wider dissemination of written music, printing made notated music available
to a broader public and thus encouraged the growth of musical literacy and of
new genres and repertoires (see sidebar, pp. 164–65).

Music printing brought changes that were as revolutionary for music in the *Effects of music*
sixteenth century as the development of notation had been for the Middle *printing*
Ages. Instead of a few precious manuscripts copied by hand and liable to all
kinds of errors and variants, a plentiful supply of new music in copies of uniform accuracy was now available—not exactly at a low price, but much less
costly than equivalent manuscripts. Throughout Europe and the Americas,
printed music spread to a broad audience the works of composers who otherwise would have been known to only a small circle. The availability of printed
music encouraged both amateurs and professionals to form vocal, instrumental, and mixed ensembles. The demand for new music went hand-in-
hand with the rise of new popular styles of music in the sixteenth century,
including distinct national styles. Printing provided a new way for composers
to make money, either directly by sale of their works to a publisher, or indirectly by making their names and compositions better known and potentially
attracting new patrons. Moreover, the existence of printed copies has preserved many works for performance and study by later generations.

MUSIC AS A RENAISSANCE ART

The Renaissance had a profound and enduring effect on music. In direct
and indirect ways, developments in music paralleled those in scholarship and

INNOVATIONS: MUSIC PRINTING

A great number of gentlemen and merchants of good account [were entertained] by the exercise of music daily used in my house, and by furnishing them with [printed] books of that kind yearly sent me out of Italy and other places.

So wrote Nicholas Yonge—a London clerk with enough means and social position to support an active amateur musical life—in the dedication to his 1588 madrigal collection *Musica transalpina* (see chapter 11). His words tell us how the music printing and publishing business completely changed the way people used and enjoyed notated music during the sixteenth century, allowing it to be cultivated not only in churches and noble courts but also in ordinary households as recreation. Until that time, only the very wealthy could think of purchasing a book of music, because the music had to be copied laboriously by hand (see

chapter 2). But the printing press made it possible to produce many copies relatively quickly with much less labor, making music available to many more people at a much lower price.

Printing from movable type, known in China for centuries and perfected in Europe by Johann Gutenberg around 1450, was first used for music in the 1470s, in liturgical books with chant notation. Using movable type meant that notes could be assembled in any order, rearranged, and reused. This method proved much more practical than other procedures, such as carving music into wood blocks.

In 1501, Ottaviano Petrucci (1466–1539) in Venice brought out the first collection of polyphonic music printed entirely from movable type, the *Harmonice musices odhecaton A* (One Hundred Polyphonic Songs, though it actually contained ninety-six). Figure 7.7, a page from this collection, shows the elegance of his work. Petrucci used a triple-impression process, in which each sheet went through the press three times: once to print the staff lines, another time to print the words, and a third to print the notes and the florid initials. His method was time-consuming, labor-intensive, and costly, but his results were models of clarity and accuracy.

Petrucci was no less clever as a businessman than he was as a craftsman. Before setting up shop, he had procured a patent on his process and a "privilege" that effectively guaranteed him a monopoly on music printing in Venice for twenty years. His first volume was an anthology of secular song, including what he judged to be among the best of his own and the preceding generations. The songs were small forms for three or four parts that could easily be performed at home or in the company of friends. He followed up with two

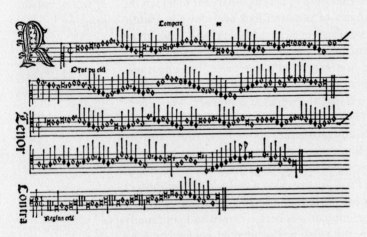

Figure 7.7: Loyset Compère's chanson Royne de ciel, *from* Harmonice musices odhecaton A, *published by Ottaviano Petrucci in 1501. The incipit of the text appears under the cantus part. The music uses the "white notation" of the Renaissance. The notes that look like diamond-shaped whole notes are semibreves; open notes with stems (akin to half notes) are minims; black notes with stems (like quarter notes) are semiminims; and flags are added to the semiminim to indicate shorter durations. The resemblance to common-practice notation is clear, except that no barlines or ties are used.*

more song collections, *Canti B* in 1502 and *Canti C* in 1504, allowing Petrucci to corner the market for the most up-to-date and popular secular music of the day. By 1523, he had published fifty-nine volumes (including reprints) of vocal and instrumental music.

Printing from a single impression—using pieces of type that printed staff, notes, and text together in one operation—was apparently first practiced by John Rastell in London about 1520 and first applied on a large scale in 1528 by Pierre Attaingnant (ca. 1494–1551/52) in Paris. Although more efficient and less costly than Petrucci's triple-impression method, the process produced much less elegant results because the staff lines were no longer continuous but part of each piece of type; inevitably, the lines were imperfectly joined and therefore appeared broken or wavy on the page, as seen in Figure 7.8. Nevertheless, the practicality of the method ensured its commercial success. Attaignant's process set the standard for all printed music until copperplate engraving became popular in the late seventeenth century.

Most ensemble music published in the sixteenth century was printed in the form of oblong **partbooks**—one small volume for each solo voice, so that a complete set was needed to perform any piece. Partbooks were intended for use at home or in social gatherings, as de-

picted in Figure 7.9. Most church choirs continued to use large handwritten choirbooks, and new ones were still being hand-copied in the sixteenth century, even as printed versions began appearing.

The economics of supply and demand for printed music grew in ever widening circles. Printing stimulated the desire for music books and increased their affordability, which in turn spurred the development of music printing and competition among publishers. By the end of the sixteenth century, Rome, Nuremberg, Lyons, Louvain, Antwerp, and London had joined Venice and Paris as centers of music publishing, and publishers and printed music had become indispensable parts of musical life.—BRH & JPB

in the other arts. The growing European economy, patronage for musicians, and the development of music printing laid the economic foundation for an increase in musical activity that continued into later centuries. Humanism and the rediscovery of ancient texts fostered a reexamination of musical aesthetics, leading to new musical styles that focused on consonance, clarity, direct appeal to the listener, natural declamation of words, and emotional expressivity. The musical language forged in this period lasted for generations and undergirds the treatment of dissonance, consonance, voice-leading, and text-setting in most later styles. The new tunings and temperaments created for Renaissance music were used through the early nineteenth century, when equal temperament began to predominate. Notions about music that developed during the Renaissance have become widely shared expectations, so that pieces that do not seek to convey emotion or appeal to a broad audience, as in some twentieth-century styles, have struck some listeners as violating basic assumptions about what music is and what it should do.

Throughout much of the seventeenth and eighteenth centuries, sixteenth-century styles endured, especially in church music, alongside the newer, more dramatic styles. Training in Renaissance counterpoint was an accepted part of learning music composition from the seventeenth century through much of the twentieth. Composers often imitated sixteenth-century polyphonic style in their choral music and as a device to suggest austerity, solemnity, or religiosity. In the late nineteenth and early twentieth centuries, Renaissance music itself was revived, and scholars began the long process of transcribing into modern notation, editing, and publishing the thousands of surviving works. Now pieces by Du Fay, Josquin, Palestrina, and other Renaissance composers are staples of the vocal repertoire, and the music of hundreds of their contemporaries is performed and recorded.

Chapter

8

England and Burgundy in the Fifteenth Century

In about 1440, French poet Martin Le Franc lauded two composers, Guillaume Du Fay and Binchois, whose beautiful melodies and "new practice of making lively consonance" made their music better than that of all their predecessors in France (see Source Reading, p. 168). He attributed the "marvelous pleasingness" of their music to their adoption of what he called the **contenance angloise** (English guise or quality) and their emulation of English composer John Dunstable. A generation later, Johannes Tinctoris looked back to these same three composers as the founders of a new art (see Source Reading in chapter 7). The influence of English music on Continental composers in the early fifteenth century has become a central theme of music history of this era, alongside the development of a new international style of polyphony and of the polyphonic mass cycle, both indebted to English influence. In this chapter, we will explore these three themes, focusing on the music of Dunstable, Du Fay, and Binchois, who from their time to ours have been considered the greatest composers of their generation. Along the way, we will examine what English elements were taken over into Continental music, what changes in values this adoption reflects, and what made the music of these three composers so appealing to their age.

ENGLISH MUSIC

The impact of English music on Continental composers in the first half of the fifteenth century had both political and artistic roots.

167

SOURCE READING

THE CONTENANCE ANGLOISE

Martin Le Franc (ca. 1410–1461) was a poet, cleric, and secretary to the duke of Savoy, who also employed Guillaume Du Fay as master of the court chapel. At the wedding of the duke's son in 1434, both had occasion to meet Binchois, who was in the retinue of the duke of Burgundy. In his poem Le champion des dames *(1440–42), Le Franc praised the music of Du Fay and Binchois in terms that have shaped our view of fifteenth-century music history.*

—— • ——

Tapissier, Carmen, Cesaris	Tapissier, Carmen, Cesaris
Na pas longtemps si bien chanterrent	not long ago sang so well
Quilz esbahirent tout paris	that they astonished all Paris
Et tous ceulx qui les frequenterrent;	and all who came to hear them.
Mais oncques jour ne deschanterrent	But never did they discant
En melodie de tels chois	such finely wrought melody—
Ce mont dit qui les hanterrent	so I was told by those who heard them—
Que G. Du Fay et Binchois.	as G. Du Fay and Binchois.
Car ilz ont nouvelle pratique	For they have a new practice
De faire frisque concordance	of making lively consonance
En haulte et en basse musique	in both loud and soft music,
En fainte, en pause, et en muance	in feigning, in rests, and in mutations.
Et ont prins de la contenance	They took on the guise
Angloise et ensuy Dunstable	of the English and follow Dunstable
Pour quoy merveilleuse plaisance	and thereby a marvelous pleasingness
Rend leur chant joyeux et notable.	makes their music joyous and remarkable.

French poem quoted in Charles Van den Borren, *Guillaume Du Fay: son importance dans l'évolution de la musique au XVe siècle* (Brussels, 1926), 53–54.

Throughout the later Middle Ages, the kings of England held territories in northern and southwestern France as dukes of Normandy and of Aquitaine. When King Charles IV of France died in 1328, his most direct heir was King Edward III of England, the son of Charles's sister, but a cousin of Charles's assumed the throne instead. In 1337, war broke out between France and England, and Edward laid claim to the French crown. The ensuing conflict lasted over a century and became known as the Hundred Years' War. During the war, especially after English king Henry V's victory at the famous battle of Agincourt in 1415, the English were intensely involved on the Continent. Henry married Catherine of Valois, daughter of French king Charles VI, and persuaded Charles to name him heir to the French throne. When both kings died in 1422, Henry's infant son succeeded him as Henry VI, while his brother John, duke of Bedford, served as regent in France. The war finally ended in 1453 with the defeat of the English and their expulsion from France.

During their long sojourn in France, the English nobility brought musicians with them, significantly increasing the numbers of English performers and composers on the Continent and of English pieces copied into Continental manuscripts. Moreover, the English sought alliances and trade with Burgundy and other lands. Cities like Bruges and Antwerp in modern-day Belgium were teeming with English diplomats and merchants, and thus the Low Countries as well as France became pathways for importing English music to the Continent.

The mere presence of English musicians and compositions might not have been enough to effect a major change in style, had Continental composers not noticed something distinctive about English music. This was the **contenance angloise**, or "English quality," referred to by Martin Le Franc. It consisted especially in the frequent use of harmonic thirds and sixths, often in parallel motion, resulting in pervasive consonance with few dissonances. Other common features included a preference for relatively simple melodies, regular phrasing, primarily syllabic text-setting, and homorhythmic textures. We observed these tendencies in thirteenth-century English polyphony (see chapter 5), and they became even stronger in English music of the fourteenth and early fifteenth centuries.

The contenance angloise

POLYPHONY ON LATIN TEXTS

The largest surviving repertory of English music from this period consists of sacred music on Latin texts, composed for religious services. One common style used a chant, sometimes lightly embellished, in the middle voice of a three-voice texture. The chants were most often from the Sarum rite, the distinctive chant dialect used in England from the late Middle Ages to the Reformation. As shown in Example 8.1, a passage from a Credo of about 1330 based on an English variant of the Credo melody in NAWM 3f, the lower voice usually moves a third below the chant, opening to a fifth at cadences and at other points for variety, while the upper voice mostly parallels the middle voice a fourth above it. The resulting sound consists primarily of $\frac{6}{3}$ sonorities (that is, a sixth and a third above the lowest note) moving in parallel motion, interspersed with open fifth-octave sonorities, especially at the ends of phrases and words. Parallel fifths, common throughout medieval music, are now avoided, and every vertical sonority is consonant.

Example 8.1: Passage from an anonymous English Credo (ca. 1330)

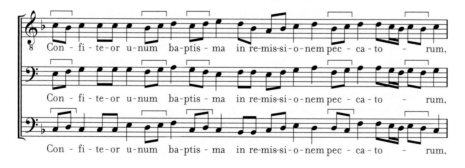

I acknowledge one baptism for the remission of sins.

Faburden   The contrapuntal style shown in this example evolved into a practice of improvised polyphony known as **faburden,** in which a plainchant in the middle voice was joined by an upper voice a perfect fourth above it and a lower voice singing mostly in parallel thirds below it, beginning each phrase and ending phrases and most words on a fifth below. Faburden was first referred to by name in about 1430 but was in use earlier, and it continued to be practiced until the English Reformation over a century later. Although some examples were written down, it was primarily a rule-based system for producing correct, sonorous polyphony that could be used even by monks and clerics who could not read polyphonic notation or compose complex counterpoint. The term "faburden" may derive from "burden," an English term for the lowest voice (used in other contexts to mean "refrain"), and the solmization syllable *fa*, since the system frequently required the singers to use B♭ ("B-fa") to harmonize with F in the chant. Faburden apparently inspired the somewhat different Continental practice known as *fauxbourdon,* described below.

Cantilena, motet,   The characteristic consonances of faburden were also found in more so-
and Mass   phisticated genres of English polyphony. **Cantilenas,** like their apparent an-
Ordinary   cestor the conductus, were freely composed, mostly homorhythmic settings of Latin texts, not based on chant. In these pieces, parallel $\frac{6}{3}$ chords are interspersed with other consonant sonorities in a texture as appealing as faburden but more varied. The most elevated genre was the motet, with the isorhythmic

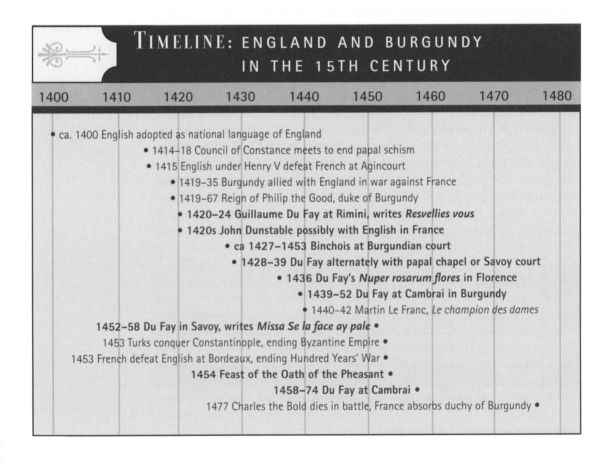

TIMELINE: ENGLAND AND BURGUNDY IN THE 15TH CENTURY

1400	1410	1420	1430	1440	1450	1460	1470	1480

- ca. 1400 English adopted as national language of England
- 1414–18 Council of Constance meets to end papal schism
- 1415 English under Henry V defeat French at Agincourt
- 1419–35 Burgundy allied with England in war against France
- 1419–67 Reign of Philip the Good, duke of Burgundy
- 1420–24 Guillaume Du Fay at Rimini, writes *Resvellies vous*
- 1420s John Dunstable possibly with English in France
- ca 1427–1453 Binchois at Burgundian court
- 1428–39 Du Fay alternately with papal chapel or Savoy court
- 1436 Du Fay's *Nuper rosarum flores* in Florence
- 1439–52 Du Fay at Cambrai in Burgundy
- 1440–42 Martin Le Franc, *Le champion des dames*
- 1452–58 Du Fay in Savoy, writes *Missa Se la face ay pale* •
- 1453 Turks conquer Constantinople, ending Byzantine Empire •
- 1453 French defeat English at Bordeaux, ending Hundred Years' War •
- 1454 Feast of the Oath of the Pheasant •
- 1458–74 Du Fay at Cambrai •
- 1477 Charles the Bold dies in battle, France absorbs duchy of Burgundy •

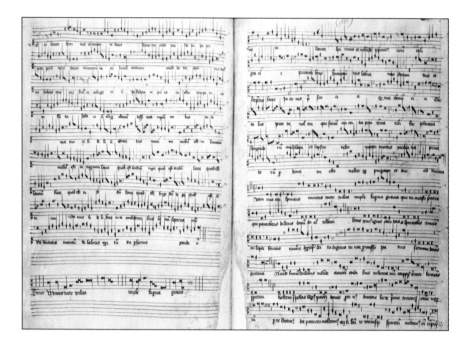

Figure 8.1: An opening from the Old Hall Manuscript. The manuscript was originally prepared in the early fifteenth century for the chapel of Thomas, duke of Clarence (d. 1421), brother of Henry V. These pages show a later addition, Dunstable's motet Veni Sancte Spiritus et emitte/Veni Sancte Spiritus et infunde/Veni Creator Spiritus/Sancti Spiritus assit. *The manuscript passed through several collectors before being donated in the late nineteenth century to the College of St. Edmund in Old Hall, near Ware, for which it is named.*

motet gradually replacing other types by 1400. By the end of the fourteenth century, settings of Mass Ordinary texts became the most common type of English polyphony, in styles from simple cantilenas to isorhythmic structures. The principal source of early-fifteenth-century English polyphony is the Old Hall Manuscript, shown in Figure 8.1, which consists primarily of settings of sections from the Mass Ordinary, along with motets, hymns, and sequences. Amid the variety of styles and genres, the English preference for thirds and sixths is always evident.

THE CAROL

The English sound is also evident in the polyphonic **carol,** a distinctively English genre. Derived from the medieval *carole,* a monophonic dance-song with alternating solo and choral sections (see chapter 4), the fifteenth-century English carol was a two- or three-part setting of a poem in English, Latin, or a mixture of the two. Most carols are on religious subjects, particularly the Christmas season and the Virgin Mary. A carol consists of a number of stanzas, all sung to the same music, and a **burden,** or refrain, with its own musical phrase, sung at the beginning and then repeated after each stanza. When, where, and by whom carols were sung is not certain, but they may have been used for dancing at religious festivals or to accompany processions.

CD 2|49

Many carols feature contrasts of texture between two- and three-part and unison writing. An example is *Alleluia: A newë work* (NAWM 31), which includes two burdens, for two and three voices respectively. The second burden, shown in Example 8.2, shows a common English texture: the top voice is most rhythmically active, while the lower voices mostly parallel it in $\frac{6}{3}$ sonorities, moving out to the octave and fifth at cadences.

Example 8.2: Second burden (refrain) from the carol Alleluia: A newë work

JOHN DUNSTABLE

Preeminent among English composers in the first half of the fifteenth century was John Dunstable (ca. 1390–1453; see biography). Among Dunstable's sixty or so compositions are examples of all the principal types of polyphony that existed in his lifetime: isorhythmic motets, Mass Ordinary sections, settings of chant, free settings of liturgical texts, and secular songs. His most celebrated motet, shown in Figure 8.1, is a four-part work that combines the hymn *Veni creator spiritus* and the sequence *Veni sancte spiritus*. It is both an impressive example of isorhythmic structure and a splendid piece of music, embodying the English preference for thirds together with fifths or sixths.

Three-voice sacred works

Dunstable's most numerous and historically important works are his three-part sacred pieces, settings of antiphons, hymns, Mass sections, and other liturgical or biblical texts. Some have a cantus firmus in the tenor, serving as the structural foundation for the upper voices. In others, a chant is elaborated in the top voice using a technique now called **paraphrase,** in which the melody is given a rhythm and ornamented by adding notes around those of the chant. Example 8.3 shows such a passage from Dunstable's *Regina*

JOHN DUNSTABLE [DUNSTAPLE] (CA. 1390–1453)

Dunstable was the most highly regarded English composer of the first half of the fifteenth century. He composed in all polyphonic genres of the time and exercised a great influence on his contemporaries and successors.

Dunstable's birthplace and early training are unknown. He was a mathematician and astronomer as well as a musician, recalling the medieval grouping of music with the mathematical sciences of the quadrivium. Apparently not a priest, he served a number of royal and noble patrons. He is listed as having been in the service of John, duke of Bedford, possibly while the latter was regent of France beginning in 1422. In about 1427–37, his patron was Joan, dowager queen of England, and subsequently he served Humphrey, duke of Gloucester.

Dunstable probably spent part of his career in France—he is the English composer most often cited as influencing Continental composers—and his compositions are preserved chiefly in manuscripts copied on the Continent. Indeed, characteristics typical of English composers in general were often credited to him by later generations.

MAJOR WORKS: *Up to 3 polyphonic mass cycles, 2 Gloria-Credo pairs, 15 other Mass Ordinary movements, 12 isorhythmic motets, 6 plainchant settings, 20 other Latin sacred works, 5 secular songs*

caeli laetare. It is characteristic of Dunstable's style that no two measures in succession have the same rhythm and that the melodies move mostly by step or steps mixed with thirds, sometimes outlining a triad.

Still other works, like Dunstable's setting of the antiphon text *Quam pulchra es* (NAWM 32), are not based on an existing melody. The three voices in this work are similar in character and nearly equal in importance. They move mostly in the same rhythm and usually pronounce the same syllables

CD 2|52   CD 1|40

Example 8.3: Cantus from Dunstable's Regina caeli laetare *compared with original plainchant*

together. The vertical sonorities are consonant, except for brief suspensions at cadences, yet show considerable variety. The streams of $\frac{6}{3}$ sonorities found in faburden appear only in a few phrases, leading into a cadence.

REDEFINING THE MOTET

As a free, mostly homorhythmic setting of a Latin text, *Quam pulchra es* could be classified as a cantilena, but in the fifteenth century it could also be called a **motet.** This term, coined in the thirteenth century for pieces that added text to the upper part of a discant clausula, gradually broadened in meaning to encompass any work with texted upper voices above a cantus firmus, whether sacred or secular. By the early fifteenth century, the isorhythmic motet was a conservative form, a century old, and by 1450 it disappeared. Meanwhile, the term *motet* was applied to settings of liturgical texts in the newer musical styles of the time, whether or not a chant melody was used. The term came to designate almost any polyphonic composition on a Latin text, including settings of texts from the Mass Proper and the Office. It was even used for settings of Mass Ordinary texts before the mass cycle became defined as a genre around the mid-fifteenth century (see below). Since the sixteenth century, the term *motet* has also been applied to sacred compositions in languages other than Latin. The changing meanings of "motet" in different eras, summarized in Figure 8.2, provide another example of musicians using familiar terms for new types of music.

THE ENGLISH INFLUENCE

English music of the early fifteenth century shows a range of styles, from improvised faburden and carols in popular style through sophisticated isorhythmic motets, chant paraphrases, and free compositions. The carols and much of the functional music for religious observances were used only in England, but the sound they exemplified, of three voices joined in a euphonious progression of sonorities dominated by thirds and sixths, pervaded

early 1200s	polyphonic piece derived from discant clausula, with words added to the upper voice
1200s–1300s	polyphonic piece with one or more upper voices, each with sacred or secular text in Latin or French, above tenor from chant or other source
ca. 1310–1450	isorhythmic motet: tenor structured by isorhythm
1400s on	used for polyphonic setting of a Latin text, especially liturgical text, other than a mass
mid-1500s on	used for some polyphonic settings of sacred texts in other languages

Figure 8.2: The changing meanings of "motet."

other English music as well. As the works of Dunstable and others and the practice of faburden became known on the Continent, this sound strongly influenced other types of composition. The English sound steered composers toward homorhythmic textures and helped win acceptance for conspicuous third and sixth sonorities in the harmonic vocabulary. It also led to the emergence on the Continent of a new way of writing for three parts: the upper voice, which has the principal melodic line as in fourteenth-century chansons, is coupled with a tenor as if in a duet, and the two parts—and eventually the contratenor as well—are more nearly equal in importance, in melodic quality, and in rhythm. In these ways, English influence was an essential element in the international style of the mid to late fifteenth century.

MUSIC IN THE BURGUNDIAN LANDS

On the European mainland, musicians connected with the court of Burgundy or trained in Burgundian lands played a particularly important role in the development of an international musical idiom in the fifteenth century.

THE DUCHY OF BURGUNDY

The duke of Burgundy was a feudal vassal of the king of France, yet for a time virtually equaled the king in power. During the late fourteenth and fifteenth centuries, successive dukes acquired large territories, partly through political marriages and diplomacy that took advantage of their kings' distress in the Hundred Years' War; indeed, for a time (1419–35) Burgundy was allied with the English against the French king. Thus to their original fiefs, the duchy and county of Burgundy in east-central France, the dukes added most of what are today Holland, Belgium, northeastern France, Luxembourg, and Lorraine, as shown in Figure 8.3. The dukes of Burgundy ruled over the whole as virtually independent sovereigns until 1477. Though their nominal capital was Dijon, the dukes had no fixed city of residence but sojourned at various places in their dominions. The main orbit of the Burgundian court by the mid-fifteenth century was around Lille, Bruges, Ghent, and especially Brussels, an area comprising modern Belgium and northeastern France. Most of the leading composers of the late fifteenth century came from the Burgundian territories, and many of them were connected with the Burgundian court.

The first duke of Burgundy, Philip the Bold (r. 1363–1404), established a chapel in 1384, and it soon became one of Europe's largest and most resplendent. Under Philip the Good (r. 1419–67), it reached twenty-three singers by 1445, surpassed only by the king of England's chapel. At first, musicians were recruited chiefly from northern France. But because Philip the Good and his successor, Charles the Bold (r. 1467–77), resided in the north rather than in Dijon, most of their musicians came from Flanders and the Low Countries (modern-day Belgium and the Netherlands). In addition to his chapel, Philip the Good maintained a band of minstrels—players of trumpets, drums, vielle, lute, harp, organ, bagpipes, and shawms—which included musicians from

Burgundian chapel and minstrels

France, Italy, Germany, and Portugal. The painting in Figure 8.4 depicts singers and instrumentalists performing at one of Philip's lavish entertainments, and the sidebar on page 177 describes another. Charles the Bold was particularly keen on music, being an amateur instrumentalist and composer. His death in 1477 left Burgundy with no male heir. The duchy itself was absorbed by the French king, but Charles's daughter Mary of Burgundy and her son Philip the Fair continued to reign over the Burgundian territories in the Low Countries and maintained the chapel.

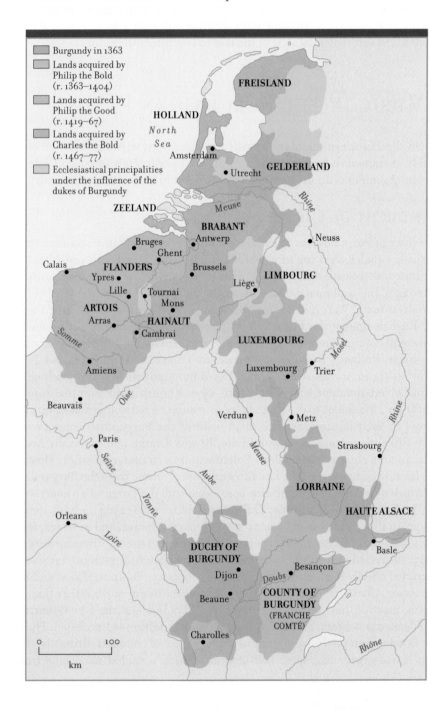

Figure 8.3: Map showing the growth of Burgundian possessions, 1363–1477.

MUSIC IN CONTEXT

The Feast of the Oath of the Pheasant

When Constantinople, the last Christian stronghold in the East, fell to Turkish Muslims in 1453, reactions at the other end of Europe were immediate and profound. The leading composer of the time, Guillaume Du Fay, wrote a lament, a motet for which he chose a cantus firmus from a Latin chant with these words from the Lamentations of Jeremiah: "All her friends have dealt treacherously with her, among all her lovers she hath none to comfort her." Duke Philip the Good of Burgundy was so troubled that he determined to launch a new crusade to rescue the eastern Church. Although the crusade never materialized, Philip created quite a stir. As leader of the wealthiest and most cultured court of Europe, he assembled hundreds of noble lords and vassals and their ladies at a huge banquet, where they took a solemn oath to come to the aid of the captive Church.

The Feast of the Oath of the Pheasant, as it is known, took place in Lille on June 17, 1454. Court chroniclers described the event in ways which suggest that every detail was designed to enhance the theme. The tables were decorated with enormous constructions that came alive as people and animals emerged from them during interludes performed between courses. Music played a large role in the spectacle. During the first interlude, a church bell rang loudly, then three choirboys and a tenor sang a song. At other moments, minstrels sang and played on portative organs, bagpipes, lutes, crumhorns, flutes, fiddles, harps, and drums. There were pantomime tableaux, each punctuated by trumpet fanfares, involving knights on horseback, a falcon slaying a heron, and scenes from the adventures of Jason, heroic patron of the Knights of the Order of the Golden Fleece.

At the climax of the banquet was staged the interlude that symbolized the reason for the entire feast. Into the huge hall a giant Arab led an elephant bearing on its back a miniature castle; within its tower was imprisoned a woman per-

Figure 8.4: An outdoor entertainment at the court of Duke Philip the Good of Burgundy. Musicians play and sing for the duke (center) and his company, while in the background hunters are chasing game. Detail from a sixteenth-century copy of an anonymous fifteenth-century painting.

sonifying Mother Church. After chanting a complainte bemoaning the fall of Constantinople, she begged the Burgundian nobles to take up her cause. At that point, the chronicles explain, a live pheasant decorated with pearls and precious gems was presented to the assembled noblemen "in order that they make useful and worthy vows." After the tables were taken out, the final episode was a joyous ballet.

The magnificence of the occasion reveals something about the extravagant lifestyle of the Burgundian court, where refinement mingled with vulgarity and chivalric ideals combined with religious sentiment. But it also shows that ceremonial music and theater were purposefully linked to meaningful action in life.—BRH

COSMOPOLITAN STYLE

The cosmopolitan atmosphere of fifteenth-century courts was constantly re-newed by visits from foreign musicians. In addition, members of the chapel themselves were continually changing, moving from one court to another in response to better opportunities. These circumstances, along with increasing trade across the Continent, fostered a common musical style. The prestige of the Burgundian court was such that the music cultivated there influenced other European musical centers: the chapels of the pope at Rome, of the em-peror in Germany, of the French and English kings, and of the various Italian courts, as well as cathedral choirs.

GENRES AND TEXTURE

Composers in the mid-fifteenth century produced four principal types of polyphonic composition: secular chansons with French texts; motets; Magni-ficats; and settings of the Mass Ordinary. Most pieces were for three voices, in a combination resembling the fourteenth-century French chanson or Italian ballata but with slightly larger ranges for each voice, the cantus spanning about a tenth or twelfth (around *a* to *c″* or *e″*) and tenor and contratenor both in a range about a sixth lower (usually *c* to *e′* or *g′*). As in fourteenth-century music, each line has a distinct role, with the main melody in the cantus, con-trapuntal support in the tenor, and harmonic filler in the contratenor.

BINCHOIS AND THE BURGUNDIAN CHANSON

In the fifteenth century, the term *chanson* encompassed any polyphonic set-ting of a French secular poem. Chansons most often set stylized love poems in the courtly tradition of *fine amour* (see chapter 4), and most followed the form of the rondeau (ABaAabAB). Ballades were written for ceremonial occasions, but gradually went out of fashion.

Binchois's chansons

CD2|54   CD 1|42

Binchois, the most important composer at the court of Philip the Good (see biography and Figure 8.5), was particularly esteemed for his chansons. His well-known rondeau *De plus en plus* (NAWM 33), from around 1425, ex-emplifies his style and the Burgundian chanson. Example 8.4 shows the opening phrase.

Example 8.4: Binchois, De plus en plus, *opening phrase*

More and more renews again, . . .

BINCHOIS [GILLES DE BINS] (CA. 1400–1460)

Gilles de Bins, known as Binchois, was along with Dunstable and Du Fay one of the three most important composers of his generation. At a time when the Burgundian court was a focus of musical activity, Binchois stood at the center of the court's musical life. His works were widely recopied and emulated by many other composers.

Binchois was probably born and trained in Mons, where he was a chorister and organist. He went to live in Lille in 1423, and apparently spent some time in the service of William Pole, earl of Suffolk, who was with the English forces occupying France. He joined the chapel of Philip the Good, duke of Burgundy, by 1427, and served at court until retiring in 1453 on a generous pension. His direct contact with English musicians and his three-decade career at the Burgundian court made him a central figure in the creation of a Burgundian style that incorporates English influences.

MAJOR WORKS: *28 mass movements (some in Gloria-Credo or Sanctus-Agnus pairs), 6 Magnificats, 29 motets, 51 rondeaux, 7 ballades*

Figure 8.5: Binchois, holding a harp (on the right), and Guillaume Du Fay, next to a portative organ, in a miniature from Martin Le Franc's poem Le champion des dames *(1440–42). Binchois, Du Fay, and Le Franc were together at Savoy in 1434 when Binchois visited with the duke of Burgundy's retinue, and the two composers may have met on other occasions as well.*

Most compositions from this era are in the equivalent of either $\frac{3}{4}$ or $\frac{6}{8}$ meter; duple meter was used mainly in subdivisions of longer works, to provide contrast. *De plus en plus* is in $\frac{6}{8}$, with occasional cross-rhythms of three quarter notes, an effect called **hemiola** (see measure 3). Like Dunstable, Binchois varies the rhythm from measure to measure, enlivening it with dotted figures and subtle syncopations. Yet the result is much less intricate than rhythms in chansons by Machaut or Ars Subtilior composers. *Meter and rhythm*

The cantus declaims the text clearly. As in most chansons of the time, the setting is mostly syllabic, especially at the beginning of each line of poetry. Groups of two to four notes provide variety, and longer melismas appear only at the most important cadences, in contrast to the more frequent melismas in fourteenth-century songs. *Music and text*

The main melody in the cantus is fluid and gently arching; the tenor is also smooth but slower; and the two voices form good two-part counterpoint, *Melody and counterpoint* mostly in sixths and thirds. The contratenor, by comparison, is full of skips and leaps, in order to fill out the harmony. The music is almost wholly consonant, with only a few dissonances, all carefully introduced as passing tones, neighbor tones, or suspensions. The upbeat opening, the full consonant harmony, and the triadic skips in cantus and contratenor reflect the influence of English music.

Cadences　　　The preferred cadence formula in the mid-fifteenth century was still a major sixth expanding to an octave between cantus and tenor, often decorated in the cantus with an under-third cadence (see Examples 6.6 and 6.7). The end of the phrase in Example 8.4 illustrates a newer version of this cadence, in which the contratenor sounds a fifth below the penultimate tenor note, then leaps up an octave to a fifth above the tenor's final note. Modern ears may hear the effect of a bass rising a fourth, as in the common-practice dominant-tonic cadence.

GUILLAUME DU FAY

Guillaume Du Fay (ca. 1397–1474) was the most famous composer of his time. He was associated with the Burgundian court, although his appointment to the ducal chapel was probably honorary. Trained at the Cathedral of Cambrai in northern France, he often traveled south, serving as a chapel musician in Italy and Savoy (now in southeastern France), but he frequently returned to Cambrai, where he spent his later career (see biography and Figure 8.6). His many travels exposed him to a wide variety of music, from his French and Italian predecessors to his English and Burgundian contemporaries and younger composers such as Johannes Ockeghem (see chapter 9), and he absorbed many of their stylistic traits into his own music, sometimes combining contrasting styles in a single piece. His music represents well the international style of the mid-fifteenth century.

CHANSONS AND THE INTERNATIONAL STYLE

CD 2|56

Du Fay's blending of national traits can be traced in his chansons. He wrote *Resvellies vous* (NAWM 34) in 1423 while in Italy at the court of Rimini and Pesaro, to celebrate his patron's wedding. French characteristics in this chanson include the ballade form (aab with refrain), many long melismas, frequent syncopation, and some free dissonances. Example 8.5 shows one phrase with cross-rhythms between the parts and several dissonant ornamental notes. Some passages recall the Ars Subtilior, with rapid notes in various divisions of the beat, including tripletlike figuration. Italian elements include relatively smooth vocal melodies, melismas on the last accented syllable of each line of text, and a meter change for the b section, paralleling the change of meter at the ritornello in the Italian madrigal.

CD 2|61　　CD 1|44

Se la face ay pale (NAWM 36a), a ballade Du Fay wrote about ten years later while at the court of Savoy, shows the strong influence of English music,

GUILLAUME DU FAY [DUFAY] (CA. 1397–1474)

Du Fay was the leading composer of his time and one of the most widely traveled. He excelled in every genre, and his music was known and sung throughout Europe.

Du Fay, the illegitimate son of a priest and an unmarried woman, was born in modern-day Belgium, probably in Beersel, near Brussels. He trained in music and grammar in the cathedral school of Cambrai in north-eastern France, where he became a choirboy in 1409. He apparently sojourned with a patron at the Council of Constance (1414–18) in southern Germany, which ended the Great Schism between rival popes in Rome, Avignon, and Pisa. He then returned to Cambrai as subdeacon at the cathedral. In 1420, he entered the service of Carlo Malatesta at Rimini, on the Adriatic coast of northern Italy. He returned north in 1424, then worked during 1426–28 for Cardinal Louis Aleman in Bologna, where he became a priest.

Du Fay served two periods in the papal chapel, first at Rome in 1428–33 and again in 1435–37 during the pope's exile in Florence and Bologna. Alternating with his service to the pope, he was chapel master in 1433–35 and 1437–39 at the court of Amadeus VIII, duke of Savoy, whose territories at the time included parts of south-eastern France, northwestern Italy, and western Switzerland. When in 1439 a church council deposed the pope and elected Amadeus pope, Du Fay escaped the conflict between his two major patrons by returning to Cambrai, by then under Burgundian control. He served as an administrator at Cambrai Cathedral and enjoyed at least an honorary appointment to the chapel of Duke Philip the Good. After the papal schism was resolved, Du Fay returned to Savoy in 1452–53 as honorary chapel master for Duke Louis. He spent his last years at Cambrai as canon of the cathedral, living in his own house and enjoying considerable wealth.

Du Fay's music survives in almost one hundred manuscripts copied between the 1420s and the early sixteenth century in regions from Spain to Poland and from Italy to Scotland, attesting to his popularity and fame as a composer.

MAJOR WORKS: *at least 6 masses, 35 other Mass movements, 4 Magnificats, 60 hymns and other chant settings, 24 motets (13 isorhythmic, 11 freely composed), 34 plainchant melodies, 60 rondeaux, 8 ballades, 13 other secular songs*

Figure 8.6: Bas-relief from Guillaume Du Fay's funeral monument, showing the composer kneeling in prayer (lower left).

Example 8.5: Du Fay, Resvellies vous, *mm. 12–15*

* = dissonant note

All lovers who love gentleness

as seen in Example 8.6. Both tenor and cantus are equally tuneful, an English trait, while the contratenor leaps around to fill in the harmony, like those in earlier French chansons. The melodies are graceful, mostly stepwise, and primarily syllabic with brief melismas, drawing on both Italian and English characteristics while leaning toward the latter with relatively brief, clearly demarked phrases. Yet the rhythmic energy of the French Ars nova is still present, in frequent syncopation and constantly varying rhythms. The harmony is consonant throughout, with prominent thirds, sixths, and full triads (as they were later called), and very few dissonances, all carefully controlled as suspensions or ornamental tones. Finally, the chanson is no longer in the fixed form of the ballade (aab), but is freely composed. The English contribution is essential, yet the music is not merely English in sound; rather, it

Example 8.6: Du Fay, Se la face ay pale, *mm. 1–10*

If my face is pale, the cause is love, that is the principal reason.

represents a blending of characteristics from all three national traditions to form a new international musical language.

MOTETS AND CHANT SETTINGS

Du Fay wrote sacred music in a variety of styles. Most works were in three voices in a texture resembling the chanson, with the main melody in the cantus supported by tenor and contratenor. The cantus might be newly composed, as in Du Fay's cantilena motets, but in many cases it was an embellished paraphrase of chant.

Fauxbourdon

Du Fay and other continental composers of the second quarter of the fifteenth century became fascinated with successions of thirds and sixths, apparently through hearing music imported from England. Twenty-four pieces by Du Fay and over a hundred by other composers use a technique called **fauxbourdon,** probably inspired by English faburden. Only the cantus and tenor were written out, moving mostly in parallel sixths, ending each phrase on an octave. A third voice, unwritten, sang in exact parallel a fourth below the cantus, producing a stream of $\frac{6}{3}$ sonorities ending on an open fifth and octave, as in faburden. The technique was used chiefly for settings of the simpler Office chants: hymns, antiphons, psalms, and canticles. Du Fay's setting of the hymn *Conditor alme siderum* (NAWM 35) uses fauxbourdon, paraphrasing the chant in the cantus. Only the even-numbered stanzas were sung polyphonically, alternating with the others in plainchant.

CD 2|59

In addition to motets in the modern chanson style and pieces using fauxbourdon, Du Fay and his contemporaries still wrote occasional isorhythmic motets for solemn public ceremonies, following the convention that an archaic musical style, like an archaic literary style, was most suitable for ceremonial and state occasions. Du Fay's *Nuper rosarum flores* was such a work, performed in 1436 at the dedication of Filippo Brunelleschi's magnificent dome for the Cathedral of Santa Maria del Fiore in Florence, shown in Figure 8.7. Du Fay's use of two isorhythmic tenors, both based on the same chant,

Isorhythmic motets

Figure 8.7: The Cathedral of Santa Maria del Fiore in Florence. Du Fay wrote the isorhythmic motet Nuper rosarum flores *for the consecration in 1436 of the dome, designed by Filippo Brunelleschi.*

may have been an allusion to Brunelleschi's use of two vaults to support the dome. Du Fay wrote the motet while serving in the chapel of Pope Eugene IV, who officiated at the dedication. Another of his motets, *Supremum est mortalibus bonum* (1433), written to commemorate the meeting of Pope Eugene with King Sigismund of Hungary, emperor-elect of the Holy Roman Empire, alternates sections in isorhythm, fauxbourdon, and free counterpoint in a masterful combination of these strongly contrasting styles.

THE POLYPHONIC MASS

Like their English colleagues, composers on the Continent wrote polyphonic settings of Mass Ordinary texts in increasing numbers during the late fourteenth and early fifteenth centuries. Until about 1420, the various items of the Ordinary were usually composed as separate pieces (Machaut's mass and a few others excepted), though occasionally a compiler would group them together. In the course of the fifteenth century, it became standard practice for composers to set the Ordinary as a coherent whole. Leading this development were English composers, notably Dunstable and his compatriot Leonel Power (d. 1445). At first, composers linked only two sections, such as a Gloria and a Credo. Gradually the practice widened to include all five main items of the Ordinary—Kyrie, Gloria, Credo, Sanctus, and Agnus Dei—in a work called a *polyphonic mass cycle*, or simply a **mass.** (In common usage, the church service—the Mass—is capitalized, but the musical genre is not.)

MASS CYCLES

Grouping music for the Mass Ordinary into cycles, with one setting for each text, goes back to the thirteenth century with cycles of Ordinary chants (see chapter 3). Scribes occasionally did the same for polyphonic settings in the fourteenth century. But such cycles were not necessarily musically related. Composers in the fifteenth century devised a variety of means to link the separate sections of a mass to each other.

Stylistic coherence   In the context of a liturgy that was mostly sung in plainchant, some sense of connection resulted simply from composing all five parts of the Ordinary in the same general style, whether freely composed, based on paraphrased chants in the upper voice, or using a chant or other melody as a cantus firmus in the tenor.

Plainsong mass   When the composer based each movement on an existing chant for that text (the Kyrie on a Kyrie chant, the Gloria on a Gloria chant, and so on), the mass gained coherence because the borrowed melodies were all liturgically appropriate, although not necessarily related musically. A mass that uses chant in this way is called a **plainsong mass.** Many plainsong masses, including Machaut's, were written to be sung during a Lady Mass, a special service dedicated to the Virgin Mary.

Motto mass   Composers could create a more noticeable musical connection by using the same thematic material in all movements of the mass. A frequent strategy early in the fifteenth century consisted of beginning each movement with the same melodic motive, in one or all voices. A mass that uses such a **head-motive** as its primary linking device is called a **motto mass.**

CANTUS-FIRMUS MASS

The use of a head-motive was soon combined with (and sometimes superseded by) another way of linking movements: constructing each one around the same cantus firmus, normally placed in the tenor. This type of mass has come to be known as a **cantus-firmus mass,** or **tenor mass.** English composers wrote the earliest such masses, but the practice was quickly adopted on the Continent, and by the second half of the fifteenth century it became the principal type of mass.

The tenor cantus firmus was written in long notes and usually in an isorhythmic pattern, as in the isorhythmic motet. When this melody was a chant, a rhythm was imposed on it. When the borrowed melody was a secular tune, the song's original rhythm was normally retained, but in successive appearances the pattern could be made faster or slower in relation to the other voices. Often composers used the tenor of a polyphonic chanson, and when they did so, they typically borrowed some elements from the other voices as well; such a mass is sometimes called a **cantus-firmus/imitation mass,** since it imitates more than one voice of the source. The mass usually derived its name from the borrowed melody. One of the melodies used most frequently was *L'homme armé* (The armed man), shown in Example 8.7. Most major

Example 8.7: L'homme armé

The armed man is to be feared. Everywhere it has been proclaimed that everyone should arm
   himself with an iron coat of mail.

composers for more than a century, including Du Fay, Ockeghem, Josquin, and Palestrina, wrote at least one *Missa L'homme armé.*

Four-voice texture

Early cantus-firmus masses were for three voices. Placing the borrowed melody in the tenor followed the motet tradition but created compositional problems. The sound-ideal of the fifteenth century needed the lowest voice to function as a harmonic foundation, particularly at cadences. Letting the lowest voice carry a chant melody that could not be altered limited the composer's ability to provide such a foundation. The solution was to add a part below the tenor, called at first **contratenor bassus** (low contratenor) and later simply **bassus,** the source of our English term **bass** for a low male voice. Above the tenor sounded a second contratenor called **contratenor altus** (high contratenor), later **altus,** hence **alto.** The highest part, the cantus (melody), was also called *discantus* (discant) or **superius** (highest); from the latter (through Italian) comes our term **soprano.** These four voice parts became standard by the mid-fifteenth century and remain so today.

Du Fay's Missa
Se la face ay pale

Du Fay's *Missa Se la face ay pale* is one of the most celebrated cantus-firmus masses. In this work, Du Fay applied the method of the isorhythmic motet on a larger scale. He used the tenor of his own ballade *Se la face ay pale* (see Example 8.6) in the tenor of the mass. He apparently wrote the mass in the 1450s while he was at Savoy, and may have borrowed the ballade, written two decades earlier for the same court, to honor or please his patron. In the Kyrie, Sanctus, and Agnus Dei, the duration of each note from the ballade is doubled. In the Gloria (NAWM 36b) and Credo, the cantus firmus is heard three times. In Example 8.8b, we see the first phrase of the song's tenor in the mass tenor at "Adoramus te," sung at triple the original duration; that is, each beat of the original tenor part (transcribed as a quarter note in Example 8.8a) corresponds to three beats here (with the beat transcribed as a half note). When the ballade melody repeats, at "Qui tollis" (8.8c), the original note values are doubled (two beats for each original beat). Only when the melody appears a third time, at "Cum sancto spiritu" (8.8d), is the melody easily recognized, because it is heard at its normal tempo. At the closing Amen, as the tenor sings the final melisma from the ballade tenor, portions of the ballade's other voices are borrowed as well, making the allusion even more recognizable. This borrowing from multiple voices makes the work a cantus-firmus/imitation mass.

CD 2|63   CD 1|46

Throughout, each voice has a distinctive function and character. The upper two voices, the superius and contratenor altus, move mostly stepwise with skips interspersed, proceed in constantly varying rhythm, and occasionally exchange motives. The tenor is the main structural voice, while the more angular contratenor bassus provides a harmonic foundation. Contrasts of sonority between textures of two, three, and four voices provide variety.

*Why the cantus-
firmus mass?*

Why did the cantus-firmus mass develop and become so widespread? Since the nineteenth century, music historians have suggested that composers sought to unify the five movements of the mass into an integrated whole, akin to the multimovement works of later centuries, and found that using the same cantus firmus in each movement was an ideal way to do so. Such a view privileges composers' initiative and musical unity, both more highly valued in the nineteenth century than in the fifteenth. More recently, scholars have shown that institutions and private patrons in the fifteenth century often commissioned settings of the Mass Ordinary for specific occasions or devotional services, just as Machaut's setting served for a Mass offered to the Virgin Mary. A particular chant or secular song used as a cantus firmus could refer to the saint to whom the mass was addressed, as in Power's *Missa Alma redemptoris Mater* on a chant to the Virgin Mary, or to the institution, family, or individual for whose benefit the mass was composed, as in Du Fay's *Missa Se la face ay pale*, linked to his Savoy patrons. Similarly, the tradition of masses on *L'homme armé* may be connected to the Order of the Golden Fleece, an association of knights at the Burgundian court, and to calls for a new crusade (see sidebar on p. 177). Musical unity resulted from using

Example 8.8: Du Fay, Missa Se la face ay pale, *Gloria*

a. Original tenor melody

b. Cantus firmus at three times original duration

We adore thee. We glorify thee. We give thee thanks

c. Cantus firmus at twice original duration

have mercy on us. Thou who takest away the sins of the world, receive [our prayer.]

d. Cantus firmus at original duration

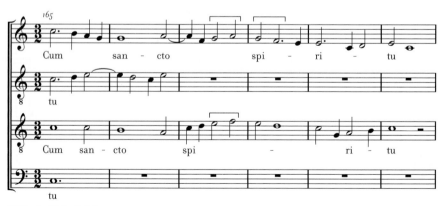

With the Holy Spirit

the same cantus firmus throughout, but the concern for diversity was at least as strong; writers such as Tinctoris praised composers for producing variety between movements, even when each was based on the same melody.

The cantus-firmus mass met multiple needs: as service music and as a work that connoisseurs such as Tinctoris could appreciate. The cyclic mass began its career as a piece written for a specific occasion or patron, replacing in many respects the function of the isorhythmic motet, and many structural elements from the latter were taken over in the cantus-firmus mass. As the motet receded in importance, the mass became the most prestigious genre of the time. The traditions that developed, in which many composers used the same melody as a cantus firmus, suggest that the mass became a proving ground for composers' abilities. We, who typically hear this music in concert or on recordings rather than in its original liturgical environment, are likely to approach a mass as we would other music, admiring the glorious sounds and composers' skill in reworking borrowed material in many varied ways.

The Musical Language of the Renaissance

The music of Dunstable, Binchois, Du Fay, and their contemporaries was regarded by Tinctoris in the 1470s as the oldest music worth listening to, and it still marks the earliest polyphonic music many Westerners may hear as familiar rather than alien. Du Fay and other composers working between the 1420s and the 1450s helped to forge a cosmopolitan musical language that blended French concern for structure and rhythmic interest, Italian emphasis on lyrical melodies, and English preference for sweetly concordant sonorities, including prominent thirds and sixths, and carefully controlled dissonance. All of these ingredients became fundamental to the musical language of the Renaissance. They remained important elements of music through the nineteenth century and beyond, and their presence in fifteenth-century music is what makes it sound more familiar to modern ears than most Medieval music does.

The musical idiom continued to evolve throughout Du Fay's career, as four-voice textures and equality between the voices became increasingly common. After his death, Du Fay was remembered as the leading composer of his era. Yet in the late fifteenth century, styles and tastes changed relatively quickly, and by the early sixteenth century, performances of the music of Du Fay or his contemporaries were rare. Their music lay unperformed and untranscribed for centuries, until rising musicological interest in the late nineteenth century led to editions and performances in the twentieth. Now works by Du Fay and other composers of his time are regularly performed and recorded, so that we can experience for ourselves the "marvelous pleasingness" Martin Le Franc heard in their music almost six centuries ago.

Franco-Flemish Composers, 1450–1520

The latter fifteenth and early sixteenth centuries saw the continuing prominence of composers from northern France, Flanders, and the Netherlands, who served courts and cities throughout France, the Low Countries, Italy, Spain, Germany, Bohemia, and Austria. The generation of composers born around 1420 and active until the 1490s inherited both the new international language and some surviving medieval traits, such as the **formes fixes,** cantus-firmus structure, and stratified counterpoint based on a structural tenor. Their newer style was marked by wider ranges, greater equality between voices, and increased use of imitation. The following generation, born around 1450 and active through about 1520, brought an end to the *formes fixes*, a growing interest in imitative and homophonic textures, and a new focus on fitting music to words with appropriate declamation, imagery, and expression.

Political Change and Consolidation

Composers in the late fifteenth and early sixteenth centuries depended as before on the support of patrons. Political and economic changes influenced the market for musicians and the flow of music.

Defeated in the Hundred Years' War in 1453, England withdrew from France and entered a period of relative insularity marked by civil war (the Wars of the Roses). But other major powers were gaining ground on the Continent, as shown in the map in Figure 9.1. After the death in 1477 of Charles the Bold, the duchy of Burgundy came under the control of the king of France, the first of several acquisitions over the next fifty years that consolidated France into a strong, centralized state. The Burgundian possessions in the Low Countries passed to Charles's daughter Mary of Burgundy, whose 1478 marriage to Maximilian of Hapsburg united her lands with his in Austria and Alsace. The marriage of Queen Isabella of Castile and Léon (northern and central Spain) to King Ferdinand of Aragon (eastern Spain, Sardinia, and Sicily) joined the two realms to create the modern kingdom of Spain. In the eventful year of 1492, Isabella and Ferdinand conquered the southern

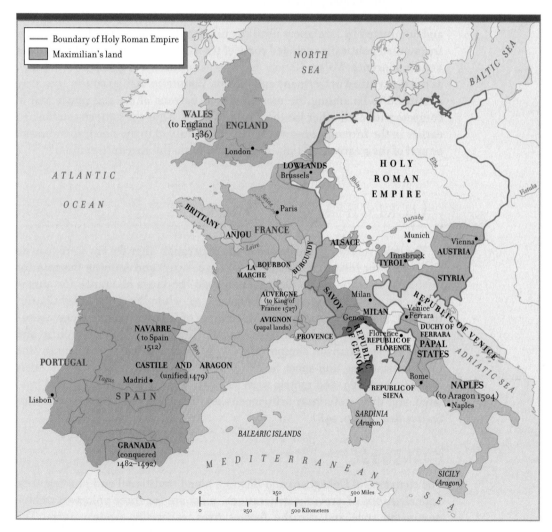

Figure 9.1: Western Europe about 1500. By this time, the Spanish rulers Isabella and Ferdinand had united Spain; the kings of France controlled several former quasi-independent fiefdoms within their borders, including Burgundy, Anjou, Brittany, and Provence; and Maximilian I, king of Germany and Holy Roman Emperor, ruled directly over Austria, Alsace, and the Low Countries.

Spanish kingdom of Granada, controlled by the Islamic Moors; forcibly expelled the Jews from Spain, ending centuries of coexistence and mutual influence between Muslims, Jews, and Christians in Spain; and sponsored Columbus's voyage west over the Atlantic Ocean, which led to the European encounter with and colonization of the New World. The marriage of Ferdinand and Isabella's daughter to the son of Mary and Maximilian (who was by then Holy Roman Emperor) ultimately brought about the unification of Austria, the Low Countries, southern Italy, Spain, and Spanish America under the Hapsburg emperor Charles V (r. 1519–1556), the most powerful European ruler since Charlemagne.

Sandwiched in between these major powers were dozens of small states and cities in Germany and Italy. When the French invaded Italy in 1494, the Italian states were unable to unite against them. The region remained divided and dominated by foreigners until the nineteenth century. Yet the areas most fragmented politically included some of the wealthiest. Italian centers such as Venice, Florence, Milan, Genoa, and Naples continued to prosper from trade, as did many cities in Germany and the Low Countries. Italian courts and cities continued to be among the most generous patrons of art and music and to compete with each other for the best musicians. Thus the pattern established earlier in the fifteenth century, of musicians trained in the north spending all or part of their careers in Italy, endured well into the sixteenth century.

OCKEGHEM AND BUSNOYS

The most renowned musicians of the generation after Du Fay were Jean de Ockeghem (or Johannes Okeghem, ca. 1420–1497) and Antoine Busnoys (or Busnois, ca. 1430–1492). Ockeghem served the kings of France for almost half a century (see biography and Figure 9.2), while Busnoys served Charles the Bold, Mary of Burgundy, and Maximilian of Hapsburg. Ockeghem was esteemed especially for his masses, and Busnoys was the most prolific and widely praised chanson composer of his time. Tinctoris lauded them as "the most outstanding and most famous professors of the art of music." Their masses, chansons, and motets were widely distributed, performed, and imitated, and they profoundly influenced the next generation of composers (see Source Reading, p. 198).

CHANSONS

The chansons of Ockeghem and Busnoys blend traditional and new features. Like chansons of previous generations, most are for three voices in treble-dominated style and use the *formes fixes*, especially rondeau form. The smooth, arching melodies, lightly syncopated rhythms, pervasive consonance, careful dissonance treatment, and prominent thirds and sixths of the Du Fay generation are still evident. New features include longer-breathed melodies, increased use of imitation, greater equality between voices, and more frequent use of duple meter.

JEAN DE OCKEGHEM [JOHANNES OKEGHEM] (CA. 1420–1497)

Ockeghem was celebrated as a singer (he is said to have had a fine bass voice), as a composer, and as the teacher of many leading composers of the next generation.

He was born and trained in the province of Hainaut in northeastern France, served briefly in Antwerp, and spent several years in France with the chapel of Charles I, duke of Bourbon. He is most closely identified with the French royal court, where he served three kings over a span of more than four decades. He was a member of the royal chapel from 1451 on, first chaplain from 1454, and master of the chapel from 1465. He was also treasurer at the royal church of St. Martin, Tours, from 1458, and became a priest around 1464. Both his career and his music are notably less cosmopolitan than those of Du Fay. He returned to his native region on occasion, where he was in touch with Du Fay, Binchois, and Busnoys, and traveled to Spain on a diplomatic mission for King Louis XI around 1470. But he seems never to have gone to Italy, and his music shows little Italian influence.

Ockeghem's known output was relatively small for a composer of his renown. Most of his works cannot be dated with any certainty. In some respects his music continues elements from previous generations, in others it typifies his time, but in certain ways it is unique, perhaps because his long

Figure 9.2: This miniature from a French manuscript of about 1530 shows Ockeghem (right foreground) and eight musicians of the French royal chapel singing from a large manuscript choirbook on a lectern, the custom of the time. Ockeghem is wearing glasses, still unusual in his day.

service in one place encouraged the development of an individual idiom.

MAJOR WORKS: *13 masses, Requiem Mass, at least 5 motets, 21 chansons*

These traits are evident in Busnoys's virelai *Je ne puis vivre*. The refrain is in triple meter, and the b section in duple. As shown in Example 9.1, the refrain opens with a long, arching melody that climbs a tenth, then cascades down an octave. Typical of Busnoys, the melody combines smooth, mostly scalar motion with interesting, constantly changing rhythms. It is imitated in the contratenor and again somewhat later in the tenor, with free counterpoint after the initial imitative entrances. The contratenor is predominantly

Example 9.1: Busnoys, Je ne puis vivre, opening

I cannot live this way forever unless I have, in my grief, [some comfort.]

smooth and singable, making it more similar in style to the other voices than are the contratenors in Du Fay's chansons. Yet the cantus and tenor still form good two-part counterpoint and would sound well alone. The music of Busnoys and Ockeghem marks a transition between the older counterpoint, in which cantus and tenor form the essential structure for the other voices, and the approach that emerged by the late fifteenth century, in which all voices play more similar roles.

Popularity and reworkings Many chansons by Busnoys and Ockeghem were immensely popular, appearing frequently in manuscripts and prints from many different countries. Chansons at this time were freely altered, rearranged, and transcribed for instruments. Some tunes were adapted in new settings by numerous composers or were used as the basis for cantus-firmus masses. The large number of reworkings of chansons by these composers testifies to their popularity.

MASSES

Although Ockeghem and Busnoys were a generation younger than Du Fay, their activity as composers overlapped his, and all three influenced each other. This is especially apparent for the masses; for example, Du Fay's *Missa L'homme armé* borrows elements from the masses by Ockeghem and Busnoys on the same cantus firmus, showing that it was composed later and drew on their achievements.

Range One distinguishing feature is range. Most of Ockeghem's thirteen masses and both of Busnoys's two surviving masses are for four voices, as are most of

Du Fay's. Yet in the masses of Ockeghem and Busnoys, the voice parts cover wider ranges than in Du Fay's. The bassus, which before 1450 was rarely notated below *c*, now extends downward to *G* or *F*, and sometimes lower. Each voice now typically extends a twelfth or thirteenth, rather than a ninth, tenth, or eleventh as in earlier polyphony. Example 9.2 compares the vocal ranges of Du Fay's *Missa Se la face ay pale* (NAWM 36b) with those of Ockeghem's *Missa De plus en plus* (NAWM 37), showing the expansion in the compass of individual voices, mostly into lower ranges. Through these changes Ockeghem creates a fuller, darker texture than we find in Du Fay's works. But like Du Fay, he varies the sonority by writing some passages or sections as trios or duets, often contrasting upper and lower voices in pairs.

CD 2|70

Example 9.2: Comparison of ranges in masses by Du Fay and Ockeghem

a. Du Fay, Missa Se la face ay pale

b. Ockeghem, Missa De plus en plus

Cantus-firmus masses

Seven of Ockeghem's masses and both of Busnoys's use a cantus firmus, often deployed in a highly individual manner. For example, *Missa De plus en plus* takes as its cantus firmus the tenor of Binchois's chanson *De plus en plus* (NAWM 33). Ockeghem follows custom by placing the cantus firmus in the tenor, with occasional echoes in the other voices. Yet unlike Du Fay's *Missa Se la face ay pale*, in which the chanson tenor appears in the original rhythm or in exact augmentation, here the cantus firmus is much more freely employed. Example 9.3 shows the opening of the Agnus Dei, where the borrowed tune appears first in augmentation, then in paraphrase, in altered rhythm and with several notes interpolated; notes taken from the chanson are numbered in the example. Ockeghem freely changes the rhythm and adds notes, giving the tenor a character much closer to the other voices than we find in most sections of Du Fay's mass (compare Example 8.8). The other parts weave free counterpoint around the tenor, with occasional moments of imitation.

Long, overlapping phrases

In Ockeghem's music, most phrases are long, and cadences are frequently elided or overlapped by other voices, creating a more continuous flow than is typical of Du Fay's music. In Example 9.3, most opportunities for cadences are avoided; even at measure 7, where the cantus and tenor form a cadence on G, the contratenor elides it by moving to E. By contrast, Du Fay's *Missa Se la face ay pale* is frequently articulated by cadences (compare Example 8.8b at measures 24, 28, 31, and 34).

Example 9.3: Cantus firmus usage in Ockeghem's Missa De plus en plus

a. Binchois, tenor from De plus en plus

b. Ockeghem, Agnus Dei from Missa De plus en plus

Missa cuiusvis	Most of Ockeghem's other masses are motto masses, unified by a common
toni *and* **Missa**	head-motive; one is a plainsong mass, as is his Requiem (Mass for the Dead).
prolationum	Two of Ockeghem's masses show exceptional compositional virtuosity. *Missa*

cuiusvis toni (Mass in any mode) can be sung in mode 1, 3, 5, or 7 by reading the music according to one of four different clef combinations and using musica ficta to avoid tritones. His *Missa prolationum*, a technical tour de force, is notated in two voices but sung in four, using the four prolations of mensural notation (see chapter 6). Example 9.4a shows the original notation and 9.4b the transcription for the opening of the second Kyrie. Each singer observes the pertinent clef and mensuration sign at the beginning of one of the two written parts. A soprano sings the notes of the superius part in the soprano clef (C-clef on the lowest staff-line) in the mensuration ₵ (imperfect time and minor prolation, like modern duple meter), while an alto reads the same line using the mezzo-soprano clef (C-clef on the second-to-lowest line) in the mensuration ◯ (perfect time, minor prolation, like modern triple meter), to produce the top two lines in Example 9.4b. The tenor and bass read the contra part in a similar fashion to produce the bottom two lines.

Example 9.4: Ockeghem, opening of Kyrie II from Missa prolationum

a. Original notation

b. Transcription

Deriving two or more voices from a single notated voice is known as **canon** (Latin for "rule"). The instruction or rule by which these further parts were derived was also called a canon. The rule might instruct the second voice to sing the same melody starting a certain number of beats or measures after the original at the same or a different pitch, as in the kind of canon most familiar today; the second voice might be the **inversion** of the first (moving by the same intervals but in the opposite direction); or it might be the original voice in **retrograde** (backward). The type of canon used in *Missa prolationum*, in

Canon

SOURCE READING

IN MEMORY OF OCKEGHEM

It was customary in the fifteenth century to compose laments on the death of famous musicians. The best known is Jean Molinet's lament for Ockeghem, set to music by Josquin des Prez, which portrays Ockeghem as the "good father" of the next generation of composers, including Josquin, Pierre de la Rue, Antoine Brumel, and Loyset Compère.

———— • ————

Nymphs of the woods, goddesses of the fountains,
Skilled singers of all nations,
Change your voices so clear and proud
To sharp cries and lamentations.
For Death, terrible despot,
Has trapped your Ockeghem in his trap.
True treasurer of music and masterpiece,
Learned, elegant in appearance, and not stout;
Great pity that the earth should cover him.
Dress yourselves in clothes of mourning,
Josquin, Piersson, Brumel, Compère,
And weep great tears from your eyes:
For you have lost your good father.
Requiescant in pace [rest in peace]. Amen.

Jean Molinet, *Déploration sur le trépas de Jean Ockeghem.*

which voices move at different rates of speed by using different mensuration signs, is known as a **mensuration canon.** Each movement is also a *double canon*, with two canons sung or played simultaneously.

Musicians valued canonic works for the ingenuity and skill they displayed. But the techniques were often artfully hidden, unlikely to be noticed by most who heard the music. Ockeghem and his contemporaries apparently believed that as far as the ordinary listener was concerned, the perfect canon, like the perfect crime, must not even be suspected, much less detected.

MEDIEVAL AND NEWER FEATURES

Some medieval traits still common in the music of Ockeghem and Busnoys, such as the *formes fixes* and reliance on a structural tenor or cantus-tenor scaffolding, disappear in the next generation; others, such as the use of a cantus firmus, continue but become less prominent. The newer elements, including greater equality of voices, more use of imitation, and expansion of range, were extended by their successors and became characteristic of the sixteenth century.

THE NEXT GENERATION

The three most eminent figures in the generation of Franco-Flemish composers born around the middle of the fifteenth century were Jacob Obrecht (1457 or 1458–1505), Henricus Isaac (or Heinrich Isaac, ca. 1450–1517), and Josquin des Prez (ca. 1450–1521). All were born and trained in the Low Countries. All traveled widely, working at courts and churches in different parts of Europe, including Italy. Their careers illustrate the lively interchange between Franco-Flemish and Italian centers, and their music combines northern and southern elements: the serious tone, focus on structure, intricate polyphony, rhythmic variety, and flowing, melismatic melodies of the north with the lighter mood, homophonic textures, more dancelike rhythms, and more clearly articulated phrases of the Italians. Characteristics of this generation can be illustrated with works by Obrecht and Isaac before considering the career and music of Josquin at greater length.

GENERAL TRAITS

Composers active around 1480–1520 shared many elements of style. The structure of vocal works was now largely determined by the text. Composers wrote polyphonic parts that were singable—even if they ended up being played—and were nearly equal in importance. The quest for full harmonies, vocal melodies, and motivic relationships between the voices made it necessary to compose all the parts phrase by phrase, rather than layering voices around the framework of a cantus-tenor duet. The foundational role of the tenor was gradually replaced by the bass, as the lowest voice in the harmony. Full triadic sonorities predominated throughout and began to replace open fifths and octaves at cadences. Borrowed melodies were still used frequently but were more often distributed among the voices, rather than confined to the tenor or superius. The mass and motet continued to be the predominant sacred genres. Breaking away from the *formes fixes*, composers cast chansons in new shapes. Pieces without text and apparently conceived for instruments became more common, although still far outnumbered by vocal works. Hidden structural devices gave way to transparent forms based on a succession of

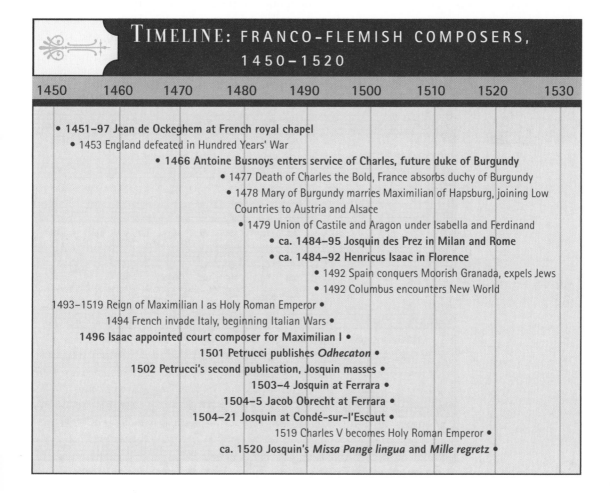

TIMELINE: FRANCO-FLEMISH COMPOSERS, 1450–1520

1450	1460	1470	1480	1490	1500	1510	1520	1530

- 1451–97 Jean de Ockeghem at French royal chapel
- 1453 England defeated in Hundred Years' War
- 1466 Antoine Busnoys enters service of Charles, future duke of Burgundy
- 1477 Death of Charles the Bold, France absorbs duchy of Burgundy
- 1478 Mary of Burgundy marries Maximilian of Hapsburg, joining Low Countries to Austria and Alsace
- 1479 Union of Castile and Aragon under Isabella and Ferdinand
- ca. 1484–95 Josquin des Prez in Milan and Rome
- ca. 1484–92 Henricus Isaac in Florence
- 1492 Spain conquers Moorish Granada, expels Jews
- 1492 Columbus encounters New World
- 1493–1519 Reign of Maximilian I as Holy Roman Emperor •
- 1494 French invade Italy, beginning Italian Wars •
- 1496 Isaac appointed court composer for Maximilian I •
- 1501 Petrucci publishes *Odhecaton* •
- 1502 Petrucci's second publication, Josquin masses •
- 1503–4 Josquin at Ferrara •
- 1504–5 Jacob Obrecht at Ferrara •
- 1504–21 Josquin at Condé-sur-l'Escaut •
- 1519 Charles V becomes Holy Roman Emperor •
- ca. 1520 Josquin's *Missa Pange lingua* and *Mille regretz* •

Figure 9.3: Jacob Obrecht in a portrait from 1496 by an anonymous Flemish painter.

clearly articulated phrases, whether imitative or homophonic in texture. These trends gave composers greater flexibility and allowed them to communicate with a wide audience.

JACOB OBRECHT

Obrecht, shown in Figure 9.3, composed about thirty masses, twenty-eight motets, and numerous chansons, songs in Dutch, and instrumental pieces. Each mass is based on a cantus firmus (sometimes two or more in combination), but he treats the borrowed material in a great variety of ways.

Like other composers of his generation, Obrecht uses imitation more frequently and extensively than did earlier composers. Example 9.5 shows the opening of the Gloria of his *Missa Fortuna desperata*, in which three voices enter at two-measure intervals with the same melody in three different octaves, then continue with free counterpoint. Such a series of imitative entrances is called a ***point of imitation.*** Throughout the mass, imitative passages are interspersed with nonimitative ones.

Despite the imitation, the music is remarkable for its clarity and transparency. The tonal center on F is clear at the outset and confirmed by a series of cadences (measures 7, 9, and 11). The

Example 9.5: Obrecht, opening of Gloria from Missa Fortuna desperata

melodic ideas are relatively short and well-defined. The rhythm is at first regular, then quickens with smaller values and mild syncopation. The counterpoint is smooth and consonant, enlivened by suspensions and passing and neighbor tones, and the last cadence is adorned by a brief run in parallel sixths (measures 11–12). All of these factors give the music immediate appeal and help to make its structure and shape easily apparent to the listener, in contrast to the concealed canons and overlapped cadences we noted in Ockeghem's music. We can draw a parallel between the clearly audible structure in music like this and the tendency in Renaissance architecture to make the structure of buildings apparent to an observer by highlighting their floors, pillars, and arches (see Figure 7.3).

HENRICUS ISAAC

Isaac worked for two of the most important patrons in Europe, serving as singer and composer for Lorenzo de' Medici (the Magnificent) in Florence from about 1484 to 1492 and as court composer for Holy Roman Emperor Maximilian I at Vienna and Innsbruck beginning in 1497, later returning to Florence. His familiarity with Italian and German music as well as French, Flemish, and Netherlandish idioms made his output more pan-European than that of his contemporaries. His sacred works include about thirty-five masses, fifty motets, and the *Choralis Constantinus*, a monumental three-volume cycle of settings of the texts and melodies of the Proper for most of the church year, comparable in its scope to the *Magnus liber organi* of Léonin. Alongside his sacred music, Isaac wrote a large number of songs with French, Italian, and German texts and many short, chansonlike pieces that appear without words in the sources and are presumably for instrumental ensemble.

In Florence, Isaac encountered songs in predominantly homophonic style, such as those sung during the festive carnival processions. He later adapted this simple Italian style for some of his German **Lieder** (songs), four-part settings of popular songs or newly composed melodies in similar style. In his setting of *Innsbruck, ich muss dich lassen* (NAWM 38) shown in Example 9.6, the melody is in the superius. As in the Italian songs, the other parts move in very similar rhythm, with rests separating each phrase, and cadences resolve to full triads rather than open sonorities. The clear structure and sweet harmony of Isaac's Lied make it immediately appealing.

Homophonic textures

CD 3|1

Homophonic texture became an important part of sixteenth-century polyphonic music, alongside and often alternating with the imitative texture seen in Obrecht's mass. It is no paradox that the music of this and later generations is both more imitative and more often homophonic than that of Ockeghem's generation; both imitation and homophony were facilitated by the greater freedom available to composers, as the traditional layering of voices around a cantus-tenor duet was replaced by composition of all voices in relation to one another.

TEXT SETTING

The pieces by Obrecht and Isaac discussed here exemplify the great concern composers of their generation had for fitting music to the words. They

Example 9.6: Isaac, Innsbruck, ich muss dich lassen, *opening*

Innsbruck, I must leave you, I am going on my way, into a foreign land.

carefully matched accents in the music to those in the text and wanted the words to be heard and understood. This meant that the task of aligning the words with the music could no longer be left to singers during a performance, as in earlier music, and thus that parts had to have the text underlaid (positioned under the music) clearly and completely. The florid lines of Ockeghem and his contemporaries gave way to more direct syllabic settings, in which a phrase of text could be grasped as an uninterrupted thought.

JOSQUIN DES PREZ

Few musicians have enjoyed higher renown or exercised greater influence than Josquin des Prez (ca. 1450–1521; see biography and Figure 9.4). He held a series of prestigious positions at courts and churches in France and Italy. His compositions appear in a large number of manuscripts and printed anthologies. Ottaviano Petrucci, the first printer of polyphonic music, published three books of Josquin masses and reprinted each to meet the demand;

JOSQUIN DES PREZ [JOSQUIN LEBLOITTE DIT DESPREZ] (CA. 1450–1521)

Josquin (known by his given name because "des Prez" was a nickname) is regarded as the greatest composer of his time. His motets, masses, and songs were widely sung, praised, and emulated in his lifetime and for decades after his death.

Josquin's biography has been clarified by recent research, but there are still gaps. Historians recently discovered his family name, Lebloitte, from a will leaving him a house and land in Condé-sur-l'Escaut, now in Belgium. His early life is undocumented, but he was probably born and trained in or near Saint Quentin in northern France, about halfway between Paris and Brussels. He served in the chapel of René, duke of Anjou, at Aix-en-Provence in the late 1470s. After René's death in 1480, his singers transferred to the service of King Louis XI at Sainte Chapelle in Paris, and Josquin may have been among them.

Josquin spent much of his career in Italy, serving the Sforza family, rulers of Milan (ca. 1484–89), and in the Sistine Chapel in Rome (1489–95 or later). Josquin may have been in France at the court of King Louis XII from 1501 to 1503. He was appointed maestro di cappella to Duke Ercole I d'Este in Ferrara in 1503 at the highest salary in the history of that chapel. A recruiter for the duke had recommended Isaac instead, noting that although Josquin was a better composer, he demanded a higher salary and composed only when he

IOSQVINVS PRATENSIS.

Figure 9.4: Josquin des Prez, in a woodcut from Petrus Opmeer, Opus chronographicum *(Antwerp, 1611). Opmeer based his portrait on an oil painting that once stood in Ste. Gudule church in Brussels but was destroyed in the 1570s.*

wanted to and not when asked; the duke hired Josquin anyway, no doubt aware of the prestige to be gained by employing the best musician available. Josquin left after a year, apparently to escape the plague. From 1504 until his death in 1521, he resided at Condé-sur-l'Escaut, where he was provost at the church of Notre Dame.

MAJOR WORKS: *18 masses, over 50 motets, about 65 chansons (about 10 for instruments), and numerous doubtfully attributed works*

no other composer received more than a single volume from Petrucci. Contemporaries hailed Josquin as "the best of the composers of our time" and "the father of musicians." In 1538, Martin Luther proclaimed that "Josquin is the master of the notes. They must do as he wills; as for the other composers, they have to do as the notes will." A generation after his death, humanist scholars compared him to Virgil and Michelangelo as an artist without peer in his art (see Source Reading). Such praise reflects not only on Josquin but on his time, for it shows the greatly increased interest in the individual artist during the Renaissance.

Composers from his time through the late sixteenth century emulated and reworked Josquin's music. Some works were recopied, published, and performed for almost a century after his death, a rare honor at a time when most music more than a few decades old was deemed unworthy of performance. His music was so esteemed and popular that publishers and copyists often attributed works of other composers to him, prompting one wag to comment that "now that Josquin is dead, he is putting out more works than when he was still alive." Historians are still sorting out which pieces are truly his.

SOURCE READINGS

PRAISE FOR JOSQUIN

Josquin had a remarkably lofty reputation throughout the sixteenth century. A generation after his death, music theorist Heinrich Glareanus compared him to the Latin epic poet Virgil, and humanist scholar Cosimo Bartoli compared him to Michelangelo, saying both were without peer.

——— • ———

No one has more effectively expressed the passions of the soul in music than this symphonist, no one has more felicitously begun, no one has been able to compete in grace and facility on an equal footing with him, just as there is no Latin poet superior in the epic to Maro [Virgil]. For just as Maro, with his natural facility, was accustomed to adapt his poem to his subject so as to set weighty matters before the eyes of his readers with close-packed spondees, fleeting ones with unmixed dactyls, to use words suited to his every subject, in short, to undertake nothing inappropriately, as Flaccus says of Homer, so our Josquin, where his matter requires it, now advances with impetuous and precipitate notes, now intones his subject in long-drawn tones, and, to sum up, has brought forth nothing that was not delightful to the ear and approved as ingenious by the learned, nothing, in short, that was not acceptable and

pleasing, even when it seemed less erudite, to those who listened to it with judgment. . . . His talent is beyond description, more easily admired than properly explained.

From Heinrich Glareanus, *Dodecachordon* (Basle, 1547), Book 3, Chapter 24. Trans. Oliver Strunk, in SR 70 (3:35), p. 430.

——— • ———

I know well that Ockeghem was, so to speak, the first who in these times rediscovered music, which had almost entirely died out—not unlike Donatello, who in his times rediscovered sculpture—and that Josquin, Ockeghem's pupil, may be said to have been, in music, a prodigy of nature, as our Michelangelo Buonarotti has been in architecture, painting, and sculpture; for, just as there has not yet been anyone who in his compositions approaches Josquin, so Michelangelo, among all those who have been active in these arts, is still alone and without peer. Both of them have opened the eyes of all those who delight in these arts or will delight in them in the future.

Cosimo Bartoli, *Ragionamenti accademici* (Venice, 1567). Trans. adapted from Gustave Reese, *Music in the Renaissance*, rev. ed. (New York: Norton, 1959), 259–60.

MOTETS

Josquin's more than fifty motets exemplify his style. While masses were normally based on existing music and always set the same text, most motets were freely composed and their texts were quite varied, drawn from the Mass Proper or other sources. Josquin's motets show the traits of the late-fifteenth-century style we have already seen, including clarity in phrasing, form, and tonal organization; fluid and tuneful melodies; transparent textures; use of imitation and homophony; and careful declamation of the text.

Beyond these widely shared traits, Josquin is especially renowned for reflecting the meaning of the words, in two ways: through **text depiction,** using musical gestures to reinforce the images in the text, and through **text expression,** conveying through music the emotions suggested by the text. Josquin has long been regarded as perhaps the first composer to use text depiction and expression in a consistent and recognizable way, although others of his generation did so as well. The idea that music is expressive of emotions is today a commonplace and was well known to the ancient Greek writers. But if Western composers before Josquin's time meant to convey feelings in their music, they did so in a code we cannot read. It would seem that humanist ideals and the revival of ancient ideas about music led to a link between music and feelings that we now take for granted but was apparently new in the late fifteenth century.

Text depiction and expression

We can see Josquin's approach in *Ave Maria . . . virgo serena* (NAWM 39) from about 1485, one of his earliest and most popular motets. The music is perfectly crafted to fit the words. Josquin delineates the form of the text by giving each segment a unique musical treatment and a concluding cadence on the tonal center C. The texture is constantly changing, as illustrated in Example 9.7. The motet opens with several overlapping points of imitation, then shifts to two, three, and all four voices in relatively homophonic phrases; later passages are equally varied. The words are declaimed naturally, giving accented syllables longer and higher notes in most cases (as at "*Do*-minus *te*-cum, *Vir*-go se-*re*-na"). Some images in the text are depicted in the music; for instance, at the words "solemni plena gaudio" (full of solemn jubilation), fullness and solemnity are suggested by the presence of all four voices singing in rhythmic unison, a texture not used previously in the motet. There are also moments when the music creates a feeling appropriate to the text. One striking example is at "Ave, cuius conceptio" (Hail to her whose conception), where the use of parallel sixths and $\frac{6}{3}$ sonorities recalls fauxbourdon, a style that by the 1480s sounded old-fashioned and thus carried associations of dignity and the sacred, evoking a reverent mood.

Ave Maria . . . virgo serena

CD 3|2   CD 1|53

This motet is excellent in many ways at once, with clear projection of the tonal center, clearly delineated phrases and sections, elegant and beautiful counterpoint, variety in texture, and sensitive declamation, depiction, and expression of the text. It is no wonder that such music established Josquin as a composer worthy of performance and emulation in his own time and later generations.

Example 9.7: Excerpt from Josquin, Ave maria . . . virgo serena

Lord be with you, serene virgin.
Hail to her whose conception, full of solemn jubilation,

MASSES

Josquin's masses are equally varied and abound in technical ingenuity. Most use a secular tune as a cantus firmus. In *Missa L'homme armé super voces musicales*, Josquin transposed the familiar tune *L'homme armé* to successive degrees of the hexachord—C for the Kyrie, D for the Gloria, and so on—and included a mensuration canon in the Agnus Dei. He wrote *Missa Hercules dux*

Ferrariae to honor Ercole (Hercules) I, duke of Ferrara, probably while serving the ducal court in 1503–4. He used as a cantus firmus a *soggetto cavato dalle vocali*, a "subject drawn from the vowels" of a phrase by letting each vowel indicate a corresponding syllable of the hexachord, thus:

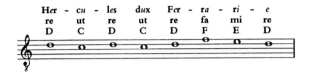

Josquin's *Missa Malheur me bat* illustrates a new approach to basing a mass on a polyphonic work. Instead of using one voice as a cantus firmus, the composer borrows extensively from all voices of the model, reworking the latter's characteristic motives, points of imitation, and general structure in each movement of the mass. This approach is especially apt when basing a mass on a motet or chanson in the new, predominantly imitative or homophonic styles of the late fifteenth and sixteenth centuries, because in such works the tenor is not the main structural voice, and no voice would function well as a cantus firmus. Typically, the resemblance to the model is strongest at the beginning and end of each movement, and the composer's craft is demonstrated by the new combinations and variations he can achieve with the borrowed material. A mass composed in this manner is termed an **imitation mass** (or *parody mass*), because it imitates another polyphonic work. Later in the sixteenth century, Josquin's mass would have been called "Mass in imitation of Malheur me bat." Around 1520, the imitation mass began to displace the cantus-firmus mass as the most common type.

Imitation mass

Missa Pange lingua (excerpted in NAWM 40), one of the last Josquin composed, represents another new type of mass, the **paraphrase mass.** It is based on the plainchant hymn *Pange lingua gloriosi.* But instead of using the hymn melody as a cantus firmus, Josquin paraphrased it in all four voices, in whole or in part, in each movement. Phrases from the hymn melody are adapted as motives that are treated in points of imitation, or occasionally in homophonic declamation.

Paraphrase mass

Thus the sound of a paraphrase mass resembles that of an imitation mass, featuring a series of independent phrases in imitative or homophonic textures without a structural cantus firmus. The two types of mass differ not in style, but in their source material, since the paraphrase mass elaborates a monophonic chant instead of a polyphonic model. Although composers continued to write cantus-firmus masses in the sixteenth century, they turned increasingly to imitation and paraphrase masses because they preferred imitative textures over the structural scaffolding of cantus-firmus technique, which came to be seen as archaic. It is likely that the source material was chosen for reasons parallel to those for the cantus-firmus mass: to suit a particular religious observance, institution, or saint; to honor a patron; to convey meanings by alluding to the original words of the chanson or motet in the context of the mass; or perhaps, in the case of an imitation mass, to pay homage to another composer through emulation.

CHANSONS

The chansons of Josquin and others of his generation represent a new style. These composers virtually abandoned the *formes fixes*, choosing instead strophic texts and simple four- or five-line poems. Rather than three voices, most chansons now use four or even five, and all voices are meant to be sung. Instead of a layered counterpoint with the cantus-tenor pair providing the skeleton and the other voices filling in, as in chansons from Machaut through most of Ockeghem's, all the parts are now equal, and the texture is suffused with imitation and homophony in varying degrees.

Mille regretz

CD 3|15

Mille regretz (NAWM 41), a chanson attributed to Josquin though perhaps not by him, illustrates the style of about 1520. In contrast to the chansons of Du Fay and Ockeghem, every voice is essential. The texture alternates between homophony and imitation and between all four voices and ever-changing combinations of two or three voices. Each phrase of text receives its own particular treatment, as illustrated in Example 9.8: four-voice homophony for "Jay si grand dueil"; a pair of voices answered by another pair for the next phrase, their descent suggesting the poet's painful sadness; and four-voice imitation for "Quon me verra."

Example 9.8: Josquin, Mille regretz

I feel so much sadness and such painful distress,
that it seems to me my days will soon dwindle away.

OLD AND NEW

The music of Ockeghem and Busnoys interweaves old and new elements. It represents the last climax of medieval thinking in their use of the *formes fixes*, in their long, winding phrases, and in such feats as the mensuration canons in *Missa prolationum*. Yet their music's expanded range, greater equality of voices, increased use of imitation, and freer treatment of borrowed material exemplify new traits that become typical of the next century.

Josquin and his generation worked with new freedom in a polyphonic idiom based on equal, vocally conceived lines, moving now in points of imitation, now in homophony, responding to the shape, accentuation, and meaning of the text. Like Ockeghem and Busnoys, Josquin was acclaimed in life and after his death. But Josquin's music continued in circulation far longer, because the stylistic changes he helped to introduce made earlier music sound old-fashioned. Josquin's works were performed and emulated through the end of the sixteenth century, no doubt aided by the new technology of music printing that emerged when he was at the peak of his career. He was less well known in the next two centuries, though never entirely forgotten, and figured prominently in histories of music written in the late eighteenth and nineteenth centuries. His complete works were transcribed and published beginning in 1921, stimulating a growing number of performances and a constant stream of scholarship. His music is now frequently performed and recorded, and he is viewed as the central composer of his time and perhaps of the entire Renaissance. The music of his contemporaries, from Ockeghem and Busnoys through Obrecht and Isaac, has also appeared in modern editions, performances, and recordings.

In some respects the musical language of Josquin's time is still with us, present in the attentive text-setting, imitative and homophonic textures, and rules of counterpoint and voice-leading practiced by composers over the next several centuries. The emotional expressivity and vivid imagery of his music set the standard for succeeding generations, so much so that the history of music from his time to the early twentieth century is more than anything else a history of musical expressivity. It is also, at least in part, the history of exemplary composers and their music. In this too we are heirs of the Renaissance, whose interest in the individual artist is shown in the way Josquin's music was singled out for praise.

Chapter

10

Sacred Music in the Era of the Reformation

When the sixteenth century began, Christians from Poland to Spain and from Italy to Scotland shared allegiance to a single church centered in Rome and supported by political leaders. By midcentury, this unity of belief and practice, inherited from the early Middle Ages, was shattered. So was the peace. European society was disrupted by the Protestant Reformation, as central and western Europe entered a century of religious wars.

Sacred music was profoundly affected. Leaders of the Reformation sought to involve worshipers more directly, through congregational singing and services presented in the vernacular rather than in Latin. These changes led to new types of religious music in each branch of Protestantism, including the **chorale** and chorale settings in the Lutheran Church, the **metrical psalm** in Calvinist churches, and the **anthem** and **Service** in the Anglican Church. The Catholic Church also undertook reforms, but continued to use Gregorian chant and polyphonic masses and motets in styles that extended the tradition of Josquin's generation. Jewish service music remained distinctive, yet absorbed some outside influences. In each tradition, the genres and styles of sacred music were determined by people's religious beliefs and aims as much as by their musical tastes.

THE REFORMATION

The Reformation began as a theological dispute and mushroomed into a rebellion against the authority of the Catholic Church. It started in Germany with Martin Luther, then spread to most of northern Europe, as shown in Figure 10.1. There were three main branches: the Lutheran movement in northern Germany and Scandinavia, the Calvinist movement led by Jean Calvin that spread from Switzerland and the Low Countries to France and Britain, and the Church of England, organized by King Henry VIII for political reasons but ultimately influenced by Reformation ideals. The theology and circumstances of each branch determined its values and choices concerning music, so knowing the religious and political issues behind each movement will help us understand why their music takes the forms it does.

MARTIN LUTHER

The instigator of the Reformation was Martin Luther (1483–1546), shown in Figure 10.2, a professor of biblical theology at the University of Wittenberg. Study of the Bible, notably St. Paul's view that "the just shall live by faith"

Figure 10.1: Religious divisions in Europe around 1560.

Figure 10.2: Martin Luther, in a portrait by Lucas Cranach.

(Romans 1:17), led Luther to conclude that God's justice consists not in rewarding people for good deeds or punishing them for sins, but in offering salvation through faith alone. His views contradicted Catholic doctrine, which held that religious rituals, penance, and good works were necessary for the absolution of sin. Luther also insisted that religious authority was derived from Scripture alone, so that if a belief or practice had no basis in the Bible it could not be true. This notion challenged the authority of the Church, which had developed a rich tapestry of teachings and practices that rested on tradition rather than Scripture.

The ninety-five theses One such practice was the sale of indulgences, credits for good deeds done by others, which one could purchase to reduce the punishment for sin. This practice raised money for the Church, but it had no Scriptural basis and violated Luther's principle that salvation was granted through faith alone, not works. So on October 31, 1517, he posted on a church door in Wittenberg a list of ninety-five theses (points or arguments) opposing indulgences. They were soon printed and disseminated widely, making Luther famous. When pressed to recant, he instead affirmed the primacy of Scripture over the Catholic hierarchy. In response, the pope charged him with heresy in 1519 and excommunicated him in 1520. By then, Luther had numerous followers in German universities and among the populace. He organized a new Evangelical Church, known in English as the Lutheran Church. Many German princes supported him and made Lutheranism the state religion, freeing them from control by Rome.

MUSIC IN THE LUTHERAN CHURCH

In creating his church, Luther sought to give the people a larger role. He made the services easier to understand by increasing the use of the vernacular. Yet he retained some Latin, which he considered valuable for educating the young. He kept much of the Catholic liturgy, some in translation and some in Latin. Similarly, Lutheran churches continued to employ a good deal of Catholic music, both chant and polyphony, whether with the original Latin texts, German translations, or new German words.

Music assumed a central position in the Lutheran Church because of Luther's own appreciation for it. He was a singer, performer on flute and lute, and composer, and he greatly admired Franco-Flemish polyphony, especially the music of Josquin. Like Plato and Aristotle, he believed strongly in the educational and ethical power of music. Through singing together, worshipers could unite in proclaiming their faith and praising God. For these reasons, he wanted the entire congregation to sing in the services, not just the celebrants and choir, as Catholic custom dictated (see Source Reading).

Luther and music

Luther never intended any formula to prevail uniformly in Lutheran churches, and various compromises between Roman usage and new practices could be found throughout sixteenth-century Germany. Large churches with trained choirs generally kept much of the Latin liturgy and its polyphonic music. Smaller churches adopted the *Deudsche Messe* (German Mass) published by Luther in 1526, which followed the main outlines of the Roman Mass but differed from it in many details and replaced most elements of the Proper and Ordinary with German hymns.

THE LUTHERAN CHORALE

The most important form of music in the Lutheran Church was the congregational hymn, known since the late sixteenth century as the **chorale.** During each service, the congregation sang several chorales, fulfilling Luther's aim of increasing worshipers' participation through music.

Chorales are known today primarily in four-part harmonized settings, but they originally consisted of only a metric, rhymed, strophic poem and a melody in simple rhythm sung in unison, without harmonization or

---

 ## SOURCE READING

MARTIN LUTHER ON CONGREGATIONAL SINGING

In early Christian services, all those present had sung hymns and psalms (see chapter 2), but by the late Middle Ages music in Catholic services was assigned to the celebrants and choir alone. When he established his new church, Luther sought to restore the congregation's role.

——— • ———

I also wish that we had as many songs as possible in the vernacular which the people could sing during Mass, immediately after the Gradual and also after the Sanctus and Agnus Dei.

For who doubts that originally all the people sang these which now only the choir sings or responds to while the bishop is consecrating the Host? The bishops may have these congregational hymns sung either after the Latin chants, or use the Latin on one Sunday and the vernacular on the next, until the time comes that the whole Mass is sung in the vernacular.

Martin Luther, "Order of Mass and Communion for the Church at Wittenberg" (1523), trans. Paul Zeller Strodach, in *Luther's Works,* vol. 53 (Philadelphia: The Fortress Press, 1965), 36.

accompaniment. Of course, chorales, like plainchants, could be enriched through harmony and counterpoint and reworked into large musical forms. Just as most medieval and Renaissance Catholic church music was based on chant, so Lutheran church music of the sixteenth through eighteenth centuries largely grew out of the chorale.

Luther and his colleagues worked quickly to provide chorales suitable for every Sunday of the church year. Luther wrote many of the poems and melodies himself. Four collections of chorales were published in 1524, and over two hundred followed in the next fifty years. The printing press played as large a role in disseminating chorales as it had in the spread of Luther's message.

Sources for chorales

There were four main sources for chorales: (1) adaptations of Gregorian chant; (2) existing German devotional songs; (3) secular songs given new words, a practice called **contrafactum**; and (4) new compositions. Recycling familiar melodies saved time and reduced the amount of new music congregations had to learn. Moreover, using Gregorian melodies and German religious songs asserted a sense of continuity with past Christian traditions.

Adaptations of chant

Example 10.1 shows the chant hymn *Veni Redemptor gentium* (NAWM 42a) and Luther's adaptation of it as a chorale, *Nun komm, der Heiden Heiland*

CD 3|16

Example 10.1: Luther's adaptation of a chorale from a chant hymn

a. *Hymn,* Veni Redemptor gentium

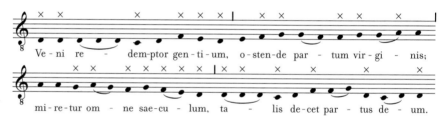

Come, Savior of nations,
display the offspring of the Virgin.
Let all ages marvel
that God granted such a birth.

b. *Luther's chorale* Nun komm, der Heiden Heiland

Now come, gentiles' Savior,
child, known to be born of the Virgin,
Let all the world marvel
that God such a birth for him ordained.

(NAWM 42b). Luther's poem is a rhymed, metrical translation of the Latin text. The notes that are shared are marked with an x, showing that Luther took over most of the melody yet made several significant alterations. Changing the first and last note in the middle phrases gives the melody a new contour with a single high point for each phrase. Although the first and last phrases in the chant hymn differ from each other, in the chorale they are the same, heightening the sense of closure. Most important, the chorale has a distinct rhythmic profile of long and short notes. The changes recast the melody in an appealing, up-to-date style that was easier for lay worshipers to sing.

CD 3|17

Religious songs in German had circulated since the ninth century, and Luther and his colleagues used many as chorales. One adapted by Luther is the Easter hymn *Christ ist erstanden* (Christ is risen), a twelfth-century song based on the Latin sequence *Victimae paschali laudes* (NAWM 5).

German devotional songs

Luther and his colleagues used many well-known secular tunes for chorales, substituting religious words. The texts were most often wholly new, but sometimes included clever reworkings of the existing poem. The most famous contrafactum (though not by Luther) is *O Welt, ich muss dich lassen* (O world, I must leave you), based on the Lied *Innsbruck, ich muss dich lassen* (NAWM 38).

Contrafacta

Finally, Luther and other composers wrote many new tunes for chorales. The best known is Luther's *Ein' feste Burg* (NAWM 42c), shown in Example 10.2, which became the anthem of the Reformation. Luther was very concerned with proper setting of text, and this chorale shows his attention to the

New melodies

CD 3|18

Example 10.2: Luther, Ein' feste Burg

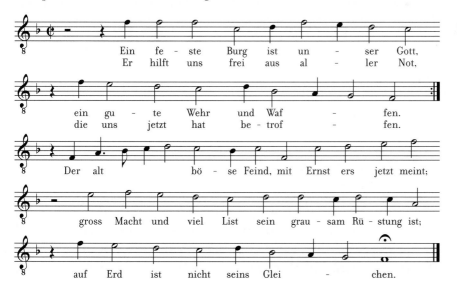

A sturdy fortress is our God, a good defense and weapon.
He helps us free from all afflictions that have now befallen us.
The old, evil enemy now means to deal with us seriously;
great power and much cunning are his cruel armaments;
on Earth is not his equal.

expression and declamation of the words. The dynamic repeated opening notes and descending scale vividly convey the images of power in the poem, which Luther adapted from Psalm 46. The original rhythm features alternating long and short notes to suit the stresses of the text. Since the eighteenth century, an altered, more even rhythm has become more common.

POLYPHONIC CHORALE SETTINGS

Lutheran composers soon began to write polyphonic settings for chorales. These served two purposes: group singing in homes and schools, and performance in church by choirs. Early published collections of chorale settings were aimed at providing music for young people to sing that was "wholesome" and could "rid them of their love ditties and wanton songs," as Luther wrote in the foreword to one such collection. These same chorale settings could also be sung in church by the choir, sometimes doubled by instruments, alternating stanzas with the congregation singing in unison without accompaniment. Such ways of performing chorales added variety and interest to the music of the services.

Composers used a variety of approaches borrowed from existing genres. Many settings adopted the traditional Lied technique, placing the unaltered

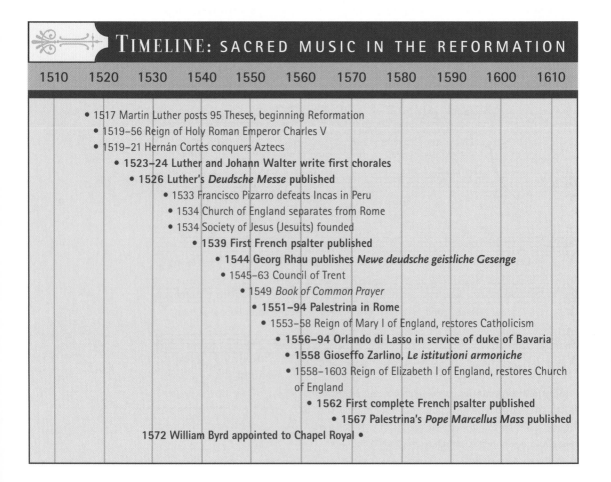

TIMELINE: SACRED MUSIC IN THE REFORMATION

1510	1520	1530	1540	1550	1560	1570	1580	1590	1600	1610

- 1517 Martin Luther posts 95 Theses, beginning Reformation
- 1519–56 Reign of Holy Roman Emperor Charles V
- 1519–21 Hernán Cortés conquers Aztecs
- 1523–24 Luther and Johann Walter write first chorales
- 1526 Luther's *Deudsche Messe* published
- 1533 Francisco Pizarro defeats Incas in Peru
- 1534 Church of England separates from Rome
- 1534 Society of Jesus (Jesuits) founded
- 1539 First French psalter published
- 1544 Georg Rhau publishes *Newe deudsche geistliche Gesenge*
- 1545–63 Council of Trent
- 1549 *Book of Common Prayer*
- 1551–94 Palestrina in Rome
- 1553–58 Reign of Mary I of England, restores Catholicism
- 1556–94 Orlando di Lasso in service of duke of Bavaria
- 1558 Gioseffo Zarlino, *Le istitutioni armoniche*
- 1558–1603 Reign of Elizabeth I of England, restores Church of England
- 1562 First complete French psalter published
- 1567 Palestrina's *Pope Marcellus Mass* published

1572 William Byrd appointed to Chapel Royal •

chorale tune in the tenor and surrounding it with three or more free-flowing parts, as in the setting by Luther's collaborator Johann Walter (1496–1570) in Example 10.3a (NAWM 42d). More elaborate settings, known as **chorale motets,** borrowed techniques from the Franco-Flemish motet. Some treated the chorale as a cantus firmus in relatively long notes surrounded by free or imitative polyphony. Others developed each phrase of the chorale imitatively in all voices. An example of the latter is Example 10.3b, in which each voice paraphrases the chorale, some more closely than others.

CD 3|19

Example 10.3: Two settings of Ein' feste Burg

a. Johann Walter, from Geistliches Gesangbüchlein

b. Lupus Hellinck, from George Rhaw's collection Newe deudsche geistliche Gesenge *(1544)*

By the last third of the century, influenced by Calvinist psalm-tune harmonizations in chordal homophony (see below), Lutheran composers most often arranged chorales with the tune in the highest voice, accompanied by block chords with little contrapuntal figuration. This is called **cantional style,** after its use in chorale collections called *Cantionale* (Latin for "songbook"). Although such settings were often sung in parts, after 1600 it became customary to have all the parts played on the organ while the congregation sang all the verses of the tune. This style of harmonization and performance has continued to the present and is embodied in hymnbooks for almost all branches of Protestantism.

THE LUTHERAN TRADITION

By 1600, Lutherans had a rich fund of over seven hundred chorale melodies and a great variety of pieces based upon them, from simple settings to complex chorale motets. Chorales were also elaborated in organ works of various types (discussed in chapter 12). The Lutheran Church had quickly gained musical independence and established a strong heritage on which later composers would build.

MUSIC IN CALVINIST CHURCHES

Outside Germany and Scandinavia, Protestantism took different forms. The largest branch was led by Jean Calvin (1509–1564). Like Luther, he rejected papal authority and embraced justification through faith alone. But Calvin believed that some people are predestined for salvation, others for

SOURCE READING

JEAN CALVIN ON SINGING PSALMS

In his preface to the psalter published at Geneva in 1542, Calvin detailed his views for how music should be used in services, and why only psalms sung by the entire congregation were appropriate.

———— • ————

We know by experience that song has great force and vigor to move and inflame people's hearts to invoke and praise God with a more vehement and ardent zeal. Care must always be taken that the song be not light and frivolous but have weight and majesty, as Saint Augustine says, and there is likewise a great difference between the music one makes to entertain people at table and in their homes, and the psalms that are sung in the Church in the presence of God and the angels.

. . . It is true that, as Saint Paul says, every evil word corrupts good manners, but when it has the melody with it, it pierces the heart much more strongly and enters within; as wine is poured into the cask with a funnel, so venom and corruption are distilled to the very depths of the heart by melody. Now what is there to do? The solution is to have songs not merely honest but also holy, which will be like spurs to incite us to pray and praise God, and to meditate on God's works in order to love, fear, honor, and glorify God. Now what Saint Augustine says is true—that we cannot sing songs worthy of God save what we have received from God. Wherefore, although we look far and wide and search in every land, we will not find better songs nor songs better suited to that end than the Psalms of David, which the Holy Spirit made and uttered through him. And for this reason, when we sing them we may be certain that God puts the words in our mouths as if God sang in us to exalt God's glory.

Jean Calvin, "Epistle to the Reader," in the Geneva Psalter (1542). Adapted from the translation by Oliver Strunk, in SR 57 (3:22), pp. 365–67.

Figure 10.3: The Calvinist Temple at Lyon, in a 1564 painting that shows the austerity of Calvinist churches. The preacher wears no elaborate vestments, there is no choir, the focus is on the pulpit rather than the altar, and the only decorations are coats of arms in the windows and above the pulpit.

damnation. He also held that all aspects of life should fall under God's law as given in the Bible, requiring of his followers lives of constant piety, uprightness, and work. From his center at Geneva, missionaries spread Calvinism across Switzerland and to other lands, establishing the Dutch Reformed Church in the Netherlands, the Presbyterian Church in Scotland, the Puritans in England, and the Huguenots in France.

Calvin and music

Seeking to focus worship on God alone, Calvin stripped churches and services of everything that might distract worshipers with worldly pleasures, including decorations, paintings, stained-glass windows, vestments, colorful ceremony, incense, musical instruments, and elaborate polyphony. Figure 10.3 shows how spare Calvinist churches were. Like Luther, however, Calvin valued congregational singing for its ability to unite worshipers in expressing their faith and praising God.

METRICAL PSALMS

Calvin insisted that only biblical texts, especially psalms, should be sung in church (see Source Reading). But psalms had verses of varying lengths, making them difficult for congregations to sing. The solution was to recast them as ***metrical psalms***—metric, rhymed, strophic translations of psalms in the vernacular that were set to newly composed melodies or tunes adapted from chant.

The French psalter

Metrical psalms were published in collections called ***psalters.*** Calvin issued several in French, beginning in 1539. A complete French psalter was published in 1562, in tens of thousands of copies printed in several cities at once, a sign of the growing importance of printing as a means for disseminating music. This psalter contained 150 psalms that were sung in church in unaccompanied unison. The melodies move mostly by step, giving them an austere simplicity. The best known is the tune for Psalm 134 (NAWM 43), shown in Example 10.4. This tune was used in English psalters for Psalm 100, becoming known as "Old Hundredth (see NAWM 43b)."

CD 3|20–21

Example 10.4: Loys Bourgeois, Psalm 134, Or sus, serviteurs du Seigneur

Arise, you servants of the Lord,
you who by night in his honor
serve him in his house,
praise him, and lift up his name.

Dutch, English, and Scottish psalters

From Switzerland and France, metrical psalms spread widely. Translations of the French psalter appeared in Germany, Holland, England, and Scotland, and the Reformed churches in those countries took over many of the French tunes. In Germany, many psalm melodies were adapted as chorales, and Lutherans and Catholics published metrical psalters to compete with the Calvinists. The French model influenced the most important English psalter of the sixteenth century, that of Thomas Sternhold and John Hopkins (1562). In 1620, the pilgrims came to New England with a combination of English and French-Dutch traditions, embodied in the psalter issued by Henry Ainsworth in Amsterdam in 1612 for English Separatists in Holland. The first book published in North America was a psalter, the *Bay Psalm Book* of 1640. Some tunes from sixteenth-century psalters are still used today, appearing in hymnals all over the world.

POLYPHONIC PSALM SETTINGS

Although singing in Calvinist churches was at first unaccompanied and monophonic, psalm tunes were set polyphonically for devotional use at home or in gatherings of amateur singers. Settings were typically in four or five parts, with the tune in either the tenor or the superius, and ranged from simple chordal style to motetlike settings in cantus-firmus style or imitation. French composers of psalm settings included Loys Bourgeois (ca. 1510–ca. 1561), Claude Goudimel (ca. 1520–1572), and Claude Le Jeune (ca. 1528–1600), and Flemish or Dutch composers included Jacobus Clemens (ca. 1510–ca. 1555) and Jan Pieterszoon Sweelinck (1562–1621). There were also settings of psalm tunes for voice and lute, for organ, and for other combinations. All told, the repertory of Calvinist polyphonic psalm settings numbers in the thousands, about as large as that of Lutheran chorale settings or of Italian madrigals (see chapter 11), as composers and printers responded to a demand for religious music that amateurs could perform for their own enjoyment and edification. If monophonic metrical psalms were church music, these polyphonic settings resembled popular music with a religious message, like modern Christian popular music.

CHURCH MUSIC IN ENGLAND

The third major branch of Protestantism in the sixteenth century was the Church of England, whose origins lay more in politics than in doctrine. King Henry VIII (r. 1509–47), shown in Figure 10.4, was married to Catherine of Aragon, daughter of Ferdinand and Isabella of Spain. Henry needed a male heir, but their only surviving child was a daughter, Mary. With Catherine past childbearing age, in 1527 Henry sought an annulment so he could marry Anne Boleyn. The pope could not grant this without offending Catherine's nephew, Emperor Charles V, so in 1534 Henry persuaded Parliament to separate from Rome and name Henry head of the Church of England.

The Church of England remained Catholic in doctrine under Henry. But during the brief reign of Edward VI (r. 1547–53), Henry's son by his third wife, Jane Seymour, the Church adopted Protestant doctrines. English replaced Latin in the service, and in 1549 the *Book of Common Prayer* was adopted as the only prayerbook permitted for public use. Edward's early death brought to the throne his half-sister Mary (r. 1553–58). Loyal to her

Figure 10.4: Henry VIII, in a portrait by Hans Holbein the Younger.

mother, Catherine, and to the pope, she restored Catholicism, but met considerable resistance. She was succeeded by Elizabeth I (r. 1558–1603), Henry's daughter by Anne Boleyn, who again broke from the papacy and brought back the liturgical reforms instituted under Edward, yet compromised enough on doctrine to make the Church of England hospitable to most Catholics as well as Protestants. The present-day Anglican Church (including the Episcopal Church in the United States) continues to blend Catholic and Protestant elements in theology, ritual, and music.

Church music

All these events had repercussions for church music. New forms were created for services in English, but Latin motets and masses were composed during the reigns of Henry, Mary, and even Elizabeth. Although most services during her reign were in English, Elizabeth provided for the use of Latin in some churches and of Latin hymns, responds, and motets in her own royal chapel. Clearly the tradition of Latin sacred polyphony was valued in itself, beyond theological issues, for its links to the past and its musical splendors.

Taverner and Tallis

The leading English composer of sacred music in the early sixteenth century was John Taverner (ca. 1490–1545). His masses and motets exemplify the English preference for long melismas, full textures, and cantus-firmus structures. The most important midcentury English composer was Thomas Tallis (ca. 1505–1585). His works encompass Latin masses and hymns, English service music, and other sacred works that reflect the religious and political upheavals in England during his lifetime. Tallis's music strikes the listener as an interplay not of abstract musical lines but of voices—so closely is the melodic curve wedded to the natural inflection of speech, and so naturally does it lie for the singer.

Service and anthem

After the Church of England adopted English as the primary liturgical language, two principal forms of Anglican music developed: the **Service** and the **anthem.** A Service consists of the music for certain portions of Matins (corresponding to Catholic Matins and Lauds), Holy Communion (Mass), and Evensong (Vespers and Compline). A contrapuntal and melismatic setting of these portions is called a *Great Service*. A *Short Service* sets the same texts, but in a syllabic, chordal style. An anthem corresponds to a Latin motet. It is a polyphonic work in English, usually sung by the choir near the end of Matins or Evensong. Many anthems set texts from the Bible or *Book of Common Prayer*. There were two main types. A **full anthem** is for unaccompanied choir in contrapuntal style. A **verse anthem** employs one or more solo voices with organ or viol accompaniment, alternating with passages for full choir doubled by instruments.

WILLIAM BYRD

The leading English composer in the late Renaissance was William Byrd (ca. 1540–1623; see biography and Figure 10.5). Although a Catholic, Byrd served the Church of England and was a member of the royal chapel. In addition to secular vocal and instrumental music (discussed in chapters 11 and 12), he wrote both Anglican service music and Latin masses and motets.

Anglican music

Byrd composed in all the forms of Anglican church music, including a Great Service, three Short Services, psalms, full anthems, and verse anthems. He was the first English composer to absorb Continental imitative techniques

WILLIAM BYRD (CA. 1540–1623)

Byrd, the most important English composer between Dunstable and Purcell, was a master of all the major genres of his time, from music for Anglican and Catholic services to secular vocal and instrumental music.

He was probably a student of Thomas Tallis and a choirboy with the Chapel Royal in London under both the Protestant Edward VI and the Catholic Queen Mary. He was a Catholic, yet he served the Church of England as organist and choirmaster at Lincoln Cathedral (1563–72) and enjoyed the patronage of Queen Elizabeth, returning to the Chapel Royal for over five decades (1572–1623). In 1575, he and Tallis were granted a twenty-one-year monopoly for the printing of music in England, and Byrd continued publishing music after Tallis's death in 1585. In trouble from time to time for his Catholic practices, Byrd was protected by the queen and other leading figures, enabling him to publish Latin masses and motets for Catholic use without fear of reprisal.

Figure 10.5: William Byrd.

MAJOR WORKS: *Over 180 motets, 3 masses, 4 Services, dozens of anthems, secular partsongs, consort songs, fantasias and other works for viol consort, and variations, fantasias, dances, and other works for keyboard*

so thoroughly that he could apply them imaginatively and without constraint. In his *Sing joyfully unto God* (NAWM 44), an energetic and vivid full anthem for six voices, points of imitation succeed one another, occasionally interspersed with more homophonic declamation. The imitation is handled freely, often with changes of interval and rhythm.

CD 3|22   CD 1|63

Byrd's Latin masses and motets are his best-known vocal compositions. He probably intended his earlier motets for the royal chapel or for private devotional gatherings. But in the 1590s he began to write music for liturgical use by Catholics who celebrated Mass in secret. His masses, one each for three, four, and five voices (ca. 1593–95), stand out as the finest by an English Renaissance composer. His two books titled *Gradualia* (1605 and 1607) contain complete polyphonic Mass Propers for the major days of the church year, a cycle as ambitious and impressive as Léonin's *Magnus liber organi* and Isaac's *Choralis Constantinus*.

Latin masses and motets

Byrd was a Catholic in an Anglican state, a loyal subject of and servant to Queen Elizabeth, protected by her from prosecution for his religious practices and yet committed to providing music for his friends and patrons to use in their clandestine services. His prolific output of both Anglican and Catholic service music, as well as his split allegiances, embody on a personal level the religious divisions throughout Europe.

CATHOLIC CHURCH MUSIC

Music in the Catholic Church was changed relatively little by the religious turbulence of the sixteenth century. Although the Church undertook some reforms, described below, the primary response to the Reformation was to stiffen the Church's resolve and reaffirm its doctrines, traditions, and practices. Church leaders did not translate services into the vernacular or invite worshipers to participate in the liturgy through singing. Instead, we find continuity in the roles played by music and in the genres and forms that were used, from chant to polyphonic masses and motets. Tradition, splendor, and a projection through music of the power and leadership of the church were valued over congregational participation. What changes appeared were primarily matters of style rather than genre or practice.

THE GENERATION OF 1520–1550

Flemish composers remained prominent in the generation active between 1520 and 1550, working in positions all over Europe. Among the best known were Adrian Willaert (ca. 1490–1562), Nicolas Gombert (ca. 1495–ca. 1560), and Jacobus Clemens. All were born in Flanders but took posts elsewhere, extending a century-old tradition. Clemens served churches in the Netherlands. Gombert spent most of his career in the chapel of Emperor Charles V, working in Madrid, Vienna, and Brussels. Willaert had positions in Rome, Ferrara, Milan, and finally Venice, where he was director of music at the principal church, St. Mark's, for thirty-five years. There he trained many eminent musicians, including theorist Gioseffo Zarlino (see chapter 7) and composers Cipriano de Rore, Nicola Vicentino, and Andrea Gabrieli (see chapters 11 and 12).

General style features   Catholic composers in this period shared several characteristics. They preserved the careful dissonance treatment and equality of voices of the preceding generation. They expanded the typical number of voices from four to five or six, which allowed a greater variety of contrasting combinations. They defined the mode of polyphonic works clearly through cadences and melodic profile. Most works were in duple meter, sometimes with brief, contrasting passages in triple meter. The prevailing texture continued to be imitative polyphony, but now voices often varied motives as they imitated them. The imitation mass became the most common type of mass, followed by the paraphrase mass, although cantus-firmus masses continued to be written. Chant melodies, usually treated freely through paraphrase in all voices, served as subjects for motets as well as masses. Canons and other intricate structural devices appeared much less often than they had in previous generations.

We can see several of these traits in Gombert's motet *Quem dicunt homines*. At the beginning of the second part, shown in Example 10.5, the six voices enter on a point of imitation, each with a slightly varied statement of the motive. As this phrase cadences, a new motive appears in closer imitation in the upper four voices (measure 106), then in all six (measures 108–10), each phrase overlapping the previous one. The succession of interlocking points of imitation continues throughout the work, creating a seamless flow without the clear breaks and strong contrasts typical of Josquin, with whom Gombert was said to have studied. At each new phrase, the voices enter in a different order and after a different interval of time, providing endless variety within a unified structure. The music reflects the value Gombert placed on combining continuity with constant variation.

Example 10.5: Gombert, Quem dicunt homines, *mm. 101–10*

Mode in polyphony   At the same time, Gombert emphasizes the mode. Renaissance composers and theorists saw the modes as a link between the Christian tradition and the emotional effects of ancient music, so making the mode clear was of vital concern. This motet is in mode 5, the Lydian mode on F. The cadences fall on F, the modal final, with subsidiary cadences on C, the tenor (see measures 106 and 109). At the beginning, the voices alternate entrances on F and C, and the melodies tend to move within ranges defined by those notes. That this is mode 5 rather than its plagal relative mode 6 is made clear by the ranges of the superius and tenor (fourth line down), which Renaissance theorists considered to be the voices that defined the mode.

Willaert and   Although they shared many characteristics, composers at this time also de-
humanism   veloped individual styles. Willaert, with his long career in Italy, was most affected by the humanist movement. He carefully suited his music to the accentuation, rhetoric, and punctuation of the text. He never allowed a rest to interrupt a word or thought within a vocal line, and he allowed a strong cadence in all voices only at significant breaks in the text. Willaert was one of the first composers to insist that syllables be printed under their notes and that scrupulous attention be paid to the stresses of Latin pronunciation. In addition to his church music, Willaert also played a significant part in the history of the Italian madrigal (see chapter 11).

CATHOLIC RESPONSE TO THE REFORMATION

As the Protestant Reformation spread, the Catholic Church responded with a series of initiatives, called the Counter-Reformation or Catholic Reformation. The loss or threatened loss of England, the Netherlands, Germany, Austria, Bohemia, Poland, and Hungary made this campaign urgent. Pope Paul III (r. 1534–49) and his successors brought austerity and asceticism to a church hierarchy formerly known for profligacy and excess. Simultaneously, Saint Ignatius Loyola (1491–1556) organized the Society of Jesus, known as the Jesuits, in 1534. Swearing strict obedience to the pope, the Jesuits founded schools and proselytized among Protestants in Europe and non-Christians in Asia and the Americas. Their work helped to restore Poland and large areas of France and Germany to Catholicism.

THE COUNCIL OF TRENT

From 1545 to 1563, with numerous interruptions, a church Council met at Trent in northern Italy to consider how to respond to the Reformation. Figure 10.6 shows the final session. After discussing possible compromises, the Council reaffirmed the doctrines and practices that Luther and Calvin had attacked. However, the Council did pass measures aimed at purging the Church of abuses and laxities.

Effects on music   Church music took up only a small part of the Council's time. As part of a move to suppress variation in local practices in favor of a uniform liturgy, tropes and most sequences were eliminated, leaving only four of the most widely used sequences, including *Victimae paschali laudes* (NAWM 5). Some reformers sought to restrict polyphonic music, complaining that basing a mass on a secular chanson profaned the liturgy or that complicated polyphony

Figure 10.6: The Council of Trent, shown at its final session in 1563, led by Pope Pius IV. Painting attributed to Titian.

made it impossible to understand the words. Some sought to eliminate poly-phonic music from convents entirely. Others argued strongly for retaining music without restrictions, noting that it had been part of Christian worship from the beginning.

In the end, the Council said little about music. The only policy adopted regarding music was this statement of 1562: "Let them keep away from the churches compositions in which there is an intermingling of the lascivious or impure, whether by instrument or by voice." It was left to local bishops to regulate music in the services. Some bishops, notably in Rome and Milan, did restrict music in convents or insist that in polyphonic works the text must always be intelligible. The prominence of their efforts led to the belief among some contemporaries and some later historians that the Council of Trent indeed had declared that polyphony was allowed only if the words remained comprehensible to all.

GIOVANNI PIERLUIGI DA PALESTRINA

The controversy around the intelligibility of words in polyphonic music became linked to Giovanni Pierluigi da Palestrina (1525/1526–1594; see biography and Figure 10.7), the leading Italian composer of church music in the sixteenth century. According to a legend already circulating soon after his death, Palestrina saved polyphony from condemnation by the Council of Trent by composing a six-voice mass that was reverent in spirit and did not

GIOVANNI PIERLUIGI DA PALESTRINA (1525/1526–1594)

Palestrina was renowned especially for his masses and motets. His music became a model for later centuries of church music and of counterpoint in strict style.

Palestrina was named after his presumed birthplace, a small town near Rome. He served as a choirboy and received his musical education at the Church of Santa Maria Maggiore in Rome. After seven years as organist and choirmaster in Palestrina (1544–51), he returned to Rome under the patronage of Pope Julius III. He spent most of his career as choirmaster at the Julian Chapel at St. Peter's (1551–55 and 1571–94) and at two other important churches in Rome, St. John Lateran (1555–60) and

Santa Maria Maggiore (1561-66). He briefly sang in the papal chapel (1555) but had to relinquish the honor because he was married. He also taught music at the new Jesuit seminary. He declined two offers that would have taken him away from Rome: one from Emperor Maximilian II in 1568 and another in 1583 from the duke of Mantua.

Most of Palestrina's music was sacred, and he wrote more masses than any other composer. His main secular works are madrigals. Late in life, he wrote that he "blushed and grieved" to have written music for love poems.

After the Council of Trent ordered changes in the liturgy, Palestrina and a colleague were commissioned to revise the official chant books to conform to the new liturgy and purge the chants of "barbarisms, obscurities, contrarieties, and superfluities." The revised edition, completed by others after Palestrina's death, was published in 1614 and remained in use until the twentieth century.

Palestrina married Lucrezia Gori in 1547, and they had three sons. After he lost two of them in the 1570s to the plague, followed by Lucrezia in 1580, Palestrina considered becoming a priest. Instead, in 1581 he married Virginia Dormoli, an affluent widow whose financial resources allowed him to publish his own music. His reputation as a composer, already high in his lifetime, grew after his death until he became an almost legendary figure.

Figure 10.7: Giovanni Pierluigi da Palestrina, in a contemporary painting.

MAJOR WORKS: *104 masses, over 300 motets, 35 Magnificats, about 70 hymns, many other liturgical compositions, about 50 spiritual madrigals with Italian texts, and 94 secular madrigals*

obscure the words. The work in question was the *Pope Marcellus Mass* (Credo and Agnus Dei I in NAWM 45), published in Palestrina's *Second Book of Masses* in 1567. While the legend is probably false, Palestrina noted in his dedication to this collection that the masses it contained were written "in a new manner," no doubt responding to the desire of some for greater clarity in setting the text.

CD 3|27-35

THE PALESTRINA STYLE

Palestrina has been called "the Prince of Music" and his works the "absolute perfection" of church style. His sober, elegant music captured the essence of the Catholic response to the Reformation in a polyphony of utter purity. Yet his music is also remarkably varied in its melodies, rhythms, textures, and sonorities and acutely sensitive to the text, making it profoundly satisfying to hear.

Palestrina's style is exemplified in his 104 masses. Fifty-one are imitation masses based on polyphonic models. Thirty-four are paraphrase masses, almost all on chant, with the borrowed melody paraphrased in all voices. Eight masses use the old-fashioned cantus-firmus method, including the first of two he wrote on *L'homme armé*. Also reminiscent of the older Flemish tradition are a small number of canonic masses. Six masses, including the *Pope Marcellus Mass*, are free, using neither canons nor borrowed material.

Masses

Palestrina's melodies have a quality almost like plainchant, no doubt influenced by the chants he often paraphrased in his masses and motets. The melodic lines in the first Agnus Dei from the *Pope Marcellus Mass* (NAWM 45b), shown in Example 10.6, are typical: long-breathed, rhythmically varied,

Melody

CD 3|35 CD 1|68

Example 10.6: Opening of Agnus Dei I from Palestrina's Pope Marcellus Mass

easily singable lines that trace a natural, elegant curve. The voices move mostly by step, with few repeated notes. Most leaps greater than a third are smoothed over by stepwise motion in the opposite direction to fill in the gap.

Counterpoint and dissonance treatment

Palestrina's counterpoint conforms in most details with the teachings of Willaert as transmitted by Zarlino in his *Le istitutione harmoniche*. The music is almost entirely in duple meter. The independent lines meet in a consonant sonority on each beat (each half note in Example 10.6), except when there is a suspension, shown by S in the example. Dissonances between beats may occur if entered and left by step, as in the passing (P) and neighbor (N) tones marked in the example. In addition, Palestrina often used the **cambiata** (Italian for "changed"), as it was later called. In this figure, marked C in Example 10.6, a voice skips down a third from a dissonance to a consonance instead of resolving by step. Where one might expect two passing tones between consonant notes, as between D and A in the cantus at measure 6, the second passing tone—here, B—is omitted, only to become the next note in the melody. This elegant gesture delays, encircles, and thus emphasizes the note.

Sonority

The smooth diatonic lines and discreet handling of dissonance give Palestrina's music transparency and serenity. At the same time, despite what might seem a limited harmonic vocabulary, he achieves an astonishing variety in sonority through different arrangements of the same few notes. For instance, in the passage in Example 10.6, each time the notes G–D or G–B–D are combined vertically their spacing is unique. These combinations, shown in Example 10.7, illustrate Palestrina's ability to produce many subtly different shadings and sonorities from the same simple harmonies, sustaining the listener's interest.

Example 10.7: Varied spacings in Palestrina's Agnus Dei

Text declamation

Palestrina strove to accentuate the words correctly and make them intelligible, in accordance with the goals of reformers. In Example 10.6, each voice declaims "Agnus Dei" clearly, with one note on each syllable except for the accented "De-," which is emphasized by an upward leap and long melisma. In the movements with longer texts, the Gloria and the Credo, Palestrina set many passages in homophony so that the words could be easily understood. Example 10.8 shows one such passage, from the Credo of the *Pope Marcellus Mass* (NAWM 45a). As a result, there is a contrast in style between these largely homophonic movements and those with shorter texts—the Kyrie, Sanctus, and Agnus Dei—which use imitative polyphony throughout.

CD 3|27

Texture

To achieve variety, Palestrina typically gave each new phrase to a different combination of voices, reserving the full six voices for climaxes, major cadences, or particularly significant words. In Example 10.8, "Genitum, non factum" (Begotten, not made) and "consubstantialem" (being of one substance) are sung by two different groups of four voices, "Patri" (with the Father) by three voices, and "per quem omnia facta sunt" (by whom all things were made) by all six. Subtle text-painting abounds: the phrase on "consubstantialem" is a variation of the previous one and thus is "of one substance" with it; "the Father" is sung by three voices, symbolizing the Trinity; and "all" in the last phrase is emphasized as all six voices sing together for the first time in the Credo.

Example 10.8: From the Credo of Palestrina's Pope Marcellus Mass

The rhythm of sixteenth-century polyphony comprises both the rhythms of the individual voices and a collective rhythm resulting from the harmonies on the beats. Within each voice, there is a great variety in durations, and no two successive measures feature the same rhythm. When each voice is barred

Rhythm

according to its own natural rhythm, as in Example 10.9, which rebars Example 10.6, we can see graphically how independent the individual lines are. But when the passage is performed, we perceive a fairly regular succession of measures in duple meter, projected by changes in harmony and suspensions on strong beats. Palestrina often uses syncopation to sustain momentum and link phrases. In Example 10.8, each phrase begins with a syncopated sonority that enters half a beat earlier than expected, just after the previous phrase cadences, and thus maintains forward motion until the end of the sentence in the text.

Example 10.9: Rhythmic independence in Palestrina's Agnus Dei

In all of these respects, Palestrina's music combines elegance, clarity, pleasingness, variety, and close attention to the words, all features that were highly valued in the Renaissance. Accordingly, his works earned praise as the pinnacle of church music.

PALESTRINA AS A MODEL

Palestrina's style was the first in the history of Western music to be consciously preserved and imitated as a model in later ages. Seventeenth-century theorists and composers looked to him as the ideal of the *stile antico* (old style). Counterpoint books from Johann Joseph Fux's *Gradus ad Parnassum* (Steps to Parnassus, 1725) to recent texts have aimed at guiding young composers to recreate this style. During the eighteenth and nineteenth centuries, through his role as a pedagogical model and the legend that his *Pope Marcellus Mass* saved church polyphony, Palestrina's reputation eclipsed all other sixteenth-century composers. Only since the late nineteenth century, when his music and that of his contemporaries has been studied, edited, and more widely performed, have we begun to see Palestrina in context and understand how his style represents just one important strand in a vast and colorful tapestry.

SPAIN AND THE NEW WORLD

In Spain, the Catholic Church was closely identified with the monarchy. Queen Isabella and King Ferdinand, joint rulers from 1479, were called the "Catholic monarchs," and they strongly promoted Catholicism in their realm. In 1480, Ferdinand launched the Spanish Inquisition, which sought to root out heresy and enforce belief in Catholic doctrine. After conquering the Moors in Granada in 1492, Ferdinand and Isabella forced Jews (and later Muslims) to accept baptism as Christians or leave Spain. Later Spanish kings Charles I (r. 1516–56, and 1519–56 as Holy Roman Emperor Charles V) and his son Philip II (r. 1556–98) were equally fervent Catholics, and together with Jesuit missionaries they made sure that the Church and its music prospered in Spain and its possessions in the Americas.

CATHOLIC MUSIC IN SPAIN

Royal family ties to the Low Countries brought Flemish musicians such as Gombert to Spain, and the Franco-Flemish tradition deeply influenced Spanish polyphony. There were also close links to Italy, through Spain's possessions in southern Italy, and directly to Rome, particularly after the election of a Spaniard as Pope Alexander VI (1492–1503). The most eminent Spanish composer of the first half of the sixteenth century, Cristóbal de Morales (ca. 1500–1553), had links to both Flemish and Italian traditions. Morales acquired fame in Italy as a member of the papal chapel between 1535 and 1545, and his masses drew on works by Josquin, Gombert, and other Franco-Flemish composers as well as on Spanish songs. Among the most widely performed Spanish composers was Morales's student Francisco Guerrero (1528–1599), chapel master at the Seville Cathedral, whose diatonic, singable melodies made his music popular throughout Spain and Spanish America.

Tomás Luis de Victoria (1548–1611) was the most famous Spanish composer of the sixteenth century. All of his music is sacred and intended for Catholic services. He spent two decades in Rome, where he almost certainly knew Palestrina and may have studied with him. Victoria was the first Spanish composer to master Palestrina's style, yet his music departs from it in several respects. Victoria's works tend to be shorter, with less florid melodies, more frequent cadences, more chromatic alterations, and more contrasting passages in homophony or triple meter. All of these characteristics are evident in his best-known work, *O magnum mysterium* (NAWM 46a). In this motet, Victoria uses a variety of motives and textures to express successively the mystery, wonder, and joy of the Christmas season.

Tomás Luis de Victoria

| CD 3|36 | | CD 1|69 |

Most of Victoria's masses are imitation masses based on his own motets, including *Missa O magnum mysterium* (Kyrie in NAWM 46b), based on this motet. Writing an imitation mass lets the composer show how existing material can be used in new ways. At the opening of the Kyrie, Victoria preserves the paired entrances of the motet but changes them from almost exact

Imitation mass

| CD 3|40 |

imitation into a dialogue between two subjects, each a distinctive variant of the original subject of the motet. In comparison with the generous length of Palestrina's Agnus Dei discussed above, Victoria's Kyrie is remarkably brief. In each movement of the mass, Victoria reworks the material from his motet in a new way, exemplifying the high value placed on variety that was a consistent feature of polyphonic mass cycles.

MUSIC IN THE SPANISH NEW WORLD

Soon after Columbus landed in the New World, Spanish *conquistadores* claimed much of its territory for Spain. Leading small bands of adventurers, Hernán Cortés overthrew the Aztec empire in present-day Mexico (1519–21), and Francisco Pizarro conquered the Incas in Peru (1527–33). The Spanish brought with them Catholic missionaries, who sought to convert the native peoples to Christianity.

Aztec and Inca music   The Aztecs and Incas had rich musical traditions, with songs in a variety of styles and a wide array of instruments, from drums to flutes. Much of their music was associated with dancing, whether for recreation or as part of religious rituals and festivals. Accounts by Spanish witnesses speak of particularly elaborate music and dances, sometimes lasting all day and into the night, to mark special occasions (see Source Reading).

SOURCE READING

A SPANIARD'S DESCRIPTION OF AZTEC FESTIVALS

Fray Toribio de Benavente (ca. 1495–ca. 1565) was one of twelve Franciscan missionaries who went to Mexico in 1524 to convert the indigenous people to Christianity. Called Motolinia ("he suffers") by the Aztecs, he admired their skill in music and described their rituals in detail.

———— • ————

Songs and dances were very important in all this land, both to celebrate the solemn festivals of the demons they honored as gods, whom they thought well served by such things, and for their own enjoyment and recreation. . . . And because in each town they put much stock in these things, each chieftain had a chapel in his house with his singers who composed the dances and songs; and these leaders sought out those who knew best how to compose songs in the meter and verses they practiced. . . .

The singers decided some days before the festivals what they would sing. In the larger towns there were many singers, and if there were to be new songs and dances they gathered in advance so there would be no imperfections on the festival day. On the morning of that day they put a large mat in the middle of the plaza where they set up their drums. Then they gathered and dressed at the house of the chieftain; from there they came singing and dancing. Sometimes they began their dances in the morning, sometimes at the hour when we celebrate High Mass. At night they returned singing to the palace, there to end their song early in the night, or when the night was well advanced, or even at midnight.

Fray Toribio de Benavente, called Motolinia (ca. 1495–ca. 1565), *Memoriales de Fray Toribio de Motolinia*, ed. Luis García Pimentel (Maxico: Casa del Editor, 1903), 339–40. Trans. Gary Tomlinson, in SR 77 (3:42), pp. 496–97.

Catholic missionaries exploited the native peoples' interest in music to spread the message of the new religion. They brought over the music used in Spanish churches and taught native musicians to sing polyphonic masses and motets and to play European instruments. The masses of Morales, Victoria, and Palestrina were sung often in New World cathedrals, and the works of Guerrero were especially popular, remaining in use for centuries. Spanish musicians moved to the Americas to serve as cathedral musicians, and many of them composed music for services, creating the first written music in the New World. Some of this sacred music was in local languages, including the first polyphonic vocal work published in the Americas, *Hanacpachap cussicuinin*, a processional in the Quechua language of Peru printed in Lima in 1631. The power of music to win converts, well known to Luther and Calvin, was used here to spread Catholicism on the other side of the globe.

Catholic music

GERMANY AND EASTERN EUROPE

Much of central and eastern Europe remained Catholic after the Reformation, including southern Germany, Austria, Bohemia, and Poland. Music in these areas reflected developments in Flanders, France, and Italy. Influences came from Franco-Flemish and other Western musicians serving at courts in the region and from local musicians trained in Italy or France. The leading eastern composers of Catholic church music were Wacław of Szamotuł (ca. 1520–ca. 1567) in Poland and Jacob Handl (1550–1591) in Bohemia.

The music of Josquin and other Franco-Flemish composers circulated in Germany beginning early in the sixteenth century, and German composers adopted their style or blended it with local traditions. The leading German composer of the late Renaissance was Hans Leo Hassler (1564–1612), who studied with Andrea Gabrieli in Venice and then held various positions at Augsburg, Nuremberg, Ulm, and Dresden. The range of his works typifies the eclecticism of German composers at the time, from settings of Lutheran chorales to Latin masses and motets for Catholic services, secular partsongs in German and Italian, and pieces for instrumental ensemble and keyboard.

Germany

ORLANDO DI LASSO

Chief among the Franco-Flemish composers in Germany was Orlando di Lasso (ca. 1532–1594), who served the duke of Bavaria for almost four decades (see biography and Figure 10.8). Lasso ranks with Palestrina among the great composers of sacred music in the sixteenth century, although unlike Palestrina, he also wrote many secular works. Whereas Palestrina became a model of the restrained church style and of strict counterpoint, Lasso was equally influential as an advocate of emotional expression and the depiction of text through music.

Lasso wrote fifty-seven masses, but his chief glory lies in his over seven hundred motets. In each motet, Lasso's rhetorical, pictorial, and dramatic interpretation of the text determines both the overall form and the details.

Motets

ORLANDO DI LASSO [ROLAND DE LASSUS] (CA. 1532–1594)

In both his career and his compositions, Lasso was one of the most cosmopolitan figures of his time. He was prolific in all genres and was a particularly imaginative composer of motets and chansons.

Lasso was born in Mons in Hainaut, the region where Du Fay, Binchois, Ockeghem, and Josquin were also born and trained. Little is known of Lasso's family or early education. Beginning at a young age, he served Italian patrons at Mantua, Sicily, Milan, Naples, and Rome, allowing him to become thoroughly familiar with Italian styles. By the age of twenty-four he had already published books of madrigals, chansons, and motets. In 1556, he entered the service of Duke Albrecht V of Bavaria. He became maestro di cappella for the ducal chapel in Munich and remained in that post until his death in 1594. He was good friends with his patron and especially with Albrecht's son, who became Duke Wilhelm V in 1579; the letters from the composer to Wilhelm reveal a witty personality capable of making jokes in four languages.

Although Lasso served almost four decades in one post, he traveled frequently and kept abreast of developments in Flanders, France, and Italy. His total production eventually amounted to more than two thousand works, and his music was well known all over Europe. The principal collection of his motets, the *Magnum opus musicum* (Great Work of Music), was published by his sons in 1604, ten years after his death.

Figure 10.8: Orlando di Lasso at the keyboard (a virginal) leading his ensemble of about twenty-five singers and fifteen instrumentalists at the Munich court of Duke Albrecht V of Bavaria. Miniature by Hans Muelich in a manuscript of Lasso's Penitential Psalms.

MAJOR WORKS: *57 masses, over 700 motets, 101 Magnificats, hundreds of other liturgical compositions, about 150 French chansons, 200 Italian madrigals, and 90 German Lieder*

CD 3|43   CD 2|1   *Tristis est anima mea* (NAWM 47), published in 1565, is one of his most deeply moving and vivid settings. The text is based on the words of Jesus before he was crucified, as reported by Matthew (26:38) and Mark (14:34). The motet's opening, shown in Example 10.10, is an evocative sound-image of sadness, depicted through a descending-semitone motive on the word "Tristis" (sad) along with carefully wrought, drawn-out suspensions. The consonant harmonization of the motive in the first two measures prepares its reappearance as a dissonant suspension in Altus 1, Cantus, and Altus 2 (marked S in the example). This use of the suspension to achieve emotional tension rather than to prepare a cadence was borrowed from the madrigal (see chapter 11) but was still rarely found in sacred music. Later in the motet, Lasso wrote a lively contrapuntal section to represent the watchful vigilance Jesus demanded of his disciples, and used a figure that circles around a note to depict "the crowd that will encircle me." At the words "you will take flight," Lasso presents eleven entrances of a running subject to portray the eleven disciples fleeing when Jesus is attacked by the twelfth disciple, Judas, and the mob. The words of the text prompted not only the rhythms, accents, and contours of the musical motives but the music's every gesture: harmonic effects, textures, suspensions, points of imitation, and the weight and placement of cadences.

Example 10.10: Lasso, Tristis est anima mea

Sad is my soul

More fully than any other sixteenth-century composer, Lasso synthesized the achievements of an epoch. He was so versatile that we cannot properly speak of a "Lasso style." He was a master of Flemish, French, Italian, and German styles, and of every genre from high church music to the bawdy secular song. His motets were especially influential, particularly on German Protestant composers. Lasso's creative use of musical devices to express the emotions and depict the images in his texts led to a strong tradition of such expressive and pictorial figures among German composers, as we will see with Heinrich Schütz (chapter 15) and Johann Sebastian Bach (chapter 19).

JEWISH MUSIC

The small but vibrant Jewish community in Europe had its own musical traditions, but they were primarily oral rather than written. Synagogue services included the singing of psalms to traditional formulas, usually performed responsorially by a leader and the congregation. Readings from Hebrew Scripture were chanted by a soloist using a system of cantillation. Melodies were not written down, but beginning in the ninth century a notation called *te'amim* was developed to indicate accents, divisions in the text, and appropriate melodic patterns. Singers were expected to improvise a melody from the notation, drawing on melodic formulas and practices handed down through oral tradition, and freely adding embellishments.

During the sixteenth century, Jewish communities began to appoint a specific person to perform the chants. This person, called the synagogue cantor, or *hazzan*, became an integral part of the community as well as the synagogue structure. Although the position of hazzan was essentially that of a professional musician, cantors did not receive formal musical training until the nineteenth century.

Over the centuries, the Ashkenazi Jews of Germany and eastern Europe and the Sephardic Jews of Spain absorbed elements from other music in their regions, and the sound and style of their music gradually diverged. Ashkenazi chants, for example, show melodic elements from Gregorian chant and German Minnelieder, while Sephardic music drew on Arab sources. Thus the threads of borrowing continued to weave through the tapestry of European music: just as early Christian chant borrowed from Jewish sources, and Lutherans based chorale tunes on Gregorian chants and German secular songs, European Jews blended styles of melody from the surrounding society with elements from their ancestral tradition.

THE LEGACY OF SIXTEENTH-CENTURY SACRED MUSIC

The religious divisions of the early sixteenth century changed Europe forever. Their echoes are still present in ongoing conflicts between Protestants and Catholics in Northern Ireland and elsewhere. Ironically, in October 1999, on the 482nd anniversary of Luther's ninety-five theses, the Lutheran and Catholic churches signed a declaration ending their dispute. But the genie is long out of the bottle, and there is no going back to the relative uniformity of doctrine and practice of fifteenth-century western Europe.

So too, the Reformation and the Catholic response utterly changed church music. The Lutheran Church developed chorales that have been sung and adapted in myriad ways for almost five hundred years. Their use as the basis for organ and choral works by Bach and other German composers has given chorales a significance for Baroque and later music equal to that of Gregorian chant. Many of the psalm tunes written for the Calvinist Reformed churches are still in use, and several, such as Old Hundredth, are sung in a wide range of Protestant churches. The Church of England and its offspring, including the Episcopal Church, continue to use the service and anthem; those of Byrd and other sixteenth-century composers are still sung, and new music is written each year in the same forms. The reformed liturgy and chant that resulted from the Council of Trent remained in use in the Catholic Church until later reforms in the twentieth century. Palestrina established a style for church music that has been emulated in all later centuries, although his music faded from regular use in the seventeenth century until its revival and publication in the nineteenth and twentieth centuries. The Palestrina revival was followed by rediscoveries of Lasso, Victoria, and others who represent different musical flavors of the High Renaissance. Only recently have we begun to hear music of this time from the Spanish New World.

In the various musical responses to theological and political disputes as described in this chapter, the political and religious content of particular musical styles is especially clear. To sing *Ein' feste Burg* or a Palestrina mass is still an act potent with meaning, even after half a millennium. This should remind us that other pieces, which we now hear simply as music, once carried equally strong associations—associations that we can learn only by studying the historical circumstances from which they emerged.

Chapter 11

Madrigal and Secular Song in the Sixteenth Century

CHAPTER OUTLINE

If fifteenth-century composers forged an international idiom, sixteenth-century musicians cultivated a new flowering of national styles, especially in secular vocal music. Poets and composers in different linguistic regions naturally developed distinctive genres and forms. Music printing fostered the creation and dissemination of music for amateurs to sing for their own pleasure. This music was usually in the vernacular, further encouraging the growth of national styles.

Among the significant national genres of the sixteenth century were the Spanish **villancico,** the Italian **frottola,** and a new kind of French chanson, all simple, strophic, mostly syllabic and homophonic, easily singable, and thus ideally suited for amateur performers. The genre that proved most significant in the long run was the Italian **madrigal,** in which Renaissance poets and composers brought to a peak their intense interests in humanism, in the individual, and in realizing in music the accents, images, and emotions of the text. Besides influencing later French chansons and German Lieder, madrigals became fashionable in England, joined around the end of the century by the **lute song.** Through the madrigal, Italy and Italian composers became the leading forces in European music for the first time, a role they would maintain for the next two centuries.

THE FIRST MARKET FOR MUSIC

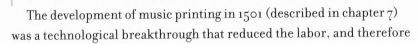

The development of music printing in 1501 (described in chapter 7) was a technological breakthrough that reduced the labor, and therefore the cost, of producing notated music in multiple copies. This made possible a much wider dissemination of music, but it also changed the economics of music. Prior to this, music was preeminently a service provided by musicians. Now for the first time music, in printed form, could be sold as a commodity.

The new supply of printed music dovetailed with a growing demand for notated music that amateurs could perform for their own enjoyment. People have always made music to entertain themselves and their friends, but for most of human history they did so without using notation. When notation was invented, it was used for church music and secular music of the aristocracy, as we have seen, leaving few written traces of the music-making of the general populace. In the sixteenth century, first among the upper classes, then among the literate urban middle classes, the ability to read notation and to perform from printed music became an expected social grace. In Baldassare Castiglione's influential *Book of the Courtier* (1528), several speakers praise those who could sing and play from notation (see Source Reading, p. 242). Many paintings from the time, such as the one in Figure 11.1, show singers or instrumentalists reading from published music, usually in the form of partbooks (described in chapter 7). In such settings, music served as a kind of social glue, an activity friends and family could join in together.

The combination of music printing with the demand for music that amateurs could sing and play created the first market for music, which ranged from relatively elite to more popular genres, styles, and forms. Published music was of course bought by professional musicians for their own use, but music suited to amateur performance sold particularly well, and composers

Amateur music-making and musical literacy

Figure 11.1: Anonymous sixteenth-century painting, showing a vocal quartet singing from partbooks. The rich costumes suggest that these are aristocratic amateurs performing for their own pleasure in the privacy of an idyllic island.

SOURCE READING

ON READING AND PERFORMING MUSIC

Baldassare Castiglione (1478–1529) was a courtier, ambassador, and poet. His most influential work was The Book of the Courtier *(1528), a manual on proper behavior at court in the guise of conversations at the ducal palace in Urbino. The ability to sing and play from notation was expected.*

———•———

The Count began again: "Gentlemen, you must know that I am not satisfied with our Courtier unless he be also a musician, and unless, besides understanding and being able to read music, he can play various instruments. For, if we rightly consider, no rest from toil and no medicine for ailing spirits can be found more decorous or praiseworthy in time of leisure than this; and especially in courts where, besides the release from vexations which music gives to all, many things are done to please the ladies, whose tender and delicate spirits are readily penetrated with harmony and filled with sweetness. Hence, it is no wonder that in both ancient and modern times they have always been particularly fond of musicians, finding music a most welcome food for the spirit."

Baldesar Castiglione, *The Book of the Courtier,* trans. Charles S. Singleton (Garden City, NY: Doubleday, 1959), 74.

worked to meet that demand. In vocal music, amateurs were most interested in singing in their own language, reinforcing an already evident trend toward diverse national genres and styles.

SPAIN

THE VILLANCICO

In the late fifteenth century, during Ferdinand and Isabella's campaign to unify and invigorate Spain, Ferdinand and others at the Spanish court encouraged the development of a uniquely Spanish music. They especially cultivated the **villancico,** which became the most important form of secular polyphonic song in Renaissance Spain. Although the name is a diminutive of *villano* (peasant), and the texts were usually on rustic or popular subjects, villancicos were composed for the aristocracy. Short, strophic, syllabic, and mostly homophonic, they reflect a growing preference for simplicity and for what were considered more authentic representations of Spanish culture, in reaction to the more complex French chanson and its Spanish relative the *canción*, written by Franco-Flemish composers in Spain.

Form and performance   The form of the villancico varies in its details but always includes a refrain (*estribillo*) and one or more stanzas (*coplas*). The stanzas typically begin with a new section (*mudanza*, "change") with two statements of a contrasting idea and conclude with a return to the music of the refrain (*vuelta*). Most often, only the last line of the refrain text recurs at the end of each stanza. The principal melody is always in the top voice; the others may have been sung or performed on instruments. During the sixteenth century, publishers issued many collections of villancicos in arrangements for solo voice with lute. In later centuries, the form was often used for sacred compositions.

Juan del Encina (1468–1529), the first Spanish playwright, was a leading composer of villancicos. His *Oy comamos y bebamos* (NAWM 48) is typical of the genre. In rather crude language, the text exhorts listeners to eat, drink, and sing because tomorrow brings the first day of Lent, a season of fasting. The music is simple in melody and harmony, with dancelike rhythms marked by frequent hemiolas.

Juan del Encina

CD 3|46

ITALY

THE FROTTOLA

An Italian counterpart to the villancico was the **frottola** (plural, *frottole*), a four-part strophic song set syllabically and homophonically, with the melody in the upper voice, marked rhythmic patterns, and simple diatonic harmonies.

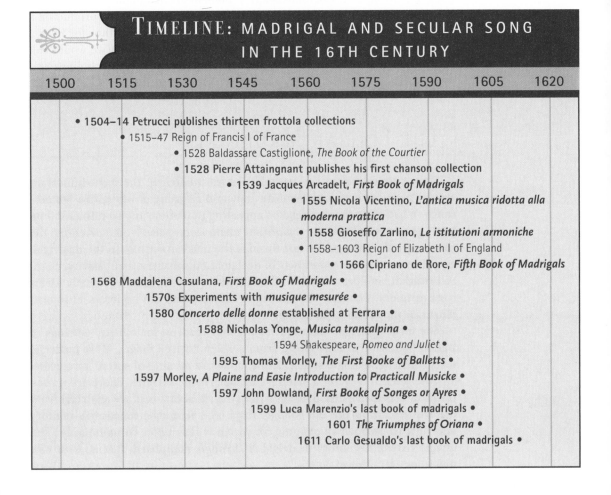

TIMELINE: MADRIGAL AND SECULAR SONG IN THE 16TH CENTURY

1500	1515	1530	1545	1560	1575	1590	1605	1620

- 1504–14 Petrucci publishes thirteen frottola collections
- 1515–47 Reign of Francis I of France
- 1528 Baldassare Castiglione, *The Book of the Courtier*
- 1528 Pierre Attaingnant publishes his first chanson collection
- 1539 Jacques Arcadelt, *First Book of Madrigals*
- 1555 Nicola Vicentino, *L'antica musica ridotta alla moderna prattica*
- 1558 Gioseffo Zarlino, *Le istitutioni armoniche*
- 1558–1603 Reign of Elizabeth I of England
- 1566 Cipriano de Rore, *Fifth Book of Madrigals*
- 1568 Maddalena Casulana, *First Book of Madrigals* •
- 1570s Experiments with *musique mesurée* •
- 1580 *Concerto delle donne* established at Ferrara •
- 1588 Nicholas Yonge, *Musica transalpina* •
- 1594 Shakespeare, *Romeo and Juliet* •
- 1595 Thomas Morley, *The First Booke of Balletts* •
- 1597 Morley, *A Plaine and Easie Introduction to Practicall Musicke* •
- 1597 John Dowland, *First Booke of Songes or Ayres* •
- 1599 Luca Marenzio's last book of madrigals •
- 1601 *The Triumphes of Oriana* •
- 1611 Carlo Gesualdo's last book of madrigals •

The music of the frottola was essentially a tune for singing the poetry, marking the end of each line with a cadence, with the lower parts providing a harmonic foundation. The genre included several subtypes, of which some had fixed forms while others were free.

Social setting   Like villancicos, frottole featured simple music and earthy and satirical texts, but were neither folk nor popular songs. Rather, they were mock-popular songs written for the amusement of the courtly elite. Fashionable in the late fifteenth and early sixteenth centuries at Italian courts such as Mantua, Ferrara, and Urbino, they were composed almost exclusively by Italian composers. Petrucci published thirteen collections of frottole between 1504 and 1514, testifying to the vogue for the genre among his well-to-do customers.

Performance   Usually the top voice was sung, while the other parts were played on instruments. Beginning in 1509, Francisco Bossinensis published collections of frottole by various composers in arrangements for voice and lute. With the lute carrying the lower parts, the solo singer could improvise melismatic flourishes at principal cadences.

Marco Cara   Among the best-known composers of frottole was Marco Cara (ca. 1465–1525), who worked at Mantua. His *Io non compro più speranza* (NAWM 49),

CD 3|47   a lighthearted complaint of a disappointed lover, appeared in Petrucci's first book of frottole and Bossinensis's first book of arrangements. The six beats to the measure alternate between duple and triple groupings, producing a characteristic hemiola pattern that remained a popular rhythm for over a century. The harmonization consists almost entirely of what we would call root-position triads, a style that influenced later music by both Italians and foreigners.

THE ITALIAN MADRIGAL

More enduring than the frottola was the **madrigal**, the most important secular genre of sixteenth-century Italy and arguably of the entire Renaissance. What made the madrigal so appealing in its time and so influential on later generations was the emphasis composers placed on enriching the meaning and impact of the text through the musical setting. In the madrigal, composers explored new effects of declamation, imagery, expressivity, characterization, and dramatization that paved the way for future dramatic forms such as opera. Through the madrigal, Italy became the leader in European music for the first time in history.

Definition and form   The term *madrigal* was used from about 1530 on for musical settings of Italian poetry of various types, from sonnets to free forms. Most madrigal texts consist of a single stanza with a moderate number of seven- or eleven-syllable lines and either a standard or free rhyme scheme. There are no refrains or repeated lines, distinguishing the sixteenth-century madrigal from the frottola, from the old *formes fixes*, and from the fourteenth-century madrigal (described in chapter 6), which it resembles in name only. The typical sixteenth-century madrigal is **through-composed**, that is, with new music for every line of poetry.

Composers frequently chose texts by major poets, including Francesco Petrarca (1304–1374), Ludovico Ariosto (1474–1533), Torquato Tasso (1544–1595), and Giovanni Battista Guarini (1538–1612). The subject matter was sentimental or erotic, with scenes and allusions borrowed from pastoral poetry. Madrigals were a form of social play, and the best poems interwove vivid imagery and description with themes of love, sex, and wit that could charm, surprise, amuse, and entertain. Poems often ended with an epigram in the last line or two that served to bring home the point of the poem.

Poetry

Madrigals dealt freely with the poetry, using a variety of homophonic and contrapuntal textures in a series of overlapping sections, each based on a single phrase of text, with all voices playing essentially equal roles. In these respects, madrigals resemble motets of the same era. Most important, madrigal composers aimed to match the artfulness of the poetry and to convey its ideas, images, and emotions to the performers and listeners.

Music

Most early madrigals, from about 1520 to 1550, were for four voices. By midcentury five voices became the rule, and six or more were not unusual. When voices were added to the traditional cantus, altus, tenor, and bassus, they were usually labeled by number in Latin: *quintus* for the fifth voice, *sextus* for the sixth. The word "voices" should be taken literally: a madrigal was a piece of vocal chamber music intended for performance with one singer to a part. As always in the sixteenth century, however, music could be adapted to the forces available, and instruments often doubled the voices or took their place. The painting by Caravaggio in Figure 11.2 shows what must have been a common manner of performing madrigals: a young man sings one line while improvising a lute accompaniment from what he remembers of the other parts, using the bass part as a guide.

Voices

Figure 11.2: Michelangelo Merisi da Caravaggio (1571–1610), The Lute Player, *painted 1595–96 for Vincenzo Giustiniani, a Roman nobleman who wrote an important* Discourse on the Music of His Times *(1628). The young man appears to be singing while accompanying himself on the lute. The bass partbook is open to* Voi sapete, *from Arcadelt's first book of madrigals (1538).*

Social roles

Madrigals were written chiefly to be sung for the enjoyment of the singers themselves, typically in mixed groups of women and men at social gatherings, after meals, and at meetings of academies (societies organized to study and discuss literary, scientific, or artistic matters). The demand for madrigals was great: counting reprints and new editions, some two thousand collections were published between 1530 and 1600, and their popularity continued well into the seventeenth century. In addition to amateur performances, by 1570 some patrons had begun to employ professional singers to perform madrigals for audiences at court. Madrigals also appeared in plays and other theatrical productions.

EARLY MADRIGAL COMPOSERS

The most important early madrigalist was Philippe Verdelot (ca. 1480/85–? 1530), a Franco-Flemish composer active in Florence and Rome, where the madrigal originated in the 1520s. Verdelot's four-voice madrigals are mostly homophonic, with line endings marked by leisurely cadences, as in the frottola; his madrigals for five and six voices are more motetlike, with frequent imitation, varying voice-groupings, and overlapping parts at cadences.

Jacques Arcadelt

CD 3|54   CD 2|4

A style mixing homophony with occasional imitation is evident in the madrigals of Jacques Arcadelt (ca. 1507–1568), a Franco-Flemish composer who worked in Florence and Rome for almost three decades before returning to France in 1551. Arcadelt's *Il bianco e dolce cigno* (NAWM 50), published in his first book of madrigals in 1538, is the most famous of the early madrigals. The text wittily contrasts a swan's mournful death with the speaker's "death that in dying fills me fully with joy and desire," an allusion to sexual climax, known in the sixteenth century as "the little death." Referring to such deaths, the poem closes with the line, "with a thousand deaths a day I would be content." Arcadelt's setting, shown in Example 11.1, is simple and ingenious: a lilting descending line suggests contentment, while the "thousand deaths a day" ("mille mort' il di") are evoked through multiple imitative entrances, especially noticeable after the largely homophonic setting of the rest of the poem.

Such madrigals were meant to be sung from partbooks. Each singer saw only his or her own line, so that the singers only discovered which sections were homophonic or imitative as they sang through the piece. One can imagine the blushes and laughs as the mixed company of men and women gradually discerned the meaning of the words and Arcadelt's witty setting.

THE PETRARCHAN MOVEMENT

The rise of the madrigal was linked to currents in Italian poetry. Led by poet and scholar Cardinal Pietro Bembo (1470–1547), poets, readers, and musicians returned to the sonnets and canzoni of Petrarch (Francesco Petrarca) and the ideals embodied in his works. In editing Petrarch's *Canzoniere* in 1501, Bembo noted that Petrarch often revised the sound of the words without changing the imagery or meaning. Bembo identified two opposing qualities

Example 11.1: Arcadelt, Il bianco e dolce cigno

If when I die no other pain I feel, with a thousand deaths a day I would be content.

that Petrarch sought in his verses: *piacevolezza* (pleasingness) and *gravità* (severity). In the pleasing category Bembo included grace, sweetness, charm, smoothness, playfulness, and wit, while in the severe he grouped modesty, dignity, majesty, magnificence, and grandeur. Rhythm, distance of rhyme, number of syllables per line, patterns of accents, lengths of syllables, and the sound qualities of the vowels and consonants all contributed to making a verse either pleasing or severe. Composers became sensitive to these sonic values. Many of the early madrigalists set Petrarch's poetry; later composers preferred his imitators and other modern poets, almost all of whom worked in Petrarch's shadow.

How composers translated Bembo's theory into musical terms can be seen in settings of Petrarch by Adrian Willaert (see chapter 10) and in the writings of Willaert's student Gioseffo Zarlino (see Source Reading, p. 248). In the sonnet *Aspro core e selvaggio*, Petrarch expressed his beloved Laura's "harsh and savage heart" in a severe line, filled with double consonants and clipped, harsh sounds; he then described her "sweet, humble, angelic face" in a

Adrian Willaert

contrasting pleasing line made up of liquid, resonant, and sweet sounds. For the first line of his remarkable setting from the mid-1540s, shown in Example 11.2a, Willaert emphasized melodic motion in whole steps and major thirds along with harmonies featuring major thirds and sixths above the bass. These major intervals were then considered harsher and more severe than semitones and minor thirds or sixths, in part because their greater size rendered melodies less smooth and harmonies brighter or sharper. For the second line, in Example 11.2b, he used more semitones and minor thirds in his melodies and chose minor thirds and minor sixths for the harmony. These intervals gave smoother and thus more charming melodies, and minor thirds and sixths were regarded as sweet harmonic intervals.

What may be surprising for modern readers, accustomed to a later convention that links major keys and triads to happiness and minor ones with sadness, is that Willaert and Zarlino associated major thirds and sixths with harshness and bitterness, and minor intervals with sweetness as well as with

SOURCE READING

SUITING THE MUSIC TO THE WORDS

Le istitutioni armoniche (The Harmonic Foundations) by Gioseffo Zarlino (1517–1590) was the most respected treatise of the mid-sixteenth century. His advice to composers on how to express emotions corresponds almost exactly to the practice of his teacher, Adrian Willaert.

———— • ————

When a composer wishes to express harshness, bitterness, and similar things, he will do best to arrange the parts of the composition so that they proceed with movements that are without the semitone, such as those of the whole tone and ditone [major third]. He should allow the major sixth and major thirteenth, which by nature are somewhat harsh, to be heard above the lowest note of the concentus, and should use the suspension of the fourth or the eleventh above the lowest part, along with somewhat slow movements, among which the suspension of the seventh may also be used. But when a composer wishes to express effects of grief and sorrow, he should (observing the rules given) use movements which proceed through the semitone, the semiditone [minor third], and similar intervals, often using minor sixths or

minor thirteenths above the lowest note of the composition, these being by nature sweet and soft, especially when combined in the right way and with discretion and judgment.

It should be noted, however, that the cause of the various effects is attributed not only to the consonances named, used in the ways described above, but also the movements which the parts make in singing. These are two sorts, namely, natural and accidental. Natural movements are those made between the natural notes of a composition, where no sign or accidental note intervenes. Accidental movements are those made by means of the accidental notes, which are indicated by the signs ♯ and ♭. The natural movements have more virility than the accidental movements, which are somewhat languid. . . . For this reason the former movements can serve to express effects of harshness and bitterness, and the latter movements can serve for effects of grief and sorrow.

Gioseffo Zarlino, *Le istitutioni harmoniche* (1558), Book III, Chapter 31, trans. Vered Cohen in Zarlino, *On the Modes,* ed. Claude V. Palisca (New Haven: Yale University Press, 1983), 95.

Example 11.2: Willaert, Aspro core e selvaggio

a. *First line*

Harsh heart and savage, and a cruel will

b. *Second line*

In a sweet, humble, angelic face

grief. This may remind us that the emotional qualities of music are a result of association, convention, and tradition, not of acoustics alone, and that in trying to understand music of an earlier time or another culture we must seek to know how those who made the music understood it, not to impose our own codes of meaning.

MIDCENTURY MADRIGALISTS

By the mid-sixteenth century, most madrigals were for five voices, with frequent changes of texture. Composers freely alternated homophony and imitative or free polyphony.

Cipriano de Rore

The leading madrigal composer at midcentury was Cipriano de Rore (1516–1565), shown in Figure 11.3. Flemish by birth, Rore worked in Italy, chiefly in Ferrara and Parma, and succeeded his teacher Willaert as music director at St. Mark's in Venice. Rore's madrigals show his profound interest in humanism and in ideas from ancient Greek music.

Figure 11.3: Cipriano de Rore, in a portrait by Hans Muelich.

Da le belle contrade d'oriente (NAWM 51) was published posthumously in 1566, in Rore's last madrigal collection. Rore imbued every detail of the music with the rhythm, sense, and feeling of the poem, a sonnet modeled on Petrarch. Throughout, accented syllables receive longer notes than do unaccented syllables, sometimes creating syncopation, as at "dolce" and "lasci" in Example 11.3. Using duration for accentuation reflects the humanists' knowledge that ancient Greek and Latin poetry had accents of quantity (length of vowel or syllable) rather than stress accents as in modern languages. Seeking to revive the Greek tradition of *ethos* (see chapter 1), Rore and other composers of his time imitated the rhythm of ancient poetry through accents of quantity.

Texture, rests, inflection, and interval

In Example 11.3, a woman expresses sorrow that her lover is about to depart. The combination of voices changes every word or two, suggesting the breathlessness of grief through frequent rests. The composer chose intervals associated with sadness and reflected natural speech inflection through the melodic contours: rising semitones for "T'en vai" (You go); falling minor thirds, semitones, and minor seventh for "haime" (alas!); and falling minor thirds on "addio" (farewell). The phrase "sola mi lasci" (alone you leave me) is sung by a single high voice, symbolizing "alone" while evoking the woman's plaintive cry. This phrase also uses two successive semitones, A–B♭–B♮, to convey grief.

Chromaticism

Direct chromatic motion—from B♭ to B♮, or any semitone between notes with the same letter name but different signs—was not possible in the Guidonian system of solmization, in which successive notes had to be part of the same hexachord (see chapter 2). Indeed, we have not seen direct chromatic motion since ancient Greek music, where it was part of the chromatic tetrachord (see chapter 1 and NAWM 2). But mid-sixteenth-century theorists embraced chromaticism, citing the authority of the Greeks. Zarlino approved of chromatic motion, along with other uses of accidentals to move temporarily beyond the notes of the diatonic mode, as ways to express sorrow (see Source Reading, p. 248). Rore frequently introduces notes outside the mode, so much so that the passage in Example 11.3 includes all twelve notes of the chromatic scale in a very brief compass.

Vicentino

Rore was not alone in appreciating chromaticism. Composer and theorist Nicola Vicentino (1511–ca. 1576) proposed reviving the chromatic and enharmonic genera of Greek music in his treatise, *L'antica musica ridotta alla moderna prattica* (Ancient Music Adapted to Modern Practice, 1555), and used chromatic motion in his madrigals, sometimes even incorporating the

Example 11.3: Rore, Da le belle contrade d'oriente

sweet desire, you go, alas! Alone you leave me! Farewell! What will [become of me?]

Greek chromatic tetrachord (see chapter 1). By the end of the century, chromaticism was no longer a special effect reminiscent of Greek antiquity, but was part of the common musical language.

WOMEN AS COMPOSERS AND PERFORMERS

Madrigals were written for mixed groups of men and women to sing in social gatherings. Yet the poets and composers were mostly male, and most madrigal texts were written from the male perspective. Professional opportunities were closed to most women, who were expected to be proper, obedient wives, servants, or nuns. Despite these limitations, several women, including Vittoria Colonna, Veronica Franco, and Gaspara Stampa, achieved fame as poets in the sixteenth century.

Female composers were comparatively rare. The first woman whose music was published, and the first to regard herself as a professional composer, was

Maddalena Casulana

Maddalena Casulana (ca. 1544–ca. 1590s). In the dedication to her *First Book of Madrigals* (1568), Casulana wrote that she was publishing them not only to honor her dedicatee, the duchess of Bracciano, but also "to expose to the world, insofar as it is given me to do so in the profession of music, the vain error of men who esteem themselves such masters of high intellectual gifts that they think women cannot share them too." Her madrigals show inventive use of all the typical devices of midcentury madrigals, including text depiction, chromaticism, surprising harmonies, and dramatic contrasts of texture.

Women's vocal ensembles   Women could more easily win renown as singers, and many did. Some were daughters and wives of the nobility, who sang in private concerts for invited audiences of their social peers, while others pursued professional careers. For example, at Ferrara in the 1570s, sisters Lucrezia and Isabella Bendidio, noblewomen by birth and marriage, won plaudits for their singing in musical evenings at court. In 1580, Duke Alfonso d'Este established the *concerto delle donne* (women's ensemble), a group of trained singers (Laura Peverara, Anna Guarini, and Livia d'Arco). Their performances at court, alone or with male singers, attracted so much attention and praise that the Gonzagas of Mantua and the Medici of Florence formed ensembles to rival that of Ferrara. Descriptions of performances by these groups (see Source Reading) make clear that the professional singers often introduced vocal ornaments and dramatized the words with appropriate gestures. Here the madrigal has been transformed, from social music for the enjoyment of the singers themselves to concert music for the pleasure of an audience.

LATER MADRIGALISTS

Important composers of madrigals in the later sixteenth century include several northerners. Orlando di Lasso and Philippe de Monte (1521–1603) both began writing madrigals while in Italy early in their careers and continued doing so during their long tenures at northern courts, Lasso in Bavaria and Monte under the Hapsburg emperors in Vienna and Prague. Lasso's madrigal collections were published in Antwerp, Nuremberg, and Munich as well as in Rome and Venice, testifying to a fashion for Italian madrigals even in the north. Giaches de Wert (1535–1596), born near Antwerp, spent nearly his entire life in Italy. Building on Rore's approach, Wert developed a dramatic style full of bold leaps, recitative-like declamation, and extravagant contrasts.

Luca Marenzio

CD 3|59

But the leading madrigalists were native Italians. Chief among them was Luca Marenzio (1553–1599), who depicted contrasting feelings and visual details with the utmost artistry. One of his most celebrated madrigals is *Solo e pensoso* (NAWM 52), based on a Petrarch sonnet and published in 1599 in Marenzio's last book of madrigals. The opening image, of the pensive poet walking alone with deliberate and slow steps, is unforgettably portrayed in the top voice by a slow chromatic ascent of over an octave, moving one half-step per measure. Later "flee" and "escape" are depicted with quickly moving figures in close imitation.

Such striking musical images, evoking the text almost literally, were so typical of madrigals that they later became known as **madrigalisms.** Although

SOURCE READING

WOMEN'S VOCAL ENSEMBLES

Vincenzo Giustiniani (1564–1637) was a well-to-do musical amateur who described contemporary musical life in Discorso sopra la musica de' suoi tempi *(Discourse on the Music of His Times, 1628). His description of the women's vocal ensembles at Ferrara and Mantua in the 1570s reveals their manner of performance and some of the reasons they were so greatly esteemed.*

———•———

These dukes [of Ferrara and Mantua] took the greatest delight in such music, especially in gathering many important gentlewomen and gentlemen to play and sing excellently. So great was their delight that they lingered sometimes for whole days in some little chambers they had ornately outfitted with pictures and tapestries for this sole purpose. There was a great rivalry between the women of Mantua and Ferrara, a competition not only in the timbre and disposition of their voices but also in ornamentation with exquisite runs joined opportunely and not excessively.... There was competition even more in moderating or enlarging the voice, loud or soft, attenuating it or fattening it as was called for, now drawing it out, now breaking it off with the accompaniment of a sweet interrupted sigh, now giving out long runs, distinct and well followed, now turns, now leaps, now long trills, now short ones, now sweet runs sung quietly, to which sometimes one suddenly heard an echo respond; and more still in the participation of the face, and of the looks and gestures that accompanied appropriately the music and conceits of the poetry; and above all, without any indecorous motions of body, mouth, or hands that might have diminished the effect of their songs, in enunciating the words so well that each one could be heard down to the last syllable and was not interrupted or overwhelmed by the runs and other ornaments. And many other particular artifices could be observed in these singers and recorded by one more expert than I. And in such noble situations these excellent singers strove with all their might to win grace from their masters, the princes, and also fame for them—wherein lay their usefulness.

Vincenzo Giustiniani, *Discorso sopra la musica de' suoi tempi* (Discourse on the Music of His Times, 1628), ed. in Angelo Solerti, *Le origini del melodramma* (Turin: Fratelli Bocca, 1903), 107–8. Trans. Gary Tomlinson, in SR 54 (3:19), pp. 353–54.

disparaged by those who preferred a naturalistic expression of feelings to the depiction of individual words, such word-painting at its best can be both clever and deeply meaningful, and it has reappeared in many kinds of vocal music over the past four centuries.

One of the most colorful figures in music history was Carlo Gesualdo, prince of Venosa (ca. 1561–1613). He is unusual among composers because he was an aristocrat, and it was rare for nobility to compose or to seek publication for their music. He was also a murderer: when he discovered his wife in bed with her lover, he killed them both. Gesualdo survived the scandal to marry Leonora d'Este, niece of Duke Alfonso II of Ferrara, in 1593.

Carlo Gesualdo

In his madrigals, Gesualdo dramatized and intensified the poetry through sharp contrasts between diatonic and chromatic passages, dissonance and consonance, chordal and imitative textures, and slow-moving and active

CD 3|65   CD 2|9

rhythms. Example 11.4 shows a passage from *"Io parto" e non più dissi* (NAWM 53), published in 1611 in his last book of madrigals, that exhibits all these types of contrast. Slow, chromatic, mostly chordal music touched with dissonance portrays the laments of the woman whose lover is about to depart. When her plaintive cries arouse him again, his return to life ("vivo son") after his "little death" is shown by a turn to faster, diatonic, imitative figures.

Example 11.4: Gesualdo, *"Io parto" e non più dissi*

["Ah, may I never cease to pine away] in sad laments." Dead I was, now I am alive,
   [for my spent spirits returned to life at the sound of such pitiable accents.]

VILLANELLA, CANZONETTA, AND BALLETTO

Alongside the relatively serious madrigal, Italian composers also cultivated lighter kinds of song. The **villanella**, a lively strophic piece in homophonic style, usually for three voices, first appeared in the 1540s and flourished especially in Naples. Composers often deliberately used parallel fifths and other harmonic crudities to suggest a rustic character and sometimes mocked the correct, more sophisticated madrigals.

Toward the end of the sixteenth century, two other light genres gained prominence: the **canzonetta** (little song) and **_balletto_** (little dance). They were written in a vivacious, homophonic style, with simple harmonies and evenly phrased sections that were often repeated. Balletti, as the name suggests, were intended for dancing as well as singing or playing. They are identifiable by their dancelike rhythms and "fa-la-la" refrains. The leading composer of canzonette and balletti was Giacomo Gastoldi (ca. 1544–1609). Both genres were imitated by German and English composers.

THE LEGACY OF THE MADRIGAL

These lighter genres continued the tradition of social singing for the pleasure of the singers themselves. While the madrigal also served this role, its purposes widened over the century to include madrigals for performance in private concerts or theatrical productions. Such venues encouraged increasing virtuosity and dramatization.

Yet a continuous thread was the ideal of conveying the text well: shaping melody and rhythm to follow the inflections and rhythms of natural speech, reflecting the poetic imagery through striking musical figures, and suiting all musical elements to the emotions in the text. The techniques developed by madrigal composers led directly to opera and other seventeenth-century forms of dramatic music. We saw in chapters 9 and 10 that sixteenth-century motets often express the emotions and illustrate the images of their texts, but the madrigal was the preeminent laboratory for such procedures. Most of our assumptions about what music should do when setting poetry were established in and for the sixteenth-century madrigal.

This emphasis on matching every aspect of the text profoundly differentiates the madrigal from earlier secular songs, such as the chansons of the fourteenth and fifteenth centuries, and it reflects the deepening impact of humanism on musical culture over the course of the Renaissance. That we still find madrigals so engaging today suggests the continuing importance of that humanist influence for our own culture and music.

FRANCE

During the long reign of Francis I (1515–47), composers in France developed a new type of chanson that was a light, fast, strongly rhythmic song for four voices. Favored subjects were pleasant, amorous situations, though more serious texts were occasionally chosen. The text is set syllabically with many repeated notes, usually in duple meter. The principal melody is in the highest voice and the musical texture largely homophonic, with occasional short points of imitation. Verse forms vary, but most pieces are divided into short sections that repeat in an easily grasped pattern, such as aabc or abca. The strophic, repetitive forms did not allow word-painting, and composers focused on tuneful melodies and pleasing rhythms rather than profound expression of the text.

Such pieces were satisfying to sing and ideally suited for amateurs. Between 1528 and 1552, Pierre Attaingnant (ca. 1494–ca. 1552), the first French music printer, brought out more than fifty collections of such chansons, about 1,500 pieces altogether, and other publishers soon followed. The great number of chansons of this type printed in the sixteenth century, including hundreds of arrangements for voice and lute or for lute alone, testifies to their popularity.

Claudin de Sermisy

CD 3|68   CD 2|12

The two principal composers in Attaingnant's early chanson collections were Claudin de Sermisy (ca. 1490–1562) and Clément Janequin (ca. 1485–ca. 1560). Sermisy's *Tant que vivray* (NAWM 54), shown in Example 11.5, is typical. The text is a lighthearted and optimistic love poem, far afield from the old tradition of courtly love. As in a frottola or villancico, the melody is in the top voice, and the harmony consists of thirds and fifths with only an occasional sixth above the bass. The voices mostly declaim the text together. One result is that accented dissonances appear where earlier chansons would have featured a syncopated suspension before a cadence, as on the third quarter note of measure 3 in the top voice. The opening long-short-short rhythm is common. The end of each line of text is marked by a relatively long note or repeated notes, emphasizing the form of the poetry.

Example 11.5: Sermisy, Tant que vivray

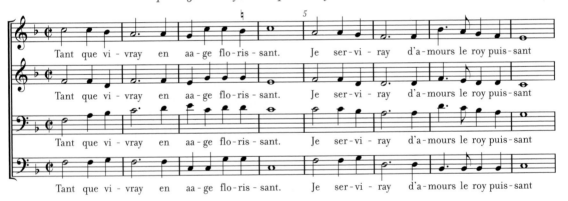

As long as I am able-bodied, I shall serve the potent king of love

Several of Sermisy's chansons were so popular that they were reprinted for decades and adapted into many new forms, from dance melodies to psalm tunes. Some even showed up in paintings, as in Figure 11.4.

Clément Janequin

Janequin wrote many kinds of chanson, including lyrical love songs, narrative songs, and bawdy songs. He was particularly celebrated for his descriptive chansons, which feature imitations of bird calls, hunting calls, street cries, and sounds of war. His most famous chanson was *La guerre* (War), supposedly about the battle of Marignan (1515). *Le chant des oiseaux* (The Song of the Birds) is filled with vocal warbles and chirping.

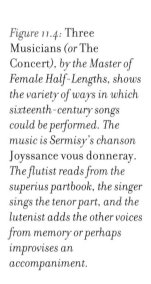

Figure 11.4: Three Musicians *(or* The Concert*), by the Master of Female Half-Lengths, shows the variety of ways in which sixteenth-century songs could be performed. The music is Sermisy's chanson* Joyssance vous donneray. *The flutist reads from the superius partbook, the singer sings the tenor part, and the lutenist adds the other voices from memory or perhaps improvises an accompaniment.*

THE LATER FRANCO-FLEMISH CHANSON

Alongside the new style of homophonic chanson, northern composers such as Gombert, Clemens, and Sweelinck (mentioned in chapter 10) maintained the older Franco-Flemish tradition of the contrapuntal chanson. Traditions mix in the chansons of Orlando di Lasso, reflecting his cosmopolitan background. While some are in the new homophonic style, others show the influence of the Italian madrigal or grow from the Franco-Flemish tradition, using a tight polyphonic texture with close imitations and sudden changes of pace in tense but often humorous settings.

MUSIQUE MESURÉE

Just as Rore and other Italian composers sought to imitate the rhythm of Greek poetry, so did the French poets and composers who cultivated **musique mesurée** (measured music). Members of the Académie de Poésie et de Musique (Academy of Poetry and Music), formed in 1570, sought to unite poetry and music as in ancient times and revive the ethical effects of ancient Greek music. By imposing their music on the general public, they hoped to improve society, an effort reminiscent of Plato.

The poet Jean-Antoine de Baïf wrote strophic French verses in ancient Greek and Latin meters, which he called *vers mesurés à l'antique* (measured verse in ancient style). Since French lacked the long and short vowels of ancient languages, Baïf assigned French vowels durations, roughly equating stress accent with length. In setting this poetry, composers such as Claude Le Jeune, the leading exponent of this genre, gave each long syllable a long note and each short syllable a note half as long. The variety of verse patterns produces a corresponding variety of musical rhythms in which duple and triple groupings alternate freely, as in Le Jeune's *Revecy venir du printans*

(NAWM 55).

Musique mesurée was too artificial to become popular. But the experiment introduced irregular rhythms into the **air de cour** (court air), a genre of song for voice and accompaniment, which became the dominant type of French vocal music after about 1580.

GERMANY

German secular song in the sixteenth century exhibits a fascinating mixture of styles. The **Meistersinger** (master singers) preserved a tradition of unaccompanied solo song, derived from the Minnesinger (see chapter 4), that became increasingly anachronistic as styles changed around them. The Meistersinger were urban merchants and artisans who pursued music as an avocation and formed guilds for composing songs according to strict rules and singing them in public concerts and competitions. The movement began in the fourteenth century, peaked in the sixteenth, and endured until the last guild dissolved in the nineteenth century. Most poems were written to fit an existing *Ton* (pl. *Töne*), a metric and rhyme scheme with its own melody. All *Töne* use bar form, and many were taken from Minnelieder. The best-known Meistersinger was Hans Sachs (1494–1576), a shoemaker in Nuremberg who composed thousands of poems and thirteen new *Töne*.

The German polyphonic Lied continued, with a popular song or leading melody in the tenor or cantus and free counterpoint in the other voices, as in Isaac's *Innsbruck, ich muss dich lassen* (NAWM 38; see chapter 9). Many collections of German Lieder were published in the first half of the century, chiefly at Nuremberg, a leading center of German culture at this time. After 1550, German taste veered toward Italian madrigals and villanelle, and the Lied declined in importance or took on Italianate characteristics. Once again a leading figure is Lasso, who composed seven collections of German Lieder. Most are madrigals in style if not in language, with close attention to the accentuation and expression of the text, alternating homophonic and imitative passages, and all parts equally important in the interplay of motives.

ENGLAND

England had its own native tradition of secular music in the sixteenth century. Both Henry VIII and his second wife, Anne Boleyn, were musicians and composers. Manuscripts from his reign (1509–47) contain a variety of songs and instrumental pieces in three and four parts that reflect many facets of court life.

From this environment, around midcentury, emerged the **consort song**, a distinctively English genre for voice accompanied by a consort of viols (a string ensemble; see chapter 12). The master of the consort song was William Byrd (see chapter 10), who raised the technical level of the medium with skillful imitative counterpoint in his collection *Psalmes, Sonets and Songs* (1588). Although composers wrote consort songs well into the seventeenth century, the genre has been overshadowed in historical memory by the English madrigal and lute song.

Consort song

ENGLISH MADRIGALS

The late sixteenth century brought a fashion for Italian culture, art, and music to England. The products of this influence most familiar today are Shakespeare's plays set in Italy, including *The Taming of the Shrew* (1593), *The Two Gentlemen of Verona* (1594), *Romeo and Juliet* (1594), *The Merchant of Venice* (1596), and *Othello* (1604). But everything from manners to clothing was affected, and music was in the vanguard.

Italian madrigals began to circulate in England in the 1560s and were sung in the homes of aristocrats and the middle class alike. In 1588, Nicholas Yonge published *Musica transalpina*, a collection of Italian madrigals translated into English. According to Yonge's preface, the anthology encompassed the repertory sung by gentlemen and merchants who met daily at his home. This and similar collections created a vogue for singing madrigals, which spurred native composers to cash in on the trend by writing their own. Leading English madrigalists include Thomas Morley (1557/8–1602), Thomas Weelkes (ca. 1575–1623), and John Wilbye (1574–1638).

Morley was the earliest and most prolific of the three. Alongside his madrigals, he wrote **canzonets** and **balletts,** borrowing the Italian genres of canzonetta and balletto. He modeled his ballett *My bonny lass she smileth* (NAWM 56) on a Gastoldi balletto, borrowing aspects of its text, rhythm, melody, and harmony. Like most balletts, it is strophic, and each verse is in two repeated sections (AABB). Each section begins with a homophonic setting of two lines of verse, with the main melody in the cantus, and concludes with a "fa-la-la" refrain that is more contrapuntal, with some imitation between the voices. The dancelike rhythms, varied textures, and occasional contrapuntal challenges made such works particularly satisfying to sing.

Thomas Morley

CD 3|79   CD 2|15

Morley described the madrigal, canzonet, ballett, and other vocal and instrumental genres in *A Plaine and Easie Introduction to Practicall Musicke* (1597). Unlike most earlier treatises, this manual was aimed at the broad public interested in music, its title inviting even the most unlearned amateur to pick it up and learn about music. The title page, shown in Figure 11.5, lists the topics to be covered: singing from notation, adding a descant to a given voice, and composing in three or more voices.

In 1601, Morley published a collection of twenty-five madrigals by twenty-three composers, modeled after a similar Italian anthology called *Il trionfo di Dori* (1592). He called his collection *The Triumphes of Oriana* in honor of

The Triumphs of Oriana

Figure 11.5: Title page of Thomas Morley's book A Plaine and Easie Introduction to Practicall Musicke *(1597). Music, in the lower right corner, is linked to the other members of the medieval quadrivium: astronomy (above music), geometry, and arithmetic (see chapter 2). As announced in the center of the page, the treatise is in three parts, covering three skills: singing from notation, improvising or composing a descant to a given voice, and composing in three or more voices.*

Queen Elizabeth. Each madrigal in Morley's collection ends with the words "Long live fair Oriana," a name often applied to Elizabeth.

Thomas Weelkes

CD 3|82   CD 2|18

One of the most famous madrigals in the collection is Weelkes's *As Vesta was* (NAWM 57), on his own poem. Elizabeth, who never married, was called the Virgin Queen, and the poem invokes both Diana, Greek goddess of virginity, and Vesta, Roman goddess of fire, hearth, and home and unmarried sister of Jupiter. Since word-painting was a strong tradition in the madrigal, Weelkes as poet provided numerous opportunities for musical depiction, and Weelkes the composer capitalized on all of them: rising scales for "ascending," falling scales for "descending" and "running down," a melodic peak for "hill," and one, two, three, or all voices for "alone," "two by two," "three by three," and "together" respectively. Most striking, and less conventional, is Weelkes's treatment of the final phrase. "Long live fair Oriana!" is set to a motive that enters almost fifty times, in all voices and in all transpositions possible in the mode, suggesting the acclamation of a vast people. The treatment is both clever and meaningful, exemplifying the mixture of wit, wordplay, sentiment, contrapuntal skill, melodiousness, and sheer pleasure for the singers that characterizes the best madrigals, English or Italian.

Like their Italian counterparts, English madrigals, balletts, and canzonets were written primarily for unaccompanied solo voices, though many printed collections indicate that the music is "apt for voices and viols," presumably in any available combination. This flexibility made these publications ideal for informal gatherings, and the music was perfectly suited for amateurs. Ability to read a vocal or instrumental part in such pieces was expected of educated persons in Elizabethan England, as it was on the Continent.

Performance

LUTE SONGS

In the early 1600s, the solo song with accompaniment became more prominent, especially the **lute song** (or **air**). The leading composers of lute songs were John Dowland (pronounced "Doe-land," 1563–1626) and Thomas Campion (1567–1620). The lute song was a more personal genre than the madrigal, with none of the latter's aura of social play. The music generally reflects the overall mood, with much less word-painting than is typical of madrigals. The lute accompaniments, always subordinate to the vocal melody, have some rhythmic and melodic independence.

Lute songs appeared in books rather than in partbooks, as madrigals did. The voice and lute parts are vertically aligned, allowing singers to accompany themselves. In some collections the songs are also printed in an alternative version, shown in Figure 11.6, with the lute accompaniment written out for three voices so arranged on the page that performers sitting around a table could all read their parts from the same book. The lute part is in **tablature**, a

Alternate formats

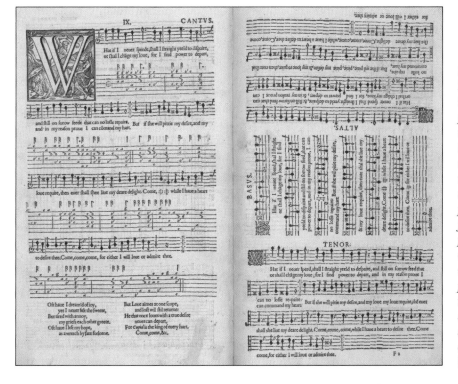

Figure 11.6: John Dowland's song What if I never speede, *as printed in his* Third and Last Book of Songs or Aires *(London, 1603). The song may be performed as a solo with lute accompaniment, reading from the left-hand page, or as a four-part arrangement, with or without lute accompaniment. The altus, tenor, and bassus are so arranged that singers around a table can read from a single book.*

notational system that tells the player which strings to pluck and where to place the fingers on the strings, rather than indicating what pitches will result.

CD 4|1   CD 2|23

The Dowland lute song best known to his contemporaries, *Flow, my tears* (NAWM 58) from his *Second Booke of Ayres* (1600), spawned a whole series of variations and arrangements (see NAWM 61). It is in the form of a pavane, a sixteenth-century Italian processional dance, with three repeated strains. The performer sings the first two stanzas of the poem to the first strain, the next two to the second, and the final stanza twice to the third strain, resulting in the musical pattern aabbCC. The repeats minimize the opportunity for depiction or expression of individual words and phrases, but Dowland's music matches the dark mood of the poetry.

The fashion in England for madrigals and lute songs was intense but relatively brief, lasting only into the 1620s. The lute song's focus on a single singer with accompaniment links it to the growing interest in solo song in the early seventeenth century, which we will explore in chapter 14.

THE MADRIGAL AND ITS IMPACT

The Italian madrigal and its offshoots, including later French chansons, German Lieder, and English madrigals, were laboratories for exploring the declamation, expression, and depiction of words. In this respect they reflect the growing influence of humanism on music over the course of the Renaissance. The importance of the text and its dramatic expression through music, especially in Italian madrigals, led directly into opera around 1600. More broadly, madrigals introduced the idea of music as a dramatic art, and over the next two centuries this concept broadened to include instrumental as well as vocal music. These developments led to the dominance of Italian music throughout the Baroque era, so that the madrigal truly made Italy the leader in European music for the first time.

The code of expression worked out by Willaert's generation is different in many respects from later codes, but is the main taproot for them. More important than the specific correspondence of certain intervals to certain moods or characters that Zarlino outlines is the broader notion that melody, harmony, rhythm, and pacing all directly communicate feelings, and that the emotions they suggest must correspond to those of the text being set. The devices that composers of operas, ballets, tone poems, and film scores have used to suggest a character's mood or manipulate the feelings of the audience have long histories, reaching back in concept and often in specific detail to the procedures that sixteenth-century composers used in their madrigals.

Madrigals themselves have varied in popularity, along with other sixteenth-century secular songs. The vogue for social singing declined after 1600 but was maintained to some extent in England. Visiting London in the 1790s, Franz Joseph Haydn heard English madrigals and wrote some of his own. The growth of amateur choral societies in the nineteenth century helped inaugurate a revival of madrigal singing, and new editions popularized English madrigals in the twentieth century, especially in schools. For the millions who have sung in school choirs or madrigal groups in Britain or North America, madrigals are often the oldest music they have performed.

From the English repertory, the revival spread to encompass Italian madrigals and French chansons. German and Spanish songs are heard less often. Of the thousands of secular songs published in sixteenth-century part-books, many have not been issued in modern editions and most have never been recorded. Madrigals and other sixteenth-century songs still serve their function admirably when amateurs sing through music together for their own pleasure, but such gatherings are rarer than they once were, and singers today have numerous more recent repertories to draw on. Like the popular songs of later times, the secular songs of the sixteenth century are known today chiefly through a few dozen hits, which are sung and reprinted repeatedly. For the avid fan, there are thousands more to explore.

Chapter 12

The Rise of Instrumental Music

Our story so far has focused on vocal music, since the great majority of pieces that survive from before the sixteenth century are for voices, alone or with instruments. Dances, fanfares, and other instrumental pieces were of course played throughout the Middle Ages and early Renaissance. But since performers played from memory or improvised, little of this music survived in notation. Instrumental music was functional: people welcomed it to accompany dancing or dining, but seldom listened to or played it for its own sake, and thus it was valued less highly than vocal music.

This limitation began to lift after 1450 and especially during the sixteenth century, when churches, patrons, and musical amateurs increasingly cultivated instrumental music. The growth in music for instruments is partly an illusion: it simply means more was being written down. But that change in itself shows that music without voices was now more often deemed worthy of preservation and dissemination in writing. It also suggests that instrumental performers were more often musically literate than in earlier eras.

The rise of instrumental music during the Renaissance is evident in the cultivation of new instruments, new roles for instrumental music, new genres, and new styles, as well as in the growing supply of written music for instruments alone, including many published collections. As in earlier times, musicians performed, improvised, and composed dance music, instrumental versions of vocal works, and settings of existing melodies. Yet they also developed important new genres that were not dependent on dancing or singing, including **variations**, **prelude**, **fantasia**, **toccata**, **ricercare**, **canzona**, and **sonata**. For the first time, composers were creating instrumental music that was as interesting and challenging as vocal music. This development set the stage for later periods, when instrumental music became increasingly important.

INSTRUMENTS

The appearance of books that describe instruments and give instructions *Books on* for playing them testifies to the growing regard for instrumental music in the *instruments* sixteenth century. Writers addressed the practicing musician, whether professional or amateur, so they wrote in the vernacular instead of in Latin. From these books we learn about pitch, tuning, and the art of embellishing a melodic line, as well as about instruments themselves.

The first such book was Sebastian Virdung's *Musica getutscht* (Music Explained, 1511). Others followed in increasing numbers. One of the richest, the second volume of *Syntagma musicum* (Systematic Treatise of Music, 1618) by Michael Praetorius, contains descriptions of instruments then in use, illustrated by woodcuts like the one in Figure 12.1.

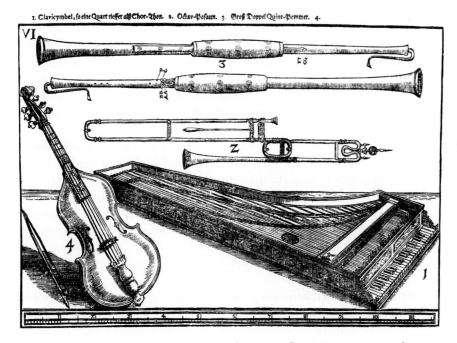

Figure 12.1: Instruments illustrated in Michael Praetorius, Syntagma musicum, *vol. 2 (Wolfenbüttel, 1618–20): (1) harpsichord, (2) sackbut or trombone, (3) tenor shawm, (4) bass viola da gamba.*

Figure 12.2: Hans Burgkmair, Maximilian I Surrounded by His Court Musicians and Instruments, *woodcut for the emperor's memoirs* Weisskunig *(1514–16). Clockwise from top left, the instruments include a cornett being played; on the table, viol, clavichord (or virginal), transverse flute, crumhorn (the curved wind instrument), three recorders, and another cornett (extending off the table); in the lower right, tromba marina (a bowed string instrument), sackbut, kettledrum, tabor (drum) with drumsticks, and lute (in its case); harp; and positive organ, being played while an assistant works the bellows.*

Renaissance musicians played an astonishing variety of instruments, some of which are pictured in Figures 12.1 and 12.2. Unlike modern performers, who typically specialize in a single instrument or two or three closely related ones, professional musicians were expected to be adept at several. Renaissance musicians maintained the distinction between *haut* (high) and *bas* (low) instruments, or relatively loud and soft instruments, that began in the Middle Ages (see chapter 6).

Instrumental families and consorts

Wind and string instruments were often built in sets or **instrumental families**, so that one uniform timbre was available throughout the entire range from soprano to bass. An instrumental ensemble, consisting of four to seven instruments, became known in England as a **consort**. Sixteenth-century musicians and listeners enjoyed the sound of a homogeneous ensemble, in which all the instruments were from the same family, but mixed ensembles (called *broken consorts*) were also common. The choice was up to the players; until the very end of the sixteenth century, composers did not specify instruments.

Wind and percussion

Most of the principal Renaissance wind instruments were already in use by the Middle Ages (see chapters 4 and 6): recorders, transverse flute, shawms, cornetts, and trumpets. Newly prominent in the Renaissance were the **sackbut,** the early form of the trombone, and the **crumhorn,** whose double reed is enclosed in a cap so the player's lips do not touch it, producing a sound like a soft bagpipe (see Figures 12.1 and 12.2). Percussion instruments also continued from the Middle Ages, often with new refinements, including the tabor, side drum, kettledrums, cymbals, triangles, and bells. Parts were never written for percussion, but performers improvised or played rhythmic patterns from memory.

The most popular household instrument in the sixteenth century was the **lute**, shown in Figure 12.3 (see also Figures 11.2 and 11.4). Lutes had been known in Europe for more than five hundred years, introduced by the Arabs into Spain. The standard lute was pear-shaped, with a rounded back, flat fingerboard, and pegbox (where the strings attached to tuning pegs) turned back at a right angle. It had one single and five double strings, usually tuned G–c–f–a–d'–g', which were plucked with the fingers. Frets, made of strips of leather wound around the neck, marked where the player stopped the string with the fingers of the left hand to raise the pitch one or more semitones. A skilled player could produce a great variety of effects, from melodies, runs, and ornaments of all kinds to chords and counterpoint. Lutenists performed solos, accompanied singing, and played in ensembles. Closely related to the lute was the Spanish **vihuela,** which had a flat back and guitar-shaped body.

Plucked strings

Figure 12.3: Young Girl Playing the Lute *(ca. 1550), by an unknown Flemish artist. The music is written in tablature, a notation that shows which strings to play and where to put the fingers on the frets to produce the right pitches.*

Figure 12.4: Consort of viols as shown on the title page of Silvestro Ganassi's manual on viol playing, Regola rubertina (1542).

Bowed strings   The **viol** or **viola da gamba** (leg viol) was developed in Spain in the mid-fifteenth century, was taken up by Italian musicians a generation later, and quickly became the leading bowed string instrument of the sixteenth century. Figure 12.4, from the title page of a manual on playing the viol, shows a consort of three viols in the three most common sizes, a bass in the middle, a tenor to our right, and a treble to the left. As seen in the illustration, the player held the instrument on or between the legs and bowed underhand. The tone, played without vibrato, was more delicate and less penetrating than a modern violin or cello. Like lutes, viols had frets, and the six strings were tuned a fourth apart with a major third in the middle; for instance, the tenor was tuned G–c–f–a–d'–g', the standard lute tuning.

A distant cousin to the viol was the **violin,** a bowed, fretless instrument tuned in fifths rather than fourths and apparently descended from the medieval fiddle. The violin first appeared in the early sixteenth century as a three-string instrument used primarily to accompany dancing. During the seventeenth century, the violin and its relatives the viola and violoncello gradually displaced the viols, in part because of their brighter tone.

The organ changed over time as organ-builders added stops (ranks of pipes) with distinctive timbres, many resembling wind instruments. By about 1500, the large church organ was essentially like the instrument we know today, although the pedal keyboard was employed only in Germany and the Low Countries and was adopted much later in other countries. The medieval portative organ had gone out of fashion, but small positive organs like the one in Figure 12.2 were common.

Keyboard   There were two main types of keyboard string instrument, the **clavichord** and the **harpsichord.** The clavichord (see Figure 12.2) was a solo instrument suitable for small rooms, while the harpsichord (see Figure 12.1) served both solo and ensemble playing in spaces of moderate size. In a clavichord, pressing a key raises a brass blade that strikes a string, making it vibrate, and remains in contact with it, sustaining the tone until the player releases the key. The position of the blade on the string determines the sounding length of the string and thus its pitch. The tone is very soft, but within limits the performer can control the volume and even effect a vibrato by changing pressure on the key. In instruments of the harpsichord family, the key moves a quill that plucks the string. Harpsichords came in different shapes and sizes and had various names, including **virginal** in England, **clavecin** in France, and *clavicembalo* in Italy. The tone was more robust than a clavichord's but could not be shaded by varying the pressure on the key. A builder could achieve different timbres and degrees of loudness by adding a second keyboard or a stop mechanism that allowed coupling with another string, usually tuned an octave higher.

Each of the instruments described here has its own qualities particularly suited to the music performed on it. Renaissance instruments are not imperfect versions of modern ones but are ideal vehicles for the music of that time. This does not mean we should not play lute music on guitar or Renaissance ensemble music on modern brass instruments, for that would deprive performers of much glorious music—and even at the time, musicians freely substituted one instrument for another. But knowing something of the sound, playing techniques, and other properties of the instruments for which a piece

Renaissance instruments and music

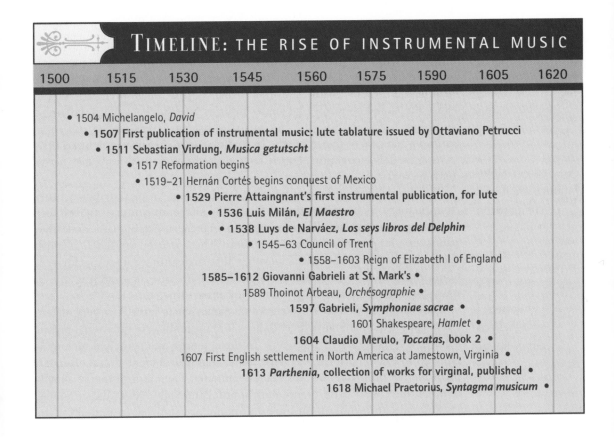

TIMELINE: THE RISE OF INSTRUMENTAL MUSIC

| 1500 | 1515 | 1530 | 1545 | 1560 | 1575 | 1590 | 1605 | 1620 |

- 1504 Michelangelo, *David*
- 1507 **First publication of instrumental music: lute tablature issued by Ottaviano Petrucci**
- 1511 Sebastian Virdung, ***Musica getutscht***
- 1517 Reformation begins
- 1519–21 Hernán Cortés begins conquest of Mexico
- **1529 Pierre Attaingnant's first instrumental publication, for lute**
- 1536 Luis Milán, *El Maestro*
- 1538 Luys de Narváez, *Los seys libros del Delphin*
- 1545–63 Council of Trent
- 1558–1603 Reign of Elizabeth I of England
- 1585–1612 Giovanni Gabrieli at St. Mark's
- 1589 Thoinot Arbeau, *Orchésographie*
- **1597 Gabrieli, *Symphoniae sacrae***
- 1601 Shakespeare, *Hamlet*
- **1604 Claudio Merulo, *Toccatas*, book 2**
- 1607 First English settlement in North America at Jamestown, Virginia
- **1613 *Parthenia*, collection of works for virginal, published**
- **1618 Michael Praetorius, *Syntagma musicum***

of music was intended can shed light on the special qualities of the music itself and how to perform it.

TYPES OF INSTRUMENTAL MUSIC

Instrumental music served many roles in the Renaissance: as accompaniment to dancing, as part of a public ceremony or religious ritual, as background to other activities, or as music for the entertainment of a small group of listeners or of the players themselves. Just as music printing created a market for music for amateur singers, it also fostered the composition and dissemination of instrumental music for amateurs to perform. Professionals also used printed music in their work, from playing for dances to playing in church.

We can divide Renaissance instrumental music into five broad categories:

- dance music
- arrangements of vocal music
- settings of existing melodies
- variations
- abstract instrumental works.

DANCE MUSIC

Social dancing was widespread and highly valued in the Renaissance, and people of breeding were expected to be expert dancers. Dancing was a way to meet people, interact with them in a formal setting, judge their fitness and social skills, and show off one's own abilities (see sidebar). With dancing a central part of social life, it is no surprise that musicians played and composed a great deal of dance music. In writing dance pieces, which owed little to vocal models, sixteenth-century composers began to develop a distinctive instrumental style.

Improvisation and composition

Performers frequently improvised dance music or played dance tunes from memory, as in earlier times. But in the sixteenth century, many dance pieces were printed in collections issued by Petrucci, Attaingnant, and other publishers, for ensemble, lute, or keyboard. These written works tell us much about improvisatory practice, showing that sixteenth-century performers often improvised by ornamenting a given melodic line or by adding one or more contrapuntal parts to a given melody or bass line.

Functional and stylized dance music

These published dances also show that dance music served two very different purposes in the Renaissance. Dances for ensemble were functional music, suitable for accompanying dancers. In these pieces, the principal melody is typically in the uppermost part, sometimes highly ornamented, but often left plain for the performer to add embellishments. The other parts are mostly homophonic, with little or no contrapuntal interplay. Most dance pieces for solo lute or keyboard, on the other hand, are stylized, intended for the

MUSIC IN CONTEXT

SOCIAL DANCE

Dancing is essential in a well-ordered society, because it allows males and females to mingle and observe one another. How else does a lady decide whom to marry? Through dancing, she can tell whether someone is shapely and fit or unattractive and lame, whether he is in good health or has unpleasant breath, and whether he is graceful and attentive or clumsy and awkward.

So writes the Renaissance dancing master Thoinot Arbeau (pen name for the astronomer Jehan Tabourot) in his *Orchésographie* (1589), the best-known dance treatise of the Renaissance. He offers these views to a young man who has just returned home from a big city where he devoted many years to studying law but where, as he confesses with some regret, he did not make time to learn how to dance. Belatedly, the young man has realized that, far from being a frivolous pastime, dancing is a pleasant and profitable activity, one that confers and preserves health provided it is practiced in moderation at suitable times and in appropriate places. It is especially recommended for those who lead sedentary lives, such as students intent upon their books and young women who spend long hours at knitting and needlework.

Most dances of the Renaissance were performed by couples who arranged themselves in rows or circles. Some, like the pavane, were elegant and dignified, involving a series of gliding steps as in a stately procession. Others, like the various branles, were executed with sideways or swaying motions. Still others, like the galliard, required such nimble steps and leaps that sometimes the man had to hoist his partner into the air. (With the ladies dressed in the elaborate costumes that we see in the illustra-

Figure 12.5: A couple dancing a galliard, accompanied by pipe and drum, fiddle, and what appears to be a viol or lute. Woodcut by Hans Hofer, ca. 1540.

tions, it is no wonder the women needed help getting off the ground!)

As the dancing master went on to suggest to his new pupil, dancing is also a kind of mute rhetoric by which persons, through movement, can make themselves understood and persuade onlookers that they are gallant or comely and worthy to be acclaimed, admired, and loved. Such attitudes help to explain the importance of social dance in the Renaissance. And although the steps may be different, the place of dance in society today remains remarkably unchanged.—BRH

Figure 12.6: Three couples dance a stately pavane at a party in the court of Duke Albrecht IV in Munich. The dancers are accompanied by a flute and drum visible in the left balcony, while the right balcony holds a kettledrum player and two trumpeters, whose instruments are hung up. In the background the duke and a lady play cards. Engraving by Matthäus Zasinger, ca. 1500.

enjoyment of the player or listeners rather than for dancing, and these often include more elaborate counterpoint or written-out decoration. The use of a very social kind of music for solitary music-making is interesting; perhaps the pleasure of solo performance was enhanced by incorporating the familiar rhythms of dance, which carried associations with social interaction or with the physical motions of dancing. Whatever the reason, from the Renaissance to the present, many instrumental works have been stylized dances.

Rhythm and form

Each dance follows a particular meter, tempo, rhythmic pattern, and form, all of which are reflected in pieces composed for it. This particularity of rhythm and form distinguishes each type of dance from the others and gives all dance music a character unlike other kinds of music. Dance pieces feature distinct sections, usually repeated, with two, three, or more sections depending on the dance. Usually the phrase structure is clear and predictable, often in four-measure groups, so that dancers can follow it easily.

Basse danse and branle

The favorite courtly dance of the fifteenth and early sixteenth centuries was the **basse danse** (low dance), a stately couple dance marked by gracefully raising and lowering the body. It featured five different kinds of steps in various combinations, including the *branle*, a sideways step. In the early sixteenth century, the branle became an independent dance, with three varieties; the branle duple and branle simple were sedate duple-time dances, while the **branle gay** was in a lively triple time. Attaingnant's second collection of *Danseries a 4 parties* (Dances in Four Parts, 1547) opens with a basse danse (NAWM 59a) and includes a branle gay (NAWM 59b). Both vary the usual long-short rhythms of triple meter by interspersing a more bouncy short-long pattern, sometimes creating a hemiola effect. Such rhythms may reflect the movements of the dancers, who at times had to move in duple rhythm against the music's triple meter. Repetition of rhythmic patterns is of course intrinsic to dance music, but these Attaingnant dances suggest that variety in both melody and rhythm was also desired.

CD 4|4–6   CD 2|26

Renaissance musicians often grouped dances in pairs or threes. A favorite combination was a slow dance in duple meter followed by a fast one in triple meter on the same tune, the music of the second dance being a variation of the first. One such pair, the **pavane** (or *pavan*) and **galliard,** was a favorite in sixteenth-century France and England. Example 12.1 presents the melody of a pavane and galliard pair by Claude Gervaise, published in 1555. The pavane was a stately dance in three repeated strains (AABBCC), and the more lively galliard follows the same form with a variant of the same melody. Figure 12.6 shows three couples dancing a pavane, clearly more reserved and less vigorous than the galliard shown in Figure 12.5. A similar pairing of dances in slow duple and fast triple meter was the *passamezzo* and *saltarello*, popular in Italy, and German and Polish sources also feature such pairs. These dances offer another instance of the Renaissance fondness for reworking existing music in new ways, as in the cantus-firmus or imitation mass.

Dance pairs

Example 12.1: Gervaise, Pavane d'Angleterre *and* Galliard

If all that people in the Renaissance were interested in had been dancing itself, a single tune for each dance would have sufficed. Yet there are hundreds of pieces for each type of dance. Clearly they prized inventiveness and variety, in their dance music as well as in church music and secular songs.

ARRANGEMENTS OF VOCAL MUSIC

Another major source for instrumental music was, paradoxically, vocal music. Instruments frequently doubled or replaced voices in polyphonic compositions. Instrumental ensembles often played vocal works, reading from the vocal parts and adding their own embellishments. Indeed, vocal music, printed in great quantities and often labeled "for singing and playing," represented the bulk of what instrumentalists played when they were not improvising or accompanying singers or dancers.

Intabulations   Lutenists and keyboard players made arrangements of vocal pieces, either improvised or written down. These arrangements were often written in tablature, so they became known as **intabulations.** Great numbers of intabulations were published during the sixteenth century, testifying to their popularity. Since plucked instruments lack the sustaining power of voices, arrangers had to recast the original work in a manner idiomatic to the instrument. The intabulations by Spanish composer Luys de Narváez (fl. 1526–49) demonstrate that such works are much closer to inventive variations than to simple transcriptions, making intabulations yet another instance of the Renaissance tendency to rework existing music. In his version of Josquin's *Mille regretz*

CD 4|7   (NAWM 60a), published in 1538, Narváez preserves the four-voice texture of the original (NAWM 41) but introduces runs, turns, and other figures, called "divisions" or "diminutions" in the terminology of the time, that enliven the rhythm and sustain the listener's interest.

SETTINGS OF EXISTING MELODIES

Instrumental music, like vocal music, sometimes incorporated existing melodies. Church organists often improvised or composed settings of Gregorian chant or other liturgical melodies for use in services, replacing portions that were normally sung.

Chant settings and   In Catholic churches, chants traditionally performed by two half-choirs
organ masses   alternating segments or verses, such as Kyries and hymns, could instead alternate between the choir singing chant and the organ playing a cantus-firmus setting or paraphrase. Such settings of short segments of chant were called *organ verses* or *versets*. Example 12.2 shows the beginning of a Kyrie by organist-composer Girolamo Cavazzoni with the chant melody (from NAWM 3b) paraphrased in the upper voice; later other voices carry phrases of the chant as well. This Kyrie is part of an **organ mass,** a compilation of all the sections of the mass for which the organ would play.

Organ chorales   In Lutheran churches, verses of chorales could alternate between the congregation singing in unison and a polyphonic setting for choir or organ.

Example 12.2: Cavazzoni, opening of Kyrie I from Missa Apostolorum

Organists typically improvised settings for their verses, but from the 1570s on, collections of chorale settings for organ appeared. These pieces varied in style, from harmonizations to more elaborate cantus-firmus settings or embellished paraphrases.

The way musical genres develop through composers imitating each other is exemplified by the *In Nomine*. Sixteenth- and seventeenth-century English composers wrote over two hundred pieces for consort or keyboard titled *In Nomine*, all but a few setting the same cantus firmus. The source for the tradition was the section on "in nomine Domini" from the Sanctus of John Taverner's *Missa Gloria tibi trinitas*, which Taverner transcribed for instruments and titled *In Nomine*. He was apparently seeking a secular use for the music at a time when England was no longer Catholic and masses were not performed. Others then wrote settings of the same melody (the chant *Gloria tibi trinitas*), and eventually *In Nomines* became one of the most popular genres of English music for viol consort, lasting through Henry Purcell's setting at the end of the seventeenth century. By then the origins of the tune and the name were long forgotten.

In Nomines

VARIATIONS

Improvising on a tune to accompany dancing has ancient roots, but the form known as **variations** or **variation form** is a sixteenth-century invention, used for independent instrumental pieces rather than as dance accompaniment. Variations combine change with repetition, taking a given **theme**—an existing or newly composed tune, bass line, harmonic plan, melody with accompaniment, or other musical subject—and presenting an uninterrupted series of variants on that theme. The goal was to showcase the variety that could be achieved in embellishing a basic idea. Variations served both to entertain the listener or amateur performer with fresh and interesting ideas and to demonstrate the skill of the performer and composer. In all these ways, playing variations paralleled an orator elaborating on a theme, suggesting a link to the Renaissance interest in the ancient art of rhetoric, or oratorical persuasion (see chapter 7).

Written variations on pavane tunes first appeared in 1508 in the lute tablatures of Joan Ambrosio Dalza, published by Petrucci, featuring either a varied repetition of each strain (AA'BB'CC') or several variants of a single strain. Composers and performers wrote and improvised variations on **ostinatos**, short bass lines repeated over and over. Several basses were used for dancing, such as the *passamezzo antico* and *passamezzo moderno*, both derived from the pavane. Composers also created sets of variations on standard airs for singing verses, such as the Spanish *Guárdame las vacas* and the Italian *romanesca* and *ruggiero*, which feature a spare melodic outline over a standard bass progression.

Example 12.3 shows the main melody and bass for *Guárdame las vacas* and the opening of each variation from a set of four variations (called *diferencias* in Spanish) by Narváez (NAWM 6ob). His 1538 collection of works for vihuela, *Los seys libros del Delphin* (The Six Books of the Dauphin), contains the first published sets of variations, including this one. In these first examples

CD 4|8

of the genre, ideas that would characterize variation form for the next five centuries are already in place: each variation preserves the phrase structure, harmonic plan, and cadences of the theme, while recasting the melody with a new figuration that distinguishes it from the other variations.

Example 12.3: Narváez, excerpts from Diferencias sobre "Guárdame las vacas"

a. Structural outline of melody and bass for Guárdame las vacas

b. First variation

c. Second variation

d. Third variation

e. Fourth variation

Other major Spanish composers of variations are the organist Antonio de Cabezón (ca. 1510–1566) and the lutenist Enríquez de Valderrábano (fl. mid-1500s). Comparing their variations on *Guárdame las vacas* with those of Narváez gives a sense of emerging differences in what was idiomatic for performers on vihuela, lute, and keyboard.

The variation enjoyed an extraordinary flowering in the late sixteenth and early seventeenth centuries among a group of English keyboard composers known as the English virginalists, after the name of their instrument. Works by the leading figure, William Byrd (see chapter 10), as well as John Bull (ca. 1562–1628) and Orlando Gibbons (1583–1625), appear in the first published collection of music for virginal, *Parthenia* (1613), shown in Figure 12.7. In addition to variations, this collection contains dances, preludes, fantasias, and other genres.

English virginalists

The English virginalists typically used dances or familiar songs of the time as themes for variation. Their interest in varying melodies distinguishes the English from earlier Spanish and Italian composers, who focused more on bass patterns and bare melodic outlines. The songs used were generally short, simple, and regular in phrasing. The melody may be presented intact throughout an entire set of variations, passing at times from one voice to another; more often, it is broken up by decorative figuration, so that its original profile is only suggested. Each variation typically uses one type of figuration, and in most variation sets the rhythmic animation increases as the work progresses, though with intermittent quieter interludes and often a slower final variation.

An example of English variation technique is Byrd's *Pavana Lachrymae* (NAWM 61), based on Dowland's lute song *Flow, my tears* (NAWM 58). The song already has the typical form of a pavane, with three strains, each repeated (AABBCC). Byrd varied each strain, then added a second, more active variation for the repetition, producing the form AA'BB'CC'. He retained the outline of the vocal melody in the right hand while adding short accompanying

CD 4|9

CD 2|29

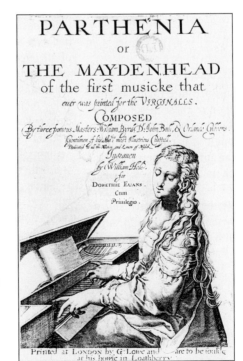

Figure 12.7: Title page of Parthenia, or The Maydenhead, *a collection of music for virginal by William Byrd, John Bull, and Orlando Gibbons presented to Princess Elizabeth and Prince Frederick on their wedding in 1613.* Parthenia *were Greek maidens' choral dances, so both title and subtitle allude whimsically to the virgin bride, the instrument's name, and the fact that this was the first such collection ever printed.*

motives or decorative turns, figurations, and scale patterns that are imitated between the hands.

ABSTRACT INSTRUMENTAL WORKS

The instrumental genres we have seen so far are all based on dance patterns or derived from song, the two traditional wellsprings of music. But beginning in the late fifteenth and early sixteenth centuries, for the first time in history, instrumentalists cultivated several types of music that were truly independent of dance rhythms or borrowed tunes. Most of these developed from habits of improvisation on polyphonic instruments such as lute or keyboard, while others drew on imitative textures derived from vocal music. Although such pieces were used as interludes in church or background music for

SOURCE READING

THE POWER OF INSTRUMENTAL MUSIC

Writers in the sixteenth century attributed great emotional powers to music, echoing the ideas of the ancient Greek writers whose works were being rediscovered and more widely read (see the excerpt from Aristotle in chapter 1). This reminiscence by a French traveler of a banquet in Milan testifies both to the abilities of Francesco da Milano (1497–1543) as an improviser and to the emotional impact of his playing. That the diners stopped conversing and listened intently demonstrates the growing esteem for purely instrumental music.

——— • ———

Among other pleasures and rare things assembled for the satisfaction of these select people was Francesco da Milano, a man considered to have attained the goal (if it is possible) of perfection in playing the lute. The tables having been cleared, he took up a lute and as though testing the tuning of his strings, sitting near one end of the table, began to search out a fantasia. He had only moved the air with three plucked sounds when his music interrupted the conversations that had begun between the guests. And having compelled them to turn their faces to him, in whole or part, he continued with such ravishing zeal, making the strings faint under his fingers through his divine manner of playing, that little by little he

transported all those who listened in such a gracious melancholy that—one resting his head in his hand supported by his elbow; another stretched out relaxed with his limbs in a careless arrangement; another, with mouth open and eyes more than half closed, fixing his gaze (one judged) on those strings; and another, with his chin fallen on his chest, concealing his face that revealed the saddest reticence one had ever seen—his listeners remained deprived of all sensations but that of hearing, as if the soul, having abandoned all the seats of the other senses, had retired to the ears in order to enjoy more at her ease such a ravishing symphony. And I believe (said Monsieur de Ventemille) that we would be there still, had not he himself, I know not how, revived the strings, and little by little invigorating his playing with a gentle force, returned our souls and our senses to the place from which he had stolen them—not without leaving as much astonishment in each of us, as if we had been picked up by an ecstatic transport of some divine frenzy.

From an account by Jacques Descartes de Ventemille as reported by Pontus de Tyard, *Solitaire second ou Prose de la musique* (Lyons: Jan de Tournes, 1555), 114–15.

conversation, they could also be played or listened to for their own sake, and improvisers and composers frequently employed unusual or highly expressive effects to attract listeners' attention (see Source Reading).

Performers on keyboard and lute often had reason to improvise: to introduce a song, to fill time during a church service, to establish the mode of a subsequent chant or hymn, to test the tuning of a lute, or to entertain themselves or an audience. Compositions that resemble such improvisations appeared early in the sixteenth century, especially in Spain and Italy, and became mainstays of the repertoire for solo players. Such pieces were given a variety of names, including **prelude, fantasia,** or **ricercare.** Not based on any preexisting melody, they unfold freely, with varying textures and musical ideas. They served the same function as an introduction to a speech, preparing the listener and establishing the tonality for what followed. The fantasias of Spanish composer Luis Milán (ca. 1500–ca. 1561) in his collection for vihuela entitled *El Maestro* (Valencia, 1536), for example, are each in the same mode as the following vocal piece, using rapid scale passages or other figuration to add tension and suspense before a strong cadence on the final of the mode.

Introductory and improvisatory pieces

The ***toccata*** was the chief form of keyboard music in improvisatory style during the second half of the century. The name, from the Italian *toccare* ("to touch"), refers to touching the keys, reminding us of the player's body and actions rather than a disembodied play of sound. The toccatas by the organist Claudio Merulo (1533–1604) exemplify the genre. His Toccata IV in the 6th Mode from his second book of toccatas (1604), excerpted in Example 12.4, shows a variety of textures and figuration. In the opening succession of slowly changing harmonies, Merulo takes advantage of the organ's power to sustain tones. The numerous suspensions and prolonged and repeated dissonances are idiomatic to the organ. Embellishments on the most active tones and scale passages in freely varied rhythms animate the texture. A contrasting middle section develops four short subjects in turn through imitation; the first of these is shown in Example 12.4b. The last third of the piece is again free, like

Toccata

Example 12.4: Merulo, Toccata IV in the 6th Mode, excerpts

a. Opening

b. Central imitative section

c. Closing

the opening, but with more spacious harmonies and even more fantastic play of brilliant running passages. The majestic slowing down of the chordal changes coupled with the increased liveliness and ever wider sweep of the runs makes an impressive climax. The closing measures appear in Example 12.4c. Pieces of this sort did not always contain fugal sections, nor were they uniformly labeled toccatas; they were also called *fantasia, prelude,* and *intonazione* (intonation).

Ricercare   One type of prelude, the **ricercare** or **ricercar,** evolved into a motetlike succession of imitative sections. The term ricercare is an Italian verb meaning both "to seek out" and "to attempt," and its application to music probably comes from lutenists' jargon for picking out notes on the instrument and testing the tuning. The earliest ricercari, for lute, were brief and improvisatory. When transferred to the keyboard, the genre acquired occasional passages of imitation. By 1540, the ricercare consisted of successive themes, each developed in imitation and overlapping with the next at the cadence—in effect, a textless imitative motet, but with embellishments that were typically instrumental. Such ricercari were written for ensemble as well as keyboard or lute. By the early seventeenth century, the ricercare was an extended fugal piece on a single subject (see chapter 15).

Canzona   The Italian **canzona** or **canzon** became one of the leading genres of contrapuntal instrumental music in the late sixteenth century, alongside the fantasia and ricercare, but had a different origin. The earliest pieces called canzona were intabulations of French chansons, after which the canzona was named. By midcentury, composers such as Girolamo Cavazzoni were writing canzonas that thoroughly reworked chansons, as in an imitation mass movement, rather than simply embellishing them. Newly composed canzonas in the style of an imitative French chanson appeared by 1580, first for ensemble and then for organ. Canzonas were light, fast-moving, and strongly rhythmic, with a fairly simple contrapuntal texture. From the chanson, composers adopted the typical opening rhythmic figure that occurs in most canzonas: a single note followed by two notes of half the value, such as a half note followed by two quarter notes. Like chansons, canzonas often feature a series of themes that differ from one another in melodic outline and rhythm. Each is worked out in turn, resulting in a series of contrasting sections.

MUSIC IN VENICE

Our discussion of instrumental music would be incomplete without considering Venice, where instrumental performers and composition reached a particularly high level in the sixteenth and early seventeenth centuries. Music in Venice exemplifies traits of the late Renaissance and also of the early Baroque period (see chapters 14 and 15), so it may serve as a point of transition between the two eras.

VENICE

Venice, the second most important Italian city after Rome, was an independent state with its own empire. Nominally a republic, it was actually an oligarchy run by several important families, with an elected leader called the doge (Venetian for "duke"). Because Venice was a city of traders and the chief port for European trade with the East, it had accumulated enormous wealth, power, and splendor by the fifteenth century. Wars and other misfortunes reduced its position in the sixteenth century, but it still controlled extensive territories on the Italian peninsula and along the Adriatic coast from Croatia to Greece.

The government had plenty of money and spent lavishly on public specta-   *Patronage of*
cle, music, and art. This was cultural propaganda on a grand scale: although   *the arts*
the empire had shrunk, the arts could still project Venice's lingering glory, and sumptuous public displays of wealth and confidence could rally the public behind the state and intimidate potential enemies at home or abroad.

CHURCH OF ST. MARK

The center of Venetian musical culture was the great eleventh-century Church of St. Mark, or Basilica San Marco, whose Byzantine domes, spacious interior, bright gold mosaics, and ostentatious Pala d'Oro, an altarpiece of solid gold and precious jewels, proclaimed the city's wealth and close links to the East. Like Venice itself, St. Mark's was independent: it was the private chapel of the doge, essentially the state church of the republic, and thus was not controlled by the church hierarchy. Many civic and religious ceremonies took place each month in the church and in the vast piazza in front of it, like the procession

Figure 12.8: Procession in Piazza San Marco *(1496) by Gentile Bellini, showing a religious or civic procession with singers and instrumentalists, with St. Mark's Church in the background.*

depicted in Figure 12.8. On each occasion, Mass and Vespers were celebrated with great pomp and elaborate music.

Music in St. Mark's was supervised by officials of the state, sparing no expense. The position of choirmaster, the most coveted musical post in all Italy, was held by Willaert, Rore, and Zarlino in the sixteenth century and by Monteverdi in the early seventeenth. Renowned artists, chosen after stringent examination, served as organists, including Claudio Merulo, Andrea Gabrieli, and his nephew Giovanni Gabrieli. Beginning in 1568, a first-rate permanent ensemble of instrumentalists was assembled, centering on cornetts and sackbuts but including violin and bassoon. Additional players were hired on major feast days, when as many as two dozen instrumentalists performed, alone or together with the choir of twenty to thirty voices.

GIOVANNI GABRIELI

The rich musical environment of Venice shaped the music of Giovanni Gabrieli (ca. 1555–1612). He served St. Mark's for almost three decades as organist, composer, and supervisor of the instrumentalists (see biography and Figure 12.9). His compositions used all the resources available at the church, resulting in works for multiple choirs and the earliest substantial collections of pieces for large instrumental ensemble.

Polychoral motets   The glory of Venetian church music is manifest in its ***polychoral motets,*** works for two or more choirs. From before the time of Willaert, composers in the Venetian region had often written for divided choirs, or *cori spezzati.* In the polychoral music of Gabrieli, the performance forces grew to new heights.

Two, three, four, even five choruses, each with a different combination of high and low voices, mingled with instruments of diverse timbres, answered one another antiphonally, and joined together in massive sonorous climaxes. Sometimes the choirs were separated spatially, with groups in the two organ lofts, one on each side of the altar, and another on the floor. Gabrieli's use of contrasting forces was a major influence on Baroque church music.

Gabrieli and other Venetian composers applied the idea of divided choirs to instruments. The *Canzon septimi toni a 8* (Canzona in Mode 7 in Eight Parts, NAWM 62) from Gabrieli's *Sacrae symphoniae* (Sacred Symphonies, 1597) resembles a double-chorus motet for two groups of four instruments, with organ accompaniment. Like other canzonas, it presents a series of contrasting sections, some imitative, others more homophonic. The two

Ensemble canzonas

CD 4|15

GIOVANNI GABRIELI (CA. 1555–1612)

Gabrieli was one of the leading composers of the late Renaissance and early Baroque periods, known today primarily for his instrumental works but equally accomplished in sacred music.

Little is known about Gabrieli's early life and training. In his teens and early twenties, he was in the service of Duke Albrecht V in Munich, where he studied with Orlando di Lasso. In 1585, he won appointment as second organist at St. Mark's, serving alongside his uncle Andrea Gabrieli until the latter's death that August. That same year, the younger Gabrieli also was elected organist to the Scuola Grande di San Rocco, one of the most prominent of the scuole (schools), or charitable confraternities, of Venice. The scuole sponsored religious observances and performances, participated in civic celebrations, and strove to outdo each other in pageantry and music, giving Gabrieli ample opportunity to compose lavish music for large forces. At St. Mark's, he was the main composer of ceremonial music, producing about a hundred motets, most for multiple choirs. As second organist, Gabrieli supervised the instrumentalists, and his ensemble canzonas and sonatas were no doubt written

for them. He served both St. Mark's and San Rocco until his death in 1612.

MAJOR WORKS: *About 100 motets, over 30 madrigals, 37 ensemble canzonas, 7 sonatas, and about 35 organ works, including ricercares, canzonas, toccatas, and intonazioni*

Figure 12.9: Portrait of Giovanni Gabrieli by Annibale Carracci (1560–1609), whose work focused on natural portraits and rejected the mannered style of the day.

instrumental groups alternate long passages, engage in more rapid dialogue, and sometimes play together, especially at the end. The form is defined by a refrain that appears three times.

Sonatas   The Venetian **sonata** (Italian for "sounded") was a close relative of the canzona, consisting of a series of sections each based on a different subject or on variants of a single subject. Both canzonas and sonatas were used at Mass or Vespers as introductions or postludes or to accompany significant rituals. The *Sonata pian' e forte* from Gabrieli's *Sacrae symphoniae* has earned a prominent place in music history because it is among the first instrumental ensemble pieces to designate specific instruments in the printed parts: in the first choir, cornett and three sackbuts, and in the second, a violin and three sackbuts. Another innovation in the printed music was indicating passages as *pian* (piano, meaning "soft") or *forte* ("loud"), one of the earliest instances of dynamic markings in music. Through contrasts of one instrumental choir against the other, single choir with both together, loud versus soft, and slow homophonic passages with faster motion and points of imitation, Gabrieli created a purely instrumental work with as much interest, variety, and depth of content as a madrigal or motet. Such pieces were the foundation from which independent instrumental music developed over the next two centuries.

INSTRUMENTAL MUSIC GAINS INDEPENDENCE

The sixteenth century saw the rise of instrumental music that was cultivated for its own sake, whether derived from dance music, related to vocal music, or conceived as abstract music independent of dance or song. The abstract types would ultimately have the most significance, leading to the sonatas and symphonies of later centuries, but links to vocal music and dance have continued in later instrumental music. Some forms of sixteenth-century instrumental music continued to be cultivated in the Baroque era and beyond, including stylized dances, organ settings of sacred tunes, variations, and preludes. Instrumental music continued to gain independence, until by the nineteenth century it reached a level of prestige higher than most vocal music. Moreover, the tradition of playing instrumental music for one's own pleasure, alone or with friends, was well established by the end of the Renaissance and has endured to this day.

Instrumental works were published in great numbers in the sixteenth century, and some were played for a generation or more until tastes changed and the old books were shelved, replaced by music in newer styles. The oldest instrumental works most listeners know today are Gabrieli's canzonas and sonatas, which were rediscovered in the early nineteenth century and have become part of the standard repertoire for modern brass instruments. The revival of most other Renaissance instrumental music had to wait until the twentieth century, when artisans began to reconstruct Renaissance instruments and produce them in increasing numbers. Scholars have transcribed a good deal of Renaissance instrumental music, but it is still far less often studied or performed than vocal music, in part because relatively few can read the complex tablatures developed for keyboard and plucked strings, which vary from each instrument to the next and from place to place. Only in recent decades have Renaissance dances and lute pieces begun to appear on recordings and classical radio stations, as performers and listeners have rediscovered the instruments, sounds, and appeal of this once very popular music.

PART OUTLINE

PART THREE

THE SEVENTEENTH CENTURY

Western culture for the last four hundred years has lived off the intellectual capital created in the seventeenth century. From discoveries about the solar system to the invention of calculus, from notions of political equality to the economic system of capitalism, Europeans in the 1600s laid the groundwork for scientific and social developments for generations to come.

The same is true in music. Familiar musical genres invented in the seventeenth century include opera, oratorio, cantata, overture, concerto, solo sonata, trio sonata, keyboard sonata, suite, fugue, chaconne, and passacaglia. During that century, Italian composers created the first recitatives, musicians in Paris and Rome organized the first orchestras, Venetian singers became the first divas, an entrepreneur in London originated the idea of public concerts, and a French girl became the first celebrated child prodigy in music. Composers in the seventeenth century responded to their contemporaries' interest in spectacle, theater, and drama by creating music that was more dramatic and spectacular than any before. Highly expressive styles developed for the stage found their way into music for religious services, forever changing the character of church music, and into instrumental music, which began for the first time to rival vocal music in importance and emotional content. Tonality, the system of major and minor keys oriented around a central pitch, emerged as the fundamental musical language of Europe, remaining so for over two centuries. These and other aspects of music first introduced in the seventeenth century are among those we encounter most often and take most for granted, making the history of that era especially interesting.

New Styles in the Seventeenth Century

Italian musicians living around 1600 knew they were inventing new ways of making music. They devised new idioms, such as **basso continuo, monody,** and **recitative**; new styles, marked by unprepared dissonance, greater focus on the solo voice or instrument, and idiomatic playing; and new genres, including **opera.** This generation saw the most deliberate cultivation of the new in music since the Ars Nova in the early 1300s.

In retrospect, we have come to see this outpouring of innovation as the beginning of a new period often called the **Baroque.** The term was employed by art historians in the nineteenth century, but only in the later twentieth century did music historians apply it to the period from about 1600 to about 1750. There are certainly elements that composers of the early seventeenth century such as Peri and Monteverdi share with early-eighteenth-century composers like Vivaldi and Bach, notably their focus on moving the **affections** (emotions). But the seventeenth century was also a period of its own, marked by continuous invention of new genres, styles, and methods, the gradual diffusion of Italian ideas, and, in response to them, the development of independent national idioms. Whichever view we take, the innovations around 1600 launched a new era in music, in which opera and theatrical styles played leading roles.

This chapter will contrast the Baroque period with its predecessor, the Renaissance. Chapter 14 traces the invention and early spread of opera in Italy. Chapter 15 takes up church, chamber, and instrumental music in the first half of the seventeenth century, and later chapters chart developments after midcentury.

EUROPE IN THE SEVENTEENTH CENTURY

The interest in innovation among musicians paralleled new ideas in science, politics, and economics. The effects of war, varying political structures, and relative wealth made circumstances for musicians different in each part of western Europe, influencing the music cultivated in the different regions.

The scientific revolution

Europe was in the midst of a scientific revolution, led by a new breed of investigators who relied on mathematics, observation, and practical experiments, not on received opinion. Johannes Kepler showed in 1609 that the planets, including the earth, move around the sun in elliptical orbits at speeds that vary with their distance from the sun. During the following decade, Galileo Galilei demonstrated the laws that control motion and used the newly invented telescope to discover sunspots and moons orbiting Jupiter. Sir Francis Bacon argued for an empirical approach to science, relying on direct observation rather than on ancient authorities. Balancing Bacon's inductive method, René Descartes put forth a deductive approach that explained the

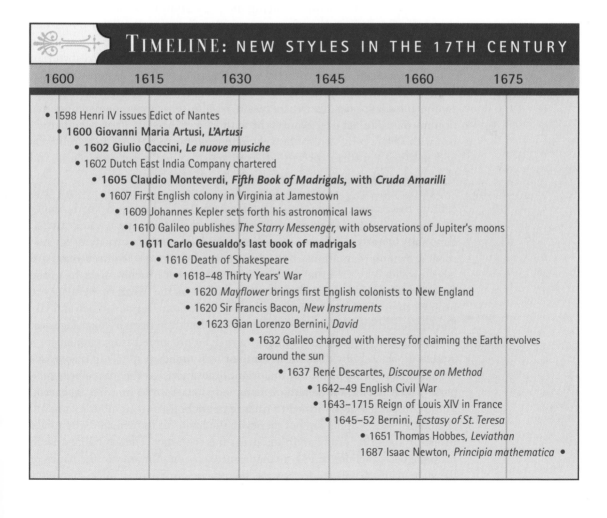

TIMELINE: NEW STYLES IN THE 17TH CENTURY

1600	1615	1630	1645	1660	1675

- 1598 Henri IV issues Edict of Nantes
- 1600 Giovanni Maria Artusi, *L'Artusi*
- 1602 Giulio Caccini, *Le nuove musiche*
- 1602 Dutch East India Company chartered
- 1605 Claudio Monteverdi, *Fifth Book of Madrigals*, with *Cruda Amarilli*
- 1607 First English colony in Virginia at Jamestown
- 1609 Johannes Kepler sets forth his astronomical laws
- 1610 Galileo publishes *The Starry Messenger*, with observations of Jupiter's moons
- 1611 Carlo Gesualdo's last book of madrigals
- 1616 Death of Shakespeare
- 1618–48 Thirty Years' War
- 1620 *Mayflower* brings first English colonists to New England
- 1620 Sir Francis Bacon, *New Instruments*
- 1623 Gian Lorenzo Bernini, *David*
- 1632 Galileo charged with heresy for claiming the Earth revolves around the sun
- 1637 René Descartes, *Discourse on Method*
- 1642–49 English Civil War
- 1643–1715 Reign of Louis XIV in France
- 1645–52 Bernini, *Ecstasy of St. Teresa*
- 1651 Thomas Hobbes, *Leviathan*
- 1687 Isaac Newton, *Principia mathematica*

world through mathematics, logic, and reasoning from first principles. These two strands joined in the work of Sir Isaac Newton, whose law of gravitation, developed in the 1660s, combined acute observation with mathematical elegance and set the pattern for scientific methods for centuries to come. The same interest in what is useful and effective, rather than what is hallowed by tradition, is apparent in seventeenth-century music of all kinds. Perception and perceived effect lay at the heart of the new styles in art and music around 1600, including the *second practice* (described below) and opera.

Politics, religion, and war The century also saw new thinking about politics, ranging from the English Levellers, who advocated democracy with equal political rights for all men, to Thomas Hobbes, whose *Leviathan* (1651) argued for an all-powerful sovereign state. Such debates were stimulated in part by struggles over religion that sometimes broke out into war. Some long-standing conflicts were resolved around the turn of the seventeenth century. In France, Henri IV issued the Edict of Nantes in 1598 guaranteeing some freedom to Protestants while confirming Catholicism as the state religion. Protestant England and Catholic Spain ended decades of war in 1604, and the Calvinist Netherlands gained independence from Spain in 1609 and became a republic. But religious conflict within the Holy Roman Empire precipitated the Thirty Years' War (1618–48), which devastated Germany, reducing the population in some areas by more than half. The English Civil War (1642–49), primarily a battle for power between the king and Parliament, also had religious aspects. The defeat of the king led to the replacement of the Church of England by a state Presbyterian church, a change that was reversed when the monarchy was restored in 1660. Italy remained entirely Catholic and thus was spared religious wars, although southern Italians staged an unsuccessful revolution against Spanish domination in 1647. Almost everywhere, the authority of the state grew, whether allied with a state religion or relatively independent from it. All these religious and political conflicts directly affected music, chiefly because rulers and church authorities remained important patrons (see below).

Colonies Meanwhile, Europeans were expanding overseas. During the seventeenth century the British, French, and Dutch established colonies in North America, the Caribbean, Africa, and Asia, in competition with Spain and Portugal. Especially lucrative imports were sugar and tobacco, new luxury items for Europe, grown on plantations in the Americas. These crops required intensive labor provided by the cruel trade in human life that brought Africans to the New World as slaves. Europeans who settled in the Western hemisphere brought their traditions with them, including Catholic service music and villancicos to the Spanish colonies and metric psalmody to British North America.

Capitalism Britain, the Netherlands, and northern Italy prospered from capitalism, a system in which individuals invested their own money (capital) in businesses designed to return a profit. An important innovation was the joint stock company, which pooled the wealth of many individuals while limiting their risk. These companies were formed to finance opera houses in Hamburg, London, and other cities. Capitalism put money in the hands of individuals, who would invest or spend it locally and thus boost the economy. The capitalist system proved a better economic engine than concentration of money in the hands of the state or the privileged few, as was the practice in Spain, France, and many smaller principalities. Among the effects on music were the rise of public opera and public concerts, as well as an increased demand between the upper and middle classes for published music, musical instruments, and music lessons.

Musicians continued to depend on patronage from court, church, or city, and the types of music that won support varied from region to region. Musicians were best off in Italy, which was wealthy from trade yet still divided between Spanish control in the south, the papal states around Rome, and several independent states in the north (see map in Figure 13.1). Rulers, cities, and leading families supported music and the arts as a way of competing for prestige. Aristocrats in Florence sponsored a brilliant series of musical and theatrical innovations around 1600, spawning similar efforts by the dukes of

Patronage

Figure 13.1: Map of Europe around 1610.

Figure 13.2: Detail of the Pamphili Palace (now Doria-Pamphili) in Rome, completed ca. 1739. Writing around 1755, Charles de Brosses criticized as "baroque" the delicate, detailed decoration of the sort he considered more suitable for silverware than for a building. His is thought to be the first use of the word in relation to one of the visual arts.

Mantua, churchmen in Rome, and the government and citizens of Venice. Their support continued Italy's reign as the dominant influence in European music through the mid-eighteenth century.

In France, power and wealth were increasingly concentrated in the king. Louis XIV (r. 1643–1715) controlled the arts, including music, and used them to assert his glory. During the seventeenth century, France replaced Spain as the predominant power on the Continent; partly as a result, French music was imitated widely, while the music of Spain had little influence beyond its borders. Civil war and parliamentary prerogative limited the wealth of the English royalty, but their patronage strongly influenced national tastes. The calamity of the Thirty Years' War sapped treasuries throughout the Holy Roman Empire, but after midcentury, German courts and free city-states built up their musical establishments, drawing on influences from both Italy and France. The church continued to support music, although its role was less important than it had been in previous centuries.

Along with aristocratic, civic, and ecclesiastical patronage, many cities had "academies," private associations that, among other functions, sponsored musical activities. Public opera houses were established in many cities, beginning in Venice in 1637. Public concerts to which one subscribed or paid admission first occurred in England in 1672, but the practice did not become widespread in Europe until the later 1700s.

From Renaissance to Baroque

THE BAROQUE AS TERM AND PERIOD

How the term *baroque*, meaning abnormal, bizarre, exaggerated, or in bad taste, came to be applied to the art and music of several generations is a story of changing tastes and values. The word is French, from the Portuguese *barroco*, a misshapen pearl. It was first applied pejoratively to music and art in the mid-eighteenth century by critics who preferred a newer, simpler style. The older, "barocque" music was deemed by one critic to be dissonant and unmelodious, with capricious and extravagant changes of key and meter, and by another as aiming "to surprise by the boldness of its sounds." The travel writer Charles de Brosses applied the term to architecture, complaining that the Pamphili Palace in Rome, shown in Figure 13.2, was decorated with filigree better suited to tableware than to buildings.

When nineteenth-century art critics began to appreciate the ornate, dramatic, and expressive tendencies of seventeenth-century painting and architecture, *baroque* took on a positive meaning. Music historians since the 1920s saw many of the same qualities of extravagance, decoration, and focus on expression in much music of the times, and by the 1950s *Baroque* was well established as a name for the period of about 1600 to around 1750. Recognizing that these 150 years encompassed a diversity of styles too great to be embraced by one word, we will speak of a Baroque period, but not a Baroque style. The boundary dates must be taken as rough approximations for a time when composers and listeners shared ideals for music and accepted common conventions for how it should behave. Most important, they prized music for its dramatic power and its capacity to move the affections (see below).

THE DRAMATIC BAROQUE

The most striking aspect of seventeenth-century literature, art, and music is its focus on the dramatic. Not since ancient Greece were there so many playwrights among the leading authors, including William Shakespeare (1564–1616) and Ben Jonson (ca. 1572–1637) in England and Pierre Corneille (1604–1684), Jean Racine (1639–1699), and Jean Baptiste Molière (1622–1673) in France. Poetry of the time often had theatrical qualities (see Source Reading), and vivid images and dramatic scenes in the poems of

SOURCE READING

THE DRAMATIZATION OF POETRY

Baroque theatricality infused poetry as well as art and music. The poem below uses the image of the poet as a fortified city attacked by the enemy, Love. Written by Giulio Strozzi (1583–1652) and set by Claudio Monteverdi in his Eighth Book of Madrigals *(1638), the poem is witty in its theatricality: As the crisis grows more intense, the protagonist shouts (at the end of each verse) to his imagined companions.*

———— • ————

The insidious enemy, Love, circles
The fortress of my heart.
Hurry up, for he is not far away.
Arm yourselves!

We must not let him approach, so he can scale
Our weak walls,
But let us make a brave sally out to meet him.
Throw on the saddles!

His weapons are no fakes, he draws nearer
With his whole army.
Hurry up, for he is not far from here.
Everyone to his post!

He intends to attack the stronghold of my eyes
With a vigorous assault.
Hurry up, for he is here without any doubt.
Everyone to his horse!

There's no more time, alas, for all of a sudden he
Has made himself the master of my heart.
Take to your heels, save yourselves if you can.
Run!

My heart, you flee in vain, you are dead.
And I hear the arrogant tyrant,
The victor, who is already inside the fortress,
Crying "Fire, slaughter!"

Giulio Strozzi, *Gira il nemico insidioso*.

Figure 13.3: Michelangelo Buonarotti's David *(1501–4), which evokes ancient Greek statuary and is endowed with the ideal traits of Renaissance human-ism, including intelligence, nobility, balance, and calm.*

Figure 13.4: Gian Lorenzo Bernini's David *(ca. 1620), embodying the Baroque virtues of drama, dynamism, and emotional expression.*

John Donne (1572–1631), the epic *Paradise Lost* of John Milton (1608–1674), and the novel *Don Quixote* by the Spaniard Miguel de Cervantes (1547–1616) at times suggest the intensity of staged performance.

Baroque art   In art and architecture, as in music, the Baroque began in Italy. The theatricality of Baroque art is seen in the sculptures of Gian Lorenzo Bernini (1598–1680), who worked for the church and other patrons in seventeenth-century Rome. Contrasting Michelangelo's famous *David* (1501–4), in Figure 13.3, with Bernini's *David* (1623) in Figure 13.4 shows the change from Renaissance to Baroque goals. Michelangelo evokes ancient Greek statuary with his standing nude, celebrates the nobility and beauty of the human figure through balance and proportion, and portrays his hero as contemplative and still, with only a furrowed brow to suggest the coming battle with Goliath. Bernini shows David winding up to sling the stone, his body dynamic, his muscles taut, his lips and face tense with exertion. The effect is dramatic, making the viewer respond emotionally rather than with detached admiration.

Even more stunning is Bernini's *Ecstasy of St. Teresa* (1645–52), shown in Figure 13.5. Teresa of Avila, a sixteenth-century Spanish nun, mystic, and leader in the Catholic Reformation, had a vision of an angel's arrow piercing her heart, overwhelming her with both pain and joy. Bernini captures that moment, with the saint in rapture, her robes wild about her, borne upward on a cloud toward a light from Heaven. The use of material is virtuosic: the heavy marble statue, fastened to the wall, seems to float in midair, lit from a hidden window above, with golden rays behind it. These were theatrical effects, designed to astonish viewers and arouse strong feelings. The Catholic Church saw such art as a persuasive instrument in its campaign to keep its flock faithful and to counteract the Reformation.

Baroque architecture could be equally theatrical, using ancient and Renaissance elements in new and astounding ways. Bernini's dramatic design for the square in front of St. Peter's Basilica at the Vatican, shown in Figure 13.6, features two semicircular colonnades, four columns deep, that seem to enfold the observer, symbolizing the Church's claim to embrace the world. While the columns, capitals, lintels, portals, and other components are traditional, the length and curve are unprecedented, and the height, width, and open space add to the spectacular effect.

Just as the central impulse of Baroque art is dramatization, the quintessential music of the Baroque era is dramatic, centered in opera but extending to songs, church music, and instrumental music.

Figure 13.5: Bernini's The Ecstasy of St. Teresa *(1645–52), in the Cornaro Chapel, church of Santa Maria della Vittoria, Rome.*

Figure 13.6: St. Peter's Square and Basilica at the Vatican in Rome, with colonnades designed by Gian Lorenzo Bernini in 1657.

THE AFFECTIONS

Most composers of the Baroque period sought musical means to express or arouse the **affections**, that is, emotions such as sadness, joy, anger, love, fear, excitement, or wonder. The affections were thought of as relatively stable states of the soul, each caused by a certain combination of spirits, or "humors," in the body. It was widely believed that experiencing a range of affections through music could bring the humors into better balance, promoting physical and psychological health, so that both vocal and instrumental works typically offered a succession of contrasting moods. Composers did not try to express their personal feelings; rather, in instrumental music, they sought to portray the affections in a generic sense, using specific conventional techniques, and in vocal music they sought to convey the emotions of the text, character, or dramatic situation.

THE SECOND PRACTICE

CD 4|23   CD 2|35

One tool for expression was to break the rules of music deliberately in order to convey the poetic text. A classic example is the madrigal *Cruda Amarilli* (NAWM 63) by Claudio Monteverdi (1567–1643; see biography and Figure 13.7); its opening is shown in Example 13.1, on page 298–99. Numerous dissonances (marked by x in the example) violate the rules of counterpoint, which forbid passing tones from falling on strong beats (see measures 2 and 6) and require dissonances to be entered and left by step (see bass, measures 2 and 6, and cantus, measure 13). Here the rule-breaking and striking dissonances serve as a rhetorical device, highlighting the words "Cruda" (cruel) and "ahi lasso" (alas) and forcing the listener of Monteverdi's time to interpret the rule-breaking music in light of the text. Precisely because the music does not follow its expected path, we are wrenched in a way that dramatizes the emotions expressed in the text, and we recognize and empathize with those feelings.

Monteverdi's madrigal was criticized in Giovanni Maria Artusi's *L'Artusi overo Delle imperfettioni della moderna musica* (The Artusi, or Of the Imperfections of Modern Music, 1600), not for its dissonances but for needlessly breaking the rules. Artusi points out, for example, that the dissonances in measure 13 would be allowed if the cantus moved by step (G–A–G–F–E) and asks why the rules are deliberately flaunted. Monteverdi wrote a brief response in 1605, filled out with more detail by his brother Giulio Cesare Monteverdi two years later (see Source Readings, pp. 298–99). They distinguished between a **prima pratica**, or **first practice**, the sixteenth-century style of vocal polyphony codified by Zarlino, and a **seconda pratica**, or **second practice**, used by modern Italians. They explained that in the first practice the music had to follow its own rules and thus dominated the verbal text, while in the second practice the text dominates the music, voice-leading rules can be broken, and dissonances can be used more freely to express the feelings evoked in the text. The second practice did not displace the first, but each was used where appropriate.

CLAUDIO MONTEVERDI (1567–1643)

Monteverdi wrote only vocal and dramatic works, including sacred pieces, madrigals, and operas, and his music is always perfectly suited to the text. He was particularly inventive in creating expressive devices and combining styles and genres to capture feelings and personalities in music.

Monteverdi was born in Cremona, in northern Italy. Trained by the cathedral's music director, he was a prodigy as a composer, publishing two volumes of sacred music by age sixteen, a collection of canzonettas at seventeen, and three books of madrigals in his early twenties.

Monteverdi was an accomplished viol and viola player by 1590, when he entered the service of Vincenzo Gonzaga, duke of Mantua. In 1601, he was appointed master of music in the ducal chapel, two years after his marriage to Claudia Cattaneo, a singer at the court. His first five books of madrigals, published between 1587 and 1605, show his mastery of the polyphonic madrigal and his evolution from late Renaissance style to a new, highly expressive language marked by unprepared dissonances, declamatory melodies, and embellishments written into the music that previously would have been improvised.

The Gonzagas commissioned Monteverdi's first operas, *L'Orfeo* (1607) and *L'Arianna* (1608; only a fragment survives). Between the two premieres, Claudia died, leaving him with three small children. He suffered a nervous breakdown in 1608, then complained bitterly to the duke that he was being mistreated. He was rewarded with an annual pension in 1609 and a generous salary increase. His *Vespro della Beata Vergine* (Vespers of the Blessed Virgin) and imitation mass on a Gombert motet, published together in 1610, may have been in-

Figure 13.7: Claudio Monteverdi, in a portrait by Bernardo Strozzi.

tended as self-advertisement, as he was unhappy in Mantua and was seeking a new position. The collection features a range of styles from modern vocal display to severe counterpoint.

The new duke dismissed Monteverdi in 1612, but the following year he became maestro di cappella at St. Mark's in Venice, the most prestigious musical post in Italy, where he remained until his death in 1643. He wrote a great deal of sacred music for St. Mark's and for the confraternities that were an important part of Venetian life. In 1632, he became a priest.

Monteverdi nevertheless remained drawn to secular music. His later madrigal collections take up the new concertato medium. His operas *Il ritorno d'Ulisse* (The Return of Ulysses, 1640) and *L'incoronazione di Poppea* (The Coronation of Poppea, 1643), written in his seventies, use a varied mixture of styles to portray the characters and their emotions.

Monteverdi died in November 1643 at the age of seventy-six. Upon his death, he was lauded in poetry and music, and his works were widely circulated.

MAJOR WORKS: *3 surviving operas,* L'Orfeo, Il ritorno d'Ulisse, *and* L'incoronazione di Poppea; *9 books of madrigals; 3 other volumes of secular songs;* Vespro della Beata Vergine; *3 masses; 4 collections of sacred music*

Example 13.1: Monteverdi, Cruda Amarilli, *mm. 1–14*

x = unprepared or incorrectly resolved dissonances

SOURCE READINGS

MUSIC AS THE SERVANT OF THE WORDS

Change to a new style often creates conflicts. One of the most famous disputes is Giovanni Maria Artusi's attack in 1600 on Claudio Monteverdi's Cruda Amarilli *for needless violations of the rules of counterpoint. In response, Monteverdi placed the madrigal first in his* Fifth Book of Madrigals *(1605) and included a brief preface suggesting that there is a "Second Practice" beyond the traditional rules. He promised a full explanation that never appeared, but his brother Giulio Cesare Monteverdi elaborated in the preface to Claudio's* Scherzi musicali *(1607), saying that in the Second Practice the music serves the words, rather than following its own rules as in the First Practice codified by Zarlino.*

———— • ————

[These passages] are contrary to what is well and good in the institution of harmony. They are harsh to the ear, rather offending than delighting it; and to the good rules left by those who have established the order and the bounds of this science, they bring confusion and imperfection of no little consequence....

I do not deny that discovering new things is not merely good but necessary. But tell me first why you wish to employ these dissonances as they employ them?... If the purpose can be attained by observing the precepts and good rules handed down by the theorists and followed by all the experts, what reason is there to go beyond the bounds to seek out new extravagances?

From Giovanni Maria Artusi, *L'Artusi overo Delle imperfettioni della moderna musica* (Venice, 1600), trans. Oliver Strunk, rev. Margaret Murata, in SR 82 (4:2), p. 532.

———— • ————

Studious Readers,

Be not surprised that I am giving these madrigals to the press without first replying to the objections that Artusi made against some very minute portions of them. Being in the service of this Serene Highness of Mantua, I am not master of the time I would require. Nevertheless I wrote a reply to let it be known that I do not do things by chance, and as soon as it is rewritten it will see the light under the title,

Cruel Amaryllis, who with your very name [teach bitterly] of love, alas!

Second Practice, or the Perfection of Modern Music. Some will wonder at this, not believing that there is any other practice than that taught by Zarlino. But let them be assured concerning consonances and dissonances that there is a different way of considering them from that already determined, which defends the modern manner of composition with the assent of reason and of the senses. I wanted to say this both so that the expression "second practice" would not be appropriated by others and so that men of intellect might meanwhile consider other second thoughts concerning harmony. And have faith that the modern composer builds on foundations of truth.

Live happily.

Claudio Monteverdi, preface to *Il quinto libro de madrigali a cinque voci* (Venice, 1605), trans. Claude V. Palisca, "The Artusi-Monteverdi Controversy," in *The New Monteverdi Companion,* ed. Denis Arnold and Nigel Fortune (London and Boston: Faber & Faber, 1985), 151–52, in SR 83 (4:3), p. 543.

——— • ———

My brother says that he does not compose his works by chance because, in this kind of music, it has been his intention to make the words the mistress [ruler] of the harmony and not the servant....

But in this case, Artusi takes certain portions, or, he calls them, "passages," from my brother's madrigal "Cruda Amarilli," paying no attention to the words [i.e., the meaning and impact of the text], but neglecting them as though they had nothing to do with the music. ... By passing judgment on these "passages" without the words, his opponent implies that all excellence and beauty consist in the exact observance of the aforesaid rules of the First Practice, which make the harmony mistress of the words. This my brother will make apparent, knowing for certain that in a kind of composition such as this one of his, ... the harmony, from being the mistress becomes the servant of the words, and the words the mistress of harmony. This is the way of thinking to which the Second Practice, or modern usage, tends.

Giulio Cesare Monteverdi, "Dichiaratione," in Claudio Monteverdi, *Scherzi musicali* (Venice, 1607), trans. Oliver Strunk, in SR 83 (4:3), p. 538.

GENERAL CHARACTERISTICS OF BAROQUE MUSIC

Beyond interest in drama and in moving the affections, music of the Baroque era tends to share several traits that distinguish it from music of other periods.

TREBLE-BASS POLARITY

The prevailing texture of Renaissance music is a polyphony of independent voices. By contrast, the new seventeenth-century music typically emphasizes homophony, featuring prominent bass and treble lines, with written-out or improvised inner parts filling in the harmony. Melody with accompaniment was not itself new; something like it appears in chansons of the fourteenth and fifteenth centuries and in homophonic partsongs in the sixteenth. What was new around 1600 was a polarity between bass and treble as the two essential lines.

Figure 13.8: A theorbo, a type of lute with long, unstopped bass strings, often used in accompanying singers. The alternate Italian name, chitarrone (large kithera), reflects Italians' interest in ancient Greek music. The instruments's first known appearance was in the Florentine intermedi of 1589 (described in chapter 14), whose theme was the power of Greek music; the theorbo may have been invented for the occasion. Detail from The Five Senses, a painting by Theodoor Rombouts (ca. 1630).

Figure 13.9: Giulio Caccini's solo madrigal Vedrò 'l mio sol, *as printed in* Le nuove musiche. *In this early example of figured bass notation, the bass is figured with the exact intervals to be sounded in the chords above it, such as the dissonant eleventh (11) resolving to the major tenth (♯10) in the first measure. In later practice, the precise octave was left to the player, so 4 and ♯ would be used instead of 11 and ♯10. A flat or sharp without a number indicates a minor or major third respectively, as in the middle of the third system.*

THE BASSO CONTINUO

Related to this polarity was the system of notation called **basso continuo** (Italian for "continuous bass") or **thoroughbass.** In this system, the composer wrote out the melody or melodies and the bass line but left it to the performers to fill in the appropriate chords or inner parts. The bass and chords were played on one or more **continuo instruments,** typically harpsichord, organ, lute, or **theorbo** (also called *chitarrone*), a large lute with extra bass strings as shown in Figure 13.8. By the later seventeenth century, the bass line was frequently reinforced by a melody instrument such as viola da gamba, cello, or bassoon. When the chords to be played were other than common triads in root position, or if nonchord tones (such as suspensions) or accidentals were needed, the composer usually added figures—numbers or flat or sharp signs—above or below the bass notes to indicate the precise notes required, as shown in Figure 13.9. Such a bass line is called a **figured bass.**

The **realization**—the actual playing—of such a bass varied according to the type of piece and the skill and taste of the player, who had considerable room

Realization

for improvisation. The performer might play only chords, or add passing tones or melodic motives that imitated the treble or bass. Example 13.2 shows two possible realizations of the first phrase of Figure 13.9—one in mostly chordal style, the other with moving parts and an embellished suspension. In choosing how to realize the bass, the continuo player was free to aid the interpretations and differing emphases of various soloists. Modern editions of works with continuo may print an editor's realization in smaller notes (compare Figure 13.9 with its realization in NAWM 64).

CD 4|26   CD 2|38

Example 13.2: Two possible continuo realizations for the opening of
Vedrò 'l mio sol

a. Chordal style

b. With figuration

I will see my sun.

Not all pieces used basso continuo; because its purpose was accompaniment, it was unnecessary in solo lute and keyboard music. Then again, old-style unaccompanied motets and madrigals were sometimes published with a continuo part, to conform with the new practice.

THE CONCERTATO MEDIUM

Seventeenth-century composers frequently combined voices with instruments that played different parts. The result was called the **concertato medium** (from Italian *concertare*, "to reach agreement"). In a musical **concerto,** contrasting forces are brought together in a harmonious ensemble. Today we think of concertos as pieces for soloists and orchestra, but the meaning was broader in the seventeenth century, embracing such genres as the **concerted madrigal** for one or more voices and continuo and the **sacred concerto,** a sacred vocal work with instruments. The use of diverse timbres in combination became characteristic of the Baroque era, in contrast to the sixteenth-century preference for homogeneous ensembles.

MEAN-TONE AND EQUAL TEMPERAMENTS

Joining voices and string instruments with keyboards and lutes created problems of tuning. As noted in chapter 7, sixteenth-century musicians used a variety of tuning systems. Just intonation was preferred by singers and violinists because it allowed the adjustments needed to keep harmonic intervals perfectly in tune. Keyboard players could not adjust pitch while performing, so they generally used mean-tone temperament, which allowed most diatonic triads to sound good but moved out of tune as the number of flats or sharps increased. Fretted instruments, like lutes and viols, needed to use equal temperament to avoid out-of-tune octaves. The combination of these three incommensurate tuning systems provoked some of Artusi's most bitter complaints against modern music.

In practice, performers worked out compromises. As composers explored a wider range of chords and keys, more-nearly-equal temperaments gradually became accepted, although many players were reluctant to give up the purer thirds possible in mean-tone temperament.

CHORDS, DISSONANCE, AND CHROMATICISM

Basso continuo composition led naturally to thinking of consonant sounds as chords rather than as sets of intervals over the bass. This idea, in turn, led to a view of dissonance less as an interval between voices than as a note that does not fit into a chord. As a result, a greater variety of dissonances was tolerated, though by the mid-seventeenth century, conventions governed how they could be introduced and resolved.

Chromaticism followed a similar development, from experimentation around the turn of the century to freedom within an orderly scheme by mid-century. Chromaticism was used especially to express intense emotions in vocal works, to suggest harmonic exploration in instrumental pieces, and to create distinctive subjects for treatment in imitative counterpoint.

HARMONICALLY DRIVEN COUNTERPOINT

The nature of counterpoint changed during the Baroque era. Treble-bass polarity and the use of continuo altered the balance among the parts, replacing the polyphony of equal voices typical of the sixteenth century with an emphasis on the bass. Even in imitative counterpoint the individual melodic lines were subordinated to a succession of chords implied by the bass, producing a counterpoint driven by harmony.

REGULAR AND FLEXIBLE RHYTHM

Music in the Baroque period was either very metric or very free. Composers used flexible rhythms for vocal recitative (see chapter 14) and improvisatory solo instrumental pieces like toccatas and preludes (see chapter 15). For other music, regular rhythms such as those found in dance music became ever more pervasive. Barlines, used in tablatures since the fifteenth century, became common in all kinds of music in the seventeenth century. At first these barlines simply demarcated phrases of equal or unequal length. But by midcentury they were used in the modern sense to mark off **measures**, recurring patterns of strong and weak beats, with the value and number of beats indicated by time signatures. The two types of rhythm, flexible and metric, were often used in succession to provide contrast, as in the pairing of recitative and aria, or toccata and fugue.

IDIOMATIC STYLES

Polyphony, playable by any combination of voices and instruments, tended to equalize vocal and instrumental styles. The prominent role of the soloist in the Baroque period encouraged composers to write music that was idiomatic for a particular medium, such as violin or solo voice. The development of the violin family was especially important because the forceful overhand bowing, in contrast to the underhand bowing on viols, produced a distinctive, penetrating sound. Lutes and keyboard instruments of course had their own idiomatic styles suited to each instrument and its playing technique. Technical improvements in wind instruments made them suitable for exposed solo performance. Famous singers and voice teachers promoted new standards of virtuosity, color, and projection. Styles for voice and for each family of instruments gradually diverged, eventually becoming so distinct that composers could consciously borrow vocal idioms in instrumental writing and vice versa.

EMBELLISHMENT AND IMPROVISATION IN PERFORMANCE

The idiomatic quality of much Baroque music relates to another trait: this music is centered on the performer and performance, not the composer and the work. Baroque musicians regarded written music as a basis for performance, not as an unalterable text. Performers were expected to add to what the composer had written. Continuo players improvised chords, melodies, and even counterpoint above the given bass. Vocal and instrumental soloists ornamented melodies while performing. Such performance practices varied from nation to nation and from one generation to another. Modern scholars and performers have tried to reconstruct these practices based on written accounts and transcribed improvisations, a task that remains complex and controversial.

Ornamentation   For us the word **ornamentation** may suggest merely adding decoration, but Baroque musicians saw it as a means for moving the affections. They recognized two principal ways of ornamenting a melodic line: (1) Brief formulas called **ornaments**, such as trills, turns, appoggiaturas, and mordents, were added to certain notes to emphasize accents, cadences, and other important points in the melody. Special signs sometimes—though not always—indicated their placement. (2) More extended embellishments, such as scales, arpeggios, and the like, were added to create a free and elaborate paraphrase of the written line. This process, sometimes called **division, diminution,** or **figuration,** was especially appropriate to melodies in slow tempo. Example 13.3 shows an excerpt from an aria in Monteverdi's opera *L'Orfeo* (see chapter 14) that was published with the original melody (top staff) in the tenor register joined by an embellished version that represents the kind of ornamentation added by a singer in one performance.

Example 13.3: Monteverdi, Possente spirto, *from* L'Orfeo, *Act III*

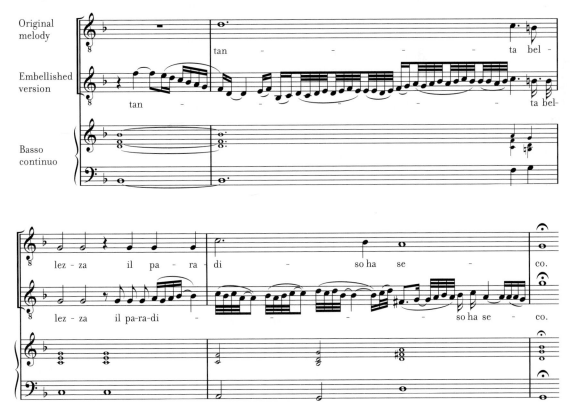

[wherever there is] so much beauty as hers is paradise.

Performers were free not only to add embellishments to a written score but also to change it in other ways. Singers often added **cadenzas**—elaborate passages decorating important cadences—to arias. Arias were omitted from operas, or different arias substituted, to suit the singers. Church organ works could be shortened to fit the service. Sections of variation sets and movements of suites could be omitted or rearranged as desired. Title pages of ensemble collections encouraged players to choose which instruments and even

Alterations

how many to use for a performance. In every respect, the written music was regarded as a script that could be adapted to suit the performers.

FROM MODAL TO TONAL MUSIC

If the above elements tend to characterize the entire Baroque period, one aspect of music that did not hold constant is harmonic organization. Musicians in the early seventeenth century still thought of themselves as working within the eight church modes or the expanded system of twelve modes codified by Glareanus (see chapter 7). By the last third of the century, Corelli, Lully, and other composers were writing music we would unhesitatingly call **tonal**, operating within the system of major and minor keys familiar from music of the eighteenth and nineteenth centuries. Rameau's *Treatise on Harmony* in 1722 offered the first complete theoretical formulation of the new system, which by then had existed in practice for over half a century.

Like the Renaissance version of the modal system, **tonality** evolved gradually. The long-standing use of certain techniques—standard cadential progressions, bass movement by a fourth or fifth, conventional bass patterns, the use of suspensions to create forward motion—eventually bred a consistent set of routines that could be codified in a theory. But the presence of such techniques does not mean that a work is tonal, and music in the first half of the century often shows the continuing influence of the modes.

ENDURING INNOVATIONS

Many of the innovations of the early seventeenth century endured for centuries, and some are still with us. Several characteristics described above remained typical of eighteenth- and nineteenth-century music, including interest in dramatic effect, emotional expressivity, rule-breaking as a rhetorical device, treble-bass polarity, chordal harmony, chromaticism, idiomatic writing, and tonality.

Others, such as basso continuo and mean-tone temperament, gradually passed from use. The performer's role as the music's "co-composer" diminished in the course of the nineteenth and early twentieth centuries when the composer came to be more important than the performer. Of course, there were star performers, but many of them also composed the music they played. In the twentieth century, faithfulness to the composer's score became a paramount virtue for music of earlier times.

Engaging with Baroque music requires us to accept, at least for a time, the values and preferences held by those who made and heard this music. Chief among them was the focus on drama and moving the affections, embodied in the development of a new genre: opera, the topic of the next chapter.

Chapter

14

The Invention of Opera

An **opera** (Italian for "work") is a drama with continuous or nearly continuous music that is staged with scenery, costumes, and action. The text for an opera is called a **libretto** (Italian for "little book"), usually a play in rhymed or unrhymed verse. The art of opera is a union of poetry, drama, and music, all brought to life through performance. From its origins around 1600, opera became the leading genre of the seventeenth and eighteenth centuries and has remained important ever since.

There are two ways to tell the tale of its creation. In one sense, opera was a new invention, an attempt to recreate in modern terms the experience of ancient Greek tragedy: a drama, sung throughout, in which music conveys the emotional effects. Yet in another sense, opera was a blend of existing genres, including plays, theatrical spectacles, dance, madrigals, and solo song. Both views are correct, because the creators of early operas drew on *ideas* about ancient tragedy and on the *content* of modern genres.

FORERUNNERS OF OPERA

The association of music with drama goes back to ancient times. The choruses and principal lyric speeches in the plays of Euripides and Sophocles were sung (see NAWM 2). Medieval liturgical dramas were sung throughout (see NAWM 6), and the religious mystery and miracle plays of the late Middle Ages included some music. Renaissance plays often incorporated songs or offstage music, as do many plays of Shakespeare.

RENAISSANCE ANTECEDENTS

Pastoral drama

One source for opera was the **pastoral drama,** a play in verse with music and songs interspersed. In a tradition derived from ancient Greece and Rome, pastoral poems told of idyllic love in rural settings peopled by rustic youths and maidens, as well as mythological figures. Simple subjects, bucolic landscapes, nostalgia for classical antiquity, and yearning for an unattainable earthly paradise made pastoral themes attractive to poets, composers, and patrons. In this imaginary world, song seemed the natural mode of discourse. The first pastoral poem to be staged was Angelo Poliziano's *Favola d'Orfeo*, on the legend of Orpheus, produced in Florence in 1471. Pastoral dramas became increasingly popular at Italian courts and academies during the sixteenth century. Their subject, style, mythological character types, and use of music and dance were all adopted by the earliest opera composers.

Madrigal and madrigal cycle

Another influence on opera was the madrigal. Some madrigals were miniature dramas, using contrasting groups of voices to suggest dialogue between characters (see NAWM 53). Madrigal composers' experience in expressing emotion and dramatizing text through music laid the foundation for opera. Occasionally, composers grouped madrigals in a series to represent a succession of scenes or a simple plot, a genre known as **madrigal comedy** or **madrigal cycle.** The best known was *L'Amfiparnaso* (The Slopes of Parnassus, 1594) by Orazio Vecchi (1550–1605).

TIMELINE: THE INVENTION OF OPERA

1590	1600	1610	1620	1630	1640	1650	1660

- ca. 1573–87 Meetings of Giovanni de' Bardi's "Camerata"
- 1581 Vincenzo Galilei, *Dialogue of Ancient and Modern Music*
- 1589 Intermedi for the play *La pellegrina* in Florence
- 1598 First opera performed, Jacopo Peri's *Dafne*
- 1598 Henri IV issues Edict of Nantes
- 1600 First surviving opera, Peri's *L'Euridice*, performed in Florence
- 1600 Giovanni Maria Artusi, *L'Artusi*
- 1602 Giulio Caccini, *Le nuove musiche*
- 1607 Claudio Monteverdi, *L'Orfeo*
- 1607 First English colony in Virginia at Jamestown
- 1618–48 Thirty Years' War
- 1620 *Mayflower* brings first colonists to New England
- 1625 Francesca Caccini, *The Liberation of Ruggiero* •
- 1632 Stefano Landi, *Sant' Alessio* •
- 1637 First public opera house opens in Venice •
- 1642–49 English Civil War •
- 1643 Monteverdi, *The Coronation of Poppea* •
- 1649 Francesco Cavalli, *Giasone* •
- 1656 Antonio Cesti, *Orontea* •

Figure 14.1: Set and costumes designed by Bernardo Buontalenti for the first intermedio *for* La pellegrina, *performed in Florence in 1589. Engraving by Agostini Carracci.*

Perhaps the most direct source for opera was the ***intermedio*** (pl. *inter-* *Intermedio* *medi*), a musical interlude on a pastoral, allegorical, or mythological subject performed between acts of a play. The genre arose from a practical need: Renaissance theaters lacked curtains that could close between acts, so something was needed to mark divisions and suggest the passage of time. Intermedi served this function. Usually there were six, performed before, between, and after a play's standard five acts and often linked by a common theme. Intermedi for important occasions were elaborate productions that combined dialogue with choral, solo, and instrumental music, dances, costumes, scenery, and stage effects: in sum, almost all the ingredients of opera except a plot and the new style of dramatic singing (described below).

The most spectacular intermedi were those for the comic play *La pellegrina* *The 1589 intermedi* (The Pilgrim Woman) at the 1589 wedding in Florence of Grand Duke Ferdinand de' Medici of Tuscany and Christine of Lorraine. Several artists who were later involved in the earliest operas worked on these intermedi, including their producer, composer and choreographer Emilio de' Cavalieri (ca. 1550–1602); poet Ottavio Rinuccini (1562–1621); and singer-composers Jacopo Peri (1561–1633) and Giulio Caccini (ca. 1550–1618). The unifying theme, conceived by Florentine count Giovanni de' Bardi (1534–1612), was the power of ancient Greek music, a consuming interest of his circle (see below). Figure 14.1 shows the set and costumes of the first intermedio, on the harmony of the spheres, giving a sense of how lavish the production was. The music was also elaborate, as illustrated by the opening piece, a madrigal for voice and three lutes sung by Vittoria Archilei, shown in Figure 14.2. It was later published as in Example 14.1 (see p. 311), with the vocal line in both its original form (the second staff) and a highly embellished version that suggests the brilliant scales, turns, and other figuration Archilei improvised in performance.

Figure 14.2: Vittoria Archilei, the most famous soprano of her time, in the role of the Dorian harmonia (one of the ancient Greek scales; see chapter 1) in the first intermedio for La pellegrina. *Costume design by Bernardo Buontalenti. In the preface to his opera* L'Euridice, *Jacopo Peri called her "the Euterpe of our age . . . who has always found my music worthy of her performance, adorning it with those ornaments and long vocal runs, both simple and double, which her lively genius invents at every moment, more to go along with the custom of our time than because she thinks that in them resides the beauty and power of our singing. She adds also those charms and graces that cannot be written and, if written, cannot be learned from the notation."*

GREEK TRAGEDY AS A MODEL

These musical and theatrical genres provided materials that composers incorporated in early operas, but opera might never have emerged without the interest of humanist scholars, poets, musicians, and patrons in reviving Greek tragedy. They hoped to generate the ethical effects of ancient music in Greece by creating modern works with equal emotional power. In this sense, opera fulfilled a profoundly humanist agenda, a parallel in dramatic music to the emulation of ancient Greek sculpture and architecture.

Music in Greek tragedy   Renaissance scholars disagreed among themselves about the role of music in ancient tragedy. One view, that only the choruses were sung, was put into practice in a 1585 performance in Vicenza of Sophocles' *Oedipus Rex* in Italian translation. For that production, Andrea Gabrieli cast the choruses in a homophonic declamatory style that emphasized the rhythm of the spoken word.

Girolamo Mei   A contrary view, that the entire text of a Greek tragedy was sung, was expressed by Girolamo Mei (1519–1594), a Florentine scholar who edited several Greek dramas. While working in Rome as a cardinal's secretary, Mei embarked on a thorough investigation of Greek music, particularly its role in the theater. After reading in Greek almost every ancient work on music that survived, he concluded that Greek music consisted of a single melody, sung by a soloist or chorus, with or without accompaniment. This melody could evoke powerful emotional effects in the listener through the natural expressiveness of vocal registers, rising and falling pitch, and changing rhythms and tempo.

THE FLORENTINE CAMERATA

Mei communicated his ideas to colleagues in Florence, notably Count Bardi and Vincenzo Galilei (ca. 1520s–1591), a theorist and composer and the father

Example 14.1: Emilio de' Cavalieri, Dalle più alte sfere, *with embellishments*

From the highest spheres

of astronomer Galileo. From the early 1570s, Bardi hosted an academy where scholars discussed literature, science, and the arts and musicians performed new music. Galilei and Giulio Caccini (and perhaps also Jacopo Peri) were part of this group, which Caccini later called the **Camerata** (circle, or association). Mei's letters about Greek music often appeared on the agenda.

In his *Dialogo della musica antica et della moderna* (Dialogue of Ancient and Modern Music, 1581), Galilei used Mei's doctrines to attack vocal counterpoint. He argued that only a single line of melody, with pitches and rhythms appropriate to the text, could express a given line of poetry. When several voices simultaneously sang different melodies and words, in different rhythms and registers, some low and some high, some rising and others descending, some in slow notes and others in fast, the resulting chaos of contradictory impressions could never deliver the emotional message of the text. Word-painting, imitations of sighing, and the like, so common in madrigals, he dismissed as childish. Only a solo melody, he believed, could enhance the natural speech inflections of a good orator or actor.

Vincenzo Galilei

MONODY, ARIA, AND SOLO MADRIGAL

Galilei was advocating a type of **monody,** a term used by modern historians to embrace all the styles of accompanied solo singing practiced in the late sixteenth and early seventeenth centuries (as distinct from monophony, which is unaccompanied melody). Solo singing was not new; soloists sang epics and other strophic poems to standard formulas with light accompaniment, composers wrote songs for voice and lute, and it was common to sing one part of a polyphonic madrigal while instruments played the other parts. But the Camerata's discussions of Greek music led several members down new paths.

Caccini's
Le nuove musiche

Caccini wrote numerous songs for solo voice with continuo in the 1590s and published them in 1602 under the title *Le nuove musiche* (The New Music). Those with strophic texts he called **arias** (Italian for "airs"), which at this time could mean any setting of strophic poetry. The others he called madrigals, showing that he considered these works to be the same type of piece as polyphonic madrigals: through-composed settings of nonstrophic poems, sung for one's own entertainment or for an audience. Today we use the term **solo madrigal** to distinguish the new type from the madrigal for several voices.

CD 4|26   CD 2|38

In his foreword, Caccini boasted that the madrigal *Vedrò 'l mio sol* (NAWM 64 and Figure 13.9) was greeted in Bardi's Camerata "with affectionate applause." Caccini set each line of poetry as a separate phrase ending in a cadence, shaping his melody to the natural accentuation of the text. He wrote into the music the kind of embellishments that singers would usually have added in performance. Faithful to the goals of the Camerata, he placed ornaments to enhance the message of the text, not just to display vocal virtuosity. His foreword to *Le nuove musiche* includes descriptions of the vocal ornaments then in use, providing a valuable resource for scholars and singers.

THE FIRST OPERAS

Peri and
Rinuccini's Dafne

After Bardi moved to Rome in 1592, discussions about new music—and performances of such works—continued under the sponsorship of another nobleman, Jacopo Corsi (1561–1602). Among the participants were two veterans of the 1589 intermedi, poet Ottavio Rinuccini and singer-composer Jacopo Peri, shown in Figure 14.3. Convinced that Greek tragedies were sung in their entirety, they set out to recreate the ancient genre in modern form. Peri's setting of Rinuccini's pastoral poem *Dafne* was performed in October 1598 at Corsi's palace. Although only fragments of the music survive, this was the first opera, modeled on the Greek plays: a staged drama, sung throughout, with music designed to convey the characters' emotions.

Cavalieri

Meanwhile, Emilio de' Cavalieri, who was in charge of theater, art, and music at the Florentine ducal court, mounted smaller scenes with his own music in a similar style. In February 1600, he produced in Rome his musical morality play *Rappresentatione di Anima et di Corpo* (Representation of the Soul and the Body), at that time the longest entirely musical stage work. These works typify the search for new expressive means that could match the power ancient writers ascribed to Greek music.

L'EURIDICE

In 1600, Peri set to music Rinuccini's pastoral drama *L'Euridice*. The subject demonstrates music's power to move the emotions: through his singing, Orfeo (Orpheus) makes even the denizens of the underworld weep and persuades them to restore his wife Euridice to life.

L'Euridice was performed in Florence that October for the wedding of Maria de' Medici, niece of the grand duke, to King Henry IV of France. Cavalieri directed, and Peri sang the role of Orfeo. The production incorporated sections of another setting of the libretto, this one by Caccini, who would not allow his singers to perform music composed by others. Both versions were soon published, and they remain the earliest surviving complete operas. Of the two settings, Caccini's is more melodious and lyrical, resembling the arias and madrigals of *Le nuove musiche.* But Peri's is better suited to the drama, because he found a new way to imitate speech and varied his approach according to the dramatic situation.

For dialogue, Peri invented a new idiom, soon known as **recitative style.** In his preface to *L'Euridice* (see Source Reading), Peri recalled the distinction made in ancient Greek theory between continuous changes of pitch in speech and intervallic, or "diastematic," motion in song (see chapter 1). He sought a kind of speech-song that was halfway between them, similar to the style that scholars thought the Greeks used for reciting heroic poems. By holding steady the notes of the basso continuo while the voice moved freely through both consonances and dissonances, he liberated the voice from the harmony enough so that it simulated free, pitchless declamation of poetry. When a syllable arrived that would be stressed in speaking—in his words, "intoned"—he formed a consonance with the bass.

Example 14.2 shows how Peri followed his own prescription for the new style. The vertical boxes identify the syllables that are sustained or accented in speech and the consonant harmonies that support them; the horizontal

The recitative style

Figure 14.3: Jacopo Peri, in a costume designed by Bernardo Buontalenti, as the legendary singer Arion in Peri and Christofano Malvezzi's fifth intermedio of 1589. Arion, returning from concerts in Corinth, sings an echo aria just before he plunges into the sea to escape his mutinous crew.

boxes contain the syllables that are passed over quickly in speech and may be set with either dissonances (marked by asterisks) or consonances against the bass and its implied chords. The ways dissonances are introduced and left often violate the rules of counterpoint, but the effort to imitate speech exempts these notes from normal musical conventions. This combination of speechlike freedom and sustained, harmonized accented syllables realized Peri's idea of a medium halfway between speech and song.

Varied styles of monody

Three excerpts from *L'Euridice* illustrate three types of monody employed by Peri. The Prologue (NAWM 65a) is modeled on the aria for singing strophic poetry as practiced throughout the sixteenth century. Each line is set to a repeated pitch and a cadential formula, and the singer varies the rhythm slightly for each strophe to fit the text. An instrumental refrain, called a **ritornello**, separates the strophes. Tirsi's song (NAWM 65b) is rhythmic and tuneful, resembling a canzonetta or dance-song. It is framed by a brief **sinfonia**, a generic term used throughout the seventeenth century for an abstract ensemble piece, especially

---

SOURCE READING

PERI'S RECITATIVE STYLE

In the preface to his opera L'Euridice, *Jacopo Peri described his search for a new kind of musical setting, midway between speech and song, that could convey a character's emotions as forcefully as did the music of ancient Greek dramas. This new style, known as recitative, became an essential part of the new genre of opera.*

———— • ————

Putting aside every other manner of singing heard up to now, I dedicated myself wholly to searching out the imitation that is owed to these poems. And I reflected that the sort of voice assigned by the ancients to song, which they called diastematic (as if to say sustained and suspended), could at times be hurried and take a moderate course between the slow sustained movements of song and the fluent and rapid ones of speech, and thus suit my purpose (just as the ancients, too, adapted the voice to reading poetry and heroic verses), approaching that other [voice] of conversation, which they called continuous and which our moderns (though perhaps for another purpose) also used in their music.

I recognized likewise that in our speech certain sounds are intoned in such a way that a harmony can be built upon them, and in the course of speaking we pass through many that are not so intoned, until we reach another that permits a movement to a new consonance.

Keeping in mind those manners and accents that serve us in our grief and joy and similar states, I made the bass move in time with these, faster or slower according to the affections. I held the bass fixed through both dissonances and consonances until the voice of the speaker, having run through various notes, arrived at a syllable that, being intoned in ordinary speech, opened the way to a new harmony. I did this not only so that the flow of the speech would not offend the ear (almost stumbling upon the repeated notes with more frequent consonant chords), but also so that the voice would not seem to dance to the movement of the bass, particularly in sad or severe subjects, granted that other more joyful subjects would require more frequent movements.

From Peri, *Le musiche sopra l'Euridice* (Florence, 1601), trans. in Claude V. Palisca, *Humanism in Italian Renaissance Musical Thought* (New Haven: Yale University Press, 1985), 428–32.

Example 14.2: Narrative recitative from Peri, Euridice

But the lovely Eurydice dancingly moved her feet on the green grass, when—O bitter, angry fate!—a snake, cruel and merciless, [that lay hidden in the grass, bit her foot.]

one that serves as a prelude. The speech in which Dafne narrates Euridice's death (NAWM 65c and Example 14.2) uses the new recitative. The bass and chords have no rhythmic profile or formal plan and are there only to support the voice's recitation, which is free to imitate the inflections and rhythms of poetic speech. At more emotional moments, Peri heightens the expressivity of his recitative, using methods from the madrigal tradition to convey a character's feelings. When Orfeo first reacts to the news of Euridice's death, as shown in Example 14.3, his breathless shock is conveyed by frequent rests (measures 1–3), and his grief by suspensions (measure 4), unprepared dissonance (measure 5), chromaticism (measures 4–6), and unexpected harmonic progressions (measures 5–6).

CD 4|30

In *L'Euridice*, Peri devised an idiom that met the demands of dramatic poetry. Although he and his associates knew they had not revived Greek music, they claimed to have realized a speech-song that was close to what had been used in ancient theater but was also compatible with modern practice. At the same time that it introduced a new style based on ancient models, Peri's opera also borrowed from the traditions of the madrigal, aria, pastoral drama, and intermedio, using what was most appropriate for each moment of the drama.

THE IMPACT OF MONODY

The various styles of monody, including recitative, aria, and madrigal, quickly made their way into all kinds of music, both secular and sacred. Monody made musical theater possible because it could convey in music everything from narration to dialogue to soliloquy, with the immediacy and flexibility needed for truly dramatic expression. The stylistic diversity Peri introduced

Example 14.3: Expressive recitative from Peri, Euridice

I do not weep and I do not sigh, O my dear Eurydice, for to sigh, to weep I cannot.

was continued and expanded in all later opera, as composers followed his lead in suiting their music to the dramatic situation.

CLAUDIO MONTEVERDI

It is sometimes not the originator of an idea, but the first person to show its full potential, who gives it a permanent place in human history. So it was with opera, whose first great composer was not Peri or Caccini but Claudio Monteverdi (see biography, p. 297).

L'ORFEO

Monteverdi's first opera, *L'Orfeo,* was commissioned by Francesco Gonzaga, heir to the throne of Mantua, and produced there in 1607. It was modeled on *L'Euridice* in subject and mixture of styles, but was musically and dramatically more effective. The librettist, Alessandro Striggio, organized the drama into the usual five acts, each centered around a song by Orfeo and ending with a vocal ensemble that comments on the situation, like the chorus in a Greek tragedy. Monteverdi brought to opera his experience composing madrigals known for expressive text-setting and intense drama. He also used a larger and more varied group of instruments than Peri had used; the score, published in 1609, calls for recorders, cornetts, trumpets, trombones, strings, double harp, and several different continuo instruments, including a regal (a buzzy-sounding reed organ) for the scenes in the underworld.

Monteverdi followed Peri in using several kinds of monody. His Prologue, *Monody* like Peri's, is a strophic aria with ritornello, although it should be noted that this aria is more declamatory than most. Monteverdi wrote out each strophe, varying the melody and the duration of the harmonies to reflect the accentuation and meaning of the text, a procedure called **strophic variation.** He used the same approach for the work's centerpiece, Orfeo's Act III aria *Possente spirto*, and included in the published score a florid ornamentation of the first four strophes (see Example 13.3). Monteverdi's recitative is more varied than Peri's, moving from narrative to songfulness to agonized expression as the drama warrants.

In addition to monody, Monteverdi included many duets, dances, and en- *Ensembles* semble madrigals and ballettos, thus providing a range of contrasting styles to reflect the varying moods in the drama. The ritornellos and choruses help to organize scenes into schemes of almost ceremonial formality. For example, Act I is an arch, framed by strophic variations in the Prologue (sung by the character personifying Music) and at the end of the act, as shown in Figure 14.4. Two choruses, a madrigal and a balletto, alternating with recitatives, precede the central impassioned recitative of Orfeo, followed by a response from Euridice and then the same balletto and madrigal in reverse order.

If Act I is a static arch, appropriate to a wedding ceremony, Act II (excerpted *Act II* in NAWM 66) is a dramatic rush forward. Orfeo and his companions salute the happy day in a series of arias and ensembles, each with its own ritornello, strung together without a break. The series culminates with a strophic aria for Orfeo, *Vi ricorda* (NAWM 66a), in which he recalls his unhappiness turning to

CD 4|34   CD 2|40

Prologue

Music: Strophic variations with ritornello, *Dal mio Permesso amato*

Act I

Shepherd: Recitative, *In questo lieto e fortunato giorno*

Chorus with instruments: Madrigal, *Vieni Imeneo*

Nymph: Recitative, *Muse, honor di Parnaso*

Chorus with instruments: Balletto with ritornello, *Lasciate i monti*

Shepherd: Recitative, *Ma tu gentil cantor*

Orfeo: Recitative, *Rosa del ciel*

Euridice: Recitative, *Io non dirò*

Chorus with instruments: Balletto with ritornello, *Lasciate i monti*

Chorus with instruments: Madrigal, *Vieni Imeneo*

Shepherd: Recitative, *Ma se'l nostro gioir*

Ensemble: Strophic variations with ritornello, *Alcun non sia*

Chorus: Madrigal, *Ecco Orfeo*

Figure 14.4: Monteverdi, L'Orfeo, Prologue and Act I.

joy as he won Euridice. The form and the lighthearted style parallel Peri's canzonetta for Tirsi, and the hemiola rhythms give it a dancelike lilt.

Ironically, at the peak of joy, a Messenger arrives to bring the tragic news that Euridice has died from a snakebite. A sudden change of continuo instrument to an organ with wooden pipes and of tonal area from Ionian mode (C major) to Aeolian (A minor) marks the Messenger's cry, *Ahi, caso acerbo* (Ah, bitter event, NAWM 66c), in an impassioned recitative. At first, Orfeo's companions do not understand and keep singing in their own tonal and timbral world as they wonder what is wrong. But after the Messenger relates her story, a shepherd repeats her opening cry, which becomes a recurring refrain for the rest of the act, as the other characters join her in grief. This use of tonal area, timbre, and formal organization to deepen the dramatic impact shows Monteverdi's skill in using all the resources at hand for expression.

CD 4|36   CD 2|41

Orfeo's lament *Tu se' morta* (NAWM 66d) attains a new height of lyricism for recitative that leaves the first monodic experiments far behind. In the opening passage, shown in Example 14.4, each phrase of music, like each phrase of text, builds on the preceding one, intensifying it through pitch and rhythm. The dissonances against sustained chords, marked with asterisks, not only enhance the illusion of speech but also express Orfeo's bitter feelings. The raw passage from an E-major to a G-minor chord (measures 3–4) underscores the irony that he still lives when Euridice—his "life"—is dead.

CD 4|40   CD 2|45

LATER DRAMATIC WORKS

Orfeo was so successful that Duke Vincenzo Gonzaga commissioned a second opera, *L'Arianna*, from Monteverdi for the next year. It won great renown, but

Example 14.4: Orfeo's lament, from Monteverdi, L'Orfeo, Act II

You are dead, my life, and I still breathe? You have departed from me.

only a fragment survives: Arianna's lament. Both *Orfeo* and *Arianna* were staged in other cities as much as three decades later, an unusual longevity for operas at the time.

Monteverdi moved to Venice in 1613 as maestro di cappella at St. Mark's. Alongside church and vocal chamber music (described in chapter 15), he continued to write operas and other dramatic works. Especially significant is *Combattimento di Tancredi e Clorinda* (The Combat of Tancred and Clorinda, 1624), a short work blending music and mime. The text, from Torquato Tasso's epic *Gerusalemme liberata* (Jerusalem Delivered, 1575), describes the combat between the crusader knight Tancred and the armored pagan heroine Clorinda. Most of the poem is narrative, which Monteverdi assigned to a tenor in recitative. The few short speeches of Tancred and Clorinda are sung by a tenor and soprano, who also mime the actions during the narrative. The instruments (strings with continuo) accompany the voices and play interludes that suggest the action, such as galloping horses and clashing swords. To convey anger and warlike actions, Monteverdi devised the **stile concitato** (excited style), characterized by rapid reiteration on a single note, whether on quickly spoken syllables or in a measured string tremolo. Other composers imitated this device, and it became a widely used convention.

Combattimento

Near the end of his life, Monteverdi composed three operas for the new public theaters in Venice (see below). Two survive: *Il ritorno d'Ulisse* (The Return of Ulysses, 1640), based on the last part of Homer's *Odyssey*, and *L'incoronazione di Poppea* (The Coronation of Poppea, 1643), a historical opera on the Roman Emperor Nero's second marriage. *Poppea*, often considered Monteverdi's masterpiece, lacks the varied instrumentation of *Orfeo* because it was written for a commercial theater instead of a wealthy court, but it surpasses *Orfeo* in depiction of human character and passions. The love scene between Nero and Poppea in Act I, scene 3 (NAWM 67), shows Monteverdi's willingness to change styles frequently to reflect the characters and their feelings: expressive recitative inflected with dissonance and chromaticism as Poppea pleads for Nero not to leave; simpler recitation for dialogue; aria styles with ritornellos, often in triple time, for declarations of love; and passages that lie somewhere between recitative and aria style, which are often called **recitativo arioso**, or **arioso.** Even for sections not in strophic verse, the composer sometimes used aria style. Content more than poetic form, and heightened emotional expression rather than the wish to charm or dazzle, determined the shifts between styles. Thus the stylistic variety in *Poppea*, though even greater than in *Orfeo*, serves the same dramatic goals.

Venetian operas

CD 4|42   CD 2|47

THE SPREAD OF ITALIAN OPERA

Operas were expensive and remained relatively rare, yet they continued to be produced in Florence and Mantua and slowly spread to other cities. As opera attracted new sponsors and audiences, it changed to reflect their tastes, from a courtly entertainment based on humanist ideals to a theatrical spectacle reminiscent of intermedi but centered on singers, much like today.

FLORENCE: FRANCESCA CACCINI

Only a few more operas were written and performed in Florence during the thirty years after *L'Euridice*, including *Dafne* (1608) by Marco da Gagliano (1582–1643). Opera had not yet gained preeminence, and the court preferred ballets and intermedi to glamorize state events. The flexibility of genres at the time is illustrated by *La liberazione di Ruggiero dall'isola d'Alcina* (The Liberation of Ruggiero from the Island of Alcina, 1625), with music by Francesca Caccini (1587–ca. 1645), staged for the visit of a Polish prince. Billed as a ballet, the work had all the trappings of opera: opening sinfonia, prologue, recitatives, arias, choruses, instrumental ritornellos, and elaborate staging, as shown in Figure 14.5. It also had dances, performed either to music sung by the chorus or to instrumental music not included in the published score. Commissioned by the archduchess, the work explores the theme of women and power, with a good and an evil sorceress, delineated by contrasting musical styles, contending over the young knight Ruggiero.

Caccini had a brilliant career as a singer, teacher, and composer, becoming the highest-paid musician employed by the grand duke of Tuscany. She came from a musical family: her father was Giulio Caccini, and she sang frequently with her sister Settimia and stepmother Margherita in a *concerto delle donne* rivaling that of Ferrara (see chapter 11). She composed music for at least fourteen dramatic entertainments, making her among the most prolific composers of dramatic music at the time.

ROME

In the 1620s, the center for new developments in opera moved to Rome, where wealthy prelates vied with each other in offering lavish entertain-

Figure 14.5: Stage design by Giulio Parigi for the second change of scene in Francesca Caccini's La liberazione di Ruggiero, produced in 1625 at the Medici Villa of Poggio Imperiale. The setting is the enchanted island of the sorceress Alcina, who holds the crusader Ruggiero captive there. The plot was based on an episode in Ludovico Ariosto's epic Orlando furioso (1532). Engraving by Alfonso Parigi.

ments. When Maffeo Barberini was elected Pope Urban VIII in 1623, his nephews were put in an advantageous position, and they became ardent sponsors of opera.

Subjects expanded from pastoral and mythological plots to include the epics of Torquato Tasso and Ludovico Ariosto, the lives of saints, and the first comic operas. The most prolific librettist was Giulio Rospigliosi (later Pope Clement IX), who helped create libretto writing as a separate craft. His most famous libretto, *Sant' Alessio* (1632), based on the life of the fifth-century Saint Alexis, was set to music by Stefano Landi (1587–1639). Operas often emphasized spectacular stage effects; for example, in the 1634 revival of *Sant' Alessio*, the devils and demons are consumed in flames.

In the Roman opera, solo singing increasingly fell into two clearly defined *Music* types, recitative and aria. The recitatives were more speechlike than Peri's or Monteverdi's, and the arias were melodious and mainly strophic. Domenico Mazzocchi (1592–1665) enlivened the recitatives in his opera *La catena d'Adone* (1626) by using short, tuneful passages that he called *mezz'arie* (half-arias) and were later termed *arioso*. The Roman operas often included vocal ensembles, developed from the madrigal tradition, and extended finales for each act, with choral singing and dancing, following the models of classical plays. Many Roman operas, including *Sant' Alessio*, open with a sinfonia in two parts, a slow chordal section followed by a lively imitative canzona; opening sinfonias of this kind became standard for seventeenth-century operas.

Because women were prohibited from the stage in Rome, female roles were *Castrati* sung by **castrati** (sing. *castrato*), males who were castrated before puberty to preserve their high vocal range. In Italy, women were not allowed to sing in church, and from the mid-sixteenth century castrati sang the high parts in church music. Later in the seventeenth and eighteenth centuries, castrati also sang in operas outside Rome, but almost always in male rather than female roles (see chapter 18).

VENICE

A decisive step in the history of opera was taken in 1637 with the opening in Venice of the first public opera house, Teatro San Cassiano. Until then musical theater depended on individual aristocratic or ecclesiastical patrons, but now it was presented for and supported in part by the paying public, with financial backing from wealthy and prominent families who rented boxes for the season.

Venice was ideal for public opera. Its reputation for freedom from reli- *Audience* gious and social restraints attracted visitors each year for Carnival, which ran for several weeks between the day after Christmas and the day before Lent. Carnival brought together diverse audiences, and producers sought to lure them to the opera. Rich merchants built and supported theaters, two to four of them each season devoted to opera. In all, nine stages existed in 1678, when Teatro San Giovanni Grisostomo, shown in Figure 14.6, opened as the last new theater of the century. The wealthier families could lease boxes, and anyone could rent a seat on the ground level for a single performance. Everyone, including box holders, had to buy admission tickets. With steady financing and a guaranteed audience for at least part of the year, artists and impresarios

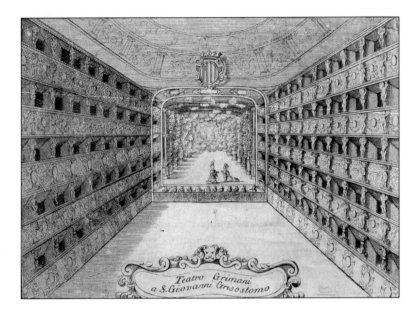

Figure 14.6: A view of the Teatro San Giovanni Grisostomo in Venice, showing the stage with sets in place, the orchestra in front of the stage, and several tiers of boxes, which offered both a better view and greater prestige for audience members than seating on the main floor. Engraving from 1709.

could count on multiple performances of an opera during the season, and many in the audience would attend the same opera numerous times.

Librettos and music

Alongside operas on mythological themes, Venetian librettists drew subjects from the epics of Homer, Virgil, Tasso, and Ariosto, and from Roman history. Plots were chosen with an eye for a wide range of emotions, dramatic conflicts, and striking stage effects, including magical transformations as well as clouds that carried singers. Three acts rather than the five of earlier times were now typical. For financial reasons, choruses and dances were mostly eliminated. The separation of recitative and aria, begun in Rome, continued in Venice and became the convention. The number of arias per act increased. No longer required to follow every nuance of the text, composers wrote melodious arias that unfold in graceful, smoothly flowing phrases supported by simple harmonies, often in triple meter with a persistent rhythmic motive. This lyrical style of vocal music was imitated all over Europe and also influenced instrumental music throughout the following centuries.

Cavalli and Cesti

Among the leading Venetian opera composers were Francesco Cavalli (1602–1676), a pupil of Monteverdi's and organist at St. Mark's, and Antonio Cesti (1623–1669). The most celebrated of Cavalli's over thirty operas was *Giasone* (Jason, 1649), whose arias exemplify the lyric style. Cesti, who also excelled in lyrical arias and duets, was Cavalli's most serious competitor but spent much of his career abroad (see below).

Singers

More important than the drama, spectacle, or composer in attracting a cosmopolitan public were the singers—especially the women and castrati—who were drawn to Venice to further their careers. Impresarios competed for the most popular singers by paying high fees. The singers Signora Girolama and Giulia Masotti earned twice to six times as much for an opera's run as Cavalli, the best-paid composer, received for writing it. The vogue of the operatic diva was inaugurated by Anna Renzi (see sidebar and Figure 14.7, pp. 324–25), and composers wrote parts expressly for her talents.

ITALIAN OPERA ABROAD

From Venice, touring companies took opera to Bologna, Naples, Lucca, Genoa, and other Italian cities. In the 1650s, permanent opera houses were established in Naples and Florence, and others soon followed.

Meanwhile, Italian opera began to reach other lands. Italian operas were staged in Paris in the 1640s, culminating in a commission to Roman composer Luigi Rossi (1597–1653) for a new version of *Orfeo* (1647). A copy of a Cavalli opera reached England, though no performance is known. Austria became a center of Italian opera. In Innsbruck, the archduke of Tyrol had a Venetian-style opera house built in 1654, and Cesti wrote four operas for that theater. When the last archduke died, Cesti moved on to the imperial court in Vienna, where his most famous opera, *Il pomo d'oro* (The Golden Apple, 1667), was performed at great expense for the wedding of Emperor Leopold I. The French turned to their own style of opera in the 1670s (although it was devised by an Italian immigrant; see chapter 16), but Italian opera reigned in German-speaking lands through the early nineteenth century.

ITALIAN OPERA AT MIDCENTURY

Cesti's *Orontea*, written for Innsbruck in 1656, was one of the most frequently performed operas in the seventeenth century, appearing all over Italy and reaching northern Germany in 1678. It epitomizes the changes opera had undergone in half a century. Instead of imitating Greek tragedy, the librettist interwove romantic and comic scenes and high and low characters, seeking first of all to entertain. The plot, based on disguise and love at first sight across social levels, is quintessentially Venetian, far from the heroics of early opera.

Cesti's Orontea

As in the typical midcentury opera, most of the action unfolds in simple recitative. Example 14.5 shows part of a scene in which Orontea, queen of

Recitative style

Example 14.5: Recitative from Cesti, Orontea, *Act II, scene 16*

If Bacchus is the cause of my delays, punish the bottle that he poured for me,
   O Lady, and not Gelone.

INNOVATIONS: SINGER-POWER AND SINGER-WORSHIP—THE DIVA

 From its very beginnings, opera was a complicated, costly, even extravagant affair requiring the collaboration of the librettist, the composer (who held a decidedly lower status than the author of the words), and the artists whose performances engaged the audience directly. In addition, it demanded the services of a vast array of crafts people and providers who worked behind the scenes. Among these silent and unseen participants—including stage managers, carpenters, painters, costume designers, tailors, hairdressers, and copyists—none was more crucial than the *impresario,* who was roughly equivalent to the modern producer. (Transferred into English from the Italian, the word *impresario* acquired its distinctive meaning with the rise of Venetian opera.) The theater's owner, head of one of the noble families of Venice, entrusted the impresario with managing the theater successfully for one season at a time, which meant bringing in a profit after all the production expenses and artists' fees were paid. Naturally, the economic outcome depended in good measure on the impresario's decisions about how many and which operas were to be performed in a given season. Competition was fierce, so the impresario also had to consider the financial risks involved in mounting spectacular scenic effects or hiring the most highly paid singers, and measure these costs against the potential gains of attracting larger audiences.

This volatile commercial atmosphere fostered, among other things, the phenomenon of the operatic *diva* (or star). Impresarios went to great lengths and expense to secure effective performers because they realized that a singer could make or break an entire opera season no matter what work was being produced. Although singer-power had been a theme in opera from its beginnings—think of Orfeo, whose legendary song persuaded supernatural forces to return his spouse to life—that power now resided with the singers themselves rather than with the characters they portrayed. Sopranos, especially those who were able to win favor through virtuosic ornamentation and persuasive interpretation, quickly achieved stardom. Once having made it to the top, a diva could demand that composers and librettists alter roles to suit her particular vocal talents and range. In so doing, she not only exercised her star-power but actually influenced the development of opera in ways that eventually affected its dramatic structure as well as its musical values.

The career of Anna Renzi, leading lady of the Venetian operatic stage in the 1640s, is a case in point and illustrates the rise in stature of the female singer. Renzi was only about twenty when her teacher brought her from Rome to Venice to perform the title role in the work that was scheduled to open the newest public opera house in that city, the Teatro Novissimo. The composer, Francesco Sacrati, undoubtedly tailored the role specifically to her in order to capitalize on her particular talents. That she played a woman pretending to be afflicted with madness on that occasion and then, a few years later, created the role of Nero's spurned empress Ottavia in Monteverdi's *Incoronazione di Poppea* speaks to her capabilities as an actress, one who could impart a certain dramatic intensity to her characters. Although her powers as a performer were by all accounts splendid, her meteoric ascent was at least in part a product of "media hype." The librettist of her first Venetian opera, Giulio Strozzi, anxious to prove that public opera employed singers as divine as those of the wealthiest courts, published a special volume of adulatory poetry in her honor in 1644.

Intima si cantum simulat præcordia mulcet,
Ipsam animam sensim si canit Anna rapit.

Jacobus Ibinus Venetus Iaciebat Ven:

Figure 14.7: The famous opera singer Anna Renzi, in an engraving from Giulio Strozzi's adulatory book The Glories of Signora Anna Renzi the Roman.

The engraving of her likeness seen in Figure 14.7 comes from that volume.

In an introductory essay, Strozzi describes Renzi's stage presence and vocal qualities, stressing the apparently spontaneous nature of her movements and gestures: "Our Signora Anna is endowed with such lifelike expression that her responses and speeches seem not memorized but born at the very moment. In sum, she transforms herself completely into the person she represents." He goes on to praise her diction and vocal delivery, extolling her "fluent tongue, smooth pronunciation, not affected, not rapid, a full, sonorous voice, not harsh, not hoarse." He also remarks on her stamina and resilience, her ability to "bear the full weight of an opera no fewer than twenty-six times, repeating it virtually every evening ... in the most perfect voice." Finally, Strozzi approaches Renzi's offstage attributes and portrays her as a person of "great intellect, much imagination, and a good memory ... ; of melancholy temperament by nature [she] is a woman of few words, but those are appropriate, sensible, and worthy." Although she did not have what might be called a "classic beauty," Renzi's qualities essentially set the standard for the **prima donna** (Italian for "first lady," the lead soprano in an opera).

Divas became larger-than-life heroines with lucrative international careers. Following her memorable Venetian years, Renzi performed roles in other Italian cities and in Innsbruck, where Queen Cristina of Sweden, who was then visiting the Austrian court, acknowledged her stunning skills by making her a present of her own medal and chain. Other prima donnas (and leading male singers) enjoyed similarly close relationships with patrons, composers, librettists, and impresarios in whose homes they sometimes lived when they were on the road. Not surprisingly, they frequently exploited these ties by insinuating themselves into the creative process, exerting their influence on such matters as the selection of a plot, the number and length of arias written for their parts, and the casting of supporting roles. Occasionally a singer even refused to participate in a production unless a particular composer was commissioned to write the music.

Singer-power and singer-worship, then, ultimately played a big part in the direction that opera took in the seventeenth century. But the story does not end there. After taking hold of the Venetian imagination, the glamorous world of opera and its stars went on to captivate all of Europe and eventually the Americas. Even today, the powerful personalities of divas and their equivalents outside of opera—rock stars and film icons—are the driving force behind much of the entertainment industry.—BRH

*Quotations from Giulio Strozzi are taken from Ellen Rosand, *Opera in Seventeenth-Century Venice: The Creation of a Genre* (University of California Press, 1991), 228–35.

CD 4|48

Egypt, meets the drunken servant Gelone rifling the pockets of the sleeping Alidoro, a young painter (NAWM 68a). This sort of recitative, with many repeated notes, mostly chord tones, and modulating harmonies with frequent secondary dominants, continued with little change for over a century.

Aria style

CD 4|49

The following scene is a soliloquy for Orontea that includes extended sections in aria, recitative, and arioso style, reflecting Orontea's conflicting emotions. Its opening aria, *Intorno all' idol mio* (NAWM 68b), in which Orontea confesses her love for Alidoro, illustrates how elaborate the aria had become by midcentury. The form is strophic, with some musical adjustments for the second stanza. The lyrical idiom reigns throughout, with smooth, mainly diatonic lines and easy rhythm gratifying to the singer, as shown in Example 14.6. The two violins, no longer restricted to ritornellos before and after the singer's strophes, play throughout the aria.

Example 14.6: Aria, Intorno all' idol mio, *from Cesti,* Orontea, *Act II, scene 17*

Around my idol breathe, just breathe, breezes sweet and pleasant.

By the middle of the seventeenth century, Italian opera had acquired the main features it would maintain without essential change for the next two hundred years: (1) concentration on solo singing, rather than ensembles and instrumental music; (2) the separation of recitative and aria; and (3) and the use of varied styles. The Florentine view of music as the servant of poetry and drama had by now been reversed; the Venetians and their imitators saw the drama and poetry as the scaffolding for the music, but their interest centered on the visual elements of scenery, costumes, and special effects and, most of all, on the arias and the stars who sang them.

OPERA AS DRAMA AND AS THEATER

Opera began as an effort to recreate ancient Greek ideals of drama, linking the new Baroque era with the first musical culture we studied in chapter 1. Yet it also had sources in theatrical spectacles like intermedi and in various types of solo song. These roots proved strong, and spectacular staging and solo singing soon became preeminent, emphasizing what might be called the theatrical side of opera at the expense of the dramatic. This tension between drama, spectacle, and vocal display has continued in all later opera and musical theater. Many operatic reform movements, including those around Gluck in the eighteenth century and Wagner in the nineteenth, sought to restore the balance in favor of drama, once again looking back to Greek tragedies for inspiration. But love of the theatrical has been a constant theme, from the elaborate costumes and dances of French Baroque opera, to the virtuosic singing of nineteenth-century Italian opera, to modern musical theater events like *Cats* and *Stomp* that emphasize everything from costumes to dancing over plot.

Most seventeenth-century operas lasted only a single season. Those that were still performed two or three decades after their composition were exceptional. Almost inevitably, a new production brought new singers and revisions to the score, often by other hands. Historians and musicians have tended to value Monteverdi most highly for his music in service of drama and have devalued other early opera, which is rarely heard today. But the focus on solo singing, separation of recitative and aria, and use of varied styles that were characteristic by 1650 continued to dominate Italian opera for the next two centuries.

Meanwhile, styles nurtured in opera also appeared in church music, vocal chamber music, and instrumental music, as we will see in the next chapter. The use of music for dramatic or theatrical effect, pioneered in the early operas, has been a constant feature of musical life ever since. Today such uses for music surround us, in songs, films, television, video games, and even commercials, and most of the emotional and dramatic effects they employ have their source in opera.

Chapter 15

Music for Chamber and Church in the Early Seventeenth Century

Seventeenth-century musicians were acutely aware of style and its relationship to the social functions music serves. Theorists of the time distinguished between church, chamber, and theater music, recognizing different styles appropriate for each. Composers continued to cultivate and expand on the forms, genres, and idioms characteristic of sixteenth-century vocal and instrumental music, giving music in each category a distinctive flavor. Yet the new styles and techniques that were developed for monody and opera quickly spread, as composers infused dramatic elements into other types of music. Thus the chamber, church, and instrumental music of 1600–1650 reveals both continuities with the past and influences from the modern theatrical style.

ITALIAN VOCAL CHAMBER MUSIC

Although opera by midcentury had become the focus of musical life in Venice, elsewhere it was still an extraordinary event. Most secular music involved ensembles with voices and was performed in private music-making or by amateurs for their own enjoyment. Different kinds of secular vocal music were cultivated in different regions and by different social groups. In Italy, canzonettas, ballettos, villanelles, and other light genres of strophic songs continued to be popular with the musically literate public (see chapter 11). Vocal chamber music for the elites appeared in many forms and styles, often combining elements of the madrigal, monody, dance songs, dramatic recitative, and aria. The concertato medium allowed varying textures, and composers used ritornellos, repeating bass patterns, and contrasts of style to create large-scale forms and enrich the expressive resources of their music. The following brief summary cannot do justice to the variety of song in the early seventeenth century, but it does focus on the three developments in Italy that had particular significance for the future: concertato works, **basso ostinato,** and the **cantata.**

SECULAR WORKS IN CONCERTATO STYLE

From the beginning of the century, Italian composers turned out thousands of pieces for solo voice or small vocal ensemble with basso continuo, sometimes including other instruments. These pieces were widely sung and were published in numerous collections. Most works were written for one to three voices, though some featured six or more. Forms and genres included madrigals, canzonettas and other strophic songs and arias, strophic variations, dialogues, and recitatives. Many of these compositions were more widely known than any of the operas, which were performed only a few times for restricted audiences, and several of the innovations crucial to opera were popularized through secular song.

The importance of the concerto medium can be gauged by its impact on the madrigal. We can trace the change from the unaccompanied polyphonic madrigal to the **concerted madrigal** with instrumental accompaniment in Monteverdi's fifth through eighth books of madrigals. Beginning with the last six madrigals of Book 5 (1605), all include a basso continuo, and some call for other instruments as well. Solos, duets, and trios are set off against the vocal ensemble, and there are instrumental introductions and ritornellos. The seventh book, titled *Concerto* (1619), includes strophic variations and canzonettas as well as through-composed madrigals. Book 8, *Madrigali guerrieri et amorosi* (Madrigals of War and Love, 1638), features a remarkable variety, encompassing madrigals for five voices; solos, duets, and trios with continuo; large pieces for chorus, soloists, and instrumental ensemble; and short dramatic works. Styles range from imitative polyphony and homophonic declamation, typical of sixteenth-century madrigals, to operatic recitative and *stile concitato* (excited style).

Concerted madrigals

OSTINATO BASSES

Many works used **basso ostinato** (Italian for "persistent bass"), or **ground bass,** a pattern in the bass that repeats while the melody above it changes. Most ostinato basses were in triple or compound meter, usually two, four, or eight measures long. There was a well-established tradition in Spain and Italy of popular songs, composed or extemporized, that were sung to familiar basso ostinato patterns such as *Guárdame las vacas* (see NAWM 60b), its close relative the *romanesca,* and the *Ruggiero* (see chapter 12). Such basses underlay many songs and instrumental works of the early seventeenth century.

CD 4|8

Descending tetrachord   Another common pattern was a descending tetrachord, a stepwise descent spanning a fourth, which Monteverdi used in his *Lamento della ninfa* (Lament of the Nymph) in his eighth book of madrigals. Its falling contour and constant repetition are suited to a lament, conveying a sense of inescapable sorrow. In the passage in Example 15.1, the recurring bass establishes a tonal center and regular phrasing, while the vocal melody conveys the nymph's distress through strong dissonances (marked with x) and phrases that overlap the four-measure groupings of the bass; notes that were dissonant in the singer's first phrase become consonant in her varied repetition and vice versa. Three male singers introduce and comment on her lament, turning this madrigal into an unstaged drama. Many composers used various forms of the descending bass pattern, especially in opera, for over a century (see NAWM 69 and 79 for examples).

Example 15.1: Monteverdi, Lamento della ninfa, *with descending tetrachord bass*

[Spoken to Love:] *Make my love return as he once was, or kill me yourself so that I will not torment myself any longer.*

Chacona   An opposite emotion was conveyed by bass patterns adapted from the **chacona** (Italian **ciaccona**), a vivacious dance-song imported from Latin America into Spain and then into Italy. The refrain followed a simple pattern of guitar chords. Example 15.2 shows the original bass pattern and the adaptation in Monteverdi's madrigal *Zefiro torna e di soavi accenti*, published in his *Scherzi musicali* (Musical Jests) of 1632. Monteverdi repeats the rising, lightly syncopated figure fifty-six times in succession while two tenors provide vivid imagery suggesting happy feelings inspired by breezes, flowers, and scenes of nature, then ironically depict the abandoned lover's torment in slow, expressive recitative.

Example 15.2: Monteverdi, Zefiro torna e di soavi accenti, *with chacona bass*

a. Chacona bass

b. Zefiro torna, *mm. 5–9*

Zephyr [the gentle breeze] returns.

CANTATA

A new genre of vocal chamber music emerged in Italy during the seventeenth century: the **cantata,** meaning a piece "to be sung." The term was applied before 1620 to a published collection of arias in strophic variation form. By midcentury, *cantata* meant a secular composition with continuo, usually for solo voice, on a lyrical or quasi-dramatic text, consisting of several sections that included both recitatives and arias. Among leading cantata composers of the mid-seventeenth century were Luigi Rossi and Antonio Cesti (see chapter 14); Giacomo Carissimi, who is remembered today for his oratorios (see below); and Barbara Strozzi (1619–1677; see biography, p. 333).

Strozzi's *Lagrime mie* (NAWM 69), published in her *Diporti di Euterpe* (Pleasures of Euterpe, 1659), is representative of the solo cantata in presenting successive sections of recitative, arioso, and aria, and of Strozzi in its focus on unrequited love. In the opening measures of the recitative, shown in Example 15.3, the long descending line, hesitations on the dissonant D♯, A, and F♯ over the opening E-minor harmony, and augmented second from D♯ to C♮ portray the weeping and sobbing lover. Throughout the cantata, Strozzi changes style and figuration frequently to capture the moods and images of the text. The overall effect, combining contrasting musical elements and emotions, is typical of the concerted style at midcentury.

CD 4|51

Example 15.3: Strozzi, Lagrime mie

My tears, [what holds you back?]

OUTSIDE ITALY

Italian styles were imitated by composers in other nations. German composers wrote villanelles, canzonettas, and other homophonic, strophic songs, which gradually displaced the older polyphonic tradition of the German Lied. The Italian style of monody spread to Germany, England, and elsewhere in northern Europe, and later in the century both German and French composers took up the cantata.

But composers outside Italy also produced songs of distinctly national character. In France, the most important genre of secular vocal music was the **air de cour** (court air), a homophonic, strophic song for four to five voices or for solo voice with lute accompaniment, sung as independent vocal music or as part of a court ballet. Simple and mostly syllabic, airs de cour differed from songs elsewhere in following the long and short syllables of the text, as in *musique mesuré* (see chapter 11), rather than a regular metrical scheme. English composers continued to write consort songs, madrigals, and lute songs in the national tradition, but they also composed songs with continuo accompaniment for court entertainment and as independent solos, ranging from recitative style and ostinato arias adopted from Italian models to dance-like airs based on native song styles or on the French air de cour. We will see the impact of Italian music on France, and of Italian and French music on England, in chapter 16.

CATHOLIC SACRED MUSIC

Just as Bernini used theatrical effects for his religious sculpture and architecture (see chapter 13), so Catholic composers adopted the theatrical idiom for church music, setting religious texts in **sacred concertos** that incorporated basso continuo, the concertato medium, monody, and operatic styles from recitative to aria. The stimulus was the same in both cases: using a dramatic, powerful art medium to convey the church's message in the most persuasive and rhetorically effective way.

Yet the church did not abandon polyphony. Indeed, Palestrina's style became the supreme model for church music, bringing associations of age, tradition, reverence, purity, and sanctity. Composers were routinely trained to write in the old contrapuntal style, known from midcentury on as the ***stile antico*** (old style), which coexisted alongside the ***stile moderno*** (modern style). A composer might utilize both styles, sometimes in a single piece, as Monteverdi did on several occasions. Over time, the *stile antico* was modernized. Composers added a basso continuo and regularized rhythms, and

Stile antico

 ## BARBARA STROZZI (1619–1677)

Strozzi was a rarity among Baroque composers, both as a woman and as a musician whose performances were intended for intimate, private gatherings rather than for large, public audiences.

Figure 15.1: Female Musician with Viola da Gamba, *almost certainly a portrait of Barbara Strozzi around 1637, painted by Bernardo Strozzi (perhaps a relative).*

She was born in Venice, the adopted (and perhaps natural) daughter of poet and librettist Giulio Strozzi. Her father nurtured her ambitions as a composer and introduced her to the intellectual elite of Venice. From her teens, she sang at the Strozzi home for gatherings of poets and other writers, formalized in 1637 as the Academy of the Unisoni. She studied with Francesco Cavalli, the leading Venetian opera composer and a student of Monteverdi's. She was supported financially by her father, by the noble patrons to whom she dedicated her publications, and probably by Giovanni Paolo Vidman, the apparent father of at least three of her four children.

Between 1644 and 1664, Strozzi published eight collections of music (one is now lost). Her publications contain over one hundred madrigals, arias, cantatas, and motets, placing her among the most prolific composers of vocal chamber music of the century. Indeed, she published more cantatas than any other composer of the time. Her choice to publish her music is unusual for women musicians in the seventeenth century and may reflect the feminist sympathies of her father and his circle.

MAJOR WORKS: *3 collections of cantatas and arias, 2 of arias, and 1 each of madrigals and motets*

church modes gave way to major-minor tonality. Johann Joseph Fux codified this quasi-Palestrinian counterpoint in his famous treatise *Gradus ad Parnassum* (Steps to Parnassus, 1725), which remained the most influential textbook on counterpoint for the next two centuries.

LARGE-SCALE SACRED CONCERTO

Major feast days—at least in the large, wealthy churches—were celebrated on a grand scale. For such observances, composers wrote Vespers, psalms, mass movements, and other works for many voices with instruments, often using *cori spezzati* (divided choirs). Giovanni Gabrieli wrote polychoral motets for St. Mark's in Venice and for the confraternity of San Rocco that included two or more choirs, vocal soloists, an instrumental ensemble, and one or more organs playing continuo. Orazio Benevoli (1605–1672) was another master of the medium and one of the major figures in seventeenth-century Catholic music. His works include psalms, motets, and masses for three or more

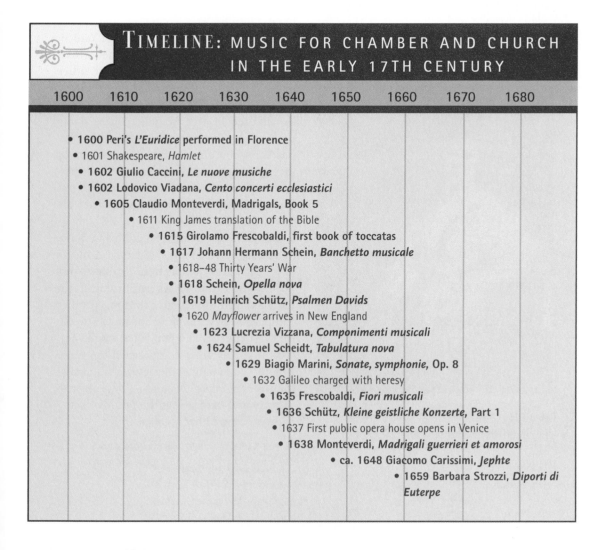

TIMELINE: MUSIC FOR CHAMBER AND CHURCH IN THE EARLY 17TH CENTURY

1600	1610	1620	1630	1640	1650	1660	1670	1680

- 1600 Peri's *L'Euridice* performed in Florence
- 1601 Shakespeare, *Hamlet*
- 1602 Giulio Caccini, *Le nuove musiche*
- 1602 Lodovico Viadana, *Cento concerti ecclesiastici*
- 1605 Claudio Monteverdi, Madrigals, Book 5
- 1611 King James translation of the Bible
- 1615 Girolamo Frescobaldi, first book of toccatas
- 1617 Johann Hermann Schein, *Banchetto musicale*
- 1618–48 Thirty Years' War
- 1618 Schein, *Opella nova*
- 1619 Heinrich Schütz, *Psalmen Davids*
- 1620 *Mayflower* arrives in New England
- 1623 Lucrezia Vizzana, *Componimenti musicali*
- 1624 Samuel Scheidt, *Tabulatura nova*
- 1629 Biagio Marini, *Sonate, symphonie*, Op. 8
- 1632 Galileo charged with heresy
- 1635 Frescobaldi, *Fiori musicali*
- 1636 Schütz, *Kleine geistliche Konzerte*, Part 1
- 1637 First public opera house opens in Venice
- 1638 Monteverdi, *Madrigali guerrieri et amorosi*
- ca. 1648 Giacomo Carissimi, *Jephte*
- 1659 Barbara Strozzi, *Diporti di Euterpe*

choirs with organ, written mostly for St. Peter's in Rome during the 1640s. Benevoli combined the sonorities with utmost skill, alternating antiphonal effects with massive climaxes.

SMALL SACRED CONCERTO

Few places had the resources to support large-scale polychoral works, but the **small sacred concerto,** with one or more soloists accompanied by organ continuo and often by one or two violins, was within the means of even small churches.

Lodovico Viadana (ca. 1560–1627) became a pioneer in using the small vocal concerto for church music, and his 1602 collection *Cento concerti ecclesiastici* (One Hundred Church Concertos) was the first volume of sacred vocal music printed with basso continuo. Viadana adapted the melodic style and imitative textures of sixteenth-century polyphony to the reduced forces of one to four singers with continuo. *Exsultate Deo*, shown in Example 15.4, is typical in suggesting more voices than are actually present. The voice imitates the bass, then both bass and voice repeat the same figure at another pitch level, creating an effect of four independent voices entering in succession. The continuo player may add further voices, as shown in the example. The presence of continuo assured a full harmony, making it unnecessary to double or replace any vocal parts with instruments; indeed, the pieces for two to four singers sound complete even if one voice is omitted. This adaptability made Viadana's collection usable by almost any church and contributed to its popularity.

Lodovico Viadana

Example 15.4: Viadana, Exsultate Deo, *from* Cento concerti ecclesiastici

Ex - sul-ta-te De - o   ex - sul - ta-te De - o   ad-ju - to-ri no - stro

Exult in God.

Alessandro Grandi (1586–1630), Monteverdi's deputy at St. Mark's in Venice in the 1620s, composed many solo motets that used the new styles of monody. His *O quam tu pulchra es* (NAWM 70), published in 1625, blends elements from recitative, solo madrigal, and lyric aria. The changing styles reflect the moods of the text, drawn from the Song of Songs, a book in the Hebrew Scriptures whose dialogue between two lovers was taken as a metaphor for God's love for the church. As shown in Example 15.5, the wonder of

Alessandro Grandi

CD 4|56

the opening line, "Oh how beautiful you are," is captured in recitative style by a sustained note in the voice, an unprepared dissonance in the bass, and a quick descent to a resolution, while parts of the text suggesting action are set in aria style in triple meter. The use of modern musical styles and the language of love parallels Bernini's sensuous depiction of St. Teresa in ecstasy (see chapter 13) in suggesting the intensity of communion with the divine. No doubt many more people encountered the modern vocal styles in church services and devotional music than in opera or in private concerts of secular vocal music.

Example 15.5: Contrasting styles in Grandi's O quam tu pulchra es

a. Recitative style

Oh how beautiful you are.

b. Aria style

Arise, hasten, arise, my bride.

MUSIC IN CONVENTS

Music in convents was mostly unheard by the public. Church administrators in Rome and other cities put many obstacles in the way of convents trying to develop a full musical life for nuns and novices. These administrators would not allow experienced male music directors, composers, or outside musicians to enter the convents for the purpose of instructing singers or joining them in rehearsals.

Lucrezia Vizzana   Despite the many regulations that made serious musical activity a clandestine operation, a lively musical culture developed in the convents throughout

Italy, especially at Santa Cristina della Fondazza in Bologna. The nuns there fought for a level of music-making equal to the standards and styles outside the convent walls. Lucrezia Vizzana (1590–1662) entered Santa Cristina as a child and was trained there by an aunt, an organist, and by the convent's music master. Her *Componimenti musicali* (Musical Compositions), published in Venice in 1623, contains twenty motets, most for one or two soprano voices with basso continuo. They incorporate elements of theatrical monody, including elaborate vocal ornamentation, declamatory phrases, and expressive use of unprepared or unresolved dissonance.

ORATORIO

Italy had a long tradition of religious music outside church services, such as the lauda. In seventeenth-century Rome, a new genre of religious dramatic music emerged, combining narrative, dialogue, and commentary. Toward midcentury, such works became known as ***oratorios,*** after the Italian word *oratorio*, or prayer hall, where lay societies met to contemplate, hear sermons, and sing laudas and other devotional songs.

Like operas, oratorios used recitatives, arias, duets, and instrumental preludes and ritornellos. But oratorios differed from operas in several ways: their subject matter was religious; they were seldom if ever staged; action was described or suggested rather than played out; there was often a narrator; and the chorus—usually an ensemble of several voices singing one to a part—could take various roles, from participating in the drama to narrating or meditating on events. Oratorio librettos were in Latin or Italian.

Oratorio versus opera

The leading composer of Latin oratorios was Giacomo Carissimi (1605–1674). His *Jephte* (ca. 1648) exemplifies the midcentury oratorio. The libretto is based on Judges 11:29–40, with some paraphrasing and added material. In recitative, the narrator introduces the story, and Jephtha, an Israelite general, vows that if the Lord gives him victory in the impending battle, he will sacrifice whatever creature first greets him on his return home. Jephtha's victory over the Ammonites is recounted by the ensemble of six singers, with appropriate effects including *stile concitato.* The narrator relates in recitative how Jephtha returns home in triumph, but the first to greet him is his daughter, so he must sacrifice her. Songs of rejoicing for victory are set as solo arias, duets, and ensembles, followed by a dialogue in recitative between father and daughter. The chorus tells how the daughter goes to the mountains with her companions to bewail her approaching death. In the final scene (NAWM 71), she sings a lament, a long, affecting recitative. Two sopranos, representing her companions, echo some of her cadential flourishes. The response by the chorus of six voices employs both polychoral and madrigalistic effects, including the descending tetrachord bass associated with laments.

Giacomo Carissimi

CD 5|1–2   CD 2|53

In the motets of Grandi and Vizzana, the oratorios of Carissimi, and in other Catholic sacred music, we see composers using a wide range of styles with both secular and religious origins to convey the church's message to their listeners. Rhetorical effectiveness was prized far above stylistic purity. In these works, the primacy of the text and its dramatic declamation was central.

LUTHERAN CHURCH MUSIC

In German-speaking regions, composers in both the Catholic and Lutheran churches soon took up the new monodic and concertato techniques. Sacred music in Austria and Catholic southern Germany remained under strong Italian influence, with Italian composers particularly active in Munich, Salzburg, Prague, and Vienna. Composers in the Lutheran central and northern regions employed the new media, sometimes using chorale tunes or texts. Alongside compositions in modern style, Lutheran composers continued to write polyphonic chorale motets and motets on biblical texts without chorale melodies.

Sacred concerto in Germany

Many biblical motets by Hans Leo Hassler, Michael Praetorius, and others in the early seventeenth century were in the large-scale concerto medium, showing Germans' admiration for the Venetian fashion. The small sacred concerto was even more common. Here the most influential figures were Viadana, whose works circulated in German-speaking lands, and Johann Hermann Schein (1586–1630), who published two important collections in 1618 and 1626 at Leipzig, both titled *Opella nova* (New Little Works). The first book consists chiefly of duets with continuo on chorales, freely paraphrasing the chorale melodies, inserting vocal embellishments, and dividing phrases among the voices. In these works, the Lutheran chorale tradition blends with the modern Italian style. The second book includes more chorale duets, but most pieces are on biblical texts and the settings are more varied, often using one or more solo instruments and contrasting solo with ensemble sections. Schein's sacred concertos set a precedent for a long series of similar works by Lutheran composers.

HEINRICH SCHÜTZ

Heinrich Schütz (1585–1672) was a master at applying the new Italian styles to church music. He studied in Venice with Giovanni Gabrieli, visited again during Monteverdi's years there, and brought their approaches back to Germany, where he was chapel master at the Saxon court in Dresden (see biography). He is particularly renowned for writing music that captures the meanings and imagery of the text.

SACRED WORKS

Schütz published most of his sacred works in a series of collections that show a remarkable variety. The first, *Psalmen Davids* (Psalms of David, 1619), combines sensitive treatment of German texts with the magnificence of the Venetian large-scale concerto for two or more choruses, soloists, and instruments, following the model of Gabrieli. *Cantiones sacrae* (Sacred Songs, 1625) contains polyphonic Latin motets, enlivened by harmonic novelties

HEINRICH SCHÜTZ (1585–1672)

Schütz is known especially for his church music and for his singular genius at conveying the meaning of words.

The son of an innkeeper, Schütz showed an early talent for music. Although his family did not want him to pursue music as a career, his singing at age twelve so impressed Moritz, the Landgrave of Hesse, that the nobleman insisted on bringing Schütz to Kassel and sponsoring his education in music and other subjects.

Schütz entered the University of Marburg to study law, but Moritz persuaded him to go to Venice in 1609 and study composition with Giovanni Gabrieli. There Schütz published his first work, a collection of five-part Italian madrigals. After Gabrieli's death in 1612, he returned to Kassel as court organist, but the elector of Saxony pressured Moritz first to lend and ultimately to grant him the young musician, showing not only that Schütz was greatly esteemed as a musician, but also that musicians were essentially servants, not entirely free to decide their own destinies.

From 1615 to his death in 1672, Schütz was chapel master for the elector's court in Dresden, although he took leaves to visit Italy and work briefly at other courts. He petitioned for reduction of his duties beginning in 1645, at age sixty, a request granted only after the elector's death in 1657.

Schütz wrote music for all major ceremonies at court, secular and sacred. The former included the first German opera (1627), several ballets, and other stage works, although almost none of this music survives. He apparently did not write independent instrumental music. What remains is a great quantity and variety of church music. Some had personal reso-

Figure 15.2: Heinrich Schütz at about age seventy, in a portrait by Christoph Spetner.

nance: his first sacred collection, *Psalmen Davids*, was published shortly before his 1619 wedding to Magdalena Wildeck, and her death in 1625 prompted simple four-part settings of a German psalter (published 1628). His *Musikalische Exequien* (1636) was funeral music for a friend and patron. But most was simply service music, each piece perfectly suited to the text at hand and the musicians at his disposal.

MAJOR WORKS: Psalmen Davids (*German polychoral psalms*), Cantiones sacrae (*Latin motets*), Symphoniae sacrae (*sacred symphonies, 3 volumes*), Musikalische Exequien (*funeral music*), Kleine geistliche Konzerte (*small sacred concertos, 2 volumes*), The Seven Last Words of Christ, Christmas History, *3 Passions* and madrigal-like word-painting. The first book of *Symphoniae sacrae* (Sacred Symphonies, 1629) presents concerted Latin motets for various small combinations of voices and instruments. Published in Venice during Schütz's second sojourn there, it shows the strong influence of Monteverdi and Grandi, combining recitative, aria, and concerted madrigal styles.

Kleine geistliche Konzerte

> CD 5|4

In 1636 and 1639, when the Thirty Years' War had reduced the number of musicians in the Dresden chapel, Schütz published his *Kleine geistliche Konzerte* (Small Sacred Concertos), motets for one to five solo voices with continuo (see Source Reading) that are perfect microcosms of his style. *O lieber Herre Gott* (NAWM 72) from the 1636 collection illustrates how Schütz matched music to text and used elements of Italian monody. The opening phrase on "O dear Lord God" is a slow, drawn-out recitative, like a prayer. The following words, "wake us up, so that we are ready," are depicted in arioso style with faster movement, upward leaps on "up" and "ready," and a rising sequence over ascending chromatic motion in the bass. A later passage conveys joy through aria style in quick triple meter with close imitation between the voices. The rapid alternation of styles is a direct reflection of Monteverdi and Grandi's influence.

Symphoniae sacrae II *and* III

> CD 5|7   CD 2|54

Two more books of *Symphoniae sacrae*, featuring sacred concertos in German, appeared in 1647 and 1650. The last installment, published after the Thirty Years' War, used the full musical resources of the Dresden chapel, now again available. The large-scale concerto *Saul, was verfolgst du mich* (NAWM 73) calls for two choirs doubled by instruments, six solo voices, two violins, and continuo and combines the polychoral style of Gabrieli with the dissonant rhetoric of Monteverdi. It brings to life the moment when Saul, on the

---

SOURCE READING

THE EFFECTS OF THE THIRTY YEARS' WAR

The Thirty Years' War (1618–48) devastated Germany and depleted the treasuries of the rulers involved. After Saxony entered the war in 1631, the elector of Saxony, Heinrich Schütz's employer, could no longer afford to keep many musicians. In response, Schütz published his Kleine geistliche Konzerte *(Small Sacred Concertos, 1636 and 1639), which could be performed with the reduced forces available. His preface acknowledged the effects of the war.*

———— • ————

The extent to which, among other liberal arts, so also praiseworthy Music has not only gone into a great decline but in many places has been altogether destroyed by the still continuing course of the war in our beloved German homeland, is clear to many eyes, along with the general ruinous conditions and deep-seated unrest which unhappy war is wont to bring with it. I myself am experiencing this with regard to several of my musical compositions, which I have had to hold back for lack of publishers up to this time and even now, until perhaps the Almighty will graciously grant us better times in which to thrive. But meanwhile, so that my God-given talent in this noble art does not remain totally idle but can create some small offering, I have composed a few small concerted pieces and have now published them as a foretaste, as it were, of my musical work in God's honor.

Heinrich Schütz, Dedication to Part One, trans. Stanley Appelbaum, in *Kleine geistliche Konzerte*, ed. Philipp Spitta (Mineola, NY: Dover, 1996), 3.

way to Damascus to fetch Christian prisoners, is stopped by a blinding flash of light and the voice of Christ calling to him, "Saul, why do you persecute me?" (Acts 26:12–18). The experience led him to convert to Christianity, change his name to Paul, and devote himself to spreading the Gospel.

This work typifies Schütz's use of **musical figures** to convey the meaning of the words. Schütz's student Christoph Bernhard (1627–1692) was one of many German theorists to catalogue figures that break the rules of traditional counterpoint but are useful to composers in interpreting the text. For example, at the end of the opening phrase, shown in Example 15.6a, the top voice leaps down from a dissonant A to a dissonant E (both against a G-minor triad). Then the two voices move in parallel seconds, the bottom voice resolving the suspension, D–C♯, at the same time the top voice anticipates the resolution by moving to D. These unusual dissonances at the cadence are what Bernhard called *cadentiae duriusculae* (harsh cadential notes), conveying the harshness of Jesus' words, "Why do you persecute me?" Later, in Example 15.6b, a

Use of musical figures

Example 15.6: Schütz, Saul, was verfolgst du mich

a. *Opening, with* cadentiae duriusculae

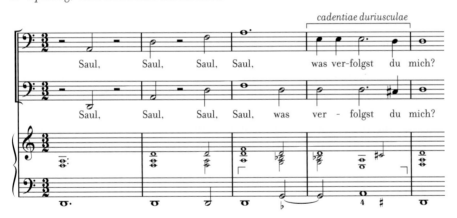

Saul, why do you persecute me?

b. *Recitative, with* saltus duriusculus

It will be hard for you to kick against the goads.

solo voice leaps down a sixth from an unresolved dissonance, a *saltus durius-culus* (harsh leap), to suggest the hard road ahead for Saul if he resists. Such figures have their roots in the text-painting of Renaissance madrigals and motets, while the attempt to codify them reflects the desire of German theorists to reconcile theory with practice.

Historia   A prominent genre in the Lutheran tradition was the **historia,** a musical setting based on a biblical narrative. In *The Seven Last Words of Christ* (1650s?), Schütz set the narrative portions as solo recitative or for chorus with continuo, while the words of Jesus, in free, expressive monody, are accompanied by strings and continuo. The whole is introduced by a short chorus and instrumental sinfonia and ends with a repetition of the sinfonia and a closing chorus. His *Christmas History* (1664) features recitatives for the narrative interspersed with scenes in the concertato medium, including arias and choruses with instrumental accompaniment.

Passions   The most common type of historia was a **Passion,** a musical setting of the story of Jesus' crucifixion. Schütz wrote three in 1666, following the accounts of Matthew, Luke, and John. For these he used not concertato style but the older German tradition of treating the narrative in plainsong and the words of the disciples, the crowd, and other groups in polyphonic motet style.

LEGACY

During his lifetime, Schütz's music was known mainly in Lutheran areas of Germany, and after his death it faded from the repertory until revived in the nineteenth and twentieth centuries. Yet he helped to establish Germany as a central part of the European tradition rather than as a peripheral region. His synthesis of German and Italian elements helped to lay the foundation for later German composers, from Bach through Brahms.

JEWISH MUSIC

The new developments in the seventeenth century extended even to Jewish music, which was among the Europeans faiths most bound by tradition. Musical practices in synagogues had remained remarkably stable for centuries, but this began to change in the early 1600s. Although cantillation was still the primary form of music in the Jewish liturgy, new techniques came into use. We know this because of several rabbinical declarations denouncing the use of popular non-Jewish tunes as the basis for improvised passages. Because of the oral nature of cantillation, no music survives to show how these secular melodies were used, but written descriptions suggest practices that resemble those still used today in Orthodox Jewish synagogues.

Polyphony   The seventeenth century also saw the introduction of polyphony into synagogue services. Through the efforts of Leon Modena (1571–1648), who was a humanist scholar as well as a rabbi and cantor, improvised polyphony was performed at the synagogue in Ferrara as early as 1604. In 1607, Modena

קינטו

השירים
אשר לשלמה

מזמורים ושירות ותשבחות אשר
חבא בחכמת הנגון והמוסיקה
לשלשה ד' ה' ו' ז' ח' קולות
כמר שלמה מהאדומים יצו
מדרי קף מאנטובה
להודו לחולהזכר לשמו עליון בכל
דבר שבקדושה חרות
בארץ:
פה ויניציאה שנת
במצות חשירים
פייטרו ולורינצו בראגאדיני
בבית יואני קאליאוני
Appresso gli Illust. Sig.
Pietro e Lorenzo Brag.

Figure 15.3: Title page of the first publication of Jewish liturgical music in polyphony, Salamone Rossi's Hashirim asher lish'lomo, *printed in Venice in 1622–23.*

became cantor at the Venice synagogue and continued to promote the use of polyphony.

Among Modena's writings on music is the preface to the first published book of polyphonic Jewish liturgical music, whose title page is shown in Figure 15.3. The thirty-three settings of Hebrew psalms, hymns, and synagogue songs were written by the Mantuan composer Salamone Rossi (ca. 1570–ca. 1630), and the collection was titled *Hashirim asher lish'lomo* (The Songs of Solomon, 1622–23), a pun on Rossi's first name. The style is that of Rossi's secular music, incorporating the influences of Monteverdi and other northern Italian composers of the time. There are also elements of Italian Jewish chant, which is the only factor, other than Hebrew texts, that identifies these works as Jewish. Rossi is equally well known for his madrigals, including the first published collection of continuo madrigals. Despite his evident skills as a composer, Rossi's Jewish faith limited his professional opportunities, and he never achieved a permanent court position. His remained one of the few attempts to write Jewish liturgical polyphony until the nineteenth century.

Salamone Rossi

INSTRUMENTAL MUSIC

The interaction of tradition and innovation typical of the first half of the seventeenth century is apparent in music for instruments as well as for voices. Instrumental music continued to gain independence from vocal music, becoming the latter's equal in both quantity and quality. Composers still practiced most sixteenth-century types of instrumental music but focused on abstract genres while neglecting those most dependent on vocal models, such as transcriptions. At the same time, instrumental composers borrowed many elements typical of the new vocal idioms, including employment of the basso continuo, interest in moving the affections, focus on the soloist, and use of virtuosic embellishment, idiomatic composition, stylistic contrast, and even specific styles such as recitative and aria. The violin, which rose to prominence in the seventeenth century, emulated the solo voice and absorbed many vocal techniques into its vocabulary.

TYPES OF INSTRUMENTAL MUSIC

There are several ways to categorize Baroque instrumental music. Four approaches are particularly helpful: by performing forces, venue, nationality, and type of composition.

Performing forces　　In considering performing forces, we find solo works, for keyboard, lute, theorbo, guitar, or harp; chamber works, for soloist or chamber group with continuo; and large-ensemble works, for two or more players on a part. The last becomes significant only after 1650, but some earlier ensemble works may have been performed with multiple players on each part.

Venue　　Baroque instrumental music can also be categorized by venue or social function. Like vocal music, instrumental works served in all three social arenas: church (e.g., organ and ensemble music in religious services), chamber (e.g., solo and small ensemble music for private entertainments and street pageants), and theater (e.g., dances and interludes in ballets and operas).

Nationality　　A third way is by nationality. Italian, French, German, English, and Spanish composers differed in the genres and stylistic elements they preferred. Part of the fascination of Baroque music is learning which traits are common in each region and watching composers borrow and blend characteristics from other lands.

Types of pieces　　Finally, a fourth way is by type of work. Until 1650, the following broad categories prevailed:

- keyboard or lute pieces in improvisatory style, called **toccata, fantasia,** or **prelude;**
- fugal pieces in continuous imitative counterpoint, called **ricercare, fantasia,** fancy, **capriccio,** or **fugue;**
- pieces with contrasting sections, often in imitative counterpoint, called **canzona** or **sonata;**
- settings of existing melodies, as in an **organ verse** or **chorale prelude;**

- pieces that vary a given melody (**variations, partita**), chorale (**chorale variations,** *chorale partita*), or bass line (**partita, chaconne, passacaglia**);
- **dances** and other pieces in stylized dance rhythms, whether independent, paired, or linked together in a **suite.**

In the second half of the century, composers more often specified the exact instrumentation, and the mix of preferred genres changed. The principal types of keyboard composition after 1650 were the prelude, toccata, fugue, chorale or chant setting, variations, and suite. Works for ensemble fell into two broad categories: sonata and related genres, and suite and similar genres. Large-ensemble music encompassed suites, sinfonias, and the new genre of the instrumental concerto.

Elements of one style or type of work often appear in another. For example, *Mixing textures* the process of varying an idea can be found in ricercares, canzonas, and dance *and styles* suites as well as in variations. Toccatas may include fugal sections, and

GIROLAMO FRESCOBALDI (1583–1643)

As one of the first composers of international stature to focus primarily on instrumental music, Frescobaldi helped to raise it to a par with vocal music. He is best known for his keyboard music, but he also wrote vocal works and ensemble canzonas.

Born in Ferrara, Frescobaldi was trained there in organ and composition. In 1608, he became organist at St. Peter's in Rome. He supplemented his income serving noble patrons and teaching keyboard, giving him an outlet for harpsichord and other chamber music. He published collections of keyboard works with dedications to various patrons. In 1628, he became organist to the Grand Duke of Tuscany in Florence, then returned to Rome and St. Peter's in 1634 under the patronage of the Barberini family, nephews of the pope. By then, his music was celebrated in France, Flanders, and Germany.

After his death, Frescobaldi remained widely admired across Europe. His keyboard music was a model for composers from his time through J. S. and C. P. E. Bach's, particularly his toccatas because of their free fantasy and his ricercares and other imitative works because of their learned counterpoint.

MAJOR WORKS: *Keyboard toccatas, fantasias, ricercares, canzonas, and partitas; Fiori musicali, with 3 organ masses; ensemble canzonas; madrigals, chamber arias, motets, and 2 masses*

Figure 15.4: Girolamo Frescobaldi in his forties, in a chalk drawing by Claude Mellan.

Figure 15.5: Toccata before Mass for Sundays, from Frescobaldi's Fiori musicali (1635), as it appeared in the original print. Frescobaldi published the work in open score rather than on two staves, as was usual for Italian keyboard music, because he considered it of great importance for performers to know how to play from open score.

canzonas may have sections in improvisatory style. For listeners at the time, the differences between national styles, between dances, or between toccata and fugal textures were as apparent as the differences between rap and country music are to modern listeners. Composers exploited these differences, using contrasts of style and texture as elements of form and expression.

TOCCATA

Toccatas and other improvisatory pieces were played on the harpsichord (as chamber music) or the organ (as service music). Although some differences can be observed between toccatas intended for organ and harpsichord, notably greater reliance on sustained tones and unusual harmonies in those for organ, most toccatas could be played on either instrument.

Girolamo Frescobaldi

The most important composer of toccatas was Girolamo Frescobaldi (1583–1643; see biography and Figure 15.4, p. 345), organist at St. Peter's in Rome. Toccata No. 3 from his first book of toccatas for harpsichord (1615; NAWM 74) is typical in featuring a succession of brief sections, each focused on a particular figure that is subtly varied. Some sections display virtuoso passage work, while others pass ideas between voices. Each section ends with a cadence, weakened harmonically, rhythmically, or through continued voice movement in order to sustain momentum until the very end. According to the composer's preface, the various sections of these toccatas may be played separately, and the player may end the piece at any appropriate cadence, reminding us that in the Baroque era written music was a platform for performance, not an unchangeable text. Frescobaldi indicated that the tempo is not subject to a regular beat but may be modified according to the sense of the music, especially by slowing at cadences.

Fiori musicali

The role of the toccata as service music is illustrated by those in Frescobaldi's *Fiori musicali* (Musical Flowers, 1635), a set of three **organ masses,** each containing all the music an organist would play at Mass. All three include a toccata before Mass and another at the Elevation of the Host before Communion, and two add another toccata before a ricercare. These toccatas are shorter than his ones for harpsichord but just as sectional, and they feature the sustained tones and harmonic surprises often found in organ toccatas. He published this collection in open score, as shown in Figure 15.5, rather than

CD 5|11   CD 3|1

on two staves, the usual notation for keyboard music, arguing in his preface that playing from a score "serves to distinguish the true gold of the actions of virtuosos from those of the ignorant."

Frescobaldi's most famous student was Johann Jacob Froberger (1616–1667), organist at the imperial court in Vienna. Froberger's toccatas tend to alternate improvisatory passages with sections in imitative counterpoint. His pieces were the model for the later merging of toccata and fugue, as in the works of Buxtehude (see NAWM 84), or their coupling, as in Bach's toccatas or preludes and fugues (see NAWM 88).

Johann Jacob Froberger

RICERCARE AND FUGUE

The seventeenth-century ricercare was typically a serious composition for organ or harpsichord in which one **subject**, or theme, is continuously developed in imitation. The Ricercare after the Credo from Frescobaldi's Mass for the Madonna in *Fiori musicali* (NAWM 75) is remarkable for the skillful handling of chromatic lines and the subtle use of shifting harmonies and dissonances, revealing a quiet intensity that characterizes much of Frescobaldi's organ music. As shown in Example 15.7, the subject has a strong profile marked by leaps and a slow chromatic ascent, making it easy to hear the subject on each entrance, while the faster diatonic countersubject offers contrast.

CD 5|13

Example 15.7: Frescobaldi, Ricercare after the Credo, from Mass for the Madonna in Fiori musicali

In the early seventeenth century, some composers, especially in Germany, began to apply the term **fugue** (from the Italian *fuga*, "flight"), formerly used for the technique of imitation itself, as the name of a genre of serious pieces that treat one theme in continuous imitation. As we will see in chapters 16 and 18, fugues became increasingly important in the late seventeenth and early eighteenth centuries.

FANTASIA

The keyboard fantasia, an imitative work on a larger scale than the ricercare, had a more complex formal organization. The leading fantasia composers in this period were the Dutch organist Jan Pieterszoon Sweelinck (1562–1621) and his German pupil Samuel Scheidt (1587–1654). In Sweelinck's fantasias, a fugal exposition usually leads to successive sections with different counter-subjects, sometimes treating the subject in rhythmic augmentation or diminution. Scheidt's *Tabulatura nova* (New Tablature, 1624) includes several monumental fantasias. He called it new, because instead of using traditional German organ tablature, Scheidt adopted the modern Italian practice of writing out each voice on a separate staff. The works of Scheidt, and his influence as a teacher, were the foundation of a remarkable development of North German organ music in the Baroque era.

English consort fantasias   In England, music for viol consort was a mainstay of social music-making in the home. The leading genre was the imitative fantasia, often called *fancy*, which could treat one or more subjects. Popular composers included Alfonso Ferrabosco the Younger (ca. 1575–1628), son of an Italian musician active at Queen Elizabeth's court, and John Coprario (ca. 1570–1626), whose Italianized name (he was born Cooper) exemplifies the English fashion for things Italian.

CANZONA

As in the sixteenth century, the canzona was an imitative piece for keyboard or ensemble in several contrasting sections, played either as chamber music or in church. Canzonas featured markedly rhythmic themes and a more lively character than ricercares. We can see in Frescobaldi's organ masses the role canzonas played in services: all include a canzona after the Epistle, and two have another after Communion. In some keyboard and most ensemble canzonas, each section treats a different theme in imitation or offers a nonimitative texture for contrast. In another type, called the *variation canzona*, transformations of a single theme appear in successive sections.

SONATA

The term *sonata* was often used early in the seventeenth century to refer broadly to any piece for instruments. It gradually came to designate a composition that resembled a canzona in form but had special characteristics. Sonatas were often scored for one or two melody instruments, usually violins, with basso continuo, while the ensemble canzona was written in four or more parts and could be played without continuo. Sonatas often exploited the idiomatic possibilities offered by a particular instrument and imitated the modern expressive vocal style, while the typical canzona displayed more of the formal, abstract quality of Renaissance polyphony.

Biagio Marini   The quality of the seventeenth-century sonata can be highlighted by examining one of the earliest sonatas for solo violin and continuo, by Biagio Marini (1594–1663). Marini served for a time as violinist at St. Mark's under Monteverdi, and then held various posts in Italy and Germany. His *Sonata IV per il*

CD 5|15

violino per sonar con due corde, from Op. 8 (NAWM 76), published in 1629, is an early example of what may be called "instrumental monody." Like the canzona, it has contrasting sections, but almost every one features idiomatic violin gestures, including large leaps, double stops, runs, trills, and embellishments. Marini's sonata opens with an expressive melody, shown in Example 15.8, that is reminiscent of a Caccini solo madrigal, then turns almost immediately to violinistic sequential figures. Rhapsodic and metrical sections alternate, recalling the contrasts of recitative and aria styles in Strozzi's cantata and Schütz's sacred concertos. One section features double stops, first in singing style and then in imitation; another leaps through a two-and-a-half-octave range.

Example 15.8: Marini, Sonata IV per il violino per sonar con due corde

By the middle of the seventeenth century the canzona and sonata had merged, and the term *sonata* came to stand for both.

SETTINGS OF EXISTING MELODIES

As in the sixteenth century (see chapter 12), organists improvised or composed settings of liturgical melodies for use in church services. These works include organ verses on Gregorian chant, like the Kyrie and Christe settings in Frescobaldi's organ masses, and various kinds of chorale settings known collectively as *organ chorales* or **chorale preludes.** Composers in middle and northern Germany produced chorale settings in large numbers and in a great variety of forms after midcentury, but examples already appear in Scheidt's *Tabulatura nova* and in the works of Sweelinck.

VARIATIONS

Keyboard and lute composers wrote sets of variations on borrowed or newly composed themes. These works were known as **variations** or **partite** (parts or divisions). The most common techniques for variations were the following:

- The melody is repeated with little change but is surrounded by different contrapuntal material in each variation and may wander from one voice to another. This type is sometimes called **cantus-firmus variations** and was practiced by Sweelinck and the English virginalists (see chapter 12).
- The melody, usually in the topmost voice, receives different embellishment in each variation while the underlying harmonies remain essentially unchanged.
- The bass or harmonic progression, rather than the melody, is held constant while the figuration changes. Sometimes, as in the case of the romanesca, a melodic outline is associated with the bass but may be obscured in the variations.

Chaconne and passacaglia
Of the last type, the forms most familiar to modern listeners are the **chaconne** and **passacaglia,** the former ultimately deriving from the chacona and the latter from the Spanish *passacalle,* a ritornello improvised over a simple cadential progression and played before and between strophes of a song. The earliest known keyboard variations on these forms are Frescobaldi's *Partite sopra ciaccona* and *Partite sopra passacagli,* both published in his second book of toccatas and partitas in 1627. Each of the first several variations from *Partite sopra ciaccona* features a different variant in the bass line, as shown in Example 15.9, indicating that Frescobaldi considered the I–V–vi–V harmonic progression to be the constant element, not the bass itself. Within a generation, *chaconne* and *passacaglia* were used in France, Germany, and elsewhere as terms for variations over a ground bass, whether traditional or newly composed, usually four measures long, in triple meter and slow tempo. Chaconnes and passacaglias appeared in solo keyboard music, chamber music, and theatrical dance music. In later centuries, the distinctions between the two faded, and the terms became interchangeable.

Example 15.9: Frescobaldi, Partite sopra ciaccona, *first three variations*

DANCE MUSIC

Dances were composed for social dancing, for theatrical spectacles, and in stylized form for chamber music for lute, keyboard, or ensemble. Dance music was so central to musical life that dance rhythms permeated other instrumental and vocal music, secular and sacred alike.

The idea of linking two or three dances together, such as pavane and galliard, was now extended to create a **suite** of several dances, used either for dancing or as chamber music. Johann Hermann Schein's *Banchetto musicale* (Musical Banquet, 1617) contains twenty suites for five instruments with continuo, each having the sequence padouana (pavane), gagliarda (galliard), courante, allemande, and tripla, the last a triple-meter variation of the allemande. Some of the suites build on one melodic idea that recurs in varied form in every dance, and others are linked by more subtle melodic similarity.

Suites

A SEPARATE TRADITION

As composers focused increasingly on abstract genres—including toccata, prelude, ricercare, fantasia, canzona, sonata, and ground bass variations—instrumental music gained stature as a tradition separate from vocal music and worthy of attention for its own sake. The toccatas, ricercares, and variations of Frescobaldi have been compared to orations, holding the listener's attention while ideas are presented and developed. This is a new role for music without words, moving beyond decoration and diversion to encompass levels of intellectual and expressive communication formerly reserved for vocal music. It was on this foundation that the fugues, sonatas, and symphonies of later generations were built.

TRADITION AND INNOVATION

The extraordinary burst of innovation in the early seventeenth century is as apparent in the chamber, church, and instrumental music of the time as in opera. Yet, like opera, these other kinds of music also drew deeply on sixteenth-century traditions, redefining existing genres and approaches by combining them with new styles and techniques.

This period is of lasting importance because it set the pattern for several generations, creating new genres such as cantata, sacred concerto, oratorio, sonata, partita, chaconne, passacaglia, and dance suite; establishing techniques such as basso continuo, the concertato medium, and ground bass; and fostering new expressive devices and an increasingly separate instrumental tradition. One especially noteworthy development was the recognition that different styles were appropriate for different purposes. Thus the older style (*stile antico*) was preserved and practiced alongside newer ones, useful for its associations with sacred music and with pedagogy. At the same time, most styles could be used outside their original contexts for expressive ends, so that, for example, theatrical styles were used in church.

But the fascination with the new that energized the music of this period implicitly guaranteed its impermanence. As tastes and styles rapidly changed, virtually all this music fell out of fashion by the end of the century. Some, like Frescobaldi's keyboard music, was known to composers but rarely played.

The music of the early seventeenth century was rediscovered in the late nineteenth century and throughout the twentieth, and much of it has been published in scholarly editions and recorded. Although nowadays performances and recordings of works by Monteverdi, Schütz, Frescobaldi, and other early-seventeenth-century composers are relatively frequent, until recent decades their music was not as well known as that of Palestrina, Vivaldi, or Bach. Perhaps this is because in the music of a Monteverdi or a Schütz styles are more fluid, the routines of melody, rhythm, harmony, and counterpoint less fixed than in sixteenth- or eighteenth-century music, so that the listener may not know what to expect. But that element of exploration is also one of the great charms of this music, as composers, thoroughly trained in a now out-of-date idiom, invented new styles at every turn, feeling their way forward in the dark to a new musical world.

Chapter

16

France, England, Spain, and the New World in the Seventeenth Century

The last two chapters focused largely on genre: how new and old ideas combined in opera, and how theatrical styles affected chamber, sacred, and instrumental music, fostering new genres such as cantata, sacred concerto, oratorio, and solo sonata. Without neglecting genre as a way of focusing our historical narrative, it becomes more useful in the middle and late Baroque period to highlight the distinctive national styles that developed, including trends within a nation's music and borrowings across borders.

National style was influenced by politics as well as by culture. Italy remained the leading musical region, but France, a centralized monarchy whose king used the arts for propaganda and social control, emerged as Italy's chief competitor. Under the king's sponsorship, musicians forged a new French idiom marked by elegance and restraint, a counterbalance to the virtuosic, expressive music of Italy. England and Germany then absorbed elements from both French and Italian styles, combining them with native traditions. The English monarch was an important musical patron but did not dominate the scene as in France, leaving room for direct support of music by the public and the invention of the public concert. Rulers of the many small German states adopted French fashions in music as in literature, art, architecture, and manners, but Italian musicians and genres remained influential. Spain largely followed its own path, including a thriving musical life in its American colonies.

In this chapter, we will explore the impact of politics on music in France and England, the adaptation of Italian genres in France, the

CHAPTER OUTLINE

THE FRENCH BAROQUE 354

THE ENGLISH BAROQUE 372

SPAIN AND THE NEW WORLD 379

FRENCH STYLE AND NATIONAL TRADITIONS 382

emergence of a distinctive French style, English assimilation of both French and Italian elements together with native traditions, and the distinctive traditions of Spain at home and in the New World. We will follow the samecategories as in the previous two chapters, in the same order: theatrical music, vocal chamber music, church music, and instrumental music.

THE FRENCH BAROQUE

The special qualities of French Baroque music were shaped by the centrality of dance and the role of the arts in an absolute monarchy. These in turn reflect the personality and policies of King Louis XIV, whose seven-decade reign changed the culture of Europe.

Figure 16.1: Louis XIV in his sixties, in a portrait by Hyacinthe Rigaud from around 1700. The king is surrounded by images that convey his grandeur: a red velvet curtain, multicolor stone column, impressive wig, and enormous ermine robe covered on one side with gold fleurs-de-lis, the symbol of French royalty. His crown is by his side, shadowed and partially obscured, as if he did not need to emphasize the sign of his power, even while his hand and staff draw the eye to it. His elongated, upright stature and exposed, perfectly shaped legs proclaim his physical strength and remind the viewer of his renown as a dancer.

Figure 16.2: Fountain on the grounds of Versailles, Louis XIV's grand country palace, showing Apollo on his chariot emerging from the sea. In Greek mythology, the sun god Apollo rode his chariot across the sky each day, descending into the sea in the west each evening and bursting out of the sea in the east each morning, ready again to arc across the sky. Louis XIV cultivated an image as "the Sun King," identifying himself with Apollo and with the rising sun.

LOUIS XIV

Louis XIV (r. 1643–1715) succeeded to the throne at age five on the death of his father. Until he was twenty-three, however, France was ruled by his mother, Anne of Austria, and her lover Cardinal Mazarin, an Italian. Resentment against the rule of foreigners provoked a series of revolts known as the Fronde. When Louis took the reins of state after Mazarin's death in 1661, he remembered those years of tumult and resolved to assert absolute authority.

In order to maintain power, Louis projected an image of himself as in supreme control, using the arts as propaganda tools. The portrait in Figure 16.1 is a fitting example: an almost theatrical performance, depicting Louis as an imposing physical specimen, surrounded by symbols of power and majesty, in complete command. *Arts as propaganda*

Louis styled himself "the Sun King," a calculated and ideal symbol for Louis as the giver of light. He identified himself with Apollo, the Greek sun god, and commissioned many depictions of Apollo, including the spectacular fountain in Figure 16.2. Apollo was also the god of music, learning, science, and the arts, and Louis wanted to be seen as the chief patron in all those fields. He centralized the arts and sciences, establishing royal academies of sculpture and painting (1648), dance (1661), literature (1663), the sciences (1669), opera (1669), and architecture (1671), and granting each academy the authority to oversee endeavors in its field. *The Sun King*

Versailles   Louis rebuilt the Louvre, the great palace in Paris (now a remarkable museum), and constructed a vast palace in the country at Versailles. Figure 16.3 shows only one part of this huge palace. The gardens are equally expansive, stretching for miles. Figure 16.4 illustrates the sculpted gardens near the palace, where everything is controlled and disciplined, and no plant is out of place or allowed to grow wild. It is a perfect image for the absolute monarchy, where all have their roles in the orderly state ruled by a single vision, and even nature must submit to the will of the king.

Versailles proclaimed Louis's power and also served a practical purpose. The monarchy was rich, but the nobility were partly independent and could be dangerous, as proven by the Fronde rebellions. By keeping the aristocracy at Versailles for large parts of the year, away from their lands and focused on court ceremonies, etiquette, and entertainment, he kept them under his firm control.

THE COURT BALLET

Dance, both social and theatrical, was particularly important in French culture and to Louis. A distinctive French genre was the **court ballet,** a substantial musical-dramatic work, staged with costumes and scenery, that featured members of the court alongside professional dancers. The typical court ballet comprised several acts, each including solo songs, choruses, and instrumental dances in styles appropriate to the characters portrayed by the dancers. Ballets had flourished at court since the *Ballet comique de la reine* (The Queen's Dramatic Ballet, 1581). Louis XIII (r. 1610–43) regularly took part in music and dance at court. His son Louis XIV won a reputation as a brilliant

Figure 16.3: Garden façade of the Palace of Versailles, designed by Louis Le Vau and built 1661–90. The columns and arches echo classical architecture, and the mythological statuary throughout the building and grounds reinforce the links Louis XIV sought to make between his reign and Greek and Roman civilization. The sheer size of the building, emphasized by the reflecting pool, was meant to impress, but was also practical, because the entire French nobility and their entourages spent much of the year here.

Figure 16.4: Part of the south garden at Versailles, with fleurs-de-lis. The carefully trimmed plantings convey an image of control over nature, and the way each garden leads to the next suggests a limitless space.

dancer, performing in ballets from the age of thirteen. His roles included Apollo in the *Ballet des fêtes de Bacchus* (Ballet of the Festivals of Bacchus, 1651) and as the Rising Sun in the *Ballet de la nuit* (Ballet of the Night, 1653), establishing his identity as the Sun King.

 Dance reinforced the state by offering a model of discipline, order, refinement, restraint, and subordination of the individual to a common enterprise. Requiring aristocrats to participate in social dancing and in ballet performances kept them busy and provided a ritualized demonstration of the social hierarchy, with the king at the top. It is no wonder that French Baroque music, so centered on dance, is marked by elegance and emotional restraint, in strong contrast to the expressivity, individuality, and showmanship typical of Italian music at the time.

Dance and political control

MUSIC AT COURT

Music for the king was as hierarchically organized as the state itself. There were 150 to 200 musicians in three divisions. The Music of the Royal Chapel included singers, organists, and other instrumentalists who performed for religious services. The Music of the Chamber, primarily string, lute, harpsichord, and flute players, provided music for indoor entertainments. The Music of the Great Stable comprised wind, brass, and timpani players, who played for military and outdoor ceremonies and sometimes joined the chapel or indoor music, adding instrumental color (see sidebar, p. 358). Louis's wind ensemble profoundly influenced the development of wind and brass music by encouraging improved instruments and playing techniques and by nurturing generations of performers, among them families of wind players such as the Hotteterres and Philidors.

MUSIC IN CONTEXT

THE MUSIC OF THE GREAT STABLE

Louis XIV's musicians of the Great Stable played at all manner of events that took place outdoors: processions occasioned by royal weddings and funerals, fireworks displays commemorating royal births, visits by foreign dignitaries, military reviews, hunts, and other types of games and pageants. Like the uniformed trumpeters who always preceded the king's coach when he rode out from his palace, stable musicians often mounted horses on these occasions, which helps to explain their association with what we now think of as an undignified place of lodging. In fact, the stable musicians were Louis XIV's best wind and brass players. They performed ceremonial music on instruments such as fifes and drums, oboes and bassoons, cornetts and trumpets, all of which could easily be heard in the open air. Stable musicians were relatively well paid and sometimes enjoyed privileges that exempted them from taxation or permitted them to pass their position on to a son.

Because employment as a stable musician offered status and job security, the institution of the Great Stable became a proving ground for several important families of wind players. A member of one such family, Jean Hotteterre (ca. 1610–ca. 1692), not only had the opportunity to perfect his playing technique but also experimented with the construction of several kinds of wind instruments. Fashioning them out of wood, he sometimes included elegant ornamental details in ivory and ebony, signs that his instruments were highly prized and appreciated at court. Lully's inclusion of woodwinds in his opera orchestra also became a factor in their improvement, since his interest in writing music for these instruments stimulated their makers and players to strive for a sweeter, more refined sound—one that merited a place alongside the *Vingt-quatre Violons du Roi* (Twenty-Four Violins of the King).

Wind players and instrument makers at the French court are generally believed to have been responsible for creating the modern oboe. This instrument differed from its predecessor, the shawm, in having a fully freestanding reed (rather than a partially enclosed one) that allowed for greater control of intonation and tone quality. Instead of being constructed out of a single piece of wood, the instrument had three sections that were fitted together in such a way as to facilitate the most delicate adjustments in tuning. It also had an expanded, two-octave range, and the instrument's improved design and smaller fingerholes allowed the player to produce more accurate chromatic pitches. Thus, despite its unpromising name, the Great Stable actually initiated the rise to prominence of woodwind instruments in today's orchestras.—BRH

Figure 16.5: Perspective view from the Chateau of Versailles of the Place d'Armes and the Stables, 1688 (oil on canvas) by Jean-Baptiste Martin (1659–1735). The musicians of the Grand Ecurie (Great Stable) provided music for the pomp and ceremony of all manner of events under Louis XIV.

Although the French often preferred the viol for chamber and solo music, they created the first large ensembles of the violin family. These became the model for the modern **orchestra**—an ensemble whose core consists of strings with more than one player performing each part. Louis XIII established the *Vingt-quatre Violons du Roi* (Twenty-Four Violins of the King), which typically played music in a five-part texture: six soprano violins, tuned like the modern violin, on the melody; twelve alto and tenor violins tuned like the modern viola, divided among three inner parts; and six bass violins, tuned a whole tone lower than the modern cello, on the bass line. In 1648, the *Petits Violons* (Small Violin Ensemble), with eighteen strings, was created for Louis XIV's personal use. These two groups accompanied ballets, balls, the king's supper, and other court entertainments. By the 1670s, the term "orchestra" was used for such ensembles, after the area in front of the stage in a theater, where the musicians were usually placed for opera and other entertainments.

String orchestras

JEAN-BAPTISTE LULLY AND FRENCH OPERA

For over three decades, Louis XIV's favorite musician was Jean-Baptiste Lully (1632–1687; see biography and Figure 16.6). Lully wrote music for ballets and religious services at court but earned his greatest success with dramatic music. In the 1670s, with Louis's support, Lully created a distinctive French kind of opera that persisted for a century.

Cardinal Mazarin had tried to establish Italian opera in France, commissioning Luigi Rossi's *Orfeo* in 1647 and Francesco Cavalli's *Ercole amante* in 1662. But the operas, which were sung in Italian, met opposition on political and artistic grounds. Lully learned operatic styles from both operas, especially from *Ercole amante*, to which he contributed ballet music. After Cavalli's departure, Lully collaborated with comic playwright Jean-Baptiste Molière to create a series of successful *comédies-ballets*, which blended elements of ballet and opera. But Lully did not yet contemplate full opera. The ballet tradition seemed too strong, as did French spoken tragedy, represented by dramatists Pierre Corneille (1606–1684) and Jean Racine (1639–1699). French literary culture demanded that poetry and drama be given priority on the stage and considered dialogue in song to lack believability. The domination of music and singing in Italian opera therefore seemed unsuitable for France.

Influences on French opera

But successful experiments by others convinced Lully that opera in French was viable. In 1672, with Louis XIV's support, he purchased a royal privilege granting him the exclusive right to produce sung drama in France and established the Académie Royale de Musique. Together with his librettist, playwright Jean-Philippe Quinault (1635–1688), Lully reconciled the demands of drama, music, and ballet in a new French form of opera, **tragédie en musique** (tragedy in music), later named **tragédie lyrique**.

Tragédie en musique

Quinault's five-act dramas combined serious plots from ancient mythology or chivalric tales with frequent **divertissements** (diversions), long interludes of dancing and choral singing. He cleverly intermingled episodes of romance and adventure with adulation of the king, glorification of France, and moral reflection. His texts were overtly and covertly propagandistic, in tune with Louis's use of the arts. Each opera included a prologue, often

Quinault's librettos

singing the king's praises literally or through allegory. The plots depicted a well-ordered, disciplined society, and the mythological characters and settings reinforced the parallels Louis sought to draw between his regime and ancient Greece and Rome. The librettos also provided opportunities for spectacles to entertain the audience, as illustrated in Figure 16.7.

JEAN-BAPTISTE LULLY (1632–1687)

Lully was renowned for creating a French type of opera, pioneering the French overture, and fostering the modern orchestra. Ironically, he was Italian, though he lived in France throughout his adult life.

Born in Florence, Lully came to Paris at age fourteen as Italian tutor to a cousin of Louis XIV. In Paris he completed his musical training and studied dance. His dancing in the *Ballet de la nuit* (1653) so impressed Louis that he appointed Lully court composer of instrumental music and director of the *Petits Violons*. In 1661, Lully became Superintendant of Music for the King's Chamber, taking over the *Vingt-quatre Violons du Roi* as well as the *Petits Violons*, and became a French citizen. His marriage the next summer to Madeleine Lambert, daughter of composer Michel Lambert, was witnessed by the king and queen, showing how high Lully had risen at court.

Lully composed music for numerous court ballets and sacred music for the royal chapel. He turned to comédies-ballets in 1664, then in 1672 to opera, where he gained his greatest fame.

The discipline Lully imposed on his orchestra, enforcing uniform bowing and coordinated use of ornaments, won admiration, was widely imitated, and became the foundation for modern orchestral practice. Although Lully conducted with a staff instead of a baton, the tradition of dictatorial leadership he introduced, modeled on the king's own absolute power, has been continued by later conductors.

Figure 16.6: Jean-Baptiste Lully, in a bronze bust by Antoine Coyzevox placed on Lully's tomb in the church of Notre Dame des Victoires in Paris.

Lully's close relationship with Louis XIV was clouded by scandal in 1685 when the king learned that Lully had seduced a young page in his service. Lully remained rich and powerful but had to rely on other patrons. He died in 1687 after he hit his foot with his staff while conducting his *Te Deum* and the injury turned to gangrene.

MAJOR WORKS: Alceste, Armide, *and 13 other operas; 14 comédies-ballets; 29 ballets (most in collaboration with other composers); numerous motets and other liturgical music*

Figure 16.7: Design for Lully's opera Armide *(1686), in an ink-wash by Jean Bérain. It shows the burning of Armide's palace, which she ordered in a fury over her failure to murder Renaud and over his escape from her power. In the foreground, Renaud, in armor, bids farewell to Armide.*

French overture

Lully's music projected the formal splendor of Louis's court. Each opera began with an **ouverture** (French for "opening"), or **overture,** marking the entry of the king (when he was present) and welcoming him and the audience to the performance. Lully's overtures were appropriately grand and followed a format that he had already used in his ballets, now known as a **French overture.** There are two sections, each played twice. The first is homophonic and majestic, marked by dotted rhythms and figures rushing toward the downbeats. The second section is faster and begins with a semblance of fugal imitation, sometimes returning at the end to the tempo and figuration of the first section. The overture to Lully's opera *Armide* (1686; NAWM 77a) exemplifies the genre.

CD 5|23   CD 2|58

A divertissement usually appeared at the center or end of every act, but its connection to the surrounding plot was often tenuous. These extended episodes, which directly continued the French ballet tradition, offered opportunities for spectacular choruses and a string of dances, each with colorful costumes and elaborate choreography. The divertissements were especially appealing to the public. Dances from Lully's ballets and operas became so popular that they were arranged in independent instrumental suites, and many new suites were composed imitating his divertissements.

Adapting recitative to French

To project drama, Lully adapted Italian recitative to French language and poetry. This was no simple task, since the style of recitative typical in Italian opera of the time was not suited to the rhythms and accents of French. Lully is said to have solved the problem by listening to celebrated French actors and closely imitating their declamation. Certainly the timing, pauses, and inflections often resemble stage speech, but Lully did not aspire to create the illusion of speech as in a recitative by Peri, and the bass is often more rhythmic and the melody more songful than in Italian recitative.

Récitatif simple,
récitatif mesuré,
and air

In what would later be called **récitatif simple** (simple recitative), Lully followed the general contours of spoken French while shifting the metric notation between duple and triple to allow the most natural declamation of the words. This style was frequently interrupted by a more songlike, uniformly measured style, **récitatif mesuré** (measured recitative), which had more deliberate motion in the accompaniment. More lyrical moments were cast as **airs**, songs with a rhyming text and regular meter and phrasing, often featuring the meter and form of a dance. Far less elaborate and effusive than arias in Italian operas, airs were typically syllabic or nearly so, with a tuneful melody, little text repetition, and no virtuosic display.

CD 5|26   CD 2|61

Armide's monologue in Act II, scene 5, of *Armide* (NAWM 77b) illustrates this mixture of styles. The scene begins with a tense orchestral prelude suffused with dotted rhythms. The sorceress, dagger in hand, stands over her

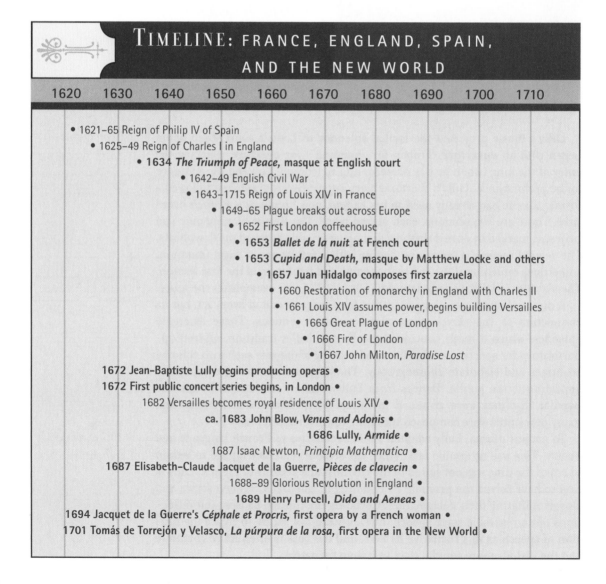

TIMELINE: FRANCE, ENGLAND, SPAIN, AND THE NEW WORLD

| 1620 | 1630 | 1640 | 1650 | 1660 | 1670 | 1680 | 1690 | 1700 | 1710 |

- 1621–65 Reign of Philip IV of Spain
- 1625–49 Reign of Charles I in England
- 1634 *The Triumph of Peace,* masque at English court
- 1642–49 English Civil War
- 1643–1715 Reign of Louis XIV in France
- 1649–65 Plague breaks out across Europe
- 1652 First London coffeehouse
- 1653 *Ballet de la nuit* at French court
- 1653 *Cupid and Death,* masque by Matthew Locke and others
- 1657 Juan Hidalgo composes first zarzuela
- 1660 Restoration of monarchy in England with Charles II
- 1661 Louis XIV assumes power, begins building Versailles
- 1665 Great Plague of London
- 1666 Fire of London
- 1667 John Milton, *Paradise Lost*
- 1672 Jean-Baptiste Lully begins producing operas •
- 1672 First public concert series begins, in London •
- 1682 Versailles becomes royal residence of Louis XIV •
- ca. 1683 John Blow, *Venus and Adonis* •
- 1686 Lully, *Armide* •
- 1687 Isaac Newton, *Principia Mathematica* •
- 1687 Elisabeth-Claude Jacquet de la Guerre, *Pièces de clavecin* •
- 1688–89 Glorious Revolution in England •
- 1689 Henry Purcell, *Dido and Aeneas* •
- 1694 Jacquet de la Guerre's *Céphale et Procris,* first opera by a French woman •
- 1701 Tomás de Torrejón y Velasco, *La púrpura de la rosa,* first opera in the New World •

captive, the sleeping warrior Renaud. In simple recitative, she speaks of her determination to kill him as revenge for freeing her captives but is prevented from acting because she has fallen in love with him. Measures of four, three, and two beats are intermixed, permitting the two accented syllables in each poetic line to fall on downbeats. Rests follow each line and are also used dramatically, as when Armide vacillates between hesitation and resolve in the excerpt shown in Example 16.1a. When she finally decides to use sorcery to make him love her, her new determination is reflected in measured recitative, in Example 16.1b. This leads to an air, shown in Example 16.1c, with the meter, rhythm, and character of a minuet (see below), a dance associated with the surrender to love. It is accompanied only by continuo, as are most of Lully's airs, but is introduced by an orchestral statement of the entire air.

Example 16.1: Excerpts from Armide's monologue in Lully's Armide

a. *Simple recitative*

What makes me hesitate? What in his favor does pity want to tell me? Let us strike . . .
Heavens! Who can stop me? Let us get on with it . . . I tremble! Let us avenge . . . I sigh!

b. *Measured recitative*

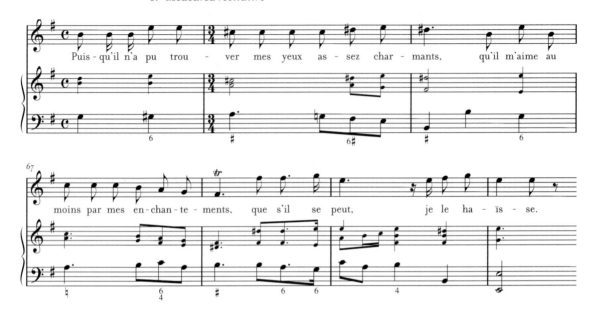

Since he could not find my eyes charming enough, let him love me at least through my sorcery, so that, if it's possible, I may hate him.

c. *Air*

Come, come, support my desires, demons, transform yourselves into friendly zephyrs.

Some typically French elements cannot be seen in the notation but were added in performance. Passages notated in even, short durations, like the eighth notes in the bass line of Example 16.1c, were often rendered by alternating longer notes on the beat with shorter offbeats, producing liltlike triplets or dotted rhythms; this practice is called **notes inégales** (unequal notes) and was considered a matter of expression and elegance, left to the players' discretion. A related practice is **overdotting,** in which a dotted note is held longer than its notated value—according to the performer's taste— while the following short note is shortened. These changes emphasize the beats and sharpen the rhythmic profile. Although the elaborate embellishments of Italian singers were considered in bad taste, performers were expected to use brief ornaments (called **agréments** in French), whether notated or not, to adorn cadences and other important notes.

Performance practice

Lully's music is **tonal,** in the new system of major and minor keys, rather than modal, the system still common earlier in the century. All the excerpts in Example 16.1 feature harmonic progressions that are typical of tonal music, moving forward in a predictable manner to close on a dominant-tonic cadence. Lully often evades the cadence by using a first-inversion tonic triad (as in measures 39, 67, and 69) to prolong the harmonic tension and make the ultimate resolution even more satisfying. This technique depends on the listener's expectations for tonal music.

Tonal organization

Armide's monologue illustrates the power of Lully's operas. The mixture of recitative, air, and orchestral interludes allowed Lully to convey emotions through simple but effective means. Limiting vocal display to tuneful melodies with a few ornaments reclaimed musical theater from the domination of singers then current in Italian opera and focused attention on the dramatic declamation of words, while making room for the sheer entertainment of divertissements, costumes, and stage effects.

Focus on drama

Lully's followers continued to write operas that imitated his style while introducing an occasional aria in Italian style, expanding the divertissements, intensifying the harmony, and increasing the complexity of the texture. Lully's own operas were performed well into the eighteenth century, in France and other countries, and his style influenced opera and instrumental music in England, Germany, and elsewhere. The French overture, which he did not invent but helped to popularize, was used across Europe through the mid-eighteenth century to introduce ballets, operas, oratorios, and instrumental works such as suites and sonatas. If every princeling wanted his own Versailles, he also wanted his own Lully, and echoes of Lully's style and of his special relationship with his patron are evident through the late eighteenth century.

Lully's influence

SONG AND CANTATA

The air was the leading genre of vocal chamber music in France, as it had been since the late sixteenth century. Composers wrote airs in a variety of styles and types, from courtly vocal music to songs of a popular cast. The air de cour (see chapter 15) gradually went out of fashion, replaced by other types like the *air sérieux* (serious air) and *air à boire* (drinking song), the former on love, pastoral, or political topics, and the latter on light or frivolous topics. Both types were typically syllabic and strophic and were scored for one to three voices with lute or continuo accompaniment. Hundreds of collections of such songs were published in Paris.

Marc-Antoine Charpentier

One of the popular composers of solo airs was Marc-Antoine Charpentier (1634–1704), a pupil of Carissimi. He used French-style embellishments and borrowed from the Italian lyric aria style to create highly melodic pieces. Beginning in the 1680s, Charpentier and other composers also adapted the Italian chamber cantata to French styles and tastes.

CHURCH MUSIC

Until about 1650, French church music was dominated by the old style of Renaissance counterpoint. In the second half of the century, in sacred as in secular vocal music, French composers borrowed genres invented in Italy, notably the sacred concerto and oratorio, but wrote in distinctively French styles.

Petit motet and grand motet

Composers in the royal chapel produced numerous motets on Latin texts. These were of two main types: the **petit motet** (small motet), a sacred concerto for few voices with continuo, and the **grand motet** (large motet) for soloists, double chorus, and orchestra, corresponding to the large-scale concertos of Gabrieli and Schütz. *Grands motets* featured several sections in different meters and tempos, encompassing preludes, vocal solos, ensembles, and choruses. Lully and Charpentier wrote outstanding *grands motets*. Louis XIV's favorite sacred composer was Michel-Richard de Lalande (1657–1726), whose more than seventy motets reveal a masterly command of the resources of the *grand motet:* syllabic solos, homophonic and fugal choruses, and operatic airs and duets, with frequent contrasts of texture and mood.

Oratorio

Charpentier introduced the Latin oratorio into France, drawing on the model of Carissimi but combining Italian and French styles of recitative and air. He usually assigned a prominent role to the chorus, often a double chorus, and his thirty-four oratorios are full of dramatic contrasts and vivid text-setting.

Organ music

A distinctive French school of organ music emerged in the seventeenth century, consisting mostly of music for church services, such as organ masses, alongside pieces resembling the overtures and expressive recitatives of French opera. National traits include the use of agréments and a strong interest in the coloristic possibilities of the organ, often specified in the title or in the score itself by indicating the combinations of organ pipes to be used in order to produce distinct tonal colors. Timbre as a compositional resource is a constant thread in French music—from these organ works and the operas of Lully to the program music of Berlioz (chapter 25) and the impressionism of Debussy (chapter 30).

LUTE AND KEYBOARD MUSIC

Lute music flourished in France during the early seventeenth century and left a permanent mark on French style. The leading lute composer was Denis

Gaultier (1603–1672), whose two published collections instructed amateurs on how to play the lute. During the seventeenth century, the **clavecin** (French for "harpsichord"), shown in Figure 16.8, displaced the lute as the main solo instrument, while harpsichord music absorbed many characteristics of lute style. Important harpsichord composers, or **clavecinists,** included Jacques Champion de Chambonnières (1601/2–1672), Jean Henry D'Anglebert (1629–1691), Elisabeth-Claude Jacquet de la Guerre (1665–1729; see biography, p. 368, and Figure 16.9), and François Couperin (1668–1733; see chapter 18). All of them served Louis XIV in various capacities but are best known today for their printed collections of harpsichord music, marketed to a growing public of well-to-do amateur performers.

Lutenists systematically developed the use of agréments, ornaments designed to emphasize important notes and give the melody shape and character. Agréments became a fundamental element of all French music, and the proper use of ornaments was a sign of refined taste. Agréments were often left to the discretion of the player, but composers also worked out ways of notating them. Figure 16.10 shows the table of agréments in D'Anglebert's *Pièces de clavecin* (Harpsichord Pieces, 1689), the most comprehensive of many such tables published in collections of harpsichord music. *Agréments*

Lute style also strongly influenced the texture of harpsichord music. Since lutenists often struck only one note at a time, they sketched in the melody, bass, and harmony by sounding the appropriate tones—now in one register, now in another—and relying on the listener's imagination to supply the *Style luthé*

Figure 16.8: Double-manual harpsichord built by Michel Richard, Paris, 1688.

continuity of the various lines. This technique, the **style luthé** (lute style), sometimes called by the modern term **style brisé** (broken style), was imitated by harpsichord composers and became an intrinsic part of French harpsichord style, as seen in Example 16.2 below.

ELISABETH-CLAUDE JACQUET DE LA GUERRE (1665–1729)

Women continued to play an active role in the music of the seventeenth century, from singers and composers to patrons of art, as well as hostesses at the salons where music was actively cultivated. One such extraordinary woman was the French composer Elisabeth-Claude Jacquet de la Guerre, born into a family of musicians and instrument makers. Trained by her father, she was the original child prodigy in music, of which Mozart is the most famous example. From the age of five, she sang and played the harpsichord at Louis XIV's court, supported by the king's mistress. In 1677, the Paris journal *Mercure galant* gushed:

> There is a prodigy who has appeared here for the last four years. She sings at sight the most difficult music. She accompanies herself, and others who wish to sing, on the harpsichord, which she plays in an inimitable manner. She composes pieces and plays them in any key one suggests.

Figure 16.9: Portrait of the composer by François de Troy (1645–1730).

Some years later the same writer called her "the marvel of our century."

In 1684, she married the organist Martin de la Guerre and moved permanently to Paris. There she taught harpsichord and gave concerts that won her wide renown. She enjoyed the patronage of Louis XIV and dedicated most of her works to him, including the first ballet (1691, now lost) and first opera (*Céphale et Procris*, 1694) written by a French woman.

Jacquet de la Guerre is best known for her two published collections of harpsichord pieces (1687 and 1707) and three books of cantatas, two on biblical subjects (1708 and 1711) and one secular (1715). Her violin and trio sonatas show an interest in the Italian instrumental style. Her output was small but encompassed a wide variety of genres, and she was recognized by her contemporaries as one of the great talents of her time.

MAJOR WORKS: Céphale et Procris (*opera*), 3 books of cantatas, 2 books of Pièces de clavecin, 8 violin sonatas, 4 trio sonatas

Figure 16.10: Table of ornaments from Pièces de clavecin (1689) *by Jean Henry D'Anglebert, showing for each ornament its notation, name, and manner of performance. "Autre" indicates another way to notate or perform the preceding ornament.*

DANCE MUSIC

Dances formed the core of the lute and keyboard repertory, reflecting their importance in French life. Composers arranged ballet music for lute or harpsichord and composed original music in dance meters and forms. Most dance music for lute or keyboard was stylized, probably intended not for dancing but for the entertainment of the player or a small audience. Paired two- and four-measure phrases are frequent in dance music, matching the patterns of many dance steps.

Earlier dances had assumed a variety of forms, such as the three repeated sections of the pavane or the repeating bass of the passamezzo. Most seventeenth-century dances were in **binary form:** two roughly equal sections, each repeated, the first leading harmonically from the tonic to close on the dominant (sometimes the relative major), the second returning to the tonic. This form was widely used for dance music and other instrumental genres over the next two centuries.

Binary form

French composers often grouped a series of stylized dances into a **suite,** as did their German counterparts (see chapter 15). The tempo and rhythm contributed to the character of each dance. A look at excerpts from Jacquet de la Guerre's Suite No. 3 in A Minor from her *Pièces de clavecin* (1687, NAWM 78), shown in Example 16.2, illustrates both the structure of a typical suite and the most common types of dance. All but two movements, the prelude and a chaconne, are in binary form. Although none of the movements would

Suites

CD 5|31–38   CD 3|3–5

have been used for dancing, the steps and associations of the dances were known to the listeners and influenced the rhythm and style of the music.

Many suites begin with a prelude in the style of a toccata or other abstract work. Here it is an **unmeasured prelude**, a distinctively French genre whose nonmetric notation allows great rhythmic freedom, as if improvising. In Example 16.2a, the whole notes indicate arpeggiated chords, the black notes show melodic passages, and the slurs show groupings or sustained notes.

The **allemande** (French for "German"), no longer danced in the seventeenth century and thus highly stylized, was usually in a moderately fast $\frac{4}{4}$ beginning with an upbeat. As shown in Example 16.2b, all voices participate in almost continuous movement, and agréments appear often. Signs of the style luthé include the opening arpeggiation of the tonic chord in the bass and staggered rhythms between the voices. The **courante** (French for "running" or "flowing") also begins with an upbeat but is in a moderate triple or compound meter ($\frac{3}{2}$ or $\frac{6}{4}$) or shifts between the two. The steps were dignified, with

Example 16.2: Movements from Jacquet de la Guerre, Pièces de clavecin, Suite No. 3 in A Minor

a. Prelude

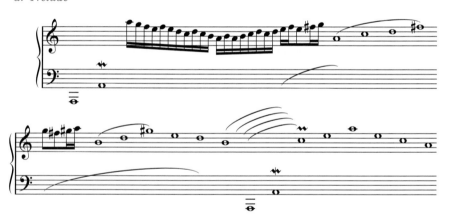

b. Allemande

c. Courante

a bend of the knees on the upbeat and a rise on the beat, often followed by a glide or step. The **sarabande** was originally a quick, lascivious dance-song from Latin America. When it came to France through Spain and Italy, it was transformed into a slow, dignified dance in triple meter with an emphasis on the second beat, as in Example 16.2d. The melodic rhythm in the first measure is especially common. The **gigue** (French for "jig") originated in the British Isles as a fast solo dance with rapid footwork. In France it became stylized as a movement in fast compound meter such as $\frac{6}{4}$ or $\frac{12}{8}$, with wide melodic leaps and continuous lively triplets. Sections often begin with fugal or quasi-fugal imitation, as in Example 16.2e.

Numerous other dances could appear in suites. Jacquet de la Guerre's suite continues with a chaconne in the form of a **rondeau,** in which a refrain alternates with a series of contrasting periods called **couplets,** then returns to close the movement. A **gavotte** follows, a duple-time dance with a half-measure upbeat, as in Example 16.2f. The dance was active, with downbeats

d. Sarabande

e. Gigue

f. Gavotte

g. Minuet

marked by a hop or jump, preceded by bending the knee and followed by one or two steps. The suite ends with a ***minuet,*** an elegant couple dance in moderate triple meter, shown in Example 16.2g. The dance used various patterns of four steps within each two-measure unit.

German versus French suites

In Germany, the suite assumed a standard order like that seen here: allemande, courante (or *corrente,* an Italian dance in $\frac{3}{4}$ time), sarabande, and gigue, often preceded by a prelude and augmented with optional dances. Each of the four standard dances had a different meter, tempo, characteristic rhythm, and national origin, providing strong contrasts between movements. But French composers allowed more variety in the dances chosen and in their order. They also often gave movements fanciful titles referring to people or moods.

EMULATION OF FRENCH STYLE

France was the leading power in Europe after the Thirty Years' War ended in 1648. Louis XIV was the most powerful monarch and the model for artistic patronage. French tastes, manners, and arts were widely regarded as the most refined and highly developed. Both admiring and envious, the English, Germans, Austrians, Poles, Russians, and others imitated French architecture, decorative arts, and music, especially keyboard styles, dances, suites, and overtures. From the 1660s on, French music was almost as influential as Italian music, and the integration of the two became one of the themes of the eighteenth century.

THE ENGLISH BAROQUE

English music drew inspiration from both Italy and France, in combination with native traditions. Royal patronage exercised a major influence, as in France, but music for the public grew increasingly important.

Limited monarchy

Unlike France, England was a limited monarchy, whose king shared rule with the Parliament. After the death of Elizabeth I in 1603, her cousin James VI of Scotland succeeded her as James I of England, uniting the two kingdoms. His son Charles I (r. 1625–49) sought to increase royal power, provoking the English Civil War (1642–49). He was executed and the monarchy was abolished in 1649, succeeded by a Commonwealth and Protectorate under Puritan leader Oliver Cromwell (1599–1658). Preferring limited monarchy to military rule, Parliament restored the monarchy in 1660 but reserved to itself the right to pass laws and levy taxes. Charles II (r. 1660–85) agreed to respect Parliament but gradually returned to his father's policy of enlarging royal power. The religious and political policies of James II (r. 1685–88), a Catholic, provoked the Glorious Revolution, which installed as sovereigns James's Protestant daughter Mary II (r. 1689–94) and her Dutch husband William of Orange (r. 1689–1702). A Bill of Rights passed that year guaranteed civil liberties and subjected the monarch to the rule of law. From then on, Parliament controlled the collection and allocation of public funds. As a consequence, the royal house had considerably less money than their French counterparts to spend on music.

MUSICAL THEATER

Despite attempts to introduce opera, the English monarchy, aristocracy, and public preferred native genres of dramatic music.

A favorite court entertainment since Henry VIII was the ***masque.*** Masques shared many aspects of opera, including instrumental music, dancing, songs, choruses, costumes, scenery, and stage machinery, but were long collaborative spectacles akin to French court ballets rather than unified dramas with music by a single composer. A highly elaborate masque, *The Triumph of Peace* (1634), included music by William Lawes (1602–1645) and others. Shorter masques were produced by aristocrats and in theaters or private schools.

Masques

Cromwell's Puritan government prohibited stage plays, but not concerts or private musical entertainments. This policy allowed the production of the first English "operas," not operas in the Italian sense, but mixtures of elements from spoken drama and the masque, including dances, songs, recitatives, and choruses. From this period comes the only seventeenth-century masque whose music survives complete, *Cupid and Death* (1653), with music by Matthew Locke (ca. 1621–1677) and Christopher Gibbons (1615–1677).

Mixed genres

After the Restoration in 1660, audiences eagerly returned to the theaters, where plays often included masques or similar musical episodes, as illustrated in Figure 16.11. Charles II had spent his exile in France, and French

Figure 16.11: Scene from "The Masque of Orpheus," with music by Matthew Locke. This masque, telling the story of Orpheus and Euridice, comprises part of Act IV of Elkanah Settle's play The Empress of Morocco, *produced in 1673 at the Dorset Garden Theatre in London. Engraving by William Dolle.*

music and court ballet became increasingly influential in England after his return. But an attempt to introduce French opera in the 1670s failed, and there was little interest in dramas set to continuous music. Only two dramas sung throughout met any success, both composed for private audiences rather than for the public: John Blow's *Venus and Adonis* (ca. 1683) and Henry Purcell's *Dido and Aeneas* (1689).

Venus and Adonis

John Blow (1649–1708) was organist of Westminster Abbey and organist and composer in the Chapel Royal. He wrote *Venus and Adonis* to entertain Charles II, and it featured Charles's former mistress Mary Davis as Venus and their daughter Mary Tudor as Cupid. Called a masque, it is really an unpretentious pastoral opera whose charming and moving music combines elements of Italian, French, and English styles. The overture and prologue are modeled on those of French operas; many of the airs and recitatives adopt the emotionally expressive style of the Italian lyric aria; other songs have English rhythms and melodic traits; and the dances and choruses stem from the masque tradition. The final chorus, *Mourn for thy servant*, is typically English in its simple, direct interpretation of the text, clear declamation, lucid part writing, and frequent harmonic audacities.

HENRY PURCELL'S DRAMATIC MUSIC

Henry Purcell (1659–1695) was England's leading composer and a royal favorite (see biography and Figure 16.12), best remembered for his dramatic music.

Dido and Aeneas

Purcell composed *Dido and Aeneas* in 1689, the year of William and Mary's coronation. The first known performance took place at an exclusive girl's boarding school in Chelsea, but the work may previously have been staged at court. Purcell's score is a masterpiece of opera in miniature: there are only four principal roles, and the three acts take only about an hour to perform. As Blow did in *Venus and Adonis*, which must have served as his principal model, Purcell incorporates elements of the English masque and of French and Italian opera.

French and Italian elements

The overture and homophonic choruses in dance rhythms resemble those of Lully, and the typical scene structure also follows Lully's example, with solo singing and a chorus leading to a dance. The most notable Italian element is the presence of several arias, rare in French opera or English masque. Three arias are built entirely over ground basses, an important type in Italian opera. The last of these, and one of the most moving arias in all opera, is Dido's lament, *When I am laid in earth* (NAWM 79b). It follows the Italian tradition of setting laments over a descending tetrachord (see chapter 15). Purcell creates great tension by rearticulating suspended notes on strong beats, intensifying the dissonance.

CD 5|40   CD 3|7

English elements

Amid these foreign influences, the English traits are still strong. The use of dance for dramatic purposes owes less to Lully than to the masque tradition. Many solos and choruses use the style of the English air: tuneful, diatonic, in the major mode, with simple, catchy rhythms. The closing chorus, *With drooping wings* (NAWM 79c), was modeled on the final chorus of *Venus and Adonis*. Equally perfect in workmanship, it is larger and conveys a more pro-

CD 5|42

found depth of sorrow. Descending minor-scale figures portray the "drooping wings" of cupids, and arresting pauses mark the words "never part."

In the recitatives, Purcell draws on precedents from Locke and Blow to fashion melodies flexibly molded to the accents, pace, and emotions of the English text. Example 16.3 shows a recitative from Act I in which Dido praises Aeneas to Belinda, her confidante. Where Lully might use simple declamation, Purcell composed florid passages to illustrate the text: upward rushes on "storms" and "fierce," and martial dotted rhythms on "valour." Descending lines filled with semitones suggest the sighs of love at "mix'd with Venus' charms, How soft in peace." Purcell catches the rhythms of English exactly with reverse-dotted rhythms on "so much" and "did he," reflecting the tendency of English speakers to shorten accented syllables. Dido's final recitative, *Thy hand, Belinda* (NAWM 79a), is a miniature masterpiece that portrays the dying Dido through a slow, stepwise, meandering descent tinged with chromaticism.

English recitatives

CD 5|39   CD 3|6

HENRY PURCELL (1659–1695)

Purcell's entire career was supported by royal patronage. His father, a member of the Chapel Royal, died just before his son's fifth birthday. Purcell joined the Chapel Royal as a choirboy and proved to be a gifted prodigy as a composer, publishing his first song at the age of eight. When his voice broke, he was apprenticed to the keeper of the king's keyboard and wind instruments. In 1677, he succeeded Matthew Locke as composer-in-ordinary for the violins, one of the more progressive positions in Britain's musical hierarchy. Purcell held a number of prestigious and simultaneous positions throughout his life, including organist of Westminster Abbey (1679), organist of the Chapel Royal (1682), and, the following year, organ maker and keeper of the king's instruments as well as composer to the court. He died at the young age of thirty-six, and his funeral was held in the hallowed Westminster Abbey, where he was also buried.

Throughout his brief life, Purcell wrote enormous amounts of music in almost all

Figure 16.12: Henry Purcell in 1695, in a portrait by John Closterman.

genres. His primary focus was vocal music: he composed songs for home performance, choral music for Anglican services and royal ceremonies, and music for the theater. Purcell's greatest gift lay in setting English words movingly yet with natural declamation.

MAJOR WORKS: Dido and Aeneas (opera), *5 semi-operas, incidental music for 43 plays, 65 anthems, 6 Services, numerous odes, songs, and catches, and chamber and keyboard music*

Example 16.3: Recitative from Purcell, Dido and Aeneas

Semi-operas *Dido and Aeneas* had no successors because the English strongly preferred spoken drama. For public theaters, Purcell wrote incidental music for almost fifty plays, most in the last five years of his life. During this period, he also wrote the music for five works in the mixed genre called **dramatic opera** or **semi-opera,** a spoken play with an overture and four or more masques or substantial musical episodes, including *The Fairy Queen* (1692), based on Shakespeare's *A Midsummer Night's Dream.*

England did not develop a native tradition of full-fledged opera until the late nineteenth century. Although Purcell died young, there is no sign that he would have inaugurated one had he lived. Without support for it from the monarchy, as in France, or from the public, as in Venice and other cities, there was no role for opera in English.

OTHER ENGLISH MUSIC

Music historians' fascination with opera in the seventeenth century has tended to obscure England, where opera never took root. But England had a lively musical culture, worth noting in its broad outlines.

Vocal music Vocal music outside the theater owed relatively little to foreign models. The royal family often commissioned large works for chorus, soloists, and orchestra for ceremonial or state occasions, such as royal birthdays, the king's return to London, or holidays. Purcell's magnificent *Ode for St. Cecilia's Day* (1692) was a direct ancestor of Handel's English oratorios (see chapter 19). In addition to hundreds of theater songs, Purcell wrote a large number of vocal solos, duets, and trios, all published for home performance. A specialty of

Purcell and other English composers in this period was the **catch**, a round or canon with a humorous, often ribald text. Catches were sung unaccompanied by a convivial group of gentlemen, in an elevated, musically intellectual parallel to the bawdy songs and coarse jokes of other all-male gatherings.

Anthems and Services remained the principal genres of Anglican church music after the Restoration. Since Charles II favored solo singing and orchestral accompaniments, Blow, Purcell, and their contemporaries produced many verse anthems for soloists with chorus. Coronation ceremonies inspired especially elaborate works. Purcell also set nonliturgical sacred texts for one or more voices with continuo, evidently for private devotional use.

The English continued to enjoy playing viol consort music, particularly In Nomines and fantasias. This was music for well-to-do amateurs to play for their own entertainment. The leading composer for viol consort at mid-century was John Jenkins (1592–1678). The principal later composers for viols were Locke and Purcell, whose viol fantasias and In Nomines, written about 1680, are the last important examples of both genres. Purcell also wrote numerous dances and other pieces for harpsichord, as well as chamber sonatas that show some Italian influences.

Instrumental music

Social dancing was an important part of English life, with strong dance traditions at court, in cities, and in rural areas. The London publisher John Playford (1623–1687) collected the tunes most commonly used for traditional English country dances and published them, along with instructions for the dances, in *The English Dancing Master* (1651). Playford's title page for his first edition is shown in Figure 16.13. This work was one of the first printed collections to include a large number of genuine folk melodies and popular airs. For us, it represents a valuable source for music that would otherwise have gone undocumented; at the time, it marked the spread of an oral tradition into urban settings where amateur performance from printed music had

Figure 16.13: Title page of the first edition of The English Dancing Master, *published by John Playford.*

been fashionable since the sixteenth century. It was one of the best-selling musical publications of the Baroque era, with new editions appearing frequently through 1728.

The public concert   Perhaps more important in the long run than the music composed in seventeenth-century England was an institution pioneered there: the public concert. Until the 1670s, concerts were private affairs, given for an invited audience by amateurs, by performers employed by a patron, or by learned academies. Then in London several trends came together: a middle class interested in listening to music, a large number of excellent musicians in the service of the royal court and the London theaters, and the inability of the king to pay his musicians well, which encouraged them to find means of supplementing their income. Impresarios rented rooms in or attached to taverns, charged an entrance fee, and paid the performers out of the proceeds (see Source Reading). Soon the first commercial concert halls were built, and modern concert life began. Public concerts gradually spread to the Continent, reaching Paris in 1725 and major German cities by the 1740s.

SOURCE READINGS

THE FIRST PUBLIC CONCERTS

Concerts that anyone can attend for the price of a ticket are so much a part of modern musical life that it is hard to imagine they are only three centuries old. The public concert is an English invention, inspired by the presence in London of excellent musicians with inadequate salaries and of middle-class audiences eager to hear music but without means to employ their own musicians. The first concert series was advertised in the London Gazette *in December 1672:*

These are to give notice, That at Mr *John Banisters* House (now called the Music-School) over against the *George Tavern* in *White Fryers*, this present Monday, will be Music performed by excellent Masters, beginning precisely at 4 of the clock in the afternoon, and every afternoon for the future, precisely at the same hour.

——— • ———

Roger North, a writer and critic, recalled the concerts:

But how and by what steps Music shot up into such request, as to crowd out from the stage even comedy itself, and to sit down in her place and become of such mighty value and price as we now know it to be, is worth inquiring after.

The first attempt was low: a project of old Banister, who was a good violin, and a theatrical composer. He opened an obscure room in a public house in Whitefriars, filled it with tables and seats, and made a side box with curtains for the music. 1^S [one shilling] apiece, call for what [food and drink] you please, pay the reckoning [the bill], and *Welcome gentlemen.*

——— • ———

Elsewhere, North noted that Banister was "one of the [King's] band of violins" whose "course of life was such as kept him poor" and who started the concert series "by way of project to get a little money." The performers, "the best hands in town," were

the mercenary teachers, chiefly foreigners, who attended for a *sportula* [a gift or share of the proceeds] at the time. Sometimes consort, sometimes solos, of the violin, flageolet (one of Banister's perfections), bass viol, lute, and song *all'Italiana,* and such varieties diverted the company, who paid at coming in.

Roger North on Music, ed. John Wilson (London: Novello, 1959), 302–3 and 352. Spelling and punctuation modernized.

Spain and the New World

The third great monarchy in western Europe was Spain. By 1600, the flood of silver from its New World colonies had made Spain the richest country in Europe. It was the most powerful nation on earth, with an empire that included Portugal (annexed in 1580), half of Italy and the Netherlands, the Philippine Islands, almost all of Central and South America, and much of North America. Ironically, Spain's great wealth led to its economic decline in the seventeenth century because it spent vast sums elsewhere in Europe for food, manufactured goods, and military adventures rather than nurturing its own industries. In the 1640s, Spain suffered defeat by France during the Thirty Years' War and revolutions in Catalonia (eastern Spain), Portugal, and southern Italy. Although Spain regained control in Catalonia and southern Italy, Portugal won its independence (taking Brazil with it). Never again was Spain a dominant military power in Europe.

Spain still ruled vast colonies in the Americas, stretching from present-day Chile and Argentina through Florida, Texas, and California. More than a century of colonization had produced an ethnically diverse society, encompassing a wide range of native peoples, Spanish immigrants and their descendents, African slaves imported to work the mines and plantations, and people of mixed race. Each group had its own music but also borrowed musical elements from other groups, a habit that has characterized music in the Americas ever since. Musicians in the Spanish colonies drew directly on Spanish and wider European traditions; in turn, dances, songs, rhythms, and musical traits popular in the colonies often found eager listeners in Spain, Italy, France, and elsewhere in Europe, as we have seen with the spread of the chacona and sarabande. For these reasons, it makes sense to consider the music of Spain and the Spanish New World together, while recognizing the different circumstances of the home country and the colonies.

Spanish colonies

OPERA, ZARZUELA, AND SONG

Spain developed its own national types of opera and musical theater. An opera in Spanish modeled on the early Florentine operas was presented at the royal court in 1627, but the style did not catch on. In 1659–60, for celebrations of peace with France and the wedding of Spanish princess Maria Teresa to Louis XIV, dramatist Pedro Calderón de la Barca and composer Juan Hidalgo (1614–1685) collaborated on two operas that inaugurated a distinctively Spanish tradition. The music survives only for the second opera, *Celos aun del aire matan;* it consists mostly of syllabic, strophic airs in Spanish styles and dance rhythms, with recitative monologues reserved for the most dramatic moments. Hidalgo also wrote music for many plays. Together with Calderón, he devised the distinctly Spanish **zarzuela,** the predominant genre of musical theater in Spain for several centuries, which was a light, mythological play in a pastoral setting that alternates between sung and spoken dialogue and various types of ensemble and solo song. Hidalgo was for Spain what Lully was for France, the founder of enduring traditions for the nation's musical theater and a composer who knew how to appeal both to his royal patrons and to a broader public.

La púrpura de la rosa

CD 5|43

The characteristics of Spanish Baroque opera are seen in *La púrpura de la rosa* (The Blood of the Rose, excerpt in NAWM 80), the first opera produced in the New World. It was staged in 1701 at the court of the viceroy of Peru in Lima to celebrate the accession to the Spanish throne of Philip V, grandson of Louis XIV and the first Bourbon king of Spain. The libretto was adapted from that of Calderón and Hidalgo's first opera; the music was by Tomás de Torrejón y Velasco (1644–1728), who may have studied with Hidalgo in Spain, went to Peru in 1667, and became *maestro di capilla* of the Lima cathedral and the most famous composer in the Americas. As was traditional in Spanish lyric theater of the time, most of the roles were played by women. The story centers on love between Venus and Adonis, threatened by the jealousy of Mars. Example 16.4 illustrates the distinctly Spanish practice of setting the dialogue, not in recitative, but rather to a strophic song. Venus and Adonis converse in the first strophe, shown here; then Venus sings three strophes to the same music, and the fifth strophe is again in dialogue. The syncopations are typical of Spanish song. The scene closes with a five-part chorus of nymphs welcoming Adonis to Venus's garden with dance and song, marked by even greater syncopations. The sound of the accompaniment was also distinctive, since the continuo in Spanish works was usually played by harps, guitars, and viols rather than by lute or keyboard as in Italy and France.

Songs

Many songs from theatrical productions also circulated in manuscript throughout Spain and Spain's possessions in Italy and the Americas. So did independent songs in genres such as the *romance*, scored for two to four voices or for solo voice with guitar or harp accompaniment, and the *tonada*, a

Example 16.4: Excerpt from Torrejón's La púrpura de la rosa

Venus: *What old-fashioned flattery!*
Adonis: *Pardon me, for I must go on following your beauty.*
Venus: *What for? If in my garden, [which now from this place lets us observe from the watchtower a laurel tree that a loving vine embraces, there are signs that all is love.]*

solo song. The many variants between manuscripts give evidence to a strong Spanish tradition of treating music as common property suitable for reworking and improvisation. Relatively few Spanish pieces were published because Spain lacked music printers, discouraging the growth of a strong amateur performing tradition as in England or France.

CHURCH MUSIC

In Spain and the Spanish colonies, many liturgical works, especially masses, continued to be composed in imitative polyphony well into the eighteenth century. But the most vibrant genre of sacred music was the villancico, sung especially at Christmas, Easter, and other important feasts. Scored for one or more choirs, soloists with choir, or solo voice with continuo, and in the vernacular rather than Latin, these works brought into church the concertato medium and the rustic style of the secular villancico (see chapter 11). The form resembled that of villancicos of the previous century, with a refrain (*estribillo*) that precedes and follows one or more stanzas (*coplas*), but the proportions were often greatly enlarged.

A typical example is the Christmas villancico *Los coflades de la estleya* (NAWM 81) by Juan de Araujo (1646–1712), who was a *maestro di capilla* in Peru and Bolivia. The two treble soloists and choir alternate in rapid dialogue over an active accompaniment. As shown in Example 16.5, both vocal and instrumental parts are full of syncopations, suggesting rhythmic influences from West Africa as well as Spain. The text speaks of poor black boys (meaning South American natives as well as Africans) going to Bethlehem to see the infant Jesus, and the music hits just the right balance of boyish exuberance with reverent awe.

CD 5|47

Example 16.5: Araujo, Los coflades de la estleya, *beginning of first copla*

Let us follow the star (Come on!), we black courtiers (Let's go!)

INSTRUMENTAL MUSIC

Few instrumental ensemble pieces survive from seventeenth-century Spain, but there were vibrant traditions of solo music for organ, harp, and guitar.

Organ music

Spanish organ music is characterized by strong contrasts of color and texture, particularly in the **tiento,** an improvisatory-style piece that often featured imitation, akin to the sixteenth-century fantasia. A striking example is the *Tiento de batalla* (Battle Tiento) of Juan Bautista José Cabanilles (1644–1712), which imitates trumpet-calls resounding from opposite sides of a battlefield. Cabanilles was the leading Spanish composer for organ, and he left us over a thousand works, including tientos, hymn-settings, and toccatas.

Harp and guitar music

The main chamber instruments were harp and guitar, and their repertory centered around dances and variations on familiar dance tunes, songs, bass ostinatos, or harmonic patterns. Compositions included the chacona, passacalle, sarabande, and other dance types that became the most widely disseminated contributions of Spain and its colonies to European music as a whole. But apart from these instrumental dances, Spanish music remained relatively little known in the rest of Europe.

FRENCH STYLE AND NATIONAL TRADITIONS

Although France, England, and Spain were all monarchies, France and its king were the most powerful and influential. French music was imitated throughout Europe, and Lully's operas were performed for more than a century after his death, a remarkable legacy for the time. The elegant, restrained manner cultivated by French composers remained strong in the eighteenth century and contributed to the distinctive flavor of later French works. The suite remained an important genre for almost a century and was revived in the twentieth century; several of the dances, especially the minuet, had long careers in other instrumental music.

Purcell represented a high water mark for English music, but in the century that followed, foreigners dominated English musical life. Because there are no institutions devoted to the performance of masques or semi-operas, English dramatic music of the seventeenth century has languished in obscurity. In part because historians have focused so intently on opera in telling the story of seventeenth-century music, *Dido and Aeneas* is renowned and widely performed, while other English music of the time is relatively unknown. Meanwhile, the public concert, an English innovation, became one of the cornerstones of musical life.

In Spain and the New World, distinctive national traditions such as Spanish opera, zarzuela, dance-songs, and villancicos continued into the next century. But influences from Italy and France became increasingly important, and Spanish music came to reflect a blending of native and more broadly European trends. The mixture of European, native American, and African characteristics in Spanish colonial music presaged later developments in the nineteenth and twentieth centuries, culminating in the worldwide enjoyment of American, Cuban, and Brazilian popular music that blends elements from all four continents.

In the late nineteenth and twentieth centuries, French, English, and Spanish musicians looked back at their respective Baroque traditions as native sources independent of the German tradition, which by then had become dominant. The works of Lully, Purcell, and others were edited and published, valued both for their intrinsic musical worth and as proof of a vibrant national musical heritage that predated Bach. Only recently have works from the New World been rediscovered, published, and appreciated for showing the early transplantation of European culture in the Americas. By the late twentieth century, Lully's operas were again being staged, and a widening range of French, English, Spanish, and New World music was performed and recorded. While politics played a role in the revival of this music, as in its creation, its ability to move and entertain us is what sustains its continuing presence.

Italy and Germany in the Late
Seventeenth Century

Unlike the centralized monarchies of France, England, and Spain, Italy and Germany were each divided into numerous sovereign states. Musical life was not concentrated in one royal court or capital city, as in Paris and London, but was supported by many rulers and cities, each competing for the best musicians. Like bees pursuing pollen, performers and composers often traveled from one center or patron to another seeking better employment, and both regions provided rich environments for exchanging ideas. In Italy, the influences were mostly native. Composers developed genres pioneered in the early seventeenth century, such as opera, cantata, and sonata, and devised the instrumental concerto. Here the story is one of stylistic evolution within an established tradition and of codifying new conventions, including the ***da capo aria*** and tonality. In German-speaking lands, by contrast, composers drew deeply on both French and Italian styles, blending elements from each with homegrown traditions. From this melting pot would come the great German and Austrian composers of the eighteenth century, from Bach and Handel to Haydn and Mozart.

ITALY

In Italy, opera continued to be the leading musical genre, and the cantata was the most prominent form of vocal chamber music. Yet the Italian musical works from this time that we remember best and perform

most often are instrumental, particularly the sonatas and concertos of Arcangelo Corelli and his contemporaries.

Figure 17.1 shows the main musical centers of Italy around 1650. Politically, the peninsula was divided among Spanish dominions in the south and
in the region around Milan; territories governed by the pope, stretching from
Rome up to Bologna and Ferrara; and numerous small states in the north.
Paradoxically, the political splintering of northern Italy bred economic and
musical strength. Outside of Rome, seat of the pope, and Naples, capital of the
southern Spanish possessions, all the major developments in Italian music
throughout the seventeenth and eighteenth centuries took place in the north.

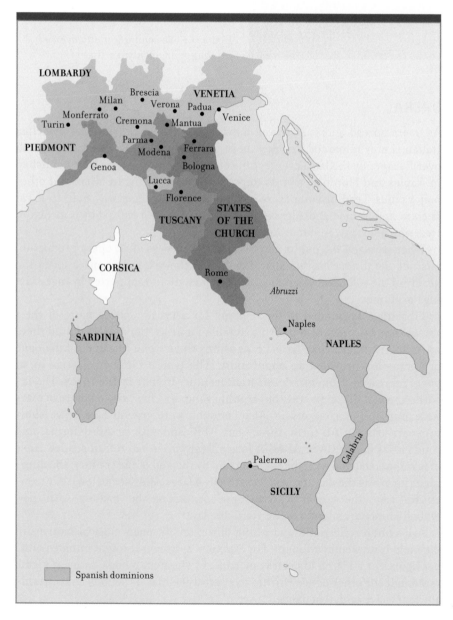

*Figure 17.1: Map of
Italy around 1650,
showing the cities that
were the main centers
for music.*

Figure 17.2: Alessandro Scarlatti, in an oil painting by an unknown artist.

OPERA

As opera spread across Italy and outward to other countries, the principal Italian center remained Venice, whose public opera houses were famous all over Europe. By the late seventeenth century, opera was also well established in Naples and Florence, and its importance was growing in Milan and other major cities. Leading composers included Giovanni Legrenzi (1626–1690) at Ferrara and Venice and Alessandro Scarlatti (1660–1725), shown in Figure 17.2, who held sway in Rome and Naples.

Arias   What attracted the public and assured the success of an opera production was not the drama but the star singers and the arias. Audiences loved the beauty of the solo voice singing an elegant melody and supported by ingratiating harmonies.

Librettists responded to the demand for arias by writing more of their verses in poetic meters and forms suitable for arias. Composers outdid them by indulging in aria-like lyrical expansions whenever a few lines of dialogue or a situation provided an opportunity. The typical number of arias in an opera increased, from two dozen at midcentury to sixty by the 1670s. The favorite form at that time was the strophic song, in which two or more stanzas were sung to the same music. Also common were ground bass arias, short two-part arias in AB form, three-part ABB′ and ABA or ABA′ forms, and rondo arias in ABACA or ABAB′A forms. Many arias had refrains, a few lines of text that recurred with the same music. By the end of the century, the dominant form was the da capo aria, essentially a large ABA (see below). Any repetition gave the singer a chance to ornament the melody with new embellishments and impressive vocal display.

Arias often reflected the meaning of the text through musical motives in the melody or accompaniment. For example, a composer might imitate trumpet figures or a march to portray martial or vehement moods, or use a gigue, sarabande, or other dance rhythm to suggest feelings or actions conventionally associated with that dance.

VOCAL CHAMBER MUSIC

The cantata had become the leading form of vocal chamber music in Italy, and the center of cantata composition was Rome. There, wealthy aristocrats and diplomats sponsored regular private parties for the elite, where the entertainment often included a cantata written expressly for the occasion. Because cantatas were meant for performance before a small discriminating audience in a room without a stage, scenery, or costumes, they invited elegance, refinement, and wit that would be lost in a spacious opera house. Moreover, the demand for a new cantata at frequent intervals offered poets and composers regular work and chances to experiment.

Cantata

Cantatas around 1650 featured many short, contrasting sections, as we find in Barbara Strozzi's *Lagrime mie* (NAWM 69). By the 1690s, poets and composers settled on a pattern of alternating recitatives and arias, normally two or three of each, totaling eight to fifteen minutes. Most cantatas were written for solo voice with continuo, though some featured two or more voices. The text, usually pastoral love-poetry, took the form of a dramatic narrative or soliloquy.

The more than six hundred cantatas of Alessandro Scarlatti mark a high point in this repertory. His *Clori vezzosa, e bella* is typical of the solo cantata around 1690–1710, with two recitative-aria pairs. The second recitative (NAWM 82a) exemplifies Scarlatti's mature style in using a wide harmonic range, chromaticism, and diminished chords. The passage in Example 17.1a moves first to the flat side, reaching an F-minor triad at "affanni miei" (my

Scarlatti cantatas

CD 5|56

Example 17.1: Recitative and aria from Scarlatti's cantata Clori vezzosa, e bella

a. *Recitative excerpt*

Because if I think that you alone are the cause of so many of my troubles, it becomes my joy, that suffering and that torture.

b. *Opening of aria* Sì, sì, ben mio

Yes, yes, my love, yes, yes, I would like, through you, still more torments for my heart.

c. *Middle section of aria*

Feeling pity at my pain, perhaps you will say one day: "Who ever saw greater faith, or a more devoted love?"

troubles), then to the sharp side, passing through A-major and E-major triads over a chromatic ascent in the bass, before cadencing on A minor. Scarlatti often used diminished seventh chords, rare for the time, to convey strong emotions or add bite to a cadence. Here a diminished seventh chord at the cadence on "il martire" (that torture) serves both purposes.

The most common form of aria in Scarlatti's operas and cantatas is the **da capo aria.** The form takes its name from the words "Da capo" (from the head) placed at the close of the second section, instructing the performers to return to the beginning of the aria and repeat the first section, producing an ABA form. Typically the A section is itself a small two-part form, with two different settings of the same text, each introduced by a brief instrumental ritornello. In Scarlatti's hands, the da capo aria was the perfect vehicle for sustaining a lyrical moment through a musical design that expressed a single sentiment, often joined with an opposing or related one in the contrasting middle section.

Da capo aria

Both arias in *Clori vezzosa, e bella* are da capo arias. The second, *Sì, sì, ben mio* (NAWM 82b) has this structure:

CD 5|57

Section:	1				2	1 repeats
	Ritornello	A1	Rit	A2	B	
Key:	Dm	Dm→ Gm	Gm	Gm→ Dm	FM→ V of Dm	

In some da capo arias, the first section closes with another ritornello, or the opening ritornello is omitted when the first section repeats.

Example 17.1b shows the first half of this aria's first section. The spritely gigue rhythm contrasts ironically with the lover's request for "more torments for my heart." The opening ritornello introduces motives that the voice takes up and develops. The first vocal statement cadences in the subdominant, the continuo states the second measure of the ritornello in that key, and the voice reenters with the second setting of the same text. The B section, shown in Example 17.1c, offers contrast in turning to a major key and more hopeful sentiments. The bass offers new variants on its opening ritornello, linking the two sections, while the voice sings a new but related melody. The cadence on G minor in measure 78 includes a chromatically altered chord that occurs often in the music of Scarlatti and his Italian contemporaries—a first-inversion triad on the flatted second degree (A♭) known as a Neapolitan sixth.

The da capo aria became the standard aria form in the eighteenth century for opera and cantata alike because it offered great flexibility in expression. The music of the B section could be as similar or contrasting as the poetry required, while the form guaranteed a contrast of key, a sense of departure and return, and harmonic and thematic closure. Singers typically introduced new embellishments on the repetition of the A section, providing the perfect opportunity to display their artistry.

Midway between cantata and opera stood the **serenata,** a semidramatic piece for several singers and small orchestra, usually written for a special occasion. Alessandro Stradella (1639–1682), an innovative composer of operas and cantatas, was one of the first to write serenatas.

Serenata

CHURCH MUSIC AND ORATORIO

Italian church composers in the second half of the seventeenth century continued to cultivate the old contrapuntal style modeled on Palestrina alongside the newer concerted styles featuring basso continuo and solo singers, sometimes mixing the two in the same work. We can see this stylistic diversity in the nearly fifty collections of sacred vocal music published by Maurizio Cazzati (1616–1678), music director at the Church of San Petronio in Bologna from 1657 to 1671. At one end of the spectrum, his *Messa a cappella* (Unaccompanied Mass) of 1670 is in a slightly modernized *stile antico*. His *Magnificat a 4* of the same year, however, alternates florid duets in the modern style with choruses in the older style. In other works he plays soloists against a full choir, as in the later instrumental concerto (see below).

Instrumental church music   San Petronio was also an important center for instrumental ensemble music, which was often played during church services. Cazzati published numerous collections of sonatas suited for use in church, including the first sonatas to include trumpet. His instrumental works, like those of other Bolognese composers, were marked by restraint and seriousness, appropriate to the setting and acoustics of San Petronio, and avoided technical display and

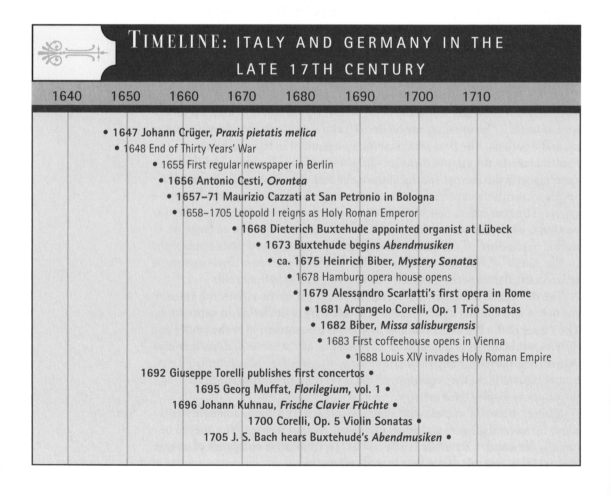

TIMELINE: ITALY AND GERMANY IN THE LATE 17TH CENTURY

1640	1650	1660	1670	1680	1690	1700	1710

- 1647 Johann Crüger, *Praxis pietatis melica*
- 1648 End of Thirty Years' War
- 1655 First regular newspaper in Berlin
- 1656 Antonio Cesti, *Orontea*
- 1657–71 Maurizio Cazzati at San Petronio in Bologna
- 1658–1705 Leopold I reigns as Holy Roman Emperor
- 1668 Dieterich Buxtehude appointed organist at Lübeck
- 1673 Buxtehude begins *Abendmusiken*
- ca. 1675 Heinrich Biber, *Mystery Sonatas*
- 1678 Hamburg opera house opens
- 1679 Alessandro Scarlatti's first opera in Rome
- 1681 Arcangelo Corelli, Op. 1 Trio Sonatas
- 1682 Biber, *Missa salisburgensis*
- 1683 First coffeehouse opens in Vienna
- 1688 Louis XIV invades Holy Roman Empire

1692 Giuseppe Torelli publishes first concertos •
1695 Georg Muffat, *Florilegium*, vol. 1 •
1696 Johann Kuhnau, *Frische Clavier Früchte* •
1700 Corelli, Op. 5 Violin Sonatas •
1705 J. S. Bach hears Buxtehude's *Abendmusiken* •

special effects. Italian organists, like their colleagues in Spain and in Catholic regions of Germany, continued to compose in existing genres, such as ricercares, toccatas, variation canzonas, and chant settings.

Although oratorios were still performed in oratories, they were also presented in the palaces of princes and cardinals, in academies, and in other institutions. They were a handy substitute for opera during Lent or at other seasons when the theaters were closed. Most oratorios were now in Italian rather than Latin, had librettos in verse, and had two sections, leaving room for a sermon or, in private entertainments, an intermission with refreshments. *Oratorios*

INSTRUMENTAL CHAMBER MUSIC

In the realm of instrumental chamber music, as in the opera and cantata, Italians remained the undisputed masters and teachers. The late seventeenth and early eighteenth centuries were the age of the great violin makers of Cremona in northern Italy: Nicolò Amati (1596–1684), Antonio Stradivari (Stradivarius, 1644–1737), and Giuseppe Bartolomeo Guarneri (1698–1744), all famed for instruments of unrivaled excellence, such as the Stradivarius shown in Figure 17.3 (see sidebar, p. 392). It was also the age of great string music in Italy, of which the two leading genres were the sonata and the instrumental concerto.

Sonatas in the first half of the seventeenth century consisted of a number of small sections differentiated by musical material, texture, mood, character, and sometimes meter and tempo, as in the Biagio Marini sonata we examined in chapter 15 (NAWM 76). As composers developed the genre, these sections gradually became longer and more self-contained. Finally, composers separated the sections into distinct movements, so that in time the sonata became a multimovement work with contrasts between movements. These contrasts were in sympathy with the theory of the affections (see chapter 13), which held that music stimulated the bodily humors and could keep them in balance by offering a diversity of moods. Some composers maintained thematic similarities between movements, as in the older variation canzona (see chapter 15), but thematic independence of movements was much more common. *Development of the sonata*

By about 1660, two main types of sonata had emerged. The **sonata da camera,** or **chamber sonata,** featured a series of stylized dances, often beginning with a prelude. The **sonata da chiesa,** or **church sonata,** contained mostly abstract movements, often including one or more that used dance rhythms or binary form but were not usually titled as dances. Church sonatas could be used in church services, substituting for certain items of the Mass Proper or for antiphons for the Magnificat at Vespers, and both types were played for entertainment in private concerts.

The most common instrumentation after 1670 for both church and chamber sonatas was two treble instruments, usually violins, with basso continuo. Such a work is called a **trio sonata** because of its three-part texture, but a performance can feature four or more players if more than one is used for the basso continuo, such as a cello performing the bass line and a harpsichord, organ, or lute doubling the bass and filling in the chords. The texture we find *Trio sonata*

MUSIC IN CONTEXT

THE VIOLIN WORKSHOP OF ANTONIO STRADIVARIUS

Just as Italian composers excelled in writing songs and arias for the solo voice from the beginning of the seventeenth century, so too it was the Italians who created new instrumental genres—solo sonata, trio sonata, and concerto—which called on the violin to imitate the subtlety, expressivity, and virtuosity of the singing voice. Not surprisingly, then, it was also the Italians—specifically, a few families of instrument builders in the town of Cremona—who developed the art of violin-making to a peak that has never been surpassed. During their heyday, the violin became the new agent of that artistic power which had previously resided only in the voice.

Antonio Stradivari (ca. 1644–1737) was the most prominent member of his universally renowned family of instrument-makers in the area of northern Italy famed for violin construction. He was possibly a pupil of Nicolò Amati, founder of another dynasty of violin-makers. During his long life, Stradivari made or supervised the production of more than 1,100 instruments—including harps, guitars, violas, and cellos—about half of which survive and are still being used today by some of the world's leading string players. Figure 17.3 shows one of the few Stradivari violins that has been restored to its original form, with a shorter fingerboard and the neck angled back only slightly from the body. Thousands of violins were made in tribute to Stradivari and modeled on his superior construction design; with no intention to deceive, these instruments bear the label "Stradivarius," although they were produced neither by the master nor his workshop, which by the mid-eighteenth century was engaged in a healthy rivalry with that of the Guarneri family.

Figure 17.3: Violin, 1693, by Antonio Stradivari, restored to its original Baroque form.

What was involved in making a "Strad" and why are these instruments so highly prized? To begin with, Stradivari selected woods of the highest possible quality—pine for the front and sides, and maple for the back of the instrument. Then he proceeded to carve the pieces, taking care to get just the right degree of arching because the body of the instrument is not flat but slightly rounded, and arrive at just the right amount of thickness because even the tiniest variation in the thickness of the wood will affect the instrument's resonance. Next he cut the elegantly shaped f-holes into the front piece to optimize the vibrations and maximize the sound. Finally, he applied the varnish to protect the instrument from dirt and to stop it from absorbing moisture. In addition to its practical function, the varnish itself added greatly to the beauty of the instrument by giving it a radiant, orange-brown sheen and highlighting the grain patterns on the wood's surface. In an effort to explain the extraordinarily rich and powerful tone of a Stradivarius violin, a popular theory held that its varnish had some sort of "magic" ingredient. However, historical research has shown that the varnish is no different from that used by furniture makers when Stradivari was alive. Other theories have advanced the idea that the wood was first soaked in water and then specially seasoned before being carved, or that the grain of the wood used is tighter than modern woods. But so far, scientists have been unable to ascertain any measurable qualities that set these instruments apart. Even if such properties are discovered, the intrinsic superiority of a Stradivarius remains a matter not only of science but also of a long-lost art.—BRH

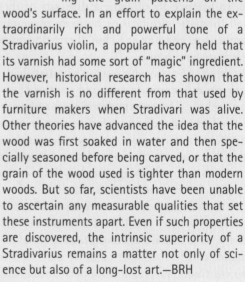

in the trio ... so continuo, served
many other ... tal.

Solo son ... uo, were at first less
numerous ... er 1700. Composers
also wrote ... ntal parts with continuo, as we ... struments.

*Solo and
ensemble sonatas*

ARCANG ...

The trio a ... 1713) represent the
crowning a ... te seventeenth century. Train ... as violinist, teacher,
and comp(... had an unparalleled
influence (

... –171**3**)

Corelli ...
ninety ...
genres ...
concer ...
standa ...
nique t ...

Bor ...
nano, ...
studied ...
beginn ...
the cra ...
Corelli ...
quickly ...
compo ...
Christi ...
As a vi(...
tor, he ...
dards t ...
foundation of most eighteenth-century
schools of violin playing. Others may have
surpassed him in bravura, but he had the
good taste to avoid empty displays of virtuosity, and no one understood the singing
qualities of the violin better than he did.

Beginning in 1681, Corelli published a
series of collections of trio sonatas, violin
sonatas, and concerti grossi that were dis-

*e 17.4: Portrait of Arcangelo Corelli (ca. 1700)
gh Howard.*

... inated across Europe, bringing him international fame.

MAJOR WORKS: *6 published collections known by
opus (work) number: Op. 1 (1681), 12 trio sonatas
(sonate da chiesa); Op. 2 (1685), 12 trio sonate da
camera (one is a chaconne); Op. 3 (1689), 12 trio
sonate da chiesa; Op. 4 (1695), 12 trio sonate da
camera; Op. 5 (1700), 12 solo violin sonatas; Op. 6
(1714), 12 concerti grossi; 6 other trio sonatas and 3
quartets for three instruments and basso continuo*

Trio sonatas   In his trio sonatas, Corelli emphasized lyricism over virtuosity. He rarely used extremely high or low notes, fast runs, or difficult double stops. The two violins, treated exactly alike, frequently cross and exchange music, interlocking in suspensions that give his works a decisive forward momentum. Example 17.2 shows a passage from the first movement of his Trio Sonata in D Major, Op. 3, No. 2 (NAWM 83), that features several typical traits of Corelli's style: a **walking bass,** with a steadily moving pattern of eighth notes, under free imitation between the violins; a chain of suspensions in the violins above a descending sequence in the bass; and a dialogue between the violins as they leapfrog over each other to progressively higher peaks.

[CD 6|1]   [CD 3|9]

Example 17.2: Passage from Corelli's Trio Sonata, Op. 3, No. 2, first movement

Church sonatas   Most of Corelli's church trio sonatas consist of four movements, often in two pairs, in the order slow-fast-slow-fast. Although there are many exceptions to this pattern, it gradually became a norm for Corelli and later composers. The first slow movement typically has a contrapuntal texture and a majestic, solemn character. The Allegro that follows normally features fugal imitation, with the bass line a full participant. This movement is the musical center of gravity for the church sonata, and it retains elements of the canzona in its use of imitation, of a subject with a marked rhythmic character, and of variation at later entrances of the subject. The subsequent slow movement most often resembles a lyric, operatic duet in triple meter. The fast final movement usually features dancelike rhythms and often is in binary form. All of these traits are true of Op. 3, No. 2. We have seen in Example 17.2 the contrapuntal web of suspensions and imitations in the first movement. As shown in Example 17.3, the opening of the second movement features exact imitation between first violin and bass and inversion in the second violin; the third movement, in the relative minor, is songlike with some imitation; and the

Example 17.3: Corelli's Trio Sonata, Op. 3, No. 2, second through fourth movements

a. *Second movement*

b. *Third movement*

c. *Fourth movement*

finale is an imitative gigue in binary form whose subject often appears in inversion, as in the second movement.

Chamber sonatas   Corelli's chamber sonatas usually begin with a prelude, after which two or three dances may follow as in the French suite. Often the first two movements resemble those of a church sonata, with a slow introduction and fugal Allegro. Some of the introductions feature dotted rhythms, recalling the French overture. The dance movements are almost always in binary form, with each section repeated, the first section closing on the dominant or relative major and the second making its way back to the tonic. Rather than sharing an almost equal role as in the church sonatas, the bass line in the chamber sonatas is almost pure accompaniment.

Solo sonatas   Corelli's solo violin sonatas are also divided between church and chamber sonatas, following similar patterns of movements but allowing considerably more virtuosity. In the Allegro movements, the solo violin sometimes employs double and triple stops to simulate the rich three-part sonority of the trio sonata and the interplay of voices in a fugue. There are fast runs, arpeggios, extended perpetual-motion passages, and cadenzas—elaborate solo embellishments at a cadence, either notated or improvised. The slow movements were notated simply but were meant to be ornamented freely and profusely. In 1710, the Amsterdam publisher Estienne Roger reissued Corelli's solo sonatas, showing for the slow movements both the original solo parts and embellished versions that, Roger claimed, represented the way the composer played the sonatas, as in Figure 17.5. The embellishments surely reflect the practice of Corelli's time, and probably of the composer himself.

Figure 17.5: A page from the first movement of Corelli's Sonata in D Major, Op. 5, No. 1, in an edition printed by Estienne Roger in Amsterdam. In the slow movements and passages, the violin part is given both as originally published and in an embellished version claimed to represent the way Corelli himself performed it.

In Corelli's sonatas, movements are thematically independent from each other (with rare exceptions) and tend to be based on a single subject stated at the outset. The music unfolds in a continuous expansion of the opening subject, with variations, sequences, brief modulations to nearby keys, and fascinating subtleties of phrasing. This steady spinning out of a single theme, in which the original idea seems to generate a spontaneous flow of musical thoughts, is highly characteristic of the late Baroque from about the 1680s on.

Thematic organization

Corelli's music is fully tonal, marked with the sense of direction or progression that, more than any other quality, distinguishes tonal music from modal music. Example 17.2, for instance, features several series of chords whose roots move down the circle of fifths, falling by a fifth or rising by a fourth (see measures 8–10 and 10–14). This is the normal direction for chord progressions in tonal music, whereas modal music may move up the circle of fifths as easily as down. In tonal progressions, the chord root also may rise by step or fall by a third before again rising by a fourth (see measures 14–15). Chord series whose roots primarily move down by a fourth or second and up by a fifth or third suggest modal thinking, as in Example 14.4 from Monteverdi's *Orfeo*. The increasing use, over the course of the seventeenth century, of directed progressions like Corelli's led gradually from modal practice to the new functional harmony we call tonality.

Tonal organization

Corelli often relied on chains of suspensions and on sequences to achieve the sense of forward harmonic motion on which tonality depends: measures 10–12 in Example 17.2 display both suspensions in the violins and a sequence in the bass, resulting in a progression down the circle of fifths. Corelli's music is almost completely diatonic; beyond secondary dominants (as in measures 8 and 12 in Example 17.2), we find only a rare diminished seventh chord or Neapolitan sixth at a cadence. His modulations within a movement— most often to the dominant and the relative minor or major—are always logical and straightforward. He either kept all movements of a sonata in the same key or, in major-key sonatas, cast the second slow movement in the relative minor.

Corelli's sonatas served as models that composers followed for the next half century. The motivic techniques and principles of tonal architecture he helped to develop were extended by Vivaldi, Handel, Bach, and other composers of the next generation. He has been called the first major composer whose reputation rests exclusively on instrumental music and the first to create instrumental works that became classics, continuing to be played and reprinted long after his death.

Influence and reputation

THE CONCERTO

Toward the end of the seventeenth century, musicians began to distinguish between music for chamber ensemble, with only one instrument for each melodic line, and music for orchestra, in which each string part was performed by two or more players. We have seen that Louis XIII of France (r. 1610–43) established a string ensemble, essentially the first orchestra, with four to six players per part. By the 1670s, similar ensembles were formed in Rome and Bologna, followed by others in Venice, Milan, and elsewhere. For

Music for orchestra

special occasions in Rome, Corelli often led a "pick-up" orchestra of forty or more, gathered from players employed by patrons throughout the city. While some pieces, like the overtures, dances, and interludes of Lully's operas, were clearly intended for orchestra, and others, like Corelli's solo violin sonatas, could be played only as chamber music, a good deal of seventeenth- and early-eighteenth-century music could be performed either way. For instance, on a festive occasion or in a large hall, each line of a trio sonata might be played by several performers.

Instrumental concerto

In the 1680s and 1690s, composers created a new kind of orchestral composition that soon became the most important type of Baroque instrumental music and helped to establish the orchestra as the leading instrumental ensemble. In the long-standing tradition of adapting old terms to new uses, the new genre was called **concerto.** Like the vocal concerto, it united two contrasting forces into a harmonious whole, in an instrumental version of the concertato medium. It combined this texture with other traits favored at the time: florid melody over a firm bass; musical organization based on tonality; and multiple movements with contrasting tempos, moods, and figuration. Concertos were closely related to sonatas and served many of the same roles: they were played at public ceremonies, entertainments, and private musical gatherings, and they could substitute for elements of the Mass.

Types of concerto

By 1700, composers were writing three kinds of concertos. The **orchestral concerto** was a work in several movements that emphasized the first violin part and the bass, distinguishing the concerto from the more contrapuntal texture characteristic of the sonata. The other two types were more numerous and, in retrospect, more important. Both systematically played on the contrast in sonority between many instruments and one or only a few. The **concerto grosso** set a small ensemble (*concertino*) of solo instruments against a large ensemble (*concerto grosso*). In the **solo concerto** a single instrument, most often a violin, contrasted with the large ensemble. The large group was almost always a string orchestra, usually divided into first and second violins, violas, and cellos, with basso continuo and bass viol either doubling the cellos or separate. In a concerto grosso, the concertino normally comprised two violins, accompanied by cello and continuo, the same forces needed to play a trio sonata, although other solo string or wind instruments might be added or substituted. In both solo concerto and concerto grosso, the full orchestra was designated **tutti** (all) or **ripieno** (full).

Predecessors of concerto style

The practice of contrasting solo instruments against a full orchestra goes back to Lully operas, where some of the dances included episodes for solo wind trio; to oratorio and opera arias by Stradella; and to sonatas for solo trumpets with string orchestra, popular in Bologna and Venice. The melodic style idiomatic to the natural trumpet, marked by triads, scales, and repeated notes, was imitated by the strings and became characteristic of concertos.

Corelli's concertos

Since Roman orchestras were typically divided between concertino and ripieno, Roman composers favored the concerto grosso. Corelli's *Concerti grossi*, Op. 6, written in the 1680s and published in revised form in 1714, are essentially trio sonatas, divided between soli and tutti. The larger group echoes the smaller, fortifies cadential passages, or otherwise punctuates the structure through doublings. Corelli's approach was widely imitated by later composers in Italy, England, and Germany. Indeed, one of the best descriptions of the Corellian concerto grosso is by a German, the composer Georg Muffat (1653–1704), introducing a collection of his own pieces that can be played either as trio sonatas or as concerti grossi (see Source Reading).

While Roman practice treated the orchestra as an expansion of the concertino, in northern Italy the soloists were adjuncts to the orchestra. Composers there focused first on the orchestral concerto, then on the solo concerto and concerto grosso. Giuseppe Torelli (1658–1709), a leading figure in the Bologna school, composed all three types, including the first concertos ever published (his Op. 5, 1692). In his concertos we can see a new notion of the concerto develop. He wrote trumpet concertos for services in San Petronio, and his Op. 6 (1698) includes two solo violin concertos, perhaps the first by any composer. Six more violin concertos and six concerti grossi appeared as his Op. 8 (1709). Most of these works follow a three-movement plan in the order fast-slow-fast, taken over from the Italian opera overture. This schema, introduced to the concerto by Venetian composer Tomaso Albinoni (1671–1750) in his Op. 2 (1700), became the standard pattern for concertos.

Giuseppe Torelli

SOURCE READING

GEORG MUFFAT ON CONVERTING SONATAS INTO CONCERTOS

Georg Muffat played a major role in introducing both Italian and French styles and genres into Germany. In the early 1680s he visited Rome, where he heard Corelli's concertos. On his return to Salzburg in 1682, he published a set of five pieces playable as sonatas but intended for full realization as concerti grossi. When he republished them in 1701 in a set of twelve concerti grossi, his foreword explained his method, making clear the roots of the concerto in the sonata.

— • —

Friendly reader:

It is very true that the beautiful concertos of a new kind that I enjoyed in Rome gave me great courage and reawakened in me some ideas that perhaps will not displease you. If nothing else, at least I tried to serve your convenience, since you may concert these sonatas in various manners with the following conditions:

1. They may be played with only three instruments, namely two violins and a cello or bass viol as a foundation. . . .

2. They may be played by four or five instruments. . . .

3. If, further, you wish to hear them as full concertos with some novelty or variety of sonority, you may form two choirs in this way. Make a small ensemble [*concertino*] of three or two violins and a cello or viola da gamba, which three solo parts, not doubled, will play throughout. From these parts you will draw the two [solo] violins as well as the violins to be doubled for the large ensemble [*concerto grosso*] when you find the letter *T,* which signifies "tutti." You will have these rest at the letter *S* [soli], when the small ensemble will play solo. The middle violas will be doubled in proportion to the other parts of the large ensemble with which they will play, except when you find the letter *S,* when it will be enough that this part be played solo and not doubled. I went to all this trouble to achieve this opportune variety.

From the Italian in *Ausserlesene Instrumental-Music* (Passau, 1701), *Denkmäler der Tonkunst in Oesterreich* XI/2, vol. 23 (Vienna, 1904), 118.

Framing ritornellos   In the fast movements of his violin concertos, Torelli often used a form that resembles and may have been modeled on the structure of the A section of a da capo aria (see above). There are two extended passages for the soloist, framed by a ritornello that appears at the beginning and end of the movement and recurs, in abbreviated form and in a different key, between the two solo passages. The solos present entirely new material, often exploiting the virtuosity of the soloist, and modulate to closely related keys, providing contrast and variety. The return of the ritornello then offers stability and resolution. Torelli's approach was developed by Antonio Vivaldi into *ritornello form,* the standard pattern for eighteenth-century concertos, as we will see in the next chapter.

THE ITALIAN STYLE

In the last third of the seventeenth century, Italian music in all genres shared common features. Composers sought to make their music pleasing to the ear, emotionally expressive, grateful to perform, and able to show off the performers to best advantage. Both voices and instruments drew on a variety of melodic styles, from lyrical song to trumpet-call arpeggiations to virtuoso passage work. The emphasis on soloists, characteristic since early in the century, continued in both vocal and instrumental music. Sacred choral music and trio sonatas featured equal voices in collaboration, but arias and solo sonatas highlighted the virtuosity and expressivity of an individual, and concertos incorporated the contrast between individual and collective voices. What we now call tonality became a strong organizing force, and many pieces followed a similar pattern of establishing the tonic, departing from it, exploring nearby keys, and returning to the tonic at the end. In arias, concertos, and other forms, the final tonic was often emphasized by a reprise of the opening material, which became a basic principle of form for the next two centuries. From all the influences across genres and among a variety of musical centers, there emerged a vibrant, exuberant, identifiably Italian style that was widely imitated and became the foundation for developments in the eighteenth century.

GERMANY AND AUSTRIA

At the end of the Thirty Years' War in 1648, much of Germany was ruined and impoverished. The Holy Roman Emperor was weak, and the empire encompassed almost three hundred essentially independent political units, from self-governing free cities such as Hamburg and Nuremberg to territories ruled by princes, dukes, counts, landgraves, margraves, electors, bishops, and archbishops. The map in Figure 17.6 can only suggest the complexity. Because states were relatively small and power decentralized, cities were smaller than those in France or Britain. The great majority of the people were farmers. Germany had neither the state-controlled industries of France, nor the robust capitalism of England and the Netherlands, and was further limited by the strong system of professional guilds left over from the Middle Ages, which discouraged innovation.

But the situation was not necessarily bleak for music. Rulers jealously guarded their sovereignty, and many imitated Louis XIV's use of the arts as a way to assert power and status. Numerous courts were eager to hire singers, instrumentalists, and composers, though the number at any one court could not rival the French court.

Court, city, and church musicians

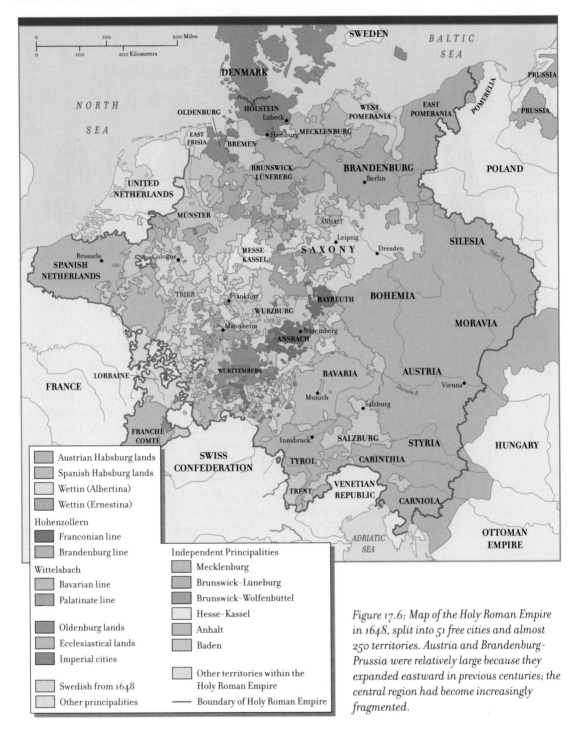

Figure 17.6: *Map of the Holy Roman Empire in 1648, split into 51 free cities and almost 250 territories. Austria and Brandenburg-Prussia were relatively large because they expanded eastward in previous centuries; the central region had become increasingly fragmented.*

Figure 17.7: Stadtpfeifer *in Nuremberg heralding the New Year. Detail of a drawing by an unknown sixteenth-century artist.*

Cities and churches also supported music. Most cities employed town musicians, called ***Stadtpfeifer*** ("town pipers"), who had the exclusive right to provide music in the city. They performed at public ceremonies, parades, weddings, and other festivities and supervised the training of apprentices. Figure 17.7 shows a small troupe in Nuremberg sounding in the New Year. Stadtpfeifer were jacks-of-all-trades, proficient at numerous wind and string instruments, and typically won their posts through auditions or family connections. The system encouraged whole families to make music their trade, among them the Bach family, already prominent in the seventeenth century and about to reach new heights in the eighteenth. In some places, chorales or sonatas called *Turmsonaten* (tower sonatas) were played daily on wind instruments from the tower of the town hall or church. In Lutheran areas, church musicians were often directly employed by the town. Some Lutheran churches sponsored concerts and recitals, as well as having music during services.

Among all these professional musicians, those at courts had the highest social standing, followed by those employed by major cities. Some spent their careers in a single place, but others moved from one position to another seeking the most advantageous circumstances.

Amateur musicians   Amateur music-making was a prominent part of social life. Many German towns had a ***collegium musicum***, an association of amateurs from the educated middle class who gathered to play and sing together for their own pleasure or to hear professionals in private performances. Such groups were also organized in schools, and some drew their members primarily from university students. In the eighteenth century, some collegia gave public concerts (see chapter 19).

German musicians and composers played and wrote music in almost all genres of the time, whether imported or homegrown. Like the English, composers in Germany drew on Italian, French, and native styles and blended them in new ways. The circulation of musicians from post to post, the presence of many foreign-born musicians, and the influence of Germans who traveled or studied abroad all combined to produce a cosmopolitan musical life that would characterize German-speaking areas for the next two centuries. As in Italy, the music in Germany from this period that is best known today is primarily instrumental, especially the great tradition of North German organ music.

Cosmopolitan styles

OPERA

As we saw in chapter 14, Italian composers were welcomed at Austrian and German courts, where opera in Italian became central to musical life. In addition to Italian composers who made opera careers in Germany—such as Carlo Pallavicino (1630–1688), who worked chiefly in Dresden, and Agostino Steffani (1654–1728), active in Munich and Hanover—German composers also took up the genre. In the eighteenth century, several of the most successful composers of Italian opera were German, from Handel and Hasse to Gluck and Mozart (see chapters 19, 20, and 22).

After scattered experiments, opera in German found a home in Hamburg with the opening in 1678 of the first public opera house in Germany. In this prosperous commercial center, the opera house was a business venture designed to turn a profit through year-round productions of works that would appeal to the middle class. In deference to Lutheran authorities, who opposed such entertainment, many operas in the early years concerned biblical subjects. Local poets translated or adapted librettos from Venetian operas and wrote new ones that were similar in subject matter and general plan. Composers adopted the recitative style of Italian opera but were eclectic in their arias. In addition to Italianate arias, usually in da capo or modified da capo form, and free ariosos, they occasionally wrote airs in the French style and in the rhythms of French dances. Also common in early German opera, especially for lower-class or comic characters, are short strophic songs in the popular style of northern Germany, displaying brisk, forthright melodies and rhythms. The foremost and most prolific of the early German opera composers was Reinhard Keiser (1674–1739), who wrote almost sixty works for the Hamburg stage.

Opera in German

SONG AND CANTATA

Keiser and his German contemporaries wrote individual songs and arias as well as cantatas in Italian and in German. The most notable song and cantata composer was Adam Krieger (1634–1666) of Dresden. His arias were mostly strophic melodies in a charmingly simple popular style with short, five-part orchestral ritornellos common in German solo songs.

CATHOLIC CHURCH MUSIC

In sacred music, composers in Catholic and Lutheran areas followed largely separate paths, responding to the very different liturgies and traditions of the two churches.

The southern German-speaking area, which included Munich, Salzburg, and Vienna, the seat of the imperial chapel, was largely Catholic. The four emperors who reigned there from 1637 to 1740 not only supported music financially but further encouraged it by their interest and actual participation as composers. Like their Italian counterparts, Catholic composers of vocal music cultivated both the older contrapuntal style and the newer concerted styles. In their masses and other liturgical works, composers at the richest courts and cathedrals intermingled orchestral preludes and ritornellos, magnificent choruses, and festive solo ensemble sections, all supported by full orchestral accompaniment. Polychoral music was especially encouraged at Salzburg, where the new cathedral had four choir lofts. For the 1,100th anniversary of the archbishopric of Salzburg in 1682, illustrated in Figure 17.8, Heinrich Biber (1644–1704) composed the monumental *Missa salisburgensis*, with sixteen singers and thirty-seven instrumentalists, each performing on a separate line of music, arranged in seven groups around the cathedral.

Figure 17.8: Interior view of the Salzburg Cathedral in 1682, during the ceremony celebrating the 1,100th anniversary of the archbishopric of Salzburg, founded in 582 by St. Rupert. Engraving by Melchior Küsel.

LUTHERAN VOCAL MUSIC

After the ravages of the Thirty Years' War, churches in the Lutheran territories of Germany quickly restored their musical forces. However, two conflicting tendencies had arisen within the church, and they inevitably affected music. Orthodox Lutherans, holding to established doctrine and public forms of worship, favored using all available resources of choral and instrumental music in their services. In contrast, Pietists emphasized private devotions and Bible readings, distrusted formality and high art in worship, and preferred simple music and poetry that expressed the emotions of the individual believer.

Lutherans possessed a common heritage in the chorale (see chapter 10). New poems and melodies continued to be composed, many of them intended not for congregational singing but for use in home devotions. The most influential Lutheran songbook of the time was Johann Crüger's *Praxis pietatis melica* (Practice of Piety in Song), issued in 1647 and reprinted in over forty editions during the next half century. Crüger set the melodies over figured bass and added accidentals to the old modal chorale melodies to make them fit emerging conventions of triadic harmony.

Chorales

Orthodox Lutheran centers provided a favorable environment for developing the sacred concerto. The backbone was the concerted vocal ensemble on a biblical text, as established by Schein, Schütz, and others in the early and mid-seventeenth century. Of more recent vintage was the solo aria, normally in Italian style, on a strophic, nonbiblical text. The chorale was the most traditional and characteristically German ingredient, set either in the concertato medium or in simple harmonies. Composers often drew on these elements in various combinations to create multimovement works. Today such works are usually referred to as cantatas, but their composers called them concertos, sacred concertos, or simply "the music" for a service.

Concerted church music

An example of the concertato chorale is the setting of *Wachet auf* by Dieterich Buxtehude (ca. 1637–1707), one of the best-known Lutheran composers of the late seventeenth century (see biography and Figure 17.9). In this work, the accompanying instruments, strings, bassoon, and continuo begin with a short festive sinfonia on motives from the chorale. Then each stanza of the chorale text is set to a new paraphrase of the melody, distinct from the others in vocal range, figuration, rhythm, texture, and relation to the original tune. The result is a series of chorale variations, a frequent procedure at the time.

Dieterich Buxtehude

LUTHERAN ORGAN MUSIC

Organ music enjoyed a golden age in the Lutheran areas of Germany between about 1650 and 1750. In the north, Buxtehude at Lübeck and Georg Böhm (1661–1733) at Lüneburg continued the tradition established by Sweelinck and Scheidt. A central group in Saxony and Thuringia included Johann Christoph Bach (1642–1703) of Eisenach, first cousin of J. S. Bach's father. One of the most notable German organ composers was Johann Pachelbel (1653–1706) of Nuremberg, composer of the now-famous canon for three violins and continuo.

The Baroque organ German organ builders of the late seventeenth and early eighteenth centuries drew on elements of French and Dutch organs, much as German composers blended Italian, French, and northern styles. The best-known builders were Arp Schnitger (1648–1718), who built the organ in Figure 17.10, and Gottfried Silbermann (1683–1753), who emulated the colorful stops used in France to play solos and contrapuntal lines. They and their colleagues adopted the Dutch practice of dividing the pipes into a main group and subsidiary groups, each with its own keyboard and pipes having a particular character and function. The main group, the *Hauptwerk,* or Great organ, sits high above the player. Other groups may include a *Rückpositiv,* mounted on the outside of the choir balcony rail behind the organist's back; a *Brustwerk,* directly above the music rack in front of

DIETERICH BUXTEHUDE (CA. 1637–1707)

Buxtehude was renowned as an organist as well as a composer of organ music and sacred vocal works. His pieces for organ, marked by strongly etched themes and virtuosic playing for both hands and the pedals, had a powerful influence on J. S. Bach and other composers.

The son of a German organist working in Denmark, Buxtehude was likely trained by his father and at the Latin School in Elsinore. He played organ in a German church there from 1660 to 1668, when he succeeded Franz Tunder as organist at St. Mary's Church in Lübeck, one of the most important and lucrative musical posts in northern Germany. He later married Tunder's younger daughter Anna Margarethe, apparently as a condition of his employment.

Buxtehude remained at St. Mary's for the rest of his life. He played for the principal services, including morning and afternoon on Sundays and feast days, and composed music to suit: organ solos as preludes to chorales and other parts of the service, and organ, ensemble, and vocal pieces for performance during Communion.

Buxtehude was famed for his *Abendmusiken,* public concerts of sacred vocal

Figure 17.9: Figure identified as Dieterich Buxtehude, from a painting (ca. 1674) by Johannes Voorhout.

music at St. Mary's on five Sunday afternoons each year before Christmas. Admission was free, subsidized by local merchants. The *Abendmusiken* attracted musicians from all over Germany. The twenty-year-old J. S. Bach attended in 1705, and is said to have walked more than two hundred miles just to hear them.

Buxtehude's works are catalogued in Georg Karstädt's *Buxtehude-Werke-Verzeichnis* (Buxtehude Works Catalogue), abbreviated BuxWV.

MAJOR WORKS: *About 120 sacred vocal works, about 40 chorale settings for organ, 22 organ preludes and toccatas, 19 harpsichord suites, numerous other keyboard pieces, 20 ensemble sonatas*

Figure 17.10: Organ built in 1695 by Arp Schnitger for the Johanniskirche in Hamburg, now in a church at Cappel. The upper chest of pipes is the Hauptwerk, *or Great organ. Below it, unseen in this photograph, are the keyboards, including the pedals, and the organist's bench. In the foreground is the* Rückpositiv, *mounted on the railing behind the organist. This organ has only* Hauptwerk, Rückpositiv, *and pedals.*

the player; an *Oberwerk*, high above the Great; and the pedal organ, whose pipes are usually arranged symmetrically on the sides of the Great. Only the largest German organs had all of these components. Even on a modest instrument, an organist could create a great variety of sounds combining variously voiced principal, flute, and reed pipes, as well as mixtures, in which pipes sounding upper harmonics add brilliance to the fundamental tone.

Most of the organ music written for Protestant churches served as a prelude to something else: a chorale, a scriptural reading, or a larger work. Such pieces were often chorale settings, or they were toccatas or preludes that contained fugues or culminated in them.

Functions of organ music

Buxtehude's toccatas typify those of seventeenth-century German composers in presenting a series of short sections in free style that alternate with longer ones in imitative counterpoint. Filled with motion and climaxes, the toccatas display a great variety of figuration and take full advantage of the organ's idiomatic qualities. Their capricious, exuberant character made them ideal vehicles for virtuosic display at the keyboard and on the pedals. The toccata as a genre and its focus on imitative counterpoint were fostered by Johann Jacob Froberger (see chapter 15), who studied with Frescobaldi and whose keyboard works had a deep impact on later German composers.

Toccatas and preludes

The free sections simulate improvisation by contrasting irregular rhythm with an unceasing drive of sixteenth notes, by using phrases that are deliberately irregular or have inconclusive endings, and by featuring abrupt changes of texture, harmony, or melodic direction. Example 17.4 shows a passage that is

CD 6|6

typical of toccata style, from Buxtehude's Praeludium in E Major, BuxWV 141 (NAWM 84). The virtuoso part for the pedals (the lowest staff in the score) includes long trills; when the pedal sustains a tone, the two hands erupt in rapid passage work with many unpredictable changes of speed, direction, and figuration. At the opposite extreme is a later, slow-paced free section marked by suspensions and passing changes of key.

Example 17.4: Buxtehude, Praeludium in E Major, BuxWV 141, toccata section

In the Praeludium in E, there are five free sections, of which the first two are the longest, the next two relatively brief transitions, and the last a climactic coda. These sections in toccata style frame four fugal sections, each on a different subject and in a different meter or tempo. The treatment is different in each case, from full-scale fugues in four voices with pedals for the first and last fugal sections, to less rigorous fugal imitation in three voices without pedals in the inner two. All four blend into the following free section.

The four subjects are shown in Example 17.5. They all share family resemblances, recalling the variation canzonas of Frescobaldi and the keyboard fantasias of Sweelinck and Scheidt, which apply variation to their fugal subjects. Here the relationships are rather subtle; while the melodic contours are similar, as shown by the vertical alignment of notes, and similar figures recur (marked a and b in the example), a theme may be reversed (see notes marked x), leaps filled in (as in the third subject), and other devices used to provide both unity and variety.

In the seventeenth century, such keyboard pieces were called "toccata," "prelude," "praeludium," or some similar name, even though they included fugal sections. In the eighteenth century, the two types of section, fugal and nonfugal, grew in length and became separate movements, so that the typical

Example 17.5: Fugue subjects from Buxtehude's Praeludium in E Major

structure consisted of a long toccata or prelude in free style followed by a fugue (see NAWM 88).

Fugue

Composers wrote fugues both as independent pieces and as sections within preludes and toccatas. By the end of the seventeenth century, "fugue" was increasingly the designation for pieces in imitative counterpoint (other than strict canons), replacing "ricercare," "fantasia," "capriccio," and other terms. Fugue subjects tend to have a more sharply chiseled melodic character and a livelier rhythm than ricercare themes. As in the ricercare, independent voices enter with the theme in turn. In a fugue a set of these entries is called an **exposition.** If the first entrance of the subject begins on the tonic note, the second entrance, referred to as the **answer,** normally begins on the dominant, and vice versa. Often the intervals of the answer are modified to fit the key. The other voices then alternate subject and answer. After a cadence, there are several more points of imitation, each differentiated from the others by the order of entries, pitch level, or some other aspect. Seventeenth-century fugues may have short **episodes**—periods of free counterpoint between statements of the subject.

Chorale settings

While toccatas, preludes, and fugues remained independent of vocal music, organ compositions based on chorales used the melodies in different ways. In *organ chorales*, the tunes were enhanced by harmony and counterpoint. A tune could serve as a theme for a set of *chorale variations*, also called *chorale partite*, or as the subject for a *chorale fantasia*.

Chorale prelude

A fourth form based on a chorale tune was the **chorale prelude.** This term, often applied to any chorale-based organ work, will be used here to denote a short piece in which the entire melody is presented just once in readily recognizable form. This form of chorale setting did not appear until the middle of the seventeenth century. The name suggests an earlier liturgical practice in which the organist played through the tune, with improvised accompaniment and ornaments, as a prelude to the congregation's or choir's singing of the chorale. Later, when they were written down, such pieces were called "chorale preludes" even if they did not serve the original purpose.

In effect, a chorale prelude is a single variation on a chorale, which may be constructed in any of the following ways:

- Each phrase of the melody serves in turn as the subject of a point of imitation.
- Phrases appear in turn, usually in the top voice, in long notes with relatively little ornamentation. Each phrase is preceded by a brief imitative development in the other voices of the phrase's beginning, in **diminution** (in shorter notes).
- The melody appears in the top voice, ornamented in an imaginative manner, and the accompanying voices proceed freely with great variety from phrase to phrase.
- The melody is accompanied in one or more of the other voices by a motive or rhythmic figure not related motivically to the melody itself.

An example of the third type is Buxtehude's chorale prelude on *Nun komm, der Heiden Heiland* (compare Example 10.1b). The opening phrase, shown in Example 17.6a, is decorated with passing and neighbor tones and with short trills that resemble French agréments in sound and function. Each phrase is progressively more elaborate in its embellishment. The last phrase, which in the original chorale is the same as the first phrase, is here presented with florid Italianate ornamentation, shown in Example 17.6b. In combining a German chorale with styles of melody and elaboration from France and Italy, this brief piece nicely illustrates the tendency for German composers to blend elements from all three regions.

OTHER INSTRUMENTAL MUSIC

By the late seventeenth century, German organists had assimilated what they could learn from Italian and French models, developed a distinctive style of their own, and established themselves as leaders in organ composition. In other realms of instrumental music, the process of assimilation was still under way, the genres practiced still largely those of Italy or France.

Harpsichord suite   The French harpsichord style was carried to Germany by Froberger, who helped to establish the allemande, courante, sarabande, and gigue as standard components of dance suites. In manuscript, Froberger ends his suites with the sarabande, a slow dance. In a later, posthumous publication of 1693, the order was revised so that each suite ends with a lively gigue, which had by then become the standard close for German suites. Many German composers, including Buxtehude, J. S. Bach, and Handel, wrote suites.

Orchestral suite   Impressed by the high standards of performance in Lully's orchestra and by the French musical style he cultivated, many German musicians sought to introduce these traits into their own country. One result of this effort was a fashion in Germany between about 1690 and 1740 for a new type of **orchestral suite.** The dances of these suites, patterned after those of Lully's ballets and operas, did not appear in any standard number or order. Among the early collections of orchestral suites were two publications titled *Florilegium* (1695 and 1698) by Georg

Example 17.6: Buxtehude, chorale prelude on Nun komm, der Heiden Heiland

a. Opening phrase, compared with original chorale

b. Final phrase

× = note from chorale melody

Muffat, who pioneered in introducing Lully's style into Germany as he had Corelli's a decade earlier. Muffat included an essay with musical examples about the French system of bowing, the playing of the *agréments*, and similar matters.

Although Muffat, Buxtehude, and other German composers took up the trio sonata, the solo sonata attracted more interest. The solo violin sonata had always been the prime vehicle for experiments in special bowings, multiple stops, and all kinds of difficult passage work. Twelve sonatas by Johann Jakob Walther (ca. 1650–1717), published in 1676 under the title *Scherzi*, built on the tradition of Biagio Marini but surpassed all others in technical brilliance. The most famous German sonatas of the seventeenth century are Heinrich Biber's *Mystery* (or *Rosary*) *Sonatas* for Violin (ca. 1675), which represent meditations on episodes in the life of Christ. These works make considerable

Sonata

Figure 17.11: Engraved title page of Johann Kuhnau's Frische Clavier Früchte, oder Sieben Suonaten, von guten Invention and Manier auff dem Claviere zu spielen *(Fresh Clavier Fruits, or Seven Sonatas, of Good Invention and Manner, to be played on the Clavier, Leipzig, 1696). In the middle we see a clavichord, the preferred instrument for home performance. Around it is an elaborate garland of grain, grapes, apples, peppers, and other fruits of the field, vine, and garden, illustrating the title.*

use of *scordatura*, unusual tunings of the violin strings to facilitate the playing of particular notes or chords. Biber was esteemed as a violin virtuoso as well as composer at the court of the archbishop of Salzburg, and he probably composed and played the sonatas as music for services at the Salzburg Cathedral, which centered each October on the Mysteries of the Rosary. Both Walther and Biber often interspersed rhapsodic movements or toccata-like sections in their sonatas, and both wrote many of their longer movements in the form of a passacaglia or theme and variations, as in Biber's Passacaglia for unaccompanied solo violin.

Seventeenth-century sonatas were strictly ensemble music until Johann Kuhnau (1660–1722) transferred the genre to the keyboard in 1692. His *Frische Clavier Früchte* (Fresh Keyboard Fruits, 1696), a title apparently calculated to herald a new genre, consists of seven multimovement sonatas. The elaborate title page, shown in Figure 17.11, was clearly designed to catch the attention of the amateur keyboard player. His six "Biblical" sonatas (1700), bearing titles such as *Saul's Madness Cured by Music* and *The Combat Between David and Goliath*, represent stories from the Old Testament cleverly and sometimes humorously told in music.

THE GERMAN SYNTHESIS

Germans had imported musical fashions from France since troubadour songs and from Italy since the sixteenth-century madrigals, each time remaking the foreign style to suit local tastes. In the seventeenth century, this trend continued with the adopted genres of opera, polychoral and concerted church music, toccata, suite, and sonata. As they mastered the styles and genres of other nations and added elements from their own traditions, composers in German-speaking lands laid the foundations for the extraordinary developments of the eighteenth century, when German and Austrian composers would play key roles in developing the sonata and concerto as vehicles for advanced musical thought and in forging a new international musical language.

SEEDS FOR THE FUTURE

In the second half of the seventeenth century, Italian music reached new heights, and Germanic composers began to come into their own. Cities and courts all over Italy and Germany sponsored Italian opera, which continued to be the most prestigious musical genre throughout the eighteenth century. The da capo aria became a convention for operas and other vocal works and lasted for almost a century. The trio sonata, solo violin sonata, and concerto, all originated by Italians, became the leading genres of ensemble music in both nations through the mid-eighteenth century. German composers also emulated French styles in vocal music and in suites for keyboard or orchestra. By the closing decades of the century, Lutheran organist-composers had surpassed their Italian and French colleagues, perhaps the first time that Germany led other nations in any field of music. It would not be the last: German musicians in the eighteenth century would make a virtue of their eclecticism and gradually outshine their Italian counterparts in the increasingly important genres of instrumental music.

This half-century saw other developments of enduring significance. Tonality as exemplified in Corelli's sonatas proved of great importance for music ever since. Among other things, the clear direction and predictable expectations characteristic of tonal music made possible more complex harmonic structures and thus longer forms. The sonata and the concerto were the first multimovement instrumental genres not based on stringing together smaller pieces, as in a suite of dances. By engaging the listener's interest for a relatively long time without the support of a text, these forms paved the way for the concert works of later centuries, designed to be listened to with complete attention.

Many pieces from this time were written for specific occasions, for local use as entertainment, or for church services, and usually received at most a few performances. These circumstances were especially true for vocal music, which was fueled by a constant demand for new operas, cantatas, and church music in preference to the old. Instrumental music had a somewhat longer life. The sonatas and concertos of Corelli continued to be played throughout the eighteenth century and influenced many composers, including Handel. German organists continued to play music of Buxtehude and his contemporaries for some time, and younger composers like J. S. Bach emulated their predecessors. But by the end of the eighteenth century, even Corelli was rarely heard. In the second half of the nineteenth century, the respect Bach and Handel showed their late-seventeenth-century forebears aroused the interest of musicians and scholars, leading to performances and editions of the music of Corelli, Buxtehude, and others from their era. Since the early twentieth century, Corelli's sonatas and concertos have found a permanent place in the repertoire, and music of the North German organists is frequently played. Other late-seventeenth-century music is available in good editions and recordings but remains less familiar than the music of the eighteenth or even the sixteenth century.

PART FOUR

THE EIGHTEENTH CENTURY

With few exceptions, the standard concert repertoire begins in the early eighteenth century with Vivaldi, Bach, and Handel. Yet there was no major change around 1700 to mark a new style, as there had been at 1300, 1400, and 1600. Rather, the new generation that reached maturity then was marked by consolidation, integrating and developing ideas and trends introduced over the previous century.

In stylistic terms, it is customary to divide the eighteenth century at 1750, regarding the first half as the late Baroque period and the second half as the Classic period, culminating in the music of Haydn and Mozart. But looked at in another way, the eighteenth century can be regarded as a period in its own right, marked not by consistency in style but by winds of change. Reading the music journals and composers' writings, one comes to see the 1700s as a century-long argument about what is most valuable in music—a contest between musical tastes. Elements of what would become the Classical style were already present at the start of the century, and echoes of the Baroque were still heard at the end.

However we view it, this century was one of the most remarkable times in the history of music. Musicians cultivated many new genres, including keyboard concerto, opera buffa, ballad opera, symphony, and string quartet, and developed new forms such as sonata form and rondo. From Vivaldi's concertos, Bach's fugues, and Handel's oratorios through Haydn's string quartets and symphonies and Mozart's piano sonatas and operas, composers of the era created exemplary works that defined their genres and today lie at the heart of the classical repertoire.

The Early Eighteenth Century in Italy and France

Composers around 1700 were not inventing new techniques, styles, and genres at the pace of their predecessors a century earlier. Rather, they continued and extended well-established traditions, and took for granted the approaches and materials developed during the seventeenth century: the doctrine of the affections, basso continuo, the concertato medium, tonality, and the genres of opera, cantata, concerto, sonata, and suite.

Interest in music of the early eighteenth century has long centered on Vivaldi, Couperin, Rameau, J. S. Bach, and Handel, each of whom established an individual style by combining elements from the mature Baroque tradition in new ways. It is fitting that we focus on them and on the patrons, institutions, tastes, and values that shaped their music, treating each composer's story as a case study of musical life at the time. This chapter will discuss Vivaldi, Couperin, and Rameau, representatives of Italy and France, still the leading musical nations at the dawn of the eighteenth century. In the following chapter, we will turn to Bach and Handel, typical of German-speaking musicians in their synthesis of elements from several national traditions. As we will see in chapter 20, even while these composers were at the peak of their careers, currents were beginning that would lead in new directions, making this the last generation of Baroque composers.

EUROPE IN A CENTURY OF CHANGE

In political and social terms, as in music, the eighteenth century moved from continuity with the past, through new currents, to radical change.

When the century began, a balance of power was emerging in Europe among several strong centralized states, each supported by a professional military and government bureaucracy. France had the biggest army, but Louis XIV's lavish spending on wars abroad and spectacles at home was depleting the treasury, and his expansionist ambitions were checked by other nations. Britain, formed by the union of England and Scotland in 1707, had the most powerful navy and used it to wrest India, Canada, and several Caribbean islands from France during the Seven Years' War (known in America as the French and Indian War, 1756–63). Having won back Hungary from the Turks in the late seventeenth century, Austria—now the Austro-Hungarian Empire—was increasing its influence, reflected by the emergence in the late eighteenth century of its capital Vienna as the leading musical city in Europe. A new power emerged when Prussia became a kingdom in 1701 and developed one of the Continent's largest and best-trained armies. Late in the century, Poland—where the nobles had resisted consolidation of power under the king—fell victim to the centralized states around it; Prussia, Russia, and Austria divided Poland's territories among themselves and erased it from the map for over a century. By then, the American Revolution (1775–83) and the French Revolution (1789) were bringing winds of change that would remake the political culture of Europe and the Americas.

Realignment and revolution

The population of Europe expanded rapidly, especially after 1750. The new mouths were fed by a growing food supply made possible through improved agricultural methods, such as crop rotation and intensive manuring, and new crops like the potato, introduced from the New World. Although roads were still bad—it took four days to travel a hundred miles—trade increased, both within Europe and with Asia and the New World. As manufacturing and trade became more lucrative, the middle class grew in size and economic clout, while the landed aristocracy became less important, though they still occupied the top of the social ladder. As the continent became more urbanized, nature was increasingly idealized. The aristocracy's nostalgia for rural life was perfectly captured in paintings by Jean-Antoine Watteau (1684–1721), such as *Embarkation for Cythera* in Figure 18.1.

Economic expansion

Many new schools were founded, both for the governmental elite—teaching the traditional Greek and Latin—and for the middle classes, providing more practical education. Frederick the Great of Prussia (r. 1740–86) and Empress Maria Theresa of Austria (r. 1740–80) sought to require primary school for every child, although they were only partially successful. By 1800, half the male population of England and France was literate, and women, usually taught at home, were catching up. Daily newspapers began in London in 1702 and quickly spread to other cities. From cheap paperbacks to leather-bound tomes, more and more books were published, purchased, read, and passed around. Novels became the most popular form of literature, including Daniel Defoe's *Robinson Crusoe* (1719) and Henry Fielding's *Tom Jones* (1749). At public coffeehouses, meetings of learned societies, and salons, gatherings in private homes hosted by well-to-do women, people avidly discussed current events, ideas, literature, and music. Amid this broadening interest in learning, thinkers such as Voltaire (1694–1778) sought to analyze social and political issues through reason and science, spawning the intellectual movement known as the Enlightenment (discussed in chapter 20).

Education and learning

Figure 18.1: Jean-Antoine Watteau's Embarkation for Cythera *(1717) was one of the most famous paintings of the eighteenth century. The setting is in an imagined Arcadian paradise of nature populated by winged infants (perhaps cupids or angels) and muscular boatmen, on the left. On the right, nearer the viewer, are several amorous couples in fashionable, modern, courtly dress. Nature is depicted by Watteau as a theater for leisure and pleasure, far from the constraints of urban society, but equally far from the reality of rural life for the poor peasants who made up most of the population of France.*

Demand for new music

In London, Paris, and other large cities, support from the middle class became increasingly important for musicians and composers. The public constantly demanded new music. Few works of any kind were performed for more than two or three seasons, and composers were expected to furnish new pieces for almost every occasion. Such unceasing pressure accounts for the vast output of many eighteenth-century composers and the phenomenal speed at which they worked.

Changing styles

The demand for new music also helps to explain the changing fashions in musical style. The eighteenth century is often divided between Baroque and Classic styles, but the two overlapped in time, as we will see in the next few chapters. Indeed, the history of this century's music can be seen as a long argument about taste and style, often literally argued in newspapers, journals, salons, and coffeehouses.

MUSIC IN ITALY

In Italy, opera remained the most prestigious—and most expensive—type of music, but instrumental music, especially the concerto, was gaining ground. Principal centers for music included Naples, Rome, and Venice, capitals of the most powerful states on the peninsula.

NAPLES

Southern Italy, a Spanish possession since the early sixteenth century, came under Austrian control in 1707, then in 1734 became an independent kingdom ruled by the son of the Spanish king. Its capital, Naples, was one of the largest cities in Italy and home to a vibrant musical life.

Naples had four **conservatories,** homes for orphaned and poor boys, that specialized in teaching music. Over the years, musical instruction gradually became as important as the original charitable purpose, and the conservatories took on paying students as well. Their pupils made musical careers all over Europe, helping to spread Italian opera and Italian instrumental music across the Continent.

Conservatories

Most conservatory students were singers, many of them castrati. By the late seventeenth century, the leading male roles in operas were almost always written for castrati, whose increased lung capacity made them ideal soloists and whose powerful, agile voices were much prized. Although most castrati

Castrati

TIMELINE: ITALY, FRANCE, AND EARLY-18TH-CENTURY EUROPE

1700	1710	1720	1730	1740	1750	1760

- 1701 Prussia becomes kingdom under Frederick I
- 1702 First daily newspaper in England
- **1703 Antonio Vivaldi appointed to the Pietà**
- 1707 Naples comes under Austrian control
- 1707 England and Scotland officially unite as Great Britain
- 1711 Charles VI crowned Holy Roman Emperor
- **1712 Vivaldi, *L'Estro armonico*, Op. 3**
- 1715–74 Reign of Louis XV
- 1717 Jean-Antoine Watteau, *Embarkation for Cythera*
- 1719 Daniel Defoe, *Robinson Crusoe,* first novel in English
- **1722 Jean-Philippe Rameau, *Treatise on Harmony***
- **1724 François Couperin, *Apotheosis of Corelli***
- **1725 Vivaldi, *The Four Seasons***
- **1725 Concert Spirituel concert series begins in Paris**
- 1726 Jonathan Swift, *Gulliver's Travels*
- 1727–60 Reign of George II of England
- **1727 Johann Sebastian Bach, *St. Matthew Passion***
- **1733 Rameau, *Hippolyte et Aricie***
- 1734 Voltaire, *Philosophical Letters*
- 1740 Frederick the Great crowned king of Prussia •
- **1742 Georg Frideric Handel, *Messiah*** •
- **1749 Rameau, *Zoroastre*** •
- 1749 Henry Fielding, *Tom Jones* •
- 1756–63 Seven Years' War (French and Indian War) •

remained church musicians, hundreds sang on opera stages across Europe. A few became international superstars and commanded huge fees, including Farinelli (Carlo Broschi, 1705–1782), who was raised and trained in Naples (see sidebar and Figure 18.2).

Opera   Opera was at the center of Neapolitan musical life, thanks to the support of its rulers and other patrons. Alessandro Scarlatti, who wrote one or more operas almost every year, was its leading composer. While new types of comic opera, sung in the Neapolitan dialect, gained popularity and inspired imitators across Europe (see chapter 20), a new kind of serious Italian opera also emerged in the 1720s, codified by the librettist Pietro Metastasio (1698–1782). Both comic and serious opera of the time continued standard practices of Baroque opera, alternating recitatives and da capo arias.

MUSIC IN CONTEXT

THE VOICE OF FARINELLI

The castrato voice resulted from the same impulse that motivates today's athletes to take hormones and steroids: the desire to control and manipulate nature in order to enhance a performer's abilities. The ever increasing demand by opera audiences for virtuosic superstars and the rise of certain castrato soloists to fame and fortune in turn stimulated the production of castrati throughout Italy, especially among poor families who saw it as a possible way of improving their miserable circumstances. However, although thousands aspired to stardom, only a few ever achieved the fame of a Farinelli, whose career took him from triumph to triumph in all the operatic capitals of Europe. His voice was legendary for its range, spanning more than three octaves, and for its breath control, which enabled him to sustain a note for a full minute before having to inhale. Charles Burney, the keen eighteenth-century observer and author, helps us understand why Farinelli became such an international star:

He was seventeen when he left [Naples] to go to Rome, where, during the run of an opera, there was a struggle every night between him and a famous player on the trumpet, in a song accompanied by that instrument; this, at first, seemed

amicable and merely sportive, till the audience began to interest themselves in the contest, and to take different sides: after severally swelling out a note, in which each manifested the power of his lungs, and tried to rival the other in brilliancy and force, they had both a swell and a shake together, by thirds, which was continued so long, while the audience eagerly awaited the event, that both seemed to be exhausted; and, in fact, the trumpeter, wholly spent, gave it up, thinking, however, his antagonist as much tired as himself, and that it would be a drawn battle; when Farinelli with a smile on his countenance, shewing he had only been sporting with him all this time, broke out all at once in the same breath, and with fresh vigour, and not only swelled and shook the note, but ran the most rapid and difficult divisions [passage work], and was at last silenced only by the acclamations of the audience. From this period may be dated that superiority which he ever maintained over all his contemporaries.*

The painting shown here depicts Farinelli as he appeared in 1734, the year of his debut in London with the Opera of the Nobility—the company that rivalled Handel's own (see p. 463)—led by Nicola Porpora, who had been Farinelli's teacher in Naples. The portrait gives us a good idea of the physical characteristics that were typical of castrati: somewhat effeminate facial features, including a smallish head and a smooth pale skin with no beard; a large chest, well-rounded hips, and narrow shoulders. Contemporary writers also commented on their fairly tall stature, which was unusual in the eighteenth century, and their tendency to obesity. In addition to illustrating these general characteristics, the portrait presents Farinelli, the singular virtuoso, as a commanding presence, exquisitely outfitted in brocade, fur-trimmed velvet, and lace, his right hand leaning on a harpsichord as if acknowledging what must have been the principal tool of his training. We may assume from his authoritative, even arrogant, pose that he had already reached the height of his powers. In fact, he retired from the stage only three years later, at age thirty-two, having been invited to Madrid, where he spent the next two decades in the service of the Spanish kings.—BRH

*Charles Burney, *The Present State of Music in France and Italy,* in Percy A. Scholes, ed., *Dr. Burney's Musical Tours in Europe,* vol. 1 (London: Oxford University Press, 1959), 153–55.

Figure 18.2: Farinelli, the most famous and widely admired of the castrato singers, in a portrait by Bartolomeo Nazari from 1734.

ROME

Opera was less central in Rome because of support for other genres and occasional strictures against opera. Rich patrons regularly sponsored academies, where their musicians performed cantatas, serenatas, sonatas, and concertos. The support of wealthy patrons attracted instrumentalists from all over Italy and Germany, making Rome a training ground for performers. Among them were violin virtuosos Francesco Geminiani (1687–1762) and Pietro Locatelli (1695–1764), who came to Rome in their teens, absorbed the Corelli tradition of performance and composition, and then made their careers in London and Amsterdam respectively, deepening the already strong impact of Corelli's style on northern Europe.

VENICE

At the beginning of the eighteenth century, Venice was declining in political and economic power but remained the most glamorous city in Europe. It was full of travelers attracted to its colorful, exuberant life. Musicians sang on the streets and canals; gondoliers had their own repertory of songs; amateurs played and sang in private academies; and opera impresarios competed for the best singers and composers.

Public festivals, more numerous in Venice than elsewhere, remained occasions of musical splendor. The city had long taken pride in its church music, chamber music, and opera. In the eighteenth century, Venice never had fewer than six opera companies, which together played thirty-four weeks of the

ANTONIO VIVALDI (1678–1741)

Vivaldi was one of the most original and prolific composers of his time, and his influence on later composers was profound.

Born in Venice, the eldest of nine children of a violinist at St. Mark's, Vivaldi trained for both music and the priesthood, a combination that was not unusual at the time. Due to his red hair, he was known as *il prete rosso* (the red priest).

In 1703, the year he was ordained, he became master of violin at the Pio Ospedale della Pietà, a home for poor or orphaned children. He was later appointed master of the concerts, a position of greater responsibility, and he remained at the Pietà until 1740, with some breaks in service.

Like most of his contemporaries, Vivaldi composed every work for a definite occasion and for particular performers. For the Pietà, he composed oratorios, sacred music, and

Figure 18.3: Antonio Vivaldi, in an engraving by François Morellon La Cave from around 1725.

especially concertos. He also fulfilled forty-nine opera commissions, most for Venice and a few for Florence, Ferrara, Verona, Rome, Vienna, and elsewhere. Between 1713 and 1719, the theaters of Venice staged more works of his than of any other composer. He usually supervised the production of his operas in person, and was often absent from the Pietà for long periods. During a two-year sojourn in Rome (1723–24), Pietà's governors asked him to compose two new concertos a month for a fee, which he did for the next six years; this arrangement is one of the most direct signs of Vivaldi's value to them as a composer, distinct from his roles as teacher and performer. He also wrote sonatas and concertos on commission and for publication.

In the 1720s, Vivaldi took the contralto Anna Girò as his singing pupil (and, some gossiped, his mistress, although he denied it). In 1737, he was censured for conduct unbecoming a priest. By then his popularity with the Venetian public had sunk, and he increasingly sought commissions elsewhere, traveling to Amsterdam in 1738 and Vienna in 1740. He earned enormous sums of money from his music, but spent almost all of it, and when he died in Vienna in 1741, he was given a pauper's funeral.

MAJOR WORKS: *About 500 concertos (including* The Four Seasons*), 16 sinfonias, 64 solo sonatas, 27 trio sonatas, 21 surviving operas, 38 cantatas, and about 60 sacred vocal works*

Figure 18.4: Women singers and string players (upper left), thought to be from the Pio Ospedale della Pietà, give a concert in Venice honoring Archduke Paul and Mary Fedorov of Russia. Painting by Francesco Guardi (1712–1793).

year. Between 1700 and 1750, the Venetian public heard ten new operas annually, and the count was even higher in the second half of the century.

ANTONIO VIVALDI

The best-known Italian composer of the early eighteenth century was Antonio Vivaldi (1678–1741), who was born and spent most of his career in Venice (see biography and Figure 18.3). A virtuoso violinist, master teacher, and popular composer of opera, cantatas, and sacred music, he is known today primarily for his concertos, which number around five hundred.

Vivaldi's main position from 1703 to 1740 was as teacher, composer, conductor, and superintendent of musical instruments at the Pio Ospedale della Pietà. The Pietà was one of four "hospitals" in Venice, homes for orphaned, illegitimate, or poor boys and girls, which were run like restrictive boarding schools and provided excellent instruction in music to those girls who showed talent. These institutions paralleled the Naples conservatories, except that careers as instrumentalists or church musicians were not open to women, and before the girls were allowed to leave they had to agree never to perform in public. Educating the girls in music served other purposes: to occupy their time; to make them more desirable as prospects for marriage or prepare them for convent life; and to earn donations for the hospitals through regular performances, such as the concert pictured in Figure 18.4. Services with music at

The Pietà

the Pietà and other places of worship in Venice attracted large audiences, and travelers wrote of these occasions with enthusiasm (see Source Reading).

Vivaldi's position required him to maintain the string instruments, teach his students to play, and constantly compose new music for them to perform. He wrote oratorios and music for Mass and Vespers, including the well-known Gloria in D major, but most of his works for the Pietà were instrumental, primarily concertos for church festivals. Concertos were uniquely well suited for players of varying abilities because the best performers could show off their skill in the solo parts, while those of lesser ability could play in the orchestra.

VIVALDI'S CONCERTOS

Vivaldi's concertos have a freshness of melody, rhythmic verve, skillful treatment of solo and orchestral color, and clarity of form that have made them perennial favorites. Working at the Pietà, having skilled performers at his disposal, and being required to produce music at a prodigious rate provided Vivaldi with a workshop for experimenting with the concerto. The secret of Vivaldi's success, and of the profound influence he exercised on other composers, was a simple but flexible recipe that allowed him to achieve extraordinary variety through ever changing combinations of a few basic elements.

SOURCE READING

CONCERTS AT THE PIO OSPEDALE DELLA PIETÀ

The Frenchman Charles de Brosses toured Italy in 1739–40 and wrote his impressions in letters to friends, later collected for publication. His account of concerts at the Pio Ospedale della Pietà, where Vivaldi had long overseen instrumental music, gives us a sense of the institution and of the concerts performed by its residents, although de Brosses was mistaken when he called them nuns.

———— • ————

A transcending music here is that of the hospitals [orphanages]. There are four, all made up of illegitimate or orphaned girls or girls whose parents are not in a condition to raise them. They are reared at public expense and trained solely to excel in music. So they sing like angels and play the violin, the flute, the organ, the violoncello, the bassoon. In short no instrument is large enough to frighten them. They are cloistered in the manner of nuns. They alone perform, and each concert is given by about forty

girls. I swear to you that there is nothing so charming as to see a young and pretty nun in her white robe, with a bouquet of pomegranate flowers over her ear, leading the orchestra and beating time with all the grace and precision imaginable. Their voices are adorable for their quality and lightness, because here they don't know about roundness or a sound drawn out like a thread in the French manner. . . .

The hospital I go to most often is that of the Pietà, where one is best entertained. It is also first for the perfection of the symphonies. What an upright performance! It is only there that you hear the first stroke of the bow—the first chord of a piece attacked as one by the strings, of which the Opéra in Paris falsely boasts.

Charles de Brosses, *L'Italie il y a cent ans ou Lettres écrites d'Italie à quelques amis en 1739 et 1740,* ed. M. R. Colomb, vol. 1 (Paris: Alphonse Levavasseur, 1836), 213–14.

Vivaldi achieved a remarkable range of colors and sonorities through different groupings of solo and orchestral instruments. His orchestra at the Pietà probably consisted of twenty to twenty-five string instruments, with harpsichord or organ for the continuo. The strings were divided in what was becoming the standard arrangement of violins I and II, violas, cellos, and bass viols (usually doubling the cellos). This was always the core group, though in many concertos Vivaldi also called for flutes, oboes, bassoons, or horns, any of which might be used as solo instruments or in the ensemble. He also used special coloristic effects, like pizzicato and muted strings.

Instrumentation

About 350 of Vivaldi's concertos are for orchestra with one solo instrument—over two-thirds of them for violin, but many also for bassoon, cello, oboe, flute, viola d'amore, recorder, or mandolin. The concertos for two violins give the soloists equal prominence, producing the texture of a duet for two high voices. The concertos that call for several solo instruments are not concerti grossi like Corelli's, in which the orchestra serves to double and reinforce the concertino of two violins and cello; rather, they feature the same opposition between virtuoso soloists and orchestra as in Vivaldi's solo concertos. There are also about sixty orchestral concertos (without solo instruments).

With occasional exceptions, Vivaldi followed the three-movement plan introduced by Albinoni: an opening fast movement; a slow movement in the same or closely related key (relative minor, dominant, or subdominant); and a final fast movement in the tonic, often shorter and sprightlier than the first. By using this format so consistently, Vivaldi helped to establish it as the standard for concertos over the next three centuries.

Three-movement structure

We saw in chapter 17 that Torelli structured the fast movements of his concertos like the A section of a da capo aria, with a ritornello at the beginning, middle, and end framing two long episodes for the soloist. Vivaldi's concertos expand on this pattern, producing what is now known as **ritornello form.** This is less a formal mold than it is an approach, or set of guidelines, that allows a great deal of variety:

Ritornello form

- Ritornellos for the full orchestra alternate with episodes for the soloist or soloists.
- The opening ritornello is composed of several small units, typically two to four measures in length, some of which may be repeated or varied. These segments can be separated from each other or combined in new ways without losing their identity as the ritornello.
- Later statements of the ritornello are usually partial, comprising only one or some of the units, sometimes varied.
- The ritornellos are guideposts to the tonal structure of the music, confirming the keys to which the music modulates. The first and last statements are in the tonic; at least one (usually the first to be in a new key) is in the dominant; and others may be in closely related keys.
- The solo episodes are characterized by virtuosic, idiomatic playing, sometimes repeating or varying elements from the ritornello, but often presenting scales, arpeggiations, or other figuration. Many episodes modulate to a new key, which is then confirmed by the following ritornello. Sometimes the soloist interrupts or plays some part of the closing ritornello.

CD 6|13   CD 3|12

All these points are illustrated by the two fast movements in Vivaldi's Concerto for Violin and Orchestra in A Minor, Op. 3, No. 6 (NAWM 85), whose forms are diagrammed in Figure 18.5. Example 18.1 shows the opening ritornello of the first movement. Each of the segments, denoted by letter, has a strongly etched, individual character that makes it easy to remember. Each is a separate harmonic unit, enabling Vivaldi to separate and recombine the segments later on. In both movements, later statements of the ritornello are only partial, and some vary motives from the original ritornello, as do some of

FIRST MOVEMENT

Measure	Forces	Section	Motives	Key	Tonal plan
1	Tutti	Ritornello	A B C C′	a	i
13	Solo	Episode	A, A′	mod to C	
21	Tutti	Ritornello	A″	a	
24	Solo	Episode	new, A′	mod to e	
35	Tutti	Ritornello	A B A‴	e	v
45	Solo	Episode	new	mod to a	
58	Tutti	Ritornello	A	a	i
60	Solo	Episode	new	mod	
68	Tutti	Ritornello	C′	a	
71	Solo	Episode	B′	a	
75	Tutti	Ritornello	C C′	a	

THIRD MOVEMENT

Measure	Forces	Section	Motives	Key	Tonal plan
95	Tutti	Ritornello	ABABCDEF	a	i
124	Solo	Episode	AB′, new	mod	
144	Tutti	Ritornello	AA	e	v
149	Solo	Episode	C′	e	
156	Tutti	Ritornello	DEF′	a	i
165	Solo	Episode	F′, new	mod to C	
185	Tutti	Ritornello	AAC′F′AAC	C, e, a	III, v, i
203	Solo	Episode	new	a	
209	Tutti	Ritornello	AB	a	i
216	Solo		C′	a	
221	Tutti		D	a	
224	Solo, Tutti		E	a	
228	Solo, Tutti		F″	a	
232	Solo	Episode	new	a	
237	Tutti	Cadence	end of F″	a	

Figure 18.5: Ritornello forms in Vivaldi's Concerto in A Minor, Op. 3, No. 6.

Example 18.1: Opening ritornello of Vivaldi's Concerto in A Minor, Op. 3, No. 6, first movement

the solo episodes. New figurations are introduced in the episodes, as shown in Example 18.2, providing even more variety within a clearly understood structure; one passage exploits the open strings of the violin (tuned *g-d'-a'-e''*) for impressive leaps. Typical of Vivaldi, the alternation between tutti and solo does not stop when the music returns to the tonic near the end of the movement; in the first movement, episodes appear between successive units of the ritornello, and in the finale, the orchestra and soloist alternate in presenting segments of the final ritornello.

Example 18.2: Examples of figuration in solo episodes of Vivaldi's Concerto in A Minor, Op. 3, No. 6, first movement

The result in each case is a movement unique in form, yet the overall strategy is clearly the same. Far from following a textbook plan, Vivaldi's ritornello structures show almost infinite variety in form and content.

Slow movements   Vivaldi was the first concerto composer to make the slow movement as important as the fast ones. His slow movement is typically a long-breathed, expressive, cantabile melody, like an adagio operatic aria or arioso, to whose already rich figuration the performer was expected to add embellishments. Some slow movements are through-composed, and others use a simplified ritornello or two-part form. The slow movement in Op. 3, No. 6, is unusual in that the bass instruments and continuo are silent, and the soloist is accompanied only by the upper strings playing sustained tones.

Economy and variety   Vivaldi once said he could compose a concerto faster than a copyist could write out the parts. One reason was that ritornello form allowed him to spin out relatively long movements from a small amount of material that he repeated, transposed, varied, and recombined. In both fast and slow movements, he frequently used sequences, generating several measures from a short motive while dramatizing a strong chord progression, as in the second segment of Example 18.1.

Despite his reliance on formulas, what is most striking about Vivaldi's concertos is their variety and range of expression. His works were known for their spontaneity of musical ideas; clear formal structures; assured harmonies; varied textures; and forceful rhythms. He established a dramatic tension between solo and tutti, not only giving the soloist contrasting figuration, as Torelli had already done, but also letting the soloist stand out as a musical personality.

Publications, titles, and programs   Vivaldi composed many of his concertos for the Pietà, but he also wrote on commission and earned money through publications. Nine collections of his concertos (Opp. 3–4 and Opp. 6–12) were published in Amsterdam, the last seven apparently printed at the publisher's expense instead of being subsidized by the composer or a patron as was common; this shows Vivaldi's value to his publisher and reflects the immense popularity of his concertos, especially in northern Europe. Several of these collections were given fanciful titles, in part to attract buyers: Op. 3, *L'estro armonico* (Harmonic Inspiration, 1711); Op. 4, *La stravaganza* (Extravagance, 1716); Op. 8, *Il cimento dell'armonia e dell'inventione* (The Test of Harmony and Invention, 1725); and Op. 9, *La cetra* (The Kithara, 1727), evoking ancient Greece. Some individual concertos were also given titles and even programs. Most famous are the first four concertos in Op. 8, known as *The Four Seasons*. Each of these is accompanied by a sonnet, perhaps written by Vivaldi himself, that describes the season, and the concertos cleverly depict the images in the poetry, taking advantage of the variety possible in ritornello forms.

VIVALDI'S POSITION AND INFLUENCE

Vivaldi's music reflects the stylistic changes of the first half of the eighteenth century. At the conservative extreme are his trio and solo sonatas, which emulate the style of Corelli. Most of his concertos were part of the stylistic mainstream, responding to and often creating contemporary trends. At the progressive extreme are the solo concerto finales, the orchestral concertos, and most of the sixteen sinfonias—works that establish Vivaldi as a founder of the Classic symphony (see chapter 21).

Range of styles

Vivaldi's influence on instrumental music equaled that of Corelli a generation earlier. His codification of ritornello form provided a model for later concerto composers. His successors admired and emulated his concise themes, clarity of form, rhythmic vitality, and logical flow of musical ideas. Among those who learned from Vivaldi was J. S. Bach, who made keyboard arrangements of at least nine Vivaldi concertos, including five from Op. 3. Later in the eighteenth century, concerto composers adopted and developed Vivaldi's dramatic conception of the soloist's role.

Influence

MUSIC IN FRANCE

While Italy had many cultural centers, France had only one: Paris, the capital and by far the largest city. Musicians in the provinces dreamed of careers in Paris, where patrons, publishers, and an eager public waited to hear and see the latest music. Only there could a composer achieve true success and a national reputation. Although other cities had concert series in which amateurs could perform, Paris was home to the most prestigious concert organizations like the Concert Spirituel, a public concert series founded in 1725. The royal court of Louis XV (r. 1715–74) continued to support musicians but no longer dominated musical life as had the court of his great-grandfather Louis XIV. In its place a wider range of patrons and institutions supported musicians and composers.

RECONCILING FRENCH AND ITALIAN STYLE

Since the seventeenth century, Italian music in France was viewed as a foreign influence, welcomed by some and resisted by others. The latest Italian music could be heard in Paris, particularly the sonatas and concertos of Corelli, Vivaldi, and others, and the relative merits of French and Italian styles were discussed constantly in salons and in print. Many French composers sought to blend the two musical styles, especially in genres pioneered in Italy. Louis Nicolas Clérambault (1676–1749), who published five books of cantatas between 1710 and 1726, alternated recitatives in the manner of Lully with Italianate arias. Jean-Marie Leclair (1697–1764), the principal French composer of violin sonatas, combined what he considered the classic purity of Corelli with French grace and sweetness of melody, perfect clarity of texture and form, and tasteful decoration.

FRANÇOIS COUPERIN

Among the most active proponents of blending French and Italian tastes was François Couperin (1668–1733), shown in Figure 18.6. His career reflects the growing diffusion of patronage in France: he was organist to the king and at the church of St. Gervais in Paris, but earned much of his money teaching harpsichord to members of the aristocracy and publishing his own music. His harpsichord *ordres*, or suites, published between 1713 and 1730, were loose aggregations of miniature pieces, most in dance rhythms and in binary form but highly stylized and refined, intended as recreation for amateur performers. Thoroughly French yet individual in style, most of these pieces carry evocative titles. Couperin's *Vingt-cinquième ordre* (Twenty-fifth Order, 1730; excerpts in NAWM 86), for example, contains *La visionaire* (The Dreamer), a rather whimsical French overture; *La misterieuse* (The Mysterious One), an allemande; *La Montflambert*, a tender gigue probably named after the wife of

Figure 18.6: François Couperin around 1695, by an unknown French painter.

SOURCE READING

COUPERIN ON THE UNION OF THE ITALIAN AND FRENCH STYLES

François Couperin was one of the leading composers in France, especially of music for harpsichord or chamber ensemble. At a time when partisans of French and Italian music debated their respective merits in conversation and print, Couperin traveled a middle road, arguing that the two styles should be joined together.

———— • ————

The Italian and French styles have long divided up the Republic of Music in France. As for me, I have always esteemed the things that deserved to be, without regard to the composer or nation. The first Italian sonatas that appeared in Paris more than thirty years ago and encouraged me to start composing some myself, to my mind wronged neither the works of Monsieur de Lully nor those of my ancestors, who will always be more admirable than imitable. Thus, by a right that my neutrality confers upon me, I sail under the happy star that has guided me until now.

Since Italian music has the right of seniority over ours, at the end of this volume you will find a grand trio sonata titled *The Apotheosis of Corelli.* A feeble spark of self-love persuaded me to present it in score. If some day my muse outdoes itself, I shall dare to undertake likewise something in the style of the incomparable Lully, although his works alone ought to suffice to immortalize him.

From François Couperin, Preface, *Les goûts-réünis* (Paris, 1724).

the king's wine merchant; *La muse victorieuse* (The Victorious Muse), a fast dance in triple time; and *Les ombres errantes* (The Roving Shadows), which reflects its title through a syncopated middle voice that shadows the top melody to form chains of suspensions. Couperin's book *L'art de toucher le clavecin* (The Art of Playing the Harpsichord, 1716) is one of the most important sources for performance practice of the French Baroque.

In his chamber music, Couperin synthesized French with Italian styles. *Chamber works* Through the titles, prefaces, and choice of contents for his published collections he proclaimed that the perfect music would be a union of the two national styles (see Source Reading). He admired the music of both Lully and Corelli, and celebrated them in suites for two violins and harpsichord: *Parnassus, or The Apotheosis of Corelli* (1724) and *The Apotheosis of Lully* (1725). In the second work, Lully is represented as joining Corelli on Mt. Parnassus to perform a French overture and then a trio sonata. Couperin was the first and most important French composer of trio sonatas, beginning in 1692. His collection *Les nations* (The Nations, 1726) contains four ordres, each consisting of a sonata da chiesa in several movements followed by a suite of dances, thus combining the most characteristic genres of France and Italy in a single set. He also wrote twelve suites he called *concerts* for harpsichord and various combinations of instruments, each consisting of a prelude and several dance movements. He titled the first four *Concerts royaux* (Royal Concerts, published 1722), because they were played before Louis XIV. Couperin published the last eight in a collection titled *Les goûts-réünis* (The Reunited Tastes, 1724), signifying that they joined French and Italian styles.

JEAN-PHILIPPE RAMEAU

Jean-Philippe Rameau (1683–1764) had an unusual career, spending two decades as an organist in the provinces, winning recognition as a music theorist around the age of forty, and achieving fame as a composer in his fifties (see biography and Figure 18.7). Attacked then as a radical, he was assailed twenty years later as a reactionary. His writings founded the theory of tonal music, and his operas established him as Lully's most important successor.

THEORY OF HARMONY

Music theory engaged Rameau throughout his life. Inspired by works of Descartes and Newton, Rameau approached music as a source of empirical data that could be explained on rational principles. He described his methodology in *Traité de l'harmonie* (Treatise on Harmony, 1722), one of the most influential theoretical works ever written.

Acoustics and chords

Rameau's debt to Descartes can be seen in his search to ground the practice of harmony in the laws of acoustics. He considered the triad and seventh chord the primal elements of music, and derived both from the natural consonances of the perfect fifth, major third, and minor third.

The fundamental bass

In Rameau's approach, each chord has a fundamental tone, equivalent in most cases to what is today called its root (the lowest note when the chord is arranged as a series of thirds). In a series of chords, the succession of these fundamental tones is the **fundamental bass.** In modern terms, Rameau was asserting that a chord keeps its identify through all its inversions and that the harmony of a passage is defined by the root progression rather than by the actual lowest note sounding. These concepts, now staples of music theory, were revolutionary at the time. Example 18.3 shows the fundamental bass for a passage from Rameau's opera *Hippolyte et Aricie* of 1733 (NAWM 87).

CD 6|35   CD 3|24

Tonal direction

For Rameau, music was driven forward by dissonance and came to rest in consonance. Seventh chords provided dissonance, triads consonance. He coined the terms **tonic** (the main note and chord in a key), **dominant** (the note and chord a perfect fifth above the tonic), and **subdominant** (the note and chord a fifth below the tonic); established those three chords as the pillars of tonality; and related other chords to them, formulating the hierarchies of functional tonality. The strongest progression between two chords in Rameau's system is from a seventh chord on the dominant to a triad on the tonic, with the dissonant notes resolving by step and the fundamental bass falling a fifth (or rising a fourth). Other falling-fifth progressions are almost as strong, and indeed motion by falling fifth is more common than any other. Through such progressions, the fundamental bass gives music coherence and direction and helps to define the key. Note in Example 18.3 that all but two of the motions in the fundamental bass are by falling fifth (marked by brackets), helping to establish the local tonics of C minor and B♭ major, and that seventh chords keep the music moving forward until the cadence is reached. Rameau recognized that a piece could change key, a process called **modulation**, but considered that each piece had one principal tonic to which other keys were secondary.

Rameau's theories have become commonplaces learned by every music student, so it takes an exercise of historical imagination to grasp how important they were at the time. Most of the elements had been described by

Rameau's impact

Example 18.3: *Recitative from Rameau's* Hippolyte et Aricie, *with fundamental bass*

Ah! if you are fair-minded, do not thunder any more at me! The glory of a hero whom injustice oppresses demands your rightful aid.

JEAN-PHILIPPE RAMEAU (1683–1764)

Practically unknown before the age of forty, Rameau emerged late in life as the most significant music theorist of his era and the leading composer in France. In his fifties and sixties, he wrote the operas and ballets that made him famous.

Rameau was born in Dijon, in Burgundy (east central France), the seventh of eleven children. From his father, an organist, Rameau received his first and, as far as we know, only formal musical instruction. He attended a Jesuit school, then visited Italy briefly as a teenager.

After two decades holding positions as organist at Clermont, Paris, Dijon, and Lyons, he moved permanently to Paris in 1722, seeking better opportunities. His pathbreaking *Traité de l'harmonie* (Treatise on Harmony), published that year, quickly won him renown as a theorist. He made a living teaching harmony and playing continuo but could not find a position as organist until 1732. In 1726, aged forty-two, he married a nineteen-year-old singer and harpsichordist, Marie-Louise Mangot, and over the next two decades they had four children.

Success as a composer came gradually and late. He published some cantatas and two books of harpsichord pieces in the 1720s. He found patrons who helped to support him, including the Prince of Carignan. His first opera, *Hippolyte et Aricie* (1733), began to build his reputation as a composer, followed by four other operas and opera-ballets in the next six years. In the mid-1730s, he won the patronage of the rich tax collector Alexandre-Jean-Joseph Le Riche de la Pouplinière, whose gatherings attracted aristocrats, artists, literary figures (Voltaire and Jean-Jacques Rousseau), adventurers (Casanova), and musicians. Rameau served his patron as organist

Figure 18.7: Jean-Philippe Rameau in about 1725. Portrait by Jacques André Joseph Aved.

and in various capacities until 1753, and members of La Pouplinière's circle became enthusiastic backers of Rameau. In 1745, the king of France granted him an annual pension. The next few years were his most productive and successful, with eleven dramatic works by 1749. Given his late start at the age of fifty, it is remarkable that over twenty-five of his ballets and operas were staged, more than by any other French composer of the eighteenth century.

Polemical writings and theoretical essays occupied Rameau's closing years. He died in Paris in 1764, at the age of eighty-one. Feisty to the end, he found strength even on his deathbed to reproach the priest administering the last rites for bad chanting.

MAJOR WORKS: 4 tragédies en musique (Hippolyte et Aricie, Castor et Pollux, Dardanus, *and* Zoroastre*), 6 other operas,* Les Indes galantes *and 6 other opera-ballets, 7 ballets, harpsichord pieces, trio sonatas, cantatas, and motets*

earlier theorists, but Rameau was the first to bring them together into a unified system. Living at a time when the notion of universal laws of nature was fashionable, Rameau found in the music of some of his contemporaries—Corelli foremost among them—harmonic practices that could be described according to universal laws. Other writers popularized his ideas, and by the late eighteenth century his approach was the primary paradigm for teaching musicians.

OPERAS

Rameau wrote several collections of keyboard music, a set of trio sonatas, and some sacred and secular vocal music but attained his greatest fame as a composer of stage works. From a young age Rameau aspired to compose opera, but the monopoly of the Académie Royale de Musique made it almost impossible to produce opera except in Paris. When he moved there in 1722, he wrote airs and dances for a few musical comedies, pieces with spoken dialogue performed at the popular theaters. Finally, in 1733, his opera *Hippolyte et Aricie* was produced in Paris, winning both admiration and controversy and establishing his reputation as a composer. A string of successes followed, including the opera-ballet *Les Indes galantes* (The Gallant Indies, 1735) and the opera *Castor et Pollux* (1737), generally considered his masterpiece. After a relatively fallow period in the early 1740s came his most productive years, from the comedy *Platée* (1745) to the tragic opera *Zoroastre* (1749), the most important of Rameau's later works.

From the first, Rameau's operas stirred up a storm of critical controversy. *Lullistes versus* The Paris intelligentsia divided into two noisy camps, one supporting Rameau *Ramistes* and the other attacking him as a subverter of the good old French opera tradition of Lully. The Lullistes found Rameau's music difficult, forced, grotesque, thick, mechanical, and unnatural—in a word, baroque. Rameau protested, in a foreword to his opera-ballet *Les Indes galantes*, that he had "sought to imitate Lully, not as a servile copyist but in taking, like him, nature herself—so beautiful and so simple—as a model." As the quarrel of the Lullistes and Ramistes raged, Rameau's increasing popularity sparked many parodies of his operas—lighthanded imitations or adaptations of the originals. By the 1750s, during the battle between critics on the relative merits of French and Italian music known as the War of the Buffoons (see chapter 20), Rameau had become the most eminent living French composer, exalted as the champion of French music by the very faction that twenty years earlier had castigated him for not writing like Lully.

Rameau's theater works resemble Lully's in several ways: both composers *Comparison* exhibit realistic declamation and precise rhythmic notation in the recitatives; *with Lully* both mix recitative with more tuneful, formally organized airs, choruses, and instrumental interludes; and both include long divertissements. But within this general framework, Rameau introduced many changes.

The melodic lines offer one notable contrast. Rameau the composer con- *Melodic and* stantly practiced the doctrine of Rameau the theorist that all melody is rooted *harmonic style* in harmony. Many of his melodic phrases are plainly triadic and make clear the harmonic progressions that must support them. Orderly relationships within the tonal system of dominants, subdominants, and modulations govern the harmony. Rameau drew from a rich palette of chords and progressions, including chromatic ones, diversifying his style much more than Lully's and achieving dramatic force through expressive, highly charged dissonances that propel the harmony forward.

Instrumental music

Rameau made his most original contribution in the instrumental sections of his operas—overtures, dances, and descriptive symphonies that accompany the stage action. The French valued music for its powers of depiction, and Rameau was their champion tone-painter. His musical pictures range from graceful miniatures to broad representations of thunder (*Hippolyte et Aricie*, Act I) or earthquake (*Les Indes galantes*, Act II). The depiction is often enhanced by novel orchestration, especially independent woodwind parts.

Airs and choruses

Like Lully and other French composers, Rameau minimized the contrast between recitative and air in comparison to Italian composers. He often smoothly moved between styles to suit the dramatic situation. Often the most powerful effects are achieved by the joint use of solo and chorus. Choruses remained prominent in French opera long after they were no longer used in Italy, and they were numerous throughout Rameau's works.

Combination of elements

CD 6|35   CD 3|24

The closing minutes of Act IV of *Hippolyte et Aricie* (NAWM 87) illustrate the high drama Rameau could achieve by combining all these elements. A divertissement of hunters and huntresses is suddenly followed by tragedy, so fast that the audience has little time to adjust. Throbbing strings depict a rough sea, while rushing scales in the flute and violins evoke high winds. A monster appears, and the chorus begs for aid from the goddess Diana, singing over the orchestra. Hippolyte steps up to fight the monster, as his beloved Aricie trembles in fear; they too sing over the orchestra, in a texture of accompanied recitative borrowed from contemporary Italian opera. The monster breathes flame and smoke, then disappears, and the orchestra stops abruptly. When the smoke clears, Aricie mournfully sees that Hippolyte is gone, and the chorus comments on the tragedy in stirring, richly dissonant homophony. The rapid juxtaposition of styles continues as Phèdre, Hippolyte's stepmother, enters, hears the news from the chorus, and laments his death, for which she feels responsible. Although no full-breathed air appears—indeed, one would be inappropriate—short segments of airlike melody are intermixed with measured and unmeasured recitative, with and without the orchestra, over varying styles of accompaniment, each element perfectly placed for maximum dramatic effect.

REPUTATION

Rameau was one of the most complex and productive musical personalities of the eighteenth century. By his sixties, he was the most honored and admired musician in France, and his operas were frequently performed years after their first productions. All his works exemplify the French traits of clarity, grace, moderation, elegance, and interest in the picturesque. He is unique among great composers in being an analyst as well as a creator.

A VOLATILE PUBLIC

By the time Vivaldi died, tastes had begun to change, the public turned elsewhere, and his music passed from the scene. In the later eighteenth century, he was virtually forgotten. But his influence on Bach was noted by nineteenth-century scholars, and his importance in the evolution of the concerto was demonstrated in the early twentieth century. Interest in Vivaldi's music, especially his concertos, was intensified by the discovery in the 1920s of what must have been Vivaldi's own collection of scores. The prominent Italian publishing house Ricordi began publishing his complete instrumental music in 1947, motivated in part by a desire to reclaim the glorious Italian Baroque tradition that had been obscured by later German composers. Vivaldi is now considered a master composer alongside Bach and Handel, and a central figure in our image of music from the Baroque. His concertos seem almost inescapable, from concerts to recordings to film and advertising scores, though his operas and other music are seldom heard.

Couperin's harpsichord music was well known in his lifetime, in England and Germany as well as in France, then slowly fell out of fashion. Rameau died famous, with several of his operas still in the repertory, but tastes changed in the 1770s and his operas gradually passed from the stage. His harpsichord music remained in circulation and was widely performed over the next several generations. In the late nineteenth century, Couperin and Rameau's compositions, especially their keyboard works, were edited and revived as exemplars of French music that could rival the Germans Bach and Handel. A complete edition of Rameau's music was issued between 1895 and 1924, followed by Couperin's complete works in 1932–33. Their music is less omnipresent than Vivaldi's but has found a secure and enthusiastic band of devotées, especially in France. Meanwhile, Rameau's reputation as a theorist never waned, and his approach became the foundation for most writings on and teaching of music theory from his day to the present.

German Composers
of the Late Baroque

In the eighteenth century, for the first time in history, the leading composers in Europe came from German-speaking lands. Telemann, Handel, members of the Bach family, Haydn, and Mozart all rose to prominence not by inventing new genres, as the Italians had done in the two previous centuries, but by synthesizing elements from Italian, French, German, and other national traditions in new, rich ways. The German secret was a balance of tastes between native trends and foreign influences. The Italians and the French generally resisted foreign ideas, and no composer in either country matched the international reputation of Vivaldi or Rameau until the nineteenth century. England became a virtual colony for foreign musicians, and it remained so until the twentieth century. Only German and Austrian composers consistently sought wide appeal by combining the best traits of several nations.

This chapter will focus on J. S. Bach and Handel, the best-known German-speaking composers of the early eighteenth century. Using them as case studies to explore conditions for music in Germany and England, we will examine how each found patronage from a variety of sources, made choices among competing tastes, values, and styles in music, and met with both success and failure.

CONTEXTS FOR MUSIC

German patrons

In the eighteenth century, German-speaking central Europe continued to be divided among hundreds of political entities, from the large states of Austria, Saxony, and Brandenburg-Prussia to tiny principalities and independent cities. Each of these supported music. Some rulers followed Louis XIV's example of displaying their power and wealth through patronage of the arts, as did the Holy Roman Emperors in Vienna, the electors of Saxony in Dresden, and King Frederick II (the Great) of Prussia (r. 1740–1786) in Berlin. City governments were also significant employers of musicians, especially in Lutheran areas, where the town council was often responsible for hiring music directors for the churches.

One interesting phenomenon in eighteenth-century Germany is the number of aristocrats who pursued music avidly as performers and as composers. Johann Ernst, prince of Weimar (1696–1715), was a violinist who composed instrumental works, of which six concertos were published. Frederick the Great, shown in Figure 19.1, regularly performed flute sonatas and concertos at private concerts in his chambers and composed flute concertos, arias, and other music. His sister Anna Amalia, princess of Prussia (1723–1787), played harpsichord and organ, composed vocal and instrumental music, and collected a large library of scores. Her niece Anna Amalia, duchess of Saxe-Weimar (1739–1807), was a keyboard player, composer, and important patron of music and literature. Her major works are two Singspiels (spoken plays with music) to texts by Goethe. Many other aristocrats were enthusiastic amateur performers, and they often made particularly generous patrons.

Aristocratic musicians

Britain was a unified monarchy, but since the revolutions in the seventeenth century the power and wealth of the royal house were quite limited. At times even the relatively low salaries of the court musicians went unpaid. In order to keep musicians in service, the king had to allow them to earn extra money outside official duties. The presence of highly skilled, underpaid, and underutilized performers in London led to the growth of the public concert. The nobility also supported music. Many nobles had visited Italy as young

English patrons

Figure 19.1: King Frederick II (the Great) of Prussia performing as flute soloist in a concerto, accompanied by a small orchestra, with Carl Philipp Emanuel Bach at the harpsichord. Painting by Adolph von Menzel, 1852.

men to learn its language, arts, and culture, a custom known as taking the "grand tour." On their return to England, they emulated Italian aristocrats in employing household musicians and helping to fund Italian opera.

Concerts and publishing

Musicians supplemented their salaried appointments through public concerts, an increasingly important part of musical life in Germany as well as England, and through the sale of their compositions to publishers. Earnings from publishing were still quite limited; the system of paying royalties on sales had not yet developed, so a composer would simply receive a set fee from a publisher for all rights to a score. Moreover, copyright laws were weak, and publishers often copied and issued pieces without paying the composer. Under these circumstances, no one could earn a living by composing alone.

MIXED TASTE

For centuries, Germans had been interested in music from other nations: Flemish polyphony; Dutch and English keyboard music; Italian madrigals, operas, and concertos; and French operas, orchestral suites, and harpsichord and lute music. German musicians were often trained in more than one style. Composers studied music from other countries when they could and imported foreign genres, styles, and techniques. This diverse background allowed German composers great flexibility to draw elements from various traditions and adapt or blend them to suit any purpose or audience. More than any other trait, this synthesis of traditions gave the music of eighteenth-century German composers its broad appeal.

Georg Philipp Telemann

A paragon of this stylistic eclecticism was Georg Philipp Telemann (1681–1767), shown in Figure 19.2, regarded by his contemporaries as one of the best composers of his era. He was also the most prolific, with over three thousand works to his credit. Writing in every genre, he produced thirty operas, forty-six Passions, over a thousand church cantatas, and hundreds of overtures, concertos, and chamber works. In 1729, he described his style as a mixture of many:

> What I have accomplished with respect to musical style is well known. First came the Polish style, followed by the French, church, chamber and operatic styles, and [finally] the Italian style, which currently occupies me more than the others do.

Figure 19.2: Georg Philipp Telemann, in an engraving by Georg Lichtensteger.

Almost every current style can be found in Telemann's music. He helped to establish the characteristic German style of his time, a synthesis of German counterpoint with traits from the other nations he mentions. His aim to please varied tastes and write for the abilities of good amateur or middle-level professional players gave Telemann's music wide appeal. His works were published in Paris as well as in Germany, and bought by musicians from Italy to England and from Spain to Scandinavia. Telemann's preference for simplicity helped make him much more popular in his time than J. S. Bach, but he was then ignored and belittled in the nineteenth century. His music was gradually revived in the twentieth century, and he is slowly regaining his stature as one of the great composers of his age.

JOHANN SEBASTIAN BACH

Posterity has raised Johann Sebastian Bach (1685–1750) to the pinnacle of composers of all time. His current position contrasts with his reputation in his own day, when he was renowned in Protestant Germany as an organ virtuoso and writer of learned contrapuntal works, but comparatively little of his music was published or circulated in manuscript. In the course of his career, Bach embraced all the major styles, forms, and genres of his time (except opera), blended them in new ways, and developed them further. The result is music of an unprecedented richness. Although some eighteenth-century listeners found his music cluttered or forced, and it was regarded as old-fashioned by the time he died, it was always esteemed by connoisseurs. The revival and publication of his works in the nineteenth century brought him legions of admirers, performers, and listeners, from the leading musicians of the day to the general public.

BACH AT WORK

Bach was a working musician who composed primarily to fulfill the needs of the positions he held (see biography and Figures 19.3 and 19.4). When he was a church organist at Arnstadt (1703–7) and Mühlhausen (1707–8) and court organist at Weimar (1708–14), he composed mostly for organ. When he became concertmaster at Weimar (1714–17), he also wrote cantatas for church. As court music director at Cöthen (1717–23), where he had no formal church music duties, he turned out mostly solo or ensemble music for domestic or court entertainment, along with some pedagogical works. At Leipzig (1723–50), in charge of music at four churches, he produced cantatas and other church music. His appointment in 1729 as director of the Leipzig collegium musicum led him to write concertos and chamber works. Numerous pieces for organ or harpsichord also date from the Leipzig period, including teaching pieces for his many private students.

Oft-told anecdotes of Bach's life remind us that musicians were not free agents but were subject to the wishes of their employers. When Bach accepted the position at Cöthen, the duke of Weimar would not let him leave at first, and imprisoned him for a month before allowing him to go. As cantor of St. Thomas's School and director of music in Leipzig, Bach was an employee of the town council, and in his contract he had to pledge himself to lead an exemplary life and not to leave town without permission from the mayor. He was the council's third choice, after Telemann—who used the offer to leverage a raise from his bosses in Hamburg—and Christoph Graupner, whose employer in Darmstadt refused to accept his resignation but increased his pay. On many occasions, Bach clashed with the council about what he saw as the prerogatives of his office, sometimes defying their authority in a bid to preserve his independence.

The position of musicians

JOHANN SEBASTIAN BACH (1685–1750)

Now considered one of the greatest composers ever, Bach regarded himself more modestly, as a conscientious craftsman doing his job to the best of his ability. He was a virtuoso organist and keyboard player, a skilled violinist, and a prolific composer in almost every genre then current except opera.

Bach came from a large family of musicians in the region of Thuringia in central Germany. Over six generations, from the late sixteenth to the nineteenth century, the Bach family produced an extraordinary number of good musicians and several outstanding ones. Johann Sebastian was born in Eisenach and attended the Latin school there, receiving a solid grounding in theology and humanistic studies. He must have learned violin from his father, a court and town musician who died when Bach was just turning ten. He then lived and studied music with his older brother Johann Christoph Bach, organist in Ohrdruf. Bach spent 1700–1702 in school at Lüneburg, where he encountered the organist Georg Böhm and experienced the French repertoire and style of the local orchestra. (For cities important in Bach's career, see Figure 19.4.)

Bach's first positions were as a church organist, beginning at Arnstadt in 1703, when he was eighteen, and then at Mühlhausen in 1707. That year he married Maria Barbara Bach, his second cousin, with whom he had seven children before her death in 1720. His second wife, Anna Magdelena Wilcke, a court singer from a family of musicians, whom he married a year later, bore him thirteen children, seven of whom died in infancy. From his time at Mühlhausen to the end of his life, Bach tutored private students in perfor-

Figure 19.3: Johann Sebastian Bach in a portrait by Elias Gottlob Haussmann (a 1748 copy of a 1746 original). Shown in Bach's hand is the manuscript of his triple canon for six voices, BWV 1076.

mance and composition, including several of his own sons, and served as an organ consultant.

In 1708, Bach became a court musician for the duke of Weimar, first as organist and later as concertmaster. He was appointed Kapellmeister (music director) at the court of Prince Leopold of Anhalt in Cöthen in 1717. After a stay of six years, Bach moved to Leipzig to become cantor of the St. Thomas School and civic music director, one of the most prestigious positions in Germany.

After a lifetime of hard work, Bach's last two years were marked by disease (probably diabetes), vision problems, and severe eye pain. At his death after a stroke, he left a small estate, split between his nine surviving children and his wife, who died in poverty ten years later.

Bach's works are identified by their number in Wolfgang Schmieder's catalogue of his works, abbreviated BWV for Bach-Werke Verzeichnis (Bach Works Catalogue).

MAJOR WORKS: St. Matthew Passion, St. John Passion, *Mass in B Minor, about 200 church cantatas and 30 secular cantatas, about 200 organ chorales and 70 other works for organ,* Brandenburg Concertos, Well-Tempered Clavier, Clavier-Übung, A Musical Offering, The Art of Fugue, *and numerous other keyboard, ensemble, orchestral, and sacred compositions*

Figure 19.4: Cities that figured in J. S. Bach's career are indicated in color on this map of modern Germany. In Bach's time, Leipzig and Dresden were in the electorate of Saxony, Lüneburg lay in the electorate of Hanover, Berlin was in Brandenburg, Hamburg was a free city, Lübeck belonged to the duchy of Holstein, and Anhalt-Cöthen and Weimar were each tiny dukedoms.

Figure 19.5: St. Thomas Church in Leipzig, where Bach regularly directed the music for services. At the far end of the square, beyond the fountain, is St. Thomas's School (after it was enlarged in 1732), where Bach taught.

Conditions in Leipzig

Bach's working conditions in Leipzig may illustrate the multiple demands on musicians in an era when no one worked solely as a composer. Leipzig was a flourishing commercial city of about 30,000, a center for publishing, and home to Germany's leading university, founded in 1409. St. Thomas's School, shown in Figure 19.5, took in both day and boarding pupils. It provided between fifty and sixty scholarships for boys and youths chosen for their musical and scholastic abilities. In return, they sang or played in the services of the four main Leipzig churches and fulfilled other musical duties. Bach's position as cantor obliged him to teach Latin and music four hours each day and to compose, copy, and rehearse music for the church services. He directed the top choir and supervised the other three, conducted by older students who were his assistants. He trained some of the best students on instruments and directed them in the church orchestra, which also included performers from the town and university. In his early years, he composed at least one major work for church each week, then gradually lessened his pace. He had further duties providing music for town ceremonies and at the university, and he received additional fees to compose and lead music for weddings, funerals, and other special occasions. For all this he was paid a comfortable middle-class income and provided with an apartment for his family in one wing of the school, including a personal study for composing and for housing his professional library.

The craft of composition

Bach learned composition primarily by copying or arranging the music of other composers, a habit maintained throughout his career. Among his pieces are adaptations of music by Torelli, Vivaldi, Telemann, and numerous others. In this way he became familiar with the methods of the foremost composers in Italy, Germany, Austria, and France.

According to his son Carl Philipp Emanuel, Bach typically composed away from the keyboard, then tested the result by playing through it. The most important step was inventing the principal theme or subject, on which Bach then elaborated using established conventions of genre, form, and harmonic structure. When working with a text, as in a recitative or aria, he wrote the vocal melody first, fitting it to the accentuation and meaning of the words. Bach's manuscripts show that he continually sought to improve his music, making small revisions as he copied out a score or performing parts, and revising afresh when he performed a piece again. He also frequently reworked his own existing pieces for new forces, new uses, or new words; many of his cantata movements are adapted from earlier cantatas, instrumental works, or other music (see Figure 19.7, p. 452).

ORGAN MUSIC

As a church organist, Bach focused on the genres employed in Lutheran services: chorale settings, played before each chorale and sometimes used to accompany the congregation as they sang; and toccatas, fantasias, preludes, and

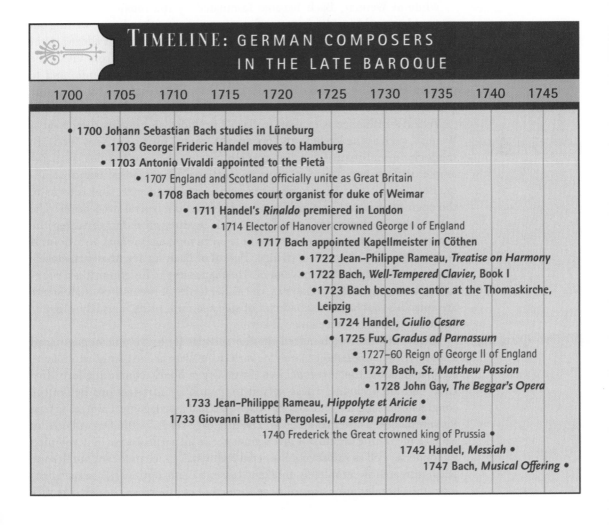

TIMELINE: GERMAN COMPOSERS IN THE LATE BAROQUE

1700	1705	1710	1715	1720	1725	1730	1735	1740	1745

- 1700 Johann Sebastian Bach studies in Lüneburg
- 1703 George Frideric Handel moves to Hamburg
- 1703 Antonio Vivaldi appointed to the Pietà
- 1707 England and Scotland officially unite as Great Britain
- 1708 Bach becomes court organist for duke of Weimar
- 1711 Handel's *Rinaldo* premiered in London
- 1714 Elector of Hanover crowned George I of England
- 1717 Bach appointed Kapellmeister in Cöthen
- 1722 Jean-Philippe Rameau, *Treatise on Harmony*
- 1722 Bach, *Well-Tempered Clavier*, Book I
- 1723 Bach becomes cantor at the Thomaskirche, Leipzig
- 1724 Handel, *Giulio Cesare*
- 1725 Fux, *Gradus ad Parnassum*
- 1727–60 Reign of George II of England
- 1727 Bach, *St. Matthew Passion*
- 1728 John Gay, *The Beggar's Opera*
- 1733 Jean-Philippe Rameau, *Hippolyte et Aricie* •
- 1733 Giovanni Battista Pergolesi, *La serva padrona* •
- 1740 Frederick the Great crowned king of Prussia •
- 1742 Handel, *Messiah* •
- 1747 Bach, *Musical Offering* •

fugues, featured as preludes or interludes at other points in the service and suitable also for recitals. (See Source Reading, p. 451, for the place of "preluding" in a Lutheran service.) From a young age, Bach was acquainted with a wide variety of organ music, by North Germans like Buxtehude and Böhm, central and southern Germans such as Pachelbel and Froberger, Italians like Frescobaldi, and French organists. While working in Arnstadt, he traveled on foot to hear Buxtehude in Lübeck, a journey of about 225 miles. By blending and then transcending his models, he developed a personal and distinctive style, marked by prolific imagination, mastery of counterpoint, assured virtuosity, and extensive use of the pedals. He was renowned as an improviser and was often called upon to test new or rebuilt organs.

Preludes
and fugues

Buxtehude had written freestanding fugues as well as preludes that alternated sections of free fantasia with fugues (see NAWM 84). By 1700, some composers were prefacing fugues with separate preludes (or toccatas or fantasias), a practice that became standard for Bach. His well-known Toccata in D Minor, BWV 565 (before 1708?), marks a middle ground; it has only one fugue but begins and ends with toccata sections and interpolates toccata-like figuration within the fugue.

Vivaldi's influence

While at Weimar, Bach became fascinated by the music of Vivaldi. He arranged several Vivaldi concertos for organ or harpsichord solo, writing out the ornaments and occasionally reinforcing the counterpoint or adding inner voices. As a consequence, Bach's own style began to change. From Vivaldi he learned to write concise themes, to clarify the harmonic scheme, and to develop subjects into grandly proportioned formal structures based on the ritornello idea.

CD 6|38   CD 3|27

Vivaldi's influence is evident in Bach's preludes and fugues composed at Weimar, such as the Prelude and Fugue in A Minor, BWV 543 (NAWM 88). In the prelude, violinistic figuration resembling that of concerto solos, as in Example 19.1a, alternates with toccata sections. Contrasting textures, sequences, circle-of-fifth progressions, clear tonal structure, and returns of the opening material in new keys all recall Vivaldi's typical procedures. The fugue subject, shown in Example 19.1b, is again violinistic, featuring the rapid oscillation between a repeated note and a moving line that on a violin is accomplished by alternating strings. Typical of Bach fugues, the form closely resembles a concerto fast movement. The fugue subject functions like a ritornello, returning in related keys as well as the tonic. Between these statements are episodes that have the character of solo sections, often marked by lighter texture, sequences, or a change of key.

Chorale settings

Bach wrote over two hundred chorale-settings for organ, encompassing all known types in a constant search for variety. At Weimar, he compiled a manuscript collection, the *Orgelbüchlein* (Little Organ Book), containing forty-five short chorale preludes. These served in church as introductions before the congregation sang the chorale. But Bach also had a pedagogical aim, as is true for several of his other collections. The title page reads "Little Organ Book, in which a beginning organist is given guidance in all sorts of ways of developing a chorale, as well as improving his pedal technique, since in these chorales the pedal is treated as completely obbligato [essential, not optional]." In each prelude, the chorale tune is heard once through, but otherwise the settings vary

Example 19.1: Opening and fugue subject from Bach, Prelude and Fugue in A Minor, BWV 543

a. Opening of prelude

b. Fugue subject

greatly. The melody may be treated in canon, elaborately ornamented, or accompanied in any number of styles. Some preludes symbolize the visual images or underlying ideas of the chorale text through musical figures, in a tradition extending back through Schütz to the Italian madrigalists. In *Durch Adams Fall* (Through Adam's fall), BWV 637 (NAWM 89b), shown in Example 19.2, while the top line carries the chorale tune, jagged descending leaps in the bass depict Adam's fall from grace, the twisting chromatic line in the alto portrays the sinuous writhing of the serpent, and the downward-sliding tenor combines with both to suggest the pull of temptation and the sorrow of sin.

CD 6|49

Example 19.2: Bach, chorale prelude on Durch Adams Fall

Bach conceived his later organ chorales in grander proportions. The settings are less intimate and subjective, replacing the vivid expressive details of the earlier works with a purely musical development of ideas.

HARPSICHORD MUSIC

Bach's music for harpsichord includes masterpieces in every current genre, including suites; preludes, fantasias, and toccatas; fugues; and variation sets.

Bach's harpsichord suites show the influence of French, Italian, and German models. He wrote three sets of six: the *English Suites*, the *French Suites*, and the Partitas. The designations "French" and "English" for the suites are

Suites

not Bach's own, and both collections blend French and Italian qualities in a highly personal style. In line with German tradition, each suite contains the standard four dance movements—allemande, courante, sarabande, and gigue—with additional short movements following the sarabande. Each of the *English Suites* opens with a prelude, in which Bach transferred Italian ensemble idioms to the keyboard. The prelude of the third *English Suite*, for example, simulates a concerto fast movement with alternating tutti and solo.

Well-Tempered Clavier   The best known of Bach's keyboard works are the two books titled the *Well-Tempered Clavier* (1722 and ca. 1740). Each book consists of twenty-four prelude and fugue pairs, one in each of the major and minor keys, arranged in rising chromatic order from C to B. Both sets were designed to demonstrate the possibilities of playing in all keys on an instrument tuned in near-equal temperament, then still novel for keyboards. Bach adapted several pieces in both books from existing works, sometimes transposing them in order to cover unusual keys.

But Bach had pedagogical aims as well. The typical prelude assigns the player a specific technical task, so that the piece functions as an étude. In addition, the preludes illustrate different types of keyboard performance conventions and compositional practices. For example, Nos. 2 and 21 of Book I are toccatas, No. 8 a sonata slow movement, No. 17 a concerto fast movement, and No. 24 a trio sonata. The fugues constitute a compendium of fugal writing, from two to five voices and from an archaic ricercare in Book I, No. 4 in C♯ minor, to techniques of inversion, canon, and augmentation in No. 8 in D♯ minor. As in the organ fugues, each subject has a clearly defined musical personality that unfolds throughout the entire fugue.

Goldberg Variations   Variety also marks the *Goldberg Variations* (1741), which raised the genre of keyboard variations to a new level of artfulness. All thirty variations preserve the bass and harmonic structure of the theme, a sarabande. Every third variation is a canon, the first at the interval of a unison, the second at a second, and so on through the ninth. The last variation is a **quodlibet,** combining two popular-song melodies in counterpoint above the bass of the theme. The non-canonic variations take many forms, including fugue, French overture, slow aria, and bravura pieces for two manuals. The result is a unique piece that draws on many existing types, like a summation of the music of his time.

Musical Offering *and* Art of Fugue   The systematic, comprehensive approach shown in the *Goldberg Variations* is evident in many of Bach's works. He often wrote several pieces of the same type in a short time, like the chorale preludes of the *Orgelbüchlein*, or sought to work out all the possibilities of a genre, technique, or idea, as in the preludes and fugues of the *Well-Tempered Clavier*. This systematic tendency is clear in two unusual works from his last years. *A Musical Offering* contains a three- and a six-part ricercare for keyboard and ten canons, all based on a theme proposed by Frederick the Great of Prussia and shown in Example 19.3. Bach improvised on the theme while visiting the king at Potsdam in 1747 and then revised and wrote out his improvisations. He added a trio sonata for flute (Frederick's instrument), violin, and continuo, in which the theme also appears, had the set printed, and dedicated it to the king. The *Art of Fugue*, composed in the final decade of Bach's life, systematically demonstrates all types of fugal writing. Written in score though intended for keyboard performance, it consists of eighteen canons and fugues in the strictest style, all based on the subject in Example 19.4 or one of its transformations, and arranged in a general order of increasing complexity. The last fugue, left incomplete at Bach's death, has four subjects, including one spelling Bach's name: B♭-A-C-B♮, or B-A-C-H in German nomenclature, B and H being the German terms for B♭ and B♮, respectively.

Example 19.3: Bach, theme from A Musical Offering

Example 19.4: Bach, theme from Art of Fugue

CHAMBER MUSIC

Bach's chief compositions for chamber ensemble are fifteen sonatas for solo instruments and harpsichord: six each for violin and flute, and three for viola da gamba. Most have four movements in slow–fast–slow–fast order, like the sonata da chiesa. Indeed, most are virtual trio sonatas, since the right-hand harpsichord part is often written out as a melodic line in counterpoint with the other instrument. These are now believed to be products of Bach's Leipzig years, when he directed the collegium musicum.

Bach's six sonatas and partitas for violin alone, six suites for cello alone, and partita for solo flute are unusual, although not unprecedented, in featuring melody instruments without accompaniment. In these works, Bach created the illusion of a harmonic and contrapuntal texture by requiring the performer to play several strings at once or jump between registers.

Works for unaccompanied instruments

ORCHESTRAL MUSIC

Bach's best-known orchestral works are the six *Brandenburg Concertos*, dedicated in 1721 to the Margrave of Brandenburg—who had requested some pieces—but composed during the previous ten or so years. For all but the first, Bach adopted the three-movement, fast–slow–fast order of the Italian concerto, as well as its triadic themes, steady driving rhythms, ritornello forms, and overall style. The Third and Sixth are orchestral concertos without featured soloists, and the others pit solo instruments in various combinations against the body of strings and continuo. In typical Bach fashion, he also expanded on his model, introducing more ritornello material into the episodes, featuring dialogue between soloists and orchestra within episodes, and enlarging the form with devices such as the astonishing long cadenza for the harpsichord (normally a continuo instrument!) in the Fifth Concerto.

Brandenburg Concertos

Most of Bach's other orchestral music was written in the 1730s when he directed the Leipzig collegium musicum, which was made up mostly of

Collegium musicum

Figure 19.6: Outdoor concert by the collegium musicum of the University of Jena in the 1740s. Bach led a similar group in Leipzig in the 1730s.

university students. By the early eighteenth century, such organizations often presented public concerts, like the outdoor concert shown in Figure 19.6; Leipzig's collegium had done so since its founding by Telemann in 1704. Bach apparently wrote his two violin concertos and Concerto in D Minor for Two Violins for such concerts. He was one of the first to write—or arrange—concertos for one or more harpsichords and orchestra, which he no doubt led in performance from the keyboard. The concerto for four harpsichords and orchestra is an arrangement of a Vivaldi concerto for four violins, and most or all of the others are arrangements of concertos by Bach or perhaps by other composers. Bach also wrote four orchestral suites, once again balancing Italian influences with French ones.

CANTATAS

In 1700, Lutheran theologian and poet Erdmann Neumeister (1671–1756) introduced a new kind of sacred work for musical setting which he called by the Italian term *cantata*. Throughout the seventeenth century, Lutheran composers had set biblical, liturgical, and chorale texts. Neumeister added poetic texts, intended to be set as recitatives, arias, and ariosos, that brought home the meaning of the day's Gospel reading. The new church cantata found widespread acceptance among Lutherans. Its poetry brought together their faith's Orthodox and Pietistic tendencies, blending objective and subjective as well as formal and emotional elements. Its musical scheme incorporated all the great traditions of the past—the chorale, the solo song, the concerted medium—and added to these the dramatically powerful elements of operatic recitative and aria. Although Bach set only five of Neumeister's texts, many of his cantatas follow a similar format.

The church cantata figured prominently in the Lutheran liturgy of Leipzig. At the two main churches, St. Nicholas's and St. Thomas's, the principal Sunday service included a motet, a Kyrie, chorales, and a cantata on alternate Sundays (see Source Reading). Bach directed the first choir, with the best singers, at the church whose turn it was to hear the cantata, while a deputy conducted the second choir at the other important church. The third and fourth choirs, made up of the less experienced singers, took care of the modest musical requirements in the two remaining churches. A 1730 memorandum from Bach to the town council set the ideal minimum requirements as twelve singers for each of the first three choirs, which sang polyphonic music, and eight for the fourth choir, which sang only monophonic chants. For the cantatas, he specified a soloist and two or three *ripienists* (from the Italian *ripieno*, "full") for each voice part (soprano, alto, tenor, and bass); the soloists sang the solo movements and were joined by the ripienists on the choral movements. Surviving performing parts suggest that at least in some cases Bach made do with only four or eight singers total. The orchestra that accompanied the cantata included strings with continuo, two or three oboes, and one or two bassoons, sometimes augmented with flutes or, on festive occasions, trumpets and timpani.

Role in church services

SOURCE READING

MUSIC IN LUTHERAN CHURCH SERVICES

In his first year as cantor and music director in Leipzig, Bach wrote out the order of events, particularly the musical ones, for the main morning service on the first Sunday in Advent. The main musical item was the cantata, which Bach refers to here as "the principal composition." The subject for the cantata was usually linked to the Gospel reading that immediately preceded it, and the sermon would often be on a similar theme. The choir also sang a motet and the Kyrie, the congregation sang chorales, and each musical item was preceded by a prelude, often improvised, on the organ.

— • —

1) Preluding
2) Motet
3) Preluding on the Kyrie, which is performed throughout in concerted manner
4) Intoning before the altar
5) Reading of the Epistle
6) Singing of the Litany

7) Preluding on [and singing of] the Chorale
8) Reading of the Gospel
9) Preluding on [and performance of] the principal composition [cantata]
10) Singing of the Creed [Luther's Credo hymn]
11) The Sermon
12) After the Sermon, as usual, singing of several verses of a hymn
13) Words of Institution [of the Sacrament]
14) Preluding on [and performance of] the composition [probably the second part of the cantata]. After the same, alternate preluding and singing of chorales until the end of the Communion, *et sic porrò* [and so on].

From *The New Bach Reader: A Life of Johann Sebastian Bach in Letters and Documents*, ed. Hans T. David and Arthur Mendel, rev. and enl. by Christoph Wolff (New York: Norton, 1998), 113.

Cantata cycles

Altogether, the Leipzig churches required fifty-eight cantatas each year, in addition to Passion music for Good Friday, Magnificats at Vespers for three festivals, an annual cantata for the installation of the city council, and occasional music such as funeral motets and wedding cantatas. Between 1723 and 1729 Bach composed at least three and possibly four complete annual cycles of about sixty cantatas each. Cantatas written during the 1730s and early 1740s may be part of a fifth cycle, but if so, many of these and of the fourth cycle have not survived. Approximately two hundred of his church cantatas have been preserved, most newly written for Leipzig, others for earlier positions at Mühlhausen or Weimar. In addition, we have about twenty secular cantatas written at Cöthen and Leipzig to celebrate birthdays of his patrons or other festive events. Since these typically could be performed only on a single occasion, Bach often reused the music for church cantatas, as shown in Figure 19.7.

Chorale cantatas

CD 6|50–64   CD 3|38

Although no single example can suggest the breadth and variety of Bach's cantatas, *Nun komm, der Heiden Heiland*, BWV 62 (NAWM 90), composed in 1724 for the first Sunday in Advent, illustrates some of his typical procedures. This work was part of his second cycle for Leipzig, which consisted of cantatas whose words and music were based on chorales. The unknown poet who wrote the texts of these cantatas used the first and last stanzas of a chorale for the opening and closing choruses and paraphrased the middle stanzas in poetry suitable for recitatives and arias. Bach then based the opening chorus on the chorale melody, ended the work with a simple four-part harmonization of the chorale for its closing stanza, and set the middle movements as recitatives and arias in operatic style for the soloists, with few if any references to the

Figure 19.7: Bach's autograph manuscript of the serenata (or secular cantata) Durchlauchtster Leopold *(Most Serene Highness Leopold), BWV 173a, written for the birthday of his patron, the prince of Anhalt-Cöthen, probably in 1722. Bach soon reused the music for his church cantata* Erhöhtes Fleisch und Blut *(Exalted Flesh and Blood), BWV 173, adding the new text beneath the original words. In the third through fifth measures, he also revised the vocal melody to better suit the revamped text and the new singer.*

chorale melody. For this cantata, Bach and the librettist used Luther's Advent chorale *Nun komm, der Heiden Heiland* (see NAWM 42b and Example 10.1b).

As we often find in Bach's choral works, the opening chorus displays an ingenious mixture of genres—here, concerto and chorale motet. The orchestra begins with a sprightly ritornello that would be at home in a Vivaldi concerto, yet features the chorale as a cantus firmus in the bass, as shown in Example 19.5. Repeated rising figures evoke the sense of welcome and anticipation in the chorale's text, which heralds the coming of the Saviour. As in a concerto, this ritornello serves as a frame for the movement, recurring three times in shortened or transposed form before its full reprise in the tonic at the end. But instead of episodes, Bach presents the four phrases of the chorale in the chorus, set in cantus-firmus style; the sopranos, doubled by the horns, sing

Example 19.5: Bach, opening ritornello of Nun komm, der Heiden Heiland, *BWV 62*

each phrase in long notes above imitative counterpoint in the other three parts, while the orchestra continues to develop motives from the ritornello. The first and fourth phrases are preceded by the lower voices in a point of imitation based on the chorale. Example 19.6 shows the fore-imitation and subsequent soprano entrance for the first chorale phrase. The mixture of secular and sacred models, and of old-style counterpoint and cantus firmus with modern Italianate style, is characteristic of Bach, creating a depth of meanings through references to many familiar types of music.

The four solo movements set sacred texts in operatic idioms. A da capo aria for tenor muses on the mystery of the incarnation; as if to show Jesus's humanity, Bach wrote the aria in minuet style with predominantly four-measure phrasing, evoking the physical body through dance. Next are a recitative and aria for bass, praising the Saviour as a hero who conquers evil. The recitative includes word-painting, such as a run on "laufen" (run). The aria follows the operatic conventions for heroic or martial arias, with the orchestra playing in octaves throughout, and the figuration emphasizing rapid motions, large leaps, and jumping arpeggios. The soprano and alto join in an accompanied recitative, moving in sweet parallel thirds and sixths as they express awe at the nativity scene. The closing chorale verse is a doxology, praising Father, Son, and Holy Spirit.

OTHER CHURCH MUSIC

Bach's church music was not confined to cantatas but included motets, Passions, and Latin service music. Most important are his Passions and Mass in B Minor.

Passions   Bach wrote two surviving Passions, telling the story of Jesus' crucifixion, for performance at Vespers on Good Friday in Leipzig. Both the *St. John Passion* (1724, later revised), based on the account of John 18–19, and the *St. Matthew Passion* (1727, revised 1736), on Matthew 26–27, employ recitatives, arias, ensembles, choruses, chorales sung by the chorus, and orchestral accompaniment. This type of setting, drawing on elements from opera, cantata, and oratorios, had replaced the older type composed by Schütz and others, which combined plainsong narration with polyphony (see chapter 15). In both Passions, a tenor narrates the biblical story in recitative, soloists play the parts of Jesus and other figures, and the chorus sings the words of the disciples, the crowd, and other groups. At other times the chorus comments on events, like the chorus in a Greek drama. The interpolated recitatives, ariosos, and arias serve a similar purpose, reflecting on the story and relating its meaning to the individual worshiper.

Although now performed as works for large choir and orchestra, recent research on the performance parts suggests that Bach's Passions were intended for just four solo and four ripieno singers, who divided the roles among them and joined together for the choral movements.

Mass in B Minor   Bach assembled the Mass in B Minor, his only complete setting of the Catholic Mass Ordinary, between 1747 and 1749. He drew most of it from music he had composed much earlier. He had already presented the Kyrie and Gloria in 1733 to the Catholic elector of Saxony, in hopes of getting an honorary

Example 19.6: Entrance of the first phrase of the chorale

a. Fore-imitation in other parts

b. Cantus firmus in soprano

Now come, Savior of the heathens

appointment to the electoral chapel, which he did receive three years later. The Sanctus was first performed on Christmas Day 1724. He adapted some of the other sections from cantata movements composed between 1714 and 1735, replacing the German text with the Latin words of the Mass and reworking the music. Of the newly composed sections, the opening of the Credo and the *Confiteor* (a later passage of the Credo) are in *stile antico*, the *Et incarnatus* (also in the Credo) and *Benedictus* (from the Sanctus) in modern styles.

Throughout the work, he juxtaposed contrasting styles, making the Mass in B Minor a compendium of approaches to church music. Since the mass was never performed as a whole during Bach's lifetime, and is too long to function well as service music, he may have intended it as an anthology of movements, each a model of its type, that could be performed separately. As a collection of exemplary works, the Mass in B Minor stands with the *Well-Tempered Clavier*, *Art of Fugue*, and *Musical Offering* as witness to Bach's desire to create comprehensive cycles that explore the furthest potential of a medium or genre.

BACH'S SYNTHESIS

Bach absorbed into his works all the genres, styles, and forms of his time and developed hitherto unsuspected potentialities in them. In his music, the

---

SOURCE READING

A CRITIQUE OF BACH'S STYLE

The composer and critic Johann Adolph Scheibe (1708–1776) considered Bach unsurpassable as an organist and keyboard composer. However, he found much of the rest of Bach's music overly elaborate and confused, preferring the more tuneful and straightforward styles of younger composers such as Johann Adolph Hasse (see chapter 20). Scheibe's critique is only one volley in the long argument between advocates of Baroque style and partisans of the new galant style.

——— • ———

This great man would be the admiration of whole nations if he had more amenity, if he did not take away the natural element in his pieces by giving them a turgid and confused style, and if he did not darken their beauty by an excess of art. Since he judges according to his own fingers, his pieces are extremely difficult to play; for he demands that singers and instrumentalists should be able to do with their throats and instruments whatever he can play

on the clavier. But this is impossible. Every ornament, every little grace, and everything that one thinks of as belonging to the method of playing, he expresses completely in notes; and this not only takes away from his pieces the beauty of harmony but completely covers the melody throughout. All the voices must work with each other and be of equal difficulty, and none of them can be recognized as the principal voice. In short, he is in music what Mr. von Lohenstein was in poetry. Turgidity has led them both from the natural to the artificial, and from the lofty to the somber; and in both one admires the onerous labor and uncommon effort—which, however, are vainly employed, since they conflict with Nature.

From an anonymous letter by "an able traveling musician" published in Scheibe's periodical review, *Der critische Musikus*, May 14, 1737, translated in *The New Bach Reader*, ed. Hans T. David and Arthur Mendel, rev. and enl. by Christoph Wolff (New York: Norton, 1998), 338.

often conflicting demands of harmony and counterpoint, of melody and polyphony, reach a tense but satisfying equilibrium. Many qualities give his works deep and lasting appeal: concentrated and distinctive themes, copious musical invention, balance between harmonic and contrapuntal forces, strong rhythmic drive, clarity of form, grand proportions, imaginative use of pictorial and symbolic figures, intensity of expression always controlled by a ruling architectural idea, and careful attention to every detail.

This recipe was too rich for some of his contemporaries, who preferred less complex, more tuneful music (see Source Reading). Throughout the 1720s and 1730s, the very decades during which Bach composed some of his most important works, the new style emanating from the opera houses of Italy invaded Germany and the rest of Europe (see chapter 20), making Bach's music seem old-fashioned. Never entirely forgotten, he was rediscovered and achieved enormous popularity in the nineteenth century, when music that could please both amateurs and connoisseurs and could keep its appeal through many performances was highly prized. Perhaps only a composer who spent most of his life teaching, wrote excellent music for students at every level from beginning to advanced, worked in positions that constantly demanded new music for immediate performance, embraced a wide variety of genres and approaches, and aspired to explore all the possibilities of every kind of music he encountered, could achieve the central position Bach now occupies in the Western musical tradition.

GEORGE FRIDERIC HANDEL

Compared to Vivaldi, Rameau, and Bach, who rarely traveled outside their countries, George Frideric Handel (1685–1759) moved comfortably among German-, Italian-, and English-speaking cities (see biography and Figure 19.8). His German music teacher gave him a thorough education in organ, harpsichord, counterpoint, and current German and Italian idioms. As a young man, three years at the Hamburg opera house and four years in Italy helped to lay the foundations of his style. He matured as a composer in England, the country then most hospitable to foreign composers. Moreover, England provided the choral tradition that made Handel's oratorios possible. Vivaldi's influence on the musical world was immediate, although he died almost totally forgotten; Rameau's was felt more slowly, and then mainly in the fields of opera and music theory; and Bach's work lay in comparative obscurity until the nineteenth century. But Handel won international renown during his lifetime, and his music has been performed ever since, making him the first composer whose music has never ceased to be performed.

Handel's music was enormously popular. When his *Music for the Royal Fireworks* was given a public rehearsal in 1749, it attracted an audience of over 12,000 people and stopped traffic in London for three hours. How could a composer gain such popularity, and why should it be Handel? The answer to the first question is that for virtually the first time, a composer was working for the public—not just for a church, a court, or a town council—and it is the public that bestows popularity. And why Handel? He was supremely adaptable, able to measure and serve the taste of the public. He could do this because of his cosmopolitan and eclectic style, drawing on German, Italian, French, and English music.

HANDEL AND HIS PATRONS

Although Handel achieved his greatest fame writing music for public performance, he was no freelancer. From his early years in Italy to the end of his life, he enjoyed the generous support of patrons. Their wishes often determined what he composed, yet their support also allowed him freedom to write operas and oratorios for the public.

GEORGE FRIDERIC HANDEL
[GEORG FRIEDERICH HÄNDEL] (1685–1759)

Handel, recognized since his own time as one of the greatest composers of his era, was a master of all types of vocal and instrumental music. He is best known for his

Figure 19.8: George Frideric Handel at his composing desk, in a portrait by Philippe Mercier.

English oratorios, a genre he invented, and for his Italian operas.

Handel was born in Halle, Germany, the son of a barber-surgeon at the local court. His father wanted him to study law, but he practiced music secretly. His organ playing at the age of nine impressed the duke, who persuaded Handel's father to let him study with Friedrich Wilhelm Zachow, composer, organist, and church music director in Halle. Under Zachow, Handel became an accomplished organist and harpsichordist, studied violin and oboe, mastered counterpoint, and learned the music of German and Italian composers by copying their scores. He entered the University of Halle in 1702 and was appointed cathedral organist. The following year, he abandoned the cantor's career for which Zachow had prepared him and instead moved to Hamburg, the center for German opera. There he played violin in the opera house orchestra and wrote his own first opera, *Almira*, performed with great success in 1705, when Handel was just twenty.

The following year, Handel traveled to Italy at the invitation of Prince Fernando de' Medici. Winning recognition as a promising

In Italy, Handel's chief patron was Marquis Francesco Ruspoli, who employed the young musician as keyboard player and composer in Rome and at his country estate. There Handel wrote Latin motets for church performance and numerous chamber cantatas for Ruspoli's weekly private music-making.

Hired in 1710 as court music director for the elector of Hanover in north central Germany, Handel used the position to establish himself in London. This is less odd than it seems: the elector was heir to the British throne, and the incumbent, Queen Anne, was in precarious health, so it was only a matter of time before Handel's patron would be in England himself. Handel spent the 1710–11 season in London, drawing his Hanover salary while he wrote *Rinaldo* for the Queen's Theatre, the new public opera house. When he came to London a second time in 1712, he found a supportive patron in the earl of

young composer, he associated with the leading patrons and musicians of Florence, Rome, Naples, and Venice. While in Italy, Handel wrote a large number of Italian cantatas, two oratorios, several Latin motets, and the operas *Rodrigo* (1707) for Florence and *Agrippina* (1709) for Venice.

Following a brief period at the court in Hanover, Germany, Handel spent the rest of his life in London, where he served numerous aristocratic patrons and enjoyed the lifelong support of the British royal family. In the 1730s, after three decades of writing Italian operas for the London theaters, Handel turned to oratorios in English, mostly on sacred subjects. He also published a considerable amount of instrumental music, from solo and trio sonatas to concertos and orchestral suites, including *Water Music* and *Royal Fireworks.*

Handel never married. In Italy and London, he lived with various patrons until 1723, when he leased a house in an upper-class neighborhood where he stayed the rest of his life. There were rumors of brief affairs with sopranos, but none has been substantiated. Recently, scholars have noted that several of his patrons moved in social circles where same-sex desire was common, and that the texts of the cantatas Handel wrote for these patrons often allude to love between men in coded terms. Whether Handel himself had intimate relationships with anyone of either sex remains open to question.

Handel's imperious, independent nature made him a formidable presence, but the rougher sides of his personality were balanced by a sense of humor and redeemed by a generous and honorable approach to life. Experiencing both successes and failures, criticism as well as praise, Handel suffered physical ailments as he aged, notably a paralytic stroke in 1737 (from which he recovered) and cataracts in his final years. By the end of his life he ranked as one of the most revered figures in London, and some three thousand people attended his funeral at Westminster Abbey.

MAJOR WORKS: Messiah, Saul, Samson, Israel in Egypt, *and about 20 other oratorios;* Giulio Cesare *and about 40 other Italian operas; numerous odes, anthems, and other sacred vocal music; about 100 Italian cantatas; about 45 concertos, 20 trio sonatas, 20 solo sonatas, numerous keyboard pieces, and the well-known* Water Music *and* Music for the Royal Fireworks

Burlington, in whose house he lived and for whom he wrote Italian cantatas and other works. Later, in 1717–19, he served a similar role for James Brydges, earl of Carnarvon, later duke of Chandos, composing during that period the large-scale Chandos Anthems for church services.

Handel's most important patrons were the British monarchs. In 1713, Queen Anne commissioned several ceremonial choral works, including a *Te Deum* and *Ode for Queen Anne's Birthday*, for which Handel took Purcell's compositions as his model. The Queen granted Handel a pension of £200 a year (roughly twice what Bach made in Leipzig). After she died in 1714 and the elector of Hanover was crowned King George I, he doubled Handel's pension to £400. George's daughter-in-law, the future Queen Caroline, increased it to £600 around 1724, when Handel undertook the musical education of her daughters. For the rest of his life, Handel could depend on this sizable income despite minimal responsibilities, a situation that contrasted with Bach's. In 1723, he won honorary appointment as composer to the Chapel Royal. He continued to supply music for important state occasions; for the coronation of King George II in 1727 he wrote four splendid anthems, including *Zadok the Priest*, performed at every British coronation since then. But while he was closely identified with the royal house, most of his activities were in the public sphere, writing and producing operas and later oratorios and composing for publication.

THE OPERAS

Handel devoted thirty-six years to composing and directing operas, which contain much of his best music. In an age when opera was the main concern of ambitious musicians, Handel excelled among his contemporaries.

International style   Handel's blending of national styles is evident from his first opera, *Almira* (1705), written for Hamburg when he was nineteen. He kept to the local fashion of setting the arias in Italian and the recitatives in German, so the audience could follow the plot. Imitating Reinhard Keiser, the dominant opera composer in Hamburg, Handel patterned the overture and dance music after French models, composed most of the arias in the Italian manner, and incorporated German elements in the counterpoint and orchestration. In Italy, he learned from Scarlatti's cantatas and operas how to create supple, long-breathed, rhythmically varied melodies that seem naturally suited for the voice, amply demonstrated in Handel's *Agrippina* (Venice, 1709). Ever after, his operatic style was uniquely international, combining French overtures and dances, Italianate arias and recitatives, and German traits, notably the tendency to double the vocal line with one or more instruments.

London operas   Handel's *Rinaldo* (1711) was the first Italian opera composed for London. Its brilliant music and elaborate stage effects made it a sensation and helped establish Handel's public reputation in England. The arias were published by John Walsh, bringing Handel additional revenue. He wrote four more operas in the 1710s, and with revivals of *Rinaldo*, a Handel opera was staged almost every season.

Royal Academy of Music   In 1718–19, about sixty wealthy gentlemen, with the support of the king, established a joint stock company for producing Italian operas. They called it

Figure 19.9: Entryway to the King's Theatre in London, where most of Handel's operas were performed. From the entrance, stairs led upward to the lobby of a sumptuous auditorium, many times larger than one might expect from this street view. Engraving from ca. 1780.

the Royal Academy of Music. The operas were staged at the King's Theatre in the Haymarket, shown in Figure 19.9. Handel was engaged as the music director. He traveled to Germany to recruit singers, mostly Italians performing in Dresden and other courts. Perhaps his biggest catch was the arrogant but widely celebrated castrato Senesino. Giovanni Bononcini (1670–1747) was brought from Rome to compose operas and to play in the orchestra. Later, the eminent sopranos Francesca Cuzzoni (1696–1778) and Faustina Bordoni (1697–1781) joined the group. For this company, which flourished from 1720 to 1728, Handel composed some of his best operas, including *Radamisto* (1720), *Ottone* (1723), *Giulio Cesare* (Julius Caesar, 1724), *Rodelinda* (1725), and *Admeto* (1727). The subjects of Handel's operas were the usual ones of the time: episodes from the lives of Roman heroes freely adapted to include the maximum number of intense dramatic situations, or tales of magic and marvelous adventure revolving around the Crusades.

The action developed through dialogue rendered in the two distinct types of recitative that emerged in Italian opera in the early eighteenth century. One type, accompanied only by basso continuo, set stretches of dialogue or monologue in as speechlike a fashion as possible (as in the Scarlatti recitative in Example 17.1a). It would later be called *recitativo semplice*, or **simple recitative**, and eventually *recitativo secco* (dry recitative). The other type, called *recitativo obbligato* and later *recitativo accompagnato*, or **accompanied recitative**, used stirring and impressive orchestral outbursts to dramatize tense situations (see Example 19.8 below). These interjections reinforced the rapid changes of emotion in the dialogue and punctuated the singer's phrases.

Recitative styles

Arias   Solo da capo arias allowed the characters to respond lyrically to their situations. Each aria represented a single specific mood or affection, or sometimes two contrasting but related affections in the A and B sections. At the singers' insistence, the arias had to be allocated according to the importance of each member of the cast and had to display the scope of each singer's vocal and dramatic powers. The **prima donna** ("first lady"), the soprano singing the leading female role, normally demanded the most and the best arias (hence the modern meaning of that phrase). Handel wrote for specific singers, seeking to show off their abilities to the best advantage.

Handel's scores are remarkable for the wide variety of aria types. They range from brilliant displays of florid ornamentation, known as **coloratura,** to sustained, sublimely expressive pathetic songs, such as *Se pietà* in *Giulio Cesare.* Arias of regal grandeur with rich contrapuntal and concertato accompaniments contrast with arias whose simple, folklike melodies suggest the French or German air. The pastoral scenes are noteworthy examples of eighteenth-century nature painting. Some arias feature the tone-color of a particular instrument to set the mood, as the French horn does in Caesar's aria *Va tacito e nascosto* from *Giulio Cesare* in which both voice and instrument imitate a hunting horn.

Instrumental   In several operas, Handel used instrumental sinfonias to mark key mo-
sections   ments in the plot such as battles, ceremonies, or incantations, and a few of his operas include ballets. The orchestra is usually fuller than for Scarlatti operas, with more use of winds, as in French operas. Vocal ensembles larger than duets are rare, as are choruses.

Scene complexes   One or both types of recitative are sometimes freely combined with arias, ariosos, and orchestral passages to make larger scene complexes that recall the freedom of Monteverdi's operas and foreshadow the methods of later composers such as Gluck (see chapter 20). Instead of presenting the plot in recitative, then the aria with orchestral ritornello as a static moment, Handel interleaves these elements so that the plot continues to move forward. In

[CD 6|65–68] [CD 3|46]

Giulio Cesare, Act II, scenes 1–2 (NAWM 91), after dialogue in simple recitative, Cleopatra's da capo aria *V'adoro pupille* is interwoven with other elements. Caesar has been brought to a grove where he overhears Cleopatra singing. An orchestral sinfonia, essentially the opening ritornello, introduces the aria's principal motive. From his hiding place, Caesar unexpectedly breaks in, expressing awe in a brief recitative. Cleopatra sings the first and middle sections of the aria, then stops; transfixed, Caesar again comments in recitative, wondering at the beauty of the song. Only then does Cleopatra take up the repetition of the A section, now not just a conventional formal device but something more profound, as we know of Caesar's entrancement.

Throughout the opera, Handel's characteristic combination of national elements is apparent. Cleopatra's aria, shown in Example 19.7, is in French sarabande rhythm, arousing the associations that dance carried with dignity, love, and seduction. Yet the da capo form of the aria is Italian, the voice is doubled by instruments in the German manner, and the orchestra is divided as in an Italian concerto, with soloists accompanying the voice and the full orchestra offering punctuation.

Handel as   Stressed by rising salaries for the singers and a scandalous dispute be-
impresario   tween the two sopranos Cuzzoni and Bordoni, the Royal Academy dissolved in

Example 19.7: Beginning of V'adoro pupille, *aria from Handel's* Giulio Cesare

1729. Although the collapse has sometimes been linked to the popular success in 1728 of *The Beggar's Opera*, John Gay's English ballad opera (see chapter 20), which satirized opera and the Academy, the main causes were financial. Handel and a partner took over the theater, formed a new company, and had several great successes with Senesino in the major roles. But Senesino found Handel dictatorial; he left in 1733 and soon joined a competing company, the Opera of the Nobility, which featured the Neapolitan composer Nicola Porpora (1686–1768) and the highest-priced singers in Europe. The two companies spent so much on singers and staging and so completely divided the London public that by 1737 both were nearly bankrupt, and the Opera of the

Nobility closed that summer. Although Handel continued to write and produce operas until 1741, none matched his earlier successes.

THE ORATORIOS

In the 1730s, Handel devised a new genre that would reward him as richly as opera had and bring his greatest popularity: the English oratorio. The Italian oratorio was essentially an opera on a sacred subject, presented in concert, usually in a religious building, rather than on stage. Handel had written such a work, *La resurrezione* (The Resurrection, 1708), during his stay in Rome. In his English oratorios, he continued aspects of the Italian tradition by setting dialogue in recitative and lyrical verses as arias. The latter resemble his opera arias in form, style, the nature of musical ideas, and techniques for expressing the affections. But Handel and his librettists brought into their oratorios elements that were foreign to Italian opera, taken from French classical drama, ancient Greek tragedy, the German Passion, and especially the English masque and full anthem.

Use of chorus   Handel's most important innovation in the oratorios was his use of the chorus. Italian oratorios had at most a few ensembles. Handel's experience with choral music led him to give the chorus much more prominence. His early training had made him familiar with Lutheran choral music and with the south German combination of chorus with orchestra and soloists. He was especially influenced by the English choral tradition, which he had absorbed and extended in his Chandos Anthems and works for the Chapel Royal. Thus, in his oratorios, the chorus makes a crucial contribution. It plays a variety of roles, participating in the action, narrating the story, or commenting on events like the chorus in Greek drama. The grand character of his choral style, drawn from the English tradition, fits the oratorio's emphasis on communal rather than individual expression.

In his choruses, Handel was a dramatist, a master of effects. He wrote for chorus in a style simpler and less consistently contrapuntal than Bach's. He alternated passages in open fugal texture with solid blocks of harmony and often set a melodic line in sustained notes against one in quicker rhythm. Everything lies well for the voices, and the orchestra usually reinforces the vocal parts, making his choral music a pleasure to sing—one factor in its enduring popularity.

Saul   Handel's first oratorio in English was *Esther*, revised from a masque of about 1718. Like his operas but unlike oratorios in Italy, Handel's oratorios were usually performed in theaters. *Esther*, which premiered at the King's Theatre in 1732, was the first in a series of oratorios Handel put on in almost every subsequent Lenten season as a way to extend his earnings from opera, which could not be staged during Lent. But the decisive move from opera to oratorio began when subscriptions to the 1738–39 opera season were insufficient, so instead of a new opera, Handel composed the oratorio *Saul* for a three-month season of choral works in early 1739.

CD 6|71–73   CD 3|49   The closing scene of Act II (NAWM 92) illustrates the blending of genres in Handel's oratorios. Saul, king of Israel, sees the young military hero David as a rival. In an accompanied recitative in martial style (NAWM 92a), shown

Example 19.8: Accompanied recitative from Handel's Saul, *Act II, scene 10*

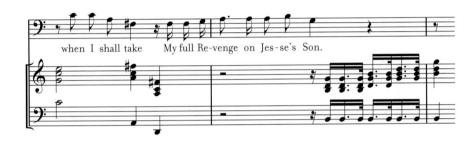

in Example 19.8, Saul resolves to have David killed. Dialogue between Saul and his son Jonathan, David's beloved friend, is rendered in simple recitative (NAWM 92b). After these two numbers in styles borrowed from opera, Handel presents not an aria, but a chorus that reflects on the morality of the situation: *O fatal Consequence of Rage* (NAWM 92c). It comprises a series of three fugues, each ending with a majestic homorhythmic passage, as illustrated in Example 19.9. In typical Handelian style, the chorus is filled with rhetorical figures that convey the meaning of the text. Here the falling tritone to express sorrow in the opening fugue subject and the use of rapid repeated notes to express rage both recall techniques first introduced by Monteverdi (see chapter 14).

CD 6|72   CD 3|50

CD 6|73   CD 3|51

Saul was well received, but Handel continued to compose and produce operas. He committed himself fully to the new genre only after remarkable success during the winter of 1741–42 with a series of oratorios and other concerts in Dublin, Ireland. The trip culminated in performances of a new oratorio, *Messiah* (1741), which would become Handel's most famous work. Its libretto is unusual: instead of telling a story, it unfolds as a series of contemplations on the Christian idea of redemption using texts drawn from the Bible, beginning with Old Testament prophecies and going through the life of Christ to his resurrection. However, the music of *Messiah* is typical of Handel, full of his characteristic charm, immediate appeal, and mixture of traditions, from the French overture to the Italianate recitatives and da capo arias, the Germanic choral fugues, and the English choral anthem style.

Messiah

Handel and a collaborator leased a theater in London to present oratorios every year during Lent. As an added attraction at these performances, the composer played an organ concerto or improvised at the organ during intermissions. Figure 19.10 on page 468 shows a contemporary sketch of an oratorio performance, perhaps led by Handel, with a chorus and orchestra each

Performing oratorios

numbering about twenty. Oratorios needed no staging or costumes and could use English singers, who were a good deal less expensive than Italian ones, so it was much easier to turn a profit. Oratorios also appealed to a potentially large middle-class public that had never felt at home with the aristocratic entertainment of opera in Italian. The English public's enthusiastic response to these concerts laid the foundation for the immense popularity that made Handel's music the prevailing influence in British musical life for more than a century.

Example 19.9: Excerpts from closing chorus of Saul, *Act II*

a. Opening fugue

b. Homophonic passage that ends the first section

Oratorios were not church music; they were intended for the concert hall and were much closer to theatrical performances than to church services—indeed, *Messiah* was advertised as a "sacred entertainment." But stories from the Hebrew Bible and Apocryphal books were well known to middle-class Protestant listeners, much more so than the historical or mythological plots of Italian opera, so most of Handel's oratorios were based on the Jewish Scriptures. Moreover, such subjects as *Saul, Israel in Egypt* (1739), *Judas Maccabaeus* (1747), and *Joshua* (1748) had an appeal based on something beyond familiarity with the ancient sacred narratives: in an era of prosperity and expanding empire, English audiences felt a kinship with what they saw as the chosen people whose heroes triumphed with the special blessing of God.

Librettos

We have seen that Bach often borrowed and reworked music by himself or by other composers. This practice was common at the time, but Handel borrowed more than most. Three duets and eleven of the twenty-eight choruses of *Israel in Egypt*, for example, were taken in whole or in part from the music of others, while four choruses were arrangements from earlier works by

Borrowing and reworking

Figure 19.10: Drawing of an oratorio performance in London around the middle of the eighteenth century, showing about twenty singers and some twenty instrumentalists. Handel may be the figure on the right or the player at the harpsichord.

Handel himself. When such instances of borrowing were discovered in the nineteenth century, Handel was charged with plagiarism, because audiences and critics at that time valued originality and demanded original themes. In Handel's time, simply presenting another composer's work as one's own was condemned, but borrowing, transcribing, adapting, rearranging, and parodying were universal and accepted practices. When Handel borrowed, he more often than not repaid with interest, finding new potential in the borrowed material.

Indeed, Handel borrowed from others or reused his own music only when the material was well suited for its new role. As an example, one of the best-known choruses in *Messiah* was adapted from a frivolous Italian duet that Handel had recently composed, but the music is perfect for its new text. The chorus sings, "All we like sheep" as a group, then "have gone astray" as single, diverging melodic lines; "we have turned" is set to a rapidly twisting, turning figure that never gets away from its starting point; and "everyone one to his own way" is rendered with stubborn insistence on a single repeated note. It is hard to imagine that these musical ideas were conceived for any other text, but they were, and the composer's cleverness is revealed in how well he makes them work in the new context. The only new material appears in the last few measures, where the point of the chorus is revealed suddenly, with dramatic force, in a slow, solemn, minor-mode setting of the words "And the Lord hath laid on Him the iniquity of us all."

INSTRUMENTAL WORKS

Although Handel made his reputation with vocal works, he wrote a great deal of instrumental music. Much of it was published by John Walsh in London, earning Handel extra income and keeping his name before the public in their home music-making. There were also unauthorized prints by other publishers, for which Handel received nothing. His keyboard works include two collections of harpsichord suites that contain not only the usual dance movements but also examples of most keyboard genres current at the time. Handel composed some twenty solo sonatas, and almost as many trio sonatas for various instruments. Corelli's influence can be heard in these works, but the sophisticated harmonies and vivacious fast movements reflect a later Italian style.

Ensemble suites

Handel's most popular instrumental works are his two suites for orchestra or winds, both composed for the king and intended for outdoor performance. *Water Music* (1717) contains three suites for winds and strings, played from a boat during a royal procession on the River Thames for the king. *Music for the Royal Fireworks* (1749), for winds (although Handel originally included strings), was composed to accompany fireworks set off in a London park to celebrate the Peace of Aix-la-Chapelle.

Concertos

Handel's concertos mix tradition and innovation but tend toward a retrospective style. His six Concerti Grossi, Op. 3 (published 1734), feature woodwind and string soloists in novel combinations. He invented the concerto for organ and orchestra, which he performed during the intermissions of his oratorios and published in three sets (1738, 1740, and 1761). His most significant concertos are the Twelve Grand Concertos, Op. 6, composed during one month in 1739 and published the next year. Instead of following Vivaldi's model, Handel adopted Corelli's conception of a sonata da chiesa for full orchestra, although he often added a movement or two to the conventional slow–fast–slow–fast pattern. The serious, dignified bearing and the prevailing full contrapuntal texture of these concertos hark back to the early part of the century, when Handel was forming his style in Italy.

HANDEL'S REPUTATION

The English came to regard Handel as a national institution, and with good reason. He passed all his mature life in London, becoming a naturalized British citizen in 1727, and wrote all his major works for British audiences. He was the most imposing figure in English music during his lifetime, and the English public nourished his genius and remained loyal to his memory. When he died in 1759, he was buried with public honors in Westminster Abbey, and three years later his monument, shown in Figure 19.11, was unveiled there.

Handel's music aged well because he adopted the devices that became important in the new style of the mid-eighteenth century. His emphasis on melody, harmony, and contrasting textures, as compared to the more strictly contrapuntal procedures of Bach, allied him with the fashions of his time. As a choral composer in the grand style he had no peer. He was a consummate master of contrast, not only in choral music but in all types of compositions.

In the oratorios he deliberately appealed to a middle-class audience, recognizing social changes that would have far-reaching effects on music. The broad, lasting appeal of his oratorios made some of them the earliest pieces by any composer to enjoy an unbroken tradition of performance down to the present.

AN ENDURING LEGACY

The careers of Bach and Handel were almost as interesting in death as in life. Burial and resurrection describe the history of Bach's music. Only a few pieces were published in his lifetime, almost all for keyboard; the rest remained in handwritten copies. Musical taste changed radically in the mid-eighteenth century, and Bach's work was quickly left behind. Bach's sons Carl Philipp Emanuel Bach and Johann Christian Bach were influenced by him but

Figure 19.11: Handel memorial in Westminster Abbey, London, sculpted by Louis-François Roubiliac. The music shows the soprano aria I know that my Redeemer liveth *from* Messiah.

went their own ways, and for a time their fame eclipsed his. Yet his music was always known to a core of musicians and connoisseurs. Some of the preludes from the *Well-Tempered Clavier* were printed, and the whole collection circulated in manuscript copies. Haydn owned a copy of the Mass in B Minor; Mozart knew the *Art of Fugue* and studied the motets on a visit to Leipzig in 1789. Citations from Bach's works appeared frequently in the musical literature of the time, and the important periodical, the *Allgemeine musikalische Zeitung,* opened its first issue (1798) with a Bach portrait.

A fuller discovery of Bach began in the nineteenth century with the publication of a biography by Johann Nikolaus Forkel in 1802. In part for reasons of nationalism, Bach was promoted by German musicians. The revival of the *St. Matthew Passion* by the composer and conductor Carl Friedrich Zelter and its performance at Berlin under Felix Mendelssohn's direction in 1829 did much to inspire interest in Bach's music. The Bach-Gesellschaft (Bach Society), founded by Robert Schumann and others in 1850 to mark the centenary of Bach's death, published a collected edition of Bach's works, completed by 1900. By the late nineteenth century, Bach had reached godlike status, and his reputation has only increased since then. His music is now everywhere, studied by every student of Western music. When twenty-seven pieces of recorded music representing the world's peoples were placed on Voyager 1 and 2, the first manmade objects to leave the solar system, eight were of European classical music, and (despite the reported objection that "that would be bragging") three of those were by Bach: movements from a *Brandenburg Concerto,* the *Well-Tempered Clavier,* and a violin partita. Composers such as Mozart, Mendelssohn, Schumann, and Brahms have emulated Bach, and he has exercised an enduring influence on modern composers as diverse as Schoenberg and Ives, Bartók and Stravinsky, Villa-Lobos and Webern.

Where Bach was resurrected, Handel never left. Some of his oratorios have been performed continually since they were written. His music was so identified with the British royalty that twenty-five years after the composer's death, King George III sponsored a large Handel festival in 1784, using the public's affection for Handel to rebuild the king's reputation after the recent unpleasantness in the American colonies. In the late eighteenth and nineteenth centuries, amateur choral societies sprang up throughout English- and German-speaking Europe, and Handel's oratorios became the core of their repertory. Through this development, Handel became the first classical composer, the first to attain a permanent place in the performing repertoire. His other music passed from the scene for awhile, then was revived, with his orchestral suites and concertos gaining a broad popularity and works in other genres receiving frequent performances. Finally, Handel's operas are now getting the attention they merit. For many listeners today, Bach and Handel *are* the Baroque.

Chapter 20

Opera and Vocal Music in the Early Classic Period

In the middle decades of the eighteenth century, composers created a new musical language based on songful, **periodic** melodies with light accompaniment. First developed in vocal music, especially comic opera, this new idiom reflected a growing taste for music that was "natural," expressive, and immediately appealing to a wide variety of listeners. It emerged during an era when many types and styles of music coexisted and the merits of each were fiercely debated. This chapter will sketch the social and intellectual background for this new language, describe its central characteristics, and trace its development in opera and vocal music. The next two chapters will examine how composers applied the new idiom to instrumental music, including several new genres and forms, and show how composers such as Haydn and Mozart enriched it with elements of other styles to form what has become known as the classical style.

EUROPE IN THE MID- TO LATE-EIGHTEENTH CENTURY

Eighteenth-century Europe was dominated politically by the great powers, centralized states with large military establishments. In the west, France had succeeded Spain as the dominant force in the seventeenth century but was outclassed in the Seven Years' War (1756–63) by Britain's more powerful navy and more vibrant economy. In central and eastern

Europe, absolutist monarchies in Prussia, Austria-Hungary, and Russia competed for influence and expanded their territories. The smaller states in Italy and Germany maintained their independence as best they could. By the end of the century, revolutions in America and France brought changes that would eventually transform political and social life throughout Europe and the Americas.

Improvements in agriculture boosted food production and made possible a rapid increase in population across Europe and North America. Capitals and other large cities expanded especially rapidly, and growth in manufacturing and trade stimulated the economy in new directions. The urban middle class rose in numbers, wealth, and social prominence, while the landed aristocracy saw their importance diminished. The poor often suffered dislocation from the land and overcrowding in the cities, victims of the very progress that helped the well-born and the lucky.

Economic change

The eighteenth century was a cosmopolitan age. Partly because of marriages between powerful families, foreign-born rulers abounded: German kings in England, Sweden, and Poland; a Spanish king in Naples; a French duke in Tuscany; a German princess (Catherine the Great) as empress of Russia. Intellectuals and artists traveled widely. The Frenchman Voltaire sojourned at the French-speaking court of Frederick II (the Great) of Prussia, the Italian poet Metastasio worked at the German imperial court in Vienna, while the German writer F. M. von Grimm gained prominence in Parisian literary and musical circles. Shared humanity mattered more than national and linguistic differences.

A cosmopolitan society

Musical life reflected this international culture. German orchestral composers were active in Paris and London, and Italian opera composers and singers worked in Austria, Germany, Spain, England, Russia, and France. Johann Joachim Quantz proposed in 1752 that the ideal musical style blended the best features of music from all nations, and by 1785 this mixed style was so universally adopted that, in the words of a French critic, there was only "one music for all of Europe" (see Source Reading). Yet nationalism, a major theme in the nineteenth century, was already beginning to emerge, especially in a growing preference for opera in the vernacular rather than in Italian.

International musical style

THE ENLIGHTENMENT

The most vibrant intellectual movement of the eighteenth century was the Enlightenment. The scientific advances of the previous century led many to believe that people could solve all kinds of problems, including social and practical ones, by reasoning from experience and from careful observation. This approach was now applied to the study of the emotions, social relations, and politics. Belief in natural law led to the notion that individuals had rights and that the role of the state was to improve the human condition. Those who subscribed to the Enlightenment valued individual faith and practical morality over the church, preferred naturalness to artificiality, and promoted universal education and a growing social equality.

The leaders of the Enlightenment were French thinkers such as Voltaire, Montesquieu, and Rousseau. Known as *philosophes*, they were social reformers

The philosophes

more than philosophers. In response to the terrible inequalities between the common people and the privileged classes, the *philosophes* developed doctrines about individual human rights. Some of these doctrines were incorporated into the American Declaration of Independence, Constitution, and Bill of Rights; indeed, Thomas Jefferson, Thomas Paine, Benjamin Franklin, and

SOURCE READINGS

THE MERGING OF NATIONAL STYLES

Throughout the seventeenth and early eighteenth centuries, Italy and France were the leading musical nations, and their distinctive styles were admired and imitated in other countries. But by the mid-eighteenth century, musicians, audiences, and critics increasingly preferred music that mixed national characteristics. Flutist and composer Johann Joachim Quantz (1697–1773), writing in his Essay on Playing the Transverse Flute *(1752), argued that the ideal music blended the best elements of many nations and appealed to the widest audience. He noted that this mixed taste was typical of German composers, and indeed many of the best-known composers of the era were German.*

—— • ——

In a style that consists, like the present German one, of a mix of the styles of different peoples, every nation finds something familiar and unfailingly pleasing. Considering all that has been discussed about the differences among styles, we must vote for the pure Italian style over the pure French. The first is no longer as solidly grounded as it used to be, having become brash and bizarre, and the second has remained too simple. Everyone will therefore agree that a style blending the good elements of both will certainly be more universal and more pleasing. For a music that is accepted and favored by many peoples, and not just by a single land, a single province, or a particular nation, must be the very best, provided it is founded on sound judgment and a healthy attitude.

Johann Joachim Quantz, *Versuch einer Anweisung, die Flöte traversiere zu spielen* (Berlin: J. F. Voss, 1752), Chapter 18, § 89.

—— • ——

Three decades later, French composer and critic Michel-Paul-Guy de Chabanon (ca. 1729–1792) observed that a single musical idiom prevailed throughout Europe. His description of music as a "universal language" resonated through the next two centuries and contributed to the growing prestige of purely instrumental music.

—— • ——

In the [present] state of civilization and mutual communication between all the peoples of Europe, there exists a commerce of the fine arts, of taste, intelligence, and enlightenment which makes the same discoveries, principles, and methods ebb and flow from one end of the continent to the other. In this free circulation, the arts lose something of their *indigenous* character; they alter it by blending it with other foreign characteristics. In this regard Europe might be considered as a mother-land of which all the arts are citizens; they all speak the same language; they all obey the same customs.

In applying what I have just said especially to music, an even more incontestable degree of truth will be found in it. There is no more than one music for all of Europe since France has overthrown the barriers of ignorance and bad taste. This universal language of our continent at the most undergoes some differences in pronunciation from one people to another, which is to say, in the manner of performing music.

From Harry Robert Lyall, "A French Music Aesthetic of the Eighteenth Century: A Translation and Commentary on Michel Paul Gui de Chabanon's *Musique considérée en elle-même et dans ses rapports avec la parole, les langues, la poésie, et la théâtre* " (Ph.D. dissertation, North Texas State University, 1975), 155–56.

other founders of the United States were as representative of the Enlightenment as were their French predecessors.

In general, the Enlightenment was interested in promoting the welfare of humankind. Rulers not only patronized arts and letters, they also promoted social reform. The century's enlightened despots, including Frederick the Great of Prussia, Catherine the Great of Russia, and Holy Roman Emperor Joseph II wanted to expand education and care for the poor. In addition, humanitarian ideals and a longing for universal brotherhood were fundamental to a popular movement known as Freemasonry, the teachings of the secret fraternal order of Masons. Founded in London early in the eighteenth century, it spread rapidly throughout Europe and North America and numbered among its adherents kings (Frederick the Great and Joseph II), statesmen (Washington), poets (Goethe), and composers (Haydn and Mozart). *Humanitarianism*

The pursuit of learning and the love of art and music became more widespread, particularly among the expanding middle class. This growing interest made new demands on writers and artists that affected both the subject matter and its manner of presentation. Philosophy, science, literature, and the fine arts all increasingly addressed a general public as well as patrons, experts, or connoisseurs. Popular treatises were written with an eye to bringing culture within the reach of all, while novelists and playwrights increasingly depicted common people in everyday situations. *Popularization of learning*

SOCIAL ROLES FOR MUSIC

While courts, city governments, and churches continued to sponsor music-making as they had for centuries, musicians increasingly depended upon support from the public. There were now public concerts in many cities (see Innovations: The Public Concert, pp. 484–85), offering opportunities for performers and composers to supplement their incomes and to reach a wider audience. Many musicians also earned money as teachers to amateur performers.

With an expanding economy, a growing middle class, and more leisure time, the number of amateurs making music continued to increase. Although women were excluded from almost all professional roles other than as singers, they were welcome as amateur performers, especially at the keyboard, as in Figure 20.3. Amateur musicians naturally bought music that they could understand and play, and music publishers catered especially to them. Most of the published music for keyboard, chamber ensemble, or voice and keyboard was designed for amateurs to perform at home for their own pleasure. In addition, from midcentury on, many amateur groups formed to sing choral music for their entertainment and for public performance, and these groups provided publishers with a rich new market. The growing enthusiasm for music also fostered the development of connoisseurs, informed listeners who cultivated a taste for the best in music. Concert life and amateur music-making reinforced each other; connoisseurs were often amateur performers themselves, and amateurs were often especially avid concertgoers. *Musical amateurs and connoisseurs*

As the musical public broadened, more people became interested in reading about music and discussing it. By midcentury, magazines devoted to musical news, reviews, and criticism began to appear, catering to both amateurs *Musical journals and histories*

INNOVATIONS: THE PUBLIC CONCERT

During the eighteenth century, public concerts and concert series arose in many cities alongside the private concerts and academies that had long been presented by wealthy individual patrons and clubs. Private concerts were by invitation only, and the aristocratic patrons who sponsored them normally assumed all the costs. Public concerts, by contrast, were usually money-making ventures for which tickets were sold. Tickets were offered by subscription to a series or for an individual event, and anyone who could pay the price could attend. But ticket prices were not readily affordable for most people, so the audience for public concerts came mostly from the upper-middle and wealthy leisure classes.

Concert halls and concert societies flourished in London starting in 1672 and especially after 1720. At pleasure gardens such as Vauxhall, shown in Figure 20.1, the public paid an entrance fee to enjoy music and other entertainment outdoors. A remarkable institution for the day was the Academy of Ancient Music, devoted to the performance of sixteenth- and seventeenth-century sacred music and madrigals and other music of earlier times; its founding in 1726 inaugurated concerts of music from the past, which became increasingly popular over the next two centuries. By the second half of the eighteenth century, musical life in London centered around public concerts, including the annual subscription series put on from 1765 to 1781 by Johann Christian Bach and Carl Friedrich Abel. Similar societies were formed in other British and North American cities, including the Edinburgh Musical Society in Scotland (1728) and the St. Cecilia Society in Charleston, South Carolina (1766).

In Paris, the composer and oboist Anne Danican Philidor founded the Concert spirituel series in 1725, which lasted until 1790. The repertoire encompassed new music from France and other na-

Figure 20.1: Outdoor concert at Vauxhall pleasure gardens in London. Mrs. Weischel sings from the balcony of the "Moorish-Gothick temple," accompanied by the orchestra behind her, while the writer Samuel Johnson and his companions eat in the supper box below. Watercolor (ca. 1784) by Thomas Rowlandson.

tions, with performers from across the continent. The presentation of sonatas and concertos by Vivaldi and other Italians fostered a growing taste for Italian music in France, and from midcentury on, performances of symphonies by German and Austrian composers spurred French composers to cultivate the symphony.

Later in the century, the movement toward public concerts spread to German-speaking lands as well. In 1763, J. A. Hiller began a concert series in Leipzig, which continued after 1781 in the new concert hall at the Gewandhaus (Clothiers' Exchange); the Gewandhaus Orchestra still exists and has become one of the most famous orchestras in the world. Similar concert organizations were founded in Vienna (1771) and in Berlin (1790).

Public concerts were advertised by word of mouth and through handbills, posters, notices in newspapers, and other printed media. Figure 20.2 shows a poster for a 1781 concert by the Concert spirituel in Paris that offers a wealth of information about the concerts of the time. The concert was presented "for the benefit of M[onsieur] Raymond, Master of Music for the performance," meaning that he directed the concert and received whatever profits were left over after paying the musicians, the hall rental, and other expenses. The price, given at the bottom of the poster, was thirty sols per person, steep enough that only the well-to-do were likely to attend. The concert was to begin "precisely at six o'clock." To judge from the announced program, it lasted about three hours, which was typical at the time.

We are accustomed today to concerts made up entirely of a single type of music, such as orchestral works, piano music, or songs. But concerts in the eighteenth and early nineteenth centuries, public or private, typically presented a variety of vocal and instrumental genres for various ensembles, as "Pops" concerts do today. The program listed here includes a symphony, two concertos, a symphonie concertante, numerous arias, and an oratorio. The composer is given only for pieces by Raymond, while in other cases, the name by each piece was that of the featured performer, showing that the performer was in most cases more impor-

Figure 20.2: Poster for the Concert spirituel from 1781.

tant than the composer. Listed ninth is "A Harpsichord Concerto, [performed] by an Amateur of this City." The unnamed amateur who played the keyboard was probably a woman, since women were not yet accepted as professional instrumentalists.

An eighteenth-century concert was a social occasion as well as an opportunity to hear music. Audience members could stroll around and converse, paying attention only to the music that interested them, without being considered rude; the silent, motionless audience was an invention of the nineteenth century. The presence of women of the right social class was essential for making the event a social success, so Raymond made sure they felt welcome by including a poem at the bottom of the poster:

TO THE LADIES.
Charming sex, whom I seek to please,
Come embellish the abode of our talents;
By your presence warm up my accents:
Just one of your looks brings me to life and
    lights me up.
Eh! what does it matter to me, this much
    vaunted Laurel
    With which genius is crowned,
    This seal of immortality,
If it is not Beauty who gives it.

—BRH & JPB

Figure 20.3: A private performance by a chamber ensemble consisting of a singer, two violins, viola, cello, and harpsichord. The presence of a woman at the keyboard and the similarity of dress and wigs worn by the musicians and listeners indicate that the performers were most likely skilled amateurs rather than professionals, who would have been dressed in servants' livery. Engraving from 1769 by Daniel Nikolaus Chodowiecki.

and connoisseurs. The public's curiosity about music extended to its origins and past styles, addressed in the first universal histories of music: Charles Burney's *A General History of Music* (1776–89), John Hawkins's *A General History of the Science and Practice of Music* (1776), and Johann Nikolaus Forkel's *Allgemeine Geschichte der Musik* (General History of Music, 1788–1801).

MUSICAL TASTE AND STYLE

Many musical styles coexisted in the eighteenth century, each supported by strong adherents and criticized by detractors. Every country had distinctive traditions and developed a national form of opera. Works in new styles, such as the operas of Pergolesi and Hasse (see below), were written at the same time as Rameau's operas, Handel's oratorios, and Bach's *Art of Fugue*, all representative of the late Baroque.

Values for music   Despite the panoply of styles, leading writers in the middle and late eighteenth century articulated the prevailing view of what was most valued in music. Instead of the contrapuntal complexity and spun-out instrumental melody of Baroque music, audiences preferred and critics praised music that featured a vocally conceived melody in short phrases over spare

TIMELINE: OPERA AND VOCAL MUSIC IN THE EARLY CLASSIC PERIOD

1720	1730	1740	1750	1760	1770	1780	1790	1800

- 1722 Leonardo Vinci, *Le zite 'ngalera*
- 1725 Concert spirituel begins in Paris
- 1728 John Gay, *The Beggar's Opera*
- 1731 Johann Adolf Hasse, *Cleofide*
- 1733 Jean-Philippe Rameau, *Hippolyte et Aricie*
- 1733 Giovanni Battista Pergolesi, *La serva padrona*
- 1734 Voltaire, *The Philosophical Letters*
- 1740–86 Reign of Frederick the Great of Prussia
- 1740 Maria Theresa crowned Holy Roman Empress
- **1742 George Frideric Handel, *Messiah***
- 1745 Francis Stephen of Lorraine elected Holy Roman Emperor
- **1749 Johann Sebastian Bach, *The Art of Fugue***
- 1751–72 Denis Diderot and collaborators publish the *Encyclopédie*
- **1752 Pergolesi's *La serva padrona* in Paris**
- **1752 *Querelle des bouffons***
- **1752 Jean-Jacques Rousseau, *Le devin du village***
- **1755 Carl Heinrich Graun, *Der Tod Jesu***
- 1760–1820 Reign of George III of England
- **1762 Christoph Willibald Gluck, *Orfeo ed Euridice***
- 1762 Rousseau, *The Social Contract*
- 1765 Joseph II becomes Holy Roman Emperor and co-ruler with Maria Theresa
- **1765–81 Bach-Abel Concerts in London**
- 1770 Thomas Gainsborough, *The Blue Boy*
- **1774 Gluck, *Orphée et Euridice* in Paris**
- 1774–92 Reign of Louis XVI of France
- 1775–83 American Revolution
- 1776 Adam Smith, *The Wealth of Nations*
- **1776 John Hawkins, *A General History of the Science and Practice of Music***
- **1776–89 Charles Burney, *A General History of Music***
- **1778 La Scala opera house opens in Milan**
- 1781 Immanuel Kant, *Critique of Pure Reason*
- **1782–93 Heinrich Christoph Koch, *Introductory Essay on Composition***
- 1789–94 French Revolution
- **1794 Johann Friedrich Reichardt, *Erlkönig***
- **1794 William Billings, *The Continental Harmony***

accompaniment. Writers held that the language of music should be universal, rather than limited by national boundaries, and should appeal to all tastes at once, from the connoisseur to the untutored. The best music should be noble as well as entertaining; expressive within the limits of decorum; and "natural"—free of technical complications and capable of immediately pleasing any sensitive listener.

TERMS FOR STYLES: GALANT, EMPFINDSAM, AND CLASSICAL

These values led to the development of a new musical idiom known today as the **classical style.** Several terms have been used to describe this style and its close relatives, and writers, both today and then, sometimes use these words with somewhat different meanings.

Galant style

During the eighteenth century, the most common term for the new style was **galant,** a French term for the courtly manner in literature that had become a catchword for everything modern, chic, smooth, easy, and sophisticated. Writers distinguished between the learned or strict style of contrapuntal writing—what we would call Baroque—and the freer, more song-like, homophonic, galant style (see Source Reading). The latter emphasized melody made up of short-breathed, often repeated gestures organized in phrases of two, three, or four measures. These phrases combined into larger units, lightly accompanied with simple harmony and punctuated by frequent cadences. Despite its French name, the galant style originated in Italian operas and concertos, and it became the foundation for the musical idiom of the mid- to late-eighteenth century.

Empfindsam style

A close relative of the galant style was the *empfindsamer Stil* (German for "sentimental style") or **empfindsam style.** Characterized by surprising turns of harmony, chromaticism, nervous rhythms, and rhapsodically free, speech-like melody, the empfindsam style is most closely associated with slow movements of Carl Philipp Emanuel Bach (see chapter 21). Yet it, too, originated in Italy and is evident in some late concertos of Vivaldi.

Classical music and classical style

The term "classical" is used at times for art music of all periods and at other times more narrowly for the style of the late eighteenth century. There is a historical reason for this ambiguity. In the nineteenth century, works of J. S. Bach, Handel, Haydn, Mozart, and Beethoven were regarded as classics of music, akin to classics of literature or art, and they formed the core of what became known as the classical repertoire (see chapter 25). During the nineteenth and twentieth centuries, the classical repertoire expanded beyond its original core, so that now "classical music" is a tradition that covers many centuries and a multitude of styles. By the mid-twentieth century, the music of Bach and Handel was called "Baroque" rather than "classical," leaving the latter as the term for the late-eighteenth-century style. Thus, from an original single meaning, "classical" evolved through use to mean two very different things in relation to music.

What is the classical style?

Some writers apply the term "classical style"—or its variant, "classic"—only to the mature music of Haydn and Mozart, while others use it more broadly

SOURCE READING

A VIEW OF THE GALANT STYLE

Keyboard teacher and composer Daniel Gottlob Türk (1750–1813) aimed his Klavierschule *(School of Clavier Playing, 1789) at the amateur who needed instruction in taste and style as well as method. He described the differences between "strict" and "free" styles—that is, between the older learned style and the new galant style.*

———— • ————

A strict (contrapuntal) style is the one in which the composer follows all the rules of harmony and modulation in the strictest manner, mixing in artful imitations and many tied notes, working out the theme carefully, and the like, in short, allowing more art to be heard than eu-

phony. In the free (*galant*) manner of composition, the composer is not so slavishly bound to the rules of harmony, modulation, and the like. He often permits bold changes, which could even be contrary to the generally accepted rules of modulation, assuming that the composer in doing this proceeds with proper insight and judgment, and with it is able to attain a certain goal. In general, the free style of writing has more expression and euphony rather than art as its chief purpose.

Daniel Gottlob Türk, *School of Clavier Playing*, trans. Raymond H. Haggh (Lincoln: University of Nebraska Press, 1982), 399. In SR 132 (5:11), p. 891.

for the entire period from the 1730s to around 1800 or 1815. The term as applied to music came by way of analogy to Greek and Roman art: at its best, classical music possessed the qualities of noble simplicity, balance, formal perfection, diversity within unity, seriousness or wit as appropriate, and freedom from excesses of ornamentation and frills. It is almost impossible to use the term without making value judgments. Is it to apply only to Haydn, Mozart, and Beethoven, in whom these qualities abound and whose works have been judged classics? Or also to their contemporaries, no matter how little known? Should it also apply to their midcentury predecessors who used a similar musical language? The latter are sometimes called *preclassic*, an unfortunate term that suggests their only value was to pave the way for Haydn and company.

The solution adapted in this book is to regard the era from about 1730 to 1815 as the Classic period, to use "Classical music" (rather than "classical style") as the all-embracing term for music of the period, and to use terms such as galant, empfindsam, and "the Haydn idiom" to identify different styles or trends current at the time. The boundaries of the Classic period overlap with the Baroque and Romantic periods, just as boundaries blur between Medieval and Renaissance and between Renaissance and Baroque, since the language, genres, and customs of music change only gradually and at different times in different places.

The Classic period

MELODY, HARMONY, TEXTURE, AND FORM

The focus on melody in the new styles led to a musical syntax quite different from the continuous motivic variation of earlier styles. J. S. Bach, for example, would typically announce at the outset of a movement the musical idea, a melodic-rhythmic subject embodying the basic affection. This idea was then spun out, using sequential repetition as a principal constructive device, within a generally irregular phrase structure marked by relatively infrequent cadences.

Periodicity

In contrast, the newer styles were characterized by **periodicity,** in which frequent resting points break the melodic flow into segments that relate to each other as parts of a larger whole. Musical ideas, rather than being persistently spun out, were articulated through distinct phrases, typically two or four measures in length (but also frequently three, five, or six measures). Two or more phrases were needed to form a **period,** a complete musical thought concluded by a cadence, and a composition was made up of two or more periods in succession. This technique creates a structure marked by frequent cadences and integrated through motivic correspondences.

Musical rhetoric

The terminology of phrases and periods was borrowed from rhetoric, the art of oration. Eighteenth-century theorists frequently compared a melody to a sentence or a musical composition to a speech. The most thorough guide to melodic composition based on rhetorical principles appears in volume 2 of the *Versuch einer Anleitung zur Composition* (Introductory Essay on Composition, 1787) by Heinrich Christoph Koch (1749–1816), one of several treatises written for amateurs who wished to learn how to compose. Here the student is shown how to construct a melody by joining short segments of melody, which Koch calls *incises*, to form phrases, and phrases to form periods. He likens the components of a musical phrase to a subject and predicate. Koch states that this kind of organization is necessary to make a melody intelligible and capable of moving our feelings, just as the sentences and clauses that break up a speech make it easier to follow the train of thought.

In Example 20.1, Koch's terminology is used to show the structure of the opening of a keyboard sonata movement by Carl Philipp Emanuel Bach (1714–1788), dating from 1742. The first incise closes weakly and is followed by a rest; the second incise completes the phrase with a more secure ending on a note of the tonic triad, forming a "I-phrase" (that is, a phrase that ends on the tonic chord). As in a sentence, the subject is completed by the predicate. The two incises are linked by the bass motion that rises a fourth, by the melodic motion that descends a fourth from its peak to the last note, and by the closing motive labeled "x." The hesitation after the first incise extends what could have been a four-measure phrase to five measures. The second phrase varies and elaborates the first, reaching a greater intensity through higher pitch in measures 8-9.

The composer then constructs a new incise from motive "x" while borrowing the bass rhythm from measure 4. This time the first incise is answered without hesitation to make a four-measure phrase. It closes on the dominant triad, making this a V-phrase. This phrase too is varied and intensified on repetition, and closes on the dominant to complete the period. Like a skilled orator, Bach holds to his subject, reinforcing it with repetition and new arguments, and carefully arranges his thoughts to make them intelligible, persuasive, and moving.

Example 20.1: C. P. E. Bach, Allegro (third movement) from Sonata in B♭, H. 32

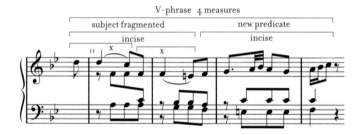

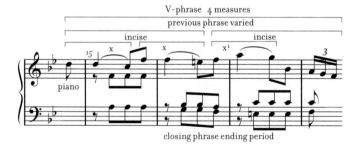

The division of the melody into phrases and periods is supported by the harmony. There is a hierarchy of cadences, with the weakest marking off internal phrases, stronger ones closing periods, and the strongest reserved for the ends of sections and movements. There is also a hierarchy of harmonic motions, with the small-scale I–V–I of a single phrase (seen here in each of the first two phrases) subsumed within a large-scale modulation from tonic to dominant and back over the course of the movement.

Harmony

Animation of texture　　Because the harmony is articulating the phrases rather than continuously driving the music forward, it tends to change less frequently than in the older Baroque style. To compensate for the slower harmonic rhythm, composers often animated the musical texture through pulsing chords (as in measures 11–17 of Example 20.1) or other rhythmic means. One of the most widely used devices in keyboard music was the **Alberti bass,** shown in Example 20.2. Named for the Italian composer Domenico Alberti (ca. 1710–1746), who used it frequently, the device broke each of the underlying chords into a simple repeating pattern of short notes that produced a discreet chordal background, setting off the melody to advantage.

Example 20.2: Alberti, opening of Sonata III from VIII sonate per cembalo, *Op. 1*

Form　　Finally, the coherence of late-eighteenth-century music was made possible by the differentiation of musical material according to its function. Each segment of music was immediately recognizable as a beginning, middle, or ending gesture. The first two measures of Example 20.1 serve well as the beginning of a phrase, period, or movement, but could not be an ending. By contrast, measures 8–10 offer an emphatic ending, but would sound out of place at the beginning of a phrase or period. Measure 12 serves well in the middle of a phrase, repeating the motive and rhythms of the previous measure; it could not be followed by a rest, as were the parallel moments in measures 2 and 7, without sounding as if the music had been interrupted midstream. Within these categories, there are levels of relative strength. The segment in measures 11–12 can begin a phrase but not a movement, since it starts in midair over an inverted chord and thus has the quality of being in the middle of a thought. Measures 13–14 are strong enough to end a phrase but not a period, as the melody rises at the end, as if asking a question. The parallel cadence in measures 17–18 is stronger, marking the end of the period, but is on the dominant, and thus cannot close the entire movement. Such distinctions allowed composers to make clear at every turn where we are in the musical form, just as an orator varies the use of emphasis and pauses to mark the beginnings and ends of sentences, paragraphs, sections, and the entire speech.

EMOTIONAL CONTRASTS

One of the most striking characteristics of Classic music resulted from a new view of human psychology. Descartes and others in the seventeenth century believed that once an emotion, such as anger or fear, was aroused, a person remained in that affection until moved by some stimulus to a different state. Accordingly, Baroque composers sought to convey a single mood in each movement, or at most to contrast conflicting moods in self-contained sections, such as the ritornello and episodes of a concerto movement. But deeper knowledge of blood circulation, the nervous system, and other aspects of human physiology led to a new understanding that feelings were constantly in flux, jostled by associations that might take unpredictable turns.

The new notion that emotions were not steady states, but were constantly changing and sometimes contradictory responses to one's experiences and thoughts, made obsolete the Baroque approach of conveying a single feeling in a movement or section. Instead, composers began to introduce contrasting moods in the various parts of a movement or even within the themes themselves. The possibilities for contrasts were heightened by the nature of the new music, with its many short phrases and its dependence on differences in the material to articulate the form.

Form and content

ITALIAN COMIC OPERA

Many stylistic traits that became typical of Classic-era music originated in Italian opera of the 1720s and 1730s. Because tradition weighed less heavily on comic opera, it was more hospitable to innovations than was serious opera. But composers, singers, and audiences for both comic and serious opera nurtured elements that would become crucial in the new style, through the value they placed on the beauty of melody and on the ability of music to portray complex characters and rapidly changing emotions.

OPERA BUFFA

Terms used in eighteenth-century Italy for comic opera included **opera buffa** (comic opera), *dramma giocoso* (jesting drama), *dramma comico* (comic drama), and *commedia per musica* (comedy in music); today *opera buffa* is often used to encompass all these types. An opera buffa was a full-length work with six or more singing characters and was sung throughout, unlike comic operas in other countries. It entertained and served a moral purpose by caricaturing the foibles of aristocrats and commoners, vain ladies, miserly old men, awkward and clever servants, deceitful husbands and wives, pedantic lawyers, bungling physicians, and pompous military commanders. These often resemble the stock characters of the *commedia dell'arte*, the improvised comedy popular in Italy since the sixteenth century. The comic cast was often complemented by serious characters around whom the main plot revolved and who interacted with the comic characters, particularly in amorous intrigues. The dialogue was set in rapidly delivered recitative accompanied by continuo, often keyboard alone.

Arias   The arias in comic operas are typically in galant style, made up of short tuneful phrases, often repeated or varied, organized into periods, and accompanied by simple harmonies and figuration. One of the pioneers of this style was Leonardo Vinci (ca. 1696–1730). His *Le zite 'ngalera* (The Spinsters in the Galley), with a libretto in Neapolitan dialect, premiered in Naples in 1722. Many of the arias are substantial, in da capo form, and accompanied by four-part string ensemble, while others are brief and supported only by continuo. One of the latter type, shown in Example 20.3, is the aria *T'aggio mmidea*, which opens a scene between Belluccia, a woman disguised as a man, and Ciommatella, a young woman who has fallen in love with "him." It begins with two one-measure phrases in an antecedent-consequent pair, repeated when the voice enters, which establishes periodic phrasing as the norm. But later

Example 20.3: Vinci, T'aggio mmidea, *from* Le zite 'ngalera, *Act I, scene 11*

Bellucia: *I envy you, beautiful bird! You disport yourself among the branches, you sing, you want to hide. And I dress up in feathers.*

Ciommatella: *Why in feathers?*

Bellucia: *Ciomma, what's the use? I told you why, but you cast my words to the sea: are you truly hard-headed?*

phrases are extended (measures 6–7 and 10) or truncated (measure 9), creating a dynamic melody that cleverly evades expectations. The surprises continue: after the usual modulation to the dominant, a deceptive cadence (measure 12) leads to a dialogue in recitative. The result is a witty musical setting that perfectly fits the text and moves the drama forward.

INTERMEZZO

Another important type of Italian comic opera, the ***intermezzo,*** was performed in two or three segments between the acts of a serious opera or play. The genre originated in the early eighteenth century when comic scenes were purged from serious operas, and the comic characters were given their own separate story in the intermezzo. These intermezzi contrasted sharply with the grand and heroic manners of the principal drama, sometimes even parodying its excesses. The plots usually presented two or three people in comic situations, and the action proceeded in alternating recitatives and arias, as in serious opera. Figure 20.4 shows an intermezzo performed in Venice.

Giovanni Battista Pergolesi (1710–1736) was one of the most original composers of his day but died young of tuberculosis. He is best known for his intermezzo *La serva padrona* (The Maid as Mistress, 1733), a classic example of opera in miniature, with only three characters: Uberto (bass), a rich bachelor;

Pergolesi's La serva padrona

Figure 20.4: Performance of an intermezzo, a short comic work given between the acts of an opera seria. This Venetian painting shows not only how such works were staged, but also how audiences behaved. Some are seated, others standing, and only some are paying attention to the performers on stage, while several are engaged in conversations. The silent attentiveness now expected of audiences for operas and classical concerts was a creation of the nineteenth century.

his maid, Serpina (soprano); and his mute valet, Vespone. Typical of comic opera, the social hierarchy is questioned as Serpina manipulates her master into proposing marriage by inventing a rival suitor (in fact, Vespone in disguise).

CD 7|1–3   CD 3|55

The scene after Serpina tells Uberto that she will marry another (NAWM 93) displays the extraordinary aptness and nimbleness of Pergolesi's music. As is typical of both comic and serious opera, the dialogue is rendered in simple recitative, accompanied only by the harpsichord and usually a sustaining bass instrument, with the words set to lively, speechlike rhythms over freely modulating harmonies. After Serpina leaves, Uberto descends into confusion when the thought of marrying her battles with concern over their difference in social class. His mutterings are rendered in accompanied recitative, in which voice and orchestra alternate freely. In serious opera, this style is reserved for the most dramatic situations; knowing this convention, Pergolesi's audience understood the effect here as comic, elevating Uberto's bewilderment to high drama. As was customary, his feelings culminate in a da capo aria. Neither the main nor the middle section of the aria develops a single musical motive, as in a Scarlatti or Handel aria. Rather, there are as many melodic ideas as there are shifting thoughts and moods in the text. In the first line, shown in Example 20.4a, Uberto exclaims that he is confused. The melody reflects his state with a nervous, jumpy motive, and its threefold repetition suggests his mental paralysis. Uberto then realizes that something mysterious is stirring in his heart (measure 15) and waxes lyrical as he asks himself whether it is love that he feels. But a sober voice within checks his ardor: he should think of himself, guarding his independence and his own interests. Here the melody, shown in Example 20.4b, is slow and deliberate. Pergolesi's depiction of character and emotion through simple, highly contrasting melodic ideas over light accompaniment made his music particularly successful and influential.

Example 20.4: Pergolesi, Son imbrogliato io già, *from* La serva padrona

a. Opening

Son im-bro-glia-to i-o già, son im-bro-glia-to i-o già, son im-bro-glia-to i-o

già! Ho un cer-to che nel co-re, che dir per me non so,—

I am all mixed up! I have a certain something in my heart; truly, I cannot tell [whether it's love or pity].

b. Later passage

U - ber - to, pen - sa a te, pen - sa a te!

[I hear a voice that tells me:] Uberto, think of yourself!

LATER COMIC OPERA

Italian comic opera changed considerably during the eighteenth century. Beginning about midcentury, the Italian dramatist Carlo Goldoni (1707–1793) introduced refinements in the comic-opera libretto. Serious, sentimental, or woeful plots began to appear alongside the traditional comic ones. An example is *La buona figliuola* (The Good Girl), adapted by Goldoni from Samuel Richardson's popular novel *Pamela* and set to music in 1760 by Niccolò Piccinni (1728–1800).

Another development was the ensemble finale, which appeared in the comic operas of Nicola Logroscino (1698–ca. 1765) and Baldassare Galuppi (1706–1785). At the end of an act, all the characters were gradually brought on stage while the action continued, becoming more and more animated until it reached a climax with all singers taking part. These ensemble finales were unlike anything in serious opera, and in writing them composers had to follow the rapidly changing action of the scene without losing coherence in the musical form.

Ensemble finales

The periodic phrasing, tuneful melodies, simple harmonies, spare accompaniment, direct expression, emotional fluidity, strong stylistic contrasts, and amusing mixtures of elements that characterized Italian comic opera became central elements of the international idiom of the later eighteenth century.

OPERA SERIA

The transparent and charming aria style of Vinci and Pergolesi soon invaded **opera seria,** or serious opera, which treated serious subjects, without comic scenes or characters.

Pietro Metastasio

Opera seria received its standard form from the Italian poet Pietro Metastasio (1698–1782). His dramas were set to music hundreds of times by many eighteenth-century composers, including Gluck and Mozart. His success in Naples, Rome, and Venice led to an appointment in 1729 as court poet in Vienna, where he remained the rest of his life. His heroic operas present conflicts of human passions, often pitting love against duty, in stories based on ancient Greek or Latin tales. His operas were intended to promote morality through entertainment and to present models of merciful and enlightened rulers, in tune with Enlightenment thought. Favorite characters are magnanimous tyrants, such as the Roman emperor Titus in *La clemenza di Tito* (The Clemency of Titus). Metastasio's librettos employ the conventional cast of two pairs of lovers surrounded by other characters. The action provides opportunities for introducing varied scenes—pastoral or martial episodes, solemn ceremonies, and the like. The resolution of the drama, which rarely has a tragic ending, often turns on a deed of heroism or sublime renunciation by one of the principal characters.

Content of opera seria

An opera seria's three acts consist almost without exception of alternating recitatives and arias. Recitatives develop the action through dialogues and monologues, set either as simple recitative or, at the most dramatic moments, as accompanied recitative. Each aria is a virtual dramatic soliloquy in which a principal character expresses feelings or reacts to the preceding scene. There are occasional duets, a few larger ensembles, and rare, simple choruses. Except in the overture, the orchestra serves mainly to accompany the singers, although as the century progressed the role of the orchestra became increasingly important.

THE ARIA

The musical interest of Italian opera is centered in the arias, which were created by eighteenth-century composers in astounding profusion and variety.

Da capo aria

The favored form in the first half of the century remained the da capo aria (see chapter 17), a basic scheme that permitted enormous variation in detail. Metastasio's two-stanza aria texts set the standard for the da capo aria of the 1720s through 1740s. The form may be represented by the following outline (in which the keys, indicated by Roman numerals, are hypothetical):

Section:	1					2	1 repeats
Music:	Ritornello	A1	Rit	A2	Rit	B	
Text:		stanza 1		stanza 1		stanza 2	
Key:	I	I → V	V	V → I	I	vi	

The opening ritornello generally announces the melodic material of the A section, sometimes simplified or embellished. The first vocal statement (A1) sets the first stanza of the text, presenting the main melodic material in the tonic and then modulating to the dominant or other closely related key. The ritornello that follows is usually short, affirming the new key with a transposed and often abbreviated passage from the opening. The second vocal statement (A2) repeats the first stanza of text. It typically begins with the principal melody or a variant of it in the new key, then wanders further afield before returning to the tonic. It often ends with a highly florid rendering of the last line or couplet, followed by a full or abbreviated return of the ritornello. The B section, heard only once, sets the second stanza of the text, most often stating it a single time or repeating only the final line or two. Normally this section is set syllabically with light accompaniment, is in a contrasting key, and may be in a different tempo or meter. There is usually a fermata just before the end of both the A and B sections, inviting the singer to execute a cadenza. Singers also added melodic embellishments throughout, especially during the repetition of the first section.

For some arias, composers shortened the repetition of the first section by omitting the opening ritornello, altering the direction "da capo" (from the beginning) to "dal segno" (from the sign, indicating that only part of the first section is repeated), or writing out an abridged return. Some arias lacked the contrasting second section and instead followed a format like a da capo aria's first section, with two vocal statements framed by ritornellos.

Abbreviated da capo

Arias written in the first decades of the century had usually projected a single affection, or mood, through the development of a single motive, or presented contrasting affections in the A and B sections. Beginning in the 1720s and 1730s, composers started to express a succession of moods, using a variety of musical material that ranged from lighthearted to tragic. Often two keys are contrasted in the first vocal statement (A1), then the material in the second key is recapitulated in the tonic at the close of the second vocal statement (A2). This repetition of material in the tonic became a central principle of form later in the century, in both vocal and instrumental music. The vocal melody dominates the music and carries it forward, and the orchestra provides harmonic support to the singer rather than adding independent contrapuntal lines. The melodies are usually in short units, most often in two- or four-measure antecedent and consequent phrases, with occasional expansions to create tension or offer variety.

New features

Figure 20.5: Johann Adolf Hasse, in a pastel portrait by Felicitas Hoffmann.

Johann Adolf Hasse (1699–1783), shown in Figure 20.5, was one of the most popular and successful opera composers in Europe around the middle of the century. He was acknowledged by most of his contemporaries as the great master of the opera seria. For most of his life he directed music and opera at the court of the elector of Saxony in Dresden, but he spent many years in Italy, married the celebrated Italian soprano Faustina Bordoni, and became so thoroughly Italian in his musical style that the Italians nicknamed him "il caro Sassone" (the dear Saxon). The great majority of his eighty operas use Metastasio librettos, some of which he set two or three times, and his music is the perfect complement to Metastasio's poetry.

CD 7|7

The famous aria *Digli ch'io son fedele* (Tell him that I am faithful) from Hasse's *Cleofide* (1731), his first opera for Dresden (NAWM 94), illustrates the elegant and judicious qualities of his music. In the first vocal statement, shown in Example 20.5, Hasse set the opening lines with a graceful motive that follows the natural rhythms and inflections of the text, highlights the parallelism between the first two lines, and reflects the earnest optimism of Cleofide, queen of India. These and several later phrases end with appoggiaturas, which lend a natural emphasis whether the line closes on a stressed or unstressed syllable. After the opening rhythmic motive appears three times, Hasse introduces syncopations and scales in measures 13–14 and reverse-dotted rhythms (called Lombardic rhythms or Scotch snaps) in measure 15.

These gently destabilizing elements give the melody interest and expressivity without sacrificing elegance. The slowly pulsing bass line stays in the background, its steadiness throwing the irregularities of the melody into relief.

The title role of Cleofide was created by Hasse's wife, Faustina Bordoni (1700–1781), who is shown in Figure 20.6. Universally admired as one of the great singer-actresses of her age, she established her reputation in Venice while still in her teens, enjoyed success at Munich and Vienna in the 1720s, then sang in Handel's opera company later that decade (see chapter 19). She married Hasse in 1730 and sang in most of his operas for Dresden, but also performed throughout Italy until her retirement from the stage in 1751. She was particularly known for her fluent articulation, trills, improvised embellishments, and expressive power.

All opera singers of Bordoni's day embellished the written vocal line, particularly in the da capo repetition. A rare surviving example of such elaboration is a version of the famous aria from *Cleofide*, as sung by the castrato Porporino (Antonio Uberti), which was written down by King Frederick the Great of Prussia, an avid musical amateur.

Figure 20.6: Faustina Bordoni, who created the title role of her husband Johann Adolf Hasse's Cleofide *(Dresden, 1731). She is shown here in a portrait by Bartolomeo Nazari (1699–1758), with an attributed date of 1734—although the date of the painting is questionable.*

Example 20.5: Hasse, Digli chi'io son fedele, *from* Cleofide

Tell him that I am faithful, Tell him that he's my treasure;
   [Tell him] to love me, that I adore him, That he should not yet despair.

This version, shown in the top staff in Example 20.5 above Hasse's melody, is ablaze with trills, mordents, rapid turns, appoggiaturas, scales, triplets, and arpeggios. It reminds us that the center of attention in an opera seria was not the composer, drama, plot, or scenery, but the singers, and displays of vocal acrobatics were certain to please the audience.

OPERA IN OTHER LANGUAGES

While opera seria maintained its character across national boundaries from Italy to England, comic opera took different forms in different countries. It usually represented people from the middle or lower classes in familiar situations and required relatively modest performing resources. Comic-opera librettos were always written in the national tongue, and the music tended to accentuate national musical idioms. From humble beginnings, comic opera grew steadily in importance after 1750, and before the end of the century many of its characteristic features had been absorbed into the mainstream of operatic composition. The historical significance of comic opera was twofold: it reflected the widespread demand for simple, clear, and "natural" singing in the second half of the eighteenth century, and it encouraged the growth of separate national traditions of opera, which became prominent in the Romantic period.

FRANCE

Querelle des bouffons   In Paris, long-simmering critical opposition to the old-fashioned, state-subsidized French opera erupted in 1752–54 in a pamphlet war known as the *Querelle des bouffons* (Quarrel of the comic actors). The dispute was prompted by the presence in Paris of an Italian comic opera troupe that for two seasons enjoyed sensational success with its performances of opere buffe and intermezzi, including *La serva padrona.* Many French intellectuals took part in the quarrel, partisans of Italian opera on one side and friends of French opera on the other.

Jean-Jacques Rousseau   One of the most vehement voices arguing for the merits of Italian opera was Jean-Jacques Rousseau (1712–1778), who praised Italian composers' emphasis on melody and their ability to express any emotion through melody. Rousseau wrote a charming little opera, *Le devin du village* (The Village Soothsayer, 1752), with airs and recitatives inspired by the new Italian melodic style. The air *J'ai perdu tout mon bonheur,* shown in Example 20.6, exhibits the balanced two-measure phrases, simple harmonies, primacy of melody, and subordinate accompaniment that Rousseau lauded in Italian opera, all of which became typical features of music in the second half of the eighteenth century. The air is interrupted by passages that imitate Italian recitative.

Opéra comique   The native French version of light opera, known as **opéra comique,** had begun around 1710 as a popular entertainment put on at suburban parish fairs. Until midcentury, the music consisted almost entirely of popular tunes, known as *vaudevilles,* or simple melodies imitating such tunes. The presence of Italian comic opera in the 1750s stimulated the production of opéras comiques in which original airs (called *ariettes*) in a mixed Italian-French style were introduced along with the older vaudevilles. The vaudevilles were gradually replaced by the ariettes until, by the end of the 1760s, all the music in an opéra comique was freshly composed. Like all the national variants of

Example 20.6: Rousseau, J'ai perdu tout mon bonheur, *from* Le devin du village

I have lost all my joy, I have lost my servant. Colin forsakes me.

light opera except the Italian, French opéra comique used spoken dialogue instead of recitative.

By the later eighteenth century, librettists and composers of opéra comique were using serious plots, some based on the social issues that agitated France during the pre- and post-Revolutionary years. The leading French opera composer of the time was the Belgian-born André Ernest Modeste Grétry (1741–1813). His *Richard Coeur-de-Lion* (Richard the Lion-Hearted, 1784) inaugurated a vogue for "rescue" operas around the turn of the century—Beethoven's *Fidelio* was one (see chapter 23)—in which the hero, in imminent danger of death for two and a half acts, is finally saved through a friend's devoted heroism. The opéra comique remained extremely popular in France throughout the Revolution and the Napoleonic era and took on even greater importance in the nineteenth century.

Serious plots

ENGLAND

In England, the popular form of opera in the local language was **ballad opera**. Like the early opéra comique, a ballad opera consisted of spoken dialogue interspersed with songs that set new words to borrowed tunes, including folk songs and dances, popular songs, and well-known airs and arias from other works for the stage. The fashion for ballad operas peaked in the 1730s, but they continued to be composed and staged over the next several decades in Britain, in its North American colonies, and later in the United States. Over

Ballad opera

time, ballad opera composers borrowed less and wrote more original music, in a development parallel to that of opera comique.

The Beggar's Opera

[CD 7|12]

The genre was spawned by the tremendous success of *The Beggar's Opera* (1728, excerpted in NAWM 95), with libretto by John Gay (1685–1732) and music arranged probably by Johann Christoph Pepusch (1667–1752). Gay's play satirized London society by replacing the ancient heroes and elevated sentiments of traditional opera with modern urban thieves and prostitutes and their crimes, as shown on the ticket in Figure 20.7. The poetry and music sometimes spoofed opera or used operatic conventions to create humor through incongruous juxtapositions. When the main character Macheath likened his roaming heart to a bee in *My heart was so free*, contemporary listeners were reminded both of the noble simile arias of serious Baroque operas (which compare a character's situation to a vivid image, portrayed in the music) and of the naive popular courting song whose tune he sings. As he and his wife Polly pledged their constancy in *Were I laid on Greenland's coast*, which would be set with great earnestness in Italian opera, the audience could not help but notice the tune, whose original text tells of a lad "run mad" by his lass, and be amused at the contrast of mood.

GERMANY AND AUSTRIA

Singspiel

Serious operas in German had been composed and produced since the seventeenth century, and a few composers continued to write such works throughout the eighteenth century, generally adopting the style and format of Italian opera mixed with French and native elements. But much more popular was the new genre called **Singspiel** (German for "singing play"), an opera with spoken dialogue, musical numbers, and usually a comic plot. The earliest examples appeared in the 1710s at the Kärntnertortheater in Vienna. The success

Figure 20.7: A ticket for a performance of The Beggar's Opera *at the Theatre Royal at Covent Garden in London. The evening's receipts were to be paid to Thomas Walker, the actor playing the central character, the notorious thief and murderer Macheath. In the engraving by renowned satirist William Hogarth (1697–1764), Polly and Lucy, both in love with Macheath, plead for his release from prison.*

of ballad operas in England inspired poets in northern Germany to translate or adapt some into German, and from the 1750s on composers were providing new music for them in a familiar and appealing melodic vein. The principal composer of Singspiel in the 1760s and 1770s was Johann Adam Hiller (1728–1804) of Leipzig. Many Singspiel tunes were published in German song collections and some achieved such lasting popularity that they virtually became folksongs, transmitted orally as well as in print.

In northern Germany, the Singspiel eventually merged with early nineteenth-century native opera. In the south, particularly in Vienna, farcical subjects and treatment became fashionable, with lively music in a popular vein influenced by Italian comic opera. The Singspiel was an important precursor of the German-language musical theater of composers such as Mozart and Weber (see chapters 22 and 26).

OPERA AND THE PUBLIC

Each of these national traditions was supported by the public rather than by well-to-do patrons. As a result, each tradition developed unique features based on what pleased audiences in that region, encouraging the growth of distinct national styles, which later became one of the strongest trends of the nineteenth century. Indeed, the increasing importance of the middle-class public for music is the main economic force behind changes in musical style and the growth of new genres in the late eighteenth century and throughout the nineteenth as well. This public support also reinforced the preference of many Enlightenment intellectuals for music that was simple, clear, direct, and had wide appeal.

OPERA REFORM

Although serious Italian opera remained dependent on aristocratic patronage, it also underwent changes that reflected Enlightenment thought. From midcentury on several composers, librettists, and patrons worked to bring opera into harmony with new ideals of music and drama. They sought to make the entire design more "natural"—that is, more flexible in structure, more expressive, less ornamented with coloratura, and more varied in musical resources. They did not abandon the da capo aria but modified it and introduced other forms as well. In order to move the action forward rapidly and more realistically, they alternated recitatives and arias more flexibly. To increase variety and heighten dramatic impact, they made greater use of accompanied recitative and ensembles. They made the orchestra more important as a vehicle for depicting scenes, evoking moods, and adding color and depth to accompaniments. They reinstated choruses, long absent in Italian opera. In all of these ways, they sought to assert the primacy of the drama and the music and subordinate the solo singers to this larger purpose, reversing the long-standing focus on star singers. The argument for such changes was articulated in *An Essay on the Opera* (1755) by Francesco Algarotti, who was influenced by the more integrated approach of French serious opera and by the tradition of classical Greek tragedy.

Jommelli and Traetta

Two of the most important figures in this reform were Niccolò Jommelli (1714–1774) and Tommaso Traetta (1727–1779). That these Italian composers worked at courts where French taste predominated—Jommelli at Stuttgart (1753–69) and Traetta in Parma (1758–65)—naturally influenced them toward a cosmopolitan type of opera. Jommelli composed some one hundred stage works and achieved wide popularity. His later operas provided models within opera seria for a more continuous dramatic flow and gave the orchestra a more important role, including more colorful use of woodwinds and horns. Traetta aimed to combine the best of French tragédie en musique and Italian opera seria in his *Ippolito et Aricia* (1759), on a libretto translated and adapted from Rameau's *Hippolyte et Aricie*. Besides borrowing some of Rameau's dance music and descriptive orchestral interludes, Traetta included a number of choruses, common in the French tradition but rare in Italian opera. For the solo roles, he used the Italian genres of recitative and aria, but deployed several forms beyond the conventional da capo aria. Thus in his own way Traetta reconciled the two main types of music drama, French and Italian.

CHRISTOPH WILLIBALD GLUCK

Christoph Willibald Gluck (1714–1787), shown in Figure 20.8, achieved a winning synthesis of French, Italian, and German operatic styles. Born of Bohemian parents in what is now Bavaria, Gluck studied under Giovanni Battista Sammartini in Italy (see chapter 21), visited London, toured in Germany as conductor of an opera troupe, became court composer to the Emperor Charles VI at Vienna, and triumphed in Paris under the patronage of Marie Antoinette. After writing operas in the conventional Italian style, he was strongly affected by the reform movement in the 1750s and collaborated with the poet Raniero de Calzabigi (1714–1795) to produce at Vienna *Orfeo ed Euridice* (1762) and *Alceste* (1767). In a preface to *Alceste*, Gluck expressed his resolve to remove the abuses that had deformed Italian opera and to confine music to what the reformers considered its proper function—to serve the poetry and advance the plot. This he wanted to accomplish without regard either to the outworn conventions of the da capo aria or the desire of singers to show off their skill in ornamental variation. He further aimed to make the overture an integral part of the opera, to adapt the orchestra to the dramatic requirements, and to lessen the contrast between aria and recitative.

Orfeo ed Euridice

Gluck aspired to write music of "a beautiful simplicity," which he achieved especially in *Orfeo ed Euridice*. In both this opera and the more monumental *Alceste*, the music is molded to the drama, with recitatives, arias, and choruses intermingled in large unified scenes. Compared to the final choruses Jommelli employed in his operas for Vienna in the early 1750s, Gluck's Chorus of Furies in Act II of *Orfeo ed Euridice* (NAWM 96) is more integral to the action. In this scene, Orfeo has descended into the underworld, where the Furies challenge him in strident tones reinforced by string tremolos, horns, and trombones. He replies with pleas for mercy, accompanied by harp and plucked strings to simulate the playing of his lyre. The opposition of per-

CD 7|14

Figure 20.8: Christoph Willibald Gluck, in a 1775 portrait by Joseph-Siffred Duplessis.

forming forces, timbres, keys, dynamic levels, and styles helps the music to deepen the dramatic conflict.

Gluck achieved his mature style in *Orfeo ed Euridice* and *Alceste*, amalgamating Italian melodic grace, German seriousness, and the stately magnificence of the French tragédie en musique. He was now ready for the climax of his career, which was ushered in with the Paris production of *Iphigénie en Aulide* (Iphigenia in Aulis) in 1774. Gluck cleverly represented himself—or was represented by his supporters—as wanting to prove that a good opera could be written to French words. In a letter to the journal *Mercure de France* in February 1773, he professed a desire for Rousseau's aid in creating "a noble, sensitive, and natural melody . . . music suited to all nations, so as to abolish these ridiculous distinctions of national styles." He thus appealed at once to the patriotism and curiosity of the French public.

French operas

Iphigénie en Aulide, with a libretto adapted from the tragedy by seventeenth-century French playwright Jean Racine, was a tremendous success. Gluck swiftly followed up with revised versions of *Orfeo* and *Alceste*, both with French texts. In a mischievously instigated rivalry with the popular Neapolitan composer Niccolò Piccinni, both composers were induced to write an opera on *Roland* by Lully's librettist Jean-Philippe Quinault. When Gluck heard that his rival was already at work on his version, Gluck set instead Quinault's *Armide* (1777), the same libretto Lully had used in 1686 (see chapter 16 and NAWM 77). Gluck's next masterpiece, *Iphigénie en Tauride* (Iphigenia in Tauris, 1779), is a work of huge proportions that displays an excellent balance of dramatic and musical interest. It uses all the resources of opera—

solo and choral singing, orchestra, and ballet—to produce a total effect of classical tragic grandeur.

Gluck's influence   Gluck's operas became models for many subsequent works, especially in Paris. His influence on the form and spirit of opera was transmitted to the nineteenth century through composers such as his erstwhile rival Piccinni, Luigi Cherubini (1760–1842), Gasparo Spontini (1774–1851), and Hector Berlioz (1803–1869).

SONG AND CHURCH MUSIC

While opera held sway in the larger public arena, solo songs, cantatas, and other types of secular vocal chamber music entertained more intimate gatherings throughout Europe. By this time, church music was a follower of secular styles rather than a focus of innovation, but it was still an important part of musical life.

SONG

Songs for home performance were composed and published in many nations, reflecting the growing interest in amateur music-making. Increasingly the accompaniment was written for a keyboard instrument, although guitar was also used. Most songs were relatively simple, usually syllabic, diatonic, and strophic, with accompaniments easy enough to be played by the singer.

Many of the songs sung at home were religious, set in a plain hymnlike style. In addition, distinctive genres of secular song emerged in different regions. In France, the *romance* was a strophic song on a sentimental text with a simple, expressive melody, almost entirely without ornamentation, over a plain accompaniment. In Britain, *ballads* were printed on single large sheets called broadsides or gathered in printed collections. Usually only the text was printed, typically a new poem about recent events or on a sentimental theme, meant to be sung to a familiar tune. Such songs were produced in Britain from the sixteenth through the early nineteenth centuries, and parallel genres were widespread on the European continent and in North America. English composers also composed new songs in popular style and in the more elegant manner cultivated in concerts at the pleasure gardens in London. In the late eighteenth century, a fashion developed for Scottish and Irish folksongs, and publishers issued hundreds of them in new settings, as well as new songs written in a similar style.

The Lied   The German song, or **Lied**, achieved a special prominence. Song was central to musical life and aesthetics in Germany. Publishers brought out more than 750 collections of Lieder with keyboard accompaniment during the second half of the century. German writers on music believed all music and musical instruments should emulate the singing voice, and insisted that song should be simple and expressive. Lyric poems were strophic, and composers setting them to music strove to create a single melody that would suit every stanza well, generally with one note per syllable. Songs were considered best when the melody was easy to sing, even by those untrained in music, and the accompaniment featured little or no figuration and was completely subordinate to the vocal line. This modest style, often (though not entirely accurately) compared to folk song, was meant to please those who performed and heard it, not to impress or astound as did the vocal display of opera. North German composers were particularly important for song composition, including Telemann in Hamburg and C. P. E. Bach and Carl Heinrich Graun (ca. 1704–1759) in Berlin. The plain style of their Lieder contrasts sharply with their more elaborate music in other genres, and probably reflects the taste of most German consumers of music.

Toward the end of the century, Johann Friedrich Reichardt (1752–1814) and other composers expanded the stylistic possibilities of the Lied, primarily by making the structure more flexible and giving the accompaniment greater independence. The most famous of Reichardt's 1,500 songs, *Erlkönig* (The Erl-King, 1794), is on the same Goethe text set by Schubert twenty years later. As shown in Example 20.7, the vocal line (identical to the top notes in the piano part) is perfectly suited to the rhythms, accents, and phrasing of the poetry, yet has the simplicity and dignity that both Reichardt and Goethe admired in folk song. The music seems folklike, yet is artfully crafted. The rhythm captures the image of the galloping horse, and frequent dynamic

Johann Friedrich Reichardt

Example 20.7: Reichardt, Erlkönig

a. Beginning

Who rides so late through night and wind? It is a father with his child. He has the boy close in his arm, he holds him tight, he keeps him warm. "My son, why do you hide your face in fear? . . ."

b. Third strophe

"You dear child, come with me; I'll play very lovely games with you."

changes enhance the drama. Although each strophe of the poem uses the same melody and harmony, the setting is varied in some way to convey the story. The second strophe begins with greater dynamic and rhythmic intensity as the father expresses his concern for his child (measure 16). In the third strophe (Example 20.7b), the wicked Erl-King speaks in a soft, eerie monotone as the melody sounds in the piano.

The virtues of song   All these genres are marked by a lack of affectation, spare accompaniment, little if any word-painting, and melodies that are simple, clear, and well suited to the accents, phrasing, and mood of the text. Although songs of the late eighteenth century are little known today, they embody values the Enlightenment held most dear. Song became a critically important genre in the nineteenth century, and the spirit of song pervades music from the late eighteenth century on.

CHURCH MUSIC

By the middle of the eighteenth century, sacred music was no longer in the center of musical culture. Once the driving force in the development of new styles, especially before 1600, church music was now valued more for its traditionalism than for innovations, or else simply adopted the current prevailing styles of secular music. As a result, church music of this era has attracted much less attention from performers and scholars than opera or instrumental music.

Catholic music   Church composers in Catholic areas conformed to the prevailing secular style, especially that of the theater. A few composers carried on the *stile antico* tradition of Palestrina or the grand polychoral style of Benevoli. But for the most part, church music took over the musical idioms and genres of opera, with orchestral accompaniment, da capo arias, and accompanied recitatives. A list of the leading eighteenth-century Italian church composers would be almost identical with the list of leading opera composers of the period. Even more than masses and motets, Italian oratorios became almost indistinguishable from operas. At the same time some composers, particularly in northern Italy, Austria, and southern Germany, affected a compromise between conservative and modern elements, influenced also by the instrumental symphonic forms of the Classic period.

Lutheran music

In Lutheran areas, the Enlightenment's focus on reason, combined with Pietism's emphasis on individual worship and the new taste for elegant simplicity, led to drastic changes in church music. The cantata and elaborate chorale-based compositions were now considered old-fashioned, and music for the service came to consist primarily of congregational hymns composed in or adapted to the new galant style. The nonliturgical genre of the oratorio became the principal medium for North German composers. The best known was the Passion oratorio *Der Tod Jesu* (The Death of Jesus, 1755) by Carl Heinrich Graun, which remained popular in Germany until the end of the nineteenth century.

English church music

In England, the enormous influence of Handel and the English interest in older music kept the Baroque styles of church music alive. Composers focused on the traditional genres of Anglican music, the service and the anthem, and on hymns for church or private devotions. William Boyce (1710–1779), more famous for his theater music, served as the official composer for the Chapel Royal. Maurice Greene (1696–1755), John Stanley (1712–1786) and Charles Avison (1709–1770), known for their orchestral and organ music, composed anthems of excellent quality. Stanley and Avison also added to the repertory of the oratorio and cantata.

New World

Church musicians in European settlements in the New World drew on their respective national styles. Villancicos and other choral music continued to be sung throughout the Spanish colonies, and French Canadian churches emulated the Catholic music of France. In British North America, diverse immigrant groups brought with them (or later imported) elements of their religious music. For example, Anglican churches in large cities presented music that differed little from that of their English cousins, featuring organs as well as choirs of men and boys. Two groups were especially notable for their music: the Puritans of New England and the Moravians of Pennsylvania and North Carolina.

New England hymnody

The Puritans who settled New England were Calvinists, and their use of music in worship centered on metrical psalm singing. The original *Bay Psalm Book* (1640; see chapter 10), the first book published in North America, contained no music, but the ninth edition of 1698 furnished thirteen melodies for singing the psalms. Congregations were taught and encouraged to read notes and not to depend simply on rote learning. In the eighteenth century, singing schools, often taught by traveling singing masters, trained a core of amateurs to sing psalm settings and anthems in parts. The availability of such singers became an invitation for composers to write new music.

William Billings

William Billings (1746–1800), the most prominent of these composers, left a significant body of music and writings. His *New-England Psalm-Singer* (1770), shown in Figure 20.9, contained 108 psalm and hymn settings and fifteen anthems and canons for chorus. His book marked two milestones—as the first published collection of music entirely composed in North America and the first music-book published in North America devoted to a single composer. Billings issued several more collections, including *The Continental Harmony* in 1794. Most of Billings's settings were "plain tunes," that is,

Figure 20.9: The frontispiece to William Billings's New England Psalm Singer (1770). Surrounding the singers at the table is a canon for six voices with a ground bass to be sung "by three or four deep voices." Engraving by Paul Revere.

homophonic four-part harmonizations of his newly invented melodies, such as *Chester*, a patriotic song from the Revolutionary War period for which he also wrote the text. But his later collections showed a preference for **fuging tunes,** like *Creation* (NAWM 97) from *The Continental Harmony*. These tunes usually open with a syllabic and homophonic section, then feature a passage in free imitation before closing with voices joined again in homophony.

CD 7|20

Billings declared his independence from the normal rules of counterpoint, writing that he had devised a set of rules better suited to his aims and method, and indeed his settings exhibit numerous parallel octaves and fifths as well as open chords without thirds. The rugged character of the music matches the colorful and eccentric personality of his writings. Other composers who contributed to the Yankee tunebooks—for example, Daniel Read (1757–1836) and Andrew Law (1748–1821)—either followed his lead or were similarly inclined. Together, these three men developed a distinctive New England idiom that stood apart from European styles.

Moravians

The Moravians, on the other hand, were thoroughly conversant with European trends. They were German-speaking Protestants from Moravia, Bohemia, and southern Germany who settled in Nazareth and Bethlehem in Pennsylvania, Salem in North Carolina, and surrounding areas. They embellished their church services with concerted arias and motets in current styles, whether imported from Europe or composed in America, and used organs, strings, and other instruments in church. Johannes Herbst (1735–1812), who came to Pennsylvania in 1786 and served as a pastor in Lancaster, Lititz, and Salem, wrote hundreds of sacred songs and anthems. Moravians also collected substantial libraries of music, both sacred and secular, and regularly played chamber music and even symphonies by the leading European composers of the time. Herbst, Johann Friedrich Peter (1746–1813), John Antes (1740–1811, the first native-born American composer of chamber music), and other Moravians wrote sacred vocal and secular instrumental works that show familiarity with and a mastery of European styles from Handel to Haydn.

OPERA AND THE NEW LANGUAGE

The new musical idioms of the mid- to late-eighteenth century had their principal sources in vocal music, especially in comic opera and vernacular song. In those genres, the urge to entertain and to reach a diverse audience led to a simplification of means and a striving for more effective and "naturalistic" expression. From Italian theaters the new styles spread through the cosmopolitan network of musicians, composers, and directors to other regions, stimulating new genres of opera and song. Seeking to serve the growing taste for a clear and universally appealing music, composers developed a spare, logically organized flow of musical ideas that could be grasped on first hearing.

The new styles were inspired by vocal music, yet they had a tremendous impact on instrumental music, creating a new approach to melody and form. But the same vocal music that led the way to a new syntax and rhetoric fell victim to changing fashion. Although *La serva padrona* was revived for several decades, and *The Beggar's Opera* lasted into the nineteenth century, other works did not fare so well. While Gluck's operas were never entirely forgotten, and *Orfeo ed Euridice* is now a permanent fixture, most other vocal music of the time quickly passed from the stage and is now little known.

Because of the way the history of music has been told, emphasizing Bach and Handel as paragons of Baroque music and Haydn and Mozart as masters of the classical style, the music of the middle eighteenth century is often seen merely as transitional. From their own perspective, musicians of the time were engaged in a vigorous argument about musical taste and style, and in a constant search to please their growing audiences. As we encounter their music today, we would be wise to measure it against their own goals and values, rather than those of an earlier or later generation.

Chapter 21

Instrumental Music: Sonata, Symphony, and Concerto at Midcentury

The new musical idiom of the mid-eighteenth century, developed primarily in opera, became pervasive in instrumental music. Periodic phrasing, songlike melodies, diverse material, contrasts of texture and style, and touches of drama, all typical of the new idiom, made it easier to follow instrumental music and to be engaged by it. As an abstract play of gestures and moods, a drama without words, the music itself absorbed the listener's attention. Paradoxically, by borrowing from vocal music, instrumental music gained new independence, rising in the next two generations to unprecedented prominence.

Instrumental music was a form of entertainment for the players and for listeners. Pleasing the performers and appealing to a wide audience became paramount for composers. The *piano* replaced the harpsichord and clavichord as the favorite keyboard instrument, and new chamber ensembles, notably the *string quartet,* were developed for social music-making. The sonata (including similar works called by other names) became the leading genre for solo and chamber music, and the concerto and *symphony* dominated orchestral music. All these genres had deep roots in Baroque music, but the new melody-centered idiom brought new forms to the individual movements, including *sonata form.*

INSTRUMENTS AND ENSEMBLES

Instrumental music served a variety of social roles in the mid- to late-eighteenth century. Much music, including keyboard, harp, or guitar music to play alone and ensemble music to perform as a social activity, was written, purchased, and performed for the enjoyment of the players themselves. Especially among the middle and upper classes, amateurs often played for family and friends.

In the houses of aristocrats and the well-to-do, musicians were employed to play during dinner or at parties. Amateur orchestras, sometimes filled out with professionals, performed in private or public concerts, and professional groups increasingly did so as well. All levels of society enjoyed music for dancing, from written-out orchestral dances for the upper echelons to folk tunes passed down by oral tradition for the peasantry.

While harpsichords and clavichords were played and manufactured *The piano* until the early nineteenth century, both gradually ceded popularity to the **pianoforte** (Italian for "soft-loud"), or **piano.** Invented by Bartolomeo Cristofori (1655–1732) in Florence in 1700, the piano uses a mechanism in which the strings are struck by hammers that then drop away, allowing each string to reverberate as long as the corresponding key is held down; this differs from the harpsichord, in which strings are plucked, and from the clavichord, where they are struck by tangents that stay in contact with the strings until the key is released. The piano allowed the player to change dynamic level and expression through touch alone, creating crescendos, diminuendos, sudden contrasts, and other effects. At first the new instrument met very slow acceptance, but from the 1760s on, makers in Austria, Germany, France, and England produced pianos in increasing quantity. There were two main types. The grand piano was shaped like a harpsichord, as shown in Figure 21.1; relatively expensive, it was used in public performances and in aristocratic homes. Most domestic instruments were square pianos, in the shape of a clavichord, like the one being played in Figure 21.2. Eighteenth-century pianos are often called *fortepianos* to distinguish them from the larger, louder forms of the piano developed in the nineteenth century.

Ensemble music was written for numerous combinations. Very common were works for one or more melody instruments, such as violin, viola, cello, or flute, together with keyboard, harp, or guitar. When the latter play basso continuo, they serve as accompaniment to the melody instruments. But whenever the keyboard has a fully written-out part in the chamber music of the 1770s and 1780s, it tends to take the lead, accompanied by the other

Figure 21.1: Piano made in 1788 by Johann Andreas Stein of Augsburg, whose instruments were typical of the age. The case resembles that of a harpsichord, and the strings are attached to a wooden frame, producing a lighter sound than the iron frames of nineteenth-century and modern pianos. The range is five octaves, from F' to f'''.

Figure 21.2: "The Cowper and Gore Families," painting by Johann Zoffany (1775), showing a square piano and a cello. Such pianos were the main domestic musical instrument from the 1760s through the mid-nineteenth century.

Figure 21.3: Table for playing string quartets, from about 1790. With the tabletop (in the background) removed and the music racks raised as shown here, the four players face one another, ideally positioned to listen to each other and engage in the "conversation" that string quartet playing was thought to embody.

parts. The reason for this dominance lies in the role this music played in domestic music-making among middle- and upper-class families. The daughters were often skilled performers at the keyboard, since music was one of the accomplishments they were expected to cultivate, while the sons—typically violinists and cellists—devoted less time to practice. Therefore an evening's entertainment required works that would highlight the woman's greater expertise, while allowing all to participate.

Chamber music for two to five strings alone was also common, especially the **string quartet** for two violins, viola, and cello. In these works, the first violin often carries most of the melodic substance, while the cello provides the bass, and the inner voices fill out the texture. However, knowing that players enjoyed hearing themselves in extended solos of several measures, composers also wrote *concertante* quartets in which the parts are of equal importance, as well as quartets in which players exchanged shorter motives as if in musical conversation.

Although now played in concerts, as they were on occasion at the time, string quartets and other chamber works were primarily intended for the enjoyment of the performers and their companions. Figure 21.3

shows a table designed for playing quartets, with a music rack for each player. The very layout, facing each other across a small table, makes clear that quartet playing was as social an activity in the late eighteenth century as card playing was in the twentieth.

The *clarinet*, a single-reed wind instrument, was invented around 1710, and by the 1780s took its place alongside the oboe, bassoon, and flute as the standard woodwind instruments. At this time, all four were typically made of wood and had one or more keys to aid in fingering. Groups of wind players had been a regular feature of courts and military establishments since the time of Louis XIV. The French ensembles often comprised only oboes, tenor oboes, and bassoons, but by the mid-eighteenth century the combination of two oboes and/or two clarinets with two horns and two bassoons was becoming common, as in Figure 21.4. There were as yet no amateur wind ensembles, and amateurs tended not to play wind instruments other than the flute.

Wind instruments and ensembles

The eighteenth-century concert orchestra was much smaller than today's. Haydn's orchestra from 1760 to 1785 rarely had more than twenty-five players, comprising flute, two oboes, two bassoons, two horns, about twelve to sixteen strings (violins I and II, violas, and cellos doubled by a bass viol), and a harpsichord, with trumpets and timpani occasionally added. Viennese orchestras of the 1790s usually numbered fewer than thirty-five players, now often including two clarinets. In the last quarter of the eighteenth century, the basso continuo was gradually abandoned in orchestral and other ensemble music because all the essential voices were present in the melody instruments. The responsibility for directing the group, formerly the job of the harpsichord player, fell to the leader of the violins.

Orchestra

The typical orchestration in the mid-eighteenth century gave all essential musical material to the strings and used the winds and horns only for doubling, reinforcing, and filling in the harmonies. Sometimes in performance woodwinds and brasses might be added to the orchestra even though the

Figure 21.4: A wind band consisting of two oboes, two clarinets, two horns, and two bassoons. Detail from an engraving of a company of grenadiers, published in London in 1753.

composer had written no parts specifically for them. Later in the century, the wind instruments were entrusted with more important and more independent material.

GENRES AND FORMS

Many of the characteristic genres of Baroque instrumental music fell out of fashion in the Classic period, including preludes, toccatas, fugues, chorale settings, and dance suites. Composers continued to write variation sets, fantasias, and individual dances for keyboard, but the major genre became the sonata in three or four movements of contrasting mood and tempo. Multimovement works similar to the keyboard sonata were also composed for a variety of chamber ensembles. These works were called sonata when written for solo instrument plus keyboard and otherwise named by the number of players: duet, trio, quartet, quintet, and so on. The main orchestral genres were the concerto, an extension of the Baroque solo concerto, and the **symphony**, derived from the Italian opera sinfonia, or overture, and the orchestral concerto. In works of three movements, typically the first and last were fast and the middle slow, often in a closely related key; later symphonies and quartets often had four movements, usually adding a minuet movement after (or sometimes before) the slow movement.

Continuity and change

The continuity of genre with earlier generations is remarkable: the concerto, the sinfonia, and the sonata for keyboard, soloist and keyboard, or chamber ensemble had all been prominent since the late seventeenth century. What is new, and quite distinct from their Baroque counterparts, however, is the content of each genre, including the forms used in each movement. All absorbed the new galant style that emphasized expressive melody in short phrases, arranged in periods, over light accompaniment.

Preference for major mode

Another difference from the Baroque era is the overwhelming preference for pieces in the major mode. More than a quarter of Vivaldi's concertos are in the minor mode, as are half of J. S. Bach's, but fewer than a tenth of those by Johann Christian Bach, Haydn, Mozart, or other composers active in the second half of the century are in minor. The major mode was considered more pleasing and natural, and was associated with more pleasant emotions. The older idea of purging negative feelings by experiencing them through music was fading. In addition, the focus on major for primary keys allowed composers to use closely related minor ones for contrast. The motion from happy stability—represented by a major-mode theme in a stable key and predictable phrasing—through dangers and trials—represented by minor keys, frequent modulation, and unstable phrasing—back to the home key and theme became a paradigm of Classic-era form.

SONATA FORM

The typical form for the first movement of a sonata, chamber work, or symphony from the Classic period is now known as **sonata form** (also called *first-movement form*). Since the nineteenth century, this form has been viewed primarily in terms of themes arranged in a three-part structure, but eighteenth-century writers understood it as a two-part form organized by phrase structure and harmony. The two views are compared in Figure 21.5.

The best contemporary account of the form is in the third and final volume of Heinrich Christoph Koch's *Introductory Essay on Composition* (1793). Building on his discussion of phrases and periods (see chapter 20), he describes first-movement form as an expanded version of binary form (see Figure 21.5). There are two large sections, each of which may be repeated, the first moving from tonic to dominant (or relative major in a minor key), the second returning to the tonic. The first section has one main period, the second two.

Koch on first-movement form

- In the first section, the principal ideas are presented, organized in a series of four phrases: the first two in the tonic; the third modulating to the dominant or relative major (often closing with a half-cadence in the new key); and the fourth in the new key, confirmed by an optional "appendix" phrase.

EIGHTEENTH-CENTURY VIEW: EXPANDED BINARY FORM

First Section		Second Section	
One Main Period		First Main Period	Second Main Period
Key: ‖: I – V :‖	‖: V – on V	I – I :‖

NINETEENTH-CENTURY VIEW: TERNARY FORM (ABA')

Exposition	Development	Recapitulation
Key: ‖: I – V :‖	X on V	I – I ‖

COMPARISON

Koch's Model		Nineteenth-Century View	
First Section		Exposition	
First and second phrase	I	First theme	I
Third phrase	mod to V	Transition	mod to V
Fourth phrase	V	Second theme	V
Appendix	V	Closing theme	V
Second Section			
First Main Period		Development	
Free	mod, often to vi, ii, iii	Develops ideas	mod
		from exposition	
Preparation for return	on V	Retransition	on V
Second Main Period		Recapitulation	
First and second phrase	I	First theme	I
Third phrase	mod	Transition	mod
Fourth phrase	I	Second theme	I
Appendix	I	Closing theme	I

Figure 21.5: Views of first-movement form.

- The first period of the second section may consist of any number of phrases. It often begins with the opening theme on the dominant, occasionally with another idea or in another key, and modulates back to the tonic by means of still another melodic idea.
- The second period of the second section parallels the first section and for the most part restates the same material, except that the third phrase ends on a half-cadence in the tonic, and the fourth phrase and appendix are now in the tonic.

For Koch, the typical phrase is four measures long, but the phrases mentioned here are often greatly expanded by repeating or varying material, inserting new material, or extending the phrase through delayed or evaded cadences. Koch notes that in symphonies, the various melodic units have a forceful and energetic character and tend to be extended and flowing, with few perceptible pauses and cadences. In sonatas and chamber works, on the other hand, melodic units are more often separated by clear phrase endings.

What Koch describes is an overall plan or set of principles for organizing a movement, not a rigid mold. His description conforms well to the great majority of first movements of the Classic period, as well as many middle movements and finales. We will see several examples in this and the next chapter.

Later view of sonata form   By the 1830s, theorists and analysts looking at works from the late 1700s and early 1800s began to describe the form in somewhat different terms. Where Koch saw a binary form, they divided the movement into three sections, corresponding to Koch's three periods (see Figure 21.5 for a comparison):

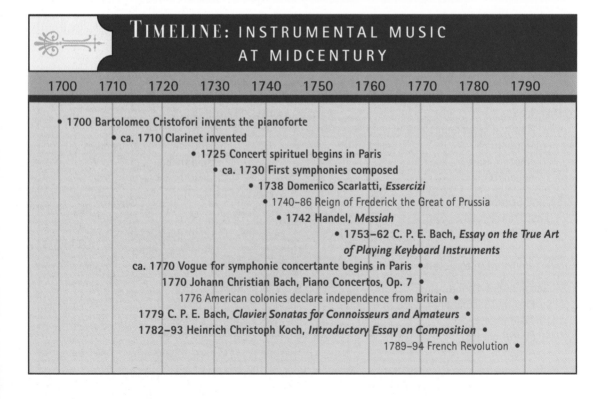

TIMELINE: INSTRUMENTAL MUSIC AT MIDCENTURY

1700	1710	1720	1730	1740	1750	1760	1770	1780	1790

- 1700 Bartolomeo Cristofori invents the pianoforte
- ca. 1710 Clarinet invented
- 1725 Concert spirituel begins in Paris
- ca. 1730 First symphonies composed
- 1738 Domenico Scarlatti, *Essercizi*
- 1740–86 Reign of Frederick the Great of Prussia
- 1742 Handel, *Messiah*
- 1753–62 C. P. E. Bach, *Essay on the True Art of Playing Keyboard Instruments*
- ca. 1770 Vogue for symphonie concertante begins in Paris •
- 1770 Johann Christian Bach, Piano Concertos, Op. 7 •
- 1776 American colonies declare independence from Britain •
- 1779 C. P. E. Bach, *Clavier Sonatas for Connoisseurs and Amateurs* •
- 1782–93 Heinrich Christoph Koch, *Introductory Essay on Composition* •
- 1789–94 French Revolution •

- an ***exposition***, usually repeated, with a first theme or group of themes in the tonic; a transition to the dominant or relative major; a second, often more lyrical theme or group in the new key; and a closing theme or cadential reinforcement in the same key;
- a ***development*** section, which modulates through a variety of keys, possibly even remote ones, and in which motives or themes from the exposition are presented in new aspects or combinations;
- a ***recapitulation***, in which the material of the exposition is restated in the original order but with all themes in the tonic.

In addition, there may be a slow introduction before the exposition, or a ***coda*** after the recapitulation that revisits one or more themes and confirms the tonic key.

Both models serve well to describe the mature works of Haydn and Mozart. But Koch's approach, emphasizing phrase structure and a specific harmonic plan, works better for music before about 1780, while the later view, focusing more on thematic content and contrast of keys, is a better fit for music after about 1800. The change came partly because movements grew longer, making themes the most obvious guideposts for listeners. Also, by the 1780s composers were moving away from the original conception of two repeated sections toward one which was more dramatically conceived, so that a second pass through the development and recapitulation would be anticlimactic; now a ternary plan (ABA′) seemed to better describe the presentation, development, and recapitulation of themes.

Changes in first-movement form

Of course, what is most interesting about any individual movement is how the composer uses the principles articulated by Koch or later theorists to create a unique piece of music. While following these principles, composers of sonata-form movements achieved a remarkable variety in form and content.

OTHER FORMS

Several of the other forms used in sonatas, chamber works, and symphonies in the Classic era also expand upon binary form, in various ways.

- Many slow movements use a variant of sonata form that omits the first period of the second section and has no repeats, but otherwise follows Koch's model; this has been called ***slow-movement sonata form*** or *sonata form without development*.
- ***Variations form***, used in some slow movements, presents a small binary form (or sometimes a single period) as a theme, followed by several embellished variants.
- ***Minuet and trio form***, often present in quartets and symphonies, joins two binary-form minuets, repeating the first after playing the second (the ***trio***) to produce an ABA pattern.
- ***Rondo form***, common in last movements, presents a small binary form or single period as a theme, then alternates it with other periods called ***episodes***, which are usually in other keys, in a pattern such as ABACA or ABACADA.

All forms of the Classic era exhibit similar compositional approaches. All depend upon grouping phrases into periods and periods into forms. All use both repetition and variation. All depend upon motion from the tonic to the dominant and back, and most confirm the tonic by restating material first presented in another key. Although expert composers scarcely had to think about these matters, it will help us to keep Koch's advice to novice composers in mind as we look at how this music is put together.

KEYBOARD MUSIC

Stimulated by the growing demand by amateurs for music that could be played at home and in private gatherings, composers of the middle and late eighteenth century produced great numbers of keyboard works, including sonatas, rondos, variations, and minuets. Sonatas were widely regarded as the most challenging for the performer and listener—and the most rewarding—so it follows that composers, especially the Italians and Germans, experimented with form, style, and expression in these works. Of the many composers active in the middle decades of the century, two are especially prominent: Domenico Scarlatti and C. P. E. Bach. In their music, we can find many elements of the new musical idiom.

DOMENICO SCARLATTI

Although he was virtually unknown throughout Europe during his lifetime, Domenico Scarlatti (1685–1757), shown in Figure 21.6, was one of the most original and creative keyboard composers of the eighteenth century. The son of Alessandro Scarlatti, and a friend and exact contemporary of Handel, he left Italy in 1719 to enter the service of the king of Portugal. When his pupil, the king's daughter, married Prince Ferdinand of Spain in 1729, Scarlatti followed her to Madrid, where he remained for the rest of his life in the service of the Spanish court, somewhat isolated from the rest of Europe.

Sonatas   Scarlatti published a collection of thirty harpsichord sonatas in 1738 under the title *Essercizi* (Exercises), but most of his 555 sonatas survive in scribal copies from his time. Each sonata is identified by its number in the standard index by Ralph Kirkpatrick. In his sonatas, Scarlatti used binary form: two sections, each repeated, the first closing in the dominant or relative major, the second modulating further afield and then returning to the tonic. The latter part of the first section invariably returns at the end of the second section, but in the tonic key, producing **rounded binary form**. Scarlatti's procedure resembles Koch's first-movement form, except that there is usually no return of the first section's opening material at any point in the second section.

Style   Scarlatti's style in the sonatas cannot be called galant because he does not emphasize melodies in short phrases over spare accompaniment, although he does have sections that resemble galant style. The harmonic scheme is paramount, and the musical material is designed mainly to activate the texture, often exhibiting the same propulsive spinning-out of motives of a Vivaldi

Figure 21.6: Domenico Scarlatti, in a portrait from about 1740 by Domingo Antonio de Velasco.

concerto. What is new, in comparison to a keyboard piece by Handel or J. S. Bach, is the sheer diversity of figuration. Example 21.1, taken from the first section of Scarlatti's Sonata in D Major, K. 119 (NAWM 98), probably composed in the 1740s, shows some of this variety. After the broken-chord opening establishes the tonic (Example 21.1a), it is confirmed by a scalar idea (Example 21.1b) and a cadence (Example 21.1c), each immediately repeated.

CD 7|22   CD 3|61

Example 21.1: Domenico Scarlatti, figures from Sonata in D Major, K. 119

a.

b.

c.

d.

e.

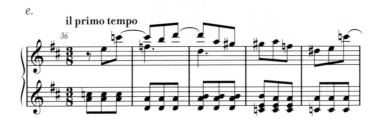

f.

A new phrase (Example 21.1d) imitates the rhythm and effect of castanets. After a modulation, a theme appears in the dominant minor (Example 21.1e); this is the first idea in the sonata to resemble the galant texture of melody with accompaniment, and it receives the most development. Scarlatti then leads us to a striking passage that builds to a climax through trills and growing dissonance, with chords of five or even six notes (Example 21.1f). The effect recalls Spanish guitar music, with the almost constant *a'* sounding like an open string strummed against those being fingered. These evocations of Spanish music are featured in a number of Scarlatti's other sonatas.

CARL PHILIPP EMANUEL BACH

Carl Philipp Emanuel Bach, shown in Figure 21.7, was one of the most influential composers of his generation. Trained in music by his father, J. S. Bach, he served at the court of Frederick the Great in Berlin from 1740 to 1768 and then became music director of the five principal churches in Hamburg. He composed oratorios, songs, symphonies, concertos, and chamber music, but most numerous and important are his works for keyboard. His *Essay on the True Art of Playing Keyboard Instruments* (1753–62) is an important source of information on the musical thought and practice of the period.

Bach's favorite keyboard instrument was the clavichord, which he prized *Sonatas* for its delicate dynamic shadings, although his late keyboard works seem to have been written with the piano in mind. He published eight sets of six keyboard sonatas (1742–79) and five sets of sonatas mixed with rondos and fantasias (1780–87). His first two sets, called the Prussian (1742) and Württemberg sonatas (1744), featured a new manner of keyboard writing and exerted a strong influence on later composers. These sets established the three-movement pattern for the sonata—with the first and last movements marked fast and the slow middle movement written in a related key—and demonstrated the possibility of expressive keyboard music outside the Baroque tradition of the suite. We have already examined a movement from the second collection (see chapter 20 and Example 20.1), which exhibited the

Figure 21.7: Carl Philipp Emanuel Bach, in a pastel portrait by his distant cousin Gottlieb Friedrich Bach, court organist and painter in Meiningen.

typical traits of the galant style: an emphasis on melody, with clear phrasing, frequent cadences, and light accompaniment. Many of his works, especially his slow movements, exemplify the empfindsam style, which adds elements that give the music greater individuality and emotional intensity.

Empfindsam characteristics

CD 7|26   CD 3|65

The main characteristics of the empfindsam style are apparent in the second movement (NAWM 99) of the fourth of his *Sechs Clavier-Sonaten für Kenner und Liebhaber* (Six Clavier Sonatas for Connoisseurs and Amateurs), composed in 1765 and published in 1779. As in the galant style, the basic texture features expressive melody in short phrases, arranged in periods, over light accompaniment. The form is slow-movement sonata form, lacking a development but otherwise conforming to Koch's description. But as shown in Example 21.2, the multiplicity of rhythmic patterns, nervously and constantly changing—turns, Scotch snaps (♬♪), short dotted figures, triplets, asymmetrical flourishes of five and thirteen notes—gives the music a restless, effervescent quality. In the opening phrase (measures 1–3), descending lines suggest sighs, and appoggiaturas and chromatic lower neighbor notes reinforce the melancholy mood. Later, Bach exploits the element of surprise, when unusual turns of melody, rests on the beat, sudden changes of dynamic

Example 21.2: C. P. E. Bach, second movement from Sonata in A Major, H. 186, Wq. 55/4

level, unexpected harmonic shifts, and a rising sequence create suspense and excitement. Bach also introduced in his instrumental works sections of musical dialogue and passages of recitative, applying the expressive tools of opera to create emotionally vibrant music.

ORCHESTRAL MUSIC

Music for orchestra grew in importance during the eighteenth century, as public and private concerts became more popular and more likely to include orchestral music.

SYMPHONY

The major orchestral genre of the mid- to late-eighteenth century was the **symphony,** a work in three or four movements, in a primarily homophonic style, without the division between orchestra and soloists that distinguishes the concerto. It originated in Italy around 1730 and spread across Europe. Throughout the century, a symphony was often the first item on a concert, followed by works in other genres. By the late 1700s, the symphony was considered the summit of instrumental music.

Like many musical genres, the symphony had more than one parent. The most obvious ancestor is the Italian *sinfonia,* or opera overture, from which the symphony takes its name. By 1700, many opera overtures used a three-movement structure in the order fast-slow-fast: an Allegro, a short lyrical Andante, and a finale in a dance rhythm, such as a minuet or gigue. These overtures, as a rule, have no musical connection with the opera they introduce and could be played as independent pieces in concerts. Yet other sources for the symphony are equally important. The orchestral concertos of Torelli and other composers (see chapter 17) also typically followed the fast-slow-fast format and were played in the same venues as concert symphonies. Church sonatas in northern Italy often had the same fast-slow-fast structure and homophonic style, and indeed throughout the eighteenth century symphonies were played in Catholic Church services, each movement at a different point in the Mass. Finally, the orchestral suite is one source for the binary forms that are common in the symphony. These similarities across genres suggest that multiple influences led to the symphony.

The first symphonies were written by composers working in Milan and the surrounding region of Lombardy in northern Italy. The most prominent was Giovanni Battista Sammartini (ca. 1700–1775), shown in Figure 21.8, whose Symphony in F Major, No. 32 (ca. 1740), is typical. It is scored for strings in four parts: violin I and II, viola, and bass, played by cellos, bass viol, and probably harpsichord and bassoon. There are three movements in the fast-slow-fast format, each relatively short; the whole piece takes less than ten minutes to play. The opening Presto (NAWM 100) follows the first-movement form described by Koch and is a concise thirty-eight measures. Each phrase of the form is given one or two distinctive ideas, and their

Italian origins

Figure 21.8: Giovanni Battista Sammartini, in an oil portrait copied in 1778 by Domenico Riccardi from a lost painting.

CD 7|28

Example 21.3: Sammartini, Symphony in F Major, No. 32, first movement, opening

diversity makes it easy to follow the form. Example 21.3 shows the first eight measures, which contain five sharply contrasting ideas: hammered octaves, a rising scale, a repeated melodic idea, rushing scalar figures, and a rising arpeggiation over throbbing bass.

Mannheim   From Italy the symphony spread north to Germany, Austria, France, and England. Especially prominent was Mannheim, where the elector Palatine's court was one of the most active musical centers in Europe. Under the leadership of Bohemian composer Johann Stamitz (1717–1757), the Mannheim orchestra became internationally famous for its impeccable discipline and technique, leading Charles Burney to call it "an army of generals." It was renowned for its unprecedented dynamic range from the softest *pianissimo* to the loudest *fortissimo* and for the thrilling sound of its crescendo, both effects that Stamitz exploited in his music.

Johann Stamitz   Stamitz was the first symphony composer to use consistently what would later become the standard plan: four movements, with a minuet and trio as the third movement, and a very fast finale, often marked Presto (quickly). He was also among the first to introduce a strongly contrasting and full-blown theme after the modulation to the dominant in the first section of an allegro movement, a practice that likewise became standard. The first movement of

CD 7|31   his Sinfonia in E♭ Major (NAWM 101), written in the mid-1750s, follows the customary plan outlined by Koch, but on a much larger scale than in Sammartini's symphony. To the four string parts, Stamitz adds two oboes and two horns, as was becoming customary. The opening phrases use several energetic ideas to emphasize the tonic. The transition to the dominant exploits the famous Mannheim crescendo, building excitement by means of string tremolos that progress from *piano* to *fortissimo*. After the arrival in the new key, a series of lyrical, graceful, and playful ideas provides a change of mood.

Other centers of symphonic activity included Vienna and Paris. In Vienna, Georg Christoph Wagenseil (1715–1777) and others wrote symphonies that feature pleasant lyricism and good humor, as well as the contrasting first-movement theme groups that later became important characteristics of Mozart's music. In Paris, an important center of composition and publication in the mid-eighteenth century, symphonies flowed from the city's presses. Foreign composers flocked to the city, including Sammartini, Stamitz, and Wagenseil. The Belgian François-Joseph Gossec (1734–1829) came to Paris in 1751 and eventually established himself as one of France's leading composers of symphonies, string quartets, and comic operas. He became one of the most popular composers of the Revolutionary period and one of the first directors of the Paris Conservatoire (see chapter 23).

Vienna and Paris

SYMPHONIE CONCERTANTE

As concert life expanded around 1770, a new genre emerged in response to the Parisian public's taste for pleasing melodies and virtuoso solos alongside big orchestral sonorities. This was the **symphonie concertante,** a concerto-like work with two or more solo instruments in addition to the regular orchestra, in which the main material is entrusted to the soloists. The format was ideal for the new concert environment because it gave composer-performers an opportunity to show off their abilities to the public, attract students, and encourage sales of their music. Hundreds of symphonies concertantes were written, performed, and published in Paris in the 1770s and 1780s, and composers in Mannheim and elsewhere soon followed suit. The genre's popularity waned by 1830, displaced by a new focus on individual virtuosity in solo recitals and concertos.

CONCERTO

Even while symphonic form gained increasing attention throughout the eighteenth century, the solo concerto remained popular as a vehicle for virtuosos, who often wrote concertos to play themselves. Among the first to compose piano concertos was Johann Christian Bach (1735–1782), shown in Figure 21.9. The youngest son of J. S. Bach, Johann Christian was trained by his father and older brother, studied and worked in Italy, and in 1762 moved to London, where he prospered as a

Figure 21.9: Johann Christian Bach, in a portrait by the renowned English painter Thomas Gainsborough (ca. 1776).

performer, teacher, impresario, and composer of concertos, symphonies, chamber music, keyboard music, and operas. His works, mostly galant in style, were performed all over Europe. He was a major influence on the young Mozart, who visited London in 1764 at age eight, met Bach, and arranged three of Bach's sonatas into concertos.

Three-movement plan

As in the early eighteenth century, concertos were typically in three movement with two fast movements around a slow middle movement. The slow movement and finale often used forms like those of other genres, but first movements followed a form unique to concertos.

Concerto first-movement form

The first movement of a typical concerto retained elements of the ritornello form of Baroque concertos, which alternates orchestral ritornellos with episodes that feature the soloist (see chapter 18), in combination with the contrasts of key and thematic material characteristic of sonata form. As Koch describes the form, there are three solo sections, structured in a way that is equivalent to the three main periods of sonata form. These sections are enclosed between four orchestral ritornellos; the first presents all or most of the main ideas while the others are relatively short. In essence, the concerto first movement is a sonata form framed by a ritornello form.

CD 7|36

To demonstrate these parallels, Figure 21.10 aligns the elements of ritornello form and of sonata form with the first movement of J. C. Bach's Concerto for Harpsichord or Piano and Strings in E♭ Major, Op. 7, No. 5 (NAWM 102), from ca. 1770. (The figure uses the more familiar nineteenth-century terminology for sonata form, although Koch's terms would be equally apt; compare Figure 21.5.) The Baroque plan of alternating ritornellos and episodes is clearly reflected in Bach's concerto, yet the three solo "episodes," in which the pianist takes the lead and the orchestra provides accompaniment and punctuation, have the shape of an exposition, development, and recapitulation of a sonata. The only long ritornello is the first, which introduces most of the movement's material in the tonic; in some modern views of concerto first-movement form, this is called the "orchestral exposition," followed by the "solo exposition." The later ritornellos can use any element from the first one, and here Bach mostly uses the closing theme. As is often the case, both the transition and the development introduce new ideas. Bach's concerto diverges from Koch's description in one significant aspect: the next-to-last ritornello is replaced by a brief orchestral articulation.

Cadenza

By Bach's time, it had become a tradition for the soloist to play a cadenza, usually improvised, just before the final orchestral ritornello. The cadenza had developed from the trills and runs that singers inserted, particularly before the return of the opening section in the da capo aria. By convention, concerto cadenzas are typically introduced by a weighty $^6_4$ chord, and the soloist signals the orchestra to reenter by playing a long trill over a dominant chord.

ENTERTAINMENT MUSIC

Finally, a great deal of music for orchestra and other ensembles was not concert music at all. Some pieces were written for background music, to be

Ritornello Form		Sonata Form		Form of J. C. Bach Movement	
Section	Key	Section	Key	Section	Key
Ritornello	I			Ritornello ("Orchestral Exposition")	
				First theme	I
				Transition	I
				Second theme	I
				Closing theme	I
Episode		Exposition		Solo ("Solo Exposition")	
		First theme	I	First theme	I
		Transition	mod	Transition, extended with new ideas	mod
		Second theme	V	Second theme	V
		Closing theme	V	Closing theme varied	V
Ritornello	V			Ritornello	
				Closing theme abbreviated	V
Episode		Development	mod	Solo ("Development")	mod
Ritornello	X			(Ritornello)	
				Brief orchestral cadence	on V
Episode		Recapitulation		Solo ("Recapitulation")	
		First theme	I	First theme	I
		Transition	mod	Transition, altered	I
		Second theme	I	Second theme	I
		Closing theme	I	Closing theme varied	I
				Cadenza	
Ritornello	I			Ritornello	
				Closing theme	I

Figure 21.10: Concerto first-movement form in J. C. Bach, Op. 7, No. 5.

played during a meal, a party, or other social occasion in an aristocratic or well-to-do home, or for performance in informal settings both indoors or out-of-doors. Genres in this category include the *divertimento, cassation,* and *serenade,* all multimovement pieces for orchestra or other combinations of winds and strings that might include a mix of dances with the types of movement common in symphonies.

THE SINGING INSTRUMENT

In the eighteenth century, instrumental music learned to sing. Composers absorbed the new styles pioneered in vocal music and blended them with existing traditions within each instrumental repertory. New genres, including piano sonata, string quartet, and symphony, as well as new forms like sonata form and concerto first-movement form, were consolidated and became the basis for much later instrumental music. In all of them, melody was paramount.

The instrumental music of this era was designed to appeal to a wide variety of people, to be understood on first hearing, and above all to please its performers and listeners. The tremendous numbers of new pieces show that they found ready audiences among middle- and upper-class amateurs and concertgoers. These numbers also confirm that consumers were eager for new music. Most of the vast quantities of instrumental music composed and published during this time passed from the stage fairly quickly, displaced by new works and styles, like popular music of later centuries.

After overshadowing their father for a generation or two, C. P. E. and J. C. Bach were in turn overshadowed by Haydn and Mozart, and their music was little played during the nineteenth century. Some of Domenico Scarlatti's sonatas circulated in the nineteenth century, and a complete edition was published early in the twentieth century. But only since the mid-twentieth century have the Bach sons, Scarlatti, Sammartini, Stamitz, and their contemporaries received enough attention from scholars, performers, and listeners for us to hear and understand them on their own terms, and be charmed once again.

Chapter 22

Classic Music in the Late Eighteenth Century

Musicians in the late eighteenth century worked mainly for courts, cities, and churches, but they also made money by teaching, performing, and composing on commission or for publication. As popularity with the public became more important, the most successful composers wrote music that pleased everyone from connoisseurs to those with little learning.

No one was better at reaching a diverse audience than Haydn and Mozart, whose music has come to exemplify the Classic period. Their careers, though exceptional in many respects, illustrate the circumstances in which professional musicians worked. Through a synthesis of styles and traditions, they created music with immediate yet deep and enduring appeal. Working for a patron in relative isolation, Haydn forged an idiom that brought him great popularity. In later years, writing for public concerts, he honed the balance of form and expression in his music, producing a series of masterpieces. Mozart achieved fame as a child prodigy, touring Europe and mastering every kind of music he encountered. In his maturity, working as a freelance pianist and composer, he blended aspects of many styles in music of unique richness. If we view these two composers in their eighteenth-century environments, we can see more clearly the problems that confronted them and the solutions they found. Haydn secured a job with a patron and lived a life of relative stability while Mozart had to find income where he could, yet both produced music that has attracted performers and listeners for over two centuries.

JOSEPH HAYDN

Joseph Haydn (1732–1809) was the most celebrated composer of his day (see biography and Figure 22.1). Prolific in every medium, he is best remembered for his numerous symphonies and string quartets, which established standards of quality, style, content, form, and expressivity that other composers emulated.

HAYDN'S PATRONS: THE ESTERHÁZY PRINCES

Haydn spent most of his career serving the Esterházy family, the most powerful noble family in Hungary. Hired in 1761 by Prince Paul Anton Esterházy, a generous patron devoted to music, Haydn had to compose whatever music the

JOSEPH HAYDN (1732–1809)

HAYDN! Great Sovereign of the tuneful art!
Thy works alone supply an ample chart
Of all the mountains, seas, and fertile plains
Within the compass of its wide domains.—
Is there an artist of the present day
Untaught by thee to think, as well as play?
Whose head thy science has not well
   supplied?
Whose hand thy labours have not fortified?

So wrote the celebrated music historian Charles Burney in 1791 on Haydn's arrival in England. Indeed, Haydn was hailed in his time as the greatest composer alive. In public life, he exemplified the Enlightenment ideals of good character, piety, and kindness. He was also an ambitious entrepreneur and skillful businessman, capable of both seriousness and humor. But above all, he had enormous talent, with which he satisfied his patrons and pleased his audiences.

Born in Rohrau, a village about thirty miles southeast of Vienna, Haydn was the son of a master wheelwright. At the age of seven he became a choirboy at St. Stephen's Cathedral in Vienna, where he acquired practical experience in music and learned singing, harpsichord, and violin. Dismissed at seventeen when his voice changed, Haydn barely supported himself as a freelance musician, composer, and teacher. He mastered counterpoint using Fux's *Gradus ad Parnassum*, studied the music of other composers, and took composition lessons from Nicola Porpora, a famous Italian composer and singing teacher.

Haydn became music director for Count Morzin in about 1757 and probably wrote his first symphonies for the count's orchestra. Three years later, he married a wigmaker's daughter, Maria Anna Keller, although he was really in love with her sister Josepha. Josepha, however, became a nun, and his long marriage was unhappy, childless, and marked by extra-marital affairs on both sides.

Figure 22.1: Franz Joseph Haydn, in an oil portrait by Thomas Hardy, painted in 1791–92 during Haydn's first sojourn in London.

In 1761, Haydn found a position that set him up for life and determined the course of his career. He entered the service of a Hungarian prince, Paul Anton Esterházy, and continued in the family's service for the rest of his life. For years Haydn was responsible for composing on demand, presenting concerts or operas weekly, and assisting with almost daily chamber music. While the position forced him to compose at a prodigious rate—just the catalog of his works, by Anthony van Hoboken, fills three hefty volumes—it allowed him to hear his music in excellent performances and to experiment with new ideas. During visits to Vienna, Haydn took part in the city's intellectual and musical life. It was there around 1784 that he met Mozart, and their mutual admiration blossomed.

The publication of Haydn's music brought him praise and fame throughout Europe and generated commissions from many other patrons. He spent most of the time between 1790 and 1795 composing, giving concerts, and teaching in London, where he had long been famous. His triumphs in London raised his reputation at home, and he was invited to return to Vienna as court music director for Prince Nikolaus II Esterházy, with minimal duties. He began to complain of weakness around 1799, and by 1802 had all but ceased to compose. He died, universally admired, in 1809.

MAJOR WORKS: *104 symphonies, 20 concertos, 68 string quartets, 29 keyboard trios, 126 baryton trios, 47 keyboard sonatas, 15 operas, 12 masses,* The Creation, The Seasons, *numerous other ensemble, keyboard, and vocal works*

prince demanded, conduct performances, train and supervise all the musical personnel, and keep the instruments in repair (see Source Reading). When Paul Anton died in 1762, his brother Nikolaus succeeded to the title; even more avid about music, he confirmed Haydn's appointment and raised his salary.

Eszterháza   At the Esterházy court, Haydn passed nearly thirty years in circumstances almost ideal for his development as a composer. Beginning in 1766, Nikolaus, whose seat was in Eisenstadt just south of Vienna, lived for most of the year at his remote country estate of Eszterháza, shown in Figure 22.2. The palace and

SOURCE READING

HAYDN'S CONTRACT

When he entered the service of Prince Paul Anton Esterházy, Haydn was named Vice-Kapellmeister, allowing the elderly Kapellmeister to retain his title but giving Haydn sole direction of orchestral, chamber, and dramatic music. His contract, excerpted below, spells out his duties and his social standing as a house officer, higher than servants yet still required to wear the court uniform. On the death of the Kapellmeister in 1766, Haydn succeeded to the title. The limits in clause 4 on circulating his music to others were later relaxed, and he earned both fame and money through performances and publications elsewhere.

———•———

2. The said Joseph Heyden [*sic*] shall be considered and treated as a member of the household. Therefore his Serene Highness is graciously pleased to place confidence in his conducting himself as becomes an honorable official of a princely house. He must be temperate, not showing himself overbearing toward his musicians, but mild and lenient, straightforward and composed. It is especially to be observed that when the orchestra shall be summoned to perform before company, the Vice-Capellmeister and all the musicians shall appear in uniform, and the said Joseph Heyden shall take care that he and all the members of his orchestra follow the instructions given, and appear in white stockings, white linen, powdered, and with either a pigtail or a tiewig. . . .

4. The said Vice-Capellmeister shall be under obligation to compose such music as his Serene Highness may command, and neither to communicate such compositions to any other person, nor to allow them to be copied, but he shall retain them for the absolute use of his Highness, and not compose for any other person without the knowledge and permission of his Highness.

5. The said Joseph Heyden shall appear daily in the antechamber before and after midday, and and inquire whether his Highness is pleased to order a performance of the orchestra. On receipt of his orders he shall communicate them to the other musicians, and take care to be punctual at the appointed time, and to ensure punctuality in his subordinates. . . .

7. The said Vice-Capellmeister shall take careful charge of all music and musical instruments, and be responsible for any injury that may occur to them from carelessness or neglect.

8. The said Joseph Heyden shall be obliged to instruct the female vocalists, in order that they may not forget in the country what they have been taught with much trouble and expense in Vienna, and, as the said Vice-Capellmeister is proficient on various instruments, he shall take care himself to practice on all that he is acquainted with.

Translated in Karl Geiringer, *Haydn: A Creative Life in Music* (New York: Norton, 1946), 52–53.

Figure 22.2: Eszterháza Palace, built 1762–66 as a summer residence on the Neusiedler Lake by the Hungarian prince Nikolaus Esterházy, whom Haydn served for almost thirty years. The palace opera house opened in 1768 with a performance of Haydn's Lo speziale. Mezzotint from 1791 by János Berkeny after Szabó and Karl Schütz, showing horsemen in formation and a Gypsy band at lower right.

grounds were designed to rival the splendor of Versailles. Eszterháza boasted two theaters, one for opera and one for marionette plays, and two large and sumptuously appointed music rooms. Haydn built up the orchestra to about twenty-five players, giving concerts every week and operas on special occasions. In almost daily chamber music sessions in the prince's private apartments, Nikolaus played cello, viola da gamba, and especially baryton, a large string instrument with sympathetic strings, shown in Figure 22.3. Through the early 1760s, Haydn composed mostly instrumental music for the prince—from orchestral works for concerts to baryton trios. After the move to Eszterháza, he also composed sacred vocal music and operas for its several theaters, while continuing to produce instrumental works.

Although Eszterháza was isolated, Haydn kept abreast of current developments in music through a constant stream of distinguished visitors and through sojourns in Vienna for one or two months each winter. He had the inestimable advantages of working with a devoted, highly skilled band of singers and players and

Figure 22.3: This baryton, shown leaning against its case, was owned by Prince Nikolaus Esterházy. A favorite instrument of the prince's, the baryton resembled a bass viola da gamba but had an extra set of resonating metal strings that could be plucked like a harp. Haydn wrote some 165 chamber works with baryton for the prince to perform, mostly trios with violin and cello.

an intelligent patron, whose requirements may have been burdensome but whose understanding and enthusiasm were inspiring. As Haydn once wrote,

> My prince was pleased with all my works, I was commended, and as conductor of an orchestra I could make experiments, observe what strengthened and what weakened an effect, and thereupon improve, substitute, omit, and try new things. I was cut off from the world, there was no one around to mislead or harass me, and so I was forced to become original.

Publication   Haydn's original contract forbade him to sell or give away his compositions, but unauthorized publications of his music in London, Paris, and elsewhere spread his reputation across Europe. A new contract in 1779 allowed Haydn to sell his music to others while continuing to direct opera and musical activities at court. He subsequently wrote most of his instrumental music with the expectation of sales to the public, in manuscript or printed copies. Since copyright at the time did not extend across national boundaries, Haydn tried to maximize his profits and to prevent pirated editions by selling the same piece simultaneously to publishers in several different countries.

TIMELINE: CLASSIC MUSIC IN THE LATE 18TH CENTURY

1760	1765	1770	1775	1780	1785	1790	1795	1800

- 1760–1820 Reign of George III of England
- **1761 Joseph Haydn hired by Prince Esterházy**
- **1762–73 Wolfgang Amadeus Mozart tours as child prodigy**
- 1765–80 Maria Theresa and Joseph II rule Austria jointly
- **1772 Haydn, Op. 20 quartets**
- **1772 Mozart concertmaster at Salzburg**
- 1774–92 Reign of Louis XVI of France
- 1776 American Declaration of Independence
- 1780 Death of Maria Theresa; Joseph II sole Hapsburg ruler
- 1781 Kant, *Critique of Pure Reason*
- **1781 Haydn, Op. 33 quartets**
- **1781 Mozart freelances in Vienna**
- **1785 Mozart, *Haydn* Quartets**
- **1787 Mozart, *Don Giovanni***
- 1788 Gibbon, *Decline and Fall of the Roman Empire*
- **1789 Haydn, *Oxford* Symphony**
- 1789–94 French Revolution
- 1790 Joseph II dies, Leopold II new emperor
- **1791 Death of Mozart**
- **1791 Haydn, first *London* Symphonies**
- **1798 Haydn, *The Creation***

SOURCE READING

HAYDN'S RECIPE FOR SUCCESS

In a brief book called Hints for Young Composers of Instrumental Music *(1805), the English gentleman composer John Marsh (1752–1828) offered tips on the use of various instruments and on other aspects of composition. Noting the revival of Handel's music in the 1780s, he credits Haydn with breathing new life into the "modern style" of galant composers.*

———— • ————

By this revival, or rather exaltation of the ancient, it seems not improbable that the modern style would have also failed in its turn (as it was about this time degenerating into a light, trivial and uniform character) had not the great Haydn, by his wonderful contrivance, by the variety and eccentricity of his modulation, by his judicious dispersion of light and shade, and happy manner of blending simple and intelligible air with abstruse and complicated harmony, greatly improved the latter species of composition, insomuch that, instead of being able, as was before the case, to anticipate in great measure the second part of any movement, from its uniform relation to the foregoing, it is

on the contrary, in his works, impossible to conceive what will follow, and a perpetual interest is kept up, in much longer pieces than any of the same kind ever composed. . . .

To conclude; in the composition of every piece of music, containing two or more movements, as well as in the selection and arrangement of pieces for a concert, let *contrast* be always attended to, as the best means of keeping the attention alive and active. For through the common neglect to relieve loud passages with soft ones, full pieces and choruses, with quartettos, songs and glees, instrumental music with vocal, and ancient music with modern, many compositions, in other respects excellent, produce but little effect; and people become fatigued, and complain of the length of concerts, which perhaps would never tire them, were they not cloyed with too much of one thing, or too great a uniformity of style.

John Marsh, *Hints to Young Composers of Instrumental Music* (London, 1805); reprinted and ed. Charles Cudworth, *The Galpin Society Journal* 18 (1965): 57–72, quoting pp. 60 and 71.

As Haydn increasingly composed for publication or for other patrons, he gained a measure of independence from his employer. His freedom grew unexpectedly in 1790 when Nikolaus died and his son Anton disbanded the orchestra. Haydn was given a pension and went to live in Vienna, but the impresario and violinist Johann Peter Salomon persuaded him to come to London for two extended stays between 1791 and 1795. There Haydn conducted concerts, taught well-to-do students, and composed many new works. His last twelve symphonies, written for London, were received there with great acclaim.

London

HAYDN'S STYLE

Haydn's style, which drew on many sources, was recognized in his time as highly individual. It was forged by his experiences trying to please his patron, his players, and the public. He sought broad and immediate appeal by devising themes that seemed familiar on first hearing and by following conventions for phrasing, form, and harmony. Yet he made his music more interesting than most by introducing the unexpected, in numerous ways (see Source Reading). In a delightful alchemy, each aspect of his style reinforced the others: the familiar was enriched by contrasts, the reliance on conventions created listener expectations that made surprises possible, the content clarified the form, and the intrinsic variety allowed him to evoke the sublime or create musical humor with equal skill.

Sources

The main source for Haydn's idiom was the galant style, the predominant language of music by midcentury, marked by songful melody in short phrases, arranged in balanced periods, over light accompaniment. Into this framework Haydn brought elements of other styles. From C. P. E. Bach, whose keyboard sonatas he studied diligently, Haydn adopted the heightened expressivity of the empfindsam style and an emphasis on making the most of each musical idea through variation and development. Also important was the learned style of counterpoint, absorbed from Baroque composers and Fux's *Gradus ad Parnassum*. Other elements came from styles associated with particular genres, nations, or social classes, from opera buffa to hymns and from military fanfares to folksongs.

Simple yet sophisticated

CD 8|1   CD 3|67

A characteristic example of Haydn's mature style is the theme for the rondo-form finale of his String Quartet in E♭ Major, Op. 33, No. 2 (*The Joke*, 1781, NAWM 103), shown in Example 22.1. The tuneful theme—a small binary form—seems simple on first hearing, but on closer examination, we find remarkable sophistication.

Economy and novelty

The theme derives entirely from a single idea presented in the first two measures (bracketed in the example). The idea contains three rhythmic motives (marked a, b, and c), which recur in various permutations in what follows. Even when the rhythm repeats exactly (at measures 3, 9, and 11), Haydn gives it a new melodic contour, so that each phrase is both familiar and fresh. Combining economy of material with constant novelty is typical of Haydn.

Rhythm, phrasing, and harmony

The opening idea does not close on the downbeat but spills over into the second half of the measure, lending it a playful, unfinished character. When it repeats at measure 5, the rhythmic momentum carries forward to the downbeat of measure 7, allowing the last motive to close on the downbeat of measure 8. Through this expansion, Haydn creates a four-measure phrase to balance the two preceding two-measure units. Because the harmony avoids root-position cadences at measures 4 and 6, the listener does not sense a relaxation until the cadence in measure 8 closes the first period. Thus rhythm and harmony work together to sustain continuity throughout the entire period, despite its short, choppy melodic units.

Expansion, delay, and drama

After the first period repeats, the second section begins on the dominant with a complementary eight-measure period that continues to vary the opening idea. After this period cadences in measure 16, a simple reprise of the first period would bring the theme to a satisfactory conclusion. But before finally granting the reprise (at measure 29), Haydn delays its arrival by inserting a long elaboration on the dominant. Louder dynamic levels, diminished chords, diminuendos and crescendos, and a pedal point all create a sense of drama. Even within this insertion there is expansion; measures 20–21 or measures 23–28 could be omitted, since the former prolongs what "should" have been a four-measure phrase and the latter confirms and extends the cadence. Such expansion of a phrase, period, or section is a basic technique in Haydn's music, used for both expressive and formal purposes.

Example 22.1: Theme from the finale of Haydn's String Quartet in E♭ Major, Op. 33, No. 2

Wit   Because this dramatization of the dominant seems exaggerated in the context of a little rondo theme, the effect is witty. The humor is produced through
incongruity of a sort that only experienced listeners and performers can notice, because in order to catch the joke we must understand the form, the
genre, and the conventions that underlie them. Haydn's wit makes his music
especially endearing to players and connoisseurs because he compliments
our perceptiveness with every joke or subtle effect he puts in his music.

This quartet earned the nickname *The Joke* because of this movement's
closing passage, shown in Example 22.2. Here Haydn inserts long rests between phrases of his theme. Through these surprising pauses, we are made
aware of our expectations for how the music will continue. When measures
5–8 of the theme (see Example 22.1) are broken into two-measure phrases
(measures 160–62 and 164–66), we suddenly realize that such two-measure
units are what we expected at the beginning, and that Haydn's original version was a witty variant. After the longest rest of all leads us to think that the
piece is over, the opening figure returns once more, suggesting yet another
go-around of the theme. But when the players relax, indicating that the piece
is finished, we are amused at the way Haydn played on our expectations. We
may also notice that the opening figure cadences on the tonic, making it a
suitable ending after all. The joke is obvious, but its fullest meaning is open
only to an experienced listener.

Differentiation   The anomaly of Haydn's converting an opening phrase into a final cadence
of function   points out a basic truth about the galant style: there is a strong differentiation
of function between elements. Familiarity with the conventions of the style

Example 22.2: Closing passage of Haydn's Op. 33, No. 2

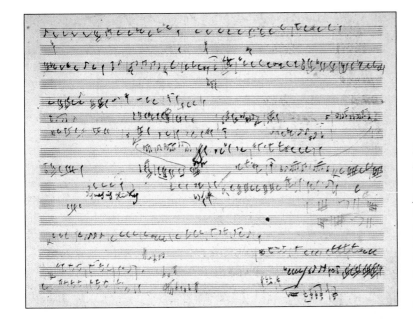

Figure 22.4: A page of Haydn's sketches for his oratorio The Seasons. *The composer notated passages in a kind of musical shorthand on one or two staves without clefs or key signatures. This was intended to jot down his thoughts, not to be read by others, and it can be difficult to follow without comparing it to the final score.*

make it easy for listeners to distinguish between musical gestures that signal the beginning, middle, or end of a phrase, period, or larger section. Even surrounded by silence, measures 164–66 clearly constitute an ending gesture, and measures 160–62 could not satisfactorily begin or end a period but must fall in the middle. Similarly, listeners can tell a theme from a transition or a cadential extension. The opening eight-measure period of Example 22.1 is immediately perceptible as thematic, marked by regular phrasing, frequent cadences, and a logical harmonic progression that stays in a single key. On the other hand, measures 17–28 could not stand alone as a theme; the relative harmonic stasis, repetitions, and continuous rhythms would sound odd in a theme but are just right for confirming a cadential arrival. Haydn exploits these differences to make his music easy to follow, but also turns gestures on their heads when he wants to amuse and surprise us.

Double appeal

When we examine Haydn's music closely, we recognize how sophisticated it is. Yet it remains simple in the best sense: clear, engaging, easy to understand. It appeals at once to the least experienced listener yet rewards the connoisseur, even after repeated hearings. This double appeal is a recipe for greatness as well as popular success, an achievement that many have tried to emulate but few have equaled.

COMPOSITIONAL PROCESS

As simple and natural as Haydn's music may sound, it was not produced without effort. According to his own report, he began a composition by improvising at the keyboard until he settled on an appropriate theme or idea. He then worked out the piece at the keyboard and on paper, usually writing down only the main melody and harmony on one or two staves. Figure 22.4, a page of sketches for his oratorio *The Seasons* (1799–1801), shows this type of musical shorthand. Often, he drafted sections in an order that was different from their appearance in the piece. Finally, he wrote out the completed score. This procedure combined improvisation and calculation, while Haydn first searched for something to say and then devised the most effective way to say it. The interplay of heart and mind this process embodies is reflected in his music's union of expressivity and craft.

SYMPHONIC FORM

Haydn has been called "the father of the symphony," not because he invented the genre but because his symphonies set the pattern for later composers through their high quality, wide dissemination, and lasting appeal. When the classical repertory was established in the nineteenth century, his were the oldest symphonies to receive regular performances. Thus he seemed to stand at the head of a great tradition.

Haydn's symphonies are traditionally identified by number, although the numbering (applied by a nineteenth-century publisher) does not precisely reflect the order in which they were written nor their total number of approximately 106. Many of his symphonies that have acquired names—few of which were bestowed by the composer himself—are among the best known. His symphonies are remarkably diverse, for he seems deliberately to have made each one an individual. Yet they have enough in common that we can distill his usual practices.

Four-movement structure

The typical Haydn symphony has four movements: (1) a fast sonata-form movement, often with a slow introduction; (2) a slow movement; (3) a minuet and trio; and (4) a fast finale, usually in sonata or rondo form. All are in the same key except the slow movement, which is in a closely related key such as the subdominant or dominant. Haydn's consistent use of this format helped to make it the standard for later composers.

Oxford Symphony

CD 7|51   CD 4|1

Haydn's Symphony No. 92 in G Major (NAWM 104) illustrates many elements that characterize his symphonic techniques. Written in 1789 for a French count, it is known as the *Oxford* because it was performed when the composer received an honorary doctorate from Oxford University in 1791.

First-movement form

As in many of Haydn's symphonies, the first movement begins with a slow introduction, whose solemn, suspenseful mood makes the ensuing Allegro sound energetic by comparison. Similarly strong contrasts delineate the components of the movement's sonata form. Thematic areas are tonally stable, with balanced phrases articulated by cadences. The themes alternate with unstable passages that serve as transitions, often scored for full orchestra and characterized by loud dynamics, sequences, modulation, dramatic rushing figures, overlapping phrases, and avoidance of cadences. The contrasts between stability and instability in phrasing and key help us follow the form. Haydn often heightens these contrasts through differences in style, texture, instrumentation, or mood, so that whichever musical elements we pay attention to, we are not likely to get lost.

Exposition

Each thematic area typically contains a variety of ideas. Example 22.3 shows the opening of the first theme group in the *Oxford* Symphony, with three distinct ideas set off by rhythm, figuration, instrumentation, and

Example 22.3: First theme from the first movement of Haydn's Symphony No. 92

dynamic level. The theme starts on the dominant seventh chord with a phrase that sounds more like a middle than a beginning (measures 21–24)—another example of Haydn playing with listener expectations. Following his usual practice, Haydn reiterates the opening material to begin the transition, introducing destabilizing turns of harmony and rhythm that steer the music in a new direction and eventually lead to the dominant. At this point, Haydn often introduces a contrasting theme, but in the *Oxford* and many other symphonies, he begins the second thematic section with the opening idea, here with a countermelody in the winds. A transition-like passage leads to the closing subject, which is typically more repetitive and cadential than the first or second themes.

Development   In the development, motives from the exposition are varied, extended, combined, or superimposed; treated in sequence, imitation, fugato, or stretto; or made into figurations for rushing passages. Enriching developments and transitions with counterpoint is one way Haydn brought the older learned style into works in the modern galant style. Abrupt changes of subject, digressions, and silences are particularly characteristic of Haydn developments.

Recapitulation   We are usually well prepared for the recapitulation, but Haydn sometimes disguises or plays down its actual appearance so that we may not recognize that it has begun until after the fact. Often the opening subject is rescored or extended in new ways. In the *Oxford* Symphony first movement, both the first and second phrases of the first theme are now imitated in the flute, introducing counterpoint where there was none in the exposition; together with the ambiguous nature of the first theme's opening idea, this makes it sound at first as if the development is continuing. The second and closing themes now appear in the tonic, but instead of curtailing the transition because he does not need to modulate, Haydn likes to intensify and animate it with a simulated modulation. He does so in this movement, where motives from the closing theme unexpectedly show up in the transition.

Slow movement   The second movement of a Haydn symphony usually offers an oasis of calm and gentle melody after the contrasts, drama, and complexity of the first movement. Many of the slow movements are in sonata form without repeats, and in later works Haydn often used theme and variations. In the *Oxford* Symphony, the slow movement is in ternary form, with a songlike theme, a dramatic middle section in the tonic minor, an abbreviated reprise, and a quiet coda that features woodwind instruments and employs colorful chromatic harmonies. Such contrasting minor sections and soft codas are common in his later symphonies.

Minuet and trio   The third movement comprises a pair of stylized minuets, with the first repeated after the second (the trio) to create an ABA form for the movement as a whole. Both minuet and trio are cast in the traditional binary dance form with repeats. The trio is usually set in the same key as the minuet (possibly with a change of mode), sometimes in a closely related key, but has a lighter orchestration and character; it takes its name from the reduced texture of three parts used for such middle dances in the seventeenth century. The minuet movement provides relaxation, since it is shorter than the previous movements, is written in a more popular style, and has a form that is easy to follow. But its very directness allowed Haydn to introduce interest and humor. In the *Oxford* Symphony, for example, the minuet has phrases of six measures rather than the usual four, and unexpected harmonies, syncopations, pauses, and changes of dynamic level keep the listener off-balance.

Finale   After the easy-going minuet, the final movement closes the symphony with a further buildup of tension, climax, and release. The finale is typically faster and shorter than the first movement, overflowing with high spirits and impish surprises. The finale of the *Oxford* Symphony, like many of Haydn's finales, is in sonata form. The playful first theme, shown in Example 22.4, also appears on the dominant in the transition to the second thematic section, returns at the end of the exposition, and predominates in the development. From the 1770s on, Haydn favored rondo finales, in which the main theme, usually a small binary form, alternates with several contrasting sections, often in the pattern ABACABA. Some are **sonata-*rondos*,** in which the A and B sections resemble the first and second themes in a sonata-form exposition, C is a modulatory development passage, and B returns near the end in the tonic.

Example 22.4: Opening theme from finale of Haydn's Symphony No. 92

THE SYMPHONIES

Haydn showed a mastery of the symphony from his first works in the genre, but his approach changed over time.

His earliest symphonies, written for Count Morzin between 1757 and 1761, were typically scored for two oboes, two horns, and strings. Most are in three movements in fast-slow-fast sequence, like earlier Italian and Austrian symphonies. For his sonata-form movements, he chose themes made of elements that were easily broken up and recombined.

Early symphonies, 1757–67

During his first years with the Esterházys, Haydn composed about thirty symphonies (1761–67), all quite diverse, as Haydn sought novelty and variety in his offerings at court. The ensemble is often augmented with flute, bassoon, or other instruments. The best-known symphonies from this time are Nos. 6 to 8, which Haydn composed soon after entering Prince Esterházy's service in 1761, titled *Le matin* (Morning), *Le midi* (Noon), and *Le soir* (Evening). Haydn included solo passages for each instrument designed to showcase the skills of his players.

Beginning about 1768, Haydn presented his symphonies at Eszterháza in the mirrored concert room shown in Figure 22.5. The twelve symphonies of the next four years show Haydn as a composer of mature technique and fertile imagination. No longer viewing the symphony as light entertainment, Haydn now regarded it as a serious work that demanded close attention. These symphonies are longer, more rhythmically complex, more contrapuntal, and more challenging to play. They are marked by greater extremes in dynamic level, more sudden contrasts between loud and soft, and more use of crescendos and sforzatos, all used to startling effect. The harmonic palette is richer than in the early symphonies, and modulations range more widely. Several

Symphonies of 1768–72

Figure 22.5: This hall in the Eszterháza Palace was used from around 1768 for concerts, at which Haydn presented his symphonies. Although in other centers symphonies were often accompanied by basso continuo and the keyboard player directed the ensemble, at Eszterháza there was no continuo, and Haydn led the ensemble while playing first violin.

symphonies from this period, particularly the six in minor keys, have an emotional, agitated character that some scholars have associated with the literary movement known as *Sturm und Drang* (storm and stress, after a 1776 play).

Symphonies of 1773–81

Beginning around 1773, Haydn turned from minor keys and experiments in form and expression to embrace a more popular style. Audiences expected symphonies to be immediately intelligible and appealing, but also serious, stirring, and impressive, and Haydn produced works that have all these traits. Symphony No. 56 in C Major (1774) is festive and brilliant, like its predecessors in the same key, but encompasses a broader emotional range, reflecting Haydn's recent experience with heightened expression. The opening theme alternates arpeggiations for the whole orchestra, suggestive of fanfares, with songlike phrases for the strings. The agitation, counterpoint, chromaticism, and dramatic surprises of *Sturm und Drang* style now serve as contrast, making the transition stand out in comparison to the themes.

Symphonies for public concerts

In the 1780s, Haydn increasingly composed for the public, selling his symphonies to patrons or publishers abroad. By now he consistently wrote for an orchestra of flute, two oboes, two bassoons, two horns, and strings, sometimes augmented by trumpets and timpani. The *Paris* Symphonies of 1785–86 (Nos. 82–87), commissioned for performance in the French capital, were his grandest so far. Queen Marie Antoinette (later guillotined during the French Revolution) is said to have especially loved No. 85, called *La Reine* (The Queen). After the six symphonies were performed again in 1787, a reviewer noted how "this great genius could draw such rich and varied developments from a single subject, so different from the sterile composers who pass continually from one idea to another." Symphonies Nos. 88–92 were also composed on commission. Like the *Paris* symphonies, they offer a combination of popular and learned styles, and of deep expression with masterful technique, that gave them immediate and lasting appeal.

The invitation from Johann Peter Salomon in 1790 to compose and conduct symphonies for the cosmopolitan and exacting audiences of London spurred Haydn to supreme efforts. Hailed by the British as "the greatest composer in the world," he was determined to live up to what was expected of him. The twelve *London* Symphonies are his crowning achievements, with more daring harmonic conceptions, intensified rhythmic drive, and, especially, more memorable thematic inventions. The orchestra is expanded, with trumpets and timpani now standard and clarinets in all but one of the last six. Woodwinds and string bass are used more independently than before, solo strings appear at times, and the whole sound achieves a new spaciousness and brilliance.

London *Symphonies*

Haydn's shrewd appraisal of London's musical tastes is evident. There is a sudden *fortissimo* crash on a weak beat in the slow movement of Symphony No. 94 that has given this work its nickname *Surprise*. It was put there because, as Haydn later acknowledged, he wanted something novel and startling to take people's minds off the rival concert series of his former pupil Ignaz Pleyel (1757–1831). The greater tunefulness may also have been prompted by this competition, since Pleyel's strong suit was melody. Haydn turned to Slovenian, Croatian, and other peasant tunes he remembered from his youth. Symphony No. 103 displays characteristic instances of folklike melodies, and the finale of No. 104, with its imitation of the bagpipe, is particularly suggestive of a peasant dance, as shown in Example 22.5. Similar allusions are the "Turkish" band effect (triangle, cymbals, bass drum) and the trumpet fanfare in the Allegretto of the *Military* Symphony (No. 100), and the ticking accompaniment in the Andante of No. 101 (the *Clock*). Such appealing features reflect Haydn's aim to please both the music lover and the expert.

Example 22.5: Opening theme from the finale of Haydn's Symphony No. 104

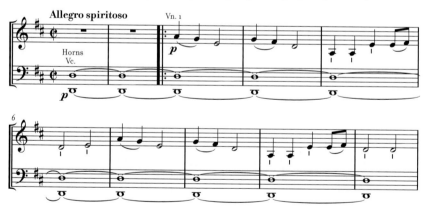

STRING QUARTETS

Haydn has been called "the father of the string quartet" with more justification than we have for the epithet "father of the symphony." Although not the first to compose quartets, he was among the earliest and was the first great master of the genre. Unlike symphonies, which were typically performed by professionals for an audience, quartets were primarily music for amateurs to play for their own pleasure. Haydn's quartets are very much addressed to the players. They are sometimes described as a conversation among the instruments: the first violin has the leading role, but the cello and inner parts often carry the melody or engage in dialogue. The evolution of his quartets parallels that of the symphonies in many respects, from early mastery, through increasing length and emotional depth, to very individual late works.

Early quartets   Haydn's first ten quartets resembled divertimentos and were so titled when they were published in his Opp. 1 (1764) and 2 (1766). From then on, Haydn tended to write quartets in groups of six, the most common number of works in a published collection.

Opp. 9, 17, and 20   The next eighteen quartets, Opp. 9 (ca. 1770), 17 (1771), and 20 (1772), established for the quartet the same four-movement pattern as in the symphony, but with the minuet often before instead of after the slow movement. In the sonata-form movements, Haydn adopted strategies unique to his quartets. After the first theme, dominated by the first violin, he usually chose a looser texture in which the primary motives pass from one instrument to another. In place of the orchestral tuttis that highlight the transitions in the symphonies, Haydn favored loud unisons or stark modulatory gestures. Several of these quartets are in minor keys, like the contemporary *Sturm und Drang* symphonies, and three from Op. 20 end with fugues. The quartets of this period made Haydn famous far beyond Austria, and their expanded proportions and expressive range set the pattern for later quartets.

Opus 33   Haydn composed the six quartets of Op. 33 in 1781 and proclaimed to two admirers that they were written in a "quite new and special way." They are lighthearted, witty, and tuneful. The minuets, here titled *scherzo* (Italian for "joke" or "trick") or *scherzando* ("joking" or "playful"), play tricks on the courtly dance by breaking normal metrical patterns, as illustrated by the heimola and sudden silence (see Example 22.6). **Scherzo** became the term for a joking or especially fast movement in minuet and trio form.

Even apart from the scherzos, Op. 33 contains some of Haydn's happiest strokes of humor, as we have seen with the rondo finale of No. 2 (see above,

Example 22.6: Scherzo from Haydn's String Quartet in G Major, Op. 33, No. 5

Examples 22.1–22.2, and NAWM 103). Haydn's playfulness in the themes themselves and in the dialogue between players added merriment to amateur quartet evenings in cities such as London, Paris, and Vienna, in the country estates of the nobility, and even in monasteries. Since quartets were normally played at sight and were not published in score, many of the jokes became apparent only in performance; there is more than one story of a player cracking up with laughter at an unexpected turn of events.

In his remaining years, Haydn composed thirty-four quartets. Especially *Later quartets* noteworthy are the six quartets of Op. 76 (ca. 1796–97), which exemplify a new approach to the quartet as a genre for performance in concerts, alongside its traditional role in private music-making. In his last quartets, Haydn expanded the harmonic frontiers, foreshadowing Romantic harmony with chromatic progressions, chromatic chords, enharmonic changes, and fanciful tonal shifts. Each quartet has individual features, as if Haydn were trying to avoid repeating himself; indeed, this had become a requirement, since he was writing primarily for publication, and amateurs and audiences were most attracted to the new. Like his late symphonies, his late quartets juxtapose the serious and jocular, the artful and folklike, the sublime and the jesting.

KEYBOARD SONATAS AND TRIOS

In Haydn's day, keyboard sonatas and trios were written for amateurs to play in private for their own enjoyment. Both genres usually featured three movements in fast-slow-fast format, and both focused on the expression of intimate or sentimental feelings, befitting their private character. Indeed, the keyboard trio was essentially a keyboard sonata accompanied by strings, the cello doubling the bass line and the violin adding background and some contrasting themes.

VOCAL WORKS

In a modest autobiographical sketch of 1776 written for an Austrian encyclopedia, Haydn named his most successful works: three operas, an Italian oratorio, and his setting of the *Stabat Mater* (1767), a work that won favor in 1780s Europe. He made no mention of the sixty symphonies he had written by then and referred to his chamber music only to complain that the Berlin critics dealt with it too harshly. In line with the aesthetic theories of the era, Haydn believed that vocal music was more important than instrumental, more effective at moving the listener, and closer to song, which he considered the natural source of all music. The enthusiastic reception of his symphonies and string quartets in Paris and London during the 1780s and 1790s showed him how highly regarded they were, and by the early nineteenth century his reputation rested primarily on his instrumental works.

Opera occupied much of Haydn's time and energy at Eszterháza. Of his fif- *Operas* teen or more Italian operas, most were comic, with music abounding in humor and high spirits. Of the three serious operas, the most famous was *Armida* (1784), remarkable for dramatic accompanied recitatives and arias on a grand scale. Although successful in their day, Haydn's operas are now rarely mounted.

Masses   Haydn's earliest surviving and last completed works were masses dating from 1749 and 1802 respectively. His last six masses (1796–1802), including *Missa in tempore belli* (Mass in Time of War, 1796), the *Lord Nelson* Mass (1798), the *Theresienmesse* (1799), and the *Harmoniemesse* (Windband Mass, 1802), are large-scale, festive works using four solo vocalists, chorus, and full orchestra with trumpets and timpani. Like the masses of Mozart and other south Germans, these works have a flamboyance that matches the architecture of the Austrian Baroque churches in which they were performed. Haydn's masses blend traditional elements, including contrapuntal writing for solo voices and the customary choral fugues at the conclusion of the Gloria and the Credo, with a new prominence for the orchestra and elements drawn from symphonic style and symphonic forms. The occasional criticism that his sacred music was too cheerful met with the composer's assurance that at the thought of God, his heart "leaped for joy" and his confidence that God would not reproach him for praising the Lord "with a cheerful heart."

Oratorios   During his stay in London, Haydn became acquainted with some of Handel's oratorios. At Westminster Abbey in 1791, Haydn was so deeply moved by the Hallelujah Chorus in a massive performance of *Messiah* that he burst into tears and exclaimed, "He is the master of us all." Haydn's appreciation for Handel bore fruit in the choral parts of his late masses and inspired him to compose his oratorios *The Creation* (completed 1798), on texts adapted from Genesis and Milton's *Paradise Lost*, and *The Seasons* (completed 1801). Both were issued simultaneously in German and English, in a nod both to Handel and to the English public, and both quickly became standards of the repertory for choral societies in German- and English-speaking areas. The German

Example 22.7: Excerpt from Haydn's Creation, *Part I*

Figure 22.6: Haydn attends a performance of his oratorio The Creation *in the Great Hall of the University of Vienna on March 27, 1808, put on to mark his seventy-sixth birthday earlier that month. This was Haydn's last public appearance before his death the following year. Watercolor by Balthasar Wigand.*

texts were written by Baron Gottfried van Swieten, the imperial court librarian in Vienna and a busy musical and literary amateur.

Haydn's instrumental introductions and interludes in both works are among the finest examples of depiction in music of the time. His *Depiction of Chaos* at the beginning of *The Creation* features confusing and disturbingly dissonant harmonies. The transition in the following recitative and chorus, with its awesome choral outburst on a C-major chord at the words "and there was Light!," shown in Example 22.7, made a profound impression on audiences and was extolled by contemporary writers as the supreme example of the sublime in music.

ACHIEVEMENT AND REPUTATION

Haydn made his last public appearance for a performance of *The Creation* to celebrate his seventy-sixth birthday in 1808, as depicted in Figure 22.6. When he died the next year, he left an enormous body of music, the fruit of over half a century of hard work. His reputation rested on a small fraction of his output, primarily the symphonies and quartets of the 1770s to 1790s and the last two oratorios. These works, which were popular with performers and audiences, greatly influenced other composers and quickly became part of the permanent repertory. In its union of opposites, its ability to hold stark contrasts together in a coherent whole, and its balance of form and expression, Haydn's best music still elicits admiration and awe. The combination he achieved of wide appeal to the public with long-lasting rewards for the connoisseur has seldom been matched.

WOLFGANG AMADEUS MOZART

Wolfgang Amadeus Mozart (1756–1791) counted Haydn as a friend, and each admired and was influenced by the other. But their lives and careers differed fundamentally. Although Mozart was twenty-four years younger than Haydn, he achieved wide renown earlier, as a touring child prodigy in the 1760s. For most of his career, Haydn worked contentedly for the Esterházy princes, while Mozart never found a suitable position and spent his mature years as a free agent in Vienna (see biography and Figure 22.7). Yet when he died at thirty-five, Mozart was seen by many (including Haydn) as Haydn's equal, and the two have come to define the music of their era.

CHILD PRODIGY

Mozart was profoundly affected by his experiences as a child prodigy. His early and thorough training gave him seemingly effortless command of the

WOLFGANG AMADEUS MOZART (1756–1791)

Mozart composed prolifically from the age of six to his premature death at thirty-five. A master of every medium, he is widely considered one of the greatest musicians of the Western classical tradition. His piano sonatas and concertos and his mature operas, symphonies, chamber, and choral works are mainstays of the repertory and epitomize the classical style.

Mozart was born in Salzburg, a quasi-independent state ruled by an archbishop. His father Leopold was a violinist and composer in the archbishop's service. When

Wolfgang and his older sister Nannerl showed remarkable talent at an early age, Leopold trained them in music and took them on tours across Europe, exhibiting their skills as child prodigies. And prodigy he was: by the age of three he had developed perfect pitch; at five he was an accomplished harpsichord player; at six he was composing; at seven he could read at sight, harmonize melodies on first hearing, and improvise on a tune supplied to him. Though arduous, these trips exposed Mozart to an enormous range of musical styles. He also composed at a stupendous rate, turning out thirty-four symphonies, sixteen quartets, five operas, and over one hundred other works before his eighteenth birthday.

Mozart spent the years 1772 to 1780 in Salzburg as third concert master at Archbishop Colloredo's court. In 1781, over his father's objections, he left the archbishop's service and settled in Vienna, convinced that he could make a living through teaching, concertizing, and composing. Indeed he quickly won success, establishing himself as the best pianist in Vienna and enjoying a triumph with his Singspiel *Die Entführung aus dem Serail*. With his father's grudging consent, he married Constanze Weber in the summer of 1782. Their marriage was happy and affectionate. Four children died in infancy, but two sons lived into adulthood, the younger becoming a composer.

Composing at a prodigious pace, teaching private students, performing in public and private concerts, and selling his works to publishers brought Mozart a good income and impressed his father. At a quartet party in Mozart's home, Haydn told Leopold, "Before God and as an honest man I tell you that your son is the greatest composer known to me either in person or by name. He has taste and, what is more, the most profound knowledge of composition." But by the late 1780s there were money troubles, apparently due more to rising family expenses than to declining income. Mozart's death at thirty-five prompted a variety of false rumors, including that he was poisoned, but it seems to have resulted from a sudden fever.

Mozart's almost six hundred compositions are listed and numbered chronologically in a thematic catalogue compiled by

Figure 22.7: Wolfgang Amadeus Mozart in an unfinished portrait from about 1789 by his brother-in-law Joseph Lange.

Ludwig von Köchel in 1862, whose "K." numbers are universally used to identify Mozart's compositions. The original numbers, which run from K. 1 to K. 626, are the most familiar and are used here, but revised numbers assigned to some pieces reflect newer information about the chronology of Mozart's music.

MAJOR WORKS: Die Entführung aus dem Serail, The Marriage of Figaro, Don Giovanni, Così fan tutte, The Magic Flute, *15 other operas and Singspiele, 17 masses, Requiem, 55 symphonies, 23 piano concertos, 15 other concertos, 26 string quartets, 19 piano sonatas, numerous songs, arias, serenades, divertimentos, dances; many other vocal and instrumental works (the traditional numbering of some Mozart works, such as symphonies 1–41 and piano concertos 1–27, assigned by publishers, excludes some compositions and includes some spurious pieces)*

Figure 22.8: Three Mozarts making music in about 1763: Leopold, violin; Wolfgang, age seven, keyboard; and Nannerl, age eleven, singing from a score. Watercolor by Louis Carrogis de Carmonetelle.

craft of composition, and his exposure at a young age to a wide range of music is reflected in his use of diverse styles to portray characters, convey moods, or heighten contrasts within a movement.

Leopold Mozart   Mozart's father, Leopold Mozart (1719–1787), was a violinist for the archbishop of Salzburg and became deputy Kapellmeister in 1763. He was a well-regarded composer and the author of a celebrated treatise on violin playing published in 1756, the year of his son's birth. From earliest childhood the boy showed such prodigious talent for music that his father sacrificed his own advancement and devoted himself to educating Wolfgang and his gifted elder sister Maria Anna, known as Nannerl (1751–1829), in music and other subjects. Both children became keyboard virtuosos, and Wolfgang was also an accomplished violinist. Father and children are pictured playing together in Figure 22.8.

Touring   From 1762 to 1773, Leopold took his children on a series of tours through Austria-Hungary, Germany, France, England, Holland, and Italy, beginning with performances for the elector of Bavaria at Munich and Empress Maria Theresa in Vienna. The map in Figure 22.9 shows some of the cities they visited. During performances in aristocratic homes and in public, Wolfgang played prepared pieces, read concertos at sight, and improvised variations, fugues, fantasias, and arias. He was repeatedly tested by experts, who published reports on his performances and improvisations as if he were a wonder of nature. Meanwhile he was composing, producing his first minuets at age five, his first symphony just before his ninth birthday, his first oratorio at eleven, and his first opera at twelve. Nannerl also composed, but none of her music survives.

Thanks to his father's excellent teaching and to his many travels, young Mozart became familiar with every kind of music being written or heard in western Europe. At each stop, he acquired music that was unavailable in

Absorbing influences

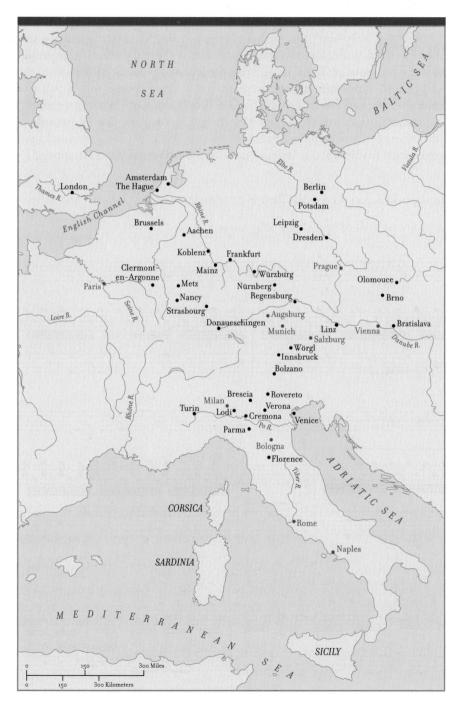

Figure 22.9: The cities that were most important in Mozart's career are indicated in color. But his travels, particularly during his younger years, include all of those in black as well.

Salzburg and met musicians who introduced him to new ideas and techniques. He absorbed it all with uncanny aptitude. The ideas that influenced him not only echoed in his youthful compositions but also continued to grow in his mind, sometimes bearing fruit years later. His work became a synthesis of national styles, a mirror that reflected the music of a whole age.

Paris   In June 1763, the whole family (including Mozart's mother Anna Maria) embarked on a three-and-a-half-year tour that included lengthy stops in Paris and London. In Paris, Mozart became interested in the music of Johann Schobert (ca. 1735–1767). In his harpsichord writing, Schobert simulated orchestral effects through rapid figuration and thick chordal textures, a technique Mozart later imitated. Example 22.8 compares passages in a Schobert sonata for harpsichord with violin accompaniment and a Mozart piano sonata that use rapid alternating notes in the right hand to simulate orchestral string tremolos.

London   Johann Christian Bach, whom Mozart met in London, had an important and lasting influence on the boy. Bach enriched his keyboard and symphonic works with features from Italian opera: songful themes, tasteful appoggia-

Example 22.8: Simulation of orchestral tremolos in sonatas by Schobert and Mozart

a. *Schobert, Sonata Op. 2, No. 1, Allegro assai*

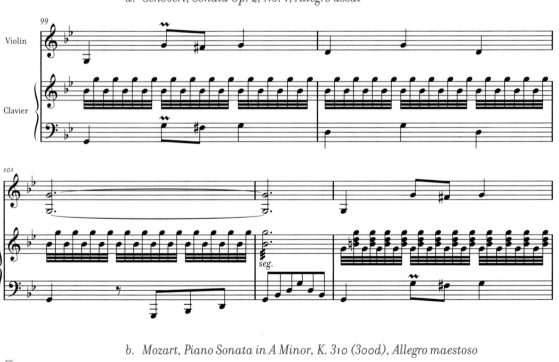

b. *Mozart, Piano Sonata in A Minor, K. 310 (300d), Allegro maestoso*

turas and triplets, and harmonic ambiguities. These traits, together with Bach's consistent use of contrasting themes in concerto and sonata-form movements, appealed to Mozart and became permanent marks of his writing. In 1772, Mozart arranged three of Bach's sonatas as piano concertos (K. 107). As we will see, Mozart's approach to concerto form has significant parallels to Bach's.

When Nannerl came of marriageable age in 1769, she bumped up against *Italy and Vienna* the prevailing attitude that women belonged in the home. Accordingly, her father insisted she stop performing in public, and she was left behind in Salzburg while father and son continued to travel. Mozart was familiar with Italian style through his father and J. C. Bach, but three trips to Italy between 1769 and 1773 left him more thoroughly Italianized than ever. He studied counterpoint with Padre Martini in Bologna and composed his first two opere serie (staged in Milan) and first string quartets. The influence of Sammartini and other Italian symphonists emerges in Mozart's symphonies written between 1770 and 1773. A visit to Vienna in 1773 acquainted him with current styles there, especially in the serenade, string quartet, and symphony. Although he may have encountered Haydn's quartets at this time, the six quartets he wrote in Vienna, K. 168–173, reflect local Viennese tastes more directly than they do Haydn's influence.

FREELANCING

If his extraordinary childhood explains the diversity of styles and genres Mozart had at his command, his adult career illustrates the growing tension between two ways musicians were now making money: steady employment with a patron or institution, and freelancing. For a musician today, the parallel choices would be to secure a salaried position—such as playing with an orchestra or teaching at a conservatory, college, or university—or to make a living by playing concerts, making recordings, teaching private students, or composing on commission or for publication. In Mozart's time, most successful musicians had paid positions and augmented their income through other activities. Few survived solely as free agents.

At age sixteen, Mozart was appointed unpaid third concertmaster at Arch- *Salzburg* bishop Colloredo's court in Salzburg, where his duties included composing church music. Much more interested in opera and instrumental music, Mozart vainly sought a position elsewhere, traveling with his father to Italy and Vienna and with his mother through Germany to Paris. The latter trip had far-reaching emotional consequences: at Mannheim he fell in love with the singer Aloysia Weber, the sister of his future wife Constanze, and in Paris his mother took ill and died. The search outside Salzburg proved fruitless, and Mozart returned home disconsolate.

After spending eight years at the Salzburg court, Mozart received a wel- *Gaining* come commission in 1780 to write an opera seria for Munich. During his sev- *independence* eral months there to compose and supervise the production of *Idomeneo* (1781), Mozart had a taste of independence. When Archbishop Colloredo summoned him back to Salzburg, Mozart dutifully went, but chafed at being

Figure 22.10: St. Michael's Square in Vienna. In the foreground is the Burgtheater, where Mozart performed several of his piano concertos in the mid-1780s and where the premieres of The Marriage of Figaro *and* Così fan tutte *took place.*

treated like a servant and soon left the archbishop's service, against his father's advice.

Vienna   For the next ten years, Mozart earned his living as a freelance musician in Vienna, with several sources of income. His Singspiel *Die Entführung aus dem Serail* (The Abduction from the Harem, 1782) was a great success and was performed repeatedly in Vienna and other German cities, and his later operas also did well. He had all the pupils he was willing to take, from wealthy amateur pianists to talented composition students, and made them pay by the month so he would not lose money if they skipped lessons. He performed in public and private concerts, quickly winning a reputation as the finest pianist in Vienna. He sometimes served as his own impresario, putting on concerts at venues such as the Burgtheater, shown in Figure 22.10, and pocketing the proceeds after expenses. He composed copiously, for his own concerts, on commission, and also for publication, as Viennese publishers issued his piano works, chamber music, piano concertos, dances, symphonies, and songs. In December 1787, Mozart was appointed chamber music composer to the emperor, giving him a steady if modest salary with light duties and a boost to his reputation; the emperor later said the job was meant to keep Mozart in Vienna, showing that it was in part a reward for his other activities.

Success or failure?   The story told soon after Mozart's death suggests that his early successes in Vienna were followed by failures: that the public deserted him, pupils fell off, commissions were few, and his finances were depleted as family expenses mounted. Some evidence supports this bleak view: a war with the Turks led to a decline in musical patronage in 1788–89; some of his ventures did not succeed; Mozart moved his family to cheaper quarters in 1788; and from then to

1791 he wrote several begging letters to his friend and brother Freemason, the merchant Michael Puchberg, who always responded generously to Mozart's appeals. Yet the Mozarts always had enough money to employ a maid and to dress appropriate to their social standing, and though Mozart gave fewer concerts, apparently by choice, receipts from publications, from his salary, and from operas and other commissions remained good. The problems do not seem to lie with the income side of the equation, but with Mozart's inability to manage his expenses, as attested by his sister Nannerl.

MATURE STYLE

Although many notable compositions date from the Salzburg years, the works that immortalized Mozart's name were composed in Vienna, when he was aged twenty-five to thirty-five and the promise of his youth came to fulfillment. In every kind of composition he achieved an extraordinary synthesis of form and content, of the galant and learned styles, of polish and charm with emotional depth.

Mozart's music was enriched by new influences from three of the century's greatest composers: Haydn, J. S. Bach, and Handel. Haydn spent every winter in Vienna, and whatever acquaintance Mozart may previously have had with his works was now deepened through intense study and personal friendship. Mozart was introduced to Bach's music by Baron Gottfried van Swieten, later the librettist for Haydn's last two oratorios. As Austrian ambassador to Berlin in 1771–78, van Swieten had become an enthusiast for the music of North German composers. In weekly reading sessions at van Swieten's home during 1782, Mozart became acquainted with Bach's *Art of Fugue, Well-Tempered Clavier*, and other works. He arranged several of Bach's fugues for string trio or quartet and composed his own Fugue in C Minor for two pianos, K. 426. Bach's deep and lasting influence makes itself known in the increased contrapuntal texture of Mozart's later works. Through van Swieten Mozart also became interested in Handel, whose *Messiah, Alexander's Feast, Acis and Galatea*, and *Ode for St. Cecilia's Day* Mozart reorchestrated in 1788–90 for private performances sponsored by van Swieten and other aristocratic patrons.

Haydn, Bach, and Handel

PIANO MUSIC

Mozart was a virtuoso pianist, and his style is well represented in his music for piano. His sonatas, fantasias, variations, rondos, and piano duets (for two players at one piano) were written for his pupils, for domestic music-making, and for publication. The nineteen piano sonatas are among his most popular works, and almost every piano student for the last two centuries has studied them. He demonstrated his command of the genre with a set of six sonatas (K. 279–284) written in 1775 while in Munich to supervise an opera, and he wrote three more while in Mannheim and Paris in 1777–78 (K. 309–311). These already show a wide variety of keys, content, and form, as if Mozart sought to explore all the possibilities of the sonata and pose diverse challenges for the player.

Sonata in
F Major, K. 332

CD 7|79

Mozart's style at the beginning of his Vienna period is exemplified by the sonata-form first movement of the Sonata in F Major, K. 332 (NAWM 105), one of three composed in 1781–83 and published as a set in 1784 (K. 330– 332). Especially characteristic of Mozart are his themes and his combination of heterogeneous styles. Example 22.9 shows the first theme and the beginning of the transition.

Example 22.9: Opening of Mozart's Piano Sonata in F Major, K. 332

Themes   While Haydn built themes by varying small motives (see Example 22.1) or forming a series of contrasting gestures (Example 22.3), Mozart's themes tend to be songlike, perhaps reflecting Italian influence. The opening idea of K. 332 (measures 1–12) is typical of his themes in seeming to unfold naturally and spontaneously, while giving evidence of careful shaping. Phrases are usually balanced between antecedent and consequent, but often the second phrase is extended—in this case through imitation between the hands. The whole melody grows out of the opening series of thirds, which are subtly paralleled in the Alberti bass accompaniment. As he often does, Mozart introduces a contrasting idea even within the first theme area (measures 12–22), but he ties it back to the opening melody by using the same cadence (measures 19–20). Every gesture reflects grace, taste, and elegance.

All composers of the time used contrast to delineate form, convey feelings, and provide variety. But Mozart's skill in using diverse styles for these purposes was unparalleled. In Example 22.9, the following styles follow in quick succession:

Contrasting styles

- the first phrase is in singing allegro style, with a songlike melody in quick tempo over broken chord figures;
- its consequent (measures 5–12) introduces imitation and counterpoint, hallmarks of the learned style;
- the second idea suggests hunting style, with a melody and bass line that can be played on the natural horn, using solely the pitches of the harmonic series (see the left hand in measures 12-20);
- the transition (beginning measure 23) is in *Sturm und Drang* style, a loud and impassioned passage in minor mode with faster rhythms, full texture, chromaticism, and strong dissonances such as diminished seventh chords.

Such frequent changes of style continue throughout the movement, outlining the form and broadening the range of expression.

Modern listeners can easily miss noticing this diversity. It all sounds like Mozart's style to us, for we are not familiar with the wide range of styles that his contemporaries would have recognized. For them, the difference between galant and learned style, or hunting style and *Sturm und Drang*, would have been as immediately apparent as the differences between swing, rock, country, rap, and military band music are today. The differing styles in Classic-era music have been referred to as **topics**, because they serve as subjects for musical discourse. Becoming aware of the many styles Mozart and other Classic composers invoke helps us understand their music and discover an intriguing and meaningful network of references we would otherwise miss.

CHAMBER MUSIC

After composing sixteen quartets in the early 1770s, Mozart did not return to the genre until his first years in Vienna. Between 1782 and 1785, he wrote six quartets (K. 387, 421, 428, 458, 464, and 465), published in 1785 as his Op. 10. He dedicated them to Haydn in gratitude for all that he had learned from the older composer. Mozart called them "the fruit of a long and laborious effort," and the many revisions in the manuscript bear witness to his exertions. Haydn's Op. 33 quartets (1781) had fully established the technique of pervasive thematic development with substantial equality between the four instruments. Mozart's six *Haydn* Quartets show his mature capacity to absorb the

Mozart's Haydn *Quartets*

essence of Haydn's achievement without becoming a mere imitator. Although the themes remain Mozartean, they are subjected to much more thorough development in an increasingly contrapuntal texture.

Quintets   Many of Mozart's other chamber works are also classics, though composed for less standardized ensembles. His string quintets, for two violins, two violas, and cello, have been praised in even stronger terms than his quartets, especially the quintets in C major and G minor (K. 515–516, 1787). Shortly after composing the Quintet for Piano and Winds, K. 452, Mozart wrote to his father, "I myself think it's the best work I've written in my entire life." His six works for solo wind and strings, including three flute quartets, oboe quartet, horn quintet, and clarinet quintet, are staples in the repertory for those instruments.

SERENADES AND DIVERTIMENTOS

Mozart composed serenades—ever popular in Salzburg—and what are now classed as divertimentos in the 1770s and early 1780s for garden parties or outdoor performances, for weddings and birthdays, or for concerts at the homes of friends and patrons. Although usually intended for background music and entertainment, they received serious treatment from Mozart. Some are like chamber music for strings with two or more wind instruments. Others, written for six or eight wind instruments in pairs, are meant for the out-of-doors, and still others approach the style of the symphony or concerto. All have in common an unaffected simplicity of both material and treatment, appropriate to their purpose. The most familiar of Mozart's serenades is *Eine kleine Nachtmusik* (A Little Night-Music, K. 525; 1787), in four movements for string quintet but now usually played by a small string ensemble.

PIANO CONCERTOS

Vienna concertos   Although Mozart wrote piano concertos in Salzburg in the 1770s, notably the impassioned Piano Concerto in E♭ Major, K. 271 (1777), the seventeen piano concertos written in Vienna occupy a central place in Mozart's output. He composed them primarily as vehicles for his own concerts and intended them to please the entire range of listeners. As he wrote to his father on December 28, 1782, the first three Vienna concertos, K. 413–415,

> are a happy medium between what's too difficult and too easy. They are Brilliant—pleasing to the ear—Natural without becoming vacuous. There are passages here and there that only connoisseurs can fully appreciate, yet the common listener will find them satisfying as well, although without knowing why.

Each of the Vienna concertos is an individual masterpiece; together they show Mozart at his best. Figure 22.11 shows a manuscript page from one of the Vienna concertos, K. 467. It reveals the composer's clarity and logic as well as a revision around the middle of the page, where he wanted to improve the textural distribution.

Figure 22.11: A page from Mozart's Piano Concerto in C Major, K. 467, dated February 1785. Mozart's rapid rate of composition is well known. In a letter to their mother, Mozart's sister Nannerl jokes that her brother was writing down a sonata while at the same time composing another in his head. It is believed that this particular concerto took Mozart around a month to finish—just to copy a concerto of this length (83 pages) would have taken many composers a full month to complete. K. 467 is surprisingly free of corrections and revisions, but around the middle of the page we can see where Mozart decided to revise some unbalanced scoring.

Mozart's concertos follow the traditional three-movement pattern in the sequence fast-slow-fast. The first movement blends elements of ritornello and sonata form as do the concertos of J. C. Bach, Mozart's primary model for these keyboard works. Comparing the first movement of Mozart's Piano Concerto in A Major, K. 488 (NAWM 106), composed in 1786, to the J. C. Bach concerto diagrammed in Figure 21.10, we see the same general outlines:

First movement

CD 8|6   CD 4|11

- the solo sections resemble the exposition, development, and recapitulation of a sonata form, with the soloist accompanied by and sometimes in dialogue with the orchestra;
- the opening orchestral ritornello introduces the movement's first theme, transition, second theme, and closing theme, but remains in the tonic;
- the ritornello returns, greatly abbreviated, to mark the end of the first solo and the end of the movement.

Like Bach, Mozart includes a cadenza for the soloist, but his cadenza usually interrupts the final ritornello, as it does here. It is also Mozart's typical practice to punctuate the long solo sections with passages for full orchestra that serve as further ritornellos. Here these include the transition in the solo exposition and recapitulation and the first two phrases of the recapitulation. The other differences are in the details that make each first movement unique. While Bach's concerto used the closing theme for later ritornellos, in K. 488 Mozart mainly uses the transition, an energetic, pulsating tutti that contrasts markedly with the quiet, lyrical themes. Mozart introduces a new idea at the beginning of the development, which becomes the focus of that section and returns at the end of the recapitulation and in the final ritornello. The resulting form follows convention in most respects yet may surprise the listener with several individual features. The movement is suffused with Mozart's characteristic wealth of melodic invention, diversity of figuration, and elegance.

Slow movement and finale   The second movement of a Mozart concerto resembles a lyrical aria. It is set in the subdominant of the principal key or, less often, in the dominant or relative minor. Its form may vary, most often sonata without development, sometimes variations or rondo. The finale is typically a rondo or sonata-rondo on themes with a popular character; these are treated in scintillating virtuoso style with opportunities for one or more cadenzas.

Balance of elements   Although the concertos were show pieces intended to dazzle an audience, Mozart never allowed display to get the upper hand. He always maintained a balance of musical interest between the orchestral and solo portions, and his infallible ear is evident in the myriad combinations of colors and textures he draws from the interplay between the piano and orchestral instruments, especially the winds. Moreover, the goal of composing for an immediate public response did not keep him from expressing profound musical ideas.

SYMPHONIES

Mozart wrote only six symphonies in the last ten years of his life, having earlier produced almost fifty, notwithstanding the traditional numbering of forty-one symphonies (introduced by a nineteenth-century publisher). The symphonies written before 1782 served most often as concert or theatrical curtain raisers; those he composed after he settled in Vienna constituted the main feature on concert programs or shared billing with concertos and arias. Many of the early symphonies followed the older Italian three-movement format, while most of the later ones have the standard four movements.

Vienna symphonies   Like Haydn, Mozart approached his mature symphonies with great seriousness, and he devoted much time and thought to their composition. The *Haffner* Symphony, K. 385, written in 1782 for the elevation to nobility of Mozart's childhood friend Sigmund Haffner, and the *Linz* Symphony, K. 425, written in 1783 for a performance in that city, typify the late symphonies in their ambitious dimensions, greater demands on performers (particularly wind players), harmonic and contrapuntal complexity, and final movements that are climactic rather than light. These symphonies are in every way as artful as the London symphonies of Haydn, and some may indeed have served as models for the older composer. The others of this group—usually recognized as his greatest—are the *Prague* Symphony in D Major (K. 504), composed in 1786 for a concert in that city, and the three Symphonies in E♭ Major (K. 543),

G minor (K. 550), and C Major (K. 551, named the *Jupiter* by an English publisher), all written in the space of six weeks during the summer of 1788.

Each of the six symphonies is a masterpiece with its own special character. Their opening gestures leave an indelible impression. The *Haffner* and *Jupiter* Symphonies both begin with loud, forceful statements in octaves followed by delicate ensemble responses. Three others (K. 425, 504, and 543) have slow introductions animated by the spirit of the French overture, with its majestic dotted rhythms, intense harmony, and anacrusis figures. Rather than intimating subtly what is to come, as Haydn sometimes did, Mozart's slow introductions create suspense, tantalizingly wandering away from the key and making its return a major event. Most unusual is the beginning of the Symphony in G Minor, which opens *piano*, rare in symphonies before this one, with a soft, undulating melody suffused with sighing gestures.

As in Haydn's late symphonies, the finales do more than send an audience away in a cheerful frame of mind. They balance the serious opening movement with a highly crafted counterweight fashioned with whimsy and humor. Most remarkable is the finale of the *Jupiter* Symphony, which takes its first theme from a fugue example in Fux's *Gradus ad Parnassum* and combines it in counterpoint with five other motives: a countersubject, two transitional figures, and two motives from the second theme of the sonata form. The coda then weaves all of these in an unsurpassed triumph of *ars combinatoria*, the art of combination and permutation derived from mathematics, which eighteenth-century theorists taught as a means of achieving melodic variety in composition. Example 22.10 shows part of this coda, with

Finales

Example 22.10: Excerpt from coda of Mozart's Jupiter *Symphony finale, showing themes in counterpoint*

> a = first theme, opening idea
> b = second theme, opening phrase
> c = countersubject to second theme
> d, e = two figures from transition that also appear in second theme

motives from the first theme (a), second theme (b and c), and transition (d and e) in counterpoint.

OPERAS

Opera was still the most prestigious musical genre, and Mozart eagerly sought opportunities to compose for the stage. On a visit to Vienna in 1768, the twelve-year-old composer wrote his first opera buffa, *La finta semplice* (The Pretend Simpleton, performed the following year at Salzburg), and first Singspiel, *Bastien und Bastienne*. During his trips to Italy in the early 1770s, he composed two opere serie that were produced in Milan, hoping they would lead to a permanent position. He composed two operas on commission for Munich, *La finta giardiniera* (1775), an opera buffa, and *Idomeneo* (1781), the best of his opere serie. In its dramatic and pictorial music, accompanied recitatives, conspicuous use of chorus, and inclusion of spectacular scenes,

SOURCE READING

MOZART'S DEPICTION OF CHARACTER AND MOOD

In his operas, Mozart portrays the personalities of the characters and conveys their feelings so perfectly through his music that listeners can immediately understand them—sometimes better than the characters understand their own predicament. In a letter to his father written while composing Die Entführung aus dem Serail, *Mozart described how he made the music of two arias fit the characters, the situation, and the singers who would premiere the roles.*

— • —

Osmin's rage will be rendered comical by the use of Turkish music. In composing the aria, I made [the singer] Fischer's beautiful deep tones really glisten.... The passage *Therefore, by the beard of the Prophet,* etc, is, to be sure, in the same tempo, but with quick notes—and as his anger increases more and more, the Allegro assai [a faster tempo]—which comes just when one thinks the aria is over—will produce an excellent Effect because it is in a different tempo and in a different key. A person who gets into such a violent rage transgresses every order, moderation, and limit; he no longer knows himself. In the same way the Music must no

longer know itself. But because passions, violent or not, must never be expressed to the point of disgust, and Music must never offend the ear, even in most horrendous situations, but must always be pleasing, in other words always remain Music, I have not chosen a key foreign to F, the key of the aria, but one that is friendly to it, not however its nearest relative in D minor, but the more remote A minor. Now about Bellmont's aria in A Major, "Oh how anxious, oh how passionate!" Do you know how I expressed it?—even expressing the loving, throbbing heart? With two violins playing in octaves. This is the favorite aria of everyone who has heard it—it's mine too. And it was written entirely for Adamberger's voice. One can see the trembling—faltering—one can see his heaving breast—which is expressed by a crescendo—one can hear the whispering and the sighing—which is expressed by the first violins with mutes and one flute playing in unison.

Letter of 26 September 1781, from *Mozart's Letters, Mozart's Life,* selected letters edited and newly translated by Robert Spaethling (New York: Norton, 2000), 286. Punctuation and spelling has been modernized.

Figure 22.12: Lorenzo Da Ponte, in a portrait by an unknown American artist. Best known for the librettos to Mozart's Marriage of Figaro, Don Giovanni, *and* Così fan tutte, *Da Ponte went to London in the 1790s and to America in 1805, where he was a grocer, private teacher, book-dealer, translator, and eventually professor of Italian at Columbia College. He became an American citizen and sought to bring Italian culture to his new nation.*

Idomeneo shows the reformist tendencies of Traetta and Gluck and the influence of French opera.

Mozart's fame in Vienna and beyond was established by *Die Entführung aus dem Serail* (1782), in which he raised the Singspiel into the realm of great art without altering its established features. The opera tells a romantic-comic story of adventure and rescue set in a Turkish harem. Such "oriental" settings and plots were popular, in part because they provided a taste of the exotic while making the Turks, long-standing enemies of Austria-Hungary, seem less threatening. But Mozart's opera transcended the genre by depicting the Turkish characters as humane and fully rounded. Mozart set the scene in the overture by using "Turkish style," meant to suggest Turkish military band music through the use of shrill winds, drums, and cymbals; exaggerated first beats; and deliberately simple harmonies, melodies, and textures. Mozart's music perfectly captures the characters and their feelings, as he had aimed (see Source Reading).

Die Entführung

Mozart's next operas were three Italian comic operas: *The Marriage of Figaro* (1786), *Don Giovanni* (Don Juan, 1787), and *Così fan tutte* (Thus Do All Women, 1790). All were set to librettos by Lorenzo Da Ponte (1749–1838), shown in Figure 22.12, poet for the imperial court theater. Da Ponte's librettos followed the conventions of opera buffa but lifted it to a higher level, giving greater depth to the characters, intensifying the social tensions between classes, and introducing moral issues. Mozart's psychological penetration and his genius for musical characterization similarly raised the genre's seriousness. Delineation of character occurs not only in solo arias but especially in duets, trios, and larger ensembles. The ensemble finales allow these characters to clash, combining realism with ongoing dramatic action and superbly

Da Ponte operas

unified musical form. Mozart's orchestration, particularly his use of winds, plays an important role in defining the characters and situations.

Don Giovanni

The Marriage of Figaro enjoyed success in Vienna but was even more enthusiastically received in Prague, leading to the commission for *Don Giovanni*, premiered there the following year. The medieval legend of Don Juan, on which the plot is based, had been treated often in literature and music since the early seventeenth century. But Da Ponte and Mozart, for the first time in opera, took the character of Don Juan seriously—not as an incongruous mixture of farcical figure, seducer, and horrible blasphemer, but as a rebel against authority, a scorner of common morality, and a supreme individualist, bold and unrepentant to the last.

Mixing styles

CD 8|24   CD 4|29

Don Giovanni incorporates opera seria characters, situations, and styles into the comic opera, as illustrated in the opening scene (NAWM 107). Leporello, Don Giovanni's servant, laments his sufferings in an opera-buffa style aria, with a touch of aristocratic horn calls when he declares his wish to live like a gentleman rather than a servant. He is interrupted by a clamor as Don Giovanni and Donna Anna emerge from her house, where he has tried to have his way with her. In furious pursuit, she sings in dramatic opera seria style and Don Giovanni replies in kind, while Leporello comments in buffo style from his hiding place. Donna Anna's father, the Commendatore, rushes in to protect her and challenges Don Giovanni to fight. They do, and the Commendatore is mortally wounded—a shocking turn of events for a comedy. In a powerful trio, he pants out his last words as Don Giovanni and Leporello comment, each in his own characteristic style. Instantly, master and servant revert to the comic banter of opera buffa in the following recitative.

Throughout the opera, there are three levels of character: Donna Anna and other nobles who emote in the elevated, dramatic tone of opera seria; Leporello and other characters, mostly lower-class, marked by the buffoonery of opera buffa (though they show both cleverness and wisdom); and Don Giovanni, who, in his character as duplicitous seducer, passes easily from one world to the other. These three levels are highlighted in the finale of Act I, where Mozart masterfully coordinates three on-stage dance bands playing simultaneously: a minuet for the nobles, a contredanse for Don Giovanni, and a rustic waltz for Leporello.

Another character with a foot in both worlds is Donna Elvira, a comic character posing as a serious one. Her attempts to depict herself as a tragic heroine abandoned by Don Giovanni are hilariously undercut by Mozart's music. For example, her rage aria *Ah fuggi il traditor,* shown in Example 22.11, is in an out-of-date style, that of Scarlatti or Handel from more than fifty years before, as if she were reading her lines out of an old book (as Leporello comments elsewhere), so she sounds fake rather than sincere. Although she attempts to be dignified, shown by her choice of sarabande rhythm, the tempo she takes is much too fast, making her sound hysterical. Such references to other styles and departures from their conventions are crucial aspects of Mozart's depiction of characters and of their feelings. Modern audiences often miss these meanings if they do not recognize the styles and conventions Mozart is evoking.

Example 22.11: Donna Elvira's aria Ah fuggi il traditor, *from Mozart's* Don Giovanni

Ah, flee the traitor, let him say nothing more

In his last year of life, Mozart wrote two final operas: an opera seria, *La clemenza di Tito* (The Mercy of Titus), for the coronation in Prague of Leopold II as king of Bohemia, and *The Magic Flute* (Die Zauberflöte) for a theater in Vienna. *The Magic Flute* is a Singspiel, with spoken dialogue instead of recitative and with some characters and scenes appropriate to popular comedy. Yet its action is filled with symbolic meaning, and its music is so rich and profound that it ranks as the first great German opera. The largely solemn mood of the score reflects the relationship between the opera and the teachings and ceremonies of Freemasonry. We know that Mozart valued his Masonic affiliation, not only from allusions in his letters but especially from the serious quality of the music he wrote for Masonic ceremonies in 1785 and for a Masonic cantata in 1791 (K. 623). In *The Magic Flute,* Mozart interwove threads of many eighteenth-century musical styles and traditions: the vocal opulence of Italian opera seria; the folk humor of the German Singspiel; the solo aria; the buffo ensemble; a new kind of accompanied recitative applicable to German words; solemn choral scenes; and even a revival of the Baroque chorale-prelude technique, with contrapuntal accompaniment. The reconciliation of older and newer styles is summed up in the delightful overture, which combines sonata form with fugue.

The Magic Flute

CHURCH MUSIC

Given that Mozart's father worked as a musician for the archbishop of Salzburg and that Mozart himself served there as concertmaster and organist, it was natural for him to compose church music from an early age. However, with notable exceptions—his Mass in C Minor, *Ave verum corpus*, and Requiem—settings of sacred texts are not counted among his major works. The masses, like Haydn's, are for the most part in the current symphonic-operatic idiom, intermingled with fugues at certain customary places, and scored for chorus and soloists in free alternation, with orchestral accompaniment.

Requiem   The Requiem, K. 626, was commissioned by a wealthy nobleman, Count Walsegg, in July 1791, but Mozart was busy with *La Clemenza di Tito* and *The Magic Flute* and made little progress until the fall. Left unfinished at Mozart's death, it was completed by his pupil and collaborator Franz Xaver Süssmayr (1766–1803), who added some instrumental parts to Mozart's draft and set the Sanctus, Benedictus, and Agnus Dei, in part repeating music that Mozart had composed for an earlier section.

ACHIEVEMENT AND REPUTATION

The unfinished Requiem has become a metaphor for Mozart's sudden, unexpected death, cutting off his career at the height of his abilities. He never found the secure position he sought, but his music eventually found a secure place among performers and listeners. His encounters with and absorption of almost every current style enabled him to extend Haydn's stylistic synthesis to an even wider range, making possible the masterful depiction of mood and character in his operas and the rich variety of his instrumental music. He equaled Haydn in balancing form and expression, immediate and long-lasting appeal. Together, the two composers ranged over all the genres practiced in the late eighteenth century, and their music represents the best that the period produced.

CLASSIC MUSIC

Since the 1790s, Haydn and Mozart have been paired as the two outstanding composers of their time. Both met with great success during their lifetimes and their music continued to be known and performed after their deaths. Haydn's and Mozart's works provided models for Beethoven and many other composers of their own generation and following ones. By the early nineteenth century, certain works of Haydn and Mozart (especially the late symphonies and some quartets of each, Haydn's late oratorios, Mozart's piano concertos and sonatas, and the five main Mozart operas) had become classics, part of the core group of works cultured people were expected to know. Their music eventually came to be known as "classical," which in turn became the name most often used for works of the late eighteenth century. Yet among the composers of their time, only Haydn and Mozart achieved widespread and enduring fame and composed such complex and heterogeneous music. It is not easy to achieve the balance between wide and deep appeal that they accomplished, and it was the unique merits of this music that led to its continued performance in the early nineteenth century and its adoption into the permanent repertory.

PART OUTLINE

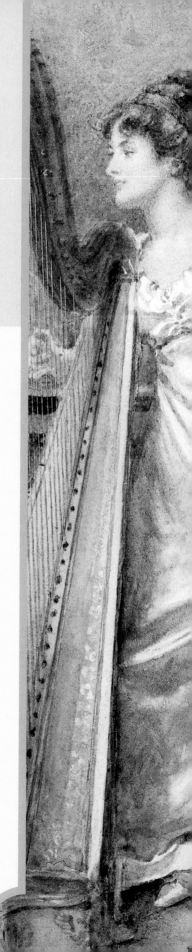

PART FIVE

THE NINETEENTH CENTURY

In the nineteenth century, the Industrial Revolution transformed the economy, bringing people from the countryside to the cities and creating a society based on mass production and distribution. The result was a large and influential middle class, who saw transformations in musical life as well. Affordable pianos and printed music broadened the market for home music, encouraging a torrent of songs and piano pieces. The audience for music expanded, and opera companies, professional orchestras, and concert halls grew in number and size.

Nineteenth-century musicians typically worked for the public—playing in orchestras, giving concerts, composing for publication, or teaching amateurs. One path to success was to specialize, becoming a virtuoso on one instrument or a composer for one medium. Another path was to create music that was novel, individual, evocative, spectacular, nationalist, exotic, or in some other way distinctive yet attractive. All of these traits are characteristic of Romanticism, a leading movement in the arts at the beginning of the 1800s and a term now associated with the entire century's music. Composers developed new styles to appeal to middle-class listeners, creating new kinds of instrumental music—from virtuoso showpieces to symphonic poems—and new operatic traditions in Italy, France, Germany, Russia, and elsewhere.

Two other developments had profound and lasting effects: the rise of a permanent repertoire of musical classics, and a growing rift between classical and popular music. These changes have shaped our modern musical culture, in which nineteenth-century music is still an enduring presence.

Chapter 23

Revolution and Change

The generation born around 1770 came of age in a whirlwind of change. From the French Revolution in 1789 through the end of the Napoleonic Wars in 1815, the old political order in Europe gave way to a new one. At the same time, a new economic order began to emerge, in which the Industrial Revolution and middle-class entrepreneurship would eventually overtake the old wealth of the landed aristocracy. One member of that generation, Ludwig van Beethoven, led a revolution of like importance in the history of music. His creation of works unprecedented in their individuality, dramatic power, wide appeal, and depth of interest to connoisseurs changed society's concept of music and of composers.

REVOLUTION, WAR, AND MUSIC, 1789–1815

THE FRENCH REVOLUTION

The French Revolution was inspired in part by Enlightenment ideas of equality, human rights, and social reform, but also had other causes. The first phase of the Revolution (1789–92) was reformist. Stimulated by King Louis XVI's ruinous fiscal policies and supported by popular uprisings like the assault on the Bastille shown in Figure 23.1, a National Assembly of well-to-do citizens forced the king to accept a new constitution for France. The Assembly abolished old privileges, adopted the Declaration of the Rights of Man and Citizen, and set up elected local governments. But after Austria and Prussia attacked France in 1792, seeking to restore the old regime, a more radical group came to power, declared France a republic, and executed the king. In this second phase (1792–94), as French armies fought off attacks, the government maintained control by executing tens of thousands of political opponents in a Reign of Terror. In the third phase (1794–99), the government adopted a more moderate constitution and sought to restore order, but opposition and economic hardships continued.

In 1799, Napoleon Bonaparte, an army general and war hero, became First Consul of the Republic. Ignoring the elected legislature, Bonaparte consolidated power and in 1804 crowned himself emperor. Through a series of military victories, he overran nearby countries, expanded French territories, ended the 840-year-old Holy Roman Empire, and created client states in Spain, Switzerland, and most of Germany and Italy, installing his own siblings as rulers. Throughout these areas as well as France, he introduced reforms that made government more efficient, the legal system more uniform, and taxation less burdensome, carrying out some of the goals of the Revolution. But a disastrous campaign to take Moscow led to Napoleon's defeat and abdication in 1814. As a congress of the major European powers met in

*Napoleon
Bonaparte*

Figure 23.1: Contemporary oil painting of The Fall of the Bastille, July 14, 1789. *The citizens of Paris stormed the old fortress, a symbol of royal authority, to obtain the guns and ammunition stored there and to protect the new municipal government from attack by royal forces. The action cost almost one hundred lives, but demonstrated the popular will for revolutionary change. The anniversary, July 14, is now celebrated as the French national holiday.*

Vienna to finalize the peace treaty, Napoleon escaped from exile in 1815, marched to Paris, and resumed power, only to suffer final defeat that summer, at Waterloo in Belgium.

Effects of the Revolution

Although the Revolution and Napoleon's wars of conquest ultimately failed, they changed European society utterly. The Revolutionary motto "liberté, egalité, fraternité" (liberty, equality, brotherhood) penetrated every stratum of French society, and French armies spread it across Europe. People everywhere saw the possibility of freedom, democratic reform, and the abolition of rank and privilege, and they sustained that vision even when its realization was delayed. Moreover, the Revolution and subsequent wars introduced a new concept of the *nation*, conceived as citizens with a common heritage and equal legal rights, not as subjects to a monarch. As the French forged an identity as a nation, so increasingly did their enemies in Germany, Italy, Spain, and Austria, giving rise to cultural and political trends that gained force throughout the nineteenth and early twentieth centuries.

MUSIC AND THE REVOLUTION

The Revolution remade every aspect of French life, including music. Composers wrote large choral works for the many government-sponsored festivals held to celebrate the Revolution. The government also supported the Opéra and Opéra-Comique, the two main opera theaters in Paris, although

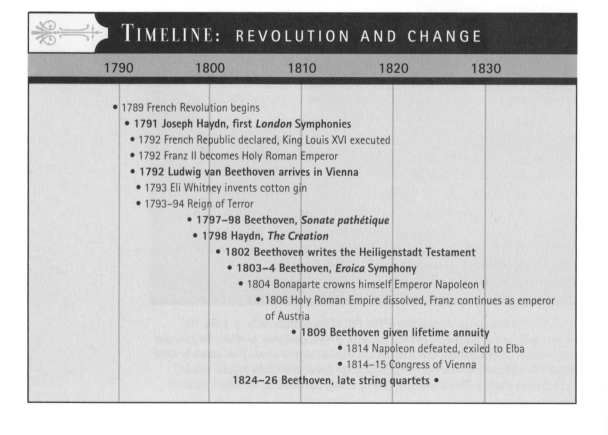

TIMELINE: REVOLUTION AND CHANGE

1790	1800	1810	1820	1830

- 1789 French Revolution begins
- **1791 Joseph Haydn, first *London* Symphonies**
- 1792 French Republic declared, King Louis XVI executed
- 1792 Franz II becomes Holy Roman Emperor
- **1792 Ludwig van Beethoven arrives in Vienna**
- 1793 Eli Whitney invents cotton gin
- 1793–94 Reign of Terror
- **1797–98 Beethoven, *Sonate pathétique***
- **1798 Haydn, *The Creation***
- 1802 Beethoven writes the Heiligenstadt Testament
- 1803–4 Beethoven, *Eroica* Symphony
- 1804 Bonaparte crowns himself Emperor Napoleon I
- 1806 Holy Roman Empire dissolved, Franz continues as emperor of Austria
- **1809 Beethoven given lifetime annuity**
- 1814 Napoleon defeated, exiled to Elba
- 1814–15 Congress of Vienna
- **1824–26 Beethoven, late string quartets** •

opera librettos were subject to censorship for political reasons. Many of the plots touched on themes of the Revolution or concerns of the time. One especially thrilling scenario (mentioned in chapter 20) centered around the rescue of a hero from unjust imprisonment.

An enduring product of the Revolutionary era was the Paris Conservatoire, a music school founded by the government in 1795 as part of the new national system of education. The Conservatoire trained singers and instrumentalists through a standard curriculum and system of examinations and offered courses in composition, theory, and music history. As the first modern conservatory, it became the model for national and regional conservatories throughout Europe. It has been a dominant force in French musical life ever since.

Paris Conservatoire

THE INDUSTRIAL REVOLUTION

Meanwhile, new technologies began to transform the economy from chiefly rural and agricultural, with most goods made by hand, to an urban economy based on manufacturing by machine. This gradual change, known as the Industrial Revolution, started in Britain during the late eighteenth century and spread across Europe and North America over the next hundred years. It began in the textile industry with inventions such as the fly shuttle (1733), spinning jenny (1764), and cotton gin (1793), leading to mass production of thread and cloth in large factories powered by water mills or by the new steam engine (invented 1769). Other industries followed suit, including the rise of instrument-making firms (see chapter 24). Mass production lowered costs and thus prices, which drove out competitors who worked by hand. Men, women, and even children came to work in the factories and the coal and iron mines that kept them running, despite long hours and often bad working conditions. The Industrial Revolution brought unprecedented prosperity, but in many ways was as disruptive as the French Revolution and Napoleonic Wars, threatening traditional ways of life and enriching the urban middle and merchant classes at the expense of the landowning aristocracy and the poor.

LUDWIG VAN BEETHOVEN

The musician whose career and music best reflect the tumultuous changes in the decades around 1800 was Ludwig van Beethoven (1770–1827; see biography and Figure 23.2). He was aware of Enlightenment ideals; absorbed the music of Haydn and Mozart; observed the French Revolution from a distance; idealized and then was disillusioned by Napoleon; and lived his last dozen years under political repression. In his youth a promising piano virtuoso and composer, he was forced to cease performing because of deafness and became the first musician to make a living almost exclusively through composition. His pieces placed new demands on listeners and performers, and in the process they redefined what listeners expected from and valued in music.

Shortly after Beethoven's death, a scholar divided his career and works into three periods, beginning a tradition that survives to this day. During the

Division into three periods

first period, which takes us from his birth in 1770 to about 1802, Beethoven mastered the musical language and genres of his time and gradually found a personal voice. In the second period, through about 1814, he developed a style that achieved a new level of drama and expression and brought him enormous popularity. In the third period, from about 1815 to his death in 1827, his music became more introspective and more difficult for performers to play and for listeners to comprehend. Such a neat framework is, of course, an

LUDWIG VAN BEETHOVEN (1770–1827)

For two centuries, composers of classical music have had to contend with an image of Beethoven—complete with flying hair, grim expression, and notorious short temper—because in the popular imagination, Beethoven epitomizes the classical composer. His symphonies, concertos, string quartets, and piano sonatas are central to the repertory of classical music, and his influence has been virtually inescapable.

Beethoven was born in Bonn in northwestern Germany, where his grandfather and father were musicians at the court of the elector of Cologne. From early childhood, Beethoven studied piano and violin with his father, Johann, who hoped to make him into a famous child prodigy like Mozart. The boy received further training from other local musicians.

Beethoven traveled to Vienna in 1787 and probably met Mozart, then moved to Vienna for good in 1792. His first teacher there was Haydn, with whom he studied counterpoint, at the same time cultivating patrons among the aristocracy. His compositions ranged widely, from music for amateurs to virtuoso works for himself and from private works for connoisseurs to public symphonies.

Confident in his own worth as an artist, Beethoven treated his aristocratic sponsors with independence and even occasional rudeness. His presumptions of social

Figure 23.2: Ludwig van Beethoven, in a portrait from around 1804 by his friend Willibrord Joseph Mähler, an amateur painter. The composer kept this painting on his wall all his life.

equality led him repeatedly to fall in love with women of noble rank, whom he as a commoner could not marry (and some of whom were already married). Especially poignant is a letter he addressed in 1812 to "Immortal Beloved." Beethoven never established a permanent home, moving more than two dozen times during his thirty-five years in Vienna.

A gradual loss of hearing provoked a crisis around 1802, from which he emerged with new resolve to compose works of unprecedented scope and depth. The music of the next dozen years established him as the most popular and critically acclaimed composer alive. Through sales to publishers and support from patrons, notably a permanent stipend set up for him in 1809, he was able to devote himself entirely to composition and write at his own pace.

On his brother's death in 1815, Beethoven became guardian for his nephew Karl, giving Beethoven the family he had long desired but also bringing years of conflict with Karl's mother Johanna. Growing deafness, bouts of illness, political repression, and the death or departure of many friends and patrons led to an increasing withdrawal from society. His music became more intense, concentrated, and difficult.

Beethoven died at fifty-six after years of ill health. His funeral procession was witnessed by over ten thousand people, and his popularity as a composer and as a cultural icon continues to this day.

MAJOR WORKS: *9 symphonies, 11 overtures, 5 piano concertos, 1 violin concerto, 16 string quartets, 9 piano trios, 10 violin sonatas, 5 cello sonatas, 32 piano sonatas, 20 piano variation sets, the opera* Fidelio, Missa solemnis, *Mass in C Major, the song cycle* An die ferne Geliebte, *over 80 songs, and numerous other works*

interpretation, a convenient way to organize a discussion of Beethoven's career and music. But it both reflects changes in his style and marks crucial turning points in his life: a crisis in 1802 over his gradual loss of hearing and a growing isolation around 1815 caused by deafness, family troubles, and, as we will see, political and economic conditions.

BONN AND THE FIRST DECADE IN VIENNA

Beethoven's first period consists of two parts: his youth in Bonn and his first decade in Vienna. In Bonn, after training by his father and other local musicians, he entered the service of Maximilian Franz, elector of Cologne, and attracted notice as a virtuoso pianist and improviser (see Source Reading). In his late teens, Beethoven began to make his mark as a composer and gained patrons among the local nobility. On a visit to Bonn, Haydn praised Beethoven's music and urged the elector to send the young man to Vienna for further study. So in November 1792, just under twenty-two years of age, Beethoven traveled from Bonn to Vienna, a five-hundred-mile journey that took a week by stagecoach.

Beethoven took lessons with Haydn, who left for London in 1794. He then studied counterpoint for a year with Johann Georg Albrechtsberger, author of a famous composition treatise. Meanwhile, Beethoven quickly established himself as a pianist and composer, with the support of generous patrons. For a while, Beethoven had rooms in a house owned by Prince Karl von Lichnowsky. At private concerts sponsored by Lichnowsky and others, Beethoven's

Teachers, patrons, and publishers

SOURCE READING

BEETHOVEN'S PLAYING AND IMPROVISING AT THE PIANO

When Beethoven's Bonn employer, the elector of Cologne, presided over a meeting of the Teutonic Order for several weeks in 1791 at Mergentheim in southern Germany, he took his musicians along. Carl Ludwig Junker, a composer and writer on music and art, came to hear them, and published a glowing account of Beethoven's playing.

———— • ————

I have also heard one of the greatest of pianists—the dear, good Bethofen.... I heard him extemporize in private; yes, I was even invited to propose a theme for him to vary. The greatness of this amiable, light-hearted man as a virtuoso may, in my opinion, be safely judged from his almost inexhaustible wealth of ideas, the highly characteristic expressiveness of his playing, and the skill he displays in performance. I do not know that he lacks anything for the making of a great artist. I have often heard Vogler play by the hour on the pianoforte—of his organ playing I cannot speak, not having heard him on that instrument—and

never failed to wonder at his astonishing ability. But Bethofen, in addition to skill, has greater clarity and profundity of ideas, and more expression—in short, he speaks to the heart. He is equally great at an *adagio* as at an *allegro*. Even the members of this remarkable orchestra are, without exception, his admirers, and are all ears when he plays. Yet he is exceedingly modest and free from all pretension. He, however, acknowledged to me that, upon the journeys which the Elector had enabled him to make, he had seldom found in the playing of the most distinguished virtuosi that excellence which he supposed he had a right to expect. His manner of treating his instrument is so different from the usual that he gives the impression of having attained his present supremacy through a path that he discovered himself.

From Bossler's *Musikalische Correspondenz* (Speyer, November 23, 1791), adapted from the translation by Henry Edward Krehbiel in Alexander Wheelock Thayer, *Thayer's Life of Beethoven*, rev. and ed. Elliot Forbes (Princeton: Princeton University Press, 1967), 105.

outstanding abilities as a pianist, and especially his improvisations, won great admiration. He also played in public concerts and taught well-to-do piano students. Aside from juvenilia published when he was twelve to fourteen years old, he started to sell works to music publishers in 1791, although his first work to bear an opus number did not appear until 1795. It was dedicated to Lichnowsky, and his Op. 2 of the following year was dedicated to Haydn. Through performing, teaching, publishing, and the generosity of patrons, Beethoven was able to make a living.

Piano sonatas   Since he was a pianist, piano works were a natural outlet for Beethoven's compositional impulses; indeed sonatas, variations, and shorter works for piano comprise the largest group of works he wrote during his first decade in Vienna. Beethoven followed the tradition of aiming solo keyboard music at the amateur market, although his early sonatas already make increasing demands on the performer. Relatively difficult passages or movements appear next to easier ones, perhaps to challenge the player. Like Mozart, Beethoven often used strong contrasts of style or topic to delineate the form and broaden the expressive range.

The title of Beethoven's *Sonate pathétique* (Sonata with Pathos or Impassioned Sonata, probably 1799), Op. 13, announced that the work would depict suffering and a tragic mode of expression. It was also likely to attract buyers, as composers and publishers found such evocative titles a useful marketing tool. The sonata, in C minor, has outer movements of a stormy, passionate character—which Beethoven's predecessors associated with that key—around a calm, profound slow movement in A♭ major. A dramatic, fantasia-like slow introduction lends the work a symphonic scope, while its unexpected recurrences before the development and again just before the end of the movement deepen the pathos that the piece conveys. The sonata-rondo finale (NAWM 108) is equally serious and intense, unlike the typically lighthearted rondos of Haydn and Mozart. Its theme recalls the second theme of the first movement, and its central episode is in A♭, the key of the second movement, creating the sort of intermovement connections that Beethoven frequently used in his later works.

Pathétique *Sonata*

CD 8|29   CD 4|34

Beethoven waited until he was well established in Vienna and confident in his craft before composing his first string quartets and symphonies. He knew these were genres in which Haydn, then regarded as the greatest composer alive, was preeminent, so that to write in them would invite a direct comparison with his former teacher. For that very reason they offered Beethoven a chance to prove his merits.

Op. 18 String Quartets

Beethoven's first six quartets, published in 1800 as his Op. 18, are indebted to both Haydn and Mozart but are no mere imitations. Beethoven's personality shows through in the individuality of every movement, the character of his themes, frequent unexpected turns of phrase, unconventional modulations, and subtleties of form. The slow movement of No. 1, which Beethoven reportedly said was inspired by the burial vault scene of *Romeo and Juliet*, is especially striking and perhaps the most dramatic—even operatic—movement yet written for string quartet. The hilarious scherzo of No. 6, shown in Example 23.1, emphasizes offbeats so convincingly that it is almost impossible to keep the beat. The finale is a rondo with a long, intense, slow introduction labeled "La Malinconia" (Melancholy), which is recalled later in the movement. The simultaneous invocation and subversion of tradition in these quartets and the stark juxtapositions of opposing emotions and styles became characteristic of Beethoven's music.

Example 23.1: Scherzo of Beethoven's String Quartet in B♭ Major, Op. 18, No. 6

First Symphony   Beethoven's Symphony No. 1 in C Major, premiered in 1800, shows his allegiance to the model of Haydn's and Mozart's late symphonies. Yet Beethoven sought to distinguish himself in distinctive ways: a slow introduction that avoids any definitive tonic cadence; careful dynamic shadings; unusual prominence for the woodwinds; a scherzo-like third movement; and long codas for the other movements.

CIRCUMSTANCES IN THE MIDDLE PERIOD

Reputation   Around 1803, Beethoven began to compose in a new, more ambitious style
and patrons   that marks a pivotal point in his career. He was free to take this step because of his reputation, the support of patrons and publishers, and, paradoxically, the predicament created by his growing loss of hearing.

By this time, Beethoven was acknowledged in German-speaking lands as the foremost pianist and composer for piano and as a symphonist on a par with Haydn and Mozart. He was befriended by the loftiest noble families of Vienna, and he had generous patrons. When Jerome Bonaparte, king of Westphalia and youngest brother of Napoleon, offered Beethoven a position in Kassel in 1808, Prince Franz Joseph von Lobkowitz, Prince Kinsky, and Archduke Rudolph, brother of Emperor Franz, joined to provide the composer a lifetime annuity just to stay in Vienna. The strong financial backing Beethoven received from his patrons meant that he could do largely what he wished as a composer. His sponsors were connoisseurs devoted to his music; indeed, Archduke Rudolph was his student in piano and composition. The

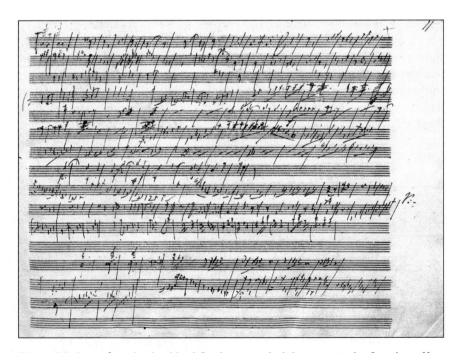

Figure 23.3: A page from the sketchbook Beethoven used while composing his Symphony No. 3 in E♭ Major (Eroica). For a partial transcription, see NAWM 109.

combination of financial, social, and creative support freed Beethoven to follow his own inspiration, a virtually unprecedented situation for a composer.

Publishers competed for Beethoven's music. He drove hard bargains, got *Publishers*
them bidding against each other, and followed Haydn's lead in publishing
works in several countries at once to preserve his rights and maximize his returns. Although he wrote on commission, he often dodged deadlines. He
could afford, as he said, to "think and think," to revise and polish a work until
it suited him.

Beethoven composed with great deliberation, one reason that he wrote so *Sketches*
much less than his predecessors—for instance, only nine symphonies compared to Haydn's one hundred-plus and Mozart's sixty-plus. He kept notebooks in which he jotted down themes and plans for compositions, worked
out the continuity of each piece, and gradually filled in details. Figure 23.3
shows a page from the sketchbook for Beethoven's Third Symphony. Thanks
to these sketchbooks, we can follow the progress of his ideas through various
stages until they reached final form (see commentary for NAWM 109). By
composing in this deliberate way, Beethoven created music in which the relation of each part to the whole was remarkably sophisticated, satisfying one of
the central tenets of nineteenth-century aesthetics.

While his status, financial position, and compositional methods made it *Deafness*
possible for Beethoven to strike out in new directions, it was apparently a
psychological crisis that made it necessary. In 1802, he realized that the hearing loss he had noticed for some time was permanent and would only get
worse. A deaf musician was as inconceivable as a blind painter. In despair,
Beethoven considered suicide, but resolved to continue for the sake of his art
(see Source Reading). He played in public less and less but kept on composing and, occasionally, conducting.

Beethoven's courageous resolve to continue composing in the face of *Music as drama*
calamity was translated into his music, as he sought with each piece to say
something new. His compositions seem to reflect the struggle of his own life,
becoming like narratives or dramas. The music gives the impression of conveying the composer's own experience and feelings rather than invoking the
stylized, objectified emotions found in earlier music. Often, the thematic
material assumes the character of a protagonist who struggles against great
odds and emerges triumphant. This new conception of instrumental music as
drama, replacing earlier notions of music as entertainment or diversion, is
part of what musicians and listeners have valued in Beethoven's music since
his own time.

This interpretation and some others to follow are only one way to view
Beethoven's output after 1802. Treating the musical elements like characters
in a drama has its detractors, but the expansiveness, dynamism, and unusual
features of many Beethoven works open them to such interpretations more
than any previous music.

The music of this period continues to build on the models of Haydn and *Style*
Mozart in most respects. The genres, forms, melodic types, phrasing, and *characteristics*
textures all draw on tradition. But the forms are often expanded to unprecedented lengths or reworked in novel ways. Typically, Beethoven is economical
in his material, adopting Haydn's focus on a few ideas subjected to intense

SOURCE READING

THE HEILIGENSTADT TESTAMENT

Beethoven began to lose his hearing in 1798, and by 1818 he could hardly hear at all. In October 1802, just before leaving his summer lodgings in the village of Heiligenstadt, he wrote about his affliction in a letter, now known as the Heiligenstadt Testament, intended to be read by his brothers after his death.

———— • ————

For 6 years now I have been hopelessly afflicted, made worse by senseless physicians, from year to year deceived with hopes of improvement, finally compelled to face the prospect of *a lasting malady* (whose cure will take years or, perhaps be impossible). Though born with a fiery, active temperament, even susceptible to the diversions of society, I was soon compelled to withdraw myself, to live life alone. If at times I tried to forget all this, oh how harshly was I flung back by the doubly sad experience of my bad hearing. Yet it was impossible for me to say to people, "Speak louder, shout, for I am deaf." Ah, how could I possibly admit an infirmity in the *one sense* which ought to be more perfect in me than in others, a sense which I once possessed in the highest perfection, a perfection such as few in my profession enjoy or ever have enjoyed.—Oh I cannot do it, therefore forgive me when you see me draw back when I would have gladly mingled with you. My misfortune is doubly painful to me because I am bound to be misunderstood; for there can be no relaxation with my fellow-men, no refined conversations, no mutual exchange of ideas. I must live almost alone like one who has been banished, I can mix with society only as much as true necessity demands. If I approach near to people a hot terror seizes upon me and I fear being exposed to the danger that my condition might be noticed. Thus it has been during the last six months which I have spent in the country. By ordering me to spare my hearing as much as possible, my intelligent doctor almost fell in with my own present frame of mind, though sometimes I ran counter to it by yielding to my desire for companionship. But what a humiliation for me when someone standing next to me heard a flute in the distance and *I heard nothing,* or someone heard a *shepherd singing* and again I heard nothing. Such incidents drove me almost to despair, a little more of that and I would have ended my life—it was only *my art* that held me back. Ah, it seemed to me impossible to leave the world until I had brought forth all that I felt was within me.

Trans. Henry Edward Krehbiel, in Alexander Wheelock Thayer, *Thayer's Life of Beethoven,* rev. and ed. Elliot Forbes (Princeton: Princeton University Press, 1967), 304–5.

development rather than Mozart's abundance of melody, yet he achieves great variety through ingenious transformations of his themes.

EROICA SYMPHONY

The first work that fully exemplifies Beethoven's new approach is his Symphony No. 3 in E♭ Major, composed in 1803–4, which he eventually named *Sinfonia Eroica* (Heroic Symphony). Longer than any previous symphony, the *Eroica* goes beyond evoking conventional moods and topics, as his First Symphony had done. The title suggests that the symphony has a subject—the celebration of a hero—and expresses in music the ideal of heroic greatness. It has been said that the heroism it depicts is Beethoven's own: that it represents in music his experience of being almost overpowered by affliction, fighting against despair, and winning back his will to create.

According to an analysis proposed by Philip G. Downs, the first movement (NAWM 109) encapsulates this story of challenge, struggle, and final victory. Within an enlarged sonata form, the main motive of the first theme, shown in Example 23.2, serves as protagonist. In its original form (Example 23.2a), it has the triadic shape of a fanfare, denoting a heroic character, but sinks down chromatically at the end to a surprising C♯, suggesting an inner weakness. Over the course of the movement, the motive undergoes a number of transformations: treated in sequence, with the chromatic tail now rising (Example 23.2b); disguised as a "new theme" in minor, with stepwise motion filling in its skips and leaps (Example 23.2c); and striving upward, only to tumble back down (Example 23.2d). By the end of the movement, it has achieved a new form, no longer falling at the end but sustaining its high note in a sign of renewed strength and final triumph (Example 23.2e).

First movement

CD 8|36   CD 4|41

Example 23.2: Main motive and its transformations in the first movement of Beethoven's Symphony No. 3

a. *Original form*

b. *In rising sequence*

c. *Disguised as a "new theme" in the development*

(* = note shared with original form)

d. *Unison statement, striving upwards*

e. *Final form*

The principal antagonist is another element from the first theme group: a leaping figure, shown in Example 23.3a, whose strong accents on weak beats create a forceful duple meter against the serene triple meter of the main motive. Offbeat accents appear in the transition, second theme, and closing theme, and near the end of the exposition they briefly threaten the equilibrium with a powerful assertion of duple time before a varied fragment of the main motive restores the proper meter, as shown in Example 23.3b.

Example 23.3: Leaping figure and associated rhythmic disturbances

a. First appearance

b. Rhythmic disruption near end of exposition

In the development, the leaping figure and offbeat accents build to a terrifying, dissonant climax. Almost overcome, the main motive gradually struggles to reassert itself. First it assumes the disguised form of Example 23.2c, in the remote key of E minor. Next it returns as in Example 23.2d, a statement in three parallel octaves without accompaniment that reaches for the heights but falls back down, deflected by another offbeat accent. Finally, as shown in Example 23.4, it achieves its new form with the sustained high note. It is now accompanied by the leaping figure, stripped of its offbeat accents so that it fits into triple meter. The transformation of both motives resolves the principal conflict of the movement in favor of the main motive. Its victory is confirmed in the recapitulation, where its return in original form (as in Example 23.2a) is immediately followed by two statements in its new form, while the leaping figure is omitted entirely. The second and closing themes unfold as before, transposed into the tonic. The long coda revisits episodes from the development, retracing the path back to victory, and reaffirms the new form of the theme. Like Beethoven in his personal crisis, the motive emerges from its struggle triumphant but changed by the experience.

Example 23.4: Main motive and leaping figure transformed and reconciled

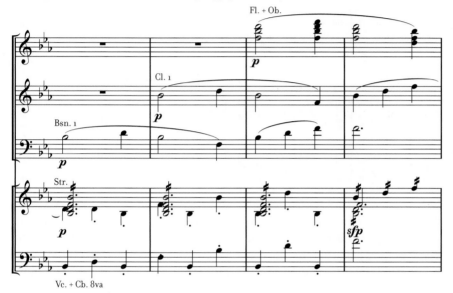

The other movements are also large and dramatic. The slow movement is a Funeral March in C minor, full of tragic grandeur and pathos. A contrasting section in C major, brimming with fanfares and celebratory lyricism, is followed by further development of the march and a varied reprise, broken up with sighs at the end. The third movement is a quick scherzo, with grandiose horn calls in the trio. The finale is a complex mixture of variations with fugal, developmental, and marchlike episodes, all based on a theme from Beethoven's ballet music for *The Creatures of Prometheus*.

Other movements

The second movement has strong links to France during the Republic, with which Beethoven was in sympathy. Thirty-second-note upbeats in the strings imitate the roll of muffled drums used in the Revolutionary processions that accompanied heroes to their final resting place. One passage strikingly parallels a famous French Revolutionary march, François-Joseph Gossec's *Marche lugubre*; see the comparison in Example 23.5. The C-major section has the character of a Revolutionary hymn, punctuated by fanfares and drum rolls and ending in unisons.

References to French Republic

Beethoven originally named the symphony "Bonaparte" in honor of Napoleon, whom he admired as a hero of the French Republic. But according to his student Ferdinand Ries, when Beethoven heard that Napoleon had crowned himself emperor, he angrily tore up the title page, disillusioned when his idol proved to be an ambitious ruler on the way to becoming a tyrant.

Example 23.5: Comparison of passages in Gossec, Marche lugubre, *and Beethoven,* Marcia funebre *from Symphony No. 3*

a. Gossec

b. Beethoven

The title page of a score containing Beethoven's corrections, shown in Figure 23.4, reveals that Bonaparte's name was violently scratched out, confirming the gist if not the details of the story. But Beethoven seems to have wavered in his opinion of Napoleon: that August he wrote to his publisher that the symphony's title was "Bonaparte," in 1809 he conducted the symphony in Vienna at a concert that Bonaparte was to have attended, and in 1810 he considered dedicating his Mass in C, Op. 86, to the emperor. In any case, Beethoven's plan to honor Napoleon may explain the strong links to music of the French Republic.

Reception   At its public premiere in 1805, the *Eroica* Symphony was recognized as an important work, but its unprecedented length and complexity made it difficult for some audience members to grasp. Beethoven had tilted Haydn and Mozart's balance between learned and less learned listeners toward the connoisseurs and had sacrificed some immediate widespread appeal in order to gain the freedom to write as he chose. This decision put Beethoven, the symphony, and indeed much music of the next two centuries on a new course, challenging listeners to engage music deeply and thoughtfully rather than merely seeking to be entertained.

OTHER WORKS OF THE MIDDLE PERIOD

Other major works over the next decade followed in the footsteps of the Third Symphony. In each, Beethoven probed new possibilities in traditional genres and forms, and several works of this period took their place among the most popular ever written in their genres.

Fidelio   Beethoven turned next to opera, still the most prestigious form of music. For a libretto, he borrowed from a French Revolutionary opera, *Léonore, ou L'amour conjugal* (Leonore, or Conjugal Love), in which Leonore, disguised as a man, rescues her husband from prison. Operas on rescue themes were embraced at the time both in France and in Vienna. Beethoven's opera, *Fidelio*, makes Leonore into an idealized figure of sublime courage and self-denial, and the last scene of the opera glorifies Leonore's heroism and the humanitarian ideals of the Revolution. The subject perfectly suited Beethoven's new heroic style, but it took him several tries to achieve the right balance between musical depth, broad appeal, and dramatic concision. The original three-act production of 1805, called *Leonore*, and a shortened revision the following year were both financial failures in part because their length and music overwhelmed the drama, and only in 1814 was a third version successful. In contrast to Mozart, for whom writing operas was almost effortless, Beethoven found it a struggle and never wrote another opera. His other dramatic music consists of overtures and incidental music for plays, notably Goethe's *Egmont*. He also wrote dozens of Lieder, often making the music as interesting as the poetry, as in later Romantic Lieder (see next chapter), rather than subordinate as in the eighteenth-century Lied.

The chamber music of the middle period abounds in fresh explorations of each genre, including two violin sonatas, Op. 47 (the *Kreutzer*) and Op. 96; the Piano Trio Op. 97 (the *Archduke*, written for Archduke Rudolph); and five string quartets. Like piano sonatas, chamber music had traditionally been intended for enjoyment in the home, but, as he did in his piano sonatas, Beethoven increasingly tested the limits of amateur players, most notably in his

Chamber music

Figure 23.4: Cover page for a score of the Eroica *Symphony containing Beethoven's corrections, which read "Sinfonia grande intitolata Bonaparte" (Grand Symphony entitled Bonaparte) before the last two words were scratched out. The date "1804 im August" was subsequently added in different ink. Below Beethoven's signature, in the middle of the page, he later added in pencil "Geschrieben auf Bonaparte" (composed about Bonaparte), not visible in this photograph.*

string quartets. Beethoven dedicated the three quartets of Op. 59 to Count Andrey Kyrillovich Razumovsky, the Russian ambassador to Vienna, who played second violin in a quartet that was said to be the finest in Europe. As a compliment to the count, Beethoven introduced Russian melodies as themes in No. 1 and No. 2. The style of these quartets was so new that musicians were slow to accept them. The first movement of No. 1, for example, is particularly charged with idiosyncrasies: single, double, and triple pedal points; frequent changes of texture; exploitation of the instruments' extreme ranges; and fugal passages.

Concertos   During his first decade in Vienna, Beethoven composed three piano concertos to play at his own concerts, following the pattern of Mozart a decade earlier. But the concertos of his middle period are, like the symphonies, composed on a grander scale. In the Piano Concerto No. 5 in E♭ Major, Op. 73 (the *Emperor*), and the Violin Concerto in D Major, Beethoven greatly expanded the music's expressive range and dimensions. The soloist is often co-equal with the orchestra, as if playing the part of a hero in a drama. In the first movement of the *Emperor* Concerto, for example, the soloist enters with a (written-out) cadenza even before the orchestra's exposition begins. Such dramatic interaction between soloist and orchestra was to become a frequent feature of nineteenth-century concertos.

Fifth Symphony   Beethoven's Fifth Symphony (1807–8) can be considered the musical projection of his resolution "I will grapple with Fate; it shall not overcome me." He symbolizes his struggle for victory by passing from C minor to C major, in a grand expansion of the move from chaos to light that he found in Haydn's

Figure 23.5: The Theater an der Wien in an anonymous engraving from 1825. At this theater on December 22, 1808, in bitter cold, Beethoven presented a four-hour concert whose program included the first public performances of the Fifth and Sixth Symphonies, the first Vienna performance of the Fourth Piano Concerto, Op. 58, with the composer as soloist, and the Choral Fantasy, Op. 80, for piano, orchestra, and chorus.

Creation (see Example 22.7). The first movement is dominated by one of the best-known motives in all of Western music: the four-note figure that is emphatically announced at the outset. (The rhythm of the motive matches that of the letter V in Morse Code—dot-dot-dot-dash—hence the theme's connection during World War II with the word and concept of *victory*.) The same rhythmic idea recurs in various guises in the other three movements. The transition from minor to major takes place in an inspired passage that begins with the timpani softly recalling the rhythm of the four-note motive and leading without a break from the scherzo into the triumphant finale. Here the entrance of the full orchestra with trombones on the C-major chord has an electrifying effect. The finale adds piccolo and contrabassoon as well as trombones to the normal complement of strings, woodwinds, horns, trumpets, and timpani.

The *Pastoral* Symphony, No. 6 in F Major, was composed immediately after the Fifth. The two were premiered on the same program in December 1808 at the Theater an der Wien, shown in Figure 23.5. Each of the *Pastoral* Symphony's five movements bears a title suggesting a scene from life in the country, following the normal sequence of movements with an extra movement (*Storm*) that serves to introduce the finale (*Thankful feelings after the storm*). In the coda of the Andante movement (*Scene by the brook*), flute, oboe, and clarinet join harmoniously in imitating bird calls—the nightingale, the quail, and the cuckoo—as shown in Example 23.6. The symphony is more a character piece than a work of program music (see chapter 24 for the distinction), marked by what Beethoven called "expression of feelings rather than description."

Pastoral Symphony

Example 23.6: Beethoven, Symphony No. 6, Scene by the brook

By 1814, Beethoven had reached the height of his of popularity. He was celebrated as the greatest living composer, his music was played regularly across Europe, and he received a steady demand from publishers for new works. The heroic style evident in some of his works, a source of controversy a decade earlier when the *Eroica* Symphony and *Razumovsky* Quartets first appeared, was now widely appreciated. He had changed audience expectations for what instrumental music can do.

Peak of popularity

CIRCUMSTANCES IN THE LATE PERIOD

Ironically, at the height of his renown, several factors forced Beethoven into greater isolation, slowed the pace of composition, and prompted a change in focus and style. His deafness became increasingly profound, until by 1818 he could hardly hear at all. Because it caused him to lose contact with others, he retreated into himself, becoming moody and morbidly suspicious even toward his friends. Family problems, ill health, and unfounded apprehensions of poverty also plagued him, and it was only by a supreme effort of will that he continued composing amid all these troubles.

Compounding these personal problems was the political and economic situation. The final defeat of Napoleon in 1815 was followed by a disastrous postwar depression, making it difficult to produce large-scale public works. That same year saw the beginning of tremendous repression instituted by Count Metternich, head of the Austrian government under the emperor. Beethoven's sympathy with the ideals of republican government as it had developed in France was now seen as a threat to the state, and he was investigated and spied on by government security forces. During these years, he did not write politically linked works like *Fidelio*, or even the *Eroica* Symphony; the heroic style itself became politically suspect and psychologically inappropriate. In his last dozen years of life, Beethoven produced only two large public works, the *Missa solemnis* and the Ninth Symphony, both completed only after the economy began to improve in the early 1820s. Otherwise, his major focus was on the last five piano sonatas (1816–21), *Diabelli Variations* for piano (1815–22), and last five string quartets (1824–26), all in genres traditionally intended for private music-making.

CHARACTERISTICS OF THE LATE STYLE

By now, Beethoven was addressing most of his compositions to connoisseurs. The publication of his late quartets in score, as in Figure 23.6, in addition to the traditional format of a set of four parts for performance, shows they were meant to be studied, not just played through for the pleasure of the performers. The urgent sense of communication to a large public was replaced by a more introspective character, and the musical language became more concentrated. Extremes meet in these pieces: the sublime and the grotesque in the *Missa solemnis* and Ninth Symphony, the profound and the apparently naïve in the last quartets. Classical forms remained, like the features of a landscape after a geological upheaval—recognizable under new contours, lying at strange angles beneath the new surface.

Variation technique   The way Beethoven used variation technique epitomizes his late style. Usually composers preserved the essential structure of the entire theme in each statement while introducing new embellishments, figurations, rhythms, and even meters and tempos. But Beethoven's late variations often go beyond this to reexamine the very substance of the theme. In the slow movement of his String Quartet in C♯ Minor, Op. 131 (1825–26), for example, only a few basic elements of the theme—a harmonic plan, a rhythmic quirk of deemphasizing the downbeat, a neighbor-note motion in the melody—are preserved through a very diverse series of variations.

Continuity   Another feature of Beethoven's late style is an emphasis on continuity. Within movements, he achieves continuity by intentionally blurring divisions

Figure 23.6: Title page of Beethoven's String Quartet in C♯ Minor, Op. 131, published by Schott in 1827 and printed in score ("en partition") to make the work easier to study. Traditionally, quartets had been printed only in separate parts, one for each player, but not in score, since only parts were needed to perform quartets. Printing this work in score made it possible for musical connoisseurs to examine the piece at leisure, play through portions at the keyboard, and explore the complex interrelationships between the elements.

between phrases or placing cadences on weak beats. He also emphasized continuity between movements, sometimes indicating that successive movements should be played without a pause in between. His *An die ferne Geliebte* (To the Distant Beloved) inaugurated the genre of the **song cycle,** a group of songs performed in succession that tell or suggest a story; earlier published song collections had little or no continuity from one song to the next.

Beethoven's search for new expressive means in his late works gave rise to new sonorities, such as the simultaneous use in all four instruments of pizzicatos or of *sul ponticello* effects (playing on the bridge to produce a thin sound) in the scherzo of the C♯-Minor Quartet. Early critics deemed some passages unsuccessful, holding that Beethoven went too far in subordinating euphony and performability to the demands of his musical conceptions, perhaps because of his deafness. But we have no reason to believe that even a

New sonorities

Beethoven with perfect hearing would have altered a single note, either to spare tender ears or to make life easier for performers. Such insistence on the composer's vision at the expense of performer freedom and audience comfort was to become an important strain in nineteenth- and, especially, in twentieth-century music, with Beethoven as the model for later composers (see Source Reading).

Use of traditional styles   In his late works, Beethoven frequently used familiar styles and genres, either for expressive purposes or to reflect on tradition. For example, the slow movement of the String Quartet in A Minor, Op. 132 (1825), titled "Holy Thanksgiving Song of a Convalescent to the Deity, in the Lydian Mode" and written after Beethoven recovered from a serious illness, opens in the style of a sixteenth-century chorale setting, each phrase simply harmonized and preceded by a brief point of imitation. The next movement has a boisterous march followed by an operatic accompanied recitative for the first violin. Other works include equally surprising references to both popular and cultivated styles.

Imitation and fugue   One of the most frequent characteristics of Beethoven's late works is his use of imitative counterpoint, especially fugue. There are numerous canonic

SOURCE READING

THE PERFORMER AS SUBORDINATE TO THE COMPOSER

Written music was traditionally viewed as a vehicle for the performer, who was at liberty to alter it in performance, for instance by adding embellishment. But the writer and critic E. T. A. Hoffmann suggested in 1813 that Beethoven was different, requiring the performer's total subordination to the vision of the composer, as if the notated music were a sacred text to be rendered with devotion and restraint. Scrupulous adherence to the composer's score gradually became a hallmark of performance in the classical tradition.

———•———

The correct and fitting performance of a work of Beethoven's asks nothing more than that one should understand him, that one should enter deeply into his being, that—conscious of one's own consecration—one should boldly dare to step into the circle of the magical phenomena that his powerful spell has evoked. He who is not conscious of this consecration, who regards sacred Music as a mere game, as a mere entertainment for an idle hour, as a momentary stimulus for dull ears, or as a means of self-ostentation—let him leave Beethoven's music alone. Only to such a man, moreover, does the objection "most ungrateful" apply. The true artist lives only in the work that he has understood as the composer meant it and that he then performs. He is above putting his own personality forward in any way, and all his endeavors are directed toward a single end—that all the wonderful enchanting pictures and apparitions that the composer has sealed into his work with magic power may be called into active life, shining in a thousand colors, and that they may surround mankind in luminous sparkling circles and, enkindling its imagination, its innermost soul, may bear it in rapid flight into the faraway spirit realm of sound.

From E. T. A. Hoffmann, "Beethovens Instrumental-Musik," *Sämtliche Werke*, ed. C. G. von Maassen, vol. 1 (Munich and Leipzig, 1908), 63–64, adapted from a review first published in March 1813. Trans. Oliver Strunk, in SR 160 (6:13), pp. 1197–98.

imitations and learned contrapuntal devices in all the late works, particularly in the fugatos that play a central role in development sections. Many movements or sections are predominantly fugal, such as the finales of the Piano Sonatas Opp. 106 and 110, the two double fugues in the finale of the Ninth Symphony, and the gigantic *Grosse Fuge* (Great Fugue) for String Quartet, Op. 133, first conceived as the finale for the Quartet in B♭ Major, Op. 130. The fugal finale has a long tradition extending back through Haydn's Op. 20 quartets to Corelli's trio sonatas. More unusual is Beethoven's use of a long, slow fugue as the first movement of the C♯-Minor Quartet, Op. 131 (NAWM 110a), shown in Example 23.7.

CD 8|52   CD 4|57

Example 23.7: Opening of Beethoven, String Quartet in C♯ Minor, Op. 131, first movement

* = prominent notes that appear as tonic of a later movement

Beethoven's reflections on tradition include reconceiving the number and arrangement of movements. Each of the last five piano sonatas has a unique succession of movement types and tempos, often linked without pause. The first and last of the late quartets (Opp. 127 and 135) have four movements, but Op. 132 has five, Op. 130 has six, and Op. 131 has seven played without breaks between them (the first two are in NAWM 110).

Reconceiving multimovement form

CD 8|52–54   CD 4|57

String Quartet in
C♯ Minor, Op. 131

The arrangement of forms, keys, and tempos in Op. 131 illustrates how Beethoven simultaneously invokes and departs from tradition in his late works:

Mvt.	Form	Key	Tempo	Time Sig.
1.	Fugue	C♯ minor	Adagio ma non troppo e molto espressivo	¢
2.	Sonata-rondo	D major	Allegretto molto vivace	6/8
3.	Recitative and transition	B min → V of A major	Allegro moderato— Adagio	C
4.	Variations	A major	Andante	2/4
5.	Scherzo	E major	Presto	¢
6.	Short rounded binary with repeats written out	G♯ minor	Adagio quasi un poco andante	3/4
7.	Sonata form	C♯ minor	Allegro	¢

Novel as this arrangement seems, it still contains the elements of the traditional four-movement quartet, much transformed: the opening sonata-form Allegro with slow introduction has been shifted to the end (nos. 6–7); the slow movement (no. 4) has a brief introduction (no. 3); the scherzo (no. 5) is in its usual place after the slow movement (but in duple rather than triple meter); and the light finale in rondo or sonata-rondo form has shifted to the beginning, preceded by a slow fugal introduction (nos. 1–2).

Unity

While Beethoven varied the traditional sequence of movements, he sought ways to integrate the movements more closely. In Op. 131, he does this through motivic and key relationships. In the finale, two motives in the first theme group permute the notes—and in one case echo the rhythm—of the fugue subject from the first movement, as shown in Example 23.8. More subtly, the keynotes of the principal movements—C♯, D, A, E, and C♯— are all prominent notes in the fugue subject or answer: the first and last, the highest, the lowest, or the most emphasized through dynamics and rhythm, marked with an asterisk in Example 23.7. These same keys play prominent roles within movements as well; for instance, the second theme in the finale is first presented in E, recapitulated in D, then repeated again in C♯.

Appeal to
connoisseurs

Like all of Beethoven's late sonatas and quartets, Op. 131 is a piece for connoisseurs. It is dramatic, emotionally rich, even funny in the scherzo, so that it appeals to audiences on many levels. But only those "in the know" about music are likely to notice and appreciate the complex relationships between

Example 23.8: Themes from finale compared to fugue subject from first movement

a. Opening of first theme

b. Lyrical idea in first theme group

the whole and the individual parts, or the crafty combination of tradition and innovation, as the old and the new are inextricably intertwined.

LAST PUBLIC WORKS

Like his late sonatas and quartets, the two large public works of Beethoven's final period reexamine the traditions of their respective genres.

Beethoven began his *Missa solemnis* as a mass to be performed at the elevation of Archduke Rudolph to archbishop of Olmütz in 1820, but it grew too long and elaborate for liturgical use. It is full of musical and liturgical symbols, reinterpreting traditional elements in new ways. The choral writing owes something to Handel, whose music Beethoven revered. But a Handel oratorio was a string of independent numbers, whereas Beethoven shaped his setting of the Kyrie, Gloria, Credo, Sanctus, and Agnus Dei as a unified five-movement symphony. As in the late masses of Haydn, choruses and solo ensembles freely alternate within each movement. Beethoven's setting was an idealized musical treatment of a well-loved text, not a liturgical work; like the late quartets, it was a concert piece in a genre that traditionally had a different function.

Missa solemnis

The Ninth Symphony was first performed in May 1824 on a program with one of Beethoven's overtures and three movements of the *Missa solemnis*, as advertised in the handbill in Figure 23.7. The large and distinguished audience applauded vociferously after the scherzo (the modern tradition of maintaining silence between movements had not yet been introduced); Beethoven

Ninth Symphony

Figure 23.7: Handbill for the concert of May 7, 1824, at the Kärntnertor Theater, advertising a "Great Musical Academy of Herr L. van Beethoven, Honorary Member of the Royal Academy of Arts and Sciences of Stockholm and Amsterdam and later Honorary Citizen of Vienna." The program promises "first: a grand overture; second: three grand hymns with solo and choral voices; third: a grand symphony with solo and choral voices entering in the finale on Schiller's Ode to Joy." The hymns were the Kyrie, Credo, and Agnus Dei of the Missa solemnis, and the symphony was the Ninth.

did not hear the applause, so one of the solo singers pulled his sleeve and pointed to the audience, and he turned and bowed.

The first three movements of the symphony are on a grand scale, and the whole takes more than an hour—even longer than the *Eroica* Symphony. But the most striking innovation is the use of solo voices and chorus in the finale. Just as Beethoven's mass was symphonic, and his quartets referred to vocal genres from recitatives and arias to the chorale motet, his last symphony looked to another genre, the choral ode. Beethoven had thought as early as 1792 of setting Schiller's *Ode to Joy,* but more than thirty years went by before he decided to incorporate a choral finale on this text in his Ninth Symphony. Consistent with his ethical ideals and religious faith, he selected stanzas that emphasize universal fellowship through joy, and its basis in the love of an eternal heavenly Father.

The apparent incongruity of introducing voices at the climax of a long instrumental symphony posed an aesthetic difficulty. Beethoven's solution determined the finale's unusual form:

- tumultuous introduction, inspired by the operatic genre of accompanied recitative;
- review and rejection (by instrumental recitatives) of the themes of the three preceding movements, then proposal and joyful acceptance of the "joy" theme;
- orchestral exposition of the theme in four stanzas;
- return of the tumultuous opening;
- bass recitative: "O Freunde, nicht diese Töne!" (O friends, not these tones! Rather let us sing more pleasant and joyful ones);
- choral-orchestral exposition of the joy theme, "Freude, schöner Götterfunken" (Joy, beautiful, divine spark), in four stanzas, varied (including

a "Turkish March"), and a long orchestral interlude (double fugue) followed by a repetition of the first stanza;
- new theme, for orchestra and chorus: "Seid umschlungen, Millionen!"
  (Be embraced, O millions!);
- double fugue on the two themes;
- a brilliant Prestissimo choral coda, bringing back the Turkish percussion, in which the joy theme is hailed in strains of matchless sublimity.

Everything here builds on tradition, but the whole is unprecedented. This
combination of innovation with reverence for the past, of disparate styles,
and of supreme compositional craft with profound emotional expression, is
characteristic of Beethoven's last period, and has been seen as a measure of
his greatness.

BEETHOVEN'S CENTRALITY

Having often celebrated heroism in his music, Beethoven himself became
a cultural hero, a reputation that grew throughout the nineteenth century. His
life story helped to define the Romantic view of the creative artist as a social
outsider who suffers courageously to bring humanity a glimpse of the divine
through art. In the twentieth century, biographers and historians began to
peel back the myth and reclaim the mere human who was Beethoven. But he
has remained a central figure in music, both because of what he accomplished
and because of how he has been regarded by critics and the public.

Many of Beethoven's compositions, particularly from the late 1790s
through the 1810s, were immediately popular and have remained so ever
since. His late works, once considered idiosyncratic, gradually came to be regarded as also great, reflecting his inner life and consummate craft even more
deeply than his more accessible music. Works of Beethoven form the core of
the symphonic repertoire and are central to the repertoires for piano, for
string quartet, and for other chamber ensembles. All later composers for
those media have had to confront him as model and competitor. His influence has been felt not only in style and technique but also in conceptions of
music and the role of the composer.

Beethoven's works invited attentive listening and probing critical interpretation. Seeking to explain his music, theorists developed new approaches
in harmonic, motivic, formal, and tonal analysis, some of which have become
standard and are applied to a wide range of music. The coherence and unity
Beethoven achieved through development, key relationships, motivic links,
and other means were highlighted in such studies and became a measure of
greatness in musical art, until challenged in recent decades by new values.

Beethoven's music was esteemed particularly for its assertion of the self.
Beethoven could afford the time to compose as he pleased, without answering
to an employer. Perhaps as a result, on occasion he put his own experiences
and feelings at the heart of a work, going beyond the long-standing traditions
of representing the emotions of a poetic text, dramatizing those of an operatic
character, or suggesting a generalized mood through conventional devices.

Such self-expression was in tune with the growing Romantic movement described in the next chapter, and it came to be expected of composers after Beethoven. Modern musicians and listeners who assume that composers before Beethoven also wrote when they felt inspired and sought to capture their own emotions in music are astonished to discover that earlier composers mostly created music to meet an immediate need, to please their employer, or to gratify their audience. Beethoven, and especially the critical reaction to Beethoven, changed everyone's idea of what a composer is and does. The image he fostered of a composer as an artist pursuing self-expression who composes only when inspired continues to hold sway.

The Romantic Generation: Song and Piano Music

Most music that survives from the Middle Ages through the eighteenth century was composed for the church or for courts. In later centuries, genres for home music-making, such as madrigals and string quartets, or for public performance, exemplified in Venetian opera, Handel's oratorios, and Haydn's late symphonies, become progressively more prominent. In the nineteenth century, music for home or public performance takes center stage. We will focus first on songs and piano music, the mainstays of home music-making and of virtuoso piano recitals, and the Romantic styles they fostered. In the following two chapters, we will examine music for the public, in the concert hall and in the theater.

THE NEW ORDER, 1815–1848

The upheavals of 1789–1815 changed the European political landscape. The French Revolution made peasants and workers into citizens instead of subjects. Napoleon's wars swept away old political boundaries and spread the revolutionary ideas of liberty, equality, and national identity across Europe. In 1814–15, the Congress of Vienna drew a new map, shown in Figure 24.1, made up of far fewer states. Although Italy and German-speaking lands were still partitioned, the inhabitants of each felt an increasing sense of a nation united by language and culture. So did the people in lands that had recently lost independence, such as Poland, or had long endured foreign domination, such as Hungary and Bohemia:

595

to them, the independent nation-state seemed an ideal. Repression held aspirations for freedom in check, until the stirring but largely unsuccessful revolutions of 1848–49. But interest in national culture grew, and composers incorporated national traits in song, instrumental music, and opera. The eighteenth-century cosmopolitan ideal was replaced by the expectation that composers write music true to their national identity.

The Americas   The Americas saw equally radical change. After Spain and Portugal were weakened by Napoleon's invasion, revolutions in 1810–24 brought independence to Latin America, and by 1838 most modern nations of the region had emerged. Between 1803 and 1848, the United States expanded west and south through purchase, treaties, and wars. Indian nations in many areas fought to retain control, but settlers moved west in increasing numbers. The United States began to create its own cultural identity in the tales of Washington Irving and Nathaniel Hawthorne, the novels of James Fenimore Cooper, and the

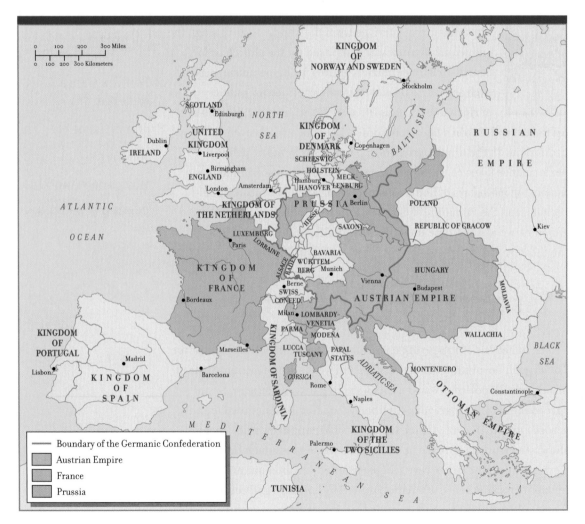

Figure 24.1: Map of Europe, 1815–48.

songs of Stephen Foster. In Canada, French and British provinces were officially united in 1841, although the two sides continued in conflict until the Canadian federation was established in 1867.

THE DECLINE OF PATRONAGE

The economic order in Europe changed along with the political, dramatically affecting musicians. War and inflation impoverished the aristocracy, and the elimination of over one hundred small states drastically reduced the number of courts supporting the arts. The typical musician no longer served a prince or church but made a living as a free agent through public performance, teaching, composing on commission, or creating music for publication. While patrons had expected their employees to play several instruments and, like Bach and Haydn, compose in most genres, musicians were now competing in an open market and often found a niche through specialization. Among the most prominent musicians of the age were *virtuosos*—performers, such as violinist Nicolò Paganini and pianist Fryderyk Chopin (see below), who specialized in one instrument and dazzled audiences with displays of technical mastery. Many composers also specialized in one medium, as Chopin did in piano music and Giuseppe Verdi in opera. Legal reforms eliminated the privileges enjoyed by the old guilds—which set standards and controlled various crafts, including music—and opened careers to anyone with talent.

As the aristocracy declined, the urban middle class grew in size and influence. The Industrial Revolution was mechanizing manufacturing, thereby reducing prices, drawing people from the country to work in factories, creating more leisure time, and allowing merchants and entrepreneurs to become the economic leaders.

MIDDLE-CLASS MUSIC-MAKING

Music-making was an important outlet for the middle classes, who had the money and leisure to purchase instruments and learn to play them. In many homes, evenings were a time for making music with family and friends, singing or playing piano, violin, flute, guitar, harp, or other instruments. Music released social pressures. It provided a way to express aspirations for equality and national freedom without risking censorship or imprisonment. It also offered an escape from wars, depressed economies, and political repression.

Music also was a means of social control. State-sponsored opera often carried political messages. Churches established amateur choirs, and factories organized wind bands for their workers, seeking to provide entertainment, elevate taste, and divert the working classes from drinking and carousing. And in an era of starkly differentiated gender roles, music kept women occupied at home.

Although many working-class women and children labored long hours in factories, women and girls of the middle and upper classes were expected to stay at home, their leisure a sign of status. The genders were assigned separate spheres: Boys went to school and men to work while women and girls

Separate spheres

maintained the home, regarded as a sacred refuge in a harsh world. When possible, servants were employed to do housework, releasing the women of the family to pursue feminine accomplishments from needlework to music.

THE PIANO

At the center of home music was the piano. Innovations in manufacturing greatly increased the availability of pianos and lowered their cost (see sidebar, pp. 600–01). Square pianos like that in Figure 24.2, small enough for parlors, found their way into many homes on both sides of the Atlantic.

The years 1820–50 saw many design improvements that allowed for new pianistic effects and a greatly expanded range. On such an instrument, a pianist could express a complete musical thought almost as well as an entire orchestra, yet more personally. These characteristics made the piano the quintessential nineteenth-century instrument, ideal both for home music and for public concerts.

Women and the piano   Women, particularly, played piano, continuing a tradition of keyboard-playing for their own and others' pleasure that stretched back to the sixteenth century. Pianist-composers such as Chopin and Liszt supported themselves in part by giving lessons to well-to-do women. Teachers expected daily practice, often for several hours, thereby keeping energetic young women occupied at home but also helping many of them achieve astonishing fluency.

Figure 24.2: Family Concert in Basle *(1849) by Sebastian Gutzwiller. This painting shows a typical domestic scene of music-making: a woman performs on a square piano while various other family members play the violin and flute. Others listen either with complete attention or while engaged in their own activities.*

There were quite a few professional women pianists in the first half of the nineteenth century—such as Clara Wieck, a formidable virtuoso who was to marry Robert Schumann—and many excellent amateurs who played at a professional level. Yet for most women, music was an accomplishment, designed to attract a spouse and serve family and friends, rather than a career. Men also played, often accompanying their wives, sisters, or daughters as they sang. A favorite format was music for two players at one piano, which offered siblings a joint recreation or a married or dating couple a structured physical and emotional intimacy.

THE MARKET FOR MUSIC AND THE NEW IDIOM

All these amateurs needed music to play, creating a boom in music publishing. In the 1770s, the largest publishers in London, Paris, and Leipzig listed hundreds of items in their catalogues, already a large number in comparison to earlier decades; in the 1820s they listed tens of thousands of pieces. The number of music stores in Europe and the New World grew rapidly in the early 1800s, increasing in London from thirty in 1794 to 150 in 1824. Technology again proved crucial: lithography, invented around 1796, let publishers print music cheaply with elaborate illustrations that helped it sell. Consumers demanded a constant flood of new music, and composers supplied it. As a result, the amount of music from the nineteenth century still available to us is overwhelming, far greater than for any previous era.

The market in sheet music gave the public at large unprecedented influence over what music was produced, because publishers had to supply what their customers wanted. Composers wrote songs, piano works, and piano duets in great quantities. Arrangers transcribed orchestral and chamber works for piano solo or duet, making concert works accessible to a large public; at a time before recordings, such arrangements were the only opportunity many people had to hear most works.

Composers writing for the public sought to make their music accessible and appealing to amateur performers by writing tuneful melodies with attractive accompaniments, little counterpoint, relatively uniform rhythm and level of difficulty from measure to measure, strong musical and extramusical imagery, evocative titles, national or exotic associations, familiar chords and progressions interspersed with dramatic or colorful harmonic contrasts, predictable four-bar phrasing, simple songlike forms, and idiomatic writing that exploited the textures, sonorities, and dynamic contrasts available on the modern piano. The most successful music offered something novel and individual that made it stand out from the crowd. Competition for sales fostered innovations in harmony such as greater use of nonharmonic tones, unexpected progressions, chromatic chords and voice leading, distant modulations, and tonal ambiguity.

The new musical idiom

These characteristics defined a new idiom, known today as the early Romantic style. The best composers of the time deepened their music's appeal to discerning players and listeners, but their styles were rooted in this idiom. The high value placed on a beautiful melody and striking harmonies within small forms such as songs and short piano pieces carried over into larger

Innovations: Musical Instruments in the Industrial Revolution

The Industrial Revolution was not a single event, but a series of inventions and applications that together radically changed the way goods were manufactured. Items that had been crafted by hand for centuries, from cloth to clocks, could now be mass produced by machine, making them much more widely available and less costly. In addition, existing products were improved and new ones developed in a continuing stream of innovation.

Music instrument making was one of many industries that became revolutionized. One profound change was in the sheer quantity of instruments that could be produced. In the 1770s, the output of even the largest piano manufacturers in Europe was only about twenty pianos a year, because every piece needed to be made by hand. By 1800, John Broadwood & Sons of London was manufacturing about four hundred pianos a year by employing a large and specialized work force, and by 1850 the firm was using steam power and mass production techniques to make over two thousand pianos a year, one hundred times as fast as eighty years before. Many were grand pianos, but most were square pianos like the one in Figure 24.2. Because they were produced in such quantity, pianos became inexpensive enough for middle-class families to afford.

The design of the piano was also improved through a number of innovations. The damper pedal, by holding all dampers off the strings, let tones continue after the keys were released, allowing greater resonance, closer imitation of orchestral sound, and new pianistic effects. The

Figure 24.3: Trumpet with piston valves (ca. 1865) by Antoine Courtois of Paris.

metal frame, introduced in England during the 1820s, allowed higher tension on the strings and thus greater volume, wider dynamic range, longer sustain, and better legato. Felt-covered hammers allowed more powerful *fortissimos* and quieter *pianissimos.* The standard range was extended to six octaves by 1820 and seven by 1850. The double-escapement action, introduced in 1821 by Parisian manufacturer Sébastien Erard, allowed quick repetition of notes and thus enabled a new level of virtuosity. All of these new capabilities were exploited by pianists and composers, and the piano became the indispensable instrument for home music-making and for public concerts. But it was clearly a modern-day machine, with thousands of separate parts and hundreds of mechanical connections.

The same spirit of innovation was applied to other instruments. Erard's firm also played an important role in creating the modern harp. Traditionally, harps were tuned to a single diatonic scale, so that they could not play chromatic passages, and even to change keys required retuning some of the strings. Several eighteenth-century harp makers had tried to solve this problem, but harps strung with all the chromatic notes were cumbersome to play, and finding a way quickly to change tuning proved difficult. Erard's solution was a new fork mechanism, operated by a set of seven pedals, that allowed the strings to be shortened, raising the pitch by one half-step. Eventually, Erard patented a harp that could be played in any key because each string could be adjusted almost instantaneously to produce any of three semitones by a double-action fork mechanism. By 1820, the firm had sold 3,500 of these instruments, whose principles are still in use by modern pedal-harp makers.

Starting in the 1810s, brass instrument makers applied the valve technology of the steam engine—in which valves controlled the flow of steam, water, or air—to the design of trumpets and horns, finally enabling these instruments to produce all the notes of the chromatic scale. Using either piston valves, as in the trumpet in Figure 24.3, or rotary valves, as on the horn in Figure 24.4, the player can open one or more lengths of pipe to extend the sounding length of the air column and thus lower the pitch one or more semitones. Only three or four valves are needed, rather than the many keys on a flute or clarinet, because brass instruments produce notes from the harmonic series, and only a few semitones separate each note in the series from the next one up or down. Many new brass instruments were invented as well, including the tuba, which became the bass of the orchestral brass section.

Wind instruments also profited from a combination of new technologies, enterprising innovators, and improved manufacturing methods. Theobald Boehm, a goldsmith and musician with experience in the steel industry, established a successful flute factory in Munich in 1828. He experimented with a number of designs for mechanisms that would achieve uniform tone production, superior volume, and better control of tuning. By 1849, he had created the modern "Boehm-system" flute, an all-metal instrument with large holes that were closed not with the bare fingers but with padded keys, linked to each other through a series of rod-axles, levers, and clutches, as shown in Figure 24.5. Louis-Auguste Buffet, working in Paris, applied some of Boehm's ideas to the clarinet, producing a design that has remained standard to the present. Adolphe Sax used a similar system of padded keys, axles, and levers to create the saxophone, a new wind instrument now familiar in marching bands and jazz.

Similar mechanical innovations brought about by the Industrial Revolution—such as interlocking

Figure 24.4: Horn with rotary valves (1835) by W. Glier of Warsaw.

rods, gears, and screws—improved the construction and tuning methods of the timpani in the early nineteenth century. By the late nineteenth century, the piano, the harp, and the wind, brass, and percussion instruments of the orchestra had almost all reached their modern form, thanks to the inventors and industrialists who applied the century's new technology to music.—JPB & BRH

Figure 24.5: Boehm system flute (1856) by Theobald Boehm.

forms as well. Originality was now marked, not by how one treated conventional material, as in the Classic era, but by the material itself.

ROMANTICISM

The new idiom, which focused on melody, emotion, novelty, and individuality, paralleled Romanticism in literature and art and came to be called **Romantic**. The term has many meanings, and tracing its history will clarify its use and implications.

"Romantic"
as a term

The word *romantic* derived from the medieval romance, a poem or tale about heroic events or persons, such as King Arthur or Charlemagne. It connoted something distant, legendary, and fantastic, an imaginary or ideal world far from everyday reality. In the nineteenth century, especially in German-speaking lands, the term was applied to literature, then to music and art. In contrast to "classic" poetry, which was deemed objectively beautiful, limited in scope and theme, and universally valid, "romantic" poetry transgressed rules and limits, expressing insatiable longing and the richness of nature. Like political liberalism and idealist philosophy, Romantic art focused on the individual and on expression of the self. By the mid-nineteenth century, works of Haydn and Mozart were regarded as classic, that is, elegant, natural, simple, clear, formally closed, and universally appealing, while Romantic music was identified with a search for the original, interesting, evocative, individual, expressive, or extreme. The music of Beethoven was regarded as straddling the two camps.

"Romantic"
as a period

By the late nineteenth century, this distinction crystallized into the notion of two style periods, Classic and Romantic, divided around the 1820s. Some later music historians considered the whole century "Romantic," while others saw the entire span from mid-eighteenth through early twentieth century as a single Classic-Romantic period in which composers shared conventions of harmony, rhythm, and form but differed in how they treated those conventions. For our purposes, the political and economic events of 1815 serve as a convenient starting point for the Romantic period because their impact on composers helps to explain the distinctive music of the era.

Romanticism
as reaction

Romanticism was a direct reaction to several of the themes explored above. Society was changing rapidly, driven in part by science and technology, and Romanticism sought refuge in the past, myth, dreams, the supernatural, and the irrational. As the new political concept of "nation" emerged, Romantics regarded "common folk" as the true embodiment of the nation. As people crowded into cities, Romantics valued rural life and looked to Nature for refuge, inspiration, and revelation. As industrialization brought about a mass society, Romantics esteemed solitude and the individual. As people in factories, shops, and homes were bound to routine, Romantics pursued novelty, boundlessness, and the exotic. And as a new capitalist economy replaced old forms of support for artists, Romantics saw artists as pursuing not money but a higher ideal of enlightening the world through access to a realm beyond the everyday. Some of these impulses are captured in the art of Caspar David

Figure 24.6: Caspar David Friedrich, Wanderer above the Sea of Fog.

Friedrich, the leading German Romantic painter, as in his *Wanderer above the Sea of Fog* (ca. 1818), shown in Figure 24.6. The same impulses suffuse the music of Romantic composers.

Romanticism encouraged composers to seek individual paths for express- *Music as the ideal* ing intense emotions, such as melancholy, longing, or joy. Composers re- *Romantic art* spected conventions of form or harmony to a point, but their imagination drove them to trespass limits and explore new realms of sound. Some writers considered instrumental music the ideal Romantic art because it was free from the concreteness of words and visual images and thus could evoke impressions, thoughts, and feelings that are beyond the power of words to express.

The idealization of instrumental music as the premier mode of artistic ex- *Absolute,* pression led Ludwig Tieck, E. T. A. Hoffmann, and other writers to formulate *characteristic, and* new distinctions among instrumental works between **absolute, characteris-** *program music* **tic** (or **descriptive**) and **program music**. A programmatic work recounts a narrative or sequence of events, often spelled out in an accompanying text called a **program**; a **character piece** depicts or suggests a mood, personality, or scene, usually indicated in its title; and absolute music offers instead an idealized play of sound and form. Program music was not a nineteenth-century invention. Composers in the seventeenth and eighteenth centuries expected their instrumental music to convey particular emotions, associations with everyday life (from dance rhythms to hunting horns), and in some cases even specific characters, scenes, or programs, as in Biber's *Mystery Sonatas* or Vivaldi's *Four Seasons*. What is truly new in the nineteenth century is the notion of absolute music, which refers to nothing but itself—a powerful idea that lay behind numerous developments in both nineteenth- and twentieth-century music.

Music and the literary   Despite the prestige of instrumental music, literature was central to the work of most composers. Many had writers as friends, and some were writers themselves; Berlioz and Schumann, for example, were professional music

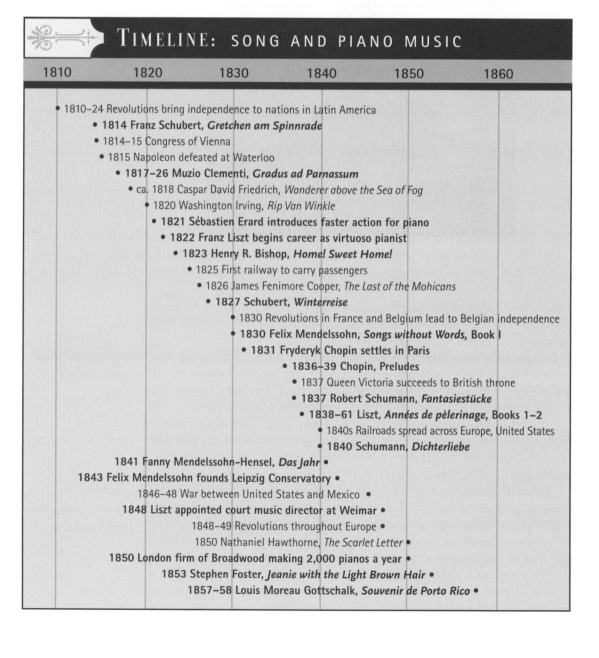

TIMELINE: SONG AND PIANO MUSIC

1810	1820	1830	1840	1850	1860

- 1810–24 Revolutions bring independence to nations in Latin America
- 1814 Franz Schubert, *Gretchen am Spinnrade*
- 1814–15 Congress of Vienna
- 1815 Napoleon defeated at Waterloo
- 1817–26 Muzio Clementi, *Gradus ad Parnassum*
- ca. 1818 Caspar David Friedrich, *Wanderer above the Sea of Fog*
- 1820 Washington Irving, *Rip Van Winkle*
- 1821 Sébastien Erard introduces faster action for piano
- 1822 Franz Liszt begins career as virtuoso pianist
- 1823 Henry R. Bishop, *Home! Sweet Home!*
- 1825 First railway to carry passengers
- 1826 James Fenimore Cooper, *The Last of the Mohicans*
- 1827 Schubert, *Winterreise*
- 1830 Revolutions in France and Belgium lead to Belgian independence
- 1830 Felix Mendelssohn, *Songs without Words*, Book I
- 1831 Fryderyk Chopin settles in Paris
- 1836–39 Chopin, *Preludes*
- 1837 Queen Victoria succeeds to British throne
- 1837 Robert Schumann, *Fantasiestücke*
- 1838–61 Liszt, *Années de pèlerinage*, Books 1–2
- 1840s Railroads spread across Europe, United States
- 1840 Schumann, *Dichterliebe*
- 1841 Fanny Mendelssohn-Hensel, *Das Jahr*
- 1843 Felix Mendelssohn founds Leipzig Conservatory
- 1846–48 War between United States and Mexico
- 1848 Liszt appointed court music director at Weimar
- 1848–49 Revolutions throughout Europe
- 1850 Nathaniel Hawthorne, *The Scarlet Letter*
- 1850 London firm of Broadwood making 2,000 pianos a year
- 1853 Stephen Foster, *Jeanie with the Light Brown Hair*
- 1857–58 Louis Moreau Gottschalk, *Souvenir de Porto Rico*

critics, Liszt wrote essays on music, and Wagner wrote his own opera librettos. From songs to choral works and opera, several leading genres required an integration of music and text. In setting words, composers sought to draw out the inner meanings and feelings suggested in the poetry or libretto. Even many instrumental works bore inseparable links to words through a descriptive title or program. The effort to find a musical effect capable of expressing an idea or program often led to innovations in harmony, melody, and instrumental color. Such novelty appealed to middle-class consumers, and the program enhanced that appeal while justifying the unusual effects. For this reason, composers and publishers often added programs or descriptive titles after a work was composed.

SONG

The trends described above are apparent in songs of the time. Voice and piano (played by the singer or an accompanist) was the preferred medium, offering a wide expressive range with minimal forces. Songs varied from simple settings with chordal accompaniment and the same melody for every verse to artful, through-composed miniature dramas in which the accompaniment rivaled the voice in importance. Only later in the century did a firm line develop between popular songs for sale to the widest possible musical public and art songs for connoisseurs.

The most influential and prestigious repertoire of nineteenth-century song was the German Lied. The Lied was in many ways the quintessential Romantic genre: a fusion of music and poetry, centering on the expression of individual feelings, with descriptive musical imagery and aspects of folk style. Another significant tradition was the British and American parlor song. Among the thousands of song composers active before midcentury, the following focuses on only a handful of the most exemplary.

THE LIED

The Romantic Lied built on a strong eighteenth-century tradition (see chapter 20). The popularity of Lieder grew after 1800. The number of German song collections published increased from about one a month in the late 1700s to over one hundred a month in 1826, when the music journal *Allgemeine musikalische Zeitung* asked "has there ever been an age more prolific in song than ours?" Changes in poetry anticipated changes in the Lied. Poets drew elements from both classical and folk traditions. A frequent theme was an individual confronting the greater forces of nature or society, vulnerable yet ennobled by the encounter; another was nature as a metaphor for human experience.

The chief poetic genre continued to be the *lyric*, a short, strophic poem on one subject expressing a personal feeling or viewpoint. The ultimate models were the lyric poets of ancient Greece and Rome, such as Sappho and Horace.

The lyric

Two collections of folk song verses, Johann Gottfried von Herder's *Volks-lieder* (Folk Songs, 1778–79) and Clemens Brentano and Achim von Arnim's *Des Knaben Wunderhorn* (The Boy's Magic Horn, 1805), influenced poets to adopt similar language and imagery. Both ancient lyrics and folk verses were meant to be sung, and the poetry written in imitation of them was ideal for setting to music, with short strophes and regular meter and rhyme.

FRANZ SCHUBERT (1797–1828)

Schubert was the first great master of the Romantic Lied and a prolific composer in all genres.

As a child, Schubert took composition lessons from the court music director, Antonio Salieri. He also studied piano, singing, violin, organ, counterpoint, and figured bass. Schubert's musical talent won him a free, first-class education at a prestigious Vienna boarding school. Although trained to follow his father's profession of schoolmaster, his heart lay in composing. For several years he taught at his father's school, all the while composing with astonishing speed and fluency; in 1815 alone he produced more than 140 songs. January 1818 saw the first publication of his music, and from then on he devoted himself entirely to composition.

By 1821, Schubert's music was widely performed in Vienna, and he was earning substantial sums from publishers. As he never secured a permanent salaried position, he gained most of his income from publication, especially of songs and piano music.

The last years of Schubert's life were clouded by illness. He died at thirty-one, possibly from syphilis he had contracted by 1823 or from its treatment with mercury. His tombstone was inscribed "Music has here buried a rich treasure but still fairer hopes." Given the brevity of his career, his output of almost one thousand works is astounding.

Figure 24.7: *Franz Schubert, in a watercolor portrait from 1825 by Wilhelm August Rieder.*

MAJOR WORKS: *Over 600 songs, including the song cycles* Die schöne Müllerin *and* Winterreise; *9 symphonies, notably No. 8 in B Minor (Unfinished) and No. 9 in C Major (The Great); about 35 chamber works, including Piano Quintet in A Major (The Trout), String Quartet in D Minor (Death and the Maiden), and String Quintet in C Major; 22 piano sonatas; many short piano pieces; 17 operas and Singspiels; 6 masses; 200 other choral works*

Figure 24.8: Sepia drawing by Schubert's friend Moritz von Schwind (1868), showing Schubert at the piano accompanying the singer Johann Michael Vogl, sitting to his right. The occasion is a Schubertiad, a gathering in a private home during which Schubert would play piano and either sing his own songs or accompany a singer.

The ballad

In the late eighteenth century, German poets cultivated a new form, the **ballad,** in imitation of the folk ballads of England and Scotland. Ballads might alternate narrative and dialogue and usually dealt with romantic adventures or supernatural incidents. Their greater length and wider palette of moods and events inspired composers to use more varied themes and textures. The ballad thus expanded the Lied both in form and in emotional content. The piano rose from accompaniment to equal partner with the voice in illustrating and intensifying the meaning of the poetry.

Song collections and song cycles

Lieder composers often grouped their songs into collections with a unifying characteristic, such as texts by a single poet or a focus on a common theme. Beethoven's *An die ferne Geliebte* (see chapter 23) introduced the concept of the *Liederkreis*, or song cycle, in which all the songs were to be performed in order, as movements of a multimovement vocal work. Using this format, composers could tell a story through a succession of songs, combining the narrative emphasis of ballads with the focused expressivity of the lyric poem.

FRANZ SCHUBERT

The characteristics of the Romantic Lied are exemplified in the songs of Franz Schubert (1797–1828; see biography and Figure 24.7). Schubert wrote over six hundred Lieder, many of which were first performed for friends in home concerts known as Schubertiads. In the picture of one such evening in Figure 24.8, many of the listeners seem transported, gazing into space with attentive expressions on their faces. The drawing conveys the intensely emotional engagement with music that was characteristic of the age.

Song texts   Schubert set poetry by many writers, including fifty-nine poems of Goethe. Some of Schubert's finest Lieder are found in his two song cycles on poems by Wilhelm Müller, *Die schöne Müllerin* (The Pretty Miller-Maid, 1823) and *Winterreise* (Winter's Journey, 1827). When Schubert wrote a song he strove to make the music the equal of the words, not merely their frame. Through melody, accompaniment, harmony, and form, he sought to embody the person speaking or characters described, the scene, the situation, and the emotions expressed.

Form   Schubert always chose forms that suited the shape and meaning of the text. When a poem sustains a single image or mood, Schubert typically uses strophic form, with the same music for each stanza, as in *Heidenröslein* (Little Heath-Rose, 1815) and *Das Wandern* (Wandering), the first song in *Die schöne Müllerin*. Contrast or change is often depicted with **modified strophic form**, in which music repeats for some strophes but others vary it or use new music; an example is *Der Lindenbaum* (The Linden Tree) from *Winterreise*, described below. Some songs use ternary form (ABA or ABA′), as in *Der Atlas* (Atlas), or bar form (AAB), as in *Ständchen* (Serenade), both from *Schwanengesang* (Swan Song, 1828). Longer narrative songs may be through-composed, with new music for each stanza, like the ballad *Erlkönig* (The Erl-King, 1815), or combine declamatory and arioso styles as in an operatic scene, like *Der Wanderer* (The Wanderer, 1816); in either case, recurring themes and a carefully planned tonal scheme lend unity.

Melody   Schubert had a gift for creating beautiful melodies that perfectly capture a poem's character, mood, and situation. Many songs use the simple, seemingly artless quality of folk song to suggest a rural setting or uncomplicated feelings, as in *Heidenröslein* and *Das Wandern*, shown in Example 24.1a–b. Others are suffused with sweetness and melancholy, as is *Ständchen*, Example 24.1c, or are declamatory and dramatic, like *Der Atlas*, Example 24.1d.

Accompaniment   The excerpts in Example 24.1 only begin to illustrate the variety of Schubert's accompaniments. The figuration always fits the poem's mood and the personality of its protagonist, from a simple alternation of bass note and chord in *Heidenröslein* to dramatic tremolos and octaves in *Der Atlas*. The accompaniment often reflects an image in the poem, especially an image of

Example 24.1: Schubert songs

a. Heidenröslein

A boy saw a rosebud standing, a rosebud on the heath

b. Das Wandern

Wandering is the miller's pleasure!

c. Ständchen

Gently my songs through the night implore you

d. Der Atlas

I, the unlucky Atlas!

movement, like the walking motion of *Das Wandern* or a serenader plucking a guitar in *Ständchen*.

In *Gretchen am Spinnrade* (Gretchen at the Spinning Wheel, 1814; NAWM 111), on an excerpt from Goethe's *Faust*, the piano suggests the spinning wheel by using a constant rising and falling sixteenth-note figure in the right hand, and the motion of the treadle, by using repeated notes in the left hand,

CD 8|62   CD 4|67

as shown in Example 24.2. These figures also convey Gretchen's agitation as she thinks of her beloved. Often, as here, the piano introduces the song's mood and central image in a short prelude before the voice enters. When Gretchen recalls her beloved's kiss, the accompaniment suddenly stops, then haltingly restarts. Although the words do not indicate her actions, we know from the music that she stops the wheel when she is overcome by emotion, then gradually returns to spinning as she regains her composure.

Example 24.2: Schubert, Gretchen am Spinnrade

My peace is gone.

Harmony   The harmony also reinforces the poetry. The simple *Das Wandern* uses only five different chords. The sweet melancholy of *Ständchen* is evoked by alternating minor and major forms of a key or triad, an effect that is almost a trademark of Schubert's style. In other songs, he underlines the poem's dramatic qualities powerfully through complex modulations. In *Der Atlas*, he uses a diminished seventh chord to move abruptly from G minor to the distant key of B major, then gradually works his way back through E minor to G minor. This extraordinary key scheme illustrates Schubert's fondness for modulation by third rather than by fifth, a trait also found in his instrumental music. His predilection for unusual harmonic relationships reflects his use of harmony as an expressive device, since the unconventional generally carries more expressive potential than the conventional, and both aspects of his harmonic practice greatly influenced later composers.

Der Lindenbaum   Schubert's mastery of all these elements is evident in *Der Lindenbaum* (NAWM 112), from *Winterreise.* Müller's cycle of twenty-four poems expresses the nostalgia of a lover revisiting in winter the haunts of a failed summer romance. In this poem, he recalls lying under a linden tree dreaming of his love. Now as he passes the tree, a chilly wind rustles the branches, which seem to call him back to find rest—or death. Fluttering triplets in the piano introduction suggest the rustling leaves of summer, a pleasant memory; later these triplets change to depict the wintry wind, with touches of chromaticism to suggest its eerie effect. A folklike melody with simple, horn-call harmony evokes the outdoor scene, the lover's past happiness, and his current nostalgia. The modified strophic form marks the progress of the story: the first strophe, remembering summer love, is in major; the second changes the mode to minor to suggest the chill of winter; the third heralds the cold wind with a new, declamatory melody; and the fourth returns to the major mode and the original melody, now sounding more spooky than comforting. The subtle ways in which the music interprets the poem, and the progress of the poem reinterprets musical elements heard previously, demonstrate how well Schubert conveys meanings through music that deepen our experience of the text.

Schubert's ability to capture the mood and character of a poem and make the music its equal in emotive and descriptive power, along with the sheer beauty of his music and the pleasure it gives to those who perform it, have endeared Schubert's songs both to his contemporaries and to generations of singers, pianists, and listeners. His songs set the standard that later song composers strove to match. *Schubert's achievement*

ROBERT AND CLARA SCHUMANN

Schubert's first important successor as a Lieder composer was Robert Schumann (1810–1856). Schumann wrote over 120 songs in 1840, which he called his "Year of Song." He focused on love songs, including the song cycles *Dichterliebe* (A Poet's Love) and *Frauenliebe und -leben* (Woman's Love and Life). He was inspired in part by his impending marriage to Clara Wieck, a renowned pianist and composer (see their joint biography and Figure 24.9). Schumann turned to song to express the passions and frustrations of love, to make money from a lucrative genre, and to synthesize music and poetry, his two great interests.

Schumann thought that music should capture a poem's essence in its own terms and that voice and piano should be equal partners. He often gave the piano relatively long preludes, interludes, or postludes, showing that the instrument is no mere accompaniment. Schumann typically used a single figuration throughout to convey the central emotion or idea of the poem. His cycle *Dichterliebe* exemplifies these precepts. He chose sixteen poems from Heinrich Heine's *Lyrical Intermezzo* and arranged them to suggest the course of a relationship from longing to initial fulfillment, abandonment, dreams of reconciliation, and resignation. *Music and poetry*

In the first song, *Im wunderschönen Monat Mai* (In the marvelous month of May; NAWM 113), the poet confesses a newborn love. His tentative feelings are expressed in the harmonic ambiguity of the opening, shown in Example 24.3, CD 8|72

Example 24.3: Schumann, Im wunderschönen Monat Mai

and his "longing and desire" through suspensions and appoggiaturas. The music signals that his love may remain unrequited by refusing to settle into a key and ending on a dominant seventh. The hint of unfulfillment is not explicit in Heine's poetry, but is Schumann's creation, revealing his success in making the piano as important as the voice, the music the equal partner of the words in conveying meaning and emotions, and the composer the cocreator with the poet.

ROBERT SCHUMANN (1810–1856)
CLARA SCHUMANN (1819–1896)

One of the most significant marriages in the history of music was that of Robert and Clara Schumann. He was a music critic and outstanding composer, especially of piano music, songs, and symphonies, and she was among the foremost pianists of her day and a distinguished composer and teacher.

Their careers intertwined, so that one is difficult to describe without the other.

Robert Schumann studied piano from age seven and soon began to compose. Son of a writer and book dealer, he had an intense interest in literature, especially Romantic writers such as Friedrich Schlegel, Jean Paul, and E. T. A. Hoffmann. After university studies in law, Schumann devoted himself to becoming a concert pianist, studying in Leipzig with Friedrich Wieck, his future father-in-law. When an injury to Schumann's right hand cut short his performing career, he turned to composition and criticism, editing the Leipzig *Neue Zeitschrift für Musik* (New Journal of Music) from 1834 to 1844. In his essays and reviews, he opposed empty virtuosity, urged the study of older music, and was among the first and strongest advocates of Chopin, Brahms, and the instrumental music of Schubert.

In his career as a composer, Schumann often focused on one medium at a time: piano music until 1840, then songs that year, symphonies in 1841, chamber music in 1842–43, oratorio in 1843, dramatic music in 1847–48, and church music in 1852.

Meanwhile, Friedrich Wieck was training his daughter Clara to become a concert pianist. Recognized as a child prodigy from her first public appearance at age nine, she

Figure 24.9: Robert and Clara Schumann in 1850. Daguerreotype (early photograph) by Johann Anton Völlner.

toured Europe and earned the praise of Goethe, Mendelssohn, Chopin, and Paganini. By the age of twenty, she was one of the leading pianists in Europe, with many published works to her credit. She and Robert became engaged, but Wieck opposed the relationship, and it took a lawsuit to permit their wedding in 1840.

Syphilis, contracted by Schumann early in his life, and depression, which ran in his family, doubtless contributed to episodes of strange behavior and aural hallucinations that climaxed in a suicide attempt in February 1854. He was confined to an asylum near Bonn, where he died in July 1856.

Although Clara Schumann curbed her concert touring after marrying Robert and while raising eight children, she continued to perform and compose. After his death, she performed and taught but ceased composing, turning instead to promoting and editing her husband's music. She continued to concertize until 1891 and to teach until her death in 1896.

MAJOR WORKS (ROBERT SCHUMANN): *Over 300 piano works, including* Papillons, Carnaval, Fantasiestücke, Kreisleriana, *and* Album for the Young; *about 300 songs; 75 partsongs for mixed, mens' or womens' voices; 4 symphonies; piano concerto; 3 piano trios; about 15 other chamber works; various works for orchestra, solo with orchestra, or voices with orchestra*

MAJOR WORKS (CLARA SCHUMANN): *Piano Trio, Op. 17; piano concerto, many piano pieces, and several collections of Lieder*

Clara Schumann also wrote several collections of Lieder, including one coauthored with Robert. Her approach to song parallels her husband's, with long preludes and postludes, similar figuration throughout each song, and voice and piano as equals in conveying the images and feelings of the poem. For example, in *Geheimes Flüstern* (Secret Whispers, 1853), from her last song cycle, the poem is dominated by an image of the forest whispering to the poet. A continuous sixteenth-note arpeggiation establishes a backdrop of rustling leaves and branches, helping to express the poet's reliance on the forest as a refuge and a communicator of life's secrets.

Clara Schumann

BRITISH AND NORTH AMERICAN SONG

A separate tradition grew in Great Britain, where songs for home performance were called *ballads* or *drawing-room ballads*, and in the United States and Canada, where they were called **parlor songs**. As the names indicate, such songs held an important place in home music-making, but they were also sung in musical theater productions and public concerts. Songs of this type are usually strophic or in verse-refrain form, with piano preludes and postludes based on phrases from the tune. Their expressivity lies almost entirely in the vocal melody. The piano supports the singer with conventional figuration, rather than dramatizing or interpreting the text as it does in many German Lieder. Like much Baroque music (see chapter 13), this type of song tended not to be treated as unalterable; rather, it served as a vehicle for the performers, who were free to adorn the melody and reshape the accompaniment.

CD 8|73

The most famous drawing-room ballad, and perhaps the best-known song of the nineteenth century, is *Home! Sweet Home!* (1823; NAWM 114) by the English composer Henry R. Bishop (1786–1855). Bishop was a renowned composer of theatrical music who is remembered today for this one song, from the opera *Clari*. It has a sentimental text in verse-refrain form, regular four-measure phrases, and the characteristic melodic style of the genre: simple, mostly diatonic, stepwise, and triadic, but also tuneful, charming, and expressive, with opportunities for embellishment. Differences between the verses show a close attention to declamation, and the accompaniment marks two places in the text: the beginning of the chorus, at "Home! Home! sweet, sweet, Home!," where it pauses in almost prayerful reverence; and the second verse, where it introduces a trill to illustrate "birds singing gaily."

Canada

Hundreds of composers all over the English-speaking world wrote parlor songs. The most notable song composer in Canada was Scottish-born church musician James P. Clarke (1807/8–1877), the first to earn a Bachelor of Music degree from a North American university, whose song cycle *Lays of the Maple Leaf* (1853) was the most substantial work yet published by a Canadian.

Stephen Foster

The leading American song composer of the nineteenth century was Stephen Foster (1826–1864). Growing up in Pittsburgh, he heard German, Italian, and Irish music. He taught himself to play several instruments but had no formal training in composition. After his 1848 song *Oh! Susanna* achieved great success, he signed a contract with a New York publisher and became the first American to earn a living solely as a composer. Like Bishop, he wrote for the stage as well as the parlor; his songs for minstrel shows are treated in chapter 26. He typically wrote his own texts, which are mostly sentimental, sometimes comic.

Foster combined elements of British ballads, American minstrel songs, German Lieder, Italian opera, and Irish folk songs. Seeking—and finding—wide popularity, he made his music easy to perform and remember. His melodies are almost wholly diatonic, mostly stepwise or pentatonic (a feature of both Irish and minstrel tunes), and progress in four-measure phrases. The harmony and accompaniment are deliberately simple, although the figuration often changes with each phrase to demarcate the form. *Jeanie with the Light*

CD 8|75

Brown Hair (1853; NAWM 115), one of his best-known songs, illustrates all these features. In the last phrase of the first verse, shown in Example 24.4, the harmonic and melodic simplicity makes the dissonances on "Jeanie," "floating," and "summer" more piquant and the faster progression at the end of phrase more expressive. There is even a touch of opera in the brief cadenza.

Continuum of taste

Today, nineteenth-century parlor songs are thought of as popular music, but they were written for the same middle-class market as German Lieder and share many of the same characteristics. The Lieder of Schubert and the Schumanns have an appeal to connoisseurs that was recognized at the time and led to their canonization as art songs by later generations. Yet in the early nineteenth century, the chasm between popular and serious music so typical of later eras had not yet opened, and all these songs coexisted on a continuum in which popular appeal and interest to the learned did not necessarily exclude one another.

Example 24.4: Foster, Jeanie with the Light Brown Hair

MUSIC FOR PIANO

If song was the most popular medium of the nineteenth century, piano music ran a close second. Piano works served three overlapping purposes: teaching, amateur enjoyment, and public performance. The first category includes graded studies such as Muzio Clementi's *Gradus ad Parnassum* (Steps to Parnassas, 1817–26), consisting of one hundred exercises of increasing difficulty, and the numerous **études** (studies) and method books by Beethoven's student Carl Czerny, many of which are still in use today. The second category encompasses dances, lyrical pieces modeled on song, character pieces, and sonatas. The third category includes bravura pieces for virtuosos. It is typical of the age that many pieces have more than one function; for example, amateur pieces were used in teaching, Chopin and Liszt pioneered the étude worthy of concert performance, and many concert artists included sonatas and small lyrical works on their programs alongside virtuoso vehicles.

SCHUBERT

Among works suitable for the amateur market, Schubert wrote dozens of marches, waltzes, and other dances. His six *Moments musicaux* (Musical Moments, 1823–28) and eight *Impromptus* (1827) are models of the short lyrical piece that creates a distinctive mood. Of his numerous works for piano duet, several challenge the most advanced amateurs, including the sublimely beautiful and moving Fantasy in F minor (1828).

Schubert's most important larger works for the piano are his eleven completed piano sonatas and the *Wanderer Fantasy* (1822), whose virtuosity and unusual form fascinated later composers. The fantasy has four linked move-

FELIX MENDELSSOHN (1809–1847)

Mendelssohn's musical precociousness equaled or even surpassed that of Mozart. He began composing seriously at age eleven and never stopped. By his fourteenth birthday he had written four Singspiele; some two dozen sacred and secular vocal works; eight string symphonies; six chamber works, including his Piano Quartet, Op. 1, published in 1823; and a raft of piano and organ pieces. At sixteen he composed his Octet for Strings, Op. 20, which is still established in the repertoire, and at seventeen the magical Overture to Shakespeare's *A Midsummer Night's Dream*.

Mendelssohn was the grandson of Moses Mendelssohn, the leading Jewish philosopher of the Enlightenment in Germany. Although Jews were slowly gaining legal rights as a spillover from the French Revolution, Felix's banker father, Abraham, had his children baptized when they were still young and then converted to Christianity himself, adding Bartholdy to the family's surname. Abraham and his wife, an amateur pianist, encouraged their children's musical interests, and both Felix and his sister Fanny were trained from an early age by excellent teachers. Thus Felix and Fanny were born into a family that was at the center of Berlin's intellectual life and received every advantage that their parents' money and position could provide.

Mendelssohn composed at an astonishing rate throughout his life, marked by frequent travel, concert tours as pianist and

Figure 24.10: Felix Mendelssohn at twenty. Water-color portrait by Warren Childe (1829).

conductor, and positions as music director in Düsseldorf, music director and conductor of the Gewandhaus Orchestra in Leipzig, and in various capacities in Berlin. In 1843, he founded the Leipzig Conservatory, whose faculty included both Robert and Clara Schumann. He died at the age of thirty-eight, after a series of strokes.

MAJOR WORKS: Oratorios St. Paul *and* Elijah; *5 symphonies, including symphony-cantata "Lobgesang"; violin concerto; 2 piano concertos; 4 overtures; incidental music to 7 plays, including* A Midsummer Night's Dream; *numerous chamber works, including 6 string quartets, 2 piano trios, 2 cello sonatas; numerous pieces for piano and for organ; choral works; and songs*

ments centered around variations on his song *Der Wanderer.* The remaining movements also use motives from the song.

Sonatas

In his sonatas, Schubert wrestled with contradictions between his song-inspired style and the demands of the sonata, with its multiple movements and extended forms. His themes typically are expansive melodies that do not lend themselves to motivic development; instead, they recur in different environments that suggest new meanings. His sonata-form movements often use three keys in the exposition rather than two (for example, tonic for the first theme, mediant for the second, and dominant for the closing theme). Some of the slow movements are particularly songful and resemble impromptus. His last three sonatas, in C minor, A major, and B♭ major, show a strong awareness of Beethoven, as in the stormy first movement of the C-minor sonata. But Schubert's lyrical style is ever present. The sonata in B♭ opens with a long singing melody, which returns throughout the movement in various guises, major and minor, complete and fragmented, as if set to new words in conflict with those of before. Schubert's approach to sonata form had a notable influence on later composers.

FELIX MENDELSSOHN

One of the leading German Romantic composers was Felix Mendelssohn (1809–1847; see biography and Figure 24.10). He blended influences from Bach, Handel, Mozart, Beethoven, and his own contemporaries in music that combined contrapuntal skill and formal clarity with Romantic expression, beautiful melodies, and interesting, often unpredictable rhythms. A virtuoso performer on both piano and organ, Mendelssohn emphasized fluent technique over bravura display. His larger piano works include three sonatas, variations, and fantasias. His *Seven Character Pieces*, published in 1827, helped to introduce that term and define the genre.

Mendelssohn's best-known piano works are his *Lieder ohne Worte* (Songs without Words), forty-eight short pieces grouped in eight books. In the first "song" (1830), shown in Example 24.5, the similarity to the Lied is immediately

Songs without Words

Example 24.5: Mendelssohn, Song without Words *No. 1, Op. 19, No. 1*

apparent. It could be written on three staves, the bass for the pianist's left hand, the arpeggiations for the right, and the melody for a singer. Having to cover all three lines with two hands produces interesting pianistic problems: how to bring out the melody and bass in a smooth legato while using mainly the weaker fourth and fifth fingers, and how to share the sixteenth-note figuration evenly between the two hands. The piece exploits the piano's ability to respond to the player's varying touch, louder for the melody and bass, softer for the accompaniment, even when they are played by fingers of the same hand. Beyond these technical matters, the piece presents an engaging melody and interesting accompaniment that convey a distinct mood, like a well-crafted song. The *Songs without Words* exemplify Mendelssohn's belief that music can express feelings words cannot (see Source Reading), reflecting the idealist philosophy that underpins Romantic thought.

CLARA SCHUMANN AND FANNY MENDELSSOHN HENSEL

The prospects for and limitations on women composers in the early nineteenth century are illustrated by the contrasting careers of Clara Schumann and Fanny Mendelssohn Hensel (1805–1847). Both were highly skilled pianist-composers, yet one played public concerts and published much of her music, while the other was confined almost entirely to the domestic sphere.

 SOURCE READING

MENDELSSOHN ON THE MEANING OF MUSIC

Mendelssohn regarded his Songs without Words *as complete in themselves, needing neither lyrics nor titles to convey their meaning. When an admirer wrote to ask what some of the individual pieces meant, Mendelssohn responded with this famous statement that argues for music's ability to express thoughts that cannot be expressed in words.*

— • —

People usually complain that music is so ambiguous, and what they are supposed to think when they hear it is so unclear, while words are understood by everyone. But for me it is exactly the opposite—and not just with entire discourses, but also with individual words; these, too, seem to be so ambiguous, so indefinite, in comparison with good music, which fills one's soul with a thousand better things than words. What the music I love expresses to me are

thoughts not too *indefinite* for words, but rather too *definite*.

Thus, I find in all attempts to put these thoughts into words something correct, but also always something insufficient, something not universal.... If you ask me what I was thinking of, I will say: just the song as it stands there. And if I happen to have had a specific word or specific words in mind for one or another of these songs, I can never divulge them to anyone, because the same word means one thing to one person and something else to another, because only the song can say the same thing, can arouse the same feelings in one person as in another—a feeling which is not, however, expressed by the same words.

Letter to Marc-André Souchay, October 15, 1842, trans. John Michael Cooper, in SR 161 (6:14), p. 1201.

Clara Schumann won fame as a pianist at a young age and was at first better known than her husband, Robert. In an era when the score was often only a starting point for a performer's embellishment, she played what was written, thus focusing attention on the composer rather than the performer. In her day, this idea was pathbreaking. Her performances also provided opportunities for improvisation, a staple of nineteenth-century concerts, and for showcasing her own music and that of her husband. Her piano compositions include polonaises, waltzes, variations, preludes and fugues, character pieces, and a Sonata in G Minor (1841–42).

Fanny Mendelssohn had equally thorough training, but for the most part performed and composed in private settings. She studied piano from a young age, and theory and composition in her teens. She was almost as talented and precocious musically as her brother Felix. After marrying painter Wilhelm Hensel, she led a salon, a regular gathering of friends and invited guests, where she played piano and presented her compositions. She wrote more than four hundred works, including at least 250 songs and 125 piano pieces. Few were published in her lifetime, because her father and brother opposed publication on the grounds that a musical career was inappropriate for a woman of her class. Their objection minimized the influence she had outside her circle and confined her mostly to the small genres appropriate for home music-making. Her masterpiece is *Das Jahr* (The Year, 1841), a series of character pieces on the twelve months, inspired by an extended trip to Italy in 1839–40. She died unexpectedly of a stroke less than a year after the publication in 1846 of her Op. 1, six songs. Only in the past thirty years or so has she become more than "Mendelssohn's sister," as scholars have discovered a trove of her works and realized the importance of her salons.

ROBERT SCHUMANN

Schumann's publications up to 1840 were all for solo piano, and they include his principal music for that instrument. Aside from a few longer works, the bulk of his piano compositions are short character pieces, often grouped in colorfully named sets such as *Papillons* (Butterflies), *Carnaval*, *Fantasiestücke* (Fantasy Pieces), *Kinderscenen* (Scenes from Childhood), and *Kreisleriana*. Attractive little pieces for children are gathered in the *Album für die Jugend* (Album for the Young).

The titles Schumann assigned to his pieces suggest that he wanted listeners to associate them with extramusical poetic fancies. This attitude is typical of the period, although Schumann claimed that he did not always know the title of a piece until the music was written. He instilled in his music the depths and contradictions of his own personality. It is by turns ardent and dreamy, vehement and visionary, whimsical and learned. In his writings, he personifies different facets of his own nature as members of the Davidsbund, a league he made up that campaigned against the Philistines of music. Florestan (from the hero of Beethoven's *Fidelio*) is the impulsive revolutionary, Eusebius (after a fourth-century pope) the contemplative dreamer, and Meister Raro ("exceptional master," as he called his teacher and Clara's father, Friedrich Wieck) the wise, mature master.

Extramusical associations

CD 8|76   CD 4|77

We can see Schumann's Florestan side in *Aufschwung* (Soaring, NAWM 116a), the second piece in his *Fantasiestücke* (1837). The work features four strongly contrasting ideas arranged in a complex ternary form with transition (ABA′ CDC Trans AB′A″), coordinating what are essentially independent blocks of music in a logical form. The impulsive A theme, shown in Example 24.6a, pounds out a dramatic motive, then soars up through four rising octaves and down in a syncopated melody; the tonic F minor, indicated by a repeated half-cadence, is evaded until the very end of the piece. The B theme, shown in Example 24.6b, soars in a different way, the melody climbing chromatically, supported by rushing figuration and an inner voice paralleling the melody.

Example 24.6: Schumann, Aufschwung

a. *Opening theme*

b. *B theme*

CD 8|84

The third piece in the set, *Warum?* (Why?, NAWM 116b), evokes Schumann's Eusebius side, contemplating an enigmatic motive through changes of register, harmony, and shape, as if weighing a question that cannot be resolved; even at the end, as the motive appears three times in the tonic, it somehow sounds unanswered. The piece remains a kind of fragment, like many of Schumann's songs and piano pieces: complete in itself, yet open to extension, as if it captured a momentary thought or experience while implying that there may be more to the story. Through gestures like these, Schumann captures the Romantic worldview in simple terms, creating music that is endlessly fascinating and rewarding for performer and listener.

FRYDERYK CHOPIN

Fryderyk Chopin (1810–1849) composed almost exclusively for piano (see biography and Figure 24.11). His entire output comprises about two hundred solo piano pieces, six works for piano and orchestra composed for his concert appearances as a young virtuoso, some twenty songs, and four chamber works. He is revered for idiomatic writing that opened new possibilities for the piano and appealed to amateurs and connoisseurs alike. The genres he cultivated range from the étude, associated with teaching, and types suitable for amateurs, such as dances and nocturnes, to longer, more challenging works, including ballades, scherzos, and sonatas, for his own performances and for other advanced players.

Chopin wrote twenty-seven études in all—twelve each in Opp. 10 (1829–32) and 25 (1832–37) and three without opus number. Because études are intended to develop technique, each one as a rule addresses a specific skill and develops a single figure. Among the problems addressed in Op. 25 are parallel diatonic and chromatic thirds (No. 6) and parallel sixths (No. 8) in the right hand, chromatic octaves in both hands (No. 10), and sixteenth-note filigree in the right hand above a vigorous march in the left (No. 11). Chopin's études were the first with significant artistic content and as such were often played in concert, inaugurating the genre of the **concert étude.**

Études

Chopin's twenty-four preludes of Op. 28 (1836–39), like the preludes in Bach's *Well-Tempered Clavier,* cover all the major and minor keys. They are brief mood pictures, less challenging than his études but like them in posing specific performance problems. They also illustrate the astounding inventiveness of his figuration. As shown in Example 24.7, No. 1 wraps arpeggiated chords around a tenor-range melody echoed an octave above; No. 2 alternates wide two-note intervals in the left hand; No. 3 has a sweeping sixteenth-note pattern; and No. 4 features pulsating chords that sink chromatically through nonfunctional sonorities on their way to more stable chords. Such rich chromatic harmonies influenced many later composers, as did the varied textures of Chopin's piano writing.

Preludes

Chopin's **waltzes, mazurkas**, and **polonaises** were often composed for his students and dedicated to them when published. All are extremely idiomatic for piano in their figuration and fingerings. The waltzes and mazurkas, although only moderately difficult, show off an amateur's ability through brilliant passage work and expression of a mood. Part of Chopin's genius was finding ways to write music that even players of limited skill could perform with satisfaction and feelings of accomplishment.

Waltzes, mazurkas, and polonaises

His waltzes evoke the ballrooms of Vienna, but his mazurkas and polonaises are suffused with the spirit of Poland. Polonaises are dances in $\frac{3}{4}$ meter often marked by a rhythmic figure of an eighth and two sixteenths on the first beat. Chopin's go beyond the stylized polonaise of Bach's time to assert a vigorous, at times militaristic, national identity.

Example 24.7: Chopin, Preludes, Op. 28

a. No. 1 in C Major

b. No. 2 in A Minor   *c. No. 3 in G Major*

d. No. 4 in E Minor

CD 8|86
The mazurka was a Polish folk dance that by Chopin's time had become an urban ballroom dance popular among high society in Paris as well as in Poland. The Mazurka in B♭ Major, Op. 7, No. 1 (1831, NAWM 117), shown in Example 24.8, illustrates the genre: $\frac{3}{4}$ meter with frequent accents on the second or third beat and often a dotted figure on the first beat; simple accompaniment; and four-measure phrases combined in periods that alternate, here in ‖:A:‖:BA:‖:CA:‖ form. The melody, which is instrumental rather than vocal in style, displays elements meant to suggest the exoticism of Polish folk music, including trills, grace notes, large leaps, and slurs beginning on the last sixteenth of a beat to imitate folk bowing. When played properly, the tempo is uneven, passing quickly through the opening ascent and then allowing extra time for the sforzando, trills, and grace notes in order to suggest the longer time required for dancers to execute a turn or a lift than to take quick steps. In the third section, shown in Example 24.8b, Chopin creates an exotic sound with drone fifths, unusual harmonies, and augmented seconds while keeping the damper pedal on to add an unusual blur. The marking **rubato** indicates a slight anticipation or delay of the right-hand melody while the accompaniment continues in strict time, or a departure from the regular pulse

in both hands at once. Like the damper pedal, rubato can be used in places where it is not marked, and nineteenth-century performers used both techniques freely as expressive devices.

Example 24.8: Chopin, Mazurka in B♭ Major, Op. 7, No. 1

a. Opening

b. Third section

The **nocturnes** are short mood pieces with beautiful, embellished melodies above sonorous accompaniments. Chopin's initial conception of the nocturne owed much to the nocturnes by Irish pianist-composer John Field (1782–1837). Both composers also drew inspiration from the vocal nocturne for two or more voices with piano or harp accompaniment, so that the nocturne for piano was essentially a song without words. The Nocturne in D♭ Major, Op. 27, No. 2 (1835, NAWM 118), has a notably expansive accompaniment and an angular melody. It also includes virtuoso elements, such as parallel thirds and sixths (a texture characteristic of the vocal nocturne); wide leaps; and triplets, quintuplets, septuplets, and cadenza-like passage work in the right hand against steady sixteenths in the left.

Nocturnes

CD 8|89   CD 4|85

Chopin's ballades and scherzos are longer and more demanding than his other one-movement piano works. Chopin was one of the first (along with Clara Schumann) to use the name **ballade** for an instrumental piece. His ballades capture the charm and fire of Polish narrative ballads, combining these qualities with constantly fresh turns in harmony and form. His scherzos are not joking or playful, as the title of the form implies, but serious and passionate. Yet they are tricky and quirky, which the term also implies, particularly in their rhythm and thematic material.

Ballades and scherzos

Sonatas   Chopin's three piano sonatas all have four movements: sonata form, minuet or scherzo, slow movement, and finale. Sonata No. 2 in B♭ Minor, Op. 35, includes the funeral march that has become Chopin's most famous piece; orchestrated, it was played at Chopin's funeral and has been heard at thousands since.

FRYDERYK CHOPIN (1810–1849)

Chopin was the Romantic composer most closely identified with the piano. His solo piano music won him enormous popularity and has been central to the repertoire ever since.

He was born near Warsaw to a French father and a Polish mother. His talent as pianist, improviser, and composer showed early, and at age seven he published his first piece and played his first public concert, as a concerto soloist. After studies at the Warsaw Conservatory, he performed in Vienna and toured Germany and Italy. His pieces with a strong Polish character were especially successful, encouraging him to write more. The national flavor of his music and its brilliant virtuosity won him a strong following in Poland. Seeking an international reputation, he returned to Vienna and to Germany. When he heard of the failed Polish revolt against Russian domination, he continued on to Paris, where he settled in 1831, never to see Poland again.

Chopin soon met the leading musicians in Paris, including Rossini, Meyerbeer, Berlioz, and Liszt, and entered the highest social circles. He became the most fashionable piano teacher for wealthy students. Their fees meant he could give up public performance and play only at private concerts and at salons hosted by the leading women of the city; in turn, the rarity of his appearances increased his cachet and allowed him to charge very high fees for lessons. He also earned considerable sums

Figure 24.11: Portrait of Fryderyk Chopin by Eugène Delacroix (1838).

from publications. He never married, but had a tempestuous nine-year affair with the novelist Aurore Dudevant, known by her pseudonym George Sand. The 1848 revolutions in Paris disrupted his teaching and forced a grueling tour of England and Scotland. By then, he was ravaged by tuberculosis and died in 1849.

MAJOR WORKS: *2 piano concertos, 3 piano sonatas, 4 ballades, 4 scherzos, 20 nocturnes, 27 études, 27 preludes, 57 mazurkas, 17 waltzes, 15 polonaises, 4 chamber works with piano, 20 songs*

The distinctive characteristics of Chopin's music stem from his life and career: Polish nationalism, the concentration on piano music, virtuosity from public performance blended with elegant lyricism for the parlor, and originality in melody, harmony, and pianism encouraged equally by the ideology of the salon and by competition in the marketplace. His works were shaped by the demand for amateur compositions yet spoke to connoisseurs as well, giving his music broad and enduring appeal. His pieces are as ingratiating to play as they are to hear. His greatest achievement was to liberate the piano from imitations of choral or ensemble textures and make it sound the way only a piano could sound, producing a whole new repertory of idiomatic sounds and figurations.

Chopin's achievement

FRANZ LISZT

Franz Liszt (1811–1886) was the most astounding piano virtuoso of his era and one of its most important composers (see biography and Figure 24.12). Already a child prodigy in Hungary and Vienna, Liszt came with his family to Paris in 1823 at age twelve. There piano manufacturer Sébastien Erard gave him a seven-octave grand piano with the new double-escapement action that allowed quick repetition, opening possibilities for virtuosity that Liszt was among the first to exploit.

As a young man, Liszt frequented the salons that formed the core of Parisian intellectual and artistic life. There he met many of the most notable writers, painters, and musicians of the day. He and Countess Marie d'Agoult became lovers and lived together in Switzerland and Italy from 1835 to 1839. He recorded impressions of both countries in piano pieces collected in *Album d'un voyageur* (Album of a Traveler, 1837–38) and *Années de pèlerinage* (Years of Pilgrimage, Books 1 and 2 composed 1838–61, Book 3, 1877–82). In many of these pieces Liszt responded to a poem (three on sonnets of Petrarch, one on Dante) or work of art (a Raphael painting, a Michelangelo sculpture).

Between 1839 and 1847 Liszt gave over one thousand solo concerts, touring Europe from Portugal and Ireland in the west to Turkey, Romania, and Russia in the east. He was the first pianist to give solo concerts in large halls, for which he pioneered the term ***recital***, still used today. He was also the first to play a range of music from Bach to his contemporaries and to play entirely from memory, two innovations that are now long-standing traditions. His reception at times rivaled the hysteria afforded rock superstars of the twentieth century, but he insisted on quiet while he played. In 1848, Liszt ceased touring and concentrated on composition. His music after 1848 is described in chapter 28.

Solo recitals

Liszt's music reflects many diverse influences. His Hungarian roots show in works based on or inspired by Hungarian or Romany (Gypsy) melodies, including nineteen *Hungarian Rhapsodies* for piano. His piano style drew on Viennese and Parisian virtuosos and added his own stunning effects. After Chopin moved to Paris in 1831, Liszt adopted Chopin's melodic lyricism, rubato, rhythmic license, and harmonic innovations.

Influences

FRANZ LISZT (1811–1886)

Liszt had an enormous impact on music, in a variety of roles. As the foremost piano virtuoso of his time, Liszt devised new playing techniques and textures for piano music. As a composer, he introduced innovations in form and harmony and invented the symphonic poem. As a conductor, he championed Bach, Beethoven, and other composers from the past, alongside Berlioz, Wagner, and other contemporaries. As a teacher, he invented the masterclass, in which students play for each other as well as for the teacher, and other approaches that remain standard practice today.

Figure 24.12: Liszt piano recital in Berlin, as depicted in an 1842 book on the city. The adulation of the audience is supported by many contemporary accounts, but two aspects of the picture are misleading: Liszt normally played from memory, and he insisted the audience be quiet while he performed.

Liszt was born in a German-speaking region of western Hungary, now in Austria. His father, an official for Prince Nikolaus Esterházy and an amateur musician, taught him piano from the age of six, then moved the family to Vienna so the boy could study piano further with Carl Czerny and theory and counterpoint with Antonio Salieri. At the age of eleven Liszt played several public concerts, inaugurating a dazzling career as a virtuoso. The next year the family moved to Paris, where Liszt studied theory and composition with private teachers.

After his father's death in 1827, Liszt earned a regular income teaching piano to children of the well-to-do. For the next two decades he pursued a brilliant career as a concert virtuoso. He left the concert stage in 1848 and devoted the rest of his career to composing, conducting, and teaching. From 1848 to 1861, he was court music director at Weimar, where he encouraged new music by conducting performances of many important works, among them the premiere of Wagner's *Lohengrin* in 1850. Several well-publicized love affairs with women of elevated social status—and honors showered upon him all over Europe—added glamour to his fame as pianist, conductor, and composer. From 1861 until about 1870, Liszt resided chiefly in Rome, where, his love affairs notwithstanding, he took minor orders in the Catholic Church. The remainder of his life was divided among Rome, Weimar, and Budapest.

MAJOR WORKS: Album d'un voyageur, Années de pèlerinage, *19* Hungarian Rhapsodies, Funerailles, *Sonata in B Minor, and hundreds of other piano pieces;* Mazeppa, Les préludes, *and 10 other symphonic poems;* Faust Symphony; *chamber music, choral music, and songs*

Perhaps Liszt's most important influence was not a pianist but the great Italian violinist Nicolò Paganini (1782–1840), one of the most hypnotic artists of the era, who raised both the technique and the mystique of the virtuoso to unprecedented heights. Stimulated by Paganini's fabulous technical prowess, Liszt resolved to accomplish similar miracles with the piano. He pushed the instrument's technique to its limits both in his own playing and in his compositions.

Paganini and virtuosity

Un sospiro (A Sigh, NAWM 119), the third of his Three Concert Études (1845–49), illustrates Liszt's virtuosic technique. It addresses the technical problem of how to project a slower moving melody outside or within rapid broken-chord figurations. At the beginning, shown in Example 24.9a, the pedal sustains harmonies while the two hands brave treacherous leaps over each other to pick out a pentatonic tune. The notation makes it look as though the pianist requires three hands, but the bottom stave is taken by the left hand, the middle by the right, and the top by whichever hand is free at the time, indicating left hand by a downward stem and right by an upward stem. Later on, the melody appears in the right hand in the middle of the texture, while the left arpeggiates below and above it. At the climax, in Example 24.9b, difficult leaps and stretches show the size of Liszt's hands (he could easily span a tenth) and lead to a chromatic cadenza in parallel sixths.

CD 9|1   CD 4|92

The last example also illustrates Liszt's use of chromatic harmony. Here a diminished seventh chord on the fourth beat of measure 36 moves to an augmented triad created by a suspension, then the following major triad moves chromatically to an augmented sixth chord (A–C♯–E–F𝄪). Chromatic movement from one chord to the next is a characteristic we already noticed in Chopin (see Example 24.7d), and it became a common element in the music of Liszt and later composers. The ensuing chromatic cadenza repeatedly decorates C♯, E, and G (F𝄪) with their neighbor notes B♯, D♯, F♯, and A, and at the end of the cadenza those neighbor notes sound together as a diminished seventh that resolves to the augmented sixth, showing that the entire cadenza served to prolong the latter chord. Such elaborate harmonic and melodic

Harmony

Example 24.9: Liszt, Un sospiro

a. Melody at opening

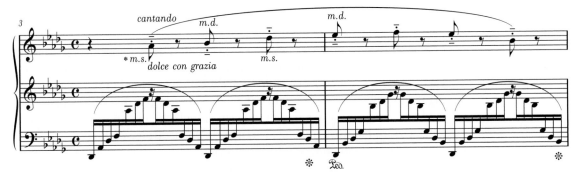

*Stems downward, left hand (*m.s.* = mano sinistra); stems upward, right hand (*m.d.* = mano destra).

b. Climax and cadenza

decoration of a dissonant sonority became a typical feature in late Romantic harmony and ultimately led Liszt to experiments that virtually abandon traditional tonality.

Character pieces and sonata

Liszt's technical innovations served both to display his skill and to allow him a vast range of expression and pictorial effects. The breadth of his poetic imagination is displayed in numerous character pieces. His only Sonata, in B minor (1853), is a masterpiece of formal innovation, using four main themes in one extended movement subdivided into three sections analogous to the movements of a Classic-era sonata. The themes are transformed and combined in a free rhapsodic order, but one that is perfectly suited to the thematic material.

Paraphrases and transcriptions

Much of Liszt's piano music consists of arrangements, of two types. His *operatic paraphrases* (some of which he called *reminiscences*) are free fantasies on excerpts from popular operas by Mozart, Bellini, Donizetti, and Verdi, often retelling the story by varying and combining the borrowed themes. His **transcriptions** of Schubert songs, Berlioz and Beethoven symphonies, Bach organ fugues, and excerpts from Wagner operas are recreations that bring important works to audiences who are either unacquainted with the originals or pleased to hear a familiar work transformed into a brilliant virtuoso vehicle.

Liszt's reputation

Liszt had a profound influence on performers and composers. As a piano virtuoso, he established most of the traditions of the modern recital, developed new playing techniques, and provided a model for others to emulate. But his contributions as a composer were equally important, opening new possibilities in harmony and form while offering deeply felt music on subjects as varied as looking at an artwork or remembering an opera. Liszt may have embodied more of the characteristics—and contradictions—of the Romantic era than any other musician.

LOUIS MOREAU GOTTSCHALK

Another pianist and composer celebrated for his audacity and showmanship was the globe-trotting American Louis Moreau Gottschalk (1829–1869), the first American composer with an international reputation. Born in New Orleans, he showed talent at a young age and studied piano and organ from the age of five. He went to Paris in 1841 for more training, and toured France, Switzerland, and Spain in 1845–52. Chopin heard him in 1845 and predicted he would become "the king of pianists." The publication of pieces based on melodies and rhythms from his mother's West Indian heritage made Gottschalk's reputation. He gave his New York debut in 1853 to wildly enthusiastic reviews, playing mostly his own compositions, and spent the rest of his life touring the United States, the Caribbean islands, and South America.

During a Caribbean tour in 1857–58, Gottschalk wrote *Souvenir de Porto Rico* (NAWM 120), which uses a theme derived from a Puerto Rican song. The piece starts soft and simple, builds to a climax full of extraordinary syncopations, and fades away, depicting a band of musicians gradually approaching, reaching a peak, and marching off into the distance. It is a perfect example of nineteenth-century piano music designed to appeal to the middle-class audience, combining an extramusical program, an exotic subject, virtuosic showmanship, and rewards for the amateur performer.

CD 9|7

THE ROMANTIC LEGACY

Home music-making, the engine that drove composers to produce a constant stream of songs and pieces, declined in the late nineteenth and early twentieth centuries, victim of new recreations for women like bicycling and of new technologies like radio and the phonograph. Young people today still practice piano, but family gatherings to make music have now all but died out, so that Lieder, parlor songs, and piano pieces rarely serve their original function. Some pieces disappeared with that change, others were established as art music, and a few became old favorites of popular music.

The Lieder of Schubert and Schumann formed the core of the art song repertoire, paralleling the Bach fugues, Handel oratorios, Haydn string quartets, and Beethoven symphonies as works that define a genre and as models for later composers. Foster's songs played a similar role for American parlor and popular song. Songs of all three composers have been sung in an unbroken tradition from their time to ours, preserving the genres they represented and opening the door for modern performers and listeners to explore music by their less well-known contemporaries.

By the 1820s, some works were already regarded as classics of piano music, including Bach's *Well-Tempered Clavier* (now played on piano) and the sonatas of Mozart and Beethoven. But Mendelssohn's *Songs without Words*, Schumann's character pieces, Chopin's études, preludes, dances, and ballades, and Liszt's études and character pieces redefined piano music and became central to the repertoire of permanent classics for the piano. The sonata and fugue became prestige genres in which composers could demonstrate their mastery of a historically important form, and the sonatas of Schubert, Chopin, Schumann, and Liszt have claimed a prominent place in the repertoire. At the same time, most of the piano music written for the home market or for virtuoso display fell out of fashion as performers, critics, and historians focused on composers and works they considered to be the greatest and dismissed pieces they judged merely entertaining.

Music by women was treated differently in a century that expected musical genius only from men and treated music as no more than a pleasing adornment for women. As these attitudes were challenged in the last decades of the twentieth century, scholars sought to unearth music by women, especially music that met the highest standards. Clara Schumann and Fanny Mendelssohn Hensel have emerged as key figures: their compositions and descriptions of their playing make clear they would have been great musicians even if Robert and Felix had never been born, and their stories function almost as parables about how social attitudes nurture and hinder talent. Current research is bringing to light music by many other talented women composers of the nineteenth century.

The melody-centered style of song and piano music affected every other genre of the nineteenth century. Never before or since were symphonies, chamber works, and choral music so full of songlike melodies. Opera composers used them too, as witnessed by, for example, Senta's ballad in Wagner's *Der fliegende Holländer* (The Flying Dutchman).

The Romantic view of music has been even more influential. We no longer view composers as artisans writing music to suit their patrons, as most earlier composers saw themselves, but as artists expressing their own ideas and feelings. Originality, fostered by competition in the marketplace and inscribed by Romantic views of individual genius, became a requirement for all later composers, encouraging an ever more rapid pace of change in musical style for the next two centuries, in popular and art music alike. Indeed, most of our attitudes about music, especially those we barely question, are those of the Romantic era.

Chapter

25

Romanticism in Classic Forms: Orchestral, Chamber, and Choral Music

 Alongside the fashion for home music-making explored in the previous chapter, the nineteenth century saw phenomenal growth in public concerts. Amateur orchestras and choral societies carried amateur performance into the public sphere, and new professional orchestras, touring virtuosos, concert societies, and entrepreneurs helped to create a vibrant concert life based on ticket sales to all classes of society. Chamber music, once primarily intended for the enjoyment of the players themselves, was now often performed as concert music.

These changes were accompanied by the gradual emergence of musical classics, pieces that continued to be performed regularly long after the composer's death. From the 1780s through the 1870s, classical repertoires formed first in choral music, starting with the oratorios of Handel and Haydn, and then in orchestral and chamber music, beginning with symphonies and string quartets of Beethoven, Haydn, and Mozart. Instead of falling out of fashion after a generation, as music had always done, some pieces attained a permanent place in musical life, akin to the classics of literature or art. Living composers in these genres could aspire to similar permanence for their own music.

In part because older music for orchestra, chamber ensemble, and chorus was still being performed, nineteenth-century composers mixed retrospective genres and forms with the new musical style. They still held onto their Romantic ideals—expressing feelings sincerely and projecting a distinctive personality—but their historical awareness was more acute than it was in piano music and songs. Composers sought to balance

631

tradition and individuality, some leaning toward innovation, others toward emulating the past. The result is a rich tension in much of this music between Romantic content and Classic genres and forms.

ORCHESTRAL MUSIC

THE NINETEENTH-CENTURY ORCHESTRA

Central to public concert life was the orchestra. The number of orchestras multiplied many times over, and concert societies played an increasingly significant role. Some orchestras, such as the Society of the Friends of Music in Vienna, were made up primarily of amateurs, while others were organized and staffed by professional musicians, including the London Philharmonic (founded 1813), New York Philharmonic (1842), and Vienna Philharmonic (also 1842). Playing in an orchestra became a profession, as it remains today. By the end of the century, most major cities in Europe and the Americas had professional orchestras that provided regular concert series, though not necessarily full-time work for the musicians.

In addition to concert orchestras (the main subject of this section), there were orchestras in opera houses, theaters, cafés, and dance halls, like the famous Viennese dance orchestras led by Joseph Lanner (1801–1843) and Johann Strauss the elder (1804–1849).

Size and composition Orchestras grew from about forty players at the beginning of the century to as many as ninety at its close. Flutes, oboes, clarinets, and bassoons acquired elaborate systems of keys by midcentury (see chapter 24), making the instruments easier to finger quickly and play in tune in most keys. Wind instruments with extended ranges, notably piccolo, English horn, bass clarinet, and contrabassoon, were occasionally used in orchestras. Valves were added to horns and trumpets, allowing players to reach all chromatic notes throughout the instruments' ranges, and the tuba joined the brass section in the 1830s.

The greater variety of instruments provided a much wider range of colors and color combinations. Composers could now treat the winds and brass more as equals to the strings, often contrasting one section with another. In some works, bass drum, triangle, and other percussion instruments joined the timpani. The new, fully chromatic pedal harp was sometimes added, often played by a woman because of the harp's long association with domestic music-making. Otherwise, orchestral players were usually all men, and with rare exceptions—including a handful of all-women orchestras—that situation did not begin to change until the mid-twentieth century, after women had won some equal rights and become more integrated generally in the work forces of Europe and the Americas.

CONDUCTORS

Eighteenth-century orchestras were led from the harpsichord or by the leader of the violins, but in the nineteenth century, this role was taken over by

Figure 25.1: Concert at Covent Garden Theatre in London, showing Louis Jullien conducting his orchestra (in front) and four military bands.

a **conductor** who used a baton to beat time and cue entrances. Although at first the conductor simply kept the orchestra together, by the 1840s conductors were drawing attention to themselves as interpreters of the music, exploiting the Romantic cult of the individual. Conductors like Louis Jullien (1812–1860), shown in Figure 25.1, formed their own orchestras and became stars on the same order as the instrumental virtuosos.

AUDIENCES AND CONCERTS

Court orchestras in the eighteenth century had played to mixed audiences of nobility and city people. The new orchestras drew a primarily middle-class audience, often the very same people whose enthusiasm for home music-making sustained the market for songs and piano music. Many orchestral pieces were available in piano transcriptions for home performance, which is often how people got to know them; the experience of hearing an orchestra was still a relatively rare event. Yet orchestral music carried a special prestige, in part because of the lasting impression of Beethoven's symphonies. The prominence given to orchestral music in this book and in most histories of music is out of proportion to the place it occupied in the activities of musicians and the public during the nineteenth century, but the emphasis is justified by the importance accorded to it by audiences, critics, and the composers themselves. *Audience*

Nineteenth-century concert programs offered a diversity of works. For example, the London Philharmonic before 1850 typically featured a symphony, *Concert programming* an aria or choral composition, a concerto or chamber work, another vocal piece, and a closing symphony or overture. Jullien's Promenade Concerts in London, less formal and aimed at a larger audience, included quadrilles and other dances (often performed jointly with military bands), choral music, and a symphony. The variety of performing forces and the alternation of instrumental and vocal music continued a tradition that went back to the first public concerts (see chapters 16 and 20). The concert of music for a single medium, inaugurated by Liszt's solo piano recitals in 1839, did not become the rule until quite late in the century.

THE RISE OF THE CLASSICAL REPERTOIRE

One of the most remarkable developments in the entire history of music is the emergence in the nineteenth century of a repertoire of musical classics by composers of the past. This process happened at different times for different genres, but it is evident in the programs of the major European orchestras. In concerts of the Leipzig Gewandhaus Orchestra, for example, about 85 percent of the pieces performed in the 1780s were by living composers; by 1820, the percentage had dropped to about 75 percent. Over the next fifty years, the situation reversed completely, so that by 1870, fully three-quarters of the reper-

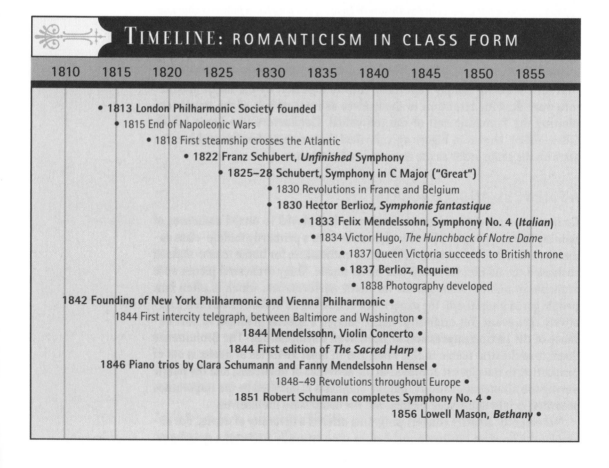

TIMELINE: ROMANTICISM IN CLASS FORM

1810	1815	1820	1825	1830	1835	1840	1845	1850	1855

- 1813 London Philharmonic Society founded
- 1815 End of Napoleonic Wars
- 1818 First steamship crosses the Atlantic
- 1822 Franz Schubert, *Unfinished* Symphony
- 1825–28 Schubert, Symphony in C Major ("Great")
- 1830 Revolutions in France and Belgium
- 1830 Hector Berlioz, *Symphonie fantastique*
- 1833 Felix Mendelssohn, Symphony No. 4 (*Italian*)
- 1834 Victor Hugo, *The Hunchback of Notre Dame*
- 1837 Queen Victoria succeeds to British throne
- 1837 Berlioz, Requiem
- 1838 Photography developed
- 1842 Founding of New York Philharmonic and Vienna Philharmonic •
- 1844 First intercity telegraph, between Baltimore and Washington •
- 1844 Mendelssohn, Violin Concerto •
- 1844 First edition of *The Sacred Harp* •
- 1846 Piano trios by Clara Schumann and Fanny Mendelssohn Hensel •
- 1848–49 Revolutions throughout Europe •
- 1851 Robert Schumann completes Symphony No. 4 •
- 1856 Lowell Mason, *Bethany* •

toire was by composers of past generations, chiefly Beethoven, Mozart, Haydn, and the early Romantics.

Several factors lay behind this change. Haydn and Beethoven achieved such popularity during their lifetimes that their music continued to be performed after their deaths, as did some works by other composers. Music by these earlier composers was often cheaper (and thus more profitable) to publish, more readily available, and easier for amateurs to perform than the newer music. Perhaps most important, influential musicians and critics actively promoted the music of the past as a counterweight to that of the present. Virtuoso performer-composers of the 1820s to 1840s, such as Paganini and Gottschalk, gained mass appeal through spectacular showmanship and heightened expressivity, often at the expense of the musical values esteemed by connoisseurs. By contrast, Haydn, Mozart, and Beethoven had aimed their music at all listeners, seeking to provide something of value for every taste. Serious musicians now championed their works as musical classics, masterpieces that combined compositional craft with emotional depth, and immediate appeal with lasting interest.

The movement to establish a classical repertoire was aided by conductors like Jullien, who saw that they could star as interpreters of the classics, and by younger virtuosos such as violinist Joseph Joachim (1831–1907) and pianist Anton Rubinstein (1829–1894), who helped to popularize the concertos of Beethoven, Mozart, and other older composers. Although most of these conductors and virtuosos also composed, the primary way to prove themselves as performers gradually shifted from performing their own music to playing the classics. This was a profound change that permanently altered the nature of performers' work and training.

The effect on performers

The rise of the permanent classical repertoire was just beginning in the 1820s, and its fullest effects were felt by composers beginning in the late nineteenth century, as we will see in later chapters. Yet even before 1850, composers of orchestral music strongly felt the presence of the old masterpieces. Most important was Beethoven, whose orchestral works were construed as artistic statements by the composer, not merely diverting entertainments, as much music had been in earlier eras. All later composers for orchestra labored in his shadow, knowing that their works would inevitably be compared to his and thus must meet a similar standard while offering something distinctive. Indeed, the history of orchestral music in the nineteenth century can be seen as a series of varied responses to Beethoven's example, as each composer explored ways to say something new and individual within the forms Beethoven had cultivated.

The effect on composers: Beethoven's legacy

THE NEW ROMANTIC STYLE: SCHUBERT

One response, pioneered by Schubert, was to maintain the outward form of the symphony while infusing it with content derived from the new Romantic style, including a greater focus on tuneful melodies, adventurous harmonic excursions, enchanting instrumental colors, strong contrasts, and heightened emotions. For Schubert and his fellow Romantics, themes were the most important element in any form, rather than the phrase and harmonic structure emphasized in eighteenth-century descriptions of form (see chapter 21). While Classic-era symphonists demonstrated their originality through the ways they treated conventional material, Schubert and his successors sought to make both their thematic material and their treatment of it as individual and memorable as possible.

Unfinished Symphony   Schubert wrote several symphonies in his teens and early twenties, but his first attempt at a large-scale symphony came in 1822 with the two movements now called the *Unfinished* Symphony, originally planned as a four-movement work in B minor. After a brief introductory subject played by the strings without accompaniment, the first movement presents a songlike melody, shown in Example 25.1a, that is quite different from the typical first themes of his predecessors and less easily fragmented into motives for symphonic development. Its soaring extension, full of anguish and longing, was also a departure. The second theme, shown in Example 25.1b, is a relaxed, graceful melody in the style of the Ländler, an Austrian country dance. These two themes share three rhythmic ideas, marked in the example, which dominate the extensions that follow each theme. Instead of centering the development section and coda on these two themes, as Haydn or Beethoven might have done, Schubert focuses on the introductory subject. In this way, Schubert was following the custom for symphonic development while devoting the main thematic areas to the presentation of memorable, lyrical melodies like those of his songs and piano works.

Example 25.1: Schubert, Unfinished *Symphony, first movement*

a. *First theme*

b. *Second theme*

The "Great" Symphony in C Major   In his Symphony No. 9 in C Major (1825–28), known as the "Great," Schubert blended his Romantic lyricism and Beethovenian drama within an expanded Classic form. The first movement opens with an unaccompanied chorale-like melody played softly in the horns, shown in Example 25.2. This melody repeats several times with varied accompaniments as in a set of variations, alternating with melodically related ideas that depart from tonic harmonies. Only in retrospect do we discover that this lyrical section is a long, slow introduction to a sonata-form Allegro, whose rhythmically charged, easily fragmented themes show the influence of Haydn and Beethoven. Typical of Schubert's approach to sonata form is

Example 25.2: Schubert, "Great" Symphony in C Major, opening of first movement

the three-key exposition, in which the second theme begins in E minor before settling into the dominant, G major. Elements of the opening chorale return during the second and closing themes, development, and coda, binding together the songlike introduction and the motivic, constantly developing Allegro.

Robert Schumann praised the C-Major Symphony's "heavenly length" (see Source Reading), appreciating the expansion of the form of all four

SOURCE READING

SCHUMANN ON SCHUBERT'S SYMPHONY IN C MAJOR

When he visited Schubert's brother Ferdinand in 1839, Robert Schumann discovered the manuscript of Schubert's 'Great" Symphony in C Major, which had never been performed in public. Through Schumann's intercession it was performed that same year at the Gewandhaus Concerts in Leipzig under the direction of Mendelssohn. In a review of the piece the following year, Schumann praised it as revealing both an unknown aspect of Schubert and a new approach to the symphony.

———— • ————

I must say at once that anyone who is not yet acquainted with this symphony knows very little about Schubert. When we consider all that he has given to art, this praise may strike many as exaggerated, partly, no doubt, because composers have so often been advised, to their chagrin, that it is better for them—after Beethoven—"to abstain from the symphonic form." . . .

On hearing Schubert's symphony and its bright, flowery, romantic life, the city [Vienna] crystallizes before me, and I realize how such works could be born in these very surroundings. . . . Everyone must acknowledge that the outer world—sparkling today, gloomy tomorrow— often deeply stirs the feeling of the poet or the

musician; and all must recognize, while listening to this symphony, that it reveals to us something more than mere beautiful song, mere joy and sorrow, such as music has ever expressed in a hundred ways, leading us into regions that, to our best recollection, we had never before explored. To understand this, one must hear this symphony. Here we find, besides the most masterly technicalities of musical composition, life in every vein, coloring down to the finest gradation, meaning everywhere, sharp expression in detail, and in the whole, a suffusing romanticism that other works by Franz Schubert have already made known to us.

And then the heavenly length of the symphony, like that of a thick novel in four volumes (perhaps by Jean Paul, who was also never able to reach a conclusion), and for the best reason—to permit readers to think it out for themselves. How this refreshes, this feeling of abundance, so contrary to our experience with others when we always dread to be disillusioned at the end and are often saddened through disappointment.

From *Neue Zeitschrift für Musik* 12 (1840): 82–83, after the translation by Paul Rosenfeld in Robert Schumann, *On Music and Musicians*, ed. Konrad Wolff (New York: Norton, 1946), 108–11.

HECTOR BERLIOZ (1803–1869)

Hector Berlioz, who created more than a dozen works that have gained the status of musical classics and who wrote the nineteenth-century "bible" on orchestration, played flute and guitar but never learned how to play piano. Born in southeastern France, he developed a fascination for music, taught himself harmony from textbooks, and began composing in his teens. His father sent him to medical school in Paris, but Berlioz frequented the opera, studied composition at the Conservatoire, and eventually abandoned medicine for a career as a composer.

After several attempts, Berlioz won the Prix de Rome in 1830, a composition prize that paid a stipend for him to live and work in Rome. By then he had become enchanted with Beethoven's symphonies, Shake-

speare's plays, and the Irish actress Harriet Smithson, whom he saw play Ophelia in *Hamlet*. His obsession for her inspired his *Symphonie fantastique* and his attempt to express his feelings in the context of a Beethovenian symphony. Its premiere in 1830 established Berlioz as a leader of the radical wing of composers in France.

Smithson spurned Berlioz for good reason: they had never met, and all she knew of him were mad love letters he sent her. Berlioz then became engaged to a nineteen-year-old piano teacher, Camille Marie Moke, but he had hardly begun his required residence in Rome when she turned around and married piano maker Camille Pleyel. In his autobiography, Berlioz recalls his response: "I must at once proceed to Paris and kill [Camille and her husband]. After that, of course, I would have to commit suicide." He made it as far as Nice, then wisely relented and returned to Italy. Back in Paris in 1832, he courted Smithson again and they married the following year. The ideal Ophelia, however, turned out to be an alcoholic, and their marriage fell apart after a few years and the birth of a son.

Although Berlioz won a few fervent advocates for his compositions, his music was too radical to win steady support from the musical institutions in Paris. He turned to music criticism as his chief profession, as Schumann did around the same time. He got his music played by putting on concerts himself, working as his own impresario, and produced a flood of important compositions.

Berlioz was one of the most literary of composers; many of his compositions were inspired by his reading of Virgil (his opera

Figure 25.2: Hector Berlioz, in a portrait by Emile Signol painted in 1832 during Berlioz's sojourn in Rome.

Les Troyens, The Trojans), Shakespeare (*Romeo and Juliet*, *King Lear Overture*, and other works), Goethe (*La damnation de Faust*), Sir Walter Scott (*Rob Roy Overture*), and other writers.

In 1835 he began to conduct, and soon became one of the first to make a career of orchestral conducting, touring across Europe presenting his own works and music by other composers.

After Smithson died in 1854, he married the singer Marie Recio, with whom he had long had an affair. In his final years, Berlioz grew ill and felt bitter at the lack of recognition for his music in France. He died at sixty-five, having outlived two wives, his son, and most of his family and friends.

MAJOR WORKS: *3 operas:* Benvenuto Cellini, Les Troyens, *and* Béatrice et Bénédict; *4 symphonies, including* Symphonie fantastique, Harold en Italie *(with viola solo), and* Roméo et Juliette *(with soloists and chorus); 4 concert overtures; over 30 choral works, including* Requiem, La damnation de Faust, Te Deum, *and* L'enfance du Christ; *orchestral song cycle* Les nuits d'été *and other songs with orchestra or piano*

movements to accommodate Schubert's beautiful melodies and orchestral effects. Schubert had found an orchestral voice that could stand any comparison. Unfortunately, neither the *Unfinished* Symphony nor the "Great" C-Major Symphony was publicly performed until many years after the composer's death.

PROGRAMMATIC ROMANTICISM: BERLIOZ

An approach different from Schubert's was reconceiving the symphony as a programmatic work and allowing it to assume unconventional form to suit the program. Following Beethoven's lead in his Fifth and Sixth Symphonies, Hector Berlioz (1803–1869; see biography and Figure 25.2) shaped his symphonies around a series of emotions that tell a story.

In the *Symphonie fantastique*, which Berlioz wrote in 1830 while still a conservatory student (finale in NAWM 121), the composer dwells on the passions aroused by his thoughts and fantasies about a woman whose love he hopes to win. He based the story on his own infatuation with the English actress Harriet Smithson. Beethoven had subjected the main theme in both his Third and Fifth Symphonies to a series of exciting adventures (see chapter 23). Berlioz followed this precedent in his device of the **idée fixe** (fixed idea), a melody that he used in each movement to represent the obsessive image of the hero's beloved, transforming it to suit the mood and situation at each point in the story. This melody, shown in Example 25.3, is introduced as the main theme of the opening movement. Instead of a brief motive inviting development, as in Beethoven's symphonies, Berlioz's theme has the long line of an operatic aria that can be extended and ornamented but resists fragmentation.

Symphonie
fantastique

CD 9|16   CD 5|1

Example 25.3: Berlioz, Symphonie fantastique, *first theme of first movement*

To ensure that his listeners would understand the feelings and experiences that inspired the symphony, Berlioz subtitled it "Episode in the Life of an Artist" and provided it with an autobiographical program (see NAWM 121). The work is thus a musical drama whose words are not spoken or sung, but read silently; Berlioz wanted listeners to regard the program "in the same way as the spoken words of an opera, serving to introduce the musical numbers by describing the situation that evokes the particular mood and expressive character of each." The situations are depicted in the passionate prose of a young and sensitive artist. Literary influences in the program include Goethe's *Faust* and Thomas De Quincey's *Confessions of an English Opium Eater.* Musical influences, besides Beethoven, are from the opera theater: Gluck, Spontini, Rossini, and Meyerbeer (see chapter 26).

The first movement, "Dreams and Passions," features a slow introduction followed by an Allegro that has the outward characteristics of sonata form, including contrasting themes and a repeated exposition. But Berlioz interrupts the "development" section with a three-measure pause heralding a full statement of the main theme in the dominant, after which he continues reworking it until a triumphant tutti *fortissimo* statement appears in the tonic that is more a resplendent clarification than a recapitulation. For the second movement, Berlioz replaced the Classic minuet with a waltz, enacting a scene at a ball where the hero catches a glimpse of his beloved. The slow third movement is a pastorale with dialogues among piping shepherds, as the hero thinks of his beloved while he walks in the country. In the fourth movement, the hero dreams of his own execution in a macabre orchestral tour de force. The fifth and final movement depicts a Witches' Sabbath, presenting transformations of the idée fixe and two other themes, first singly, then in combination. One of the themes is the chant sequence *Dies irae*, part of the Mass for the Dead; this movement inaugurated a long tradition of using the *Dies irae*, especially its opening phrase, as a symbol of death, the macabre, or the diabolical.

The *Symphonie fantastique* is original not only in bending the symphony to serve narrative and autobiographical purposes but also in Berlioz's astounding ability to express the emotional content of his drama in music of great communicative power. Berlioz unified the symphony by introducing a recurring theme and by developing the dramatic idea through the five movements, extending procedures Beethoven had used in his Fifth, Sixth, and Ninth Symphonies. Equally important is the variety he created by transforming his themes and using an astonishing array of instrumental colors, which lend a distinctive character to each passage. These include muted strings to suggest dreaming, harps for the ball, English horn and an offstage oboe imitating shepherds' pipes, snare drum and cymbals for the march to the scaffold, tubular bells standing in for church bells, and violins played with the wood of the bow to create a dry, eerie sound for the witches' dance. Berlioz's vivid aural imagination and his inventive orchestral sonorities shine through in nearly every measure.

For his second symphony, *Harold en Italie* (Harold in Italy, 1834), Berlioz drew its title from Lord Byron's poem *Childe Harold* and its substance from recollections of the composer's sojourn in Italy. The piece features a solo viola, though less prominently than in a concerto—which is why Paganini, who commissioned the work as a showpiece for viola, refused to play it. A recurring theme in the viola appears in each movement and is combined contrapuntally with the other themes. The finale sums up the themes of the preceding movements, as in Beethoven's Ninth Symphony, but does not end with a triumphant chorale. Indeed, the viola remains largely passive, like Byron's antihero Harold, so that the work inverts the heroism of Beethoven's symphonies.

Harold en Italie

In his later symphonies, Berlioz departed even further from the traditional model. In *Roméo et Juliette* (1839, revised ca. 1847), which he called a "dramatic symphony," he combined orchestra, soloists, and chorus in an unstaged concert drama, building in its conception on the precedent set by Beethoven's Ninth Symphony. The *Grande symphonie funèbre et triomphale* (Grand Funeral and Triumphant Symphony, 1840) for military band with optional strings and chorus is one of the early masterpieces of band music.

Berlioz's *Symphonie fantastique* and other symphonic works made him the leader of the Romantic movement's radical wing. All subsequent composers of program music would be indebted to him. He enriched orchestral music with new resources of harmony, color, expression, and form. The idée fixe and his device of bringing back a theme in different movements gave impetus to the cyclical symphony of the later nineteenth century (see chapter 29). His orchestration initiated a new era in which instrumental color rivaled harmony and melody as an expressive tool for composers. He codified his practice in the first book on the subject, his *Treatise on Instrumentation and Orchestration* (1843).

Berlioz's achievement

CLASSICAL ROMANTICISM: MENDELSSOHN

Mendelssohn's works, compared with those of Berlioz written during the same period, have a much more Classic sound. For one thing, Mendelssohn was rigorously trained in Classic forms in his youth, writing thirteen string symphonies that gave him a mastery of form, counterpoint, and fugue and helped to determine his personal style. For another, his mature symphonies (which are numbered by date of publication rather than composition) follow Classic models, although with departures that show the strong impact of Romanticism. In line with Romantic interest in the past, he wrote his Symphony No. 5 (*Reformation*, 1830) to celebrate the Protestant Reformation and concluded it with a movement based on Luther's chorale *Ein' feste Burg*. In his Symphony No. 2, titled *Lobgesang* (Song of Praise, 1840), he adds solo voices, chorus, and organ, following the pattern of Beethoven's Ninth Symphony while blending the genres of symphony and cantata. Mendelssohn's two most frequently performed symphonies both carry geographical subtitles: the *Italian* (No. 4, 1833) and the *Scottish* (No. 3, 1842). They preserve impressions he gained of sounds and landscapes on trips to Italy and the British Isles, which he also recorded in drawings and paintings like the one in Figure 25.3.

Italian *Symphony*   The *Italian* Symphony celebrates the sunny and vibrant south, with a slow movement suggesting a procession of chanting pilgrims and a finale suggesting people dancing a spirited *saltarello*. Mendelssohn opens the first movement with a melody, shown in Example 25.4, whose sighing lurches, many

Figure 25.3: Watercolor painting by Felix Mendelssohn, titled Amalfi *in May 1831. Mendelssohn sketched, drew, and painted throughout his journeys in Italy and Britain. This is a view of the Gulf of Salerno from Amalfi, near Naples, in southern Italy.*

sequences, and repeated postponement of closure are inspired by Italian opera, though its character is instrumental rather than vocal. The second theme is similarly constructed, giving both thematic areas more the quality of well-shaped tunes than of material for future development. As a consequence, the development section dwells on a new melodic idea, a motive that gradually builds to a new theme in combination with the opening figure of the first theme. All three themes are recalled in the recapitulation, binding the movement together. In this way, Mendelssohn neatly accommodates his tuneful themes within the developmental structure of sonata form.

Example 25.4: Mendelssohn, Symphony No. 4 (Italian), *opening theme*

Mendelssohn's genius for musical landscapes is evident in his overtures *The Hebrides* (also called *Fingal's Cave*, 1832), on another Scottish topic, and *Meerestille und glückliche Fahrt* (Becalmed at Sea and Prosperous Voyage, 1828–1832). His masterpiece in the genre is the *Midsummer Night's Dream Overture*, inspired by Shakespeare's play. Written in 1826 when he was seventeen, it set the standard for all subsequent concert overtures. The picture he presents at the start of the overture of the fairies dancing is a brilliant example of perpetual motion for a full orchestra trained to tiptoe like a chamber ensemble. The Classic overture structure of sonata form without repeats is perfectly clear, but the listener's attention is drawn to Mendelssohn's imaginative use of musical figuration and orchestral color to evoke everything from fairy dust to the braying of the character Bottom after his head is magically transformed into that of a jackass. Seventeen years later, Mendelssohn wrote additional incidental music, including the famous *Wedding March*, for a production of the play.

Overtures

Mendelssohn, a virtuoso pianist, wrote four concertos for his own performances, the last two of which were published in his lifetime: No. 1 in G Minor (1831) and No. 2 in D Minor (1837). Although the showpieces composed by most virtuosos of the time revel in startling effects and technical display—more for their own sakes than for their musical inspiration—Mendelssohn

Piano concertos

emphasized the musical content, seeking to achieve the same balance of audience appeal and lasting value that connoisseurs praised in the concertos of Mozart and Beethoven. Indeed, for Mendelssohn as for Beethoven, a concerto was an expression of the composer that almost incidentally showed off the skills of the soloist.

Violin Concerto

CD 9|30   CD 5|15

The same could be said for Mendelssohn's Violin Concerto in E Minor (1844, finale in NAWM 122). The three movements are linked by thematic content and connecting passages: a transition leads from the opening Allegro molto appassionato to the lyrical Andante, and an introduction to the last movement alludes to the first movement's opening theme. In the first movement, Mendelssohn has the soloist state the main theme at the outset, skipping the usual orchestral exposition, and places the cadenza just before rather than after the recapitulation, allowing him to omit the closing ritornello. Essentially, he reworked concerto form into a variant of sonata form with a featured soloist, a reformulation that is typical of Mendelssohn and of his age in finding new ways to reinterpret yet continue tradition. The middle movement, in ABA' form, is a romance for violin and orchestra driven by a slowly unfolding melody. The sonata-rondo finale has the lightness of a scherzo. Although there are plenty of opportunities for the soloist to show off, the concerto always seems motivated by a greater expressive purpose. The violin and orchestra share equally in the finale, while, at the same time, the leading melodies move seamlessly from soloist to orchestra and back.

NEW WINE IN OLD BOTTLES: ROBERT SCHUMANN

In the eyes of many composers and listeners, the prestigious status that Beethoven had conferred on the symphony made it a rite of passage to full recognition. For example, Clara Schumann believed that composers were judged by their symphonies and operas, and she wrote in her diary, "My greatest wish is that [Robert] should compose for orchestra." When he did so, Robert Schumann applied the same lofty idealism as in his piano music and music criticism. His primary orchestral models were Schubert's "Great" C-Major Symphony and the symphonies and concertos of Mendelssohn, which showed how songlike themes could be integrated into developmental forms.

Schumann completed his First Symphony in B♭ Major in the spring of 1841 and drafted another that same year—his "symphony year," after the "Lieder year" of 1840. The music of the First, known as the *Spring* Symphony, is appropriately fresh and spontaneous, and is driven by inexhaustible rhythmic energy. The four movements of the other symphony, in D Minor (later revised as Symphony No. 4), are played without a break, joined by harmonic links and by a transitional passage leading to the finale, as in Beethoven's Fifth Symphony. Moreover, each movement contains themes derived from the slow introduction, making the entire work an integrated cycle. The result is an extended symphonic fantasia that encompasses the standard four movements of the symphony yet recalls the succession of linked fragments in Schumann's song cycle *Dichterliebe* and in piano pieces like *Fantasiestücke* (see chapter 24). Like the melodies in these works, Schumann's symphonic themes typically dwell on one rhythmic figure, as in Example 25.5, rather than embracing contrasting patterns as in most Classic-era themes. In place of the balance of opposing elements within a theme, Schumann creates variety through constantly changing presentations of the theme, providing a dynamic experience for the listener. Such an approach to the symphony exemplifies the strong interest of the Romantic generation in offering something new and distinctive in each individual work while drawing strong connections to inherited tradition.

Example 25.5: Schumann, Symphony No. 4 in D Minor, first movement, opening of first theme

THE ROMANTIC LEGACY

Schubert, Berlioz, Mendelssohn, and Schumann each found a distinctive solution to the problem of how to write symphonic music after Beethoven. But while they won a place beside Beethoven in the repertoire, they did not displace him, and orchestral composers in the second half of the century continued to struggle against his potentially overwhelming influence (see chapters 28 and 29). New genres like the symphonic poem, pioneered by Liszt, offered one path, while composers like Brahms and Bruckner engaged the symphony tradition directly. All these later composers drew on models in the Romantic generation, finding in them a rich treasure of new possibilities: Berlioz's symphonies and Mendelssohn's overtures for programmatic and descriptive music, Mendelssohn and Schumann for links and continuities between movements, Berlioz and Schumann for transformation of themes, and all of them for ways to integrate the Romantic emphasis on melody, surprising harmonies, and novel orchestral effects into the symphonic tradition.

CHAMBER MUSIC

In chamber as in orchestral music, the masterpieces of the past proved inescapable for nineteenth-century composers. Chamber music continued to serve as a form of home music-making for the enjoyment of the players. But string quartets and other chamber works were increasingly played in concerts by professional ensembles, like the one shown in Figure 25.4. Composers often treated chamber music as seriously as symphonies, especially in genres that were identified with Haydn, Mozart, and Beethoven, like the string quartet, violin sonata, and piano trio. These came to be seen as classic forms that required an engagement with the past, and composers increasingly aspired to match the individuality of Beethoven's middle and late quartets.

Figure 25.4: String quartet concert. Playing first violin is Wilma Norman-Neruda, one of the few women to make a career as a professional violinist in the nineteenth century.

Schubert　　In his teens, Schubert wrote several string quartets for his friends and family to play, modeling them on works by Mozart and Haydn. He achieved an individual and appealing style in the five-movement Quintet for piano, violin, viola, cello, and bass (1819), known as the *Trout* Quintet because the fourth movement presents variations on his song *Die Forelle* (The Trout). But his most important chamber works came only in his last five years of life: the String Quartets in A Minor (1824), D Minor (1824, nicknamed "Death and the Maiden"), and G Major (1826), and the String Quintet in C Major (1828). All attain the "heavenly length" Schumann admired in the C-Major Symphony. In mood, difficulty, style, and conception, Schubert's late chamber works are conceived more as dramatic pieces of concert music than as entertaining diversions for amateur players.

The String Quintet in C Major, which Schubert composed in the last two months of his life, is often considered his chamber music masterpiece. To the standard four instruments of the quartet, he added a second cello, whose rich sound appealed to Romantic sensibilities. Schubert obtains exquisite effects and constantly varying textures from this combination. He treats all five instruments as equals and groups them in ever-changing ways, often with one instrument pitted against two pairs. For example, the beautiful E♭-major melody of the second theme in the first movement, shown in Example 25.6, appears first in the cellos in parallel thirds, with the viola providing a pizzicato bass line and violins an offbeat accompaniment. Later the parts exchange ideas, with the melody in the violins, and in the recapitulation, the melody appears in the first cello and viola. Throughout, the ideas are set forth and developed in a truly symphonic way. There are strong contrasts of mood and of style within and between movements, from the profound slow movement to the playful finale, and from learned counterpoint to rustic vernacular styles.

Example 25.6: Schubert, String Quintet in C Major, first movement, opening of second theme

Mendelssohn wrote a large amount of chamber music, and in it we can trace his evolution from a talented boy, to a maturing composer testing his skill against Beethoven, to mastery on his own terms. He wrote numerous chamber works in his youth, using Haydn, Mozart, and Bach as his principal models. His first published compositions, written in 1822–25, were three piano quartets and a violin sonata, and his earliest recognized masterpiece was his Octet for strings, Op. 20 (1825). After the appearance of Beethoven's late quartets, Mendelssohn absorbed their influence in his String Quartets in A Minor, Op. 13 (1827), and E♭ Major, Op. 12 (1829). Following Beethoven's lead, Mendelssohn integrated the movements through thematic connections, while giving each movement a distinctive, highly contrasting character. His most characteristic works are the Piano Trios in D Minor, Op. 49, and in C Minor, Op. 66. Both are full of tuneful, attractive themes and idiomatic writing, and both feature slow movements in the manner of his *Songs without Words* and scherzos in his typical pixyish style. In pieces like these, the Classic genre and forms serve as vessels for the Romantic material, emphasizing expressive melody over the motivic economy and taut development typical of Beethoven.

Mendelssohn

Robert Schumann followed his "Lieder year" and "symphony year" with a "chamber music year" in 1842–43. After studying the quartets of Haydn and Mozart, he composed three string quartets, published together as Op. 41, followed by a piano quintet and a piano quartet. In his critical writings, he had argued that string quartets should resemble a four-way conversation, and his own quartets meet this ideal, with fluid interchange among the parts. He also insisted that quartet composers should build on the tradition of Haydn, Mozart, and Beethoven without simply imitating them, and indeed Schumann's quartets reflect the influence of these three composers more strongly than his works in other genres yet still project his own distinctive style.

Robert Schumann

Influenced by his study of Bach, Schumann introduced a new, more poly-phonic approach to chamber music in 1847 with his Piano Trios No. 1 in D Minor, Op. 63, and No. 2 in F Major, Op. 80. The two contrast markedly in mood, the first somber, the second warm and cheerful, but both balance intellectual rigor in form and counterpoint with expressive depth and origi-nality in the themes and their development. This combination of elements made them his most influential chamber works, especially on Brahms and other German composers.

BEYOND WOMEN'S DOMAINS

Women were discouraged from composing large public concert works like symphonies, which were considered the proper domain only of men. Pieces with piano were accepted as extensions of private music-making, yet rela-tively few women composed for chamber ensemble.

Fanny Mendelssohn Hensel

Fanny Mendelssohn Hensel wrote several chamber works, but only her Piano Trio, Op. 11, was published during the nineteenth century (in 1850, four years after she composed it and three years after her death). It demon-strates an assured mastery of the genre, full of idiomatic writing for all three instruments, expressive themes, and convincing development of the ideas. A long, dramatic sonata-form movement with virtuosic passage work for the piano is followed by an Andante espressivo and a song without words. The fi-nale begins, most unusually, with a recitative and nocturne-like passage for unaccompanied piano before the other instruments join in an impassioned sonata form. In all movements, the instruments frequently trade roles, with one taking the melody while the others accompany, thus fulfilling the ideal of chamber music as conversation among peers.

Clara Schumann

Clara Schumann composed what she regarded as her best work, the Piano Trio in G Minor, in 1846, the same year Hensel wrote her trio, and the work may have inspired her husband's trios of the following year. The first and last movements, in sonata form, combine traits from Baroque, Classic, and Romantic models: memorable songlike themes, rich poly-phonic treatment, development through motivic fragmentation and imita-tion, fugue (in the finale's development), and rousing codas. Schumann specified minuet tempo for the second movement but labeled it Scherzo to highlight its subtle rhythmic tricks, such as Scotch snaps and syncopa-tions. The slow third movement (NAWM 123) is outwardly simple in form, a modified ABA with a nocturne-like, somewhat melancholy first section and a more animated B section. But the effect is enriched by constantly changing textures. As we see in Example 25.7, the opening melody appears three times, each time in a different instrument and with ever more com-plex accompanying figuration.

CD 9|41   CD 5|26

CHAMBER MUSIC AND THE CLASSICAL TRADITION

By midcentury, chamber music was regarded as a conservative medium strongly linked to classical models, cultivated by those who saw themselves as

Example 25.7: Clara Schumann, Piano Trio, Op. 17, third movement

a. Opening melody in piano

b. Restatement in violin

c. Reprise in cello

continuing the classical tradition but shunned by more radical composers such as Berlioz and Liszt. Yet in creating new twists on Classic forms and expressing Romantic passions in genres long associated with private music-making and intimate listening, chamber music composers of the early nineteenth century offered something new and distinctive.

CHORAL MUSIC

While the nineteenth-century orchestra was becoming a professional institution, the choir was heading in the opposite direction. Church choirs were increasingly made up of amateurs, and most choruses outside of church were organized primarily for the enjoyment of the singers themselves. In part because of their amateur status, choruses were less prestigious than orchestras and opera houses, and much of the music written for them has been neglected. The choral repertoire was one of the first to be dominated by music of the past, and as a result nineteenth-century choral music is often retrospective in genre and format, though not necessarily in style.

There were three main types of choral music in the nineteenth century:

- oratorios and similar works for large chorus and orchestra, often with one or more solo vocalists, on dramatic, narrative, or sacred texts but intended for concert rather than stage performance;
- short choral works on secular texts, usually homophonic with the melody in the upper voice, with or without accompaniment by a piano or organ;
- liturgical works, anthems, hymns, and other sacred pieces written for church choirs, congregations, or home performance.

Choral music was a particularly lucrative field for publishers, since each choir member needed a separate copy of the music for every piece, and most works were also suitable for home music-making. Publishers recognized the potential of the market and issued great quantities of music for amateur and church choirs at low prices.

AMATEUR CHOIRS

Amateur choruses were typically organized as **choral societies**, with members paying dues to purchase music, pay the conductor, and meet other expenses. One of the first choral societies, the Berlin Singakademie, began as a singing class for wealthy women. In 1791 men were accepted as well, and the group gave its first concert. By 1800, under the direction of Carl Friedrich Zelter (Felix and Fanny Mendelssohn's teacher), the chorus had quintupled in size to almost 150 members. Zelter added an orchestra to allow the group to sing oratorios, and by his death in 1832 the chorus had over 350 singers.

Similar organizations sprang up in Leipzig, Dresden, Zurich, Liverpool, Manchester, Boston, and other cities all over Germany, Switzerland, England, and the United States. All-male choruses, often composed of working-class men, were especially popular in France, Germany, and American cities with large German populations. Choral singing was seen as a way to occupy leisure time, develop a sense of unity, elevate musical tastes, and encourage spiritual and ethical values (see Source Reading, p. 652). In addition, choral societies were often self-governing with elected managing boards, providing practice in democratic processes—one reason they were forbidden in autocratic Austria until later in the century.

Figure 25.5: Handel Festival at the Crystal Palace in London in 1857, with an orchestra of over three hundred and a chorus of almost two thousand, as shown in The Illustrated London News.

Large amateur choruses also played a central role at music festivals, where singers from across a region gathered to perform. The first such festivals centered on Handel's works, beginning in England in 1759, the year of his death. Festivals were held in France during the Revolutionary era, and in the nineteenth century the tradition spread across Germany, Austria, and North America. Festival choruses made up of hundreds of singers were even larger than local choral societies. Figure 25.5 shows the Handel Festival in London's Crystal Palace in 1857, with an immense choir and orchestra in a huge performing space. Not to be outdone, bandleader Patrick S. Gilmore organized the World Peace Jubilee (1872) in Boston with an orchestra numbering two thousand and a chorus of twenty thousand.

Festivals

ORATORIOS AND OTHER LARGE WORKS

The Handel and Haydn oratorios formed the core of the repertoire for the large choruses, a pairing immortalized in the name of the Handel and Haydn Society, founded in Boston in 1815 and the oldest music organization in the United States that is still active today. Another composer was added in 1829, when the twenty-year-old Mendelssohn conducted the Berlin Singakademie in the first performance of J. S. Bach's *St. Matthew Passion* since the composer's death in 1750. Bach's *St. John Passion* and Mass in B Minor followed in 1833 and 1834. These performances began the revival of Bach's vocal music, although they converted pieces Bach wrote for performance in church by eight to twelve singers and an orchestra of about fifteen into concert works for large chorus and orchestra.

While performing music of the past, the choral societies and festivals also encouraged the composition of new works in the same mold. The most successful new oratorios were Mendelssohn's *St. Paul* (1836) and *Elijah* (1846),

Mendelssohn's oratorios

which themselves became standards of the choral repertoire. Both were composed for choral festivals, treated biblical subjects, and received great acclaim in Europe and North America. In *Elijah*, Mendelssohn used chorales to mark structural divisions and offer commentary, as Bach had done in his passions; employed a wide variety of styles and textures for choral movements, as Handel had done in his oratorios; and used unifying motives and links between movements to integrate the work into a cohesive whole, following the practice of his own time. In these ways, Mendelssohn rooted his oratorios in Baroque tradition while creating something new and up-to-date.

The final chorus of *Elijah* (NAWM 124) is Handelian in spirit, with a powerful homorhythmic opening, vigorous fugue, culminating statement of the fugue theme in chordal harmony, and contrapuntal Amen, while contrasts of minor and major and touches of chromaticism draw on more recent styles. The fugue lends an appropriate solemnity to the close of the oratorio through the use of an old, familiar form.

Berlioz's Requiem and Te Deum   The availability of large forces encouraged a grandiosity that reached a pinnacle in two choral works by Berlioz, the Requiem (*Grande Messe des Morts*, 1837) and the *Te Deum* (1855). They belong not to an ecclesiastical but

---

SOURCE READING

THE VALUE OF AMATEUR CHOIRS

The choral society movement was encouraged not only by a love of music but by the belief that the right kind of music promoted ethical values, a view that goes back to Plato. Richard Wagner commented that for the English "an evening spent listening to an oratorio may be regarded as a sort of service and is almost as good as going to church." George Hogarth, Secretary of the London Philharmonic Society, praised choral singing as an instrument of moral reform.

———— • ————

The cultivation of a taste for music furnishes to the rich a refined and intellectual pursuit, which excludes the indulgence of frivolous and vicious amusements, and to the poor, a *laborem dulce lenimen*, a relaxation from toil, more attractive than the haunts of intemperance.... In the densely populated districts of Yorkshire, Lancashire, and Derbyshire, music is cultivated among the working classes to an extent unparalleled in any other part of the kingdom. Every town has its choral society, supported by the amateurs of the place and its neighbourhood, where the works of Handel, and the more modern masters, are performed with precision and effect, by a vocal and instrumental orchestra consisting of mechanics and workpeople.... Their employers promote and encourage so salutary a recreation by countenancing, and contributing to defray the expenses, of their musical associations; and some provide regular musical instruction for such of their workpeople as show a disposition for it.... Wherever the working classes are taught to prefer the pleasures of the intellect, and even of taste, to the gratification of sense, a great and favorable change takes place in their character and manners.... Sentiments are awakened in them which makes them love their families and homes; their wages are not squandered in intemperance, and they become happier as well as better.

George Hogarth, *Musical History, Biography and Criticism* (London, 1835), 430–31, as quoted by Henry Raynor, *Music and Society Since 1815* (New York: Schocken Books, 1976), 98.

to a patriotic tradition inspired by the massive music festivals of the French Revolution. Both works are of huge dimensions, not only in length and number of performers but also in grandeur of conception. The Requiem requires an orchestra of 140 players, four brass choirs distributed around the performance space, four tam-tams, ten pairs of cymbals, and sixteen kettledrums, all used to achieve brilliant musical effects from representing the thunderous clamor of the Day of Judgment to the pianissimo strokes of bass drum and cymbals that punctuate the *Sanctus*.

PARTSONGS

The staple of smaller mixed, men's, and women's choirs was the ***partsong***, the choral parallel to the Lied or parlor song. Like solo songs, partsongs were also used in domestic music-making. Schubert, Mendelssohn, Schumann, Liszt, Hensel, and nearly every other composer in Europe produced partsongs and choruses on patriotic, sentimental, convivial, and other kinds of verse. Nature was a favorite subject. Example 25.8 shows the refrain from one of the most popular English partsongs, *All among the Barley* (1849) by Elizabeth Stirling (1819–1895), a renowned organist and composer in London. Such music is perfectly suited for amateurs performing for their own pleasure: it is simple and easy to sing, the melodies are attractive, the lower parts also have

Example 25.8: Elizabeth Stirling, refrain from All among the Barley

melodic interest, and the harmony is spiced with occasional dissonances (for instance at "not" and "on") and surprises (at the first "scythe").

Although the most popular partsongs were sung and reprinted for decades, the amateur choruses and home music-making that supported the genre declined after the nineteenth century, and no permanent repertoire of classics developed for the partsong as there did for oratorios and Lieder. This music served its immediate purpose and has been largely forgotten.

CHURCH MUSIC

Church music remained a vehicle for worship, but in some areas it also served as music for amateur singers at home and in public gatherings.

Catholic music   Instead of using amateur choirs for services, Catholic churches tended to employ clerics and choirboys; women were normally excluded from performing in church. Catholic composers continued to produce concerted liturgical music. Schubert's Masses in A♭ and E♭ are exemplary settings of the Ordinary. Elaborate works like Gioachino Rossini's *Stabat Mater* (1832, revised 1841) brought up-to-date operatic styles into church. But in the second quarter of the century, renewed interest in music of the past brought about a revival of the sixteenth-century choral style of Palestrina's masses and motets. The phrase **a cappella** had been used since the seventeenth century to denote the old contrapuntal style known as *stile antico*, but in the nineteenth century it came to mean "unaccompanied," because of the mistaken belief that it referred to the lack of any instrumental accompaniment in the papal chapel where Palestrina worked. By the mid-nineteenth century, the Catholic Church was actively promoting the composition of unaccompanied choral music in a Palestrina-inspired style. In German-speaking areas especially, the Cecilian movement, named after St. Cecilia, encouraged a cappella performances of older music and of new works in similar styles.

Protestant churches   Protestant churches also saw new developments building on music of the past. The performances of Bach's passions at the Berlin Singakademie took place during a general revival of Lutheran music. Lutheran composers produced a flood of new music for services or home devotions that often used Bach as a model, as in numerous psalm settings by Mendelssohn. Anglican musicians recovered classics from their tradition. Among new works, the anthems of Samuel Sebastian Wesley (1810–1876) were especially acclaimed. Women, encouraged by their participation in choral societies, began to sing in church choirs, and some, like Elizabeth Stirling, served as professional church organists. Yet in some corners of the church the Oxford Movement, begun in 1841, sought to restore all-male choirs of boys and men and to revive sixteenth-century unaccompanied polyphony.

Russian Orthodox music   In Russia, Dmitri Bortnyansky (1751–1825), chapel master and then director of the imperial chapel choir at St. Petersburg, was the first in a long line of composers who developed a new style of Russian church music. Inspired by the modal chants of the Orthodox liturgy, they used free rhythm and unaccompanied voices in single or double choruses with octave doublings in a rich and solemn texture.

In the United States, church music divided not only by sect but by race. *The United States*
African-American churches developed their own styles of music that would
later have enormous influence. In the 1790s, Reverend Richard Allen organized
the first congregation of the African Methodist Episcopal Church and published
a hymn book designed specifically for his all-black congregation. In the predominantly white churches, choirs sang music like their European brethren.
Congregational singing continued to be central, and here two trends diverged.

Singing masters spread the music of the Yankee tunesmiths throughout the *Shape-note singing*
South, composed new tunes and harmonizations in a similar style, and published both old and new songs in collections such as *Kentucky Harmony*
(1816), *The Southern Harmony* (1835), and *The Sacred Harp* (1844). The last,
the most popular of its kind, included some spiritual songs and others used in
Southern revival meetings. The tradition of performing this music is known
as **shape-note singing** after the notation used in these collections, in which
the shape of the noteheads indicates solmization syllables, allowing for easy
sight-reading in parts. This notational system is an inventive American
reconception of the syllables introduced by Guido of Arezzo (see chapter 2).
Figure 25.6 shows a song from *The Sacred Harp*, which uses four syllables and
shapes. The major scale is sung to the syllables *fa-sol-la-fa-sol-la-mi-fa*,
using *fa* (shown with a triangle) for the notes just above a half-step and *sol*
(round), *la* (square), and *mi* (diamond) for the following whole steps. Ordinary folks sang from these collections in church and in local and regional
gatherings, using the solmization syllables the first time through each song
and then singing all the verses.

The tune in Figure 25.6, found in the tenor part (the middle line), is *New
Britain*, a melody of unknown origin sung since the early nineteenth century
to John Newton's poem "Amazing Grace." The harmonization is typical of the
shape-note songbooks, with many open fifths (as in measures 1, 5, and 8),
dissonant fourths above the bass (measures 4, 7, and 10–11), and parallel
fifths and octaves (measures 4–5, 6–7, 7–8, 9–11, and 13–14) that give this
music its characteristic sound.

The style of the Yankee tunesmiths and shape-note singers was considered *Lowell Mason*
crude and primitive by musicians who knew European music. Especially

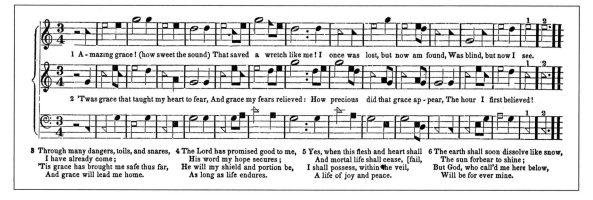

Figure 25.6: *The hymn tune* New Britain *(in the middle voice), set to the text "Amazing
Grace" by John Newton, as it appears in the* The Sacred Harp, *3rd edition (1859).*

significant was Lowell Mason (1792–1872), born in Massachusetts and trained
in harmony and composition by a German emigrant musician in Savannah,
Georgia. Mason returned to Boston in 1827, became president of the Handel
and Haydn Society, and helped found the Boston Academy of Music to provide musical instruction for children. As superintendent of music for the
Boston public schools, he introduced music into the regular curriculum,
prompting other cities to follow suit and thereby establishing the American
tradition of music education in schools. He deplored what he regarded as the
crude music of the Yankee tunesmiths and championed a correct, modest European style, in which he composed some 1,200 original hymn tunes and
arranged many others. Even today, many Protestant hymnals contain several
of his melodies and arrangements. Among his most famous tunes is *Bethany*
(1856), set to Sarah Flower Adams's 1841 poem "Nearer, My God, to Thee,"
shown in Example 25.9. The melody is largely pentatonic and in modified
AABA form, like *New Britain*, but the harmony follows the rules of proper European music of the time.

THE TRADITION OF CHORAL MUSIC

From Gregorian chant through the oratorios of Handel, music for choirs often
led stylistic development in music. But choral music in the nineteenth cen-

Example 25.9: Lowell Mason, Bethany

tury either looked back to previous eras or emulated other genres of the time, such as solo song. In histories of music that focus on the evolution of musical style, nineteenth-century choral music need hardly be mentioned. But enormous numbers of people participated in or heard choral music in concert or church, and it has exercised a significant and enduring influence on musical tastes.

ROMANTICISM AND THE CLASSICAL TRADITION

The first half of the nineteenth century was a paradoxical age in music. The period saw astonishing growth in concert life, music publishing, instrument manufacture, amateur music-making, touring virtuosos, and professional orchestras and chamber ensembles, all of which reinforced each other and spurred composers to produce a torrent of new music. These same factors also helped to establish a repertoire of classical masterpieces from Handel and Bach through Haydn, Mozart, and Beethoven. Composers of music for symphony orchestra, chamber ensemble, or large chorus could see this process at work and aspired to similar greatness. They competed for performances, recognition, and sales with the masters of the past—and with their contemporaries—by introducing something new and individual into genres and forms that were hallowed by tradition. In varying degrees, they blended elements of Romanticism into Classic frameworks from the eighteenth century.

Many of the works they produced—including Schubert's *Unfinished* and "Great" C-Major Symphonies and late chamber works; Berlioz's *Symphonie fantastique* and Requiem; Mendelssohn's *Italian* and *Scottish* Symphonies, Violin Concerto, and *Elijah;* and Schumann's symphonies—won wide popularity and became classics in their own right. Pieces by these and other composers of their time have become staples of the repertoire. For many of these works in eighteenth-century genres and forms, their relationship to past music is an important aspect of their meaning, part of what makes the music interesting, distinctive, and worth hearing many times over. In other compositions, the tension between new and old is no less strong, but what is innovative seems more significant than the references to tradition. As we will see in later chapters, composers defining themselves in relation to the classical tradition is a theme that grew stronger for at least the next century and produced a remarkable variety of responses.

Of course, few pieces attained a permanent place in the repertoire during their composer's lifetime. Most works were printed, performed, and eventually forgotten, the typical fate of music in earlier centuries. But with music of the past playing an increasing role, some composers were lucky enough to find performers or critics to champion their works after their deaths, as Mendelssohn had done for Bach, Schumann for Schubert, and Clara Schumann for her husband. Berlioz, for example, had to wait until the second half

of the twentieth century for full acceptance, aided by recordings of his monumental works. The music of Clara Schumann and Fanny Mendelssohn Hensel
passed out of view for over a hundred years, until it was revived in the late
twentieth century when musicians sought out deserving pieces by women
composers.

Meanwhile, some of the utilitarian music of the day won a surprising permanence. The orchestral waltzes and other dances of Joseph Lanner and Johann Strauss the elder, the Orthodox choral music of Bortnyansky, numerous
hymns by Lowell Mason and his contemporaries, and the music of *The Sacred
Harp* have all been performed continuously since they first appeared, sustained by living traditions in which their music is useful and even revered. As
we will see in later chapters, the nineteenth and twentieth centuries spawned
many such repertoires of classic works from the past, even while new styles
and types of music emerged at a dizzying pace.

Chapter

26

Romantic Opera and Musical Theater to Midcentury

While purely instrumental music gained prestige, opera continued to be a central part of musical life, especially in Italy and France. Opera served as elite entertainment and also as the source of music that was popular with audiences of all classes and professions. Composers followed national trends, even while they developed new forms and approaches and borrowed ideas across national boundaries. Italian composers dominated the field, but new types of opera that were cultivated in France and Germany also exercised a lasting influence. In addition, a lively operatic life emerged in the Americas, centered on the performance of European operas. At the same time, a new form of musical theater—the minstrel show—sprang up in the United States and became the first musical export from North America to Europe.

THE ROLES OF OPERA

The first half of the nineteenth century was in many ways a golden age for opera. New opera theaters were erected all over Western Europe. The craze even jumped the Atlantic and took root in the New World. Most opera theaters were run for profit by an impresario, usually backed by government subsidies or private support. Members of the upper and middle classes attended fully staged opera, and for some people, being seen at the opera asserted their social status even more than their love of music. Outside the opera house, excerpts from opera cropped up everywhere, comprising an important part of popular as well as elite

659

culture. Individual numbers and complete scores were published in versions for voices and piano and were performed in salons and by amateurs at home; selections from operas were transcribed for piano; overtures and arias appeared on concert programs in original form or arrangements; operas were abridged and parodied in burlesques, puppet shows, and other forms of popular theater; and melodies from opera arias became staples of café orchestras and even barrel organs. All types of opera from the period embody this dual appeal to the elite and to the public at large.

Subjects and settings for operas varied widely during the nineteenth century, from grand historical epics to folk tales, and from plots with strong political overtones to stories that centered on private emotions and personal relationships. Librettists sought to reflect the concerns of the broader audience that was now attending operas, not so much by putting middle-class characters on stage—although that would become more common over the course of the century—as by addressing issues that spoke to them: how to balance love with loyalty to family (as in Meyerbeer's *Les Huguenots*) or nation (Bellini's *Norma*), women's growing desire for independence (Rossini's *Barber of Seville* and Donizetti's *Lucia di Lammermoor*), the struggle for freedom (Rossini's *William Tell* and Auber's *La muette de Portici*), and the fear of evil (Weber's *Der Freischütz*).

Although the libretto and spectacular stage effects continued to be significant factors in an opera's success, the music itself now became the most important element. Star singers were still paid more than composers, but the composer was increasingly the dominant force. New operas by the leading composers became major events, and successful ones were performed numerous times and restaged in many cities. By 1850, a permanent repertory of operas began to emerge, paralleling the classical repertoire in the concert hall. At the center of this repertory were operas by Rossini, Bellini, Donizetti, Meyerbeer, and Weber, alongside the late Mozart operas.

ITALY

In the early nineteenth century, Rossini, Donizetti, and Bellini created a new Italian tradition in opera and composed works that have been performed across Europe and in the New World almost every year since their first performances.

GIOACHINO ROSSINI

If asked who was the most famous and important living composer, many people in Europe around 1825 would have answered not Beethoven but rather Gioachino Rossini (1792–1868; see biography and Figure 26.1). He is best known today for his comic operas such as *L'Italiana in Algeri* (The Italian Woman in Algiers; Venice, 1813) and *Il Barbiere di Siviglia* (The Barber of Seville; Rome, 1816). Yet Rossini's reputation during his lifetime rested as much on his serious operas such as *Otello* (Naples, 1816), *Mosè in Egitto*

GIOACHINO ROSSINI (1792–1868)

Rossini's reputation rests chiefly on his operas, which include some of the most popular ever written.

Born in Pesaro on the Adriatic coast of Italy, Rossini was the son of a horn and trumpet player and an operatic singer. He studied music as a child and performed professionally as a violist, singer, and pianist. In 1806, he enrolled in the Bologna Conservatory, where his studies of counterpoint and the music of Haydn and Mozart deepened his craft.

Rossini was commissioned to write his first opera in 1810, at age eighteen, and the great success three years later of *Tancredi* and *L'Italiana in Algeri* established his international reputation. In 1815, he was appointed musical director of the Teatro San Carlo in Naples, and a year later his most successful opera, *The Barber of Seville*, was produced. For the next eight years, Rossini composed numerous operas for Naples and other cities. Because copyright protection did not exist in Italy, he could earn money from operas only when he participated in the performances. As a result, he constantly had to produce new works, composing very rapidly (sometimes writing an opera in a month or less), often borrowing or reworking overtures and arias from his own previous works. He always wrote for particular singers, creating music to suit their talents.

In 1822, Rossini married the soprano Isabella Colbran, with whom he had worked since coming to Naples. After *Semiramide* (1823), Rossini's last opera for Italy, they

Figure 26.1: Gioachino Rossini around 1816, the year he composed The Barber of Seville. *Painting by Vincenzo Camuccini.*

traveled to London, then settled in Paris, where he became director of the Théâtre Italien. He reworked some of his Italian operas to French librettos translated or adapted from the Italian and wrote one entirely new opera in French, *Guillaume Tell*, in 1829. Then suddenly and mysteriously, at barely forty years old, he ceased writing operas, turning to sacred works and short songs and piano pieces.

The remaining forty years of his life were marred by illness—some say hypochondria, others bipolar disorders—but he was financially comfortable, entertaining every Saturday night in his villa outside Paris, eating to excess, and inventing recipes that he exchanged with some of the most famous chefs in Europe. He began an affair with Olympe Pélissier in the 1830s and married her in 1846 after his first wife's death. In his last decade, he produced witty piano pieces and songs—often parodies of other music—that influenced Saint-Saëns, Satie, and others and anticipate French neoclassicism of the twentieth century. He died in 1868, known best for music written four decades earlier.

MAJOR WORKS: *39 operas, including* Tancredi, L'Italiana in Algeri, The Barber of Seville, Otello, La Cenerentola, Mosè in Egitto, Semiramide, *and* Guillaume Tell; Stabat Mater, Petite messe solonelle, *and other sacred vocal works; and smaller vocal and instrumental pieces collected in* Soirées musicales *and* Péchés de vieillesse *(Sins of Old Age)*

(Moses in Egpyt; Naples, 1818), and *Guillaume Tell* (William Tell; Paris, 1829). He was the most popular and influential opera composer of his generation, in part because he blended aspects of opera buffa and opera seria into both his comic and his serious operas, making them all more varied, more appealing, and more true to human character. The new conventions he established for Italian opera would endure for over half a century.

Bel canto style   Rossini helped establish a style of Italian opera known as **bel canto**—literally, "beautiful singing." The term refers to the elegant style characterized by lyrical lines, seemingly effortless technique, and florid delivery. In bel canto operas, the most important element is the voice, even more important than the story, the orchestra, and the visuals.

General style   Rossini's operas are known for their irrepressible tunefulness combined with snappy rhythms and clear phrases. His spare orchestration supports rather than competes with the singers, while featuring individual instruments, especially winds, for color. His harmonic schemes are not complex but often original, and he shares with other early-nineteenth-century composers a fondness for bringing third-related keys into close juxtaposition with the tonic. One of his characteristic devices, both simple and effective, became known as the "Rossini crescendo"—building up excitement by repeating a phrase, louder each time and often at a higher pitch, sometimes giving the effect of a world about to spin out of control.

Scene structure   The action in earlier operas was confined to dry recitative dialogue, while arias were dramatically static, expressing only one or two moods. But Rossini and his librettists developed a scene structure that distributed the story throughout an act and integrated new plot developments or changes of mood within an aria or ensemble. A continuous succession of orchestrally accompanied recitatives, solo arias, duets, ensembles, and choruses all contributed to advancing the plot, with both orchestra and chorus playing more significant roles than they had in previous Italian operas.

As shown in Figure 26.2, a typical scene begins with an instrumental introduction and a recitative section (called a *scena*, Italian for "scene") that is accompanied by the orchestra. The ensuing aria has two main sections, a slow, lyrical **cantabile** and a lively and brilliant **cabaletta.** The cantabile expresses relatively calm moods such as pensiveness, sadness, or hope, and the cabaletta more active feelings such as anger or joy. Part or all of the cabaletta is repeated, perhaps with improvised embellishments. Some arias, like *Una voce poco fa* from *The Barber of Seville* (NAWM 125), have these two sections only, but in most arias, we also find a middle section between the cantabile and the cabaletta called the **tempo di mezzo** (middle movement), which is usually some kind of transition or interruption by other characters and in which something happens to alter the situation or the character's mood. A duet or ensemble has a similar form (as in the duet from Verdi's *La traviata* in NAWM 127), but the cantabile is usually preceded by an opening section (called *tempo d'attacco*) in which the characters trade melodic phrases. The finale of an act, which brings together most or all of the characters, is organized along similar lines, although different terms were used for the sections, as shown in Figure 26.2. Rossini's basic format could be flexibly applied to suit almost any dramatic situation, and

CD 9|48

a. Aria (solo or with chorus)					
Orchestral introduction	*Scena*		*Cantabile*	*Tempo di mezzo* (middle section)	*Cabaletta*
	recitative		usually slow	changes tempo, modulates; may be transition, ensemble, or chorus	usually fast

b. Duet or ensemble					
Orchestral introduction	*Scena*	*Tempo d'attacco* (opening section)	*Cantabile*	*Tempo di mezzo*	*Cabaletta*

c. Finale					
Orchestral introduction	*Scena*	Dialogue	*Largo concertato* (concerted slow section)	Dialogue	*Stretta* (fast section)

Figure 26.2: Scene structures in Rossini operas.

his structure created a dramatic progression from one mood or idea to another while allowing more than two contrasting moods to be presented within a coherent form.

Considered today Rossini's most popular opera, *The Barber of Seville* combines features of opera buffa with bel canto tradition. The main character, the town's barber and resident schemer, helps a count (disguised as Lindoro, a poor soldier) to win the hand of the beautiful and wealthy Rosina, who has been locked away by her guardian, Dr. Bartolo—a man intent on marrying her for her inheritance. Secret messages, drunken brawls, and mistaken identities are all part of the chaotic plot.

Rosina's justly famous aria *Una voce poco fa* (NAWM 125) conveys her character through changes of style, as shown in Example 26.1. The orchestral introduction presents ideas that will reappear later. There is no opening recitative, but the first part of her cantabile—as she narrates being serenaded by and falling in love with Lindoro—is broken into small phrases punctuated by orchestral chords, a style that recalls orchestral recitative, appropriate to narration (Example 26.1a). When she swears to outwit her guardian, the style briefly changes to a comic patter song (Example 26.1b), which is preceded and followed by elaborate embellishments and runs as she vows to marry Lindoro. Rossini proceeds directly to the cabaletta, where the music reveals Rosina's true nature. She claims to be both docile and obedient—singing a winning, lyrical melody (Example 26.1c)—as well as a viper and trickster—showing off her sudden vocal leaps and rapid passage work in buffo style (Example 26.1d). The aria is a cunning portrayal of the different facets of Rosina's character and a masterful combination of bel canto melody, wit, and comic description.

The Barber of Seville

CD 9|48

Example 26.1: Changes of style in Una voce poco fa, *from Rossini's* The Barber of Seville

a. Quasi-recitative

A voice a short while ago here in my heart resounded.

b. Patter song

The guardian will refuse, I shall sharpen my wits.

Serious operas

The lasting appeal of Rossini's comic operas has overshadowed his serious ones, but they were equally significant in his day. Many of the serious operas have enjoyed successful revivals in recent decades, showing that his style and approach have a far wider range in delineating characters, capturing situations, and conveying emotions than is represented in the comic operas alone.

Guillaume Tell

The best known of his serious operas was his last, *Guillaume Tell*, which was written for the Paris Opéra in 1829 and had five hundred performances there during the composer's lifetime. The libretto, based on Friedrich von Schiller's *Wilhelm Tell* (1804), celebrates a folk hero who led a rebellion of

c. *Cabaletta, lyrical opening*

I am docile, I am respectful. . . .

d. *Contrasting comic style*

But if they touch my weaker side, I can be a viper. . . .

three Swiss cantons against an Austrian governor. The theme was timely—revolution and struggles for national unity were in the air—but it also subjected the work to censorship in Milan, London, Berlin, and St. Petersburg. While continuing the conventions he had helped to establish in Italian opera, Rossini's setting includes many choruses, ensembles, dances, processions, and atmospheric instrumental interludes, all in the manner of French grand opera (see below).

Rossini's opera overtures have found a second career in the concert hall, as gems of the orchestral repertoire. Most are in two parts, a long,

Overtures

slow introduction with a lyrical melody for wind instruments followed by a fast sonata-form movement without development. The most famous is the overture to *Guillaume Tell*, which has four sections: a slow pastoral introduction; a musical depiction of a storm; another slow section featuring a *ranz de vaches*— a Swiss cowherd's call—played by an English horn and repeated throughout the opera; and a galloping allegro (used in the twentieth century as the theme for the television show *The Lone Ranger*). Combining simplicity in melody, harmony, and form with vivacious rhythms, exciting dynamics, and unusual orchestral effects has made Rossini's overtures perennial favorites.

VINCENZO BELLINI

Vincenzo Bellini (1801–1835) was a younger contemporary of Rossini's who came to prominence after Rossini had retired from opera composition. Bellini preferred dramas of passion, with fast, gripping action. His favorite librettist, Felice Romani, did not limit action to recitative passages but built it into the arias and provided opportunities for lyrical moments within the recitatives. Of Bellini's ten operas—all serious—the most important are *La Sonnambula* (The Sleepwalker, 1831), *Norma* (1831), and *I Puritani* (The Puritans, 1835).

Style   Bellini is known for long, sweeping, highly embellished, intensely emotional melodies. Among the most famous is the cantabile section of Norma's *cavatina*, or entrance aria, *Casta diva* (Chaste goddess) from *Norma*, shown in Example 26.2. When Norma, high priestess of the Druids, prays to the moon for peace with the Romans, her vocal line seems to be in constant motion,

Example 26.2: Casta diva, from Bellini's Norma

Chaste goddess, who plates with silver [these sacred ancient plants]

creating a deeply expressive and unpredictable melody. The secret of such melodies is that an underlying simple structure, often stepwise motion (A–G–F in the first phrase, A–B♭ in the second), is embellished with ever-changing figuration that draws our attention and plays with our expectations. The scene follows Rossini's typical pattern, beginning with orchestrally accompanied recitative, followed by the cantabile section, a declamatory tempo di mezzo, and a brilliant cabaletta. In each section, the chorus plays an important role, responding to Norma's pleas for peace. The constant interaction of the principal protagonists with subordinate characters and the chorus creates a sense of continuous action, which Bellini reinforces through frequent changes of style, texture, and figuration.

GAETANO DONIZETTI

One of the most prolific Italian composers during the second quarter of the century was Gaetano Donizetti (1797–1848), who composed oratorios, cantatas, chamber and church music, about one hundred songs, and several symphonies in addition to some seventy operas. His most enduring works were the serious operas *Anna Bolena* (Milan, 1830) and *Lucia di Lammermoor* (Naples, 1835); the opéra comique *La Fille du regiment* (The Daughter of the Regiment; Paris, 1840); and the buffo operas *L'elisir d'amore* (The Elixir of Love; Milan, 1832) and *Don Pasquale* (Paris, 1843).

Donizetti, like Rossini, had an instinct for the theater and for melody that effectively captures a character, situation, or feeling. His comic operas often mix sentimentality with comedy. In his serious operas, Donizetti constantly moves the drama forward, occasionally averting cadences that would entice applause and thus sustaining dramatic tension until a major scene is finished. The beginnings and endings of the formal components of a scene, such as the orchestral introduction, cantabile, and cabaletta, are sometimes disguised by choral or recitative episodes so that the music seems to possess an almost seamless continuity.

One of Donizetti's most famous operas, *Lucia di Lammermoor*, set in the lonely cliffs and ancient feuds of the Scottish highlands, offers a prime example of this kind of transparent continuity. Lucia is tricked by her brother into thinking that the man she loves, Edgardo, has been unfaithful. She reluctantly agrees to marry someone else, but on her wedding night, she murders him on their nuptial bed. Lucia then begins to hallucinate, imagining she hears Edgardo's voice calling to her, and she goes mad. Her "mad scene" in the last act creates an unbroken flow of events through numerous entrances and tempo changes.

Lucia di Lammermoor

The scene begins with a short chorus that comments on Lucia's deathly and disheveled appearance as she enters after murdering her husband. We then hear foreboding music that first appeared in the opera's prelude, played by a quartet of horns. Against this and a syncopated flute motive, Lucia begins an impassioned recitative, calling out to Edgardo. The flutes and clarinets recollect the theme of her love duet with him from Act I; such hearkening back to an earlier theme or motive became known as a ***reminiscence motive***. Lucia's recitative continues through several tempo changes and overlaps the introduction to her cantabile, the blurring of boundaries serving as a sign of her madness. Lucia's tutor, a captain of the guards, and her brother, having learned of the murder, break in to pray for the Lord's mercy. At the tempo di mezzo, she is joined by her brother and tutor and later the chorus. After a pause and orchestral introduction, Lucia begins the cabaletta. But before she can sing the anticipated repetition, the chorus and other characters break in, joining her again as she brings the repetition to a close and faints. Such flexible adaptation of Rossini's standard scene-structure to suit the course of the drama is typical of Donizetti and served as a model for Giuseppe Verdi in the next generation (see chapter 27).

CLASSICS OF ITALIAN OPERA

The most successful operas of Rossini, Bellini, and Donizetti were performed in opera houses all over Italy and at theaters in other nations that specialized in Italian opera or presented Italian operas in translation. Their most famous arias became popular tunes heard by large segments of the public. By midcentury, these operas were becoming part of a core repertory, staged repeatedly wherever opera was performed. Rossini's *The Barber of Seville*, Bellini's *Norma*, and Donizetti's *Lucia di Lammermoor* were among the first operas ever to reach the status of permanent classics, akin to Handel's *Messiah* or Beethoven's symphonies. In part due to the phenomenal success of these operas, Italian musical life was dominated by opera for several more generations, during which the most noted composers specialized in opera, while instrumental genres, choral music, and even solo song were overshadowed.

FRANCE

Throughout the nineteenth century, opera remained the most prestigious musical genre in France, whose musical culture was second only to Italy's in its focus on the genre.

French opera under Napoleon

From its founding by Lully in the late seventeenth century, French opera was centered in Paris and shaped by politics. The French Revolution had ended aristocratic patronage, bringing new laws that allowed anyone to open a public theater. But Napoleon again restricted theaters, allowing only three to present operas. The Opéra, which focused on tragedy, was the most prestigious, staging new works, revivals by Gluck and others, and French versions of foreign operas by composers such as Mozart. The Opéra-Comique gave operas with spoken dialogue instead of recitative; despite the name, many of these opéras comiques had serious plots. The Théâtre Italien presented operas in Italian, including works composed for Paris and older operas by Mozart and others. Other Paris theaters featured plays, comedies, vaudevilles (comedies with songs interspersed), pantomimes (scenes acted out silently), and ballets, most of which included music. Although Paris was the center for producing new works, theaters and opera houses in other French cities were also active.

Figure 26.3: The new Paris Opéra building on Rue Le Peletier, which opened August 16, 1821. The illustration shows its interior during a performance in the 1840s of Meyerbeer's Robert le diable. *The stage scenery is of a new kind, with a curved backdrop shell designed to look more realistic than previous flat canvasses could. Lithograph by Jules Arnout.*

Following the defeat of Napoleon, the French monarchy was restored under Louis XVIII, brother of Louis XVI. A new theater for the Opéra, shown in Figure 26.3, was built in 1821. Gas lighting was introduced the next year, allowing much more spectacular and subtle stage effects. The Théâtre Italien mounted operas by Rossini, who became the director there in 1824. But Charles X (r. 1824–30) failed to gain the support of the growing and powerful middle class, and the bloodless "July Revolution" of 1830 put his distant cousin Louis Philippe on the throne as a constitutional monarch. The government continued to subsidize opera and concerts, and the royal family contributed informally to opera and benefit concerts rather than sponsoring them directly. The Opéra theater was leased to a businessman, Louis Véron, who found wealthy sponsors. Anyone could purchase tickets, but the boxes were rented at high prices.

Restoration and the July Revolution

GRAND OPERA

With the decline of royal patronage, a new kind of opera came into being, designed to appeal to the newly well-to-do middle-class audiences who thronged the opera theaters looking for excitement and entertainment. **Grand opera**, as this type came to be called, was as much spectacle as music, consistent with the fashion that had prevailed in France ever since Lully. Writers created librettos that exploited every possible occasion for ballets, machinery, choruses, and crowd scenes, while flattering the middle class by painting aristocrats as wicked and their opponents as virtuous. Two early examples of grand opera were Rossini's *Guillaume Tell* (1829), featuring an onstage lake across which Tell rows to safety, and *La muette de Portici* (The Mute of Portici, 1828) by Daniel-François-Esprit Auber (1782–1871), which ends with the eruption of the volcano Vesuvius—and ironically has a title role that is danced, not sung, since she is a mute. Both operas were on themes of rebellion against foreign repression. Indeed, a performance in Brussels of *La muette de Portici* in 1830—about a peasant revolt two centuries earlier—resonated enough with the viewing public that it sparked a riot, depicted in Figure 26.4, that ultimately led to Belgium's independence.

Eugène Scribe and Giacomo Meyerbeer

Along with Véron, the director of the Paris Opéra, the leaders of grand opera were the librettist Eugène Scribe (1791–1861) and the composer Giacomo Meyerbeer (1791–1864). Scribe, who coauthored the libretto to *La muette de Portici*, created the mix of formality, spectacle, and historical, political, or religious themes that defined the new genre. Meyerbeer's *Robert le diable* (Robert the Devil, 1831, shown in Figure 26.3) and *Les Huguenots* (1836), both on Scribe librettos, set the pattern for the musical treatment, using every available technique to dramatize the action and please the public. Meyerbeer had a command of varied musical styles forged from his earlier experiences: born to a German-Jewish family in Berlin, he was a child prodigy, as a pianist, then spent nine successful years as an opera composer in Italy, where he Italianized his first name (originally Jakob).

Figure 26.4: Riot at the Théâtre de la Monnaie in Brussels, on August 25, 1830, during a performance of Auber's La muette de Portici. *The stage design includes the erupting volcano Vesuvius at the conclusion of the opera. The plot centered on liberation from foreign domination; this particular performance inflamed the Belgians to rebel against their Dutch rulers. Engraving by Hébert after a drawing by Henri Hendricks.*

Les Huguenots is typical of French grand opera. It has five long acts, an enormous cast, a ballet, and dramatic scenery and lighting effects. Embedded in the historical event of the St. Valentine's Day Massacre—a culmination of the conflict between the Catholics and the Protestants (Huguenots) in sixteenth-century France and one of the crucial events in French history—is the tragic fate of a pair of lovers. In the closing scene of Act II, Meyerbeer illustrates his ability to integrate crowd scenes, public ceremonies, and confrontations on stage with deep personal emotions. Here Queen Marguerite de Valois tries to reconcile the two sides through a peace-making marriage of a Catholic woman, Valentine, to the Protestant Raoul. A timpani solo introduces the oath of peace, sung in unison, unaccompanied and *pianissimo*, by the leaders of the two factions. The chorus, with orchestra, interjects *fortissimo* "Nous jurons" (We swear) three times. In an extended unaccompanied ensemble in four parts, the leaders hail the benefits of harmony among all people. Only the militant Protestant Marcel defies the others, vowing to make war on Rome and its soldiers. As the orchestra rejoins the singers on a diminished seventh chord, Marguerite's voice floats above all the others, crowning the scene with coloratura. Later, when Raoul rejects Valentine as a prospective wife, and the truce between the opposing factions breaks down, Marcel in the midst of the fury triumphantly booms out a phrase of the Lutheran chorale *Ein' feste Burg ist unser Gott* (A Mighty Fortress Is Our God). The scene exemplifies the conception of grand opera as a combination of entertaining spectacle and glorious singing with a serious artistic statement.

Les Huguenots

Meyerbeer's approach to grand opera was admired and emulated by later composers. Other grand operas, like *La Juive* (The Jewess, 1835) by Jacques Halévy (1799–1862) with a libretto by Scribe, follow a similar formula. Donizetti's *La Favorite* (1840) was a grand opera written for Paris, as were Verdi's *Les Vêpres Siciliennes* (1855) and *Don Carlos* (1867). The genre spread, with productions in Germany, London, and elsewhere. Particularly significant is Meyerbeer's profound influence on Richard Wagner (see chapter 27), whose *Rienzi* (1842) is grand opera pure and simple, and whose later operas were heavily influenced by *Les Huguenots*.

Impact of grand opera

Hector Berlioz's great five-act opera *Les Troyens* (1856–58, partial premiere in 1863) drew on grand opera but also on the older French opera tradition of Lully, Rameau, and Gluck. The text, by Berlioz himself, is based on the second and fourth books of Virgil's *Aeneid*. Berlioz condensed the narrative in a series of powerful scene-complexes and used appropriate occasions to introduce ballets, processions, and other musical numbers. Like Meyerbeer's *Huguenots*, *Les Troyens* can be classified as an "epic opera"—a work in which the story of a nation is more significant than the passions and emotions of individual characters.

Berlioz, Les Troyens

OPÉRA COMIQUE

Side by side with grand opera, opéra comique continued to be fashionable. As in the eighteenth century, the technical difference between the two was that opéra comique used spoken dialogue instead of recitative. Apart from this, the differences were primarily questions of size and subject matter. Opéra

Figure 26.5: Marie Taglioni, clad in the new costume of the Romantic ballerina, with a close-fitting bodice and sheer, almost translucent skirt. Her position, rising "on point" (on the toes, in special shoes that allow this), typifies the light, airy effect ballet dancers sought to achieve. Lithograph from the 1830s by James Henry Lynch after Alfred Edward Chalon.

comique was less pretentious than grand opera and required fewer singers and players. Its plots, as a rule, presented straightforward comedy or semi-serious drama instead of the historical pageantry typical of grand opera. Two kinds of opéra comique existed in the early part of the nineteenth century, the romantic and the comic, although many works shared characteristics of both types.

BALLET

Another form of musical theater popular in France was the ballet. French operas since the seventeenth century had often included ballets, but in the late eighteenth century dance troupes began to present independent ballets that had a series of dance scenes linked together by a narrative. A new style, now known as Romantic ballet, was introduced by Marie Taglioni (1804–1884), shown in Figure 26.5. In this style, still common in modern performances, ballerinas became preeminent, moving with a new lightness, grace, and freedom exemplified by sheer, translucent skirts and by shoes that allowed them to stand on point. Having triumphed throughout Europe and Russia in the 1830s, Taglioni toured North America for two years in 1840–42, introducing European ballet and scoring a phenomenal success.

Composers typically wrote music for ballets after the dance had already been choreographed, so they had to fit their music to the timing, rhythms, movements, and mood of the dance. One of the highlights of Romantic ballet was *Giselle*, premiered at the Paris Opéra in 1841, with music by Adolphe Adam (1803–1856) that used recurring motives and recollection of earlier material to highlight the progress of the drama, as in an opera.

GERMANY

The interaction between music and literature, so typical of nineteenth-century Romanticism, was developed most fully by composers in the German-speaking lands, in opera as well as song and instrumental music. At the root of German opera was the Singspiel, whose composers in the early nineteenth century soaked up Romantic elements from French opera while intensifying the genre's specific national features.

CARL MARIA VON WEBER

The work that established German Romantic opera was *Der Freischütz* (The Rifleman, first performed in Berlin in 1821), by Carl Maria von Weber (1786–1826), depicted in Figure 26.6. What made *Der Freischütz* so daring for its time was not only Weber's unusual orchestration and harmonies, but also his idea of putting ordinary folk center stage, talking and singing about their concerns, their loves, and their fears.

The libretto of *Der Freischütz* exemplifies the characteristics of German Romantic opera. Plots are drawn from medieval history, legend, or fairy tale. The story involves supernatural beings and happenings set against a background of wilderness and mystery, but scenes of humble village or country life are frequently introduced. Supernatural incidents and the natural setting are not incidental or decorative but are intertwined with the fate of the human protagonists. Mortal characters act not merely as individuals, but as agents or representatives of superhuman forces, whether good or evil. The triumph of good is a form of salvation or redemption, a vaguely religious concept of deliverance from sin and error through suffering, conversion, or revelation. In *German Romantic opera* giving such importance to the physical and spiritual background, German opera differs sharply from contemporary French and Italian opera. But its musical styles and forms draw directly from those of other countries, while the use of simple folklike melodies introduces a distinctly German national element. German opera also displays increasingly chromatic harmony, the use of orchestral color for dramatic expression, and an emphasis on the inner voices, in contrast to the Italian stress on melody.

All these facets are illustrated in *Der Freischütz*. Rustic choruses, marches, dances, and airs mingle in the score with multisectional arias in the Italian style. The somber forest background is depicted idyllically by the horns at the beginning of the overture and diabolically in the eerie midnight scene in the Wolf's Glen, shown in Figure 26.7.

Figure 26.6: Carl Maria von Weber, in a portrait by Carline Bardua.

Figure 26.7: Setting by Carl Wilhelm Holdermann for the Wolf's Glen Scene in Weber's Der Freischütz *as performed at Weimar in 1822. In the magic circle, Caspar casts the magic bullets, while Max looks around with growing alarm at the frightening apparitions aroused by each bullet cast.*

In a story line derived from folklore, Max, a young ranger, loves Agathe, but in order to win her hand in marriage, he must pass a test of marksmanship. He has had bad luck for a few days, failing target practice. Caspar, a fellow ranger, persuades Max that he can obtain some magic bullets, which will guarantee that Max will win the trial. In the dead of night, the two men meet in the Wolf's Glen, where Caspar casts the magic bullets. But unbeknownst to Max, Caspar has sold his soul to the devil, Samiel, who controls the final bullet cast and has destined it to kill Agathe. Max uses up three bullets to impress the prince before the contest begins and has only one left—that guided by Samiel—for the fateful trial. Agathe unexpectedly appears in the line of fire as Max shoots, but she is protected by an old hermit's magical wreath, and the bullet kills Caspar instead.

Wolf's Glen Scene

CD 9|55

The Wolf's Glen Scene (finale of Act II, NAWM 126), during which the seven bullets are cast, incorporates elements of the **melodrama**, a genre of musical theater that combined spoken dialogue with background music. Melodramas had been popular in France and in German-speaking areas since the 1770s, and scenes in melodrama had appeared in operas by Mozart, Beethoven, and others. Speaking his lines over continuous orchestral music, Caspar first invokes Samiel. Then, as he casts each bullet, with Max cowering beside him, Caspar counts *one, two, three,* and so on, while the mountains echo each count. For each casting, Weber paints a different picture of the terrifying dark forest. Throughout, he ingeniously exploits the resources of the orchestra: timpani, trombones, clarinets, and horns in the foreground, often against string tremolos. Diminished and augmented intervals and daring chromaticism depict evil, and an offstage chorus reinforces the shadowy and supernatural elements of the plot.

Der Freischütz was immensely popular because of its appeal to national sentiment and the beauty of its music. It was soon produced in many other cities and has seen continuous performances ever since.

THE UNITED STATES

If the history of opera composition in the first half of the nineteenth century focuses on Italy, Paris, and Germany, the history of opera performance must include London, Spain, eastern Europe and the Americas, where opera became an important part of musical life.

In North America, theater companies in major cities and touring troupes *Theater companies* that traveled across the continent performed not only spoken plays but also ballad operas such as John Gay's *The Beggar's Opera* (see chapter 20) and English versions of foreign-language operas, which typically replaced recitative with spoken dialogue and simplified the ensembles and arias. These companies presented operas as entertainment accessible to all, in a time before the gulf had opened up between high and low (popular) culture.

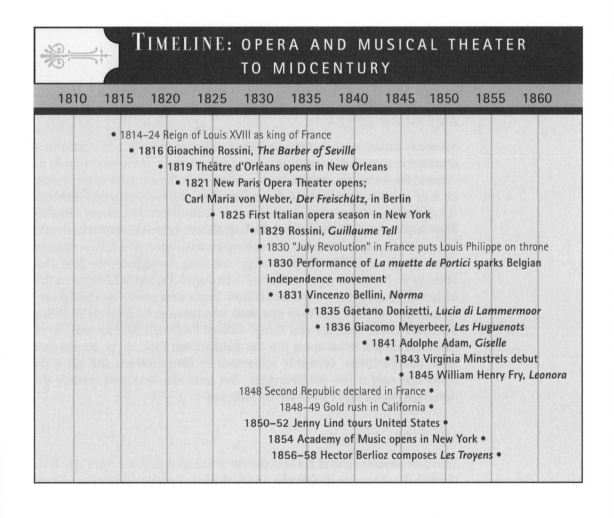

TIMELINE: OPERA AND MUSICAL THEATER TO MIDCENTURY

1810	1815	1820	1825	1830	1835	1840	1845	1850	1855	1860

- 1814–24 Reign of Louis XVIII as king of France
- 1816 Gioachino Rossini, *The Barber of Seville*
- 1819 Théâtre d'Orléans opens in New Orleans
- 1821 New Paris Opera Theater opens; Carl Maria von Weber, *Der Freischütz*, in Berlin
- 1825 First Italian opera season in New York
- 1829 Rossini, *Guillaume Tell*
- 1830 "July Revolution" in France puts Louis Philippe on throne
- 1830 Performance of *La muette de Portici* sparks Belgian independence movement
- 1831 Vincenzo Bellini, *Norma*
- 1835 Gaetano Donizetti, *Lucia di Lammermoor*
- 1836 Giacomo Meyerbeer, *Les Huguenots*
- 1841 Adolphe Adam, *Giselle*
- 1843 Virginia Minstrels debut
- 1845 William Henry Fry, *Leonora*
- 1848 Second Republic declared in France •
- 1848–49 Gold rush in California •
- 1850–52 Jenny Lind tours United States •
- 1854 Academy of Music opens in New York •
- 1856–58 Hector Berlioz composes *Les Troyens* •

European opera

Opera in foreign languages took hold more slowly. In New Orleans, formerly a French colonial city, French operas helped to preserve a distinctive cultural identity. Active between 1819 and 1866, the Théâtre d'Orléans performed primarily French and Italian operas in the original languages, giving many American premieres and touring the East Coast several times. In New York, a European troupe presented a season of Italian operas in 1825–26, including Rossini's *Barber of Seville* and Mozart's *Don Giovanni*. Several attempts were made to establish a permanent Italian opera house; one in 1833 involved Mozart's librettist Lorenzo da Ponte, then professor of Italian at Columbia University. The first opera company to last more than a few years was the Academy of Music, which opened in 1854 with *Norma* and presented regular opera seasons until 1886. By the 1850s, opera in Italian and English was also established in San Francisco, newly wealthy with Gold Rush money.

Opera as popular entertainment

While foreign-language operas attracted a relatively small, elite audience, a much wider public heard the music of opera. Overtures, arias, and other excerpts were arranged and published as sheet music, performed in parlors, and included in concerts. When Swedish soprano Jenny Lind toured the United States in 1850–52, singing before tens of thousands of people, her programs included opera overtures and Italian arias (especially Bellini's *Casta diva*) alongside familiar songs such as *Home! Sweet Home!* The music and plots of operas were so well known that operatic parodies had a ready audience; for example, New York's Olympic Theater offered opera burlesques like *Mrs. Normer* (on *Norma*) and *Fried Shots* (on *Der Freischütz*). Thus, although few Americans saw operas in their original form, operatic music was widespread as popular entertainment.

AMERICAN OPERA

American audiences that supported opera in Italian, French, or German were attracted in part by its prestige as a European art form. There was virtually no demand for American composers to produce opera on a similar scale because no local product carried the same cachet. Two ambitious attempts illustrate the difficulties of creating a native opera. William Henry Fry, son of a wealthy Philadelphia family, believed that the English and American tradition of mixing spoken dialogue with arias and ensembles was a corruption of the operatic ideal. His *Leonora* (Philadelphia, 1845) was sung throughout, the first such opera by an American-born composer to be staged. Fry based his style on that of European composers, especially Bellini. There were several successful performances, but his opera soon vanished; why listen to an imitator of Bellini when one could hear the real thing? George Frederick Bristow took up an American subject in his opera *Rip Van Winkle* (New York, 1855), but the style again was European, primarily influenced by Mendelssohn, and again the opera had only a few performances. Not until the twentieth century did American operas find a more secure audience.

MINSTREL SHOWS

The most popular form of musical theater in the United States from the 1830s through the 1870s was **minstrelsy**, in which white performers blackened their faces with burnt cork and impersonated African Americans in jokes, skits, songs, and dances. Figure 26.8 illustrates scenes from a typical minstrel show by one of the most successful troupes, Christy's Minstrels. Audiences today would find these shows offensive for trading on racial stereotypes. Yet in its day, minstrelsy was a response to the ambivalent feelings white Americans held toward blacks, a blend of fascination and fear. Like drag shows today (in which men dress as women) or eighteenth-century comic operas in which servants got the better of their masters, minstrel shows explored issues of social and political power and of proper and improper behavior through inversions of normal social roles. White performers playing black characters had license to behave outside accepted norms and to comment candidly on social, political, and economic conditions.

Minstrelsy grew from the solo comic performances of Daddy Rice as Jim Crow, a naive plantation slave, and of George Washington Dixon as Zip Coon, a boastful black urban dandy. Their theme songs were among the best sellers of their day; Rice's *Jump Jim Crow* was the first American piece of music to be a hit overseas, and *Zip Coon* (to the same tune as *Turkey in the Straw*) was almost as popular. Rice developed a genre he called "Ethiopian opera," interspersing sketch comedy with songs, performed between or after the acts of a play. The first full independent minstrel shows, consisting of dialogue, songs, banjo and fiddle playing, and dances loosely strung together, were given in 1843 by the Virginia Minstrels in New York, who then continued their shows throughout the East Coast and the British Isles. This group gave their name to the genre and made minstrelsy the first musical export from the United States to Europe, where it remained popular for over a century; "The Black and

Origins

Figure 26.8: Cover of a collection of music sung in shows by Christy's Minstrels. The troupe's founder and leader, Edwin P. Christy (1815–1862), is at top, followed by scenes in which white actors, singers, and musicians made up in blackface and dressed as stylish urban blacks or as plantation slaves imitate the dances, songs, and dialogue of African Americans.

White Minstrel Show," featuring white singers in blackface, ran on British television from 1958 to 1978.

Although minstrel shows long ago passed out of fashion, some of the songs written for them have proven remarkably durable. The Virginia Minstrels' violinist, Dan Emmett (1815–1902), was the composer of *Dixie* (1860), whose theme of longing for the South is common in minstrel songs. Many of Stephen Foster's best-known songs were written for Christy's Minstrels, including *Oh! Susanna* (1848), *Camptown Races* (1850), *Old Folks at Home* (1851), and *My Old Kentucky Home* (1853). The first two are fast comic numbers, the latter two are slow, sentimental plantation ballads, and most share the black dialect, pentatonic melodies, and occasional syncopation that were typical of minstrel songs.

Minstrel songs   Minstrel songs were not direct imitations of African-American music but did borrow elements characteristic of African and African-American traditions, from the banjo (a folk instrument based on African predecessors) to call-and-response, in which a lead singer alternates with a chorus or with instruments. Thus minstrelsy was the first of many forms of entertainment in which white musicians have borrowed from the music of African Americans, one of the strongest and most distinctive strands of American music.

OPERA AS HIGH CULTURE

Most musical theater in the early 1800s was aimed at mixed tastes. Composers and producers of all kinds of opera in every country could assume that their audience included wealthy elites, educated connoisseurs, musical amateurs, and the public at large. The librettists and composers of *The Barber of Seville*, *Norma*, *Lucia di Lammermoor*, *Les Huguenots*, and *Der Freischütz* sought to include elements that would appeal to all possible listeners.

By the middle of the nineteenth century, these and other works had become part of a repertory of operas that were performed repeatedly. In the later nineteenth and early twentieth centuries, new operas were staged less frequently, and the standard repertory came to predominate worldwide. Over time, the works that have survived, and opera itself as a medium, have become music for the elite; perhaps only in Italy, where some audience members still sing along with their favorite arias and choruses, has opera kept one foot in the world of popular music. Meanwhile, the vaudevilles, pantomimes, musical comedies, minstrel shows, and other lighter forms of musical theater from the period have been almost completely forgotten, yet their descendents—variety shows, cabarets, musicals, and the like—have formed a vital part of musical life for the last two centuries.

Today opera is a very expensive art form that depends on government support and wealthy private donors. It attracts devoted fans from all classes of society, but attending live opera still serves as a status symbol. Most listeners know operas primarily through recordings and radio broadcasts. Wherever opera is heard, most of the operas that are performed come from the nineteenth century, eclipsing all earlier periods, and the composers studied in this chapter are particularly well represented.

Chapter

27

Opera and Musical Theater in the Later Nineteenth Century

The second half of the nineteenth century saw a continuation of strong national traditions in Italian, German, and French opera, the rise of a vibrant Russian school in opera and ballet, and growing traditions of musical theater in other lands. *Nationalism* was an increasingly important force, linking opera to broader political and cultural currents. Sources for plots varied, from ancient legends to modern love affairs, and from European history to exotic tales in foreign lands. As the market for theatrical music grew larger and more diverse, elite and popular audiences diverged and new forms of comic opera and musical theater emerged to satisfy popular tastes. Verdi and Wagner dominated Italian and German opera respectively, while composers in France, Bohemia, Russia, and elsewhere developed new national styles.

TECHNOLOGY, POLITICS, AND NATIONALISM

Europe and the United States became industrial powerhouses during the latter nineteenth century. Railroads spread across both continents, transporting people and goods more rapidly. New products and technologies such as chemical soaps and dyes, steel manufacture, the electric lightbulb, and the telephone spawned new industries and altered daily life. Workers streamed to the cities to work in factories, and labor unions formed to represent their interests. With improved agriculture,

Figure 27.1: The Uprising (1848) by French artist Honoré Daumier. Renowned for his satirical drawings that lampooned those in power, Daumier here paints a sincere portrait of the passion that united workers (in shirtsleeves) and middle class (in top hat), men, women, and children in the 1848 Paris revolution.

sanitation, and medicine, life expectancy and population rose dramatically. Literacy also increased, and newspapers and magazines proliferated, made cheaper by advertising. With new laws that limited investors' risk to the amount they owned in stock, the modern corporation emerged, employing legions of office workers and middle managers. Mass consumption became a driving force for the economy, evident in the new institutions of the brand name, the department store, and the mail-order catalogue.

1848 revolutions   A growing movement for political reform in the 1840s culminated in a series of popular uprisings that swept Europe in 1848–49. The first revolution, pictured in Figure 27.1, was in France, toppling King Louis Philippe and establishing the Second French Republic. Its gains were short-lived, since the desire for order overcame the push for reform. Napoleon's nephew was elected president and in 1852 made himself Emperor Napoleon III (1852–70). Similar revolts in German, Italian, and Austro-Hungarian cities failed to produce permanent changes, due in part to the disunity among revolutionary leaders and lack of support from peasants.

Political reforms   Over the next half century, however, most European governments granted more political rights to their people, including constitutional limits on the monarch, direct election of parliamentary assemblies, greater freedom of the press, and voting rights for most men. Russia abolished serfdom in 1861, and in the United States the Civil War of 1861–65 brought the abolition of slavery. France established its Third Republic in 1875. In the 1880s, Germany granted workers national health care, limits on the working day, and old-age pensions that formed a model for other countries. Beginning in 1848 with the Seneca Falls Convention in upstate New York, women began pushing for equal treatment under the law, including the rights to make contracts, get a divorce, and cast a vote. Although women in most areas would not win the vote until the twentieth century, they made substantial gains by the end of the nineteenth. But improved rights for the many went hand in hand with exploitation of others, as expropriation of Native American lands continued in the Americas, the Russian Empire expanded south and east, and the European powers divided up Africa and much of Asia into colonies.

Nationalism

The French Revolution and Napoleonic Wars had helped to popularize the concept of a nation as a group of citizens with a common heritage rather than as subjects of a ruler. The influence of this idea continued to grow throughout the nineteenth century. **Nationalism** in the political realm was the attempt to unify a particular group of people by creating a national identity through characteristics such as a common language, shared culture, historical traditions, and national institutions and rituals. Not all of these elements had to be present; the Swiss achieved a sense of nationhood through shared history and institutions despite speaking four different languages, while elsewhere people sought to create a sense of commonality based on language and culture that crossed existing political boundaries. Although later generations would take it as a given, national identity was in almost every case intentionally created and channeled to achieve social and political goals.

National unification

Nationalism could be used to support the status quo or to challenge it. In France, Britain, and Russia, which had long been unified states, expressions of nationalism could rally support for the government. But German and Italy had been divided since the Middle Ages, and in both regions nationalist sentiment supported unification. The 1848 revolutionaries in Germany tried to unify through negotiation, but failed. Then between 1864 and 1871, Prussia under prime minister Otto Bismarck forged the German Empire through a combination of war and diplomacy. In Italy, the 1848 revolts against foreign rule brought democratic reforms and inspired the movement known as the Risorgimento (resurgence), which sought to unite Italy and reclaim the leading role it played in Roman antiquity and the Renaissance. Unification came in 1859–61: after the armies of Sardinia expelled Austrian rulers from northern Italy and conquered most of the papal states in central Italy, revolutionaries under Giuseppe Garibaldi overthrew the Bourbon monarchy in Sicily and southern Italy and then acknowledged the king of Sardinia, Victor Emmanuel II, as king of united Italy.

Cultural nationalism

Literature, music, and the other arts played important roles in promoting nationalism, and in turn nationalism had a profound influence on the arts (see sidebar, p. 682). In both Germany and Italy, cultural nationalism—teaching a national language in the schools rather than local dialects, creating national newspapers and journals, and cultivating a national identity through the arts—was crucial in forging a new nation. By contrast, in Austria-Hungary, cultural nationalism worked against political unity, for the empire encompassed ethnic Germans, Czechs, Slovaks, Poles, Hungarians, Romanians, Serbs, Croats, Slovenians, and Italians, and those promoting independence for their people could buttress their case by speaking their own language, emphasizing their distinctive traditions, and creating nationalist art and music.

Other themes
in the arts
Nationalism was not the only common theme in the arts. There was a strong tradition of *realism* in art and literature. Novels by Charles Dickens, Gustave Flaubert, and Feodor Dostoevsky; plays by Henrik Ibsen; and paintings and illustrations by Honoré Daumier and Gustave Courbet all showed the real suffering of the poor and the hypocrisies of the political and economic

MUSIC IN CONTEXT

NATIONALISM AND EXOTICISM

Nationalism became a kind of religion in the nineteenth century, in both political and cultural realms. In music, nationalism meant that some composers cultivated melodic and harmonic styles or chose subjects that carried associations with their own ethnic group. Sometimes this involved using native folk songs and dances or imitating their musical characteristics, but composers also invented "national" styles by introducing novel sounds or by deliberately shunning the conventions of the common international musical language. In a similar way, artists and architects looked to native handicrafts, ornamentation, and building styles to develop a distinctive national style, as in the onion domes and intricate decoration on the Russian church shown in Figure 27.2.

The search for an independent native voice was especially keen in Russia and eastern Europe, where the dominance of Austro-German instrumental music and Italian opera was felt as a threat to homegrown musical creativity.

For many, composing in a recognizably national style was a sign of authenticity. Norwegian composer Edvard Grieg insisted that "the spirit of my native land, which has long found a voice in the traditional songs of its people, is a living presence in all I give forth."

Many composers also wrote music associated with a nation or region other than their own, as when French and Russian composers wrote music on Spanish or Asian topics. Such evocation of a distant land or foreign culture was called *exoticism*. Some works borrowed actual melodies or stylistic features, but authenticity was not required. More important was creating a sense of difference that combined strangeness and allure.

Musical exoticism has a long history. In the eighteenth century, Rameau's opera-ballet *Les indes galantes* (see chapter 18) featured scenes from Asia and the New World, and Turkish-style sounds and instruments were all the rage in the late 1700s (see chapter 22). By the nineteenth century, exoticism reached new heights, especially in opera, and Puccini's operas *Madama Butterfly* (set in Japan) and *Turandot* (set in China) carried the tradition into the twentieth century.

Figure 27.2: Church of the Resurrection in St. Petersburg, built 1883–1907.

elite. There were also escapes from modern city life through exoticism, fantasy, and the distant past in works by Pre-Raphaelites such as English poet and painter Dante Gabriel Rossetti, or enjoyment of the outdoors in paintings by Claude Monet, John Singer Sargent, and other impressionists.

OPERA

Throughout the later nineteenth century, opera became increasingly associated with nationalism as an ideology, whether intentionally or by circumstance. But just as many composers blended traditions.

Rise of the operatic repertory

Especially significant was a growing tendency to stage operas that had already been successful rather than gambling on new works. Gradually a core repertory emerged, varying somewhat in each country, and the number of new operas produced each year declined. As a result, composers took longer to write each opera; instead of composing two or more each year and being paid only for the first production of each, as Rossini and Donizetti had done, composers could take years to compose an opera, hoping to earn royalties from productions around the globe. Sticking to conventions became less important than creating something original that would stand out against the competition.

Other changes

As the audience for opera grew, so did the performing spaces. Orchestras became larger and louder, and singers now needed more powerful and intense voices to be heard, rather than the flexibility prized in earlier generations. Naturally, composers adapted to the new type of singer, writing melodies that were more syllabic and less ornamented. Perhaps seeking to contribute something new to the repertory, composers set ever more varied plots; greater realism in many operas, focusing on the private emotional lives of common people, was balanced by stories based on exoticism, fantasy, legend, fairy tales, or the supernatural. New genres of light opera emerged, including **opera bouffe** in France, **operetta** in Austria, England, and the United States, and *zarzuela* in Spain. Late in the century, electric lighting replaced gas, allowing new lighting effects. When electricity made it possible to dim the house lights almost completely, the traditional convivial atmosphere of opera, in which conversation was acceptable between and even during arias, was gradually replaced by reverent silence. These changes, especially the creation of the permanent repertory, made the world of opera in the late nineteenth century very similar to what it is today.

GIUSEPPE VERDI

Giuseppe Verdi (1813–1901; see biography and Figure 27.3) was the dominant figure in Italian music for the fifty years after Donizetti. The first of his twenty-six operas was produced in 1839 when he was twenty-six, the last in 1893 when he was eighty.

GIUSEPPE VERDI (1813–1901)

Verdi's music has been called the epitome of Romantic drama and passion. He worked within the traditions of his predecessors but during his long life continually refined his techniques.

The son of an innkeeper in a village near Busseto in northern Italy, Verdi studied music as a child, and by age nine was a church organist. After studying privately in Milan, he returned home and took a position as music director in Busseto, where he married Margherita Barezzi in 1836. Their two children died in infancy before her own early death in 1840, devastating events to Verdi.

He returned to Milan, pouring himself into his music and aiming for a career composing operas. The success of his first, *Oberto*, won him a contract for three more operas. One of those, *Nabucco* (1842), was a triumph and launched Verdi as a star composer. The next eleven years were the busiest of his career, and he wrote one or two new operas each year for houses in Milan, Venice, Rome, Naples, Florence, London, Paris, and Trieste. This period culminated in *Rigoletto* (1851), *Il trovatore* (1853), and *La traviata* (1853), which quickly became part of the permanent opera repertory.

During these years he met soprano Giuseppina Strepponi, who became his life partner. After spending most of 1847–49 in Paris, he acquired land near Busseto and moved back there with Strepponi, where he and his lover put up with much gossip about their unsanctioned union. In 1851, they settled on a nearby farm, where they lived for the rest of their lives, with frequent sojourns to Paris, Milan, and other cities. They married in secret in 1859.

After *La traviata*, Verdi slowed his production of new operas, writing only six in

Figure 27.3: Giuseppe Verdi at seventy-two, in a pastel portrait by Giovanni Boldoni.

the sixteen years from *Les vêpres siciliennes* (1855) to *Aida* (1871). Then he retired from the stage, focusing on his farm and living off royalties from his music, until his publisher Giulio Ricordi persuaded him to write two last operas, *Otello* (1887) and *Falstaff* (1893). Strepponi died in 1897, and Verdi followed in early 1901. A month later, escorted by a procession of thousands of admirers, his remains—along with Strepponi's—were interred in Milan at the home for retired musicians he had helped to found. According to his wishes, the funeral was a very quiet affair, "without music or singing."

MAJOR WORKS: *26 operas, including* Nabucco, Macbeth, Luisa Miller, Rigoletto, Il trovatore, La traviata, Les vêpres siciliennes, Simon Boccanegra, Un ballo in maschera, La forza del destino, Don Carlos, Aida, Otello, *and* Falstaff; *Requiem and other Latin sacred choral works*

Although Verdi supported and became identified with the Italian Risorgimento, overt nationalism was not a component of his operas. But a few of his early operas contain choruses that some heard as thinly disguised appeals against foreign domination, and by 1859, his name had become a patriotic symbol and rallying cry: "Viva Verdi!" to Italian patriots stood for "**Viva** Vittorio **E**manuele **R**e **d**'**I**talia!"—Long live Victor Emmanuel, king of Italy.

Nationalism

APPROACH TO OPERA

The secret to Verdi's popularity was his ability to capture character, feeling, and situation in memorable melodies that sound both fresh and familiar. Many use a simple form such as AABA, making them easy to follow, and combine regular phrasing and plain harmony with an intriguing rhythmic and melodic motive that catches the listener's attention. So aware was Verdi of the appeal of his melodies that he strove to keep a new opera's best tunes from being leaked to the public before the premiere. But his craft did not stop at melody; he had strict training in harmony and counterpoint, a wide knowledge of the music of his predecessors, and a keen ear for orchestration that adds color and atmosphere without overpowering the singers.

Verdi usually chose the opera's subject himself. He preferred stories that had succeeded as spoken dramas, drawing on plays by authors like Shakespeare, Friedrich Schiller, and Victor Hugo. He expected fast action, striking contrasts, unusual characters, and strong emotional situations from his librettos.

Librettos

STYLE

Verdi's early operas built on the conventions of Rossini, Bellini, and especially Donizetti. His first great success was *Nabucco* (Milan, 1842), on the biblical story of Nebuchadnezzar; the unison chorus *Va pensiero* later became an emblem of Italian opposition to foreign oppression. *Luisa Miller* (Naples, 1849) marked a turn toward finer psychological portrayal of character. Musical characterization, dramatic unity, and melodic invention unite in *Rigoletto* (Venice, 1851), in which the central characters are delineated by their styles of singing and relation to musical convention. This and the next two operas, *Il trovatore* (The Troubadour; Rome, 1853) and *La traviata* (The Fallen Woman; Venice, 1853), reach new heights of dramatic compression and have remained among the most popular operas ever composed. Verdi often uses reminiscence motives, as Donizetti had done in *Lucia di Lammermoor*, recalling at crucial points in the drama distinctive themes from earlier scenes in order to reinforce connections and deepen the dramatic impact. In both *Il trovatore* and *La traviata*, Verdi replaced the overture with a briefer prelude that sets the scene and introduces important themes to come.

Many features of Verdi's mature works are embodied in *La traviata*. The resources he commanded are evident in the scene of the final act in which Violetta, the "fallen woman" of the title, and her lover Alfredo reconcile after she had left him to save his family's reputation (NAWM 127). The scene follows the structure Rossini had standardized for duets—scena (recitative), tempo

La traviata

CD 9|69   CD 5|30

d'attacco (opening section), slow cantabile, tempo di mezzo (contrasting dramatic section), and fast cabaletta—yet each element is in a new style characteristic of Verdi. Instead of recitative punctuated by the orchestra, the scena presents a complete musical texture in the orchestra, a skipping melody in four-measure phrases, over which Violetta and her maid engage in recitative-like dialogue. When Alfredo enters, their conversation is set not as recitative but as a tuneful song (the tempo d'attacco) that alternates phrases between them. The following cantabile, in which Alfredo and Violetta look forward to life together as she recovers her health, is almost as simple and direct as a popular song, both in its form (AABB with coda) and in the tunefulness of its A section, shown in Example 27.1. The tempo di mezzo offers a series of startling contrasts in mood and style, as Violetta collapses, insists she is well, collapses again, and finally despairs that her illness will overtake her just as happiness is so near. These emotions intensify in the cabaletta, where Violetta bewails her ironic misfortune and Alfredo begs her to calm herself. This final section follows a common form for Verdi, AABA' with coda, which allows him to introduce contrast and end on an emotional climax. Throughout the scene, Verdi takes every opportunity for stark contrasts, strong emotions, and catchy melodies while keeping the action moving.

Example 27.1: Excerpt from Verdi's La traviata, *Act IV*

Paris, my dear, we shall forsake; our life, united, we shall pass together.

LATER OPERAS

Now famous and well off, Verdi could afford to work even more carefully, writing only six new operas in the next two decades. In these operas, the action is more continuous; solos, ensembles, and choruses are more freely combined; harmonies become more daring; and the orchestra is treated with great originality. Verdi still used traditional forms but often reshaped them to suit the dramatic situation. An important influence was French grand opera, especially Meyerbeer. Verdi wrote *Les vêpres siciliennes* (The Sicilian Vespers, 1855) as a grand opera, for Paris, to a libretto by Meyerbeer's collaborator Eugène Scribe, blending French and Italian elements. He introduced comic roles in *Un ballo in maschera* (A Masked Ball; Rome, 1859), which borrows elements of opéra comique. And in *Aida* (1871), commissioned for the

Figure 27.4: The title character of Verdi's Falstaff—*adventurer, swindler, and rogue—as pictured by Giuseppe d'Amato on the cover of a special number of* L'Illustrazione Italiana *issued for the opera's premiere in 1893.*

Cairo opera, Verdi treated an Egyptian subject, which gave him the opportunity to introduce exotic color and spectacle.

Verdi wrote only two more operas after *Aida*, highly individual master-pieces based on plays by his favorite dramatist, Shakespeare. Both feature librettos by poet and composer Arrigo Boito (1842–1918).

Otello *and* Falstaff

In 1879, Verdi's publisher Giulio Ricordi, eager for another opera, pro-posed adapting Shakespeare's *Othello*. Verdi began *Otello* in 1884, and it was finally produced in Milan in 1887. Like Donizetti before him, Verdi often sought continuity in music and action, and here he realized it most com-pletely, through unifying motives in the orchestra and in the unbroken flow of music within each act. The traditional scheme of declamatory and lyrical solos, duets, ensembles, and choruses is still present, but the units are arranged in larger scene-complexes, and the orchestra develops themes in a more symphonic manner, often independent of the voices.

Two years after the premiere of *Otello*, Boito suggested an opera on scenes from Shakespeare's *The Merry Wives of Windsor* and *Henry IV* involving the character Falstaff, shown in Figure 27.4. If *Otello* was the consummation of Italian tragic opera, *Falstaff* (Milan, 1893) holds a parallel place in comic opera. While Verdi reshaped dramatic lyrical melody for *Otello*, for *Falstaff* he transformed that characteristic element of opera buffa, the ensemble. Carried along over a nimble, endlessly varied orchestral background, the comedy speeds to its climaxes in the finales of the second and third acts, culminating in a fugue for the entire cast on the words "All the world's a joke. We are all born fools."

VERDI'S RECEPTION

Verdi experienced phenomenal success in his own lifetime. By the 1850s, his operas were performed more often than those of any other Italian composer. In the twentieth century, even his operas that had not been performed in decades were revived, and in recent decades there have been more operas in the permanent repertory by Verdi than by any other composer.

LATER ITALIAN COMPOSERS

Verdi was such a central figure that later Italian opera composers struggled to escape his shadow. As opera houses increasingly performed works already in the repertory rather than new ones, few operas by composers after Verdi found a permanent place there.

Verismo   Two operas that did enter the repertory are *Cavalleria rusticana* (Rustic Chivalry, 1890) by Pietro Mascagni (1863–1945) and *I Pagliacci* (The Clowns, 1892) by Ruggero Leoncavallo (1858–1919), often paired with each other in performance. Both are examples of **verismo** (from Italian *vero*, "true"), an operatic parallel to realism in literature. Instead of treating historical figures or faraway places, verismo presents everyday people, especially the lower classes, in familiar situations, often depicting events that are brutal or sordid. Though short-lived, verismo had parallels or repercussions in France and Germany, and the veristic impulse lives on in television and movie dramas.

GIACOMO PUCCINI

The most successful Italian opera composer after Verdi was Giacomo Puccini (1858–1924). The son of a church organist and composer, he was slated to follow in his father's footsteps but chose instead to focus on opera. After studying at the conservatory in Milan, Puccini attracted attention with his first opera in 1884. His third opera, *Manon Lescaut* (1893), catapulted him to international fame and established him as one of the rising stars of his generation.

Puccini created a highly individual personal style by blending Verdi's focus on vocal melody with elements of Wagner's approach (see below), notably the use of recurring melodies or *leitmotives*, less reliance on conventional operatic forms, and a greater role for the orchestra in creating musical continuity. Puccini often juxtaposed different styles and harmonic worlds in order to suggest his contrasting characters, such as impoverished artists and other residents of the Parisian Latin Quarter in *La bohème* (1896); the idealistic singer Tosca and the evil Scarpia in *Tosca* (1900); a Japanese woman and her American lover in *Madama Butterfly* (1904); or various levels of ancient Chinese society in *Turandot* (1926).

In Puccini's operas, arias, choruses, and ensembles are usually part of a continuous flow rather than set off as independent numbers. The standard scene structure pioneered by Rossini and observed in most of Verdi's operas is replaced by a fluid succession of sections in different tempos and characters. Musical ideas grow out of the dramatic action, blurring the distinction between recitative and aria. Example 27.2 shows a key moment in *La bohème*, after the poet Rodolfo, having just met Mimi, touches her hand for the first time. The melody begins on a single note, as if in recitative, then blossoms in a series of short phrases, each initiated by a large upward leap; simple and understated, it conveys Rodolfo's surging emotions under a placid exterior. The accompaniment is also simple, with a violin melody above offbeat pulsations, yet the harmony never entirely comes to rest, as each tonic chord is colored either by an added sixth on B♭ (measures 2, 5, and 9) or by a bass note on the dominant (measures 2 and 6). The lyrical melody becomes a recurring theme, yet it does not stand apart as a separate aria. Through these very simple means, Puccini responds directly to the text and the situation. His melody-centered, colorful, and emotionally direct style has won his operas a permanent place in the repertory and has exercised a strong influence on scoring for film and television.

Example 27.2: From Puccini, La bohème, *Act I*

What a frozen little hand! Let me warm it up. What's the use of searching [for your key]?
In the dark we won't find it.

RICHARD WAGNER

The outstanding composer of German opera, and one of the crucial figures in nineteenth-century culture, was Richard Wagner (1813–1883; see biography and Figure 27.5). Several of his ideas had an enormous impact on all of the arts, notably his belief in the interrelationships between the arts and his view of art as a kind of religion. Within music, his significance is threefold: he brought German Romantic opera to a new height; he created what he considered a new genre, the **music drama**; and in his late works he developed a rich chromatic idiom that influenced composers to attenuate and even abandon tonality.

RICHARD WAGNER (1813–1883)

Wagner was one of the most influential musicians of all time. His emphasis on music as the servant of drama, his use of leitmotives as an organizing principle, and his chromatic harmonies had a profound and far-reaching impact on many later composers.

He was born in Leipzig, Germany, the ninth child of a police actuary. Soon after Richard's birth his father died, and his mother married Ludwig Geyer, an actor and playwright whom Wagner suspected not only was his real father but also might have been Jewish. At the age of fifteen, Wagner attended a performance of Beethoven's Ninth Symphony, which he claimed had a profound effect on him. He studied music in Dresden and Leipzig, and his student works include piano pieces, overtures, and a symphony that show a firm grasp of compositional technique and a devotion to Beethoven.

In the early 1830s, Wagner began writing operas and held positions with regional opera companies in southern Germany and Latvia. By then, he had met the soprano Minna Planer, whom he married in 1836.

Figure 27.5: Richard Wagner in 1867.

They spent 1839–42 in Paris, where Wagner worked as a music journalist while trying to secure performances for his operas, with no success despite support from Meyerbeer. In 1842, Wagner moved back to Dresden, where his *Rienzi* was a great success, followed by *Der fliegende Holländer* in early 1843. That year he was appointed second Kapellmeister for the king of Saxony in

Dresden, directing the opera, conducting the orchestra, and composing for occasions at court.

Wagner supported the 1848–49 insurrection and had to flee Germany after a warrant was issued for his arrest. He settled in Switzerland, where he wrote his most important essays and began his massive cycle of four music dramas, *Der Ring des Nibelungen*. He was supported by a stipend from two wealthy female patrons. After several years of travel, in 1864 he found a new patron in the young King Ludwig II of Bavaria, who paid his debts, granted him an annual pension, and sponsored the production of his operas *Tristan und Isolde* and *Die Meistersinger* and the first two operas in the *Ring* cycle.

Although Wagner would stay married to Minna until her death in 1866, he maintained relationships with numerous other women. After an affair with Mathilde Wesendonck—he set five of her poems for his *Wesendonck-Lieder*—he formed a new union with Cosima von Bülow, daughter of Liszt and wife of the conductor Hans von Bülow. He had three children with her, but Cosima did not marry him until 1870, after her marriage to von Bülow was annulled.

Wagner dreamed of a permanent festival of his operas, and in 1872 he began to build the festival theater at Bayreuth. The first festival was held in 1876, with the premiere of the complete *Ring* cycle, and the second in 1882, with performances of his last opera, *Parsifal*. He died the next year of a heart attack and was buried at his beloved Bayreuth.

MAJOR WORKS: *13 operas*, notably Der fliegende Holländer, Tannhäuser, Lohengrin, *the four-opera cycle* Der Ring des Nibelungen (Das Rheingold, Die Walküre, Siegfried, Götterdämmerung), Tristan und Isolde, Die Meistersinger von Nürnberg, *and* Parsifal

WRITINGS

For Wagner, the function of music was to serve dramatic expression. He presented his ideas in a series of essays, including *The Artwork of the Future* (1850) and *Opera and Drama* (1851, revised 1868). He believed that Beethoven had done everything that could be done in instrumental music and had shown in his Ninth Symphony the path to the future by joining music to words (see Source Reading). Wagner saw himself—not the composers of symphonies and quartets—as Beethoven's true successor.

Wagner believed in the absolute oneness of drama and music—that the two are organically connected expressions of a single dramatic idea. Poetry, scenic design, staging, action, and music work together to form what he called a **Gesamtkunstwerk** (total or collective artwork). The orchestra conveys the inner aspect of the drama, while the sung words articulate the outer aspect— the events and situations that further the action. The orchestral web is the chief factor in the music, and the vocal lines are part of the musical texture. This conception is basic to the definition of music drama: in a traditional opera, the voices lead and the orchestra supports, punctuates, and comments; in a music drama, the dramatic thread is in the music itself, led by the orchestra, and the voices give it definition and precision through words.

Gesamtkunstwerk

Anti-Semitism   Wagner's published writings address not only music but also literature, drama, and even political and moral topics. He believed that music drama could help reform society and that art should not be undertaken for profit. He was a musical and philosophical nationalist, claiming that German art was pure, spiritual, and profound, as opposed to the superficiality of Italian and French music. Most controversial is his abhorrent anti-Semitic tract *Das Judentum in der Musik* (Jewishness in Music), which appeared under a pseudonym in 1850 and under Wagner's name in 1869. What drove him to write this essay, he explained to Liszt, was his antipathy toward Meyerbeer, whose

SOURCE READING

THE ARTWORK OF THE FUTURE

In The Artwork of the Future *(1850), Richard Wagner argued that Beethoven strove to discover the full potential of music and found it in his Ninth Symphony by rooting his music in the* word. *Thus for Wagner purely instrumental music after Beethoven was sterile ("the* last *symphony had already been* written"), *and only the artwork that combined all the arts was worthwhile.*

———— • ————

This *last symphony* of Beethoven's is the redemption of music out of its own element as a *universal art.* It is the *human* gospel of the art of the future. Beyond it there can be no *progress,* for there can follow on it immediately only the completed artwork of the future, *the universal drama,* to which Beethoven has forged for us the artistic key.

Thus from within itself music accomplished what no one of the other arts was capable of in isolation. Each of these arts, in its barren independence, helped itself only by taking and egoistic borrowing; not one was capable of being *itself* and of weaving from within itself the all-uniting bond. The art of tone, by being wholly *itself* and by moving from within its own primeval element, attained strength for the most tremendous and most generous of all self-sacrifices—that of self-control, indeed of self-denial—thus to offer to its sister arts a redeeming hand. . . .

Man as artist can be fully satisfied only in the union of all the art varieties in the *collective* artwork [*Gesamtkunstwerk*]; in every *individualization* of his artistic capacities he is *unfree,* not wholly that which he can be; in the collective artwork he is *free,* wholly that which he can be.

The *true* aim of art is accordingly *all-embracing;* everyone animated by the true artistic impulse seeks to attain, through the full development of his particular capacity, not the glorification of *this particular capacity,* but the glorification *in art of mankind in general.*

The highest collective artwork is the *drama;* it is present in its *ultimate completeness* only when *each art variety, in its ultimate completeness,* is present in it.

True drama can be conceived only as resulting from the *collective impulse of all the arts* to communicate in the most immediate way with a *collective public;* each individual art variety can reveal itself as *fully understandable* to this collective public only through collective communication, together with the other art varieties, in the drama, for the aim of each individual art variety is fully attained only in the mutually understanding and understandable cooperation of all the art varieties.

From *Das Kunstwerk der Zukunft: Sämtliche Schriften und Dichtungen,* 6th ed. (Leipzig, 1912–14). Translation by Oliver Strunk, in SR 153 (6:6), pp. 1108–9 and 1112.

music he once admired and who had used his influence to help Wagner. But Wagner turned against the elder composer when critics wrote how much Meyerbeer influenced his own music. Seeking to establish his independence, Wagner attacked Meyerbeer's music, arguing that it was weak because he was Jewish and therefore lacked national roots, without which a composer could not have an authentic style. Wagner implied that the same problem affected Mendelssohn, whom he had revered in his younger days, despite Mendelssohn's conversion to Christianity. In this essay, Wagner drew on and strengthened an anti-Semitic strain in German culture, while attempting to obscure his deep debt to both Meyerbeer and Mendelssohn.

OPERAS

Before formulating his conception of music drama, Wagner composed several operas that drew directly on his predecessors. His first triumph came with *Rienzi*, a five-act grand opera in the Meyerbeer mold, performed at Dresden in 1842. The following year Dresden saw a production of *Der fliegende Holländer* (The Flying Dutchman), a Romantic opera in the tradition of Weber.

Characteristics that became typical of Wagner's later music were established in *The Flying Dutchman*. The libretto—written, like those of all his operas, by the composer himself—is based on a Germanic legend, and the hero is redeemed through the unselfish love of a heroine (in this case, Senta), a common theme in Romantic literature as well as for Wagner. Themes from Senta's ballad, the central number of the opera, appear in the overture and recur throughout the opera, functioning like reminiscence motives in Weber, Donizetti, and Verdi.

The Flying Dutchman

In *Tannhäuser* (Dresden, 1845), Wagner again adapted a Germanic legend about sin and redemption. For Tannhäuser's narrative in Act III, Wagner introduced a new kind of flexible, semi-declamatory vocal line that became his normal method of setting text. *Lohengrin*, first performed under Liszt's direction at Weimar in 1850, embodies several other elements that foreshadow the music dramas that followed. In this work, Wagner's treatment of medieval legend and German folklore is both moralizing and symbolic, suffused with nationalism while aspiring to universality. Wagner's new style of declamatory melody appears more often, and the technique of recurring themes is further developed.

Tannhäuser *and* Lohengrin

MUSIC DRAMAS

From 1848 to 1852, around the time he was formulating and publishing his ideas on music drama, Wagner wrote the verse librettos for a cycle of four dramas with the collective title *Der Ring des Nibelungen* (The Ring of the Nibelungs). The music of the first two—*Das Rheingold* (The Rhine Gold) and *Die Walküre* (The Valkyrie)—and part of the third, *Siegfried*, was finished by 1857, and the entire cycle was completed with *Götterdämmerung* (The Twilight of the Gods) in 1874. The first complete performance took place two

Der Ring des Nibelungen

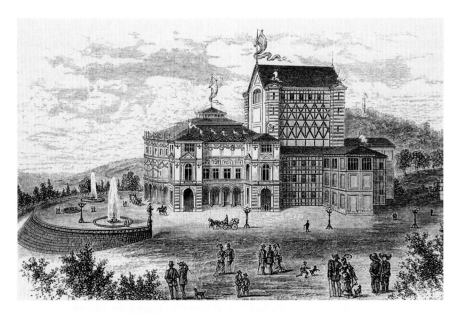

Figure 27.6: The Bayreuth Festival Theater, designed by Otto Brückwald, incorporated Wagner's ideals for the production of music drama. Here he was able to produce the Ring *cycle in its entirety for the first time in August 1876.* Parsifal *(1882) was written for this theater, which continues to be the stage for the Bayreuth Festival today.*

years later in a theater built in Bayreuth according to Wagner's specifications, shown in Figure 27.6. The four dramas, a kind of German national epic, are woven out of stories from Teutonic and Nordic legends and linked by common characters and musical motives. The cycle is largely about the value of love and people's willingness to abandon it for worldly ends. The "Ring" of the title refers to a ring that the gnome Alberich fashions out of gold he stole from the river Rhine, where it was guarded by three Rhine maidens. In time, the ring is also stolen from Alberich, who puts a curse of misery and death on anyone who wears it. In the course of the four dramas—about nineteen hours of music—the curse is fulfilled and the Rhine maidens reclaim the ring.

Tristan, Meistersinger, *and* Parsifal

During breaks from composing *Siegfried*, Wagner wrote *Tristan und Isolde* (1857–59), discussed below, and *Die Meistersinger von Nürnberg* (The Meistersingers of Nuremberg, 1862–67). His final work was *Parsifal* (1882), which was based on the legend of the Holy Grail and used the opposition between diatonic and chromatic music to suggest the polarity of redemption and corruption.

The Leitmotiv

Each music drama—and indeed the entire *Ring* cycle as a group—is organized around numerous themes and motives that are each associated with a particular person, thing, emotion, or idea. Analysts of Wagner's music dramas have called such a theme or motive a **Leitmotiv** (leading motive), often rendered as *leitmotif* or *leitmotive* in English. The association is established by sounding the leitmotive (usually in the orchestra) at the first appearance or mention of the subject, and by its repetition during subsequent appearances or citations. Often the significance of a leitmotive can be recognized from the words to which it is first sung. Thus the leitmotive is a musical label, but it becomes more than that through its symphonic treatment in the music drama: it accumulates significance as it recurs in new contexts; it may recall an object in situations where the object itself is not present; it may be varied, developed, or transformed as the plot develops; similar motives may suggest a connection between the objects to which they refer, especially if one leitmotive morphs into another; motives may be contrapuntally combined; and, through their repetition, motives unify a scene or opera as recurrent themes unify a symphony. In principle, there is a complete correspondence between the symphonic web of leitmotives and the dramatic web of the action, though at times motives seem to appear more for musical than dramatic reasons.

Wagner's idea of music drama and the use of leitmotives can be illustrated through *Tristan und Isolde.* The story—of a secret love, brought about by a love potion, that leads to the lovers' death—comes from a thirteenth-century romance by Gottfried von Strassburg. Example 27.3 shows several leitmotives in the order they appear in the last section of Act 1, scene 5 (NAWM 128), in which Tristan and Isolde drink the potion and fall in love. The text sung at each leitmotive's most characteristic appearance is given along with the motive.

Leitmotives in Tristan und Isolde

[CD 9|78]   [CD 5|39]

In Wagner's hands, leitmotives differ from the use of reminiscence motives by Weber, Verdi, and his own earlier operas. His leitmotives are for the most part short, concentrated, and intended to characterize their subject at various levels of meaning. The first motive of Example 27.3d, for example, is identified with the longing that Tristan and Isolde feel for each other, now intensified by the love potion. At the same time, the harmonic progression from the dominant seventh in A minor to the chord on the sixth degree—a deceptive-cadence pattern first heard in the prelude—symbolizes the very essence of the drama, a love doomed to remain unfulfilled. Leitmotives are often characterized by particular instruments, registers, harmonies, or keys, which may also suggest meanings or associations.

A more important difference is that Wagner's leitmotives are the basic musical material of the score. He uses them not once in a while but constantly, in intimate alliance with every step of the action. They also serve as elements for forming melodies, replacing the four-square phrases set off by pauses and cadences of earlier composers. The leitmotives, their development, their restatements and variants, and the connective tissue linking these, form the stuff of "musical prose" Wagner used to replace the "poetic" rhythms of symmetrical phrases. The impression of "endless melody" observed by many commentators results from the continuity of line, unbroken by the stops and restarts of Classic musical syntax.

Act I, scene 5, of *Tristan* demonstrates the intertwining of action, scenery, and music. The ship, sails, lines, Isolde's quarters, and nearby shore objectify Tristan's assigned mission, to deliver the reluctant Isolde to King Mark as his bride. As the crew drops anchor and hails the king on shore (Example 27.3g), Tristan and Isolde, who are oblivious to the excitement around them, succumb to the love potion her companion Brangäne substituted for the poison Isolde had demanded. The chorus's realistic shouts interrupt the sometimes speechlike, sometimes lyrical and passionate declamation of Tristan and

Example 27.3: Leitmotives from Wagner's Tristan und Isolde, *Act I, scene 5*

Isolde. The large orchestra maintains continuity, elaborating motives that il-lustrate the content of the speech or the underlying emotions and associa-tions. Thus action, dialogue, musical scene-painting, and lyrical expression are not parceled out to different moments, as in traditional opera, but all constantly mingle and reinforce one another.

Some details will illustrate how the motives acquire and convey meaning. As Isolde prepares to drink the potion, she sings "Ich trink' sie dir!" (I drink to you) to a motive of a rising sixth and descending semitones (Example 27.3b), from then on associated with the love potion. The orchestra takes up the motive and provides a new twist through ascending semitones (Example 27.3c), suggesting mutual longing. The lovers stand motionless as the orchestra repeats their motive of longing (Example 27.3d), with the deceptive resolution suggesting the impossibility of fulfillment. Now a new melody is developed as they call to each other, the harmony groping forward (Example 27.3e). The words "Sehnender Minne" (passionate love), which they pronounce together, identify a new motive in the orchestra (Example 27.3f), which is churned through a series of rising sequences. The celebratory music hailing the king (Example 27.3g) competes for attention with the rapture of the lovers until the curtain falls at the end of Act I. Throughout, the open-ended leitmotives allow Wagner to string them together in whatever sequence makes sense to convey the actions and emotions of the drama, while their constant variation conveys an impression of the developing dramatic situation and the fluid feelings of the characters.

WAGNERIAN HARMONY

In *Tristan*, complex chromatic alterations of chords, constant shifting of key, telescoping of resolutions, and blurring of progressions by means of suspensions and other nonchord tones all combine to produce a novel, ambiguous kind of tonality that expresses yearning and unfulfilled desire by evoking yet evading traditional harmonic expectations.

Several of these traits are evident in Example 27.3. The motive in Example 27.3b closes on a half-diminished seventh chord on F, a chromatic alteration of the seventh chord on the second degree of Eb major. Instead of cadencing in that key, Wagner respells the chord as F–B–D♯–G♯ (Example 27.3c), the famous "Tristan chord" that is the first chord in the opera, and treats it as an augmented sixth chord in A minor (F–B–D♯–A) with a very long chromatic appoggiatura on G♯. Thus a chord that does not occur naturally in either key, Eb major or A minor, is used to pivot between them. The resolution to the dominant seventh of A minor is inflected by a piquant chromatic neighbor (A♯), so that we hear four dissonant sonorities in a row, each of which "resolves" the previous one without itself resolving to consonance. The passage in Example 27.3d includes blistering appoggiaturas on the first two chords (E♯ over E, B over F and C), suggesting a melody that yearns to struggle free of its harmonic context, and a sequence of chords that evades cadences on A minor, G major, and C major before settling temporarily on D minor. At other times, as in Example 27.3f, the dissonances are mostly ornamental, adding sensuous inflections to a relatively stable passage in a major key.

Contrasts between chromatic and diatonic music (as here between Examples 27.3c and 27.3g) and between tonally stable and unstable passages were basic elements of Wagner's expressive palette. Such oppositions have long histories, stretching back to the madrigals of the mid- to late-sixteenth century. Wagner's formulation was particularly powerful and has had an enduring influence on later opera and on film and television scores.

WAGNER'S INFLUENCE

Wagner's ideas and music were enormously influential. More has been written about Wagner than about any other musician. His writings, and the success of his music dramas, regained for dramatic and representational music the prestige that some had argued belonged to absolute music alone. His ideal of opera as a drama with music, words, staging, and action all intimately linked affected virtually all later opera. Almost as important was his method of minimizing divisions within an act and charging the orchestra with maintaining continuity by developing pregnant musical motives while the voices sang in free, arioso lines rather than in the balanced phrases of the traditional aria. Wagner was a master of orchestral color, and here also his example bore fruit. Many musicians became Wagnerians, while others kept their distance or opposed his ideas, but few escaped his influence.

Wagner also had an impact on the other arts and on culture at large. Paul Verlaine, Stéphane Mallarmé, and other poets associated with the symbolist movement drew on Wagner's use of leitmotives and symbols, an influence that carried over to many writers of the early twentieth century. Visual artists including Gustav Klimt and Aubrey Beardsley transferred to their realm Wagner's interest in legends and symbols, and his re-creations of national legends inspired imitators everywhere.

Regrettably, his anti-Semitic writings and nationalist mythologizing also found supporters. The National Socialist (Nazi) movement in Germany appropriated Wagner's music as a symbol of the best of German culture. Several critics have found anti-Semitic undercurrents in the operas themselves, and for decades his music was not welcome in Israel. Such controversies helped to dim the cult of Wagnerism, but his music remains pervasive and influential.

FRANCE

In France, no one figure was as dominant as Verdi and Wagner were in their respective lands, but Paris remained the main center for the production of new works. State subsidies for the main opera houses brought with them occasional attempts to dictate policy, including an insistence on performing new works by French composers. Although these efforts to support French music have nationalist origins, relatively few operas had overtly nationalist plots.

Particularly notable is the variety of offerings in the Parisian musical theaters, ranging from old genres to new ones and from serious to light entertainment.

GRAND OPERA, BALLET, AND LYRIC OPERA

Grand opera continued its prominence through Meyerbeer's *L'Africaine* (1865) and Verdi's *Don Carlos* (1867)—written for the Paris Opéra—then began to fade in importance and to blend with other types of serious opera.

But ballet, long a part of grand opera, grew in popularity as an independent art. The leading ballet composer was Leo Delibes (1836–1891), whose *Coppélia* (1870) and *Sylvia* (1876) were premiered at the Opéra and became standards of the ballet repertoire.

The romantic type of opéra comique developed into a genre that might best be termed **lyric opera**, after the Théâtre Lyrique founded in 1851. Lyric opera lies somewhere between light opéra comique and grand opera. Like opéra comique, its main appeal is through melody. The subject matter is usually romantic drama or fantasy, and the scale is larger than that of the opéra comique, although not so huge as that of the typical grand opera.

The most famous lyric opera is *Faust* by Charles Gounod (1818–1893), the most frequently performed opera in the last third of the nineteenth century. First staged at the Théâtre Lyrique in 1859 as an opéra comique (that is, with spoken dialogue), it was later arranged by the composer in its now familiar form with recitatives. The result is a well-proportioned work in an elegant lyric style, with melodies that balance Classic clarity with Romantic expressivity.

Gounod's Faust

Other popular lyric operas include Gounod's *Roméo et Juliette* (1867) and the many successful operas of Jules Massenet (1842–1912)—*Manon* (1884), *Werther* (1892), and *Thaïs* (1894).Their suave, sensuous, and often sentimental melodies are characteristic of the French style, along with unobtrusive harmonies and a rich orchestral palette.

EXOTICISM

Several operas exploited an interest in exoticism, including *The Pearl Fishers* (1863) by Georges Bizet (1838–1875), set in ancient Ceylon; the biblical opera *Samson et Dalila* (1877) by Camille Saint-Saëns (1835–1921); and Delibes's *Lakmé* (1883), on the doomed relationship between an Indian priestess of Brahma and an officer in the English army occupying India.

Exoticism and realism combine in Bizet's *Carmen*, premiered at the Opéra-Comique in 1875. It was set not in Asia but in Spain, considered as exotic by Parisians despite its proximity. Originally classified as an opéra comique (although Bizet never called it that) because it contained spoken dialogue (later set in recitative), it was a stark, realistic drama ending with a tragic murder. That such an opera could be called "comique" shows that the distinction between opera and opéra comique had become a mere technicality.

The Spanish flavor was embodied especially in the character of Carmen, shown in Figure 27.7 as portrayed by the singer who created the role. Carmen is a Gypsy who works in a cigarette factory and lives only for pleasures of the moment. Her suggestive costume and behavior, her provocative

Figure 27.7: The first Carmen, Célestine Galli-Marié. Her costume and gestures combined with Bizet's music to evoke her exotic allure as a Spanish Gypsy.

sexuality and language, and Bizet's music all characterize her as outside of normal society, making her both dangerous and enticing. Bizet borrowed three authentic Spanish melodies, including Carmen's famous habanera *L'amour est un oiseau rebelle* (Love is a rebellious bird). But most of the Spanish-sounding music is Bizet's own invention, blending elements associated with Gypsy or Spanish music with the modern French style. As shown in Example 27.4, a motive linked to Carmen's fate emphasizes augmented seconds, considered a trademark of Gypsy music, and a variant of the same motive accompanies Carmen's first entrance. She seduces Don José, an upright army corporal, by singing a seguidilla (NAWM 129), a type of Spanish song in fast triple time. The accompaniment pattern imitates the strumming of a guitar, the vocal melody features melismas and grace notes, and the harmony suggests the Phrygian mode, all features conventionally linked to Spanish music.

CD 10|1   CD 5|47

Example 27.4: Augmented second motives from Bizet's Carmen

a. *Motive associated with Carmen's fate*

b. *Carmen's entrance motive*

The plot provoked outrage among some at the premiere—one critic wrote that Bizet "had sunk to the sewers of society" to create his heroine—but the opera won success and has become one of the most popular of all time.

LIGHTER FARE

Opéra bouffe While the serious theaters were controlled by the government, the **opéra bouffe** could satirize French society more freely. This new genre emerged in the 1850s during the Second Empire and emphasized the smart, witty, and satirical elements of comic opera. Its founder was Jacques Offenbach (1819–1880), who even managed to introduce a can-can dance for the gods in his *Orphée aux enfers* (Orpheus in the Underworld, 1858). His work influenced developments in comic opera in England, Vienna, the United States, and elsewhere (see below). The perennial charm of Offenbach's music owes much to its appealing melody and rhythm, simple textures and harmonies, and conventional formal patterns. But the deceptively naïve quality often clothes a rapier wit, satirizing operatic as well as social conventions.

Paris was also famous for its popular musical theaters. **Cabarets** like Chat Noir (Black Cat, opened 1881) were night clubs that offered serious or comic sketches, dances, songs, and poetry, often with the intent to foster innovation and draw together artists and the public. A **café-concert** joined the food and beverage service of a café with musical entertainment, usually songs on sentimental, comic, or political topics. The Folies-Bergère, Moulin Rouge, and other large music halls offered various kinds of entertainment including **revues,** shows that strung together dances, songs, comedy, and other acts, often united by a common theme. From grand opera to music halls, the range of offerings in Paris was vast, and listeners with broad tastes might sample the Opéra, a cabaret, and the Moulin Rouge, all in the same weekend.

Cabarets and revues

RUSSIA

Having spread across Western Europe in the seventeenth century and to the New World in the early eighteenth, opera finally arrived in Russia in 1731 with a performance in Moscow by a visiting Italian troupe. Five years later a permanent opera company was formed at the Imperial Court in St. Petersburg, and in 1755 it gave the first opera in Russian, using spoken dialogue. But until the nineteenth century, most of the star singers and composers were foreigners, primarily Italians.

RUSSIAN NATIONALISM

When nationalism began to affect Russian artists, opera proved valuable as a genre in which a distinctive Russian identity could be proclaimed through subject matter, set design, costumes, and music. Ironically, while nationalism was a force for unification in Germany and Italy and for liberation struggles in Austria-Hungary, in Russia it was primarily a tool of propaganda for the absolutist government under the czar.

The first Russian composer recognized both by Russians and internationally as an equal of his Western contemporaries was Mikhail Glinka (1804–1857), who established his reputation in 1836 with the patriotic, pro-government historical drama *A Life for the Tsar*, the first Russian opera sung throughout. Some of the recitative and melodic writing has a distinctive Russian character, attributable to modal scales, quotation or paraphrasing of folk songs, and a folklike idiom. Glinka based his second opera, *Ruslan and Lyudmila* (1842), on a poem by Russia's leading poet, Aleksander Pushkin (1799–1837). It contains many imaginative uses of the whole-tone scale (see below), chromaticism, dissonance, and variation technique applied to folk songs.

Mikhail Glinka

Glinka is valued in the West for the Russian flavor of these operas, which satisfied Western tastes for both the national and the exotic. But he was more important to his countrymen as the first to claim a place for Russia in the international musical world. This paradox pervades the reception of Russian music: foreign audiences and critics often prize what is recognizably national in it above all other characteristics, which is often not what the composers themselves or their compatriots most esteemed.

LOOKING WEST

When Czar Alexander II emancipated the serfs in 1861, he did so as part of a broader effort to modernize Russia and catch up to Western Europe. There were two main approaches to modernization: the nationalists, or "Slavo-philes," idealized Russia's distinctiveness, while the internationalists, or "westernizers," sought to adapt Western technology and education. This di-chotomy has often been applied to schools of Russian composers, but it is misleading, because all who composed operas, ballets, symphonies, or sonatas were adopting Western genres and approaches, whatever their style. Rather, a distinction might be made between composers who pursued profes-sional training in the Western mode and those who opposed academic study as a threat to their originality.

Rubinsteins and conservatories   Among the former, a key figure was Anton Rubinstein (1829–1894), virtuoso pianist and prolific composer, who founded the St. Petersburg Conservatory in 1862 with a program of training on the Western model. His pianist brother Nikolay Rubinstein (1835–1881) founded the Moscow Conservatory in 1866 on similar lines. Their work raised the standards of musicianship all over Russia and led to a strong tradition of Russian pianists, violinists, composers, and other musicians that continues today.

Figure 27.8: Piotr Il'yich Tchaikovsky in 1893, the last year of his life, in an oil portrait by Nikolay Kuznetzov.

PIOTR IL'YICH TCHAIKOVSKY

The leading Russian composer of the nineteenth century was Piotr Il'yich Tchaikovsky (1840–1893), shown in Figure 27.8. He studied with Anton Rubinstein at the St. Petersburg Con-servatory, was one of its first students to graduate, and taught at the Moscow Conservatory for twelve years. From 1878 on, he made his living solely as a composer, aided until 1890 by a generous stipend from a wealthy and mysterious widow, Nadezhda von Meck, whom he never met. Tchaikovsky sought to reconcile the nationalist and internationalist tendencies in Russian music, drawing models from Beethoven, Schubert, Schumann, and other Western composers as well as from Russian folk and popular music. He wrote a great deal of music for the stage, including incidental music, ballets, and operas. His other works are discussed in chapter 29.

Tchaikovsky's two most important operas were both based on Pushkin. *Eugene Onegin* (1879) is notable for penetrating the passions of its characters and for the way numerous themes are generated from a germ motive first announced in the orchestral prelude. The opera includes folklike music for the peasant chorus, but also features another kind of national music: its main characters are landed gentry, and they sing in a style modeled on the domestic music-making of that class of Russian society. In *The Queen of Spades* (1890), Tchaikovsky matched the ghoulish atmosphere of Pushkin's story and recreated the spirit of the eighteenth-century Russia of Catherine the Great by borrowing musical ideas from that period. These operas show that the styles and materials composers used in order to provide national flavor were not limited to folk music, although Westerners may not recognize the allusions to other kinds of Russian music.

Tchaikovsky won spectacular success with his ballets *Swan Lake* (1876), *The Sleeping Beauty* (1889), and *The Nutcracker* (1892), the most famous and frequently performed ballets in the permanent repertory. For his ballets, Tchaikovsky found a style that combined hummable melodies with colorful orchestration perfectly suited to the fairy-tale atmosphere of the stories and to the gestures of classical ballet.

Ballets

THE MIGHTY HANDFUL

Standing against the professionalism of the conservatories were five composers dubbed *moguchaya kuchka* or the Mighty Handful (or Mighty Five): Mily Balakirev (1837–1910), Aleksander Borodin (1833–1887), César Cui (1835–1918), Modest Musorgsky (1839–1881), and Nikolay Rimsky-Korsakov (1844–1908). Only Balakirev had conventional training in music, but it would be wrong to call the others amateurs. They admired Western music but studied it on their own (see Source Reading), outside the academic musical

SOURCE READING

THE MIGHTY HANDFUL

In a 1909 memoir, critic and composer César Cui recalled the gatherings almost fifty years earlier when the circle around Mily Balakirev met to pore over scores and argue about music. They opposed academic correctness, prized the most progressive composers of Western Europe, and saw themselves as part of that international current.

———— • ————

We formed a close-knit circle of young composers. And since there was nowhere to study (the conservatory didn't exist) our *self-education* began. It consisted of playing through everything that had been written by all the greatest composers, and all works were subjected to criticism and analysis in all their technical and creative aspects. We were

young and our judgments were harsh. We were very disrespectful in our attitude toward Mozart and Mendelssohn; to the latter we opposed Schumann, who was then ignored by everyone. We were very enthusiastic about Liszt and Berlioz. We worshipped Chopin and Glinka. We carried on heated debates (in the course of which we would down as many as four or five glasses of tea with jam), we discussed musical form, program music, vocal music, and especially operatic form.

From César Cui, "Pervye kompozitorskie shagi Ts. A. Kiui," in *Isbrannye stat'l* (Leningrad: Muzgiz, 1952), 544. Trans. Richard Taruskin in *Defining Russia Musically: Historical and Hermeneutical Essays* (Princeton: Princeton University Press, 1997), xv.

establishment whose exercises and prizes they scorned. It was because of their enthusiasm for Schumann, Chopin, Liszt, Berlioz, and other progressive composers in the West that they sought a fresh approach in their own music. As part of that new approach they incorporated aspects of Russian folk song, modal and exotic scales, and folk polyphony, but they also extended traits from the Western composers they most admired. Their theatrical music is covered here; their songs and instrumental works are treated in chapter 29.

Mily Balakirev and César Cui

Balakirev was the leader of their circle and an informal teacher for the others, but wrote little for the stage. He published two collections of folk songs in his own arrangements (1866 and 1899) that were sources for many later composers. Cui completed fourteen operas, including four for children, but none entered the permanent repertory.

Aleksander Borodin

Borodin, though devoted to music from a young age, was a chemist by profession and had difficulty finding time to compose. He left many works unfinished, including *Prince Igor* (1869–87), a four-act opera in the French grand opera tradition. It was completed after his death by Rimsky-Korsakov and Aleksander Glazunov and premiered in 1890. In it Borodin contrasted two musical styles to evoke the two ethnic groups, depicting his Russian characters with melodies modeled on Russian folk song and providing the Polovtsians, a central Asian people, with an exotic style laced with vocal melismas, melodic chromaticism and augmented seconds, double-reed instruments, and other signifiers Europeans associated with Asian music. The *Polovtsian Dances* in Act II are often performed separately. Indeed, already viewed as exotic in the West, Russian composers often found as much success at home and abroad with exoticist works as with nationalist ones.

MODEST MUSORGSKY

Widely considered the most original of the Mighty Handful, Musorgsky earned a living as a clerk in the civil service and received most of his musical training from Balakirev. His principal stage works were the operas *Boris Go-*

Figure 27.9: Portrait of Modest Musorgsky by Ilya Repin, painted in early March 1881, only two weeks before the composer's death from complications of alcoholism. Artist and composer shared a devotion to nationalism, reflected in the peasant shirt Musorgsky wears, and to realism, evident in the unblinking depiction of his unkempt hair, watery eyes, and red nose.

Figure 27.10: Set design by Mikhail Il'yich Bocharov for the Coronation Scene from Musorgsky's Boris Godunov *in its first production at the Mariinsky Theater in St. Petersburg in early 1874.*

dunov (1868–69, revised 1871–74), based on a Pushkin play, and *Khovanshchina* (The Khovansky Affair, 1872–80, completed after Musorgsky's death by Rimsky-Korsakov). The realism so prominent in nineteenth-century Russian literature echoes especially in *Boris Godunov*, in the way Musorgsky imitated Russian speech, in his lifelike musical depiction of gestures, and, in the choral scenes, the sound and stir of the crowds. Both realism and nationalism are reflected in the composer's famous portrait, shown in Figure 27.9.

Musorgsky's individuality shines through every aspect of his music, as illustrated by the famous Coronation Scene from *Boris Godunov* (NAWM 130), shown in Figure 27.10 as it was staged for the opera's 1874 premiere in St. Petersburg. Example 27.5a shows Boris's first statement in the scene, after he is hailed as the new czar. The vocal melody exemplifies Musorgsky's approach. He set words naturalistically, following the rhythm and pacing of speech as closely as possible: almost always syllabic, with accented syllables on strong beats, often higher and louder than the surrounding notes. As a result, his vocal music tends to lack lyrical melodic lines and symmetrical phrasing, but at the same time he avoided the conventions of recitative. He sought a melodic profile closer to Russian folk songs, which typically move in a relatively narrow range, rise at the beginning of phrases and sink to cadences, and often repeat one or two melodic or rhythmic motives. All these characteristics are apparent here.

Melodic style

CD 10|6

Musorgsky's harmony is essentially tonal, projecting a clear sense of the key, but in many respects it is highly original, even revolutionary. He often juxtaposes distantly related or coloristic harmonies, usually joined by a com-

Harmony

mon tone. One such progression is the sequence of C minor, A♭ minor, and G major in Example 27.5a, which includes two pairings that became staples of eerie or gloomy movie music in the twentieth century: two minor triads whose roots are a major third apart (C and A♭ minor, which share E♭), and a minor and a major triad with a common third degree (A♭ minor and G major share C♭/B). Other examples, shown in Example 27.5b and c, are the Coronation

Example 27.5: Excerpts from the Coronation Scene from Musorgsky's Boris Godunov

a. Boris's speech

My soul suffers. Some kind of involuntary fear has stifled my heart with ominous premonitions.

b. Opening chords (the "Boris" chords)

c. Third-related triads harmonizing a repeated note

Long live Tsar Boris Feodorovich!

Scene's opening chords, two dominant seventh chords that have roots a tritone apart and two notes in common (here, C and G♭/F♯), and three major triads related by thirds (here, E, C, and A major) that have a common tone and
are used in succession to harmonize it. These types of chord progression are
not the result of naïve experimentation, as some have imputed to Musorgsky,
but show his intellectual approach to composition and his familiarity with
Liszt, Glinka, and other composers who had used such progressions.

Another trait that is characteristic of Musorgsky and of much Russian
music is composition in large blocks of material. This is true of the opera as a
whole: rather than continuously developed action, *Boris Godunov* is a series
of episodes held together by an epic thread and the central figure of the czar.
But juxtaposition of blocks is also evident in the Coronation Scene. The opening section elaborates the two chords shown in Example 27.5b, twice building
to a peak of activity and intensity. Then Example 27.5c begins a section of
rapid juxtapositions in which every few measures Musorgsky changes figuration and apparent key, until the chorus sings a folk song in C major accompanied by the first traditional harmony in the scene. Musorgsky rarely uses
actual folk melodies; this tune adds an element of realism, as do the bells that
ring constantly up to this point, like the church bells of Moscow.

Block construction

NIKOLAY RIMSKY-KORSAKOV

Rimsky-Korsakov studied music with private teachers and with Balakirev
while pursuing a career in the Russian Navy. In 1871, he became a professor at
the St. Petersburg Conservatory, abandoning the anti-academic stance of the
Balakirev circle. He quickly became aware of how much he still had to learn
before he could teach music theory; he burned the midnight oil to keep ahead
of his students and later described himself as one of the Conservatory's best
students. He also became an active orchestral conductor and a master of
orchestration.

Ironically, Rimsky-Korsakov's professionalism guaranteed the continuation of a distinctively Russian school. He edited, completed, and orchestrated
works by Glinka, Musorgsky, Borodin, and others, helping to ensure their

Professionalism

survival. As a conductor at home and in western Europe, he championed Russian music. He also wrote the harmony text most frequently used in Russia and a manual on orchestration, and he taught some of the most important composers of the next generation, including Aleksander Glazunov and Igor Stravinsky.

Operas   Rimsky-Korsakov proved his abiding interest in national music by arranging and editing two collections of folk songs (1875–82) and by incorporating folk tunes and their melodic characteristics into his own compositions. Although best known in the West for his orchestral works, he was primarily an opera composer. Several of his fifteen operas draw on Russian history, plays, epics, or folk tales. In many of them, including the epic *Sadko* (1895–97) and the fairy-tale operas *Tsar Saltan* (1899–1900) and *The Golden Cockerel* (1906–7), he alternated a diatonic, often modal style used for the everyday world with a lightly chromatic, "fantastic" style that suggested the world of supernatural beings and magical occurrences.

Whole-tone and octatonic collections   A key element of the fantastic style was the use of scales or pitch collections in which the same sequence of intervals occurs several times, so that there is more than one possible tone center. The simplest such scale is the **whole-tone scale** (or *whole-tone collection*), consisting of only whole steps; another is the **octatonic scale** (or *octatonic collection*), which alternates whole and half steps. Both are shown in Example 27.6. While each of the twelve major scales contains a unique collection of seven notes, there are only two whole-tone collections and three octatonic collections, shown in the example; any other transposition of these scales will simply reproduce the same notes as one of the scales shown here (assuming enharmonic equivalence). Because they lack the strong gravitation toward a tonic that is characteristic of diatonic scales, the whole-tone and octatonic scales create a sense of floating or otherworldliness. Their secret is to divide the octave in equal units; as the example shows, the whole-tone scale comprises two augmented triads (which divide the octave into three major thirds), and the octatonic scale contains two diminished seventh chords (which divide the octave into four minor thirds). Such scales are found already in the music of Liszt, but they became trademarks of Russian music in the late nineteenth and early twentieth centuries.

Example 27.6: Scales based on equal divisions of the octave

a. *Whole-tone scales*

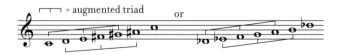

b. *Octatonic scales*

Example 27.7 shows an example from the second scene of *Sadko*, depicting a fantastic realm under the sea. The rising octatonic scale in the bass is harmonized by the major triads and dominant seventh chords available in the scale, whose roots are related by minor thirds (A, C, E♭, and F♯). The floating harmonies here contrast strongly with the diatonic, folklike song Sadko has just sung, marking him as a human amid the magical surroundings.

Example 27.7: From Rimsky-Korsakov's Sadko, *scene 2*

RUSSIAN INFLUENCE

Tchaikovsky and the Mighty Five developed musical styles that were strongly individual, markedly national, yet suffused with elements from the West. In turn, they influenced Western composers of the very late nineteenth and early twentieth century, who were especially drawn to the Russians' block construction, orchestral colors, use of modality, and artificial scales. In less than a century, Russian music went from being peripheral to being a major current in Western music.

OTHER NATIONS

Opera continued to spread to other nations, often—though not always—allied with nationalist movements.

BOHEMIA

In Bohemia (now the Czech Republic), opera was a specifically nationalist project. Bohemia had for centuries been an Austrian crown land and so, unlike Russia, had always been in the mainstream of European music. Education was in German, the official state language and the primary language of the middle and upper classes and city-dwellers. Opera had long been heard in the capital, Prague, but in Italian (Mozart's *Don Giovanni* was premiered there) or in German. In the 1860s, in an attempt to foster a national tradition of stage works in Czech, the provincial government established a Czech national theater, and a nobleman sponsored a contest for the best historical and comic operas in Czech.

The contest was won by the national theater's conductor, Bedřich Smetana (1824–1884), whose eight operas form the core of the Czech operatic repertory and whose comic opera *The Bartered Bride* (1866) secured his

Bedřich Smetana

international reputation. Smetana chose Czech subjects, and the sets and costumes drew on national traditions. Within a personal idiom heavily influenced by Liszt, Smetana created a Czech national style by using folklike tunes and popular dance rhythms like the polka and by avoiding many of the stylistic conventions of Italian and German opera.

Antonín Dvořák   Smetana was succeeded by Antonín Dvořák (1841–1904), whose twelve operas include plots based on Czech village life, Czech fairy tales, and Slavic history. Most important are *Dmitrij* (1882, revised 1894), a historical music drama influenced by Meyerbeer and Wagner, and *Rusalka* (1900), a lyric fairy-tale opera in which he adopted Rimsky-Korsakov's dichotomy between

TIMELINE: OPERA AND MUSICAL THEATER IN LATER 19TH CENTURY

1830	1840	1850	1860	1870	1880	1890	1900

- 1836 Mikhail Glinka, *A Life for the Tsar*
- 1843 Richard Wagner, *Der fliegende Holländer*
- 1848 Revolutions in European cities
- 1848 Karl Marx and Friedrich Engels, *Communist Manifesto*
- 1848 Seneca Falls Convention, beginning of women's suffrage movement
- 1848–49 California Gold Rush
- 1852–70 Second French Empire under Napoleon III
- 1853 Giuseppe Verdi, *Il trovatore* and *La traviata*
- 1854 Academy of Music opens in New York
- 1857–59 Wagner composes *Tristan und Isolde*
- 1858 Jacques Offenbach, *Orpheus in the Underworld*
- 1859 Charles Darwin, *The Origin of Species*
- 1861 Victor Emmanuel crowned king of Italy
- 1861 Russia abolishes serfdom
- 1861–65 Civil War in United States
- 1866 Bedřich Smetana, *The Bartered Bride*
- 1869 John Stuart Mill, *On the Subjection of Women*
- 1870–71 Franco-Prussian War
- 1871 German Empire unites German states outside Austria
- 1874 Premiere of Modest Musorgsky's *Boris Godunov*
- 1875 Georges Bizet, *Carmen*
- 1876 Wagner, premiere of complete *Ring* cycle
- 1879 Thomas Edison invents the electric lightbulb
- 1879 Piotr Il'yich Tchaikovsky, *Eugene Onegin*
- 1879 Gilbert and Sullivan, *The Pirates of Penzance*
- 1887 Verdi's *Otello* premieres
- 1896 Giacomo Puccini, *La bohème*
- 1898 Spanish-American War

the diatonic world of humanity and the fantastic style for the nature spirits. Both Smetana and Dvořák are better known in the West for their instrumental music, which is discussed in chapter 29.

OPERA IN OTHER LANDS

The shape that opera took in each nation depended on its individual circumstances. In Poland, which was ruled by Russia, opera was part of a national cultural revival. Stanisław Moniuszko (1819–1872) inaugurated a tradition of Polish national opera with *Halka* (1848, revised 1858). Spain, on the other hand, had been independent for centuries but had become peripheral to currents in France, Italy, and Germany. Felipe Pedrell (1841–1922) sparked a nationalist revival with his editions of sixteenth-century Spanish composers and his operas, chief of which was *Los Pirineos* (The Pyrenees, 1891). Britain was dominated by foreign opera, despite repeated attempts to create a national opera tradition in the vernacular. Among the most important British operas were the six of Ethel Smyth (1858–1944), best known for *The Wreckers* (1904). In New York, the Metropolitan Opera Company opened in 1883, performing the entire range of European opera, but almost no native composers attempted opera. The first internationally recognized composer of opera from the New World was Antônio Carlos Gomes (1836–1896) of Brazil, who had early success with two operas in Portuguese, although neither entered the permanent repertoire. His later operas were written in Italy and in Italian. His masterpiece is *Il Guarany* (1870), on a Brazilian subject centering on reconciliation between the native Indians and the Portuguese colonists, but the style is essentially Italian.

Germany achieved independence from the Italian and French operatic traditions first, followed by Russia and Bohemia, but the impression elsewhere is inescapably one of outsiders looking in, like small planets orbiting a sun.

OPERETTA

In lighter forms of musical theater, however, that is not the case, and these forms flourished in nearly every country. ***Operetta***—a new kind of light opera with spoken dialogue, originating in the opéra bouffe of Offenbach—was manifestly an entertainment, in which nationalism was beside the point. It could be both funny and romantic, spoofing the conventions of opera yet using them sincerely when appropriate. The great masters of operetta in the generation after Offenbach were the Viennese Johann Strauss the Younger (1825–1899), known for *Die Fledermaus* (The Bat, 1874), and in England, the team of W. S. Gilbert (librettist) and Arthur Sullivan (composer, 1842–1900). Sullivan wanted to be known as a serious composer, but his opera on Walter Scott's *Ivanhoe* (1891) was nowhere near the success of his collaborations with Gilbert, especially *HMS Pinafore* (1878), *The Pirates of Penzance* (1879), and *The Mikado* (1885).

The chorus and ensemble *When the foeman bares his steel* from *The Pirates of Penzance* (NAWM 131) illustrates the humor of Gilbert and Sullivan.

CD 10|12

Everything follows convention yet goes oddly wrong. As the policemen prepare to march on a band of pirates, they sing a rousing chorus set in a martial dotted rhythm. The men, however, freely admit they are terrified at the prospect of battle and are simply covering up their fears. Mabel—a beautiful young woman—and a women's chorus, singing a stirring melody, urge the policemen to suffer death for glory's sake. The police are not happy with this message, but decide it would be too impolite to protest. At the climax, the two choruses sing their melodies in counterpoint, a hilarious juxtaposition of opposing styles and a send-up of the conventions of opera ensembles in which everyone on stage sings together. When the police continue to sing about marching off to the fray, the Major General notes that they have not left yet ("Yes, but you *don't* go!," he observes with some irritation). The standard roles of men and women in opera, appeals to glory, the tendency to sing at length about taking action before doing it, and other familiar traits are all mocked mercilessly. Throughout, Sullivan matches style and gesture to the text in a satire that shows his command of a wide range of styles.

THE VARIETY OF MUSICAL THEATER

In addition to opera and related forms, other kinds of musical theater flourished throughout Europe and the Americas. Ballet in France and Russia has already been mentioned, along with the cabarets, cafés, and night clubs of Paris.

The particular forms of entertainment varied from place to place, but the variety of musical theater may be illustrated with a snapshot of the United States in the second half of the nineteenth century. European opera was heard in several major cities, both in the original languages and in translation. Minstrel shows continued (see chapter 26), now including all-black troupes as well as white entertainers in blackface. Operettas were imported from Europe—indeed, *The Pirates of Penzance* was premiered in New York—and homegrown composers wrote their own, including *El capitan* by John Philip Sousa (1854–1932). A pastiche called *The Black Crook* (1866) combined a melodrama with a visiting French ballet troupe to score a tremendous financial success, and it toured for years, constantly interpolating new material to keep up with fashion. Another great success was *Evangeline* (1874), with music by Edward E. Rice, the first "musical comedy" and an ancestor to the modern musical (see chapter 30). Singing comics Ned Harrigan (1844–1911) and Tony Hart (1855–1891) collaborated with composer David Braham on comic sketches and musical plays, often focused on Irish, Italian, or other ethnic characters. By bringing variety shows out of the saloons and into music halls that respectable women could attend, New York theater impresario Tony Pastor (1837–1908) invented what became known as **vaudeville,** the major form of theatrical entertainment in the United States until talking movies took over in the late 1920s.

In all these endeavors, the focus was on pleasing the audience and making as much money as possible. In that respect, if in few others, these forms of musical theater could trace their heritage back to the public opera theaters seventeenth-century Venice (see chapter 14).

MUSIC FOR THE STAGE AND ITS AUDIENCES

Verdi and Wagner brought the opera of their nations to a peak never surpassed. Even in their lifetimes, they achieved a permanence and centrality in the opera repertory akin to Handel's for oratorio and Beethoven's for the symphony. Excerpts from Wagner operas also became staples of orchestral concerts, beginning during his lifetime when full productions were still rare, and several excerpts are perhaps best known in that form. Puccini alone of the Italians after Verdi holds a major place in the international opera repertory. Opera composers in other lands found room in their national traditions, and some of their works also entered the permanent international repertory, most notably Gounod's *Faust*, Bizet's *Carmen*, Tchaikovsky's *Eugene Onegin* and *The Queen of Spades*, Musorgsky's *Boris Godunov*, and Smetana's *The Bartered Bride*.

Nationalism was a major concern in nineteenth-century opera, and it continues to affect the reception of much of this music in both positive and negative ways. The most nationalist of nineteenth-century composers, Wagner, obscured his nationalism by a claim to universality, and the enthusiastic response of German, English, and even French critics has made it seem that nationalism can be heard only when composers deliberately depart from the German "mainstream." Composers from "peripheral" countries, from Russia to Latin America, are expected to write national music, and those who do are rewarded with an international audience; yet in some respects this keeps their products exotic and means they can never be as central as composers from Germany, Austria, France, or Italy.

Meanwhile, the split between elite and popular musical theater became irreparable in this period and has continued to widen. Verdi was still capable of attracting connoisseurs while pleasing the public at large, but the high seriousness of Wagner and much other opera did not aim for popular entertainment. The popular genres created in reaction, from operetta to vaudeville, became increasingly important and underlie much of the music of the last century. Yet opera is a constant reference as well, since it was for opera that almost every expressive device in the musical language was first created, and those devices still carry meaning today in music for film, television, and other media.

Late Romanticism in Germany and Austria

During the second half of the nineteenth century, the Western musical world diversified as the audience for music broadened and became more segmented. Increasing interest in music of the past was balanced by the emergence of new styles of concert music, and a growing seriousness in the concert hall and new forms of entertainment music widened the gulf between classical and popular music. We will focus in this chapter on the classical tradition in Germany, examining how a debate between partisans of Johannes Brahms and of Richard Wagner crystallized divisions within German music. The following chapter treats national traditions in France and eastern and northern Europe and explores the division into classical and popular streams primarily through musical life in the United States.

DICHOTOMIES AND DISPUTES

Music since 1850 may appear more varied than that of earlier eras simply because the historical evidence is more complete and a wider range of music survives. But that greater diversity is not just an illusion. Several factors combined to make the later nineteenth century the most varied period yet, surpassed only by the even more diverse twentieth century.

Classical repertoire   Before the nineteenth century, most music that was performed had been composed in living memory, except for the chants, chorales, and hymns of the church. By 1850, orchestral, chamber, choral, and other concerts increasingly focused on a repertoire of musical classics, and with each decade the proportion of older works grew (see chapter 25). The establishment of a permanent classical repertoire may be the most important fact about music in the late nineteenth century, for it had many effects beyond concert programming.

In tandem with the rise of the classical repertoire, interest in music of the past intensified. The new field of musicology was created in order to study and make available the music of previous generations. Scholars unearthed and published music by the great composers of past eras, issuing editions of the complete works of Bach, Handel, Palestrina, Mozart, Schütz, and Lasso, as well as the early-nineteenth-century masters Beethoven, Mendelssohn, Chopin, Schumann, and Schubert. These editions and numerous less comprehensive performing editions helped to form a canon of composers whose music comprised the center of the repertoire and the mainstream of music history. Most of these composers were German, and their editions were issued by German scholars and publishers, linking the revival of past music to nationalism; the German editions of Palestrina and Chopin were notable for granting those composers canonic status despite their nationality. Less widely known music of the Renaissance and Baroque was collected in series such as Denkmäler der Tonkunst (Monuments of Musical Art, begun 1869), Denkmäler deutscher Tonkunst (Monuments of German Music, begun 1892),

Revival of past music

TIMELINE: LATE ROMANTICISM IN GERMANY AND AUSTRIA

1840	1850	1860	1870	1880	1890	1900

- 1848 Revolutions in European cities
- 1848–1916 Franz Joseph reigns as emperor of Austria
- 1851 Complete edition of J. S. Bach's works begun
- 1854 Franz Liszt, *Les Préludes*
- 1854 Edward Hanslick, *On the Musically Beautiful*
- 1857–59 Richard Wagner, *Tristan und Isolde*
- 1861 William I becomes king of Prussia
- 1862 Otto von Bismarck appointed premier of Prussia
- 1867 Austrian Empire reorganized as Austro-Hungarian monarchy
- 1868 Johannes Brahms, *A German Requiem*
- 1870–71 Franco-Prussian War
- 1871 German Empire proclaimed, William I becomes emperor
- 1874–80 Anton Bruckner, Fourth Symphony (*Romantic*) •
- 1885 Brahms, Fourth Symphony •
- 1889 Hugo Wolf, Mörike Lieder •
- 1897 Richard Strauss, *Don Quixote* •

and Denkmäler der Tonkunst in Österreich (Monuments of Music in Austria, begun 1894). Belatedly, scholars and publishers outside Germany began to produce editions of music by their own historical masters, including Purcell in England and Grétry and Rameau in France.

Old versus new   Thus in the later nineteenth century, performers and audiences had available to them not only new music and works in the standard repertoire but an increasing supply of older music that, paradoxically, was new to them and satisfied some of the desire to hear new pieces as well as familiar ones. When a choir's repertoire could include music culled from four centuries, and a pianist might perform works ranging from Bach to the present in a single concert, it is safe to say that nothing approaching this variety of styles had ever before been present simultaneously in the performing tradition.

Brahms versus Wagner   The continuing presence of older music posed problems for living composers. How do you craft new works to appeal to an audience that is primarily accustomed to hearing music already familiar to them, most of it composed a generation or more ago? Composers responded in varying ways. Some, like Brahms, competed with the classical masters on their own ground, writing symphonies and chamber works worthy of a place next to Beethoven and songs and piano pieces that rival the achievements of Schubert, Schumann, and Chopin. Others, like Wagner and Liszt, saw the legacy of Beethoven as pointing in a different direction, toward new genres such as music drama and symphonic poems. In German-speaking lands, the dispute polarized around Brahms and Wagner and around the dichotomies between absolute and program music, between tradition and innovation, and between classical genres and forms and new ones. What is clear in retrospect is that partisans on both sides shared the common goals of linking themselves to Beethoven, appealing to audiences familiar with the classical masterworks, and securing a place for their own music in the increasingly crowded permanent repertoire. All such music became known as ***classical music*** because it was written for similar performing forces as works represented in the classical repertoire and was intended to be performed alongside them.

Nationalism and internationalism   Although the classical repertoire centered around German-speaking composers, it was performed to varying degrees in concert halls across Europe and the Americas. As a result, composers in other lands also found themselves competing with the classics and addressing issues of national identity.

Nationalism was as strong a force in instrumental music, song, and choral music as in opera. National flavor was prized as evidence of a composer's authenticity and distinctiveness. The search for a musical past was in part nationalist. German and French composers found it in their written tradition as well as in folklore; for example, Brahms drew inspiration from Schütz, Bach, Beethoven, and other German predecessors. Eastern and northern Europeans found a usable past primarily by incorporating aspects of the unwritten tradition of folk music in their own lands (see chapter 29). Nationalism was not an attempt to break free of the Western tradition, but a way to join it by presenting a distinctive flavor that could be welcomed as part of the international repertoire. Composers everywhere had the choice of whether and how to emphasize their nationality. In the nations farthest from the center, such as Russia and the United States, composers fell at different points on a continuum

Figure 28.1: Scene outside the coffeehouse at the Volksgarten, a large outdoor pleasure garden in Vienna, in 1898. In the background, Johann Strauss the younger leads his orchestra, heard and enjoyed but not attended to with the concentration a classical concert orchestra would have commanded at the time.

between nationalist and internationalist orientations, depending on how much they emphasized distinctly national elements in their music.

We saw in chapter 27 how, as opera grew more serious, lighter theatrical entertainment sprang up in response, from operetta to cabaret and vaudeville. In instrumental music, song, and choral music, there was likewise a growing gulf between classical music and music intended for popular consumption, both in concert and in publications for music-making at home. The dichotomy has been expressed in various terms, with different shades of meaning: classical versus popular, serious versus light, cultivated versus vernacular, high versus low. Although at the beginning of the nineteenth century Beethoven could write both kinds of music—symphonies and string quartets on one side, light rondos and folk-song arrangements on the other—this wide range was rare for composers later in the century, who tended to specialize in one kind of music. While Brahms and Bruckner were writing their symphonies in Vienna, Johann Strauss the younger, known as "The Waltz King," was in the same city composing hundreds of waltzes, galops, and other dances to be performed at balls and in concerts, like the open-air concert in Figure 28.1. Classical and popular styles gradually diverged, until there was much less in common between the musical idioms of a symphony and a popular song in the early twentieth century than there had been in Mozart's day.

All of these dichotomies—between old and new musical works and styles, absolute and program music, nationalist and internationalist elements, and

Classical versus popular music

Negotiating the fault lines

classical and popular music—were fault lines in the musical landscape. Listeners and amateurs often enjoyed all the possibilities, piling German Lieder and popular songs or sonatas and marches side by side on their piano racks, but composers had to make choices. The composers treated in this chapter and in the following one include the most successful of their day and represent a wide range of strategies for meeting the challenges of their time.

Johannes Brahms

Johannes Brahms (1833–1897; see biography and Figure 28.2) matured as a composer just as the classical repertoire came to dominate concert life. By the time he was twenty, three-fifths of the music played in orchestral concerts was by dead composers, and by the time he was forty, that proportion had risen beyond three-quarters. Brahms fully understood what it meant to compose for audiences whose tastes were formed by the classical masterpieces of the last two centuries: one had to create pieces that were like those already enshrined in the repertoire in function and aesthetic yet were different enough to offer something new and attractive. He worked slowly and was severely self-critical, knowing that his reputation hinged on the high quality of every piece. He was well-versed in music of the past, from Beethoven and the early Romantics back to Renaissance and Baroque composers, and he synthesized elements from their music with current classical and folk idioms to create a unique personal style. Like Schubert before him, Brahms used virtually all musical languages of his time, from church styles to Hungarian-Gypsy music, and integrated them into his music to achieve a very varied and expressive idiom of his own. At the same time, his erudition was combined with a deeply Romantic sensibility, so that his music appealed at once to listeners who appreciated its lyrical beauty and sincere expressivity and to connoisseurs who admired its integrity and elegant craft.

ORCHESTRAL WORKS

Brahms knew that his symphonies would have to match the standards established by Beethoven. "I shall never compose a symphony!" he exclaimed in 1870. "You have no idea how someone like me feels when he hears such a giant marching behind him all the time." In fact, by his fortieth year, he had completed only four orchestral pieces: two serenades, the Piano Concerto No. 1 in D Minor (1861), and Variations on a Theme of Haydn, Op. 56a (1873). When he did finally produce a symphony, he deliberately invoked Beethoven's model yet carved out a fresh path.

Symphonies   Brahms wrote four symphonies. The first, Symphony No. 1 in C Minor, Op. 68, was finally completed in 1876, after Brahms worked on it for over twenty years. The symphony's success prompted Brahms immediately to write another, No. 2 in D Major, Op. 73, in 1877. Two more followed: Symphony No. 3 in F. Major, Op. 90, in 1883; and Symphony No. 4 in E Minor, Op. 98, in 1885.

JOHANNES BRAHMS (1833–1897)

Brahms was the leading German composer of his time in every field except opera and an important influence on twentieth-century music.

He was born in Hamburg to a family of modest means. His father played horn and double bass in dance halls and local ensembles. Brahms studied piano, cello, and horn as a child, and through lessons in piano and music theory developed a love for music of Bach, Haydn, Mozart, and Beethoven. He earned money playing popular music at restaurants and taverns, which fostered a lifelong taste for folk and popular music. He was especially fond of the Hungarian-Gypsy style and used it in many compositions.

In 1853, Brahms met the violinist Joseph Joachim and Robert and Clara Schumann, who became his strongest supporters. Schumann praised Brahms in print, launching his career, and helped him secure a publisher. After Schumann's suicide attempt and confinement for mental illness, Brahms helped take care of the family while Clara returned to her life as a performer. He fell in love with her, but whether they had more than a platonic relationship, even after Schumann's death in 1856, is not known. He had a series of attachments with other women but chose to remain a bachelor, surrounding himself with a close circle of friends.

Brahms made his living by concertizing as a pianist and conductor and from sales of his music to publishers. He conducted the Singakademie in Vienna in 1862–63 and settled there permanently in 1868. From 1872 to 1875, he directed the chorus and

Figure 28.2: Johannes Brahms in about 1862. Portrait by Carl Jagemann.

orchestra of the Gesellschaft der Musikfreunde, programming mostly German music from the sixteenth century through his own day. He was also active as an editor for music by C. P. E. Bach, François Couperin, Schumann, Schubert, and Chopin. In his last two decades he traveled widely as a conductor, performing mostly his own works, and was awarded numerous honors. He died of liver cancer less than one year after Clara Schumann's death and was buried in Vienna's Central Cemetery near Beethoven and Schubert.

MAJOR WORKS: *4 symphonies, 2 piano concertos, Violin Concerto, 2 overtures, 2 serenades, 3 string quartets, 21 other chamber works, 3 piano sonatas, numerous piano pieces,* A German Requiem, *choral works, vocal ensembles, and about 200 Lieder*

First Symphony

Brahms's First Symphony carried the weight and history of the genre, yet for every similarity to Beethoven there is a departure. It has the conventional sequence of movements—fast, slow, a light movement, and fast. Yet the third movement is not a scherzo but a lyrical intermezzo or character piece, a substitution Brahms repeated in his other symphonies. Brahms echoes Beethoven's Fifth Symphony by moving from C minor to C major and from struggle to triumph, but the overall key scheme of the four movements—C minor, E major, A♭ major with a B-major middle section, and C minor and major—is characteristic of later composers in defining a circle of major thirds. The presence in both first and last movements of slow introductions that gradually unfold the principal thematic material before the Allegro begins is unlike any Beethoven model but recalls the earliest version of Schumann's Fourth Symphony. The main theme of the finale is a hymnlike melody, which immediately suggests a parallel to the finale of Beethoven's Ninth Symphony. Yet there are no voices, as if to say that for Brahms, Beethoven's recourse to words is not necessary. The symphony fully absorbs Beethoven's influence—the conductor Hans von Bülow dubbed it "Beethoven's Tenth"—but also blends in other models and includes much that is new, as it must if it is to stand comparison with Beethoven's constant innovations.

Third Symphony

The opening measures of Symphony No. 3, shown in Example 28.1, illustrate three frequent characteristics in Brahms's music: wide melodic spans; cross-relations between major and minor forms of the tonic triad; and metric ambiguity between triple and duple divisions of the bar. Here, the rests on the fourth beat invite hearing the theme in $\frac{3}{2}$, but the next phrase makes the $\frac{6}{4}$ meter clear. The conflict between major and minor recurs in the finale, which begins in F minor and settles in F major only in the coda. The finale's second theme, shown in Example 28.2, features another metric effect that is virtually a Brahms trademark: the clash of simultaneous triple and duple meters.

CD 10|18   CD 5|52

The finale of Brahms's Fourth Symphony (NAWM 132), shown in Figure 28.3, is a chaconne, a form that reflects Brahms's fascination with Baroque

Example 28.1: Opening theme of Brahms's Symphony No. 3, first movement

Example 28.2: Second theme of Brahms's Symphony No. 3, finale

Figure 28.3: Autograph score of the opening of the finale of Brahms's Symphony No. 4 in E Minor, Op. 98.

music. It is at once a set of variations on a bass ostinato and on a harmonic pattern. Brahms drew the rising bass figure from the final chorus of Bach's cantata *Nach dir, Herr, verlanget mich*, BWV 150, but he may have had other models in mind as well, such as Buxtehude's Ciacona in E Minor. The use of a variation movement to end a symphony recalls Beethoven's *Eroica* Symphony, one of the few to feature such a finale; like Beethoven, Brahms first presents his bass line as a melody in the upper register and only works it into the bass after several variations. Another possible model is the chaconne finale to Bach's Partita for Unaccompanied Violin in D Minor, which Brahms had transcribed in 1877 as a left-hand exercise for piano; when the ostinato finally reaches the bass, the melodic figuration is a sarabande rhythm exactly like Bach's, and subsequent variations often parallel Bach's, from dotted rhythms to bariolage (rapidly alternating stopped and open strings). All three variation finales are laid out in a broad three-part form with a contrasting middle section, another link between them.

The rich web of allusion is typical of Brahms. To fully understand what he is drawing from the past, we would have to know the music of three centuries as deeply as he did. And yet the Fourth Symphony finale is perfectly clear and coherent without recognizing a single reference to other music. What is most important is that by blending elements from the recent and the more distant past within a contemporary idiom, Brahms was able to create music that sounds wholly original, new, and individual.

Brahms brought the same distinctiveness to his concertos. The Violin Concerto in D Major, Op. 77 (1878), ranks with Beethoven's in its

Concertos

seriousness, scope, and popularity. Perhaps his greatest concerto is his Piano Concerto No. 2 in B♭ Major, Op. 83 (1881), whose four movements and close integration between piano and orchestra make it the most symphonic of concertos.

CHAMBER MUSIC

In chamber music as in orchestral music, Brahms was the true successor of Beethoven. Not only is the quantity of his production impressive—twenty-four works in all—but the quality as well, including at least a half-dozen masterpieces. As in his symphonies, there are echoes of earlier composers integrated into music that could only have been written by Brahms.

Piano Quintet   Seven of Brahms's chamber works feature piano with strings, including three piano trios and three piano quartets. Most popular is his Quintet for Piano and Strings in F Minor, Op. 34 (1864). His treatment of the first movement's opening idea, shown in Example 28.3a, illustrates his use of a method, prevalent throughout his works, of continuously building on germinal ideas, which Schoenberg called ***developing variation***. The theme itself is a series of variants of its opening measure. In diminution, the theme becomes a piano figure against string chords (Example 28.3b); a transformation of the theme's first measure blossoms into a new lyrical melody (28.3c); then a more distant

Example 28.3: Developing variation in Brahms's Piano Quintet in F Minor, first movement

variant of the second measure is subjected to close imitation in the two violins (28.3d). The last three ideas have little in common, yet all derive from a common ancestor.

PIANO MUSIC

Brahms developed a highly individual piano style characterized by full sonority; broken-chord figuration; frequent doubling of the melodic line in octaves, thirds, or sixths; multiple chordlike appoggiaturas; and frequent use of cross-rhythms. He was extraordinarily imaginative in developing simple ideas into innovative textures, using arpeggiations, repeated notes, contrasting rhythms in different lines, and other means to increase the number of attacks while maintaining transparent clarity.

As a young man in 1852–53, Brahms wrote three large sonatas in the tradition of Beethoven that also incorporate the chromatic harmony of Chopin and Liszt and the songlike style of Schumann's character pieces. In his twenties and thirties, Brahms began to focus on variations, culminating in the Variations and Fugue on a Theme of Handel, Op. 24 (1861) and the difficult, étude-like Variations on a Theme of Paganini, Op. 35 (1863). Brahms did not simply ornament the melody or change the accompanimental figuration but set out his variations as a string of short character pieces based on the formal and harmonic plan of the theme. The twenty-five variations on Handel's theme, for instance, include evocations of Chopin and Mozart, canons, études, character pieces, hunting-horn style, a miniature Hungarian rhapsody, a siciliana, a chromatic fantasia, a musette, a scherzo, and a march, all culminating with a Beethovenian fugue.

In his last two decades, Brahms issued six collections of intermezzos, rhapsodies, and other short pieces that are perhaps his greatest contribution to keyboard literature. Most are in ABA' form and have songlike melodies, resembling songs without words or character pieces. The varied textures, surprising harmonies, and deft counterpoint show Brahms's familiarity with keyboard music from Bach to his own time, while the pianistic idiom remains within reach of the amateur performer, and the attractive melodies delight the listener.

SONGS

Brahms's used Schubert as his model for songwriting, making the voice the primary partner and the piano rich with supporting figuration. Many of his 260 Lieder, like Schubert's, follow a strophic or modified strophic form, and some, like the familiar *Wiegenlied* (Lullaby, 1868), imitate the style of folk songs. Brahms often chose texts that suggest emotional restraint or an introspective, elegiac mood. Yet he still expresses passion, which becomes all the more effective because it is controlled.

The first strophe of *Wie Melodien zieht es mir* (1886), shown in Example 28.4, illustrates several characteristics of Brahms's songwriting. The melody is beautiful and not difficult to sing, but it frequently surprises with unexpected

Example 28.4: Brahms, Wie Melodien zieht es mir

Like melodies a thought drifts lightly through my mind, like spring flowers it blooms and hovers in the air like fragrance.

changes of direction, chromaticism, and strong appoggiaturas (see measures 2, 3, 7, and 11). The harmony is fundamentally simple, which makes the vocal dissonances and the chromatic twists (as in measures 4 and 9–10) all the more poignant. Some of Brahms's favorite figurations appear, including extended arpeggiation, syncopated rhythms, and melodies in parallel thirds or sixths. The piano is greatly varied in texture, changing figuration about every two measures; this trait distinguishes Brahms's Lieder from those of Schumann or Schubert while recalling Mozart's frequent changes of figure and topic (see chapter 22). In his songs, as in his piano music, Brahms was one of the rare composers of the late nineteenth century who wrote music that is both accessible for amateur performers and interesting for the connoisseur, reviving the alchemy of Haydn and Mozart a century earlier.

CHORAL WORKS

The same alchemy pervades Brahms's choral music, which was all composed for amateur performers. He arranged German folk songs for chorus and wrote many short, unaccompanied songs for women's, men's, or mixed voices, as well as larger pieces for chorus with orchestra.

His greatest choral work is *Ein deutsches Requiem* (A German Requiem, 1868), for soprano and baritone soloists, chorus, and orchestra, whose title page is shown in Figure 28.4. The text is not the liturgical words of the Latin Requiem (Mass for the Dead), but rather passages in German, chosen by the composer, from the Old Testament, Apocrypha, and New Testament. Brahms's music draws on Schütz and Bach in its use of counterpoint and expressive text-setting and echoes their concern with mortality and the hope for salvation. In the *German Requiem*, these solemn thoughts are clothed with opulent colors of nineteenth-century harmony, regulated by spacious formal architecture and guided by Brahms's unerring judgment for choral and orchestral effect.

A German
Requiem

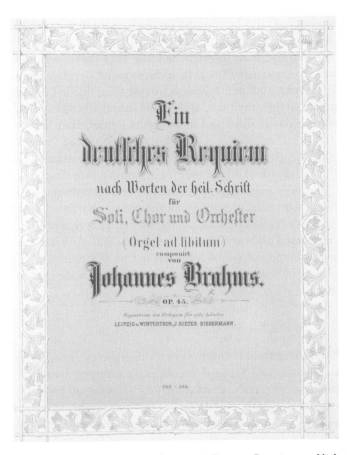

Figure 28.4: Title page of the first edition of Brahms's German Requiem, *published 1869. Performances of this work across Europe won enthusiastic responses from audiences and critics and established Brahms as a major composer.*

BRAHMS'S PLACE

Brahms has often been called conservative, but he was actually a pathbreaker. He was among the first to view the entire range of music of the present and past as material to draw upon in composing his own new and highly individual music—a stance we see repeatedly in composers of the twentieth century. By introducing new elements into traditional forms and trying to meet the master composers on their own ground, he was arguably pursuing a more difficult course than those who simply made their mark through innovation. Yet he never lost sight of the average listener or musical amateur and succeeded in creating pieces that please on first hearing and continue to engage us after many more.

THE WAGNERIANS

The New German School

In 1859, music critic Franz Brendel proposed the term "New German School" for the composers he felt were leading the new developments, primarily Wagner, Liszt, and Berlioz and their disciples in the next generation. Although he acknowledged that neither Liszt nor Berlioz was German, he claimed they were German in origin because they took Beethoven as their model. The term crystallized the polarization among German composers between Liszt, Wagner, and their followers on one side, who believed that music could be linked to the other arts, and on the other side the advocates of absolute music such as Brahms and music critic Eduard Hanslick (see Source Reading).

Composers identified with the Wagnerian side of the debate include Liszt himself after he abandoned his career as a virtuoso (see chapter 24); Anton Bruckner, Brahms's contemporary; and two in the next generation, Hugo Wolf and Richard Strauss. Wagner's view that music should subordinate itself in a collective artwork with drama, poetry, and other arts posed problems for those who composed orchestral music, songs, and choral works. Each of these four composers found individual solutions to this dilemma—and to the more general problem of how to compose for an audience now steeped in the classical tradition.

LISZT

In 1848, Liszt retired from his career as a touring pianist, became court music director at Weimar, and focused increasingly on composition. From this point on, his music was no longer a vehicle for showing off his virtuosity, and the poetic idea and logical development of the material became more important. Although he still aimed for the stunning immediate effect, he clearly understood the shift toward the classical repertoire (a shift he had aided by including earlier composers in his recitals) and presented himself as a composer worthy of comparison to his peers and predecessors.

SOURCE READINGS

ABSOLUTE AND PROGRAM MUSIC

The most articulate proponent of absolute music was music critic Eduard Hanslick (1825–1904). He claimed that music should be understood and appreciated on its own terms rather than for its ties to anything outside music.

——— • ———

What kind of beauty is the beauty of a musical composition?

It is a specifically musical kind of beauty. By this we understand a beauty that is self-contained and in no need of content from outside itself, that consists simply and solely of tones and their artistic combination. . . .

Nothing could be more misguided and prevalent than the view which distinguishes between beautiful music which possesses ideal content and beautiful music which does not. This view has a much too narrow conception of the beautiful in music, representing both the elaborately constructed form and the ideal content with which the form is filled as self-sufficient. Consequently this view divides all compositions into two categories, the full and the empty, like champagne bottles. Musical champagne, however, has the peculiarity that it grows along with the bottle.

Eduard Hanslick, *On the Musically Beautiful*, trans. and ed. Geoffrey Payzant (Indianapolis: Hackett, 1986), 32, in SR 162 (6:15), p. 1203.

——— • ———

Liszt, on the other hand, argued in defending Berlioz's Harold in Italy *that a program could clarify the composer's intentions.*

——— • ———

The program asks only acknowledgment for the possibility of precise definition of the psychological moment which prompts the composer to create his work and of the thought to which he gives outward form. If it is on the one hand childish, idle, sometimes even mistaken, to outline programs after the event, and thus to dispel the magic, to profane the feeling, and to tear to pieces with words the soul's most delicate web, in an attempt to *explain* the feeling of an instrumental poem which took this shape precisely because its content could not be expressed in words, images, and ideas; so on the other hand the master is also master of his work and can create it under the influence of definite impressions which he wishes to bring to a full and complete realization in the listener. The specifically musical symphonist carries his listeners with him into ideal regions, whose shaping and ornamenting he relinquishes to their individual imaginations; in such cases it is extremely dangerous to wish to impose on one's neighbor the same scenes or successions of ideas into which our imagination feels itself transported. The painter-symphonist, however, setting himself the task of reproducing with equal clarity a picture clearly present in his mind, of developing a series of emotional states which are unequivocally and definitely latent in his consciousness—why may he not, through a program, strive to make himself fully intelligible? . . .

Through song there have always been *combinations* of music with literary or quasi-literary works; the present time seeks a *union* of the two which promises to become a more intimate one than any that have offered themselves thus far.

Franz Liszt (with Carolyne von Sayn-Wittgenstein), "Berlioz und seine Haroldsymphonie," *Neue Zeitschrift für Musik* 43 (1855): 49–50 and 77. Trans. Oliver Strunk, in SR 158 (6:11), pp. 1168–69 and 1171.

Symphonic poems   Between 1848 and 1858, Liszt composed twelve orchestral works he called **symphonic poems** (or *tone poems*), adding a thirteenth in 1881–82. Each is a one-movement programmatic work with sections of contrasting character and tempo, presenting a few themes that are developed, repeated, varied, or transformed. These pieces are symphonic in sound, weight, and developmental procedures and are "poems" by analogy to literary poems. Often the form has vestiges of traditional patterns such as sonata form or the contrasts in mood and tempo found in a four-movement symphony.

The content and form of symphonic poems were usually suggested by a picture, statue, play, poem, scene, personality, or something else, identified by the title and usually by a program. Thus Liszt's *Prometheus* (1850–55) relates to a myth and to a poem by Herder, *Mazeppa* (1852–54) to a poem by Victor Hugo, and *Orpheus* (1853–54) to Gluck's opera *Orfeo ed Euridice* and to an Etruscan vase in the Louvre Museum depicting Orpheus singing to the lyre. The two works that Liszt called symphonies—the *Faust Symphony* (1854) and *Dante Symphony* (1856)—are also programmatic, essentially consisting of a linked series of symphonic poems. Liszt's symphonic poems thus parallel for orchestral music Wagner's concept of the collective artwork, formulated around the same time.

Thematic   Liszt devised a method of providing unity, variety, and narrative-like logic
transformation   to a composition by transforming the thematic material to reflect the diverse moods needed to portray a programmatic subject. In his symphonic poem *Les Préludes* (The Preludes, 1854), he applied this method, known as **thematic transformation**, with notable artistic success. We can see how this works in Example 28.5. A three-note motive (28.5a) that is initially tentative, like a prelude, is modified and expanded to take on different characters: flowing yet somewhat amorphous (28.5b), resolute (28.5c), lyrical (28.5d), stormy (28.5e and f), excited (28.5g, an inverted form of the motive), and martial (28.5h). A more distant metamorphosis (28.5i) serves as a contrasting theme and is itself subjected to transformations. Liszt linked *Les Préludes* to a poem of that title by Alfonse-Marie de Lamartine, following the same sequence of moods: introductory, with pizzicato chords and arpeggios in the strings and harp to suggest a poet summoning his Muse with lyre and song; amorous (measure 47, Example 28.5d); troubled and pessimistic about human destiny (measure 131, Example 28.5f); peaceful and pastoral (measure 200); bellicose (measure 344, Example 28.5h); and a return to the initial mood (measure 405). Liszt also used thematic transformation in works without an overt program. The four movements of his Piano Concerto No. 1 in E♭ Major (completed 1855), for example, are linked by themes that are transformed within and between movements.

Sonata in B Minor   In his Piano Sonata in B Minor (1853), Liszt works out four themes in one extended movement lasting about a half-hour. The form can be seen from one perspective as a gigantic sonata form, from another as four movements— fast sonata, slow movement, fugue, and fast finale—played without pause. The themes are transformed in a multiplicity of ways, arriving at an apotheosis in the coda. This is one of the outstanding piano compositions of the nineteenth century, a fitting response to Beethoven's sonatas and a model for later com-

Example 28.5: *Thematic transformation in Liszt's* Les Préludes

posers. It shows Liszt's engagement with the past tradition in a way that reconceives conventions in a radically new manner and points to the future.

The choral works offer another kind of accommodation between past and present. Most important are the two oratorios, *St. Elisabeth* (1857–62), on St. Elisabeth of Hungary, and *Christus* (1866–72), on the life of Christ. Both derive much of their thematic material from melodies of plainchants related to their subjects, paraphrased and treated in the style of modern times.

Choral music

Liszt was perhaps even more influential as a composer than he was as a virtuoso. The symphonic poem was taken up by many composers, including Smetana, Franck, Saint-Saëns, Tchaikovsky, Rimsky-Korsakov, Richard Strauss, and Ives. Liszt's chromatic harmonies helped to form Wagner's style after 1854, and his interest in even divisions of the octave, such as the augmented triad, had a strong impact on Russian and French composers. His

Liszt's influence

Figure 28.5: Anton Bruckner in 1891, around the time he was awarded an honorary Doctor of Philosophy by the University of Vienna. Bronzed plaster of Paris sculpture by Viktor Tilgner.

practice of thematic transformation had parallels in Wagner's treatment of leitmotives and Brahms's developing variation and had many later echoes in the late nineteenth and twentieth centuries.

ANTON BRUCKNER

If Liszt showed how to compose purely orchestral music in a Wagnerian spirit, Anton Bruckner (1824–1896), shown in Figure 28.5, tried the more daunting tasks of absorbing Wagner's style and ethos into the traditional symphony and of writing church music that united the technical resources of nineteenth-century music with a reverent, liturgical approach to the sacred texts. Profoundly religious, Bruckner was thoroughly schooled in counterpoint and served as organist of the cathedral at Linz, and as court organist in Vienna from 1867 to his death.

Symphonies   Bruckner wrote nine numbered symphonies and two early unnumbered ones. He frequently revised them, and as a result most exist in two or three versions. All are in the conventional four movements, and none is explicitly programmatic, though he did at one time furnish descriptive tags for the Fourth (*Romantic*) Symphony in E♭ Major (1874–80).

Influences   Bruckner looked to Beethoven's Ninth Symphony as a model for procedure, purpose, grandiose proportions, and religious spirit. Beethoven's first movement, in which the theme emerges from inchoate intervals and rhythms, suggested an opening gambit, while Beethoven's fourth-movement hymn served as a model for the chorale-like themes in most of Bruckner's finales, although he never used voices. As in Beethoven's Ninth, Bruckner's finales often recycle subjects from earlier movements. Bruckner's debt to Wagner is evident in large-scale structures, the great length of the symphonies, lush harmonies, sequential repetition of entire passages, and the huge orchestra. Bruckner's experience as an organist informed his orchestration, in which instruments or groups are brought in, opposed, and combined, just like the contrasting keyboards of an organ are, and the massive blocks of sound, piled one on top of the other, suggest an organist's improvisation.

Bruckner's symphonies typically begin, like Beethoven's Ninth, with a vague agitation in the strings out of which a theme gradually condenses and then builds up in a crescendo, conveying a sense of coming into being. For example, the Fourth Symphony opens with a quiet tonic-triad tremolo in the strings against horn calls with falling and rising fifths (occasionally altered to sixths and octaves) and a triple-dotted rhythm, shown in Example 28.6a. After some striking modulations, the intervals are filled in with scalar passages, and the theme in Example 28.6b emerges *fortissimo*, forcefully proclaiming the tonic with a favorite rhythmic figure that alternates duple and triple divisions. Development of this idea leads to the key of D♭, where a bird call—as Bruckner identified it—is heard against a lyrical melody in the viola, shown in Example 28.6c. Both themes are reworked until the development section combines them in a dreamlike sequence resembling Wagner's orchestral interludes. A return to the main key ushers in a recapitulation that reviews material from the exposition in the expected order, with the bird-call section in B major, followed by a long coda. Although we can view this movement in terms of sonata form, the continuous development of musical ideas, characteristic of Beethoven and Wagner, gives the work a monumental dimension.

Fourth Symphony

Example 28.6: Motives from Bruckner, Symphony No. 4 (Romantic), first movement

Bruckner's religious choral music blends modern elements with influences from the Cecilian movement, which promoted a revival of the sixteenth-century a cappella style. His motets for unaccompanied chorus reflect these Cecilian ideals, yet their harmonic palette ranges from the strictly

Choral music

modal *Os justi* to the quickly modulating harmonies of *Virga Jesse.* His Mass No. 2 in E Minor (1866) is a unique neo-medieval work for eight-part chorus and fifteen wind instruments (paired oboes, clarinets, bassoons, and trumpets, four horns, and three trombones). Bruckner designed his sacred music to function equally well as part of the liturgy or as concert music and to project a sense of timelessness while incorporating up-to-date harmony, balancing these competing requirements perhaps better than any of his contemporaries.

HUGO WOLF

Hugo Wolf (1860–1903) is best known for adapting Wagner's methods to the German Lied. He also wrote piano pieces, a string quartet, symphonic works, choruses, and an opera, but none shared the success of his songs.

Lieder   Wolf produced most of his 250 Lieder in short periods of intense creative activity between 1887 and 1897, when he was incapacitated by a mental breakdown, probably caused by syphilis. He published five principal collections of Lieder, each devoted to a single poet or group: Eduard Mörike (1889), Joseph Freiherr von Eichendorff (1889), Goethe (1890), and German translations of Spanish poems (1891) and Italian poems (1892 and 1896). By concentrating

Example 28.7: Wolf, Lebe wohl!

"Farewell!" You are not aware of what it means, this word of pain; with a confident face
[and light heart you said it.]

on one poet or group at a time and placing the poet's name above his own in the titles of his collections, Wolf indicated a new ideal of equality between words and music, derived from Wagner's music dramas. Wolf had little use for the folk-song type of melody and strophic structures characteristic of Brahms. Instead, he judiciously applied to the Lied Wagner's notion of a collective artwork, achieving a fusion of poetry and music, and of voice and piano, without subordinating either to the other.

A good illustration of Wolf's approach is *Lebe wohl!* from the Mörike songbook, shown in Example 28.7. The vocal line adapts Wagner's arioso style, presenting a speechlike rhythm and pitch contour. As in Wagner's operas, continuity is sustained by the instrumental part rather than the voice, which often parallels melodies in the piano. The chromatic voice-leading, appoggiaturas, anticipations, and wandering tonality are clearly inspired by the idiom of *Tristan und Isolde* (compare NAWM 128). Dissonances resolve to other dissonances, pure triads are rare, and phrases end more often on dissonant than on consonant chords. A measure of the intense chromaticism is that all twelve chromatic notes appear in the first phrase (measures 1–4) and again in measures 5–6, an effect later termed **chromatic saturation** (see chapter 31). The music is a perfect reflection of the text in declamation and in emotion, aptly conveying the despairing feelings of a rejected lover.

RICHARD STRAUSS

Richard Strauss (1864–1949), shown in Figure 28.6, was a dominant figure in German musical life for most of his career. He was celebrated as a conductor, holding positions in the opera houses of Munich, Weimar, Berlin, and Vienna, and conducting most of the world's great orchestras during numerous tours. As a composer, he is remembered especially for his symphonic poems, most written before 1900; his operas, all but one of which came later (see chapter 30); and his Lieder.

Strauss's chief models for program music were Berlioz and Liszt, drawing on their colorful orchestration, transformation of themes, and types of program. Like theirs, some of Strauss's programs are based on literature, including *Don Juan* (1888–89), after a poem by Nikolaus Lenau; *Macbeth* (1888, revised 1891), on Shakespeare; *Also sprach Zarathustra* (Thus Spoke Zoroaster, 1896), after a prose-poem by philosopher-poet Friedrich Nietzsche; and *Don Quixote* (1897), on the picaresque novel by Miguel Cervantes. Other works drew on his personal experience, as Berlioz had done in his *Symphonie fantastique. Tod und Verklärung* (Death and Transfiguration, 1888–89) was inspired by Strauss's recovery from a life-threatening illness, and *Ein*

Figure 28.6: *Richard Strauss in the 1890s, at the peak of his career as a composer of symphonic poems.*

Heldenleben (A Hero's Life, 1897–98) is openly autobiographical, caricaturing his critics in cacophonous passages while glorifying his own triumphs with citations from his early works.

Program music covers a broad spectrum, from representing specific events, as in Berlioz's *Symphonie fantastique*, to a more general evocation of ideas and emotional states, as in several of Liszt's symphonic poems. Strauss's symphonic poems fall at varying places on this spectrum, from the representational to the philosophical.

Don Juan

Don Juan is Strauss's first complete mature work, and its success established his reputation while still in his twenties. Events in Don Juan's career as a roving lover are pictured, including wooing a new romantic interest, a rather graphic sexual climax followed by a search for his next conquest, and his death at the end. Yet most of the piece evokes general moods of activity, boldness, and romance, rather than following a specific plot.

Till Eulenspiegel

If *Don Juan* falls in the middle of the spectrum, *Till Eulenspiegel* (1894–95) tends toward the representational, telling the comic tale of a trickster's exploits. The realistic details of Till's adventures are specified by marginal notes the composer added to the printed score. Two themes for Till are used and developed like leitmotives, changing to suggest his activities and situation. Yet the specific events are so thoroughly blended into the musical flow that the work could be heard simply as a character sketch of a particularly appealing rascal, or just as a piece of musical humor. This illustrates an important point about program music in the nineteenth and early twentieth centuries: as in opera, the suggestion of events and ideas outside music allows and explains the use of novel musical sounds, gestures, and forms, but in most cases the music still makes sense on its own terms, presenting, developing, and recalling themes and motives in ways that both parallel and diverge from the processes and forms of earlier music. Strauss indicated that the piece is "in rondo form." It is not a rondo in the Classic sense, but rondo-like because the two Till themes keep recurring in a variety of guises, enlivened by shrewd touches of instrumentation. Rondo is appropriate to Till, who remains the same fool after each prank.

Also sprach
Zarathustra

Also sprach Zarathustra is a musical commentary on Nietzsche's long prose-poem, which proclaimed that the Christian ethic should be replaced by the ideal of a superman who is above good and evil. Although the general course of the program is philosophical, moments are directly representational. Zarathustra's address to the rising sun in the prologue inspired the splendid opening, with a deep C in the organ pedal and contrabassoon, a rising brass fanfare, opposing C minor and C major triads, thumping timpani, and triumphant orchestral culmination for full orchestra. The passage became one of Strauss's most famous when it was used in the soundtrack of the film *2001: A Space Odyssey* to accompany both the sunrise and a scene meant to suggest the birth of reasoning.

Don Quixote

As the rondo suits *Till Eulenspiegel*, so variation form fits the adventures of the knight Don Quixote and his squire Sancho Panza, shown in Figure 28.7, whose personalities are shaped by their frustrating experiences. We are no longer in a world of merry pranks but in one of split personalities and double meanings. The wry humor and cleverness in *Don Quixote* (see excerpt in

Figure 28.7: Page from a nineteenth-century translation of Miguel Cervantes' Don Quixote, *first published in Spanish in 1605, showing Don Quixote (right), who imagines himself a knight, with his servant Sancho Panza, playing the role of his squire.*

NAWM 133) lie not so much in the apt depiction of real things as in the play with musical ideas. Much of this work has a chamber-music sound, because it is conceived in contrapuntal lines, and its themes attach to particular solo instruments, notably the cello for Don Quixote and bass clarinet, tenor tuba, and viola for Sancho Panza. "Variations" here does not mean preserving a melody or harmonic progression and its form through a number of statements. Rather, the themes of the two main characters are transformed so that the beginnings of the themes sprout new melodic characters, building on Liszt's technique of thematic transformation.

CD 10|25   CD 5|59

REACHING THE AUDIENCE

Each of the composers examined in this chapter pursued a different path, but all succeeded in reaching an audience and securing a permanent place in the classical repertoire. Brahms wrote music in a wide range of traditional forms and genres, and of all late-nineteenth-century composers came closest to achieving the broad appeal to performers, amateurs, listeners, and connoisseurs alike that was characteristic of his great predecessors Bach, Handel, Haydn, Mozart, and Beethoven. Brahms was seen first as a conservative opposed to Wagner and Liszt, then as a cerebral composer of demanding music, but by his death in 1897 he was considered a classic—the third of the "three

B's" after Bach and Beethoven—and the central figure of classical music in his time, outside the field of opera.

The composers of the Wagnerian wing of the German tradition, like Wagner himself, tended to focus more narrowly on a few genres. The symphonic poems of Liszt and especially of Strauss found a ready audience among lovers of classical music because these works offered something essentially new that was both deeply connected to the symphonic tradition, through procedures of thematic presentation, development, and return, and appealing to first-time listeners, through the programs and novel effects. The choral music of Liszt and Bruckner, Bruckner's symphonies, and Wolf's songs had a harder time competing against the well-established classics in these genres, but they too found a devoted audience of connoisseurs—particularly in Germany and Austria—and now have an enduring place in the repertoire. From our perspective more than a century later, the dispute between the partisans of Brahms and those of the New German School seems like an argument among close relatives, for all traced their heritage back to Beethoven and the early Romantics and sought to add something of their own to an already rich common tradition.

Diverging Traditions in the Later Nineteenth Century

We have seen how German and Austrian composers in the second half of the nineteenth century responded in different ways to their common heritage, and in the process each created a distinctive personal style. Composers in other lands drew both on the German tradition and on the music of their own nations. Often—but not always—they sought to assert a specifically national style, as well as an individual one. French composers debated whether to assimilate Bach, Beethoven, and Wagner or to pursue a more national idiom. In Russia, Bohemia, and Scandinavia, nationalist schools emerged in instrumental music as well as in opera. Yet in Britain and the Americas, many composers avoided overt nationalism, choosing instead to speak in what they regarded as the universal common language of music.

All these competing currents contributed to the growing diversity of classical music in the later nineteenth century. But classical music was only one of several streams in musical life, alongside entertainment music, popular song, utilitarian music, and folk music. Through a look at trends in the United States, we can gain a sense of the variety of musical traditions at the time.

FRANCE

In concert music as in opera, Paris was the center of French musical life. Concert-giving institutions balanced interest in German music with concern for France's musical heritage and encouragement of its native

Concert life in Paris

composers. Beginning in 1852, an orchestra of the best Paris Conservatoire students gave concerts focused on symphonic music of Haydn, Mozart, Beethoven, Mendelssohn, and Schumann, and on new French works in the same vein, such as Gounod's symphonies. Other organizations presented a similar repertoire to audiences numbering in the thousands. Figure 29.1 shows the program of the first Concert National (founded 1873), split equally between German classics and new French works. Conductor Edouard Colonne focused his 1885–86 concert series on surveying the history of music and introduced explanatory program notes, which became standard in Paris by the end of the century and are now part of concerts everywhere.

Politics   French music was linked to politics, a tradition that stretched back to royal control of music in the seventeenth century (see chapter 16). Concert series, composers, and even musical styles were often associated with political movements. One notable political effect was an increasing activity in musical life after the Franco-Prussian War of 1870–71, when the government and the Parisian elite sought to assert the vibrancy of French culture in the face of an embarrassing defeat. For example, the Société Nationale de Musique (National Society of Music), founded in 1871, gave performances of works by French composers and sought to revive the great French music of the past through editions and performances of Rameau, Gluck, and sixteenth-century composers.

Schools   Music schools reflected competing visions. The Conservatoire stressed technical training with an emphasis on opera. It was still the most prestigious school, and a first prize there could guarantee a successful career. The École Niedermeyer, founded in 1853, gave general instruction but focused on

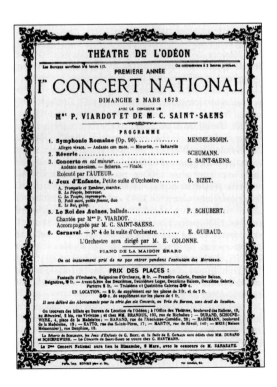

Figure 29.1: Handbill for the first Concert National, conducted by Edouard Colonne on March 2, 1873. The program is split between German music from earlier generations—Mendelssohn's Italian Symphony, a short Schumann piece, and a Schubert song—and new music by living French composers Saint-Saëns, Bizet, and Ernest Guiraud, all then in their thirties. Many of the seats were so inexpensive (at one franc or less) that almost anyone could afford to attend, and audiences were often very large.

church music; by teaching students to sing Gregorian chant and to accompany it with modal chords, the school influenced many French composers to use modal melody and harmony. The Schola Cantorum, founded in 1894 by Vincent d'Indy (1851–1931) and others, introduced broad historical studies in music, allied with conservative politics.

The growth in concert activity, proliferation of music schools, revival of past traditions, and encouragement of new music created a stimulating climate that helped Paris regain a leading position in music. Two main strands in composition can be identified before the emergence of impressionism (discussed in chapter 30): a cosmopolitan tradition, transmitted through César Franck (1822–1890) and his pupils, and a more specifically French tradition, embodied in the music of Gabriel Fauré (1845–1924) and passed on to countless twentieth-century composers through his students, especially the famous pedagogue Nadia Boulanger (1887–1979).

Renewal

CÉSAR FRANCK

Franck was born in Belgium, came to Paris to study at the Conservatoire, and became a professor of organ there in 1871. Working mainly in instrumental genres and oratorio, he achieved a distinctive style by blending traditional counterpoint and classical forms with Liszt's thematic transformation, Wagner's harmony, and the Romantic idea of cyclic unification through thematic return.

Typical of Franck's approach is the *Prelude, Chorale, and Fugue* (1884) for piano, which emulates a Baroque toccata in the prelude; introduces a chorale-like melody in distant keys; presents a fugue on a chromatic subject that has been foreshadowed in both previous sections; and closes by combining the opening toccata texture with the chorale melody and fugue subject in counterpoint. It is a piece that could only have been written by someone who had absorbed the thematic and harmonic methods of Liszt and Wagner and also the organ music of Bach and the French Baroque. Franck's organ music took a similar approach, often combining original melodies in chorale style with richly developed fantasias and full chordal finales, as in his *Three Chorales* (1890). His improvisatory style inaugurated a new type of organ music in France, one dominated by lyrical themes, contrapuntal development, and orchestral color. The design of the organ in France changed completely during this period in order to accommodate this new approach.

Keyboard music

Franck has been called the founder of modern French chamber music. His chief chamber works are a Piano Quintet in F Minor (1879), a String Quartet in D Major (1889), and the Violin Sonata in A Major (1886). All are cyclic, featuring themes that recur or are transformed in two or more movements. His Symphony in D Minor (1888), a model of cyclic form, is perhaps the most popular French symphony after Berlioz.

Chamber and symphonic music

GABRIEL FAURÉ AND THE FRENCH TRADITION

The other tendency in French music drew primarily on earlier French composers from Couperin to Gounod and approached music more as sonorous

Figure 29.2: Gabriel Fauré in a portrait by John Singer Sargent (1889).

form than as expression. Order and restraint are fundamental. Instead of emotional displays and musical depiction, we hear subtle patterns of tones, rhythms, and colors. The music sounds more lyric or dancelike than epic or dramatic. It is economical, simple, and reserved rather than profuse, complex, or grandiloquent.

The refined music of Gabriel Fauré, who is shown in Figure 29.2, embodies the qualities of the French tradition. He studied under Saint-Saëns at the École Niedermeyer, held various posts as an organist, and was a founder of the Société Nationale. He became professor of composition at the Paris Conservatoire in 1896 and was its director from 1905 to 1920. Fauré wrote some music in larger forms, including his best-known work, the Requiem (1887), and two operas. But he was primarily a composer of songs; of piano music, chiefly preludes, impromptus, nocturnes, and barcarolles; and of chamber music.

Harmony   Fauré began by composing songs in the manner of Gounod, and lyrical melody, with no display of virtuosity, remained the basis of his style. But in his maturity, from about 1885, he developed a new language in which melodic lines are fragmented and harmony becomes much less directional. *Avant que tu ne t'en ailles* from the song cycle *La bonne chanson* (The Good Song, 1892) illustrates these characteristics. Each phrase of melody is a declamatory fragment in its own tonal world, joined to the others only by subtle motivic echoes. In the passage shown in Example 29.1, the chords consist mainly of dominant sevenths and ninths, but the tension melts as one chord fades into another, linked through common tones. In each of the first three measures, for example, the dominant seventh on G♯ is succeeded by an E♯-major triad, which neutralizes the leading tone B♯ in the vocal line as the fifth of the new chord and treats the seventh F♯ as an appoggiatura. Such harmonic successions dilute the need for resolution and undermine the pull of the tonic, creating a sense of repose or even stasis that is the opposite of the emotional unrest in Wagner's music. Here the chromaticism that is the lifeblood of so much expressive music in the nineteenth century becomes instead a means to achieve equilibrium and restraint, attributes that have long been esteemed in French music.

Example 29.1: Excerpt from Fauré's Avant que tu ne t'en ailles

EASTERN AND NORTHERN EUROPE

The instrumental repertoire centered on works by German and Austrian composers from Bach to Brahms, but some composers from eastern and northern Europe active in the later nineteenth century were able to secure a place in the classical canon. Inevitably, their works were perceived as offering a different voice, colored as much by their nationality as by their individual character.

TCHAIKOVSKY

Tchaikovsky was by far the most successful of these composers, and his ballets (discussed in chapter 27), piano concertos, Violin Concerto (1878), and symphonies won a place so near the heart of the repertoire that they transcended nationalism. His best-known symphonies are his last three: No. 4 in F Minor (1877–78); No. 5 in E Minor (1888); and No. 6 in B Minor, the *Pathétique* (1893).

Fourth Symphony   Tchaikovsky wrote his patron Nadezhda von Meck that the Fourth Symphony had a private program in which the horn-call from the introduction symbolizes inexorable fate. The horn motive is recalled after the exposition and before the coda of the final movement, unifying the symphony through cyclic return while conveying the program. The outer movements are dramatic, suffused with high emotion; the second movement is wistful, and the third an airy scherzo of a type that became a Russian specialty. Especially novel is the key scheme of the first movement, organized by a circle of minor thirds: the first theme group is in F minor and the second in A♭ major, as expected, but the closing theme appears in B major, a tritone from the tonic; then the recapitulation begins in D minor for the first and second themes, modulates to F major for the closing theme, and returns to F minor for the coda. As we saw in chapter 27, such circles of minor or major thirds were common in Russian music, though the three-key exposition and the recapitulation that begins away from the tonic suggest the influence of Schubert.

Sixth Symphony   In his Sixth Symphony, Tchaikovsky replaces the usual scherzo with a $\frac{5}{4}$ Russian waltz. The order of movements is novel: the dance comes second, then a vivacious rondo in march character, and the piece ends extraordinarily with a despairing slow movement that fades away at the end over a low pulse in the strings, like the beating of a dying heart. The darkly passionate character of the first movement (which quotes the Russian Orthodox Requiem), together with the pessimistic finale, led Tchaikovsky's brother to nickname the symphony *Pathétique*.

THE MIGHTY HANDFUL

Tchaikovsky was the most prominent Russian composer of his time, but others also found a place in the repertoire. The five composers known as the Mighty Handful—Balakirev and Cui, as well as Borodin, Musorgsky, and Rimsky-Korsakov (discussed below)—were active in instrumental music as well as in opera, and indeed their instrumental music is better known in the West.

Borodin   Borodin's principal instrumental works are his two string quartets (1874–79 and 1881), Symphony No. 2 in B Minor (1869–76), and a symphonic sketch, *In Central Asia* (1880). Alone among the Mighty Handful, he was a devotee of chamber music and an admirer of Mendelssohn. Although he seldom quoted folk tunes—as Balakirev and Cui did—his melodies reflect their spirit. His chamber and orchestral works are characterized by songlike themes, transparent orchestral texture, modally tinged harmonies, and his original method of spinning out an entire movement from a single pregnant thematic idea, as in the first movement of the Second Symphony.

Musorgsky   Musorgsky's principal nonoperatic works are a symphonic fantasy, *Night on Bald Mountain* (1867); a set of piano pieces, *Pictures at an Exhibition* (1874; later orchestrated by Ravel); and the song cycles *The Nursery* (1872), *Sunless* (1874), and *Songs and Dances of Death* (1875). *Pictures at an Exhibition* is a suite of ten pieces inspired by an exhibition Musorgsky saw of over four hundred sketches, paintings, and designs by his late friend Viktor Hartmann, who shared with the composer an interest in finding a new artistic language that was uniquely Russian. Several of the paintings are rendered in

Figure 29.3: Design for Kiev City Gate, Main Façade, *by Viktor Hartmann.*

character pieces, sewn together by interludes that vary a theme meant to represent the viewer walking through the gallery. Figure 29.3 shows Hartmann's design for a commemorative gate to be built at Kiev that combined classical columns, capitals, and arches with decoration modeled on Russian folk art. In Example 29.2, Musorgsky translates this image into a grand processional hymn that similarly combines Western and Russian elements, blending classical procedures with a melody that resembles a Russian folk song and harmonies that suggest the modality and parallel motion of folk polyphony.

Example 29.2: The Great Gate of Kiev, *from Musorgsky's* Pictures at an Exhibition

Rimsky-Korsakov is best known for his programmatic orchestral works, although he also wrote symphonies, chamber music, choruses, and songs as well as operas. The *Capriccio espagnol* (1887), the symphonic suite *Sheherazade* (1888), and the *Russian Easter Overture* (1888) display his genius for orchestration and musical characterization. The first two typify exoticism, based on Spanish themes and on tales from the *Arabian Nights* respectively,

Rimsky-Korsakov

and the third is nationalist, incorporating Russian Orthodox liturgical melodies. The four movements of *Sheherazade*, each on a different story, are woven together by the themes of the Sultan and his wife Sheherazade, the storyteller, portrayed by a solo violin.

BOHEMIA: SMETANA AND DVOŘÁK

Like the Russians, Smetana and Dvořák are better known outside their native land for their instrumental music than for their operas, no doubt because instrumental music can leap over the language barrier.

Smetana — Smetana sought to create a national music in his String Quartet No. 1, *From My Life* (1876), and in his cycle of six symphonic poems collectively titled *Má vlast* (My Country, ca. 1872–79). Of the latter, the best known is *The Moldau*, a picture of the river that winds through the Czech countryside on its way to Prague. But the most stirring is *Tábor*, named after the city where followers of radical religious reformer Jan Hus (ca. 1369–1415) built a fortress that became a symbol of Czech resistance to outside oppression. *Tábor* falls into two sections, like the slow introduction and Allegro of a symphonic first movement. In each half, fragments of a Hussite chorale are presented and developed until the entire chorale theme appears in full for the first time at the end. Smetana uses this process to embody the legend that the Hussite warriors will gather strength and emerge from their stronghold in the Czech people's time of need.

Dvořák — Dvořák wrote nine symphonies, four concertos, including the Cello Concerto in B Minor (1894–95), numerous dances and other works for orchestra, and many chamber works, piano pieces, songs, and choral works. Many of his pieces are in an international style; for example, his Symphony No. 6 in D Major (1880), premiered in Vienna, is full of allusions to Beethoven and Brahms symphonies, as Dvořák claimed a place in the Viennese symphonic tradition. But in pieces like the *Slavonic Dances* for orchestra (1878 and 1886–87) and the *Dumky* Piano Trio (1890–91), he used elements from Czech traditional music to achieve a national idiom.

Dvořák's best-known symphony is No. 9 in E Minor (*From the New World*), which he wrote in 1893 during an extended sojourn in the United States as artistic director of the National Conservatory of Music in New York. He had been hired with the expectation that as a nationalist composer he would show how to create a new national style of art music for the United States. Believing that a truly national music could derive only from folk traditions, Dvořák looked to the music of American Indians and African Americans (see Source Reading). After studying Indian melodies and hearing an African-American student at the Conservatory, Harry T. Burleigh, sing plantation songs and spirituals, Dvořák took the elements of those musical idioms, including pentatonic melodies, syncopated rhythms, drones, and plagal cadences, and applied them to his symphony. These sounds also suffuse his String Quartet No. 12 in F Major (*American*), written in the summer of 1893 while at a Czech settlement in Spillville, Iowa. As we will see below, Americans differed on whether Dvořák's approach was the right one.

NORWAY: EDVARD GRIEG

At the same time that the Mighty Five were forging a distinct Russian idiom, Edvard Grieg (1843–1907) was writing a series of songs, short piano pieces, and orchestral suites that incorporated the modal melodies and harmonies as well as the dance rhythms of his native Norway. An ethnic character emerges most clearly in his songs on Norwegian texts, his *Peer Gynt* Suite (1875), and especially the *Slåtter*, Norwegian peasant dances that Grieg arranged for the piano from transcripts of country fiddle playing. His piano style, with its delicate grace notes and mordents, owes something to Chopin, but the all-pervading influence in his music is that of Norwegian folk songs and dances, reflected in his modal turns of melody and harmony (Lydian raised fourth, Aeolian lowered seventh, alternative major-minor third); frequent drones in

SOURCE READING

DVOŘÁK ON AN AMERICAN NATIONAL MUSIC

Recognized as a nationalist composer, Dvořák was often asked during his sojourn in America about how to create an American national music. This passage is from a magazine article written in 1895, a few months before he returned to Europe, and includes revealing comments about his own situation as well as American music.

———•———

A while ago [in an 1893 interview] I suggested that inspiration for truly national music might be derived from the Negro melodies or Indian chants. I was led to take this view partly by the fact that the so-called plantation songs are indeed the most striking and appealing melodies that have yet been found on this side of the water, but largely by the observation that this seems to be recognized, though often unconsciously, by most Americans. All races have their distinctively national songs, which they at once recognize as their own, even if they have never heard them before. . . .

Undoubtedly the germs for the best in music lie hidden among all the races that are commingled in this great country. The music of the people is like a rare and lovely flower growing amidst encroaching weeds. Thousands pass it, while others trample it under foot, and thus the chances are that it will perish before it is seen by the one discriminating spirit who will prize it above all else. The fact that no one has as yet arisen to make the most of it does not prove that nothing is there.

Not so many years ago Slavic music was not known to the men of other races. A few men like Chopin, Glinka, Moniuszko, Smetana, Rubinstein, and Tchaikovsky, with a few others, were able to create a Slavic school of music. Chopin alone caused the music of Poland to be known and prized by all lovers of music. Smetana did the same for Bohemians. Such national music, I repeat, is not created out of nothing. It is discovered and clothed in new beauty, just as the myths and the legends of a people are brought to light and crystallized in undying verse by the master poets. All that is needed is a delicate ear, a retentive memory, and the power to weld the fragments of former ages together in one harmonious whole. . . . The music of the people, sooner or later, will command attention and creep into the books of composers.

Antonín Dvořák, "Music in America," *Harper's* 90 (February 1895), as excerpted in *Composers on Music: Eight Centuries of Writings,* ed. Josiah Fisk (Boston: Northeastern University Press, 1997), 163.

the bass or middle register (suggested by the drone strings on Norwegian stringed instruments); and the fascinating combination of $\frac{3}{4}$ and $\frac{6}{8}$ rhythm in the *Slåtter*. Not all Grieg's music was nationalist; among his best-known pieces is the Piano Concerto in A Minor (1868, revised 1907), a bravura work that remains a favorite.

BRITAIN: EDWARD ELGAR

Edward Elgar (1857–1934) was the first English composer in more than two hundred years to enjoy wide international recognition. The English in the late nineteenth century did not strive for a distinctive national style, preferring to adopt what seemed the universal language of the classical tradition. Accordingly, Elgar's music is untouched by folk songs or any other noticeable national tradition. He derived his harmonic style from Brahms and Wagner and drew from Wagner the system of leitmotives in his oratorios. The oratorio *The Dream of Gerontius* (1900), on a Catholic poem by John Henry Newman,

TIMELINE: DIVERGING TRADITIONS IN THE LATER 19TH CENTURY

1840	1850	1860	1870	1880	1890	1900	1910

- 1848–49 California Gold Rush
- 1852–70 Second French Empire under Napoleon III
- 1855–81 Reign of Czar Alexander II of Russia
- **1860s First African-American spirituals published**
- 1861–65 Civil War in United States
- 1862 Victor Hugo, *Les Misérables*
- **1865 Theodore Thomas Orchestra founded**
- 1866 Fyodor Dostoyevsky, *Crime and Punishment*
- 1870–71 Franco-Prussian War
- **1872–79 Bedřich Smetana, *Má vlast***
- **1874 Modest Musorgsky, *Pictures at an Exhibition***
- 1875 Third French Republic
- **1877–78 Piotr Il'yich Tchaikovsky, Fourth Symphony**
- 1879 Thomas Edison invents the electric lightbulb
- **1880s Tin Pan Alley becomes center for popular song publishers**
- 1884 César Franck, Symphony in D Minor •
- 1889 Eiffel Tower erected •
- **1893 Antonín Dvořák, *New World* Symphony •**
- **1897 John Philip Sousa, *The Stars and Stripes Forever* •**
- 1898 Spanish-American War •
- **1907 Amy Beach, Piano Quintet •**

influenced by Wagner's *Parsifal*, gives the orchestra an expressive role as important as the chorus. His symphonic output includes the *Enigma Variations* (1899) and two symphonies.

FINDING A NICHE

This sampling of a few composers can give only a taste of the variety of national and individual styles in Europe in the second half of the nineteenth century. Composers often first found a niche for their music within a local, regional, or national performing tradition. A lucky few won a broader audience, often by capitalizing on their national identity, especially when that nation was not yet represented in the international repertoire. This remained true for composers in the early twentieth century, as we will see in the next two chapters.

THE UNITED STATES

In the United States, national identity was complicated by the country's ethnic diversity. Immigrants from many different regions in Europe, Africa, Latin America, and Asia brought their own musical traditions, from folk to classical. American musical life became not exactly a melting pot but perhaps a stewpot, where each group maintained its own music while lending a flavor to the whole.

Superimposed on these ethnic divisions were the rapidly emerging distinctions among classical, popular, and folk music. In theory, these three categories represented different attitudes toward notation, composition, and performance. The classical tradition centered on the composer and the work and required scrupulous adherence to the notated score. Popular music was written down and sold as a commodity but centered on the performer and the performance, allowing considerable leeway in rearranging the notated music. Folk music was independent of notation, passed on through oral tradition. But in practice, the categories overlapped. Folk tunes were written down and sold as popular music, arranged for concert performance, or incorporated into classical pieces; classical works were transcribed and altered for performance in popular venues; and some popular songs (such as *Turkey in the Straw*) became so well known they were passed down orally, like folk songs.

Of all these trends, we will look at four: music in the classical tradition; band music, affected strongly by the growing split between classical and popular music; popular songs; and music of African Americans, drawing on oral traditions but becoming a strand of both popular and classical music.

THE CLASSICAL TRADITION

Beginning in the 1840s, crop failures and the 1848 Revolution spurred many Germans to emigrate to the United States, following others who had come over the previous century. Many of the immigrants were musicians and music

Immigration and institutions

teachers with a strong commitment to classical music, and they contributed to an extraordinary growth in performing institutions, music schools, and university departments of music in the second half of the nineteenth century. German musicians filled positions in orchestras, taught music at all levels, and—along with Americans who had studied in Germany—dominated the teaching of composition and music theory in conservatories and universities. The new immigrants and the institutions they helped to found fostered an increasingly sharp divide between classical music and popular music. Not surprisingly, German tastes and styles dominated American music in the classical tradition until World War I.

Theodore Thomas   One of the most famous immigrant musicians was Theodore Thomas (1835–1905), who came over with his family in 1845, played violin with the New York Philharmonic and the Academy of Music, conducted the Brooklyn Philharmonic, and in 1865 founded his own professional orchestra. Through constant performing and touring, the Theodore Thomas Orchestra became the best and the most financially successful in the United States. Thomas was devoted to the classical masterworks but recognized that there was not a large enough demand for them to pay his musicians' salaries. So his orchestra gave both concert hall programs centered on works in the classical tradition and outdoor concerts that interspersed dances and lighter music between overtures and symphonic movements, pleasing the public while introducing them to the classics in small doses. In 1890, he became the first conductor of the Chicago Symphony Orchestra, one of a new breed of full-time professional orchestras backed by wealthy donors and focused almost entirely on classical music.

American composers   As classical music became well established, native-born composers were able to pursue careers that combined composition with performing and teaching, especially in the region from Boston to New York. Among them were John Knowles Paine (1839–1906), trained by a German immigrant, who became Harvard's first professor of music; George Whitefield Chadwick (1854–1931), who studied at the New England Conservatory in Boston and became its director; Chadwick's student Horatio Parker (1863–1919), who taught at Yale and was the first dean of its School of Music; and Edward MacDowell (1860–1908), a New Yorker who was the first professor of music at Columbia University in New York. All studied in Germany as well as the United States, and all pursued styles deeply rooted in the German tradition (primarily the Brahms wing for the Boston composers, Wagner and Liszt for MacDowell).

However, these composers had varying attitudes about nationalism. Parker believed American composers should simply write the best music they could; his Latin oratorio *Hora novissima* (1893), the piece that made his reputation, is in a universal style modeled on German and English oratorios. Chadwick, on the other hand, developed an idiom laced with American traits such as pentatonic melodies and characteristic rhythms from Protestant psalmody and African-Caribbean dances, used in his Symphony No. 2 in B♭ Major (1883–85) and *Symphonic Sketches* (1895–1904). MacDowell opposed jingoistic nationalism, but like most Europeans he saw a national identity as an important aspect of any composer's claim to international attention. Among his overtly nationalist works is his Second (*Indian*) Suite for orchestra (1891–95), based on American Indian melodies.

Another Boston composer, Amy Marcy Beach (1867–1944), shown in Figure 29.4, could not study or teach at the top universities because they excluded women. A child prodigy, she studied piano, harmony, and counterpoint privately, then taught herself to compose by studying and playing works of composers she admired. Married to a wealthy physician, she was freed of financial concerns and devoted herself to composition. At the time, women were considered incapable of composing in longer forms. As if to prove them wrong, she wrote large-scale works such as her Mass in E♭ (1890), *Gaelic* Symphony (1894–96), Piano Concerto (1899), and Piano Quintet (1907), all of them well received. She also wrote about 120 songs and dozens of piano and

Figure 29.4: Amy Beach in about 1903.

choral pieces, many of them very popular. Beach was internationally recognized as one of America's leading composers, and she inspired many women in later generations.

Some of Beach's music had an ethnic flavor, like the *Gaelic* Symphony on Irish tunes and the String Quartet (1929) on American Indian melodies. But most of her works engaged the traditions of the German classics. She based the themes of the first and third movements of her own Piano Quintet on a theme from Brahms's Piano Quintet, Op. 34, which she had performed in 1900. Her individual voice emerges forcefully in the third and last movement (NAWM 134), moving beyond the Brahmsian music of the first movement to embrace late-nineteenth-century chromatic harmony, with unusual inversions, augmented triads, and colorful nonchord tones.

CD 10|31

BAND MUSIC

While orchestras gradually moved toward greater concentration on the classics, wind and brass bands maintained the mix of serious and popular music that had once been common to all concerts.

The earliest American bands were attached to military units, but in the nineteenth century local bands became common everywhere. One important factor was the invention of brass instruments with valves, pistons, or keys, allowing these instruments to play melodies throughout their range (instead of just notes from the harmonic series) and making them easier for amateurs to play. Soon the brass were the backbone of the band, either joining or replacing the winds. Amateur bands were formed in communities across the country; some of the earliest are still active, including the Allentown Band (founded 1828) and Repasz Band (1831) in Pennsylvania. Bands played indoors or outdoors, seated or on parade, in concerts but also at dances, holiday celebrations, fairs, picnics, parties, ball games, political rallies, store openings, sales events, weddings, funerals, and other public and private gatherings.

Spread of bands

The Civil War was called the most musical war in history because almost every regiment on both sides had its own band, which entertained the troops, led marches, performed in parades, and played during battles to hearten the soldiers. After the war, community bands continued to proliferate, becoming such a fixture of American life that by the 1880s there were some ten thousand bands that performed at every opportunity.

Professional bands   The period between the Civil War and World War I was the heyday of professional bands. The Irish-born conductor Patrick S. Gilmore (1829–1892) founded his own band in 1858, enlisted together with them in the Union Army, and led them in concerts after the war. Inspired by patriotism, finances, and fame, he organized two mammoth music festivals: a five-day National Peace Jubilee in Boston in 1869, featuring a thousand-piece band and a chorus of ten thousand, and a World Peace Jubilee in 1872 to celebrate the end of the Franco-Prussian War, with more than twenty thousand performers, including Johann Strauss. Gilmore's Band toured the nation in 1876, traveling from New York to San Francisco, and two years later they made an international tour. His success led to a flood of professional touring bands. The most successful bandmaster was John Philip Sousa (1854–1932), whose years conducting the United States Marine Band (1880–92) raised it to national prominence through tours and savvy promotion. In 1892, he organized his own band, shown in Figure 29.5, which made annual tours of the United States, several European tours, and a world tour.

Repertory   The repertory of nineteenth-century bands consisted of marches; quicksteps (fast marches); dances including two-steps, waltzes, polkas, galops, and schottisches; arrangements of opera arias and songs, including medleys;

Figure 29.5: John Philip Sousa with the Sousa Band at a fashionable outdoor concert.

a. Standard March Form		
March	Trio	March (da capo)
Intro ‖: A :‖: B :‖	(Optional Intro) ‖: C :‖: D :‖	Intro ‖: A :‖ B :‖

b. Nonrepetitive March Form			
March	Trio	Break Strain	Trio
Intro ‖: A :‖: B :‖	C	‖: D	C :‖

Figure 29.6: March forms

transcriptions of pieces by classical composers from Rossini to Wagner; and virtuosic display pieces often featuring famous soloists. Except for the instrumentation, this was essentially the same fare played by orchestras in the mid-nineteenth century, such as those conducted by Louis Jullien (see chapter 25) and Theodore Thomas. Bands, whose first purpose was entertainment, retained this formula far longer. Sousa's programming was especially astute. After every selection listed on the program, the band played an encore, usually a light, quick piece guaranteed to please. Yet he also performed the European classics from Bach to Richard Strauss, introducing Wagner's music to more Americans than anyone else. The same variety is evident in the music Sousa composed for band, which varies from programmatic fantasias to more than a hundred marches, including his most famous march, *The Stars and Stripes Forever* (1897; NAWM 135). Not limited to a single genre or medium, Sousa also wrote more than a dozen operettas and some seventy songs.

CD 10|38

Marches

The staple of the band repertory was and still is the **march**. Figure 29.6a shows the standard march form at midcentury: a brief introduction, usually of four measures; two **strains** or periods, each repeated; a trio in a contrasting key, most often in the subdominant, with an optional introduction and two repeated strains; and then a da capo repetition of the march up to the trio. The strains are typically sixteen measures long, and often the second half of a strain varies its first half. The first strain of the trio tends to be soft and lyrical, in contrast to the dynamism of the other strains.

This form was well suited to parades, when the band may be blocks away by the time the first strain returns, but Sousa sensed that concert performance required a more dramatic effect, building to a climax rather than returning to the beginning. So in most of his marches, including *The Stars and Stripes Forever*, he dropped the da capo repetition and instead alternated the lyrical trio with a more aggressive break strain, producing the form in Figure 29.6b. In performances, if not always in the score, Sousa added countermelodies or increased the instrumentation or dynamic level with each repetition of the trio. Just as Beethoven and Brahms had done in their symphonies, Sousa shifted the weight to the end to create a sense of forward progress. This

Sousa marches

dramatic flair, combined with catchy melodies, lively rhythms, and strong contrasts of instruments and textures, helped to make Sousa marches the most widely known ever and to earn him the nickname "The March King" (after Johann Strauss, "The Waltz King").

POPULAR SONG

While bands embraced a wide repertoire from marches to classics, the world of song was splintering. Schubert's Lieder and Stephen Foster's parlor songs had served similar purposes, intended primarily for home music-making and occasionally performed in concerts. But in the later nineteenth century, there was a widening gulf between **art songs** and **popular songs**. Art songs, such as those of Fauré and Wolf, had precisely notated piano parts, tended to be through-composed rather than strophic, were meant to engage listeners on a high artistic plane, and required high professional standards of both pianist and singer. Composers of popular songs sought instead to entertain their audience, accommodate amateur performers, and sell as many copies of the sheet music as possible, so immediate appeal and stick-in-your-head catchiness were the most important attributes.

Subjects   Topics for popular songs included love, heartbreak, birth, death, racial and ethnic satire, new inventions like the bicycle and telephone, sentimental thoughts of mother and the old family home, and America's favorite pastime, baseball. Songs were pressed into service for every possible cause: abolition, the Civil War, temperance (the campaign against drunkenness), labor organizing, political campaigns, and evangelism, as in gospel songs such as *In the Sweet Bye and Bye.*

Conventions   Popular art depends upon the interplay of convention and novelty, and both are evident in the best popular songs. The standard form remained verse and refrain, with a four- or eight-measure introduction for the piano; an eight-, sixteen-, or thirty-two-measure verse; and a refrain of similar size. Often the refrain was scored in parts for chorus (or four solo singers), so that **chorus** came to be used as a term for refrain. Both verse and refrain typically had internal repetitions, falling into forms such as AABA; in some songs the verse and refrain shared material, and in others the chorus was wholly new, occasionally even in a different meter. The key to success was creating a catchy phrase, sometimes called the *hook*, that could grab the listener's attention and then be repeated and varied over the course of the song. The chorus of Charles K. Harris's *After the Ball* (1892), shown in Example 29.3, begins with a motive that is simple yet has enough unusual features to make it intriguing: it begins and ends away from the tonic note, avoids stepwise motion, twice rocks back and forth on a minor third, and has its high point early in the phrase on an unstressed beat and syllable. Linked with the waltz rhythm, all these features convey a lack of balance, suggesting the intoxication of dancing at a ball. The motive is varied many times in succession, then is replaced by a more stable, stepwise phrase at the close (producing AA'A"B form). The lilting waltz suits the subject of the text, and the move from giddiness to steadiness drives home the lesson the words convey.

Example 29.3: Chorus from Charles K. Harris's After the Ball

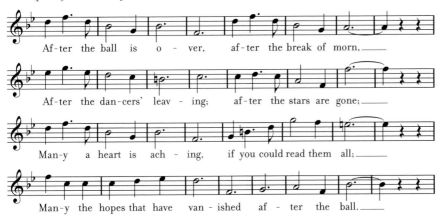

Af-ter the ball is o - ver, af-ter the break of morn,_____

Af-ter the dan-cers' leav - ing; af-ter the stars are gone;_____

Man-y a heart is ach - ing, if you could read them all;_____

Man-y the hopes that have van - ished af - ter the ball._____

Tin Pan Alley

Harris's song was enormously popular, selling millions of copies and—since he had published it himself—making him rich. It typifies the products of **Tin Pan Alley,** the jocular name for a district on West 28th Street in New York where, beginning in the 1880s, numerous publishers specializing in popular songs were located. Harris's strategy for promoting the song also became typical. He paid a singer to introduce the song in a show, and when it became a hit with the audiences, people went out in droves to buy a copy of the sheet music. The link between success on stage and in sales of printed music harkens back to Baroque opera, includes the minstrel show tunes of Stephen Foster and others in the nineteenth century, and remained important in the twentieth century.

MUSIC OF AFRICAN AMERICANS

The one immigrant group that came to the United States against their will was Africans. Imported as slaves in inhuman conditions, they came from many ethnic groups with different languages and customs. Mixed together on plantations or as domestic servants, they would have had a difficult time maintaining their original languages and cultures even if their owners had not actively worked to prevent this. But elements of their music were easier to preserve, because they had been widely shared among African societies and because white slaveowners did not consider singing a threat. Indeed, work songs were actively encouraged as a way to keep up the pace and the spirits. Among the many traits of African-American music that have been traced back to Africa are these:

- alternating short phrases between a leader and the group, called **call and response**;
- improvisation, usually based on a simple formula that allows wide-ranging variation;
- syncopation;
- repetition of short rhythmic or melodic patterns;

- multiple layers of rhythm, with beats in some instruments (or hand clapping or foot stomping) and offbeats in others;
- bending pitches or sliding from one pitch to another;
- moans, shouts, and other vocalizations; and
- instruments like the banjo, based on a West African stringed instrument.

We will see these and other traits in ragtime, blues, jazz, rhythm and blues, and other twentieth-century styles based on African-American traditions.

Spirituals   The African-American form of music with the greatest impact in the nineteenth century was the ***spiritual,*** a religious song of southern slaves, passed down through oral tradition. The texts were usually based on images or stories from the Bible, but they often carried hidden meanings of the slaves' yearning for freedom. The first to appear in print was *Go Down, Moses,* which uses the story of Israel's deliverance from Egypt as a symbol for the liberation of the slaves. The song was published in 1861, during the first year of the Civil War, after a missionary heard it sung by refugee slaves.

The first publications of spirituals tried to document the songs as former slaves sang them, though the editors admitted that they could not notate the bent pitches and other aspects of performance. But soon dozens of spirituals were arranged as songs with piano accompaniments that anyone could play and in four-part harmony for choirs. The Fisk Jubilee Singers, depicted in Figure 29.7, popularized spirituals in the 1870s through polished performances in concert tours on both sides of the Atlantic. By the end of the nineteenth century, spirituals were simultaneously folk music for those who had

Figure 29.7: The original Fisk Jubilee Singers, photographed in 1873 in London, during their European tour. Founded at Fisk University in Nashville, Tennessee, the group consisted of black student musicians who performed spirituals and other songs in four-part harmony.

learned them from oral tradition, popular songs for those who bought them in collections or as sheet music or heard them in popular venues, and a source of melodic material for classical composers.

RECEPTION AND RECOGNITION

By the end of the nineteenth century, what seemed in retrospect like a mainstream of musical development in the late eighteenth century had broken into many smaller currents, like a great river forming a delta as it heads toward the sea. The split between classical and popular music had widened and was becoming irrevocable, but even within those two broad traditions there were many competing strands.

Most of the classical composers we have studied found a place in the permanent repertoire. National flavor helped many gain a niche, from Fauré at Europe's center to Tchaikovsky, Grieg, and others on the periphery. Some were admitted into the canon of classical masters on the strength of relatively few works, as were Franck, Smetana, and Elgar. In each case, performers, audiences, and critics tended to favor works that brought a distinctive new personality into the tradition, a trend that would become even stronger in the twentieth century.

Divisions between classical and popular streams existed everywhere in Europe and the Americas, not only in the United States. Yet the American case is especially interesting because the hierarchy of permanence is the opposite of Europe's. In the United States, the late-nineteenth-century composers in the classical tradition won respect and renown in their lifetimes, but then faded from view, and despite recent revivals their music is still relatively little known. By contrast, some popular traditions produced works that have never ceased being played and enjoyed. These pieces—including Sousa's best-known marches, popular songs such as *The Battle Cry of Freedom* and *The Band Played On*, and dozens of African-American spirituals—have every reason to be called "classics." The twentieth century in turn saw other types of popular music develop their own repertories of classics and their own legions of connoisseurs. More than in most other nations, the permanent repertoire of American classics grew from indigenous popular traditions, rather than as an offshoot of the international classical mainstream.

PART OUTLINE

PART SIX

THE TWENTIETH CENTURY AND AFTER

We know more about musical culture in the twentieth century than in any other period. Recalling the four types of evidence discussed in chapter 1 for reconstructing the music of the past—physical remains, visual images, writings about music and musicians, and music itself—we have far more of all of these for music since 1900 than for all previous eras combined. The new technologies of sound recording, photography, film, television, and computers have preserved and made available every kind of music-making from almost every nation and social group, giving us a more complete picture than for earlier times, when music survived only in notation. On the other hand, the sheer amount of music from the past century can seem overwhelming, and our historical closeness can make it difficult to discern what is of greatest or most lasting importance.

The music from the twentieth century was also more diverse than in previous generations. Throughout each decade, musicians reexamined their basic assumptions about music and created new works that did astonishing things. New traditions emerged such as ragtime, jazz, musicals, film music, rock, rap, and other types of popular music. In the classical realm, some composers continued to write tonal music, while others devised new systems of organizing pitch, such as atonality, polytonality, neotonality, and twelve-tone methods. It was a time of competing styles, from impressionism and expressionism to neoclassicism, minimalism, and neo-Romanticism, and of exploring new sounds and approaches, including experimental music, spatial music, electronic music, indeterminacy, chance, and collage. These trends are still with us, and more come each year, making today's musical life the most varied the world has ever known.

The Early Twentieth Century

The early twentieth century was a time of rapid change in technology, society, and the arts, including music. American popular music developed new currents in *ragtime* and *jazz* that won the world's attention. Composers in the classical tradition, forced to compete for space on concert programs with the classics of the past, sought to to win an audience in the present and secure a place in the permanent repertoire of the future by offering a unique style and perspective that balanced tradition and novel elements. Faced with common problems, they created highly individual solutions, differing in what they valued most in the tradition, what they discarded, and what innovations they introduced. Most continued to use tonality, but many wrote ***post-tonal*** music, and a few took up the banner of the ***avant-garde.*** As a result, music became increasingly diverse in style and approach, a process that accelerated throughout the twentieth century.

MODERN TIMES, 1898–1918

Few eras have been as self-consciously "modern" as the early twentieth century. The pace of technological and social change was more rapid than in any previous era, prompting both an optimistic sense of progress and a nostalgia for a simpler past.

New technologies   One symbol of progress was the electrification of industry, businesses, and homes. Electric lighting increasingly replaced gas lighting, and electrical appliances were produced for the home market. Internal combustion engines fueled by petroleum gradually replaced coal engines in steamships and factories. By streamlining production and distribution, Henry Ford made his Model T the first widely affordable automobile, launching the modern world's love affair with the car. Wilbur and Orville Wright flew the first working airplane in 1903, and by the end of the next decade airplanes were used for both military and commercial purposes. New products, improved transportation, and new marketing techniques combined to expand the mass market for manufactured goods. Of crucial importance for music were new technologies for reproducing music, from player pianos to phonographs (see sidebar). Meanwhile, moving picture shows—the movies—offered a new form of theatrical entertainment with musical accompaniment.

The growth of industry fostered an expanding economy. People continued to migrate from rural areas to cities, although not without regret; Tin Pan Alley songs and Mahler symphonies alike expressed a yearning for home and the countryside. Economic inequalities prompted workers to organize in labor unions to fight for better conditions, inspired social reformers such as Jane Addams to work with the poor, and aroused revolutionary movements in Russia and elsewhere. International trade continued to increase. European nations grew rich importing raw materials and food, and marketing manufactured goods to the world. The great powers—Britain, France, and the German, Austro-Hungarian, Russian, and Ottoman Empires—competed for dominance, while the peoples of eastern Europe, from the Balkans to Finland, agitated for their own freedom. Increasing tensions and complex political issues culminated in World War I (1914–18). The modern, efficient machinery of war killed millions of soldiers, ending the hope that technological improvements would lead inevitably to the betterment of humankind. The collapse of widespread faith in human progress left deep disillusionment in its wake.

Economy and social conflicts

During these years, the United States emerged as a world power. It easily defeated Spain in the Spanish-American war of 1898, taking over Puerto Rico, Cuba, the Philippines, and other Spanish colonies. American industries and overseas trade expanded rapidly, growing to rival the industrial powerhouses of Britain and Germany. The United States' entrance into World War I in April 1917 on the side of Britain and France tipped the scales against Germany and Austria-Hungary, and President Woodrow Wilson played a leading role in negotiating the peace.

United States

As in Europe, rapid economic development brought social conflict. The Progressive movement created reforms to reduce the dominance of large corporations. Immigrants continued to stream to the United States, now increasingly from southern and eastern Europe, and their presence in cities caused strains with earlier immigrant groups. Looking for new opportunities, African Americans from the South moved to the large northern cities but because of racist attitudes settled into segregated neighborhoods. Here a black urban culture began to develop, in which music was a major cultural force.

Psychologists raised new questions about what it meant to be human. Sigmund Freud developed psychoanalysis, theorizing that human behavior springs from unconscious desires that are repressed by cultural restraints and that dreams are windows into a person's internal conflicts. Ivan Pavlov showed that dogs accustomed to being fed after a bell was rung would salivate

New views on the human mind

INNOVATIONS: RECORDED SOUND AND ITS IMPACT

The advent of recording technology had the most significant impact on musical culture of any innovation since the printing press. It completely revolutionized the way we experience and share music as listeners, performers, or composers. When Thomas Edison made the first sound recording in his laboratory in Menlo Park, New Jersey, in 1877, using his tinfoil cylinder phonograph shown in Figure 30.1, he intended his new device as a dictation machine for offices. He had no idea that his invention would catapult some musicians to fame and fortune, deliver their product to huge audiences, and spawn a multibillion-dollar industry.

Edison's phonograph recorded sound by a mechanical process. The sound waves, collected by a horn, moved a diaphragm that transmitted its motions to a needle. The needle cut a groove in the cylinder as the latter rotated, turned by a hand crank. The undulations in the groove corresponded to the motions of the diaphragm. To play back the record, the process was reversed: as the crank rotated the cylinder, the shape of the groove made the needle move, which in turn moved the diaphragm, and its vibrations sent the recorded sounds moving through the air.

Edison soon replaced his fragile tinfoil cylinders with wax cylinders, which could be mass-produced by a molding process. Adding a motor to the machine made it possible to maintain a steady speed of rotation, necessary for recording music. Members of John Philip Sousa's band and other artists made recordings that were sold commercially, but quantities were limited because each cylinder had to be recorded separately.

In 1887, Emile Berliner invented a more practical system that recorded on a flat disc, which could be used as a mold to make any number of duplicates. Record players like the one in Figure 30.2 became available in the 1890s, and ten-inch discs with a capacity for four minutes of music were sold for a dollar each, the equivalent of about twenty dollars today.

The early discs featured famous artists, such as the great Italian tenor Enrico Caruso (1873–1921), who made his first recording in 1902 and whose many records encouraged the medium's acceptance as suitable for opera. Because he became one of the recording industry's earliest superstars, it has been said that "Caruso made the phonograph and it made him." His recordings also preserved his performances beyond the grave. The new technology allowed performers to achieve for the first time the kind of immortality previously available only to composers.

Mechanical recording was well suited for voices, but the limited range of frequencies it could reproduce made orchestra music sound tinny. For years, the only symphony available was Beethoven's Fifth, recorded in 1913 by the Berlin Philharmonic for His Master's Voice. Because it was such a long piece, the company had to issue it

Figure 30.1: Thomas Edison with his original phonograph, which recorded sounds through impressions on a tinfoil cylinder.

Figure 30.2: The "Trademark Model" of the phonograph by His Master's Voice, available beginning in 1898. The firm's name and the dog's pose implied that the device reproduced sound so faithfully that a dog would recognize a recording of his owner's voice.

on eight discs gathered in an "album," which became the standard format for longer works.

In the 1920s, new methods of recording and reproduction using electricity—including the electric microphone—allowed a great increase in frequency range, dynamic variation, and fidelity, making the medium still more attractive to musicians and music lovers. Falling prices and continuing improvement of the recording process stimulated a growing market for recordings, from popular songs and dance numbers to the classical repertoire. Record companies competed to record the most popular performers, and by the late 1940s most of the better-known orchestral works had been recorded more than ten times each.

Encouraged by competition, companies continued to develop new improvements. In 1946, Columbia Records introduced the long-playing record, or LP, which rotated at 33-1/3 revolutions per minute instead of 78, used smaller grooves, and thus allowed twenty-three minutes of music per side instead of four. Music lovers bought the LPs by the millions and got rid of their old 78s. High-fidelity and stereophonic records were introduced in the 1950s, which also saw the debut of an entirely new recording technology: magnetic tape. Philips introduced cassette tapes in 1963, and by the 1970s tape sales were rivaling those of records. Then in 1983, Philips and Sony unveiled the Compact Disc, or CD, which stored recorded sound in digital code etched onto a four-inch plastic disc and read by a laser. Even as listeners were replacing all their LPs with CDs, new technologies were being developed that made it possible to download music from the Internet onto a personal computer or portable device.

The development of recordings irrevocably altered the way people listen to music. No longer did they have to get themselves to a concert hall or gather around a bandstand. They could now sit in their homes and order up a favorite singer or an entire orchestra at their convenience, listening to a single performance repeatedly if it pleased them. The visual element of music-making suddenly disappeared; listeners heard performers without seeing them, and musicians played in recording studios for invisible audiences. Listening to recordings often replaced amateur music-making at home, with the paradoxical effect that people devoted less time and effort to engaging actively with music as participants. For many people, listening to music became no longer a communal activity but a largely solitary pursuit. People also used recorded music as a background to other activities, rather than listening with focused concentration.

Along with performers and listeners, composers too have been influenced by the new technologies, being able to avail themselves of musical styles and ideas outside of their ordinary experience. Exotic musics from Africa, India, Asia, and elsewhere became available via recording without the hardships or expense of travel, and the entire history of Western music, from the singing of plainchant by monks in a faraway monastery to the most recent pop tune, may be heard on disc. Furthermore, composers since the 1940s have used recorded sounds to make music, allowing them to incorporate an unprecedented variety of sounds.

—BRH & JBP

at the sound of the bell even if no food was present and that humans could likewise be conditioned to respond to stimuli in predictable ways. These approaches challenged the Romantic view of individuals as protagonists of their own dramas, seeming instead to portray humans as subject to internal and social forces of which they were only dimly aware. Such changing views of human nature played a strong role in literature and the other arts.

The arts Sustained by Romantic notions of art as a window on the divine and of the artist as an enlightened visionary, artists increasingly regarded their work as an end in itself to be appreciated for its own sake. Success was measured not by wide popular appeal but by the esteem of intellectuals and fellow artists. Many artists searched for new and unusual content or techniques. Symbolist poets such as Paul Verlaine, Stéphane Mallarmé, Paul Valéry, and Stefan George, for example, used intense imagery, symbols, and disrupted syntax to evoke an indefinite, dreamlike state and to suggest feelings and experiences rather than describing them directly.

From In the late nineteenth century, French painters known as *impressionists—*
impressionism named after Claude Monet's painting *Impression: Sunrise* (1872), shown in
to cubism Figure 30.3—inaugurated the first in a series of artistic movements that

Figure 30.3: Claude Monet, Impression: Sunrise *(1872). Monet entered this work and eight others in an exhibition he helped to organize in 1874. A critic headlined his mocking review "Exhibition of the Impressionists," picking up on Monet's title and coining a term that would encompass an entire artistic movement. Instead of mixing his colors on a palette, Monet juxtaposed them on the canvas to capture a fleeting moment of the early light of day. Apart from the rowboats and the sun reflecting from the water in the foreground, the tall ships, smokestacks, and cranes blend into the misty blue-gray background against a reddish sky.*

Figure 3o.4: Paul Cézanne, Mont Sainte-Victoire *(1906). Cézanne painted many versions of this scene visible from his house in Aix-en-Provence in southern France, rendering the massive mountain and the details of the city and countryside as juxtaposed blocks of color in geometrical arrangements.*

utterly changed styles and attitudes toward art. The impressionists sought not to depict things realistically but to capture the impressions they gave to the artist, adopting a stance of detached observation rather than direct emotional engagement. In Monet's paintings, objects and people are suggested by a few brush strokes, often of starkly contrasting colors, leaving it to the viewer's eyes and mind to blend the colors and fill in the missing details. The effect of light on an object is often as much the subject of a painting as is the object itself. Although impressionist paintings are widely popular today, they were at first poorly received, derided as lacking in artistic skill and opposed to traditional aesthetics. Such reactions would also greet other modern styles of painting and music.

Each impressionist painter had a highly individual style, and later artists extended their ideas in unique ways. Paul Cézanne depicted natural scenes and figures as orderly arrangements of geometrical forms and planes of color, as in his painting of Mont Sainte-Victoire (1906) in Figure 30.4. Pablo Picasso and Georges Braque further abstracted this idea in *cubism,* a style in which three-dimensional objects are represented on a flat plane by breaking them down into geometrical shapes, such as cubes and cones, and juxtaposing or overlapping them in an active, colorful design. Figure 3o.5

Figure 30.5: Pablo Picasso, The Treble Clef *(1912). This cubist painting includes a violin on the right, broken into its various components and planes, and a clarinet on the left, stylized as multiple bars (gray, blue, brown, and black-and-white), most with fingerholes, and concentric circles and a cone to represent the instrument's bell.*

shows an example, one of a series Picasso painted in 1912 that used the violin as a subject.

The revolution begun by impressionism stimulated new ways of making, seeing, and thinking about paintings, giving birth to movements such as expressionism (discussed in chapter 31) and abstract art. In most of these new movements, artists and their approving critics no longer placed a high value on beauty or on pleasing the viewer, as had painters from the Renaissance to the Romantics. Instead, they valued originality and substance, demanding that the viewer work to understand and interpret the image.

Effects on music   We will see all these trends reflected in music in this and the next several chapters. Music was directly affected by the expanding economy, new technologies, the devastation of World War I, the emergence of the United States on the world stage, the role of African-American urban culture as a breeding ground for new musical styles, new thinking about human nature, and the new artistic movements, with particularly close parallels to symbolism, impressionism, expressionism, and cubism.

Vernacular Musical Traditions

The impact of prosperity and technology on music, and the growing importance of the United States and especially African Americans, are apparent in the varied and vibrant musical traditions outside the classical concert hall and opera house.

POPULAR SONG AND STAGE MUSIC

The most ubiquitous music was popular song, performed in cabarets, cafés, music halls, and theaters and published for the home market. Each linguistic region had its own repertoire and styles of popular song, although growing trade and travel enabled some songs to reach an international market. British songs had found audiences in the United States since the eighteenth century, and in the twentieth century American songs became increasingly popular in Britain. Tin Pan Alley was in its heyday, and some hits of the time became classics that are still familiar, such as *Take Me Out to the Ball Game* (1908) by Jack Norworth and Albert Von Tilzer and *Over There* (1917) by George M. Cohan (1878–1942).

Operettas and revues

Many of the best-known popular songs came from stage shows. Revues spread from Paris to London, New York, and elsewhere, increasingly centered around song and dance numbers, often with flashy costumes and sets. Franz Léhar (1870–1948) gave the Viennese operetta new life with *The Merry Widow* (1905) and other works, while in the United States Victor Herbert (1859–1924) achieved successes with his operettas *Babes in Toyland* (1903) and *Naughty Marietta* (1910).

Musicals

A significant new genre, the *musical comedy* or **musical**, featured songs and dance numbers in styles drawn from popular music in the context of a spoken play with a comic or romantic plot. English theater manager George Edwardes established the genre by combining elements of variety shows, comic operas, and plays in a series of productions at the Gaiety Theatre in London in the 1890s. British musicals were soon staged in the United States, and the New York theater district on Broadway became the main center for musicals, along with London's West End. George M. Cohan inaugurated a distinctive style of American musical with his *Little Johnny Jones* (1904), which brought together American subject matter and the vernacular sounds of vaudeville and Tin Pan Alley with the romantic plots and European styles of comic opera and operetta. That show included two of the most famous and enduring popular songs of the era, *Give My Regards to Broadway* and *The Yankee Doodle Boy* (whose chorus begins "I'm a Yankee Doodle Dandy"). From these roots would grow the musicals of Jerome Kern, Irving Berlin, George Gershwin, Rodgers and Hammerstein, and Andrew Lloyd Webber, among many others.

MUSIC FOR SILENT FILMS

Moving picture shows began to compete with live theater in the 1890s and became enormously popular in the twentieth century. Films were silent until the late 1920s but were always accompanied by music, just as dance and other spectacles had been. The first such public display was Emile Reynaud's *Pantomimes lumineuses* (Luminous Mime Shows, 1892), presented in Paris, with music by Gaston Paulin. Music covered up the noise of the projector, provided continuity to the succession of scenes and shots, evoked appropriate moods, and marked dramatic events. Often the music was performed by a pianist or organist, who might improvise or play excerpts from memory, draw-

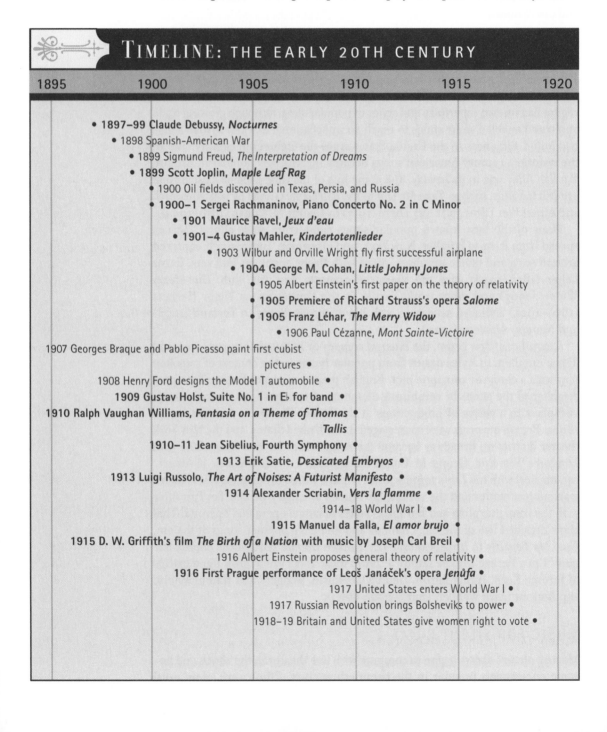

TIMELINE: THE EARLY 20TH CENTURY

| 1895 | 1900 | 1905 | 1910 | 1915 | 1920 |

- 1897–99 Claude Debussy, *Nocturnes*
- 1898 Spanish-American War
- 1899 Sigmund Freud, *The Interpretation of Dreams*
- 1899 Scott Joplin, *Maple Leaf Rag*
- 1900 Oil fields discovered in Texas, Persia, and Russia
- 1900–1 Sergei Rachmaninov, Piano Concerto No. 2 in C Minor
- 1901 Maurice Ravel, *Jeux d'eau*
- 1901–4 Gustav Mahler, *Kindertotenlieder*
- 1903 Wilbur and Orville Wright fly first successful airplane
- 1904 George M. Cohan, *Little Johnny Jones*
- 1905 Albert Einstein's first paper on the theory of relativity
- 1905 Premiere of Richard Strauss's opera *Salome*
- 1905 Franz Lehár, *The Merry Widow*
- 1906 Paul Cézanne, *Mont Sainte-Victoire*

1907 Georges Braque and Pablo Picasso paint first cubist pictures •

1908 Henry Ford designs the Model T automobile •

1909 Gustav Holst, Suite No. 1 in E♭ for band •

1910 Ralph Vaughan Williams, *Fantasia on a Theme of Thomas Tallis* •

1910–11 Jean Sibelius, Fourth Symphony •

1913 Erik Satie, *Dessicated Embryos* •

1913 Luigi Russolo, *The Art of Noises: A Futurist Manifesto* •

1914 Alexander Scriabin, *Vers la flamme* •

1914–18 World War I •

1915 Manuel da Falla, *El amor brujo* •

1915 D. W. Griffith's film *The Birth of a Nation* with music by Joseph Carl Breil •

1916 Albert Einstein proposes general theory of relativity •

1916 First Prague performance of Leoš Janáček's opera *Jenůfa* •

1917 United States enters World War I •

1917 Russian Revolution brings Bolsheviks to power •

1918–19 Britain and United States give women right to vote •

ing on both classical and popular pieces. In larger theaters, instrumental ensembles played music arranged or composed for the film by the resident music director. Opera and operetta were important influences on film music. These genres had already established conventions for enhancing drama through musical accompaniment, and music for films borrowed many of them, including loud, rapid passages for moments of excitement, tremolos to suggest tension or high drama, and soft, romantic themes for love scenes. Strongly contrasting excerpts or styles, from Wagner to popular song, were used side by side to evoke changes of scene or dramatic situation and to delineate characters.

Because the music affected the audience's reactions to the movie and thus its profitability, filmmakers made efforts to standardize the music for their films. Beginning in 1909, studios issued cue sheets that showed the sequence of scenes and events in a movie and suggested appropriate music. Music publishers saw a market niche and printed anthologies of pieces and excerpts grouped by mood or situation, of which Giuseppe Becce's *Kinothek* (Berlin, 1919) was among the most widely used. Saint-Saëns's score for *L'assassinat du duc de Guise* (1908) inaugurated the era of the film score, composed to accompany a particular film. This idea was popularized especially by the orchestral score Joseph Carl Breil (1870–1926) created for D. W. Griffith's *The Birth of a Nation* (1915), a film with a racist message whose success highlighted the immense social impact of the movies. Breil interwove excerpts arranged from Wagner, Tchaikovsky, popular songs, and other sources with his own music. Later composers increasingly wrote original scores that evoked the styles and conventions of Romantic or popular composers.

Cue sheets and film scores

BAND MUSIC

The tradition of military and amateur wind bands remained strong across Europe and North America. In the United States and Canada, bands increasingly found a home in colleges and schools as well, playing at sporting events and in concerts. Sousa's band continued to tour and became a pioneer in making phonograph recordings. Among the many other professional bands was Helen May Butler's Ladies Brass Band, one of several all-female ensembles formed in response to the exclusion of women from most bands.

The twentieth century saw a growing effort among bandleaders to establish a repertoire of serious works for band worthy of comparison to the orchestral repertoire. Because of the band's long association with the military and with amateur performance, there were very few original pieces for band by the major Classic and Romantic composers, who were represented on band concerts mostly by transcriptions. In the first decades of the century, a new seriousness of purpose emerged in pieces that soon formed the core of a developing classical repertoire for band, notably Suites No. 1 in E♭ (1909) and 2 in F (1911) by English composer Gustav Holst (1874–1934); *Dionysiaques* (1914–25) by French composer Florent Schmitt (1870–1958); *Irish Tune from County Derry* (1917) and *Lincolnshire Posy* (1937) by Australian composer Percy Grainger (1882–1961); and *English Folk Song Suite* (1923) and *Toccata marziale* (1924) by Ralph Vaughan Williams (discussed below). Holst,

Concert repertoire

Grainger, and Vaughan Williams drew on folk songs for themes, distributed the melodic content more evenly between winds and brass, used modal harmonies within a tonal context, and developed a symphonic style of instrumentation.

African-American bands

Brass bands were one of the main training grounds for African-American musicians, along with black churches and dance orchestras. During the late nineteenth century and early twentieth centuries, black bands occupied an important place in both black and white social life in many big cities, including New Orleans, Baltimore, Memphis, Newark, Richmond, Philadelphia, New York, Detroit, and Chicago. Among the bandleaders and composers who attracted national and international attention were James Reese Europe, Tim Brymn, William H. Tyers, and Ford Dabney. Their bands performed from notation and did relatively little improvising, but they played with a swinging and syncopated style that distinguished them from white bands. Europe's band created a sensation in Paris during and after World War I, and the French Garde Républicaine tried in vain to imitate its sound.

RAGTIME

Among the dances played by both brass and concert bands were pieces in **ragtime,** a style popular from the 1890s through the 1910s that featured syncopated (or "ragged") rhythm against a regular, marchlike bass. This syncopation apparently derived from the clapping *Juba* of American blacks, a survival of African drumming and hand clapping. The emphasis on offbeats in one rhythmic layer against steady beats in another reflects the complex cross-rhythms common in African music.

Ragtime is today known mostly as a style of piano music, but in the late nineteenth and early twentieth centuries the term also encompassed ensemble music and songs. Ragtime was originally a manner of improvising or performing, "ragging" pieces notated in even rhythms by introducing syncopations. One vehicle was the cakewalk, a couples dance derived from slave dances and marked by strutting and acrobatic movements. Music for cakewalks was printed without syncopations until 1897, when syncopated figures characteristic of ragtime began to appear. Beginning that year, instrumental works called **rags** were published, especially for piano, and cakewalks and rags were soon among the best-selling forms of instrumental music. Classically trained African-American composer Will Marion Cook (1869–1944) introduced the new rhythms into the Broadway tradition with *Clorindy, or The Origin of the Cakewalk* (1898), and his *In Dahomey,* produced in New York in 1902 and London in 1903, brought the cakewalk and ragtime style to Europe. Many popular songs were also written with ragtime rhythms. Both black and white composers, songwriters, and performers embraced the style; indeed, the Sousa band made some of the first ragtime recordings.

Figure 30.6: Scott Joplin in a photograph printed on the cover of his rag The Cascades *(1904).*

The leading ragtime composer was Scott Joplin (1867–1917), shown in Figure 30.6. Son of a former slave, he studied music in his home town of Texarkana, Texas, and worked in Sedalia and St. Louis, Missouri, before moving to New York in 1907. His most ambitious work was the opera *Treemonisha*, completed in 1910 though not staged until 1972. But he was best known for his piano rags, especially *Maple Leaf Rag* (1899; NAWM 136a). Like most rags, it is in $\frac{2}{4}$ meter and follows the form of a march, with a series of sixteen-measure strains, each repeated. The second strain, excerpted in Example 30.1, shows several rhythmic features typical of ragtime. The left hand keeps up a steady pulse in eighth notes, alternating between bass notes and chords, while the right-hand figures syncopate both within and across the beat. The notes in octaves, which receive extra stress, occur every three sixteenth notes, momentarily creating the impression of $\frac{3}{16}$ meter in the right hand against $\frac{2}{4}$ in the left. Essentially the same rhythmic idea appears in each two-measure unit. Such repetition of a short rhythmic pattern, like syncopation and multiple rhythmic layers, is a characteristic of African-American music that can be traced back to Africa. So while the form, left-hand pattern, harmony, and chromatic motion all ultimately derive from European sources, the rhythmic elements have African roots, and the resulting mixture is quintessentially African-American.

Scott Joplin

CD 10|43

Example 30.1: Second strain from Joplin's Maple Leaf Rag

EARLY JAZZ

The 1910s also saw the early development of another type of music from African-American roots: ***jazz.*** Jazz evolved into a diverse tradition encompassing many styles, genres, and social roles but seems to have begun as a mixture of ragtime and dance music with elements of the blues (described in chapter 32).

New Orleans has long been considered the "cradle of jazz," although recent research has uncovered early jazz in other regions as well. The cultural and social environment of New Orleans nurtured the development of early jazz.

New Orleans

The French and Spanish background of the city gave it a flavor different from other cities in the United States. Before Emancipation, New Orleans was the only place in the South where slaves were allowed to gather in public. As a result, music in New Orleans retained some African traditions that were lost elsewhere. Moreover, the city had close connections to the Caribbean, and rhythms from Haitian, Cuban, and Creole music also influenced early jazz. The dance bands of New Orleans interwove these strands with European styles, gradually producing a new kind of music.

The new style had no name at first, or was simply known as the New Orleans style of ragtime. But when bands from New Orleans began playing in Chicago, New York, and elsewhere, they used the term "jazz." Bands who popularized the term included a black group that toured in 1913–18 as the New Orleans Jazz Band, and a white band that in 1917 performed in New York and made recordings as the Original Dixieland Jazz Band.

Manner of performance

Jazz differed from ragtime particularly in the way it was performed. Instead of playing the music "straight," observing the rhythms and textures of a fully notated piece, players extemporized arrangements that distinguished one performer or performance from another. Listening to early jazz pianist and composer and New Orleans native Jelly Roll Morton (1890–1941) play Joplin's *Maple Leaf Rag* in a recording from 1938 (NAWM 136b), we recognize that this is unmistakably jazz and not ragtime because of the anticipations of beats, the swinging, uneven rendering of successions of equal note values, the grace notes, the enriched harmony, and the weaving of ragtime's brief motivic units into a more continuous line.

CLASSICS OF VERNACULAR MUSIC

Many of the pieces discussed above became classics in their own traditions, from the hit songs of George M. Cohan to the Holst suites for band and the Joplin piano rags. The proliferation of traditions, styles, and genres makes it difficult to write a single coherent narrative of musical developments in the twentieth century. Yet one of the recurring themes is that very proliferation of styles, apparent in the classical tradition as well.

MODERN MUSIC IN THE CLASSICAL TRADITION

By the turn of the twentieth century, the permanent repertoire of musical classics dominated almost every field of concert music, from piano, song, or chamber music recitals to operas and orchestral concerts. The change from a century before was enormous. In the eighteenth century, performers and listeners demanded new music all the time, and "ancient music" included anything written more than twenty years earlier. But musicians and audiences in the early 1900s expected that most concert music they performed or heard would be at least a generation old, and they judged new music by the standards of the classics already enshrined in the repertoire. In essence, concert halls and opera houses had become museums for displaying the musical artworks of the past two hundred years. The repertoire varied according to the performing medium and from region to region, but the core was largely the same throughout most of Europe and the Americas, including operas and operatic excerpts from Mozart through Verdi, Wagner, and Bizet; orchestral and chamber music from Haydn through the late Romantics; and keyboard music by J. S. Bach, Haydn, Mozart, Beethoven, and prominent nineteenth-century composers.

Living composers increasingly found themselves in competition with the music of the past. This is the great theme of modern music in the classical tradition, especially in the first half of the century: in competing with past composers for the attention of performers and listeners who loved the classical masterworks, living composers sought to secure a place for themselves by offering something new and distinctive while continuing the tradition. They combined individuality and innovation with emulation of the past, seeking to write music that would be considered original and worthy of performance alongside the masterworks of earlier times.

Their choices of what to preserve and what to change varied, reflecting differences in what they valued, or did not value, in the tradition. The search for an original, individual style made the use of conventional gestures, including standard cadences and other routines of tonal harmony, problematic. Some composers abandoned tonality, while others attenuated it or extended it in new directions. As part of the heritage from Romanticism, composers were expected to write music that was true to their national identity and drew on regional traditions yet spoke to an international audience. Each composer synthesized a personal style from the diverse mix of national and foreign influences and of old and new music that surrounded them.

The result was music of tremendous variety. The most successful modern composers offered something unique, a style and a viewpoint that were not previously represented in the repertoire. The wide range of styles and approaches produced many currents and unique figures, precluding a single stylistic mainstream of twentieth-century classical music. The following account of some of the best-known composers active early in the century, together with a closer look at six modernist composers in chapter 31, can only suggest the rich variety of the era.

GERMANY AND AUSTRIA

German-speaking composers faced a particular challenge because their national tradition was already so central to the repertoire. The two most successful German composers of their generation, Gustav Mahler and Richard Strauss, both found ways to intensify elements from their heritage and create music at once familiar and radically new.

GUSTAV MAHLER

Mahler (1860–1911) was the leading Austro-German composer of symphonies after Brahms and Bruckner and one of the great masters of the song for voice and orchestra. He made his living as a conductor, renowned for his dynamism, precision, and expressivity—traits that are depicted in Figure 30.7. After conducting at numerous opera houses, including Prague, Leipzig, Budapest, and Hamburg, he directed the Vienna Opera from 1897 to 1907, the Metropolitan Opera in New York from 1907 to 1910, and the New York Phil-

Figure 30.7: Caricature of Gustav Mahler as conductor, by Hans Schliessmann in the Fliegende Blätter *of March 1901. The German captions (not shown) read (top) "A hypermodern conductor" and (bottom) "Kapellmeister Kappelmann conducts his Diabolical Symphony." The face, glasses, haircut, stature, and gestures are all those of Mahler, whose dynamic gestures and expressive style made him a favorite with the public and have influenced many later conductors.*

harmonic from 1909 to 1911. Composing mainly in the summers between busy seasons of conducting, he completed five orchestral song cycles and nine symphonies, leaving a tenth unfinished. He revised most of his works repeatedly, including the first seven symphonies. As a composer, Mahler inherited the Romantic traditions of Berlioz, Schumann, Liszt, Wagner, and especially the Viennese branch of Haydn, Mozart, Beethoven, Schubert, Brahms, and Bruckner, and he was a prime influence on Schoenberg, Berg, Webern, and other Viennese composers.

Mahler the symphonist cannot be separated from Mahler the song composer. Themes from his *Lieder eines fahrenden Gesellen* (Songs of a Wayfarer, 1883–85, revised 1891–96) appear in the opening and closing movements of the First Symphony (1884–88, revised 1893–96 and 1906). Following the examples of Beethoven, Berlioz, and Liszt, Mahler used voices in four of his symphonies, most extensively in the Second (1888–94, revised 1906) and Eighth (1906–7). The Second, Third (1893–96, revised 1906), and Fourth (1892–1900, rev. 1901–10) incorporate melodies from his cycle of twelve songs on folk poems from the early-nineteenth-century collection *Des Knaben Wunderhorn* (The Boy's Magic Horn, 1892–98) and introduce texts of some of the songs in the vocal movements.

Songs in the symphonies

Mahler extended Beethoven's concept of the symphony as a bold personal statement. He once observed that to write a symphony was to "construct a world," and his symphonies often convey a sense of life experience, as if telling a story or depicting a scene. To create the impression of events occurring in a variegated world, he used musical styles as topics, just as Mozart had done (see chapter 22). For example, in the slow introduction to Mahler's First Symphony, the strings softly sustain the note A in seven octaves, producing an effect of vast space, filled in at times by ideas in other instruments—a melody in the winds, clarinets with hunting horn calls, a trumpet fanfare, a cuckoo call, a Romantic horn theme in parallel thirds—like the sounds of humans and nature heard across a great landscape. In this and other works, he often drew on the styles and rhythms of Austrian folk songs and dances, using them at times to suggest his urban audience's nostalgia for rural scenes and simpler times.

Symphony as world

Another source of variety is Mahler's instrumentation. His works typically require an enormous number of performers. The Second Symphony calls for a huge string section, seventeen woodwinds, twenty-five brasses, six timpani and other percussion, four harps, organ, soprano and alto soloists, and a large chorus; the Eighth demands an even larger array of players and singers, earning its nickname "Symphony of a Thousand." But the size of the orchestra tells only part of the story. Mahler showed great imagination in combining instruments, achieving effects ranging from the most delicate to the gigantic. Often only a few instruments are playing while he creates many different chamber-orchestra groupings from his vast palette of sounds. Mahler was one of the first composers to envision music as an art not just of notes but of sound itself, an approach that became more common over the course of the twentieth century.

Instrumentation and sound

In accord with Mahler's interest in presenting a world, his symphonies often imply a program. For the first four symphonies, he wrote detailed

Programmatic content

programs in the manner of Berlioz and Liszt but later suppressed them. No such clues exist for the Fifth, Sixth, and Seventh Symphonies (composed between 1901 and 1905), yet the presence of pictorial details, material borrowed from his own songs, and the overall plan of each work combine to suggest that the composer had extramusical ideas in mind like those ascribed to Beethoven's Third and Fifth Symphonies. Thus Mahler's Fifth moves from a funereal opening march to triumph in the scherzo and a joyous finale. The Sixth is his "tragic" symphony, culminating in a colossal finale in which heroic struggle seems to end in defeat and death. The Ninth, Mahler's last completed symphony (1908–9), conjures up a mood of resignation mixed with bitter satire, a strange and sad farewell to life.

Fourth Symphony   The Fourth Symphony, one of Mahler's most popular, illustrates several of his compositional techniques. Each movement strongly differs from the others, exaggerating the contrasts in a traditional four-movement symphony, as if to suggest the world's variety. The work begins in one key (G major) and ends in another (E major), implying that life's adventures do not always bring us back home.

The first movement recalls the late-eighteenth-century symphony, through references to Haydn and Mozart's styles and by using sonata-form conventions, and contrasts it with Romantic styles. The exposition has clearly articulated themes, shown in Example 30.2: a principal theme in the tonic G major, a lyrical second theme on the dominant, and a playful closing theme. In the first theme, Mahler follows Mozart in using contrasting rhythmic and melodic figures (compare Example 22.9), but outdoes him in the number and variety of motives. There are surprises and deceptions that recall Classic-era wit: unexpected sforzandos, dynamic changes, and harmonic twists; portions of the theme used to accompany or interrupt other portions; and figures expanded to the point of pomposity (like the dotted figure in measure 6 as extended in measures 8–9), played upside down (that same figure in measure 12, in contrary motion with itself in the cellos), or varied in other surprising ways.

Example 30.2: Themes from Mahler's Symphony No. 4, first movement

a. First theme

b. Second theme

c. Closing theme

By contrast to these Classic-era elements, the second theme resembles a Romantic song and is introduced in the cellos and later joined by the horn, two quintessentially Romantic instruments. The development is fantasy-like and tonally daring, a Romantic outburst in a Classic frame, as Mahler shows how the two idioms can be blended in a single movement. When motives from the themes are reassigned to different instruments and recombined in new ways, they sound ironic and self-parodying, suggesting a feverish dream in which remembered images pop up from the subconscious in strange and distorted guises. The effect is as if the rational order of the eighteenth-century Enlightenment were displaced by the irrational dreams analyzed by Freud. The recapitulation restores lucidity and logic, but there is no going back to the innocence of the opening; the movement achieves balance by embracing all the possibilities it includes rather than trying to resolve all the potential conflicts, in a musical metaphor for the compromises required of us by the complexities and contradictions of modern life. This movement's interweaving of classical references, Romantic fantasy, and modern style has a close counterpart in the paintings of Mahler's friend and fellow Viennese, Gustav Klimt, whose painting entitled *Music* appears in Figure 30.8.

Irony also haunts the *Kindertotenlieder* (Songs on the Death of Children, 1901–4), an orchestral song cycle on poems of Friedrich Rückert. The first song, *Nun will die Sonn' so hell aufgeh'n* (NAWM 137), achieves the transparency of chamber music through its spare use of instruments. Mahler's characteristic post-Wagnerian harmony intensifies the emotion through stark contrasts of dissonance with consonance and of chromaticism with diatonicism. Thin textures and simple melodies and rhythms produce an effect of understated restraint, ironic for a song about the death of one's child. The irony is heightened at times by an emotional mismatch between text and music: the opening line, "Now will the sun so brightly rise again," is sung to a woeful, descending, D-minor melody, while the next phrase rises chromatically to a sunny D major on the words "as if no misfortune occurred during the night."

Das Lied von der Erde (The Song of the Earth, 1908) rivals the Ninth Symphony as the high point of Mahler's late works. It is a song cycle for tenor and

Kindertotenlieder

Das Lied von der Erde

Figure 30.8: Music *(1895), by Gustav Klimt (1862–1918), a leader of the Secessionist group of artists in Vienna, who challenged the narrow realism supported by the art establishment. This painting, for the music room of a wealthy industrialist, combines allusions to the classical past—notably the ancient Greek kithara (see Figure 1.9)—with a sensuous modern style influenced by symbolism.*

alto soloists with orchestra based on poems translated from the Chinese. The texts alternate between frenzied grasping at the dreamlike whirl of life and sad resignation at having to part from all its joys and beauties. Just as Mahler called on the human voice in his symphonies to complete his musical thought with words, here he calls on the orchestra to sustain and supplement the singers, both in accompaniment and in extensive connecting interludes. The exotic atmosphere of the words is lightly suggested by instrumental color and the use of the pentatonic scale. In no other work did Mahler so perfectly define and balance the two sides of his personality, ecstatic pleasure and deadly foreboding.

STRAUSS OPERAS

While Mahler focused on the symphony and song cycle, Richard Strauss followed a different course. Having established himself in the 1880s and 1890s as the leading composer of symphonic poems after Liszt (see chapter 28), Strauss turned to opera, seeking to inherit Wagner's mantle. After an early failure with *Guntram* in 1893 and moderate success with *Feuersnot* (The Fire Famine) in 1901, he scored a triumph in 1905 with *Salome*, and from then on the powers of depiction and characterization that he had honed in his symphonic poems went almost exclusively into opera. His primary models were Wagner and Mozart, composers from the Austro-German tradition whose operas he enjoyed conducting most of all and who—despite the great differences between them—were both adept at using contrasting styles to capture their characters' personalities, articulate their emotions, and convey the dramatic situation. Like Wagner, Strauss heightened both musical coherence and dramatic power through the use of leitmotives and the association of certain keys with particular characters.

Salome is a setting of a one-act play by Oscar Wilde in German translation. Strauss adapted the libretto himself, as illustrated in Figure 30.9. In this decadent version of the biblical story, Salome performs her famous Dance of the Seven Veils and entices Herod to deliver the head of John the Baptist on a silver platter so that she can kiss his cold lips. The subject, actions, and emotions were stranger than any attempted in opera before, and they stimulated Strauss to create harmonically complex and dissonant music that greatly influenced later composers.

Salome

Example 30.3 shows a passage just after Herod has reluctantly agreed to Salome's demand. Strauss achieves a blistering level of dissonance by superimposing ideas, using all twelve chromatic notes in quick succession and harmonies with up to seven notes. At times the music seems to be in two keys at once. Yet a simple concept holds the passage together: a fundamental dissonance, the tritone D–A♭, is prolonged and intensified by other notes until it

Figure 30.9: Richard Strauss's copy of Oscar Wilde's play Salome *(1896) in the German translation by Hedwig Lachmann. On the left-hand page is an illustration by British artist Aubrey Beardsley, whose decadent style captures the macabre situation as Salome speaks to the severed head of John the Baptist. On the right-hand page, Strauss edited the play to arrive at his own libretto. He also made sketches for musical ideas in the text's margins.*

Example 30.3: Dissonance prolongation in a passage from Strauss's Salome

a. *Opening of passage*

b. Closing resolution

I am sure a disaster will happen.

resolves tonally to E♭. The tritone is clad in different guises, allowing Strauss to create a sense of ambiguity and foreboding while hinting toward the ultimate resolution. The lowest staff of the example presents a simplified outline of the harmony. Throughout the entire passage, the note D is sustained as a drone together with a G–A♭ trill. In the third measure of the example, adding a B♭–C dyad gives the notes for a dominant ninth in E♭ (B♭-D–A♭–C) under a scale in that key in parallel seconds, foreshadowing the eventual resolution. In the next measure, superimposed over this sonority is an embellished diminished seventh chord (E–G–B♭–D♭), which a measure later resolves chromatically upwards to a bright E-major triad projected through numerous motives; together with the drone D, this forms a kind of augmented sixth chord (equivalent to F♭–A♭–C♭–D). Both the latter chord and the B♭-D–A♭–C chord, despite the strong dissonances between them, contain the tritone D–A♭ and herald a resolution to E♭. But that resolution is delayed for more than a minute as other chords are overlaid in a chromatically shifting surface above the sustained dissonance. At the end of the passage, shown in Example 30.3b, the D–A♭ tritone finally resolves to E♭, through chromatic motion that sums up the preceding chromaticism while obscuring the underlying dominant-to-tonic progression.

Such fiercely dissonant music inspired some later composers to abandon tonality altogether. But other passages in this opera sound as sweetly diatonic, consonant, and clearly key-centered as this passage is chromatic, dissonant, and ambiguous. The intense effect Strauss achieves here is predicated on our expectations that the dissonances will resolve. For his purposes of musical dramatization Strauss needed the polarities inherent in tonal music between dissonance and consonance, chromaticism and diatonicism, instability and stability, tension and resolution.

Elektra

With *Elektra* (1906–8), Strauss began a long and fruitful collaboration with the Viennese playwright Hugo von Hofmannsthal (1874–1929) that would result in seven operas. Adapted from a play by Sophocles, *Elektra* dwells on the emotions of insane hatred and revenge. Accordingly, Strauss intensified the chromaticism, dissonance, and tonal instability at times even beyond *Salome*, offset at other times by serene, diatonic, and tonally stable passages.

Der Rosenkavalier

Der Rosenkavalier (The Cavalier of the Rose, 1909–10) takes us into a sunnier world of elegant, stylized eroticism and tender feeling in the aristocratic, powdered-wig milieu of eighteenth-century Vienna. Here deceptively simple diatonic music dominates, while chromaticism, novel harmonic twists, unpredictably curving melodies, and magical orchestral colors suggest sensuality and enchantment. The whole score, with its mingling of sentiment and comedy, overflows with the lighthearted rhythms and melodies of Viennese waltzes—a witty anachronism, since the waltz craze began in the early nineteenth century, well after the events in the opera.

Style and rhetoric

Strauss's later operas also exhibit his cunning use of musical styles and his intensification of the polarities inherent in tonality to depict characters and convey the drama. Ultimately, Strauss's art is rhetorical, seeking to engage the audience's emotions directly, as a film composer might do, and he needed just as wide a range of style and effect.

CLAUDE DEBUSSY

While Mahler and Strauss extended Wagnerian harmony to new levels of rhetorical intensity, their French contemporary Claude Debussy (1862–1918; see biography and Figure 30.10) took it in a different direction: toward pleasure in the moment. His admiration for Wagner's works, especially *Tristan* and *Parsifal*, was coupled with revulsion against Wagner's bombast and his attempts to expound philosophy in music. Debussy drew from the French tradition a preference for sensibility, taste, and restraint, admiring particularly his older contemporary Emmanuel Chabrier (1841–1894). He found new ideas in Russian composers, especially Balakirev, Rimsky-Korsakov, Borodin, and Musorgsky; in medieval music, notably parallel organum; and in music from Asia. Blending these and other influences, he produced works of striking individuality that had a profound impact on almost all later composers.

Impressionism and symbolism

Debussy's music is often called impressionist, by analogy to the impressionist painters, but it is closer to symbolism, a connection reinforced by his friendships with symbolist poets and his use of their texts for songs and dramatic works. One trait shared with both trends is a sense of detached observation: rather than expressing deeply felt emotion or telling a story, as did Romantic music, Debussy's typically evokes a mood, feeling, atmosphere, or

CLAUDE DEBUSSY (1862–1918)

Debussy exercised an enormous influence on his contemporaries and later generations, creating music of new sounds and delicate colors.

Debussy was born in a suburb of Paris to a middle-class family. He began studying at the Paris Conservatoire at the age of ten, first piano and then composition. In the early 1880s he worked for Tchaikovsky's patron Nadezhda von Meck and twice traveled to Russia, where he encountered the recent works of Rimsky-Korsakov and others that deeply influenced his style and orchestration. He won the coveted Prix de Rome in 1884 and spent two years in Italy. Returning to Paris in 1887, he became friends with several symbolist poets and other artists. He made the pilgrimage to Bayreuth to hear Wagner's operas in 1888 and 1889, but came away recognizing both the power of the music and his own need to avoid being overly influenced by it.

In the 1890s, Debussy lived with his lover Gabrielle Dupont in Montmartre, the "Bohemian" neighborhood that had become a center for the new artistic movements. He found his own voice in composing a series of songs, his early piano music, the *Prelude to "The Afternoon of a Faun,"* and especially his opera *Pelléas et Mélisande,* whose 1902 premiere made him a star overnight. He made a living as a music critic and through an income from his publisher.

After Gabrielle left him in 1898, Debussy married Lilly Texier the next year. But in 1903 he fell in love with Emma Bardac, with whom he had a child in 1905 and whom he married in 1908. By then he was well estab-

Figure 30.10: Portrait of Claude Debussy by Jacques-Emile Blanche, completed in 1902.

lished as France's leading modern composer, producing orchestral works like *La mer* and *Images* and piano pieces that soon entered the standard repertory. Although depressed by World War I and a diagnosis of cancer in 1914, he soon regained his productivity and composed his Études and three chamber sonatas before his death in 1918.

MAJOR WORKS: Pelléas et Mélisande *(opera)*; Prelude to "The Afternoon of a Faun," Nocturnes, La mer, Images, Jeux, *and other orchestral works;* Preludes, Études, Images, Children's Corner, *and many other piano pieces; string quartet, sonatas, and other chamber works*

scene. As in symbolist poetry, the normal syntax is often disrupted, and our attention is drawn instead to individual images that carry the work's structure and meaning. He creates musical images through motives, harmony, exotic scales (such as the whole-tone, octatonic, and pentatonic scales), instrumental timbre, and other elements, then composes by juxtaposing them. Motives need not develop, but may repeat with small changes, like an object viewed from different perspectives; dissonances need not resolve; sonorities may move in parallel motion; contrasts of scale type underlie the articulation of phrases and sections; and instrumental timbres are intrinsic to the musical content rather than simple coloration.

PIANO MUSIC

These traits are evident in Debussy's piano music. In the passage from *L'isle joyeuse* (The Joyous Isle, 1903–4) in Example 30.4, each motive is associated with a particular figuration, chord or succession of chords, scale type, dynamic level, and range on the piano, producing a succession of images that remain distinct from one another even as each flows into the next: (a) a rising major third motive in a whole-tone environment; (b) an upward sweep in the B Dorian diatonic scale; (c) a partially chromatic motive based on undulating thirds; (d) a pentatonic filigree; and (e) chromatic lines in contrary motion

Example 30.4: Debussy, L'isle joyeuse, *mm. 23–29*

over a pedal A (combined with c). In the motion from each segment to the next, some notes remain the same and some change, producing the effect of a harmonic progression.

The harmonic styles of Wagner and Liszt influenced Debussy's use of chromatic and whole-tone chords, but the urgency to resolve is absent. Instead, we are content to enjoy each moment as it comes. Debussy usually maintained a tonal focus—a kind of key center, here A—but he defied the conventional tonal relationships between chords and allowed each chord a degree of independence. This changed attitude toward harmony, inviting us to take pleasure in each event rather than yearn for resolution, gives his music a feeling of detached observation. Debussy once said of his music, "There is no theory. You merely have to listen. Pleasure is the law." Of course pleasure can lead to exuberance or even ecstasy, as it does in the climactic conclusion of this piece, so it should not be imagined that Debussy's music is without feeling.

Many of Debussy's other piano pieces also have evocative titles, often suggesting a visual image, like *Estampes* (Engravings or Prints, 1903) and the two sets of *Images* (1901–5 and 1907). *Children's Corner* (1906–8) depicts a child's world, including a sly poke at Czerny's piano exercises in *Dr. Gradus ad Parnassum* and a salute to American ragtime (with a satirical quotation from Wagner's *Tristan*) in *Golliwogg's Cake-Walk*. The twenty-four Preludes (two books, 1909–10 and 1911–13) are character pieces whose picturesque titles are placed at the end rather than the beginning of each piece to allow listeners or performers to form their own images. Other works are relatively abstract, although unmistakably in Debussy's style: *Suite bergamasque* (ca. 1890) and *Pour le piano* (1894–1901) update the French tradition of the keyboard suite, and the late Études (1915) explore pianistic timbre as well as technique in the tradition of Chopin.

ORCHESTRAL MUSIC

Debussy's orchestral music shows the same characteristics as his piano works, with the added element of instrumental timbre. Often a particular instrument is associated with a certain motive, and different musical layers are separated through tone color. His works require a large orchestra, which is seldom used to make a loud sound but instead offers a great variety of tone colors and textures. Even more than Mahler, Debussy treated music as an art of sound and reveled in the wide range of sounds available in the orchestra.

Debussy based his celebrated *Prélude à "L'après-midi d'un faune"* (Prelude to "The Afternoon of a Faun," 1891–94) on a symbolist poem by Mallarmé, and he treats the subject the same way that French symbolist poets did: by evoking a mood through suggestion, connotation, and indirection rather than through intense emotional expression. Debussy's orchestral technique is well represented by the three *Nocturnes* (1897–99), with subdued, imagist instrumentation in *Nuages* (Clouds), the brilliance of the full ensemble in *Fêtes* (Festivals), and the blending of orchestra with wordless female chorus in *Sirènes* (the Sirens of Greek mythology). *La Mer* (The Sea, 1903–5), subtitled "three symphonic sketches," captures the movements of the sea through rapidly alternating musical images.

Nuages

CD 10|59   CD 5|73

Nuages (NAWM 138) from *Nocturnes* exemplifies the interaction of timbre with motive, scale type, and other elements to create a musical image. There are three sections in modified ABA′ form. The piece begins with an oscillating pattern of fifths and thirds, adapted from a Musorgsky song, that conveys an impression of movement but no harmonic direction, an apt analogy for slowly moving clouds. Each time the pattern appears in the A section, it features different tone colors or pitches, or both, sometimes changing into a series of parallel triads or ninth chords. In the abbreviated A′ section the pattern practically disappears, giving the impression of dispersing clouds. Juxtaposed with this figure's inconstancy is one that changes little: an English-horn motive that quickly rises and slowly falls through a segment of the octatonic scale. The English horn sometimes omits or repeats some of its final notes, but the motive is never developed, transposed, or given to another instrument, and the English horn never plays anything else; there is complete identification between timbre and motive. The motive is usually answered by horns playing a tritone or other figures from the same octatonic scale (in the A section) or a whole-tone scale (in the A′ section). It is not clear what, if anything, these musical images represent; they are themselves, lending coherence to the music and helping to convey a sense of stillness and contemplation.

SONGS AND STAGE MUSIC

Debussy's lifelong engagement with texts—he was also a music critic—made him particularly interested in the written word. Notable among his songs are settings of several major French poets, including Charles Baudelaire, Paul Verlaine, and the ballades of fifteenth-century poet François Villon. He repeatedly sought out dramatic projects, from incidental music to Gabriele d'Annunzio's mystery play *The Martyrdom of Saint Sebastian* (1910–11) and the ballet *Jeux* (1912–13) to several unfinished works. His only completed opera, *Pelléas et Mélisande* (1893–1902), was his response to Wagner's *Tristan und Isolde*, and made his reputation when it premiered at the Paris Opéra-Comique. The veiled allusions and images of the text, a symbolist play by Maurice Maeterlinck, are matched by the strange, often modal harmonies, subdued colors, and restrained expressiveness of the music. The voices, set in fluent recitative that matches the flow of the French language, are supported but never dominated by a continuous orchestral background, while the instrumental interludes connecting the scenes carry on the mysterious inner drama.

DEBUSSY'S INFLUENCE

The changes that Debussy introduced in harmonic and orchestral usage made him one of the seminal forces in the history of music. The composers who at one time or another came under his influence include nearly every distinguished composer of the early and middle twentieth century, from Ravel, Messiaen, and Boulez in France to Puccini, Janáček, Strauss, Scriabin, Ives, Falla, Bartók, Stravinsky, Berg, and others from many national traditions, as well as American jazz and popular musicians. His emphasis on sound itself as an element of music opened doors to new possibilities later explored by Varèse, Cage, and many composers.

THE FIRST MODERN GENERATION

The careers and music of Mahler, Strauss, and Debussy exemplify the search by those in the first generation of modern composers for a personal style that absorbed what was useful from the past, was true to their national identity, yet was distinctive and individual. As we survey a number of major composers from nations across Europe, we will see this interplay between tradition and innovation and between national identity and personal style at work.

FRANCE: RAVEL

Maurice Ravel (1875–1937) is often grouped with Debussy as an impressionist, and some of his works seem to fit the label. But he might better be called a superb assimilater, whose music encompasses a variety of influences while carrying his distinctive stamp marked by consummate craftsmanship, traditional forms, diatonic melodies, and complex harmonies within an essentially tonal language.

The impressionist side of Ravel, and some differences from Debussy, are illustrated in the piano piece *Jeux d'eau* (Fountains, 1901). In it Ravel drew on Liszt's pianistic techniques and in turn gave Debussy ideas for his own watery music. The passage in Example 30.5 includes many innovative textures, such as parallel dissonant chords under rushing scales, and chords and arpeggiated figures that emphasize opens fifths and fourths. This passage juxtaposes whole-tone with diatonic music, as in *L'isle joyeuse* (Example 30.4). But unlike Debussy, Ravel treats his whole-tone sonorities as dissonant harmonies that must resolve, culminating in a complex reworking of the traditional ii–V–I tonal cadence: a progression from an F♯ ninth chord (drawn from one whole-tone scale) through an F–A–B–D♯ augmented sixth chord (drawn from the other whole-tone scale) to a resolution on the tonic E major. Also characteristic of Ravel are the prominent major sevenths he attaches to the tonic and subdominant chords in measure 7, creating a spiky dissonance that Debussy normally avoided.

Distinctive traits

Example 30.5: Ravel, Jeux d'eau, *mm. 6–7*

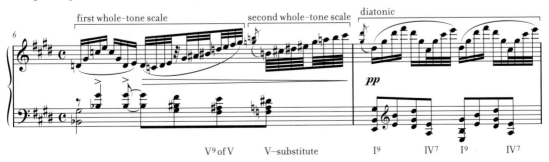

Varied influences   The descriptive piano pieces in the sets *Miroirs* (Mirrors, 1904–5) and *Gaspard de la nuit* (1908), the orchestral suite *Rapsodie espagnole* (Spanish Rhapsody, 1907–8), and the ballet *Daphnis et Chloé* (1909–12) likewise invoke impressionism in their strong musical imagery, brilliant instrumental technique, and colorful harmonies. But Ravel also absorbs ideas from older French music and from the Classic tradition. He borrows from the French Baroque tradition of stylized dances and suites in his piano pieces *Menuet antique* (1895), *Pavane pour une infante défunte* (Pavane for a Dead Princess, 1899), and *Le tombeau de Couperin* (Memorial for Couperin, 1914–17), all of which he later orchestrated. His songs draw on French art and popular traditions and range in topic from humorous and realistic characterizations of animal life in *Histoires naturelles* (1906) to three symbolist poems by Stéphane Mallarmé for voice and chamber ensemble (1913). Ravel's settings closely reflect the natural accents of French, often dropping final syllables that were truncated in normal speech and music hall songs but had traditionally been set in art songs. His interest in Classic forms is clear in works such as the Sonatine for piano (1903–5), String Quartet in F (1902–3), Piano Trio (1914), and Violin Sonata (1923–27). Ravel also looked to popular traditions outside France, using Viennese waltz rhythms in the orchestral poem *La valse* (1919–20); Gypsy style in *Tzigane* for violin and piano or orchestra (1924); blues in the Violin Sonata; and jazz elements in the Piano Concerto for the Left Hand (1929–30), composed for pianist Paul Wittgenstein, who had lost his right arm in World War I. Many works featured Spanish idioms, including Ravel's famous *Bolero* (1928), an orchestral rumination on a single idea varied by changes of instrumentation and a gradual crescendo. Working in a classical tradition that esteemed originality, Ravel avoided repeating himself by drawing on a wide range of sources and giving each piece its individual stamp.

SPAIN: FALLA

French, Russian, and other composers had often used Spanish elements to create an exotic atmosphere. In the early twentieth century, Spanish composers sought to reclaim their national tradition, using authentic native materials in order to appeal to their own people and to gain a foothold in the international repertoire. The principal Spanish composer of the time, Manuel de Falla (1876–1946), developed a diverse nationalism that resisted the merely exotic. He collected and arranged national folk songs, introducing a wider public to the variety in the folk tradition. His earlier works—such as the opera *La vida breve* (Life Is Short, 1904–13) and the ballets *El amor brujo* (Love, the Sorcerer, 1915) and *El sombrero de tres picos* (The Three-Cornered Hat, 1916–19)—are imbued with the melodic and rhythmic qualities of Spanish popular music. His finest mature works are *El retablo de maese Pedro* (Master Pedro's Puppet Show, 1919–23), based on an episode from the great Spanish novel *Don Quixote*, and the concerto for harpsichord with five solo instruments (1923–26), which harks back to the Spanish Baroque. Both works combine specific national elements with the neoclassic approach popular after World War I to produce music that is both nationalist and more broadly modern.

ENGLAND: VAUGHAN WILLIAMS AND HOLST

The English musical renaissance begun by Elgar took a nationalist turn in the twentieth century, when composers sought a distinctive voice for English art music after centuries of domination by foreign styles. Cecil Sharp (1859–1924), Ralph Vaughan Williams (1872–1958), and others collected and published hundreds of folk songs, leading to the use of these melodies in compositions such as Vaughan Williams's *Norfolk Rhapsodies* (1905–6) and *Five Variants of "Dives and Lazarus"* (1939) as well as Holst's *Somerset Rhapsody* (1906–7). These two composers, shown together in Figure 30.11, had become close friends as students at the Royal Conservatory of Music, and they became the leaders of a new English school.

Gustav Holst

Holst, who contributed notable works for stage, chorus, orchestra, and band (see above), was influenced not only by English song but also by Hindu sacred texts, which he set in *Choral Hymns from the Rig Veda* (1908–12). But he is best known for a non-nationalist work, the orchestral suite *The Planets* (1914–16), which became the source for many conventions of scoring for movies and television shows set in space.

Ralph Vaughan Williams

Vaughan Williams was more national in style than Holst. His works include nine symphonies and other orchestral pieces, film scores, works for band, songs, operas, and many choral pieces. He drew inspiration not only from folk song but also from English hymnody and earlier English composers such as Thomas Tallis and Henry Purcell. He also studied with Ravel and absorbed strong influences from Debussy, Bach, and Handel.

Figure 30.11: Gustav Holst (seated) and Ralph Vaughan Williams in 1921, during a walking tour of the scenic Malvern Hills in the English Midlands.

Vaughan Williams exemplified a trait common to several modern English composers: he wrote both art music and practical or utilitarian music, using elements from each tradition in the other. He gained a profound knowledge of hymnody as musical editor of the new *English Hymnal* in 1904–6, writing later that "Two years of close association with some of the best (as well as some of the worst) tunes in the world was a better musical education than any amount of sonatas and fugues." He also composed a half-dozen hymn tunes, arranged over forty folk songs as hymns, and resurrected forgotten sixteenth-century tunes for the hymnal. Throughout his long career, he conducted local amateur singers and players, for whom he wrote a number of pieces. Such links with amateur music-making kept Vaughan Williams and other English composers from cultivating an esoteric style addressed only to elite listeners.

The national quality of Vaughan Williams's music comes from his incorporation or imitation of British folk tunes and his assimilation of the modal harmony of sixteenth-century English composers. One of his most popular works, *Fantasia on a Theme of Thomas Tallis* (1910) for double string orchestra and string quartet, is based on a Tallis hymn in the Phrygian mode that Vaughan Williams had revived for the *English Hymnal*. The piece introduces fragments of the tune, states it simply once, and develops motives from it in a free fantasy, using antiphonal sonorities and triads in parallel motion in a modal framework. Like his teacher Ravel, Vaughan Williams found ways to write varied but always national and recognizably individual music.

CZECH NATIONALISM: JANÁČEK

Spain and Britain were independent nations for whom nationalism was primarily a cultural issue. But for the peoples of eastern Europe under the Austro-Hungarian and Russian Empires, it was also an urgent political concern. Music that reflected a people's language and traditions was valuable at home as an assertion of an independent national identity and abroad as an appeal for international recognition as a nation.

The leading twentieth-century Czech composer, Leoš Janáček (1854–1928), worked in the genres of Western art music, especially opera, but sought a specifically national style. Beginning in the 1880s, he collected and edited folk music from his native region of Moravia, studied the rhythms and inflections of peasant speech and song, and devised a highly personal idiom based on them. He asserted his independence from Austria not only in melodic style but also in his characteristic procedures. His music relies on contrasting sonorities, harmonies, motives, and tone colors, and it proceeds primarily by repeating and juxtaposing ideas in a manner akin to Musorgsky or Debussy rather than developing them as in the Germanic tradition.

After winning local renown for his folk song and dance collections and for choral music in Czech, Janáček gained wider prominence in his sixties when his opera *Jenůfa*, based on a Moravian subject and premiered in Brno in 1904, was performed in Prague in 1916 and again in Vienna in 1918, the year that Czechoslovakia gained independence after the dissolution of Austria-Hungary. With new confidence from both personal and political triumphs, in his last decade Janáček produced a string of operas that dominated the Czech stage between

Alexander Scriabin (1872–1915), shown in Figure 30.13, traveled a different path. He began by writing nocturnes, preludes, études, and mazurkas in the manner of Chopin, then gradually absorbed the chromaticism of Liszt and Wagner; the octatonic scale and other exotic elements from Rimsky-Korsakov; and the juxtapositions of texture, scale, and figuration from Debussy and Russian composers. He gradually evolved a complex harmonic vocabulary all his own. Besides piano music, he wrote symphonies and other orchestral works, notably *Poem of Ecstasy* (1908) and *Prometheus* (1910). During performances of the latter, the composer wanted the concert hall to be flooded with changing colored light; his own *synaesthesia* caused him to link particular pitches to colors, and he aspired to a synthesis of all the arts with the aim of inducing states of mystic rapture.

The changes in his musical language can be followed in his ten piano sonatas, of which the last five, composed 1912–13, dispense with key signatures and tonality. He replaced conventional tonal harmony by choosing for each work a complex chord that serves as a kind of tonic and as the source of a work's melodic and harmonic material. The referential chord typically contains one or two tritones and is usually part of an octatonic scale, sometimes with one added note. These chords resemble Wagner's Tristan chord (see chapter 27), yet they are treated as static objects and do not project a yearning toward resolution; instead of the desire Wagner sought to invoke, they suggest a transcendence of desire, which can be read as erotic or mystic depending on the context. Scriabin creates a sense of harmonic progression by transposing and altering the referential chord, enlivening the texture with vigorous figuration, until the chord returns at the end, sometimes with alterations. Such pieces cannot be described as tonal, but the novel harmony serves most of the functions of tonality, establishing a home tonal region, departing from it, and returning.

Figure 30.13: Alexander Scriabin, in a portrait by A. Y. Golovin.

Example 30.8 illustrates this process in *Vers la flamme* (Toward the Flame), Op. 72 (1914, NAWM 140), a one-movement "poem" for piano. The opening (Example 30.8b) establishes a referential sonority of two tritones, E–A♯–G♯–D, decorated melodically by C♯ and F♯. With the exception of F♯, these are all notes from the octatonic scale shown in Example 30.8a. When the sonority is transposed up a minor third in measure 5, the remaining notes of the scale appear, and the whole passage repeats in the new position. Such octatonic sonorities and chord successions occur throughout, interspersed with other types of harmonies. As shown in Example 30.8c–e, the opening chord returns periodically in new guises, acquiring B as well as C♯ and F♯ along the way; all these variants also appear in transposition, usually by major or minor third or tritone. At the climactic ending (Example 30.8f), the D becomes D♯, creating a resonant chord based mostly on fourths that serves as a final tonic equivalent. The predominant figuration changes from section to section, producing an effect of static blocks of sound that are juxtaposed, as in Musorgsky's and Debussy's music.

Vers la flamme

CD 10|72

Example 30.8: Excerpts from Scriabin, Vers la flamme

a. Octatonic scale on E-F

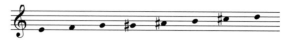

b. Opening

c. Measures 41–42

d. Measures 77–78

e. Measures 107–8

f. Measure 125

TONAL AND POST-TONAL MUSIC

Of all the composers in the classical tradition we have surveyed here, Scriabin traveled the furthest from common-practice tonal harmony, Rachmaninov the least far. The others can be arrayed at different points along a spectrum between them. For all composers of the time, tonality was an unavoidable issue: the demand for originality made conventional chord progressions seem stale, yet if they strayed too far they might lose their audience.

That it was still possible to compose tonal music in the twentieth century is clear from the careers of Strauss, Ravel, Vaughan Williams, Rachmaninov, and many younger composers active through the 1930s and beyond, who found new flavors and possibilities within tonality but never abandoned it. Even today, every music student learns the rules of tonal music, and it remains the common language against which others are judged. Yet other composers, including Debussy, Falla, Janáček, and Scriabin, moved beyond tonal practice in the early 1900s, as each developed a personal musical language that followed its own rules. Even when a tonal center can be identified, whether a single pitch as in Debussy's *L'isle joyeuse* or a chord complex as in Scriabin's *Vers la flamme*, it no longer makes sense to describe the music as tonal, because the harmonic language diverges too far from common practice. The most general term for such music is ***post-tonal,*** which embraces all the new ways composers found to organize pitch, from atonality to neotonality (see chapters 31 and 33). The new possibilities of post-tonal idioms were part of the marvelous diversity of twentieth-century music in the classical tradition, but so were the individual approaches to tonality.

THE AVANT-GARDE

While all these modern composers were devising ways to say something new within the classical tradition, the years before World War I also brought the first stirrings of a movement that directly challenged that tradition and would grow in importance over the course of the century: the **avant-garde.** The French military used the term to describe an advance group that prepared the way for the main army. The term was then adopted in the mid-nineteenth century for and by French artists who saw themselves as a vanguard exploring new territory. Although sometimes applied to anyone who departs from convention, or to modernists such as Schoenberg (see chapter 31), the term is most helpful when used more narrowly for art that is iconoclastic, irreverent, antagonistic, and nihilistic—for art that seeks to overthrow accepted aesthetics and start fresh. Rather than attempt to write music suited for the classical repertoire, avant-garde composers have challenged the very concept of deathless classics, asking their listeners to focus instead on what is happening in the present. Their movement is marked not by shared elements of style but by shared attitudes, particularly an unrelenting opposition to the status quo.

ERIK SATIE

One side of the avant-garde is exemplified by the music of Erik Satie (1866–1925), which wittily upends conventional ideas. His three *Gymnopédies* (1888) for piano, for example, challenged the Romantic notions of expressivity and individuality. Instead of offering variety, as expected in a set of pieces, they are all ostentatiously plain and unemotional, using the same slow tempo, the same accompanimental pattern, virtually the same melodic rhythm, and similar modal harmonies and puzzling dynamics. Satie's use of modal and unresolved chords opened new possibilities for Debussy and Ravel, who turned them to different uses but did not follow his avant-garde tendencies.

Piano works   Between 1900 and 1915, Satie wrote several sets of piano pieces with surrealistic titles like *Three Pieces in the Form of a Pear* (1903, which actually has seven pieces) and *Automatic Descriptions* (1913). Most had running commentary and tongue-in-cheek directions to the player, such as "withdraw your hand and put it in your pocket," "that's wonderful!," or "heavy as a sow." These satirized the titles and directions of Debussy and other composers of descriptive and programmatic music. Moreover, by printing the commentary on the music rather than in a program, so that only the player was aware of it, Satie critiqued the idea of concert music and reclaimed the fading tradition of music for the player's own enjoyment. But the comic and critical spirit resides also in the music itself—spare, dry, capricious, brief, repetitive, parodistic, and witty in the highest degree. The classical masterworks are a particular target: the three *Dessicated Embryos* (1913) include a mocking "quotation from the celebrated mazurka of Schubert" (actually Chopin's funeral march), marked "they all begin to cry," and a long "obligatory cadenza (by the composer)" that pounds on the tonic repeatedly, a jibe at the similar passages that close several Beethoven symphonies. Clearly Satie was not out to create masterpieces that would take their place in the great tradition; rather, he was challenging the very bases of that tradition.

Larger works   In his larger pieces, Satie sought to create music that would fix our attention on the present. His "realistic ballet" *Parade* (1916–17), with a scenario by the writer Jean Cocteau, choreography by Léonide Massine, and scenery and

Figure 30.14: Costume for the Paris Manager in the first production of Satie's ballet Parade *(1917). The sets and costumes for this ballet, designed by Pablo Picasso, brought his cubist style to the stage.*

costumes by Picasso, introduced cubism to the stage, as illustrated in Figure 30.14. In the cubist spirit of including fragments of everyday life, Satie's score incorporated jazz elements, a whistle, a siren, and a typewriter. It caused a scandal, as did his later ballet with film, *Relâche* (No Show Tonight, 1924). His "symphonic drama" *Socrate* (1920), for soloists and chamber orchestra on texts from Plato, attains in its last scene, on the death of Socrates, a poignancy that is intensified by the stylistic monotony and the studied avoidance of a direct emotional appeal. Satie intended his *Musique d'ameublement* (Furniture Music, 1920), written to be played during the intermissions of a play, as background music that should *not* be listened to. Each work by Satie questioned the listener's expectations, no two pieces were alike, and whenever he gained followers, he abandoned them by doing something radically different. His biting, antisentimental spirit, economical textures, and severe harmony and melody influenced the music of his younger compatriots Milhaud and Poulenc, among others, and he was a significant inspiration for the American avant-garde, notably Virgil Thomson and John Cage.

FUTURISM

Although Satie questioned traditional assumptions about expressivity, individuality, seriousness, masterworks, and the very purpose of music, he used traditional instruments and musical pitches. The Italian **futurists** rejected even those. In *The Art of Noises: Futurist Manifesto* (1913; see Source Reading), the futurist painter Luigi Russolo argued in dead earnest that musical sounds had become stale and that the modern world of machines required a new kind of music based on noise. He divided noises into six families, then he and his colleagues built new instruments called *intuonarumori* (noise-makers), each capable of producing a particular kind of noise over a range of at least an octave and a half. They composed pieces for these instruments,

SOURCE READING

THE ART OF NOISES

Futurism began in 1909 as a literary and artistic movement in Italy celebrating the dynamism, speed, machines, and violence of the twentieth century. Luigi Russolo (1885–1947) was a futurist painter who turned his attention to music in 1913. In The Art of Noises: A Futurist Manifesto, *Russolo laid out his argument for music based on noise rather than musical pitches.*

———— • ————

The art of music at first sought and achieved purity and sweetness of sound; later, it blended diverse sounds, but always with intent to caress the ear with suave harmonics. Today, growing ever more complicated, it seeks those combinations of sounds that fall most dissonantly, strangely, and harshly upon the ear. We thus approach nearer and nearer to the *music of noise.*

This musical evolution parallels the growing multiplicity of machines, which everywhere are assisting mankind. Not only amid the clamor of great cities but even in the countryside, which until yesterday was ordinarily quiet, the machine today has created so many varieties and combinations of noise that pure musical sound—with its poverty and monotony—no longer awakens any emotion in the hearer. . . .

We must break out of this narrow circle of pure musical sounds, and conquer the infinite variety of noise-sounds.

Everyone will recognize that every musical sound carries with it an incrustation of familiar and stale sense associations, which predispose the hearer to boredom, despite all the efforts of innovating musicians. We futurists have all deeply loved the music of the great composers. Beethoven and Wagner for many years wrung our hearts. But now we are satiated with them and derive much greater pleasure from ideally combining the noises of street-cars, internal-combustion engines, automobiles, and busy crowds than from re-hearing, for example, the "Eroica" or the "Pastorale." . . .

Every manifestation of life is accompanied by noise. Noise is therefore familiar to our ears and has the power to remind us immediately of life itself. Musical sound, a thing extraneous to life and independent of it, an occasional and unnecessary adjunct, has become for our ears what a too familiar face is to our eyes. Noise, on the other hand, which comes to us confused and irregular as life itself, never reveals itself wholly but reserves for us innumerable surprises. We are convinced, therefore, that by selecting, co-ordinating, and controlling noises we shall enrich mankind with a new and unsuspected source of pleasure. Despite the fact that it is characteristic of sound to remind us brutally of life, the Art of Noises must not limit itself to reproductive imitation. It will reach its greatest emotional power through the purely acoustic enjoyment which the inspiration of the artist will contrive to evoke from combinations of noises.

Translated by Stephen Somervell in Nicolas Slonimsky, *Music Since 1900,* 4th ed. (New York: Charles Scribner's Sons, 1971), 1299–1301. In SR 177 (7:8), pp. 1330–32.

alone or with traditional instruments, and presented them in concert between 1913 and 1921 in Italy, London, and Paris.

In opposition to the constant recycling of classics in the concert halls, futurist music was impermanent, perhaps deliberately so; only one fragment of Russolo's music survives, and the instruments were destroyed during World War II. But the movement continued in various forms in Italy, France, and Russia during the 1920s and 1930s, and it anticipated or stimulated many later developments, including electronic music, microtonal composition, and the pursuit of new instrumental timbres. As different as futurist music was from Satie's, they shared a focus on the experience of listening in the present moment and an iconoclastic rejection of the music and aesthetics of the past, both attributes that remained central to avant-garde music throughout the twentieth century.

LATE ROMANTIC OR MODERN?

The music of the early twentieth century was remarkably diverse, and its reception has been equally varied. Few operettas and virtually no musicals of the time were performed for more than a few seasons, and modern productions are rare, though some of the popular songs of the time have endured. Music for silent films was always an art for the moment, not for the ages, but from the 1960s on, the tradition of improvised accompaniment was revived along with silent movies themselves, and in recent decades a few of the full scores have been performed again with their films. The band works of Holst, Vaughan Williams, and Grainger have remained classics of the concert band repertoire. Ragtime fell out of fashion in the 1920s, was revived after World War II, and regained wide popularity in the 1970s. All these musical traditions now receive increasing attention from historians, as reflected in this book, whose first four editions ignored them completely.

Opinions have changed about the period's classical composers as well. Their position between the lions of late Romanticism, discussed in chapters 27–29, and the modernist composers discussed in chapter 31 can make their music hard to classify. The first edition of this book in 1960 treated Debussy as a late-Romantic figure, but by the 1973 second edition he was regarded as a seminal force for modern music. All the composers of this generation have aspects of both eras, combining nineteenth-century elements with twentieth-century sensibilities. Perhaps that is why much of this music—especially that of Mahler, Strauss, Debussy, Ravel, Sibelius, and Rachmaninov—has proven extremely popular with listeners.

Critical disputes about what is most valuable in music have been especially acute in the twentieth century, and as a result, critical esteem for these composers has changed over time, often dramatically. Mahler, in his own day known outside Vienna mostly as a conductor, was established by the 1960s as a major composer through the advocacy of conductors like Bruno Walter and Leonard Bernstein, aided by arguments that he was a herald of modernism through his close connections to Schoenberg, Webern, and Berg.

Similar efforts after World War II raised Janáček from local to international fame. Meanwhile, when critics and scholars increasingly came to view tonality as old-fashioned, the reputations of Strauss and Sibelius declined, only to be rescued later in the century when their innovations became better understood and when increasing numbers of living composers turned back to the sounds and methods of tonal music. While some music by composers of this generation may sound late Romantic in spirit or technique, what makes all of it modern is this overwhelming sense of measuring oneself against the past.

Chapter 31

Modernism and the Classical Tradition

Modern composers in the classical tradition all faced a common challenge—how to secure a place in an increasingly crowded repertoire by writing works that performers, audiences, and critics deemed worthy of performance alongside the classics of the past. To succeed, their music had to meet the criteria established by the classics: to be works of high quality that participated in the tradition of serious art music; that had lasting value, rewarding both performers and listeners through many rehearsals and close study; and that proclaimed a distinctive musical personality. These criteria were broad enough that composers as diverse as Mahler, Debussy, Vaughan Williams, Sibelius, Rachmaninov, and Scriabin could each win an enduring position in the repertoire, as we saw in the previous chapter.

In the years just before and after World War I, a younger group of composers carried out a more radical break from the musical language of the past than their predecessors or contemporaries, while maintaining strong links to the tradition. These composers, known as ***modernists***, reassessed inherited conventions as profoundly as the modernists in art who pioneered expressionism, cubism, and abstract art. Modernists in both art and music did not aim to please viewers or listeners on first sight or first hearing, an attribute that had always been considered essential. Instead, they sought to challenge our perceptions and capacities, providing an experience that would be impossible through traditional means. Modernists offered an implicit critique of mass culture and easily digested art, and their writings often show it. These composers saw no contradiction in claiming the masters of the past as models. In fact, they saw their own work as continuing what the pathbreaking classical composers had started, not as overthrowing that tradition. The paradox of all modern classical music, that it must partake of the tradition yet offer something new, is especially acute in the work of modernist composers, who are often most radical in the ways they interpret and remake the past.

Rather than taking up the topics in this chapter one by one, we will introduce them in the context of discussing six modernist composers who are among the best known and most influential of the entire century. Arnold Schoenberg and Igor Stravinsky were leaders of two branches of modernism that often seem to be at opposite poles but that faced common concerns. Schoenberg's students Alban Berg and Anton Webern took their teacher's ideas in individual directions. Béla Bartók and Charles Ives both developed unique combinations of nationalism and modernism within the classical tradition. Born between 1874 and 1885, all six began by writing tonal music in late Romantic styles, then devised new and distinctive post-tonal idioms that won them a central place in the world of modern music.

ARNOLD SCHOENBERG

Arnold Schoenberg (1874–1951; see biography and Figure 31.1) was committed to continuing the German classical tradition, and for that very reason he felt compelled to move beyond tonality to *atonality*—a term for music that avoids establishing a tonal center—and then to the ***twelve-tone method***, a form of atonality based on systematic orderings of the twelve notes of the chromatic scale. His innovations made him famous in some quarters and—because the resulting music was both dissonant and difficult to follow—notorious in others.

TONAL WORKS

Like other modernists of his generation, Schoenberg began by writing tonal music in late Romantic style. The chromatic idiom of his first important work, a tone poem for string sextet titled *Verklärte Nacht* (Transfigured Night, 1899), grew from that of Wagner's *Tristan und Isolde*, while the symphonic poem *Pelleas und Melisande* (1902–3) draws on Mahler and Strauss. The huge cantata *Gurrelieder* (Songs of Gurre, 1900–1, orchestration completed 1911) outdoes Wagner in emotional fervor, and Mahler and Strauss in the complexity of its scoring.

Developing variation   Schoenberg soon turned away from late Romantic gigantism and toward chamber music. He found in Brahms the principle of *developing variation* (see chapter 28) and applied it in his own works, such as the String Quartet No. 1 in D Minor, Op. 7. In the quartet all the themes and most subsidiary voices evolve from a few germinal motives through variation and combination. The form of the one-movement work, combining an enlarged sonata form with the four standard movements of a quartet, owes much to Liszt's

ARNOLD SCHOENBERG (1874–1951)

Schoenberg was one of the most influential composers of the twentieth century, best known for his atonal and twelve-tone music.

Schoenberg was born in Vienna, the son of a Jewish shopkeeper. He began violin lessons at age eight, then taught himself to compose by imitating the music he played. When his father died in 1891, Schoenberg had to leave school and work as a bank clerk. His instruction in theory and composition was minimal, although the composer Alexander von Zemlinsky served for a time as sounding board and teacher.

Schoenberg married Zemlinsky's sister Mathilde in 1901, and they moved to Berlin, where he worked at a cabaret until Richard Strauss got him a job teaching composition at the Stern Conservatory. Two years later he returned to Vienna and taught privately, attracting his two most famous students, Alban Berg and Anton Webern. He had the support of Mahler and other progressive musicians, but his works met stormy receptions, especially after he adopted atonality in 1908. He took up painting in an expressionist style—see the striking self-portrait in Figure 31.1—and developed friendships with several expressionist painters (one of whom had an affair with Mathilde, who briefly left him before returning for the sake of their two children).

After World War I, Schoenberg founded and directed the Society for Private Musical Performances in Vienna, which between 1919 and 1921 gave about 350 performances of music by himself and his students and colleagues. After a creative impasse, he formulated the twelve-tone method used in the Piano Suite (1921–23) and most of his later works.

Mathilde died in 1923, and a year later Schoenberg married Gertrud Kolisch, with

Figure 31.1: Self-portrait by Arnold Schoenberg from 1910, showing his interest in expressionism in painting as well as in music.

whom he had three more children and moved back to Berlin. But in 1933 the Nazis came to power and announced their intention to remove all Jewish instructors from faculty appointments. Although he had become a Lutheran when he was twenty-four to avoid anti-Semitism, he converted back to Judaism after moving with his family to France. He then traveled on to the United States, finally arriving in Los Angeles in 1934. He was appointed to a professorship at UCLA and retired in 1944 at age seventy. He died in Los Angeles in 1951 on July 13, having always feared the number 13.

MAJOR WORKS: *4 operas:* Erwartung, Die glückliche Hand, Von heute auf morgen, *and* Moses und Aron; Pierrot lunaire, Gurrelieder, *and numerous songs and choral works; 2 chamber symphonies, Five Orchestral Pieces, Variations for Orchestra, and other orchestral works; 5 string quartets, Verklärte Nacht, Wind Quintet, and other chamber works; Piano Suite and several sets of piano pieces*

SOURCE READINGS

NEW MUSIC AND TRADITION

Arnold Schoenberg saw no contradiction between tradition and innovation. For him, the tradition of classical music was a legacy of innovation, and it was his job as a composer to weave threads from the past and the present into something truly new. He returned to this theme constantly in his writings.

———— • ————

In higher art, only that is worth being presented which has never before been presented. There is no great work of art which does not convey a new message to humanity; there is no great artist who fails in this respect. This is the code of honor of all the great in art, and consequently in all great works of the great we will find that newness which never perishes, whether it be of Josquin des Prés, of Bach or Haydn, or of any other great master.

Because: Art means New Art.

* * *

My teachers were primarily Bach and Mozart, and secondarily Beethoven, Brahms, and Wagner....

I also learned much from Schubert and Mahler, Strauss and Reger too. I shut myself off from no one, and so I could say of myself:

My originality comes from this: I immediately imitated everything I saw that was good, even when I had not first seen it in someone else's work.

And I may say: often enough I saw it first in myself. For if I saw something I did not leave it at that; I acquired it, in order to possess it; I worked on it and extended it, and it led me to something new.

I am convinced that eventually people will recognize how immediately this "something new" is linked to the loftiest models that have been granted us. I venture to credit myself with having written truly new music which, being based on tradition, is destined to become tradition.

From "New Music, Outmoded Music, Style and Idea" and "National Music (2)," in *Style and Idea: Selected Writings of Arnold Schoenberg,* ed. Leonard Stein, trans. Leo Black (London: Faber & Faber, 1975), 114–15 and 173–74.

Piano Sonata in B Minor, demonstrating Schoenberg's willingness to blend influences in order to create something new.

Nonrepetition   The quartet exemplifies Schoenberg's intertwined goals for his music: to continue the tradition and to say something that had never been said before (see Source Reading). He believed that the great composers of the past had all contributed something new and therefore of permanent significance, while preserving and extending what was of highest value in the music of their predecessors. He sought to do likewise, hoping to achieve similar immortality. In essence, his entire career was a process of developing variation on the ideas and procedures he found in the Austro-German tradition of classical music from Bach to Mahler and Strauss. He asked of each work that it not simply repeat but build on the past. Remarkably, he required the same *within* each piece: except for marked repeats in binary forms, nothing should repeat exactly. As he wrote, "With me, variation almost completely takes the place of repetition." This principle of *nonrepetition* between and within pieces helps explain how Schoenberg's music would evolve.

ATONAL MUSIC

In 1908, Schoenberg began to compose pieces that avoided establishing any note as a tonal center. Others called such music *atonal*, although Schoenberg disliked the term. He felt compelled to abandon tonality in part because the heightened chromaticism, distant modulations, and prolonged dissonances of music since *Tristan* had weakened the pull of the tonic, making its declaration at the end of a piece seem increasingly arbitrary. Schoenberg emulated Strauss and others in devising novel progressions and avoiding conventional cadences, as the principle of nonrepetition demanded, but it became harder and harder to find new ways to arrive at the tonic convincingly. Moreover, in music with complex chromatic chords, we cannot easily determine which notes are the dissonant ones that have to resolve. The ambiguities led

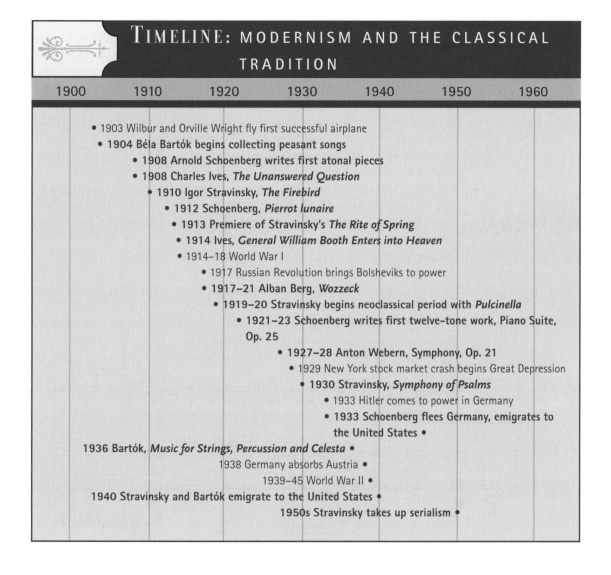

TIMELINE: MODERNISM AND THE CLASSICAL TRADITION

1900	1910	1920	1930	1940	1950	1960

- 1903 Wilbur and Orville Wright fly first successful airplane
- 1904 Béla Bartók begins collecting peasant songs
- 1908 Arnold Schoenberg writes first atonal pieces
- 1908 Charles Ives, *The Unanswered Question*
- 1910 Igor Stravinsky, *The Firebird*
- 1912 Schoenberg, *Pierrot lunaire*
- 1913 Premiere of Stravinsky's *The Rite of Spring*
- 1914 Ives, *General William Booth Enters into Heaven*
- 1914–18 World War I
- 1917 Russian Revolution brings Bolsheviks to power
- 1917–21 Alban Berg, *Wozzeck*
- 1919–20 Stravinsky begins neoclassical period with *Pulcinella*
- 1921–23 Schoenberg writes first twelve-tone work, Piano Suite, Op. 25
- 1927–28 Anton Webern, Symphony, Op. 21
- 1929 New York stock market crash begins Great Depression
- 1930 Stravinsky, *Symphony of Psalms*
- 1933 Hitler comes to power in Germany
- 1933 Schoenberg flees Germany, emigrates to the United States •
- 1936 Bartók, *Music for Strings, Percussion and Celesta* •
- 1938 Germany absorbs Austria •
- 1939–45 World War II •
- 1940 Stravinsky and Bartók emigrate to the United States •
- 1950s Stravinsky takes up serialism •

Schoenberg to what he called "the emancipation of the dissonance"—freeing dissonance from its need to resolve to consonance, so that any combination of tones could serve as a stable chord that did not require resolution. Once this idea was accepted, he believed that atonality was inevitable.

Coherence in atonal music   Without a tonal backbone, how was music to be organized? Schoenberg relied on three methods: developing variation, the integration of harmony and melody, and chromatic saturation. All had been used in tonal music, but now he drew on them more fully to provide structure. In addition, he often used gestures from tonal music, forging links to tradition and making his music easier to follow. One of Schoenberg's first entirely atonal pieces, dating from March 1908, will illustrate: *Saget mir, auf welchem Pfade* (Tell me on which path), the fifth song from a cycle of fifteen on poems from *The Book of the Hanging Gardens* by symbolist poet Stefan George (Op. 15, 1908–9). The sense of floating in tonal space created by music that does not gravitate to a tonic is perfectly suited to the vague eroticism of the poetry, which expresses, through outward symbols, the inner feelings of a love affair.

Example 31.1 shows the first two phrases. Much about the music is familiar from earlier German Lieder, including the texture of voice with piano, the rise and fall of the vocal melody, the division into phrases, the use of dynamics to shape each phrase, and the descending gestures to mark the ends of phrases. Developing variation is apparent in both voice and accompaniment. The opening vocal motive of a descending semitone changes in measure 2 to a falling whole tone, is inverted in measure 3 as a rising major seventh, and reappears in measure 4 as a descending semitone, though in a new rhythm. Similar development of a semitone motive can be traced in the piano. Meanwhile, the chords in measure 1 are varied in measure 2, and elements from them—such as the combination of a tritone with a perfect fourth or major third—are echoed in measures 3 and 4. Everything that follows is derived in some way from these opening measures. A variant of measures 3–4 closes the piece, providing a traditional sense of return and closure despite the lack of a key.

Example 31.1: Schoenberg, Saget mir, auf welchem Pfade, *No. 5, from* The Book of the Hanging Gardens, *Op. 15*

Red boxes indicate set 016 as melody or harmony.

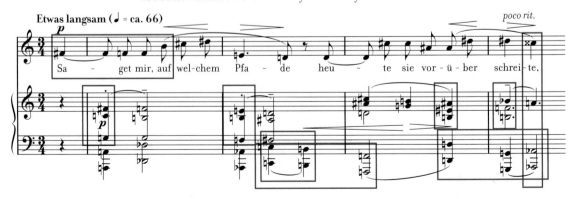

Tell me, on which path she stepped along today

Schoenberg integrated melody and harmony through a process he called *Pitch-class sets* "composing with the tones of a motive," which springs directly from developing variation. In this process, he manipulated the notes and intervals of a motive to create chords and new melodies. One way this worked was to treat the notes of a motive containing three or more pitches just as we might a triad or other tonal chord: as a collection of pitches that could be transposed, inverted, and arranged in any order and register to generate melodies and harmonies. Theorists later termed such a collection a *set* or, more formally, **pitch-class set,** using **pitch-class** to mean one of the twelve notes of the chromatic scale and its enharmonic equivalents in any octave. A convenient way to label sets is to arrange the notes in the most compact array from lowest to highest and number each pitch-class by the number of semitones above the first one. In this song, the first three notes in the vocal line form the set 016 (counting F as 0, F♯ as 1 semitone higher, and B as 6 semitones higher). In the example, this and all later occurrences of this set are enclosed in red boxes. The first chord in the piano also contains this set, transposed and arranged as a perfect fourth and tritone within a major seventh. It reappears, often transposed or inverted, in several later chords and melodically in the bass. Other sets are used in similar fashion. Using a limited number of sets gives the music a consistent sound. Schoenberg tended to use sets that formed strong dissonances, because those sets are most distinctive and therefore easier to follow as the music unfolds. This integration of melody and harmony harks back to music of earlier eras.

Atonal music can also be shaped through **chromatic saturation,** the ap- *Chromatic* pearance of all twelve pitch-classes within a segment of music. We saw this *saturation* method at work in Example 28.7, a song of Hugo Wolf that is highly chromatic but still tonal, where all twelve chromatic notes are stated in the first phrase and again in the next two measures. The appearance of a note that has not recently been sounded can give a sense of moving forward harmonically. As a corollary, once the twelfth chromatic note has appeared, there can be a sense of fullness and completion, which Wolf in a tonal context and Schoenberg in an atonal context to reinforce the feeling of completing a phrase. In Example 31.1, all twelve notes occur in the first two-measure phrase, the last two (D and A♯) stated in the piano chord on the second beat of measure 2. Simultaneously, the other notes in that sonority (C and F♯ in the piano and E in the voice) initiate another round of all twelve, completed at the end of the next phrase with the arrival of A and A♭ in the piano. The coordination of chromatic saturation with phrasing is not always this exact; sometimes one or more notes are saved for the next phrase, helping to create longer spans.

Through these means, Schoenberg sought to write atonal music that was as *Atonal works* logical as tonal music. In 1909, he completed *The Book of the Hanging Gardens;* Three Piano Pieces, Op. 11; Five Orchestral Pieces, Op. 16; and *Erwartung* (Expectation), Op. 17, a one-character opera for soprano. In the works with orchestra, he followed Mahler in treating instruments soloistically and in swiftly alternating timbres to produce a great variety of colors. *Erwartung,* the height of **expressionism** in music, uses exaggerated gestures, angular melodies, and unrelenting dissonance to convey the tortured emotions of the protagonist (see sidebar, p. 808). In this opera, Schoenberg

MUSIC IN CONTEXT

EXPRESSIONISM

In the early twentieth century, several groups of German and Austrian painters embraced an international movement called *expressionism*, which also extended to literature, music, dance, theater, and architecture. Expressionism developed from the subjectivity of Romanticism but differed from it in the introspective experience it aimed to portray and how it chose to portray it.

Expressionist painters such as Ernst Ludwig Kirchner and Richard Gerstl rejected traditional Western aesthetic values by representing real objects or people in grossly distorted ways, characterized by an intensely expressive use of pure colors and dynamic brushstrokes as in Gerstl's portrait of the Schoenberg family (Figure 31.2). These artists and others drew on contemporary themes involving the dark side of city life, in which people lived under extreme psychological pressure, as well as bright scenes from the circus and music-halls that masked a more gloomy reality. They aspired to represent inner experience, to explore the hidden world of the psyche and to render visible the stressful emotional life of the modern person—isolated, helpless in the grip of poorly understood forces, prey to inner conflict, tension, anxiety, and fear, and tormented by elemental, irrational drives including an eroticism that often had morbid overtones. That is also how the Viennese doctor Sigmund Freud, founder of psychoanalysis, described the deepest level of memory and emotional activity in his *Interpretation of Dreams* (1900). In short, expressionism sought to capture the human condition as it was perceived in the early twentieth century.

Arnold Schoenberg and his pupil Alban Berg were two leading exponents of expressionism in music, which paralleled expressionist art by adopting a similarly desperate and revolutionary style. Its characteristics are evident in Schoenberg's *Erwartung*, an opera in which a lone protagonist—emblematic of the artist's alienation from society and its conventions—

pushed nonrepetition to an extreme: the work is not only atonal, it has no themes or motives that return and lacks any reference to traditional forms. The fluid, constantly changing music suits the nightmare-like text.

Return to form   Composers, however, can go only so far in avoiding repetition: Schoenberg could not write another piece like *Erwartung* without repeating himself. Instead, he turned back to tradition, using motives, themes, and long-range repetition and evoking traditional forms and the functions of tonality in new ways.

Pierrot lunaire   Early stages of this return can be seen in *Pierrot lunaire* (Moonstruck Pierrot, 1912), a cycle of twenty-one songs drawn from a larger poetic cycle by the Belgian symbolist poet Albert Giraud. Schoenberg scored the text, translated into German, for a woman's voice with a chamber ensemble of five performers who play nine different instruments. In keeping with the principle of nonrepetition, the combination of instruments in each movement is unique. The voice declaims the text in **Sprechstimme** ("speaking voice"), approximating the written pitches in the gliding tones of speech, while following the notated rhythm exactly—an innovative idea that blends the traditional no-

gives voice to what the composer described as a dream of *Angst*, an overwhelming feeling of dread or anxiety. Its distorted melodies and fragmented rhythms, violently graphic musical images, and discordant harmonies create the quasi-hysterical atmosphere typical of the style. In none of Schoenberg's expressionist pieces, nor in Berg's opera *Wozzeck*, did these composers try to create music that is pretty or naturalistic (as the impressionists did); rather, they deployed the most direct—even drastic—means, no matter how unappealing, to convey extreme and irrational states of mind.

Schoenberg was also an amateur painter and took lessons from Gerstl, one of the leading exponents of expressionism in Austria. Schoenberg's most impressive pictures, a series of "gazes" in the form of faces, not only emphasize the act of looking but also suggest the same feelings of claustrophobia and *Angst* as those portrayed in *Erwartung*. With other Viennese expressionists Schoenberg also shared an interest in producing self-portraits (see Figure 31.1); they indicate, perhaps, his constant questioning, both of his own identity and of his place among the modernists.—BRH

Figure 31.2: Richard Gerstl, portrait of the Schoenberg family.

tions of song and melodrama. The inexact pitches evoke an eerie atmosphere for the symbolist text, in which the clown Pierrot suffers gruesome visions provoked by a moonbeam that takes many shapes.

Expressionist features of the work aside, Schoenberg highlights many traditional elements. Each poem has a refrain, and Schoenberg typically sets the repeated lines of text with a variant of their original music at the same pitch level, thereby creating a sense of departure and return, as in tonal music. We find varied repetition at all levels, from motives and chords to themes, sections, and one entire song: No. 7 is recast as an instrumental epilogue at the end of No. 13, *Enthauptung* (Beheading, in NAWM 141b). The cycle includes several traditional forms and genres, including a waltz, a serenade, a barcarolle, and an aria over a walking bass, reminiscent of Bach. Schoenberg called No. 8, *Nacht* (Night, NAWM 141a), a passacaglia, but it is an unusual one because the unifying motive—a rising minor third followed by a descending major third—reappears in various note values in all parts, often treated in canon. The constant repetition of this motive, whose contour in original and

CD 11|4   CD 6|4

CD 11|1   CD 6|1

inverted forms resembles wings, fittingly illustrates Pierrot's obsession with the giant moths that enclose him in a frightening trap and shut out the sun. Even *Enthauptung*, which appears to abandon thematic development for anarchic improvisation, unfolds by constantly varying the initial ideas to capture the images and feelings in the text.

TWELVE-TONE METHOD

Schoenberg still faced a problem: with his atonal methods, he could not match the formal coherence of tonal music and had to rely on a text to sustain pieces of any length. He found the solution in the **twelve-tone method**.

The method   He formulated what he called his "method of composing with twelve tones that are related only to one another" (rather than to a tonic) in the early 1920s, after several years during which he published no music. The basis of a twelve-tone composition is a **row** or **series** consisting of the twelve pitch-classes arranged in an order chosen by the composer and producing a particular sequence of intervals. The tones of the series may be used both successively, as melody, and simultaneously, as harmony or counterpoint, in any octave and with any desired rhythm. The row may be used not only in its original, or **prime**, form but also in **inversion**, in **retrograde** order (backward), and in **retrograde inversion**, and may appear in all twelve possible transpositions of any of the four forms. The twelve-note series is often broken into segments of three to six notes, which are then used as sets to create melodic motives and chords. As a rule, the composer states all twelve pitches of the series before going on to use the series in any of its forms again (unless two or more statements occur simultaneously).

Sets, saturation,   Stated this way, the method may sound arbitrary. But for Schoenberg, it
and structure   was a systematic way to accomplish what he was already doing in his atonal music: integrating harmony and melody by composing with a limited number of sets (here, those defined by segments of the row), marking off phrases and subphrases with chromatic saturation (regulated by the appearance of all twelve notes in each statement of the row), and relying on developing variation. Moreover, Schoenberg recreated by analogy the structural functions of tonality, using the transposition of his rows as an analogue to modulation in tonal music. After focusing on vocal works in his atonal period, he turned to traditional instrumental forms, as if to demonstrate the power of his method to reconstitute tonal forms in a new musical language. Among these works, composed between 1921 and 1949, are the Piano Suite, Op. 25, modeled on the keyboard suites of Bach; Variations for Orchestra, Op. 31; Third and Fourth String Quartets, Opp. 30 and 37; Violin Concerto, Op. 36; and Piano Concerto, Op. 42. In these pieces, motives and themes are presented and developed, using the tonal forms and genres of Classic and Romantic music, but twelve-tone rows stand in for the keys.

Piano Suite   The Piano Suite (excerpted in NAWM 142) illustrates some of Schoenberg's methods. Throughout the work, the row appears in only eight forms, shown in Example 31.2a: the untransposed prime form (P–0); the prime transposed up six semitones (P–6); the inversion in the same two transpositions (I–0 and I–6); and their retrogrades (R–0, R–6, RI–0, and RI–6).

CD 11|8   CD 6|8

Schoenberg designed the row so that each of these begins on either E or B♭ and ends on the other, and all the primes and inversions have G and D♭ as the second pair of notes (see orange box in Example 31.2a). The recurrence of E, B♭, G, and D♭ in the same places creates a consistency that Schoenberg saw as an analogue to staying in a single key throughout, the normal practice in a Baroque keyboard suite, although it is much more difficult for a listener to hear. The first four notes of R–0 give a nod to Schoenberg's model, J. S. Bach, by spelling his name: B♭-A-C-B♮ (B-A-C-H, in German nomenclature).

Example 31.2b shows the rows deployed at the beginning of the Prelude (NAWM 142a). P–0 is in the right hand as melody, divided into motives of

CD 11|8

CD 6|8

Example 31.2: Schoenberg, Piano Suite, Op. 25

a. Row forms

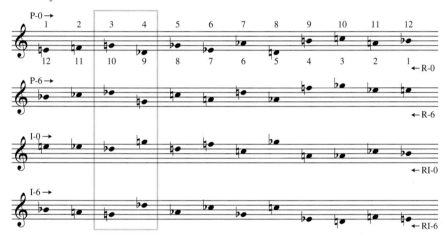

b. Prelude

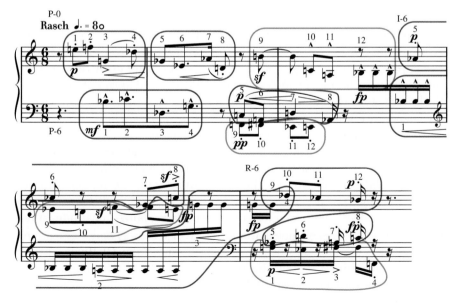

c. Minuet

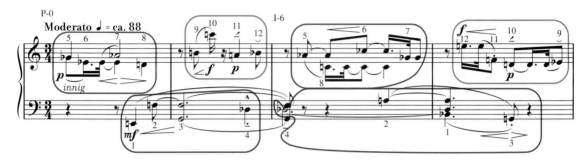

four notes each (in brown, blue, and green circles respectively). Twelve-tone theorists call such groups of four consecutive notes from the row **tetrachords**, using the ancient Greek term in a new sense (see chapter 1). In the left hand as accompaniment we find P–6, using the same division into tetrachords and presenting the last two simultaneously. Each tetrachord is a different type of set, containing different intervals, so in featuring them Schoenberg continued his earlier practice of composing with sets. There is an intervallic canon between the two hands, recalling Bach's contrapuntal practice. At the end of measure 3, I–6 begins, presenting all three tetrachords simultaneously, each in its own rhythm. The last two notes of its first tetrachord overlap the statement of R–6 in measure 5, which also presents the tetrachords simultaneously. Here the left-hand texture is less contrapuntal and more like accompanimental chords.

CD 11|9   CD 6|9

In the Minuet (NAWM 142b), shown in Example 31.2c, P–0 in the first two measures is answered by I–6 in the second two. Again both are divided into tetrachords, with the first accompanying the others. But Schoenberg starts the melody before the accompaniment, so that the first note of the row does not appear first, and he sometimes reorders the notes within the tetrachords. Thus he was still composing with motives and sets, as in his atonal music. Again, the end of each two-measure phrase is coordinated with the end of a row, so that chromatic saturation is still helping to demarcate phrasing. Developing variation is clearly at work, since the second phrase varies the first and develops its dotted rhythmic motive. Also, there are many references to tonal music, including the meter of the dance, the foursquare phrasing, and the leading-tone melodic gestures at the end of each two-measure phrase. All the factors we saw in the atonal music are just as important here.

Twelve-tone regions and modulation

The Piano Suite stays in the same "key" throughout, but for a sonata form or other Classic-era form Schoenberg had to find an analogue to modulation. He created it in his Fourth String Quartet and many other works by devising a way to establish twelve-tone regions containing only one transposition of each row form. Example 31.3 shows the row for the quartet. Schoenberg designed it so that the last six notes—the second **hexachord**—constitute an inverted form of the first six notes, in a different order. As a result, there is one inversion of the row, I–5, whose first hexachord has the same notes as the second hexachord of P–0, and vice versa. If the two rows are combined contrapuntally, by the time the first half of each has been stated, all twelve chromatic notes will have been heard exactly once; every other inversion would duplicate at least one note. This special relationship prompted Schoenberg to treat each transposition of the prime form, its related inversion, and their retrogrades as a tonal region analogous to a key. In the first movement of the quartet, a sonata form, the P–0/I–5 region serves as "tonic"—the region in which the piece begins and ends, which occupies the largest number of measures, and which is used for the first theme in the exposition and coda. The region a fifth higher is used for the second theme in the exposition, serving as a sort of "dominant" region, and the other ten transpositions are used as contrasting "keys." Thus through his twelve-tone method, Schoenberg sought to recreate the forms of tonal music in an entirely new language.

Example 31.3: Row forms used in Schoenberg's Fourth String Quartet, Op. 37

LATE TONAL WORKS

Twelve-tone music was not Schoenberg's only strategy for looking back at the tradition. Some of his works from the 1930s and 1940s are tonal, and in two works he "recomposed" eighteenth-century music, by Matthias Georg Monn and by Handel. These "arrangements" highlight the wide stylistic gulf between Schoenberg's modernism and the tonal tradition by juxtaposing them directly. In their own way, these works are as radical as the twelve-tone music.

SCHOENBERG AS MODERNIST

We have discussed Schoenberg at much greater length than his place in the repertoire seems to warrant. Yet he merits the space, not only because his music is complex, takes time to understand, and influenced others enormously, but because the problems he chose to address as a modern composer and the way he faced them did much to shape the course of musical practice in the twentieth century. His desire to match the achievements of his forebears pressed him both backward—to reclaim the genres, forms, procedures, and gestures of the past—and onward toward a new musical language. Ironically, his music won him both a central place in the modernist tradition as well as an enduring unpopularity with most listeners and a great many performers, who valued the familiar musical language and conventions that he felt compelled to abandon. The disconnection between audiences and connoisseurs in their evaluation of music, evident already in the reception of Beethoven's late quartets, reached a new intensity with Schoenberg and many other modernists and became a principal theme of twentieth-century music.

The Second
Viennese School

Schoenberg attracted many devoted students. The two most notable, Alban Berg and Anton Webern, were both natives of Vienna and are often grouped with Schoenberg as members of the Second Viennese School, drawing an implicit connection to the first Viennese threesome, Haydn, Mozart, and Beethoven.

ALBAN BERG

Alban Berg (1885–1935), shown in Figure 31.3, began studies with Schoenberg in 1904 at age nineteen. Although he adopted his teacher's atonal and twelve-tone methods, listeners found his music more approachable. He achieved much greater popular success than his teacher, especially with his

Figure 31.3: Alban Berg around 1910, in a portrait by Arnold Schoenberg.

opera *Wozzeck*, premiered in 1925. His secret lay in infusing his post-tonal idiom not only with the forms and procedures of tonal music, as Schoenberg had done, but also with its expressive gestures, characteristic styles, and other elements that quickly conveyed meanings and feelings to his hearers. In this respect he was a direct heir of Mahler and Strauss.

Wozzeck is the outstanding example of expressionist opera. The libretto, arranged by Berg from a fragmentary play by Georg Büchner (1813–1837), presents the soldier Wozzeck as a hapless victim of his environment, despised by his fellow men, forced by poverty to submit to a doctor's experiments, betrayed in love, and driven finally to murder and suicide. The music is atonal, not twelve-tone, and includes Sprechstimme in some scenes. Each of the three acts has continuous music, with the changing scenes (five in each act) linked by orchestral interludes.

Berg highlights the drama and organizes the music through the use of leitmotives, pitch-class sets identified with the main characters, and traditional forms that wryly comment on the characters and situation. Wozzeck's outburst in the first scene, "Wir arme Leut!" (We poor people!), shown in Example 31.4a, is one of his leitmotives and contains his characteristic set. The first act includes a Baroque suite, suggesting the formality of Wozzeck's captain; a rhapsody, suiting Wozzeck's fantastic visions; a march and lullaby for a scene with his mistress Marie and their child; a passacaglia for the doctor's constant prattling about his theory; and a rondo for Marie's seduction by a rival suitor, who tries repeatedly until she gives in. The second act, the heart of the drama, is a symphony in five movements, including a sonata form, a fantasia and fugue, a ternary slow movement, a scherzo, and a rondo. The third act presents six inventions, reflecting Wozzeck's

Example 31.4: Motives from Berg's Wozzeck

a. Wozzeck's leitmotive and characteristic set, from Act I, scene 1

b. Tavern piano in Act III, scene 3, with rhythmic pattern and Wozzeck's set

growing obsession: on a theme (seven variations and a fugue); on a note (B); on a rhythm; on a chord; on a key; and on a duration (the eighth note). Especially notable is the invention on a key, the last and longest interlude between scenes, when, as Berg put it, the composer steps in front of the curtain and comments on the tragedy we have witnessed. It sounds at times like a Mahler slow movement in D minor, especially at the beginning and end. But it is entirely organized by atonal principles, in a masterly demonstration of Berg's ability to touch the hearts of his listeners with familiar gestures and sounds while speaking in atonal language.

The invention on a rhythm in Act III, scene 3 (NAWM 143), illustrates Berg's approach. Just after murdering Marie, Wozzeck sits in a tavern drinking and singing, then dances briefly with Marie's friend Margret; she sits on his lap and sings a song, but when she spies blood on his hand, Wozzeck becomes agitated and rushes out. The scene begins with an onstage, out-of-tune tavern piano playing a wild polka, shown in Example 31.4b. The music is atonal—the notes in the first two measures comprise the set associated with Wozzeck—but it instantly conveys the impression of a popular dance tune, through triadic accompaniment under a melody that moves by step and by skip. Just as the singers on stage are acting their parts, so too the atonal music is acting the part of tonal music, and its meaning is immediately clear. The melody lays out the rhythmic theme for the scene, which is then obsessively reiterated at various levels of augmentation and diminution, so that it is almost always present. By constantly repeating the rhythm, Berg unifies the scene through developing variation and also reveals Wozzeck's preoccupation with his guilt, which he cannot escape. When Wozzeck sings a folk song and Margret a popular song with piano accompaniment, Berg imitates recognizable tonal styles in an atonal idiom. The almost constant references to tonality and to familiar styles and genres help to keep listeners engaged, while the atonality heightens the dramatic impact.

Soon after Wozzeck was premiered, Berg adopted twelve-tone methods, turning them to his own ends. He often chose rows that allowed for tonal-sounding

CD 11|12   CD 6|12

Twelve-tone works

chords and chord progressions, connecting the new style with the past and investing his music with immediate emotional impact. His chief twelve-tone works are his *Lyric Suite* for string quartet (1925–26), his Violin Concerto (1935), and a second opera, *Lulu* (1928–35), whose orchestration was not quite complete when he died.

Violin Concerto   Berg designed the row of the Violin Concerto with four interlocking minor and major triads, marked with square brackets in Example 31.5a, which permits frequent references to tonal chords while using twelve-tone procedures. The piece includes evocations of a violin tuning its open strings (using notes 1, 3, 5, and 7 of the row), tonal chord progressions, Viennese waltzes, a folk song, and a Bach chorale. The last of these, *Es ist genug* (It is enough), which ends Bach's Cantata No. 60, alludes to the death of Manon Gropius, to whose memory the concerto is dedicated; she was the daughter of Berg's close friend Alma Mahler (widow of Gustav Mahler) and died at eighteen of polio. As shown in Example 31.5b, the chorale melody begins with three rising whole steps, like the last four notes of Berg's row, and Bach's harmonization highlights chords that can be derived from the row. Thus the quotation of the chorale is not something foreign, but stems directly from the row itself.

Example 31.5: Row from Berg's Violin Concerto and Bach's Es ist genug

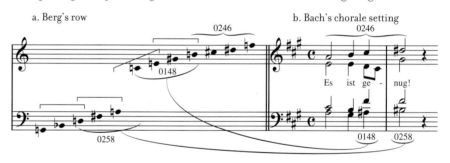

It is enough!

Berg's concerto can be understood on first hearing by anyone familiar with tonal music, yet its structure is wholly determined by twelve-tone procedures. Berg understood that because twelve-tone music was unfamiliar, it could be incomprehensible to the listener, yet it also had the capacity to imitate any style or emotional gesture, just as an actor may play any role. Thus his music accommodates innovation with the past, reworking the music's inner structure just as radically as in Schoenberg's music but keeping more of the familiar on the surface of the music.

ANTON WEBERN

Anton Webern (1883–1945), shown in Figure 31.4, began lessons with Schoenberg in 1904, at the same time as Berg. He was already studying musicology under Guido Adler at the University of Vienna, where he received a Ph.D. in 1906 and absorbed ideas about music history that influenced his own (and perhaps also Schoenberg's) development.

Webern believed that music involves the presentation of ideas that can be expressed in no other way; that it operates according to rules of order based on natural law rather than taste; that great art does what is necessary, not arbitrary; that evolution in art is also necessary; and that history, and thus musical idioms and practices, can move only forward, not backward. After Schoenberg had formulated, and Webern and Berg had adopted, the twelve-tone method, Webern argued in a series of lectures published posthumously as *The Path to the New Music* that twelve-tone music was the inevitable result of music's evolution because it combined the most advanced approaches to pitch (using all twelve chromatic notes), musical space (integrating the melodic and harmonic dimensions), and the presentation of musical ideas (combining Classic forms with polyphonic procedures and unity with variety, deriving every element from the thematic material). With his view of history, Webern regarded each step along the way from tonality to atonality to twelve-tone music as an act of discovery, not invention. This gave him—and Schoenberg—total confidence in their own work, despite the incomprehension and opposition they encountered from performers and listeners. Webern's concept of the composer as an artist expressing new ideas, yet also as a researcher making new discoveries, sprang from his training in musicology, and it became enormously influential in the mid- to late-twentieth century. The contrast to the servant-artisan composer of the fifteenth to eighteenth centuries, or the nineteenth-century composer working to satisfy the public taste, is huge.

View of music history

Webern, like Schoenberg and Berg, passed through the stages of late Romantic chromaticism, atonality, and twelve-tone organization, the last beginning in 1925 with the three songs of Op. 17. His works, about equally divided between instrumental and vocal, are mostly for small chamber ensembles.

Webern was at heart a Romantic who sought to write deeply expressive music. Yet because he believed great art should do only what is necessary, his music is extremely concentrated. When writing his Six Bagatelles for String Quartet, Op. 9 (1911–13), he remarked that once he had incorporated all twelve notes, he often felt that the piece was finished. Another atonal work, No. 4 of his Five Pieces for Orchestra, Op. 10, runs to only six measures, and the last of his Three Little Pieces for Cello and Piano, Op. 11, to just twenty notes. Even larger works, like the Symphony, Op. 21 (1927–28), and the String Quartet, Op. 28 (1936–38), are only eight or nine minutes long, and his entire mature output takes less than four hours to play. Textures are stripped to the bare essentials; his music has

Figure 31.4: Anton Webern in 1908, in a portrait by Max Oppenheimer.

sometimes been described as pointillistic, since it often features only one to three or four notes at once or in the same instrument in succession. The dynamics, specified down to the finest gradations, seldom rise above *forte*. Perhaps influenced by his musicological studies—for his dissertation he edited volume 2 of Henricus Isaac's *Choralis Constantinus*—he often used techniques of Renaissance polyphony, including canons in inversion or retrograde. Unlike Berg, he avoided using sets or rows with tonal implications.

Symphony, Op. 21

CD 11|15

The first movement of the Symphony, Op. 21 (NAWM 144), illustrates Webern's use of twelve-tone procedures, canons, instrumentation, and form. The entire movement is a double canon in inversion. Example 31.6 shows the beginning, with canon 1 in the top two staves and canon 2 in the bottom two staves. Instead of highlighting the canonic lines by setting each as a continuous melody in a distinctive timbre and range, Webern deliberately integrates them. Each line is filled with rests, changes timbre frequently, and weaves back and forth through the same three-octave range. The succession of timbres is as much part of the melody as are the pitches and rhythms, and

Example 31.6: Double canon at the opening of Webern's Symphony, Op. 21

the changes of instrument in the leading voice of each canon are echoed in the following voice. Here Webern applies Schoenberg's concept of **Klangfarbenmelodie** (tone-color melody), in which changes of tone color are perceived as parallel to changing pitches in a melody.

The double canon is nestled within a reinterpretation of sonata form, showing Webern's integration of Classic formal principles with procedures from Renaissance polyphony. The exposition contains not two contrasting themes, but a contrast of character between canon 1 and canon 2. After the exposition repeats exactly, the development is a palindrome, and the recapitulation presents the same succession of rows as the exposition, but in new rhythms and registers. The development and recapitulation then repeat, as in an early Classic symphony. Thus through analogy, Webern recreates the tonal structure of a Classic symphonic first movement in twelve-tone terms. Like Schoenberg's twelve-tone analogies to tonal structure, Webern's is beyond the capacity of most listeners. What can be heard more readily is the exact repetition of each half of the movement; given the origins of twelve-tone music in the principle of nonrepetition and developing variation, such deliberate repetition makes a strong reference to the forms of the past.

Although Webern received little acclaim during his lifetime and has never gained wide popularity, recognition of his work among scholars and composers grew steadily in the years after World War II. His music had an abiding influence on some composers in Italy, Germany, France, and the United States, especially in the first two decades after the war.

Influence

IGOR STRAVINSKY

While Schoenberg, Berg, and Webern worked inside the Austro-German tradition, Igor Stravinsky (1882–1971; see biography and Figure 31.5) started as a Russian nationalist and became a cosmopolitan—and arguably the most important composer of his time. He created an individual voice by developing several style traits, most derived from Russian traditions, into his distinctive trademarks: undermining meter through unpredictable accents and rests or through rapid changes of meter; frequent ostinatos; layering and juxtaposition of static blocks of sound; discontinuity and interruption; dissonance based on diatonic, octatonic, and other collections; and dry, antilyrical, but colorful use of instruments. He forged these traits during his "Russian" period (to about 1918) and used them again in his later periods. Through Stravinsky, elements of Russian music became part of a common international modernist practice.

RUSSIAN PERIOD

Stravinsky wrote his most popular works early in his career: the ballets *The Firebird* (1910), *Petrushka* (1910–11), and *The Rite of Spring* (*Le sacre du printemps*, 1911–13), all commissioned by Sergei Diaghilev for the Ballets Russes in Paris.

IGOR STRAVINSKY (1882–1971)

Stravinsky participated in the most significant trends in modern music during his lifetime, wrote some of the most successful and enduring music of the twentieth century, and had an enormous influence on three generations of composers.

Stravinsky was born in Orianenbaum, near St. Petersburg in Russia, to a well-to-do musical family. He began piano lessons at age nine and studied music theory in his later teens but never attended the Conservatory. His most important teacher was Rimsky-Korsakov, with whom he studied composition and orchestration privately.

Figure 31.5: Photograph of Igor Stravinsky in Paris in May 1913, the month of the premiere of The Rite of Spring.

In 1906, Stravinsky married his cousin Catherine Nosenko, with whom he had four children.

Stravinsky demonstrated his command of his teacher's rich, colorful style in *Scherzo fantastique* and *Fireworks*. After hearing these two pieces in 1909, the impresario Sergei Diaghilev commissioned Stravinsky to compose for the Ballets Russes (Russian Ballet), which reigned in Paris from 1909 to 1929. For Diaghilev, Stravinsky wrote the ballets that made him famous and that are still his most popular works: *The Firebird, Petrushka,* and *The Rite of Spring.* He collaborated on them with choreographers Mikhail Fokine, founder of the modern ballet style, and Vaclav Nijinsky, one of the greatest dancers of the early twentieth century.

Stravinsky moved to Paris in 1911, then to Switzerland in 1914. Six years later, after becoming stranded in the West by World War I and the 1917 Russian Revolution, he returned to France, having already begun to compose in the neoclassical idiom that would characterize his music for the next three decades. The commotion at the *Rite of Spring* premiere bestowed on him a delicious notoriety, and because he performed tirelessly, first as a pianist and then as a conductor, Stravinsky was well known in 1920s Europe and America. He continued to work with the Ballets Russes but also wrote abstract instrumental works. One of his favorite collaborators was the choreographer George Balanchine.

Catherine died in March 1939. In September, just weeks after the outbreak of World War II, Stravinsky moved to the United States. In March 1940, he married

Vera Sudeikin, with whom he had been having an affair since the early 1920s. He settled in Hollywood, not far from Schoenberg and Rachmaninov, and wrote several pieces that referred to American styles, such as the *Ebony Concerto* for the jazz clarinetist Woody Herman and his band. His last major neoclassical work was the opera *The Rake's Progress*, premiered in Venice in 1951.

In 1948 Stravinsky met Robert Craft, who became his assistant. Craft was enthusiastic about the twelve-tone music of Schoenberg and Webern. By the mid-1950s, Stravinsky had absorbed twelve-tone methods into his own idiom. Most of his late works are serial and many are religious, from *Canticum sacrum* in 1955 through the *Requiem Canticles* in 1965–66. Stravinsky and his wife moved to New York in 1969. He died there two years later and was buried in Venice.

MAJOR WORKS: The Firebird, Petrushka, The Rite of Spring, L'histoire du soldat, *Symphonies of Wind Instruments*, Les noces, *Octet, for wind instruments*, Oedipus rex, Symphony of Psalms, *Symphony in C, Symphony in Three Movements*, The Rake's Progress, Agon, Requiem Canticles

The Firebird, based on Russian folk tales, stems from the Russian nationalist tradition and especially from the exoticism of Rimsky-Korsakov. Throughout, humans are characterized by diatonic music, while supernatural creatures and places are cast in octatonic or chromatic realms, following Rimsky's standard practice.

The Firebird

In *Petrushka*, Stravinsky introduced several of the stylistic traits that became closely identified with him. The opening scene of the ballet depicts a fair in St. Petersburg during the final week of carnival season. Here we find Stravinsky's characteristic blocks of static harmony with repetitive melodic and rhythmic patterns as well as abrupt shifts from one block to another. Each group of dancers receives its distinctive music: a band of tipsy revelers, an organ grinder with a dancer, a music-box player with another dancer, the puppet theater where Petrushka stars. Seemingly unconnected musical events interrupt each other without transition and then just as suddenly return, creating a sharp juxtaposition of diverse textures that has been compared to the cubism of Pablo Picasso (see chapter 29 and Figure 29.4). The interruption and juxtaposition of blocks, which Stravinsky absorbed from the Russian practice of Musorgsky and Rimsky-Korsakov, is here linked to the visual juxtapositions of ballet.

Petrushka

Stravinsky enhanced the Russian and popular carnival atmosphere throughout the ballet by borrowing and elaborating several Russian folk tunes, a popular French song, and Viennese waltzes. Rather than smoothing out these borrowings, Stravinsky preserved their contexts, heightening the differences between their styles to make each block of sound as distinctive as possible. The passage in Example 31.7, which accompanies the drunken merrymakers, is based on a folk song from Rimsky-Korsakov's 1877 collection of traditional songs. But Stravinsky avoids the dominant-tonic harmony of Rimsky's version; instead, he places the melody in the bass and simulates folk harmony, in which voices sing in parallel fifths and octaves, often against drones. In contrast to the diatonic folk songs, Stravinsky uses octatonic music for the supernatural, but the harmony is now more biting than in *The Firebird*. The puppet Petrushka, who has been brought to life by a magician, is characterized in the famous "Petrushka chord" that combines F♯ and C major triads, both part of the same octatonic scale, as shown in Example 31.8.

Example 31.7: Passage from Stravinsky's Petrushka *based on Russian folk song*

Example 31.8: "Petrushka" chord, with octatonic scale from which it derives

Stravinsky's distinctive style crystallized in *The Rite of Spring*. The subject was still Russian, but now it was an imagined fertility ritual set in prehistoric Russia, during which an adolescent girl is chosen for sacrifice and must dance herself to death. Although Stravinsky again borrowed folk melodies, the scenario, choreography, and music were marked by primitivism, a deliberate representation of the elemental, crude, and uncultured, and cast aside the sophistication and stylishness of modern life and trained artistry. Figure 31.6 shows one of the costumes from the original production. The audience at the premiere was shocked, breaking out in a notorious riot (see Source Reading, p. 824). Later, the piece became one of the most frequently performed compositions of its time.

The characteristics of Stravinsky's mature idiom can be heard in the first scene, *Danse des adolescentes* (Dance of the Adolescent Girls, NAWM 145a), whose opening measures are shown in Example 31.9.

Despite the regular barring, each pulse in the first two measures is played with the same strength, negating the hierarchy of beats and offbeats that is essential to meter. Then accented chords, doubled by eight horns, create an unpredictable pattern of stresses that destroy any feeling of metrical regularity. Yet while the listener is utterly disoriented metrically and rhythmically, the music is cleverly conceived for ballet; the passage makes an eight-measure period, and the dancers can count four-measure phrases. This re-

Figure 31.6: Costume sketch by Nikolai Roerich of a peasant girl from the original production of Stravinsky's The Rite of Spring.

duction of meter to mere pulsation was the element that most strongly conveyed a sense of primitivism in the music. In the final dance of the ballet, the *Danse sacrale* (Sacrificial Dance, NAWM 145b), Stravinsky adopted two additional strategies that reduce meter to pulse: rapidly changing meters, and unpredictable alternation of notes with rests.

CD 11|23

The entire passage in Example 31.9 is built from ostinatos, including pounded or arpeggiated chords and the melodic ostinato in the English horn. Stravinsky uses these repeating figures to create static blocks of sound, which he juxtaposes. Here one block is replaced by another, then returns. Within each block, and indeed throughout the piece, there is no development of motives or themes as traditionally understood, but rather repetition and unpredictable variation.

Ostinatos and juxtaposed blocks

Example 31.9: Opening of Danse des adolescentes, *from Stravinsky's* The Rite of Spring

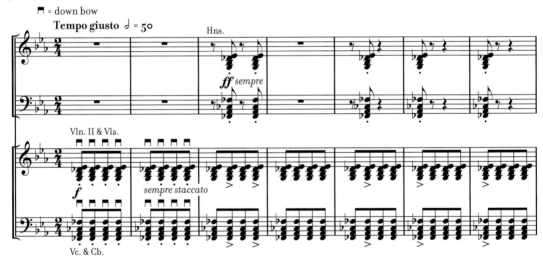

Layering   Often Stravinsky builds up textures by layering two or more independent strands of music on top of each other. The material at measure 9 is composed of three layers distinguished by timbre and figuration, with the top line also set off by register and pitch collection.

Discontinuity and connection   In typical Stravinsky fashion, the patterns within successive blocks are quite different, creating discontinuity. Yet the collection of pitches being used differs by only one new note (*c*), lending a strong sense of continuity. Stravinsky plays off the obvious surface discontinuities of his music with more subtle connections, somewhat like Mozart did when he joined a varied series of topics by using harmony and form (see chapter 22).

Dissonance   Most dissonance in Stravinsky's music is based on the scales used in Russian classical music, such as the diatonic and octatonic collections. Here the dissonant chords in measures 1–8 combine an F♭-major triad in the lower strings with a first-inversion dominant seventh chord on E♭ in the upper strings to produce a sonority that has all seven notes of the A♭ harmonic minor scale.

Timbre linked with motive and variation   Stravinsky often identified a musical idea with a particular timbre. Here the pounding chords are always in the strings with horn reinforcements, and the English horn ostinato recurs only in that instrument throughout the first

SOURCE READING

THE PREMIERE OF *THE RITE OF SPRING*

The first performance of Igor Stravinsky's The Rite of Spring *on May 29, 1913, was greeted by a riot. As he told the story almost half a century later, he was as shocked by the audience's reaction as some listeners were by the spectacle. Apparently it was the choreography, more than the music, that provoked the audience, and ever since the piece has usually been performed in concert rather than as a ballet.*

———•———

That the first performance of *Le Sacre du printemps* was attended by a scandal must be known to everybody. Strange as it may seem, however, I was unprepared for the explosion myself. The reactions of the musicians who came to the orchestra rehearsals were without intimation of it and the stage spectacle did not appear likely to precipitate a riot. . . .

Mild protests against the music could be heard from the very beginning of the performance. Then, when the curtain opened on the group of knock-kneed and long-braided Lolitas jumping up and down [*Danses des adolescentes*], the storm broke. Cries of "Ta

gueule" ["Shut up!"] came from behind me. I heard Florent Schmitt shout "Taisez-vous garces du seizième" ["Be quiet, you bitches of the sixteenth"]; the "garces" of the sixteenth arrondissement [the most fashionable residential district of Paris] were, of course, the most elegant ladies in Paris. The uproar continued, however, and a few minutes later I left the hall in a rage; I was sitting on the right near the orchestra, and I remember slamming the door. I have never again been that angry. The music was so familiar to me; I loved it, and I could not understand why people who had not yet heard it wanted to protest in advance. I arrived in a fury backstage, where I saw Diaghilev flicking the house lights in a last effort to quiet the hall. For the rest of the performance I stood in the wings behind Nijinsky holding the tails of his *frac*, while he stood on a chair shouting numbers to the dancers, like a coxswain.

From Igor Stravinsky and Robert Craft, *Expositions and Developments* (New York: Doubleday, 1962), 159–64.

Figure 31.7: Title page designed by Picasso for Stravinsky's piano arrangement of Ragtime, *originally for eleven instruments.*

half of the dance. In the second half, it migrates through several other instruments. In music without motivic development, such changes of timbre are one means to provide variety, a technique Stravinsky learned from Glinka and Rimsky-Korsakov.

Stravinsky's preference for dry rather than lush or resonant timbres is reflected in his use of instruments. Here this sound is evident in the staccato string chords, which are all played with a down-bow to create even emphasis and natural separations; in the pizzicato cellos; and in the staccato English horn and bassoons. *Stark timbres*

Having developed these techniques, Stravinsky continued to use them throughout his career. During World War I, the wartime economy forced him to turn away from the large orchestra of his early ballets toward small combinations of instruments to accompany stage works. For *L'histoire du soldat* (The Soldier's Tale, 1918), he called for six solo instruments in pairs (violin and double bass, clarinet and bassoon, cornet and trombone) and one percussionist to play interludes in a spoken narration and dialogue. In the marches, tango, waltz, and ragtime movements of *L'histoire*, and in *Ragtime* (1917–18), shown in Figure 31.7, Stravinsky discovered ways to imitate familiar styles while using the devices that had become his trademarks. Stranded in the West by the war and then by the Bolshevik Revolution in his home country, he began to move away from Russian topics while retaining the distinctive traits that stemmed largely from his Russian training. *Small-ensemble works*

NEOCLASSICAL PERIOD

In 1919, Diaghilev asked Stravinsky to orchestrate pieces by the eighteenth-century composer Pergolesi (including music erroneously attributed to him) to accompany a new ballet, *Pulcinella*. Stravinsky applied his distinctive stylistic traits to the music, reworking a number of pieces so that they retained the original music faithfully yet sounded more like Stravinsky than Pergolesi. He later spoke of this experience as his "discovery of the past, the epiphany through which the whole of my late work became possible." In the same year of 1920, he completed the *Symphonies of Wind Instruments*, which applied the methods distilled in *The Rite of Spring* to an entirely abstract composition.

Neoclassicism defined

Thus was launched **neoclassicism**, a new stage in Stravinsky's career. Although the term has gone through many shades of meaning, it has come to represent a broad movement from the 1910s to the 1950s in which composers revived, imitated, or evoked the styles, genres, and forms of pre-Romantic music, especially that of the eighteenth century, then called Classic ("Baroque" as a term for early-eighteenth-century music became widely used only after 1940). Neoclassicism grew in part from a rejection of Romanticism, whose associations with high emotions, irrationality, yearning, individualism, and nationalism were all suspect in the wake of the wanton destruction of World War I. Stravinsky was widely recognized as the leader of the neoclassical movement. His neoclassical period, from 1919 to 1951, marks a turn away from Russian folk music and toward earlier Western art music as a source for imitation, quotation, or allusion.

Uses of neoclassicism

This step was useful to Stravinsky because the fashion in the West for Russian nationalism was beginning to fade, in part because the political and cultural ties between France and Russia had dissolved after the Bolshevik Revolution. In technical terms, imitating and alluding to music in the classical tradition was hardly different from what he had been doing all along in making use of folk and popular materials, so neoclassicism in effect gave him new subject matter without requiring him to retool completely. Neoclassicism also addressed the dilemma of establishing a place in the crowded classical repertoire. Stravinsky had already solved the problem of creating an individual style. He now used his distinctive idiom, forged in the Russian traditions, to establish fresh links to the Western classical tradition, just as Schoenberg used his modernist twelve-tone procedures to resurrect the forms and genres of the classical past. Yet even as Stravinsky became thoroughly cosmopolitan, he always remained something of an outsider, and instead of Schoenberg's expressionism, we find in Stravinsky's music an emotional detachment. Thus his neoclassical music adopts an anti-Romantic tone, reflecting a preference for balance, coolness, objectivity, and absolute (as opposed to program) music.

Symphony of Psalms

Stravinsky's neoclassicism and its continuity with his earlier style are both evident in his *Symphony of Psalms* (1930) for mixed chorus and orchestra on psalms from the Latin Vulgate Bible. Stravinsky said he used Latin because the ritualistic language left him free to concentrate on its phonetic qualities, but its use also refers back to the long tradition of Latin texts in Western church music. Baroque features include almost perpetual motion, frequent ostinatos (also a Stravinsky trademark), and the fully developed fugue of the second movement. Stravinsky avoids a Romantic orchestral sound and emphasizes what he called an "objective" rather than emotional sound palette by omitting violins, violas, and clarinets.

In the first movement (NAWM 146), excerpted in Example 31.10, traditional elements are reinterpreted in new ways, and Stravinsky's personal idiom is much in evidence. At the opening (Example 31.10a), the sense of meter is kept unsteady by changing meters and unexpected rests. One sound block, an E-minor triad in full orchestra, alternates with another, sixteenth-note arpeggiations in oboe and bassoon. Discontinuity between the two blocks is heightened by differences in pitch, yet both draw notes from the same octatonic scale (Example 31.10b), thereby *creating* continuity. At the first vocal entrance (Example 31.10c), the melody is restricted to two pitches, E and F, suggesting a simple Gregorian chant. It is accompanied by three

CD 11|31

Example 31.10: Excerpts from Stravinsky's Symphony of Psalms

a. Opening

b. Octatonic scale

c. Vocal entrance

Hear my prayer

layers of ostinatos sounding the full octatonic scale. The scoring for double-reed instruments alone creates an unusual sound, evoking a Renaissance consort. Later, the opening E-minor triad returns in a diatonic rather than octatonic context. Such alternation between these two collections has been characteristic of Stravinsky since his early works.

Neotonality   Although E is emphasized as a tonal center in all three of these passages, it is established simply through assertion, using three different methods. At the beginning (Example 31.10a), the E-minor triad is the only harmony; at the vocal entrance (Example 31.10c), E is the focus of the melody, and an E-minor triad occurs on every downbeat; at the later diatonic passage, E is sustained in the bass. Such assertion of a tonal center through reiteration is very different from Schoenberg's atonality. Yet this music cannot be described as tonal, since it does not follow the rules of traditional harmony. Music like this is **neotonal**—the composer is finding new ways to establish a single pitch as a tonal center.

Schoenberg and   Partly because his music was based on tonal centers as well as on recogniz-
Stravinsky   able genres and styles, performers and audiences found Stravinsky's neoclassical works easier to play and to follow than Schoenberg's twelve-tone compositions. Both composers attracted supporters, who argued about music's need to adhere to tradition versus the need to find new methods, in an echo of the Brahms-Wagner disputes of the nineteenth century. In recent decades, musicians and scholars have come to see how much in common the two composers had, especially in their music of the 1920s–1940s, when both sought to revivify traditional forms in an entirely new and personal musical language.

SERIAL PERIOD

After Schoenberg's death in 1951, the twelve-tone methods he had pioneered were as much a part of past history as sonata form. They were also becoming popular with younger composers, who extended the principles to series in parameters other than pitch, such as rhythm (see chapter 34). Such music based on series was no longer simply twelve-tone, and it became known as **serial music,** a term that has also been applied retrospectively to Schoenberg and his students.

In part to encompass yet another branch of the classical tradition, and in part to keep up with the times, Stravinsky—already in his seventies—adapted serial techniques in his music from about 1953 on. His best-known serial works include the song cycle *In memoriam Dylan Thomas* (1954); *Threni* (1957–58), for voices and orchestra on texts from the Lamentations of Jeremiah; and *Movements* (1958–59), for piano and orchestra. All of them show his characteristic idiom of juxtaposed blocks, disrupted meter, and his other signature traits, although the pitch content is increasingly chromatic.

Stravinsky's particular genius lay in finding stylistic markers, derived from Russian sources yet distinctly his own, that proved so recognizable and adaptable that he could assimilate or allude to any style while putting his personal stamp on the music. By drawing on everything from early music to the serial music of his time, he claimed the entire tradition as his own.

INFLUENCE

Stravinsky's impact on other composers was in a league with that of Wagner and Debussy. Through Stravinsky, elements that had been nurtured in Russian music (ostinatos, juxtaposition of blocks, interruption, lack of development) and traits he had introduced (such as frequent changes of meter, unpredictable accents and rests, and dry orchestration) became commonplaces of modern music, used by composers employing many different styles. Stravinsky popularized neoclassicism, setting an example that many others imitated. His serial music was less well known, but his support for serialism helped it gain a strong following among composers and academics. His willingness to change styles encouraged others to do the same, though few if any matched his ability to project a single personality in any style he adopted. His writings were also important, including his *Poetics of Music* and a series of conversation books written with Robert Craft between 1959 and 1972. For some, his pronouncements on music had the effect of words and ideas handed down from an oracle.

BÉLA BARTÓK

Modernists other than Stravinsky found elements in their own national music that allowed them to create a distinctive voice while continuing the classical tradition. Two of the most significant, the Hungarian Béla Bartók and the American Charles Ives, did so in part by paying attention to musical traditions and qualities that had been ignored or disdained.

Béla Bartók (1881–1945; see biography and Figure 31.8) created an individual modernist idiom by synthesizing elements of Hungarian, Romanian, Slovak, and Bulgarian peasant music with elements of the German and French classical tradition. He arrived at this synthesis only after thorough grounding in both traditions and exposure to several modern trends.

Born in the Austro-Hungarian Empire and trained as a pianist, Bartók started composing at a young age, progressing from short character pieces to longer works modeled on the music of Bach, Mozart, Beethoven, Brahms, and Liszt. Encounters with the tone poems of Richard Strauss in 1902, with Debussy's music over the following decade, and with Schoenberg's and Stravinsky's works in the 1910s and 1920s inspired Bartók to write music that emulated and ultimately absorbed their idioms.

Classical and modern influences

Bartók's search for an innately Hungarian music led him to collect and study peasant music, often in collaboration with fellow composer Zoltán Kodály (1882–1967). Bartók published nearly two thousand Hungarian, Romanian, Slovak, Croatian, Serbian, and Bulgarian song and dance tunes—only a small part of the music he had collected in expeditions ranging over central Europe, Turkey, and North Africa. He used the new technology of audio recording, as shown in Figure 31.9 on page 831, which preserved the unique and unfamiliar characteristics of each folk singer and style far better than the older method of transcribing music by ear into conventional notation. He

Peasant music

BÉLA BARTÓK (1881–1945)

Bartók was a virtuoso pianist, piano teacher, and ethnomusicologist, and is renowned as one of the leading composers of the early twentieth century.

Bartók was born in the Austro-Hungarian Empire, in a small Hungarian city now in Romania. His parents were teachers and amateur musicians, and he took piano lessons from age five and composed from age nine. He studied piano and composition at the Hungarian Royal Academy of Music in Budapest, returning there in 1907 to teach piano. As a virtuoso pianist, he performed all over Europe and edited keyboard music of Bach, Scarlatti, Haydn, Mozart, Beethoven, and others.

In 1904, Bartók overheard the singing of a woman from Transylvania (a region then in Hungary and now in Romania), which sparked a lifelong interest in folk music of Hungary, Romania, and nearby lands. He collected thousands of songs and dances, edited them in collections, and wrote about folk music. He arranged many folk tunes, wrote pieces based on them, and borrowed elements from various folk traditions for use in his concert music.

In 1909, Bartók married his student Márta Ziegler, who assisted him in his work. Their son was born in 1910. In 1923, he divorced Márta and married Ditta Pásztory, who bore him a second son the next year.

In 1934, Bartók left the Academy of Music and moved to a full-time position as ethnomusicologist at the Academy of Sciences, where he joined Zoltán Kodály and others in preparing a critical edition of Hungarian folk music. His compositions over the next five years, including the last two string quartets and *Music for Strings, Percussion and Celesta,* marked the high point of his career. Yet the rise of the Nazis in Germany and their 1938 takeover of Austria brought the threat of fascism in Hungary. Bartók arranged to send his manuscripts to the United States, then followed with his family in 1940, settling in New York. His last years were difficult financially and physically. Friends procured jobs and commissions for him, sometimes without his knowledge, but he was already suffering from leukemia, which took his life in 1945.

MAJOR WORKS: Bluebeard's Castle, The Miraculous Mandarin, Dance Suite, *Concerto for Orchestra,* Music for Strings, Percussion and Celesta, *3 piano concertos, 2 violin concertos, 6 string quartets, 2 violin sonatas, 1 piano sonata,* Mikrokosmos, *numerous other works for piano, songs, choral works, and folk song arrangements*

Figure 31.8: Béla Bartók in 1936.

Figure 31.9: Bartók in 1907, recording Slovakian folk songs on an acoustic cylinder machine in the village of Zobordarázs.

then analyzed the collected specimens using techniques developed in the new discipline of ethnomusicology, and he edited collections and wrote books and articles that established him as the leading scholar of this music. Bartók argued that Hungarian peasant music represented the nation better than the urban popular music that had long been identified as "Hungarian." This position was politically radical at a time when Hungary was still ruled by an urban, German-speaking elite, but his views eventually won the day.

Bartók arranged many peasant tunes and created original works based on them. In other pieces, he blended rhythmic, melodic, or formal characteristics of peasant music with those of classical and modern music.

He first achieved a distinctive personal style around 1908, with compositions such as the First String Quartet and the one-act opera *Bluebeard's Castle*, composed in 1911 and premiered in 1918, which combines Hungarian folk elements with influences from Debussy's *Pelléas et Mélisande*. His *Allegro barbaro* (1911) and other piano works introduced a new approach to the piano, treating it more as a percussive instrument than as a spinner of cantabile melodies and resonant accompaniments. His compositions from the decade after World War I show him pushing toward the limits of dissonance and tonal ambiguity, reaching the furthest point with his two Violin Sonatas of 1921 and 1922. Other works of this decade include the expressionist pantomime *The Miraculous Mandarin* and the Third and Fourth String Quartets. His later works, which seem in comparison more accessible to a broad audience, have become the most widely known, including the Fifth and Sixth Quartets, *Music for Strings, Percussion and Celesta*, (1936), and the Concerto for Orchestra (1943). His *Mikrokosmos* (1929–39)—153 piano pieces in six books of graded difficulty—is a work of great pedagogical value

Stylistic evolution

that also summarizes Bartók's own style and presents, in microcosm, the development of European music in the first third of the twentieth century.

BARTÓK'S SYNTHESIS

In synthesizing peasant with classical music, Bartók emphasized what the traditions have in common and, at the same time, what is most distinctive about each. In both traditions, pieces typically have a single pitch center, use diatonic and other scales, and feature melodies built from motives that are repeated and varied. Then, from the classical tradition, Bartók retained its elaborate contrapuntal and formal procedures, such as fugue and sonata form. From the peasant tradition, he drew rhythmic complexity and irregular meters, common especially in Bulgarian music; modal scales and mixed modes; and specific types of melodic structure and ornamentation. By intensifying these distinctive qualities, Bartók wrote music that can be simultaneously more complex in its counterpoint than Bach's and more ornamented and rhythmically complex than his folk models. In addition, Bartók's use of dissonance, his harmony, and his love of symmetry result partly from mixing concepts and materials taken from the two traditions; for instance, his frequent use of seconds and fourths in chords derives both from their prominence in folk melodies and from the practice of his fellow modernists. His synthesis preserves the integrity of both traditions. He never used folk elements merely for color, nor did he compromise their individuality for smoothness, yet his music always remains grounded in the classical tradition.

Use of neotonality

Music for Strings, Percussion and Celesta illustrates Bartók's synthesis and several characteristics of his personal style. The combination of peasant and classical elements to create a modernist idiom is seen in his use of neotonality. Each of the four movements establishes a tonal center by methods analogous to the modal melodies of folk song and to the chordal motion and tonic-dominant polarities of classical music, while avoiding common-practice harmony. The tonal center of the first and last movements is A, with an important secondary center at the tritone E♭/D♯, a post-tonal analogue to the conventional dominant E. The second movement is in C, with a similar tritone pole on F♯, those two tones being each a minor third on either side of A; the

CD 11|36   CD 6|19

slow third movement (NAWM 147) has the opposite arrangement, centering on F♯ with C as the competing pole. Some of the principal themes of the four movements and all of the final cadences clearly bring out this tritone relationship, as shown in Example 31.11. In addition, the cadences evoke standard procedures in tonal music, from counterpoint in contrary motion (Example 31.11b) to a mock dominant-tonic cadence (Example 31.11d). There are also strong similarities to peasant music. Peasant melodies often rise from and return to the tonal center, as in the first movement theme (Example 31.11a); center around a tone, as in the second movement theme (Example 31.11c); or descend to the tonal center from its upper octave, as in the finale (Example 31.11f). Here the synthesis of the two traditions to create a modernist idiom is rich in allusions to music in both traditions.

Melodic structure

The themes are created by varying small motives, a typical procedure both in classical music, from Bach and Haydn to Schoenberg and Stravinsky, and

Example 31.11: Bartók, Music for Strings, Percussion and Celesta

a. First movement theme

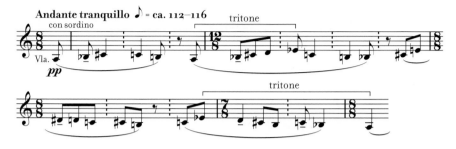

b. Final cadence of first movement

c. Second movement theme

d. Final cadence of second movement

e. Final cadence of third movement

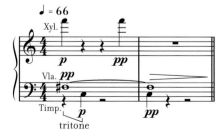

f. Fourth movement theme

g. Final cadence

in the peasant music of central and southeastern Europe. Many Hungarian tunes use short phrases and repeat motives with slight variations, like the AA′BB′ pattern of the first-movement theme (Example 31.11a), while Bulgarian dance tunes typically spin out a rhythmic-melodic motive, as in the finale's theme (Example 31.11f). The latter is diatonic, like many classical themes, but clearly in the Lydian mode, which is used in some peasant songs. Hungarian songs can mix modes, an effect Bartók borrows at the end of the second-movement theme (Example 31.11c), where the melodic rise and fall suggests Lydian, then Phrygian, modes.

Form and counterpoint   The complex forms and contrapuntal procedures used by Bartók come strictly from the classical tradition. The first movement is an elaborate fugue, with entrances that successively rise and fall around the circle of fifths in both directions, meeting in a climax at the opposite pole of E♭. The second movement is a sonata form; the third movement a modified arch form (ABCB′A′) in which the phrases of the first-movement fugue theme are embedded; and the finale a rondo that includes a modified reprise of the fugue theme. Such thematic references to the first movement recall the cyclic symphonies of Berlioz, Franck, and Tchaikovsky, among others. Each movement includes canon and imitation, often in inversion. The palindromic form of the third movement is foreshadowed in the opening xylophone solo, shown in Example 31.12, which from the midpoint at the beginning of measure 3 is identical going in both directions. Bartók was very fond of such symmetries, as we can see in the mirror counterpoint at the end of the first movement (Example 31.11b).

Example 31.12: Xylophone solo from opening of third movement

Elements from traditional peasant styles are also evident. Bulgarian dance meters feature long and short beats rather than strong and weak beats, with the longs half again as long as the short. In Western notation, this translates into irregular groupings of twos and threes, as in, for example, the 2 + 3 pattern of a *paidushka*, 3 + 2 + 2 of a *chetvorno*, or 2 + 2 + 2 + 3 of a *svornato*. Bartók adopts this effect in the 2 + 3 + 3 pattern in the fourth movement theme (Example 31.11f) and, more abstractly, in the groups of twos and threes in the first-movement fugue theme (Example 31.11a). The heavily ornamented, partly chromatic type of Serbo-Croatian song in Example 31.13a, which Bartók described as *parlando-rubato* (speechlike, in free tempo), is echoed near the beginning of the third movement, shown in Example 31.13b. Melodies over drones, as in this example, are also a feature of peasant music. String glissandos, snapped pizzicatos, percussive chords laced with dissonant seconds, and other characteristics of Bartók's personal style do not derive directly from peasant music but can convey a rough, vibrant effect that suggests a source other than art music.

Peasant elements

Example 31.13: Evocation of peasant ornamentation in the third movement

a. *Serbo-Croatian song*

b. *Passage near beginning of third movement*

BARTÓK AS MODERNIST

Like his fellow modernists, Bartók aspired to create masterpieces like those of the classical masters he took as models, emulated their music, and sought new methods and materials in order to distinguish his music from that of other composers. The new elements he found were those of another tradition, the peasant music of his and other nations. Through his synthesis of both

CHARLES IVES (1874–1954)

Like the archetypal artist in countless movies, Ives worked in obscurity for most of his career but lived to be recognized as one of the most significant classical-music composers of his generation.

Ives was born in Danbury, a small city in Connecticut where his father, George, was a bandmaster, church musician, and music teacher. Ives studied piano and organ, showing prodigious talent—at age fourteen he became the youngest professional church organist in the state. His father taught him theory and composition and encouraged an experimental approach to sound.

In college at Yale, he took liberal arts courses and studied music theory and com-

Figure 31.10: Charles Ives in New York, around 1913.

position with composer, teacher, and organist Horatio Parker. While in college, Ives wrote marches and songs for his fraternity brothers and church music for his position as organist at Centre Church in New Haven.

After graduating in 1898, he settled in New York, where he worked as a church organist, got a job in the insurance business, and lived with fellow Yale graduates in an apartment they called "Poverty Flat." When his cantata *The Celestial Country* failed to garner strongly positive reviews, Ives quit his organist position and focused on insurance. His firm, Ives & Myrick, became one of the most successful agencies in the nation, as Ives pioneered the training of agents (his classes are one source for the modern business school) and the idea of estate planning.

His courtship with Harmony Twichell, whom he married in 1908, inspired a new confidence, and the next decade brought an outpouring of music, including most of the pieces that later made Ives's reputation. Composing evenings and weekends, he prepared finished copies of his less radical pieces, such as the first three symphonies and the violin sonatas, but published nothing and left many works in sketch or partial score.

After trying vainly for over a decade to interest performers and publishers in his music, Ives was spurred in 1918 by a health crisis to edit and self-publish *114 Songs* and his Second Piano Sonata (*Concord, Mass., 1840–60*), which was accompanied by a book, *Essays Before a Sonata*. He devoted the 1920s to completing several large pieces. The remaining three decades of his life saw the premieres and publication of most of his major works. Although accused—

despite his thorough musical training—of amateurism because he was a businessman, Ives won a number of advocates among younger composers, performers, and conductors, who promoted his music. By the time of his death at age seventy-nine, he was widely regarded as the first to create a distinctly American body of art music, and his reputation has continued to grow.

MAJOR WORKS: *4 symphonies*, Holidays Symphony, Three Places in New England, The Unanswered Question, *2 string quartets, 4 violin sonatas, 2 piano sonatas, about 200 songs*

traditions, he created new works with a strong personal identity and a rich connection to the music of the past.

CHARLES IVES

Charles Ives (1874–1954; see biography and Figure 31.10), like Bartók, created a personal modernist idiom by synthesizing international and regional musical traditions. Ives was a fluent composer in four distinct spheres: American vernacular music, Protestant church music, European classical music, and experimental music (see below), of which he was the first major exponent. In his mature music, he combined elements from all four, using the multiplicity of styles as a rhetorical device to convey rich musical meanings.

Ives grew up surrounded by American vernacular music, from parlor songs and minstrel show tunes to the marches and cornet solos his father performed as leader of the town band. In his teens and his college years at Yale, Ives wrote numerous marches and parlor songs in the styles of the day, including a presidential campaign song for William McKinley and a march played at McKinley's inauguration in 1897. At Yale he also composed part-songs for the glee club and stage music for fraternity shows.

Vernacular music

Ives sang and heard hymns in church and at revival meetings, and he played them as a professional church organist for most of his teens and twenties (1888–1902). During those years, he improvised organ preludes and postludes, and composed solo songs and sacred choral works representing all the styles then prominent in American Protestantism, from simple hymnody to the cultivated manner of his composition teacher at Yale, Horatio Parker.

Church music

As a teenager, Ives played major organ works by Bach, Mendelssohn, and contemporary French and American composers, along with transcriptions from sonatas and symphonies of Beethoven, Schubert, Brahms, and other composers in the classical tradition. With Parker, he intensified his study of art music, writing exercises in counterpoint, fugue, and orchestration and composing in genres from art song to symphony. His First Symphony, which

Classical music

he began in his last year in college, was directly modeled on Dvořák's *New World* Symphony, with elements from Schubert, Beethoven, and Tchaikovsky.

Experimental works

In his **experimental music,** Ives's typical approach was to preserve most of the traditional rules but change others to see what would happen. As a youth, he practiced drumming on the piano, devising dissonant chords that would suggest the sound of drums. In his teens, he wrote several pieces that were **polytonal,** with the melody in one key and the accompaniment in another, or with four imitative voices, each in its own key, asking "If you can play a tune in one key, why can't a feller, if he feels like [it], play one in two keys?" Polytonality was later developed independently by other composers, but Ives was the first to use it systematically.

After his studies with Parker sharpened his craft, Ives wrote numerous short pieces whose main purpose was to try out new techniques. Two are excerpted in Example 31.14. *Processional* for chorus and organ, sketched around 1902, is an essay in possible chord structures. Ives presents over a C pedal point a series of chords, each a stack of one or two intervals, gradually expanding from seconds to thirds, fourths, fifths, sixths, and sevenths and finally resolving to octaves at the end of the phrase. *Scherzo: All the Way Around and Back* (ca. 1908) for chamber ensemble is an almost perfect palindrome, building up layers of dissonant ostinatos until at the climax units of two, three, five, seven, and eleven equal divisions of the measure are sounding simultaneously, then proceeding in retrograde. The choice of these units was not arbitrary; they represent the first five prime numbers—numbers not divisible by any other. Like many of his experiments, these pieces introduced unprecedented levels of dissonance and rhythmic complexity, although they usually preserved the idea of a tonal center.

None of Ives's experimental pieces was published or performed in public until long after they were written; they were essentially ways of trying out ideas, and they made Ives aware of new possibilities that he could use in other, less systematic pieces for purposes of expression or representation. But one experimental work became one of Ives's best known pieces because his novel means fit the inspired program so perfectly: *The Unanswered Question* (1908). Slowly moving strings in G major represent "the silences of the Druids—who know, see and hear nothing," while over them a trumpet poses

Example 31.14: New techniques in Ives's experimental compositions

a.   *Organ chords in* Processional *made of stacked similar intervals*

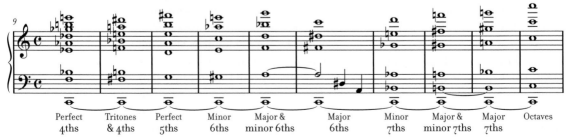

| Perfect 4ths | Tritones & 4ths | Perfect 5ths | Minor 6ths | Major & minor 6ths | Major 6ths | Minor 7ths | Major & minor 7ths | Major 7ths | Octaves |

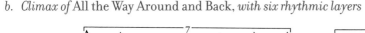

b. Climax of All the Way Around and Back, *with six rhythmic layers*

"the perennial question of existence" and four flutes attempt ever more energetic and dissonant answers until they give up in frustration, leaving the
question to sound once more, unanswered. The trumpet and flute parts are
atonal, making Ives one of the first composers to use atonality (roughly contemporary with Schoenberg but independent of him) and the first to combine
tonal and atonal layers in the same piece.

SYNTHESES

From 1902 on, Ives wrote only in classical genres, but he brought into his
music the styles and sounds of the other traditions he knew. Typically, he employed them to suggest extramusical meanings, whether in a character piece
or programmatic work. In his Second Symphony, Ives used themes paraphrased from American popular songs and hymns, borrowed transitional
passages from Bach, Brahms, and Wagner, and combined all of these in a
symphonic form and idiom modeled on Brahms, Dvořák, and Tchaikovsky.
Through this synthesis, Ives proclaimed the unity of his own experience as an
American familiar with the vernacular, church, and classical traditions and
claimed a place for distinctively American music in the symphonic repertoire. Doing so was a radical act, for although classical audiences accepted
folk melodies as sources for concert works, they tended to regard the hymn
tunes and popular songs Ives used as beneath notice and entirely out of place
in the concert hall.

Ives's Third Symphony, four violin sonatas, and First Piano Sonata all feature movements based on American hymn tunes. Here Ives uses procedures

Cumulative form

of thematic fragmentation and development from European sonata forms and symphonies, but reverses the normal course of events so that the development happens first and the themes appear in their entirety only at the end. This procedure, akin to Smetana's structure in *Tábor* (see chapter 29) and Sibelius's teleological genesis (see chapter 30), has been called **cumulative form.** In the Second Symphony, Ives had paraphrased the American melodies so they would work well as themes in standard European forms. Here he reshapes the form so the simple American tune appears as the culmination of the previous development, making a place for American melody within the European tradition. While not overtly programmatic, these pieces suggest the coming together of individual voices and the fervent spirit of hymn-singing

SOURCE READING

AMERICANISM IN MUSIC

Dvořák had advised American composers to use African-American or American Indian music as sources for a distinctively national music, and many did so. Charles Ives felt that for himself, as a white New Englander, a more appropriate source was the music regularly heard and sung by people in his own region, from hymns to popular song. No matter what sources are used, he argued, the composer must understand the music from the inside and know what it meant to the people who heard and performed it.

———— • ————

If a man finds that the cadences of an Apache war-dance come nearest to his soul—provided he has taken pains to know enough other cadences, for eclecticism is part of his duty; sorting potatoes means a better crop next year—let him assimilate whatever he finds highest of the Indian ideal so that he can use it with the cadences, fervently, transcendentally, inevitably, furiously, in his symphonies, in his operas, in his whistlings on the way to work, so that he can paint his house with them, make them a part of his prayer-book—this is all possible and necessary, if he is confident that they have a part in his spiritual consciousness. With this assurance, his music will have everything it should of sincerity, nobility, strength, and beauty, no matter how it sounds; and if, with this, he is true to none but the highest of American ideals (that is, the ideals only that coincide with his

spiritual consciousness), his music will be true to itself and incidentally American, and it will be so even after it is proved that all our Indians came from Asia.

The man "born down to Babbitt's Corners" may find a deep appeal in the simple but acute Gospel hymns of the New England "camp meetin'" of a generation or so ago. . . . If the Yankee can reflect the fervency with which "his gospels" were sung—the fervency of "Aunt Sarah," who scrubbed her life away for her brother's ten orphans, the fervency with which this woman, after a fourteen-hour work day on the farm, would hitch up and drive five miles through the mud and rain to "prayer meetin'," her one articulate outlet for the fullness of her unselfish soul—if he can reflect the fervency of such a spirit, he may find there a local color that will do all the world good. If his music can but catch that spirit by being a part with itself, it will come somewhere near his ideal—and it will be American too—perhaps nearer so than that of the devotee of Indian or negro melody. In other words, if local color, national color, any color, is a true pigment of the universal color, it is a divine quality, it is a part of substance in art—not of manner.

From Charles Ives, *Essays Before a Sonata, The Majority, and Other Writings*, ed. Howard Boatwright (New York: Norton, 1970), 79–81.

at the camp-meeting revivals of Ives's youth. In these works, Ives is a musical nationalist, but he is also asserting the universal value of his country's music (see Source Reading).

Many of Ives's later pieces are programmatic, celebrating aspects of American life. *Three Places in New England* presents orchestral pictures of the first African-American regiment in the Civil War, a band playing at a Fourth of July picnic, and a walk by a river with his wife during their honeymoon. *A Symphony: New England Holidays* captures the sounds, events, and feelings of Washington's Birthday, Decoration Day (later renamed Memorial Day), the Fourth of July, and Thanksgiving. His Second Piano Sonata, titled *Concord, Mass. 1840–60,* characterizes in music the literary contributions of writers associated with that city and time: Emerson, Thoreau, Hawthorne, and the Alcotts. Other works are more philosophical, such as the Fourth Symphony, an extraordinary, complex work that poses and seeks to answer "the searching questions of What? and Why?" In all of these, Ives uses references to American tunes or musical styles, from Stephen Foster to ragtime, to suggest the meanings he wanted to convey. In some pieces he uses multiple tunes, layered on top of each other in a musical **collage** or woven together like a patchwork quilt, to invoke the way experiences are recalled in memory. He also uses techniques developed in his experimental music, often to represent certain kinds of sounds or motions, such as exploding fireworks or mists over a river.

American program music

With such a wide range of styles at his command, Ives frequently mixed styles—whether traditional or newly invented—within a single piece. Like Mozart's use of contrasting topics (see chapter 22), Mahler's references to various styles, and the juxtapositions of different blocks of material in the music of Debussy, Scriabin, and Stravinsky, this heterogeneity of styles provided a way for Ives to evoke a wide range of extramusical references and also to articulate the musical form, distinguishing each phrase, section, or passage from the next through stylistic contrast. He also used style, alongside timbre, rhythm, figuration, register, and other more traditional means, to differentiate layers heard simultaneously, as we saw in *The Unanswered Question.*

Stylistic heterogeneity

Ives synthesized all four traditions his music encompassed in his song *General William Booth Enters into Heaven* (1914, NAWM 148), on a poem by Vachel Lindsay that pictures the founder of the Salvation Army leading the poor and downtrodden into heaven. It is an art song, but the musical content is drawn primarily from American vernacular music, church music, and experimental music. At the opening, shown in Example 31.15, Ives evokes Booth's bass drum through the experimental technique of piano-drumming, using a standard rhythmic pattern of American drummers. The vocal line is derived from the hymn *There Is a Fountain Filled with Blood,* just as Lindsay took his meter and rhythm from *Are You Washed in the Blood?,* a hymn full of similar imagery. Each group of Booth's followers described in the poem receives a different musical characterization, using polytonality, novel chord structures, dissonant ostinatos, and other techniques Ives first explored in his experimental works. At the line "Big-voiced lassies made their banjos bang," Ives paraphrases in the piano a minstrel-show tune, *Oh, Dem Golden Slippers* (by the pioneer black composer James A. Bland), a song about going

General Booth

to heaven whose second verse begins "Oh my ole banjo." At the climax of the poem, Jesus blesses the marchers, and all are immediately transformed. Having hinted at it repeatedly, Ives now presents the entire verse of *There Is a Fountain Filled with Blood* over the drum patterns in the piano for this moment of transformation, completing the cumulative form. Thus Ives combines the art-song framework with the American vernacular tradition (drum pattern and minstrel song), church music (hymn tune), and experimental techniques (piano-drumming) to convey the experience of the poem.

Example 31.15: Ives, General William Booth Enters into Heaven

IVES'S PLACE

Ives was isolated as a composer. Among his contemporaries, he was influenced by the music of Strauss, Debussy, and Scriabin, but he encountered that of Stravinsky only late in his career, after arriving independently at similar methods, and that of Schoenberg and other modernists only after he had ceased to compose. Nor did they know his music; except for some early vernacular and church works, most pieces were performed and published only long after he had written them. Thus his direct influence was felt mostly after World War II, when his departures from the conventional were taken as an example by postwar composers, encouraging them to experiment and providing models for some novel procedures. He could justifiably be called the founder of the experimental-music tradition in the United States that includes, among others, Henry Cowell, Edgard Varèse, and John Cage. In most of his works, Ives was a modernist who, like Bartók, Stravinsky, and Berg, drew on his own nation's music to develop a distinctive idiom within the classical tradition. In all of these ways, his work has been of incalculable importance to younger generations of American musicians.

COMPOSER AND AUDIENCE

Modernism intensified the split between popular and classical music that had grown wide in the nineteenth century. One secret of Haydn, Mozart, and Beethoven was their ability to appeal both to inexperienced listeners, who enjoyed the music's surface features on first hearing, and to well-trained connoisseurs, who could fully understand its intricacies. Modernism tipped the balance toward the latter, with music targeted especially to those willing to study it, hear it repeatedly, and explore its rich structure and references to other music. Such works have become favorites of composers themselves, adventurous performers, academics, theorists, and historians. Modernist composers have a central place in the canon of music, but they are more admired by critics, composers, and scholars than they are loved by audience members, who prefer their less radical contemporaries such as Strauss, Sibelius, and Rachmaninov. Some of the canonic works of musical modernism still arouse disdain or incomprehension among certain performers and concertgoers, who find them "too modern" even now, a century after they were composed.

On the other hand, the dissonance, atonality, multiple layers, sudden juxtapositions, unpredictability, and startling stylistic contrasts that offended audiences generations ago are now familiar from repeated performances and recordings, and from their use in more recent music, especially music for films. Bartók's *Music for Strings, Percussion and Celesta* turns up in *The Shining*, and Ives's *The Unanswered Question* in *The Thin Red Line*, but a much longer list of film scores use sounds and techniques pioneered by modernist composers for their strong emotional effect.

The music of all six composers discussed in this chapter has found a small but growing and apparently permanent niche in the repertoire. All are performed and recorded more and more, and interest in their music has tended to increase with every passing decade.

Between the World Wars: Jazz and Popular Music

The period between World Wars I and II saw a remarkable series of changes in musical life and continued diversification in musical styles. The spread of phonographs, improved recording techniques, and the new technologies of radio and sound films fostered a mass market for music in sound as well as in notation. Classical concert music and opera remained the most prestigious musical traditions, but the varieties of popular music were better known and usually more lucrative. Especially prominent were trends from the United States, notably jazz. Music, always an accompaniment to "silent" movies, became an integral part of sound films, and composers of opera, classical concert music, musicals, and popular songs all found a place in the movie industry. Styles of classical music grew ever more varied, as composers responded in individual ways to musical trends from modernism to the avant-garde, and to political and economic conditions in their respective nations. After examining the historical background to the period, we will focus in this chapter on developments in popular music between the wars, especially in the United States. In the next chapter, we will address the classical tradition.

BETWEEN THE WARS

When World War I began in 1914, most Europeans and North Americans had enjoyed a generation of peace and prosperity and had a strong faith in progress and the benefits of modernity. By the time the war ended in 1918, they had been profoundly disillusioned. New technologies of warfare, from artillery to poison gas, produced staggering losses of human life and material resources. Over nine million soldiers were killed, and economies across Europe were wrecked. The losses were compounded by a worldwide influenza epidemic in 1918 that killed twenty million people. Modern life no longer seemed benign, and music and other forms of entertainment provided an escape. In this context, popular music and jazz flourished as never before. So did interest in music of earlier times, manifest in neoclassicism and in a growing movement to revive music from before 1750.

New nations and ideologies

The war brought an end to the Austro-Hungarian, German, Russian, and Ottoman empires, and independence to Finland, Estonia, Latvia, Lithuania, Poland, Czechoslovakia, Hungary, and Yugoslavia. In Russia the Bolsheviks—radical Marxist revolutionaries—seized power in late 1917 and set up a dictatorship, forming the Soviet Union. In several other nations, democratic governments gave way to totalitarian rule. Benito Mussolini and the fascists took over the Italian government in 1922, and the Spanish Civil War (1936–39) brought Francisco Franco to power. In Germany, the democracy formed after the World War I, known as the Weimar Republic for the city where the constitution was drafted, proved too weak to deal with mounting economic problems. After the National Socialists (Nazis) won an electoral plurality, their leader Adolf Hitler was appointed chancellor in 1933 and soon established a dictatorship. In a fierce anti-Semitic campaign, the Nazis passed laws to deprive people of Jewish background of their citizenship and all other rights, driving into exile countless writers, artists, composers, and scholars, many of whom—like Arnold Schoenberg—settled in the United States.

Economy

After World War I, the nations of Europe were faced with war debt, crippling inflation, and a shattered infrastructure. The United States and Canada, which suffered far fewer casualties, enjoyed a financial boom. Increased prosperity and leisure time helped make this a golden age for music in America, both popular and classical. American culture and music, especially jazz, had a profound influence on Europeans during the 1920s. But in October 1929, the New York stock market crashed, sparking a worldwide depression. Unemployment approached fifty percent in some areas, producing unprecedented turmoil. In response, governments in Europe and the Americas undertook relief and public works programs, such as the New Deal in the United States. The economies in most nations were still recovering when Germany invaded Poland in September 1939, beginning World War II.

Roles for women

During the 1920s, women increasingly took their place in the public sphere. The need during World War I to replace men in staffing offices and factories had brought women new freedom of movement and economic independence. After the war, women won the right to vote in Britain, the United States, and Germany. Birth control and rising levels of education gave women greater access to careers. The 1930s, however, saw a backlash in some countries against women's freedoms on economic and ideological grounds, especially under the Nazis and other totalitarian regimes.

THE ARTS

The 1920s were a time of freewheeling experimentation in the arts. We have already encountered the avant-garde efforts of Satie, the twelve-tone music of Schoenberg, and the neoclassicism of Stravinsky, and other new trends in music are described in the next chapter. In literature, the decade saw T. S. Eliot's modernist poem of disillusionment, *The Waste Land*, with its many references to literature of the past; James Joyce's stream-of-consciousness novel *Ulysses*; Marcel Proust's multivolume novel of time and memory,

TIMELINE: JAZZ AND POPULAR MUSIC
BETWEEN THE WARS

1910	1915	1920	1925	1930	1935	1940

- 1913–27 Marcel Proust, *Remembrance of Things Past*
- 1914–18 World War I
- 1917 Russian Revolution
- 1919 Women win right to vote in United States
- **1920 King Oliver forms the Creole Jazz Band**
- 1922 T. S. Eliot, *The Waste Land*
- 1922 James Joyce, *Ulysses*
- 1922 First sponsored radio broadcast in the United States
- 1922 Fascists take over government in Italy
- **1924 George Gershwin, *Rhapsody in Blue***
- **1925 Electric microphones introduced** •
- 1927 Charles Lindbergh flies solo across the Atlantic •
- **1927 Jerome Kern, *Show Boat*** •
- **1927 Bessie Smith, *Back Water Blues*** •
- **1927 *The Jazz Singer*, first talking picture** •
- **1927–31 Duke Ellington at the Cotton Club** •
- **1928 Louis Armstrong and His Hot Five record *West End Blues*** •
- 1929 New York stock market crash begins Great Depression •
- 1933 Hitler comes to power in Germany •
- **1933 Max Steiner, score for *King Kong*** •
- 1933 Thomas Hart Benton, Indiana Murals •
- 1933–45 Franklin Delano Roosevelt, president of the United States •
- **1935 Irving Berlin, score for *Top Hat*** •
- **1935 Gershwin, *Porgy and Bess*** •
- 1936–39 Spanish Civil War •
- 1938 Germany absorbs Austria •
- 1939 John Steinbeck, *The Grapes of Wrath* •
- 1939–45 World War II •
- **1940 Ellington, *Cotton Tail*** •

Figure 32.1: Electric Power, Motor-Cars, Steel, *panel from the murals by American painter Thomas Hart Benton (1889–1975) for the Indiana Hall at the 1933 World's Fair in Chicago. This panel celebrates workers and designers in the steel mills of northwest Indiana, electric power generation, and the automobile industry.*

Remembrance of Things Past; the politically engaged plays of Bertolt Brecht; and the feminist novels and essays of Virginia Woolf. The Dadaist movement in art promoted the absurd; Marcel Duchamp's *Fountain* (a urinal on its back) contradicted some of art's most basic assumptions. Surrealist painters like Salvador Dalí and René Magritte explored the dreamlike world of the unconscious opened up by Freud. Architects from Werner Gropius in Germany to Frank Lloyd Wright in the United States were pioneering new, less decorated forms with an insistence that the function of a building be reflected in its design.

The 1930s

Impelled by the worldwide depression of the 1930s, many artists reexamined their role and sought to make their work relevant to the economic and social problems of the time. John Steinbeck, in his novel *The Grapes of Wrath*, wrote about farmers impoverished by the Dust Bowl in the American plains and by exploitation in California. Artists such as George Grosz and Käthe Kollwitz in Germany, Diego Rivera in Mexico, and Thomas Hart Benton in the United States pictured social conditions in simple, direct, yet modern styles that could be understood by everyone, as we can see, for example, in Figure 32.1. Many classical composers likewise sought to write music that was accessible to all, hoping to catch the imagination of ordinary working people.

NEW TECHNOLOGIES

The rapid growth of diverse musical styles between the world wars was due in part to new technologies. Recordings, radio broadcasting, and the introduction of sound to film enabled the preservation and rapid distribution of music in performance, not just in score. Now a musical performance, formerly as impermanent as a moment in time, could be preserved, admired, and replayed many times. This change created a new mass market and new commercial possibilities, allowed performers to share in the benefits of mass distribution, and vaulted some performers—whether of classical, jazz, or popular music—to international stardom.

Recordings   The popular music industry had revolved around sheet music from the 1890s through the 1910s, but after the war publishers realized that recordings offered a market of potentially unlimited size. Songwriters and bandleaders also turned to recordings, often tailoring their pieces to fit the three-to-four-minute limit of a record side. New technology affected performance styles. For example, before 1925, recording technology was acoustic, and only opera singers and "belters" could make an effective vocal recording. The introduction of electric recording in 1925 allowed for more sensitive recording of "crooners," encouraging songwriters to compose songs suitable for a more intimate singing style and leading to the rise of singers like Bing Crosby and Frank Sinatra. The new electric microphones were also more sensitive to the nuances of orchestral music.

Radio   Musicians also profited from exposure over the radio, since music proved to be a good way of filling large periods of airtime. Radio caught on quickly; by 1924 there were over 1,400 radio stations around North America, and during the 1920s national broadcasting systems were developed in all the major European nations. Recordings were still too poor in quality to be played successfully over the radio, so stations relied primarily on live performers in their own studios and on regional or national transmissions of live shows. Stations in Europe and the Americas sponsored orchestras, such as the BBC Symphony Orchestra (founded 1930) in London and the NBC Symphony Orchestra (1937) in New York. Dance bands also made use of the new medium to gain wider exposure. Benny Goodman and his band, for example, hosted two radio shows, *Let's Dance* (1934–35) and *The Camel Caravan* (1936–39).

Diffusion of music   Recordings and radio spawned an unparalleled growth in the size of the audience for all kinds of music. Music was now available to almost everyone, no matter what their level of musical training. These technologies brought about widespread dissemination of the classical repertoire from Bach to Bartók and began to make available less well-known music from the remote past to the present. They also furthered the growth of a huge body of popular music, blues, and jazz. Most of the latter originated in the United States, and it is there our story will focus for most of this chapter.

AMERICAN MUSICAL THEATER AND POPULAR SONG

The period between the two world wars, and especially the 1920s, was a rich time for American popular music. Music for stage shows of all kinds enjoyed great popularity: vaudeville troupes toured the continent, and operettas, revues, and musicals attracted large audiences. Popular songs from

Tin Pan Alley also proliferated. The period roughly from 1920 to 1955—before the advent of rock and roll and the demise of the sheet music industry—is known as the "Golden Age" of Tin Pan Alley.

In the 1920s, as in the previous two decades, popular song and music for theater were inextricably linked. In large part, it was the attractiveness of the songs that drove the popularity of a musical and its composer. Many of the best-known songs, made familiar in hit shows, were then sold as sheet music, often with a picture of the performer who introduced the song on the cover. Yet there were changes in the popular song industry. Sheet music of Tin Pan Alley songs still circulated in American parlors, but publishers and songwriters increasingly counted on recordings to popularize their tunes. And with the arrival of sound technology for films in the late 1920s, the Hollywood musical was born, creating another important venue for popular songwriters. The most successful songwriters of this period—such as Irving Berlin (1888–1989), Jerome Kern (1885–1945), and George Gershwin (1898–1937)—were equally at home writing music for Tin Pan Alley, musical theater, and Hollywood musicals.

MUSICAL THEATER

Revues

Vaudeville shows, loose collections of variety acts, were still very popular, but the craze in larger cities such as New York was for revues, conceived as complete shows made up primarily of musical numbers that often included many performers. The premier series of revues was the Ziegfeld Follies, assembled each year by producer Florenz Ziegfeld, which included variety entertainment, star performers, and troupes of beautiful female dancers. Important popular song composers such as Irving Berlin wrote music for these shows. Berlin's contributions to the 1919 Ziegfeld Follies included *A Pretty Girl Is Like a Melody*, which was sung by a bevy of scantily-clad women, each costumed as a particular piece of classical music.

Musicals

Several new operettas were successful in the 1920s, such as Sigmund Romberg's *The Student Prince*, but the genre was rapidly being replaced by the musical. Like all forms of musical theater, musicals were complex collaborations, with different artists responsible for the music, lyrics (the texts set to music), book (the spoken words of the play), choreography, staging, sets, and costumes. Some musicals were primarily vehicles for star entertainers, featuring new popular songs that were framed by a loose plot, a structure reminiscent of the singer-centered and aria-focused Italian opera of the mid-seventeenth to early eighteenth centuries. Yet there was an increasing interest in creating more integrated musicals, shows in which the musical numbers are closely related to the story, which is plot-driven rather than focused on the performers. Like reform opera of the late eighteenth century (see chapter 20), such musicals were valued for their dramatic impact, in addition to their appeal as entertaining spectacle.

Show Boat

Jerome Kern's masterpiece, *Show Boat* (1927), with book and lyrics by Oscar Hammerstein II, best exemplifies this new integrated approach. *Show Boat* brings together a number of traditions (such as opera, operetta, musical comedy, revues, and vaudeville) and musical styles (including ragtime,

Figure 32.2: Scene from the 1946 revival of Show Boat, *showing the end of the first act.*

spirituals, sentimental ballads, and marches), but the multiple styles all serve dramatic ends. The score is operatic in scope, with interwoven referential themes and motives, much like the operas of Richard Wagner (whose music dramas Kern greatly admired). Based on a novel by Edna Ferber, *Show Boat* dealt with serious social issues, such as racism and miscegenation, and captured recent historic events, such as the 1893 Chicago World's Fair. It was a tremendous success, toured the country after its Broadway run, and enjoyed numerous revivals, among them the 1946 New York production shown in Figure 32.2.

TIN PAN ALLEY: THE GOLDEN AGE

By the 1910s, several types of Tin Pan Alley songs had solidified, including waltz, ragtime, and novelty songs. Most Tin Pan Alley songs followed a standard form of one or more verses followed by a thirty-two measure chorus in an AABA, ABAB, or ABAC pattern. The focus was increasingly on the chorus, where songwriters placed their catchiest rhythms and melodic ideas. Many songwriters worked with lyricists as songwriting teams, although some composers, such as Irving Berlin, wrote both words and music for their songs.

Irving Berlin   Irving Berlin's lengthy career and prodigious output position him as one of America's most prolific and best-loved popular songwriters. Widely known for his sentimental and patriotic tunes that seem to capture the American spirit, like *God Bless America* and *White Christmas*, Berlin mastered all current popular song genres and was involved in every aspect of the music business. It was said that America could not fight a war or celebrate a holiday without a song from this Russian-born son of a Jewish cantor. In the early teens, Berlin was known as America's chief ragtime composer, primarily because of the smashing success of his song *Alexander's Ragtime Band* (1911). Many of his songs were written for revues, such as *Face the Music* and *As Thousands Cheer*; movies, like *Top Hat* and *Holiday Inn*; or musicals, such as *Call Me Madam*.

Cole Porter (1891–1964), like Irving Berlin, wrote both lyrics and music for his songs. Educated in music at Yale, Harvard, and the Schola Cantorum in Paris, Porter is remembered for his suave, urbane, sophisticated lyrics that revel in innuendo and double-entendre and for his irresistibly catchy and memorable tunes. Examples in which the music greatly complements the inventive text include *Let's Do It, I Get a Kick Out of You, It's De-lovely,* and *You're the Top.* Porter wrote exclusively for theater and Hollywood musicals, producing gems such as *Night and Day* from the theater production *Gay Divorce,* which later became a Hollywood musical, *The Gay Divorcee. Night and Day* was popularized by dancer and singer Fred Astaire, who starred in many theater and film productions of Porter's musicals.

Cole Porter

THE JAZZ AGE

Revues, musicals, and Tin Pan Alley songs continued traditions that had been imported from Europe or arose among Americans of European descent. But African-American music and musicians played an increasingly influential role in American musical life, and in the 1920s two related traditions of African-American origin gained wide currency: blues and jazz. Indeed, the 1920s became known as "The Jazz Age," and jazz became the emblematic music for that period when a new generation was cultivating a spirit of social liberation.

BLUES

One of the most influential genres of music to come out of early-twentieth-century America was the **blues.** The origin of the blues is obscure, likely stemming from a combination of rural work songs and other African-American oral traditions. The lyrics typically speak of disappointments, mistreatment, or other troubles that produce the state of mind known since the early nineteenth century as "the blues." Yet the words also convey defiance and a will to survive abandonment by a faithless lover, a lost job, oppression, or disaster. Often touches of humor suggested the knife-edge separation between sorrow and laughter, tragedy and comedy. The music expresses the feelings suggested by the words through melodic contours, freely syncopated rhythms, and distinctive vocal or instrumental effects (such as a slide, rasp, or growl) that evoke the sound of a person expressing pain, sorrow, or frustration. Blues often feature flatted or bent (slightly lowered or sliding) notes, sometimes called **blue notes,** on the third, fifth, and seventh scale degrees, which add to the emotional intensity. Yet the conventional framework of the

Figure 32.3: Bessie Smith, "Empress of the Blues," in the mid-1920s, when she was the most successful and prominent African-American musician of the decade.

CD 11|49

blues allows the performers to display their artistry, in a musical parallel to the defiance implied in the lyrics. Ultimately the blues are not about *having* the blues, but about *conquering* them through a kind of catharsis embodied in the music.

Two distinct blues traditions emerged in the 1910s and 1920s, now known as *classic blues* and *delta blues*.

Classic blues were performed primarily by African-American women singers such as Ma Rainey (1886–1939); Bessie Smith (1894–1937), shown in Figure 32.3; and Alberta Hunter (1895–1984). Typically accompanied by a piano or small combo, these women popularized the blues on black variety circuits, on minstrel circuits, in clubs, and on many recordings. The recording by Mamie Smith (1883–1946) of *Crazy Blues* (1920), the first recording by an African-American singer of a blues song, sold 75,000 copies in a few months, earning her a small fortune. Her success prompted record companies to begin marketing their products to black audiences, in the same way they were already targeting other ethnic groups, selling Irish records to Irish audiences and Yiddish records to Jewish audiences. Records targeted to blacks became known as "race records."

The classic blues singers joined aspects of oral tradition with elements of popular song, thanks in part to W. C. Handy (1873–1958), known as the "father of the blues." Handy did not invent the blues, but as a publisher, he introduced blues songs in sheet music form as early as 1912, thus taking advantage of both the genre's new popularity and the booming sheet music industry. With his publications, Handy solidified what we now think of as standard **twelve-bar blues** form. In this form, illustrated by Bessie Smith's *Back Water Blues* (1927, NAWM 149) in Example 32.1, each poetic stanza has three lines; the second line typically restates the first, and the third completes the thought. Each line of text is sung to four measures of music over a set harmonic pattern, in which the first four-measure phrase remains on the tonic chord; the second phrase begins on the subdominant and ends on the tonic; and the third phrase starts on the dominant and moves back to the tonic, as illustrated in the table below:

Measure:	1	2	3	4	5	6	7	8	9	10	11	12
Harmony:	I	I(IV)	I	I	IV	IV	I	I	V	V(IV)	I	I
Poetic structure:	A				A				B			

After a brief piano introduction, each of the seven stanzas of *Back Water Blues* follows the same form and general melodic outline. The form may be simple, but in Smith's recorded performance, the musical possibilities seem infinite. She enlivens each stanza with unique timbres, phrasing, and melodic sensibility. The melody shows the typical traits of the blues, with

Example 32.1: First stanza of Bessie Smith's Back Water Blues

prominent blue notes on the third and seventh degrees of the scale (E/E♭ and B/B♭) and a tendency to place stressed syllables just before rather than on the strong beats of the measure. The vocal melody cadences in the third measure of each phrase, allowing a call-and-response interchange between the voice and the piano accompaniment, played by African-American composer and pianist James P. Johnson (1891–1955). In its use of improvisation on a simple formula, syncopation, repetition of short patterns, bent pitches, and call and response, this song embodies many of the characteristics of African-American music that apparently originated in Africa (see chapter 29).

Delta blues came primarily from the Mississippi Delta region and is asso- *Delta blues*
ciated primarily with male African-American singers and guitarists. In comparison to classic blues, which tended to conform to the conventions of popular song genres, delta blues are more directly rooted in oral traditions, resulting in greater flexibility of textual and musical form and harmonic choices. Blues singers gained national exposure through collectors such as Alan Lomax, who traveled to remote, rural parts of the south and recorded blues artists as they sang and accompanied themselves on guitar. Delta blues recordings from the 1920s and 1930s reveal a wealth of expressive devices. The singing style is rough, rich in timbre and nuance, and rhythmically flexible, and each section of a blues song features alternation between the voice and accompanying guitar in the style of call and response.

During the first half of the twentieth century, when an unprecedented number of African-Americans moved from the rural south to northern urban centers, many blues singers followed the same path. Many of the Mississippi Delta blues singers landed in Chicago, already a burgeoning center of new recording technology, which would greatly extend their influence on future performers. Legendary bluesman Robert Johnson (1911–1938), for example, recorded only twenty-nine songs in his brief career, yet his musical legacy extended well into the 1960s, when British rock musicians rediscovered his recordings.

JAZZ IN THE 1920s

Jazz was already established and growing in popularity during the late 1910s (see chapter 30). The essence of 1920s jazz was syncopated rhythm, combined with novel vocal and instrumental sounds and an unbridled spirit that seemed to mock earlier social and musical properties. Improvisation was an important element of jazz, but often melodies in the style of an improvisation were worked out in rehearsals, played from memory, or written down and played from notation. Jazz was very much a player's art, so the rise of the recording industry and of radio played a key role in fostering its growth and dissemination.

New Orleans jazz   The leading style of jazz in the period just after World War I is now known as **New Orleans jazz.** This style, named after the city where it originated, centers on group variation of a given tune, either improvised or in the same spontaneous style. The result is a counterpoint of melodic lines, alternating with solos during which the rest of the ensemble provides a rhythmic and harmonic background. It incorporates the African idiom of call and response, as well as the ecstatic outpourings of the African-American Gospel tradition. The development of the style in New Orleans was enhanced by the healthy rivalry between musically literate Creoles and musically untutored African Americans, who possessed great improvisational skill. Leading musicians, including cornettist Joe "King" Oliver (1885–1938), trumpeter Louis Armstrong (1901–1971), and pianist Jelly Roll Morton (1890–1941), developed the style playing in clubs in Storyville, the city's red-light district. In the late 1910s, many New Orleans jazz performers left the city when professional opportunities elsewhere in the country beckoned, spreading the style to other regions.

King Oliver and   King Oliver moved north to Chicago in 1918 and formed his own band in *Louis Armstrong*   1920. In 1922, Oliver invited Louis Armstrong, whom he had mentored in New Orleans, to come north and join his band, by then named King Oliver's Creole Jazz Band. The next year the band began recording for OKeh Records in Chicago and for Gennett in Richmond, Indiana, both among the most important record labels in jazz history, and posed for the publicity photograph in Figure 32.4 (see p. 856). Armstrong later assembled his own band for making recordings, calling it the Hot Five or Hot Seven, depending on the current number of musicians. With these groups he cut several dozen recordings for OKeh between 1925 and 1928.

CD 11|50   The recordings of these two bands embody the classic New Orleans style. Armstrong's recording of Oliver's tune *West End Blues* (NAWM 150), recorded with his Hot Five in Chicago in 1928, exemplifies the conventions of the style. The ensemble is small and is divided into two groups: the "front line" of melodic instruments—trumpet, clarinet, and trombone—and the **rhythm section** that keeps the beat and fills in the background—drums, piano, and banjo. New Orleans jazz typically takes twelve-bar blues, a sixteen-measure strain from ragtime, or a thirty-two-bar popular song form (usually AABA) as a starting point. A tune is presented at the beginning over a particular harmonic progression, then that same progression repeats several times while various soloists or combinations of instruments play over it. Each such repetition is called a **chorus** (not to be confused with the chorus in a song with verse and chorus). Typically each chorus features different instruments and some new musical ideas, producing a kind of theme-and-variation form.

As the title suggests, *West End Blues* is built on twelve-bar blues form. The published sheet music (NAWM 150a) adapts the blues to Tin Pan Alley verse-refrain form, presenting the blues progression once in the verse, shown in Example 32.2a, and twice in the refrain. But the recording (NAWM 150b) follows the conventions of jazz, presenting a blazing trumpet introduction by Armstrong and five choruses of the twelve-bar blues pattern. In the first, Armstrong varies the published verse as shown in Example 32.2b, progressing from a fairly straight performance of the tune to increasingly fanciful acrobatics. In the second chorus, the trombonist plays off the first half of the published refrain, and in the rest, he improvises freely. The third chorus

Example 32.2: Verse of King Oliver's West End Blues *with Louis Armstrong's variation*

Figure 32.4: King Oliver's Creole Jazz Band in a 1923 publicity photograph. Left to right: Honoré Dutrey, trombone; Baby Dodds, drums; King Oliver, cornet; Louis Armstrong (kneeling), slide trumpet; Lillian Hardin (later Armstrong's wife), piano; Bill Johnson, banjo; and Johnny Dodds, clarinet. The drums, piano, and banjo served as a rhythm section.

features the clarinet alternating in call and response with Armstrong who, to tenderly expressive effect, sings syllables rather than playing notes on his instrument, a technique known as **scat singing**.

BIG BANDS

Although Armstrong's feats as a soloist inspired virtuosity in other jazz musicians, the main function of jazz was to accompany dancing. A fashion for larger bands began in the 1920s, propelled partly by the availability of larger performance spaces for jazz, including supper clubs, ballrooms, auditoriums, and theaters. African-American bandleaders, such as Armstrong, Fletcher Henderson, Duke Ellington, and Count Basie, as well as white musicians like Paul Whiteman and Benny Goodman, organized **big bands**. By 1930, the typical dance band was divided into three sections: brass, reeds, and rhythm. Brasses might include three trumpets and two trombones; the reed section was made up of clarinets and saxophones; and the rhythm section consisted of piano, drums, guitar (replacing the banjo), and double bass. These sections interacted as units and alternated with soloists, providing a great variety of sounds. Although solos might still be improvised, the piece was written down by an arranger, who was sometimes the leader (as in the case of Ellington) but more often a member of the band or a skilled orchestrator. Successful arrangers captured in notation the spontaneous spirit of improvised playing. Preparing arrangements in advance made possible a wider variety of effects, including rhythmic unisons of the entire band or of a section, coordinated dialogue between sections and soloists, and more complex chromatic harmonies, all of which added to the emotional impact and polished sound of the music. With the creation of fully or largely notated jazz pieces, jazz composers who made their own arrangements came increasingly to resemble their counterparts in the classical music world. They also borrowed sounds from modern classical music, especially the four-note sonorities (such as seventh chords and added sixth chords) and chromatic harmonies of Debussy and Ravel.

In addition to playing instrumental pieces, the typical big band also featured a vocalist, who might sing through the entire piece or come in on one of the later choruses. Much of the big-band repertory comprised popular songs in which the band both accompanied a singer and elaborated on the song through clever, harmonically adventurous arrangements that highlighted one or another of the band's sections. The combination of stylish, well-executed arrangements with hard-driving jazz rhythms produced a music that became known as **swing**. Swing was an immediate hit with the American public, igniting a dance craze across the country. The number of swing bands exploded during the 1930s, boosted by new white bands entering the jazz world, especially those led by Tommy Dorsey and Glenn Miller. In an era still marked by racial prejudice and segregation, the white bands had an easier time establishing themselves.

The swing era

GEORGE GERSHWIN

Some American composers, such as George Gershwin, shown in Figure 32.5, were quick to recognize the potential of jazz and blues to add new dimensions to art music. Gershwin's most famous piece, *Rhapsody in Blue* (1924), billed

Jazz in art music

Figure 32.5: George Gershwin at the piano in 1937, during rehearsals for the film Shall We Dance? His brother, lyricist Ira Gershwin, is to his left. Seated, to his right, are Fred Astaire and Ginger Rogers.

as a "jazz concerto," had its premiere as the climactic number of an extravagant concert organized by bandleader Paul Whiteman as "An Experiment in Modern Music." Scored for solo piano and jazz ensemble, and influenced by popular song forms, blue notes, and other elements of jazz and blues, the *Rhapsody* met with immediate approval and pointed the way for other American composers to incorporate jazz into their art music. Gershwin himself continued to fuse the seemingly disparate traditions, producing compositions like the Piano Concerto in F (1925), the second movement of which is constructed over a twelve-bar blues harmonic pattern stretched to fit a sixteen-measure theme. Gershwin's *Porgy and Bess* (1935), which he called a folk opera, draws elements from both the operatic and Broadway traditions. The music is continuous and features recurring motives like those in Verdi or Wagner operas. Yet in part because the characters are all African-American, the musical style is heavily influenced by African-American idioms such as spirituals, blues, and jazz. This blending of traditions is part of Gershwin's appeal, and it makes his music especially rich in reference and in meaning.

Musicals and popular songs

Gershwin was a writer of popular songs and musicals as well as a composer of jazz-influenced classical music. Like Irving Berlin, Gershwin got his start writing for revues. And like Kern and Porter, Gershwin moved increasingly toward integrated musicals, even venturing into social commentary. *Of Thee I Sing* (1931), a satire of the American presidential election process, was the first musical to win the Pulitzer Prize for drama. Gershwin's musicals catapulted several new performers to fame; *Lady, Be Good!* (1924) featured the singing and dancing brother-and-sister team of Fred and Adele Astaire, while *Girl Crazy* (1930) made stars of Ethel Merman and Ginger Rogers. In *Girl Crazy*, Ethel Merman sang the song *I Got Rhythm* (NAWM 151), which became an instant hit and soon began a long career as a vehicle for jazz improvisation. The harmonic progression of the song's chorus (in jazz terminology, its "changes") was adopted for so many new jazz tunes that this progression itself came to be known as "rhythm changes."

CD 11|55   CD 6|32

JAZZ IN EUROPE

Jazz spread quickly in the 1920s throughout North America, Latin America, and Europe. European musicians and music lovers encountered American jazz through imported recordings, sheet music, and traveling jazz ensembles. African-American musician-soldiers serving in Europe during World War I, such as the band led by James Reese Europe (see chapter 30), had helped to introduce the new style. By the 1920s, jazz groups were forming in Europe, and a European jazz tradition was well established by the 1930s. Jazz also became a frequent topic in European literature and arts, as illustrated by Figure 32.6.

In 1934, Gypsy guitarist Django Reinhardt (1910–1953) formed one of the most successful and musically innovative European jazz bands, the Quintette du Hot Club de France. The group toured throughout Europe until the outbreak of World War II. The first European to become an outstanding jazz performer and composer, Reinhardt demonstrated the international potential of

Figure 32.6: The Three Musicians *(1920), by Henri Hayden (1883–1970). Born in Poland, Hayden came to Paris in 1907 and painted in a cubist style for many years. The three instruments—banjo, saxophone, and guitar—mark the music of this group as jazz, all the rage in Paris after World War I.*

the American-born tradition, blending it with his own Gypsy heritage to create a highly individual and appealing style.

DUKE ELLINGTON

One of the leading composers of the Jazz Age and after, and one of the most influential American composers ever, was Duke Ellington (see biography and Figure 32.7).

Ellington developed his individual style and began to garner national attention during the years 1927–31, when his group was house band at the Cotton Club in Harlem, the vibrant and famous African-American area in New York. The Cotton Club was Harlem's preeminent nightclub, offering alcohol (illegal because of Prohibition, yet readily available) and entertainment. It featured black performers, including Ellington's band and a bevy of beautiful, light-skinned female dancers, but its clientele was white. The Cotton Club period was crucial to the development of Ellington's sound. Because his was the house band, the personnel was relatively stable, they had time to rehearse, and Ellington could use the band as a workshop to try out new pieces and new effects, testing the unusual timbres and voicings that became his trademark. Picking up where Gershwin had left off, he started experimenting with longer jazz works, such as *Creole Rhapsody* and *Reminiscing in Tempo*.

Cotton Club years

Rather than relying primarily on improvisation, the group moved more and more to arrangements worked out in advance that contrasted ensemble passages with solos, whether scored or improvised. When hiring players, Ellington looked for excellent musicians with very individual sounds, then capitalized on the unique talents of his band members by writing specifically

DUKE ELLINGTON (1899–1974)

Edward Kennedy ("Duke") Ellington, the most important composer of jazz to date, was an influential innovator who expanded what was possible in jazz and sought to break down barriers between it and art music. He admired the great jazz musicians, but his favorite composers were Debussy, Stravinsky, and Gershwin.

Born in Washington, D.C., Ellington was the son of a White House butler. He studied piano, including ragtime, from the age of seven and received a good education in music and other subjects. Known for his regal bearing and sartorial splendor, he

Figure 32.7: Duke Ellington at the piano in the mid-1930s.

earned the nickname "Duke" while still in high school. By the age of seventeen, Ellington was playing throughout the Washington area with his own group. In 1923, he moved to New York with his band the Washingtonians, playing at clubs on Broadway and at the Cotton Club in Harlem and making recordings.

During the 1930s and early 1940s, Ellington was the leading figure in jazz, and in later years he continued to play a prominent role, especially in efforts to have jazz recognized as a kind of art music, not merely as entertainment. He and his band made several international tours in the 1950s and 1960s, sponsored by the State Department and intended to create good will toward the United States. By the 1960s he was regarded as a national treasure. He won thirteen Grammy awards, was awarded seventeen honorary degrees, was granted the Presidential Medal of Honor in 1969, and in the early 1970s was named a member of the National Institute of Arts and Letters and of the Swedish Royal Academy of Music, the first jazz musician to be so honored. He played and toured with his band until his death at age seventy-five, when his son, Mercer Ellington, took over the band and continued to tour.

MAJOR WORKS: East St. Louis Toodle-oo; Black and Tan Fantasy; Mood Indigo; Creole Rhapsody; Concerto for Cootie; Ko-Ko; Cotton Tail; Black, Brown and Beige; *and more than 1,300 other compositions*

for them or collaborating with them, as in *Black and Tan Fantasy* (1927) with trumpeter Bubber Miley and *Mood Indigo* (1930) with clarinet and saxophone player Barney Bigard. His band grew from ten to twelve players, made about two hundred recordings, and appeared regularly on radio broadcasts.

From 1931 on, Ellington and his band spent most of their time on the road. *Touring* The band continued to grow, reaching fourteen players in the late 1930s and eighteen in 1946. The group's repertoire consisted largely of Ellington's own tunes, but they also played popular songs and dance favorites. Many of Ellington's tunes were given lyrics and sold as popular songs, including *Sophisticated Lady* and *Don't Get Around Much Anymore.* Ellington often wrote and recorded smaller ensemble pieces to highlight the skills of individual players, keeping his stars happy by giving each a little piece of the limelight.

The early 1940s is widely considered the peak of Ellington's creative abili- *The 1940s* ties and of the performing rapport among the band members. In 1939–40, he added three important new members: Jimmie Blanton on bass, Ben Webster on tenor saxophone, and Billy Strayhorn as second pianist, composer, and arranger. Ellington took advantage of their talents and wrote a number of new pieces to display their gifts. *Cotton Tail* (1940, NAWM 152) was written for [CD 11|58] [CD 6|35] Webster, and his solo became a classic. Strayhorn shared composing duties with Ellington, producing standards such as *Take the A Train* (1941), which became one of the band's signature tunes.

Cotton Tail illustrates Ellington's music from this era. It follows the typical form for jazz performances, with a tune at the beginning followed by a series of choruses over the same progression. *Cotton Tail* is a **contrafact,** a new tune composed over a harmonic progression borrowed from a particular song—in this case, the chorus of Gershwin's *I Got Rhythm* (NAWM 151). Ellington's melody—fast, angular, highly syncopated, and full of unexpected twists—is nothing like Gershwin's, even though the harmonic progression is the same. The first two choruses feature Ben Webster soloing on tenor saxophone accompanied by the rhythm section with occasional punctuation from the rest of the band. Example 32.3 compares the opening measures of Ellington's tune with those of Webster's choruses. The solo plays off the same chord

Example 32.3: Duke Ellington's Cotton Tail *and Ben Webster's solo*

progression as the tune but does not vary or develop the tune; rather, the music at each chorus presents new ideas and may or may not use melodic or rhythmic ideas from earlier in the piece. The remaining three choruses feature various combinations of instruments playing together or in call-and-response fashion, and the first eight bars of Ellington's tune return to bring the piece to a close.

Beyond category   Throughout his career, Ellington fought the label "jazz composer," preferring to consider his music (and all good music) "beyond category." He believed that jazz could serve not only as dance or entertainment music but also as art music, listened to for its own sake. He frequently pushed against the boundaries of technology and convention. Until the introduction of long-playing records in the late 1940s, a piece could only be about three minutes long in order to fit on one side of a 78-rpm record; longer pieces had to be split up on several record sides, making them more difficult to market. Ellington composed longer pieces anyway and convinced the record companies to record the pieces on multiple sides. Later in his career, he composed suites, such as *Black, Brown, and Beige* (1943), *Harlem* (1950), and *Suite Thursday* (1960), and collaborated with Billy Strayhorn in rescoring for jazz band classical favorites such as Tchaikovsky's *Nutcracker Suite* and Grieg's *Peer Gynt Suite.* In asserting the value of jazz as an art music, he was declaring it worthy of attentive listening and of a permanent place in American culture. In both respects, his view has won out.

FILM MUSIC

Sound in film   In the same way that recordings and radio fostered the explosive growth of jazz, new technologies transformed film music. In the late 1920s, methods were invented to synchronize recorded sound with film, opening up new possibilities for the use of music as part of a film, not merely as live accompaniment to it. The first "talking picture" (so called because it featured recorded dialogue) was *The Jazz Singer* (1927) starring Al Jolson, which included scenes of Jolson singing and other scenes in which music was used to accompany the action, as in earlier silent films. These two types of scene exemplify the two categories of music in film that have continued to the present:

(1) music that is heard or performed by the characters themselves, known as **diegetic music** or **source music,** and

(2) background music that conveys to the viewer a mood or other aspects of a scene or character, known as **nondiegetic music** or **underscoring**.

On-screen performances   The advent of sound film put many theater musicians out of work, an economic downturn made disastrous by the Great Depression. Yet it did open a new window of opportunity. By the mid-1930s, the major Hollywood studios each employed composers, orchestrators, arrangers, and editors to create music for films and orchestras to perform it, and filmmakers abroad assembled similar units. Both dramas and comedies often included musical numbers as interludes or for dramatic reasons. One of the earliest movies to use music dramatically was the Austrian film *Der blaue Engel* (simultaneously released in English as *The Blue Angel*, 1930). In it Marlene Dietrich as a cabaret singer performs songs by Friedrich Hollaender (a.k.a. Frederick Hollander), among them her signature song, *Falling in Love Again*, which in the German version has entirely different and racier words.

Beginning in 1929, Hollywood studios produced numerous musicals com- *Movie musicals* posed for film. Romberg (*Viennese Nights*), Gershwin (*Delicious* and *Shall We Dance?*), Berlin (*Top Hat*), Kern (*Swing Time*), and Porter (*Born to Dance*) all wrote music for movie musicals during the 1930s, considered the "Golden Age" of the Hollywood musical. The spectacular choreography of Busby Berkeley enlivened *Gold Diggers of 1933* and many other films, and the singing and dancing of Bing Crosby, Fred Astaire, and Ginger Rogers in many movie musicals made them international stars. Movie musicals were enormously popular; they offered escape from the Great Depression, their level of talent was high, and they were inexpensive compared to Broadway shows. *The Wizard of Oz* (1939), with songs by Harold Arlen, introduced color photography to film musicals and launched the career of Judy Garland. A parallel development in Germany was the film operetta, including scores by Franz Lehár (*Where Is This Lady?*) and other prominent composers, but the rise of the Nazis in 1933 forced many of the leading figures to emigrate.

The Hollywood studios also fostered the rise of film scores that were fully integrated into the dramatic action, like the music for an opera—"opera without singing," in the memorable phrase of composer Erich Wolfgang Korngold. Many of the composers working in Hollywood were European immigrants, and they applied the language of Wagner, Strauss, and Debussy to music for film. Max Steiner (1888–1971), an immigrant from Vienna who had worked on Broadway for fifteen years as an arranger, orchestrator, and composer, established the model for the Hollywood film score with his music for *King Kong* (1933). The movie, whose poster is shown in Figure 32.8, centered on a giant gorilla discovered in Africa and brought to New York, where it threatens the city. Steiner's score is organized around leitmotives for characters and ideas, as in a Wagner opera, and coordinates the music with actions on screen, often marking particular movements with musical effects. The music conveys mood, character, and place through styles with strong associations, from primitivism for the African setting to orchestral Romanticism for dramatic moments, and it uses modernist techniques when appropriate, such as intense dissonance for fright and other extreme emotions. All of these traits became characteristic of film scoring.

Steiner continued writing film scores through the 1960s, his credits including *Gone with the Wind* (1939) and

Figure 32.8: Poster for King Kong *(1933), whose score by Max Steiner set the paradigm for Hollywood film music.*

Casablanca (1943). Other leading Hollywood film composers include Erich Wolfgang Korngold (1897–1957), who brought his experience as a Viennese composer of opera and classical concert works to scores for the Errol Flynn swashbucklers *Captain Blood* (1935) and *The Adventures of Robin Hood* (1938), and Alfred Newman (1900–1970), the first major native-born American film composer, known for scores to *Wuthering Heights, The Song of Bernadette, How the West Was Won, Airport,* and more than two hundred other films. Music also played a prominent role in animated films, from shorts like Walt Disney's pioneering cartoon *Steamboat Willie* (1928) and the Bugs Bunny cartoons scored by Carl Stalling to full-length features, beginning with Disney's *Snow White and the Seven Dwarfs* (1937) with a score by Frank Churchill. Music became integral to all these types of film, guiding the viewer's emotional responses and giving depth to the events on screen.

MASS MEDIA AND POPULAR MUSIC

Through the new technologies of recordings, radio, and sound on film, American popular music, jazz, and film music reached audiences throughout the Western world. Music could now be preserved and enjoyed year after year, for decades to come. As a result, much of this music maintained its popularity, and within a generation or two many of these pieces achieved the status of classics: widely known, heard and reheard, and highly valued. By the 1970s, canons of classics had developed for popular song, blues, jazz, and film music, in parallel with the canon of classical music that had emerged in the nineteenth century. The central core of those canons—parallel to Bach, Mozart, and Beethoven in the classical world—is in most cases formed by composers and performers whose music was popular between the world wars, including Berlin, Kern, Gershwin, Porter, Bessie Smith, King Oliver, Armstrong, Ellington, Steiner, Korngold, and Newman.

Today, in addition to recordings and movies, live ensembles perform Tin Pan Alley songs, Broadway musicals, blues, New Orleans jazz, swing, big-band jazz, and even movie scores from the 1920s and 1930s. This music is admired both for its original value as entertainment and because it is considered artful, worth listening to with attention, and capable of offering musical experiences available nowhere else—the same reasons that music of earlier generations was preserved and revived in the nineteenth century. There are now many traditions of musical classics, and all have a share in our richly varied musical life.

Chapter

33

Between the World Wars:
The Classical Tradition

Music in the classical tradition continued to diversify in style and concept between the world wars, as composers sought individual solutions to the common problem of finding a place in the crowded classical repertoire. In all nations and regions, music composition became increasingly—or perhaps only more overtly—tied to political concerns and ideologies. Government regulation of music was especially strong in the Soviet Union and Nazi Germany. Some composers in the classical tradition—reacting to social and political pressures, to the economic crisis of the Depression, to their older modernist colleagues, or to the perceived loss of a listening public for modern music—sought to reconnect with a large audience, while others pursued new ideas with little concern for popularity. Throughout the Americas a growing number of composers won international reputations with music that represented their nations on the world stage. An experimental or "ultramodernist" tradition emerged in the United States alongside a growing nationalist trend, both representing assertions of independence from Europe.

MUSIC, POLITICS, AND THE PEOPLE

Music has long been linked to politics. Aristotle discussed music in his *Politics*, and he and Plato described the appropriate uses of music for the ideal society. Charlemagne's desire to unify his large empire led to the codification of Gregorian chant. Louis XIV asserted control through

865

dance and opera. And an opera performance in 1830 sparked the revolution that won independence for Belgium.

Classical music as autonomous   But in the nineteenth century, some writers claimed that classical music was an autonomous art that transcended politics and should be composed, performed, experienced, and admired for its own sake, separate from political or social concerns. The new "science" of musicology that emerged during the nineteenth century reinforced this view, focusing more on the styles and procedures of past music than on its social functions. To some extent, treating

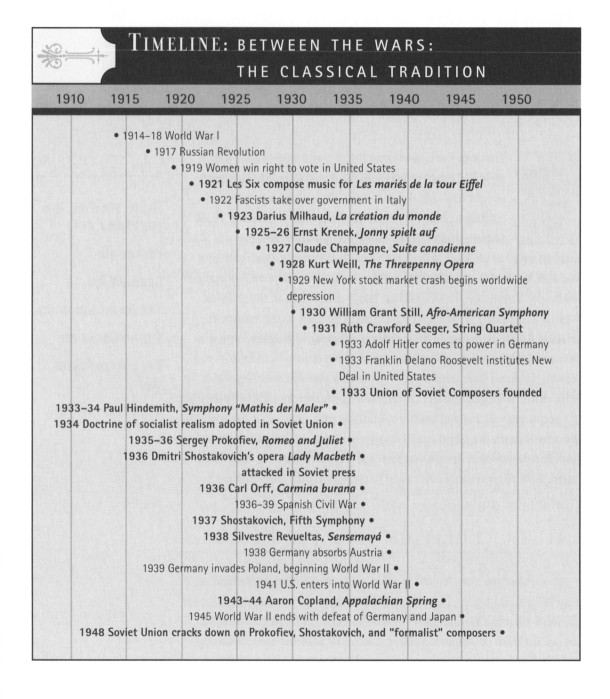

TIMELINE: BETWEEN THE WARS:
THE CLASSICAL TRADITION

1910	1915	1920	1925	1930	1935	1940	1945	1950

- 1914–18 World War I
- 1917 Russian Revolution
- 1919 Women win right to vote in United States
- 1921 Les Six compose music for *Les mariés de la tour Eiffel*
- 1922 Fascists take over government in Italy
- 1923 Darius Milhaud, *La création du monde*
- 1925–26 Ernst Krenek, *Jonny spielt auf*
- 1927 Claude Champagne, *Suite canadienne*
- 1928 Kurt Weill, *The Threepenny Opera*
- 1929 New York stock market crash begins worldwide depression
- 1930 William Grant Still, *Afro-American Symphony*
- 1931 Ruth Crawford Seeger, String Quartet
- 1933 Adolf Hitler comes to power in Germany
- 1933 Franklin Delano Roosevelt institutes New Deal in United States
- 1933 Union of Soviet Composers founded
- 1933–34 Paul Hindemith, *Symphony "Mathis der Maler"*
- 1934 Doctrine of socialist realism adopted in Soviet Union
- 1935–36 Sergey Prokofiev, *Romeo and Juliet*
- 1936 Dmitri Shostakovich's opera *Lady Macbeth* attacked in Soviet press
- 1936 Carl Orff, *Carmina burana*
- 1936–39 Spanish Civil War
- 1937 Shostakovich, Fifth Symphony
- 1938 Silvestre Revueltas, *Sensemayá*
- 1938 Germany absorbs Austria
- 1939 Germany invades Poland, beginning World War II
- 1941 U.S. enters into World War II
- 1943–44 Aaron Copland, *Appalachian Spring*
- 1945 World War II ends with defeat of Germany and Japan
- 1948 Soviet Union cracks down on Prokofiev, Shostakovich, and "formalist" composers

music on its own terms was an admirable ideal, allowing many listeners to enjoy music for its own sake and as a respite from the concerns of the day. But in other respects, from its cultivation by the economic and social elite to its association with nationalism, classical music never fully escaped politics.

The period between the world wars brought new links between music and politics. In democracies such as Britain, France, Germany under the Weimar Republic, and the United States, economic troubles and political conflicts led many composers to believe that art which set itself apart from social needs was in danger of becoming irrelevant to society at large. As the gap widened between the unfamiliar sounds of modernist music and the ability of listeners to understand it, composers tried to bring contemporary music closer to the general public by crafting widely accessible concert works or by writing music for films, theater, and dance. Convinced that music performed by amateurs and school groups was as important as art music, composers wrote works that were within the capabilities of amateurs and rewarding to perform, yet were modern in style. Many composers used music, especially musical theater, to engage current social, political, and economic issues. Nationalism continued as a strong force in most countries, exemplified in the musical styles of individual composers and in efforts to edit, publish, and perform music of the nation, including both folk music and the written music of earlier times.

Links to politics

Most governments sponsored musical activities directly. Public schools increasingly included music in the curriculum. Hungarian composer Zoltán Kodály devised a method of teaching music to children through the use of folk songs, musical games, and graded exercises—a method that was eventually adopted by many schools across Europe and North America. Throughout most of Europe, radio was controlled by the government and was a major employer of composers and performers. During the New Deal in the United States, the federal government established programs to employ out-of-work musicians and composers. Totalitarian governments insisted that music under their regimes support the state and its ideologies. In the 1930s, the Soviet Union and Nazi Germany attempted to suppress the composition and performance of modernist music, which was condemned in one country as bourgeois decadence, in the other as cultural Bolshevism. This last example illustrates a point worth bearing in mind. Although musical styles were often identified with particular ideologies, these links were contingent on the unique political situation in each nation; the same style, even the same piece, could be seen as progressive or socialist in one place and conservative or fascistic in another.

Government sponsorship

FRANCE

In France, and especially in Paris, musical life had long been intertwined with politics. Groups across the political spectrum sponsored concerts that supported their points of view. In the early 1900s, the conservative nationalist Ligue de la Patrie Française (League of the French Homeland) joined with

Vincent d'Indy and his Schola Cantorum to present concerts and lectures that showcased the French tradition—particularly composers from the Middle Ages to the 1789 Revolution and the classically oriented composers since Franck—as the embodiment of authentic French culture based on religious principles and respect for authority. In response, the government, then dominated by left-wing parties, promoted French composers since the Revolution, especially those like Berlioz and Saint-Saëns who, their advocates argued, freed French music from the bonds of tradition. In this way, not only new music but the music of the past was politically contested.

Notions of classicism   During and after World War I, nationalists asserted that French music was intrinsically classic, as opposed to the Romanticism of the Germans. Thus neoclassicism—the use of classical genres and forms, tonal centers, and common-practice or neotonal harmonies, allied with emotional restraint and a rejection of Romantic excess—became the prevailing trend in France after the war, associated with patriotism. But exactly how the "classic" was to be defined became a point of contention. Conservatives like d'Indy identified it with balance, order, discipline, and tradition, contrasting with the irrationality and individualism of Romanticism. Composers on the left, like Ravel (see chapter 30), saw the classic as encompassing the universal and not merely the national. His music included elements from Viennese waltzes (*La valse*), Spain (*Bolero*), Gypsy style (*Tzigane*), blues (Violin Sonata), and jazz (Concerto for the Left Hand), all rejected by the conservative nationalists.

LES SIX

A younger group of composers absorbed the strong influence of neoclassicism but sought to escape the old political dichotomies. Arthur Honegger (1892–1955), Darius Milhaud (1892–1974), Francis Poulenc (1899–1963), Germaine Tailleferre (1892–1983), Georges Auric (1899–1983), and Louis Durey (1888–1979) were dubbed "Les Six" (The Six), in a parallel to the Mighty Five in Russia (see chapter 27), by a French journalist who saw them as seeking to free French music from foreign domination. They drew inspiration from Satie and were hailed by writer Jean Cocteau, who called for new music that would be fully French and anti-Romantic in its clarity, accessibility, and emotional restraint.

The group, pictured in Figure 33.1, collaborated in joint concerts, an album of piano music, and Cocteau's absurdist play-with-ballet *Les mariés de la tour Eiffel* (Newlyweds on the Eiffel Tower, 1921). But the group did not remain together long—Durey left even before the ballet project started—and none of them fully conformed to Cocteau's program. Instead, they each wrote highly individual works that drew on a wide range of influences, including but not limited to neoclassicism. Tailleferre was the most in tune with neoclassical ideals, drawing on Couperin and Rameau (see chapter 18) in her Piano Concerto (1923–24) and other works. Auric was the most taken with Satie's avant-garde approach. But the most individual were Honegger, Milhaud, and Poulenc, who achieved success independent of the group and found ways to make their music distinctive within the broad outlines of neoclassicism.

Figure 33.1: The Group of the Six (Hommage à Satie) *by Jacques-Emile Blanche (1922–23). This group portrait shows five of the composers known as Les Six and three of their collaborators. Clockwise from bottom left are Germaine Tailleferre, Darius Milhaud, Arthur Honegger, conductor Jean Wiéner, pianist Marcelle Mayer, Francis Poulenc, writer Jean Cocteau, and Georges Auric. Not shown is Louis Durey, who left the group in 1921.*

Honegger excelled in music of dynamic action and graphic gesture, expressed in short-breathed melodies, strong ostinato rhythms, bold colors, and dissonant harmonies. His symphonic movement *Pacific 231* (1923), a translation into music of the visual and physical impression of a speeding locomotive, was hailed as a sensational piece of modernist descriptive music. Honegger won an international reputation in 1923 with his oratorio *King David*, which combined the tradition of music for amateur chorus with allusions to styles from Gregorian chant to Baroque polyphony to jazz. The evocations of pre-Romantic styles, use of traditional forms and procedures, and prevailing diatonic language all reveal the impact of neoclassicism.

Arthur Honegger

Milhaud produced an immense quantity of music, including piano pieces, chamber music (his eighteen string quartets are especially notable), suites, sonatas, symphonies, film music, ballets, songs, cantatas, operas, and music for children. His works are diverse in style and approach, ranging from the comic frivolity of the ballet *Le boeuf sur le toit* (The Ox on the Roof, 1919) to the earnestness of the opera-oratorio *Christophe Colomb* (1928) and the religious devotion of the *Sacred Service* (1947), which reflects Milhaud's Jewish heritage. He was especially open to sounds and styles from the Americas. Saxophones, ragtime syncopations, and the blues find their way into his ballet

Darius Milhaud

La création du monde (The Creation of the World, 1923). Brazilian folk melodies and rhythms appear in *Le boeuf sur la toit* and in the orchestral dances *Saudades do Brasil* (Souvenirs of Brazil, 1920–21), illustrated in Example 33.1. In addition to the syncopated rhythms and diatonic melodies of Brazilian dance, the latter uses polytonality, in which two lines of melody and planes of harmony, each in a distinct and different key, sound simultaneously. This procedure would become associated with Milhaud, although many used it before and since. In all his music, Milhaud blended ingenuity, freshness, and variety with the clarity and logical form he had absorbed from neoclassicism. Yet his openness to foreign influences, from jazz to Schoenberg, was a far cry from the program of nationalist classical purity favored by d'Indy.

Example 33.1: Milhaud, "Copacabaña," from Saudades do Brasil

Francis Poulenc

Poulenc drew especially on the Parisian popular chanson tradition sustained in cabarets and revues. This too violated the strictures of d'Indy, who rejected influence from "lower" forms of music. Poulenc's compositions revel in an ingratiating harmonic idiom, draw grace and wit from popular styles, and wed satirical mimicry to fluent melody, as in his surrealist opera *Les mamelles de Tiresias* (The Breasts of Tiresias, 1940). The *Concert champêtre* (Pastoral Concerto) for harpsichord or piano and small orchestra (1928) evokes the spirit of Rameau and Domenico Scarlatti, and his sonatas and chamber works for various groups of instruments bring an expressive, song-influenced melodic idiom and fresh, mildly dissonant harmonies into classical genres and forms. Among his other compositions are a Mass in G for a cappella chorus (1937), several motets, other choral works, and numerous songs. His three-act opera *Dialogues of the Carmelites* (1956) is an affecting meditation on the execution of Carmelite nuns during the French Revolution, raising issues of religion, politics, allegiance, and personal choice that had deep resonances in French political life.

GERMANY

Germany under the Weimar Republic (1919–1933) was a hotbed of political contention, which echoed in the musical world. After the Nazis came to power in 1933, they attacked most modern music as decadent, banned the political left and Jews from participating in public life, and persecuted Jews and other minorities. As a result, many leading musicians took refuge abroad.

NEW OBJECTIVITY

In opposition to the emotional intensity of the late Romantics and the expressionism of Schoenberg and Berg, a new trend emerged in the 1920s under the slogan *Neue Sachlichkeit*, meaning **New Objectivity** or New Realism. The phrase was first used in art criticism and quickly adopted by musicians. As articulated by the composer Ernst Krenek (1900–1991) and others, the New Objectivity opposed complexity and promoted the use of familiar elements, borrowing from popular music and jazz or from Classical and Baroque procedures. In their view, music should be objective in its expression, as in the Baroque concept of the affections (see chapter 13), rather than subjective or extreme. The notion of music as autonomous was rejected. Instead, it should be widely accessible, communicate clearly, and draw connections to the events and concerns of the time.

Krenek's *Jonny spielt auf*, premiered in Leipzig in 1927, was the embodiment of these ideals, an opera set in the present time that used the interaction of a European composer and an African-American jazz musician to examine dichotomies between contemplation and pleasure and between a seemingly exhausted and inward-looking European tradition and a new and energetic American one. The music drew on jazz and on a simplified harmonic language. The opera was an immediate success, was produced on over seventy stages during the next three years, and established Krenek's reputation. But almost from the start it was vociferously attacked by the Nazis as "degenerate" for its use of African-American elements. Krenek later adopted the twelve-tone method and emigrated to the United States after Nazi Germany absorbed his native Austria in 1938.

Ernst Krenek

KURT WEILL

Kurt Weill (1900–1950), an opera composer in Berlin, was also an exponent of the New Objectivity. Sympathetic to the political left, he sought to offer social commentary and to entertain everyday people rather than the intellectual elites.

Weill collaborated with the playwright Bertolt Brecht on the allegorical opera *Aufstieg und Fall der Stadt Mahagonny* (Rise and Fall of the City of Mahagonny, premiered 1930). In the opera, fugitives from justice build a town dedicated to pleasure, free of legal or moral taboos, but soon find that they have created a hell rather than a paradise on earth. Weill's score incorporates elements of popular music and jazz and makes witty references to a variety of styles. The pit orchestra includes instruments typical of jazz bands—two saxophones, piano, banjo, and bass guitar—as well as winds and timpani, while three saxophones, zither, a bandoneon (a kind of accordion), strings, and brass play in the stage orchestra. Through satire in both libretto and music, Brecht and Weill sought to expose what they regarded as the failures of capitalism, which the city of Mahagonny exemplified.

Mahagonny

Figure 33.2: Lotte Lenya in a scene from Kurt Weill's The Threepenny Opera *in a New York production from the mid-1950s.*

The Threepenny Opera

The most famous collaboration between Weill and Brecht was *Die Dreigroschenoper* (The Threepenny Opera, premiered 1928). Brecht based the libretto on *The Beggar's Opera* by John Gay (see chapter 20 and NAWM 95), although Weill borrowed only one air from the score. The cast included Lotte Lenya, shown in Figure 33.2, whom Weill had married in 1926; she became his favorite interpreter and after his death a champion of his work. The music parodied rather than imitated American hit songs, then the rage in Europe. Weill juxtaposed in a surreal manner the eighteenth-century ballad texts, European dance music, and American jazz. The original Berlin production ran for over two years, and within five years *The Threepenny Opera* enjoyed more than ten thousand performances in nineteen languages. The Nazis banned it as decadent in 1933, when Weill and Lenya left for Paris and then for the United States.

Career on Broadway

In New York, Weill began his second career as a composer for Broadway musicals. The most successful were *Knickerbocker Holiday* (1938), *Lady in the Dark* (1940), and the musical tragedy *Lost in the Stars* (1948), about apartheid in South Africa. The spirit of the New Objectivity lived on in these works, crafted by a classically trained modernist yet addressed to a broad musical public and meant to be immediately grasped by mind and heart.

PAUL HINDEMITH

Paul Hindemith (1895–1963) was among the most prolific composers of the century. At the Berlin School of Music (1927–37), Yale University (1940–53), and the University of Zurich (1951–57), he taught two generations of musicians. He thought of himself primarily as a practicing musician, performing professionally as violinist, violist, and conductor and able to play many other instruments. The experience of performance became central to his music, whether intended for amateurs or professionals.

In the fragmented world of new music between the wars, Hindemith changed his approach several times. He began composing in a late Romantic style, then developed an individual expressionist language in works like the one-act opera *Murder, Hope of Women* (1919). Soon he adopted the aesthetic stance later dubbed the New Objectivity, which in his music was exemplified by an avoidance of Romantic expressivity and a focus on purely musical procedures, especially motivic development and a polyphony of independent lines. The seven works he titled simply *Kammermusik* (Chamber Music, 1922–27) included a piece for small orchestra and six concertos for solo instrument and chamber orchestra, which encompassed a variety of movement types from neo-Baroque ritornello forms to military marches and dances. All his music was neotonal, establishing pitch centers through techniques from simple reiteration of a note to complex contrapuntal voice-leading.

By the late 1920s, Hindemith was disturbed by the widening gulf between modern composers and an increasingly passive public. In response, he began composing what was known as **Gebrauchsmusik**—"music for use," as distinguished from music for its own sake. His goal was to create for young or amateur performers that was high in quality, modern in style, and challenging yet rewarding to perform.

After the Nazis came to power, they attacked Hindemith in the press and banned much of his music as "cultural Bolshevism." He began to examine the role of the artist in relation to politics and power, and from his questioning emerged the opera *Mathis der Maler* (Matthias the Painter, 1934–35; premiered 1938 in Zurich) and *Symphony "Mathis der Maler"* (1933–34), his best-known work, composed while he was writing the libretto of the opera. The opera is based on the life of Matthias Grünewald, painter of the famous Isenheim alterpiece shown in Figure 33.3. Mathis, the opera's main character, leaves his calling as a painter to join the peasants in their rebellion against the nobles during the Peasants' War of 1525. In despair after their defeat, he comes to realize that by abandoning his art he betrayed his gift and his true obligation to society, which is to paint. Yet Hindemith does not portray art as entirely autonomous, since Mathis's experiences inform his moral vision. The opera can be read as an allegory for Hindemith's own career.

For *Mathis* and his other works from the 1930s on, Hindemith developed a new, neo-Romantic style, with less dissonant linear counterpoint and more systematic tonal organization. He devised a new harmonic method that he called "harmonic fluctuation": fairly consonant chords progress toward combinations containing greater tension and dissonance, which are then resolved either suddenly or by slowly moderating the tension until consonance is again reached. We can see this technique in Example 33.2, the beginning of the second movement of the symphony (and the seventh scene of the opera), representing Mathis painting the entombment of Christ shown in Figure 33.3 (see p. 875). From an open fifth, the harmony adds fourths and major seconds, with some parallel-fourth motion leading to a cadence on a fifth-octave sonority. An answering phrase in the winds adds minor thirds, reaching a height of

Works of the Weimar period

Gebrauchsmusik

Mathis der Maler

dissonance on a minor ninth before returning to the initial sonority with octave doublings. A similar use of parallel fourths and harmonic fluctuation can be found in many of Hindemith's later works, such as his choral setting of Rilke's *Un cygne* (A Swan, 1939; NAWM 153), part of a set of six pieces for a cappella chorus that exemplifies his music for amateur or school performers.

CD 11|64

Example 33.2: Hindemith, Symphony "Mathis der Maler," *opening of second movement*

Later works

In 1936, the Nazi government forbade performances of Hindemith's music. *Mathis der Maler* had to be premiered in Switzerland, and Hindemith moved there in 1938. He emigrated to the United States in 1940 after the outbreak of World War II and stayed for over a decade, returning to Switzerland in 1953. Having found his mature style in *Mathis*, he applied it to a series of sonatas for almost every orchestral instrument (1935–55). *Ludus tonalis* (Tonal Play, 1942) for piano evokes the model of Bach's *Well-Tempered Clavier* with twelve fugues, each centered on a different note in the chromatic scale, linked by modulating interludes and framed by a prelude (modulating from C to F♯) and postlude (F♯ to C). Other notable later works include *Symphonic Metamorphosis after Themes of Carl Maria von Weber* (1943) and the Symphony in B♭ for band (1951).

MUSIC UNDER THE NAZIS

Krenek, Weill, and Hindemith all fled to the United States, but other composers stayed in Germany during the Nazi era. The Nazis established a Reich Chamber of Culture under Joseph Goebbels, which included a Reich Music Chamber to which all musicians had to belong. Richard Strauss, the grand old man of German music, was appointed its first president, but was soon forced to resign when he continued to collaborate on operas with a Jewish librettist, Stefan Zweig.

The Nazis' requirements for music were mostly expressed in negatives: music must not be dissonant, atonal, twelve-tone, "chaotic," intellectual, Jewish, jazz-influenced, or left-wing, which excluded all modernist and most modern music. Composers had to cooperate with the regime in order to have their music performed, and most did. But many German composers continued to write in personal idioms influenced by Schoenberg, Stravinsky, Hindemith, or Weill, whose music the Nazis had attacked as decadent or banned outright. As a result, no coherent Nazi style of new music emerged. Rather, the government focused more on performance than on composition, exploiting the great German composers of the nineteenth century from Beethoven to Bruckner as symbols of the alleged superiority of the German people. They

Figure 33.3: Three panels from the Isenheim Altarpiece, *painted by Matthias Grünewald between 1512 and 1516 for the chapel of a hospital and monastery. On the top right is the* Nativity *with Mary holding the newborn Jesus; on the left is the* Concert of Angels, *the inspiration for the first movement of Hindemith's Symphony "Mathis der Maler," and below is the* Entombment, *evoked in the second movement. Both movements were reused in the opera* Mathis der Maler, *about Grünewald's life.*

especially fostered a cult of Wagner, whose anti-Semitic views supported their own and whose *Ring* cycle embodied a German mythology they could embrace.

Carl Orff   The one German composer who won an international reputation during the Nazi era was Carl Orff (1895–1982), who was far from sympathetic with the regime. His best-known work, *Carmina burana* (1936) for chorus and orchestra, set medieval poems akin to goliard songs (see chapter 4) in an attractive, deceptively simple neo-modal idiom. Drawing on Stravinsky, folk songs, chant, and medieval secular song, Orff created a monumental pseudo-antique style based on drones, ostinatos, harmonic stasis, and strophic repetition. His *Carmina burana* is distinctive yet immediately comprehensible and has been much imitated, especially by composers for film and television. Like Kodály, Orff also developed methods and materials for teaching music in schools, calling for movement, singing, and playing on percussion and other instruments, leading children in a natural way to experience a great variety of scales and rhythms and to arrive at a broadly based understanding of music.

THE SOVIET UNION

In the Soviet Union, the government controlled the arts along with every other realm of life. The arts were seen as ways to indoctrinate the people in Marxist-Leninist ideology, enhance their patriotism, and venerate the leadership. Soon after the Revolution, theaters, conservatories, concert halls, performing ensembles, publishers, and other musical institutions were all nationalized, and concert programming and the opera and ballet repertories were strictly regulated.

Composers'
organizations   Civil war in 1918–20 and an economic crisis through the early 1920s preoccupied the government and forced some relaxation of state control over the arts. During this period of relative freedom, divergent tendencies emerged among composers and crystallized in two organizations founded in 1923. The Association for Contemporary Music sought to continue the modernist trends established by Scriabin and others before the war and promoted contacts with the West, sponsoring performances of music by Stravinsky, Schoenberg, Hindemith, and others. The Russian Association of Proletarian Musicians, on the other hand, considered such music elitist and instead encouraged simple tonal music with wide appeal, especially "mass songs" (songs for group unison singing) to socialist texts. After Joseph Stalin consolidated total power in 1929, dissent was quashed. The competing composers' groups were replaced in 1933 by a single new organization, the Union of Soviet Composers.

Socialist realism
versus formalism   A 1934 writers' congress promulgated **socialist realism** as the ideal for Soviet arts. In literature, drama, and painting, this doctrine called for using a realistic style (as opposed to abstraction or symbolism) in works that portrayed socialism in a positive light, showing signs of progress for the people under the Soviet state and celebrating revolutionary ideology and its heroes. What this meant for music was the use of a relatively simple, accessible language, centered on melody, often drawing on folk or folklike styles, and used

for patriotic or inspirational subject matter. Interest in music for its own sake or in modernist styles was condemned as "formalism." But the definitions of socialist realism and formalism were so vague and arbitrary that composers often ran afoul of the authorities, including the two leading Soviet composers of the time, Sergey Prokofiev and Dmitri Shostakovich.

SERGEY PROKOFIEV

Prokofiev (1891–1953) made his initial reputation as a radical modernist, combining striking dissonance with motoric rhythms. He left Russia after the Revolution and spent almost two decades residing and touring in North America and western Europe, composing solo piano works and concertos for himself to play, and fulfilling commissions for larger compositions, among them an opera for Chicago, *The Love for Three Oranges* (1921), and ballets for Serge Diaghilev's Ballets Russes in Paris.

His career at a low ebb, Prokofiev succumbed to promises from the Soviet regime of commissions and performances. He returned to Russia permanently in 1936, having already fulfilled Soviet commissions for the film *Lieutenant Kijé* (1934), later arranged as a concert suite, and for the ballet *Romeo and Juliet* (1935–36). Both became among his most popular works and entered the standard repertory. So did his symphonic fairy tale for narrator and orchestra, *Peter and the Wolf* (1936)—one of many pieces he wrote in response to the Soviet demand for high-quality music for children—and a cantata drawn from music for the film *Alexander Nevsky* (1938). Prokofiev's pieces for state occasions, like his cantatas for the twentieth and thirtieth anniversaries of the Russian Revolution, were less successful and were ignored outside of the Soviet Union.

World War II again brought a relaxation of government control, and Prokofiev turned to absolute music in classical genres, notably the Piano Sonatas Nos. 6–8 (1939–44) and the Fifth Symphony (1944). These works are largely tonal, with the unexpected harmonic juxtapositions and the alternation of acerbic dryness, lyricism, and motoric rhythms that had been features of his personal style since the 1910s. But after the war, the authorities again cracked down in a 1948 resolution that condemned the works of Prokofiev and other leading composers as "formalist." He tried to write more simply, but never recovered the balance of wit with feeling and of convention with surprise that marks his best music. He died in 1953—ironically, on the same day as Stalin, whose brutal regime had so circumscribed his freedom.

DMITRI SHOSTAKOVICH

Shostakovich (1906–1975), shown in Figure 33.4, received his education and spent his entire career within the Soviet system. He studied at the Conservatory in Petrograd (later Leningrad, now St. Petersburg), cultivating a combination of traditional discipline with experimentation. In the 1920s, he was more aligned with the modernist than with the proletarian wing in Russia. The premiere of his First Symphony in 1926, when he was nineteen, and subsequent performances in the West rocketed him to international prominence.

Figure 33.4: Portrait of Dmitri Shostakovich by T. Salakhov.

Lady Macbeth of Mtsensk   Shostakovich's opera *Lady Macbeth of the Mtsensk District* was premiered in 1934 in both Leningrad and Moscow and scored a great success, with subsequent performances throughout the Soviet Union and abroad. But Stalin saw it in January 1936 and was angered by its discordant modernist music and surrealistic, often grotesque, portrayal of violence and sex. Shortly thereafter, the newspaper *Pravda* printed an unsigned article attacking the opera as "Chaos Instead of Music" (see Source Reading). In its wake the production was closed down and the opera withdrawn. Shostakovich temporarily lost his favored status and may have feared for his life: the previous year Stalin had begun a campaign of repression known as the Purges, during which many political figures, intellectuals, and artists were executed or banished to prison camps.

Fifth Symphony   It is hard not to see the Fifth Symphony, written and premiered to great acclaim in 1937, as his response to the criticism of his opera; indeed, he endorsed a description of the work as "a Soviet artist's reply to just criticism." The symphony embodies a new approach Shostakovich had been developing, inspired by close study of Mahler's symphonies, that encompassed a wide range of styles and moods, from lyricism to dynamism and from deep feeling and high tragedy to bombast and the grotesque. It is framed as a heroic symphony in the grand manner of Beethoven and Tchaikovsky and in the traditional four movements. A dynamic opening movement in sonata form, suggestive of struggle, is followed by a scherzo-like Allegretto (NAWM 154), an intensely sad slow movement, and a boisterous finale. The symphony outwardly conformed to the tenets of socialist realism, infusing the most prestigious nineteenth-century instrumental genre with an optimistic, populist outlook and adopting a clear, easily understood tonal language. For that reason, it provided the vehicle for Shostakovich's rehabilitation with the state. Yet it was also possible to hear in it messages of bitterness and mourning in the face of totalitarian repression. The Allegretto adopts the jarring contrasts of a Mahler scherzo, juxtaposing passages that evoke a variety of popular styles from waltz to fanfare. The sorrowful slow movement evokes traditional Russian funeral music; it prompted open tears at the premiere and has been seen by some as expressing sorrow at the Purges. The triumphalism of the final movement could also be interpreted as false enthusiasm. Such double meanings do not mean that Shostakovich was a dissident—there was no room for dissidence under Stalin—but by composing multivalent music, he could at once please the Party bosses and provide an outlet for emotions that had to remain unspoken.

CD 11|66

All of Shostakovich's works were created in a politicized context, and the search for double meanings has been widespread in the West and in Russia

Seventh Symphony

SOURCE READING

CENSURING SHOSTAKOVICH

After Shostakovich's opera Lady Macbeth of the Mtsensk District *had been performed widely to great acclaim, Stalin's government singled it out for censure with a negative review in* Pravda (Truth), *the Communist Party newspaper. Through this attack on the nation's leading composer, they signaled a crackdown on composers' artistic freedoms.*

———— • ————

From the first minute, the listener is shocked by deliberate dissonance, by a confused stream of sounds. Snatches of melody, the beginnings of a musical phrase, are drowned, emerge again, and disappear in a grinding and squealing roar. To follow this "music" is most difficult; to remember it, impossible.

Thus it goes practically throughout the entire opera. The singing on the stage is replaced by shrieks. If the composer chances to come on the path of a clear and simple melody, then immediately, as though frightened at this misfortune, he throws himself back into a wilderness of musical chaos—in places becoming cacophony. The expression which the listener demands is supplanted by wild rhythm. Passion is here supposed to be expressed by musical noise. All this is not due to lack of talent, or to lack of ability to depict simple and strong emotions in music. Here is music turned deliberately inside out in order that nothing will be reminiscent of classical opera, or have anything in common with symphonic music or with simple and popular musical language accessible to all. . . . The power of good music to infect the masses has been sacrificed to a petty-bourgeois, "formalist" attempt to create originality through cheap clowning. It is a game of clever ingenuity that may end very badly.

From "Chaos Instead of Music," as translated in Victor Seroff, *Dmitri Shostakovich: The Life and Background of a Soviet Composer* (New York: Alfred A. Knopf, 1943), 204–5. In SR 188 (7:19), pp. 1397–98.

after the fall of the Soviet Union. The Seventh Symphony (*Leningrad,* 1941) deals programmatically with the heroic defense of Leningrad against Hitler's armies, although some hear in its depiction of the totalitarian invaders a complaint against Stalin's repression as well. It was performed in London and New York in 1942 and immediately became a symbol of the war against Nazi Germany, in which the United States, Britain, and the Soviet Union were allies.

Later works   In the 1948 crackdown, Shostakovich was denounced along with Prokofiev and others, and he had to write patriotic film scores and choral paeans to the regime to gain rehabilitation. He wrote some of his music "for the drawer"—with no expectation of performance until the political atmosphere changed. In an assertion of individuality, he musically signed the third movement of the Tenth Symphony (1953, the year of Stalin's death) with a motive drawn from the German spelling of his name, D–E♭–C–B–in German nomenclature, D–Es–C–H, or D–S–C–H, from **D**mitri **SCH**ostakovich. He used the same motive in the Fifth and Eighth String Quartets (1952 and 1960) and the concertos for violin and for cello.

The ambivalence in Shostakovich's music reflects the accommodations he had to make to survive in a state where one could never say precisely what one felt, and thus where the arts—especially music—offered an outlet for what was otherwise inexpressible. The relative accessibility of his music combined with its impression of giving voice to inner feelings has won Shostakovitch many devoted listeners not only in Russia but throughout the world.

THE AMERICAS

In the New World, the interwar period saw the emergence of composers who gained prominence in their own countries and recognition in Europe, placing their homelands on the international stage for the first time. As with composers in the "peripheral" nations of Europe, these composers of the Americas found that creating a distinctive national style was often the only way to gain attention from an international audience. Their nationalism was sometimes infused with national politics but always linked to the cultural politics of securing for themselves and their countries a niche in the performing repertoire.

CANADA

Canada had a thriving musical life that developed along patterns similar to those in the United States. In both nations, performance of the European classical repertoire was far more central than playing music of homegrown composers in the classical tradition. Performing spaces, concert societies, bands, professional chamber ensembles, choral societies, and conservatories all emerged in Canada during the nineteenth century, and the twentieth century brought the founding of orchestras in most large cities, beginning with symphonies in Quebec (1903) and Toronto (1906).

The first Canadian composer to achieve an international reputation was Claude Champagne (1891–1965). He learned French-Canadian fiddle music and dance tunes in his youth, then as a young man was deeply influenced by Russian composers, from Musorgsky to Scriabin. During studies in Paris in 1921–28, he encountered Renaissance polyphony, Fauré, and Debussy, and saw in their modal practice links to the folk tunes of Canada. He developed a distinctive nationalist style in his *Suite canadienne* (Canadian Suite, 1927) for chorus and orchestra, blending elements from French-Canadian folk music and polyphonic French chansons with the symphonic tradition. His best-known piece, *Dance villageoise* (Village Dance, 1929), evokes both French-Canadian and Irish folk styles, acknowledging another ethnic strain in Canada and in his own heritage.

Claude Champagne

BRAZIL

Art music was well established in Brazil by the late nineteenth century, with successful operas by Gomes (see chapter 27) and others and with several composers of concert music who developed their own nationalist styles.

The most important Brazilian composer was Heitor Villa-Lobos (1887–1959), who drew together traditional Brazilian elements with modernist techniques. He spent the years 1923–30 mostly in Paris, where performances of his music won widespread praise and established him as the most prominent Latin American composer. He returned to Brazil in 1930 and, with government support, instituted a national effort to promote music in the schools and through choral singing. He was criticized for his collaboration with Brazil's nationalist dictatorship, akin to the totalitarian regimes of Europe at the time, but it is not clear whether he shared its ideology.

Heitor Villa-Lobos

The series of fourteen pieces titled *Chôros* (1920–28), after a type of popular ensemble music Villa-Lobos played in the streets of Rio de Janeiro in his youth, are among his most characteristic works. For various media, from solo guitar or piano to orchestra with chorus, each *Chôros* blends one or more vernacular styles of Brazil, typified by syncopated rhythms and unusual timbres, with modernist techniques such as ostinatos, polytonality, polyrhythms, and vivid orchestration to create a remarkably distinctive sound. Another series, the nine *Bachianas brasileiras* (1930–45), pays tribute to Bach and thus to the neoclassical trend of the times. Each is a suite of two to four movements combining elements of Baroque harmony, counterpoint, genres, and styles with Brazilian folk elements and long, lyrical melodic lines. This unique blend is exemplified in Villa-Lobos's most famous work, *Bachianas brasileiras No. 5* (1938–45) for solo soprano (mostly wordless) and eight or more cellos.

Chôros and Bachianas brasileiras

MEXICO

Beginning in 1921, the Mexican government began to support bringing the arts to a wide public and promoted a new nationalism that drew on native Indian cultures, especially from before the Spanish Conquest. As part of this effort, Diego Rivera and other artists were commissioned to paint murals in

Figure 33.5: The Day of the Dead Man *(1923–24), a fresco by Diego Rivera (1886–1957) for the Ministry of Public Instruction in Mexico City. This picture portrays a Mexican festival in a style that draws on pre-Columbian art.*

public buildings that illustrated Mexican life, such as the fresco shown in Figure 33.5.

Carlos Chávez   The first composer associated with the new nationalism was Carlos Chávez (1899–1978), who also served as conductor of Mexico's first professional orchestra and director of the national conservatory. He wrote two ballets on Aztec scenarios, and his *Sinfonía india* (Indian Symphony, 1935–36) uses Indian melodies in a modernist, primitivist idiom also apparent in his Piano Concerto (1938–40). Other works are not overtly nationalist, including his *Sinfonía romantica* (Symphony No. 4, 1953).

Silvestre Revueltas   Silvestre Revueltas (1899–1940) studied in Mexico and then in America before returning to assume the post of assistant conductor under Chávez. His compositions do not use folk songs but combine melodies modeled on Mexican folk and popular music with a modernist idiom. Characteristic is his *Sensemayá* (1938, NAWM 155), a symphonic poem—really a song without words—based on a poem by Cuban poet Nicolás Guillén. The poetic text, though never sung, is rendered syllabically by strings and trombones in three sections of the work, framed by interludes. Both poem and piece tell of an African-Cuban magical rite in which a large figure representing a snake is carried by a dancer and ritualistically put to death. Borrowing methods and textures from Stravinsky's *Rite of Spring*, Revueltas builds up a layered fabric

CD 11|74   CD 6|41

of ostinatos in irregular meters (mostly $\frac{7}{8}$) over which he juxtaposes melodies of contrasting characters and timbres and slowly builds to the climax.

THE UNITED STATES

American composers and performers developed new links with Europe between the wars, due in part to the immigration of many of Europe's leading composers for political or professional reasons. By the early 1940s, these refugees included Rachmaninov, Schoenberg, Stravinsky, Bartók, Milhaud, Krenek, Weill, and Hindemith. Americans had studied in Germany since the mid-nineteenth century, but World War I helped to foster a reorientation of American music away from Germany and toward France. Starting in the early 1920s, a steady stream of Americans went to France to study with Nadia Boulanger (1887–1979), renowned pedagogue and promoter of Fauré and Stravinsky, who taught classes in Paris and Fontainebleau until her death. Among those studying with her were Aaron Copland, Virgil Thomson, Roy Harris, Walter Piston, Ross Lee Finney, and Elliott Carter.

The interwar period also saw several new currents among American composers. Two of the most salient were an experimentalist or ultramodernist trend, focused on developing new musical resources, and an Americanist trend, blending nationalism with a new populism inspired by the Depression and by President Roosevelt's New Deal policies. The former group included Edgard Varèse, Henry Cowell, and Ruth Crawford Seeger, and the latter encompassed Aaron Copland, William Grant Still, Cowell's later works, and many others. Both currents asserted independence from Europe while still drawing on the European tradition. In order to secure performances for their music in a concert culture that focused on European masterworks, American composers formed their own organizations, including the International Composers Guild founded by Varèse, the League of Composers headed by Claire Reis, and Cowell's *New Music*.

EDGARD VARÈSE

The French-born Edgard Varèse (1883–1965) studied at the Schola Cantorum and Conservatoire, had a brief career in Paris and Berlin as a composer and as a conductor of early and contemporary music, and then moved to New York in 1915. Varèse celebrated his adopted country in his first major work, *Amériques* (1918–21). Its fragmentary melodies and loose structure betray links to Debussy. He was also influenced by Schoenberg, notably in the use of strong dissonance and chromatic saturation, and by Stravinsky, including the association of a musical idea with instrumental color, the avoidance of linear development, and the juxtaposition of disparate elements through layering and interruption.

Next came a series of works that laid down a new agenda: *Offrandes* (1921), *Hyperprism* (1922–23), *Octandre* (1923), *Intégrales* (1924–25), *Ionisation* (for percussion only, 1929–31), and *Ecuatorial* (1932–34). In these works,

Spatial music and sound-masses

Varèse aimed to liberate composition from conventional melody, harmony, meter, regular pulse, recurrent beat, and traditional orchestration. For Varèse, sounds as such were the essential structural components of music, which he defined as "organized sound," and he considered all sounds acceptable as raw material. He imagined music as **spatial,** akin to an aural ballet in which what he called **sound masses** moved through musical space, changing and interacting. A sound mass is a body of sounds characterized by a particular timbre, register, rhythm, and melodic gesture, which may be stable or may gradually be transformed. In Varèse's compositions, these sound masses collide, intersect, speed up, slow down, combine, split up, diffuse, and expand and contract in range, volume, and timbre. A great variety of percussion instruments, some drawn from non-Western cultures and others (such as the siren) from city life, play key roles, acting independently as equals to the winds and strings. For Varèse, form was not something you start with, but what results as you work with the material; typically, his pieces are organized as series of sections, each centered around a few sound-masses, some of which may carry over to later sections. In Varèse's entirely new conception of music, the listener must put aside expectations that music will be rhetorical or will develop organically, as in earlier styles, and must simply observe the interaction of "intelligent bodies of sound moving in space."

Electronic music   Since his music depended on sound itself, especially unusual ones, Varèse sought new instruments from the 1920s on. Only after World War II did the new resources of electronic sound generation and the tape recorder (discussed in chapter 34) make possible the realization of the sounds he heard in his mind, in his *Déserts* (1950–54) for winds, percussion, and tape and in the tape piece *Poème electronique* (1957–58).

HENRY COWELL

A native Californian, Henry Cowell (1897–1965) began composing as a teenager with little training in European music, and from the start he sought out new resources for music. Many of his early pieces are experimental, designed to try out a new technique. *The Tides of Manaunaun* (ca. 1917) uses **tone clusters,** chords of diatonic or chromatic seconds produced by pressing the keys with the fist or forearm, to represent the tides moved by Manaunaun, the legendary Irish sea-god. He used the technique so often, including in his Piano Concerto (1928), that it became identified as his invention, and Bartók once wrote Cowell asking permission to use clusters. In *The Aeolian Harp* (1923), the player strums the piano strings while holding down three- and four-note chords on the keyboard, as if playing a grand autoharp. In *The Banshee* (1925), an assistant holds the damper pedal down so that the strings can resonate freely while the pianist strums the strings, plucks some, and rubs along the length of the lower, wire-wound strings with the fingertips to create an eerie, voicelike howl similar to that of a banshee, a spirit in Irish legend. Besides new playing techniques, Cowell also explored new textures and procedures, such as giving each voice a different subdivision of the meter. He summarized his new ideas in his book *New Musical Resources* (1930).

Throughout his career, Cowell was interested in non-Western musics. He took an eclectic approach to composition, trying out everything that interested him rather than developing a single identifiable style. During and after the 1930s, Cowell turned from experimentalism to a more accessible language, often incorporating American, Irish, or Asian elements. He wrote a series of works called *Hymn and Fuguing Tune* for band or for orchestra, modeled on the style of William Billings and his contemporaries, alongside symphonies and other traditional genres. In the years after World War II, several pieces show his interest in Asian music and incorporate instruments such as the Indian tabla and the Japanese koto.

Cowell promoted music by his contemporaries as well as his own through concerts and through the periodical *New Music*, in which he published scores by Ives and other modernist and ultramodernist composers. His adventurous search for new resources and his interest in non-Western music had an enormous impact on younger composers, especially in the United States.

RUTH CRAWFORD SEEGER

Among the composers whose works Cowell published was Ruth Crawford (1901–1953), shown in Figure 33.6, the first woman to win a Guggenheim Fellowship in music. She was most active as a composer in Chicago between 1924 and 1929 and in New York between 1929 and 1933. In New York, she studied composition with the composer and musicologist Charles Seeger, whom she married in 1932. Seeger had developed theories about dissonant counterpoint, rhythmic freedom between contrapuntal voices, and other modern techniques that Crawford helped to refine and then applied in her own music. In her New York period she experimented with serial techniques, including their application to parameters other than pitch. Influenced by the New Deal, she became convinced that preserving folk songs would be a greater contribution to the nation's musical life than writing modernist works that few would hear or appreciate. She collaborated with writer Carl Sandburg and folklorists John and Alan Lomax, editing American folk songs from field recordings. She also published many transcriptions and arrangements in which she sought to be faithful to the songs' native contexts. Crawford stands out for her advocacy in preserving American traditional music and for being one of the very few women in the ultramodernist group.

Crawford's best-known work is the String Quartet (1931), composed while in Europe on a Guggenheim Fellowship. Each movement is different, embodying Crawford's constant search for new procedures. In the first movement, four thematic ideas unfold in dissonant counterpoint; rarely do two instruments attack a note at the same time, creating a sense of great independence between

Figure 33.6: Ruth Crawford in the 1920s, in a photograph by Fernand de Gueldre.

the parts. The second movement develops a short motive through counterpoint and convergence, creating rapid changes of accent and implied meter. The third movement features "heterophony of dynamics": while all four instruments sustain long tones, one instrument at a time comes to the fore through a crescendo, and the dynamically prominent notes are heard as a composite melody that builds to an intense climax. The finale (NAWM 156), shown in Example 33.3, is laid out in two-part counterpoint, pitting the first violin against the three other instruments playing in parallel octaves with mutes on. The first violin plays a single note, then two, three, four, and so on, adding one note with each phrase until it reaches twenty-one, gradually getting softer. In between its phrases, the other instruments, using a ten-note series, play rapid sixteenth-notes groups that decline from twenty notes to one, gradually getting louder, so that the two voices head in opposite directions in density and dynamics. At the end of this process, each part sustains its last tone, and then the entire musical fabric is repeated in retrograde, transposed up a semitone, to create a nearly perfect palindrome. Through four highly contrasting movements, Crawford simultaneously embraces the tradition of the string quartet and satisfies the ultramodernist desire for something truly new.

CD 11|83   CD 6|50

Example 33.3: Opening of the finale of Crawford's String Quartet

AARON COPLAND

Aaron Copland (1900–1990), shown in Figure 33.7, moved from stringent dissonance in the 1920s to a streamlined style in the 1930s and 1940s that combined modernism with national American idioms. Copland's Jewish faith, his homosexuality, and his leftist politics made him something of an outsider, yet he became the most important and central American composer of his generation through his own compositions and his work for the cause of American music. He organized concert series and composer groups and promoted works of his predecessors and contemporaries, including Ives, Chávez, and Virgil Thomson. Through encouragement, counsel, and by example, he influenced many younger American composers, among them Leonard Bernstein, Elliott Carter, and David Del Tredici.

Early works

Growing up in a Jewish immigrant family in Brooklyn, Copland was exposed to ragtime and popular music from a young age, while studying piano, theory, and composition in the European tradition. He was the first of many American composers to study in Paris with Nadia Boulanger, from whom he learned to write music that was clear, logical, and elegant. Jazz elements and strong dissonances figure prominently in his early works, such as *Music for the Theatre* (1925) and the Piano Concerto (1927).

Americanist style

Recognizing the growing number of radio and record listeners, Copland sought to appeal to a larger audience. At the same time, the Depression had

Figure 33.7: Aaron Copland in the 1930s, composing in his studio.

deepened his belief in socialism, and he turned to writing music in a language the broad masses of people could understand, on subjects that were relevant to their lives and concerns. He developed a new style by reducing his modernist technique to its essence of counterpoint, dissonance, and juxtaposition, then combining it with simple textures and diatonic melodies and harmonies. In some works, he borrowed traditional songs to suggest place and atmosphere. He incorporated Mexican folk songs in the orchestral suite *El Salón México* (1932–36) and cowboy songs in the ballets *Billy the Kid* (1938) and *Rodeo* (1942), which reflected the American frontier experience. His opera *The Second Hurricane* (1936)—written for schools—and his scores for a number of films including *Our Town* (1940) represent music composed specifically "for use."

Appalachian Spring

CD 11|86   CD 6|53

Copland's Americanist idiom is exemplified in *Appalachian Spring* (1943–44), first written as a ballet with an ensemble of thirteen instruments but better known in the arrangement as an orchestral suite (excerpt in NAWM 157). The work incorporates variations on the Shaker hymn *'Tis the Gift to Be Simple*. Example 33.4 shows two variations on the hymn's third phrase. The song is subtly transfigured and its essence is absorbed in music that sincerely and simply expresses the spirit of rural life in American terms. Copland's use of transparent, widely spaced sonorities, empty octaves and fifths, and diatonic dissonances creates a distinctive sound that has been frequently imitated and has become the quintessential musical emblem of America, used especially in music for film and television.

Later works

Copland's later works encompassed a variety of styles. His Americanist idiom continued in the Third Symphony (1946), but in the Piano Quartet (1950), the Piano Fantasy (1957), and the orchestral *Inscape* (1967), he

Example 33.4: Passages from Copland's Appalachian Spring, *showing two variations of the Shaker hymn's third phrase*

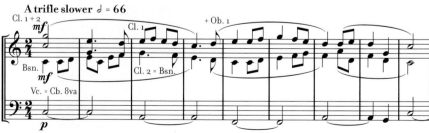

Figure 33.8: William Grant Still in an undated photograph.

adopted some features of twelve-tone technique. Perhaps he sought to cultivate a more abstract language during the 1950s, when the left-wing political
sympathies that lay behind his Americanist music came under attack. Despite
the range of styles he employed, Copland retained an unmistakable artistic
identity. His music preserves a sense of a tonal center, though seldom by traditional means. His rhythms are lively and flexible, and he was adept at obtaining new sounds from simple chords by exploiting instrumental color and
spacing.

WILLIAM GRANT STILL

William Grant Still (1895–1978), shown in Figure 33.8, also incorporated
specifically American idioms into art music. He drew on a diverse musical
background, including composition studies with George Whitefield Chadwick and Edgard Varèse and work as an arranger for W. C. Handy's dance
band. Still's success as a composer, when blacks were still largely excluded
from the field of classical music, earned him the sobriquet "Dean of Afro-
American Composers." He broke numerous racial barriers and earned many
"firsts" for his race—the first African American to conduct a major symphony orchestra in the United States (the Los Angeles Philharmonic, 1936);
the first to have an opera produced by a major company in the United States
(*Troubled Island* at New York's City Center, 1949); and the first to have an
opera televised over a national network. He composed over 150 compositions, including operas, ballets, symphonies, chamber works, choral pieces,
and solo vocal works.

Still established his reputation with the *Afro-American Symphony* (1930),
the first symphonic work by an African-American composer to be performed

Afro-American
Symphony

CD 12|1   CD 6|63

by a major American orchestra. The symphony encompasses African-American musical elements within the traditional framework of a European four-movement symphony. The opening movement (NAWM 158) is in sonata form, with a first theme in twelve-bar blues structure and a second theme that suggests a spiritual. It also features numerous other traits from African-American traditions: call and response, syncopation, varied repetition of short melodic or rhythmic ideas, jazz harmonies, dialogue between groups of instruments as in a jazz arrangement, and instrumental timbres common in jazz, such as trumpets and trombones played with Harmon mutes.

VIRGIL THOMSON

Virgil Thomson (1896–1989) was a witty and caustic critic for the *New York Herald-Tribune* (1940–54) as well as a composer. During studies at Harvard and in Paris with Nadia Boulanger, he fell under the influence of Satie, whom he met in 1922. Thomson later described Satie as the only influential composer of the time "whose works can be enjoyed and appreciated without any knowledge of the history of music," noting that "the only thing really hermetic and difficult to understand about the music of Erik Satie is the fact that there is nothing hermetic about it at all." Rejecting modernism's complexity, unfamiliarity, and obsession with the past classical tradition, Thomson adopted Satie's branch of avant-gardism and sought to write music that was simple, direct, playful, and focused on the present.

Four Saints in Three Acts   Between 1925 and 1940 Thomson lived in Paris. There he found a kindred soul in another American expatriate, Gertrude Stein, with whom he collaborated on the opera *Four Saints in Three Acts* (1927–28). Stein's libretto on the life of St. Teresa of Avila (see Figure 13.5) seems absurdist—for example, there are four acts, not three, and many more than four saints. Yet the words are not without meaning: "Pigeons on the grass, alas" is about a visitation of the Holy Spirit, often shown as a dove. The libretto's use of simple words in complex arrangements is precisely reflected in Thomson's music, which mixes dance rhythms from waltz to tango, hymnlike melodies, simple diatonic chords and progressions, evocations of marches and patriotic tunes, and other familiar elements and styles, often in wild and surprising juxtapositions. Throughout, the setting of texts shows an uncanny facility for turning American speech into fluid musical lines.

Other works   Much of Thomson's other music is more overtly Americanist. He evoked the simplicity of nineteenth-century hymnody in his *Variations on Sunday School Tunes* (1926–27) for organ and the *Symphony on a Hymn Tune* (1928). He wrote a series of "portraits" of friends and acquaintances, most for piano, some for chamber groups. His second opera, *The Mother of Us All* (1947), also a collaboration with Stein, is based on the life of the women's suffrage leader Susan B. Anthony. Its mix of hymnody, marches, and waltzes is direct and familiar but encompasses moments of deep sentiment. Like Copland, Thomson also wrote film scores, using American folk elements from cowboy songs to spirituals; indeed, he claimed that Copland had borrowed the Americanist style from him.

DIVERSITY OF STYLES

In addition to the composers mentioned here, the interwar period saw the emergence of George Gershwin as a composer in classical genres (see chapter 32) and the first publications and performances of the mature music of Charles Ives (see chapter 31), who was seen both as an ultramodernist and as an Americanist and thus was promoted by both Cowell and Copland. Other composers wrote in styles ranging from the neoclassical to the Romantic. The variety of American idioms between the wars illustrates the general point we have already seen in chapters 30 and 31. Most composers of art music sought a place in the crowded classical repertoire by writing music that was individual and distinctive yet drew on past traditions and genres. Meanwhile, the most radical composers—like Varèse, Cowell, and (in his own way) Thomson—each forged a new concept of music. For them, the best solution to the problem of competing with the past was to ignore it and focus on creating something fundamentally new.

WHAT POLITICS?

Art music between the wars includes some of the most widely performed classical works of the twentieth century. By now, listeners and musicians have largely forgotten the political circumstances in which most of this music was created. Audiences like Poulenc's sonatas, Orff's *Carmina burana*, Shostakovich's Fifth Symphony, or Copland's Americanist ballets without regard to the politics that shaped their creation. Indeed, the insistence on immediate wide appeal by authorities in totalitarian states seems to have helped the popularity of some works such as Prokofiev's *Romeo and Juliet* and *Peter and the Wolf*, which lack the dissonance and satire of his pieces composed in the West. Today Milhaud, Poulenc, Weill, and Thomson are admired for their wit and clarity, Hindemith for his summation of the German tradition from Bach through Brahms in a novel musical language, Shostakovich and Prokofiev for their highly emotional and passionate symphonic styles, and composers in the Americas for giving their national traditions a place in the classical tradition—all with little thought to the ideologies that swirled around these composers and the constraints under which they labored. Yet politics still shapes the reception of some of this music, as shown by the continuing controversy about whether Shostakovich meant his music to convey a dissident message.

The postwar depoliticizing of art music composed between the wars resulted in part from the idea that classical music is a thing apart, an idealized, autonomous art, a notion that continues today but has come under increasing scrutiny from historians and musicians. With historical distance comes a greater focus on the music itself and fading memories of the circumstances in which it was born. Moreover, the period after World War II saw a reaction in the West against not only Nazism but also communism and political ideologies in general, making overt links to politics a potentially embarrassing distraction for listeners. Copland's turn from populist Americanism to abstract twelve-tone music in the 1950s illustrates this reaction. Indeed, the least overtly political trend discussed in this chapter, the experimental tradition exemplified by Varèse, Cowell, and Crawford. grew in strength after the war, leading directly to postwar trends in North America and Europe.

In the long run, what seems most important about classical music between the wars, including that of the composers previously discussed in chapters 29 through 31, is its great variety. Most composers still sought a place in the permanent repertoire and tried to secure it by combining elements from the classical tradition with individual and innovative traits that distinguished their music from that of their peers. The varied styles that emerged resulted in part from different views of what was valuable in the past classics and in part from composers' differing circumstances. They transformed their ways of thinking, from the political to the personal, into music of unprecedented diversity. Among their works, there are riches for every taste.

Chapter 34

Postwar Crosscurrents

The central theme of Western music history since the mid-nineteenth century is a growing pluralism. With each generation, new popular traditions emerged in response to changes in society, and the heirs to the classical tradition created more diverse styles of art music at an ever increasing rate. This process accelerated in the twenty-five years after the end of World War II, propelled by an economic boom in the United States and most of western Europe, by ever more rapid communications, and by a desire among younger generations to explore new possibilities. Musicians developed new styles, trends, and traditions, including forms of popular music aimed principally at young people, such as **rock and roll** and its offshoots; styles of jazz, from **bebop** to **free jazz**, that demanded more concentrated listening; increasingly complex approaches to serial composition; music built of sound itself that employed new instruments, **electronic music**, or new sounds on orchestral instruments; applications of **indeterminacy** and **chance** in composition; and pieces based on **quotation** and **collage** of past music. In Europe, new music was often supported by governments, through radio stations and institutes, while in North America colleges and universities became major patrons of music, training young performers and music educators and supporting composers, new music ensembles, **wind ensembles**, and jazz programs.

CHAPTER OUTLINE

THE COLD WAR AND THE SPLINTERING TRADITION

The postwar expansion was achieved by generations who had suffered through the Depression and the most global and destructive war the

893

world had ever seen. Germany, Italy, and Japan were defeated by the Allies, but at great cost. Millions were dead: soldiers killed in action, civilians in bombing raids, and Jews and other victims in the Nazi death camps. Much of Europe lay in ruins, and many of the buildings, artworks, and musical scores Europeans had created over the centuries were destroyed. By dropping atomic bombs on Hiroshima and Nagasaki, the United States forced Japan to capitulate but inaugurated the atomic age, and in response the Soviet Union, Britain, France, and other nations developed their own nuclear arsenals. The horrors of war, the Holocaust, and nuclear weapons provoked a wide range of cultural reactions, from the French existentialist literature of Jean-Paul Sartre and Albert Camus to a growing fashion for horror and science fiction films.

The Cold War   At war's end, the Soviet Union occupied most of eastern Europe. By 1948, it reabsorbed Lithuania, Latvia, and Estonia, which were independent between the wars, and installed communist regimes under its control in Poland, Czechoslovakia, Hungary, Romania, and Bulgaria. Communist governments also took power in Yugoslavia, Albania, and China. Western nations responded with attempts to contain the expansion of communism. Interna-

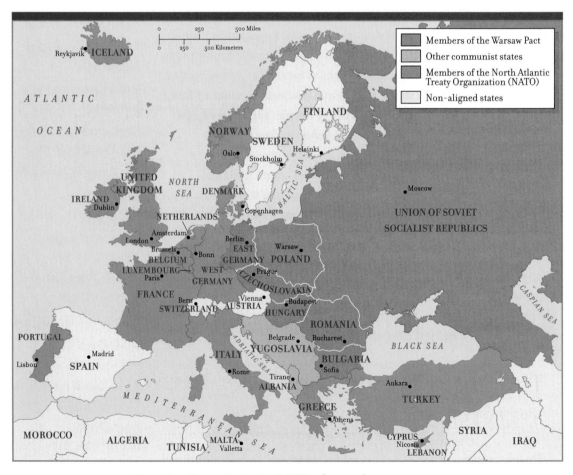

Figure 34.1: Europe during the Cold War (1945–91).

tional relations for the next two generations were framed by the political conflict, known as the Cold War, between the United States and the Soviet Union and their respective allies. Figure 34.1 shows the map of postwar Europe, divided between the North Atlantic Treaty Organization—an alliance of the United States, Canada, and European democracies—and the Soviet Union's parallel organization, the Warsaw Pact. Symbolic of the conflict was the division of Germany between a democratic, pro-Western government in West Germany and a communist government in East Germany.

New international institutions such as the United Nations, founded in 1945, furthered cooperation but could not defuse all tensions. At times the Cold War heated up, as in the Korean War (1950–53), Cuban missile crisis (1962), and Vietnam War (1954–75). It also played out in other types of competition, such as the race into space, won by the United States with the first moon landing in 1969. Music performance and composition, along with Olympic sports, chess, and other cultural fields, were used by both sides as arenas for competition.

The United States, least damaged by the war among the active participants, *Economic* enjoyed rapid economic growth. Technological innovations and expanded *expansion* manufacturing capacity boosted productivity, resulting in historically high incomes for factory and office workers that lifted most Americans into the middle class. Returning soldiers created both a baby boom and a housing boom, raising consumer demand. The G.I. Bill paid for veterans to go to college, producing a tremendous expansion of colleges and universities and of the numbers of citizens with university degrees, which further fueled economic growth. The number of families owning their own homes soared, and they bought cars, furniture, household appliances, and other goods at growing rates. Western Europe and Japan underwent similar economic growth, aided by investments from the United States. Cooperation through the Common Market and NATO wove western Europe together, making old nationalist tensions increasingly obsolete.

The expansion of higher education in North America and Europe was *Greater access* linked with growing access to the arts, and attendance at museums, concerts, *to music* and other cultural venues increased along with government and private support. Television and home stereo systems increasingly brought entertainment and music into the home. The 78-rpm records (disks rotating 78 times per minute) that were the mainstay of recordings before the war were replaced by long-playing records (LPs), which could accommodate more than twenty minutes of music per side, and 45-rpm "singles" became the main medium for popular songs. The invention of the transistor led to miniature, portable radios that could go anywhere, bringing broadcast music into cars and the outdoors. "Disc jockeys" played recordings of popular songs on the radio, replacing most of the live-music shows of previous decades. Tape recorders, invented during the 1930s and widely available from the 1950s on, improved the sound of recorded music, made electronic music possible, and put into the hands of individuals the tools for preserving and manipulating sounds.

Starting with British India in 1947, European colonies throughout Asia and *Independence* Africa won independence and emerged as new nations. The growing political *and civil rights* and economic significance of Asia and Africa encouraged cultural exchanges, leading to a rising interest in music of the non-Western world in the West and in American popular music throughout the world. The nonviolent strategies Mohandas Gandhi developed to win independence for India were adopted by Martin Luther King Jr. and others in the effort to win equal civil rights for African Americans, a movement in which music played a significant role as unifier and inspiration. The Civil Rights movement in turn inspired others in the 1960s and 1970s, from student organizations and protests against the Vietnam War to the women's and gay liberation movements.

Musical pluralism   The victory over fascism, the economic boom, new technologies, and the winds of freedom helped to inspire a period of unprecedented experimentation and diversification in music. Popular music splintered into traditions for different regions, ethnicities, affinity groups, and ages, each owing something to earlier popular song, blues, jazz, or swing while forging a distinctive identity. Composers of art music went in numerous directions, sharing less common ground as they explored new possibilities. Urban centers, mass media, and colleges and universities allowed musicians to find a small but devoted audience that would support specialized types of music, creating niche markets in which everything from early music groups to avant-garde rock bands could thrive. Musicians, critics, and listeners engaged in strident debates about music: whether rock music was a bad influence on the young or a source of freedom, whether jazz should hold to its traditions or search out new methods, whether classical composers should seek to appeal to a broad public or pursue a hermetic ideal in isolation. Among the dizzying number and variety of trends in this period, this chapter will describe some of the most important and distinctive.

POPULAR MUSIC

In the interwar years, popular music in the United States was closely allied to Broadway musicals and to jazz. But after the war, musicians took these traditions in separate directions.

Identity through music   Economic growth in the postwar years gave young people greater leisure time and more disposable income. For the first time, teenagers became significant for the marketing industry, and clothing, cosmetics, magazines, movies, and entertainment were designed for and marketed to them. Increasingly, young people had their own radios and record players, and they listened to and bought recordings of music that reflected their own tastes. Record companies responded by marketing specific kinds of music to the teen and young adult market that became known as ***pop music.*** Some types of music, like rock and roll, united most teenagers in the late 1950s and early 1960s, creating a "generation gap" between them and older generations. But as popular music continued to split into niche markets, people of all ages found that the music they listened to marked their identity as strongly as the clothes they wore and the ways they behaved. Each type of music had its own stars, fans, and radio programs, and the popularity of songs in each category was tracked on ***charts,*** weekly rankings by sales of 45-rpm singles.

COUNTRY MUSIC

One tradition, associated primarily with white southerners, was **country music** (also called *country-and-western*), a type of popular music with folk-music roots that began between the wars, spread through radio shows and recordings, and grew in popularity after World War II. As suggested by the painting in Figure 34.2, country music was a blend of many sources: the hill-country music of the southeast, based on traditional Anglo-American ballads and fiddle tunes; western cowboy songs and styles popularized by Gene Autry and other movie cowboys; popular songs of the nineteenth and early twentieth centuries; blues, banjo music, and other African-American traditions; big-band swing; and gospel songs. Such a combination of traditions across social and ethnic lines is typically American. Country music was valued for its energy, its sincere sentiments, its witty wordplay (part of its heritage from Tin Pan Alley), and its ability to articulate the experience of rural and working-class Americans in a rapidly changing world.

Typically country music centers on a singer strumming a guitar accompaniment, often joined by others singing in close harmony or backed by a band dominated by fiddles and guitars (eventually electric and pedal steel guitars).

Figure 34.2: The Sources of Country Music *(1975)*, *mural by Thomas Hart Benton for the Country Music Hall of Fame and Museum in Nashville, Tennessee. The sources depicted include (counter-clockwise from lower left) traditional Anglo-American ballads accompanied by Appalachian dulcimer, fiddle tunes played for dancing, cowboy songs with guitar accompaniment, African-American song and banjo traditions, popular songs (represented by the shows in the distant steamboat), traveling songs (represented by the train), and gospel songs and hymns.*

Several distinctive styles developed, including *western swing, honky-tonk,* and *bluegrass.* Two stars of postwar country music, Hank Williams (1923–1953) and Johnny Cash (1932–2003), reached both country and mainstream audiences. Nashville became the center of country music in part because of important venues such as the Grand Ol' Opry, made famous through radio and later television broadcasts. By the 1970s, there were country music stations all over the United States, and country became a nationwide style with continuing regional, racial, and class associations, much as New Orleans jazz had done fifty years earlier.

RHYTHM-AND-BLUES AND ROCK AND ROLL

In urban areas, a new sound known as **rhythm-and-blues** developed in the years just after World War II. Rhythm-and-blues groups typically included a vocalist or vocal quartet, a piano or organ, electric guitar, bass, and drums, and they performed mostly new songs built on twelve-bar blues or thirty-two-bar popular song formulas. Rhythm-and-blues is distinguished from traditional blues by insistent rhythm, with emphasis on the second and fourth beats—called the *back beats*—in $\frac{4}{4}$ meter; whining guitar; and a repetitive amplified bass line.

At first intended for an African-American audience, rhythm-and-blues reached white teenagers through radio and recordings. The teens were attracted to the sexual themes of the lyrics, the strong rhythms, and the intensity of the performances. Recognizing an opportunity, record companies produced *covers,* recordings by white singers of songs already popular in performances by black singers. For example, *Hound Dog,* a twelve-bar blues by the white songwriting duo Jerry Leiber and Mike Stoller, was a hit for black blues-singer Willie Mae "Big Mama" Thornton (1926–1984) in 1952, but sold millions more copies in the 1956 recording by Elvis Presley (1935–1977). In a time when African Americans were struggling for equal rights, the popularity of a black urban style of music among white teenagers was a force for change.

Rock and roll   Alan Freed, a popular radio disc jockey in Cleveland, is credited with coining **rock and roll** as a name for a new style that blended black and white traditions of popular music. Rock and roll combined the unrelenting beat of rhythm-and-blues with the milder guitar background of country music. The instrumentation consisted of amplified or electric guitars for both rhythm and melody, backed by electric bass and drums and sometimes augmented by other instruments. Song forms drew on Tin Pan Alley as well as blues, and rhythms and vocal styles encompassed everything from boogie-woogie to country twangs and gospel shouts. The words, most often concerned with love or sex, were often delivered in a raucous, sometimes wailing voice, although there were also gentle romantic ballads sung in a deliberately subdued mode. Both the words and the varied styles spoke directly to teens' experiences, creating a close identification between the listeners and their music.

Rock and roll was launched nationally in the 1955 film *Blackboard Jungle* with the hit song *Rock Around the Clock* by Bill Haley and the Comets. The first mega-star was Elvis Presley, who enjoyed phenomenal success with his hip-swiveling blend of country and rhythm-and-blues. By 1960, rock and

Figure 34.3: The British rock group the Beatles performing on the television series "The Ed Sullivan Show" on February 9, 1964. Already well-known in England, the Beatles became a worldwide cultural phenomenon. Their appearance on American television ushered in what became known as Beatlemania.

roll—soon simply called **rock**—was being heard all over the world, especially in English-speaking areas, and was outselling every other kind of music. Black rock-and-roll singer-songwriter Chuck Berry (b.1926) caught the bravado of the young displacing their elders in his 1956 hit *Roll Over, Beethoven:* "Roll over, Beethoven, and dig these rhythm and blues."

THE SIXTIES

By the early 1960s, many of rock's earliest stars had fallen off the pop charts. Into the void stepped the Beatles, a quartet from Liverpool, England, composed of two creative singer-songwriters, John Lennon (1940–1980) and Paul McCartney (b.1942); guitarist and songwriter George Harrison (1943–2001); and drummer Ringo Starr. "Beatlemania," already taking hold in the United Kingdom in 1963, reached the United States in February 1964 when the Beatles began an American tour, shown in Figure 34.3. After a few years of touring, the Beatles began devoting their energy to studio recordings, experimenting with techniques impossible to produce in a live setting. The resulting albums, especially *Sgt. Pepper's Lonely Hearts Club Band* (1967), embraced a wide variety of musical styles, from British music hall songs to Indian sitar music, in songs whose level of interest to connoisseurs began to rival that of classical music. Their example encouraged other rock bands to experiment with recording technology and to create rock-based music of depth.

The Beatles

Rock branches out

The Beatles' 1964 American tour began the "British Invasion," an influx into North America of British bands such as the Rolling Stones, the Kinks, the Animals, the Who, and Cream. Many of these bands were blues-based, influenced by African-American bluesmen such as Robert Johnson. The emphasis on blues and an increasing focus on electric guitar solos gave rock a harder edge. Guitar virtuosos such as Jimi Hendrix (1942–1970) and Cream's Eric Clapton (b. 1945) became for the electric guitar what Paganini and Liszt were for the nineteenth-century violin and piano; Hendrix's stunning solo on *The Star-Spangled Banner* at the outdoor rock festival Woodstock (1969) was both a protest against knee-jerk patriotism and an assertion of virtuosic prowess. As bands sought an individual sound, they developed many new styles within the broad tradition of rock: the California style of the Beach Boys; Steppenwolf's *heavy metal* style; the *hard rock* of Led Zeppelin and Aerosmith; the *acid rock* or *psychedelic rock* of Jefferson Airplane; and the *avant-garde rock* of Frank Zappa. Music and lyrics were youth-oriented, often expressing opposition to the prevailing political culture or social expectations.

Folk and protest music

In the postwar decades, rising interest in American folk songs led to a new kind of popular music that drew on folk traditions. Groups like the Weavers and Peter, Paul, and Mary performed genuine folk songs alongside new songs in similar styles. Although the latter by definition were popular songs (newly composed by known authors and sold through sheet music and recordings) rather than folk songs (which have unknown origins and are passed down orally), the whole tradition became known as **folk music.** In opposition to the increasing sophistication and professionalism of most other popular music, folk music was deliberately simple, featuring one or more singers with guitar or banjo accompaniment, and often the audience was encouraged to join in the singing. Like rock and roll, folk music was an important musical voice for expressing identity and ideology. Since the nineteenth century, singer-songwriters had adapted folk, popular, and hymn tunes to political ends by writing new texts in support of labor unions and other social causes. Many such songs were created for the Civil Rights movement, including the movement's anthem *We Shall Overcome*, adapted from a hymn. In the 1940s and 1950s, Woody Guthrie (1912–1967) and Pete Seeger (b. 1919), stepson of Ruth Crawford Seeger, were especially prominent as singers and songwriters of folk and protest songs.

In the 1960s, the struggles for civil rights and against the Vietnam War galvanized younger musicians such as Joan Baez (b. 1941) and Bob Dylan (b. 1941) who voiced the protests of their generation in their songs. Dylan's songs *Blowin' in the Wind* (1962) and *The Times They Are A-Changin'* (1963) combined traditional folk styles with simple guitar harmonies, a rough voice, blues harmonica, and a keen sense of poetry. By the mid-sixties, Dylan was using electric guitar in a blend of folk and rock traditions. His complex lyrics, marked by unusual rhymes, puns, alliteration, and apparently deep or hidden meanings, captivated a generation and inspired many other pop artists.

Soul

The leading African-American tradition of popular music in the 1960s was **soul,** a descendant of rhythm-and-blues in which the intense expression, melismas, and ecstatic vocalizations of gospel singing were brought over to songs on love, sex, and other secular subjects. Among the leading exponents

Figure 34.4: Ray Charles shown performing at the piano, in a photograph taken around 1960.

were singer-songwriter Ray Charles (1930–2004), shown in Figure 34.4, who popularized the new trend from the mid-1950s on; James Brown (b. 1928), the "King of Soul"; Otis Redding (1941–1967); and Aretha Franklin (b. 1942). Soul became closely associated with the struggle for African-American equality through Brown's *Say It Loud—I'm Black and I'm Proud* (1968) and Franklin's recording of Redding's *Respect* (1967).

Motown

The sounds of Motown—a Detroit-based record company founded and owned by African-American entrepreneur Berry Gordy (b. 1929)—dominated the soul charts of the 1960s and often crossed over to top the pop charts as well. Gordy's intention was to create popular music that would appeal to both black and white audiences. In-house songwriting teams and studio musicians produced a consistent, groomed sound for groups like Smokey Robinson and the Miracles, the Supremes, the Temptations, the Four Tops, and Martha and the Vandellas. Other significant performer-composers who got their start at Motown include Marvin Gaye (1939–1984), Stevie Wonder (b. 1950), and Michael Jackson (b. 1958).

Tex-Mex and salsa

Latino-Americans produced their own styles of music, drawing on traditions from Central or Latin America. In Texas and the southwestern United States, *Tex-Mex* combined Mexican mariachi music with American country music. In New York City and Puerto Rico, a distinctive type of dance music called **salsa** emerged in the 1960s. Salsa is a mix of Cuban dance styles with jazz, rock, and Puerto Rican musical elements. A typical salsa ensemble includes ten to fourteen members on vocals, piano, Cuban percussion (such as timbales, claves, and conga drums), bass, and brass. Each instrument plays a distinctive rhythm, forming a driving dance beat of interlocking, polyrhythmic ostinatos. Championed by Tito Puente (1923–2000) and other performers, salsa embodied the rich ethnic mix of New York's music scene and offered the Puerto Rican immigrant community a distinct musical identity.

Pluralism and hybrids   The diversity of popular traditions shows the pluralism of modern society but also its common threads. Although identified with a particular group of people, each of these traditions represents a blend of elements from several sources, including common roots in prewar popular song, jazz, and blues. Popular music in other nations likewise blended local and regional traditions with elements absorbed from American popular styles. Although the traditional music of a culture or region once helped provide a sense of common identity for all generations, the emergence of new styles of popular music in each region reflected and reinforced tensions between older and younger generations and between rural and urban populations.

BROADWAY AND FILM MUSIC

Musicals   Broadway musicals maintained their traditions after World War II, mostly separate from trends in popular music. The emphasis on integrated musicals that began with *Show Boat*—in which all aspects of the production support the plot—continued. As in the past, most Broadway shows were collaborations, and the great songwriting teams produced hit tunes well into the 1960s. Composer Richard Rodgers (1902–1979) initially collaborated with lyricist Lorenz Hart (1895–1943) and later with Oscar Hammerstein II (1895–1960), and Frederick Loewe (1904–1988) wrote music for the books and lyrics of Alan Jay Lerner (1918–1986). Irving Berlin was still active, producing classics such as *Annie Get Your Gun* (1946) and *Call Me Madam* (1950), and Cole Porter had one of his biggest hits with *Kiss Me, Kate* (1948), based on Shakespeare's *The Taming of the Shrew*. Successful musicals tended to find their way to Hollywood films within a few years and were also quickly disseminated to the public through recordings and productions by touring, amateur, and, in later years, high school theater groups.

Rodgers and Hammerstein   Rodgers and Hammerstein produced some of Broadway's best-loved shows, including *Oklahoma!* (1943), *Carousel* (1945), *South Pacific* (1949), *The King and I* (1951), and *The Sound of Music* (1959). Shown in Figure 34.5, their first collaboration, *Oklahoma!*, not only enjoyed a record-breaking run of over two thousand performances but also marked a pivotal moment in the development of the integrated musical. Set in the Oklahoma territory around 1900, the story is richly textured, filled with both dramatic and comedic subplots. The characters are developed not only through dialogue but also through song. Dance, choreographed by famed dancer Agnes de Mille, also played a crucial dramatic role. The story's emphasis on American folk history and the simple pleasures of rural life appealed greatly to Americans during war time and the early postwar years.

Figure 34.5: The original Broadway cast from the 1943 musical production of Oklahoma!, *the first collaboration between Richard Rodgers and Oscar Hammerstein II.*

Leonard Bernstein

Leonard Bernstein (1910–1990) was a major presence both on Broadway and in classical music. Initially known as a classical composer, he became an overnight celebrity in 1944 after brilliantly conducting the New York Philharmonic as a last-minute replacement. That same year, his Broadway musical *On the Town* opened for a run of 463 performances. In addition to his career as a conductor and composer of symphonies and vocal music, Bernstein enjoyed enormous success with his musical *West Side Story* (1957), with lyrics by Stephen Sondheim (b. 1930) and book by Arthur Laurents. Set in gang-ridden New York City of the 1950s, *West Side Story* is a retelling of Shakespeare's *Romeo and Juliet*, substituting rival gangs for the warring families of the original. The setting provided Bernstein with rich opportunities for including a variety of musical styles, including Afro-Caribbean dance styles, jazz, and soaring melodies in Tin Pan Alley AABA formulas.

Later Broadway

In the 1960s, Broadway musicals diversified their subject matter and therefore adapted styles from other traditions. Jerry Bock evoked Jewish folk music for *Fiddler on the Roof* (1964), set in a Russian Jewish village, and Galt MacDermot's *Hair* (1967), a picture of urban hippie life, uses a rock band and emulates Motown, acid rock, and folk music alongside traditional Broadway styles.

TIMELINE: POSTWAR CROSSCURRENTS

1935	1940	1945	1950	1955	1960	1965	1970	1975

- 1939 Germany invades Poland, beginning World War II
- **1941 Olivier Messiaen, *Quartet for the End of Time***
- **1943 Rodgers and Hammerstein's *Oklahoma!* opens on Broadway**
- **1944–45 Benjamin Britten, *Peter Grimes***
- 1945 World War II ends with defeat of Germany and Japan
- **1945 Charlie Parker and Dizzy Gillespie, *Anthropology***
- 1948 United States launches Marshall Plan for economic development of western Europe
- 1949 North Atlantic Treaty Organization formed
- 1949 George Orwell, *1984*
- **1949–50 Miles Davis, *Birth of the Cool***
- **1950 First piece of musique concrète**
- 1950–53 Korean War
- **1951 John Cage, *Music of Changes***
- **1952–53 Samuel Barber, *Hermit Songs***
- 1953 United States and Soviet Union both test hydrogen bombs
- 1953 Francis Crick and James Watson discover structure of DNA
- **1955 Bill Haley and the Comets, *Rock Around the Clock***
- 1958 European Common Market formed
- **1960 Bernard Herrmann, film score to *Psycho* •**
- **1960 Ornette Coleman, *Free Jazz* •**
- **1960 Krzysztof Penderecki, *Threnody* •**
- 1962 Cuban missile crisis •
- **1962 Bob Dylan, *Blowin' in the Wind* •**
- 1963 President John F. Kennedy assassinated •
- **1964 The Beatles' first American tour •**
- **1964 Milton Babbitt, *Philomel* •**
- **1966 Moog and Buchla synthesizers introduced •**
- **1967 Aretha Franklin records *Respect* •**
- **1967 The Beatles, *Sgt. Pepper's Lonely Hearts Club Band* •**
- 1968 Students riot in Paris, antiwar protests in United States •
- **1968 Karel Husa, *Music for Prague 1968* •**
- 1969 Neil Armstrong and Buzz Aldrin are first humans on the moon •
- **1969 Half a million people attend Woodstock outdoor rock festival in Bethel, •** New York
- **1970 George Crumb, *Black Angels* •**

FILM MUSIC

Film music also diversified in the postwar years, as composers chose styles and sounds that were appropriate to the subject and mood. Miklós Rózsa (1907–1995) developed several different styles, from an angular, contrapuntal, yet tonal modernism that helped to define the movie genre of *film noir* to a mock-ancient style for historical epics such as *Ben Hur* (1959). The score to *A Streetcar Named Desire* (1951) by Alex North (1910–1991) popularized the use of jazz to represent urban settings, sexual situations, and social ills from alcoholism to crime. Leonard Bernstein used a dissonant modernist style in his score for *On the Waterfront* (1954), and others adopted atonal and serial music where their tense emotional qualities were appropriate. Bernard Herrmann (1911–1975) was famous for his scores to Orson Welles's *Citizen Kane* (1941) and Alfred Hitchcock's *Vertigo* (1958), *North by Northwest* (1959), and *Psycho* (1960), whose dissonant tonal language drew on Ives, Berg, Hindemith, and other modernists. Westerns often featured music in the diatonic Americanist style championed by Copland in his ballets and film scores, but the Italian composer Ennio Morricone (b. 1928) created a new, pop-influenced style for his Western scores, including *The Good, the Bad and the Ugly* (1967). National and ethnic traditions helped to establish place and atmosphere, from Mikis Theodorakis's score for *Zorba the Greek* (1964) to the blend of traditional and Western elements in the film music of India, China, and Japan. Electronic music was used frequently for psychologically upsetting events, the strange or supernatural, and space aliens.

Popular music continued to be a strong element in postwar film. In his jazz-influenced score to *Laura* (1944), David Raksin (1912–2004) introduced a theme song that was woven throughout the film and became a hit song in its own right. Many later films also featured theme songs, whose presence on the pop charts could earn additional income and advertise the film. Rock and other forms of pop music appeared in movies aimed at the teen market, from *The Blackboard Jungle* and a series starring Elvis Presley to the beach movies of the 1960s. The Beatles' *A Hard Days Night* (1964) was a financial success both as a film and as a soundtrack recording, and many other movies followed a similar model of marketing the film and soundtrack together.

FROM BEBOP TO FREE JAZZ

The three decades from 1940 to 1970 witnessed the emergence of several new styles of jazz, the continuation of older styles, and a growing consciousness of jazz history and a desire to preserve it. Jazz lost its role as a form of popular music when it was replaced by rhythm-and-blues and other styles. Instead, jazz was increasingly regarded as music that demanded concentrated listening. Although most of the major jazz artists were African American, many of the performers and the great majority of the audience for jazz were white.

In the years immediately following the end of World War II, financial support for big bands declined sharply. More musicians now joined smaller groups, called *combos*. The styles they played differed from region to region and group to group.

BEBOP

A new style of jazz built around virtuosic soloists fronting small combos, known as **bebop** or **bop,** emerged in the early 1940s during the waning years of the swing craze. In New York City, soloists playing with swing bands began to meet in after-hours clubs after their regular engagements finished for the evening. Clubs such as Minton's Playhouse and Monroe's Uptown House offered these musicians the opportunity to pit their skills against each other in "cutting contests," playing standards at blistering speed or in difficult keys to weed out the less-talented musicians. Out of these cutting contests grew a new musical language that became known as bebop.

Characteristics   Bebop was rooted in standards from the swing era, in blues progressions, and in other popular sources for contrafacts, but it was newly infused with extreme virtuosity, harmonic ingenuity, unusual dissonances, chromaticism, complicated rhythms, and a focus on solo voices and improvisation. A typical bebop combo featured a rhythm section of piano, drums, bass, and one or more melody instruments, such as trumpet, alto or tenor saxophone, or trombone. In contrast to big-band music, bebop was meant not for dancing but for attentive listening. The focus was on the star performers and their prowess as improvisers. Performances in which one of the players was essentially the composer are preserved on recordings that have become classics, listened to over and over again, analyzed, and reviewed in critical essays.

Anthropology   A characteristic example of bebop is *Anthropology* (NAWM 159), by alto saxophonist Charlie Parker (1920–1955, nicknamed "Bird") and trumpeter Dizzy Gillespie (1917–1993), shown in Figure 34.6. Like many other bebop standards, *Anthropology* is a contrafact on the "rhythm changes"; that is, it features a new melody over the chord progression for Gershwin's *I Got Rhythm* (see chapter 32 and NAWM 151 and 152). A bebop performance normally begins with an introduction and then the *head*, the primary tune, played in unison or octaves by the melody instruments. Players perform from an abbreviated score called a lead sheet (shown in NAWM 159a), which includes only the head, with chord symbols indicating the harmony. The tune for *Anthropology* is typical in consisting of short, rapid bursts of notes separated by surprising rests, creating a jagged, unpredictable melody. The head is followed by several choruses, solo improvisations over the harmony, and the piece ends with a final statement of the head. In the classic recording of *Anthropology,* Parker played a sizzling solo of unusual length (transcribed in NAWM 159b), taking up three choruses while he surrounded the chord changes with a flurry of chromatic alterations. This solo has been learned by countless younger saxophonists who sought to emulate Parker's sound and style.

In addition to Gillespie and Parker, prominent bebop musicians included trumpeter Miles Davis (1926–1991) and in their early careers saxophonist

CD 12|8   CD 6|70

Figure 34.6: Alto saxophonist Charlie Parker and trumpeter Dizzy Gillespie performing with bassist Tommy Potter and tenor saxophonist John Coltrane, in a photograph taken on stage at the legendary Birdland in New York City, ca. 1950.

John Coltrane (1926–1967); pianists Thelonious Monk (1917–1982) and Bud Powell (1924–1966); and drummers Kenny Clarke (1914–1985) and Max Roach (b. 1924).

AFTER BEBOP

Many of these musicians pioneered new jazz styles in the 1950s, seeking paths for individual expression by extending the methods and ideas of bebop. Miles Davis was behind a series of innovations, beginning with his album *Birth of the Cool* (1949–50). Its softer timbres, more relaxed pace, and rhythmic subtleties inaugurated the trend that became known as *cool jazz*, soon taken up by the Modern Jazz Quartet, Dave Brubeck (b. 1920), and many others. Whereas bebop had begun as an improvising soloists' music, *Birth of the Cool* put the composer-arranger front and center.

A contrasting style was *hard bop*, dominated by drummers such as Kenny Clarke, Max Roach, and Art Blakey (1919–90), which focused on the percussive and propulsive side of jazz. Miles Davis (*Kind of Blue*, 1959) explored yet another new style known as *modal jazz*, which featured slowly unfolding melodies over stable, relatively static modal harmonies. The new jazz styles from bebop on have been compared by some historians to the multiplicity of modern styles in twentieth-century classical music, and they derive from a similar source: a desire to say something new in a distinctive style that remained rooted in the tradition.

In the 1960s, Ornette Coleman (b. 1930) and his quartet introduced a more radically new jazz language known as **free jazz**, named after their

Avant-garde jazz

landmark album *Free Jazz* (1960). This experimental style moved away from jazz standards and familiar tunes, turning instead to a language built of melodic and harmonic gestures, innovative sounds, atonality, and free forms using improvisation that was carried on outside the strictures and structures of standard jazz forms. John Coltrane developed a personal avant-garde style based on very fast playing, motivic development, new sonorities, and greater dissonance and density of sound. Like avant-garde composers, creators of free jazz and other avant-garde jazz styles question some of the basic assumptions of the tradition yet clearly draw from it.

JAZZ AS A CLASSICAL MUSIC

While some jazz performers were pursuing new alternatives, others maintained older styles, reviving ragtime and New Orleans jazz or continuing to play swing. In a striking parallel to the rise of the classical concert repertoire over a century earlier, by 1970 the jazz world had developed its own roster of classics that were treasured on recordings and kept alive in performance. A sense of history was inculcated by written histories and recorded anthologies of jazz. As younger listeners turned to rhythm-and-blues and other new traditions, jazz increasingly became music for the well-informed listener. Jazz critics and historians began to describe jazz as a kind of classical music. Jazz ensembles were formed at many schools, colleges, and universities beginning in the 1950s and 1960s, and jazz history became part of the curriculum. Now respected as an art music, jazz nonetheless retained some of the aura of the rebellious popular music it had been half a century before.

HEIRS TO THE CLASSICAL TRADITION

The tradition of classical music performance became stronger than ever during the postwar years. Audiences grew, government support in many nations rose, schools of music expanded, and music education in primary and secondary schools increased in quantity and quality. But the living composers who saw themselves as participants in the tradition shared less and less common ground, with little consensus on style, aesthetic, or purpose. Some composers sought to preserve and extend particular aspects of the tradition, from audience appeal to modernist complexity, while others focused on the new. After two world wars, nationalism had come to seem a dangerous relic of the past, and neoclassicism an inadequate response to modernity. In every nation there was a diversity of styles and approaches, and ideas that began in one place were often imitated elsewhere. Thus it makes sense to divide our survey, not by nation, but by large trends, using individual composers as case studies.

THE NEW PATRONAGE

A few composers, such as Stravinsky and Copland, were able to support themselves with commissions, royalties, and income from conducting or performances. Other composers required patronage, but without the kings and aristocracy of earlier times, it had to come in new forms. In Europe, composers were supported by the state, through radio stations, annual subsidies, grants, arts agencies, or educational institutions.

In the United States and Canada, many composers were employed as teaching faculty in universities, colleges, and conservatories, giving them time to compose, a ready audience, and access to performing organizations, including ensembles set up to perform new music. Since colleges and universities prize academic freedom, the music coming from academic composers has been diverse, varying from traditional styles to avant-garde and experimental. Indeed, the safety of tenure and the ivory tower tended to isolate composers from the public and make them independent of its support. To a great extent, the type of music encouraged at a school varied with the composers who taught there. Among many refugees from Europe, Schoenberg taught at the University of California at Los Angeles, Milhaud at Mills College in Oakland, California, and Paul Hindemith at Yale. Walter Piston, a Nadia Boulanger student who taught at Harvard, encouraged a neoclassical approach, while Princeton was dominated by approaches derived from Schoenberg and Webern, particularly through the influence of Roger Sessions and his student and colleague Milton Babbitt. The Universities of Illinois and Michigan were also important centers, where annual festivals of contemporary music served as forums for both avant-garde and traditional approaches.

The university as patron

TRADITIONAL MEDIA

Although critical discussion has often focused on new sounds and techniques, many postwar composers used traditional media. Like their forebears, they sought an individual voice within the classical tradition.

OLIVIER MESSIAEN

Olivier Messiaen (1908–1992), shown in Figure 34.7, was the most important French composer born in the twentieth century. A native of Avignon in southern France, he studied organ and composition at the Paris Conservatoire, was organist at St. Trinité in Paris from 1931 on, and became professor of harmony at the Conservatoire in 1941. After the war, he taught many important composers of the younger generation, including his fellow Frenchman Pierre Boulez (b. 1925), the German Karlheinz Stockhausen (b. 1928), the Italian Luigi Nono (b. 1924), and the Netherlander Ton de Leeuw (b. 1926). It is a tribute to the quality and impartiality of Messiaen's teaching that each pupil went his own way.

A devout Catholic, Messiaen composed many pieces on religious subjects, such as the *Quatuor pour la fin du temps* (Quartet for the End of Time) for violin, clarinet, cello, and piano, written at a German military prison camp in 1941 for performance by the composer and three fellow prisoners; *Vingt regards sur l'Enfant-Jésus* (Twenty Looks at the Infant Jesus, 1944) for piano;

Figure 34.7: Olivier Messiaen.

Example 34.1: *Messiaen*, Liturgie du cristal *from* Quatuor pour la fin du temps

a. *Opening measures*

* Glissando bref; id. aux passages similaires.

b. Durational pattern in piano

c. Durational pattern in cello, with nonretrogradable rhythms

his opera *Saint Francis of Assisi* (1975–83); and numerous works for his own instrument, the organ. Other principal compositions include *Turangalîla-symphonie* (1946–48) and *Catalogue d'oiseaux* (Catalogue of Birds, 1956–58) for piano.

Messiaen sought to embody in music a stance of ecstatic contemplation. His works typically present an experience of concentrated meditation on a few materials, like a musical mantra. Rather than developing themes, he juxtaposes static ideas, showing his heritage from Debussy and Stravinsky. Messiaen used several characteristic devices, described in his book *The Technique of My Musical Language* (1944), that helped him achieve his goal of writing meditative music. The opening movement of the *Quatuor pour la fin du temps*, titled *Liturgie de cristal* (Crystal Liturgy, NAWM 160), illustrates several of them, as shown in Example 34.1.

Music as contemplation

CD 12|16   CD 6|75

Messiaen often wrote down birdsongs in musical notation and used them in several compositions, where they convey a sense of contemplating the gifts of nature and the divine. In Example 34.1, both the violin and clarinet play figures that suggest birdcalls, repeating them at irregular intervals.

Birdcalls

What Messiaen called *modes of limited transposition* are collections of notes, like the whole tone and octatonic scales, that do not change when transposed by certain intervals; for example, an octatonic scale transposed a minor third, tritone, or major sixth will yield the same set of notes. Such scales lack the differentiation of diatonic scales and so do not create a strong desire for resolution, making them well suited for music designed to suggest contemplation and a negation of desire. In *Liturgie de cristal*, the cello notes are all from a single whole tone scale, in a repeating sequence of five notes (C–E–D–F♯–B♭).

Modes of limited transposition

Messiaen's harmony also avoids moving forward to a resolution. Rather, chord series are simply repeated to create a sense of stasis or meditation. In this movement, the piano plays a succession of twenty-nine chords six times (the last incomplete); the second statement begins in measure 8.

Harmonic stasis

Messiaen treats rhythm as a matter of duration, not meter. Meter, as a se-ries of beats organized in measures, is a human or worldly thing, associated with dance and heartbeats. When we respond to music metrically, we are in our bodies, but when we attend instead to durations we are in the realm of time, ruled by the divine In Example 34.1, the changing note-lengths in the cello and piano do not create a sense of syncopation against a metric frame-work; instead, the smooth, legato playing style makes us hear patterns of shorter and longer durations. Throughout the movement both piano and cello

Duration, not meter

play repeated patterns of durations that resemble the *talea*, or repeating rhythmic pattern, of medieval isorhythm (see chapter 6). The piano features a series of seventeen durations played ten times, of which the first two statements appear in the example. Against this talea, the twenty-nine-chord series acts like the *color* in medieval isorhythm. Similarly, the cello has a talea of fifteen durations, framing its five-note color. These repeating pitch and rhythmic series create cyclic repetition, which again invites contemplation.

Additive and nonretrogradable rhythms

Example 34.1b and c show the piano and cello taleae written out in integral note values (without ties). The piano talea features a device Messiaen used to emphasize duration over meter: what he called *added values*, such as the dotted eighth note amid even eighths or the lone sixteenth note, which add a small durational value to produce units of irregular length. The cello part includes another Messiaen trademark that he dubbed *nonretrogradable rhythms*, which are the same forwards and backwards; as shown by brackets, the first three notes form one such rhythm, the next twelve another. Such patterns preserve their identity outside of time—whether heard in normal time or reverse time, they are the same—and thus symbolize the eternal, that which exists outside of time.

Beautiful sounds

Finally, Messiaen preferred beautiful timbres and colorful harmonies. Here, the cello plays in high harmonics (sounding two octaves above the notated pitches), creating an ethereal sound, augmented by the gentle birdcalls in the high violin and clarinet, over soft dissonances in the piano. Messiaen invites us to meditate on these sonorous objects as they constantly recombine in new ways yet remain the same, like colorful shapes in a kaleidoscope.

BENJAMIN BRITTEN

If Messiaen focused on music of contemplation, English composer Benjamin Britten (1913–1976) was concerned primarily with communication. After studying privately and at the Royal College of Music, Britten spent several years in the late 1930s writing music for films, an experience that shaped his style by teaching him to communicate through the simplest means. Like Copland, he tempered modernism with simplicity to achieve a clear and widely appealing idiom. Maturing in the 1930s, he was deeply influenced by humanitarian concerns and ideals of public service, manifest in his interest in writing music for children and amateurs, his allegorical pleas for tolerance, and his pacifism.

Music for amateurs

The English choral tradition was nurtured in church and cathedral choirs, schools, and amateur choruses. Most of Britten's choral music was conceived for such groups, and works such as *Hymn to St. Cecilia* (1941–42), *A Ceremony of Carols* (1942), and *Missa brevis* (1959) have become standards. His one-act opera *Noye's Fludde* (Noah's Flood, 1957–58), on the text of a medieval miracle play, is intended for a mixture of professional performers with children of various ages and includes hymns that the audience is invited to sing. These and his other works for nonprofessionals are melodious, challenging pieces that suit their performers' abilities yet are not limited by them.

Homosexuality

Britten was a homosexual and was the life partner of the tenor Peter Pears (1910–1986). Shown in Figure 34.8, the two met in 1936 and lived together

Figure 34.8: Benjamin Britten (right) and Peter Pears on the balcony of the Old Mill Snape, ca. 1944, when Britten was working on his opera Peter Grimes.

until Britten's death four decades later. Britten wrote most of his tenor roles for Pears, and the two collaborated as performers and as producers of the annual music festival at Aldeburgh in England. Several of Britten's operas have themes that relate to homosexuality, including *Billy Budd* (1950–51) and *Death in Venice* (1971–74).

Peter Grimes (1944–45), which established Britten's reputation and became the first English opera since Purcell to enter the international repertory, centers on a fisherman who is disliked by the other residents of his village, pursued by mobs, and ultimately driven to suicide. The theme of the individual persecuted by the crowd can be read as an allegory for the condition of homosexuals in a hostile society. Tellingly, Grimes is not a sympathetic character; we are meant to see ourselves, not in him, but in the ugly crowd that unthinkingly persecutes outsiders on the basis of suspicions and misinformation, forcing a poignant catharsis in the final tragedy. In the last scene (NAWM 161), as a search party pursues him calling his name, Grimes raves and mocks them in an unmeasured recitative, until his friend Balstrode urges him to sail his boat out to sea and sink it. The opera ends with a stunning depiction of the uncaring sea and equally uncaring townsfolk in a most successful application of bitonality: strings, harp, and winds arpeggiate thirds that encompass all the notes of the C-major scale, depicting the shimmering sea, as the town's citizens go about their business, singing a slow hymn to the sea in A major. The entire scene displays the eloquent dramatic effects Britten creates out of simple means.

Peter Grimes

CD 12|17

War Requiem

Britten's pacifism—his conscientious objection to war in any form—is expressed in his choral masterpiece, the *War Requiem* (1961–62). Commissioned for the consecration of the new cathedral at Coventry, a city destroyed in a German bombing raid during World War II, the work weaves together the Latin text of the Requiem Mass with verses by Wilfred Owen, English soldier and poet killed in France in 1918 just days before the end of World War I. The Latin texts are set for soprano soloist, chorus, boys' choir, and full orchestra, the Owen for alternating tenor and baritone soloists with chamber orchestra. Ironies abound. As the chorus sings "Requiem aeternam" (Grant them eternal rest), they hammer home a tritone (F♯–C), the least restful of intervals but the tonal axis of the entire work. Britten interleaves the English texts so that they comment on the Latin, as in the "Lacrimosa," where the melodic links between the soprano's Latin and the tenor's English verses highlight the futility he feels at the death of a friend in battle.

Britten's commitment—to pacifism, to tolerance, to including all ages and talents in music-making—gives his music a quality of social engagement that has attracted many performers and listeners and has inspired later composers.

TONAL TRADITIONALISM

Many twentieth-century composers developed individual styles without departing radically from the past. Tonality or neotonality often, though not necessarily, characterizes their music. Seeking to communicate with as varied a public as possible, these composers offered listeners a thread that can be followed through identifiable themes, readily audible forms, and programmatic subjects or titles. The most successful also discovered the secret of inspiring performers to champion their music, creating works that musicians are eager to play more than once.

Samuel Barber

Of the American composers who remained committed to tonality, one of the most successful was Samuel Barber (1910–1981). His tonal romanticism is fully expressed in his best-known work, *Adagio for Strings* (arranged from the slow movement of his String Quartet, 1936), and in his Violin Concerto (1939) and Piano Concerto (1962). He often incorporated modernist resources into his tonal music; for example, his Piano Sonata (1949) uses twelve-tone rows in a tonal framework. Barber was renowned for his vocal music, including *Dover Beach* (1931) for voice and string quartet, *Knoxville: Summer of 1915* (1950) for voice and orchestra, and three operas. The songs in his cycle *Hermit Songs* (1952–53), on texts by medieval Irish monks and hermits, are always tonally centered, yet each offers a novel blend of traditional tonality with modern resources. For instance, the eighth song, *The Monk and His Cat* (NAWM 162), shown in Example 34.2, is solidly in F major yet features almost no consonant harmonies. Barber uses open fifths in the bass line to suggest a medieval atmosphere and dissonant augmented unisons (B♭–B♮ and E–E♭) in the piano to suggest the cat. Against the steady rhythm of the piano, the vocal melody projects the natural text accentuation in a syncopated, flexible line. This song shows Barber's ability to write music that sounds fresh, like no other music, while using only traditional resources.

CD 12|23   CD 6|76

Example 34.2: Barber, The Monk and His Cat, from Hermit Songs

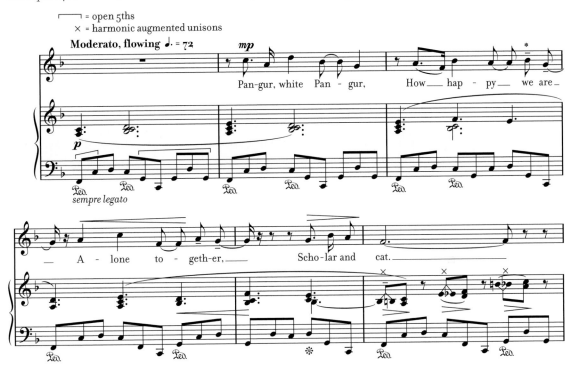

*Notes marked (–) in these two measures should be slightly longer, pochissimo rubato.

STYLISTIC MIXTURES

The wide dissemination of music from all over the world encouraged composers to mix styles and traditions. Some blended their own national or regional traditions with international ones, while other composers incorporated elements from distant lands.

Alberto Ginastera (1916–1983) of Argentina, the most prominent Latin American composer after Villa-Lobos, drew on both nationalism and international sources. He divided his own career into three periods. His "objective nationalism" (to 1947), typified in *Danzas argentinas* for piano (1937), is characterized by tonal music infused with traditional Argentine folk elements. In the second period, "subjective nationalism" (1947–57), he forged an original style through a Bartók-like synthesis of native and international elements, as in *Pampeanas No. 1* for violin and piano (1947) and *No. 2* for cello and piano (1950). His "neo-expressionism" (after 1957) combines earlier traits with twelve-tone and avant-garde techniques, as in his operas *Don Rodrigo* (1963–64), *Bomarzo* (1966–67), and *Beatrix Cenci* (1971). Ginastera's turn from nationalism to a more abstract style is typical of the postwar era.

Latin America: Ginastera

In the 1950s and 1960s, as jazz was being taken more and more seriously, some American composers who were conversant with both jazz and classical

Third Stream

music sought consciously to merge the two. One of the most successful of these, Gunther Schuller (b. 1925), called this combination "third stream." In his *Transformation* (1957), a pointillistic twelve-tone context with elements of Schoenberg's *Klangfarbenmelodie* is transformed into a full-blown modern jazz piece.

Michael Tippett   Englishman Michael Tippett (1905–1998) represents a different kind of synthesis, remarkably open to historical, ethnic, and non-Western styles and

---

SOURCE READING

COMPOSITION AS RESEARCH

Milton Babbitt, professor of music and of mathematics at Princeton University, argued that composers, like scientists, engage in research that advances knowledge and should be supported for that work, even if it lies beyond most people's comprehension. His view extends in new terms the nineteenth-century view of music as an autonomous art to be pursued for its own sake. This excerpt is from an essay he wrote under the title "The Composer as Specialist," changed by an editor at the magazine where it first appeared to the more provocative "Who Cares If You Listen?"

———— • ————

Why should the layman be other than bored and puzzled by what he is unable to understand, music or anything else? It is only the translation of this boredom and puzzlement into resentment and denunciation that seems to me indefensible. After all, the public does have its own music, its ubiquitous music: music to eat by, to read by, to dance by, and to be impressed by. Why refuse to recognize the possibility that contemporary music has reached a stage long since attained by other forms of activity? The time has passed when the normally well-educated man without special preparation can understand the most advanced work in, for example, mathematics, philosophy, and physics. Advanced music, to the extent that it reflects the knowledge and originality of the informed composer, scarcely can be expected to appear more intelligible than these arts and sciences to the person whose musical education usually has been even less extensive than his back-

ground in other fields. But to this, a double standard is invoked, with the words "music is music," implying also that "music is *just* music." Why not, then, equate the activities of the radio repairman with those of the theoretical physicist, on the basis of the dictum that "physics is physics"? . . .

. . . I dare suggest that the composer would do himself and his music an immediate and eventual service by total, resolute, and voluntary withdrawal from this public world to one of private performance and electronic media, with its very real possibility of complete elimination of the public and social aspects of musical composition. By so doing, the separation between the domains would be defined beyond any possibility of confusion of categories, and the composer would be free to pursue a private life of professional achievement, as opposed to a public life of unprofessional compromise and exhibitionism.

But how, it may be asked, will this serve to secure the means of survival for the composer and his music? One answer is that after all such a private life is what the university provides the scholar and the scientist. It is only proper that the university, which—significantly—has provided so many contemporary composers with their professional training and general education, should provide a home for the "complex," "difficult," and "problematical" in music.

From Milton Babbitt, "Who Cares If You Listen?," *High Fidelity* 8, no. 2 (February 1958): 39–40. In SR 174 (7:5), 1305–11.

materials. The rhythmic and metrical independence Tippett assigned to instrumental parts derived partly from English Renaissance music. The Piano Concerto (1953–55) and the Triple Concerto for violin, viola, and cello (1979) reveal Tippett's admiration for Javanese gamelan music, the first in its textures and instrumental combinations, the second in its use of a Javanese melody with rippling figuration and sounds such as gongs in the accompaniment of the slow movement. As we will see below, many other composers drew on Asian music as part of their exploration of new sounds and textures.

SERIALISM

After World War II, young composers in Germany and elsewhere embraced music that the Nazi regime had condemned, especially that of Schoenberg and Webern. By the early 1950s, many composers had adopted twelve-tone methods, adapting them to their own purposes. We have seen that established composers like Stravinsky and Ginastera took up serialism, but it had its most profound impact on the generation of composers who were just beginning their careers at the end of the war. Their interest was partly musical, reflecting enthusiasm for new possibilities, and partly political, expressing a rejection of the Nazi and communist ideologies that had opposed such dissonant and esoteric music.

The new developments were encouraged by government-sponsored musical institutions, such as the courses for new music held in Darmstadt, West Germany each summer beginning in 1946 (with the secret assistance of the United States' occupying forces). At a memorial concert of his works at Darmstadt in 1953, Webern was hailed as the father of a new movement. In the United States, serialism was adopted by many university composers and others, even Copland, as a way to achieve a music free of nationalist, fascist, or leftist ideology and thus escape the taint of politics many styles had acquired during the 1930s and early 1940s. Government and university support was crucial, since there was never a large or enthusiastic audience for serial music. Some saw that as a virtue, allowing music to advance in its own terms, like physics, without having to please the untutored listener (see Source Reading). *Politics and institutional support*

The ideas fostered at Darmstadt and other centers for new music inspired experiments by composers in many countries. But every composer worked independently, striking out in new directions, cultivating a personal language and style. Pierre Boulez of Paris and Karlheinz Stockhausen of Cologne, both pupils of Messiaen, became the two principal composers of the Darmstadt group, and Milton Babbitt (b. 1916; see Figure 34.11 below) became the leading serial composer and theorist in the United States. *Individualism*

EXTENSIONS OF SERIALISM

Beginning in the late 1940s, composers applied the principle of Schoenberg's tone rows to musical parameters other than pitch, giving rise to what has been called ***total serialism.*** If the twelve notes of the chromatic scale could be serialized, so could durations, intensities, timbres, and other elements, although typically only some nonpitch elements are treated serially, and the rest are used to highlight the serial structure. Other new extensions included methods of deriving subsidiary rows from the main series of a work, using fragments of a row, and subjecting rows to various other transformations.

Milton Babbitt   Babbitt combined series of pitches and of durations and manipulated them by the usual operations of inversion and retrograde in his Three Compositions for Piano (1947), the first piece to apply serial principles to duration. His music quickly grew more complex, as he went beyond the practices of Schoenberg and his circle to realize new potentials of the twelve-tone system.

The opening bars of Babbitt's Third String Quartet (1970), shown in Example 34.3, illustrate the complexity of his approach. There are eight layers or voices, each instrument having two voices, arco (bowed) and pizzicato (plucked). At the beginning, each voice has its own row form and transposition, as marked in the example. Babbitt so arranged it that each of four groups of voices—the arco voices, the pizzicato voices, the violins, and the lower strings—features one of each type of row form (prime, inversion, retrograde, and retrograde inversion). Moreover, although none of the rows is completely stated in this passage, each segment of approximately two measures includes all twelve pitch-classes (the E of the second segment is delayed to measure 5 in violin I), in an extension of Schoenberg's principle of combinatorial rows (see chapter 31).

Rhythm is serialized by analogy to the pitch series. The basic row, shown in Example 34.3a, can be stated as a series of numbers, indicating the number of semitones each note lies above the first note, F. Babbitt translates these numbers into what he called "time-points" within the measure, with 0 indicating the first sixty-fourth note of the $\frac{3}{8}$ bar and 11 the last. In this opening passage, these time-points are expressed by the dynamics. The notes marked *forte* (in any instrument) occur at time-points 0, 11, 6, 7, and 5, the first five elements of P-0, in that order. Meanwhile, the notes marked *piano* occur at time-points 1, 9, and 8, corresponding to the opening of R-5 (F♯–D–D♭, respectively 1, 9, and 8 semitones above F); the *fff* notes at time-points 2 and 10, the opening of R-6 (G–E♭); and the *ppp* notes at time-points 4 and 3, the opening of P-4 (A–A♭). The four row segments articulated in this way by the dynamics are the same four that appear in the pitches of the first two measures of the piece: the first five notes of P-0 are in violin II, the first three notes of R-5 in the viola, and the first two notes of R-6 and P-4 in violin I and cello respectively. In addition to these connections, there are many other intervallic and rhythmic relationships that weave the instrumental strands into a unified texture, achieving maximum interrelatedness of material.

Pierre Boulez   Composers in Europe explored similar ideas, independent of Babbitt. In *Mode de valeurs et d'intensités* (Mode of Durations and Intensities), the third of *Quatre études de rythme* (Four Rhythmic Studies, 1949) for piano, Messiaen created a "mode" comprising thirty-six pitches, each assigned a specific duration, dynamic level, and articulation to be used every time that

Example 34.3: Babbitt, String Quartet No. 3

a. Basic row

b. Measures 1–6, with row forms and time-points indicated

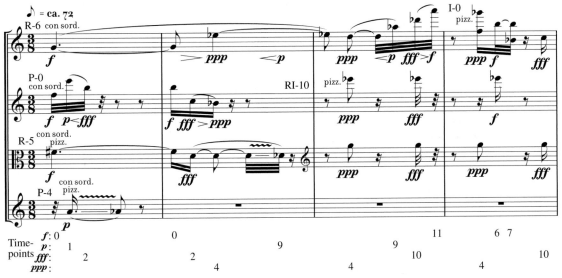

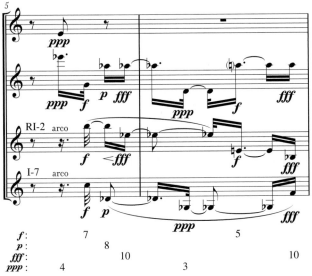

pitch occurred. Although the pitches were arranged in three divisions, each including all twelve chromatic notes, the piece itself was not serially organized. But it inspired Messiaen's former pupil, Pierre Boulez, to write the first European work of total serialism, *Structures* (1952) for two pianos, in which pitches and durations are both serial and dynamics and articulation are used to distinguish rows from one another.

Boulez soon relaxed the rigidity of total serialism. In *Le marteau sans maître* (The Hammer without a Master, 1954, revised 1957), he fused the pointillist style and serial method with sensitive musical realization of the text. This work in nine short movements is a setting of verses from a cycle of surrealist poems by René Char, interspersed with instrumental "commentaries." The ensemble—a different combination in each movement, as in Schoenberg's *Pierrot lunaire*—comprises alto flute, xylorimba, vibraphone, guitar, viola, and a variety of soft percussion instruments. The ensemble produces a translucent scrim of sound, all in the middle and high registers, with effects often suggestive of Balinese gamelan music. The contralto vocal line is characterized by wide melodic intervals, glissandos, and occasional Sprechstimme.

The listener   A totally serial composition may give a listener an impression of randomness, because music based on these principles typically lacks readily perceived themes, a distinct rhythmic pulse, and a sense of progression toward points of climax. Instead, the listener hears only unrepeated and unpredictable musical events. To be sure, the totality of these events in a well-constructed work does form a logical pattern, but it will inevitably be unique, likely resembling nothing the listener has heard before, and therefore difficult to perceive. As a result, postwar serial music has enjoyed an enduring unpopularity, appealing principally to a small set of enthusiasts.

NONSERIAL COMPLEXITY AND VIRTUOSITY

The music of total serialism was extraordinarily difficult to perform. For the structure to be clear in a work like Babbitt's Third Quartet, not only must the pitches and rhythms be absolutely accurate, but the dynamics must be exact—every *ff* exactly that and not *f* or *fff*. In the postwar years, a new generation of technically proficient performers emerged who were capable of playing such works and who made careers as champions of the newest music. Their presence encouraged composers to write pieces to challenge the skills of these new virtuosos. Much of this new music was not serial, but drew on sounds and textures like those explored in serial music.

Luciano Berio   The new virtuosity is well represented by the series of works by Italian composer Luciano Berio (1925–2003) titled *Sequenza*, each for an unaccompanied solo instrument from flute (1958) to accordion (1995–96) and each composed for a specific performer. The excerpt from *Sequenza IV* for piano

(1965–66) in Example 34.4 shows the rapid gestures and sudden changes of register and dynamic level that are typical of the work. The atonal language, figuration, and textures Berio uses here resemble those of his earlier serial music. Throughout, he uses the sustain pedal (which holds the dampers off the strings for notes that are being held when the pedal is pressed) to allow open strings to continue sounding or to catch harmonics from other notes, creating an unusual effect.

Example 34.4: Berio, passage from Sequenza IV *for piano*

The American composer Elliott Carter (b. 1908) also wrote for virtuoso performers, using a complex, nonserial style characterized by innovations in rhythm and form. Beginning with his Cello Sonata (1948), Carter developed what he called *metric modulation*, in which a transition is made from one tempo and meter to another through an intermediary stage that shares aspects of both, resulting in a precise proportional change in the value of a durational unit.

Elliott Carter

The passage from his String Quartet No. 2 (1959) in Example 34.5 illustrates Carter's methods. In this work, each instrumental part takes on a distinctive personality that interacts with the others as if in a dramatic work. The instruments are differentiated by their most prominent intervals: the first violin dwells on minor thirds and perfect fifths, the second violin on major sixths and sevenths, the viola on tritones and ninths, the cello on perfect fourths and minor sixths. They are also distinguished by rhythm: rapid even notes in the first violin, regular punctuations in the second violin, triplets in the viola, and a notated accelerando in the cello, with a dotted arrow indicating license to speed up smoothly rather than exactly as notated. The first violin effects the metric modulation: what was a sixteenth-note quintuplet in measures 57–58 is renotated as a sixteenth note in measure 59, then in measure 60 the dotted eighth (equal to three sixteenths) becomes the beat, creating a 3:5 proportion in tempo, from 112 beats per minute to 186.7. There is also a proportion of 8:5 between the first violin and the second violin, whose chords articulate a tempo of 70 attacks per minute. The result is a counterpoint of sharply differentiated lines, inspired in part by the multilayered textures in the music of Ives, whom Carter knew in his youth.

Example 34.5: Carter, metric modulation in String Quartet No. 2

The performance difficulties of works like these has meant that they are seldom performed and are known mainly through recordings. Yet, like nineteenth-century virtuoso showpieces, the best of these pieces attract some of the top performers and are likely to endure.

NEW SOUNDS AND TEXTURES

One prominent strand in twentieth-century music was the exploration of new musical resources, including new sounds and new conceptions of music. In the postwar period, the search for new resources intensified. Among all the variety, at least four overlapping trends can be identified: the use of new instruments, sounds, and scales; incorporation of non-Western sounds and instruments; electronic music; and music of texture and process.

NEW INSTRUMENTS, SOUNDS, AND SCALES

In their effort to offer something new and distinctive in art music, many composers sought out new sounds, sometimes building new instruments or reconfiguring traditional ones, and some explored scales featuring intervals smaller than a semitone.

Over the course of a long and influential career, John Cage (1912–1992) sought to bring into music sounds, approaches, and ideas that previously had been excluded. He repeatedly challenged the core concepts of music itself and thereby played a leading role in the postwar avant-garde (see below). His music in the late 1930s and 1940s focused on new sounds, building on the work of his teacher Henry Cowell. He wrote numerous works for percussion ensemble, using both traditional instruments and untraditional ones, such as tin cans of varying size and pitch in *Third Construction in Metal* (1941) and an electric buzzer and electronically amplified noises in *Imaginary Landscape No. 3* (1942).

John Cage

Cage's experimentation with timbre culminated in his invention of the **prepared piano,** in which various objects—such as pennies, bolts, screws, or pieces of wood, rubber, plastic, weather stripping, or slit bamboo—are inserted between the strings, resulting in delicate, complex percussive sounds when the piano is played from the keyboard. Essentially, the prepared piano is a one-person percussion ensemble, with sounds that resemble drums, woodblocks, gongs, and other standard or unusual instruments. Cage's *Sonatas and Interludes* (1946–48) is his best-known work for prepared piano, consisting of twenty-six "sonatas"—movements in two repeated parts, as in a Scarlatti sonata, but without thematic returns—and four interludes. The pianist prepares the piano in advance, following detailed instructions concerning what objects to place between the strings and where to put them, and each movement explores a different set of timbres and figurations.

Prepared piano

One composer who combined the exploration of new instrumental sounds with a new approach to pitch was Harry Partch (1901–1974), who undertook an individualistic, single-minded search for new sonic media. He repudiated equal temperament and Western harmony and counterpoint to seek a wholly new system inspired partly by Chinese, Native American, Jewish, Christian, African, and rural American music. His writings speak of a "monophonic" musical ideal, harking back to the ancient Greeks. Partch devised a new scale with forty-three notes to the octave based on just intonation, in which notes relate to each other through pure intervals from the harmonic series. He then built new instruments that could play in this scale, including modified guitars, marimbas, tuned cloud-chamber bowls (large glass containers used in early particle physics), a large string instrument like the ancient Greek kithara, and the gourd tree, shown in Figure 34.9. In his multimedia works of the 1950s and 1960s, these instruments accompany speaking and chanting voices and dancing by singer-actor-dancers. *Oedipus—A Music-Dance Drama* (1951) and *Revelation in the Courthouse Park* (1962), based on Euripides' *The Bacchae*, aspired to the ideal of Greek tragedy.

Harry Partch

George Crumb (b. 1929) has been most imaginative in coaxing new sounds out of ordinary instruments and objects. In *Ancient Voices of Children* (1970), a cycle of four songs on poems by Federico García Lorca with two

George Crumb

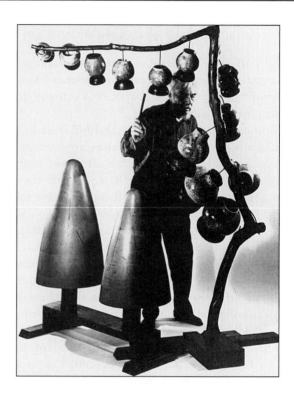

Figure 34.9: Harry Partch playing the gourd tree, one of the instruments he invented to realize his music based on his forty-three-note untempered scale. Beside him are two cone gongs.

instrumental interludes, unusual sound sources include toy piano, musical saw, harmonica, mandolin, Tibetan prayer stones, Japanese temple bells, and electric piano. He obtained special effects also from conventional instruments: for example, players must bend the pitch of the piano by applying a chisel to the strings, thread paper in the harp strings, and tune the mandolin a quarter tone flat. In *Black Angels* (1970, NAWM 163), a string quartet is electronically amplified to produce surrealistic dreamlike juxtapositions. The composer explored unusual means of bowing, such as striking the strings near the pegs with the bow and bowing between the left-hand fingers and the pegs. The new and unusual effects in Crumb's music always have a musical purpose, providing material for juxtaposition and variation, and usually evoke extramusical associations as well. Here, they help to express his reactions to the Vietnam conflict, the social unrest in the United States, and the horrors of war.

CD 12|26

NON-WESTERN STYLES AND INSTRUMENTS

Growing sensitivity to the perspectives of other cultures led to an exploration of their music with respect for its uniqueness, rather than invoking the "foreign" for its sheer otherness as in nineteenth-century exoticism.

Asian influences

Several Western composers became fascinated with Asian instruments, sounds, and textures. We have seen that Tippett, Cage, and Partch drew on ideas from Asian music. Canadian-American composer Colin McPhee (1900–1964) studied music in Bali in the 1930s, transcribed gamelan music for Western instruments, and composed *Tabuh-tabuhan* (1936) for orchestra and many other pieces that drew on Balinese materials. Henry Cowell's lifelong interest in Asian music grew after World War II, and travels to Iran, India, and Japan led to several works that blended Asian and Western elements, including *Persian Set* (1957) for chamber orchestra, Symphony No. 13 "Madras" (1956–58), *Ongaku* (1957) for orchestra, and two concertos for the Japanese koto (a plucked string instrument) and orchestra (1961–62 and 1965). Cowell's student and friend Lou Harrison (1917–2003) combined interests in just intonation and inventing new instruments, inspired by Partch, with enthusiasm for the music of Asia. After visiting Korea and Taiwan in 1961–62, Harrison wrote several works that combine Western and Asian instruments, including *Pacifika Rondo* (1963) and *La Koro Sutro* (1972), and beginning in the 1970s he composed dozens of pieces for traditional Javanese gamelan.

Interest in linking Asian and Western traditions extended as well to Asian composers familiar with European styles. Western music, both classical and popular, became well known in Asia over the course of the twentieth century, and by midcentury many Asians were writing music in the European classical tradition. Among the most inventive and best-known was Tōru Takemitsu (1930–1996), who wrote music for Western ensembles and inspired by European influences, such as *Requiem* for strings (1957), before turning in the 1960s to the music of his native Japan and blending the two traditions. His *November Steps* (1967) is a sort of double concerto, contrasting the sonorities of the Japanese shakuhachi (a bamboo flute) and biwa (a pear-shaped lute) with those of a Western orchestra. Takemitsu often combined Japanese and Western instruments and techniques in his many film scores, such as the score for Akira Kurosawa's *Ran* (1985).

Japan: Takemitsu

ELECTRONIC MUSIC

As new technologies developed, musicians explored their potential. No technology promised more far-reaching changes for music than the electronic recording, production, and transformation of sounds. These technologies were first exploited in art music but ultimately became more significant for popular music, especially after 1970 (see chapter 35).

One approach was to work with recorded sounds, taking the entire world of sound as potential material for music, manipulating the chosen sounds through mechanical and electronic means, and assembling them into collages. Pierre Schaeffer (1910–1995), who pioneered music of this type at Radiodiffusion Française (French Radio) in Paris in the 1940s, named it **musique concrète** because the composer worked concretely with sound itself rather than with music notation. He and his collaborator Pierre Henry created the first major work of musique concrète, *Symphonie pour un homme seul* (Symphony for One Man), premiered in a 1950 radio broadcast. Tape recorders, which became widely available around that year, made it possible to record, amplify, and transform sounds, then superimpose, juxtapose, fragment, and arrange them as desired to produce pieces of music.

Musique concrète

Another source for new sounds was to produce them electronically. Most electronic sounds are created by oscillators, invented in 1915. The first successful electronic instrument was the Theremin, invented around 1920 by Lev Termen, which changed pitch according to the distance between the

Electronic sound

instrument's antenna and the performer's hand. The Ondes Martenot, invented in 1928 by Maurice Martenot, was controlled by a wire, ribbon, or keyboard. Both instruments produced only one note at a time, were capable of glissandos along the entire pitch continuum, and projected a haunting, almost voice-like sound. Featured in some orchestral works, they became common in film scores like Hitchcock's *Spellbound,* where they lent an eerie or futuristic effect, but they were not used in electronic music itself.

Electronic music studios   Between 1951 and 1953, studios to create electronic music were founded at Columbia University in New York and at radio stations in Cologne (Germany), Milan (Italy), and Tokyo (Japan), followed by many others across Europe and the Americas. At most studios, composers focused on producing sounds electronically and manipulating them through electronic devices and on tape. A whole new realm of possible sounds became available, including sounds not producible by any "natural" means.

Gesang der Jünglinge *and* Poème electronique   Karlheinz Stockhausen and others often used recorded sounds alongside electronic ones, as in his *Gesang der Jünglinge* (Song of the Youths, 1955–56), which incorporated a boy's voice. This was the first major electronic piece to use multiple tracks, played in concert through several loudspeakers placed in various positions relative to the audience, which created a sense of the music coming from numerous directions and moving through space. Varèse's *Poème electronique* (Electronic Poem, 1957–58) also combined electronic sounds with recorded ones, from noises to a singer, and represented a pinnacle of his concept of spatial music. Commissioned by the Philips Radio Corporation for the Brussels Exposition in 1958, the eight-minute piece was projected by 425 loudspeakers ranged all about the interior space of the pavilion designed by Le Corbusier, shown in Figure 34.10, accompanied by moving colored lights and projected images. Fifteen thousand people a day experienced this multimedia piece over a six-month period, so that it was probably heard by more people than any other serious work of electronic music.

Figure 34.10: The Philips Pavilion at the 1958 World's Fair in Brussels, Belgium. Edgard Varèse collaborated with the architect Le Corbusier to fill this building with the sound of Poème electronique, *composed at the Philips laboratories at Eindhoven in the Netherlands.*

Figure 34.11: Milton Babbitt at the console of the Mark II RCA Synthesizer at the Columbia-Princeton Electronic Music Center in New York.

Synthesizers

Electronic music was at first produced by combining, modifying, and controlling in various ways the output of oscillators, then recording these sounds on tape. The composer had to splice the tapes and mix their output, sometimes in combination with recorded sounds of physical objects in motion or of musicians, speakers, or singers. Electronic sound synthesizers were developed to make the process much easier. The composer could call on pitches from a music keyboard and with switches and knobs control harmonics, waveform (which determines timbre), resonance, and location of sound sources. The RCA Mark II Synthesizer, shown in Figure 34.11, was developed at the joint Columbia-Princeton Electronic Music Center in the late 1950s and used by many composers from the United States and abroad.

In the mid-1960s, Robert Moog and Donald Buchla each developed far simpler and more compact synthesizers based on voltage-controlled oscillators. When these became commercially available in 1966, they were adopted by electronic music studios and individual composers around the world. One of the early works created on the Buchla synthesizer was *Silver Apples of the Moon* (1967) by Morton Subotnick (b. 1933), the first electronic piece to be commissioned by a record company, designed to fill two sides of an LP and to be played at home rather than in concert. The new synthesizers were also adopted by popular artists such as the Beatles, and electronic synthesizers soon became a familiar sound in pop music.

The electronic medium gave composers complete, unmediated control over their compositions. Much of the new music already demanded complex rhythms and minute shadings of pitch, intensity, and timbre that could barely be realized by human performers, but in the electronic studio, every detail could be accurately calculated and recorded. Yet the absence of performers hindered the acceptance of purely electronic music, since audiences expect to

Role of performers

have performers to watch and respond to, and since performers are the main promoters and advocates for new music.

Tape and live performance

CD 12|28   CD 6|79

Recognizing this, composers soon began to create works that combined prerecorded tape with live performers. One of the most moving early examples was Milton Babbitt's *Philomel* (1964, first section in NAWM 164), for soprano soloist with a tape that includes altered recorded fragments of the singer as well as electronic sounds. The live voice and the voice on tape engage in dialogue, accompanied by synthesized sounds, all worked out according to Babbitt's usual serial procedures.

MUSIC OF TEXTURE AND PROCESS

Varèse's conception of music as spatial, with sound-masses moving through musical space and interacting with each other like an abstract ballet in sound, opened the door to music that centered not on melody, harmony, or counterpoint but on sound itself. Moreover, the exploration of electronic sounds stimulated the invention of new sound effects obtainable from conventional instruments and voices, often imitating electronic music. Composers now wrote pieces whose material consists primarily of striking sound combinations that create interesting and novel textures, organized by gradual or sudden processes of change.

Iannis Xenakis

One of the first to write such music for acoustic instruments was Iannis Xenakis (1922–2001). A Greek who spent most of his career in France, Xenakis was an engineer and architect as well as a composer. Like the ancient Greeks, he saw mathematics as fundamental to both music and architecture, so he based his music on mathematical concepts. In *Metastaseis* (1953–54), he gave each string player in the orchestra a unique part to play. In many sections of the work, each player has a glissando, moving slowly or quickly in comparison to the other parts. In Figure 34.12, Xenakis plotted out the glissandos as straight lines on a graph that add up to create an effect of curves in musical space. He then transferred the lines to standard musical notation. The resulting motions, of a chromatic cluster gradually closing to a unison or a unison expanding to a cluster, resemble changes achievable in electronic music through the use of pitch filters. The overall effect is very strongly visual, although the materials are musical. Indeed, Xenakis later applied the same idea of straight lines creating a curving effect in the design for the Philips Pavilion (see Figure 34.10), on which he worked with Le Corbusier.

Krzysztof Penderecki

CD 12|33

One of the best-known pieces based on texture and process is *Threnody: To the Victims of Hiroshima* (1960, NAWM 165) for fifty-two string instruments by Polish composer Krzysztof Penderecki (b. 1933). The score gives few definite pulses or note values, and instead measures time by seconds. Again each instrument has a unique part to play. Each section focuses on a particular kind of sound, using newly invented notation that shows the effect graphically but not imprecisely. At the beginning, four to six instruments enter at a time, each playing its highest possible note, like a scream of very high clusters. This gradually gives way to a section in which each player rapidly repeats a series of sound effects—such as bowing or arpeggiating behind the bridge (producing high pitches), striking the soundboard, or bowing or plucking the highest possible note. The players may choose one of four patterns, they may move at different speeds (each as fast as possible), and the exact sounds each produces are indeterminate, but the overall effect is essentially the same in each performance, creating a prickly, interesting texture. Next is a section based on sustained tones, quarter-tone clusters, and glissandos between them, shown graphically in the score in Example 34.6 and notated precisely in the parts. The entire pitched and unpitched world, animate and inanimate, wailing and weeping at once, often in polychoral and antiphonal calls and responses, seems to mourn in this dirge. Remarkably, Penderecki originally conceived the work as a purely abstract play of sound and titled it *8′37″* (its timing); the evocative final title has won it a much larger audience than it would otherwise have had, by connecting the new musical resources it uses to the tradition of expressive instrumental music extending back to the eighteenth century.

Penderecki used similar techniques in many other pieces, including the *St. Luke Passion* (1963–66) and his opera *The Devils of Loudon* (1968), which

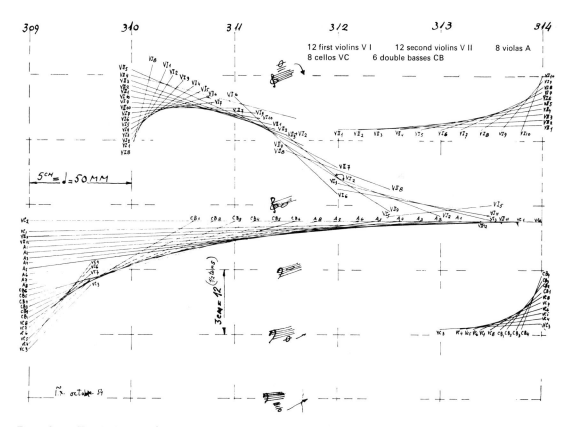

Figure 34.12: Xenakis's graph for a passage in Metastaseis, *with pitch as the vertical axis and time as the horizontal axis. The lower half of the graph represents the lower strings attacking a chromatic cluster together, then curving upward as the lowest pitches in the cluster rise in rapid glissandos and the higher ones move progressively more slowly. A measure later, the upper strings enter on another cluster, then rise and fall in their own pattern. Toward the end of the passage, groups of strings enter on the same note one after another, each successively rising in a faster glissando until all end together in a chromatic cluster.*

Example 34.6: Penderecki, Threnody

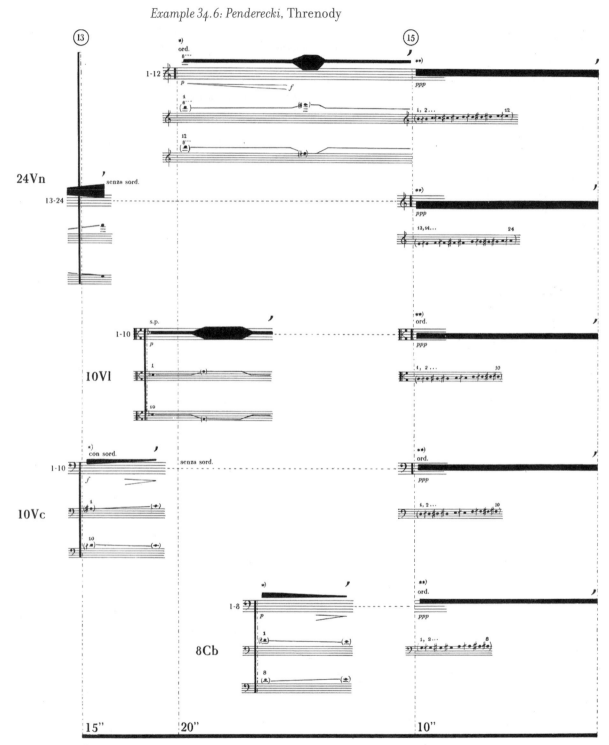

*) * patrz uwaga na s. 6 / vgl. Anmerkung auf Seite 6 / cp. note on page 6 / voir note page 6

**) ** Każdy instrumentalista wykonuje przeznaczony dla niego dźwięk;L, co w rezultacie daje równoczesne brzmienie całej skali ćwierćtonowej między podanym dolnym a górnym dźwiękiem.
Jeder Instrumentalist spielt den seinem Instrument zugeordneten Ton, so daß gleichzeitig die ganze Vierteltonskala zwischen den angegebenen unteren und oberen Grenztönen erklingt.
Each instrumentalist plays the tone allocated to his instrument, so that the whole quarter-tone scale between the indicated lowest and highest tone sounds simultaneously.
Chaque exécutant joue uniquement le son dévolu à son instrument de façon à ce qu'on entende en même temps toute l'échelle des quarts de ton comprise entre les hauteurs extrêmes indiquées.

show how the new resources can be used dramatically. But in these works he already began to incorporate elements of more traditional styles, and in the mid-1970s he turned to a personal style of neo-Romanticism (see chapter 35).

The music of Hungarian composer György Ligeti (b. 1923) achieved world renown through Stanley Kubrick's science fiction film *2001: A Space Odyssey*, which uses excerpts from three of his works: *Atmosphères* (1961), *Requiem* (1963–65), and *Lux aeterna* (1966). This music is in constant motion, yet static both harmonically and melodically. *Atmosphères* begins with fifty-six muted strings, together with a selection of woodwinds and horns, playing simultaneously all the chromatic notes through a five-octave range. Instruments imperceptibly drop out until only the violas and cellos remain. An orchestral tutti follows with a similar panchromatic layout, but out of it emerge two clusters: one, in the strings, made up of the seven notes of a diatonic scale, contrasts with the other, a pentatonic cluster of the remaining five notes of the chromatic scale, in the woodwinds and horns. While one group crescendos, the other diminuendos, then the two reverse, creating changing sonorities that suggest the play of light and shadow on clouds. At times Ligeti uses what he called "micropolyphony," canons with many lines moving at different rates to create the effect of a mass of sound slowly moving through space. In one spectacular passage, these lines gradually rise until they reach the top of the orchestra, with four piccolos sounding *fortissimo* notes a half-step apart high in their range; at such a high register, the differences in pitch create resultant tones octaves lower. This eerily electronic-sounding effect is then cut off by a low cluster in the basses.

György Ligeti

NEW THINKING

Whether using new instruments, traditional instruments, modified instruments (such as prepared piano or amplified string quartet), non-Western instruments, electronic instruments, or tape, composers using new sounds had to make choices about how to construct their music to incorporate the new materials. The spectrum of choices earlier composers had made, from the precise determinism of Schoenberg's twelve-tone music to Varèse's use of sound-masses, inspired the younger generation to explore these and other possibilities. Much of this music requires listeners to forego traditional expectations for melody, harmony, and form and to engage each work instead as an experience of sound itself. These pieces demand new thinking about music from their listeners as much as from their composers, and the questions and new insights they stimulate are part of what many have valued in these works.

THE AVANT-GARDE

In some discussions of twentieth-century music, total serialism, the new virtuosity, the exploration of new sounds, electronic music, music of texture and process, and other postwar developments are all lumped together as

Modernist, experimentalist, avant-garde

manifestations of the avant-garde. But this obscures an important distinction. Many of the composers discussed here intended their music (or at least some of it) to find a place in the permanent classical repertoire alongside the masterpieces of the past, and they designed their works to function in the same way as the established classics, drawing on the art music tradition, proclaiming a distinctive musical personality, and rewarding rehearings. Even as they introduced radical new methods, as Babbitt, Carter, and Crumb did in their string quartets discussed above, these composers continued the goals of modernism. Other works were experimental, intended to try out new methods for their own sake.

As noted in our discussion of Satie and futurism in chapter 30, avant-garde composers have quite different motivations: they challenge accepted aesthetics, even the very concept of permanent classics, and invite listeners to focus on what is happening in the present. The distinction does not lie in what techniques are used, but in the music's purpose. It is sometimes hard to figure out a composer's motivations: did Penderecki intend his *Threnody* as an experiment in new musical sounds and resources, as a challenge to the basic concepts of concert music, or as a piece to be heard repeatedly, admired, and played alongside the classics? That it has been performed and recorded many times suggests the last, but the very question shows how entangled the three streams have become in postwar music.

JOHN CAGE

The leading composer and philosopher of the postwar avant-garde was John Cage, shown in Figure 34.13. From his earlier experimentation with percussion music and the prepared piano (described above), he turned in the 1950s and 1960s to ever more radical reconceptions of music. In his writings, he strongly opposed the museum-like preservation of music from the past and argued for music that focused the listener's attention on the present moment. He did not seek to write works that expressed emotions, conveyed images, developed material, revealed a coherent structure, or unfolded a logical series of events, as music had done for centuries. Instead, influenced by Zen Buddhism, he created opportunities for experiencing sounds as themselves, not as vehicles for the composer's intentions (see Source Reading, p. 934). His three main strategies for accomplishing this were **chance, indeterminacy,** and the blurring of boundaries between music, art, and life.

Chance   By leaving some of the decisions normally made by a composer to chance, Cage created pieces in which the sounds did not convey his intentions, but simply were. His approach varied from piece to piece but typically involved choosing a gamut of elements to be included, planning how they were to be selected, and then using chance operations to do the selection. *Music of Changes* for piano (1951, Book I in NAWM 166) took its name from the ancient Chinese book of prophecy *I-Ching* (*Book of Changes*), which offers a method of divination by tossing coins six times to determine the answer from a list of sixty-four possibilities. For *Music of Changes*, Cage devised charts of possible sounds (half were silences), dynamics, durations, and tempos and used the method from the *I-Ching* to select which were to be used, filling in a formal structure

CD 12|40   CD 6|84

Figure 34.13: John Cage working on his Sonatas and Interludes *for prepared piano, 1947.*

based on units of time. The result is a piece in which sounds occur (and may recur) randomly and at random volumes, durations, and speeds.

Chance is a way to determine certain aspects of the music without impos- *Indeterminacy*
ing the composer's intentions. Another approach Cage pioneered is what he called *indeterminacy*, in which the composer leaves certain aspects of the music unspecified. He drew the idea in part from the work of his friend Morton Feldman (1926–1987), who in pieces such as *Projection 1* for cello (1950) used graphic notation to indicate register, timbre, and timing in general terms rather than specifying precise notes and durations. Cage's *Concert* for piano and orchestra (1957–58) includes sixty-three pages containing various kinds of graphic notation, intended to be realized by the players according to instructions in the score; the exact sounds produced vary considerably from one performance to another. Cage's most extreme indeterminate work—and his most famous piece—was *4′33″* (Four Minutes Thirty-Three Seconds, 1952), in which the performer or performers sit silently at their instruments for a span of time specified in the title (subdivided into three "movements"), while whatever noises can be heard in the concert hall or from outside constitute the music. The piece implies that silence is simply openness to ambient sound and that there are always environmental sounds worth contemplating.

In chance music, some elements are determined by chance; in indeterminate music, some elements are left unspecified by the composer. In both, Cage invites the listener simply to hear sounds as sounds, whether notated in the music or not, whether generated by the performers or occurring as part of the ambient sounds, experiencing each sound as it comes along, not trying to connect it to what precedes or follows it, not expecting the music to communicate feelings or meanings of any kind, but listening as intently as we would listen to any art music, so that we learn to extend our attention beyond music to the world itself. Value judgments become irrelevant; as Cage observes, there can be no "mistakes" in such music, "for once anything happens it authentically is."

SOURCE READING

MUSIC IN THE PRESENT MOMENT

John Cage articulated his views about music in a series of lectures given at Darmstadt, Germany, in 1958, and published in his first book of writings, Silence *(1961). The lecture "Changes," from which the following is excerpted, was interleaved in its presentation with excerpts from Cage's* Music of Changes.

——— • ———

[In my recent works,] the view taken is not of an activity the purpose of which is to integrate the opposites, but rather of an activity characterized by process and essentially purposeless. The mind, though stripped of its right to control, is still present. What does it do, having nothing to do? And what happens to a piece of music when it is purposelessly made?

What happens, for instance, to silence? That is, how does the mind's perception of it change? Formerly, silence was the time lapse between sounds, useful towards a variety of ends, among them that of tasteful arrangement, where by separating two sounds or two groups of sounds their differences or relationships might receive emphasis; or that of expressivity, where silences in a musical discourse might provide pause or punctuation; or again, that of architecture, where the introduction or interruption of silence might give definition either to a predetermined structure or to an organically developing one. Where none of these or other goals is present, silence becomes something else—not silence at all, but sounds, the ambient sounds. The nature of these is unpredictable and changing. These sounds (which are called silence only because they do not form part of a musical intention) may be depended upon to exist. The world teems with them, and is, in fact, at no point free of them. He who has entered an anechoic chamber, a room made as silent as technologically possible, has heard there two sounds, one high, one low—the high the listener's nervous system in operation, the low his blood circulation. There are, demonstrably, sounds to be heard and forever, given ears to hear. Where these ears are in connection with a mind that has nothing to do, that mind is free to enter into the act of listening, hearing each sound just as it is, not as a phenomenon more or less approximating a preconception. . . .

The early works have beginnings, middles, and endings. The later ones do not. They begin anywhere, last any length of time, and involve more or fewer instruments and players. They are therefore not preconceived objects, and to approach them as objects is to utterly miss the point. They are occasions for experience. . . . The mind may be used either to ignore ambient sounds, pitches other than the eighty-eight [keys on a piano], durations which are not counted, timbres which are unmusical or distasteful, and in general to control and understand an available experience. Or the mind may give up its desire to improve on creation and function as a faithful receiver of experience.

From John Cage, "Changes," in *Silence: Lectures and Writings* (Middletown, CT: Wesleyan University Press, 1961), 22–23 and 31–32.

Beginning in the late 1950s, Cage moved toward complete openness in every aspect of composition and performance. *Variations IV* (1963), for instance, uses both indeterminacy and chance (transparent plastic sheets with lines, dots, and other symbols are superimposed randomly and then read as graphic notation) to create a piece "for any number of players, any sounds or combinations of sounds produced by any means, with or without other activities." The "other activities" might include speech, theater, dance, and activities of daily life. Including these in "musical" works blurred the boundaries between music, other arts, and the rest of life. *Musicircus* (1967) is an open-ended "happening," consisting of any number of musicians and ensembles, each performing different music, all playing at once in a large space while the audience wanders freely. Through such events, Cage sought to focus our attention on whatever is happening in the present, experiencing it without prejudice.

Blurring the boundaries

INDETERMINACY IN WORKS OF OTHER COMPOSERS

Many composers adopted indeterminacy in some form under Cage's influence. Inspired by the mobiles of Alexander Calder, Earle Brown (b. 1926) wrote *Available Forms I* (1961) for eighteen players and *Available Forms II* (1962) for large orchestra, in which the musicians play completely scored fragments—with some leeway in the choice of pitches—in the order and tempos determined by the conductor. The score to Karlheinz Stockhausen's *Klavierstück XI* (Piano Piece No. 11, 1956) consists of a single large sheet with nineteen short segments of music that are to be played in succession as the player's eye happens to light on one after another. Directions are given for choosing and linking the segments; not all need be played, any may be repeated, and the piece ends after the pianist plays any segment for a third time. In such works the piece will vary considerably from performance to performance, while its overall character remains within a certain range. As we have seen, Penderecki used indeterminate graphic notation in sections of *Threnody*, although the effect is similar in each performance.

The Polish composer Witold Lutosławski (1913–1994) made selective use of indeterminacy, while insisting on his authorship of the entire composition—a stance quite at odds with Cage's, suggesting an orientation more modernist than avant-garde. In his String Quartet (1964), pitches and rhythms are specified but not the coordination of parts; the players begin a section together, but each plays independently, changing tempo as desired, until the next checkpoint is reached, when at a signal from one of the players they begin together again. Symphony No. 3 (1983) applies this method with great subtlety. Some sections invite individual players to dwell upon a figure in the manner of a soloist playing a cadenza; at other times, eight stands of violins, guided by prescribed pitches but only approximate durations, go their own ways like tendrils of a vine. These passages achieve a freedom and eloquence hardly possible through precise notation and show the power of limited indeterminacy within a traditional genre.

Witold Lutosławski

One by-product of indeterminacy is the variety of new kinds of notation. Scores range all the way from fragments of conventional staff notes through

Significance of indeterminacy

purely graphic suggestions of melodic curves, dynamic ranges, rhythms, and the like to even more slippery and meager directives. Another consequence of indeterminacy is that no two performances of a piece are identical. In effect, a composition does not exist as such, but only as a performance, or as the sum of possible performances. Through the reconsideration of "the musical work" that indeterminacy and related notions stimulated, musicians in the late twentieth century became increasingly aware of the openness of early music as well, coming to understand that a medieval song or an early Baroque aria is also a platform for performance open to a variety of choices within a stylistically appropriate range, not a rigidly defined, unchanging work.

MUSIC AS THEATER AND PERFORMANCE ART

Cage's embrace of indeterminacy and of all types of sounds and actions as possible material for composition inspired others to challenge accepted definitions of music and art.

Fluxus   **Performance art,** in which performing an action in a public place constitutes a work of art, came into its own in the 1960s, spearheaded by Fluxus, a loose group of avant-garde artists in Europe and the United States who cooperated to produce concerts and publications of their pieces. For example, *Composition 1960 No. 2* by La Monte Young (b. 1935) instructs the performer to "Build a fire in front of the audience." *Grapefruit* (1964) by Yoko Ono (b. 1933) is a collection of such pieces, many of them conceptual, aimed as much at the performer as at any observers; in her *Earth Piece* (1963), the performer is directed to "listen to the sound of the earth turning." Ono brought her avant-garde approach into rock music in collaboration with John Lennon of the Beatles after their marriage in 1969. Some Fluxus pieces were never intended to be performed, but their very composition challenges received concepts of music, the concert, performance, and the audience. Such a piece is *An Anti-Personnel Bomb* (1969) by Philip Corner (b. 1933), which asks the performer to throw into the audience "an anti-personnel-type CBU bomb"—a type used in the Vietnam War, against which the piece obliquely protests. One of the central figures of the Fluxus movement, Korean-born Nam June Paik (b. 1932), devised exhibits with multiple television sets that blended music, video, performance art, and sculpture.

Temporary art   Performance art is intended to be temporary, experienced in the moment and essentially unrepeatable. Such pieces had no place in the concert repertoire because they proceeded from wholly different assumptions. But they left lingering questions about what music is and is for, opening up possibilities that are still being explored.

QUOTATION AND COLLAGE

A resource used by many composers of varying orientations was **quotation** of existing music, including a **collage** of multiple quotations. The reworking of borrowed material by earlier composers from Bach and Handel to modernists like Schoenberg, Ives, and Stravinsky served as inspiration, as did quotations in modern poetry and collage in modern art. But postwar composers turned borrowing to new purposes, using evocations of older music to carry meanings that were not available by other means.

English composer Peter Maxwell Davies (b. 1934) drew on chant and English Renaissance music for many works, emphasizing the gulf between modern times and the distant past by distorting the source material or transforming it through modern procedures. His opera *Taverner* (1962–70), on the life of Renaissance composer John Taverner, reworks the latter's *In Nomine* in a variety of ways before finally presenting it in recognizable form at the end, recalling Ives's cumulative form.

Peter Maxwell Davies

American composer George Rochberg (1918–2005), who had written mostly serial music, found it inadequate to express his feelings on the death of his son in 1964, and turned the next year to works based on borrowed material. *Contra mortem et tempus* (Against Death and Time) quotes passages from Boulez, Berio, Varèse, and Ives, and *Music for a Magic Theater* incorporates music of Mozart, Beethoven, Mahler, Webern, Varèse, Stockhausen, and his own earlier works, seeking in both pieces to evoke "the many-layered density of human existence." *Nach Bach* (After Bach, 1966) for harpsichord is a "commentary" on Bach's Keyboard Partita No. 6 in E Minor, BWV 830, in which fragments of the Bach, altered to varying degrees, emerge from Rochberg's own atonal music to create a dialogue between composers and styles. A similar work is *Baroque Variations* (1967) by Lukas Foss (b. 1922), whose three movements subject pieces by Handel, Domenico Scarlatti, and Bach respectively to a variety of transformations from adding clusters to fading out to inaudibility, creating what the composer called "'dreams' about these pieces." George Crumb also often reflects on music of the past; for example, his *Black Angels* quotes the chant *Dies irae* and Schubert's *Death and the Maiden* Quartet for their affective associations.

Rochberg, Foss, Crumb

Stockhausen used borrowed material in several works, notably *Gesang der Jünglinge, Telemusik* (1966), *Hymnen* (1967), and *Opus 1970* (1970). *Hymnen* incorporates words and melodies of many different national anthems in a performance combining electronic sounds with voices and instruments. The intention, Stockhausen claimed, was "not to interpret, but to hear familiar, old, preformed musical material with new ears, to penetrate and transform it with a musical consciousness of today." This aim represents a new way of relating music of the present to that of the past. *Opus 1970*, written for the Beethoven bicentenary in that year, includes transformed but recognizable fragments from Beethoven's works, assembled on tape and played from four loudspeakers alongside live music; the older composer's music is distorted and overwhelmed in an act more of violent conquest than of homage.

Stockhausen

One of the richest pieces based on borrowed material is the third movement of Luciano Berio's *Sinfonia* (Symphony, 1968–69). Berio incorporated most of the scherzo movement of Mahler's Second Symphony and superimposed on it an amplified verbal commentary by an eight-voice ensemble and a musical commentary by a large orchestra. The bar-to-bar continuity of the Mahler is mostly maintained, although at times it disappears temporarily or

Berio's Sinfonia

appears with parts of the texture omitted. Overlaid on the Mahler are quotations from over one hundred other works, including Richard Strauss's *Der Rosenkavalier*, Ravel's *La Valse*, Berg's *Wozzeck*, and Debussy's *La Mer*. Each quotation connects in some way to the Mahler or to the spoken texts, drawn mostly from Samuel Beckett's *The Unnamable*, an interior monologue of a man who has just died. Both words and music suggest a stream of consciousness, as the memories of a lifetime emerge and slip away.

Role of the familiar   Music based on quotation can carry many meanings, but often it gives the audience something familiar to grasp—either the quoted piece itself or the style or type of piece it represents—and provides a new experience drawing on what the listener already knows. As a result, many listeners find it much more approachable than the unfamiliar sounds of serialism, electronic music, the avant-garde, and other postwar trends. For some composers, using borrowed material has been a way to rediscover styles and methods of the past, including tonality. This is one origin for the recent trends of neoromanticism and postmodernism, discussed in the next chapter.

BAND AND WIND ENSEMBLE MUSIC

Band music, traditionally viewed as a kind of popular music, underwent a striking transformation in the postwar era with the creation of a large repertoire of serious works for winds, especially in North America. This change in focus resulted from the convergence of several factors.

Concert bands   Over the previous century, the wind band had grown in popularity to become one of the fixtures of American life. There were amateur bands in most towns of any size, along with several professional bands. The most famous bandmaster after Sousa was Edwin Franko Goldman (1878–1956). He and his son, Richard Franko Goldman (1910–1980), continued the tradition of outdoor band concerts through the nationally broadcast Goldman Band summer series from New York's Central Park. Bands were especially important in the schools; virtually every high school and college had one, and by the 1960s there were fifty thousand wind bands in schools across the country. The American Bandmasters Association (founded 1930) and College Band Directors National Association (CBDNA, founded 1942) promoted bands and band music, including professional training for conductors and standardization of ensembles. Most important, they promoted the concept of the **concert band** (or *symphonic band*) as a vehicle for serious concert music. In purpose, role, performing context, and repertoire, a concert band is more like an orchestra than like the marching bands of holiday parades and football games.

Commissioning serious works   Goldman, the CBDNA, and various conductors were eager to broaden the repertoire for winds, building on the foundation laid by Holst, Schmitt, Grainger, and Vaughan Williams early in the century (see chapter 30) to create a body of works parallel in weight and seriousness to music for orchestra. They embarked on ambitious programs to commission works for concert band. Major composers contributed pieces for the medium, including

Schoenberg's *Theme and Variations*, Op. 43a (1943), Milhaud's *Suite Fran-çaise* (1944), and Hindemith's Symphony in B♭ (1951).

Then in 1952, Frederick Fennell (1914–2005) founded the Eastman Wind Ensemble at the Eastman School of Music in Rochester, New York. The **wind ensemble** was a group dedicated solely to serious music, rather than the mix of marches and other fare typically played by bands. Band pieces were traditionally scored for multiple players on each instrumental part and with each musical line in more than one instrument so that substitutions could be made to suit the available players. But the wind ensemble was different: each instrumental part became essential and all or most were played by soloists, as in a large chamber ensemble. Wind ensembles quickly spread to other schools, and there are now several professional wind ensembles such as the Detroit Winds. The notion of specific rather than variable instrumentation influenced band scoring as well.

Wind ensemble

The presence of serious concert ensembles, well-funded commissions, and the prospect of enjoying widespread performances and earning continuing income from their music attracted many composers to write for winds, particularly at a time when orchestras were playing few works by living composers. Many composers who worked in a variety of media achieved their most frequent performances and most enduring success with music for winds, such as Vincent Persichetti (1915–1987; *Divertimento*, 1950, and Symphony No. 6, 1956) and William Schuman (1910–1992; *George Washington Bridge*), or have written one or more pieces that are now part of the permanent repertoire of serious classical music for winds, including Copland's *Emblems* (1964), Penderecki's *Pittsburgh Overture* (1967), and *. . . and the mountains rising nowhere* (1977) by Joseph Schwantner (b. 1943).

Works for winds

These works for band or wind ensemble reflect the same wide range of styles and concerns as do contemporary orchestral works. An example is *Music for Prague 1968* (1968, first movement in NAWM 167) by Karel Husa (b. 1921), originally composed for concert band and later arranged for orchestra. Indeed, this piece could serve as a summary for our entire consideration of classical music in this chapter because it unites a number of trends. It was written by a university composer (Husa taught at Cornell) and commissioned by a college ensemble (the Ithaca College Concert Band). It was prompted by political concerns, as a response to the occupation of Czechoslovakia (Husa's native country) and overthrow of its liberalizing government by the Soviet Union in August 1968. It combines quoted material with obvious meanings—the same Czech hymn Smetana had used in his *Tábor* (see chapter 29)—with abstract procedures and uses a variety of modern resources, including twelve-tone methods, indeterminacy (indicating gestures while leaving the choice of pitches or exact rhythm to the players), a focus on texture, and an all-percussion movement.

Music for Prague 1968

CD 12|43

Finally, the career of *Music for Prague 1968* suggests a continuing problem for wind music: although this piece has received over seven thousand performances, more than any other Husa work and more than the great majority of twentieth-century classical compositions, Husa's music in standard classical genres has won him more prestige, including prizes for his String Quartet No.

The problem of prestige

3 (awarded the Pulitzer Prize in 1969) and his Cello Concerto (winner of the Grawemeyer Award for 1983). Despite the tremendous growth in quantity and quality of the repertoire, wind music still lacks the status of music for strings or orchestra, due to its longstanding associations with marches, entertainment music, and amateur performers.

ROLL OVER, BEETHOVEN

In the years since 1970, popular music has grown ever more central to musical life. The teenagers who listened to Elvis Presley, the Beatles, Bob Dylan, or Aretha Franklin grew up but held onto the music they loved. There are now classics in pop music as surely as in classical music—nurtured and introduced to new generations by the "golden oldies" radio stations that emerged in the 1970s—and it is the music of the 1950s and 1960s that lies at the heart of that repertoire.

Repertoires of classics emerged also in Broadway and jazz. Musicals by Rodgers and Hammerstein and others from the postwar decades are staged every year by touring companies and in schools, and jazz numbers by Charlie Parker, Miles Davis, and John Coltrane have become as standard as earlier works by Armstrong, Gershwin, and Ellington. Film music has of course endured in its role as accompaniment to the movies themselves, but in recent years it has received attention for its own sake as well. In each of these musical traditions, the music from the postwar era has never ceased being played (at least in recorded form) and is now among the most frequently heard and deeply loved of the entire tradition.

Postwar classical or art music has not fared as well. Some works have become established in the permanent repertoire, such as the postwar symphonies and quartets of Shostakovich and the operas and choral music of Britten, and a few others are part of the canon that well-educated classical musicians and listeners know, including Messiaen's *Quartet for the End of Time* and Penderecki's *Threnody*. But most art music of the era, whether traditional or innovative, found few listeners when it was new and has no larger an audience today. Some of the experiments in total serialism, electronic music, indeterminacy, performance art, and other new ideas now seem dated, and works whose impact depended in part on the unfamiliarity of their sounds or techniques do not always stand up well to rehearings. Yet many of those sounds and techniques have become common currency for later composers of classical, popular, and film music, from electronics and Asian instruments to variegated textures and quotation, and Cage's philosophy of music has opened up new possibilities that have borne fruit in recent decades, from minimalism to dance theater events like *Stomp*. Virtually everything is fair game now.

The End of the Millennium

Chapter

35

In the last three decades of the twentieth century and the first years of the twenty-first, the Western musical tradition continued to diversify. New institutions were created to preserve the history of jazz and popular music, while new types such as punk and rap emerged to meet new functions. Digital synthesizers and computers provided new resources for electronic music in both classical and popular traditions. New forms of ***mixed media*** challenged old distinctions between art and popular music and between music, theater, dance, and other arts. Among composers in the classical tradition, an increased interest in reaching a broad audience produced a number of new currents, including ***minimalism*** and ***neo-Romanticism***. At the same time, almost all the trends discussed in the previous chapter continued, and many composers pursued individual paths.

Because this chapter cannot do justice to all the varied music of this era, we will look at only a few salient issues. We will begin with a survey of the changing world of music, noting especially the broadening conception of music as an art, the influence of new digital technologies, and the increasing importance of mixed media. We will then examine four trends that seem especially prominent in these decades: the fragmentation of popular music; minimalism and its offshoots; a rising concern among classical composers for writing immediately accessible music; and the impact of non-Western musics on musicians in Western traditions.

941

A GLOBAL CULTURE

The late 1960s and 1970s brought a series of political and economic shocks to Western nations. Student protests symbolized a growing gulf between younger and older generations. In the United States, urban riots, growing discord over the Vietnam War, and the assassinations of Martin Luther King Jr. and Robert F. Kennedy marked increasing social strife. The Organization of Petroleum Exporting Countries cut oil production in 1973 to force up prices, leading to economic disruptions and inflation for the next decade. The Watergate scandal, over a political burglary and subsequent cover-up, led to the impeachment and resignation of President Richard Nixon in 1974 and greatly diminished Americans' faith in their government.

Detente and democracy   Meanwhile, Cold War tensions began to ease during the 1970s. Under the policy of *detente*, the United States and the Soviet Union sought greater cultural contacts and signed treaties to reduce nuclear arms. European leaders reached across the East-West divide. President Nixon initiated diplomatic

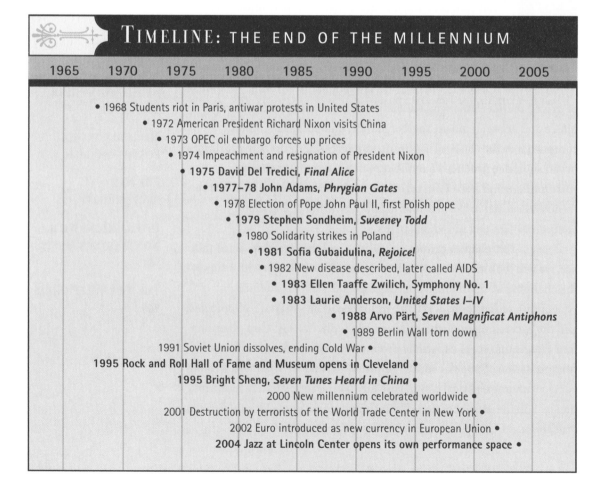

TIMELINE: THE END OF THE MILLENNIUM

1965	1970	1975	1980	1985	1990	1995	2000	2005

• 1968 Students riot in Paris, antiwar protests in United States
• 1972 American President Richard Nixon visits China
• 1973 OPEC oil embargo forces up prices
• 1974 Impeachment and resignation of President Nixon
• **1975 David Del Tredici, *Final Alice***
• **1977–78 John Adams, *Phrygian Gates***
• 1978 Election of Pope John Paul II, first Polish pope
• **1979 Stephen Sondheim, *Sweeney Todd***
• 1980 Solidarity strikes in Poland
• **1981 Sofia Gubaidulina, *Rejoice!***
• 1982 New disease described, later called AIDS
• **1983 Ellen Taaffe Zwilich, Symphony No. 1**
• **1983 Laurie Anderson, *United States I–IV***
• **1988 Arvo Pärt, *Seven Magnificat Antiphons***
• 1989 Berlin Wall torn down
1991 Soviet Union dissolves, ending Cold War •
1995 Rock and Roll Hall of Fame and Museum opens in Cleveland •
1995 Bright Sheng, *Seven Tunes Heard in China* •
2000 New millennium celebrated worldwide •
2001 Destruction by terrorists of the World Trade Center in New York •
2002 Euro introduced as new currency in European Union •
2004 Jazz at Lincoln Center opens its own performance space •

relations with the communist government in China after years without formal contact. Authoritarian regimes in Spain and Portugal, the last dictatorships in western Europe, were peacefully replaced by democratic governments.

Increasing contacts with the West and the election of a Polish pope, the first from a communist country, helped to inspire movements for change in eastern Europe. Beginning with the 1980 strike by the Solidarity movement in Poland, and climaxing with the fall of the Berlin Wall in 1989 and the union of East and West Germany the following year, the people of central and eastern Europe freed themselves from Soviet domination with remarkably little bloodshed. In the Soviet Union itself, Mikhail Gorbachev's policies of *glasnost* (openness) and *perestroika* (restructuring) encouraged freer expression and a more entrepreneurial economy. Although he sought to reform the Soviet Union, the ultimate result was its dissolution in 1991. Its fifteen constituent republics, from massive Russia to tiny Armenia, became independent nations, with governments ranging from democratic to authoritarian.

Collapse of European communism

The Soviet Union's collapse ended the Cold War that had defined the postwar world. It did not end the fear of a nuclear attack, however, because the knowledge and technology for manufacturing nuclear weapons was spreading. In the post-Soviet era, regional conflicts from the Middle East to the Korean peninsula became more urgent, and civil wars proliferated from the Balkans and Africa to the Philippines. Extremists increasingly turned to terror as a tactic, whether directed at their own government, as in the 1995 Oklahoma City bombing, or other lands, as in Al Qaeda's attack on the World Trade Center in New York City and the Pentagon in Washington, D.C., on September 11, 2001.

New conflicts

In the economic realm, the end of the Cold War encouraged a trend toward integration across national boundaries. The Common Market became the European Union, absorbing new members from eastern Europe and pursuing a unified European economic system, symbolized by the euro, a new international currency introduced in 2002. Asian countries enjoyed rapid growth, sustained by increasing trade with the rest of the world. Reductions in trade barriers and new technologies led to rising productivity in the Western democracies, producing an economic boom in the 1990s. By then, almost every country was part of an interwoven global economy.

Global economy

News, entertainment, and the arts became global as well. The spread of communications satellites and cable television, and the advent in the 1980s and 1990s of personal computers, fax machines, cell phones, and the Internet, put people around the world in immediate touch with one another. Many issues, from the environment to the drug trade to terrorism, crossed national boundaries, requiring countries to work together. With easy travel, diseases from flu to AIDS spread rapidly across the globe, prompting international cooperation in response. The new global culture was symbolized by New Year's Day in 2000, when television showed celebrations of the new millennium all over the world, as midnight moved across time zones from New Zealand to Alaska.

Global links

Improved communications and travel also fostered a global market for the arts. Many forms of entertainment now reach audiences all over the world, from Hollywood movies to touring groups of traditional artists such as the

Global arts

Bulgarian Women's Choir and Tuvan throat-singers. From Seiji Ozawa to Tan Dun, Asians have become prominent as musicians in the Western classical tradition, while some Americans and Europeans have become proficient performers of Indian, Javanese, or other Asian musics. Music from around the world is now easily accessible through recordings, the Internet, and live performances. The diversity of the world's music has brought a growing awareness in Europe and the Americas that each musician's work is but one strand in a global tapestry.

THE CHANGING WORLD OF MUSIC

In the multidimensional world of music since the 1970s, most people cross musical boundaries every day. A person might attend live concerts and collect recordings of classical music, jazz, rock, and non-Western music, and hear pop songs at the gym, country music on the radio, and background music of various types in shops, elevators, and offices. Musicians live in the same fluid environment, and their work reflects it; for example, country musicians who grew up in the 1960s and 1970s have found it natural to incorporate electric guitar and drum sounds from the rock music they heard in their youth. Crossing and blending traditions have become commonplace.

BROADENING THE MEANING OF "ART MUSIC"

The idea of art music—music listened to with rapt attention, valued for its own sake, and preserved in a repertoire of classics—began in the tradition of concert music, but by the late twentieth century it had spread to other traditions.

Jazz repertory   Each style of jazz has continued to attract performers and listeners even after the "next" style had emerged, so that jazz of all eras is available in performance and on recordings, just like classical music. The reissuing of old recordings on LPs and compact discs (see sidebar, p. 947) has made the entire history of jazz readily accessible. In the 1980s, new institutions were created to preserve and present classic works of former times. The Smithsonian Jazz Orchestra, led by David Baker, gives live performances of jazz from past generations, scrupulously transcribed from recordings or reconstructed from the original charts. Jazz at Lincoln Center, founded by Wynton Marsalis in 1987 as an ensemble and concert series for historically accurate jazz performances at the complex shared by the New York Philharmonic and Metropolitan Opera, got its own hall in 2004, a short walk from Lincoln Center. By then it was widely accepted that jazz was an art music with its own repertory of classics.

Rock museums   In a similar vein, academic musicians from the generation that grew up listening to rock music began in the 1980s to teach courses on rock history and embrace it as a subject for study alongside classical music and jazz. Wealthy donors funded new institutions dedicated to preserving the rock legacy, notably the Rock and Roll Hall of Fame and Museum in Cleveland, shown in Figure 35.1, and the Experience Music Project in Seattle. These institutions, together with the enduring popularity of rock and pop songs from the 1950s on (as shown by sales figures and "golden oldies" radio stations), indicate that this music has become a tradition of classics, akin to jazz and classical music. Country music is not far behind; the Country Music Hall of Fame and Museum, which dates back to the 1960s, opened a spectacular new building in Nashville in 2001, and interest in preserving older styles is growing.

The musical, too, became recognized as a tradition of classics, marked by academic books and courses if not yet by museums or performing institutions. New productions of shows by Rodgers and Hammerstein, Lerner and Loewe, Kern, Porter, Berlin, and others have been staged on Broadway and around the world. Musicals that have not been seen since their original runs decades ago have been revived with the same commitment shown by those who rediscovered, edited, and performed works of earlier centuries.

Musicals

New musicals often aspire to the level of art music more than entertainment. The dominant figure in the American musical has been Stephen Sondheim, whose musicals include the plotless social commentary of *Company* (1970); the melodramatic *Sweeney Todd* (1979), about a murderous London barber; *Sunday in the Park with George* (1984), based on a famous pointillist painting by Georges Seurat; and *Assassins* (1991), featuring successful and would-be assassins of American presidents—all subjects earlier musicals would not likely have touched. Sondheim's lyrics are witty and poetic, and his songs draw on Broadway and popular styles while often breaking from convention, sounding a bit like art songs in a semi-popular idiom. Andrew Lloyd Webber (b. 1948) is the leading English composer of musicals, including *Jesus Christ Superstar* (1970–71), a rock-music retelling of Jesus' life; *Evita* (1976–78), about Eva Peron, wife of Argentinian dictator Juan Peron; *Cats* (1981), on poetry by T. S. Eliot; and *The Phantom of the Opera* (1986), one of

Figure 35.1: The Rock and Roll Hall of Fame and Museum in Cleveland, Ohio. The building, on the shores of Lake Erie, was designed by internationally famous architect I. M. Pei and opened in September 1995.

the first musicals to be based on a classic film, reversing the usual direction taken by adaptation. Like film composers, Webber has drawn on a wide range of styles to suit the dramatic situation, while retaining the musical's traditional focus on lyrical, affecting melody. Also remarkably successful with audiences were the musicals of French composer Claude-Michel Schönberg (b. 1944), notably *Les Misérables* (1980; English version, 1985), a setting of Victor Hugo's novel of poverty in Paris, and *Miss Saigon* (1989), retelling Puccini's *Madame Butterfly* in the context of the Vietnam War. Other musicals based on operas followed, such as *Rent* (1996) by Jonathan Larson (1960–1996), which adapted the plot of Puccini's *La bohème* to the pop music styles of New York in the era of AIDS. Many of these musicals resemble operas in their serious tone, use of spectacle, and almost continuous music.

Asian classical music   Western listeners have increasingly become aware of Asian classical traditions, including those of Japan, China, Indonesia, India, and Iran. Now Western classical music is no longer the only, or even the most, prestigious musical tradition, but one of many.

NEW TECHNOLOGIES

Since the 1970s, new technologies have altered the ways musicians work with music and listeners consume it. Among the most important new inventions are the **digital** synthesis, recording, and reproduction of sound (see sidebar), which have given creators of music new tools and listeners new flexibility.

Sampling   One significant technique is **sampling**, a process of creating new compositions by patching together digital chunks of previously recorded music. Although sampling raises copyright concerns, it has been used extensively in rap (see below) and other forms of pop music, as well as in experimental, avant-garde, and classical concert music.

Computer music   Advances in computing and the miniaturization of the computer have offered many new possibilities, explored by composers whose music is part experimentation with technology and part sound sculpture. One of the pioneers of computer music is Charles Dodge (b. 1942), whose *Speech Songs* (1972) features computer-synthesized vocal sounds, mixing lifelike imitations of speech with transformations that change vowels into noise or natural inflections into melodies to create a word-based music well suited to the surrealistic poetry he uses as a text. Paul Lansky (b. 1944) developed his own software to create computer works. He manipulates recorded sounds, such as speech in *Six Fantasies on a Poem by Thomas Campion* (1979) and *Smalltalk* (1988) or highway traffic noises in *Night Traffic* (1990), transforming them beyond immediate recognition and using them as a kind of pitched percussion. Despite the unusual sound sources, his music draws on pop traditions, with tonal harmonies, regular meter, propulsive beat, and layered syncopated rhythms. A very different aesthetic is pursued at the Institut de Recherche et Coordination Acoustique/Musique (Institute for Acoustic and Musical Research and Coordination) in Paris, founded by Pierre Boulez, one of the premier centers for computer music in Europe. In *Inharmonique* (1977) and other works written during his time as director of the IRCAM computer music department, Jean-Claude Risset (b. 1938) uses the computer to mediate between live

MUSIC IN CONTEXT

DIGITAL TECHNOLOGIES

In the early 1970s and early 1980s, music joined the digital revolution. Inventors devised a method for translating sound into a coded series of on-off pulses, or 1s and 0s, in the same way that computers stored and transmitted data. Soon digital processes were replacing older ones, known as *analog* because they rely on creating an analogue of the soundwaves, such as the undulations in the groove of a record.

By the 1980s, musicians were using digital synthesizers, as in Figure 35.2, instead of the older analog devices that produced sounds generated from or processed by electrical circuits. Because digital processes produced and recorded sounds as streams of numbers, musical sounds could be reproduced and controlled precisely. Electronic keyboards combined with computers made synthesized music accessible to musicians everywhere. Through computers, composers could control all the parameters of pitch, timbre, dynamics, and rhythm, and the characteristics thus digitally encoded could be translated directly into music through MIDI (Musical Instrument Digital Interface).

Figure 35.2: Keyboard console of the Synclavier II digital synthesizer from 1981.

Some musicians combined live performers with synthesized or computer-generated music into a performance medium that is now commonplace. Using software programs that respond to music, the composer devises formulas that are then played on a synthesizer, digital piano, or acoustic instrument. In this way, a musician can generate imitative or nonimitative polyphony, rhythmic or melodic ostinatos, heterophony, and a variety of other textures by playing on a synthesizer keyboard in "real time"—that is, as actually played and heard, rather than laboriously prepared in advance and tape-recorded.

Vinyl records, the primary means of distribution for decades, gave way in the 1980s to compact discs (CDs) which were smaller, more durable, and able to reproduce music digitally, offering greater fidelity. Thousands of recordings first released on 78- or 33-rpm records were reissued on CDs, making an entire century of recorded sound more widely accessible than ever before. Portable playback devices with headphones or earbuds have made it possible to carry music of one's own choice everywhere. By the twenty-first century, CDs were themselves rivaled by newer digital technologies. Using mp3 files, computers and portable players can store and play thousands of songs. Individual consumers swap digital music files on peer-to-peer file-sharing Internet sites, some of which have been shut down because of copyright infringement lawsuits. More recently, various Web sites have begun to offer legal downloads, as recording companies have begun to find ways to make money through the Internet. Many musicians use their own Web sites to gain exposure, offering free downloads of excerpts or entire works. Thousands of radio stations are now also available via the Internet. The way we interact with music is being transformed by digital technology, bringing changes that are hard to describe and harder to predict.

voices or acoustic instruments and synthesized or electronically processed sound. He has continued to design new sounds, exploring the interaction of sound waves, harmonics, timbre, and other basic elements of sound. The work of these three composers only begins to illustrate the potential of computer music.

MIXED MEDIA

Music in the late twentieth century has grown closer to other performance arts, as it increasingly has become part of **mixed media** artworks.

Stage shows and music videos

A pop music concert in the 1960s typically consisted of a group playing music, perhaps with some exaggerated physical gestures to charge up the audience. But by the 1980s, stage shows for performers like Michael Jackson or Madonna, though still called concerts, involved elaborate sets and costumes, intricate choreography, and visual effects such as lighting, fog machines, and pyrotechnics. The spectacle was almost as important as the music, which was only one component in a multimedia extravaganza. **Music videos,** short films that provide a visual accompaniment to songs, came of age in the early 1980s, serving as the mainstay of the cable channel MTV (Music Television) and quickly becoming a primary form of contact for popular music consumers. Most were elaborate productions, with sets, costumes, dancing, and rapid-fire editing all calculated to catch the eye, draw attention to the song, and promote sales.

Laurie Anderson

While pop music was becoming more visual, performance art was becoming more musical. One of the leading performance artists, Laurie Anderson (b. 1947), shown in Figure 35.3, incorporates a wide range of media, including singing, violin playing, poetry, speaking, electronics, film, slides, and lighting. Her single *O Superman* (1981), which featured her synthesizer-

Figure 35.3: Performance artist Laurie Anderson playing an electronic violin during a concert.

Figure 35.4: Scene from the London production of STOMP.

processed voice in a simple, repetitive song with light electronic accompaniment, was an unexpected pop hit, winning her additional audiences and reinforcing the musical element in her work. She has released several albums of songs, but the heart of her art has remained in her stage shows. Most ambitious was *United States I–IV* (1983), a seven-hour extravaganza that used all the tools of modern media to comment ironically on the alienation and social ills of the culture that invented them.

Spectacle works

A new genre of musical theater emerged in the 1990s in which the process of making music itself became a visual spectacle. *STOMP* (1991), created by Luke Cresswell and Steve McNicholas in England and on Broadway and on tour since 1994, has no dialogue or plot, but consists entirely of a troupe of performers using everyday objects from matchbooks to brooms to garbage can lids to produce elaborate percussion music carried out with stunning choreography, as in Figure 35.4. Jim Mason's *Blast!* (2001) took the routines of a marching band halftime show and drum corps performance, souped them up with new choreography, and put them on the Broadway stage.

Film music

Film is a multimedia format of long standing, and although music played an important role from the start—so-called silent films always had piano, organ, or orchestral accompaniment—its significance in recent decades has heightened. In a growing number of movies, music no longer serves as background accompaniment. It has become as much a part of the total art work as the music in an opera or musical. Many films use existing music; George Lucas's *American Graffiti* (1973) set a pattern by employing pop music of the late 1950s and early 1960s to accompany a teen drama set in that era. But most striking was the return to full-scale symphonic scores organized around leitmotives. The music by John Williams (b. 1932) for the six *Star Wars* movies (1977–2005) was arguably as important as the actors in conveying the dramatic action. Symphonic movie soundtracks became hot-selling recordings, outpacing all other orchestral music and raising the stature of film composers.

TRENDS

The broadening conception of music as an art, the proliferation of new technologies, and the growing interaction of music with other media are only three of many trends in recent music, but they are characteristic in crossing boundaries between traditions.

Other trends resulted from pressures within traditions. The strong identification of 1950s and 1960s teenagers with rock and pop music prompted a search by smaller social groups for a music to call their own. They were abetted by a popular music industry that was eager, as always, to exploit new markets. As a result, the popular tradition has become fragmented. Meanwhile, the desire of classical composers to connect with listeners who were unsympathetic to modernist or avant-garde music has prompted a search for more accessible languages, including minimalism. Blending Western with non-Western traditions combines these trends by acknowledging the emerging global culture.

NICHES IN POPULAR MUSIC

As the supply of music has increased and choices have became more varied, the amount of music common to all members of a society has diminished. The days are over when all of America heard the songs of Irving Berlin, or the Beatles were famous around the world. Instead, popular music has splintered into niche markets and competing trends, each identified with particular social groups. Some trends won widespread, though usually brief, popularity, while others remained the property of specific groups. The following sampling of popular music trends in North America and Europe since 1970 suggests the ways various segments of society built a group identity by sharing a common music.

Disco   In the 1970s, a new style of dance music known as *disco* developed in New York clubs that catered primarily to African-Americans, Latinos, and gay men, then become an international craze. Club-goers valued the steady $\frac{4}{4}$ meter and uniform dance tempo of disco songs, which allowed disk jockeys to move smoothly from song to song and the dancers to keep moving without interruption. Lush orchestrations and slick production pleased the ear while the relentless beat moved the body, joining glamour, fun, and sexuality in an intoxicating brew. Disco reached its height of popularity with the film *Saturday Night Fever* (1977) and the accompanying soundtrack by the Bee Gees.

Punk, New Wave, alternative rock, and grunge   Another 1970s trend was *punk,* a hard-driving style voicing teenage alienation. The most notorious punk band, the Sex Pistols, popularized edgy fashions such as safety pins through flesh and preached nihilism in their lyrics. Most punk musicians were largely untutored, preferring raw, unskilled sounds to the virtuosity and smooth production of rock and disco. *New Wave* musicians like Blondie and Talking Heads followed closely on the heels of punk, sharing some of its nihilism without disdaining musical skill, and won wider commercial success. *Alternative rock*, a catch-all term for rock music set apart from the mainstream, was nurtured by college and independent radio stations and performing venues, then came to dominate in the early 1990s thanks to *grunge* rockers from Seattle, such as Nirvana, Soundgarden, and Pearl Jam. Grunge combined the nihilism of punk and the electric-guitar-laden sound of heavy metal with intimate lyrics and dressed-down fashions (especially flannel). Nirvana's 1991 song *Smells Like Teen Spirit* brought grunge to national attention. Each of these styles became an emblem for youth of a certain age, having the great merit of offending or being incomprehensible to most of their elders.

Rap, with rhymed lyrics chanted over repeated dance beats, began in the 1970s as part of African-American urban youth culture. From its origins as a party music in New York, rap has branched out into multiple types, including *gangsta rap*, celebrating lawlessness, and *conscious rap*, which voiced the woes of inequality and racism. With songs like *Fight the Power*, the rap group Public Enemy, shown in Figure 35.5, led the ranks of conscious rap in the late 1980s and early 1990s. In a parallel to the discovery of rhythm-and-blues by white teens in the 1950s, rap became the popular music of a generation of white suburban teenagers, especially males attracted to its heavy beat and themes of male dominance. By the late 1990s, styles adapted from rap were practiced in western Europe, Africa, and around the world.

Rap

Other types of music have served to foster group feeling among particular segments of society but have rarely attracted the attention of outsiders. For example, the movement called *women's music* encompasses songs in various styles, often folk-influenced, with texts that reflect a feminist perspective. More widely known is *Christian rock*, which uses current popular styles to

Musical subcultures

Figure 35.5: Rap group Public Enemy, featuring soloists Terminator X (front left), Flavor Flav (center, with his trademark giant watch), and Chuck D (right).

convey evangelical Christian themes. As is true for women's music, the message is more important than the style.

The types of popular music listed here only begin to suggest the varieties current since 1970. Wherever there is a group with distinctive tastes or needs, there is a market niche and musicians to fill it, from polka bands in Milwaukee to Bollywood singers in India.

MINIMALISM AND POSTMINIMALISM

Composers of art music have also cultivated a varied range of styles and approaches. One of the most prominent new trends has been **minimalism,** in which materials are reduced to a minimum and procedures simplified so that what is going on in the music is immediately apparent. Minimalism began as an avant-garde aesthetic focused on the musical processes themselves but over time became a widely used and popular technique, capable of a wide range of expressive content. Composers of minimalist works absorbed influences from rock, African music, Asian music, tonality, and finally Romanticism, to create what has been called the leading musical style of the late twentieth century.

Minimalism in art   Art critic Richard Wollheim coined "minimal art" in 1965 as a term for art that reduced materials and form to fundamentals and was not intended to express feelings or convey the artist's state of mind. Minimalist artworks often feature a repetitive pattern of simple elements. For example, Carl Andre's *64 Copper Squares* (1969) consists of sixty-four square copper plates laid on the floor in a square, and Frank Stella's painting *Hyena Stomp* (1962), shown in Figure 35.6, forms a spiral pattern from straight lines and bands of bright color. Such art focused on its materials, making it part of the avant-garde concept art of the 1960s.

Early minimalism   A parallel movement was nurtured among musicians in New York City and
in music   in the California counterculture. One of the pioneers of musical minimalism was La Monte Young (b. 1935), whose *The Tortoise: His Dreams and Journeys* (1964) was an improvisation in which instrumentalists and singers come in and out on various harmonics over a fundamental played as a drone by a synthesizer. Terry Riley (b. 1935), who once performed in Young's ensemble, experimented with tape loops, short segments of magnetic tape spliced into loops that when fed through a tape recorder play the same recorded sounds again and again. His tape piece *Mescalin Mix* (1962–63) piled up many such loops, each repeating a short phrase, over a regular pulse. His most famous work, *In C* (1964), uses a similar procedure with live instruments. It can be performed by any number of instruments, each playing the same series of brief repeated figures over a quickly pulsing octave C, with the number of repetitions in each part and the coordination of parts left indeterminate. The resulting sound combines a steady pulsation with a process of slow change from consonance to diatonic dissonance and back. The concept and materials are simple and the process immediately audible, but the multilayered texture is complex and like nothing ever heard before.

Figure 35.6: Hyena Stomp *by Frank Stella (b. 1936). Stella reduced painting to its fundamentals, intending that his work be understood as only a play of form and color, not as an expression of feelings. The title, from a jazz piece by Jelly Roll Morton, reflects Stella's interest in translating syncopation into visual form in this painting.*

FROM AVANT-GARDE TO WIDESPREAD APPEAL

While Young remained an avant-garde experimentalist and Riley moved toward rock music, three other Americans brought minimalist procedures into art music intended for a broad audience.

Steve Reich (b. 1936) developed a quasi-canonic procedure in which musicians play the same material out of phase with each other. Like Riley, he began in the electronic studio, superimposing tape loops of the same spoken phrase in such a way that one loop was slightly shorter and thus gradually moved ahead of the other, an effect called *phasing.* In *Piano Phase* (1967), shown in Example 35.1, Reich applied a similar idea to a work for two pianos. Both pianists repeat the same figure in unison several times, then one gradually pulls ahead until he is exactly one eighth-note ahead of the other, and they repeat the figure several times in rhythmic synchronization but melodically out of phase. This process is repeated twelve times, producing a different series of harmonic combinations each time the parts slip into synchrony, until the two parts are again in melodic unison; then the same process is used for a figure of eight notes and then one of four notes. The fascination in music like this lies in observing gradual changes and the many possible permutations of very simple ideas. The processes that underlie the composition are revealed for every listener to hear and experience.

Steve Reich

Example 35.1: Opening of Reich's Piano Phase

Reich formed his own ensemble and was able to make a living by performing, touring, and recording his works. Much of his music in the 1970s was percussive, superimposing layers of figuration in ways that parallel African drumming, one source of his inspiration. He attracted a wide range of listeners, drawing audiences accustomed to jazz, rock, and pop music as well as classical, as the diatonic material and rapid pulsation gave his music wide appeal. By the 1980s, he no longer subscribed to a minimalist aesthetic, instead using minimalist techniques to create large-scale works with significant emotional content, often drawing on his Jewish heritage. *Tehillim* (1981) is a setting of psalm texts in the original Hebrew for four singers and orchestra, using rhythmic and melodic canons at the unison. The texture in each section gradually becomes more complex, with all four soloists singing the same melody in close succession. As it becomes harder to follow a single part, we can shift our focus to hear the salient points of each. A piece as rich and complex as this can hardly be called minimalist, but it shows the application of minimalist techniques in the realm of art music.

Philip Glass   Philip Glass (b. 1937) had published twenty works by the time he completed degrees at the University of Chicago and The Juilliard School and finished studies with Nadia Boulanger, but withdrew all of them after working with the Indian sitarist Ravi Shankar in Paris. Glass's works since the mid-1960s have been deeply influenced by the rhythmic organization of Indian music. They emphasized melodiousness, consonance, and the simple harmonic progressions and abundant amplification of rock music, and have won Glass a large and diverse following from rock enthusiasts to classical listeners. Like Reich, he initially wrote mainly for his own ensemble, but he has secured his reputation with a series of major works, including symphonies, concertos, and operas.

His one-act, four-and-a-half-hour opera *Einstein on the Beach*, premiered at the Metropolitan Opera House in 1976, was a collaboration with avant-garde director Robert Wilson, who wrote the scenario. The opera avoids narrative, has no sung text other than solfège syllables (the modern descendents of solmization syllables; see chapter 2), and involves mostly nonsensical stage action. The music consists primarily of repeated figures, mostly arpeggiated triads, performed by an orchestra of electronic keyboard

Figure 35.7: American composer and conductor John Adams conducting the BBC Symphony Orchestra in London, five days before the 9/11 attack on the World Trade Center in New York.

instruments, woodwinds, and a solo violinist. Other operas followed, including *Satyagraha* (1980), about Gandhi's nonviolent struggle for Indian independence, and *Akhnaten* (1984), about an Egyptian pharoah martyred for his monotheistic worship of the sun god. *The Voyage* (1992), commissioned by the Metropolitan Opera to commemorate the five hundredth anniversary of Columbus's voyage to the New World, blends his signature style of multi-layered ostinatos, rapid pulse, and slowly changing tonal or modal harmonies with the standard orchestra, recitatives, and arias of the operatic tradition.

John Adams (b. 1947), shown in Figure 35.7, has traced a path from minimalism to a personal style that blends minimalist techniques with a variety of other approaches. His *Phrygian Gates* for piano (1977–78; opening excerpt in NAWM 168) is representative of the period when minimalism was moving beyond its avant-garde origins to become a style rather than an aesthetic. Except for a middle section of shifting sustained chords, this twenty-four-minute piece relies almost entirely on quick repetitive figurations, primarily in diatonic modes. The music goes through what Adams calls "gates," changing from one set of notes to another: from the Lydian scale on A to the Phrygian scale on A, as shown in Example 35.2, then the Lydian and Phrygian scales on E, and so on. These changes give the work its title, and they convey the sense of a journey through a gradually changing environment.

Adams continued to use minimalist techniques in his later works, but also embraced elements from popular and classical music. *Harmonielehre* (1985),

John Adams

CD 12|50

Example 35.2: A gate change from Adams's Phrygian Gates

a symphonic poem that draws on Romantic and modernist styles, was greeted by one news magazine with the enthusiastic headline, "The Heart Is Back in the Game." The first movement begins with loud, repeated E-minor chords, then moves through a minimalist landscape to arrive at a middle section in which twittering ostinatos in the upper register accompany a tragic, almost expressionist, long-breathed melody that recalls late Mahler or Berg. Adams's opera *Nixon in China* (1987), on Nixon's 1972 trip to China to open relations with the communist regime, treats its up-to-date subject with the formality of a Baroque historical opera while applying minimalist techniques. Short, driving, pulsating ideas, insistently repeated, constantly evolve, using an orchestra dominated by brass, winds, and percussion. Over time, Adams has relied less on minimalist techniques and more on traditional harmonic and contrapuntal means. He has embraced a wide range of topics, from celebrating Jesus' Nativity, in the oratorio *El Niño* (1999–2000), to mourning the deaths in the terrorist attacks of September 11, 2001, in *On the Transmigration of Souls* (2002).

THE NEW ACCESSIBILITY

In the late twentieth century, composers in the classical tradition faced a new reality. While they were able to make a living teaching at universities or conservatories, obtaining performances for their music was increasingly difficult. It was often easier to win a commission for a new piece than to secure a second or third performance of an existing work. Few compositions entered the repertory, and few listeners heard a piece more than once. In some respects, the situation was like that of the eighteenth century, when a concerto or symphony was seldom heard twice by the same listeners. Moreover, at a time when music was growing more plentiful and easy to access, the audience for classical music seemed to be shrinking.

Some composers took this situation as the price of artistic freedom and continued writing as they had before. Others sought to attract wider interest by writing music that could be understood on first hearing. Composers like Reich, Glass, and Adams found one solution in minimalism. Other composers used a variety of approaches, often in tandem: modifying their modernist idiom to make it more accessible; radically simplifying their material and procedures; quoting from and alluding to past styles; resurrecting nineteenth-century tonal Romanticism; and invoking extramusical meanings and imagery.

ACCESSIBLE MODERNISM

Some composers writing in a modernist idiom have made their music accessible by keeping the ideas and procedures relatively simple and easy to grasp.

Ellen Taaffe Zwilich (b. 1939), shown in Figure 35.8, joins continuous variation with older formal devices of recurrence and contrast. Like Schoenberg, she presents the main idea at the outset, then elaborates it through developing variation in which everything grows logically from the initial seed. Yet the basic idea is usually simple and the textures clear, making her music much easier to follow than Schoenberg's. A prime example is her Symphony No. 1 (1982), which won the first Pulitzer Prize in Music awarded to a woman. In the first movement (NAWM 169), all the melodic material derives through variation from the initial interval of a rising minor third, and the harmonies combine thirds to produce dissonant sonorities. The soft opening gesture, a threefold rising third with an accelerando, serves as a motto that generates a gradual increase in tempo, dynamics, and density to a central Allegro, then toward the end the music slows and thins to a quiet close. The gradual process of development is easy to hear and the experience of listening both intellectually and emotionally satisfying.

Ellen Taaffe Zwilich

CD 12|59

RADICAL SIMPLIFICATION

Other composers combined a radical simplification of material and procedures with a return to diatonic music. One strain can be found in minimalism, discussed above, but not all music of this type fits the minimalist category.

Estonian composer Arvo Pärt (b. 1935) forged a highly individual, instantly recognizable style using the simplest materials. Following early neoclassical and serial works, and others that contrasted modernist with Baroque styles,

Arvo Pärt

Figure 35.8: Ellen Taaffe Zwilich in a photograph from ca. 2003.

he turned to a study of Gregorian chant and early polyphony. In the 1970s, he devised a method he called *tintinnabuli*, after the bell-like sonorities it produced. Its essence lies in counterpoint between a pitch-centered, mostly stepwise diatonic melody and one or more other voices that sound only notes of the tonic triad, with the placement of each note determined by a preset system. The technique is exemplified in Pärt's *Seven Magnificat Antiphons* (1988, rev. 1991, excerpts in NAWM 170) and illustrated in Example 35.3, which shows the opening of No. 6, *O König aller Völker*. The second tenor (the lower part on the tenor staff) presents a plain modal tune that is centered on A and that moves no more than a fourth away in either direction. Its rhythm is restricted to quarter and half notes, and measures change length to fit the text accentuation. The tenor melody is echoed by the second soprano to form an augmentation canon. The altos recite the text, phrase by phrase, on D. The other parts sound notes of the D minor triad, following strict but simple rules reminiscent of early polyphony (see chapter 5). The bass and first tenor surround the second-tenor melody, each singing the note of the D minor triad that is second closest to the melody note: thus, at the outset, we find the D below and the F above the melody's opening A. Meanwhile, the first soprano sings the note from the triad that is nearest above the second soprano melody. The resulting texture alternates between consonance and diatonic dissonance, allowing for variety and dramatic climaxes within a stripped-down, pitch-centered style.

CD 12|65

Example 35.3: O König aller Völker, *No. 6 of Pärt's* Seven Magnificat Antiphons

O king of all peoples, their expectation [and hope]

QUOTATION AND POLYSTYLISM

Another approach was to extend quotation and collage (see chapter 34) to include combining past and present styles. Such blending of styles in music has been compared to the architecture of Philip Johnson, Robert Venturi, Cesar Pelli, and others, who left behind the bare glass façades of mid-twentieth century modernism by incorporating elements of earlier styles into essen-

Figure 35.9: The AT&T building in New York City, recently renamed the Sony Building. The architect, Philip Johnson, blends elements from the past, such as the columns and slanted roofline, together with modern elements of glass and concrete in his design. This blending of elements from different periods, sometimes called postmodernism, *rejects the stark glass walls and undecorated façades of many mid-twentieth-century buildings.*

tially modern designs as in Figure 35.9, a mixture that came to be called **post-modernism**. A central aspect of postmodernism is a turning away from the belief, crucial to modernist thought, that history progresses irreversibly in one direction. In music, this idea means abandoning the notion that musical idioms develop continuously, as if according to a plan or some inner necessity. To the postmodernist, history gives the artist more freedom than that; the styles of all epochs and cultures are equally available as musical material, to be employed as the composer sees fit.

A composer who quoted from and borrowed past styles effectively was Alfred Schnittke (1934–1998). He worked in the Soviet Union, where he was known chiefly for his film music, before moving to Germany in 1990. The Soviet government began to relax its control over culture in the 1960s under Nikita Khrushchev, exposing Schnittke and other young composers to Western trends such as serial, chance, and electronic music. After writing several works based on serialism, indeterminacy, and new instrumental sounds, Schnittke turned to what he called **polystylism**, a combination of new and older styles created through quotation or stylistic allusion. His Symphony No. 1 (1969–72) incorporates passages from works by Haydn, Beethoven, Chopin, Tchaikovsky, Grieg, Johann Strauss, and Schnittke himself. For listeners familiar with works of these composers, such music embodies a contrast not only of styles but of historical periods. Schnittke's later works—including

Alfred Schnittke

eight more symphonies, numerous concertos, and chamber music—depend less on stark juxtapositions than on integrating a small number of ideas borrowed from or modeled on earlier music.

John Corigliano   Like Schnittke, the American composer John Corigliano (b. 1938) frequently juxtaposes styles to convey meanings, drawing on a stylistic continuum from Baroque and Classic to avant-garde. His opera *The Ghosts of Versailles* (1987) centers around ghosts in the French royal palace, including Queen Marie Antoinette and others slain during the Revolution, and a play staged for their entertainment; the ghosts are rendered with modern serial music and timbral effects, while the play is set in a style based on Mozart operas. Corigliano's Symphony No. 1 (1989), a memorial to friends who died of AIDS, incorporates quotations from some of their favorite pieces framed by deeply expressive, often angry or tragic music drawing on a variety of modern techniques.

Peter Schickele and   The wittiest and most popular composer to use quotation and stylistic allu-
P. D. Q. Bach   sion is Peter Schickele (b. 1935). His works, such as his five string quartets (1983–98), are mostly tonal. They draw on a wide variety of styles, from Stravinsky to jazz and rock, and create form and expression through contrasts of style, mood, texture, figuration, timbre, dynamics, and other factors, sometimes using quotation for humorous effect. He is best known for his music under the guise of P. D. Q. Bach, the supposed youngest son of J. S. Bach who inherited none of his father's talent. This persona allows Schickele to spoof old music, its performing practice, and musicologists. Performing conventions go awry, as in the long-winded continuo accompaniment in the cantata *Iphigenia in Brooklyn* (1964); bizarre instruments are featured, like the double-reed slide music stand, parodying the unfamiliar instruments called for in early music; and every stylistic expectation is violated, with hilarious results. For example, in the *"Howdy"* Symphony (1982)—a response to Haydn's *Farewell* Symphony—the first movement Allegro uses contrasts of style to delineate form, as in Classic-era music (see chapter 22), but here the styles range from Classic to vaudeville, big-band jazz, and modernist dissonance; the witty incongruities and surprises typical of Haydn become burlesque.

NEO-ROMANTICISM

In their search for expressive tools that connect directly with listeners, some composers adopted the familiar tonal idiom of nineteenth-century Romanticism or incorporated its sounds and gestures, a trend known as **neo-Romanticism**.

Krzysztof   For example, after making his reputation with pieces based on texture and
Penderecki   process (see chapter 34), Krzysztof Penderecki focused increasingly on melody and drew on past styles, genres, and harmonic practice in neo-Romantic works of the mid-1970s and beyond, such as the Violin Concerto No. 1 (1976–77) and the opera *Paradise Lost* (1975–78). The struggles of the trade union Solidarity to achieve democracy in Poland inspired the *Polish Requiem* (1980–84), in which Penderecki combined neo-Romanticism, ele-

ments from Renaissance and Baroque styles, and his signature textures from the 1960s in a new synthesis of styles.

Having turned from serialism to quotation in the 1960s (see chapter 34), George Rochberg moved on in the 1970s to use Romantic and early modernist styles for their expressive potential. His String Quartet No. 5 (1978) is neo-Romantic in three of its five movements. Each movement is written in a consistent style, but the styles differ considerably between movements. The first movement is a sprightly sonata form in A major reminiscent of late Beethoven or Schubert; the second, a sad E♭-minor slow movement whose canons and loosely dissonant harmonies recall early Bartók; the third, a Beethovenian scherzo in A minor with a Mahlerian trio; the fourth, an atonal serenade that resembles works of Schoenberg or Berg; and the finale, an energetic, constantly developing, rapidly modulating yet tonal rondo in late Romantic style, akin to Schoenberg's First Quartet. The mixture of idioms challenged the traditional expectation that music be stylistically uniform, but even more radical was Rochberg's choice to reclaim styles of the past and use them in a wholehearted effort to make their resources his own without the distancing effects notable in Stravinsky's neoclassicism or Schnittke's polystylism.

Rochberg

David Del Tredici (b. 1937) embraced neo-Romanticism for a different reason. After using atonal and serial methods in the 1960s, he changed his style radically when he started to set excerpts from Lewis Carroll's stories for children, feeling that their whimsy called for a direct, comprehensible presentation. *Final Alice* (1975), to a text from the final chapters of *Alice's Adventures in Wonderland*, is scored for amplified soprano and orchestra, with a "folk group" of banjo, mandolin, accordion, and two soprano saxophones. The soprano narrates, plays all the parts, and sings a series of arias. The central motive of the piece, a rising major sixth introduced by the saxophones, is taken up by other instruments and becomes the fundamental interval of "The Accusation" sung by the White Rabbit, shown in Example 35.4; a greater concentration of rising sixths in a melody is hard to imagine. Through this and other arias, the orchestra and folk group accompany in a kind of nonsense tonality, with slightly off-kilter dance rhythms and multiple layers in differing tempos. Most of the music is tonal, ranging from folklike episodes to an idiom reminiscent of Richard Strauss. But when Alice begins to grow larger, Del Tredici suggests the strange occurrence with atonal music, a twelve-tone

David Del Tredici

Example 35.4: "The Accusation," from Del Tredici's Final Alice

motive, and the electronic sounds of the Theremin. By using tonal and atonal styles side by side for their expressive effect, Del Tredici renounced the modernist ideology of progress. In its place, he returned to eighteenth- and nineteenth-century ideals of music, mixing diverse styles in a coherent whole that is comprehensible on first hearing to an untrained listener yet holds hidden delights for the connoisseur (see Source Reading).

EXTRAMUSICAL IMAGERY AND MEANINGS

Composers using various styles invoked extramusical meanings and imagery, hoping that listeners would accept unusual sounds if their meanings were clear. Spirituality was a frequent theme, continuing music's long association with religion and the transcendent.

Sofia Gubaidulina   Despite the official atheism of her native Soviet Union, almost all the works of Sofia Gubaidulina (b. 1931) have a spiritual dimension, often suggested in the title. The five movements of her sonata for violin and cello, *Rejoice!* (1981), were inspired by eighteenth-century devotional texts.

SOURCE READINGS

ON REACHING AN AUDIENCE

David Del Tredici's Final Alice *won immediate praise from listeners, as noted in the reviews of its premiere in October 1976.*

———— • ————

When the last stroke of *Final Alice* died away at the Chicago Symphony concert, the audience broke into sustained applause which quickly grew into a standing ovation. Cheers and bravos mingled with the handclaps. . . . It was the most enthusiastic reception of a new work that I have ever heard at a symphony concert.

Thomas Willis, *Chicago Tribune*, October 9, 1976.

But some of his fellow composers viewed the piece as a betrayal of the tenets of modernism, and Del Tredici found himself having to defend his success.

———— • ————

About halfway through [composing] the piece, I thought, "Oh my God, if I just leave it like this, my colleagues will think I'm crazy." But then I thought, "What else can I do? If nothing else occurs to me I can't go against my instincts." But I was terrified my colleagues would think I was an idiot. . . . People think now that I wanted to be tonal and have a big audience. But that was just not true. I didn't want to be tonal. My world was my colleagues—my composing friends. . . . The success of *Final Alice* was very defining as to who my real friends were. I think many composers regard success as a kind of threat. It's really better, they think, if nobody has any success, to be all in one boat. Composers now are beginning to realize that if a piece excites an audience, that doesn't mean it's terrible. For my generation, it is considered vulgar to have an audience really, really like a piece on a first hearing. But why are we writing music except to move people and to be expressive? To have what has moved us move somebody else?

Right now, audiences just reject contemporary music. But if they start to like one thing, then they begin to have perspective. That will make a difference, it always has in the past. The sleeping giant is the audience.

From an interview with John Rockwell, in *The New York Times*, Sunday, October 26, 1980, Section D, pp. 23, 28.

According to the composer, the sonata expresses the transcendence from ordinary reality to a state of joy and relies particularly on the passage from a
fundamental note to its harmonics to embody this journey of consciousness.
The fifth movement (NAWM 171), inscribed with the text "Listen to the still
small voice within," is a study in chromatics, tremolos, and harmonics, particularly glissandos from low fundamental notes in the cello to their higher
harmonics.

CD 12|67

The music of English composer John Tavener (b. 1944) also has centered
on spiritual concerns. After writing works influenced by Stravinsky's serialism and block construction, he joined the Orthodox Church in 1977 and
began to incorporate elements from its liturgical music, as in *Liturgy of St.
John Chrysostom* (1977) for unaccompanied chorus. He made his reputation
with sacred choral works in a harmonically simple, chant-derived idiom,
then applied a similar style in a series of instrumental works on religious
subjects that won international renown, of which *The Protecting Veil* for cello
and string orchestra (1987) is best known.

John Tavener

R. Murray Schafer (b. 1933), the leading Canadian composer of the era,
traversed a wide variety of styles from neoclassical to avant-garde, yet most of
his pieces are based on extramusical inspirations. His orchestral works
Dream Rainbow Dream Thunder (1986) and *Manitou* (1995), for example,
reflect ideas from the culture of the Inuits, natives of Canada. His most striking innovation is what he calls *environmental music*, pieces that break out of
the concert hall and require more than passive attention from listeners.
Music for Wilderness Lake (1979) is to be performed at sunrise and sunset at
a small lake away from human settlements, with twelve trombonists positioned around its shores playing meditative melodies to one another across
the water, cued by a conductor in a raft, and joined by animal sounds. Ideally,
listeners would participate in the event by experiencing the lake, its stillness,
its sounds, and its surrounding wilderness as the music is performed; in fact,
most can only watch the event on film.

R. Murray Schafer

Many works by American composer Joan Tower (b. 1938) are based on images. *Silver Ladders* (1986) for orchestra features rising lines (the "ladders"
of the title), either stepwise or leaping by fourths, moving at different speeds
amid a variety of textures. The "silver" in the title is meant to evoke the metal
in both its solid state, embodied in the dense orchestral sections, and its
molten state, represented through freely-flowing solos for clarinet, oboe,
marimba, and trumpet. The piece offers an abstract play of musical ideas, but
the imagery offers the listener a welcome hook that makes the work easier to
follow.

Joan Tower

DIRECT COMMUNICATION

The pieces discussed here represent only a few of the many strategies composers have used to communicate directly with listeners. By the 1990s, most
composers sought to write music that nonspecialist audiences could grasp, by
employing familiar idioms, gestures, and other elements drawn from the entire range of music history, popular styles, and musics of the world. These familiar elements were often juxtaposed or blended in unprecedented ways in

order to provide a new experience and achieve a distinctive profile. Thus, composers sought to uphold the high value placed on individuality since the nineteenth century while seeking to reclaim the immediate appeal that, many felt, had been lost in the modernist era.

INTERACTIONS WITH NON-WESTERN MUSICS

Minimalism was only one of many currents in Western music to be inspired by the musics of Asia and Africa.

Classical composers

Some composers drew directly on Asian musics. Bright Sheng (b. 1955), born and trained in China, moved to New York in 1982 for further study and has made his career in the United States. He seeks to integrate elements of Asian and Western music while respecting the integrity of each, inspired by the attempts of Bartók to do the same with eastern European folk and Western classical music. In the solo cello suite *Seven Tunes Heard in China* (1995; No. 1 in NAWM 172), Sheng joins the European tradition of the Bach cello suites—with sequences, double stops, and implied polyphony—to the playing style of Chinese bowed string instruments, marked by grace notes, glissandos, sudden dynamic changes, and flexible rhythm. The mostly pentatonic Chinese tune used as a source is fragmented and spun out using both Baroque and modernist methods, including polytonality. The result blends together fundamental aspects of Chinese, Western classical, and modern music. A similar union of Western and non-Western styles and sensibilities can be found in the music of South African native Kevin Volans (b. 1949), much of which draws on African traditions, and in some works by Australian composer Peter Sculthorpe (b. 1929) that incorporate or imitate Aboriginal melodies.

CD 12|75   CD 6|87

World Beat

Also linked to the globalization of music was *World Beat*, a term referring to African popular musics that reached international audiences. African musicians like the Nigerian Fela Kuti (1938–1997) merged popular styles from the United States and elsewhere with local traditions to create new sounds. Their music in turn began during the 1980s to be heard worldwide, and pop artists in Europe and America incorporated World Beat into their own music. Paul Simon's African-infused, Grammy-award-winning album *Graceland* (1986) raised the issue of cultural appropriation; one hit song from that album, *Diamonds on the Soles of Her Shoes*, featured Simon on lead vocals, backed by Ladysmith Black Mambazo (a traditional South African unaccompanied group) and a band of South African musicians.

In the final analysis, all the works described in this section are quintessentially Western, representing new instances of the centuries-old capacity of European music to absorb foreign elements and arrive at a new synthesis, as in the merging of French, Italian, and English traditions into an international language in the fifteenth century (see chapter 8) or of various styles and habits into the cosmopolitan idiom of the Classic era (see chapters 20–22).

But these recent works go beyond nineteenth-century exoticism in the respect they show for the intrinsic value of the non-Western traditions on which they draw.

THE NEW MILLENNIUM

It is too early to know what music from the late twentieth or early twenty-first century will be remembered, performed, and listened to in the future or will influence later music. Trends change too quickly to give a balanced or complete overview of recent music. But it seems clear that there is a continuing tension in all types of music between finding a niche of committed listeners whose support will endure and finding a wide audience. There are few pieces that everyone knows; perhaps national anthems and film music come closest to providing the shared musical experiences that seem to have been more common in the past. The immediate success and enduring place enjoyed by Beethoven in orchestral music, Verdi in opera, Duke Ellington in jazz, or the Beatles in popular music no longer seems possible for musicians working today because the audience is so divided that such unanimity of opinion is unlikely to be achieved.

Yet perhaps the relative lack of dominant figures may be a good thing. Music of the past and of the entire world is more available now than ever. Thanks to radio, recordings, and marketing, most of the music we have studied is heard by more people each year today than it was during the composer's lifetime. There is no need to focus our interest on a few great composers when there is so much variety to enjoy. The choices we have for music to hear and perform have become almost limitless. So too are the possibilities for new music. With new computer software and the collage approach found in both classical and rap music, it is now possible for all of us with access to technology to make our own music, without performance training. In some respects, we are surrounded by more music than we can ever consume. But perhaps we are also returning to something akin to the condition of music long ago, when every singer sang his or her own song.

Glossary

Within a definition, terms that are themselves defined in this glossary are printed in SMALL CAPITALS. Terms defined in general dictionaries are not included here. Pronunciation of foreign words is approximate and is given only when the spelling makes mispronunciation likely; "nh" stands for a final "n" in French, which nasalizes the preceding vowel (as in "chanson," rendered here as "shanh-SONH").

Abgesang (pronounced AHP-ge-zong)   See BAR FORM.

absolute music   Music that is independent of words, drama, visual images, or any kind of representational aspects.

a cappella (Italian, "in chapel style")   Manner of choral singing without instrumental accompaniment.

accidental   Sign that calls for altering the pitch of a NOTE: a sharp (♯) raises the pitch a semitone, a flat (♭) lowers it a semitone, and a natural (♮) cancels a previous accidental.

accompanied recitative   RECITATIVE that uses ORCHESTRAL accompaniment to dramatize the text.

act   Main division of an OPERA. Most operas have two to five acts, although some have only one.

affections   Objectified or archetypal emotions or states of mind, such as sadness, joy, fear, or wonder; one goal of much BAROQUE music was to arouse the affections.

Agnus Dei (Latin, "Lamb of God")   Fifth of the five major musical items in the MASS ORDINARY, based on a litany.

agrément (French, "charm"; pronounced ah-gray-MANH)   ORNAMENT in French music, usually indicated by a sign.

air   English or French song for solo voice with instrumental accompaniment, setting rhymed poetry, often STROPHIC, and usually in the METER of a dance.

air de cour (French, "court air")   Type of song for voice and accompaniment, prominent in France from about 1580 through the seventeenth century.

Alberti bass   Broken-CHORD accompaniment common in the second half of the eighteenth century and named after Domenico Alberti, who used the FIGURATION frequently.

Alleluia   Item from the MASS PROPER, sung just before the Gospel reading, comprising a RESPOND to the text "Alleluia," a verse, and a repetition of the respond. CHANT alleluias are normally MELISMATIC in style and sung in a RESPONSORIAL manner, one or more soloists alternating with the CHOIR.

allemande (French for "German")   Highly stylized DANCE in BINARY FORM, in moderately fast quadruple METER with almost continuous movement, beginning with an upbeat. Popular during the RENAISSANCE and BAROQUE; appearing often as the first dance in a SUITE.

alto (from ALTUS)   (1) Relatively low female voice, or high male voice. (2) Part for such a voice in an ENSEMBLE work.

altus (Latin, "high")   In fifteenth- and sixteenth-century POLYPHONY, a part in a range between the TENOR and the SUPERIUS; originally CONTRATENOR ALTUS.

Ambrosian chant   A repertory of ecclesiastical CHANT used in Milan.

answer   In the EXPOSITION of a FUGUE, the second entry of the SUBJECT, normally on the DOMINANT if the subject was on the TONIC, and vice versa. Also refers to subsequent answers to the subject.

anthem   A POLYPHONIC sacred work in English for Anglican religious services.

antiphon   (1) A LITURGICAL CHANT that precedes and follows a PSALM or CANTICLE in the OFFICE. (2) In the MASS, a chant originally associated with ANTIPHONAL PSALMODY; specifically, the COMMUNION and the first and final portion of the INTROIT.

antiphonal   Adjective describing a manner of performance in which two or more groups alternate.

Aquitanian polyphony   Style of POLYPHONY from the twelfth century, encompassing both DISCANT and FLORID ORGANUM.

aria (Italian, "air")   (1) In the late sixteenth and early seventeenth centuries, any section of an Italian STROPHIC poem for a solo singer. (2) Lyrical monologue in an OPERA or other vocal work such as CANTATA and ORATORIO.

arioso   (1) RECITATIVO ARIOSO. (2) Short, ARIA-like passage. (3) Style of vocal writing that approaches the lyricism of an ARIA but is freer in form.

arpeggio (from Italian *arpa*, "harp")   Broken-CHORD FIGURE.

Ars Nova (Latin, "new art")   Style of POLYPHONY from fourteenth-century France, distinguished from earlier styles by a new system of rhythmic NOTATION that allowed duple or triple division of NOTE values, SYNCOPATION, and great rhythmic flexibility.

Ars Subtilior (Latin, "more subtle art")   Style of POLYPHONY from the late fourteenth or very early fifteenth centuries in southern France and northern Italy, distinguished by extreme complexity in rhythm and NOTATION.

art music   Music that is (or is meant to be) listened to with rapt attention, for its own sake. Compare POPULAR MUSIC.

art song   A song intended to be appreciated as an artistic statement rather than as entertainment, featuring precisely notated music, usually THROUGH COMPOSED, and requiring professional standards of performance. Compare POPULAR SONG.

atonal, atonality   Terms for music that avoids establishing a central pitch or tonal center (such as the TONIC in TONAL music).

aulos   Ancient Greek reed instrument, usually played in pairs.

authentic mode   A MODE (2) in which the RANGE normally extends from a STEP below the FINAL to an octave above it. See also PLAGAL MODE.

avant-garde   Term for music (and art) that is iconoclastic, irreverent, antagonistic, and nihilistic, seeking to overthrow established aesthetics.

ballad   (1) Long narrative poem, or musical setting of such a poem. (2) Late-eighteenth-century German poetic form that imitated the folk ballad of England and Scotland and was set to music by German composers. The ballad expanded the LIED in both FORM and emotional content.

ballad opera   GENRE of eighteenth-century English comic play featuring songs in which new words are set to borrowed tunes.

ballade   (a) French FORME FIXE, normally in three stanzas, in which each stanza has the musical FORM aab and ends with a REFRAIN. (2) Instrumental piece inspired by the GENRE of narrative poetry.

ballata (from Italian *ballare*, "to dance"; pl. *ballate*)   Fourteenth-century Italian song GENRE with the FORM AbbaA, in which A is the *ripresa* or REFRAIN, and the single stanza consists of two *piedi* (bb) and a *volta* (a) sung to the music of the ripresa.

ballet   In sixteenth- and seventeenth-century France, an entertainment in which both professionals and guests danced; later, a stage work danced by professionals.

balletto, ballett (Italian, "little dance")   Sixteenth-century Italian (and later English) song GENRE in a simple, dancelike, HOMOPHONIC style with repeated sections and "fa-la-la" refrains.

band   Large ENSEMBLE of winds, brass, and percussion instruments, or of brass and percussion instruments without winds.

bar form   Song FORM in which the first section of MELODY is sung twice with different texts (the two STOLLEN) and the remainder (the ABGESANG) is sung once.

bard   Medieval poet-singer, especially of epics.

Baroque (from Portuguese *barroco*, "a misshapen pearl")   PERIOD of music history from about 1600 to about 1750, overlapping the late RENAISSANCE and early CLASSIC periods.

bas (French, "low"; pronounced BAH)   In the fourteenth through sixteenth centuries, term for soft instruments such as VIELLES and HARPS. See HAUT.

bass (from BASSUS)   (1) The lowest part in an ENSEMBLE work. (2) Low male voice. (3) Low instrument, especially the string bass or bass VIOL.

basse danse (French, "low dance")   Type of stately couple DANCE of the fifteenth and early sixteenth centuries.

basso continuo (Italian, "continuous bass")   (1) System of NOTATION and performance practice, used in the BAROQUE PERIOD, in which an instrumental BASS line is written out and one or more players of keyboard, LUTE, or similar instruments fill in the HARMONY with appropriate CHORDS or IMPROVISED MELODIC lines. (2) The bass line itself.

basso ostinato (Italian, "persistent bass") or **ground bass**   A pattern in the BASS that repeats while the MELODY above it changes.

bassus (Latin, "low")   In fifteenth- and sixteenth-century POLYPHONY, the lowest part; originally CONTRATENOR BASSUS.

bebop (or **bop**)   A style of JAZZ developed in New York in the 1940s that had a diversified rhythmic texture, enriched HARMONIC vocabulary, and an emphasis on IMPROVISATION with rapid MELODIES and asymmetrical PHRASES.

bel canto (Italian, "beautiful singing")   Elegant Italian vocal style of the early nineteenth century marked by lyrical, embellished, and florid melodies that show off the beauty, agility, and fluency of the singer's voice.

big band Type of large JAZZ ENSEMBLE popular between the world wars, featuring brass, reeds, and RHYTHM SECTIONS, and playing prepared arrangements that included rhythmic unisons and coordinated dialogue between sections and soloists.

binary form A FORM comprised of two complementary sections, each of which is repeated. The first section usually ends on the DOMINANT or the relative major, although it many end of the TONIC or other KEY; the second section returns to the tonic.

blue note Slight drop or slide in pitch on the third, fifth, or seventh degree of a MAJOR SCALE, common in BLUES and JAZZ.

blues (1) African-American vocal GENRE that is based on a simple repetitive formula and characterized by a distinctive style of performance. (2) TWELVE-BAR BLUES.

bop See BEBOP.

branle gay RENAISSANCE DANCE in a lively triple METER based on a sideways swaying step.

breve (from Latin *brevis*, "short") In medieval and RENAISSANCE systems of RHYTHMIC NOTATION, a NOTE that is normally equal to half or a third of a LONG.

bull lyre Sumerian LYRE with a bull's head at one end of the soundbox.

burden (1) In English medieval POLYPHONY, the lowest voice. (2) In the English CAROL, the REFRAIN.

Byzantine chant The repertory of ecclesiastical CHANT used in the Byzantine RITE and in the modern Greek Orthodox Church.

cabaletta In the operatic scene structure developed by Gioachino Rossini in the early nineteenth century, the last part of an ARIA or ENSEMBLE, which was lively and brilliant and expressed active feelings, such as joy or despair. See also CANTABILE and TEMPO DI MEZZO.

cabaret Type of nightclub, first introduced in nineteenth-century Paris, that offered serious or comic sketches, dances, songs, and poetry.

caccia (Italian, "hunt"; pronounced CAH-cha; pl. *cacce*) Fourteenth-century Italian FORM featuring two voices in CANON over a free untexted TENOR.

cadence MELODIC or HARMONIC succession that closes a musical PHRASE, PERIOD, section, or COMPOSITION.

cadenza (Italian, "cadence") Highly embellished passage, often IMPROVISED, at an important CADENCE, usually occurring just before the end of a piece or section.

café-concert Type of dining establishment, prominent in late-nineteenth- and early-twentieth-century Pans, that combined the food and drink of a café with musical entertainment, usually songs on sentimental, comic, or political topics.

call and response Alternation of short PHRASES between a leader and a group; used especially for music in the African-American tradition.

cambiata (Italian, "changed") Figure in sixteenth-century POLYPHONY in which a voice skips down from a DISSONANCE

to a CONSONANCE instead of resolving by STEP, then moves to the expected NOTE of resolution.

Camerata (Italian, "circle" or "association") Circle of intellectuals and amateurs of the arts that met in Florence, Italy, in the 1570s and 1580s.

canon (Latin, "rule") (1) Rule for performing music, particularly for deriving more than one voice from a single line of notated music, as when several voices sing the same MELODY, entering at certain intervals of time or singing at different speeds simultaneously. (2) COMPOSITION in which the voices enter successively at determined pitch and time intervals, all performing the same MELODY.

cantabile (Italian, "songlike") (1) Songful, lyrical, in a songlike style. (2) In the operatic scene structure developed by Gioachino Rossini in the early nineteenth century, the first section of an ARIA or ENSEMBLE, somewhat slow and expressing a relatively calm mood. See also CABELETTA and TEMPO DI MEZZO.

cantata (Italian, "to be sung") (1) In the seventeenth and eighteenth centuries, a vocal chamber work with CONTINUO, usually for solo voice, consisting of several sections or MOVEMENTS that include RECITATIVES and ARIAS and setting a lyrical or quasi-dramatic text. (2) Form of Lutheran church music in the eighteenth century, combining poetic texts with texts drawn from CHORALES or the Bible, and including RECITATIVES, ARIAS, chorale settings, and usually one or more CHORUSES. (3) In later eras, a work for soloists, CHORUS, and ORCHESTRA in several MOVEMENTS but smaller than an ORATORIO.

canticle HYMN-like or PSALM-like passage from a part of the Bible other than the Book of Psalms.

cantiga Medieval MONOPHONIC song in Spanish or Portuguese.

cantilena (Latin, "song") POLYPHONIC song not based on a CANTUS FIRMUS; used especially for polyphonic songs by English composers of the late thirteenth through early fifteenth centuries.

cantillation Chanting of a sacred text by a solo singer, particularly in the Jewish synagogue.

cantional style (from Latin *cantionale*, "songbook") Manner of setting CHORALES in CHORDAL HOMOPHONY with the MELODY in the highest voice.

cantor In Jewish synagogue music, the main solo singer. In the medieval Christian church, the leader of the CHOIR.

cantus (Latin, "melody") In POLYPHONY of the fourteenth through sixteenth centuries, the highest voice, especially the texted voice in a polyphonic song.

cantus firmus (Latin, "fixed melody") An existing MELODY, often taken from a GREGORIAN CHANT, on which a new POLYPHONIC work is based; used especially for MELODIES presented in long NOTES.

cantus-firmus mass POLYPHONIC MASS in which the same CANTUS FIRMUS is used in each MOVEMENT, normally in the TENOR.

cantus-firmus/imitation mass POLYPHONIC MASS in which each MOVEMENT is based on the same polyphonic work, using that work's TENOR (sometimes the SUPERIUS) as a CANTUS FIRMUS, normally in the tenor, and borrowing some elements from the other voices of the model to use in the other voices of the mass.

cantus-firmus variations Instrumental GENRE of the late 1500s and early 1600s, comprising a set of VARIATIONS in which the MELODY repeats with little change but is surrounded by different CONTRAPUNTAL material in each variation.

canzona (canzon) (Italian, "song") (1) Sixteenth-century Italian GENRE, an instrmental work adapted from a CHANSON or composed in a similar style. (2) In the late sixteenth and early seventeenth centuries, an instrumental work in several contrasting sections, of which the first and some of the others are in IMITATIVE COUNTERPOINT.

canzonetta, canzonet (Italian, "little song") Sixteenth-century Italian (and later English) song GENRE in a simple, mostly HOMOPHONIC style. Diminutive of CANZONA.

capriccio (Italian, "whim") (1) In the BAROQUE period, a FUGAL piece in continuous IMITATIVE COUNTERPOINT. (2) In the nineteenth century, a short COMPOSITION in free FORM, usually for PIANO.

carol English song, usually on a religious subject, with several stanzas and a BURDEN, or REFRAIN. From the fifteenth century on, most carols are POLYPHONIC.

carole Medieval circle or line dance, or the MONOPHONIC song that accompanied it.

castrati (sing. castrato) Male singers who were castrated before puberty to preserve their high vocal RANGE, prominent in the seventeenth and early eighteenth centuries, especially in OPERA.

catch English GENRE of CANON, usually with a humorous or ribald text.

cauda (Latin, "tail"; pl. *caudae*) MELISMATIC passage in a POLYPHONIC CONDUCTUS.

centonization (from Latin *cento*, "patchwork") A process of composing a new MELODY by combining standard MOTIVES and formulas, used in BYZANTINE CHANT.

chacona (Italian, **ciaccona**) A vivacious dance-song imported from Latin America into Spain and then into Italy, popular during the seventeenth century

chaconne (or **ciaccona**) BAROQUE GENRE derived from the CHACONA, consisting of VARIATIONS over a BASSO CONTINUO.

chamber sonata See SONATA DA CAMERA.

chance Approach to composing music pioneered by John Cage, in which some of the decisions normally made by the composer are instead determined through random procedures, such as tossing coins. Chance differs from INDETERMINACY but shares with it the result that the sounds in the music do not convey an intention and are therefore to be experienced only as pure sound.

chanson (French, "song"; pronounced shanh-SONH) Secular song with French words; used especially for POLYPHONIC songs of the fourteenth through sixteenth centuries.

chanson de geste (French, "song of deeds") Type of medieval French epic recounting the deeds of national heros, sung to MELODIC formulas.

chansonnier (French, "songbook") Manuscript collection of secular songs with French words; used both for collections of MONOPHONIC TROUBADOUR and TROUVÈRE songs and for collections of POLYPHONIC songs.

chant (1) Unison unaccompanied song, particularly that of the Latin LITURGY (also called PLAINCHANT). (2) The repertory of unaccompanied liturgical songs of a particular RITE.

chant dialect One of the repertories of ecclesiastical CHANT, including GREGORIAN, BYZANTINE, AMBROSIAN, and OLD ROMAN CHANT.

chapel A group of salaried musicians and clerics employed by a ruler, nobleman, church official, or other patron, who officiate at and furnish music for religious services.

character piece A piece of CHARACTERISTIC MUSIC, especially one for PIANO.

characteristic (or **descriptive**) **music** Instrumental music that depicts or suggests a mood, personality, or scene, usually indicated in its title.

charts In postwar POPULAR MUSIC, weekly rankings of songs by sales or other measures of popularity.

choir A group of singers who perform together, singing either in unison or in parts. Used especially for the group that sings in a religious service.

choral society Amateur CHORUS whose members sing for their own enjoyment and may pay dues to purchase music, pay the CONDUCTOR, and meet other expenses.

chorale (pronounced ko-RAL) STROPHIC HYMN in the Lutheran tradition, intended to be sung by the congregation.

chorale motet CHORALE setting in the style of a sixteenth-century MOTET.

chorale prelude Relatively short setting for organ of a CHORALE MELODY, used as an introduction for congregational singing or as an interlude in a Lutheran church service.

chorale variations A set of VARIATIONS on a CHORALE MELODY.

chord Three or more simultaneous NOTES heard as a single entity. In TONAL music, three or more notes that can be arranged as a succession of thirds, such as a TRIAD.

chorus (1) Group of singers who perform together, usually with several singers on each part. (2) A MOVEMENT or passage for such a group in an ORATORIO, OPERA, or other multimovement work. (3) The REFRAIN of a POPULAR SONG. (4) In JAZZ, a statement of the HARMONIC PROGRESSION of the opening tune, over which one or more instruments play variants or new musical ideas.

chromatic (from Greek *chroma*, "color") (1) In ancient Greek music, adjective describing a TETRACHORD comprising a minor third and two SEMITONES, or a MELODY that uses such tetrachords. (2) Adjective describing a melody that uses two or more successive semitones in the same direction, a SCALE consisting exclusively of semitones, an INTERVAL or CHORD that draws NOTES from more than one DIATONIC scale, or music that uses many such melodies or chords.

chromatic saturation   The appearance of all twelve PITCH-CLASSES within a segment of music.

chromaticism   The use of many NOTES from the CHROMATIC SCALE in a passage or piece.

church calendar   In a Christian RITE, the schedule of days commemorating special events, individuals, or times of year.

church sonata   See SONATA DA CHIESA.

ciaccona   See CHACONA.

Classic period   In music history, the era from about 1730 to about 1815, between and overlapping the BAROQUE and ROMANTIC PERIODS.

classical music   (1) Common term for ART MUSIC of all PERIODS, as distinct from POPULAR MUSIC OR FOLK MUSIC. (2) Music in the tradition of the repertoire of musical masterworks that formed in the nineteenth century, including lesser works in the same GENRES (such as OPERA, ORATORIO, SYMPHONY, SONATA, STRING QUARTET, and ART SONG) or for the same performing forces and newly composed works intended as part of the same tradition. (3) Music in the CLASSIC PERIOD.

classical style   Musical idiom of the eighteenth century, generally characterized by an emphasis on MELODY over relatively light accompaniment; simple, clearly articulated harmonic plans; PERIODIC phrasing; clearly delineated FORMS based on contrast between THEMES, between KEYS, between stable and unstable passages, and between sections with different functions; and contrasts of mood, style, and figuration within MOVEMENTS as well as between them.

clausula (Latin, "clause," pl. *clausulae*)   In NOTRE DAME POLYPHONY, a self-contained section of an ORGANUM that closes with a CADENCE.

clavecin   French term for HARPSICHORD. A person who performs on or composes works for the clavecin is known as a **clavecinist**.

clavichord   Keyboard instrument popular between the fifteenth and eighteenth centuries. The loudness, which depends on the force with which a brass blade strikes the strings, is under the direct control of the player.

clos   See OPEN AND CLOSED ENDINGS.

coda (Italian, "tail")   A supplementary ending to a COMPOSITION or MOVEMENT; a concluding section that lies outside the FORM as usually described.

collage   Work or passage that uses multiple QUOTATIONS without following a standard procedure for doing so, such as QUODLIBET or medley.

collegium musicum   An association of amateurs, popular during the BAROQUE PERIOD, who gathered to play and sing together for their own pleasure. Today, an ensemble of university students that performs early music.

color (Latin rhetorical term for ornament, particularly repetition, pronounced KOH-lor)   In an ISORHYTHMIC COMPOSITION, a repeated MELODIC pattern, as opposed to the repeating rhythmic pattern (the TALEA).

coloratura   Florid vocal ORNAMENTATION.

Communion   Item in the MASS PROPER, originally sung during communion, comprising an ANTIPHON without verses.

composition   The act or process of creating new pieces of music, or a piece that results from this process and is substantially similar each time it is performed; usually distinguished from IMPROVISATION and performance.

concert band   Large ENSEMBLE of winds, brass, and percussion instruments that performs seated in concert halls, like an ORCHESTRA.

concert étude   See ÉTUDE

concertato medium (from Italian *concertare*, "to reach agreement")   In seventeenth-century music, the combination of voices with one or more instruments, where the instruments do not simply double the voices but play independent parts.

concerted madrigal   Early-seventeenth-century type of MADRIGAL for one or more voices accompanied by BASSO CONTINUO and in some cases by other instruments.

concerto (from Italian *concertare*, "to reach agreement")   (1) In the seventeenth century, ENSEMBLE of instruments or of voices with one or more instruments, or a work for such an ensemble. (2) COMPOSITION in which one or more solo instruments (or instrumental group) contrasts with an ORCHESTRAL ENSEMBLE. See also SOLO CONCERTO, CONCERTO GROSS, and ORCHESTRAL CONCERTO.

concerto grosso   Instrumental work that exploits the contrast in sonority between a small ENSEMBLE of solo instruments (*concertino*), usually the same forces that appeared in the TRIO SONATA, and a large ENSEMBLE (RIPIENO or *concerto grosso*).

concitato   See STILE CONCITATO.

conductor   A person who leads a performance, especially for an ORCHESTRA, BAND, CHORUS, or other large ENSEMBLE, by means of gestures.

conductus   A serious medieval song, MONOPHONIC or POLYPHONIC, setting a rhymed, rhythmic Latin poem.

conjunct   (1) In ancient Greek music, adjective used to describe the relationship between two TETRACHORDS when the bottom NOTE of one is the same as the top note of the other. (2) Of a MELODY, consisting mostly of STEPS.

conservatory   School that specializes in teaching music.

consonance   INTERVAL or CHORD that has a stable, harmonious sound. Compare DISSONANCE.

consort   English name (current ca. 1575–1700) for a group of instruments, either all of one type (called a *full consort*), such as a consort of VIOLS, or of different types (called a *broken consort*).

consort song   RENAISSANCE English GENRE of song for voice accompanied by a CONSORT of VIOLS.

contenance angloise (French, "English guise") Characteristic quality of early-fifteenth-century English music, marked by pervasive CONSONANCE with frequent use of HARMONIC thirds and sixths, often in parallel motion.

continuo BASSO CONTINUO.

continuo instruments Instruments used to REALIZE a BASSO CONTINUO, such as HARPSICHORD, organ, LUTE, or THEORBO.

contrafact In JAZZ, a new MELODY composed over a HARMONIC PROGRESSION borrowed from another song.

contrafactum (Latin, "counterfeit"; pl. *contrafacta*) The practice of replacing the text of a vocal work with a new text while the music remains essentially the same; or the resulting piece.

contrapuntal Employing COUNTERPOINT, or two or more simultaneous MELODIC lines.

contratenor (Latin, "against the tenor") In fourteenth- and fifteenth-century POLYPHONY, voice composed after or in conjunction with the TENOR and in about the same RANGE, helping to form the HARMONIC foundation.

contratenor altus, contratenor bassus (Latin) In fifteenth-century POLYPHONY, CONTRATENOR parts that lie relatively high (ALTUS) or low (BASSUS) in comparison to the TENOR. Often simply written as "altus" or "bassus," these are the ancestors of the vocal ranges ALTO and BASS.

cornett Wind instrument of hollowed-out wood or ivory, with finger holes and a cup mouthpiece, blown like a brass instrument.

counterpoint The combination of two or more simultaneous MELODIC lines according to a set of rules.

country music (also known as *country-and-western*) A type of POPULAR MUSIC associated primarily with white southerners, that blends elements of FOLK MUSIC, POPULAR SONG, and other traditions.

couplet In a RONDO or seventeenth- or eighteenth-century RONDEAU, one of several PERIODS or passages that alternate with the REFRAIN.

courante A DANCE in BINARY FORM, in triple METER at a moderate tempo and with an upbeat, featured as a standard MOVEMENT of the BAROQUE dance SUITE.

court ballet Seventeenth-century French GENRE, an extensive musical-dramatic work with costumes, scenery, poetry, and dance that featured members of the court as well as professional dancers.

courtly love See FINE AMOUR.

Credo (Latin, "I believe") Third of the five major musical items in the MASS ORDINARY, a creed or statement of faith.

crumhorn RENAISSANCE wind instrument, with a double reed enclosed in a cap so the player's lips do not touch the reed.

cumulative form FORM used by Charles Ives and others in which the principal THEME appears in its entirety only at the end of a work, preceded by its DEVELOPMENT.

cycle A group of related works, comprising MOVEMENTS of a single larger entity. Examples include cycles of CHANTS for the MASS ORDINARY, consisting of one setting each of the KYRIE, GLORIA, SANCTUS, and AGNUS DEI (and

sometimes also *Ite, missa est*); the POLYPHONIC MASS cycle of the fifteenth through seventeenth centuries; and the SONG CYCLE of the nineteenth century.

da capo aria ARIA FORM with two sections. The first section is repeated after the second section's close, which carries the instruction *da capo* (Italian, "from the head"), creating an ABA FORM.

dances Pieces in stylized dance rhythms, whether independent, paired, or linked together in a SUITE.

descriptive music See CHARACTERISTIC MUSIC.

developing variation Term coined by Arnold Schoenberg for the process of deriving new THEMES, accompaniments, and other ideas throughout a piece through variations of a germinal idea.

development (1) The process of reworking, recombining, fragmenting, and varying given THEMES or other material. (2) In SONATA FORM, the section after the EXPOSITION, which MODULATES through a variety of KEYS and in which THEMES from the exposition are presented in new ways.

diastematic Having to do with INTERVALS. In diastematic motion, the voice moves between sustained pitches separated by discrete intervals; in diastematic NOTATION, the approximate intervals are indicated by relative height (see HEIGHTED NEUMES).

diatonic (1) In ancient Greek music, adjective describing a TETRACHORD with two WHOLE TONES and one SEMITONE. (2) Name for a SCALE that includes five whole tones and two semitones, where the semitones are separated by two or three whole tones. (3) Adjective describing a MELODY, CHORD, or passage based exclusively on a single diatonic scale.

diegetic music or **source music** In film, music that is heard or performed by the characters themselves.

digital Relating to methods for producing or recording musical sounds by translating them into a coded series of on-off pulses, or 1s and 0s, in the same way that computers store and transmit data.

diminution (1) Uniform reduction of NOTE values in a MELODY or PHRASE. (2) Type of IMPROVISED ORNAMENTATION in the sixteenth and seventeenth centuries, in which relatively long notes are replaced with SCALES or other FIGURES composed of short notes.

direct Pertaining to a manner of performing CHANT without alternation between groups (see ANTIPHONAL) or between soloist and group (see RESPONSORIAL).

discant (Latin, "singing apart") (1) Twelfth-century style of POLYPHONY in which the upper voice or voices have about one to three NOTES for each note of the lower voice. (2) TREBLE part.

disjunct (1) In ancient Greek music, adjective used to describe the relationship between two TETRACHORDS when the bottom NOTE of one is a whole tone above the top note of the other. (2) Of a MELODY, consisting mostly of skips (thirds) and leaps (larger INTERVALS) rather than STEPS.

dissonance (1) Two or more NOTES sounding together to produce a discord, or a sound that needs to be resolved to a CONSONANCE. (2) A NOTE that does not belong to the CHORD that sounds simultaneously with it; a nonchord TONE.

diva A leading and successful female OPERA singer. See also PRIMA DONNA.

divertissement In TRAGÉDIE EN MUSIQUE, a long interlude of BALLET, solo AIRS, choral singing, and spectacle, intended as entertainment.

division See DIMINUTION (2).

dominant In TONAL music, the NOTE and CHORD a perfect fifth above the TONIC.

double leading-tone cadence CADENCE popular in the fourteenth and fifteenth centuries, in which the bottom voice moves down a WHOLE TONE and the upper voices move up a SEMITONE, forming a major third and major sixth expanding to an open fifth and octave.

double motet Thirteenth-century MOTET in three voices, with different texts in the DUPLUM and TRIPLUM.

Doxology A formula of praise to the Trinity. Two FORMS are used in GREGORIAN CHANT: the Greater Doxology, or GLORIA, and the Lesser Doxology, used with PSALMS, INTROITS, and other chants.

dramatic opera Seventeenth-century English mixed GENRE of musical theater, a spoken play with an OVERTURE and four or more MASQUES or long musical interludes. Today often called SEMI-OPERA.

drone NOTE or notes sustained throughout an entire piece or section.

duplum (from Latin *duplus*, "double") In POLYPHONY of the late twelfth through fourteenth centuries, second voice from the bottom in a four-voice TEXTURE, above the TENOR.

dynamics Level of loudness or softness, or intensity.

echos (Greek; pl. *echoi*) One of the eight MODES associated with BYZANTINE CHANT.

electronic music Music based on sounds that are produced or modified through electronic means.

empfindsam style (German, "sensitive style" or "sentimental style") Close relative of the GALANT style, featuring surprising turns of HARMONY, CHROMATICISM, nervous RHYTHMS, and speechlike MELODIES.

enharmonic (1) In ancient Greek music, adjective describing a TETRACHORD comprising a major third and two quartertones, or a MELODY that uses such tetrachords. (2) Adjective describing the relationship between two pitches that are notated differently but sound alike when played, such as G♯ and A♭.

ensemble (1) A group of singers or instrumentalists who perform together. (2) In an OPERA, a passage or piece for more than one singer.

episode (1) In a FUGUE, a passage of COUNTERPOINT between statements of the SUBJECT. (2) In RONDO FORM, a section between two statements of the main THEME. (3) A subsidiary passage between presentations of the main thematic material.

equal temperament A TEMPERAMENT in which the octave is divided into twelve equal SEMITONES. This is the most commonly used tuning for Western music today.

estampie Medieval instrumental DANCE that features a series of sections, each played twice with two different endings, OUVERT and CLOS.

ethos (Greek, "custom") (1) Moral and ethical character or way of being or behaving. (2) Character, mood, or emotional effect of a certain TONOS, MODE, METER, or MELODY.

étude (French, "study") An instrumental piece designed to develop a particular skill or performing technique. Certain nineteenth-century études that contained significant artistic content and were played in concert were called CONCERT ÉTUDES.

exoticism Nineteenth-century trend in which composers wrote music that evoked feelings and settings of distant lands or foreign cultures.

experimental music A trend in twentieth-century music that focused on the exploration of new musical sounds, techniques, and resources.

exposition (1) In a FUGUE, a set of entries of the SUBJECT. (2) In SONATA FORM, the first part of the MOVEMENT, in which the main THEMES are stated, beginning in the TONIC and usually closing in the DOMINANT (or relative major).

expressionism Early-twentieth-century term derived from art, in which music avoids all traditional forms of "beauty" in order to express deep personal feelings through exaggerated gestures, angular MELODIES, and extreme DISSONANCE.

faburden English style of IMPROVISED POLYPHONY from the late Middle Ages and RENAISSANCE, in which a CHANT in the middle voice is joined by an upper voice moving in parallel a perfect fourth above it and a lower voice that follows below the chant mostly in parallel thirds, moving to a fifth below to mark the beginning and end of phrases and the ends of most words.

fantasia (Italian, "fantasy"), **fantasy** (1) Instrumental COMPOSITION that resembles an IMPROVISATION or lacks a strict FORM. (2) IMITATIVE instrumental piece on a single subject.

fauxbourdon (pronounced FOH-boor-donh) Continental style of POLYPHONY in the early RENAISSANCE, in which two voices are written, moving mostly in parallel sixths and ending each PHRASE on an octave, while a third unwritten voice is sung in parallel perfect fourths below the upper voice.

figuration, figure MELODIC pattern made of commonplace materials such as SCALES or ARPEGGIOS, usually not distinctive enough to be considered a MOTIVE or THEME.

figured bass A form of BASSO CONTINUO in which the BASS line is supplied with numbers or flat or sharp signs to indicate the appropriate CHORDS to be played.

final The main NOTE in a MODE; the normal closing note of a CHANT in that mode.

finale   Last MOVEMENT of a work in three or more movements, or the closing portion of an ACT in an OPERA.

fine amour (French, "refined love"; pronounced FEEN ah-MOOR; *fin' amors* in Occitan; also called **courtly love**)   An idealized love for an unattainable woman who is admired from a distance. Chief subject of the TROUBADOURS and TROUVÈRES.

first practice   See PRIMA PRATICA.

florid organum   Twelfth-century style of two-voice POLYPHONY in which the lower voice sustains relatively long NOTES while the upper voice sings note-groups of varying length above each note of the lower voice.

folk music   (1) Music of unknown authorship from a particular region or people, passed down through oral tradition. (2) In the decades after World War II, a type of POPULAR MUSIC that drew on folk traditions, which included both genuine FOLK SONGS and POPULAR SONGS.

folk song   Song of unknown authorship from a particular region or people, passed down through oral tradition.

form   The shape or structure of a COMPOSITION or MOVEMENT.

formes fixes (French, "fixed forms"; pronounced form FEEX)   Schemes of poetic and musical repetition, each featuring a REFRAIN, used in late medieval and fifteenth-century French CHANSONS; in particular, the BALLADE, RONDEAU, and VIRELAI.

Franconian notation   System of NOTATION described by Franco of Cologne around 1280, using noteshapes to indicate durations.

free jazz   An experimental JAZZ style introduced in the 1960s by Ornette Coleman, using IMPROVISATION that disregards the standard forms and conventions of jazz.

free organum   Style of ORGANUM in which the ORGANAL voice moves in a free mixture of contrary, oblique, parallel, and similar motion against the CHANT (and usually above it).

French overture   Type of OVERTURE used in TRAGÉDIE EN MUSIQUE and other GENRES, that opens with a slow, HOMOPHONIC, and majestic section, followed by a faster second section that begins with IMITATION.

frottola (pl. *frottole*)   Sixteenth-century GENRE of Italian POLYPHONIC song in mock-popular style, typically SYLLABIC, HOMOPHONIC, and DIATONIC, with the MELODY in the upper voice and marked rhythmic patterns.

fugal   Resembling a FUGUE; featuring fugue-like IMITATION.

fuging tune   Eighteenth-century American type of PSALM or HYMN tune that features a passage in free IMITATION, usually preceded and followed by HOMOPHONIC sections.

fugue (from Italian *fuga*, "flight")   COMPOSITION or section of a composition in IMITATIVE TEXTURE that is based on a single SUBJECT and begins with successive statements of the subject in voices.

full anthem   ANTHEM for unaccompanied CHOIR in CONTRAPUNTAL style.

fundamental bass   Term coined by Jean-Philippe Rameau to indicate the succession of the roots or fundamental tones in a series of CHORDS.

futurism, futurists   Twentieth-century movement that created music based on noise.

galant (French, "elegant")   Eighteenth-century musical style that featured songlike MELODIES, short PHRASES, frequent CADENCES, and light accompaniment.

galliard   Sixteenth-century dance in fast triple METER, often paired with the PAVANE and in the same FORM (AABBCC).

gamut   The entire range of pitches normally written in the Middle Ages (see p. 47).

gavotte   BAROQUE duple-time dance in BINARY FORM, with a half-measure upbeat and a characteristic rhythm of short-short-*long*.

Gebrauchsmusik (German "utilitarian music" or "music for use")   Term from the 1920s to describe music that was socially relevant and useful, especially music for amateurs, children, or workers to play or sing.

genre   Type or category of musical COMPOSITION, such as SONATA or SYMPHONY.

genus (Latin, "class"; pronounced GHEH-noos; pl. *genera*)   In ancient Greek music, one of three forms of TETRACHORD: DIATONIC, CHROMATIC, and ENHARMONIC.

Gesamtkunstwerk (German, "total artwork" or "collective artwork")   Term coined by Richard Wagner for a dramatic work in which poetry, scenic design, staging, action, and music all work together toward one artistic expression.

gigue (French for "jig")   Stylized DANCE movement of a standard BAROQUE SUITE, in BINARY FORM, marked by fast compound METER such as $\frac{6}{4}$ or $\frac{12}{8}$ with wide MELODIC leaps and continuous triplets. The two sections usually both begin with IMITATION.

Gloria (Latin, "Glory")   Second of the five major musical items in the MASS ORDINARY, a praise formula also known as the Greater DOXOLOGY.

goliard songs   Medieval Latin songs associated with the goliards, who were wandering students and clerics.

Gradual (from Latin *gradus*, "stairstep")   Item in the MASS PROPER, sung after the Epistle reading, comprising a RESPOND and VERSE. CHANT graduals are normally MELISMATIC in style and sung in a RESPONSORIAL manner, one or more soloists alternating with the CHOIR.

grand motet   French version of the large-scale SACRED CONCERTO, for soloists, double CHORUS, and ORCHESTRA.

grand opera   A serious form of OPERA, popular during the ROMANTIC era, that was sung throughout and included BALLETS, CHORUSES and spectacular staging.

Greater Perfect System   In ancient Greek music, a system of TETRACHORDS spanning two octaves.

Gregorian chant   The repertory of ecclesiastical CHANT used in the Roman Catholic Church.

ground bass   BASSO OSTINATO.

half step (or **semitone**)   The smallest INTERVAL normally used in Western music, equivalent to the interval between any two successive NOTES on the PIANO keyboard; half the size of a WHOLE STEP.

harmonia (pl. *harmoniai*)   Ancient Greek term with multiple meanings: (1) the union of parts in an orderly whole; (2) INTERVAL; (3) SCALE type; (4) style of MELODY.

harmonic progression A logical succession of CHORDS with a sense of direction; especially, the succession of chords used to accompany a MELODY or used as the basis for VARIATIONS.

harmony Aspect of music that pertains to simultaneous combinations of NOTES, the INTERVALS and CHORDS that result, and the correct succession of chords.

harp Plucked string instrument with a resonating soundbox, neck, and strings in roughly triangular shape. The strings rise perpendicular from the soundboard to the neck.

harpsichord Keyboard instrument in use between the fifteenth and eighteenth centuries. It was distinguished from the CLAVICHORD and the PIANO by the fact that its strings were plucked, not struck.

haut (French, "high"; pronounced OH) In the fourteenth through sixteenth centuries, term for loud instruments such as CORNETTS and SACKBUTS. See BAS.

head-motive Initial passage or MOTIVE of a piece or MOVEMENT; used especially for a motive or PHRASE that appears at the beginning of each movement of a MOTTO MASS or CANTUS-FIRMUS MASS.

heighted neumes In an early form of NOTATION, NEUMES arranged so that their relative height indicated higher or lower pitch. Also called DIASTEMATIC neumes.

hemiola (from Greek *hemiolios*, "one and a half") A metrical effect in which three duple units substitute for two triple ones, such as three successive quarter NOTES within a MEASURE of $\frac{6}{8}$, or three two-beat groupings in two measures of triple METER. Hemiola may occur between voices or successive measures.

heterophony Music or musical TEXTURE in which a MELODY is performed by two or more parts simultaneously in more than one way, for example, one voice performing it simply, and the other with embellishments.

hexachord (from Greek, "six strings") (1) A set of six pitches. (2) In medieval and RENAISSANCE SOLMIZATION, the six NOTES represented by the syllables *ut, re, mi, fa, sol, la*, which could be transposed to three positions: the "natural" hexachord, C–D–E–F–G–A; the "hard" hexachord, G–A–B–C–D–E; and the "soft" hexachord, F–G–A–B♭–C–D. (3) In TWELVE-TONE theory, the first six or last six notes in the ROW.

historia In Lutheran music of the sixteenth to eighteenth centuries, a musical setting based on a biblical narrative. See PASSION.

hocket (French *hoquet*, "hiccup") In thirteenth- and fourteenth-century POLYPHONY, the device of alternating rapidly between two voices, each resting while the other sings, as if a single MELODY is split between them; or, a COMPOSITION based on this device.

homophony Musical TEXTURE in which all voices move together in essentially the same RHYTHM, as distinct from POLYPHONY and HETEROPHONY. See also MELODY AND ACCOMPANIMENT.

homorhythmic Having the same RHYTHM, as when several voices or parts move together.

humanism Movement in the RENAISSANCE to revive ancient Greek and Roman culture and to study things pertaining to human knowledge and experience.

hurdy-gurdy An instrument with MELODY and DRONE strings, bowed by a rotating wheel turned with a crank, with levers worked by a keyboard to change the pitch on the melody string(s).

hymn Song to or in honor of a god. In the Christian tradition, song of praise sung to God.

idée fixe (French, "fixed idea") term coined by Hector Berlioz for a MELODY that is used throughout a piece to represent a person, thing, or idea, transforming it to suit the mood and situation.

imitate (1) To repeat or slightly vary in one voice or part a segment of MELODY just heard in another, at pitch or transposed. (2) To follow the example of an existing piece or style in composing a new piece.

imitation (1) In POLYPHONIC music, the device of repeating (imitating) a MELODY or MOTIVE announced in one part in one or more other parts, often at a different pitch level and sometimes with minor MELODIC or rhythmic alterations. Usually the voices enter with the element that is imitated, although sometimes imitation happens within the middle of a segment of melody. (2) The act of patterning a new work after an existing work or style; especially, to borrow much of the existing work's material.

imitation mass (or **parody mass**) POLYPHONIC MASS in which each MOVEMENT is based on the same polyphonic model, normally a CHANSON or MOTET, and all voices of the model are used in the mass, but none is used as a CANTUS FIRMUS.

imitative counterpoint CONTRAPUNTAL TEXTURE marked by IMITATION between voices.

imperfect (or **minor**) **division** In medieval and RENAISSANCE NOTATION, a division of a NOTE value into two of the next smaller units (rather than three). See MODE, TIME, and PROLATION.

impresario During the BAROQUE PERIOD, a businessman who managed and oversaw the production of OPERAS; today, someone who books and stages operas and other musical events.

impressionism Late-nineteenth-century term derived from art, used for music that evokes moods and visual imagery through colorful HARMONY and instrumental TIMBRE.

improvisation, improvising Spontaneous invention of music while performing, including devising VARIATIONS, embellishments, or accompaniments for existing music.

indeterminacy An approach to composition, pioneered by John Cage, in which the composer leaves certain aspects of the music unspecified. Should not be confused with CHANCE.

instrumental family Set of instruments, all of the same type but of different sizes and RANGES, such as a VIOL CONSORT.

intabulation　Arrangement of a vocal piece for LUTE or keyboard, typically written in TABLATURE.

intermedio　Musical interlude on a pastoral, allegorical, or mythological subject performed before, between, or after the acts of a spoken comedy or tragedy.

intermezzo　Eighteenth-century GENRE of Italian comic OPERA, performed between acts of a serious OPERA or play.

interval　Distance in pitch between two NOTES.

intonation　The first NOTES of a CHANT, sung by a soloist to establish the pitch for the CHOIR, which joins the soloist to continue the chant.

Introit　(from Latin *introitus*, "entrance")　First item in the MASS PROPER, originally sung for the entrance procession, comprising an ANTIPHON, PSALM verse, Lesser DOXOLOGY, and reprise of the ANTIPHON.

inversion　(1) In a MELODY or TWELVE-TONE ROW, reversing the upward or downward direction of each INTERVAL while maintaining its size; or the new melody or row form that results. (2) In HARMONY, a distribution of the NOTES in a CHORD so that a note other than the ROOT is the lowest note. (3) In COUNTERPOINT, reversing the relative position of two melodies, so that the one that had been lower is now above the other.

isorhythm　(from Greek *iso-*, "equal," and *rhythm*) Repetition in a voice part (usually the TENOR) of an extended pattern of durations throughout a section or an entire COMPOSITION.

jazz　A type of music developed mostly by African Americans in the early part of the twentieth century that combined elements of African, popular, and European music, and that has evolved into a broad tradition encompassing many styles.

jongleur　(French)　Itinerant medieval musician or street entertainer.

jubilus　(Latin)　In CHANT, an effusive MELISMA, particularly the melisma on "-ia" in an ALLELUIA.

just intonation　A system of tuning NOTES in the SCALE, common in the RENAISSANCE, in which most (but not all) thirds, sixths, perfect fourths, and perfect fifths are in perfect tune.

key　In TONAL music, the hierarchy of NOTES, CHORDS, and other pitch elements around a central note, the TONIC. There are two kinds of keys, major and minor.

kithara　Ancient Greek instrument, a large LYRE.

Klangfarbenmelodie　(German, "tone-color melody") Term coined by Arnold Schoenberg to describe a succession of tone colors that is perceived as analogous to the changing pitches in a MELODY.

Kyrie　(Greek, "Lord")　One of the five major musical items in the MASS ORDINARY, based on a BYZANTINE litany.

lauda　(from Latin *laudare*, "to praise")　Italian devotional song.

Leitmotiv, leitmotive　(German, "leading motive")　In an OPERA or MUSIC DRAMA, a MOTIVE, THEME, or musical idea associated with a person, thing, mood, or idea, which returns in original or altered form throughout.

Lesser Doxology　See DOXOLOGY.

libretto　(Italian, "little book")　Literary text for an OPERA or other musical stage work.

Lied　(German, "song"; pl. *Lieder*)　Song with German words, whether MONOPHONIC, POLYPHONIC, or for voice with accompaniment; used especially for polyphonic songs in the RENAISSANCE and songs for voice and PIANO in the eighteenth and nineteenth centuries.

ligature　NEUME-like noteshape used to indicate a short RHYTHMIC pattern in twelfth- to sixteenth-century NOTATION.

liturgical drama　Dialogue on a sacred subject, set to music and usually performed with action, and linked to the LITURGY.

liturgy　The prescribed body of texts to be spoken or sung and ritual actions to be performed in a religious service.

long　In medieval and RENAISSANCE systems of RHYTHMIC NOTATION, a NOTE equal to two or three BREVES.

lute　Plucked string instrument popular from the late Middle Ages through the BAROQUE PERIOD, typically pear- or almond-shaped with a rounded back, flat fingerboard, frets, and one single and five double strings.

lute song　English GENRE of solo song with LUTE accompaniment.

lyre　Plucked string instrument with a resonating soundbox, two arms, crossbar, and strings that run parallel to the soundboard and attach to the crossbar.

lyric opera　ROMANTIC OPERA that lies somewhere between light OPÉRA COMIQUE and GRAND OPERA.

madrigal　(Italian *madrigale*, "song in the mother tongue") (1) Fourteenth-century Italian poetic form and its musical setting having two or three stanzas followed by a RITORNELLO. (2) Sixteenth-century Italian poem having any number of lines, each of seven or eleven syllables. (3) POLYPHONIC or CONCERTATO setting of such a poem or of a sonnet or other nonrepetitive VERSE form. (4) English polyphonic work imitating the Italian GENRE.

madrigal comedy, madrigal cycle　In the late sixteenth and early seventeenth centuries, a series of MADRIGALS that represents a succession of scenes or a simple plot.

madrigalism　A particularly evocative—or, if used in a disparaging sense, a thoroughly conventional—instance of TEXT DEPICTION or WORD-PAINTING; so called because of the prominent role of word-painting in MADRIGALS.

major scale　DIATONIC succession of NOTES with a major third and major seventh above the TONIC.

march　A piece in duple or 6/8 METER comprising an introduction and several STRAINS, each repeated. Typically there are two strains in the initial key followed by a TRIO in a key a fourth higher; the opening strains may or may not repeat after the trio.

masque Seventeenth-century English entertainment involving poetry, music, DANCE, costumes, CHORUSES, and elaborate sets, akin to the French COURT BALLET.

Mass (from Latin *missa*, "dismissed") (1) The most important service in the Roman church. (2) A musical work setting the texts of the ORDINARY of the Mass, typically KYRIE, GLORIA, CREDO, SANCTUS, and AGNUS DEI. In this book, as in common usage, the church service is capitalized (the Mass), but a musical setting of the Mass Ordinary is not (a mass).

mazurka A type of Polish folk dance (and later ballroom dance) in triple METER, characterized by accents on the second or third beat and often by dotted figures on the first beat, or a stylized PIANO piece based on such a DANCE.

mean-tone temperament A type of TEMPERAMENT in which the fifths are tuned small so that the major thirds sound well; frequently used for keyboard instruments from the RENAISSANCE through the eighteenth century.

measure (1) A unit of musical time consisting of a given number of beats; the basic unit of METER. (2) Metrical unit set off by barlines.

mediant In a PSALM TONE, the CADENCE that marks the middle of the PSALM verse.

Meistersinger (German, "master singer") Type of German amateur singer and poet-composer of the fourteenth through seventeenth centuries, who was a member of a guild that cultivated a style of MONOPHONIC song derived from MINNELIEDER.

melisma A long MELODIC passage sung to a single syllable of text.

melismatic Of a MELODY, having many MELISMAS.

melodrama A genre of musical theater that combined spoken dialogue with background music.

melody (1) Succession of tones perceived as a coherent line. (2) Tune. (3) Principal part accompanied by other parts or CHORDS.

melody and accompaniment A kind of HOMOPHONIC TEXTURE in which there is one main MELODY, which is accompanied by CHORDS or other FIGURATION.

mensuration canon A CANON in which voices move at different rates of speed by using different MENSURATION SIGNS.

mensuration signs In ARS NOVA and RENAISSANCE systems of rhythmic NOTATION, signs that indicate which combination of time and prolation to use (see MODE, TIME, AND PROLATION). The predecessors of TIME SIGNATURES.

meter Recurring patterns of strong and weak beats, dividing musical time into regularly recurring units of equal duration.

metrical psalm Metric, rhymed, and STROPHIC vernacular translation of a PSALM, sung to a relatively simple MELODY that repeats for each strophe.

minim In ARS NOVA and RENAISSANCE systems of rhythmic NOTATION, a NOTE that is equal to half or a third of a SEMIBREVE.

minimalism One of the leading musical styles of the late twentieth century, in which materials are reduced to a minimum and procedures simplified so that what is going on in the music is immediately apparent. Often characterized by a constant pulse and many repetitions of simple RHYTHMIC, MELODIC, or HARMONIC patterns.

Minnelieder (German, "love songs") Songs of the MINNESINGER.

Minnesinger (German, "singer of love"; also pl.) A poet-composer of medieval Germany who wrote MONOPHONIC songs, particularly about love, in Middle High German.

minor scale DIATONIC SCALE that begins with a WHOLE STEP and HALF STEP, forming a minor third above the TONIC. The sixth and seventh above the tonic are also minor in the natural minor scale but one or both may be raised.

minstrel (from Latin *minister*, "servant") Thirteenth-century traveling musician, some of whom were also employed at a court or city.

minstrelsy Popular form of musical theater in the United States during the mid-nineteenth century, in which white performers blackened their faces and impersonated African Americans in jokes, skits, songs, and dances.

minuet DANCE in moderate triple METER, two-measure units, and BINARY FORM.

minuet and trio form FORM that joins two BINARY-FORM MINUETS to create an ABA pattern, where A is the minuet and B the TRIO.

mixed media Trend of the late twentieth century that combines two or more of the arts, including music, to create a new kind of PERFORMANCE ART or musical theater.

mixed parallel and oblique organum Early form of ORGANUM that combines parallel motion with oblique motion (in which the ORGANAL VOICE remains on the same NOTE while the PRINCIPAL VOICE moves) in order to avoid tritones.

modal Making use of a MODE. Compare TONAL.

mode (1) A SCALE or MELODY type, identified by the particular INTERVALLIC relationships among the NOTES in the mode. (2) In particular, one of the eight scale or melody types recognized by church musicians and theorists beginning in the Middle Ages, distinguished from one another by the arrangement of WHOLE TONES and SEMITONES around the FINAL, by the RANGE relative to the final, and by the position of the TENOR or RECITING TONE. (3) RHYTHMIC MODE. See also MODE, TIME, AND PROLATION.

mode, time, and prolation (Latin *modus, tempus, prolatio*) The three levels of rhythmic DIVISION in ARS NOVA NOTATION. Mode is the division of LONGS into BREVES; time the division of breves into SEMIBREVES; and prolation the division of semibreves into MINIMS.

modernists Twentieth-century composers who made a radical break from the musical language of their predecessors and contemporaries while maintaining strong links to the tradition.

modified strophic form Variant of STROPHIC FORM in which the music for the first stanza is varied for later stanzas, or in which there is a change of KEY, RHYTHM, character, or material.

modulation   The TONAL music, a gradual change from one KEY to another within a section of a MOVEMENT.

monody   (1) An accompanied solo song. (2) The musical TEXTURE of solo singing accompanied by one or more instruments.

monophonic   Consisting of a single unaccompanied MELODIC line.

monophony   Music or musical TEXTURE consisting of unaccompanied MELODY.

motet (from French *mot*, "word")   POLYPHONIC vocal COMPOSITION; the specific meaning changes over time. The earliest motets add a text to an existing DISCANT CLAUSULA. Thirteenth-century motets feature one or more voices, each with its own sacred or secular text in Latin or French, above a TENOR drawn from CHANT or other MELODY. Most fourteenth- and some fifteenth-century motets feature ISORHYTHM and may include a CONTRATENOR. From the fifteenth century on, any polyphonic setting of a Latin text (other than a MASS) could be called a motet; from the sixteenth century on, the term was also applied to sacred compositions in other languages.

motive   Short MELODIC or RHYTHMIC idea that recurs in the same or altered form.

motto mass   POLYPHONIC MASS in which the MOVEMENTS are linked primarily by sharing the same opening MOTIVE or PHRASE.

movement   Self-contained unit of music, complete in itself, that can stand alone or be joined with others in a larger work. Some types of COMPOSITION typically consist of several movements (such as the four movements common in the SYMPHONY).

music drama   Nineteenth-century GENRE created by Richard Wagner in which drama and music become organically connected to express a kind of absolute oneness. See also GESAMTKUNSTWERK.

music video   Type of short film popularized in the early 1980s that provides a visual accompaniment to a POP SONG.

musica ficta (Latin, "feigned music")   (1) In early music, NOTES outside the standard GAMUT, which excluded all flatted and sharped notes except B♭. (2). In POLYPHONY of the fourteenth through sixteenth centuries, the practice of raising or lowering by a semitone the pitch of a written note, particularly at a CADENCE, for the sake of smoother HARMONY or motion of the parts.

musica mundana, musica humana, musica instrumentalis (Latin, "music of the universe," "human music," and "instrumental music")   Three kinds of music identified by Boethius (ca. 480–ca. 524), respectively the "music" or numerical relationships governing the movement of stars, planets, and the seasons; the "music" that harmonizes the human body and soul and their parts; and audible music produced by voices or instruments.

musical   GENRE of musical theater that features songs and dance numbers in styles drawn from POPULAR MUSIC

in the context of a spoken play with a comic or romantic plot.

musical figure   In BAROQUE music, a MELODIC pattern or CONTRAPUNTAL effect conventionally employed to convey the meaning of a text.

musique concrète (French, "concrete music")   Term coined by composers working in Paris in the 1940s for music composed by assembling and manipulating recorded sounds, working "concretely" with sound itself rather than with music NOTATION.

musique mesurée (French, "measured music")   Late-sixteenth-century French style of text-setting, especially in CHANSONS, in which stressed syllables are given longer NOTES than unstressed syllables (usually twice as long).

mutation   In SOLMIZATION, the process of changing from one HEXACHORD to another.

nationalism   (1) In politics and culture, an attempt to unify or represent a particular group of people by creating a national identity through characteristics such as common language, shared culture, historical traditions, and national institutions and rituals. (2) Nineteenth- and twentieth-century trend in music in which composers were eager to embrace elements in their music that claimed a national identity.

neoclassicism   Trend in music from the 1910s to the 1950s in which composers revived, imitated, or evoked the styles, GENRES, and FORMS of pre-ROMANTIC music, especially those of the eighteenth century.

neo-Romanticism   A trend of the late twentieth century in which composers adopted the familiar tonal idiom of nineteenth-century ROMANTIC music and incorporated its sounds and gestures.

neotonal   Term for music since the early 1900s that establishes a single pitch as a tonal center, but does not follow the traditional rules of TONALITY.

neumatic   In CHANT, having about one to six NOTES (or one NEUME) sung to each syllable of text.

neume   A sign used in NOTATION of CHANT to indicate a certain number of NOTES and general MELODIC direction (in early forms of notation) or particular pitches (in later forms).

New Objectivity   Term coined in the 1920s to describe a kind of new realism in music, in reaction to the emotional intensity of the late ROMANTICS and the EXPRESSIONISM of Schoenberg and Berg.

New Orleans jazz   Leading style of JAZZ just after World War I, which centers on group VARIATION of a given tune, either IMPROVISED or in the style of improvisation.

nocturne   Type of short PIANO piece popular during the ROMANTIC PERIOD, marked by highly embellished MELODY, sonorous accompaniments, and a contemplative mood.

nondiegetic music or **underscoring**   In film, background music that conveys to the viewer a mood or other aspect of a scene or character but is not heard by the characters themselves. Compare DIEGETIC MUSIC.

notation A system for writing down musical sounds, or the process of writing down music. The principal notation systems of European music use a staff of lines and signs that define the pitch, duration, and other qualities of sound.

note (1) A musical TONE. (2) A symbol denoting a musical tone.

notes inégales (French, "unequal notes"; pronounced NOTS an-ay GALL) Seventeenth-century convention of performing French music in which passages notated in short, even durations, such as a succession of eighth notes, are performed by alternating longer notes on the beat with shorter offbeats to produce a lilting rhythm.

Notre Dame polyphony Style of POLYPHONY from the late twelfth and thirteenth centuries, associated with the Cathedral of Notre Dame in Paris.

octatonic scale (or *octatonic collection*) A SCALE that alternates WHOLE and HALF STEPS.

Offertory Item in the MASS PROPER, sung while the COMMUNION is prepared, comprising a RESPOND without VERSES.

Office (from Latin *officium*, "obligation" or "ceremony") A series of eight prayer services of the Roman church, celebrated daily at specified times, especially in monasteries and convents; also, any one of those services.

Old Roman chant A repertory of ecclesiastical CHANT preserved in eleventh- and twelfth-century manuscripts from Rome representing a local tradition; a near relative of GREGORIAN CHANT.

open and closed endings (French, *ouvert* and *clos*) In an ESTAMPIE, BALLADE, or other medieval form, two different endings for a repeated section. The first ("open") closes on a pitch other than the FINAL, and the second ("closed") ends with a full CADENCE on the final.

opera (Italian, "work") Drama with continuous or nearly continuous music, staged with scenery, costumes, and action.

opera buffa (Italian, "comic opera") Eighteenth-century GENRE of Italian comic OPERA, sung throughout.

opéra bouffe ROMANTIC operatic GENRE in France that emphasized the smart, witty, and satirical elements of OPÉRA COMIQUE.

opéra comique (French, "comic opera") (1) In the eighteenth century, light French comic OPERA, which used spoken dialogue instead of RECITATIVES. (2) In nineteenth-century France, opera with spoken dialogue, whether comic or tragic.

opera seria (Italian, "serious opera") Eighteenth-century GENRE of Italian OPERA, on a serious subject but normally with a happy ending, usually without comic characters and scenes.

operetta Nineteenth-century kind of light OPERA with spoken dialogue, originating in OPÉRA BOUFFE.

opus (Latin, "work") Work or collection of works in the same GENRE, issued as a publication.

oratorio GENRE of dramatic music that originated in the seventeenth century, combining narrative, dialogue, and commentary through ARIAS, RECITATIVES, ENSEMBLES, CHORUSES, and instrumental music, like an unstaged OPERA. Usually on a religious or biblical subject.

orchestra ENSEMBLE whose core consists of strings with more than one player on a part, usually joined by woodwinds, brass, and percussion instruments.

orchestral concerto Orchestral GENRE in several MOVEMENTS, originating in the late seventeenth century, that emphasized the first VIOLIN part and the BASS, avoiding the more CONTRAPUNTAL TEXTURE of the SONATA.

orchestral suite Late-seventeenth-century German SUITE for ORCHESTRA patterned after the groups of DANCES in French BALLETS and OPERA.

Ordinary (from Latin *ordinarium*, "usual") Texts of the MASS that remain the same on most or all days of the CHURCH CALENDAR, although the tunes may change.

organ mass Setting for organ of all sections of the MASS for which the organ would play, including ORGAN VERSES and other pieces.

organ verse Setting for an organ of an existing MELODY from the Roman Catholic LITURGY.

organal voice (Latin, *vox organalis*) In an ORGANUM, the voice that is added above or below the original CHANT MELODY.

organum (Latin; pronounced OR-guh-num) (1) One of several styles of early POLYPHONY from the ninth through thirteenth centuries, involving the addition of one or more voices to an existing CHANT. (2) A piece, whether IMPROVISED or written, in one of those styles, in which one voice is drawn from a CHANT. The plural is *organa*.

organum duplum In NOTRE DAME POLYPHONY, an ORGANUM in two voices.

ornament A brief, conventional formula, such as a TRILL or turn, written or IMPROVISED, that adds expression or charm to a MELODIC line.

ornamentation The addition of embellishments to a given MELODY, either during performance or as part of the act of COMPOSITION.

ostinato (Italian, "obstinate") Short musical pattern that is repeated persistently throughout a piece or section. See BASSO OSTINATO.

ouvert See OPEN AND CLOSED ENDINGS.

ouverture (French, "opening") (1) OVERTURE, especially FRENCH OVERTURE. (2) SUITE for ORCHESTRA, beginning with an OVERTURE.

overdotting Performing practice in French BAROQUE music in which a dotted NOTE is held longer than written, while the following short note is shortened.

overture (1) An ORCHESTRAL piece introducing an OPERA or other long work. (2) Independent ORCHESTRAL WORK in one movement, usually descriptive.

parallel organum Type of POLYPHONY in which an added voice moves in exact parallel to a CHANT, normally a perfect fifth below it. Either voice may be doubled at the octave.

paraphrase Technique in which a CHANT or other MELODY is reworked, often by altering rhythms and adding NOTES, and placed in a POLYPHONIC setting.

paraphrase mass POLYPHONIC MASS in which each MOVEMENT is based on the same MONOPHONIC MELODY, normally a CHANT, which is PARAPHRASED in most or all voices rather than being used as a CANTUS FIRMUS in one voice.

parlor song Song for home music-making, sometimes performed in public concerts as well.

parody mass IMITATION MASS.

partbook A manuscript or printed book containing the music for one voice or instrumental part of a POLYPHONIC COMPOSITION (most often, an anthology of pieces); to perform any piece, a complete set of partbooks is needed, so that all the parts are represented.

partita BAROQUE term for a set of VARIATIONS on a MELODY or BASS line.

partsong (1) A song for more than one voice. (2) In the nineteenth century, a song for CHORUS, parallel in function and style to the LIED or PARLOR SONG.

passacaglia BAROQUE GENRE of VARIATIONS over a repeated BASS line or HARMONIC PROGRESSION in triple METER.

Passion A musical setting of one of the biblical accounts of Jesus' crucifixion, the most common type of HISTORIA.

pastoral drama Play in verse with incidental music and songs, normally set in idealized rural surroundings, often in ancient times; a source for the earliest OPERA LIBRETTOS.

pavane (pavan) Sixteenth-century dance in slow duple METER with three repeated sections (AABBCC). Often followed by a GALLIARD.

perfect (or **major**) **division** In medieval and RENAISSANCE NOTATION, a division of a note value into three (rather than two) of the next smaller unit. See MODE, TIME, and PROLATION.

perfection (1) What we all strive for. (2) In medieval systems of NOTATION, a unit of duration equal to three TEMPORA, akin to a MEASURE of three beats.

performance art A type of art that first came to prominence in the 1960s, based on the idea that performing a prescribed action in a public place constitutes a work of art.

period (1) In music history, an era whose music is understood to have common attributes of style, conventions, approach, and function, in contrast to the previous and following eras. (2) In musical FORM, especially since the eighteenth century, a complete musical thought concluded by a CADENCE and normally containing at least two PHRASES.

periodic Organized in discrete PHRASES or PERIODS.

periodicity The quality of being PERIODIC, especially when this is emphasized through frequent resting points and articulations between PHRASES and PERIODS.

petit motet (French, "little motet") French version of the SMALL SACRED CONCERTO, for one, two, or three voices and CONTINUO.

phrase A unit of MELODY or of an entire musical TEXTURE that has a distinct beginning and ending and is followed by a pause or other articulation but does not express a complete musical thought. See PERIOD (2).

Phrygian cadence CADENCE in which the bottom voice moves down a semitone and upper voices move up a whole tone to form a fifth and octave over the cadential NOTE.

piano or **pianoforte** A keyboard instrument invented in 1700 that uses a mechanism in which the strings are struck, rather than plucked as the HARPSICHORD was, and which allowed for crescendos, dimuendos, and other effects.

pipe and tabor Two instruments played by one player, respectively a high whistle fingered with one hand and a small drum beaten with a stick or mallet.

pitch-class Any one of the twelve NOTES of the CHROMATIC SCALE, including its ENHARMONIC equivalents, in any octave.

pitch-class set (or **set**) A collection of PITCH-CLASSES that preserves its identity when transposed, inverted, or reordered and used MELODICALLY or HARMONICALLY.

plagal mode A MODE (2) in a which the RANGE normally extends from a fourth (or fifth) below the FINAL to a fifth or sixth above it. See also AUTHENTIC MODE.

plainchant, plainsong A unison unaccompanied song, particularly a LITURGICAL song to a Latin text.

plainsong mass A MASS in which each MOVEMENT is based on a CHANT to the same text (the KYRIE is based on a chant Kyrie, the GLORIA on a chant Gloria, and so on).

point of imitation Passage in a POLYPHONIC work in which two or more parts enter in IMITATION.

polonaise A stately Polish processional DANCE in triple METER, or a stylized piece in the style of such a dance.

polychoral For more than one CHOIR.

polychoral motet MOTET for two or more choirs.

polyphony Music or musical TEXTURE consisting of two or more simultaneous lines of independent MELODY. See also COUNTERPOINT.

polystylism Term coined by Alfred Schnittke for a combination of newer and older musical styles created through QUOTATION or stylistic allusion.

polytonality The simultaneous use of two or more KEYS, each in a different layer of the music (such as MELODY and accompaniment).

pop music Term coined in the 1950s for music that reflected the tastes and styles popular with the teen and young adult market.

popular music Music, primarily intended as entertainment, that is sold in printed or recorded form. It is distinguished from FOLK MUSIC by being written down and marketed as a commodity, and from CLASSICAL MUSIC by being centered on the performer and the performance, allowing great latitude in rearranging the notated music.

popular song Song that is intended primarily to entertain an audience, accommodate amateur performers, and sell as many copies as possible. Compare ART SONG.

portative organ Medieval or RENAISSANCE organ small enough to be carried, played by one hand while the other worked the bellows.

positive organ Organ from the medieval through BAROQUE PERIODS that was small enough to be moved, usually placed on a table.

postmodernism Trend in the late twentieth century that blurs the boundaries between high and popular art, and in which styles of all epochs and cultures are equally available for creating music.

post-tonal General term for music after 1900 that does not adhere to TONALITY but instead uses any of the new ways that composers found to organize pitch, from ATONALITY to NEOTONALITY.

prelude Introductory piece for solo instrument, often in the style of an IMPROVISATION, or introductory MOVEMENT in a multimovement work such as an OPERA or SUITE.

prepared piano An invention of John Cage in which various objects—such as pennies, bolts, screws, or pieces of wood, rubber, plastic, or slit bamboo—are inserted between the strings of a PIANO, resulting in complex percussive sounds when the piano is played from the keyboard.

prima donna (Italian, "first lady") A soprano singing the leading female role in an OPERA. See also DIVA.

prima pratica (Italian, "first practice") Claudio Monteverdi's term for the style and practice of sixteenth-century POLYPHONY, in contradistinction to the SECONDA PRATICA.

prime In TWELVE-TONE music based on a particular ROW, the original form of the row, transposed or untransposed, as opposed to the INVERSION, RETROGRADE, or RETROGRADE INVERSION.

principal voice (Latin, *vox principalis*) In an ORGANUM, the original CHANT MELODY.

program Text to accompany an instrumental work of PROGRAM MUSIC, describing the sequence of events depicted in the music.

program music Instrumental music that tells a story or follows a narrative or other sequence of events, often spelled out in an accompanying text called a PROGRAM.

prolation See MODE, TIME, AND PROLATION.

Proper (from Latin *proprium*, "particular" or "appropriate") Texts of the MASS that are assigned to a particular day in the CHURCH CALENDAR.

psalm A poem of praise to God, one of 150 in the Book of Psalms in the Hebrew Scriptures (the Christian Old Testament). Singing psalms was a central part of Jewish, Christian, Catholic, and Protestant worship.

psalm tone A MELODIC formula for singing PSALMS in the OFFICE. There is one psalm tone for each MODE.

psalmody The singing of PSALMS.

psalter A published collection of METRICAL PSALMS.

psaltery A plucked string instrument whose strings are attached to a frame over a wooden sounding board.

Pythagorean intonation A system of tuning NOTES in the SCALE, common in the Middle Ages, in which all perfect fourths and fifths are in perfect tune.

quadruplum (Latin, "quadruple") (1) In POLYPHONY of the late twelfth through fourteenth centuries, fourth voice from the bottom in a four-voice TEXTURE, added to a TENOR, DUPLUM, and TRIPLUM. (2) In NOTRE DAME POLYPHONY, an ORGANUM in four voices.

quodlibet (Latin, "whatever you please) COMPOSITION or passage in which two or more existing MELODIES, or parts of melodies, are combined in COUNTERPOINT.

quotation Direct borrowing of one work in another, especially when the borrowed material is not reworked using a standard musical procedure (such as VARIATIONS, PARAPHRASE, or IMITATION MASS) but is set off as a foreign element.

rag Instrumental work in RAGTIME style, usually in the FORM of a MARCH.

ragtime Musical style that features SYNCOPATED rhythm against a regular, marchlike BASS.

range A span of NOTES, as in the range of a MELODY or of a MODE.

realization Performing (or creating a performable edition of) music whose NOTATION is incomplete, as in playing a BASSO CONTINUO or completing a piece left unfinished by its composer.

recapitulation In SONATA FORM, the third main section, which restates the material from the EXPOSITION, normally all in the TONIC.

recital Term popularized by Franz Liszt for his solo piano performances and used today for any presentation given by a single performer or a small group.

récitatif mesuré (French, "measured recitative") In French BAROQUE OPERA, RECITATIVE in a songlike, measured style, in a uniform METER, and with relatively steady motion in the accompaniment.

récitatif simple (French, "simple recitative") In French BAROQUE OPERA, RECITATIVE that shifts frequently between duple and triple METER to allow the natural speechlike declamation of the words.

recitation formula In CHANT, a simple outline MELODY used for a variety of texts.

recitative A passage or section in an OPERA, ORATORIO, CANTATA, or other vocal work in RECITATIVE STYLE

recitative style (from Italian *stile recitativo*, "recitational style") A type of vocal singing that approaches speech and follows the natural rhythms of the text.

recitativo arioso A passage or selection in an OPERA or other vocal work in a style that lies somewhere between RECITATIVE STYLE and ARIA style.

reciting tone (also called TENOR) The second most important NOTE in a MODE (after the FINAL), often emphasized in CHANT and used for reciting text in a PSALM TONE.

recorder End-blown wind instrument with a whistle mouthpiece, usually made of wood.

refrain In a song, a recurring line (or lines) of text, usually set to a recurring MELODY.

reminiscence motive In an OPERA, a MOTIVE, THEME, or MELODY that recurs in a later scene, in order to recall the events and feelings with which it was first associated. Compare LEITMOTIV.

Renaissance (French, "rebirth") PERIOD of art, cultural, and music history between the Middle Ages and the BAROQUE PERIOD, marked by HUMANISM, a revival of ancient culture and ideas, and a new focus on the individual, the world, and the senses.

respond The first part of a RESPONSORIAL CHANT, appearing before and sometimes repeated after the PSALM verse.

responsorial Pertaining to a manner of performing CHANT in which a soloist alternates with a group.

responsory RESPONSORIAL CHANT used in the OFFICE. Matins includes nine Great Responsories, and several other Office services include a Short Responsory.

retrograde Backward statement of a previously heard MELODY, passage, or TWELVE-TONE ROW.

retrograde inversion Upside-down and backward statement of a MELODY or TWELVE-TONE ROW.

revue Type of musical theater that includes a variety of dances, songs, comedy, and other acts, often united by a common theme.

rhythm (1) The pattern of music's movement in time. (2) A particular pattern of short and long durations.

rhythm section In a JAZZ ENSEMBLE, the group of instruments that keeps the beat and fills in the background.

rhythm-and-blues African-American style of POPULAR MUSIC, originating in the 1940s, that featured a vocalist or vocal quartet, PIANO or organ, electric guitar, bass, and drums, and songs built on TWELVE-BAR BLUES or POPULAR SONG formulas.

rhythmic modes System of six durational patterns (for example, mode 1, long-short) used in POLYPHONY of the late twelfth and thirteenth centuries, used as the basis of the rhythmic NOTATION of the Notre Dame composers.

ricercare (ricercar) (Italian, "to seek out" or "to attempt") (1) In the early to mid-sixteenth century, a PRELUDE in the style of an IMPROVISATION. (2) From the late sixteenth century on, an instrumental piece that treats one or more SUBJECTS in IMITATION.

ripieno (Italian, "full") In a SOLO CONCERTO or CONCERTO GROSSO, designates the full ORCHESTRA. All called TUTTI.

rite The set of practices that defines a particular Christian tradition, including a CHURCH CALENDAR, a LITURGY, and a repertory of CHANT.

ritornello (Italian, "refrain") (1) In a fourteenth-century MADRIGAL, the closing section, in a different METER from the preceding verses. (2) In sixteenth- and seventeenth-century vocal music, instrumental introduction or interlude between sung stanzas. (3) In an ARIA or similar piece, an instrumental passage that recurs several times, like a refrain. Typically, it is played at the beginning, as interludes (often in modified form), and again at the end, and it states the main THEME. (4) In a fast MOVEMENT of a CONCERTO, the recurring thematic material played at the beginning by the full orchestra and repeated, usually in varied form, throughout the movement and at the end.

ritornello form Standard FORM for fast MOVEMENTS in CONCERTOS of the first half of the eighteenth century, featuring a RITORNELLO (4) for full ORCHESTRA that alternates with EPISODES characterized by virtuosic material played by one or more soloists.

rock and roll (or **rock**) A musical style that emerged in the United States in the mid-1950s as a blend of black and white traditions of POPULAR MUSIC, primarily RHYTHM-AND-BLUES, COUNTRY MUSIC, POP MUSIC, and TIN PAN ALLEY.

Romantic Term applied to music of the nineteenth century. Romantic music had looser and more extended FORMS, greater experimentation with HARMONY and TEXTURE, richly expressive and memorable MELODIES, improved musical instruments, an interest in musical NATIONALISM, and a view of music as a moral force, in which there was a link between the artists' inner lives and the world around them.

rondeau (pl. *rondeaux*) (1) French FORME FIXE with a single stanza and the musical FORM ABaAabAB, with capital letters indicating lines of REFRAIN and lowercase letters indicating new text set to music from the refrain. (2) FORM in seventeenth- and eighteenth-century instrumental music in which a repeated STRAIN alternates with other strains, as in the pattern AABACA.

rondellus Technique in medieval English POLYPHONY in which two or three PHRASES of music, first heard simultaneously in different voices, are each sung in turn by each of the voices.

rondo Piece or MOVEMENT in RONDO FORM.

rondo form Musical FORM in which the first or main section recurs, usually in the TONIC, between subsidiary sections or EPISODES.

root The lowest NOTE in a CHORD when it is arranged as a succession of thirds.

rota FORM of medieval English POLYPHONY in which two or more voices sing the same MELODY, entering at different times and repeating the melody until all stop together. See CANON.

rounded binary form BINARY FORM in which the latter part of the first section returns at the end of the second section, but in the TONIC.

row In TWELVE-TONE MUSIC, an ordering of all twelve PITCH-CLASSES that is used to generate the musical content.

rubato (from Italian *tempo rubato*, "stolen time") Technique common in ROMANTIC music in which the performer holds back or hurries the written NOTE values.

sackbut RENAISSANCE brass instrument, an early form of the trombone.

sacred concerto   In the seventeenth century, a COMPOSITION on a sacred text for one or more singers and instrumental accompaniment.

salsa   A type of dance music that emerged in the 1960s combining elements of Cuban dance styles with JAZZ, ROCK, and Puerto Rican music.

sampling   A process of creating new COMPOSITIONS by patching together snippets of previously recorded music.

Sanctus (Latin, "Holy")   One of the five major musical items in the MASS ORDINARY, based in part on Isaiah 6:3.

sarabande   (1) Originally a quick dance-song from Latin America. (2) In French BAROQUE music, a slow DANCE in BINARY FORM and in triple METER, often emphasizing the second beat; a standard MOVEMENT of a SUITE.

scale   A series of three or more different pitches in ascending or descending order and arranged in a specific pattern.

scat singing   Technique in JAZZ in which the performer sings nonsense syllables to an IMPROVISED or composed MELODY.

scherzo (Italian, "joke")   A joking or particularly fast MOVEMENT in MINUET AND TRIO FORM.

score notation   A type of NOTATION in which the different voices or parts are aligned vertically to show how they are coordinated with each other.

seconda pratica or **second practice**   Monteverdi's term for a practice of COUNTERPOINT and COMPOSITION that allows the rules of sixteenth-century counterpoint (the PRIMA PRATICA) to be broken in order to express the feelings of a text. Also called *stile moderno*.

semibreve   In medieval and RENAISSANCE systems of rhythmic NOTATION, a NOTE that is normally equal to half or a third of a BREVE.

semiminim   In ARS NOVA and RENAISSANCE systems of rhythmic NOTATION, a NOTE that is equal to half of a MINIM.

semi-opera   Modern term for DRAMATIC OPERA.

semitone (or **half step**)   The smallest INTERVAL normally used in Western music; half of a TONE.

sequence (from Latin *sequentia*, "something that follows")   (1) A category of Latin CHANT that follows the ALLELUIA in some MASSES. (2) Restatement of a pattern, either MELODIC or HARMONIC, on successive or different pitch levels.

serenata (Italian, "serenade")   A semidramatic piece for several singers and small ORCHESTRA, usually written for a special occasion.

serial music   Music that uses the TWELVE-TONE METHOD; used especially for music that extends the same general approach to SERIES in parameters other than pitch.

series   (1) A ROW. (2) An ordering of specific durations, dynamic levels, or other non-pitch elements, used in SERIAL MUSIC.

Service   A setting of Anglican service music, encompassing specific portions of Matins, Holy Communion, and Evensong. A *Great Service* is a MELISMATIC, CONTRAPUNTAL setting of these texts; a *Short Service* sets the same text in SYLLABIC, CHORDAL style.

set   PITCH-CLASS SET.

shape-note singing   A tradition of group singing that arose in nineteenth-century America, named after the NOTATION used in song collections in which the shape of the noteheads indicates the SOLMIZATION syllables, allowing for easy sight-reading in parts.

shawm   Double reed instrument, similar to the oboe, used in the medieval, RENAISSANCE, and BAROQUE PERIODS.

sinfonia   (1) Generic term used throughout the seventeenth century for an abstract ENSEMBLE piece, especially one that serves as an introduction to a vocal work. (2) Italian OPERA OVERTURE in the early eighteenth century. (3) Early SYMPHONY.

simple recitative   Style of RECITATIVE scored for solo voice and BASSO CONTINUO, used for setting dialogue or monologue in as speechlike a fashion as possible, without dramatization.

Singspiel (German, "singing play")   German GENRE of OPERA, featuring spoken dialogue interspersed with songs, CHORUSES, and instrumental music.

sketch   General term for a compositional idea jotted down in a notebook, or an early draft of a work.

slow-movement sonata form   Classic-era variant of SONATA FORM that omits the DEVELOPMENT.

small sacred concerto   Seventeenth-century GENRE of sacred vocal music featuring one or more soloists accompanied by organ CONTINUO (or modest instrumental ENSEMBLE).

socialist realism   A doctrine of the Soviet Union, begun in the 1930s, in which all the arts were required to use a realistic approach (as opposed to an abstract or symbolic one) that portrayed socialism in a positive light. In music this meant use of simple, accessible language, centered on MELODY, and patriotic subject matter.

solmization   A method of assigning syllables to STEPS in a SCALE, used to make it easier to identify and sing the WHOLE TONES and SEMITONES in a MELODY.

solo concerto   CONCERTO in which a single instrument, such as a VIOLIN, contrasts with an ORCHESTRA.

solo madrigal   In the late sixteenth and early seventeenth centuries, a THROUGH-COMPOSED setting of a nonstrophic poem for solo voice with accompaniment, distinguished from an ARIA and from a MADRIGAL for several voices.

sonata (Italian, "sounded")   (1) A piece to be played on one or more instruments. (2) BAROQUE instrumental piece with contrasting sections or MOVEMENTS, often with IMITATIVE COUNTERPOINT. (3) GENRE in several movements for one or two solo instruments.

sonata da camera or **chamber sonata**   BAROQUE SONATA, usually a SUITE of stylized DANCES, scored for one or more TREBLE instruments and CONTINUO.

sonata da chiesa or **church sonata**   BAROQUE instrumental work intended for performance in church; usually in four MOVEMENTS—slow-fast-slow-fast—and scored for one or more TREBLE instruments and CONTINUO.

sonata form FORM typically used in first MOVEMENTS of SONATAS, instrumental chamber works, and SYMPHONIES during the CLASSIC and ROMANTIC PERIODS. An expansion of ROUNDED BINARY FORM, it was described in the nineteenth century as consisting of an EXPOSITION, DEVELOPMENT, and RECAPITULATION based on a limited number of THEMES.

sonata-rondo A FORM that blends characteristics of SONATA FORM and RONDO FORM. One frequent structure is ABACABA, in which A and B correspond to the first and second THEMES of SONATA FORM and B appears first in the DOMINANT and returns in the TONIC.

song cycle A group of songs performed in succession that tells or suggests a story.

soprano (from SUPERIUS) (1) High female voice. (2) Part for such a voice in an ENSEMBLE work.

soul The leading African-American tradition of POPULAR MUSIC in the 1960s that combined elements of RHYTHM-AND-BLUES and gospel singing in songs on love, sex, and other secular subjects.

sound mass Term coined by Edgard Varèse for a body of sounds characterized by a particular TIMBRE, register, RHYTHM, or MELODIC gesture, which may remain stable or may be transformed as it recurs.

source music See DIEGETIC MUSIC.

spatial Pertaining to a conception of music as sounds moving through musical space, rather than as the presentation and VARIATION of THEMES or MOTIVES.

species The particular ordering of WHOLE TONES and SEMITONES within a perfect fourth, fifth, or octave.

spiritual African-American type of religious song that originated among southern slaves and was passed down through oral tradition, with texts often based on stories or images from the Bible.

Sprechstimme (German, "speaking voice") A vocal style developed by Arnold Schoenberg in which the performer approximates the written pitches in the gliding tones of speech, while following the notated rhythm.

Stadtpfeifer (German, "town pipers") Professional town musicians who had the exclusive right to provide music within city limits.

step INTERVAL between two adjacent pitches in a DIATONIC, CHROMATIC, OCTATONIC, or WHOLE-TONE SCALE; WHOLE STEP or HALF STEP.

stile antico (Italian, "old style") Style used in music written after 1600, in imitation of the old contrapuntal style of Palestrina, used especially for church music.

stile concitato (Italian, "excited style") Style devised by Claudio Monteverdi to portray anger and warlike actions, characterized by rapid reiteration of a single NOTE, whether on quickly spoken syllables or in a measured string tremolo.

stile moderno (Italian, "modern style") Seventeenth-century style that used BASSO CONTINUO and applied the rules of COUNTERPOINT freely. See SECONDA PRATICA.

Stollen See BAR FORM.

stop (1) Mechanism on an organ to turn on or off the sounding of certain sets of pipes. (2) The particular set of pipes controlled by such a mechanism.

string quartet (1) Standard chamber ENSEMBLE consisting of two VIOLINS, viola, and cello. (2) Multimovement COMPOSITION for this ENSEMBLE.

strain In a MARCH or RAG, a PERIOD, usually of sixteen or thirty-two measures.

strophic Of a poem, consisting of two or more stanzas that are equivalent in form and can each be sung to the same MELODY; of a vocal work, consisting of a strophic poem set to the same music for each stanza.

strophic variation Early seventeenth-century vocal GENRE, a setting of a STROPHIC poem, in which the MELODY of the first stanza is varied but the HARMONIC plan remains essentially the same, although the duration of harmonies may change to reflect the accentuation and meaning of the text.

style luthé (French, "lute style") or **style brisé** (French, "broken style") Broken or ARPEGGIATED TEXTURE in keyboard and LUTE music from seventeenth-century France. The technique originated with the lute, and the FIGURATION was transferred to the HARPSICHORD.

subdominant In TONAL music, the NOTE and CHORD a fifth below the TONIC.

subject THEME, used especially for the main MELODY used in a RICERCARE, FUGUE, or other IMITATIVE work.

substitute clausula In NOTRE DAME POLYPHONY, a new CLAUSULA (usually in DISCANT style) designed to replace the original polyphonic setting of a particular segment of a CHANT.

suite A set of pieces that are linked together into a single work. During the BAROQUE, a suite usually referred to a set of stylized DANCE pieces.

superius (Latin, "highest") In fifteenth- and sixteenth-century POLYPHONY, the highest part (compare CANTUS).

suspension DISSONANCE created when a NOTE is sustained while another voice moves to form a dissonance with it; the sustained voice descends a STEP to resolve the dissonance.

syllabic Having (or tending to have) one NOTE sung to each syllable of text.

symphonic poem (or **tone poem**) Term coined by Franz Liszt for a one-movement work of PROGRAM MUSIC for orchestra that conveys a poetic idea, story, scene, or succession of moods by presenting THEMES that are repeated, varied, or transformed.

symphonie concertante A CONCERTO-like GENRE of the late eighteenth and early nineteenth centuries for two or more solo instruments and ORCHESTRA, characterized by its lightheartedness and MELODIC variety.

symphony Large work for ORCHESTRA, usually in four MOVEMENTS.

swing A style of JAZZ originating in the 1930s that was characterized by large ENSEMBLEs and hard-driving jazz rhythms.

synchopation Temporary disruption of METER by beginning a long NOTE on an offbeat and sustaining it through the beginning of the next beat.

synthesizer Electronic instrument that generates and processes a wide variety of sounds.

tablature A system of NOTATION used for LUTE or other plucked string instrument that tells the player which strings to pluck and where to place the fingers on the strings, rather than indicating which NOTES will result. Tablatures were also used for keyboard instruments until the seventeenth century.

tabor See PIPE AND TABOR.

talea (Latin, "cutting"; pronounced TAH-lay-ah) In an ISORHYTHMIC COMPOSITION, an extended rhythmic pattern repeated one or more times, usually in the TENOR. Compare COLOR.

temperament Any system of tuning NOTES in the SCALE in which pitches are adjusted to make most or all INTERVALS sound well, though perhaps not in perfect tune.

tempo (Italian, "time") Speed of performance, or relative pace of the music.

tempo di mezzo (Italian, "middle movement") The operatic scene structure developed by Gioachino Rossini in the early nineteenth century, the middle section of an ARIA or ENSEMBLE, usually an interruption or a TRANSITION, that falls between the CANTABILE and the CABALETTA.

tempus (Latin, "time"; pl. *tempora*) In medieval systems of NOTATION, the basic time unit. See also MODE, TIME, and PROLATION.

tenor (from Latin *tenere*, "to hold") (1) In a MODE or CHANT, the RECITING TONE. (2) In POLYPHONY of the twelfth and thirteenth centuries, the voice part that has the chant or other borrowed MELODY, often in long-held NOTES. (3) Male voice of a relatively high range.

tenor mass CANTUS-FIRMUS MASS.

termination In a PSALM TONE, the CADENCE that marks the end of the PSALM VERSE.

ternary form A FORM in three main sections, in which the first and third are identical or closely related and the middle section is contrasting, creating an ABA pattern.

tetrachord (from Greek, "four strings") (1) In Greek and medieval theory, a SCALE of four NOTES spanning a perfect fourth. (2) In modern theory, a SET of four pitches or PITCH-CLASSES. (3) In TWELVE-TONE theory, the first four, middle four, or last four notes in the ROW.

text depiction Using musical gestures to reinforce or suggest images in a text, such as rising on the word "ascend."

text expression Conveying or suggesting through musical means the emotions expressed in a text.

texture The combination of elements in a piece or passage, such as the number and relationship of independent parts (as in MONOPHONY, HETEROPHONY, POLYPHONY, or HOMOPHONY), GROUPS (as in POLYCHORAL MUSIC), or

musical events (as in relatively dense or transparent sonorities).

theme Musical subject of a COMPOSITION or section, or of a set of VARIATIONS.

thematic transformation A method devised by Franz Liszt to provide unity, variety, and a narrative-like logic to a composition by transforming the thematic material into new THEMES or other elements, in order to reflect the diverse moods needed to portray a PROGRAMMATIC subject.

theorbo Large LUTE with extra BASS strings, used especially in the seventeenth century for performing BASSO CONTINUO as accompaniment to singers or instruments.

thoroughbass BASSO CONTINUO.

through-composed Composed throughout, as when each stanza or other unit of a poem is set to new music rather than in a STROPHIC manner to a single MELODY.

tiento Spanish IMPROVISATORY-style instrumental piece that features IMITATION, akin to the sixteenth-century FANTASIA.

timbre or **tone color** Characteristic color or sound of an instrument or voice.

time signature Sign or numerical proportion, such as $\frac{3}{4}$, placed at the beginning of a piece, section, or MEASURE to indicated the METER.

Tin Pan Alley (1) Jocular name for a district in New York where numerous publishers specializing in POPULAR SONGS were located from the 1880s through the 1950s. (2) Styles of American popular song from that era.

toccata (Italian, "touched") Piece for keyboard instrument or LUTE resembling an IMPROVISATION that may include IMITATIVE sections or may serve as a PRELUDE to an independent FUGUE.

tonal Operating within the system of TONALITY.

tonality The system, common since the late seventeenth century, by which a piece of music is organized around a TONIC NOTE, CHORD, and KEY, to which all the other notes and keys in the piece are subordinate.

tone (1) A sound of definite pitch. (2) See WHOLE STEP.

tone cluster Term coined by Henry Cowell for a CHORD of DIATONIC or CHROMATIC seconds.

tone color See TIMBRE.

tone poem SYMPHONIC POEM, or a similar work for a medium other than ORCHESTRA.

tonic (1) The first and central NOTE of a MAJOR or MINOR SCALE. (2) The main KEY of a piece or MOVEMENT, in which the piece or movement begins and ends and to which all other keys are subordinate.

tonos (pl. *tonoi*) Ancient Greek term used with different meanings by various writers; one meaning is a particular set of pitches within a certain RANGE or region of the voice.

topics Term for the different and contrasting styles in Classic-era music that serve as subjects for musical discourse.

total serialism The application of the principles of the TWELVE-TONE METHOD to musical parameters other than pitch, including duration, intensities, and TIMBRES. See SERIAL MUSIC.

Tract (from Latin *tractus*, "drawn out")   Item in the MASS PROPER that replaces the ALLELUIA on certain days in Lent, comprising a series of PSALM VERSES.

tragédie en musique (French, "tragedy in music"; later **tragédie lyrique**, "lyric tragedy")   French seventeenth- and eighteenth-century form of OPERA, pioneered by Jean-Baptiste Lully, that combined the French classic drama and BALLET traditions with music, DANCES, and spectacles.

transcription   Arrangement of a piece for an instrumental medium different from the original, such as a reduction of an ORCHESTRAL score for PIANO.

transition   (1) In the EXPOSITION of a MOVEMENT in SONATA FORM, the passage between the first and second THEMES that effects the MODULATION to a new KEY. (2) More generally, a passage between two MOVEMENTS or SECTIONS of a work.

transverse flute   Flute blown across a hole in the side of the pipe and held to one side of the player; used for medieval, RENAISSANCE, and BAROQUE forms of the flute to distinguish it from the RECORDER, which is blown in one end and held in front.

treble (French, "triple")   (1) A high voice or a part written for high voice, especially the highest part in three-part POLYPHONY of the fourteenth and fifteenth centuries. (2) Pertaining to the highest voice.

treble-dominated style   Style common in the fourteenth and fifteenth centuries, in which the main MELODY is in the CANTUS, the upper voice carrying the text, supported by a slower-moving TENOR and CONTRATENOR.

Trecento (Italian, short for *mille trecento*, "one thousand three hundred"; pronounced treh-CHEN-toh)   The 1300s (the fourteenth century), particularly with reference to Italian art, literature, and music of the time.

triad   CHORD consisting of two successive thirds (for instance, C–E–G), or any INVERSION of such a chord.

trill   Rapid alternation between a NOTE and another HALF STEP or WHOLE STEP above.

trio   (1) Piece for three players or singers. (2) The second of two alternating DANCES, in the Classic-era MINUET AND TRIO FORM. (3) The second main section of a MARCH.

trio sonata   Common instrumental GENRE during the BAROQUE PERIOD, a SONATA for two TREBLE instruments (usually VIOLINS) above a BASSO CONTINUO. A performance featured four or more players if more than one was used for the continuo part.

triple motet   Thirteenth-century MOTET in four voices, with a different text in each voice above the TENOR.

triplum (from Latin *triplus*, "triple")   (1) In POLYPHONY of the late twelfth through fourteenth centuries, third voice from the bottom in a three- or four-voice TEXTURE, added to a TENOR and DUPLUM. (2) In NOTRE DAME POLYPHONY, an ORGANUM in three voices.

tritone   INTERVAL spanning three WHOLE TONES or six SEMITONES, such as F to B.

trobairitz (from Occitan *trobar*, "to compose a song")   A female TROUBADOUR.

trope   Addition to an existing CHANT, consisting of (1) words and MELODY; (2) a MELISMA; or (3) words only, set to an existing melisma or other melody.

troubadour (from Occitan *trobar*, "to compose a song")   A poet-composer of southern France who wrote MONOPHONIC songs in Occitan (*langue d'oc*) in the twelfth or thirteenth century.

trouvère (from Old French *trover*, "to compose a song")   A poet-composer of northern France who wrote MONOPHONIC songs in Old French (*langue d'oïl*) in the twelfth or thirteenth century.

tutti (Italian, "all")   (1) In both the SOLO CONCERTO and the CONCERTO GROSSO, designates the full ORCHESTRA. Also called RIPIENO (Italian, "full"). (2) Instruction to an ENSEMBLE that all should play.

twelve-bar blues   Standard formula for the BLUES, with a HARMONIC PROGRESSION in which the first four-measure PHRASE is on the TONIC, the second phrase begins on the SUBDOMINANT and ends on the tonic, and the third phrase starts on the DOMINANT and returns to the tonic.

twelve-tone method   A form of ATONALITY based on the systematic ordering of the twelve notes of the CHROMATIC scale into a ROW that may be manipulated according to certain rules.

unmeasured prelude   A French BAROQUE keyboard GENRE, usually the first MOVEMENT in a SUITE, whose nonmetric NOTATION gives a feeling of IMPROVISATION.

underscoring   See NONDIEGETIC MUSIC.

variation   The process of reworking a given MELODY, song, THEME, or other musical idea, or the resulting varied FORM of it.

variations (variations form)   FORM that presents an uninterrupted series of variants (each called a VARIATION) on a THEME; the theme may be a MELODY, a BASS line, a HARMONIC plan, or other musical subject.

vaudeville   In late-nineteenth- and early-twentieth-century America, a type of variety show including musical numbers, but without the common theme of a REVUE.

verismo (Italian, "realism")   Nineteenth-century operatic MOVEMENT that presents everyday people in familiar situations, often depicting sordid or brutal events.

verse   (1) Line of poetry. (2) Stanza of a HYMN or STROPHIC song. (3) Sentence of a PSALM. (4) In GREGORIAN CHANT, a setting of a Psalm verse or similar text, such as the verses that are part of the INTROIT, GRADUAL, and ALLELUIA.

verse anthem   ANTHEM in which passages for solo voice(s) with accompaniment alternate with passages for full CHOIR doubled by instruments.

verse-refrain form   A FORM in vocal music in which two or more stanzas of poetry are each sung to the same music (the VERSE) and each is followed by the same REFRAIN.

versus (Latin, "verse") A type of Latin sacred song, either MONOPHONIC or POLYPHONIC, setting a rhymed, rhythmic poem.

vielle Medieval bowed string instrument, early form of the fiddle and predecessor of the VIOLIN and VIOL.

vihuela Spanish relative of the LUTE with a flat back and guitar-shaped body.

villancico (from Spanish *villano*, "peasant"; pronounced vee-yan-THEE-co) Type of POLYPHONIC song in Spanish, with several stanzas framed by a REFRAIN; originally secular, the FORM was later used for sacred works, especially associated with Christmas or other important holy days.

villanella Type of sixteenth-century Italian song, generally for three voices, in a rustic HOMOPHONIC style.

viol (viola da gamba) Bowed, fretted string instrument popular from the mid-fifteenth to the early eighteenth centuries, held between the legs.

violin Bowed, fretless string instrument tuned in fifths (*g-d′-a′-e″*).

virelai French FORME FIXE in the pattern A bba A bba A bba A, in which a REFRAIN (A) alternates with stanzas with the musical FORM bba, the a using the same music as the refrain.

virginal (1) English name for HARPSICHORD, used for all types until the seventeenth century. (2) Type of HARPSICHORD that is small enough to place on a table, with a single keyboard and strings running at right angles to the keys rather than parallel with them as in larger harpsichords.

virtuoso Performer who specializes in one instrument and dazzles audiences with his or her technical prowess.

voice exchange In POLYPHONY, technique in which voices trade segments of music, so that the same combination of lines is heard twice or more, but with different voices singing each line.

walking bass BASS line in BAROQUE music—and later in JAZZ—that moves steadily and continuously.

waltz Type of couple dance in triple meter, popular in the late eighteenth and nineteenth centuries, or a short, stylized work for the PIANO in the style of such a dance.

whole step (or **whole tone**) An interval equivalent to two SEMITONES.

whole-tone scale (or *whole-tone collection*) A SCALE consisting of only WHOLE STEPS.

wind ensemble Large ENSEMBLE of winds, brass, and percussion instruments, mostly with one player per part, dedicated solely to serious music, rather than to the mix of MARCHES and other fare typically played by BANDS.

word-painting TEXT DEPICTION.

zarzuela Spanish GENRE of musical theater, a light, mythological play in a pastoral setting that alternates between sung and spoken dialogue and various types of ENSEMBLE and solo song.

For Further Reading

ABBREVIATIONS

AIM   American Institute of Musicology; publications include CEKM, CMM, CSM, and MSD. For lists, see *Musica Disciplina* (1988): 217–56.

CDMI   *I Classici della Musica Italiana*, 36 vols. (Milan: Istituto Editoriale Italiano, 1918–20; Società Anonima Notari la Santa, 1919–21).

CEKM   *Corpus of Early Keyboard Music* (AIM, 1963–).

CHWMT   *The Cambridge History of Western Music Theory*, ed. Thomas Christensen (Cambridge: Cambridge University Press, 2002).

CMM   *Corpus mensurabilis musicae* (AIM, 1948–).

DdT   *Denkmäler deutscher Tonkunst*, 65 vols. (Leipzig: Breitkopf & Härtel, 1892–1931; repr. Wiesbaden, 1957–61).

DTB   *Denkmäler der Tonkunst in Bayern* (Augsburg, 1900–38; new series, Leipzig: Breitkopf & Härtel, 1967–).

DTO   *Denkmäler der Tonkunst in Oesterreich* (Vienna: Artaria, 1894–1904; Leipzig, Breitkopf & Härtel, 1905–13; Vienna: Universal, 1919–38; Graz: Akademische Druck- und Verlaganstalt, 1966–).

EMH   *Early Music History*, 1981–.

EP   R. Eitner, ed., *Publikationen älterer praktischer und theoretischer Musikwerke, vorzugsweise des XV. und XVI. Jahrhunderts*, 29 vols. in 33 Jahrgänge (Berlin: Bahn & Liepmannssohn; Leipzig: Breitkopf & Härtel, 1873–1905; repr. 1967).

JAMS   *Journal of the American Musicological Society*, 1948–.

JM   *Journal of Musicology*, 1982–.

MB   *Musica Britannica* (London: Stainer & Bell, 1951–).

MQ   *The Musical Quarterly*, 1915–.

MSD   *Musicological Studies and Documents* (AIM, 1951–).

NG2   *New Grove Dictionary of Music and Musicians*, 2nd ed., ed. Stanley Sadie (London: Macmillan, 2001). Online at www.grove.com.

NOHM   *New Oxford History of Music* (London: Oxford University Press, 1954–).

PAM   *Publikationen älterer Musik* (Leipzig: Breitkopf & Härtel, 1926–40).

PMFC   *Polyphonic Music of the Fourteenth Century* (Monaco: Oiseau-Lyre, 1956–).

PMMM   *Publications of Medieval Music, Manuscripts* (Brooklyn: Institute of Mediaeval Music, 1957–).

SR   *Source Readings in Music History*, rev. ed., ed. Oliver Strunk, gen. ed. Leo Treitler (New York: Norton, 1998). Readings in SR are referred to by their number in the entire collection and, when different, their number in the individual paperback volumes published separately: vol. 1, *Greek View of Music*, ed. Thomas J. Mathiesen; vol. 2, *The Early Christian Period and the Latin Middle Ages*, ed. James McKinnon; vol. 3, *The Renaissance*, ed. Gary Tomlinson; vol. 4, *The Baroque Era*, ed. Margaret Murata; vol. 5, *The Late Eighteenth Century*, ed. Wye Jamison Allanbrook; vol. 6, *The Nineteenth Century*, ed. Ruth Solie; vol. 7, *The Twentieth Century*, ed. Robert P. Morgan. Thus "SR 14 (2:6)" means number 14 in the single-volume hardback and number 6 in volume 2 of the paperbacks.

The following is not a comprehensive listing of resources available on each topic but rather a collection of the most significant or helpful recent publications, which can serve as a starting point for further exploration.

GENERAL

The New Grove Dictionary of Music and Musicians, 2nd ed. [NG2], ed. Stanley Sadie (London: Macmillan, 2001), is the first source to consult for almost any subject related to music. NG2 articles are listed below when they offer an exceptional survey or summary of a significant topic; articles on individual composers, theorists, performers, other musicians, instruments, genres, terms, cities, and national traditions are not listed separately but are authoritative and highly recommended. The same content, in some cases updated, is available from Grove Music Online at www.grovemusic.com.

Richard Taruskin, *The Oxford History of Western Music* (New York: Oxford University Press, 2005) is a new six-volume comprehensive survey. *The New Oxford History of Music* [NOHM] (London: Oxford University Press, 1954–) is a multivolume history by numerous experts. *Reader's Guide to Music: History, Theory, Criticism*, ed. Murray Steib (Chicago: Fitzroy Dearborn, 1999), lists and summarizes the most useful and authoritative books on numerous composers, genres, countries, and topics.

Women and Music

The role of women in music has been underrepresented in standard music history texts. Useful correctives are *Women and Music: A History*, ed. Karin Pendle (Bloomington: Indiana University Press, 1991; 2nd ed., 2001), and *Women Making Music: The Western Art Tradition, 1150–1950*, ed. Jane Bowers and Judith Tick (Urbana: University of Illinois Press, 1986). Primary source documents by and about women in music are collected in *Women in Music: An Anthology of Source Readings from the Middle Ages to the Present*, rev. ed., ed. Carol Neuls-Bates (Boston: Northeastern University Press, 1996). Works by women are contained in *Historical Anthology of Music by Women*, ed. James R. Briscoe (Bloomington: Indiana University Press, 1987) and *New Historical Anthology of Music by Women*, ed. Briscoe (Bloomington: Indiana University Press, 2004), and in the series Women Composers: Music through the Ages, ed. Martha Furman Schleifer and Sylvia Glickman (New York: G. K. Hall, 1996–).

Social and Intellectual History of Music

Pioneering treatments of music in its social and economic contexts are Henry Raynor's, *A Social History of Music: From the Middle Ages to Beethoven* (New York: Schocken, 1972) and *Music and Society since 1815* (New York: Schocken, 1976), still stimulating though out of date. On music and aesthetics in history, see Edward A. Lippman, *A History of Western Musical Aesthetics* (Lincoln: University of Nebraska Press, 1992). For a history of the use of music for healing, see the essays in *Music as Medicine: The History of Music Therapy since Antiquity*, ed. Peregrine Horden (Aldershot: Ashgate, 2000).

Music Theory

On the history of music theory, see *The Cambridge History of Western Music Theory*, ed. Thomas Christensen (Cambridge: Cambridge University Press, 2002) [CHWMT]. For bibliography, see David Damschroder and David Russell Williams, *Music Theory from Zarlino to Schenker: A Bibliography and Guide* (Stuyvesant, NY: Pendragon, 1990).

Musical Instruments

For musical instruments, see *The New Grove Dictionary of Musical Instruments*, ed. Stanley Sadie (London: Macmillan, 1984), and Mary Remnant, *Musical Instruments: An Illustrated History from Antiquity to the Present*, gen. ed. Reinhard G. Pauly (Portland, OR: Amadeus Press, 1989).

Performance Practice

See Colin Lawson and Robin Stowell, *The Historical Performance of Music: An Introduction* (Cambridge: Cambridge University Press, 1999); Howard Mayer Brown and Stanley Sadie, eds., *Performance Practice*, 2 vols. (New

York: Norton, 1990); and *Readings in the History of Music in Performance*, trans. and ed. Carol MacClintock (Bloomington: Indiana University Press, 1979).

Source Readings

A rich, annotated compendium of writings about music from ancient Greece to modern America is Oliver Strunk's *Source Readings in Music History*, rev. ed. [SR], gen. ed. Leo Treitler (New York: Norton, 1998); it is also available in seven paperback volumes, each on a separate historical period. While Strunk and Treitler print entire texts or sections, smaller items and passages are collected in *Music in the Western World: A History in Documents*, ed. Piero Weiss and Richard Taruskin (New York: Schirmer, 1984), and *Composers on Music: Eight Centuries of Writings*, 2nd ed., ed. Josiah Fisk (Boston: Northeastern University Press, 1997).

For writings on music and aesthetics, see *Musical Aesthetics: A Historical Reader*, 3 vols., ed. Edward A. Lippman (New York: Pendragon, 1986), and *Contemplating Music: Source Readings in the Aesthetics of Music*, 4 vols., ed. Carl Dahlhaus and Ruth Katz (New York: Pendragon, 1987–93). On systems and principles of music education, see *Music Education: Source Readings from Ancient Greece to Today*, ed. Michael L. Mark (New York: Routledge, 2002). *Music, Mysticism, and Magic: A Sourcebook*, ed. Joscelyn Godwin (London: Routledge and Kegan Paul, 1986), offers materials on these often overlooked sides of music.

PART I: THE ANCIENT AND MEDIEVAL WORLDS

An outstanding survey of medieval music appears in *The Early Middle Ages to 1300*, ed. Richard Crocker and David Hiley (Oxford: Oxford University Press, 1990), and *Music as Concept and Practice in the Late Middle Ages*, ed. Reinhard Strohm and Bonnie J. Blackburn (Oxford: Oxford University Press, 2001), which replace older volumes of NOHM. Other surveys include David Fenwick Wilson, *Music of the Middle Ages: Style and Structure*, paired with his *Music of the Middle Ages: An Anthology for Performance and Study* (New York: Schirmer, 1990); Jeremy Yudkin, *Music in Medieval Europe* (Upper Saddle River, NJ: Prentice Hall, 1989), which includes an integrated anthology; and Richard H. Hoppin, *Medieval Music*, paired with his *Anthology of Medieval Music* (New York: Norton, 1978). Another anthology is *Medieval Music: The Oxford Anthology of Music*, ed. W. Thomas Marrocco and Nicholas Sandon (London: Oxford University Press, 1977).

The social and cultural contexts for music for this period are treated in *Antiquity and the Middle Ages: From Ancient Greece to the 15th Century*, ed. James McKinnon (London: Macmillan, 1990; Englewood Cliffs, NJ: Prentice Hall, 1991), a collection of chapters by various authorities. Philosophical and aesthetic perspectives on music are

traced in Herbert M. Schueller, *The Idea of Music: An Introduction to Musical Aesthetics in Antiquity and the Middle Ages* (Kalamazoo: Medieval Institute Publications, Western Michigan University, 1988). *A Companion to Medieval and Renaissance Music*, ed. Tess Knighton and David Fallows (Berkeley: University of California Press, 1992), offers a variegated collection of essays by performers and scholars on performance practice, aesthetics, genre, style, instruments, and other matters.

An annotated bibliography on medieval musical scholarship is Andrew Hughes, *Medieval Music: The Sixth Liberal Art* (Toronto: University of Toronto Press, 1980).

Performance Practice

On performance issues, see *A Performer's Guide to Medieval Music*, ed. Ross W. Duffin (Bloomington: Indiana University Press, 2000); Timothy J. McGee, *The Sound of Medieval Song: Ornamentation and Vocal Style According to the Treatises* (Oxford: Clarendon, 1998); *Performance Practice: Music Before 1600*, ed. Howard Mayer Brown and Stanley Sadie (London: Macmillan, 1989); Timothy J. McGee, *Medieval and Renaissance Music: A Performer's Guide* (Toronto: University of Toronto Press, 1985); and *Singing Early Music: The Pronunciation of European Languages in the Late Middle Ages and Renaissance*, ed. McGee, with A. G. Rigg and David N. Klausner (Bloomington: Indiana University Press, 1996), which includes a CD. Daniel Leech-Wilkinson addresses the modern idea of medieval music, especially with respect to performance practice, in *The Modern Invention of Medieval Music: Scholarship, Ideology, Performance* (Cambridge: Cambridge University Press, 2002).

CHAPTER 1

The categorization in chapter 1 of evidence relating to music of the past into four main types (instruments and other physical remains, images, writings, and music itself) is based on the first chapter of Thomas J. Mathiesen's *Apollo's Lyre* (cited below).

Music before Historical Records

Essays speculating on music's origins are collected in *The Origins of Music*, ed. Nils L. Wallin, Björn Merker, and Steven Brown (Cambridge, MA: MIT, 2000).

The prehistory of European music is summarized in Ellen Hickmann, "Europe, pre- and proto-historic," in NG2. Pictures of instruments unearthed from prehistoric through historic times are collected in Annemies Tamboer, *Ausgegrabene Klänge: Archäologische Musikinstrumente aus allen Epochen* (Oldenburg: Isensee, 1999).

Mesopotamia

See Anne Draffkorn Kilmer, "Mesopotamia," in NG2. On Enheduanna, see William W. Hallo and J. J. A. van Dijk, *En-*

heduanna: The Exaltation of Inanna (New Haven: Yale University Press, 1968). On Babylonian notation, see M. L. West, "The Babylonian Musical Notation and the Hurrian Melodic Texts," *Music and Letters* 125 (1993–94): 161–79. For other ancient cultures, see NG2 articles on "Anatolia" and "Egypt."

Greece and Rome

The most comprehensive survey of Greek music, its history, instruments, practice, and theory is Thomas J. Mathiesen, *Apollo's Lyre: Greek Music and Music Theory in Antiquity and the Early Middle Ages* (Lincoln: University of Nebraska Press, 1999). See also his "Greece, I," in NG2; his "Greek Music Theory," in CHWMT, 109–35; Warren D. Anderson, *Music and Musicians in Ancient Greece* (Ithaca, NY: Cornell University Press, 1994); and M. L. West, *Ancient Greek Music* (Oxford: Clarendon, 1992). For a discussion of ethos, see Anderson, *Ethos and Education in Greek Music* (Cambridge, MA: Harvard University Press, 1966), or Anderson and Mathiesen, "Ethos," in NG2.

Surveys that cover both Greek and Roman music include John G. Landels, *Music in Ancient Greece and Rome* (London: Routledge, 1999), and Giovanni Comotti, *Music in Greek and Roman Culture*, trans. Rosaria V. Munson (Baltimore: Johns Hopkins University Press, 1989). See also "Rome," in NG2.

Transcriptions of the extant Greek melodies and fragments are given in Egert Pöhlmann and Martin L. West, *Documents of Ancient Greek Music: The Extant Melodies and Fragments* (Oxford: Clarendon, 2001).

Most of the Greek writings referred to in this chapter are available in English translation. SR includes excerpts from Plato's *Republic* and *Timaeus* and Aristotle's *Poetics* (SR 1–3) along with theoretical writings by Cleonides, Aristides Quintilianus, and Gaudentius (SR 4–6); the latter three list the note names in the Greek system, the last two describe Greek notation, and Gaudentius includes the story of Pythagoras's discovery of the ratios underlying the octave, fifth, and fourth.

A large portion of Greek and Latin literature is contained in the Loeb Classical Library, with translations on facing pages with the originals. The views of Plato and Aristotle described here are summarized from Plato's *Republic* 3, 4, and 10; his *Laws* 2, 3, and 7; and Aristotle's *Politics* 8 and *Poetics* 1. Writings specific to music are gathered in *Greek Musical Writings*, 2 vols., ed. Andrew Barker (Cambridge: Cambridge University Press, 1984–89), with useful explanatory notes; volume 1 contains writings by poets, dramatists, and philosophers, and volume 2 has complete English translations of Aristoxenus, Nicomachus, Ptolemy, and Aristides Quintilianus and excerpts from Plato, Aristotle, and other writers.

The following translations of individual treatises are also available: Aristoxenus, *The Harmonics of Aristoxenus*, ed. and trans. Henry S. Macran (Oxford: Clarendon, 1902); *The Euclidian Division of the Canon*, ed. and trans. André Barbera (Lincoln: University of Nebraska Press,

1991); Sextus Empiricus, *Against the Musicians*, ed. and trans. Denise Davidson Greaves (Lincoln: University of Nebraska Press, 1986); Aristides Quintilianus, *On Music in Three Books*, trans. Mathiesen (New Haven: Yale University Press, 1983); Nicomachus of Gerasa, *The Manual of Harmonics of Nicomachus the Pythagorean*, trans. and commentary by Flora R. Levin (Grand Rapids, MI: Phanes, 1994); Claudius Ptolemy, *Harmonics*, trans. and commentary by Jon Solomon (Leiden: Brill, 2000).

CHAPTER 2

Judaism

The classic work on Jewish music is A. Z. ldelsohn, *Jewish Music in Its Historical Development* (New York, 1929; repr. New York: Schocken, 1967). See also Joachim Braun, "Jewish Music, §II: Ancient Israel/Palestine," in NG2.

On the connections between Jewish music and the music of the early Christian Church, see James W. McKinnon, *The Temple, the Church Fathers and Early Western Chant* (Brookfield, VT: Ashgate, 1998), and Peter Jeffery, *Re-Envisioning Past Musical Cultures: Ethnomusicology in the Study of Gregorian Chant* (Chicago: University of Chicago Press, 1992). See also Eric Werner's seminal study, *The Sacred Bridge: The Interdependence of Music and Liturgy in Synagogue and Church during the First Millennium*, 2 vols. (London: D. Dobson; New York: Columbia University Press, 1959–84).

Early Christian Music

See McKinnon, "Christian Church, music of the early," in NG2. For an important collection of patristic and pagan source readings on music in early Christian worship and society, see *Music in Early Christian Literature*, ed. McKinnon (Cambridge: Cambridge University Press, 1987). For an overview of monastic life, see James C. King and Werner Vogler, *The Culture of the Abbey of St. Gall* (Stuttgart: Belser, 1991). Excerpts from the writings of St. Basil, St. John Chrysostom, St. Jerome, and St. Augustine are in SR 9–13 (2:1–5).

Byzantine Chant

See Dimitri E. Conomos, *Byzantine Hymnography and Byzantine Chant* (Brookline, MA: Hellenic College Press, 1984); Oliver Strunk, *Essays on Music in the Byzantine World* (New York: Norton, 1977); and Egon Wellesz, *A History of Byzantine Music and Hymnody*, 2nd ed. (Oxford: Clarendon, 1971). Giulio Cattin, *Music of the Middle Ages I*, trans. Steven Botterill (Cambridge: Cambridge University Press, 1984), focuses on Byzantine and Latin chant.

Dialects of Western Chant

The standard work on Western dialects of chant, including Gregorian chant, is David Hiley, *Western Plainchant*

(Oxford: Clarendon, 1993). See also Giulio Cattin, *Music of the Middle Ages I*. For a study in depth of one of the chant dialects, see Thomas F. Kelly, *The Beneventan Chant* (Cambridge: Cambridge University Press, 1989). The ancient Gallican rite is described by a contemporary in SR 18 (2:10).

The Creation of Gregorian Chant

An eighth-century description of the Roman liturgy is in SR 19 (2:11).

On the oral transmission and written codification of Gregorian Chant, see Leo Treitler, *With Voice and Pen: Coming to Know Medieval Song and How It Was Made* (Oxford: Oxford University Press, 2003), with accompanying CD; McKinnon, *The Advent Project: The Later-Seventh-Century Creation of the Roman Mass Proper* (Berkeley: University of California Press, 2000); Kenneth Levy, *Gregorian Chant and the Carolingians* (Princeton: Princeton University Press, 1998); Jeffery, *Re-Envisioning Past Musical Cultures* ; James Grier, "Adémar de Chabannes, Carolingian Musical Practices, and *Nota Romana*," JAMS 56 (2003): 43–98; and McKinnon, "The Emergence of Gregorian Chant in the Carolingian Era," in *Antiquity and the Middle Ages*, 88–119.

Notation

Isidore of Seville's comment about notation is from his *Etymologies*, Book 3, excerpted in SR 16 (2:8). Near-contemporary accounts of melodies being corrupted in transmission from Rome to Frankish lands are in SR 21–22 (2:13–14). Guido of Arezzo describes his new notation in the Prologue to his Antiphoner, in SR 27 (2:19), and points out its benefits in *Epistle on an Unknown Chant*, in SR 28 (2:20), which also introduces his solmization syllables.

For an overview of notation, see "Notation" in NG2. Facsimiles of many of the earliest manuscripts of plainchant are published in *Paléographie musicale: les principaux manuscrits de chant Grégorien, Ambrosien, Mozarabe, Gallican* (Solesmes: Imprimerie St-Pierre; Tournai: Desclée, Lefebure, 1889–), two series. Color reproductions from various manuscripts appear in *Schriftbild der einstimmigen Musik*, Musikgeschichte in Bildern 3/4, ed. Bruno Stäblein (Leipzig: Deutscher Verlag für Musik, 1975).

Theory

Martianus Capella, *De nuptiis Philologiae et Mercurii*, trans. with commentary in William Harris Stahl et al., *Martianus Capella and the Seven Liberal Arts* (New York: Columbia University Press, 1971). On music in the trivium and quadrivium, see *The Seven Liberal Arts in the Middle Ages*, ed. David L. Wagner (Bloomington: Indiana University Press, 1983).

Boethius, *Fundamentals of Music (De institutione musica libri quinque)*, trans. with intro. and notes by Calvin M. Bower, ed. Claude V. Palisca (New Haven: Yale University Press, 1989); excerpts in SR 14 (2:6). See also the useful collection of essays contained in *Boethius and the Liberal Arts*, ed. Michael Masi (Berne: Paul Lange, 1981).

Musica enchiriadis and Scolica enchiriadis, trans. with intro. and notes by Raymond Erickson, ed. Palisca (New Haven: Yale University Press, 1995); excerpt from the former in SR 24 (2:16).

Texts of original sources of most theoretical treatises in Latin, both manuscript and printed, can be accessed online through the Thesaurus Musicarum Latinarum at www.music.indiana.edu/tml.

On medieval theory, see Bower, "The Transmission of Ancient Music Theory into the Middle Ages"; Jan Herlinger, "Medieval Canonics"; and David E. Cohen, "Notes, Scales, and Modes in the Earlier Middle Ages," in CHWMT, pp. 136–67, 168–92, and 307–63 respectively. See also Thomas J. Mathiesen, *Apollo's Lyre*, chapter 7, "The Tradition in the Middle Ages." For an overview of medieval theories of mode, see Harold S. Powers and Frans Wiering, "Mode, §II: Medieval Modal Theory," in NG2.

CHAPTER 3

Liturgy

An eighth-century form of the Mass liturgy, *Ordo romanus XVII*, appears in SR 19 (2:11), and the description of the Office in *The Rule of St. Benedict* is in SR 17 (2:9). On liturgy, see John Harper, *The Forms and Orders of Western Liturgy from the Tenth to the Eighteenth Century* (Oxford: Clarendon, 1991); and Cheslyn Jones, Geoffrey Wainwright, and Edward Yarnold, SJ, *The Study of Liturgy*, 2nd ed. (New York: Oxford University Press, 1992). On the psalms, see *The Place of the Psalms in the Intellectual Culture in the Middle Ages*, ed. Nancy van Deusen (Albany: State University of New York, 1999). On the Office, see the valuable essays gathered in *The Divine Office in the Latin Middle Ages: Methodology and Source Studies, Regional Developments, Hagiography*, ed. Margot E. Fassler and Rebecca A. Baltzer (Oxford: Oxford University Press, 2000).

The quotation from St. Basil on p. 53 is from SR 9 (2:1).

Gregorian Chant

The Liber Usualis with Introduction and Rubrics in English (New York: Desclée, 1961) is the practical reference for chant use in the modern Catholic liturgy. It presents an idealized version that attempts to account for diverse sources and changes over the centuries. The chants of the Mass in plainsong notation with facsimiles of original neumes above and below are in *Graduale triplex* (Solesmes: Abbaye Saint-Pierre de Solesmes, 1979). On the work of the Benedictine monks of Solesmes in researching and editing chant, see Katherine Bergeron, *Decadent Enchantments: The Revival of Gregorian Chant at Solesmes* (Berkeley: University of California Press, 1998).

The standard work on chant is David Hiley, *Western Plainchant*. A useful shorter guide is Richard L. Crocker, *An Introduction to Gregorian Chant* (New Haven: Yale University Press, 2000), with accompanying CD with numerous examples.

Three treatises relevant to chant, including Guido of Arezzo's *Micrologus*, are translated by Warren Babb in *Hucbald, Guido and John on Music*, ed. Claude V. Palisca (New Haven: Yale University Press, 1978).

Trope

See Alejandro Enrique Planchart, "Trope (i)," in NG2, and Hiley, *Western Plainchant*. Two complete troped masses from eleventh-century France, including the Mass for Christmas Day, appear in *Festive Troped Masses from the Eleventh Century: Christmas and Easter in Aquitaine*, ed. Charlotte Roederer (Madison, WI: A-R Editions, 1989).

Sequence

See Margot Fassler, *Gothic Song: Victorine Sequences and Augustinian Reform in Twelfth-Century Paris* (Cambridge: Cambridge University Press, 1993), and Crocker, *The Early Medieval Sequence* (Berkeley: University of California Press, 1977).

Liturgical Drama

Major studies include William L. Smoldon, *The Music of the Medieval Church Dramas*, ed. Cynthia Bourgeault (London and New York: Oxford University Press, 1980), and Susan Rankin, *The Music of the Medieval Liturgical Drama in France and England*, 2 vols. (New York: Garland, 1989), who collates music for most of the dramas.

Hildegard of Bingen

A letter from Hildegard appears in SR 23 (2:15). Studies of her and her music include Fiona Maddocks, *Hildegard of Bingen: The Woman of Her Age* (New York: Doubleday, 2001); Sabina Flanagan, *Hildegard of Bingen, 1098–1179: A Visionary Life*, 2nd ed. (London: Routledge, 1998); *Voice of the Living Light: Hildegard of Bingen and Her World*, ed. Barbara Newman (Berkeley: University of California Press, 1998); and *The 'Ordo virtutum' of Hildegard of Bingen: Critical Studies*, ed. Audrey Ekdahl Davidson (Kalamazoo: Medieval Institute Publications, Western Michigan University, 1992). For Hildegard's music, see *Symphonia: A Critical Edition of the "Symphonia armonie celestium revelationum,"* 2nd ed., with intro., trans., and commentary by Newman (Ithaca, NY: Cornell University Press, 1998).

Music in Convents

See Anne Bagnall Yardley, "'Ful weel she soong the service dyvyne': The Cloistered Musician in the Middle Ages," in *Women Making Music: The Western Art Tradition, 1150–1940*, ed. Jane Bowers and Judith Tick (Urbana: University of Illinois Press, 1986), 15–38.

CHAPTER 4

Song

An excellent study of monophonic settings of various kinds of texts, both sacred and secular, is John Stevens, *Words and Music in the Middle Ages: Song, Narrative, Dance and Drama, 1050–1350* (Cambridge: Cambridge University Press, 1986). On secular monophony, see Margaret L. Switten, *The Medieval Lyric* (South Hadley, MA: Mount Holyoke College, 1987–) and accompanying cassettes. The CD-ROM and CD set directed by Switten, *Teaching Medieval Lyric with Modern Technology: New Windows on the Medieval World* (South Hadley, MA: Mount Holyoke College, 2001), includes manuscript facsimiles, transcriptions, texts, translations, commentary, and performances of Latin songs, troubadour and trouvère songs, and the *Cantigas de Santa Maria*.

David Wulstan argues for a rhythmic interpretation of all medieval song in *The Emperor's Old Clothes: The Rhythm of Mediaeval Song* (Ottawa: Institute of Mediaeval Music, 2001). For a collection of essays devoted to women and song in medieval society, see *Medieval Woman's Song: Cross-Cultural Approaches*, ed. Anne L. Klinck and Ann Marie Rasmussen (Philadelphia: University of Pennsylvania Press, 2002).

Latin Song

Bryan Gillingham reassesses the roles and origins of Latin secular monophonic song in *The Social Background to Latin Medieval Secular Song* (Ottawa: Institute of Mediaeval Music, 1998). For a critical evaluation of the music, see his *A Critical Study of Secular Medieval Latin Song* (Ottawa: Institute of Mediaeval Music, 1995). Almost the entire repertoire appears in *Secular Medieval Latin Song: An Anthology*, ed. Gillingham (Ottawa: Institute of Mediaeval Music, 1993).

France

Two excellent studies are Christopher Page, *Voices and Instruments of the Middle Ages: Instrumental Practice and Songs in France, 1100–1300* (Berkeley: University of California Press, 1986), and Hendrik van der Werf, *The Chansons of the Troubadors and Trouvères: A Study of the Melodies and Their Relation to the Poems* (Utrecht: A. Oosthoek, 1972), from which the translation of Bernart de Ventadorn's *Can vei la lauzeta mover* on p. 79 is taken. Christopher Page, *The Owl and the Nightingale: Musical Life and Ideas in France 1100–1300* (London: Dent, 1989) is a valuable contribution to the social history of music in France in the twelfth and thirteenth centuries. See also Page, "Court and City in France, 1100–1300," in *Antiquity* and the Middle Ages, ed. James W. McKinnon, 197–217. On court life and manners, see C. Stephen Jaeger, *The Origins of Courtliness: Civilizing Trends and the Formation of Courtly Ideals, 939–1210* (Philadelphia: University of Pennsylvania Press, 1985). John Haines, *Eight Centuries of Troubadours and Trouvères: The Changing Identity of Medieval Music* (Cambridge: Cambridge University Press, 2004), examines changing historical perspectives on the troubadours and trouvères. For bibliography, see Margaret L. Switten, *Music and Poetry in the Middle Ages: A Guide to Research on French and Occitan Song, 1100–1400* (New York: Garland, 1995).

The standard work on the music, history, and cultural context of the troubadours is Elizabeth Aubrey, *The Music of the Troubadours* (Bloomington: Indiana University Press, 1996). Their *vidas* (life stories) are translated by Margarita Egan, *The Vidas of the Troubadours* (New York and London, 1984); *razos*, describing particular songs, are translated by William E. Burgwinkle, *Razos and Troubadour Songs* (New York: Garland, 1992). An edition of troubadour songs is *The Extant Troubadour Melodies: Transcriptions and Essays for Performers and Scholars*, ed. Hendrik van der Werf, texts ed. Gerald A. Bond (Rochester, NY: Author, 1984). Troubadour and trouvère songs appear in *Songs of the Troubadours and Trouvères: An Anthology of Poems and Melodies*, ed. Samuel N. Rosenberg, Margaret L. Switten, and Gérard Le Vot (New York: Garland, 1998). On the trobairitz, see *Songs of the Women Troubadours*, ed. Matilda Tomaryn Bruckner, Laurie Shepard, and Sarah White (New York: Garland, 1995).

Trouvère songs are in *Trouvères-Melodien*, ed. Hendrik van der Werf, in Monumenta musicae medii aevi, 11–12 (Kassel: Bärenreiter, 1977–79). For works of Adam de la Halle, see *The Lyrics and Melodies of Adam de La Halle*, ed. and trans. Deborah Hubbard Nelson, music ed. van der Werf (New York: Garland, 1985), and *Le jeu de Robin et Marion*, ed. and trans. Shira I. Schwam-Baird, music ed. Milton G. Scheuermann, Jr. (New York: Garland, 1994). For the women trouvères, see *Songs of the Women Trouvères*, ed. Eglal Doss-Quinby et al. (New Haven: Yale University Press, 2001).

Chansonniers in facsimile include Pierre Aubry, *Le Chansonnier de l'Arsenal* (Paris: P. Geuthner, 1909), facsimile and partial transcription; Jean Beck, *Le Chansonnier Cangé*, 2 vols. (Philadelphia: University of Pennsylvania Press, 1927) (vol. 2 has transcriptions); Beck, *Le Manuscrit du Roi*, 2 vols. (Philadelphia: University of Pennsylvania Press, 1938); and Alfred Jeanroy, *Le Chansonnier d'Arras* (Paris, 1925; repr. New York: Johnson, 1968).

England

On English song, see E. J. Dobson and F. L. Harrison, *Medieval English Songs* (London: Faber & Faber, 1979), and Harrison, *Music in Medieval Britain* (Buren, Netherlands: Knuf, 1980).

Germany

For the Minnesinger, see James V. McMahon, *The Music of Early Minnesang* (Columbia, SC: Camden House, 1990).

Italy

On Italian song and its relation to the tradition of the troubadours, see F. Alberto Gallo, *Music in the Castle: Troubadours, Books, and Orators in Italian Courts of the Thirteenth, Fourteenth, and Fifteenth Centuries*, trans. Anna Herklotz (Chicago: University of Chicago Press, 1996). On the lauda in general, see Blake Wilson, "Lauda," in NG2. For the lauda repertory, see *The Earliest Laude: The Cortona Hymnal*, ed. Hans Tischler (Ottawa: Institute of Mediaeval Music, 2002), and *The Florence Laudario: An Edition of Florence, Biblioteca nazionale centrale, Banco rari 18*, music ed. Wilson, texts ed. and trans. Nello Barbieri (Madison, WI: A-R Editions, 1995). On the medieval Florentine lauda tradition, see Wilson, *Music and Merchants: The Laudesi Companies of Republican Florence* (Oxford: Oxford University Press, 1992). On the Venetian tradition in the Middle Ages and later, see Jonathan Glixon, *Honoring God and the City: Music at the Venetian Confraternities, 1260–1807* (Oxford: Oxford University Press, 2003). Other regional traditions are examined by Cyrilla Barr, *The Monophonic Lauda and the Lay Religious Confraternities of Tuscany and Umbria in the Late Middle Ages* (Kalamazoo: Medieval Institute Publications, Western Michigan University, 1988).

Spain

For the cantigas, see Joseph F. O'Callaghan, *Alfonxo X and the Cantigas de Santa Maria: A Poetic Biography* (Leiden and Boston: Brill, 1998). The music is edited in Alfonso X El Sabio, *Cantigas de Santa María: Nueva transcripción integral de su música según la métrica latina*, ed. Roberto Pla (Madrid: Música Didáctica, 2001), the texts in Afonso X, O Sábio, *Cantigas de Santa Maria*, ed. Walter Mettmann (Edicións Xerais de Galicia, 1981), and translations in *Songs of Holy Mary of Alfonso X, The Wise*, trans. Kathleen Kulp-Hill (Tempe: Arizona Center for Medieval and Renaissance Studies, 2000). An older edition with complete facsimile is Higinio Anglès, *La música de las cantigas de Santa Maria del Rey Alfonso el Sabio*, 3 vols. in 4 (Barcelona: Biblioteca Central, Sección de Musica, 1943–64). On Muslim and Jewish song, especially in Spain, see Amnon Shiloah, "Muslim and Jewish Musical Traditions of the Middle Ages," in *Music as Concept and Practice in the Late Middle Ages*, ed. Reinhard Strohm and Bonnie J. Blackburn, 1–30.

Instruments and Dance

On individual instruments, see *A Performer's Guide to Medieval Music*, ed. Ross W. Duffin (Bloomington: Indiana University Press, 2000). On the music, see Howard

Mayer Brown and Keith Polk, "Instrumental Music, *c. 1300–c.* 1520," and Walter Salmen, "Dances and Dance Music, *c.* 1300–*c.* 1530," in *Music as Concept and Practice in the Late Middle Ages*, ed. Strohm and Blackburn, 97–161 and 162–90. For transcriptions of all the extant dances, along with a useful commentary, see Timothy McGee, *Medieval Instrumental Dances* (Bloomington: Indiana University Press, 1989).

CHAPTER 5

General

The Early Middle Ages to 1300, ed. Richard L. Crocker and David Hiley, contains excellent surveys of early polyphony by Sarah Fuller, Notre Dame polyphony by Janet Knapp, and French and English thirteenth-century polyphony by Crocker. F. Alberto Gallo, *Music of the Middle Ages II*, trans. Steven Botterill (Cambridge: Cambridge University Press, 1985), focuses on polyphony in the Latin West. See also Sarah Fuller, "Organum-*discantus-contrapunctus* in the Middle Ages," in CHWMT, 477–502; and "Organum," "Discant," "Conductus," and "Motet, §I: Middle Ages" in NG2.

A view of the social roles for polyphonic music is offered in Marion S. Gushee, "The Polyphonic Music of the Medieval Monastery, Cathedral and University," in *Antiquity and the Middle Ages*, ed. James W. McKinnon, 143–69. In *Discarding Images: Reflections on Music and Culture in Medieval France* (Oxford: Clarendon, 1993), Christopher Page challenges conventional views of the thirteenth century as rationalistic, constructive, and ascetic, and pleads for a more intuitive understanding of its human qualities.

Early Organum

For a translation of *Musica enchiriadis* and *Scolica enchiriadis*, see above under chapter 2; for Guido of Arezzo's *Micrologus*, see under chapter 3. The major study in English of the Winchester Troper, which includes transcriptions of some of the music, is Alejandro Planchart, *The Repertory of Tropes at Winchester*, 2 vols. (Princeton: Princeton University Press, 1977). For free organum, see *Ad Organum Faciendum & Item de Organo*, ed. and trans. Jay A. Huff (Brooklyn: Institute of Mediaeval Music, 1969).

Aquitanian Polyphony

See Fuller, "St. Martial, §III: Polyphony," in NG2. *Codex Calixtinus de la Catedral de Santiago de Compostela* (n.p.: Kaydeda Ediciones, 1993) provides a color facsimile of the entire codex. Theodore Karp, *The Polyphony of St. Martial and Santiago de Compostela*, 2 vols. (Oxford: Clarendon, 1992), argues for a rhythmic transcription of this repertory and provides an edition, but his principles have not been widely accepted. Editions without rhythms are Hendrik van der Werf, *The Oldest Extant Part Music and the Origin of Western Polyphony*, 2 vols. (Rochester, NY: Author, 1993), and Bryan Gillingham, *Saint Martial Polyphony* (Henryville, PA: Institute of Mediaeval Music, 1984).

Notre Dame Polyphony

Craig Wright reviews the history of music at Notre Dame during the Middle Ages and early Renaissance with fascinating detail in *Music and Ceremony at Notre Dame of Paris: 500–1500* (Cambridge: Cambridge University Press, 1989). On the performance of Notre Dame polyphony, see Edward H. Roesner, "The Performance of Parisian Organum," *Early Music* 7 (April 1979): 174–89; Rebecca A. Baltzer, "The Geography of the Liturgy at Notre-Dame of Paris," in *Plainsong in the Age of Polyphony*, ed. Thomas Forrest Kelly (Cambridge: Cambridge University Press, 1992), 45–64; and Baltzer, "How Long was Notre-Dame Organum Performed?" in *Beyond the Moon: Festscrift Luther Dittmer*, ed. Gillingham and Paul Merkley (Ottawa: Institute of Mediaeval Music, 1990), 118–43.

The standard index of the Notre Dame repertory is Friedrich Ludwig, *Repertorium organorum recentioris et motetorum vetustissimi stili* (Brooklyn: Institute of Mediaeval Music, 1964–78). A more up-to-date catalogue in English is van der Werf, *Integrated Directory of Organa, Clausulae, and Motets of the Thirteenth Century* (Rochester, NY: Author, 1989). See also Gillingham, *Indices to the Notre-Dame Fascimiles* (Ottawa: Institute of Mediaeval Music, 1994).

The three major sources believed to be the most complete descendants of the *Magnus liber organi* are the manuscripts Wolfenbüttel, Helmstedt 628 (formerly 677), called W1; Wolfenbüttel, Helmstedt 1099 (1206), called W2; and Florence, Biblioteca Medicea-Laurenziana, pluteo 29.1, called F. All three are published in facsimile: W1 in *An Old St. Andrews Music Book*, ed. J. H. Baxter (London: St. Andrews University Publications, 1931), or *Die mitteralterliche Musik-Handschrift W1*, ed. Martin Staehelin, (Wiesbaden, 1995), with introduction in both English and German; W2 in *Wolfenbüttel 1099*, ed. Luther A. Dittmer, PMMM 2 (1960); and F in *Firenze, Biblioteca Mediceo-Laurenziana, pluteo 29.1*, 2 vols., ed. Dittmer, PMMM 10–11 (1966–67).

The organa and clausulae are transcribed in *Le Magnus liber organi de Notre-Dame de Paris*, 6 vols., gen. ed. Edward H. Roesner (Monaco: Oiseau-Lyre, 1993–), with an introductory note on performance in vol. 1. Hans Tischler, *The Parisian Two-Part Organa: The Complete Comparative Edition*, 2 vols. (New York, 1988), transcribes the repertoire in the rhythmic modes throughout, as does the partial edition included in William G. Waite, *The Rhythm of Twelfth-Century Polyphony: Its Theory and Practice* (New Haven: Yale University Press, 1954).

For an overview of Notre Dame notation and its rhythmic interpretation, see Gillingham, *Modal Rhythm* (Ottawa: The Institute of Mediaeval Music, 1986). See also

Roesner, "Rhythmic modes"; Hiley and Thomas B. Payne, "Notation, II"; and Margaret Bent, "Notation, III"; in NG2.

Relevant theorists include Anonymous IV, *De mensuris et discantu*, trans. Jeremy Yudkin, MSD 41 (Neuhausen-Stuttgart: AIM/Hänssler, 1985), and Joannes de Garlandia, *Concerning Measured Music (De mensurabili musica)*, trans. Stanley H. Birnbaum (Colorado Springs: Colorado College Music Press, 1978). An excerpt from the latter is in SR 30 (2:22).

Conductus

See Robert Falck, *The Notre Dame Conductus: A Study of the Repertory* (Henryville, PA: Institute of Mediaeval Music, 1981), and Page, *Latin Poetry and Conductus Rhythm in Medieval France* (London: Royal Musical Association, 1997). Editions of conductus include *The Conductus Collection of MS Wolfenbüttel 1099*, 3 vols., ed. Ethel Thurston (Madison, WI: A-R Editions, 1980), and *Notre-Dame and Related Conductus: Opera omnia*, 10 vols., ed. Gordon Anderson (Henryville, PA: Institute of Mediaeval Music, 1979–).

Motet

Hearing the Motet of the Middle Ages and Renaissance, ed. Dolores Pesce (New York: Oxford University Press, 1997), is a fascinating collection of essays on motets of different eras. Engaging recent studies of the motet include van der Werf, *Hidden Beauty in Motets of the Early Thirteenth Century* (Tucson: Author, 1998); Sylvia Huot, *Allegorical Play in the Old French Motet: The Sacred and the Profane in Thirteenth-Century Polyphony* (Stanford: Stanford University Press, 1997); and Mark Everist, *French Motets in the Thirteenth Century: Music, Poetry, and Genre* (Cambridge: Cambridge University Press, 1994). Tischler, *The Style and Evolution of the Earliest Motets (to circa 1270)*, 3 vols. (Henryville, PA: Institute of Mediaeval Music, 1985), is a companion to his edition and includes a comprehensive catalogue.

The most complete edition of early motets, which presents each motet in several versions from various manuscripts, is *The Earliest Motets (to circa 1270): A Complete Comparative Edition*, 3 vols., ed. Tischler (New Haven: Yale University Press, 1982). Editions of particular manuscripts include *The Latin Compositions of Fasciles VII and VIII of the Notre Dame Manuscript Wolfenbüttel Helmstedt 1099 (1206)*, 2 vols., ed. Gordon Anderson (Brooklyn: Institute of Mediaeval Music, 1968); *The Montpellier Codex*, Recent Researches in the Music of the Middle Ages and Early Renaissance 2–8, ed. Tischler (Madison, WI: A-R Editions, 1978–85); *Compositions of the Bamberg Manuscript*, CMM 75, ed. Anderson (Neuhausen-Stuttgart: Hänssler, 1977); and Higini Anglès, *El codex musical de Las Huelgas*, 3 vols. (Barcelona: Institut d'estudis catalans, Biblioteca de Catalunya, 1931).

Notation

For details of the notation of twelfth- and thirteenth-century polyphonic music, consult Carl Parrish, *The Notation of Medieval Music* (New York: Norton, 1978); Willi Apel, *The Notation of Polyphonic Music*, 5th ed. (Cambridge, MA: Medieval Academy of America, 1961); and Waite, *The Rhythm of Twelfth-Century Polyphony*. An excerpt from Franco of Cologne's *Ars cantus mensurabilis* is in SR 31 (2:23).

English Polyphony

Peter M. Lefferts, "Medieval England, 950–1450," in *Antiquity and the Middle Ages*, ed. McKinnon, 170–96, offers an overview and contexts for English polyphonic and monophonic music. See also Lefferts, *The Motet in England in the Fourteenth Century* (Ann Arbor: UMI Research Press, 1996). Shai Burstyn, "Gerald of Wales and the *Sumer* Canon," JM 2 (1983): 135–50, argues for folk polyphony as an influence on English music and against a firm division between improvisation and composition.

Surviving works are collected in *English Music of the Thirteenth and Early Fourteenth Centuries*, ed. Ernest H. Sanders, PMFC 14 (Monaco: Oiseau-Lyre, 1979). The Worcester fragments are edited in PMMM 5 and in *The Worcester Fragments: A Catalogue Raisonné and Transcription*, ed. Dittmer, MSD 2.

CHAPTER 6

General

Polyphonic Music of the Fourteenth Century [PMFC] (Monaco: Oiseau-Lyre, 1956–91) is a comprehensive edition of fourteenth-century music from France, Italy, and England: vol. 1: *Roman de Fauvel*, Vitry, and French Mass Ordinary cycles; 2–3: Machaut; 4: Landini; 5: motets of French provenance; 6–11: Italian secular music; 12–13: Italian sacred and ceremonial music; 14: English music of the thirteenth and fourteenth centuries; 15: English motets; 16–17: English Mass, Office, and ceremonial music; 18–22: French secular music; 23: French sacred music; 24: Ciconia.

On rhythmic notation from the thirteenth through fifteenth centuries, see Anna Maria Busse Berger, "The Evolution of Rhythmic Notation," in CHWMT, 628–56. On theory in general, see Jan Herlinger, "Music Theory of the Fourteenth and Early Fifteenth Centuries," in *Music as Concept and Practice in the Late Middle Ages*, ed. Reinhard Strohm and Bonnie J. Blackburn (Oxford: Oxford University Press, 2001), 244–300.

Roman de Fauvel

See the facsimile in François Avril, Nancy Regaldo, and Edward H. Roesner, *Le Roman de Fauvel and Other Works: Facsimile with Introductory Essay* (New York:

Broude, 1986), and the edition in *Le premier et le secont livre de Fauvel*, ed. Paul Helmer (Ottawa: Institute of Mediaeval Music, 1997). A diverse collection of essays devoted to *Fauvel* is *Fauvel Studies: Allegory, Chronicle, Music, and Image in Paris, Bibliothèque nationale de France, MS francais 146*, ed. Margaret Bent and Andrew Wathey (Oxford: Clarendon, 1998). See also Emma Dillon, *Medieval Music-Making and the Roman de Fauvel* (Cambridge: Cambridge University Press, 2002).

Ars nova and Vitry

See the treatise attributed to Philippe de Vitry known as *Ars nova*, ed. Gilbert Reaney, André Gilles, and Jean Maillard, Corpus scriptorum de musica 8 (American Institute of Musicology, 1964), trans. Leon Plantinga in *Journal of Music Theory* 5 (1961): 204–23. Excerpts from Jehan de Murs's *Notitia artis musicae* are in SR 34 (2:26), and Jacques de Liège's critique from *Speculum musicae* is in SR 35 (2:27).

On Vitry as composer, see Daniel Leech-Wilkinson, *Compositional Techniques in the Four-Part Isorhythmic Motets of Philippe de Vitry and His Contemporaries*, 2 vols. (New York: Garland, 1989). Motets attributed to Vitry appear in PMFC 1 and 5 (see above) and in Philippe de Vitry, *Complete Works*, ed. Leo Schrade, with new introduction and notes by Roesner (Monaco: Oiseau-Lyre, 1984).

Machaut

Lawrence Earp, *Guillaume de Machaut: A Guide to Research* (New York: Garland, 1995) provides a comprehensive biography, bibliography, and discography, and is the best source for Machaut research. On the mass, see Daniel Leech-Wilkinson, *Machaut's Mass: An Introduction* (Oxford: Clarendon, 1990). Anne Walters Robertson, *Guillaume de Machaut in Reims: Context and Meaning in His Musical Works* (New York: Cambridge University Press, 2002) illuminates his music by placing it in context and establishes a date and purpose for Machaut's mass.

The standard Machaut edition is by Leo Schrade in PMFC 2–3. A newer, partial edition is *Guillaume de Machaut 1300–1377: Oeuvres complètes*, ed. Sylvette Leguy (Paris: Le Droict Chemin de Musique, 1977–). An edition of the mass is in CMM 2, and other fourteenth-century Mass music in France appears in CMM 13 (Mass of Tournai) and CMM 29. Machaut's *Le Jugement du roy de Behaigne and Remede de Fortune*, ed. and trans. James I. Wimsatt and William W. Kibler, music ed. Rebecca A. Baltzer (Athens and London: University of Georgia Press, 1988), illustrates how French secular song functioned in court culture. See also Machaut's *Le livre dou voir dit*, ed. Daniel Leech-Wilkinson, trans. R. Barton Palmer (New York: Garland, 1998).

Other French Composers and Ars Subtilior

Editions of the music appear in PMFC 18–24 (see above) and in CMM 36–37 (Codex Reina), 39 (Manuscripts of Chantilly, Musée Condé, and Modena), and 53 (*French Secular Compositions of the Fourteenth Century*, 3 vols., ed. Willi Apel).

Trecento

A good account of the musical scene is Michael Long, "Trecento Italy," in *Antiquity and the Middle Ages*, ed. James W. McKinnon (Englewood Cliffs, NJ: Prentice Hall, 1991), 241–68. On Landini, see Long, "Francesco Landini and the Florentine Cultural Elite," EMH 3 (1983): 83–99. Several important articles by Nino Pirrotta on the unwritten tradition are collected in his *Music and Culture in Italy from the Middle Ages to the Baroque: A Collection of Essays* (Cambridge, MA: Harvard University Press, 1984). For general bibliography, see Viola L. Hagopian, *Italian Ars Nova Music: A Bibliographic Guide to Modern Editions and Related Literature*, rev. ed. (Berkeley: University of California Press, 1973).

Editions include *The Music of Jacopo da Bologna*, ed. W. Thomas Marrocco (Berkeley: University of California Press, 1954), and *Fourteenth-Century Italian Cacce*, 2nd rev. ed., idem. (Cambridge, MA: Medieval Academy of America, 1961). The standard Landini edition is by Leo Schrade in PMFC 4. For the Squarcialupi Codex, see the edition by Johannes Wolf, *Der Squarcialupi Codex* (Lippstadt: Kistner & Siegel, 1955), and the facsimile in *Il codice Squarcialupi: Ms. Mediceo Palatino 87, Biblioteca laurenziana di Firenze* (Florence: Giunti Barbèra, 1992). Other editions of Trecento music appear in PMFC 6–13 and in CMM 8, *Music of Fourteenth-Century Italy*, ed. Nino Pirrotta.

On Italian theorists, see Prosdocimo de' Beldomandi, *Contrapunctus (Counterpoint)*, trans. Jan Herlinger (Lincoln: University of Nebraska Press, 1984), and Herlinger, *The Lucidarium of Marchetto of Padua* (Chicago: University of Chicago Press, 1985). The Italian notational system is described by Marchetto of Padua in SR 33 (2:25).

Instrumental Music

Keyboard music from the Robertsbridge Codex (British Library, MS Add. 28550) and other manuscripts appears in *Keyboard Music of the Fourteenth and Fifteenth Centuries*, ed. Apel, CEKM 1. Keyboard music from the Faenza Codex (Faenza, Biblioteca comunale, MS 117), ed. and trans. Dragan Plamenac, CMM 57, appears in facsimile in MSD 10.

Musica Ficta

Karol Berger, *Musica Ficta: Theories of Accidental Inflections in Vocal Polyphony from Marchetto da Padova to Gioseffo Zarlino* (Cambridge: Cambridge University Press, 1987). For an aesthetic assessment of chromaticism and ficta in the Middle Ages, see Thomas Brothers, *Chromatic Beauty in the Late Medieval Chanson: An Interpretation of Manuscript Accidentals* (Cambridge: Cambridge University Press, 1997).

PART II: THE RENAISSANCE

Excellent surveys of music in the fifteenth and sixteenth centuries include Allan Atlas, *Renaissance Music* (New York: Norton, 1998); Leeman Perkins, *Music in the Age of the Renaissance* (New York: Norton, 1998); Howard M. Brown and Louise Stein, *Music in the Renaissance*, 2nd ed. (Upper Saddle River, NJ: Prentice Hall, 1999); and Reinhard Strohm, *The Rise of European Music, 1380–1500* (Cambridge: Cambridge University Press, 1993).

The social, cultural, and historical contexts for music for this period are treated in *The Renaissance: From the 1470s to the End of the 16th Century*, ed. Iain Fenlon (London: Macmillan, 1989; Englewood Cliffs, NJ: Prentice Hall, 1989). On performance practice, see *A Performer's Guide to Renaissance Music*, ed. Jeffrey T. Kite-Powell (New York: Schirmer, 1994). See also *A Companion to Medieval and Renaissance Music*, ed. Tess Knighton, David Fallows, and Timothy J. McGee, *Medieval and Renaissance Music: A Performer's Guide*.

CHAPTER 7

The Renaissance and Music

A classic essay on the relation of music to the Renaissance is Edward E. Lowinsky, "Music in the Culture of the Renaissance," *Journal of the History of Ideas* 15 (1954): 509–53, in Lowinsky, *Music in the Culture of the Renaissance and Other Essays*, ed. Bonnie J. Blackburn (Chicago: University of Chicago Press, 1989), 19–39. A more recent study on the meaning of "Renaissance" in music studies is Jessie Ann Owens, "Music Historiography and the Definition of 'Renaissance,'" *Notes* 47 (December 1990): 305–30. See also the relevant chapters in Allan Atlas, *Renaissance Music*, and Leeman Perkins, *Music in the Age of the Renaissance*.

Humanism

On humanism, see Ann E. Moyer, *Musica scientia: Musical Scholarship in the Italian Renaissance* (Ithaca, NY: Cornell University Press, 1992); Claude V. Palisca, *Humanism in Italian Renaissance Musical Thought* (New Haven: Yale University Press, 1985); and Palisca, "Humanism and Music," in Albert Rabil, Jr., *Renaissance Humanism: Foundations, Forms, and Legacy*, vol. 3: *Humanism and the Disciplines* (Philadelphia: University of Pennsylvania Press, 1988), 450–85.

Patronage

The role of patronage is examined in *Music in Medieval and Early Modern Europe: Patronage, Sources, and Texts*, ed. Iain Fenlon (Cambridge: Cambridge University Press, 1981). Several studies examine musical activities in the context of Renaissance culture and society and the rela-

tionship between patronage and musical production in specific geographic locations. Strohm, *Music in Late Medieval Bruges*, rev. ed. (Oxford: Clarendon, 1990), offers a vivid picture of musical life in a Flemish community of the fifteenth century, particularly strong in documenting the role of the churches and confraternities as patrons of music. Others include Paul A. Merkley and Lora L. M. Matthews, *Music and Patronage in the Sforza Court* (Turnhout: Brepols, 1999); Frank A. D'Accone, *The Civic Muse: Music and Musicians in Siena during the Middle Ages and the Renaissance* (Chicago: University of Chicago Press, 1997); Christopher A. Reynolds, *Papal Patronage and the Music of St. Peter's, 1380–1513* (Berkeley: University of California Press, 1995); Lewis Lockwood, *Music in Renaissance Ferrara, 1400–1505: The Creation of a Musical Center in the Italian Renaissance* (Cambridge, MA: Harvard University Press, 1987); Atlas, *Music at the Aragonese Court of Naples* (Cambridge: Cambridge University Press, 1985); William Prizer, "Music and Ceremonial in the Low Countries: Philip the Fair and the Order of the Golden Fleece," *EMH* 5 (1985): 113–35; Fenlon, *Music Patronage in Sixteenth-Century Mantua*, 2 vols. (Cambridge: Cambridge University Press, 1980 and 1984); and David Price, *Patrons and Musicians of the English Renaissance* (Cambridge: Cambridge University Press, 1981).

Compositional Practice

On various aspects of composition and performance, see the collected essays and introduction in Margaret Bent, *Counterpoint, Composition, and Musica ficta* (New York: Routledge, 2002). On techniques of music composition as both a mental practice and physical act, see Owens, *Composers at Work: The Craft of Musical Composition, 1450–1600* (New York: Oxford University Press, 1997); and Blackburn, "On Compositional Process in the Fifteenth Century," *JAMS* 40 (1987): 210–84. An important reconsideration of fifteenth-century compositional process from a performative perspective is Rob C. Wegman, "From Maker to Composer: Improvisation and Musical Authorship in the Low Countries, 1450–1500," *JAMS* 49 (Fall 1996): 409–79.

Tuning and Temperament

See Jan Herlinger, "Medieval Canonics," and Rudolf Rasch, "Tuning and Temperament," in CHWMT, 168–92 and 193–222; Mark Lindley, "Tuning" and "Temperament," in NG2; and J. Murray Barbour, *Tuning and Temperament: A Historical Survey* (New York: Da Capo, 1972).

Theory and Theorists

For a brief survey of Renaissance theory, see Palisca, "Theory, theorists," sections 8–9, in NG2. On mode, see Cristle Collins Judd, "Renaissance Modal Theory: Theoretical, Compositional, and Editorial Perspectives," in CHWMT, 364–406; Harry S. Powers and Frans Wiering,

"Mode," chapter III, in NG2; and Bernhard Meier, *The Modes of Classical Vocal Polyphony*, trans. Ellen S. Beebe (New York: Broude, 1988). On counterpoint, see Peter Schubert, "Counterpoint Pedagogy in the Renaissance," in CHWMT, 503–33. See also David Damschroder and David Russell Williams, *Music Theory from Zarlino to Schenker: A Bibliography and Guide* (Stuyvesant, NY: Pendragon, 1990).

Several of the treatises mentioned or quoted in this chapter have been translated into English:

Johannes Tinctoris, *Liber de arte contrapuncti*, trans. Albert Seay as *The Art of Counterpoint*, MSD 5 (American Institute of Musicology, 1961). Excerpts in SR 67 (3:32).

Gioseffo Zarlino, *Le istitutioni harmoniche*, part 3, in *The Art of Counterpoint*, trans. Guy A. Marco Palisca (New Haven: Yale University Press, 1968; New York: Norton, 1976; Da Capo, 1983); part 4, in *On the Modes*, trans. Vered Cohen, ed. Palisca (New Haven: Yale University Press, 1983); excerpts in SR 37 (3:2) and SR 71 (3:36).

Pietro Aaron, *Toscanello in musica*, trans. Peter Bergquist (Colorado Springs: Colorado College Music Press, 1970). *Treatise on the Nature and Recognition of All the Tones of Figured Song*, excerpts in SR 69 (3:34).

Bartolomé Ramis de Pareia, *Musica practica*, trans. Clement A. Miller (American Institute of Musicology, 1993). Excerpts in SR 68 (3:33).

Franchino Gaffurio, *Theorica musice*, trans. with introduction and notes by Walter K. Kreyszig as *The Theory of Music*, ed. Palisca (New Haven: Yale University Press, 1993); *De Harmonia musicorum instrumentorum opus*, trans. Miller, MSD 33 (Stuttgart: American Institute of Musicology/Hänssler, 1977); *Practica musicae*, trans. Miller, MSD 20 (American Institute of Musicology, 1968), also trans. Irwin Young in *The Practica musicae of Franchinus Gafurius* (Madison: University of Wisconsin Press, 1969).

Heinrich Glarean, *Dodekachordon*, trans. Miller, MSD 6 (American Institute of Musicology, 1965). Excerpts in SR 70 (3:35).

Words and Music

For theories of text underlay as discussed in contemporary treatises, see Don Harrán, *Word-Tone Relations in Musical Thought from Antiquity to the Seventeenth Century*, MSD 40 (American Institute of Musicology, 1986).

Music Printing

For an overview from the origins of music printing to the present, see Stanley Boorman, Eleanor Selfridge-Field, and Donald W. Krummel, "Printing and publishing of music," in NG2. See also *Music Printing and Publishing*, eds. Donald W. Krummel and Stanley Sadie (New York: Norton, 1990).

A detailed study of Italian printers is offered by Fenlon, *Music, Print and Culture in Early Sixteenth-Century Italy* (London: British Library, 1995). For more detailed

regional studies of Italian publishing, see Jane A. Bernstein, *Print Culture and Music in Sixteenth-Century Venice* (Oxford: Oxford University Press, 2001); Richard J. Agee, *The Gardano Music Printing Firms, 1569–1611* (Rochester: University of Rochester, 1998); and Tim Carter, *Music, Patronage and Printing in Late Renaissance Florence* (Aldershot: Ashgate, 2000).

Petrucci's first three song collections are available in facsimile: *Harmonice Musices Odhecaton A*, 3rd ed. (1504; repr. New York: Broude, 1973); *Canti B numero cinquanta* (1502; repr. New York: Broude, 1975); and *Canti C numero cinquanta* (1504; repr. New York: Broude, 1978). The first two also are available in transcription: *Harmonice Musices Odhecaton A*, ed. Helen Hewitt with literary texts ed. by Isabel Pope (Cambridge, MA: Medieval Academy of America, 1946); and *Canti B numero cinquanta*, ed. Hewitt, Monuments of Renaissance Music 2 (Chicago: University of Chicago Press, 1967).

Accounts of the earliest music printers in France are in Daniel Heartz, *Pierre Attaingnant, Royal Printer of Music* (Berkeley: University of California Press, 1968). Essays on music printing in the Low Countries are collected in *Music Fragments and Manuscripts in the Low Countries: Alta capella: Music Printing in Antwerp and Europe in the 16th Century*, ed. Eugeen Schreurs and Henri Vanhulst (Leuven: Alamire, 1997).

Chapter 8

English Music

For a concise survey of Dunstable's music, see Margaret Bent, *Dunstaple* (London: Oxford University Press, 1980). For social roles of music, see Peter M. Lefferts, "Medieval England, 950–1450," and Frank L. Harrison, *Music in Medieval Britain*, listed above under chapter 4.

Editions of English music of the fourteenth and fifteenth centuries include John Dunstable, *Complete Works*, ed. Manfred F. Bukofzer, rev. ed. by Bent, Ian Bent, and Brian Trowell, in MB 8 (1970); Leonel Power, *Complete Works*, ed. Charles Hamm, in CMM 50; Walter Frye, *Collected Works*, ed. Sylvia W. Kenney, in CMM 19; *The Old Hall Manuscript*, 4 vols., ed. Andrew Hughes and Bent, in CMM 46; *Mediaeval Carols*, ed. John E. Stevens, in MB 4; *The Eton Choir Book*, ed. Harrison, in MB 10–12; and *Fifteenth-Century Liturgical Music*, ed. Andrew Hughes, Bent, and Gareth Curtis, in *Early English Church Music*, vols. 8, 22, 34, and 42 (London: Stainer & Bell, 1968–2001).

Burgundy

Craig Wright, *Music at the Court of Burgundy, 1364–1419* (Henryville, PA: Institute of Mediaeval Music, 1979). On choral performance in fifteenth-century Burgundy, see David Fallows, "Specific Information on the Ensembles for Composed Polyphony, 1400–1474," in *Studies in the Performance of Late Mediaeval Music*, ed. Stanley Boorman

(Cambridge: Cambridge University Press, 1983), 109–60. See also Reinhard Strohm, *Music in Late Medieval Bruges.*

On the Burgundian chanson during this period see, Walter H. Kemp, *Burgundian Court Song in the Time of Binchois: The Anonymous Chansons of El Escorial, MS V.III.24* (Oxford: Oxford University Press, 1990).

Critical essays on Binchois appear in *Binchois Studies*, ed. Andrew Kirkman and Dennis Slavin (Oxford: Oxford University Press, 2000). Binchois's chansons are transcribed in *Die Chansons von Gilles Binchois (1400–1460)*, ed. Wolfgang Rehm (Mainz: B. Schott, 1957). For his sacred works, see *The Sacred Music of Gilles Binchois*, ed. Philip Kaye (Oxford: Oxford University Press, 1992).

Du Fay

Much new information on Du Fay, including his birthdate, appeared in Alejandro Enrique Planchart, "Guillaume Du Fay's Benefices and His Relationship to the Court of Burgundy," EMH 8 (1988): 117–71. See also his article on Du Fay in NG2; Fallows, *Dufay* (New York: Vintage, 1987); and Julie E. Cumming, *The Motet in the Age of Du Fay* (Cambridge: Cambridge University Press, 1999). On Du Fay's compositional techniques, see Kevin N. Moll, *Counterpoint and Compositional Process in the Time of Dufay: Perspectives from German Musicology* (New York: Garland, 1997). On his attention to text-setting, see Don Michael Randel, "Dufay the Reader," in *Music and Language* (New York: Broude, 1983), 38–78.

Du Fay's works appear in his *Opera omnia*, ed. Heinrich Besseler, in CMM 1, vol. 6 (Chansons); rev. ed. by Fallows, 1995.

Works by Du Fay and his contemporaries are preserved in a large number of manuscripts, mostly of Italian origin. Several of the most important ones are available in facsimile and modern editions. A manuscript copied in northern Italy in about 1460 that contains 325 works dating from about 1400 to 1440 is *Oxford, Bodleian Library, MS. Canon. Misc. 213*, ed. with intro. and inventory by Fallows (Chicago: University of Chicago Press, 1995). The Trent Codices are seven volumes now in the library of the National Museum in the Castello del Buonconsiglio in Trent, containing more than 1,600 compositions written between 1400 and 1475; a facsimile appears in *Codex Tridentinus 87–93* (Rome: Bibliopola, 1969–70), and portions are transcribed in DTO, vols. 14/15, 22, 38, 53, 61, and 76. Canons from the Trent Codices, ed. Richard Loyan, appear in CMM 38. The Chansonnier El Escorial, which contains pieces attributed to Dunstable, Du Fay, Binchois, and others, appears in an edition by Martha K. Hanen, *The Chansonnier El Escorial*, 3 vols. (Henryville, PA: Institute of Mediaeval Music, 1983).

Polyphonic Mass

Contrary to earlier scholarship, Kirkman argues that the recognition of the mass cycle as a genre came only around 1450; see "The Invention of the Cyclic Mass," JAMS 54 (Spring 2001): 1–47. The major work on cantus-firmus use in masses and other liturgical works is Edgar H. Sparks, *Cantus Firmus in Mass and Motet, 1420–1520* (Berkeley: University of California Press, 1963). On *L'homme armé*, see Alejandro Planchart, "The Origins and Early History of *L'homme armé*," JM 20 (Summer 2003): 305–57.

Many early masses appear in the Trent Codices (see above). See also *Monumenta polyphoniae liturgicae*, ed. Laurence Feininger (Rome: 1947–74), Series I, Ordinary of the Mass (vol. 1 contains ten early masses on *L'homme armé*), and Series II, Proper of the Mass (scholarly editions preserving all features of the original manuscripts).

CHAPTER 9

Ockeghem

Ockeghem's masses are in *Johannes Ockeghem: Masses and Mass Sections*, ed. Jaap van Benthem (Utrecht, 1994–) and in *Johannes Ockeghem: Collected Works*, vols. 1 and 2, 2nd ed., ed. Dragan Plamenac (New York: American Musicological Society, 1959–66). For his other works, see *Collected Works*, vol. 3: *Motets and Chansons*, eds. Richard Wexler and Plamenac (Philadelphia: American Musicological Society, 1992). On Ockeghem's mass music and musical borrowing, see Fabrice Fitch, *Johannes Ockeghem: Masses and Models* (Paris: H. Champion, 1997). For a bibliography, see Martin Picker, *Johannes Ockeghem and Jacob Obrecht: A Guide to Research* (New York: Garland, 1988).

Busnoys

Antoine Busnoys: Method, Meaning, and Context in Late Medieval Music, ed. Paula Higgins (Oxford: Clarendon, 1999), is an excellent collection of essays. The incomplete *Collected Works* has only the Latin-texted works, ed. Richard Taruskin (New York: Broude, 1990).

Obrecht

The major study is Rob C. Wegman, *Born for the Muses: The Life and Masses of Jacob Obrecht* (Oxford: Clarendon, 1994). Obrecht's works are published in *New Obrecht Edition*, ed. Chris Maas et al. (Utrecht, 1983–99); *Werken*, 8 vols., ed. Johannes Wolf (Amsterdam: G. Alsbach; Leipzig: Breitkopf & Härtel, 1912–21; repr. 1968); and *Opera Omnia*, 5 vols., ed. Marcus van Crevel (Amsterdam: G. Alsbach, 1953–). For a bibliography, see under Ockeghem.

Isaac

Isaac's complete works are published in *Henrici Isaac Opera omnia*, 7 vols., ed. Edward R. Lerner, CMM 65 (1974–84). See also *Choralis Constantinus*, Books I and

II, in DTO, vols. 10 and 32; Book III, ed. Louise Cuyler (Ann Arbor: University of Michigan Press, 1950); *Five Polyphonic Masses*, ed. Cuyler (Ann Arbor: University of Michigan Press, 1956); *Messen*, ed. Martin Staehelin, Musikalische Denkmäler, 7–8 (Mainz: B. Schott, 1971–73). For a bibliography, see Martin Picker, *Henricus Isaac: A Guide to Research* (New York: Garland, 1991).

Josquin

Recent archival discoveries have considerably altered the chronicle of Josquin's life. Paul Merkley, "Josquin at Ferrara," JM 18 (2001): 544–83, summarizes many of the recent discoveries before reporting new finds and embarking upon an account of Josquin's time in Ferrara. See especially Lora Matthews and Merkley, *Music and Patronage in the Sforza Court* (Turnhout: Brepols, 1999), and Pamela Starr, "Josquin, Rome, and a Case of Mistaken Identity," JM 15 (1997): 43–65. Outstanding collections of articles on Josquin appear in *The Josquin Companion*, ed. Richard Sherr (Oxford: Oxford University Press, 2000) and in *Josquin des Prez, Proceedings of the International Josquin Festival-Conference, New York, 1971*, ed. Edward E. Lowinsky and Bonnie J. Blackburn (London: Oxford University Press, 1976). Andrew Kirkman, "From Humanism to Enlightenment: Reinventing Josquin," JM 17 (1999): 441–58, examines changing perspectives on Josquin's reputation from early in his lifetime through the nineteenth century. For a bibliography, see Sydney Robinson Charles, *Josquin des Prez: A Guide to Research* (New York: Garland, 1983).

Josquin's works are published in *New Josquin Edition*, ed. Willem Elders et al. (Utrecht: Vereeniging voor Nederlandse Muziekgeschiedenis, 1987–), in progress, and *Werken*, 13 vols., ed. Albert Smijers et al. (Amsterdam: Vereeniging voor Nederlandse Muziekgeschiedenis, 1921–69).

Chapter 10

Lutheran Music

The basic work on Lutheran church music is Friedrich Blume, *Protestant Church Music* (New York: Norton, 1974). For printed sources and translations of individual chorales, consult *Dictionary of Hymnology*, 2 vols., ed. John Julian (Grand Rapids, MI: Kregel, 1985). For an examination of the role of music in Lutheran Germany, see Rebecca Wagner Oettinger, *Music as Propaganda in the German Reformation* (Aldershot: Ashgate, 2001).

Luther's *Deudsche Messe* (1526) is published in facsimile by Bärenreiter (Kassel, 1934). Johann Walter's *Geystliche gesangk Buchleyn* of 1524 is published in EP, vol. 7 (Year 6), and his complete works in *Sämtliche Werke*, ed. Otto Schröder (Kassel: Bärenreiter, 1953–73). Georg Rhau's 1544 collection *Newe deudsche geistliche Gesenge CXXIII* is in DdT, vol. 34. Luther's foreword to the *Wittemberg Gesangbuch* is in SR 55 (3:20).

Metrical Psalms

On metrical psalms, see Waldo Selden Pratt, *The Music of the French Psalter of 1562* (New York: Columbia University Press, 1939), and Robin A. Leaver, *Goostly Psalmes and Spirituall Songes: English and Dutch Metrical Psalms from Coverdale to Utenhove, 1535–1566* (Oxford: Oxford University Press, 1991). A facsimile reprint of the Bay Psalm Book has been published by the Chicago University Press, 1956. See also Richard G. Appel, *Music of the Bay Psalm Book*, 9th ed. (Brooklyn: Institute for Studies in American Music, 1975).

Polyphonic psalm settings by Claude Goudimel and Claude Le Jeune are in their collected works: for Goudimel, *Oeuvres complètes*, ed. Pierre Pidoux et al., Gesamtausgaben 3 (Brooklyn: Institute of Medieval Music, 1967–83), and *Maîtres musiciens de la Renaissance française*, ed. Henry Expert, 2, 4, and 6; for Le Jeune, *Maîtres musiciens de la Renaissance française*, ed. Expert, 11, 21, 22, and 23. For psalm settings by Jacobus Clemens, see below; for Jan Pieterszoon Sweelinck, see chapter 15.

Church Music in England

See Peter Le Huray, *Music and the Reformation in England, 1549–1660*, corr. ed. (New York: Cambridge University Press, 1978), and Colin Hand, *John Taverner: His Life and Music* (London: Eulenburg, 1978). A number of important articles on music and choirs in the English church are gathered in Roger Bowers, *English Church Polyphony: Singers and Sources from the 14th to the 17th Century* (Aldershot: Ashgate Press, 1999). For other sources, see Richard Turbet, *Tudor Music: A Research and Information Guide, with an Appendix Updating William Byrd* (New York: Garland, 1994). A relevant anthology is *The Treasury of English Church Music II, 1545–1650*, corr. ed., ed. Peter Le Huray (Cambridge: Cambridge University Press, 1982).

Byrd

Major books on Byrd include Joseph Kerman, *The Masses and Motets of William Byrd* (Berkeley: University of California Press, 1980), and Oliver W. Neighbor, *The Consort and Keyboard Music of William Byrd* (Berkeley: University of California Press, 1978). See also John Harley, *William Byrd: Gentleman of the Chapel Royal* (Aldershot: Scolar, 1997), and *Byrd Studies*, ed. Alan Brown and Turbet (Cambridge: Cambridge University Press, 1992).

Byrd's works are published in *The Collected Works of William Byrd*, ed. Edmund H. Fellowes (London: Stainer & Bell, 1937–50); rev. ed., gen ed. Thurston Dart (1964–70). A new edition is in progress: *The Byrd Edition*, gen. ed. Philip Brett (London: Stainer & Bell, 1976–). The dedications for his *Gradualia* are in SR 63 (3:28).

The Generation of 1520–1550

Willaert's works are in CMM 3, ed. Hermann Zenck, Walter Gerstenberg, and Bernhard Meier; Gombert's in CMM 6, ed. Joseph Schmidt-Görg; and Clemens's in CMM 4, ed. K. Ph. Bernet Kempers.

Catholic Music in Italy

On the Council of Trent, see Craig A. Monson, "The Council of Trent Revisited," JAMS 55 (Spring 2002): 1–37. On Italian church music, see Jerome Roche, *North Italian Church Music in the Age of Monteverdi* (Oxford: Clarendon, 1984). Though now somewhat dated, a classic study in Counter-Reformation Italy remains Lewis Lockwood, *The Counter-Reformation and the Masses of Vincenzo Ruffo* (Vienna: Universal, 1970).

Palestrina

The classic work in English on Palestrina is Knud Jeppesen's *The Style of Palestrina and the Dissonance*, 2nd ed., trans. Edward J. Dent (London: Oxford University Press, 1946), which offers detailed analysis of Palestrina's music. For a bibliography, see Clara Marvin, *Giovanni Pierluigi da Palestrina: A Guide to Research* (New York: Routledge, 2002). On the imitation masses, see Quentin W. Quereau, "Aspects of Palestrina's Parody Procedure," JM 1 (1982): 198–216. Lockwood's edition of the *Pope Marcellus Mass*, Norton Critical Scores (New York: Norton, 1975), includes studies on the work and the legend surrounding it. Palestrina's dedication to his *Second Book of Masses* is in SR 60 (3:25). Palestrina's works are in *Giovanni Pierluigi da Palestrina: Le opere complete*, ed. Raffaele Casimiri et al. (Rome: Fratelli Scalera, 1939–87).

Spain and the New World

See Robert Stevenson, *Spanish Cathedral Music in the Golden Age* (Berkeley: University of California Press, 1961). Accounts of Aztec and Inca music are in SR 77–78 (3:42–43). For a recent interpretation of the possible role of song in Aztec society, see Gary Tomlinson, "Montaigne's Cannibal Songs," *repercussions* 7–8 (Spring–Fall 1999–2000): 209–35; see also the more broadly conceived but related article, "Ideologies of Aztec Song," JAMS 48 (Fall 1995): 343–79.

For modern editions of Spanish music of the sixteenth century, see the series *Monumentos de la musica española*, gen. ed. Higini Anglès (1941–); the music of Morales is in vols. 11, 13, 15, 17, 20, 21, 24, and 34; that of Guerrero in vols. 16 and 19, ed. Miguel Querol Gavaldá; and that of Victoria in vols. 25, 26, 30, and 31. Victoria's works are also in his *Opera omnia*, ed. Felipe Pedrell (Leipzig: Breitkopf & Härtel, 1902–13; repr. 1965).

Germany and Eastern Europe

A varied collection of essays on music in fifteenth- and sixteenth-century Germany is *Music in the German Renaissance: Sources, Styles and Contexts*, ed. John Kmetz (Cambridge: Cambridge University Press, 1994). Hassler's works are in *Sämtliche Werke*, ed. C. Russell Crosby (Wiesbaden: Breitkopf & Härtel, 1961–). Handl's are in a *Collected Edition*, ed. Dragotin Cvetko (Ljubljana, 1966–), and in DTO, vols. 12, 14, 30, 40, 48, 51, 52, 78, 94, 95, 118, and 119.

Lasso

For an overview, see Jerome Roche, *Lassus*, Oxford Studies of Composers (London: Oxford University Press, 1982). A detailed study of his Magnificats is David Crook, *Orlando di Lasso's Imitation Magnificats for Counter-Reformation Munich* (Princeton: Princeton University Press, 1994). See also the useful collection of essays in *Orlando di Lasso Studies*, ed. Peter Bergquist (Cambridge: Cambridge University Press, 1999). For bibliography, see James Erb, *Orlando di Lasso: A Guide to Research* (New York: Garland, 1990). His complete works are available in two editions: *Sämtliche Werke*, ed. Franz X. Haberl and Adolf Sandberger (Leipzig: Breitkopf & Härtel, 1894–1927; repr. 1974), and *Sämtliche Werke*, new series, ed. Siegfried Hermelink et al. (Kassel: Bärenreiter, 1956–). The motets are edited by Bergquist in *The Complete Motets* (Madison, WI: A-R Editions, 1995–).

Jewish Music

See Edwin Seroussi, Eliyahu Schleifer et al., "Jewish Music, §III: Liturgical and paraliturgical," in NG2; Hanoch Avenary, *The Ashkenazi Tradition of Biblical Chant between 1500 and 1900: Documentation and Musical Analysis* (Tel Aviv: Tel Aviv University, 1978); and Idelsohn, *Jewish Music in Its Historical Development*.

CHAPTER 11

Spain

On the importance and longevity of the villancico in both Spain and the Americas, see Paul R. Laird, *Toward a History of the Spanish Villancico* (Warren, MI: Harmonie Park, 1997). See the edition by Jesus Bal y Gay of the Cancionero de Upsala (Mexico: El Colegio de México, 1944), with a historical essay on the polyphonic villancico by Isabel Pope. See also *Madrigales españoles ineditos del siglo XVI*, ed. Miguel Querol Gavalda (Barcelona: Instituto Español de Musicologia, 1981).

Italian Frottola

See William Prizer, *Courtly Pastimes: The Frottole of Marchetto Cara* (Ann Arbor: UMI Research Press, 1981), and idem., "Isabella d'Este and Lucretia Borgia as Patrons of

Music: The Frottola at Mantua and Ferrara," JAMS 38 (1985): 1–33. For a reassessment and critique of the modern use of the term *frottola*, as well as of the various genres under which the term is now subsumed, see Nino Pirrotta, "Before the Madrigal," JM 12 (Summer 1994): 237–52.

Examples of the frottola and related forms are in Alfred Einstein's *The Italian Madrigal* (Princeton: Princeton University Press, 1949), vol. 3, nos. 1–14. See also Rudolf Schwarz's edition of Petrucci's first and fourth books of frottole in PAM 8, and *Frottole nell'edizione principe di O. Petrucci*, ed. Raffaello Monterosso (Cremona: Athenaeum Cremonense, 1954).

Italian Madrigal

The definitive study on Italian madrigals is Alfred Einstein, *The Italian Madrigal* (Princeton: Princeton University Press, 1949; reprinted with additions, 1971). A shorter survey is Jerome Roche, *The Madrigal*, 2nd ed. (New York: Oxford University Press, 1990). Major studies of the madrigal since Einstein's work include Martha Feldman, *City Culture and the Madrigal in Venice* (Berkeley: University of California Press, 1995); Iain Fenlon and James Haar, *The Italian Madrigal in the Early Sixteenth Century* (Cambridge: Cambridge University Press, 1988); Haar, *Essays on Italian Poetry and Music in the Renaissance, 1350–1600* (Berkeley: University of California Press, 1986); and Anthony Newcomb, *The Madrigal at Ferrara, 1579–1597* (Princeton: Princeton University Press, 1980). Studies on individual madrigal composers include Haar, "Toward a Chronology of the Madrigals of Arcadelt," JM 5 (1987): 28–54; Henry W. Kaufmann, *The Life and Works of Nicola Vicentino, 1511–ca. 1576*, MSD 11 (American Institute of Musicology, 1966); Thomasin LaMay, "Madalena Casulana," in *Gender, Sexuality, and Early Music*, ed. Todd M. Borgerding (New York: Routledge, 2002); Denis Arnold, *Marenzio* (London: Oxford University Press, 1965); James Chater, *Luca Marenzio and the Italian Madrigal, 1577–1593* (Ann Arbor: UMI Research Press, 1981); Marco Bizzarini, *Luca Marenzio: The Career of a Musician between the Renaissance and the Counter-Reformation*, trans. Chater (Aldershot: Ashgate, 2003); and Glenn Watkins, *Gesualdo: The Man and His Music*, 2nd ed. (Oxford: Clarendon, 1991). For a hermeneutic approach to several important madrigal composers and their work, see Susan McClary, *Modal Subjectivities: Self-Fashioning in the Italian Madrigal* (Berkeley: University of California Press, 2004).

The madrigals of most composers mentioned here are in their collected works: Verdelot in CMM 28, ed. Anne-Marie Bragard; Arcadelt in CMM 31, ed. Albert Seay; Willaert in CMM 3, ed. Hermann Zenck, Walter Gerstenberg, and Bernhard Meier; Rore in CMM 14, ed. Bernhard Meier; Vicentino in CMM 26, ed. Henry W. Kaufmann; Casulana in *I madrigali di Maddalena Casulana*, ed. Beatrice Pescerelli (Florence: L. S. Olschki, 1979); Wert in CMM 24, ed. Carol

MacClintock and Melvin Bernstein; and Gesualdo in *Sämtliche Werke*, ed. Glenn E. Watkins and Wilhelm Weismann (Hamburg: Ugrino, 1957–67). Marenzio's madrigals are available in three editions: CMM 72, ed. Meier and Roland Jackson; PAM 4, 6, ed. Einstein; and *The Secular Works*, ed. Steven Ledbetter and Patricia Myers (New York: Broude, 1977–). Modern anthologies of Italian madrigals include *The Oxford Book of Italian Madrigals*, ed. R. Alec Harman (London: Oxford University Press, 1983).

Nicolà Vicentino's treatise *L'antica musica ridotta alla moderna prattica* is available in an annotated translation as *Ancient Music Adapted to Modern Practice*, trans. with notes by Maria Rika Maniates, ed. Claude V. Palisca (New Haven: Yale University Press, 1996). Two sonnets by Gaspara Stampa are translated in SR 49 (3:14), and Maddalena Casulana's preface to her first book of madrigals is in SR 50 (3:15).

France

On the sixteenth-century French chanson, see Lawrence Bernstein, "The 'Parisian Chanson': Problems of Style and Terminology," JAMS 31 (1978): 193–240, and idem., "Notes on the Origin of the Parisian Chanson," JM 1 (1982): 275–326. On Attaingnant, see Daniel Heartz, *Pierre Attaingnant, Royal Printer of Music* (Berkeley: University of California Press, 1970). On Lasso's chansons and their place in Protestant France, see Richard Freedman, *The Chansons of Orlando di Lasso and their Protestant Listeners: Music, Piety, and Print in Sixteenth-Century France* (Rochester: University of Rochester, 2001).

Modern editions include Sermisy's works in CMM 52, ed. Gaston Allaire and Isabelle Cazeaux; Janequin, *Chansons polyphoniques: oeuvres complètes*, ed. A. Tillman Merritt and François Lesure (Monaco: Oiseau-Lyre, 1965–71); and Le Jeune, *Airs*, ed. D. P. Walker (AIM, Miscellanea 1). For examples of the French chanson from the first half of the sixteenth century, see *Anthologie de la chanson parisienne au XVIᵉ siècle*, ed. Lesure (Monaco: Oiseau-Lyre, 1953), and *Chanson Albums of Marguerite of Austria*, ed. Martin Picker (Berkeley: University of California Press, 1965).

Germany

German Lieder of the first half of the sixteenth century are in EP, Years 1–4, 7–8, 33; late sixteenth-century Lieder are in EP, Years 23 (Regnart) and 25 (Eccard).

England

For English secular music before the madrigal, see the relevant chapters in David Wulstan, *Tudor Music* (London: J. M. Dent, 1985). An English manuscript containing secular music from the time of Henry VIII is edited by John Stevens in MB 18; also from this period is the *Early Tudor Songs and Carols*, MB 36, ed. Stevens.

On the English madrigal, see Joseph Kerman, *The Elizabethan Madrigal* (New York: American Musicological Society, 1962). On Weelkes, see David Brown, *Thomas Weelkes* (London: Faber & Faber, 1969). On the solo song, see Ian Spink, *English Song: Dowland to Purcell* (London: Batsford, 1974; rev. ed., 1986). Morley's *A Plaine and Easie Introduction to Practicall Musicke* (1597) has been published in a modern edition by R. Alec Harman (London: Dent, 1952; 2nd ed., New York: Norton, 1973), with excerpts in SR 75 (3:40).

A good modern sampling of English madrigals is *The Oxford Book of English Madrigals*, ed. Philip Ledger (London: Oxford University Press, 1979). More complete collections are those of madrigals in *The English Madrigal School*, 36 vols., ed. Edmund H. Fellowes (London: Stainer & Bell, 1913–24), and of lute songs in *The English School of Lutenist Song Writers*, 16 vols., ed. Fellowes (London: Winthrop Rogers, 1920–32); second series, 16 vols. (1925–27). See also Allison Hall, *E. H. Fellowes, An Index to the English Madrigalists and the English School of Lutenist Song Writers* (Boston: Music Library Association, 1984).

Chapter 12

Instruments

Many Renaissance instruments, their playing techniques, and repertoires are covered in individual chapters of *A Performer's Guide to Renaissance Music*, ed. Jeffrey T. Kite-Powell.

Sebastian Virdung's *Musica getutscht* has been published in facsimile (Kassel: Bärenreiter, 1970) and in translation by Beth Bullard (Cambridge and New York: Cambridge University Press, 1993). Michael Praetorius's *Syntagma musicum* has appeared in facsimile (Kassel: Bärenreiter, 1958–59), and volume 2, *De organographia* (On Instruments), is available in two translations, by David Z. Crookes (Oxford: Clarendon, 1986) and by Harold Blumenfeld (New York: Bärenreiter, 1962; repr. New York: Da Capo, 1980).

Instrumental Music in General

On musical culture and performance in fifteenth-century Germany, see Keith Polk, *German Instrumental Music of the Late Middle Ages: Players, Patrons, and Performance Practice* (Cambridge: Cambridge University Press, 1992). On music at the court of Maximilian, see Louise Cuyler, *The Emperor Maximilian and Music* (London: Oxford University Press, 1973). On the violin and violin bands in Tudor and Stuart England, see Peter Holman, *The Violin at the English Court, 1540–1690* (Oxford: Oxford University Press, 1993). For a listing of sixteenth-century prints, see Howard M. Brown, *Instrumental Music Printed before 1600* (Cambridge, MA: Harvard University Press, 1965).

Lute and Vihuela Music

Lute music published by Attaingnant appears in *Preludes, Chansons and Dances for Lute Published in Paris 1529–30*, ed. Daniel Heartz (Neuilly-sur-Seine: Société de Musique d'Autrefois, 1964). Examples of Italian lute music are found in *The Lute Music of Francesco Canova da Milano*, ed. Arthur J. Ness (Cambridge, MA.: Harvard University Press, 1970).

Luys de Narváez's *Los seys libros del Delphin* is transcribed in Monumentos de la Música Española 3 (Barcelona: Consejo Superior de Investigaciones Cientifica, 1945). Luis Milan's *Libro de musica de vihuela de mano intitulado El Maestro*, ed. Leo Schrade, is in PAM, Year 2, part 1 (repr. Hildesheim: Olms, 1967).

For performance practice, see *Performance on Lute, Guitar, and Vihuela: Historical Practice and Modern Interpretation*, ed. Victor Anand Coelho (Cambridge: Cambridge University Press, 1997).

Keyboard Music

Regional repertoires and performance practices are examined in *Keyboard Music before 1700*, 2nd ed., ed. Alexander Silbiger (New York: Routledge, 2004). A classic survey is Willi Apel, *The History of Keyboard Music to 1700*, trans. Hans Tischler (Bloomington: Indiana University Press, 1972).

Organ pieces based on cantus firmi are contained in *Deux Livres d'orgue parus chez Pierre Attaingnant*, ed. Yvonne Rokseth (Paris: E. Droz, 1925), and in *The Mulliner Book* (see below). Transcriptions of vocal pieces for organ are found in *Die italienische Orgelmusik am Anfang des Cinquecento*, ed. Knud Jeppesen (Copenhagen: E. Munksgaard, 1943; 2nd ed., 1960).

Organ works by Girolamo Cavazzoni appear in his *Orgelwerke*, ed. Oscar Mischiati (Mainz: B. Schott's Söhne, 1961). Those of Claudio Merulo appear in his complete works in progress, CMM 51; his toccatas, ed. Sandro Dalla Libera (Milan: Ricordi, 1959); his ricercares, ed. John Morehen (Madison, WI: A-R Editions, 2000), and ed. Andrea Marcon and Armin Gaus (Zimmern ob Rottweil: Edition Gaus, 1995); his canzonas, ed. Walter Cunningham and Charles McDermott (Madison, WI: A-R Editions, 1992), and ed. Pierre Pidoux (Kassel: Bärenreiter, 1954); and his organ masses, ed. Robert Judd in CEKM 47 (1991), and ed. Rudolf Walter, 4 vols. (Vienna: Doblinger, 1992–95).

English Instrumental Music

On English Renaissance keyboard music, see John Caldwell, *English Keyboard Music before the Nineteenth Century* (New York: Praeger, 1979), and Virginia Brookes, *British Keyboard Music to c. 1660: Sources and Thematic Index* (London: Oxford University Press, 1996).

Parthenia, the first printed collection of virginal music, has appeared in a facsimile edition by Otto Erich

Deutsch (London: Chiswick, 1942). The earliest manuscript collection of sixteenth-century English keyboard music was *The Mulliner Book* (ca. 1540–85), ed. Denis Stevens, MB 1. The most comprehensive is *The Fitzwilliam Virginal Book* (1609–19), copied by Francis Tregian, which contains nearly three hundred works, including transcriptions of madrigals, contrapuntal fantasias, dances, preludes, descriptive pieces, and many sets of variations; 2 vols., ed. J. A. Fuller Maitland and W. Barclay Squire (New York: Dover, 1963). Other manuscript collections in modern editions include *The Dublin Virginal Manuscript* (ca. 1570), ed. John M. Ward (Wellesley, 1954), and Byrd's *My Ladye Nevells Booke*, ed. Hilda Andrews (New York: Dover, 1969). Editions of works grouped by composer include Byrd, MB 27 and 28, and *Forty-five Pieces for Keyboard Instruments*, ed. Stephen D. Tuttle (Paris: Oiseau-Lyre, 1939); Bull, MB 14 and 19; Tomkins, MB 5; Gibbons, MB 20, and *Complete Keyboard Works*, 5 vols., ed. Margaret Glynn, (London: Stainer & Bell, 1922–25); and Giles Farnaby, MB 24.

Venice

On music in Venice, see H. C. Robbins Landon and John Julius Norwich, *Five Centuries of Music in Venice* (New York: Schirmer, 1991). On cori spezzati, see James H. Moore, "The *Vespro delle Cinque Laudate* and the Role of *Salmi spezzati* at St. Mark's," JAMS 34 (1981): 249–78; and, on the relationship between the architecture and the musical style, David Bryant, "The 'Cori Spezzati' of St. Mark's: Myth and Reality," EMH 1 (1981): 165–86. On musical culture in Venice, see Iain Fenlon, "Magnificence as Civic Image: Music and Ceremonial Space in Early Modern Venice," in *Music and Culture in Late Renaissance Italy* (Oxford: Oxford University Press, 2002), 1–23.

On Gabrieli, see Denis Arnold, *Giovanni Gabrieli and the Music of the Venetian High Renaissance* (London: Oxford University Press, 1979); idem., *Giovanni Gabrieli* (London: Oxford University Press, 1974); and Richard Charteris, *Giovanni Gabrieli: A Thematic Catalogue of His Music* (Stuyvesant, NY: Pendragon, 1996). On Gabrieli's instrumental music, see Eleanor Selfridge-Field, *Venetian Instrumental Music from Gabrieli to Vivaldi*, 3rd ed. (New York: Dover, 1994). Gabrieli's complete works are in CMM 12, ed. Arnold and Charteris. Compositions by Andrea and Giovanni Gabrieli are published in the first two volumes of *Istituzioni e monumenti dell'arte musicale italiana* (Milan: Ricordi, 1931–41).

PART III: THE SEVENTEENTH CENTURY

Excellent surveys of Baroque music include John Walter Hill, *Baroque Music: Music in Western Europe, 1580–1750* (New York: Norton, 2005); George J. Buelow,

A History of Baroque Music (Bloomington: Indiana University Press, 2004); David Schulenberg, *Music of the Baroque* (New York: Oxford University Press, 2001), and Claude V. Palisca, *Baroque Music*, 3rd ed. (Englewood Cliffs, NJ: Prentice Hall, 1991). Anthologies include Hill, *Anthology of Baroque Music* (New York: Norton, 2005), and Schulenberg, *Music of the Baroque: An Anthology of Scores* (New York: Oxford University Press, 2001). More focused surveys are Tim Carter, *Music in Late Renaissance and Early Baroque Italy* (London: Batsford, 1992), and Lorenzo Bianconi, *Music in the Seventeenth Century*, trans. David Bryant (Cambridge: Cambridge University Press, 1982).

The social and cultural contexts for music of the Baroque period are treated in *The Early Baroque Era: From the Late 16th Century to the 1660s*, ed. Curtis Price (Basingstoke: Macmillan, 1993), and *The Late Baroque Era: From the 1680s to 1740*, ed. Buelow (Basingstoke: Macmillan, 1993).

For a bibliography on the period, see John Baron, *Baroque Music: A Research and Information Guide* (New York: Garland, 1993), and Julie Anne Sadie, *Companion to Baroque Music* (London: Dent, 1990).

On performance practice, see *A Performer's Guide to Seventeenth-Century Music*, ed. Stewart Carter (New York: Schirmer, 1997).

CHAPTER 13

Baroque as Term

On the term *baroque*, see Claude V. Palisca, "Baroque," in NG2. The early uses of the word *baroque* for music can be found in "Lettre de M *** à Mlle *** sur l'origine de la musique," *Mercure de France*, May 1734, 868–70, and Noël Antoine Pluche, *Spectacle de la nature*, vol. 7 (Paris: Veuve Estienne, 1746), and for architecture in Charles de Brosses, *L'Italie li y a cent ans ou Lettres écrites d'Italie à quelques amis en 1739 et 1740*, ed. M. R. Colomb, vol. 2 (Paris: Alphonse Levavasseur, 1836), 117–18.

The Second Practice

On Monteverdi and the second practice, see Massimo Ossi, *Divining the Oracle: Monteverdi's seconda prattica* (Chicago: University of Chicago Press, 2003). Artusi's attack on Monteverdi is excerpted in SR 82 (3:2), and Giulio Cesare Monteverdi's reply is in SR 83 (4:3).

Basso Continuo

F. T. Arnold, *The Art of Accompaniment from a Thorough-Bass as Practiced in the XVIIth and XVIIIth Centuries*, 2 vols. (New York: Dover, 1965), is the basic work on basso continuo, with copious quotations and examples from the sources. A very useful introduction, both scholarly and practical, is Peter F. Williams, *Figured Bass Accompaniment*, 2 vols. (Edinburgh: Edinburgh University Press,

1970). For contemporary advice, see Agostino Agazzari's brief treatise *Of Playing upon a Bass with All Instruments and of Their Use in a Consort*, in SR 102 (4:22).

Temperaments

See under chapter 7, above.

Performance

An important source for performance practice for singers around 1600 is Giulio Caccini's preface to *Le nuove musiche* (1602), excerpted in SR 100 (4:20). An anonymous treatise, *The Choragus, or, Some Observations for Staging Dramatic Works Well* (1630), is excerpted in SR 103 (4:23). Pietro della Valle offers contemporary testimony on performance practices, including improvised embellishment, in his *Of the Music of Our Time*, excerpted in SR 84 (4:4).

On ornamentation, see Frederick Neumann, *Ornamentation in Baroque and Post-Baroque Music, with Special Emphasis on J. S. Bach*, 3rd ed. (Princeton: Princeton University Press, 1983).

From Modal to Tonal Music

See Harold S. Powers and Frans Wiering, "Mode, §III, 5: Transition to Major and Minor Keys," in NG2, and Gregory Barnett, "Tonal Organization in Seventeenth-Century Music Theory," in CHWMT (Cambridge: Cambridge University Press, 2002), 407–55.

CHAPTER 14

Forerunners of Opera

On the 1589 Florentine intermedi, see James M. Saslow, *The Medici Wedding of 1589: Florentine Festival as Theatrum Mundi* (New Haven: Yale University Press, 1996). The music appears in *Les fêtes du mariage de Ferdinand de Médicis et de Christine de Lorraine, Florence, 1589*, vol. 1: *Musique des intermèdes de "la Pellegrina,"* ed. D. P. Walker (Paris: Éditions du Centre national de la recherche scientifique, 1963).

Andrea Gabrieli's choruses for the 1585 production of Sophocles' *Oedipus Rex* in Vicenza are published in Leo Schrade, *La représentation d'Edipo Tiranno au Teatro Olimpico (Vicenza, 1585)* (Paris: CNRS, 1960).

The Florentine Camerata

For a description of the Florentine Camerata by Giovanni de' Bardi's son, see SR 81 (4:1). See *The Florentine Camerata: Documentary Studies and Translations*, ed. Claude V. Palisca (New Haven: Yale University Press, 1989); Girolamo Mei, *Letters on Ancient and Modern Music to Vincenzo Galilei and Giovanni Bardi*, 2nd ed., ed. Palisca (Stuttgart: Hänssler/AIM, 1977); and Vincenzo Galilei, *Dialogue on Ancient and Modern Music*, trans. with notes by Palisca (New Haven: Yale University Press, 2003).

Monody

Giulio Caccini's monodies appear in *Le nuove musiche*, ed. H. Wiley Hitchcock (Madison, WI: A-R Editions, 1970), preface excerpted in SR 100 (4:20), and in *Nuove musiche e nuova maniera di scriverle*, ed. Hitchcock (Madison, WI: A-R Editions, 1978). Those of Jacopo Peri are in *Le varie musiche and Other Songs*, ed. Tim Carter (Madison, WI: A-R Editions, 1986). Other monody publications are available in facsimile, such as those in *Italian Secular Song, 1606–1636*, 7 vols., ed. Gary Tomlinson (New York: Garland, 1986).

Opera

A rich source of information, interpretation, and bibliography in the entire field of opera is the *New Grove Dictionary of Opera*, 4 vols. (New York: Grove's Dictionaries of Music, 1992). Key articles from the general *New Grove* are assembled in Stanely Sadie, ed., *History of Opera* (New York: Norton, 1990). For a chronological survey consult Donald J. Grout, *A Short History of Opera*, 3rd ed., with Hermine Weigel Williams (New York: Columbia University Press, 1988). An up-to-date survey is Jean Grundy Fanelli, *Opera for Everyone: A Historic, Social, Artistic, Literary, and Musical Study* (Lanham, MD: Scarecrow, 2004). See also Richard Somerset-Ward, *The Story of Opera* (New York: Abrams, 1998); and John Bokina, *Opera and Politics: From Monteverdi to Henze* (New Haven: Yale University Press, 1997). On Italian opera, see *The History of Italian Opera*, 5 vols., ed. Lorenzo Bianconi and Giorgio Pestelli (Chicago: University of Chicago Press, 1998). For primary source readings, see *Opera: A History in Documents*, ed. Piero Weiss (New York: Oxford University Press, 2002). A useful bibliography is Guy A. Marco's *Opera: A Research and Information Guide*, 2nd ed. (New York: Garland, 2001). On early opera, see Frederick W. Sternfeld, *The Birth of Opera* (Oxford: Clarendon, 1993). Robert Donington, *The Rise of Opera* (London: Faber & Faber, 1981) covers opera from the beginning to Lully. On Peri, see Tim Carter, *Jacopo Peri, 1561–1633: His Life and Works*, 2 vols. (New York: Garland, 1989).

Peri's *Euridice* is available in a modern performing edition by Howard Mayer Brown (Madison, WI: A-R Editions, 1981) and in two facsimile editions (New York: Broude, 1973; Florence: Edizioni Musicali OTOS, 1970). Modern editions of Caccini's *Euridice* include a critical edition by Angelo Coan (Florence: Edizioni Musicali OTOS, 1980) and a facsimile (Bologna: Forni, 1976). Peri's preface is translated in SR 107 (4:27), Caccini's in SR 99 (4:19). Emilio de' Cavalieri's *Rappresentatione di Anima et di Corpo* is available in an edition by Eike Funck (Wolfenbüttel: Möseler, 1979) and in facsimile (Bologna: Forni, 1967 and 2000).

Claudio Monteverdi

On Monteverdi, see Paolo Fabbri, *Monteverdi*, trans. Carter (Cambridge: Cambridge University Press, 1994); Silke Leopold, *Monteverdi: Music in Transition* (Oxford: Clarendon, 1991); Denis Arnold, *Monteverdi*, 3rd ed., rev.

Carter (London: J. M. Dent, 1990); and Gary Tomlinson, *Monteverdi and the End of the Renaissance* (Berkeley: University of California Press, 1987). See also Ossi, *Divining the Oracle*, on the seconda prattica; Carter, *Monteverdi's Musical Theatre* (New Haven: Yale University Press, 2002), on the theatrical works; on *Orfeo*, *Monteverdi: Orfeo*, ed. John Whenham (Cambridge: Cambridge University Press, 1986); on the Vespers, Jeffrey G. Kurtzman, *The Monteverdi Vespers of 1610: Music, Context, Performance* (Oxford: Oxford University Press, 1999); and on the Venetian period, Denis Stevens, *Monteverdi in Venice* (Madison, NJ: Fairleigh Dickinson University Press, 2001). The premiere of *Orfeo* is described in Thomas Forrest Kelly, *First Nights: Five Musical Premieres* (New Haven: Yale University Press, 2000), 2–59. For an extensive bibliography and detailed studies, see *The New Monteverdi Companion*, ed. Arnold and Nigel Fortune (London: Faber & Faber, 1985). His correspondence is compiled in *The Letters of Claudio Monteverdi*, rev. ed., trans. with intro. by Stevens (Oxford: Clarendon; New York: Oxford University Press, 1995). For Monteverdi's description of the *stile concitato*, see SR 109 (4:29).

Monteverdi's complete works appear in *Tutte le opere*, 16 vols., ed. Gian Francesco Malipiero (Asolo: G. F. Malipiero, 1926–42; rev. and repr. Vienna: Universal Edition, 1967–68). More recent editions of the operas are those of Stevens, *L'Orfeo* (London: Novello, 1967; rev. ed. Gregg International, 1972, with intro. by Stevens) and Edward H. Tarr (Paris: Éditions Costallat, 1974); of Alan Curtis, *Il ritorno d'Ulisse in patria* (London: Novello, 2002); and of Curtis, *L'incoronazione di Poppea* (London: Novello, 1989). A new critical edition is in progress under Raffaello Monterosso (Cremona: Fondazione Claudio Monteverdi, 1970–).

The Spread of Italian Opera

Francesca Caccini's *La liberazione di Ruggiero* is available in an edition by Doris Silbert (Northampton, MA: Smith College, 1945) and in facsimile (Florence: Studio per Edizioni Scelte, 1998).

On early opera in Rome, see Margaret Murata, *Operas for the Papal Court, 1631–1668* (Ann Arbor: UMI Research Press, 1981). Stefano Landi's *Sant' Alessio* is available in facsimile (Bologna: Forni, 1970).

For a comprehensive history of Venetian opera, see Ellen Rosand, *Opera in Seventeenth-Century Venice: The Creation of a Genre* (Berkeley: University of California Press, 1991). On female roles in Venetian operas, see Wendy Heller, *Emblems of Eloquence: Opera and Women's Voices in Seventeenth-Century Venice* (Berkeley: University of California Press, 2003). On the singer Anna Renzi, see Beth L. Glixon, "Private Lives of Public Women: Prima donnas in Mid-Seventeenth-Century Venice," *Music and Letters* 76 (November 1995): 509–31. A sample contract for Renzi to perform for a season at a Venetian opera house is in SR 89 (4:9).

Francesco Cavalli's *Giasone* (Prologue and Act I only) is in EP, vol. 12, and modernized performing versions by Raymond Leppard (London: Faber Music; New York: Schirmer) are available for *La Calisto* (1975), *Egisto* (1977), and *Ormindo* (1969). Antonio Cesti's *Orontea*, ed. William C. Holmes, is in the Wellesley Edition, no. 11 (Wellesley College, 1973); *Il pomo d'oro*, ed. Guido Adler, in DTO, 3/2 and 4/2 (1896; repr. 1959), and a new edition of Acts 3 and 5 by Carl B. Schmidt (Madison, WI: A-R Editions, 1982). Facsimiles of Italian operas from the mid-seventeenth century, including Cavalli and Cesti, are found in *Italian Opera, 1640–1770*, gen. ed. Howard Mayer Brown (New York: Garland, 1977–84).

CHAPTER 15

Vocal Chamber Music

On the cantata in Rome, see John Walter Hill, *Roman Monody, Cantata, and Opera from the Circles Around Cardinal Montalto*, 2 vols. (Oxford: Oxford University Press, 1997). On Barbara Strozzi, see Glixon, "New Light on the Life and Career of Barbara Strozzi," MQ 81 (Summer 1997): 311–35; idem., "More on the Life and Death of Barbara Strozzi, MQ 83 (Spring 1999): 134–41; and Ellen Rosand, "The Voice of Barbara Strozzi," in *Women Making Music: The Western Art Tradition, 1150–1950*, ed. Jane Bowers and Judith Tick (Urbana: University of Illinois Press, 1986), 168–90. Facsimiles of cantatas by Carissimi, Cesti, Strozzi, and others appear in *The Italian Cantata in the Seventeenth Century*, gen. ed. Carolyn Gianturco (New York: Garland, 1986). On the chaconne, see the book by Richard Hudson below, under "Instrumental Music." For a collection of airs de cour, see *Air de cour pour voix et luth (1603–1643)*, ed. André Verchaly (Paris: Heugel, 1961).

Catholic Church Music

On Italian church music, see Jerome Roche, *North Italian Church Music in the Age of Monteverdi* (Oxford: Clarendon, 1984). Gabrieli's motets are in his *Opera omnia*, ed. Arnold and Richard Charteris, CMM 12. Orazio Benevoli's polychoral works are in *Horatii Benevoli Opera Omnia* (Rome and Trent: Societas Universalis Sanctae Ceciliae, 1966–73). A modern edition of Lodovico Viadana's *Cento concerti ecclesiastici* is in his *Opere*, ser. 1, vol. 1 (Kassel: Bärenreiter, 1964). A translation of Viadana's preface appears in SR 101 (4:21).

On music at the convent of Santa Cristina della Fondazza in Bologna, see Craig A. Monson, *Disembodied Voices: Music and Culture in an Early Modern Italian Convent* (Berkeley: University of California Press, 1995).

Oratorio

An excellent comprehensive study is Howard E. Smither, *A History of the Oratorio*, 4 vols. (Chapel Hill: University of

North Carolina Press, 1977–2000). Giacomo Carissimi's *Jephte* is available in editions by Adelchi Amisano (Milan: G. Ricordi, 1977) and by Gottfried Wolters (Wolfenbüttel: Möseler, 1969); most of his other oratorios are available in editions by Lino Bianchi (Rome: Istituto Italiano per la Storia della Musica, 1951–).

Lutheran Church Music

Johann Hermann Schein's *Opella nova* is in vols. 4–5 of the new complete edition, *Neue Ausgabe sämtlicher Werke*, ed. Adam Adrio and Siegmund Helms (Kassel: Bärenreiter, 1963–).

Heinrich Schütz

Schütz describes his career in SR 86 (4:6), one of several letters he wrote asking to retire. Allen Skei's *Heinrich Schütz: A Guide to Research* (New York: Garland, 1981) is an indispensable reference tool.

Schütz's complete works are in his *Sämtlicher Werke*, 18 vols., ed. Philipp Spitta and Arnold Schering (Leipzig: Breitkopf & Härtel, 1885–1927), using original clefs, and *Neue Ausgabe sämtlicher Werke* (Kassel: Bärenreiter, 1955–), which transposes many works. Consult also *Heinrich Schütz: A Bibliography of the Collected Works and Performing Editions*, comp. D. Douglas Miller and Anne L. Highsmith (New York: Greenwood, 1986).

On musical figures, see Dietrich Bartel, *Musica poetica: Musical-Rhetorical Figures in German Baroque Music* (Lincoln: University of Nebraska Press, 1997). Christoph Bernhard's writings are translated by Walter Hilse in "The Treatises of Christoph Bernhard," *The Music Forum* 3 (1973): 31–179.

Jewish Music

On Rossi, see Don Harrán, *Salamone Rossi: Jewish Musician in Late Renaissance Mantua* (Oxford: Oxford University Press, 1999). Rossi's complete works, ed. Harrán, are in CMM 100 (1995). See also Seroussi, Schleifer et al., "Jewish Music, §III: Liturgical and paraliturgical," in NG2; Avenary, *The Ashkenazi Tradition of Biblical Chant between 1500 and 1900* ; and Idelsohn, *Jewish Music in Its Historical Development*.

Instrumental Music

Surveys of particular repertoires include Andrew Dell'Antonio, *Syntax, Form and Genre in Sonatas and Canzonas 1621–1635* (Lucca: Libreria musicale italiana, 1997); *Keyboard Music Before 1700*, ed. Alexander Silbiger; Willi Apel, *The History of Keyboard Music to 1700*; William S. Newman, *The Sonata in the Baroque Era*, 4th ed. (New York: Norton, 1983); David D. Boyden, *The History of Violin Playing from Its Origins to 1761* (London: Oxford University Press, 1965). Modern editions of printed and manuscript keyboard collections can be found in the series *17th Century Keyboard Music* (New York: Garland, 1987–89).

On Girolamo Frescobaldi, see Frederick Hammond, *Girolamo Frescobaldi* (Cambridge, MA: Harvard University Press, 1983), and *Frescobaldi Studies*, ed. Silbiger (Durham, NC: Duke University Press, 1987). Frescobaldi's music is available in his *Opere complete* (Milan: Edizioni Suvini Zerboni, 1975–).

Johann Jacob Froberger's harpsichord works appear in *Oeuvres complètes pour clavecin*, ed. Howard Schott, Le pupitre 57–58 (Paris: Heugel, 1979–2000). His harpsichord and organ works are appearing in a new critical edition, ed. Siegbert Rampe (Kassel: Bärenreiter, 1993–).

On Jan Pieterszoon Sweelinck, see Alan Curtis, *Sweelinck's Keyboard Music: A Study of English Elements in Seventeeth-Century Dutch Composition*, 3rd ed., with bio. note (Leiden: E. J. Brill, 1987). His keyboard works are in his *Opera omnia*, vol. 1: *The Instrumental Works*, 2nd rev. ed., ed. Gustav Leonhardt et al. (Amsterdam: Vereeniging voor Nederlandse Muziekgeschiedenis, 1974). Samuel Scheidt's *Tabulatura nova* is available in an edition by Harald Vogel (Wiesbaden: Breitkopf & Härtel, 1994–).

Biagio Marini's sonatas for strings appear in Marini, *String Sonatas from Opus 1 and Opus 8*, ed. Thomas D. Dunn (Madison, WI: A-R Editions, 1981). His complete Op. 8 has been edited by Maura Zoni (Milan: Edizioni Suvini Zerboni, 2004).

On the history of the chaconne and passacaglia, in both instrumental and vocal music, see Richard Hudson, *The Folia, the Saraband, the Passacaglia, and the Chaconne*, 4 vols., MSD 35 (Neuhausen-Stuttgart: Hänssler, 1982), and Silbiger, "Passacaglia and Ciaccona: Genre Pairing and Ambiguity from Frescobaldi to Couperin," *Journal of Seventeenth-Century Music* 2.1 (1996), at www.sscm-jscm.org/ v2no1.html.

Schein's *Banchetto musicale* is in vol. 9 of the new complete edition (see above).

CHAPTER 16

French Opera and Ballet

On Lully and French opera, see Caroline Wood, *Music and Drama in the tragédie en musique, 1673–1715: Jean Baptiste Lully and His Successors* (New York: Garland, 1996), and *French Baroque Opera: A Reader*, ed. Wood and Graham Sadler (Aldershot: Ashgate, 2000). Two classic treatments of French music of this period in its political and social context are Robert M. Isherwood, *Music in the Service of the King: France in the Seventeenth Century* (Ithaca, NY: Cornell University Press, 1973), and James R. Anthony, *French Baroque Music from Beaujoyeulx to Rameau*, rev. ed. (Portland, OR: Amadeus, 1997). See also *French Musical Thoughts, 1600–1800*, ed. Georgia Cowart (Ann Arbor: UMI Research Press, 1989).

Most of Lully's works are collected in *Oeuvres complètes*, 10 vols., ed. Henry Prunières (Paris: Éditions de La Revue musicale, 1930–39; repr. New York: Broude, 1966–74). For a thematic catalogue, see Herbert Schneider, *Chronologisches-thematisches Katalog sämtlicher Werke von Jean-Baptiste Lully* (Tutzing: Hans Schneider, 1981). Vocal scores of operas by Lully and other composers, mostly French, of the seventeenth and eighteenth centuries are in the series *Les Chefs d'oeuvres classiques de l'opéra français*, 40 vols. (Paris: T. Michaelis, ca. 1880; repr. New York: Broude, 1972).

On rhythm in French Baroque music, see Stephen E. Hefling, *Rhythmic Alteration in Seventeenth- and Eighteenth-Century Music: Notes inégales and Overdotting* (New York: Schirmer, 1993). For a contemporary French view of ballet, see SR 110 (4:30).

Other French Vocal Music

On Charpentier, see H. Wiley Hitchcock, *Marc-Antoine Charpentier* (Oxford: Oxford University Press, 1990), and Hitchcock's catalogue, *Les oeuvres de Marc-Antoine Charpentier* (Paris: Picard, 1982). Charpentier's cantatas and oratorios appear in his *Oeuvres*, 15 vols. (incomplete), ed. Guy Lambert (Paris, 1948–53).

French Lute and Keyboard Music

See David Ledbetter, *Harpsichord and Lute Music in 17th-Century France* (Bloomington: Indiana University Press, 1987). On Elisabeth-Claude Jacquet de la Guerre, see Edith Borroff, *An Introduction to Elisabeth-Claude Jacquet de la Guerre*, Musicological Studies 12 (Brooklyn: Institute of Mediaeval Music, 1966). *Her Pièces de clavecin* are edited by Carol Henry Bates (Paris: Heugel, 1986). Selected clavecin pieces and the cantata *Semelé* are in *Historical Anthology of Music by Women*, ed. James R. Briscoe (Bloomington: Indiana University Press, 1987), 57–76.

English Stage Music

See Eric W. White, *A History of English Opera* (London: Faber & Faber, 1983).

Excerpts from incidental music for English plays and masques (1616–1641) are in *La musique de scène de la troupe de Shakespeare, The King's Men, sous le règne de Jacques I*, 2nd rev. ed., ed. John P. Cutts (Paris: Éditions du Centre national de la recherche scientifique, 1971). Three masques with music by William Lawes are in *Trois masques à la cour de Charles 1er d'Angleterre*, ed. Murray Lefkowitz (Paris: CNRS, 1970). Anthony Lewis has edited John Blow's *Venus and Adonis* (Monaco: Oiseau-Lyre, 1949).

Henry Purcell

The best recent biography is Peter Holman, *Henry Purcell* (Oxford: Oxford University Press, 1994). His works are catalogued in Franklin B. Zimmerman, *Henry Purcell, An Analytical Catalogue of His Music* (New York: St. Martin's,

1963). On *Dido and Aeneas*, see Ellen T. Harris, *Henry Purcell's "Dido and Aeneas"* (Oxford: Clarendon, 1987), and *Purcell, Dido and Aeneas*, Norton Critical Scores, ed. Curtis Price (New York: Norton, 1986). A complete edition, now undergoing revision, is *The Works of Henry Purcell*, 32 vols. (London: Novello, 1878–1965; rev. 1957–).

Other English Music

See *The Blackwell History of Music in Britain*, vol. 3: *The Seventeenth Century*, ed. Ian Spink (Oxford: Blackwell, 1992).

On song, see Spink, *English Song: Dowland to Purcell*, rev. ed. (New York: Taplinger, 1986). A good selection of catches may be found in *The Catch Club; or Merry Companions*, 1733, facs., ed. Joel Newman (New York: Da Capo, 1965); or 1762, facs., consisting of pieces by Purcell, Blow, et al. (Farnborough, England: Gregg International, 1969).

On Anglican church music, see Peter Le Huray, *Music and the Reformation in England, 1549–1660*, and Christopher Dearnley, *English Church Music, 1650–1750* (London: Barrie & Jenkins, 1970). John Blow's Coronation Anthems are in MB 7. Anthologies of English church music are *The Treasury of English Church Music II, 1545–1650*, ed. Le Huray and Christopher Dearnley, and *The Treasury of English Church Music III, 1650–1760* (London: Blandford, 1965).

On English chamber music, see Ernst H. Meyer, *Early English Chamber Music from the Middle Ages to Purcell*, 2nd ed., with Diana Poulton (London: Lawrence & Wishart, 1982). John Jenkins's consort music is in MB 26 and 39, and other volumes contain consort and viol music by other English composers of this period. See the excerpt from Christopher Simpson's *The Division-Viol* in SR 104 (4:24) for instructions to viol players on improvising above a ground bass.

The tunes from John Playford's *The English Dancing Master* are edited by Jeremy Barlow in *The Complete Country Dance Tunes from Playford's Dancing Master, 1651–ca. 1728* (London: Faber, 1985), and facsimiles of the first edition have been edited by Margaret Dean-Smith (London: Schott, 1957).

The musical scene in England is well observed in the writings of writer and amateur musician Roger North, collected in *Roger North on Music*, ed. John Wilson (London: Novello, 1959), with excerpts in SR 94, 95, and 98 (4:14, 15, and 18).

Spain and the New World

See Louise K. Stein, *Songs of Mortals, Dialogues of the Gods: Music and Theatre in Seventeenth-Century Spain* (Oxford: Oxford University Press, 1993), and Maurice Esses, *Dance and Instrumental Diferencias in Spain During the 17th and Early 18th Centuries* (Stuyvesant, NY: Pendragon, 1992). Robert Stevenson, *Christmas Music from Baroque México* (Berkeley: University of California Press, 1974), and Stevenson, *Music in Mexico: A Historical Survey* (New York: Crowell, 1971).

Editions include Tomás de Torrejón y Velasco, *La púrpura de la rosa*, series A, vol. 25: Musica Hispana, ed. Stein (Madrid: Instituto Complutense de Ciencias Musicales, 1999), and Juan de Araujo, *Antología*, Colección de Música Colonial Americana 7, ed. Carmen Garcia Muñoz (Buenos Aires: Institutio de Investigación Musicologica Carlos Vega, 1991).

CHAPTER 17

Italian Opera

For Italian opera in the second half of the seventeenth century, consult *The History of Italian Opera*, ed. Bianconi and Pestelli; *A History of Opera*, ed. Stanley Sadie; Donald J. Grout, *A Short History of Opera*; Robert Donington, *The Rise of Opera*; and Ellen Rosand, *Opera in Seventeenth-Century Venice*, all listed above under chapter 14. See also the contemporary report on opera in Venice in SR 91 (4:11).

On Alessandro Scarlatti and his music, see Grout, *Alessandro Scarlatti: An Introduction to His Operas* (Berkeley: University of California Press, 1979), and Carole Franklin Vidali, *Alessandro and Domenico Scarlatti: A Guide to Research* (New York: Garland, 1993).

Nine of Alessandro Scarlatti's operas have been edited in *The Operas of Alessandro Scarlatti*, gen. ed. Donald J. Grout (Cambridge, MA: Harvard University Press, 1974–85). Facsimiles of several late-seventeenth-century operas are in *Italian Opera, 1640–1770*, gen. ed. Howard M. Brown (New York: Garland, 1977–84).

Italian Cantata and Serenata

Editions of several Scarlatti cantatas appear in Alessandro Scarlatti, *Three Cantatas for Voice and Cello with Keyboard*, ed. Peter Foster, Nona Pyron, and Timothy Roberts (Fullerton, CA: Grancino, 1982), and in CDMI, vol. 30. Facsimiles of cantata manuscripts and prints by Scarlatti and others are in *The Italian Cantata in the Seventeenth Century*, gen. ed. Carolyn Gianturco (New York: Garland, 1986). On Stradella, see Carolyn Gianturco, *Alessandro Stradella, 1639–1682: His Life and Music* (Oxford: Clarendon, 1994), and Carolyn Gianturco and Eleanor McCrickard, *Alessandro Stradella (1639–1682): A Thematic Catalogue of His Compositions* (Stuyvesant, NY: Pendragon, 1991).

Italian Sacred Music

Facsimiles of solo motets are in *Solo Motets from the Seventeenth Century*, ed. Anne Schnoebelen (New York: Garland, 1987); motets by Maurizio Cazzati are in volumes 6 and 7. Editions of selected sacred works are in *Seventeenth-Century Italian Sacred Music*, gen. ed. Schnoebelen (New York: Garland, 1995–); vols. 1–10 contain music for the Mass, vols. 11–20 music for Vespers and Compline. Facsimiles of Italian oratorios are found in *The Italian Oratorio: 1650–1800*, ed. Joyce Johnson and Howard Smither (New York: Garland, 1986).

Italian Instrumental Music

Selfridge-Field, *Venetian Instrumental Music from Gabrieli to Vivaldi*, noted above under chapter 12, considers the history of instrumental genres in addition to music performance in Venice. Also relevant are David D. Boyden, *The History of Violin Playing from its Origins to 1761*, noted under chapter 14; Newman, *The Sonata in the Baroque Era*, which is the best comprehensive study of the genre; and Peter Allsop, *The Italian "Trio" Sonata from Its Origins until Corelli* (Oxford: Clarendon, 1992).

Instrumental ensemble works by various Italian composers can be found in *Anthology of Instrumental Music from the End of the Sixteenth to the End of the Seventeenth Century*, ed. J. W. von Wasielewski (New York: Da Capo, 1974). Examples of the trio sonata before Corelli include Giovanni Legrenzi's *Sonatas, Op. 2, Op. 10*, ed. Stephen Bonta (Cambridge, MA: Harvard University Press, 1984, 1992). See also the anthologies *The Italian Trio Sonata* and *The Trio Sonata Outside Italy*, both ed. Erich Schenk (Cologne: Arno Volk, 1955, 1970), and *The Solo Sonata*, ed. Franz Giegling (Cologne: A. Volk, 1960).

Arcangelo Corelli

There are two editions of Corelli's complete works: *Historisch-kritische Gesamtausgabe der musikalischen Werke*, gen. ed. Hans Oesch (Cologne: A. Volk, 1976–), and *Oeuvres*, ed. Joseph Joachim and Friedrich Chrysander (London: Augener, 1888–91; repr. 1952; solo and trio sonatas repr. New York: Dover, 1992).

The Concerto

On the birth and development of the orchestra, see John Spitzer and Neal Zaslaw, *The Birth of the Orchestra: History of an Institution, 1650–1815* (Oxford: Oxford University Press, 2004), and idem., "Orchestra," in NG2. For a detailed study of the concerto, see Arthur Hutchings, *The Baroque Concerto*, rev. ed. (New York: Scribner, 1979).

There are several editions of concertos by Giuseppe Torelli, including Op. 6, ed. John G. Seuss (Middleton, WI: A-R Editions, 2002); Op. 8, 12 nos., ed. Maxwell Sobel (Indianapolis: Concerto, 1999); individual concertos from Opp. 5 and 8, ed. Walter Kolneder (Vienna: Doblinger, 1979–87); and two trumpet concertos, ed. Mathias Siedel (Hamburg: H. Sikorski, 1971). Tomaso Albinoni's concertos from Op. 2 are edited by Fabrizio Ammetto and Gioia Filocamo (Bologna: UT Orpheus, 2003); Op. 10 by Maxwell Sobel (Indianapolis: Concerto, 1999); and other concertos by Walter Kolneder (Adliswil-Zurich: Kunzelmann, 1980–).

German Opera and Song

Several Reinhard Keiser operas exist in modern editions, and others are available in facsimile in *Handel Sources: Material for the Study of Handel's Borrowing*, ed. John H. Roberts (New York: Garland, 1986–). Adam Krieger's *Neue Arien* are in DdT, vol. 19.

Dieterich Buxtehude

An exemplary study of Buxtehude and his environment is Kerala J. Snyder, *Dieterich Buxtehude: Organist in Lübeck* (New York: Schirmer, 1987; repr. 1993).

The eight-volume collected edition *Dietrich Buxtehudes Werke* (Hamburg: Ugrino, 1925–37; repr. New York: Broude, 1977–) contains only vocal works. A new edition is underway, Dietrich Buxtehude, *The Collected Works* (New York: Broude, 1987–). There are several editions of the organ music, including *Sämtliche Orgelwerke*, ed. Klaus Beckmann (Wiesbaden: Breitkopf & Härtel, 1971–72; rev. ed., 1995–97), and *Sämtliche Orgelwerke*, ed. Josef Hedar (Copenhagen: Hansen, 1952).

For a thematic catalogue, see Georg Karstädt, *Thematisch-systematisches Verzeichnis der musikalischen Werke von Dietrich Buxtehude: Buxtehude-Werke-Verzeichnis* (Wiesbaden: Breitkopf & Härtel, 1974; rev. ed., 1985).

German Organ Music

A useful catalogue listing organ preludes and composers has been compiled by J. E. Edson, *Organ Preludes: An Index to Compositions on Hymn Tunes, Chorales, Plainsong Melodies, Gregorian Tunes, and Carols*, 2 vols. (Metuchen, NJ: Scarecrow, 1970).

Editions include Georg Böhm, *Klavier- und Orgelwerke*, ed. Gesa Wolgast (Wiesbaden: Breitkopf & Härtel, 1952), and Johann Pachelbel, *Orgelwerke*, ed. Traugott Fedtke (Frankfurt: Litolff; New York: C. F. Peters, 1972–73).

Other German Instrumental Music

Harpsichord suites by Johann Pachelbel are in DTB, Vol. 2/i. Georg Muffat's *Florilegium* appears in DTO, vols. 2 and 4. Excerpts from the prefaces, with many guides to performance practice, are in SR 106 (4:26). Concertos and other instrumental ensemble pieces by Muffat are in DTO, vols. 1, 23, and 89.

Johann Jakob Walther's *Scherzi* are published in *Das Erbe deutscher Musik*, series 1, vol. 17. Heinrich Biber's Mystery Sonatas are available in editions by Ernst Kubitschek with Marianne Rônez (Vienna: Doblinger, 2000), and by William P. Tortolano (Chicago: GIA, 1993). A facsimile of the manuscript appears in Biber, *Mysterien-Sonaten ("Rosenkranz-Sonaten"): Bayerische Staatsbibliothek München Mus. Ms. 4123*, ed. Ernst Kubitschek (Bad Reichenhall: Comes, 1990).

Johann Kuhnau, *The Collected Works for Keyboard*, ed. C. David Harris (New York: Broude, 2003).

PART IV: THE EIGHTEENTH CENTURY

For overviews of Baroque music, see under part III above. For surveys of the Classic period, see under chapter 20 below.

For social and cultural contexts, see Richard D. Leppert, *Music and Image: Domesticity, Ideology, and Socio-Cultural Formation in Eighteenth-Century England* (Cambridge: Cambridge University Press, 1988); the articles in *The Late Baroque Era: From the 1680s to 1740*, ed. George J. Buelow (Basingstoke: Macmillan, 1993); and the source readings in *Music and Culture in Eighteenth-Century Europe: A Source Book*, ed. Enrico Fubini and Bonnie J. Blackburn, trans. Wolfgang Fries et al. (Chicago: University of Chicago Press, 1994). On the business aspects of composition, see Frederic M. Scherer, *Quarter Notes and Bank Notes: The Economics of Music Composition in the Eighteenth and Nineteenth Centuries* (Princeton: Princeton University Press, 2004).

Joel Lester, *Compositional Theory in the Eighteenth Century* (Cambridge, MA: Harvard University Press, 1992), offers an overview of eighteenth-century theoretical treatises. The association of particular keys with specific meanings is studied in Rita Steblin, *A History of Key Characteristics in the Eighteenth and Early Nineteenth Centuries*, 2nd ed. (Rochester, NY: University of Rochester Press, 2002). For performance practice, see Peter Le Huray, *Authenticity in Performance: Eighteenth-Century Case Studies* (Cambridge: Cambridge University Press, 1990).

CHAPTER 18

Music in Italy

On the history of the castrati, see "Castrato," in NG2. On singers, see the comments by Pierfrancesco Tosi in SR 85 (4:5). On musical life in Naples in the eighteenth century, see Carolyn Gianturco, "Naples: A City of Entertainment," in *The Late Baroque Era: From the 1680s to 1740*, ed. George J. Buelow. For a contemporary view of the Venetian *ospedali*, see SR 87 (4:7).

Antonio Vivaldi

The best recent study of Vivaldi is Michael Talbot, *Vivaldi* (New York: Oxford University Press, 2000). Another good biography is Karl Heller, *Antonio Vivaldi: The Red Priest of Venice*, trans. David Marinelli (Portland, OR: Amadeus, 1997). Patrick Barbier, *Vivaldi's Venice* (London: Souvenir, 2003), and H. C. Robbins Landon, *Vivaldi: Voice of the Baroque* (London: Thames & Hudson, 1993), place Vivaldi in its Venetian context. Talbot, *Venetian Music in the Age of Vivaldi* (Aldershot: Ashgate, 1999), and Eleanor Selfridge-Field, *Venetian Instrumental Music from Gabrieli to Vivaldi*, link Vivaldi to the Venetian musical tradition. For a bibliography, see Talbot, *Antonio Vivaldi: A Guide to Research* (New York: Garland, 1988).

Paul Everett, *Vivaldi: The Four Seasons and Other Concertos, Op. 8* (Cambridge: Cambridge University Press, 1996), offers a guide to Vivaldi's most famous concertos. Simon McVeigh and Jehoash Hirshberg examine the origins, development, and later influence of Vivaldi's concerto procedures in *The Italian Solo Concerto, 1700–1760: Rhetorical Strategies and Style History* (Rochester, NY: Boydell, 2005).

A helpful collection of primary sources is *Antonio Vivaldi: Documents of His Life and Works*, ed. Walter Kolneder, trans. Kurt Michaelis (New York: Heinrichshofen/C. F. Peters, 1982). For an eighteenth-century view of the Vivaldi concerto, see the excerpt from Johann Joachim Quantz's *Essay on a Method for Playing the Transverse Flute* in SR 125 (5:4).

Vivaldi's instrumental works appear in *Le opere di Antonio Vivaldi*, ed. Gian Francesco Malipiero et al. (Milan: Ricordi, 1947–72) and are catalogued in Antonio Fanna, *Opere strumentale di Antonio Vivaldi (1678–1741)* (Milan: Ricordi, 1986). A new scholarly edition, which includes vocal works, is in preparation by the Istituto Italiano Antonio Vivaldi, ed. Paul Everett and Talbot (Milan: Ricordi, 1982–). There are several thematic catalogues; the most definitive is Peter Ryom, *Verzeichnis der Werke Antonio Vivaldis (RV)*, 2nd ed. (Leipzig: Deutscher Verlag für Musik VEB, 1979).

Music in France

On French Baroque music, see James R. Anthony, *French Baroque Music from Beaujoyeulx to Rameau*, and *French Baroque Opera: A Reader*, ed. Caroline Wood and Graham Sadler. A useful resource is Bruce Gustafson and David Fuller, *A Catalogue of French Harpsichord Music, 1699–1780* (Oxford: Clarendon, 1990). For comparisons of French and Italian music from around 1700, see SR 111–112 (4:31–32).

A complete edition of four books of sonatas for violin and basso continuo by Jean-Marie Leclair, ed. Robert E. Preston, are in *Recent Researches in the Music of the Baroque Era*, 4–5 and 10–11 (New Haven, CT and Madison, WI: A-R Editions, 1969–95).

François Couperin

For a broader view of Couperin's life and work, see David Tunley, *François Couperin and the "Perfection of Music"* (Aldershot: Ashgate, 2004); Wilfrid Mellers, *François Couperin and the French Classical Tradition* (London: Faber, 1987), and Tunley, *Couperin* (London: BBC, 1982). Couperin's treatise on playing the harpsichord, *L'Art de toucher le clavecin* (1716), is in English translation by Margery Halford (New York: Alfred, 1974).

François Couperin's works are in his *Oeuvres complètes*, 12 vols., ed. Maurice Cauchie (Paris: Oiseau-Lyre, 1932–33), and a new critical edition by Kenneth Gilbert and André Schaeffner (Monaco: Oiseau-Lyre, 1980–). For Couperin's *Pièces de clavecin*, consult the new edition by Davitt Moroney (Monaco: Oiseau-Lyre, 2004). For a thematic catalog, see Maurice Cauchie, *Thematic Index of the Works of François Couperin* (Monaco: Lyrebird, 1949; repr. New York: AMS, 1976).

Jean-Philippe Rameau

On Rameau and his operas, see Charles William Dill, *Monstrous Opera: Rameau and the Tragic Tradition* (Princeton: Princeton University Press, 1998). For Rameau as theorist, see Thomas Christensen, *Rameau and Musical Thought in the Enlightenment* (Cambridge: Cambridge University Press, 1993); Joel Lester, "Rameau and Eighteenth-Century Harmonic Theory," in CHWMT; and Jairo Moreno, "The Complicity of the Imagination: Representation, Subject, and System in Rameau," in *Musical Representations, Subjects, and Objects: The Construction of Musical Thought in Zarlino, Descartes, Rameau, and Weber* (Bloomington: Indiana University Press, 2004). A useful bibliography is Donald Foster, *Jean-Philippe Rameau: A Guide to Research* (New York: Garland, 1989).

Rameau's writings on theory can be found in *The Complete Theoretical Writings of Jean-Philippe Rameau*, 6 vols., ed. Erwin Jacobi (AIM, Series Misc. 3), and in *Treatise on Harmony*, trans. with intro. and notes by Philip Gossett (New York: Dover, 1971). An excerpt from *Treatise on Harmony* is also found in SR 115 (4:35).

Rameau's musical works can be found in *Oeuvres complètes*, 18 vols. in 20; incomplete, ed. Camille Saint-Saëns (Paris: A. Durand et fils, 1895–1924; repr. New York, 1968). A new edition, *Opera omnia*, ed. Sylvie Boisseau, is in progress (Paris: G. Billaudot, 1996–).

CHAPTER 19

Georg Philipp Telemann

Telemann's description of his stylistic development is from a 1729 letter to Johann Walther, translated in Steven Zohn, "Telemann, Georg Philipp, §5 Influence and reputation," in NG2. See Richard Petzoldt, *Georg Philipp Telemann*, trans. Horace Fitzpatrick (New York: Oxford University Press, 1974), for a biography.

Telemann's works appear in *Georg Philipp Telemann: Musikalische Werke*, ed. Gesellschaft für Musikforschung (Kassel: Bärenreiter, 1950–). Two partial but complementary thematic catalogs exist: for instrumental works, see Martin Ruhnke, *Georg Philipp Telemann, Thematisch-systematisches Verzeichnis seiner Werke: Instrumentalwerke* (Kassel: Bärenreiter, 1984); for vocal works, see Werner Menke, *Thematisches Verzeichnis der Vokalwerke von Georg Philipp Telemann*, 2nd ed. (Frankfurt: Klostermann, 1988).

Johann Sebastian Bach

The most authoritative Bach biography in English is Christoph Wolff, *Johann Sebastian Bach: The Learned Musician* (New York: Norton, 2000). Shorter studies include Malcolm Boyd, *Bach*, 3rd ed. (New York: Oxford University Press, 2000), and Peter F. Williams, *The Life of Bach* (Cambridge: Cambridge University Press, 2004).

An invaluable documentary anthology is Hans David and Arthur Mendel, *The New Bach Reader*, rev. and enlarged by Wolff (New York: Norton, 1998); it contains in English translation important sources from which our knowledge of Bach's life and reputation is drawn, as well as essays on Bach's music and public reception. A useful and comprehensive reference book, containing over 900 entries by forty contributors, is *J. S. Bach*, ed. Boyd (Oxford: Oxford University Press, 1999). On Bach and his family, see Wolff et al., "Bach," in NG2. See Daniel R. Melamed and Michael Marissen, *An Introduction to Bach Studies* (New York: Oxford University Press, 1998), for a rich guide to the tools of Bach research.

Other books on Bach and his music: Williams, *The Organ Music of J. S. Bach*, 2nd ed. (New York: Cambridge University Press, 2003), which gives a piece-by-piece commentary; David Ledbetter, *Bach's Well-Tempered Clavier: The 48 Preludes and Fugues* (New Haven: Yale University Press, 2002); Meredith Little and Natalie Jenne, *Dance and the Music of J. S. Bach*, expanded ed. (Bloomington: Indiana University Press, 2001); Laurence Dreyfus, *Bach and the Patterns of Invention* (Cambridge, MA: Harvard University Press, 1996); Wolff, *Bach: Essays on His Life and Music* (Cambridge, MA: Harvard University Press, 1991); and Robert L. Marshall, *The Music of Johann Sebastian Bach: The Sources, the Style, the Significance* (New York: Schirmer, 1989).

On Bach's specifications for performing forces in Leipzig, see his "Short but Most Necessary Draft for a Well-Appointed Church Music," in SR 88 (3:8). Two of the cantatas are available with notes and commentary: *Cantata No. 4, Christ lag in Todesbanden*, ed. Gerhard Herz (New York: Norton, 1967), and *Cantata No. 140, Wachet auf*, ed. Herz (New York: Norton, 1972), which contains a table showing a revised chronology of Bach's vocal music. Analytical discussions can be found in Eric Chafe, *Analyzing Bach Cantatas* (New York: Oxford University Press, 2000), and in Alfred Dürr, *Bach's Cantatas*, trans. Richard Jones (Oxford: Oxford University Press, 2003). For a study of Bach's compositional methods, see Marshall, *The Compositional Process of J. S. Bach: A Study of the Autograph Scores of the Vocal Works* (Princeton: Princeton University Press, 1972).

Melamed, *Hearing Bach's Passions* (New York: Oxford University Press, 2005), examines the Passions from several perspectives and argues that the *St. Matthew Passion* was a work for eight soloists rather than double chorus. For the Mass in B Minor, see George B. Stuaffer, *Bach: The Mass in B Minor* (New Haven: Yale University Press, 2004).

The first critical edition of Bach's complete works was his *Werke*, 61 vols., in 47 Jahrgänge (Leipzig: Bach-Gesellschaft, 1851–99; supp. 1926; repr. Ann Arbor, MI: J. W. Edwards, 1947; in miniature format, 1969). A newer edition of the complete works, in progress, is *Neue Ausgabe sämtlicher Werke* (Kassel: Bärenreiter, 1954–). Facsimiles of his manuscripts are available in *Faksimile-Reihe Bachser Werke und Schriftstücke* (Leipzig: Deutscher Verlag für Musik, 1955–).

The standard thematic catalogue is *Thematisch-systematisches Verzeichnis der musikalischen Werke von Johann Sebastian Bach (BWV)*, 2nd rev. and expanded ed., ed. Wolfgang Schmieder (Wiesbaden: Breitkopf & Härtel, 1990), with references to the Bach Gesellschaft edition and to other standard modern editions. An abridged version is *Bach-Werke-Verzeichnis: Nach der von Wolfgang Schmieder vorgelegten 2. Ausgabe*, ed. Alfred Dürr and Yoshitake Kobayashi with Kirsten Beisswenger (Wiesbaden: Breitkopf & Härtel, 1998). See also Hans-Joachim Schulze and Wolff, *Bach Compendium: Analytisch-bibliographisches Repertorium der Werke Johann Sebastian Bachs* (Leipzig and Dresden: Peters, 1985–), for source, bibliographic, and analytical information on Bach's entire output, supplementing the BWV.

For the Voyager recordings, see voyager.jpl. nasa.gov/spacecraft/music.html.

George Frideric Handel

Recommended books include Donald Burrows, *Handel* (New York: Oxford University Press, 1996); H. C. Robbins Landon, *Handel and His World* (London: Weidenfeld & Nicolson, 1984; repr. London: Flamingo, 1992); and *The Cambridge Companion to Handel*, ed. Burrows (Cambridge: Cambridge University Press, 1997).

On Handel's operas, see Winton Dean and J. Merrill Knapp, *Handel's Operas, 1704–1726*, rev. ed. (Oxford: Clarendon, 1995); Reinhard Strohm, *Essays on Handel and Italian Opera* (Cambridge: Cambridge University Press, 1985), which includes studies on A. Scarlatti and Vivaldi; and Ellen T. Harris, *Handel and the Pastoral Tradition* (London: Oxford University Press, 1980). Handel usually had particular singers in mind when composing his operas, and their impact on his music is described in Carl Steven LaRue, *Handel and His Singers: The Creation of the Royal Academy Operas, 1720–1728* (New York: Oxford University Press, 1995). The long chapter, "Origin of the Italian Opera in England and Its Progress There during the Present Century," in Charles Burney's *General History of Music* (pp. 651–904 in the modern edition cited under chapter 20), includes a detailed account of Handel's operas in London and many observations on the music. For a contemporary reaction to Handel's first London opera, see Joseph Addison's comments in SR 113 (3:33).

For the oratorios and masques, see David Ross Hurley, *Handel's Muse: Patterns of Creation in His Oratorios and Musical Dramas, 1743–1751* (Oxford: Oxford University Press, 2001); Ruth Smith, *Handel's Oratorios and Eighteenth-Century Thought* (Cambridge: Cambridge University Press, 1995); and Dean, *Handel's Dramatic Oratorios and Masques* (Oxford: Clarendon, 1990). The premiere of *Messiah* is described in Thomas Forrest Kelly, *First Nights: Five Musical Premieres* (New Haven: Yale University Press, 2000), 60–107.

Themes of same-sex desire among Handel's patrons, and in the texts of his cantatas, are explored by Harris, *Handel as Orpheus: Voice and Desire in the Chamber Cantatas* (Cambridge, MA: Harvard University Press, 2001). See also Gary C. Thomas, "'Was George Frideric

Handel Gay?': On Closet Questions and Cultural Politics," in *Queering the Pitch: The New Gay and Lesbian Musicology*, ed. Philip Brett, Elizabeth Wood, and Thomas (New York: Routledge, 1994), 155–203.

A useful bibliographic guide is Mary Ann Parker-Hale, *G. F. Handel: A Guide to Research* (New York: Garland, 1988).

The first critical edition was Georg Friedrich Händel, *Werke*, ed. Friedrich Chrysander (Leipzig: Breitkopf & Härtel, 1858–1903; repr. Ridgewood, NJ: Gregg International, 1965–66). A new edition is in progress: *Hallische Händel-Ausgabe*, ed. Max Schneider and Rudolf Steglich (Kassel: Bärenreiter, 1955–). For a complete listing of Handel's compositions, see A. Craig Bell, *Chronological-Thematic Catalogue*, 2nd ed. (Darley: Grian-Aig, 1972); see also the thematic catalogue by Bernd Baselt in the *Händel-Handbuch*, vols. 1–3 (Kassel: Bärenreiter, 1978–86). Handel's musical manuscripts are catalogued by Burrows and Martha J. Ronish, *A Catalogue of Handel's Musical Autographs* (Oxford: Clarendon, 1994).

CHAPTER 20

Music of the Classic Period

An excellent survey is Philip G. Downs, *Classical Music: The Era of Haydn, Mozart, and Beethoven* (New York: Norton, 1992), accompanied by the *Anthology of Classical Music*, ed. Downs (New York: Norton, 1992). See also Reinhard G. Pauly, *Music in the Classic Period*, 4th ed. (Upper Saddle River, NJ: Prentice Hall, 2000), and Giorgio Pestelli, *The Age of Mozart and Beethoven*, trans. Eric Cross (Cambridge: Cambridge University Press, 1984). For chronology, see Charles J. Hall, *An Eighteenth-Century Musical Chronicle: Events 1750–1799* (Westport, CT: Greenwood, 1990), updated in Hall, *Chronology of Western Classical Music*, vol. 1: *1751–1900* (New York: Routledge, 2002).

For readings on the general cultural scene in various countries and cities, consult *The Classical Era: From the 1740s to the End of the 18th Century*, ed. Neal Zaslaw (Englewood Cliffs, NJ: Prentice Hall, 1989). On the Enlightenment, see Cynthia Verba, *Music and the French Enlightenment: Reconstruction of a Dialogue, 1750–1764* (Oxford: Clarendon, 1993).

Important sources of information about eighteenth-century musical life are Charles Burney's two travel books, *The Present State of Music in France and Italy* (London, 1771; facs. repr. New York: Broude, 1969) and *The Present State of Music in Germany, The Netherlands, and the United Provinces*, 2 vols. (London, 1773; facs. repr. New York: Broude, 1969). An edition of the former appeared under the title *Music, Men and Manners in France and Italy, 1770*, ed. H. Edmund Poole (London: Folio Society, 1969), and an excerpt appears in SR 144 (5:23). Percy Scholes edited both books under the title *Dr. Burney's Musical Tours in Europe* (London: Oxford University Press, 1959).

On performing practice, see Clive Brown, *Classical and Romantic Performing Practice 1750–1900* (Oxford: Oxford University Press, 1999).

Public Concerts

A rich study of concert life is Simon McVeigh's *Concert Life in London from Mozart to Haydn* (Cambridge: Cambridge University Press, 1993).

One aspect of concert-giving, especially in London, was the performance of music from the past, which eventually led to the creation of a repertoire of musical classics. For the early stages of this development, see William Weber, *The Rise of Musical Classics in Eighteenth-Century England: A Study in Canon, Ritual, and Ideology* (Oxford: Clarendon, 1992).

Histories of Music

The first general histories of music appeared in the last quarter of the eighteenth century, reflecting contemporary views of music and offering primary source material for the music of the time. All are available in modern reprints or editions: Burney, *A General History of Music*, 2 vols. (London, 1776–89), modern edition with critical and historical notes by Frank Mercer (London: G. T. Foulis, 1935; repr. New York: Dover, 1957); Sir John Hawkins, *A General History of the Science and Practice of Music* (London, 1776; repr. New York: Dover, 1963); Johann Nicolaus Forkel, *Allgemeine Geschichte der Musik* [A General History of Music], 2 vols. (Leipzig, 1788–1801; repr. Graz: Akademische Druck- und Verlagsanstalt, 1967). Part of Forkel's introduction is translated in SR 146 (5:25).

Musical Taste and Style

On terms for style, see Daniel Heartz and Bruce Alan Brown, "Classical," "Empfindsamkeit," and "Galant," in NG2, s.v. On the galant style, see Heartz, *Music in European Capitals: The Galant Style, 1720–1780* (New York: Norton, 2003).

A stimulating summary of musical language and style in the Classic period, based on the theorists of the time, is Leonard G. Ratner, *Classic Music: Expression, Form, and Style* (New York: Schirmer, 1980). Excerpts from individual treatises are translated in SR 122–132 (5:1–11). The portions of Heinrich Christoph Koch's *Versuch einer Anleitung zur Composition* on melodic composition are translated as *Introductory Essay on Composition: The Mechanical Rules of Melody, Sections 3 and 4*, trans. with an intro. by Nancy Kovaleff Baker (New Haven: Yale University Press, 1983), with excerpts in SR 124 (5:3).

Daniel Webb's comments on emotions are in his *Observations on the Correspondence between Poetry and Music* (London: J. Dodsley, 1769; repr. New York: Garland, 1970), 47. For more on expression and imitation in music, see the excerpts from writings by Jean-Jacques Rousseau, Johann Jakob Engel, and Michel-Paul-Guy de Chabanon in SR 138, 139, and 141 (5:17, 18, and 20).

Opera

On the varieties of opera in the later eighteenth century, see Heartz, *From Garrick to Gluck: Essays on Opera in the Age of Enlightenment*, ed. John Rice (Hillsdale, NY: Pendragon, 2004); see also the volumes by Sadie (ed.); Grout, Fanelli, Bianconi, and Pestelli (eds.); Weiss; and Marco listed above under chapter 14.

Italian Comic Opera

A useful resource on Pergolesi is Marvin E. Paymer with Hermine W. Williams, *Giovanni Battista Pergolesi: A Guide to Research* (New York: Garland, 1989). Pergolesi's collected works are in *Opera omnia*, ed. Francesco Caffarelli (Rome: Gli Amici della Musica da Camera, 1939–42; repr. 1943). Vocal works have accompaniments in piano score with instrumental cues. The edition contains many works that are not by Pergolesi and omits a number of authentic works. See Marvin E. Paymer, *A Thematic Catalogue of the Opera Omnia, with an Appendix Listing Omitted Compositions* (New York: Pendragon, 1977). A few volumes of a new edition have appeared: *Complete Works*, gen. ed. Barry S. Brook, Francesco Degrada, and Helmut Hucke (New York: Pendragon; Milan: G. Ricordi, 1986–).

Italian comic operas by other composers are published in CDMI, vols. 13 (Galuppi) and 20 (Paisiello).

Opera Seria

A central work on the Italian opera of this period is Eric Weimer, *Opera seria and the Evolution of Classical Style, 1755–1772* (Ann Arbor: UMI Research, 1984).

Burney's comments on Hasse are from *The Present State of Music in Germany*, 2nd ed., vol. 1 (London, 1775), 238–39. An embellished version of the soprano line for *Digli ch'io son fedele*, improvised by or composed for Faustina Bordoni, is published in Hellmuth Christian Wolff, *Original Vocal Improvisations from the 16th–18th Centuries* (Cologne: Arno Volk Verlag Hans Gerig, 1972), 143–68. The version sung by Porporino and transcribed by Frederick the Great is there as well, and a facsimile of the original manuscript is in Friedrich II, *Auszierung zur Arie Digli ch'io son fedele aus der Oper Cleofide von Johann Adolf Hasse*, ed. Wolfgang Goldhan (Wiesbaden: Breitkopf & Härtel, 1991).

A large number of operas from this period are published in facsimiles of manuscript copies in the series *Italian Opera 1640–1770*, ed. with intros. by Howard Mayer Brown (New York: Garland, 1977–83). Among the composers are J. C. Bach, Galuppi, Gluck, Graun, Hasse, Jommelli, Pergolesi, Piccinni, Traetta, Vinci, and many others. There are also companion volumes of librettos, *Italian Opera Librettos, 1640–1770*, with intros. by H. M. Brown (New York: Garland, 1978–84).

French, English, and German Opera

On the opéra comique, see David Charlton, *Grétry and the Growth of Opéra-comique* (Cambridge: Cambridge University Press, 1986). The Belgian government sponsored the edition of Grétry's operas, *Collection complète des oeuvres de Grétry* (Leipzig: Breitkopf & Härtel, 1884–1936; repr. New York, 1970–). For Jean-Jacques Rousseau's comparison of French and Italian opera, see the excerpt from *Letter on French Music* in SR 133 (5:12).

On ballad opera, see Roger Fiske, *English Theatre Music in the Eighteenth Century* (Oxford: Oxford University Press, 1986). See the fascimiles of texts and music in *The Ballad Opera*, 28 vols., ed. Walter H. Rubsamen (New York: Garland, 1974).

On German opera, see John Hamilton Warrack, *German Opera: From the Beginnings to Wagner* (Cambridge: Cambridge University Press, 2001), and Thomas Bauman, *North German Opera in the Age of Goethe* (Cambridge: Cambridge University Press, 1985). Facsimiles of German and Austrian operas are found in *German Opera, 1770–1800*, ed. Bauman (New York: Garland, 1985–86). Composers include Hiller, Benda, Reichardt, Zumsteeg, Süssmayr, Salieri, and others. Modern editions of German Singspiele include, from Vienna, *Die Bergknappen* (The Miners) by Ignaz Umlauf (DTO 36) and *Der Dorfbarbier* (The Village Barber) by Johann Schenk (DTO 48); and, from North Germany, *Der Jahrmarkt* (The Fair) by Georg Benda (DdT 64). See also the songs from Viennese Singspiele in DTO 64.

Opera Reform

An excerpt from Francesco Algarotti, *An Essay on the Opera*, is in SR 134 (5:13). Niccolò Jommelli's *Fetonte* is published in DdT 32–33, and selections from Tommaso Traetta's operas are in DTB 14/1 and 17.

On Christoph Willibald Gluck, see Patricia Howard, *Gluck: An Eighteenth-Century Portrait in Letters and Documents* (Oxford: Clarendon, 1995). On Gluck's operas, see B. A. Brown, *Gluck and the French Theatre in Vienna* (Oxford: Clarendon, 1991). *C. W. von Gluck: Orfeo*, comp. Howard (Cambridge: Cambridge University Press, 1981), is a handbook on *Orfeo ed Euridice*. Gluck articulates the principles of his reform in the dedication to his Alceste in SR 136 (5:15). A useful bibliography is Howard, *Christoph Willibald Gluck: A Guide to Research*, 2nd ed. (New York: Routledge, 2003). An edition of the complete works, ed. Rudolf Gerber et al., is in progress (Kassel: Bärenreiter, 1951–), and Alfred Wotquenne's thematic catalogue was published in French and German (Leipzig: Breitkopf & Härtel, 1904; repr. Hildesheim: Georg Olms, 1967).

Song and Church Music

An excellent source on the eighteenth-century German Lied is *The Cambridge Companion to the Lied*, part 2, ed. James Parsons (Cambridge: Cambridge University Press, 2004). The second part of vol. 1 of Max Friedländer's *Das deutsche Lied im 18. Jahrhundert* (Stuttgart: J. G. Cotta, 1902) contains 236 songs, mostly from eighteenth-century collections. See also DTO 54 and 79 and DdT 35–36 and 57. For British song, see *The Blackwell History of Music in Britain*, vol. 4, *The Eighteenth Century*, ed. H. Diack Johnstone and Roger Fiske (Oxford: Blackwell, 1990).

Viennese church music of the late eighteenth century is in DTO 62 and 83. Hasse's oratorio *La Conversione di S. Agostino* is in DdT 20, and Jommelli's *Passione di Gesu Cristo* in CDMI 15.

For William Billings, see David P. McKay and Richard Crawford, *William Billings of Boston: Eighteenth-Century Composer* (Princeton: Princeton University Press, 1975), and *Catalog of the Musical Works of William Billings*, comp. Karl Kroeger (New York: Greenwood, 1991). His music appears in *The Complete Works of William Billings*, ed. Kroeger and Hans Nathan (Boston: American Musicological Society and Colonial Society of Massachusetts, 1977–90).

CHAPTER 21

Instruments and Ensembles

For the history of the piano, see "Pianoforte, §I: History of the instrument," in NG2; *Piano: An Encyclopedia*, 2nd ed., ed. Robert and Margaret W. Palmieri (New York: Routledge, 2003); Edwin M. Good, *Giraffes, Black Dragons, and Other Pianos: A Technological History from Cristofori to the Modern Concert Grand*, 2nd ed. (Stanford: Stanford University Press, 2001); Michael Cole, *The Pianoforte in the Classical Era* (Oxford: Clarendon, 1998); Richard Maunder, *Keyboard Instruments in Eighteenth-Century Vienna* (Oxford: Clarendon, 1998); Stewart Pollens, *The Early Pianoforte* (Cambridge: Cambridge University Press, 1995); and R. E. M. Harding, *The Piano-forte: Its History to the Great Exhibition of 1851*, 2nd ed. (Old Woking, England: Gresham, 1978; repr. London: Heckscher, 1989). An excellent social history of the piano is in James Parakilas et al., *Piano Roles: Three Hundred Years of Life with the Piano* (New Haven: Yale University Press, 1999). The classic by Arthur Loesser, *Men, Women, and Pianos* (New York: Simon & Schuster, 1954; repr. New York: Dover, 1990), is also still valuable.

Two useful guides to music for the piano (and other keyboard instruments) are Stewart Gordon, *A History of Keyboard Literature: Music for the Piano and Its Forerunners* (New York: Schirmer, 1996), and John Gillespie, *Five Centuries of Keyboard Music: An Historical Survey of Music for Harpsichord and Piano* (New York: Dover, 1972). Selected essays by various experts on eighteenth-century keyboard instruments, composers, and music can be found in *Eighteenth-Century Keyboard Music*, 2nd ed., ed. Robert L. Marshall (New York: Routledge, 2003). For issues of performance, see Sandra P. Rosenblum, *Performance Practices in Classic Piano Music* (Bloomington: Indiana University Press, 1988). For a bibliography, see Robert Palmieri, *Piano Information Guide: An Aid to Research* (New York: Garland, 1989).

A helpful guide to literature on chamber music is John H. Baron, *Chamber Music: A Research and Information Guide*, 2nd ed. (New York: Routledge, 2002).

On the string quartet, see Robin Stowell, *The Cambridge Companion to the String Quartet* (Cambridge: Cambridge University Press, 2003); Mara Parker, *The String Quartet, 1750–1797: Four Types of Musical Conversation* (Aldershot: Ashgate, 2002); and Paul Griffiths, *The String Quartet* (New York: Thames & Hudson, 1983).

There is still relatively little written on the history of wind ensembles and music for them. See David Whitwell, *The History and Literature of the Wind Band and Wind Ensemble*, 11 vols. (Northridge, CA: Winds, 1982–84); *Wind Ensemble Sourcebook and Biographical Guide*, ed. Marshall Stoneham, Jon A. Gillaspie, and David Lindsey (Westport, CT: Greenwood, 1997); and Barbera Secrist-Schmedes, *Wind Chamber Music for Two to Sixteen Winds: An Annotated Guide* (Lanham, MD: Scarecrow, 2002). See also "Band" and "Harmoniemusik," in NG2.

Genres and Forms

For the symphony, see below.

On the sonata and sonata form, see William S. Newman, *The Sonata in the Classic Era*, 3rd ed. (New York: Norton, 1983), and Charles Rosen, *Sonata Forms*, rev. ed. (New York: Norton, 1988). For classical form in general, see William E. Caplin, *Classical Form: A Theory of Formal Functions for the Instrumental Music of Haydn, Mozart, and Beethoven* (New York: Oxford University Press, 1998). Mark Evan Bonds, *Wordless Rhetoric: Musical Form and the Metaphor of the Oration* (Cambridge, MA: Harvard University Press, 1991), shows how theorists from the 1720s to the 1830s used metaphors from grammar and rhetoric to describe form in instrumental works.

To contrast eighteenth- and nineteenth-century views of sonata form, see the excerpts from Heinrich Christoph Koch's *Introductory Essay on Composition* (1782–93) and from Adolf Bernhard Marx's *The Theory of Musical Composition* (1868) in SR 126 (5:5) and 164 (6:17) respectively. See also Scott Burnham, "Form," in CHWMT, 880–906.

Domenico Scarlatti

Studies include Malcolm Boyd, *Domenico Scarlatti—Master of Music* (New York: Schirmer, 1986), and Ralph Kirkpatrick's classic *Domenico Scarlatti* (Princeton: Princeton University Press, 1953; new ed., 1983). On the sonatas, see W. Dean Sutcliffe, *The Keyboard Sonatas of Domenico Scarlatti and Eighteenth-Century Musical Style* (Cambridge: Cambridge University Press, 2003). For a bibliography, see Carole F. Vidali, *Alessandro and Domenico Scarlatti: A Guide to Research* (New York: Garland, 1993). For a thematic catalogue, see *Domenico Scarlatti Thematic Index According to Ralph Kirkpatrick and Emilia Fadini*, ed. Laurette Goldberg and Patrice Mathews with William Glennon (Berkeley: MusicSources, 1999).

Two critical editions of the sonatas are available: *Sonates*, ed. Kenneth Gilbert (Paris: Heugel, 1971–84), and *Sonate per clavicembalo*, ed. Emilia Fadini (Milan: Ricordi, 1978–). Facsimiles of the sonatas in manuscript are in *Sonate per cembalo* (Florence: Studio per Edizioni Scelte, 1985–1992), and *Complete Keyboard Works*, ed. Kirkpatrick (New York: Johnson Reprint, 1972).

Carl Philipp Emanuel Bach

See Hans-Günter Ottenberg, *C. P. E. Bach*, trans. Philip J. Whitmore (Oxford: Oxford University Press, 1987), and David Schulenberg, *The Instrumental Music of C. P. E. Bach* (Ann Arbor: UMI Research, 1984). Bach's correspondence has been published in *The Letters of C. P. E. Bach*, ed. and trans. Stephen Lewis Clark (Oxford: Oxford University Press, 1997). For a bibliography, see Doris Bosworth Powers, *Carl Philipp Emanuel Bach: A Guide to Research* (New York: Routledge, 2002).

A planned complete edition, *Carl Philipp Emanuel Bach Edition*, gen. ed. Rachel W. Wade, coord. ed. E. Eugene Helm (New York: Oxford University Press, 1989–), was never completed; a new one is underway. *Collected Works for Solo Keyboard*, 6 vols., ed. Darrell Berg (New York: Garland, 1985), is a facsimile edition of eighteenth-century prints and manuscripts.

The current thematic catalogue is Helm, *Thematic Catalogue of the Works of Carl Philipp Emanuel Bach* (New Haven: Yale University Press, 1989); an older thematic catalogue is by Alfred Wotquenne (Leipzig and New York: Breitkopf & Härtel, 1905; repr. Wiesbaden, 1964), and both numbering systems are still used.

C. P. E. Bach's treatise *Versuch über die wahre Art, das Clavier zu spielen* was first published in 1753 (Part 1) and 1762 (Part 2) and is available in a facsimile edition by L. Hoffmann-Erbrecht (Leipzig: Breitkopf & Härtel, 1957); the translation by William J. Mitchell as *Essay on the True Art of Playing Keyboard Instruments* (New York: Norton, 1949) combines the original and revised editions of the eighteenth century. Excerpt in SR 129 (5:8).

Symphony

Preston Stedman, *The Symphony* (Englewood Cliffs, NJ: Prentice Hall, 1979; 2nd ed. 1992), and Louise Cuyler, *The Symphony* (New York: Harcourt Brace Jovanovich, 1973; 2nd ed. Warren, MI: Harmonie Park, 1995), offer general histories of the symphony. For a bibliography, see Preston Stedman, *The Symphony: A Research and Information Guide* (New York: Garland, 1990). A comprehensive collection of approximately 600 symphonies in full score begun under the editorship of Barry S. Brook, *The Symphony: 1720–1840* (New York and London: Garland, 1979–85), consists of six series, A–F, each corresponding to a geographical region.

On Sammartini, see the essays in *Giovanni Battista Sammartini and His Musical Environment*, ed. Anna Cat-

toretti (Turnhout: Brepols, 2004). Some of Sammartini's symphonies appear in *The Symphonies of G. B. Sammartini*, vol. 1, ed. Bathia Churgin (Cambridge, MA: Harvard University Press, 1968). His works are catalogued in Newell Jenkins and Churgin, *Thematic Catalogue of the Works of Giovanni Battista Sammartini: Orchestral and Vocal Music* (Cambridge, MA: Harvard University Press, 1976).

Concerning the symphony in Mannheim in general and Johann Stamitz in particular, consult Eugene K. Wolf, *The Symphonies of Johann Stamitz: A Study in the Formation of the Classic Style* (Utrecht/Antwerp: Bohn, Scheltema & Holkema; The Hague: M. Nijhoff, 1981), which includes a thematic catalogue of the orchestral works. Wolf's *Manuscripts from Mannheim, ca. 1730–1778: A Study in the Methodology of Musical Source Research*, in collaboration with Jean K. Wolf and Paul Corneilson (Frankfurt: Peter Lang, 2002), uses symphonies and other music from Mannheim as case studies in musicological research on sources. Symphonies by Mannheim composers are found in DTB, vols. 3/1, 7/2, and 8/2; a reprint of the music in 2 volumes is entitled *Mannheim Symphonists*, ed. Hugo Riemann (New York: Broude, 1956). Symphonies by Viennese composers are in DTO, vols. 31 and 39; North German symphonies, DdT, vols. 51–52; symphonies by C. P. E. Bach, Das Erbe deutscher Musik, series 1, vol. 18. Instrumental works of Michael Haydn in DTO, vol. 29; of Carl Ditters von Dittersdorf, in DTO, vol. 81.

Johann Christian Bach

See Heinz Gärtner, *Johann Christian Bach: Mozart's Friend and Mentor*, trans. Reinhard G. Pauly (Portland, OR: Amadeus, 1994). On the keyboard concertos, see Jane R. Stevens, *The Bach Family and the Keyboard Concerto: The Evolution of a Genre* (Warren, MI: Harmonie Park, 2001). *The Collected Works of Johann Christian Bach, 1735–1782*, 48 vols., gen. ed. Ernest Warburton (New York: Garland, 1984–99) is a facsimile edition that includes a *Thematic Catalogue* and volume of *Sources & Documents*. The symphonies are also in Das Erbe deutscher Musik, series 1, vols. 3 and 30.

CHAPTER 22

Haydn, Mozart, and Others

Daniel Heartz, *Haydn, Mozart, and the Viennese School, 1740–1780* (New York: Norton, 1995), sets their work in the context of eighteenth-century Viennese culture and society. Charles Rosen, *The Classical Style: Haydn, Mozart, Beethoven*, expanded ed. (New York: Norton, 1997), seeks to define the distinctive traits of these three composers' music. On their symphonies, see A. Peter Brown, *The Symphonic Repertoire*, vol. 2: *The First Golden Age of the Viennese Symphony: Haydn, Mozart, Beethoven, and Schubert* (Bloomington: Indiana University Press, 2002).

Joseph Haydn

For Joseph Haydn's life and works, see James Webster and Georg Feder, *The New Grove Haydn* (New York: Palgrave/Grove, 2002); *Haydn*, ed. David Wyn Jones (Oxford: Oxford University Press, 2002); Rosemary Hughes, *Haydn*, 6th ed. (London: Dent, 1989); H. C. Robbins Landon and Jones, *Haydn: His Life and Music* (Bloomington: Indiana University Press, 1988); and Karl Geiringer, *Haydn: A Creative Life in Music* (New York: Norton, 1946; 3rd rev. ed. 1982). See also Landon, *Haydn: A Documentary Study* (New York: Rizzoli, 1981), and Landon's compendium *Haydn: Chronicle and Works*, 5 vols. (Bloomington: Indiana University Press, 1976–80). *The Cambridge Companion to Haydn*, ed. Caryl Clark (Cambridge: Cambridge University Press, 2005), is a helpful guide.

For a fresh look at Haydn's methods of composition, see James Webster, *Haydn's "Farewell" Symphony and the Idea of Classical Style: Through-Composition and Cyclic Integration in His Instrumental Music* (Cambridge: Cambridge University Press, 1991). The central role of variation is explored in Elaine R. Sisman, *Haydn and the Classical Variation* (Cambridge, MA: Harvard University Press, 1993). For a serious consideration of Haydn's proverbial humor, see Gretchen A. Wheelock, *Haydn's Ingenious Jesting with Art: Contexts of Musical Wit and Humor* (New York: Schirmer, 1992). On the social setting for Haydn's concert music and its critical reception, see Mary Sue Morrow, *Concert Life in Haydn's Vienna: Aspects of a Developing Musical and Social Institution* (Stuyvesant, NY: Pendragon, 1989). Two recent collections of provocative essays are *Haydn and His World*, ed. Sisman (Princeton: Princeton University Press, 1997), and *Haydn Studies*, ed. W. Dean Sutcliffe (Cambridge: Cambridge University Press, 1998).

Recent studies of Haydn's symphonies include Brown, *The First Golden Age of the Viennese Symphony* (see above); Richard Will, *The Characteristic Symphony in the Age of Haydn and Beethoven* (Cambridge: Cambridge University Press, 2002); Bernard Harrison, *Haydn: The "Paris" Symphonies* (Cambridge: Cambridge University Press, 1998); Ethan Haimo, *Haydn's Symphonic Forms: Essays in Compositional Logic* (Oxford: Clarendon, 1995); and David P. Schroeder, *Haydn and the Enlightenment: The Late Symphonies and Their Audience* (Oxford: Clarendon, 1990; repr. 1997), on the social and intellectual background of the Paris and London symphonies. *Haydn, Symphony No. 103 in E-flat*, Norton Critical Scores, ed. Geiringer (New York: Norton, 1974), includes a score with numerous essays related to the piece. Donald F. Tovey's classic analytical program notes for several of Haydn's symphonies are included in his *Essays in Musical Analysis*, vol. 1 (London: Oxford University Press, 1935; repr. 1972).

On the quartets, see William Drabkin, *A Reader's Guide to Haydn's Early String Quartets* (Westport, CT: Greenwood, 2000), and Rosemary Hughes, *Haydn String Quartets* (Seattle: University of Washington Press, 1969; rev. 5th ed. 1975). On performance issues, see Hans Keller, *The Great Haydn Quartets: Their Interpretation* (London: Dent, 1993).

On Haydn's keyboard works, see A. Peter Brown, *Joseph Haydn's Keyboard Music: Sources and Style* (Bloomington: Indiana University Press, 1986); László Somfai, *The Keyboard Sonatas of Joseph Haydn: Instruments and Performance Practice, Genres and Styles*, trans. by the author with Charlotte Greenspan (Chicago: University of Chicago Press, 1995); and Bernard Harrison, *Haydn's Keyboard Music: Studies in Performance Practice* (Oxford: Oxford University Press, 1997).

An illuminating study of a Haydn choral work in performance is Brown, *Performing Haydn's "The Creation": Reconstructing the Earliest Renditions* (Bloomington: Indiana University Press, 1986).

Source material is in *The Collected Correspondence and London Notebooks of Joseph Haydn*, ed. Landon (London and New York: Barrie & Rockliff, 1959). For a bibliography, see Floyd K. Grave with Margaret G. Grave, *Franz Joseph Haydn: A Guide to Research* (New York: Garland, 1990).

The definitive edition of Haydn's works, published by the Joseph Haydn Institute of Cologne, is *Joseph Haydn: Werke*, ed. Jens Peter Larsen et al. (Munich: G. Henle, 1958–). The thematic catalogue is Anthony van Hoboken, *Joseph Haydn: Thematisch-bibliographisches Werkverzeichnis*, 3 vols. (Mainz: B. Schott's Söhne, 1957–78). See Stephen C. Bryant and Gary W. Chapman, *A Melodic Index to Haydn's Instrumental Music* (New York: Pendragon, 1982), to identify the titles of works for which only the melody is known and to locate them in Hoboken's thematic catalogue.

Wolfgang Amadeus Mozart

There have been many biographies of Mozart. Recent ones include Robert W. Gutman, *Mozart: A Cultural Biography* (New York: Harcourt Brace, 1999); Peter Gay, *Mozart* (New York: Lipper/Viking, 1999), by a renowned cultural historian; John Rosselli, *The Life of Mozart* (Cambridge: Cambridge University Press, 1998), a good brief biography; Maynard Solomon, *Mozart: A Life* (New York: HarperCollins, 1995), a psychological treatment; and Wolfgang Hildesheimer, *Mozart*, trans. Marion Faber (New York: Farrar, Straus, Giroux, 1981), a stimulating psychological portrait. Useful for presenting original sources are Otto Erich Deutsch, *Mozart, a Documentary Biography*, 2nd ed., trans. E. Blom et al. (Stanford: Stanford University Press, 1965), and a supplement, *New Mozart Documents: A Supplement to O. E. Deutsch's Documentary Biography*, comp. by Cliff Eisen (Stanford: Stanford University Press, 1991).

Useful for the life and works are *The Cambridge Companion to Mozart*, ed. Simon P. Keefe (New York: Cambridge University Press, 2003); *The Mozart Compendium: A Guide to Mozart's Life and Music*, ed. Landon (New York: Schirmer, 1990); and *The Compleat Mozart: A Guide to the Musical Works of Wolfgang Amadeus Mozart*, ed. Neal Zaslaw with William Cowdery (New York: Norton, 1990).

On the Mozart family, see Ruth Halliwell, *The Mozart Family: Four Lives in a Social Context* (Oxford: Clarendon, 1998), and David P. Schroeder, *Mozart in Revolt: Strategies of Resistance, Mischief, and Deception* (New Haven: Yale University Press, 1999), on Mozart's relationship to his father. For the correspondence, see A. Hyatt King and Monica Carolan, *Letters of Mozart and His Family*, 3rd ed., ed. and trans. Emily Anderson (London: Macmillan, 1985), and the excerpts from Mozart's letters in SR 140 (5:19). Leopold Mozart's treatise *Gründliche Violinschule* (1756) has been published as *A Treatise on the Fundamental Principles of Violin Playing*, 2nd ed., trans. Editha Knocker (London and New York: Oxford University Press, 1951); an excerpt in a different translation appears in SR 130 (5:9).

John Jenkins, *Mozart and the English Connection* (London: Cygnus Arts, 1998), gives an account of Mozart's first visit to London in 1764–65 and its historical significance.

On the Vienna years, see Volkmar Braunbehrens, *Mozart in Vienna, 1781–1791*, trans. Timothy Bell (New York: Grove Weidenfeld, 1990); Landon, *Mozart and Vienna* (New York: Schirmer, 1991); idem., *Mozart, The Golden Years, 1781–1791* (London: Thames & Hudson, 1989); idem., *Mozart's Last Year* (London: Thames & Hudson, 1988; repr. 1999); and idem., *Mozart and the Masons: New Light on the Lodge, "Crowned Hope"* (New York: Thames & Hudson, 1983; repr. 1991).

For bibliographies and research guides, see *The Mozart Repertory: A Guide for Musicians, Programmers, and Researchers*, ed. Neal Zaslaw and Fiona Morgan Fein (Ithaca, NY: Cornell University Press, 1991), and Baird Hastings, *Wolfgang Amadeus Mozart: A Guide to Research* (New York: Garland, 1989).

The notion of "topics" in Classic-era music was introduced and explained by Leonard G. Ratner, "Topics," in *Classic Music: Expression, Form, and Style* (New York: Schirmer, 1980), 9–30.

Guides to the instrumental works include John Irving, *Mozart's Piano Sonatas: Contexts, Sources, Style* (Cambridge: Cambridge University Press, 1997); idem., *Mozart: The "Haydn" Quartets* (Cambridge: Cambridge University Press, 1998); A. Hyatt King, *Mozart Chamber Music* (Seattle: University of Washington Press, 1969; repr. London: Ariel, 1986); and Erik Smith, *Mozart Serenades, Divertimenti and Dances* (London: BBC, 1982).

On the concertos, see John Irving, *Mozart's Piano Concertos* (Aldershot: Ashgate, 2003); Simon P. Keefe, *Mozart's Piano Concertos: Dramatic Dialogue in the Age of Enlightenment* (Rochester, NY: Boydell, 2001); *Mozart's Piano Concertos: Text, Context, Interpretation*, ed. Neal

Zaslaw (Ann Arbor: University of Michigan Press, 1996); A. Hyatt King, *Mozart String and Wind Concertos* (London: BBC, 1978); and *Mozart, Piano Concerto in C major, K. 503*, Norton Critical Scores, ed. Joseph Kerman (New York: Norton, 1970).

On the symphonies, see A. Peter Brown, *The First Golden Age of the Viennese Symphony* (above), and Neal Zaslaw, *Mozart's Symphonies: Context, Performance Practice, Reception* (Oxford: Clarendon, 1989). Studies of individual symphonies include Elaine Sisman, *Mozart: The "Jupiter" Symphony, No. 41 in C Major, K. 551* (Cambridge: Cambridge University Press, 1993), and *Mozart, Symphony in G Minor, K. 550*, Norton Critical Scores, ed. Nathan Broder (New York: Norton, 1967).

For the operas, see *Mozart and His Operas*, ed. Stanley Sadie (New York: St. Martin's, 2000); Mary Hunter, *The Culture of Opera Buffa in Mozart's Vienna* (Princeton: Princeton University Press, 1999); Nicholas Till, *Mozart and the Enlightenment: Truth, Virtue, and Beauty in Mozart's Operas* (New York: Norton, 1993); Heartz, *Mozart's Operas*, ed. Bauman (Berkeley: University of California Press, 1990); Andrew Steptoe, *The Mozart-Da Ponte Operas* (Oxford: Clarendon, 1988); Carolyn Gianturco, *Mozart's Early Operas* (London: Batsford, 1981); Julian Rushton, *W. A. Mozart: "Don Giovanni"* (Cambridge: Cambridge University Press, 1981), a useful handbook; and Peter Gammond, *The Magic Flute: A Guide to the Opera* (London: Breslich & Foss, 1979). Wye J. Allanbrook, *Rhythmic Gesture in Mozart: Le nozze di Figaro and Don Giovanni* (Chicago: Chicago University Press, 1983), applies Ratner's theory of topics to the first two Da Ponte operas. Two new studies on the symbolism in *The Magic Flute* in connection with Viennese Freemasonry and Masonic rituals are Matheus Franciscus Maria von den Berk, *The Magic Flute/Zauberflöte: An Alchemical Allegory* (Boston: Brill, 2004), and Michael Besack, *Which Craft?: W. A. Mozart and the Magic Flute* (Oakland: Regent, 2001). Mary Du Mont, *The Mozart-Da Ponte Operas: An Annotated Bibliography* (Westport, CT: Greenwood, 2000), is a good research guide on the subject.

On performance practice, see *Perspectives on Mozart Performance*, ed. R. Larry Todd and Peter Williams (Cambridge: Cambridge University Press, 1991), and Frederick Neumann, *Ornamentation and Improvisation in Mozart* (Princeton: Princeton University Press, 1986).

The standard collected edition is the *Neue Ausgabe sämtlicher Werke* (Kassel: Bärenreiter, 1955–). An older edition of his works is *Wolfgang Amadeus Mozart's Werke* (Leipzig: Breitkopf & Härtel, 1876–1907; repr. Ann Arbor: Edwards, 1951–56; repr. in miniature format New York: Kalmus, 1969). The thematic catalogue is Ludwig Köchel, *Chronologisch-thematisches Verzeichnis* (Leipzig, 1862); 6th ed., ed. Franz Giegling, Alexander Weinmann, and Gerd Sievers (Wiesbaden: Breitkopf & Härtel, 1964).

PART V: THE NINETEENTH CENTURY

Leon Plantinga, *Romantic Music* (New York: Norton, 1984), offers a comprehensive survey, accompanied by *Anthology of Romantic Music*, ed. Plantinga (New York: Norton, 1984). Briefer surveys include Jon W. Finson, *Nineteenth-Century Music: The Western Classical Tradition* (Upper Saddle River, NJ: Prentice Hall, 2002); Rey M. Longyear, *Nineteenth-Century Romanticism in Music*, 3rd ed. (Englewood Cliffs, NJ: Prentice Hall, 1988); and Arnold Whittall, *Romantic Music: A Concise History from Schubert to Sibelius* (New York: Thames & Hudson, 1987). Carl Dahlhaus, *Nineteenth-Century Music*, trans. J. Bradford Robinson (Berkeley: University of California Press, 1989), considers not only the music but criticism, historiography, and sociological issues. Topical chapters by various experts appear in *The Cambridge History of Nineteenth-Century Music*, ed. Jim Samson (Cambridge: Cambridge University Press, 2001), and NOHM, vol. 9: *Romanticism (1830–1890)*, ed. Gerald Abraham (Oxford: Oxford University Press, 1990). For chronology, see Charles J. Hall, *A Nineteenth-Century Musical Chronicle: Events 1800–1899* (Westport, CT: Greenwood, 1989), updated in Hall, *Chronology of Western Classical Music*, vol. 1: *1751–1900* (New York: Routledge, 2002).

For excellent essays on the political, social, and historical background of music centers in Europe and the Americas, see *The Early Romantic Era: Between Revolutions, 1789 and 1848*, ed. Alexander Ringer (Englewood Cliffs, NJ: Prentice Hall, 1991), and *The Late Romantic Era from the Mid-19th Century to World War I*, ed. Samson (Englewood Cliffs, NJ: Prentice Hall, 1991). On the business aspects of composition, see Frederic M. Scherer, *Quarter Notes and Bank Notes: The Economics of Music Composition in the Eighteenth and Nineteenth Centuries* (Princeton: Princeton University Press, 2004). For music in relation to German culture, see David Gramit, *Cultivating Music: The Aspirations, Interests, and Limits of German Musical Culture, 1770–1848* (Berkeley: University of California Press, 2002). On the United States, see Nicholas E. Tawa, *High-Minded and Low-Down: Music in the Lives of Americans, 1800–1861* (Boston: Northeastern University Press, 2000).

A source book for the musical vocabulary of the period is Leonard G. Ratner, *Romantic Music: Sound and Syntax* (New York: Schirmer, 1992). One thread of musical style, the Hungarian or Gypsy style, is explored by Jonathan Bellman, *The Style Hongrois in the Music of Western Europe* (Boston: Northeastern University Press, 1993). On music theory of the time, see *Music Theory in the Age of Romanticism*, ed. Ian Bent (Cambridge: Cambridge University Press, 1996), and David W. Bernstein, "Nineteenth-Century Harmonic Theory: The Austro-German Legacy," in CHWMT, 778–811. Christopher Alan Reynolds, *Motives for Allusion: Context and Content in Nineteenth-Century Music* (Cambridge, MA: Harvard University Press, 2003), provides a theoretical framework for musical allusions in nineteenth-century music, when one piece quotes or echoes another.

On performing practice, see Clive Brown, *Classical and Romantic Performing Practice 1750–1900* under part IV above. An essential stylistic feature of nineteenth-century music is the variation in tempo known as *rubato*; a history of its development is Richard Hudson, *Stolen Time: The History of Tempo Rubato* (Oxford: Clarendon, 1994).

CHAPTER 23

French Revolution

On music in the Revolutionary era, see Laura Mason, *Singing the French Revolution: Popular Culture and Politics, 1787–1799* (Ithaca, NY: Cornell University Press, 1996); *Music and the French Revolution*, ed. Malcolm Boyd (Cambridge: Cambridge University Press, 1992); and Jean Mongrédien, *French Music from the Enlightenment to Romanticism: 1789–1830* (Portland, OR: Amadeus, 1996).

Ludwig van Beethoven

Of the numerous Beethoven biographies, the best recent ones are Lewis Lockwood, *Beethoven: The Music and the Life* (New York: Norton, 2003); Barry Cooper, *Beethoven* (Oxford: Oxford University Press, 2000); David Wyn Jones, *The Life of Beethoven* (New York: Cambridge University Press, 1998), a short biography; and Maynard Solomon, *Beethoven*, 2nd rev. ed. (New York: Schirmer, 1998), which has many original interpretations. William Kinderman, *Beethoven* (Berkeley: University of California Press, 1995), treats the musical works in a biographical context. Tia DeNora, *Beethoven and the Construction of Genius: Musical Politics in Vienna, 1792–1803* (Berkeley: University of California Press, 1995), focuses on Beethoven's crucial first decade in Vienna.

A classic biography is Alexander Wheelock Thayer, *Life of Beethoven*, rev. and ed. Elliott Forbes (Princeton: Princeton University Press, 1964). *Beethoven the First Biography, 1827*, is a recent edition of the first Beethoven biography, by Johann Aloy Schlosser, trans. Reinhard G. Pauly, ed. Cooper (Portland, OR: Amadeus, 1996). Although the truthfulness of Schlosser's account is questionable, it provides a contemporary view of Beethoven as person and artist. The same can be said for Anton Schindler, *Beethoven as I Knew Him*, ed. Donald W. MacArdle, trans. Cynthia S. Jolly (New York: Norton, 1972; repr. Mineola, NY: Dover, 1996). See also *Beethoven: Impressions by His Contemporaries*, ed. Oscar G. Sonneck (New York: G. Schirmer, 1926; repr. New York: Dover, 1967). Russell Martin, *Beethoven's Hair: An Extraordinary Historical Odyssey and a Musical Mystery Solved* (London: Bloomsbury, 2000), concludes after testing a lock of Beethoven's hair that he died from lead poisoning.

Helpful essays on Beethoven appear in *The Beethoven Companion*, ed. Glenn Stanley (Cambridge: Cambridge

University Press, 2000); *Beethoven and His World*, ed. Scott G. Burnham and Michael P. Steinberg (Princeton: Princeton University Press, 2000); and Solomon, *Beethoven Essays* (Cambridge, MA: Harvard University Press, 1988).

For analytical approaches, see especially Carl Dahlhaus, *Ludwig van Beethoven: Approaches to His Music*, trans. Mary Whittall (Oxford: Oxford University Press, 1991); Robert Hatten, *Musical Meaning in Beethoven: Markedness, Correlation, and Interpretation* (Bloomington: Indiana University Press, 1994); and Fred Everett Maus, "Music as Drama," *Music Theory Spectrum* 10 (1988): 56–73. The analysis given here of Beethoven's *Eroica* Symphony, first movement, though different in detail, is based on Philip G. Downs, "Beethoven's 'New Way' and the *Eroica*, " *MQ* 56 (October 1970): 585–604, reprinted in *The Creative World of Beethoven*, ed. Paul Henry Lang (New York: Norton, 1971), 83–102.

The reception of Beethoven's work in and shortly after his lifetime is considered in Robin Wallace, *Beethoven's Critics* (Cambridge: Cambridge University Press, 1986). On his American critics, see Ora Frishberg Saloman, *Beethoven's Symphonies and J. S. Dwight: The Birth of American Music Criticism* (Boston: Northeastern University Press, 1995). Burnham, *Beethoven Hero* (Princeton: Princeton University Press, 1995), discusses the cultural value of Beethoven's heroic style and its critical reception. A compilation and discussion of writings on Beethoven in German periodicals in the years 1783–1820 appears in *The Critical Reception of Beethoven's Compositions by His German Contemporaries*, ed. William Meredith, Wayne M. Senner, and Wallace (Lincoln: University of Nebraska Press, 1999).

For Beethoven's piano works, see Charles Rosen, *Beethoven's Piano Sonatas: A Short Companion* (New Haven: Yale University Press, 2002); Kenneth Drake, *The Beethoven Sonatas and the Creative Experience* (Bloomington: Indiana University Press, 2000); Timothy Jones, *Beethoven: The "Moonlight" and Other Sonatas, Op. 27 and Op. 31* (Cambridge: Cambridge University Press, 1999); Donald Francis Tovey, *A Companion to Beethoven's Pianoforte Sonatas: Bar-by-bar Analysis*, preface and notes by Cooper (London: Associated Board of the Royal Schools of Music, 1998); and George Barth, *The Pianist as Orator: Beethoven and the Transformation of Keyboard Style* (Ithaca, NY: Cornell University Press, 1992).

On the string quartets, see *The Beethoven Quartet Companion*, ed. Robert Winter and Robert Martin (Berkeley: University of California Press, 1994), and Joseph Kerman, *The Beethoven Quartets* (New York: Knopf, 1967; repr. Norton, 1979).

Discussions of Beethoven's symphonies within the larger stylistic contexts of his time can be found in A. Peter Brown, *The Symphonic Repertoire*, vol. 2: *The First Golden Age of the Viennese Symphony: Haydn, Mozart, Beethoven, and Schubert* (Bloomington: Indiana Univer-

sity Press, 2002), and Richard Will, *The Characteristic Symphony in the Age of Haydn and Beethoven* (Cambridge: Cambridge University Press, 2002). Guides to specific symphonies include Thomas Sipe, *Beethoven, Eroica Symphony* (New York: Cambridge University Press, 1998); David Wyn Jones, *Beethoven, Pastoral Symphony* (New York: Cambridge University Press, 1995); Nicholas Cook, *Beethoven: Symphony No. 9* (New York: Cambridge University Press, 1993); and David Benjamin Levy, *Beethoven: The Ninth Symphony*, rev. ed. (New Haven: Yale University Press, 2003). The premiere of the Ninth Symphony is described in Thomas Forrest Kelly, *First Nights: Five Musical Premieres* (New Haven: Yale University Press, 2000), 108–79.

For Beethoven's concertos, see Leon Plantinga, *Beethoven's Concertos: History, Style, Performance* (New York: Norton, 1999); Robin Stowell, *Beethoven: Violin Concerto* (New York: Cambridge University Press, 1998); and Antony Hopkins, *The Seven Concertos of Beethoven* (Brookfield, VT: Ashgate, 1997).

On Beethoven's late period, see Stephen Rumph, *Beethoven After Napoleon: Political Romanticism in the Late Works* (Berkeley: University of California Press, 2004), and Solomon, *Late Beethoven: Music, Thought, Imagination* (Berkeley: University of California Press, 2003), who argues that Beethoven's late works reflect changes in his beliefs about nature, the divine, and humanity as recorded in his daily diary.

The standard edition of Beethoven's complete works is *Neue Ausgabe sämtlicher Werke*, ed. Joseph Schmidt-Görg and Martin Staehelin (Munich: Henle, 1961–84). The first such edition was *Ludwig van Beethovens Werke*, 24 series and supp. (Leipzig: Breitkopf & Härtel, 1864–90; repr. Ann Arbor: J. W. Edwards, 1949; repr. in miniature format New York: Kalmus, 1971); works omitted from this edition are in *Supplemente zur Gesamtausgabe*, ed. Willy Hess (Wiesbaden: Breitkopf & Härtel, 1959–).

The traditional count and numbering of Beethoven's symphonies and other genres omit certain compositions, such as his "Battle Symphony" (also titled *Wellington's Victory*, Op. 91, 1813), several early piano sonatas, and a piano concerto of 1784. In the standard thematic catalogue of Beethoven's music, *Das Werk Beethovens* (Munich, 1955), Georg Kinsky and Hans Halm list his Opp. 1–136 followed by 204 works labeled "WoO" (*Werk ohne Opuszahl*—work without opus number); additional material is in *Studien und Materialien zum Werk-verzeichnis von Kinsky-Halm*, ed. Kurt Dorfmüller (Munich: Henle, 1979). A number of additional works are listed in Hess, *Verzeichnis der nicht in der Gesamtausgabe veröffentlichten Werke Ludwig van Beethovens* [Index of Works by Ludwig van Beethoven Not in the Collected Edition] (Wiesbaden, 1957), updated and trans. James F. Green as *The New Hess Catalog of Beethoven's Works* (West Newbury, VT: Vance Brook, 2003).

For Beethoven's letters, see *The Letters of Beethoven*, 3 vols., trans. and ed. Emily Anderson (New York: St.

Martin's, 1961; repr. London: Macmillan, 1985); *Letters to Beethoven and Other Correspondence*, 3 vols., ed. and trans. Theodore Albrecht (Lincoln: University of Nebraska Press, 1996); and *New Beethoven Letters*, ed. MacArdle and Ludwig Misch (Norman: University of Oklahoma Press, 1957).

On Beethoven's autographs, sketches, and sketchbooks, see Douglas Johnson, Alan Tyson, and Robert Winter, *The Beethoven Sketchbooks: History, Reconstruction, and Inventory* (Berkeley: University of California Press, 1985), and Lockwood, *Beethoven: Studies in the Creative Process* (Cambridge, MA: Harvard University Press, 1992). Sketches of a single composition are exhaustively treated in Winter, *Compositional Origins of Beethoven's Opus 131* (Ann Arbor: UMI Research, 1982). An older study, but important because it contains sketches not published elsewhere, including many for the *Eroica* Symphony, is Gustav Nottebohm, *Two Beethoven Sketchbooks*, trans. Jonathan Katz (London: Gollancz, 1979).

CHAPTER 24

The Piano and the Market for Music

On the piano, see chapter 21 above, especially James Parakilas et al., *Piano Roles*. On social and business aspects of music, see *The Early Romantic Era*, ed. Alexander Ringer; Henry Raynor, *Music and Society since 1815*; and Frederic M. Scherer, *Quarter Notes and Bank Notes*, all under Part V above.

Romanticism

John Daverio, *Nineteenth-Century Music and the German Romantic Ideology* (New York: Schirmer, 1993), places music in the context of the Romantic movement in Germany. On the aesthetics of Romanticism and the concept of Romantic Genius, see Charles Rosen, *Romantic Poets, Critics and Other Madmen* (Cambridge, MA: Harvard University Press, 1998). Rosen's *The Romantic Generation* (Cambridge, MA: Harvard University Press, 1995), combines a study of musical forms and styles of composers active in the 1830s with an exploration of the attitudes and literary background of Romanticism. Excerpts from the Romantic writers Jean Paul and Wilhelm Wackenroder appear in SR 148–149 (6:1–2). E. T. A. Hoffmann's famous essay on Beethoven is excerpted in SR 160 (6:13).

On absolute and program music in the nineteenth century, see Daniel K. L. Chua, *Absolute Music and the Construction of Meaning* (Cambridge: Cambridge University Press, 1999); Carl Dahlhaus, *The Idea of Absolute Music*, trans. Roger Lustig (Chicago: University of Chicago Press, 1989); and Berthold Hoeckner, *Programming the Absolute: Nineteenth-Century German Music and the Hermeneutics of the Moment* (Princeton: Princeton University Press, 2002).

The Lied

For overviews of the Lied, see *The Cambridge Companion to the Lied*, ed. James Parsons (Cambridge: Cambridge University Press, 2004), and *German Lieder in the Nineteenth Century*, ed. Rufus Hallmark (New York: Schirmer, 1996). Lawrence D. Snyder, *German Poetry in Song: An Index of Lieder* (Berkeley: Fallen Leaf, 1995), is an index to 9,800 Lieder composed since 1770.

Franz Schubert

Recent studies of Schubert's life and music include Brian Newbould, *Schubert: The Music and the Man* (Berkeley: University of California Press, 1997); John Reed, *Schubert*, 2nd ed. (New York: Oxford University Press, 1997); Elizabeth Norman McKay, *Franz Schubert: A Biography* (Oxford: Clarendon, 1996); and Christopher H. Gibbs, *The Life of Schubert* (Cambridge: Cambridge University Press, 2000), a brief biography. See also *The Cambridge Companion to Schubert*, ed. Gibbs (Cambridge: Cambridge University Press, 1997). Original sources are in *The Schubert Reader: A Life of Franz Schubert in Letters and Documents*, ed. Otto E. Deutsch, trans. Eric Blom (New York: Norton, 1947), and *Schubert: Memoirs by His Friends*, ed. Deutsch (London: A. and C. Black, 1958). John Daverio, *Crossing Paths: Schubert, Schumann, and Brahms* (Oxford: Oxford University Press, 2002), is a study of the connections between art and life of three major Romantic composers.

For general overviews of Schubert's Lieder, see Reed, *The Schubert Song Companion* (New York: Universe, 1985), and Michael Hall, *Schubert's Song Sets* (Aldershot, England: Ashgate, 2003). For the cultural context of Schubert's songs, see Susan Youens, *Schubert's Late Lieder: Beyond the Song Cycle* (New York: Cambridge University Press, 2002), and Lawrence Kramer, *Franz Schubert: Sexuality, Subjectivity, Song* (Cambridge: Cambridge University Press, 1998). Other notable studies include Youens, *Schubert's Poets and the Making of Lieder* (Cambridge: Cambridge University Press, 1996); Richard Kramer, *Distant Cycles: Schubert and the Conceiving of Song* (Chicago: University of Chicago Press, 1994); Marjorie Wing Hirsch, *Schubert's Dramatic Lieder* (Cambridge: Cambridge University Press, 1993); Youens, *Schubert, Die schöne Müllerin* (Cambridge: Cambridge University Press, 1992); and Youens, *Retracing a Winter's Journey: Schubert's Winterreise* (Ithaca, NY: Cornell University Press, 1991). Schubert's manuscript for *Winterreise* is available in facsimile: Franz Schubert, *Winterreise: The Autograph Score*, with an introduction by Youens (New York: Pierpont Morgan Library with Dover, 1989).

On the piano music, consult Charles Fisk, *Returning Cycles: Contexts for the Interpretation of Schubert's Impromptus and Last Sonatas* (Berkeley: University of California Press, 2001).

For Schubert's orchestral and chamber music, see chapter 25.

The modern critical edition of Schubert's collected works is *Neue Ausgabe sämtlicher Werke*, ed. Walther Dürr et al. (Kassel and New York: Bärenreiter, 1964–). An earlier edition is *Kritisch durchgesehene Gesamtausgabe*, ed. Eusebius Mandyczewski et al. (Leipzig: Breitkopf & Härtel, 1888–97; repr. New York: Dover, 1964–69; in miniature format New York: Kalmus, 1971), 21 series in 41 vols., 10 separate *Revisionsberichte*. The Lieder are also published in a complete edition by C. F. Peters in 7 vols. The thematic catalogue is *Schubert: A Thematic Catalogue of His Works* by Deutsch (London: Dent, 1951); rev. and trans. by Dürr et al. as *Franz Schubert: Thematisches Verzeichnis seiner Werke in chronologischer Folge von Otto Erich Deutsch* (Kassel: Bärenreiter, 1978).

Robert Schumann

For an introduction to Schumann's life and work, see Daverio, *Robert Schumann: Herald of a "New Poetic Age"* (New York: Oxford University Press, 1997). Other biographies include Eric Frederick Jensen, *Schumann* (Oxford: Oxford University Press, 2001); Joan Chissell, *Schumann*, 5th ed. (London: Dent, 1989); and Peter Ostwald, *Schumann: The Inner Voices of a Musical Genius* (Boston: Northeastern University Press, 1985). See also Daverio, *Crossing Paths: Schubert, Schumann, and Brahms* (above). On rhythm in Schumann's music, see Harald Krebs, *Fantasy Pieces: Metrical Dissonance in the Music of Robert Schumann* (New York: Oxford University Press, 1999).

Schumann's writings are examined in Leon Plantinga, *Schumann as Critic* (New Haven: Yale University Press, 1967), and excerpts are in SR 157 (6:10), including his famous appreciation of Brahms, "New Paths" (1853). His relationship with Clara Schumann and their lives in music are brought to life in *The Complete Correspondence of Clara and Robert Schumann*, ed. Eva Weissweiler, trans. Hildegard Fritsch and Ronald L. Crawford (New York: P. Lang, 1994–), and *The Marriage Diaries of Robert and Clara Schumann: From Their Wedding Day through the Russia Trip*, ed. Gerd Neuhaus, trans. Ostwald (Boston: Northeastern University Press, 1993).

Studies of Schumann's Lieder include Beate Julia Perrey, *Schumann's Dichterliebe and Early Romantic Poetics: Fragmentation of Desire* (Cambridge: Cambridge University Press, 2002); David Ferris, *Schumann's Eichendorff Liederkreis and the Genre of the Romantic Cycle* (New York: Oxford University Press, 2000); Eric Sams, *The Songs of Robert Schumann*, 3rd ed. (Bloomington: Indiana University Press, 1993); and Rufus Hallmark, *The Genesis of Schumann's Dichterliebe: A Source Study* (Ann Arbor: UMI Research, 1979).

On Schumann's piano music and its intimate association with literature, see Erika Reiman, *Schumann's Piano Cycles and the Novels of Jean Paul* (Rochester, NY: University of Rochester Press, 2004). Nicholas Marston, *Schumann, Fantasie, Op. 17* (Cambridge: Cambridge Uni-

versity Press, 1992), offers an intensive study of an extended work.

For Schumann's orchestral and chamber music, see chapter 25.

The first collected edition was *Robert Schumanns Werke* (Leipzig: Breitkopf & Härtel, 1881–93; repr. in miniature format New York: Kalmus, 1971). A new edition is in progress: *Robert Schumann: Neue Ausgabe sämtlicher Werke*, ed. Akio Mayeda, KlausWolfgang Niemoller, and others (Mainz: Schott, 1991–). For a thematic catalogue, see *Robert Schumann: Thematisches Verzeichnis sämtlicher im Druck erschienenen musikalischen Werke*, ed. Kurt Hoffman and Siegmar Keil, 5th ed. (Hamburg: Schuberth, 1982).

Clara Schumann

See Nancy B. Reich, *Clara Schumann: The Artist and the Woman*, rev. ed. (Ithaca, NY: Cornell University Press, 2001), and Chissell, *Clara Schumann, a Dedicated Spirit: A Study of Her Life and Work* (London: Hamilton, 1983). For her correspondence and diaries with Robert Schumann, see above.

Stephen Foster

On Foster, see Ken Emerson, *Doo-dah!: Stephen Foster and the Rise of American Popular Culture* (New York: Simon & Schuster, 1997), and William W. Austin, *"Susanna," "Jeanie," and "The Old Folks at Home": The Songs of Stephen C. Foster from His Time to Ours*, 2nd ed. (Urbana: University of Illinois Press, 1987). For bibliography, consult Calvin Elliker, *Stephen Collins Foster: A Guide to Research* (New York: Garland, 1988).

Music for Piano

See *Nineteenth-Century Piano Music*, 2nd ed., ed. R. Larry Todd (New York: Routledge, 2004). For piano music by Schubert, Robert Schumann, and Clara Schumann, see above. R. Allen Lott, *From Paris to Peoria: How European Piano Virtuosos Brought Classical Music to the American Heartland* (Oxford: Oxford University Press, 2003), recounts the North American concert tours of legendary pianists such as Leopold de Meyer, Henri Herz, Sigismund Thalberg, Anton Rubinstein, and Hans von Bülow.

Felix Mendelssohn

A magisterial new biography is R. Larry Todd, *Mendelssohn: A Life in Music* (Oxford: Oxford University Press, 2003). Others include Clive Brown, *A Portrait of Mendelssohn* (New Haven: Yale University Press, 2003); Philip Radcliffe, *Mendelssohn*, rev. ed. Peter Ward Jones (Oxford: Oxford University Press, 2000); Peter Mercer-Taylor, *The Life of Mendelssohn* (Cambridge: Cambridge University Press, 2000); and Roger Nichols, *Mendelssohn Remembered* (London: Faber & Faber, 1997), which highlights primary documents. For his correspondence, see *Felix Mendelssohn: A Life in Letters*, ed. Rudolf Elvers, trans. Craig Tomlinson (New York: Fromm International, 1986). *The Cambridge Companion to Mendelssohn*, ed. Mercer-Taylor (New York: Cambridge University Press, 2004), and *The Mendelssohn Companion*, ed. Douglass Seaton (Westport, CT: Greenwood, 2001), include articles on the composer, his times, and his works in individual genres. For bibliography, see John Michael Cooper, *Felix Mendelssohn Bartholdy: A Guide to Research, with an Introduction to Research Concerning Fanny Hensel* (New York: Routledge, 2001).

For Mendelssohn's orchestral and chamber music, see chapter 25.

The modern critical edition is *Leipziger Ausgabe der Werke*, ed. Internationale Felix-Mendelssohn-Gesellschaft (Leipzig: Deutscher Verlag für Musik, 1960–). The first complete works edition was the *Kritisch durchgesehene Ausgabe* (Leipzig: Breitkopf & Härtel, 1874–77; repr. Farnborough, England: Gregg International, 1967; miniature format New York: Kalmus, 1971), 19 series in 35 vols.

Fanny Mendelssohn Hensel

For a biography, see Françoise Tillard, *Fanny Mendelssohn* (Portland, OR: Amadeus, 1996). See also Fanny Mendelssohn Hensel, *The Letters of Fanny Hensel to Felix Mendelssohn*, ed. and trans. Marcia J. Citron (Stuyvesant, NY: Pendragon, 1987). The songs are catalogued in Annette Maurer, *Thematisches Verzeichnis der klavierbegleiteten Sololieder Fanny Hensels* (Kassel: Furore, 1997). For a research guide, see above under Felix Mendelssohn.

Fryderyk Chopin

The standard study is Jim Samson, *Chopin* (New York: Oxford University Press, 1996). Perspectives from his own time are gathered in Pierre H. Azoury, *Chopin through His Contemporaries: Friends, Lovers, and Rivals* (Westport, CT: Greenwood, 1999), and Jean-Jacques Eigeldinger, *Chopin: Pianist and Teacher as Seen by His Pupils*, trans. Krysia Osostowics and Naomi Shohet, ed. Roy Howat (Cambridge: Cambridge University Press, 1987). For Chopin's musical life in Paris and the cultural and social environment of the city, see William Atwood, *The Parisian Chopin* (New Haven: Yale University Press, 1999), and Tad Szulc, *Chopin in Paris: The Life and Times of the Romantic Composer* (New York: Da Capo, 2000). Recent studies of Chopin in his times are in *The Age of Chopin: Interdisciplinary Inquiries*, ed. Halina Goldberg (Bloomington: Indiana University Press, 2004). See also Chopin's *Selected Correspondence*, ed. and trans. A. Hedley (London: Heinemann, 1962).

On Chopin's music, see John S. Rink, *Chopin: The Piano Concertos* (Cambridge: Cambridge University Press, 1997); Jeffrey Kallberg, *Chopin at the Boundaries: Sex,*

History, and Musical Genre (Cambridge, MA: Harvard University Press, 1996); *The Cambridge Companion to Chopin*, ed. Samson (Cambridge: Cambridge University Press, 1992); and *Chopin, Preludes, Op. 28*, Norton Critical Scores, ed. Thomas Higgins (New York: Norton, 1973). For bibliography, see William Smialek, *Frédéric Chopin: A Guide to Research* (New York: Garland, 2000).

The modern critical edition is *Complete Works*, ed. Jan Ekier (Cracow: Polskie Wydawn. Muzyczne, 1967–). The first was his *Werke*, 14 vols. (Leipzig: Breitkopf & Härtel, 1878–80; supplements and reports, 1878–1902), catalogued in *An Annotated Catalogue of Chopin's First Edition*, ed. Christophe Grabowski and John Rink (Cambridge: Cambridge University Press, 2003). For thematic catalogues, see Maurice J. E. Brown, *Chopin: An Index of His Works in Chronological Order*, 2nd ed. (London: Macmillan, 1972), and K. Kobylańska, *Frédéric Chopin: Thematisch-bibliographisches Werkverzeichnis* (Munich: Henle, 1979).

Franz Liszt

The standard biography is Alan Walker, *Franz Liszt*, 3 vols. (Ithaca, NY: Cornell University Press, 1987–97). See also Derek Watson, *Liszt*, rev. ed. (Oxford: Oxford University Press, 2000), and Dana Gooley, *The Virtuoso Liszt* (Cambridge: Cambridge University Press, 2004). On Liszt as a piano teacher and virtuoso, see August Göllerich, *The Piano Master Class of Franz Liszt, 1884–1886: Dairy Notes of August Göllerich*, ed. Wilhelm Jerger and Richard Louis Zimdars; trans. and enlarged by Richard Louis Zimdars (Bloomington: Indiana University Press, 1996).

The Cambridge Companion to Liszt, ed. Kenneth Hamilton (Cambridge: Cambridge University Press, 2004), and *The Liszt Companion*, ed. Arnold Ben (Westport, CT: Greenwood, 2002), include various studies of Liszt and his work in musical and historical context. On the piano music, see Hamilton, *Liszt: Sonata in B Minor* (Cambridge, Cambridge University Press, 1996), and Samson, *Virtuosity and the Musical Work: The Transcendental Studies of Liszt* (New York: Cambridge University Press, 2003). For consideration of Liszt as an important cultural figure, see *Liszt and the Birth of Modern Europe: Music as a Mirror of Religious, Political, Cultural and Aesthetic Transformation*, ed. Michael Saffle and Rossana Dalmonte (Hillsdale, NY: Pendragon, 2003). For bibliography, see Saffle, *Franz Liszt: A Guide to Research*, 2nd ed. (New York: Routledge, 2004).

For Liszt's orchestral music, see chapter 28.

A number of compilations of Liszt's own writings and correspondence are available, including *Selected Letters*, ed. and trans. Adrian Williams (Oxford: Clarendon, 1998), and *An Artist's Journey: Lettres d'un bachelier ès musique, 1835–1841*, trans. Charles Suttoni (Chicago: University of Chicago Press, 1989).

A new scholarly edition of Liszt's works is in progress, as his *Neue Ausgabe sämtlicher Werke*, ed. I. Sulyok et al.

(Kassel and Budapest: Bärenreiter, 1970–). The first critical edition, left incomplete, was his *Musikalische Werke*, 34 vols. (Leipzig: Breitkopf & Härtel, 1907–36; repr. 1967).

Louis Moreau Gottschalk

S. Frederick Starr, *Bamboula!: The Life and Times of Louis Moreau Gottschalk* (New York: Oxford University Press, 1995), is an excellent biography. Gottschalk's memoirs are published as *Notes of a Pianist*, ed. Jeanne Behrend (New York: Knopf, 1964; repr. Da Capo, 1979). For a bibliography, see James E. Perone, *Louis Moreau Gottschalk: A Bio-Bibliography* (Westport, CT: Greenwood, 2002).

CHAPTER 25

Rise of the Classical Repertoire

A seminal article is William Weber, "Mass Culture and the Reshaping of European Musical Taste, 1770–1870," *International Review of the Aesthetics and Sociology of Music* 8 (1977): 5–21; repr. 25 (1994): 175–90. See also Weber, "The Rise of the Classical Repertoire in Nineteenth-Century Orchestral Concerts," in *The Orchestra: Origins and Transformations* (see below), 361–86, and *Music and the Middle Class: The Social Structure of Concert Life in London, Paris, and Vienna between 1830 and 1848*, 2nd ed. (Aldershot: Ashgate, 2004). Lydia Goehr, *The Imaginary Museum of Musical Works: An Essay in the Philosophy of Music* (Oxford: Clarendon, 1992), explores the development of the concept of the musical work, a central part of the idea of musical classics, and its effects on musical culture. Admiration for the great composers of the past—Bach, Handel, Haydn, Mozart, and Beethoven—is evident in the 1841 essay by American Transcendentalist writer Margaret Fuller in SR 150 (6:3).

Orchestral Music

The Orchestra: Origins and Transformations, ed. Joan Peyser (New York: Scribner, 1986; repr. Billboard, 2000), is a useful compendium of articles about the orchestra and orchestral music since the late eighteenth century, including development of instruments, conductors, concert life, and repertoire. For a broad treatment of the symphony in the Romantic era, see D. Kern Holoman, *The Nineteenth-Century Symphony* (New York: Schirmer, 1997). The impact of Beethoven's symphonies on later symphony composers is discussed in Mark Evan Bonds, *After Beethoven: Imperatives of Originality in the Symphony* (Cambridge, MA: Harvard University Press, 1996). On piano concertos, see Stephen D. Lindeman, *Structural Novelty and Tradition in the Early Romantic Piano Concerto* (Stuyvesant, NY: Pendragon, 1999).

Franz Schubert

On the symphonies, see A. Peter Brown, *The Symphonic Repertoire*, vol. 2: *The First Golden Age of the Viennese Symphony: Haydn, Mozart, Beethoven, and Schubert* (Bloomington: Indiana University Press, 2002); Brian Newbould, *Schubert and the Symphony: A New Perspective* (Surbiton, England: Toccata, 1992); and *Schubert, Symphony in B minor ("Unfinished")*, Norton Critical Scores, ed. Martin Chusid (New York: Norton, 1968). See also the bibliography for chapter 24.

Hector Berlioz

Excellent studies of Berlioz's life and works include David Cairns, *Berlioz*, 2 vols. (Berkeley: University of California Press, 2000); Hugh Macdonald, *Berlioz* (New York: Oxford University Press, 2000); and D. Kern Holoman, *Berlioz* (Cambridge, MA: Harvard University Press, 1989). For a shorter introduction, see Peter A. Bloom, *The Life of Berlioz* (Cambridge: Cambridge University Press, 1998). On the music, see Julian Rushton, *The Music of Berlioz* (New York: Oxford University Press, 2001), and *Berlioz, Romeo et Juliette* (New York: Cambridge University Press, 1994); and Daniel Albright, *Berlioz's Semi-operas, Romeo et Juliette and La Damnation de Faust* (Rochester, NY: Rochester University Press, 2001). Other useful books include *The Cambridge Companion to Berlioz*, ed. Bloom (Cambridge: Cambridge University Press, 2000); Rushton, *The Musical Language of Berlioz* (Cambridge: Cambridge University Press, 1983); and Holoman, *The Creative Process in the Autograph Musical Documents of Hector Berlioz, ca. 1818–1840* (Ann Arbor: UMI Research, 1980). For further references, see Jeffrey Langford and Jane Denker Graves, *Hector Berlioz: A Guide to Research* (New York: Garland, 1989), and Michael G. H. Wright, *A Berlioz Bibliography: Critical Writing on Hector Berlioz from 1825 to 1986* (Farnborough: Saint Michael's Abbey, 1988).

A recent translation of Berlioz's treatise on instrumentation and orchestration is *Berlioz's Orchestration Treatise: A Translation and Commentary*, trans. Hugh Macdonald (Cambridge: Cambridge University Press, 2002). Berlioz's critical writings on music are in *Berlioz, Evenings with the Orchestra*, trans. Jacques Barzun, forward by Bloom (Chicago: University of Chicago Press, 1999). His other writings include *The Memoirs of Berlioz*, trans. and ed. David Cairns (New York: Knopf, 2002), and *Selected Letters of Berlioz*, ed. Macdonald and trans. Roger Nichols (New York: Norton, 1997). Writings of Berlioz's contemporaries and colleagues are in Michael Rose, *Berlioz Remembered* (New York: Faber & Faber, 2001).

Berlioz, *Fantastic Symphony*, Norton Critical Scores, ed. Edward T. Cone (New York: Norton, 1971), is a score of the *Symphonie fantastique* with many related sources and articles. See also Brian Richardson, *Berlioz, Symphonie fantastique* (Leeds: Mayflower, 1990). On the symphony's premiere, see Thomas Forrest Kelly, *First Nights: Five Musical Premieres* (New Haven: Yale University Press, 2000), 180–255.

The modern critical edition is *New Berlioz Edition*, ed. Macdonald et al. (Kassel: Bärenreiter, 1967–). An earlier incomplete edition is his *Werke* (Leipzig: Breitkopf & Härtel, 1900–1907; repr. New York: Kalmus, 1971), 9 series in 20 vols. The standard catalogue is Holoman, *Catalogue of the Works of Hector Berlioz* (Kassel: Bärenreiter, 1987).

Felix Mendelssohn and Robert Schumann

For a close look at Mendelssohn's most popular symphony, see John Michael Cooper, *Mendelssohn's "Italian" Symphony* (Oxford: Oxford University Press, 2003). Jon W. Finson, *Robert Schumann and the Study of Orchestral Composition: The Genesis of the First Symphony, Op. 38* (Oxford: Clarendon, 1989), offers a fascinating look at the composition process. See also the bibliography for chapter 24.

Chamber Music

On chamber music by Beethoven, Schubert, Mendelssohn, Robert Schumann, Brahms, and other nineteenth-century composers, see *Nineteenth-Century Chamber Music*, ed. Stephen E. Hefling (New York: Routledge, 2004).

Choral Music

Henry Raynor traces the history of choral societies in "Choral Music in Germany and England," in *Music and Society since 1815* (above under part IV), 86–99. On men's choirs in France, see "Orphéon," in NG2; on men's choirs in Germany, see "Liedertafel," in NG2.

On the nineteenth-century oratorio tradition, see volume 4 of Smither, *A History of the Oratorio* (above under chapter 15). On Mendelssohn's oratorio *Paulus*, see Siegward Reichwald, *The Musical Genesis of Felix Mendelssohn's Paulus* (London: Scarecrow, 2001).

A selection of partsongs can be found in *English Romantic Partsongs*, ed. Paul Hillier (Oxford: Oxford University Press, 1986).

James Garrat, *Palestrina and the German Romantic Imagination: Interpreting Historicism in Nineteenth-Century Music* (Cambridge: Cambridge University Press, 2002), discusses Palestrina's influence on nineteenth-century church music and how his style affected composers of the Romantic era, including Mendelssohn.

The United States

On music in the United States, including early nineteenth-century church music, see especially Richard Crawford, *America's Musical Life: A History* (New York: Norton, 2001); H. Wiley Hitchcock, *Music in the United States: A Historical Introduction*, 4th ed. with Kyle Gann (Upper Saddle River, NJ: Prentice Hall, 2000); *The Cambridge History of American Music*, ed. David Nicholls (Cambridge: Cambridge University Press, 1998); Gilbert Chase, *America's Music: From the Pilgrims to the Present*, 3rd ed. (Urbana: University of Illinois Press, 1987); and Charles Hamm, *Music in the New World* (New York: Nor-

ton, 1983). For New England, see Nicholas E. Tawa, *From Psalm to Symphony: A History of Music in New England* (Boston: Northeastern University Press, 2001).

On the shape-note tradition, see John Bealle, *Public Worship, Private Faith: Sacred Harp and American Folksong* (Athens: University of Georgia Press, 1997), and Buell Cobb, *The Sacred Harp: A Tradition and Its Music* (Athens: University of Georgia Press, 1978). *The Sacred Harp* has appeared in many editions and continues to be revised, most recently in 1991 (Bremen, GA: Sacred Harp, 1991); a modern facsimile is available of the third edition of 1859 (Nashville: Broadman, 1968).

On Lowell Mason, see Carol A. Pemberton, *Lowell Mason: His Life and Work* (Ann Arbor: UMI Research, 1985), and *Lowell Mason: A Bio-Bibliography* (New York: Greenwood, 1988).

CHAPTER 26

Opera

For general works on opera, see chapter 14. Particularly pertinent to this chapter are *The Cambridge Companion to Grand Opera*, ed. David Charlton (New York: Cambridge University Press, 2003); Edward J. Dent, *The Rise of Romantic Opera*, ed. Winton Dean (Cambridge: Cambridge University Press, 1976); and Joseph Kerman, *Opera as Drama*, rev. ed. (Berkeley: University of California Press, 1988). For some provocative recent approaches, see Mary Ann Smart, *Mimomania: Music and Gesture in Nineteenth-Century Opera* (Berkeley: University of California Press, 2004), and Carolyn Abbate, *Unsung Voices: Opera and Musical Narrative in the Nineteenth Century* (Princeton: Princeton University Press, 1991).

For facsimiles of operas by early Romantic composers, see the series *Early Romantic Opera*, ed. Philip Gossett and Charles Rosen (New York: Garland, 1977–).

Italian Opera

See Danièle Pistone, *Nineteenth-Century Italian Opera from Rossini to Puccini*, trans. E. Thomas Glasgow (Portland, OR: Amadeus, 1995), and Charles Osbourne, *The Bel Canto Operas of Rossini, Donizetti, and Bellini* (London: Methuen, 1994). On the business of opera, see John Rosselli, *The Opera Industry in Italy from Cimarosa to Verdi: The Role of the Impresario* (Cambridge: Cambridge University Press, 1984). See also *Italian Opera: 1810–40*, 58 vols., ed. Gossett (New York: Garland, 1986–), for facsimiles of printed editions of complete operas and excerpts by contemporaries of Rossini, Bellini, and Donizetti.

Gioachino Rossini

For biography, see Richard Osborne, *Rossini* (Oxford: Oxford University Press, 2001), and David Mountfield, *Rossini* (New York: Simon & Schuster, 1995). Still of interest is an 1824 book by a hero-worshiping contemporary, Stendhal [Marie Henri Beyle], *Life of Rossini*, trans. Richard N. Coe (Seattle: University of Washington Press, 1972), who gives delightful insights though not accurate information. An appreciative review of Rossini's *William Tell* by Berlioz is in SR 156 (6:9). See also *The Cambridge Companion to Rossini*, ed. Emanuele Senici (Cambridge: Cambridge University Press, 2004); and Denise P. Gallo, *Gioachino Rossini: A Guide to Research* (New York: Routledge, 2002).

The collected edition of Rossini's operas is *Edizione critica delle opere di Gioachino Rossini* (Pesaro: Fondazione Rossini, 1979–). Non-operatic works of Rossini appear in the *Quaderni Rossiniani* (Pesaro: Fondazione Rossini, 1954–).

Vincenzo Bellini

See Rosselli, *The Life of Bellini* (Cambridge: Cambridge University Press, 1996), and Simon Maguire, *Vincenzo Bellini and the Aesthetics of Early Nineteenth-Century Italian Opera* (New York: Garland, 1989).

Bellini's complete works are in Vincenzo Bellini, *Edizione nazionale delle opere, 1801–1835* (Cremona: Fondazione Claudio Monteverdi, 2002–). A useful research tool is Stephen A. Willier, *Vincenzo Bellini: A Guide to Research* (New York: Routledge, 2002).

Gaetano Donizetti

On various aspects of Donizetti's life and works, see William Ashbrook, *Donizetti and His Operas* (Cambridge: Cambridge University Press, 1982); Gossett, *Anna Bolena and the Artistic Maturity of Gaetano Donizetti* (Oxford: Clarendon, 1985); and John Allitt, *Donizetti in the Light of Romanticism and the Teaching of Johann Simon Mayr* (Shaftesbury: Element, 1991). See also James P. Cassaro, *Gaetano Donizetti: A Guide to Research* (New York: Garland, 2000).

The critical edition is Gaetano Donizetti, *Collected Works* (London: Published under the auspices of the Donizetti Society by Egret House, 1973–); see Series I for the operatic works.

French Opera and Ballet

For opera in Revolutionary France, see Emmet Kennedy, *Theatre, Opera, and Audiences in Revolutionary Paris: Analysis and Repertory* (Westport, CT: Greenwood, 1996); and *Music and the French Revolution*, ed. Malcolm Boyd (Cambridge: Cambridge University Press, 1992). For the general history of French opera in the first half of the nineteenth century, see Patrick Barbier, *Opera in Paris, 1800–1850: A Lively History*, trans. Robert Luoma (Portland, OR: Amadeus, 1995), and Anselm Gerhard, *The Urbanization of Opera: Music Theater in Paris in the Nineteenth Century*, trans. Mary Whitall (Chicago: University of Chicago Press, 1998).

On French grand opera, consult Hervé Lacombe, *The Keys to French Opera in the Nineteenth Century*, trans. Edward Schneider (Berkeley: University of California Press, 2001); Jane F. Fulcher, *The Nation's Image: French Grand Opera as Politics and Politicized Art* (Cambridge: Cambridge University Press, 1987); and Mark Everist, *Giacomo Meyerbeer and Music Drama in Nineteenth-Century Paris* (Aldershot: Ashgate, 2004). For *Les Troyens*, see *Hector Berlioz, Les Troyens*, ed. Ian Kemp (Cambridge: Cambridge University Press, 1988).

On French ballet, see Ivor Forbes Guest, *Ballet under Napoleon* (Alton, England: Dance, 2002), and Susan Leigh Foster, *Choreography and Narrative: Ballet's Staging of Story and Desire* (Bloomington: Indiana University Press, 1996).

German Opera

See Warrack, *German Opera*, under chapter 17 above.

Carl Maria von Weber

The standard biography is John H. Warrack, *Carl Maria von Weber*, 2nd ed. (Cambridge: Cambridge University Press, 1976). A new and important study is Stephen C. Meyer, *Carl Maria von Weber and the Search for a German Opera* (Bloomington: Indiana University Press, 2003). See also Weber's *Collected Writings on Music*, trans. Martin Cooper, ed. John H. Warrack (Cambridge: Cambridge University Press, 1981), and Donald G. Henderson, *Carl Maria von Weber: A Guide to Research* (New York: Garland, 1990).

Collected works are in Carl Maria von Weber, *Gesamtausgabe* (Mainz: Schott, 1997–). Thematic catalogue comp. by Friedrich W. Jähns (Berlin: Robert Lienau, 1871; repr. 1967).

The United States

On the history of performing European operas and classical music in the United States, see Joseph Horowitz, *Classical Music in America: A History of Its Rise and Fall* (New York: Norton, 2005); Karen Ahlquist, *Democracy at the Opera: Music, Theater and Culture in New York City, 1825–60* (Urbana: University of Illinois Press, 1997); several of the essays in *Opera and the Golden West: The Past, Present, and Future of Opera in the U.S.A.*, ed. John L. DeGaetani and Josef P. Sirefman (Rutherford, NJ: Fairleigh Dickinson University Press, 1993); John Dizikes, *Opera in America: A Cultural History* (New Haven: Yale University Press, 1993); Katherine K. Preston, *Opera on the Road: Traveling Opera Troupes in the United States, 1825–60* (Urbana: University of Illinois Press, 1993; repr. 2001); Michael Broyles, *Music of the Highest Class: Elitism and Populism in Antebellum Boston* (New Haven: Yale University Press, 1992); and Lawrence W. Levine, *Highbrow/Lowbrow: The Emergence of Cultural Hierarchy in America* (Cambridge, MA: Harvard University Press, 1988). See also Peter G. Davis, *The*

American Opera Singer: The Lives and Adventures of America's Great Singers in Opera and Concert, from 1825 to the Present (New York: Doubleday, 1997).

On all types of American theatrical music, see Julian Mates, *America's Musical Stage: Two Hundred Years of Musical Theatre* (Westport, CT: Greenwood, 1985).

American Opera

On the development of opera by American composers since the nineteenth century, see Elise K. Kirk, *American Opera* (Urbana: University of Illinois Press, 2001), and several essays in *Opera and the Golden West*, ed. DeGaetani and Sirefman.

Minstrel Shows

On minstrelsy, see William J. Mahar, *Behind the Burnt Cork Mask: Early Blackface Minstrelsy and Antebellum American Popular Culture* (Urbana: University of Illinois Press, 1999); Dale Cockrell, *Demons of Disorder: Early Blackface Minstrels and Their World* (Cambridge: Cambridge University Press, 1997); and Robert C. Toll, *Blacking Up: The Minstrel Show in Nineteenth Century America* (New York: Oxford University Press, 1974).

CHAPTER 27

Nationalism

The best overview of nationalism is Richard Taruskin, "Nationalism," in NG2. See also *Musical Constructions of Nationalism: Essays on the History and Ideology of European Musical Culture 1800–1945*, ed. Harry White and Michael Murphy (Cork: Cork University Press, 2001), and Philip V. Bohlman, *The Music of European Nationalism: Cultural Identity and Modern History* (Santa Barbara: ABC-CLIO, 2004).

Giuseppe Verdi

For Verdi's biography, see John Rosselli, *The Life of Verdi* (New York: Cambridge University Press, 2000); Mary Jane Phillips-Matz, *Verdi: A Biography* (New York: Oxford University Press, 1993); and Julian Budden, *Verdi* (London: Dent, 1985). Surveys of his operas include *Verdi and His Operas*, ed. Stanley Sadie (London: Macmillan Reference; New York: St. Martin's, 2000), and Budden, *The Operas of Verdi*, 3 vols. (New York: Praeger, 1973–82). Guides to individual works include David Rosen, *Verdi: Requiem* (Cambridge: Cambridge University Press, 1995); James A. Hepokoski, *Giuseppe Verdi, Otello* (Cambridge: Cambridge University Press, 1987); and Hepokoski, *Giuseppe Verdi, Falstaff* (Cambridge: Cambridge University Press, 1983).

Other useful books: *The Cambridge Companion to Verdi*, ed. Scott L. Balthazar (Cambridge: Cambridge University Press, 2003); Gilles de Van, *Verdi's Theater: Creating Drama through Music*, trans. Gilda Roberts (Chicago:

University of Chicago Press, 1998); *Verdi's Middle Period: Source Studies, Analysis, and Performance Practice*, ed. Martin Chusid (Chicago: University of Chicago Press, 1997); Pierluigi Petrobelli, *Music in the Theater: Essays on Verdi and Other Composers* (Princeton: Princeton University Press, 1994); *Analyzing Opera: Verdi and Wagner*, ed. Carolyn Abbate and Roger Parker (Berkeley: University of California Press, 1989); David Kimbell, *Verdi in the Age of Italian Romanticism* (Cambridge: Cambridge University Press, 1981); *The Verdi Companion*, ed. William Weaver and Chusid (New York: Norton, 1979); and Weaver, *Verdi: A Documentary Study* (London: Thames & Hudson, 1977).

For a bibliography, see Gregory W. Harwood, *Giuseppe Verdi: A Guide to Research* (New York: Garland, 1998).

Verdi's complete works edition is *The Works of Giuseppe Verdi*, ed. Philip Gossett (Chicago: University of Chicago Press; Milan: Ricordi, 1983–).

Verismo

See Carl Dahlhaus, *Realism in Nineteenth-Century Music*, trans. Mary Whittall (Cambridge: Cambridge University Press, 1985), and Matteo Sansone, *Verismo from Literature to Opera* (Edinburgh: University of Edinburgh, 1987).

Giacomo Puccini

See Budden, *Puccini: His Life and Works* (Oxford and New York: Oxford University Press, 2002); Phillips-Matz, *Puccini: A Biography* (Boston: Northeastern University Press, 2002); *Puccini and His Operas*, ed. Sadie (London: Macmillan; New York: St. Martin's, 2000); Mosco Carner, *Puccini: A Critical Biography*, 3rd ed. (New York: Holmes and Meier, 1992); Howard Greenfield, *Puccini* (New York: Putnam, 1980), which contains an extensive bibliography; and William Ashbrook, *The Operas of Puccini* (New York: Oxford University Press, 1968). For programmatic notes on all the operas, with musical examples, see *The Puccini Companion*, ed. William Weaver and Simonetta Puccini (New York: Norton, 1994).

The thematic catalogue is Dieter Schickling, *Giacomo Puccini: Catalogue of the Works* (New York: Bärenreiter, 2003). For bibliography, see Linda B. Fairtile, *Giacomo Puccini: A Guide to Research* (New York: Garland, 1999).

Richard Wagner

Biographical studies include Barry Millington, *The New Grove Wagner* (New York: Palgrave/Grove, 2002); Michael Tanner, *Wagner* (Princeton: Princeton University Press, 1996); Martin Gregor-Dellin, *Richard Wagner*, trans. J. Maxwell Brownjohn (San Diego: Harcourt Brace Jovanovich, 1983); and Derek Watson, *Richard Wagner: A Biography* (New York: Schirmer, 1981). The monumental biography by Ernest Newman, *Life of Richard Wagner*, 4 vols. (London: Cassell, 1933–47; repr. New York: Cambridge University Press, 1976), is still worth consulting.

Useful general studies include *Wagner and His Operas*, ed. Sadie (London: Macmillan; New York: St. Martin's, 2000); Charles Osbourne, *The Complete Operas of Richard Wagner* (New York: Da Capo, 1993); *Wagner Handbook*, ed. Ulrich Müller and Peter Wapnewski, trans. John Deathridge (Cambridge, MA: Harvard University Press, 1992); *The Wagner Companion*, ed. Peter Burbridge and Richard Sutton (Cambridge: Cambridge University Press, 1979); and Carl Dahlhaus, *Richard Wagner's Music Dramas*, trans. Arnold Whittall (Cambridge: Cambridge University Press, 1979). Robert Bailey, *Prelude and Transfiguration from "Tristan and Isolde,"* Norton Critical Scores (New York: Norton, 1985), gives historical background, views and comments, and analytical essays on the work.

Concerning Wagner's anti-Semitism, see Marc A. Weiner, *Wagner and the Anti-Semitic Imagination* (Lincoln: University of Nebraska Press, 1995), and Jacob Katz, *The Darker Side of Genius: Richard Wagner's Antisemitism* (Hanover, NH: University Press of New England, 1986). See also Gottfried Wagner, *Twilight of the Wagners: The Unveiling of a Family's Legacy* (New York: Picador, 1999).

On Wagner's compositional process, see Curt von Westernhagen's *The Forging of the "Ring": Richard Wagner's Composition Sketches for "Der Ring des Nibelungen,"* trans. Arnold and Mary Whittall (Cambridge: Cambridge University Press, 1976); and Warren Darcy, *Wagner's Das Rheingold* (New York: Oxford University Press, 1993).

See also Lawrence Kramer, *Opera and Modern Culture: Wagner and Strauss* (Berkeley: University of California Press, 2004); Joachim Köhler, *Richard Wagner: The Last of the Titans*, trans. Stewart Spencer (New Haven: Yale University Press, 2004); Philip Kitcher and Richard Schacht, *Finding an Ending: Reflections on Wagner's "Ring"* (New York: Oxford University Press, 2004); Fred Brigham, *Wagner and Nineteenth-Century Culture* (Basingstoke: Palgrave Macmillan, 2003); Dieter Borchmeier, *Drama and the World of Richard Wagner*, trans. Daphne Ellis (Princeton: Princeton University Press, 2003); Bryan Magee, *The Tristan Chord: Wagner and Philosophy* (New York: Metropolitan, 2001); and *Analyzing Opera: Verdi and Wagner*, ed. Carolyn Abbate and Roger Parker (Berkeley: University of California Press, 1989).

For a bibliography, see Michael Saffle, *Richard Wagner: A Guide to Research* (New York: Routledge, 2002).

Wagner's writings are published in his *Prose Works*, 8 vols., trans. William Ashton Ellis (London, 1892–99; repr. New York: Broude, 1966); especially relevant are vol. 1 (*Art and Revolution* and *The Artwork of the Future*) and vol. 2 (*Opera and Drama*). Commentary on these is in Dieter Borchmeyer, *Richard Wagner, Theory and Theatre*, trans. Spencer (Oxford: Clarendon, 1991), and Thomas S. Grey, *Wagner's Musical Prose: Text and Contexts* (Cambridge: Cambridge University Press, 1995). An excerpt from *The Artwork of the Future* is in SR 153 (6:6).

Documentary material includes Wagner, *My Life*, ed. Whittall, trans. Andrew Grey (Cambridge: Cambridge University Press, 1983), and Cosima Wagner's *Diaries*, ed. Martin

Gregor-Dellin and Dietrich Mack, trans. Geoffrey Skelton, 2 vols. (New York: Harcourt Brace Jovanovich, 1978–80). Wagner's correspondence is catalogued in *Wagner-Briefe-Verzeichnis: WBV: Chronologisches Verzeichnis der Briefe von Richard Wagner*, ed. Werner Breig, Martin Dürrer, and Andreas Mielke (Wiesbaden: Breitkopf & Härtel, 1998).

A new complete edition of Wagner's is in progress: *Sämtliche Werke*, ed. Dahlhaus et al. (Mainz: B. Schott's Söhne, 1970–). An earlier edition, *Musikalische Werke*, ed. Michael Balling (Leipzig: Breitkopf & Härtel, 1912–29; repr. New York: Da Capo, 1971), was incomplete. The catalogue of works is *Richard Wagner Werk-Verzeichnis: Verzeichnis der musikalischen Werke Richard Wagners und ihrer Quellen*, ed. John Deathridge, Martin Geck, and Egon Voss (Mainz: Schott, 1986).

Charles Gounod

See Stephen Huebner, *The Operas of Charles Gounod* (Oxford: Clarendon; New York: Oxford University Press, 1990), and James Harding, *Gounod* (New York: Stein and Day, 1973).

Georges Bizet

The standard biography in English is Winton Dean, *Georges Bizet, His Life and Work*, 3rd ed. (London: Dent, 1975). Susan McClary, *Georges Bizet: Carmen*, Cambridge Opera Handbooks (New York: Cambridge University Press, 1992), offers insightful views on the opera's portrayal of women and the exotic, among other topics.

Russian Opera

On operas by Glinka and other Russian composers through the 1860s, see Richard Taruskin, *Opera and Drama in Russia as Preached and Practiced in the 1860s* (Ann Arbor: UMI Research, 1981). The influences of Wagner's music and literary writings on generations of Russian musicians and writers are discussed in Rosamund Bartlett, *Wagner and Russia* (Cambridge: Cambridge University Press, 1995). See also items listed under chapter 29, below.

Mikhail Glinka

For biography, see Alexandra Orlova, *Glinka's Life in Music: A Chronicle*, trans. Richard Hoops (Ann Arbor: UMI Research, 1988), and Aleksandr S. Rozanov, *M. I. Glinka: His Life and Times* (Neptune City, NJ: Paganiniana, 1988). See also Glinka's *Memoirs*, trans. R. B. Mudge (Norman: University of Oklahoma Press, 1963).

Piotr Il'yich Tchaikovsky

The most comprehensive biography of Tchaikovsky is by David Brown, in four volumes: *Tchaikovsky: The Early Years, 1840–1874* (New York: Norton, 1978); *The Crisis*

Years, 1874–1878 (1982); *The Years of Wandering, 1878–1885* (1986); and *The Final Years* (1992). See also Edward Garden, *Tchaikovsky* (Oxford: Oxford University Press, 2000); Anthony Holden, *Tchaikovsky: A Biography* (New York: Random House, 1995); and Alexander Poznansky, *Tchaikovsky: The Quest for the Inner Man* (New York: Schirmer, 1991). Primary documents are in *Tchaikovsky: A Self-Portrait*, comp. Alexandra Orlova, trans. R. M. Davison (Oxford: Oxford University Press, 1990), and *Tchaikovsky, Letters to His Family: An Autobiography*, trans. Galina von Meck (New York: Stein & Day, 1981). Other studies include Henry Zajaczkowski, *Tchaikovsky's Musical Style* (Ann Arbor: UMI Research, 1987), and the essays in *Tchaikovsky and His World*, ed. Leslie Kearney (Princeton: Princeton University Press, 1998).

The new critical edition is *P. I. Chaykovsky: Novoye polnoye sobraniye sochineniy* [New Edition of the Complete Works] (Moscow: Muzyka; New York: Schott, 1993–). An older collected works edition is *P. I. Chaykovsky: Polnoye sobraniye sochineniy* [Complete Works], ed. B. V. Asaf'yev and others (Moscow: Gos. muzykal'noe izd-vo, 1940–90). *The Tchaikovsky Handbook: A Guide to the Man and His Music*, comp. Poznansky and Brett Langston (Bloomington: Indiana University Press, 2002), includes a thematic catalogue, catalogues of photographs and letters, autobiography, and bibliography.

Modest Musorgsky

Biographies include Brown, *Musorgsky: His Life and Works* (Oxford: Oxford University Press, 2002), and Caryl Emerson, *The Life of Musorgsky* (Cambridge and New York: Cambridge University Press, 1999). Documents are collected in *The Musorgsky Reader: A Life of M. P. Musorgsky in Letters and Documents*, ed. Jay Leyda and Sergei Bertensson (New York: Norton, 1947; repr. 1970); *Musorgsky Remembered*, comp. and ed. Alexandra Orlova, trans. Véronique Zaytzeff and Frederick Morrison (Bloomington: Indiana University Press, 1991); and Orlova, *Musorgsky's Works and Days*, trans. Roy E. Guenther (Ann Arbor: UMI Research, 1983). Important critical studies are Richard Taruskin, *Musorgsky: Eight Essays and an Epilogue* (Princeton: Princeton University Press, 1993), and Caryl Emerson and Robert William Oldani, *Modest Musorgsky and Boris Godunov: Myths, Realities, Reconsiderations* (Cambridge: Cambridge University Press, 1994).

Nikolai Rimsky-Korsakov

Rimsky-Korsakov's *Principles of Orchestration*, trans. Edward Agate (New York: Dover, 1964), describes his approach, with examples from his own works. His memoirs appear in *My Musical Life*, trans. Judah A. Joffe, 3rd U.S. ed. (London: Faber, 1989); see also *Reminiscences of Rimsky-Korsakov*, ed. V. V. Yastrebtsev, ed. and trans. Florence Jonas (New York: Columbia University Press, 1985). For bibliography, see Gerald R. Seaman, *Nikolai Andreevich Rimsky-Korsakov: A Guide to Research* (New York: Garland, 1988). His works are collected in *Polnoe sobranie sochinenii* [Complete Works] (Moscow: Gos. muzykal'noe izd-vo, 1946–70; individual volumes repr. Melville, NY: Belwin Mills, 1981–84).

Bedřich Smetana

See John Clapham, *Smetana* (London: Dent, 1972), and John Tyrell, *Czech Opera* (Cambridge: Cambridge University Press, 1988). The most complete collected edition is *Studijní vydání del Bedřicha Smetany* [Study Scores of Smetana's Works] (Prague: Museum Bedřicha Smetany, 1940–77).

Antonín Dvořák

The best biography in English is John Clapham's *Antonín Dvořák*, rev. ed. (New York: Norton, 1979). See also Michael B. Beckerman, *New Worlds of Dvořák: Searching in America for the Composer's Inner Life* (New York: Norton, 2003); *Rethinking Dvořák: Views from Five Countries*, ed. David R. Beveridge (Oxford: Clarendon, 1996); *Dvořák and His World*, ed. Michael Beckerman (Princeton: Princeton University Press, 1993); and Dvořák's *Letters and Reminiscences*, ed. Otakar Šourek, trans. Roberta Samsour (Prague: Artia, 1958; repr. New York: Da Capo, 1983).

Dvořák's works are collected in *Kritickévydání podle skladatelova rukopisu* [Critical Edition of the Complete Works] (Prague: Artia, 1955–). Recent catalogues are Peter J. F. Herbert, *Antonín Dvořák: Complete Catalogue of Works* (Tadley: Dvořák Society, 2004), and Jarmil Burghauser and John Clapham, *Thematic Catalogue*, 2nd ed. (Prague: Bärenreiter, Editio Supraphon, 1996).

Operetta

For a general history, see Richard Traubner, *Operetta: A Theatrical History*, rev. ed. (New York: Routledge, 2003). On Strauss, see Camille Crittenden, *Johann Strauss and Vienna: Operetta and the Politics of Popular Culture* (Cambridge: Cambridge University Press, 2000). On Gilbert and Sullivan, see Michael Ainger, *Gilbert and Sullivan: A Dual Biography* (Oxford: Oxford University Press, 2002), and Gayden Wren, *A Most Ingenious Paradox: The Art of Gilbert and Sullivan* (New York: Oxford University Press, 2001). Philip H. Dillard, *Sir Arthur Sullivan: A Resource Book* (Lanham, MD: Scarecrow, 1996), includes work list, bibliography, discography, filmography, and other research aids; see also Dillard's *How Quaint the Ways of Paradox!: An Annotated Gilbert & Sullivan Bibliography* (Metuchen, NJ: Scarecrow, 1991).

CHAPTER 28

Revival of Past Music

Harry Haskell, *The Early Music Revival: A History* (London: Thames & Hudson, 1988), traces the rise of historical concerts and the historical performance movement from its origins through the late twentieth century. On editions, see "Editions, historical," in NG2.

Johannes Brahms

Recommended biographies are Jan Swafford, *Johannes Brahms: A Biography* (New York: Knopf, 1997), and Malcolm MacDonald, *Brahms* (New York: Schirmer, 1990). *A Brahms Reader*, ed. Michael Musgrave (New Haven, CT: Yale University Press, 2000), includes letters, reviews, early biographies, reminiscences, and commentaries from his friends and contemporary critics. See also *Johannes Brahms: His Life and Letters*, ed. Styra Avins, trans. Josef Eisinger and Avins (New York: Oxford University Press, 1997).

On the music, see *The Compleat Brahms: A Guide to the Musical Works of Johannes Brahms*, ed. Leon Botstein (New York: Norton, 1999), and John Daverio, *Crossing Paths: Schubert, Schumann, and Brahms* (Oxford: Oxford University Press, 2002). On developing variation, see Walter Frisch, *Brahms and the Principle of Developing Variation* (Berkeley: University of California Press, 1984), which draws from Arnold Schoenberg's "Brahms the Progressive" and other essays in *Style and Idea* (see under chapter 31). Daniel Beller-McKenna, *Brahms and the German Spirit* (Cambridge, MA: Harvard University Press, 2004), studies the interpretations of nationalism and religion in Brahms's instrumental and vocal works. See also *The Cambridge Companion to Brahms*, ed. Michael Musgrave (New York: Cambridge University Press, 1999), and *Brahms and His World*, ed. Frisch (Princeton: Princeton University Press, 1990).

Studies of Brahms's symphonies include Frisch, *Brahms: The Four Symphonies* (New Yaven: Yale University Press, 2003); A. Peter Brown, *The Second Golden Age of the Viennese Symphony: Brahms, Bruckner, Dvořák, Mahler, and Selected Contemporaries* (Bloomington: Indiana University Press, 2003); Raymond Knapp, *Brahms and the Challenge of the Symphony* (Stuyvesant, NY: Pendragon, 1997); David Brodbeck, *Brahms, Symphony No. 1* (New York: Cambridge University Press, 1997); Reinhold Brinkmann, *Late Idyll: The Second Symphony of Johannes Brahms* (Cambridge, MA: Harvard University Press, 1995); and *Symphony No. 4 in E Minor, Op. 98*, ed. Kenneth Hull, Norton Critical Scores (New York: Norton, 2000). On the finale of the Fourth Symphony, see also Knapp, "The Finale of Brahms's Fourth Symphony: The Tale of the Subject," *19th-Century Music* 13 (Summer 1989): 3–17, and J. Peter Burkholder, "Brahms and Twentieth-Century Classical Music," *19th-Century Music* 8 (Summer 1984): 75–83.

For the other instrumental music, see the relevant chapters in *Nineteenth-Century Chamber Music*, ed. Stephen E. Hefling (New York: Routledge, 2004), and *Nineteenth-Century Piano Music*, ed. Larry Todd, 2nd ed. (New York: Routledge, 2004). For the vocal music, see A. Craig Bell, *Brahms: The Vocal Music* (London: Associated University Press, 1996), and Musgrave, *Brahms, A German Requiem* (New York: Cambridge University Press, 1996).

For bibliography, see Thomas Quigley with Mary I. Ingraham, *Johannes Brahms: An Annotated Bibliography of the Literature from 1982 to 1996 with an Appendix on Brahms and the Internet* (Lanham, MD: Scarecrow, 1998).

Brahms's complete works are in his *Sämtliche Werke*, 26 vols. (Leipzig: Breitkopf & Härtel, 1926–27; repr. Ann Arbor, MI: Edwards, 1949; repr. in miniature format New York: Kalmus, 1970). Thematic catalogue: Donald and Margit McCorkle, *Johannes Brahms: Thematisch-bibliographisches Werkverzeichnis* (Munich: Henle, 1984).

Franz Liszt

See under chapter 24 above. For Liszt's orchestral music, consult Keith Thomas Johns, *The Symphonic Poems of Franz Liszt*, ed. Michael Saffle (Stuyvesant, NY: Pendragon, 1997). For Liszt's views of program music, see SR 158 (6:11); for Eduard Hanslick's argument for a specifically musical beauty, rather than programmaticism, see the excerpt from *On the Musically Beautiful* in SR 162 (6:15).

Anton Bruckner

Derek Watson, *Bruckner* (New York: Oxford University Press, 1996), surveys Bruckner's life and works. Stephen Johnson, *Bruckner Remembered* (Boston: Faber & Faber, 1998), is a psychological biography. Various topics are treated in *The Cambridge Companion to Bruckner*, ed. John Williamson (Cambridge: Cambridge University Press, 2004), and in *Bruckner Studies*, ed. Timothy L. Jackson and Paul Hawkshaw (New York: Cambridge University Press, 1997).

On the symphonies, see Julian Horton, *Bruckner's Symphonies: Analysis, Reception and Cultural Politics* (Cambridge: Cambridge University Press, 2004); Brown, *The Second Golden Age of the Viennese Symphony* ; and Benjamin M. Korstvedt, *Anton Bruckner: Symphony No. 8* (Cambridge: Cambridge University Press, 2000). For Bruckner's wind and choral music, see Keith William Kinder, *The Wind and Wind-Chorus Music of Anton Bruckner* (Westport, CT: Greenwood, 2000).

The critical edition is the *Sämtliche Werke, kritische Gesamtausgabe*, ed. Leopold Nowak (Vienna: Musikwissenschaftlicher Verlag, 1951–). An older collected works edition is *Sämtliche Werke*, 11 vols., ed. R. Haas et al. (Augsburg: B. Filser, 1930–44).

Macmillan, 1993). Watkins, *Pyramids at the Louvre: Music, Culture, and Collage from Stravinsky to the Postmodernists* (Cambridge, MA: Harvard University Press, 1994), places modern music within a broader culture of borrowing, reference, and eclecticism.

Nicolas Slonimsky's *Music since 1900*, 5th ed. (New York: Schirmer, 1994), is a compendium of useful resources, including a timeline of musical events and numerous primary documents; it has been updated by Laura Kuhn, 6th ed. (New York: Schirmer/Gale, 2001). Another timeline is Charles J. Hall's *A Twentieth-Century Musical Chronicle: Events, 1900–1988* (Westport, CT: Greenwood, 1989), updated in Hall, *Chronology of Western Classical Music*, vol. 2: *1901–2000* (New York: Routledge, 2002). *Music of the Twentieth-Century Avant-Garde: A Biocritical Sourcebook*, ed. Larry Sitsky (Westport, CT: Greenwood, 2002), offers resources for research.

Composers' writings and other primary documents are collected in SR2; *Modernism and Music: An Anthology of Sources*, ed. Daniel Albright (Chicago: University of Chicago Press, 2004); *Composers on Modern Musical Culture: An Anthology of Readings on Twentieth-Century Music*, ed. Simms (New York: Schirmer, 1999); and *Contemporary Composers on Contemporary Music*, expanded ed., ed. Elliott Schwartz and Barney Childs with Jim Fox (New York: Da Capo, 1998).

Compositions by twentieth-century women composers are collected in *Contemporary Anthology of Music by Women*, ed. James R. Briscoe (Bloomington: Indiana University Press, 1997).

CHAPTER 30

Recorded Sound

On the history and technology of recorded sound, see Jerome F. Weber, John Borwick, et al., "Recorded sound," in NG2. For a fascinating discussion of its impact on musical life, see Mark Katz, *Capturing Sound: How Technology Has Changed Music* (Berkeley: University of California Press, 2004).

Popular Song and Stage Music

For sources on popular song in the United States, see chapter 29, above, and chapters 32 and 34, below. For English popular song, see Dave Russell, *Popular Music in England, 1840–1914: A Social History* (Montreal: McGill-Queen's University Press, 1987). On musical theater and Broadway, see chapter 32, below.

Music for Silent Films

Mervyn Cooke, "Film music," in NG2, briefly surveys the entire history of film music. The best study of the silent era is Martin Miller Marks, *Music and the Silent Film, Contexts and Case Studies, 1895–1924* (New York and Oxford: Oxford University Press, 1997). See also *The Sounds of Early Cinema*, ed. Richard Abel and Rick Altman (Bloomington: Indiana University Press, 2001). *Film Music 1*, ed. Clifford McCarty (New York: Garland, 1989), includes several chapters on the music of silent films and early cinema. A good research guide is Gillian Anderson, *Music for Silent Films, 1894–1929: A Guide* (Washington, DC: Library of Congress, 1988).

Band Music

For English bands, see Roy Newsome, *Brass Roots: A Hundred Years of Brass Bands and their Music, 1836–1936* (Aldershot: Ashgate: 1998), and *The British Brass Band: A Musical and Social History*, ed. Newsome (Oxford: Oxford University Press, 2000). On bands in the United States, see Frank L. Battisti, *The Winds of Change: The Evolution of the Contemporary American Wind Band/Ensemble and Its Conductor* (Galesville, MD: Meredith Music, 2002), and *The Twentieth Century American Wind Band/Ensemble: History, Development and Literature* (Ft. Lauderdale: Meredith Music, 1995). On Holst, see Jon C. Mitchell, *From Kneller Hall to Hammersmith: The Band Works of Gustav Holst* (Tutzing, Germany: H. Schneider, 1990).

Ragtime

Studies of ragtime include David A. Jasen, *That American Rag: The Story of Ragtime from Coast to Coast* (New York: Schirmer, 2000); *Ragtime: Its History, Composers, and Music*, ed. John Edward Hasse (New York: Schirmer, 1985); and the classic history by Edward A. Berlin, *Ragtime: A Musical and Cultural History* (Berkeley: University of California Press, 1980). On Joplin, see Berlin, *King of Ragtime: Scott Joplin and His Era* (New York: Oxford University Press, 1994), and Susan Curtis, *Dancing to a Black Man's Tune: A Life of Scott Joplin* (Columbia: University of Missouri Press, 1994).

Early Jazz

The detailed and insightful "Jazz" essay by Mark Tucker (text) and Travis Jackson (bibliography), in NG2, is an excellent place to begin any study of jazz. NG2 contains articles on every aspect of jazz, and coverage is even more thorough in its companion, *The New Grove Dictionary of Jazz*, 2nd ed., ed. Barry Kernfeld (New York: Grove's Dictionaries, 2002). Gunther Schuller's classic text, *Early Jazz: Its Roots and Musical Development*, rev. ed. (Oxford: Oxford University Press, 1986), traces the history of jazz from its origins through Duke Ellington. Gary Giddins, *Visions of Jazz* (Oxford: Oxford University Press, 1998), is a comprehensive history of jazz from the early days to modern jazz. Frank Tirro, *Jazz, A History*, 2nd ed. (New York: Norton, 1993), offers a historical survey.

For personal accounts of the history of jazz, see Nat Shapiro and Nat Hentoff, *Hear Me Talkin' to Ya: The Story of Jazz as Told by the Men Who Made It*, 2nd ed. (New York: Dover, 1966). *Keeping Time: Readings in Jazz History*, ed.

Robert Walser (Oxford: Oxford University Press, 1999), is a useful collection of source readings. Based on interviews with Jelly Roll Morton, Alan Lomax's *Mister Jelly Roll: The Fortunes of Jelly Roll Morton, New Orleans Creole and "Inventor of Jazz,"* 3rd ed. (Berkeley: University of California Press, 2001), is a valuable study of Morton and the earliest days of jazz. For more on jazz, see chapter 32.

Modern Music

The view of modern music sketched here was first outlined in J. Peter Burkholder, "Museum Pieces: The Historicist Mainstream in Music of the Last Hundred Years," JM 2 (Spring 1983): 115–34, and "The Twentieth Century and the Orchestra as Museum," in *The Orchestra: Origins and Transformations*, ed. Joan Peyser (New York: Charles Scribner's Sons, 1986; repr. Billboard Books, 2000), 408–33.

Gustav Mahler

Excellent studies of Mahler and his music include Donald Mitchell, *Gustav Mahler: The Early Years*, rev. ed., ed. Paul Banks and David Matthews (Berkeley: University of California Press, 1980); Mitchell, *Gustav Mahler: The Wunderhorn Years* (Boulder, CO: Westview, 1976; repr. Woodbridge: Boydell, 2003); and Henry-Louis de La Grange, *Mahler* (vol. 1, New York: Doubleday, 1973; vols. 2 and 3, Oxford: Oxford University Press, 1984 and 1995). See also Peter Franklin, *The Life of Mahler* (Cambridge: Cambridge University Press, 1997); Kurt Blaukopf, *Mahler: A Documentary Study* (New York: Oxford University Press, 1976); and Deryck Cooke, *Gustav Mahler: An Introduction to His Music* (London: Faber & Faber, 1980).

For detailed studies of Mahler's music, see Raymond Knapp, *Symphonic Metamorphoses: Subjectivity and Alienation in Mahler's Re-cycled Songs* (Middletown, CT: Wesleyan University Press, 2003); Constantin Floros, *Gustav Mahler: The Symphonies* (Portland, OR: Amadeus, 1993); Mitchell, *Gustav Mahler, Songs and Symphonies of Life and Death: Interpretations and Annotations* (Berkeley: University of California Press, 1985); and the essays in *The Mahler Companion*, ed. Mitchell and Andrew Nicholson (Oxford: Oxford University Press, 1999). Studies of individual symphonies include Peter Franklin, *Mahler: Symphony No. 3* (Cambridge: Cambridge University Press, 1991); James L. Zychowicz, *Mahler's Fourth Symphony* (New York: Oxford University Press, 2000); and Robert Samuels, *Mahler's Sixth Symphony: A Study in Musical Semiotics* (Cambridge: Cambridge University Press, 1995).

A critical edition of Mahler's works is in progress, ed. Internationale Gustav Mahler Gesellschaft (Vienna, 1960–).

Richard Strauss

See chapter 28, above. On the operas, see Lawrence Kramer, *Opera and Modern Culture: Wagner and Strauss* (Berkeley: University of California Press, 2004), and

Joanna Bottenberg, *Shared Creation: Words and Music in the Hofmannsthal-Strauss Opera*, with foreword by Steven Paul Scher (New York: P. Lang, 1996).

Claude Debussy

The standard biography in English is Edward Lockspeiser, *Debussy: His Life and Mind*, 2 vols. (New York: Macmillan, 1962–65); a shorter version is *Debussy*, 5th ed. (London: Dent, 1980). See also Roger Nichols, *The Life of Debussy* (Cambridge: Cambridge University Press, 1998), and *Debussy Remembered* (Portland, OR: Amadeus, 1992).

Richard S. Parks, *The Music of Claude Debussy* (New Haven: Yale University Press, 1989), shows Debussy's coordination of changes in pitch collection with figuration, phrasing, and form. Roy Howat, *Debussy in Proportion: A Musical Analysis* (Cambridge: Cambridge University Press, 1983), proposes that proportions, including the Golden Section, are important aspects of Debussy's forms. For more on the music and the composer, see *The Cambridge Companion to Debussy*, ed. Simon Trezise (Cambridge: Cambridge University Press, 2003); *Debussy and His World*, ed. Jane F. Fulcher (Princeton: Princeton University Press, 2001); *Debussy Studies*, ed. Richard Langham Smith (Cambridge: Cambridge University Press, 1997); and Arthur B. Wenk, *Claude Debussy and Twentieth-Century Music* (Boston: Twayne, 1983).

On particular works and genres, see Paul Roberts, *Images: The Piano Music of Claude Debussy* (Portland, OR: Amadeus, 1996); Nichols and Smith, *Claude Debussy, Pelléas et Mélisande* (Cambridge: Cambridge University Press, 1989); David A. Grayson, *The Genesis of Debussy's Pelléas et Mélisande* (Ann Arbor: UMI Research, 1986); Robert Orledge, *Debussy and the Theatre* (Cambridge: Cambridge University Press, 1982); and Debussy, *Prelude to "The Afternoon of a Faun,"* Norton Critical Scores, ed. William W. Austin (New York: Norton, 1970).

For cultural and political background to music in France in Debussy's lifetime, see Fulcher, *French Cultural Politics and Music: From the Dreyfus Affair to the First World War* (New York: Oxford University Press, 1999).

On performance practice, see *Debussy in Performance*, ed. James R. Briscoe (New Haven: Yale University Press, 1999). For bibliography and other aids, see Briscoe, *Claude Debussy: A Guide to Research* (New York: Garland, 1990).

Debussy's essays are published in *Debussy on Music: The Critical Writings of the Great French Composer*, ed. François Lesure, trans. Smith (New York: Knopf, 1977), excerpted in SR 197 (7:28).

Maurice Ravel

Recent biographies include Benjamin Ivry, *Maurice Ravel: A Life* (New York: Welcome Rain, 2000), and Nichols, *Ravel Remembered* (New York: Norton, 1988). *The Cambridge Companion to Ravel*, ed. Deborah Mawer (New York: Cambridge

University Press, 2000), contains many helpful essays. Primary documents appear in *A Ravel Reader: Correspondence, Articles, Interviews*, ed. Arbie Orenstein (New York: Columbia University Press, 1990; repr. Dover, 2003). For bibliography, see Stephen Zank, *Maurice Ravel: A Guide to Research* (New York: Routledge, 2005).

Manuel de Falla

Especially significant are two recent books by Carol A. Hess, *Sacred Passions: The Life and Music of Manuel de Falla* (New York: Oxford University Press, 2005), and *Manuel de Falla and Modernism in Spain, 1898–1936* (Chicago: University of Chicago Press, 2001). See also Nancy Lee Harper, *Manuel de Falla: His Life and Music* (Lanham, MD: Scarecrow, 2005), and Burnett James, *Manuel de Falla and the Spanish Musical Renaissance* (London: Gollancz, 1979). There are two research guides: Harper, *Manuel de Falla: A Bio-bibliography* (Westport, CT: Greenwood, 1998), and Gilbert Chase and Andrew Budwig, *Manuel de Falla: A Bibliography and Research Guide* (New York: Garland, 1985). The thematic catalogue is Antonio Ruiz-Pipó, *Catalogue de l'oeuvre de Manuel de Falla* (Paris: M. Eschig, 1993).

Ralph Vaughan Williams

Biographies include Simon Heffer, *Vaughan Williams* (London: Weidenfeld & Nicolson, 2000); James Day, *Vaughan Williams* (Oxford: Oxford University Press, 1998); Jerrold Northrup Moore, *Vaughan Williams: A Life in Photographs* (Oxford: Oxford University Press, 1992); and Ursula Vaughan Williams, *R.V.W.: A Biography of Ralph Vaughan Williams* (Oxford: Oxford University Press, 1964; repr. 1988). On the music, see Lionel Pike, *Vaughan Williams and the Symphony* (London: Toccata, 2003); Michael Kennedy, *The Works of Ralph Vaughan Williams*, rev. ed. (London: Oxford University Press, 1982); and Kennedy, *A Catalogue of the Works of Ralph Vaughan Williams*, 2nd ed. (Oxford: Oxford University Press, 1996). Vaughan Williams's writings include *National Music and Other Essays*, 2nd ed. (Oxford: Clarendon, 1996), and *The Making of Music* (Ithaca, NY: Cornell University Press, 1955; repr. Westport, CT: Greenwood, 1976).

Gustav Holst

For biography, see Michael Short, *Gustav Holst: The Man and His Music* (Oxford: Oxford University Press, 1990), and Imogen Holst, *Gustav Holst: A Biography*, 2nd ed. (Oxford: Oxford University Press, 1969; repr. 1988). On the music, see A. E. F. Dickinson, *Holst's Music: A Guide*, ed. Alan Gibbs (London: Thames, 1995); Richard Green, *Holst: The Planets* (Cambridge: Cambridge University Press, 1995); Holst, *The Music of Gustav Holst*, 2nd ed. (Oxford: Oxford University Press, 1968); and idem., *A Thematic Catalogue of Gustav Holst's Music* (London: Faber & Faber, 1974).

Leoš Janáček

See Mirka Zemanová, *Janáček* (Boston: Northeastern University Press, 2002); Jaroslav Vogel, *Leoš Janáček: His Life and Works*, rev. ed., ed. Karl Janovicky (New York: Norton, 1981); and Zdenka Janáček, *My Life with Janáček*, ed. and trans. John Tyrrell (London: Faber, 1998). On the operas, see *Janáček's Operas: A Documentary Account*, ed. Tyrrell (Princeton: Princeton University Press, 1992), and Tyrrell, *Leoš Janáček: Kát'a Kabanová* (Cambridge: Cambridge University Press, 1982). The catalogue is Nigel Simeone et al., *Janáček's Works: A Catalogue of the Music and Writings of Leoč Janáček* (Oxford: Clarendon, 1997). The complete works are published (Prague/Kassel: Supraphon/Bärenreiter, 1979–).

Jean Sibelius

The classic biography is Erik Tawastjerna, *Sibelius*, rev. ed., trans. and ed. Robert Layton (London: Faber & Faber, 1976). Other recommended biographies are Guy Rickards, *Jean Sibelius* (London: Phaidon, 1997), and Layton, *Sibelius* (New York: Schirmer, 1993).

The terms "rotational form" and "teleological genesis" are James A. Hepokoski's, from his *Sibelius, Symphony No. 5* (New York: Cambridge University Press, 1993). Other studies include *The Cambridge Companion to Sibelius*, ed. Daniel M. Grimley (Cambridge: Cambridge University Press, 1993); *The Sibelius Companion*, ed. Glenda Dawn Goss (Westport, CT: Greenwood, 1996); and Burnett James, *The Music of Jean Sibelius* (Rutherford, NJ: Fairleigh Dickinson University Press, 1983). For a bibliography, see Glenda Dawn Goss, *Jean Sibelius: A Guide to Research* (New York: Garland, 1998). The thematic catalogue is Fabian Dahlström, *Jean Sibelius: Thematisch-bibliographisches Verzeichnis seiner Werke* (Wiesbaden: Breitkopf & Härtel, 2003).

On Finnish and Scandinavian music in general, see Ruth-Esther Hillila and Barbara Blanchard Hong, *Historical Dictionary of the Music and Musicians of Finland* (Westport, CT: Greenwood, 1997); *Music and Nationalism in 20th-century Great Britain and Finland*, ed. Tomi Mäkelä (Hamburg: Von Bockel, 1997); and Antony Hodgson, *Scandinavian Music: Finland and Sweden* (Rutherford, NJ: Fairleigh Dickinson University Press, 1984).

Sergei Rachmaninov

Biographies include Geoffrey Norris, *Rachmaninoff* (Oxford: Oxford University Press, 2001); Sergei Bertensson and Jay Leyda, *Sergei Rachmaninoff: A Lifetime in Music* (Bloomington: Indiana University Press, 2001); and Barrie Martyn, *Rachmaninoff: Composer, Pianist, Conductor* (Aldershot: Scolar Press, 1990). On the music, see David Butler Cannata, *Rachmaninoff and the Symphony* (Innsbruck: Studien Verlag; Lucca: LIM Editrice, 1999).

Alexander Scriabin

See Faubion Bowers, *Scriabin, A Biography*, 2 vols., rev. ed. (New York: Dover, 1996), and Boris de Schloezer, *Scriabin: Artist and Mystic*, trans. Nicolas Slonimsky (Berkeley: University of California Press, 1987), an account by a friend and relative. On the music, see especially Peter Deane Roberts, *Modernism in Russian Piano Music: Skriabin, Prokofiev, and Their Russian Contemporaries* (Bloomington: Indiana University Press, 1993). James M. Baker, *The Music of Alexander Scriabin* (New Haven: Yale University Press, 1986), offers a theoretical approach and several analyses. The thematic catalogue is Daniel Bosshard, *Thematisch-chronologisches Verzeichnis der musikalischen Werke von Alexander Skrjabin* (Ardez: Ediziun Trais Giats, 2003).

Erik Satie

On Erik Satie as exemplar of the avant-garde, see Alan M. Gillmor, *Erik Satie* (Boston: Twayne, 1988), and "Erik Satie and the Concept of the Avant-Garde," MQ 69 (Winter 1983): 104–19, which draws on Renato Poggioli, *The Theory of the Avant-Garde*, trans. Gerald Fitzgerald (New York: Harper & Row, 1971). See also Steven Moore Whiting, *Satie the Bohemian: From Cabaret to Concert Hall* (Oxford: Oxford University Press, 1999); Orledge, *Satie Remembered*, trans. Nichols (London: Faber & Faber, 1995); Nancy Perloff, *Art and the Everyday: Popular Entertainment and the Circle of Erik Satie* (Oxford: Clarendon, 1991); and Orledge, *Satie the Composer* (Cambridge: Cambridge University Press, 1990).

Satie's writings have been published in *A Mammal's Notebook: Collected Writings of Erik Satie*, ed. Ornella Volta, trans. Antony Melville (London: Atlas, 1996), and *The Writings of Erik Satie*, ed. and trans. Nigel Wilkins (London: Eulenberg, 1980). His *Memoirs of an Amnesiac*, excerpted in SR 208 (7:39), illustrate his satire of convention.

Alternative uses of the term "avant-garde" in music are briefly surveyed in Jim Samson, "Avant garde," in NG2.

Futurism

Luigi Russolo's essay "The Art of Noises: Futurist Manifesto" appears in SR 177 (7:8). See also Marjorie Perloff, *The Futurist Moment: Avant-Garde, Avant Guerre, and the Language of Rupture* (Chicago: University of Chicago Press, 1986).

CHAPTER 31

Modernism in Music

See "Modern Music" under chapter 30, above. Joseph N. Straus, *Remaking the Past: Music Modernism and the Influence of the Tonal Tradition* (Cambridge, MA: Harvard University Press, 1990), discusses the music of five of the composers in this chapter in terms of their competition

with the past. See also Leon Botstein, "Modernism," in NG2.

The best introduction to set theory, used for analyzing atonal works by the composers featured in this chapter and many others, is Straus, *Introduction to Post-Tonal Theory*, 2nd ed. (Englewood Cliffs, NJ: Prentice Hall, 2000). The seminal work is Allen Forte, *The Structure of Atonal Music* (New Haven: Yale University Press, 1973).

Arnold Schoenberg

For a short biography, see Charles Rosen, *Arnold Schoenberg* (Chicago: University of Chicago Press, 1996). A classic biography is Willi Reich, *Schoenberg: A Critical Biography*, trans. Leo Black (New York: Praeger, 1971; repr. Da Capo, 1981).

Important studies of the man and his music include Bryan R. Simms, *The Atonal Music of Arnold Schoenberg, 1908–1923* (New York: Oxford University Press, 2000); Walter Frisch, *The Early Works of Arnold Schoenberg, 1893–1908* (Berkeley: University of California Press, 1993); Ethan Haimo, *Schoenberg's Serial Odyssey: The Evolution of His Twelve-Tone Method, 1914–1928* (Oxford: Clarendon, 1990); Alexander L. Ringer, *Arnold Schoenberg: The Composer as Jew* (Oxford: Clarendon, 1990); Carl Dahlhaus, *Schoenberg and the New Music*, trans. Derrick Puffett and Alfred Clayton (Cambridge: Cambridge University Press, 1987); and Joan A. Smith, *Schoenberg and His Circle: A Viennese Portrait* (New York: Schirmer, 1986).

Insightful essays and other useful materials can be found in *Schoenberg and His World*, ed. Frisch (Princeton: Princeton University Press, 1999); *Schoenberg, Berg, and Webern: A Companion to the Second Viennese School*, ed. Simms (Westport, CT: Greenwood, 1999); *The Arnold Schoenberg Companion*, ed. Walter B. Bailey (Westport, CT: Greenwood, 1998); and *Constructive Dissonance: Arnold Schoenberg and the Transformations of Twentieth-Century Culture*, ed. Juliane Brand and Christopher Hailey (Berkeley: University of California Press, 1997). For *Pierrot lunaire*, see Jonathan Dunsby, *Schoenberg, Pierrot lunaire* (Cambridge: Cambridge University Press, 1992). Theodor W. Adorno, *Philosophy of Modern Music*, trans. Anne G. Mitchell and Wesley V. Blomster (New York: Seabury, 1973; repr. Continuum, 2003), argues that Schoenberg's music is a true (and Stravinsky's a false) reflection of modern times.

Schoenberg's most influential essays appear in the collection *Style and Idea: Selected Writings of Arnold Schoenberg*, ed. Leonard Stein, trans. Black (New York: St. Martins, 1975; repr. Berkeley: University of California Press, 1984). His "Composition with Twelve Tones" is excerpted in SR 181 (7:12). Other theoretical writings include *Theory of Harmony*, trans. Roy E. Carter (Berkeley: University of California Press, 1978); *The Musical Idea and the Logic, Technique, and Art of Its Presentation*, ed. and trans. Patricia Carpenter and Severine Neff (New York:

Columbia University Press, 1995); and *Coherence, Counterpoint, Instrumentation, Instruction in Form*, ed. Neff, trans. Charlotte M. Cross and Neff (Lincoln: University of Nebraska Press, 1994). Writings, paintings, and other documents are collected in *A Schoenberg Reader: Documents of a Life*, ed. Joseph Auner (New Haven: Yale University Press, 2003). For correspondence, see his *Letters*, ed. Erwin Stein, trans. Eithne Wilkins and Ernst Kaiser (London: Faber & Faber, 1964; repr. Berkeley: University of California Press, 1987); *The Berg-Schoenberg Correspondence*, ed. and trans. Brand, Hailey, and Donald Harris (New York: Norton, 1987); and two letters in SR 170 (7:1).

The complete works appear in *Sämtliche Werke*, ed. Josef Rufer and Dahlhaus (Mainz: B. Schott; Vienna: Universal, 1966–85). For catalogues, see *Arnold Schönberg: Catalogue Raisonné* (Vienna: Arnold Schönberg Center, 2005), and Rufer, *The Works of Arnold Schoenberg: A Catalogue of His Compositions, Writings, and Paintings*, trans. Dika Newlin (London: Faber & Faber, 1962).

Alban Berg

For a biography, see Mosco Carner, *Alban Berg: The Man and the Work*, 2nd ed. (New York: Holmes & Meier, 1983). On the operas, see Patricia Hall, *A View of Berg's Lulu through the Autograph Sources* (Berkeley: University of California Press, 1996); Douglas Jarman, *Alban Berg, Lulu* (Cambridge: Cambridge University Press, 1991), and *Alban Berg, Wozzeck* (Cambridge: Cambridge University Press, 1989); George Perle, *The Operas of Alban Berg*, 2 vols. (Berkeley: University of California Press, 1980–85); and Janet Schmalfeldt, *Berg's Wozzeck: Harmonic Language and Dramatic Design* (New Haven: Yale University Press, 1983). Other studies include *Schoenberg, Berg, and Webern: A Companion to the Second Viennese School*, ed. Simms; *The Cambridge Companion to Berg*, ed. Anthony Pople (Cambridge: Cambridge University Press, 1997); Dave Headlam, *The Music of Alban Berg* (New Haven: Yale University Press, 1996); *Alban Berg: Historical and Analytical Perspectives*, ed. David Gable and Robert P. Morgan (Oxford: Clarendon, 1991); Adorno, *Alban Berg, Master of the Smallest Link*, trans. Brand and Hailey (Cambridge: Cambridge University Press, 1991); Pople, *Berg, Violin Concerto* (Cambridge: Cambridge University Press, 1991); *The Berg Companion*, ed. Jarman (Boston: Northeastern University Press, 1990); and Jarman, *The Music of Alban Berg* (Berkeley: University of California Press, 1979). See also *The Berg-Schoenberg Correspondence*, and Simms, *Alban Berg: A Guide to Research* (New York: Garland, 1996).

Anton Webern

The standard biography is Hans and Rosaleen Moldenhauer, *Anton von Webern* (New York: Knopf, 1979). Recent shorter biographies are Kathryn Bailey, *The Life of Webern* (Cambridge: Cambridge University Press, 1998), and Malcolm Hayes, *Anton von Webern* (London: Phaidon, 1995). Studies of the music include Kathryn Bailey, *The Twelve-Note Music of Anton Webern: Old Forms in a New Language* (Cambridge: Cambridge University Press, 2004); Julian Johnson, *Webern and the Transformation of Nature* (Cambridge: Cambridge University Press, 1999); *Schoenberg, Berg, and Webern: A Companion to the Second Viennese School*, ed. Simms; and Forte, *The Atonal Music of Anton Webern* (New Haven: Yale University Press, 1998).

Webern's lectures on the evolution of music, which argue that twelve-tone music is the inevitable result of historical development, are collected in *The Path to New Music*, trans. Black (Bryn Mawr, PA: Theodore Presser, 1963). For a research guide, see Zoltan Roman, *Anton von Webern: An Annotated Bibliography* (Detroit: Information Coordinators, 1983).

Igor Stravinsky

Biographical studies include Stephen Walsh, *The New Grove Stravinsky* (New York: Grove, 2002); Charles M. Joseph, *Stravinsky Inside Out* (New Haven: Yale University Press, 2001); Walsh, *Stravinsky: A Creative Spring: Russia and France, 1882–1934* (New York: Knopf, 1999); Michael Oliver, *Igor Stravinsky* (London: Phaidon, 1995); Mikhail S. Druskin, *Igor Stravinsky: His Life, Works, and Views*, trans. Martin Cooper (Cambridge: Cambridge University Press, 1983); and Eric Walter White, *Stravinsky: The Composer and His Works*, 2nd ed. (Berkeley: University of California Press, 1979). See also Vera Stravinsky and Robert Craft, *Stravinsky in Pictures and Documents* (New York: Simon & Schuster, 1978).

Richard Taruskin, *Stravinsky and the Russian Traditions: A Biography of the Works through Mavra* (Berkeley: University of California Press, 1996), is the most comprehensive and important study of Stravinsky's development, tracing the salient characteristics of his music to their origins in his Russian background. On *The Rite of Spring*, see Peter Hill, *Stravinsky: The Rite of Spring* (Cambridge: Cambridge University Press, 2000); Pieter van den Toorn, *Stravinsky and "The Rite of Spring": The Beginnings of a Musical Language* (Berkeley: University of California Press, 1987); and Forte, *The Harmonic Organization of "The Rite of Spring"* (New Haven: Yale University Press, 1978). The premiere of *The Rite of Spring* is described in Thomas Forrest Kelly, *First Nights: Five Musical Premieres* (New Haven: Yale University Press, 2000), 256–359.

Other significant recent books on the music include *The Cambridge Companion to Stravinsky*, ed. Jonathan Cross (Cambridge: Cambridge University Press, 2003); Charles M. Joseph, *Stravinsky and Balanchine: A Journey of Invention* (New Haven: Yale University Press, 2002); Maureen A. Carr, *Multiple Masks: Neoclassicism* in *Stravinsky's Works on Greek Subjects* (Lincoln: University of Nebraska Press, 2002); Joseph N. Straus, *Stravinsky's Late Music* (New York: Cambridge University Press, 2001); Cross, *The Stravinsky Legacy* (New York: Cambridge University Press, 1998); Louis Andreissen, *The Apollonian Clockwork: On Stravinsky* (Oxford: Oxford University Press, 1989); *Stravinsky Retrospectives*, ed. Ethan Haimo and Paul Johnson (Lincoln: University of Nebraska Press, 1987); *Confronting Stravinsky: Man, Musician, and Modernist*, ed. Jann Pasler (Berkeley: University of California Press, 1986); van den Toorn, *The Music of Igor Stravinsky* (New Haven: Yale University Press, 1983); and Paul Griffiths, *Igor Stravinsky, The Rake's Progress* (New York: Cambridge University Press, 1982).

Stravinsky's writings, even when credited to him alone, were almost always the result of collaboration (some would say ghost-writing). These include *An Autobiography* (New York, 1936; repr. Norton, 1962); *Poetics of Music in the Form of Six Lessons*, trans. Arthur Knodel and Ingolf Dahl (Cambridge, MA: Harvard University Press, 1970), excerpted in SR 172 (7:3); and a series of books with his assistant Robert Craft, which contain many penetrating observations on music and musicians in the twentieth century: *Conversations with Igor Stravinsky* (Garden City, NY: Doubleday, 1959); *Memories and Commentaries* (Garden City, NY: Doubleday, 1960; repr. Berkeley: University of California Press, 1981); *Expositions and Developments* (Garden City, NY: Doubleday, 1962); *Themes and Episodes* (New York: Knopf, 1966); *Dialogues and a Diary* (New York: Knopf, 1968; rev. ed. as *Dialogues*, Berkeley: University of California Press, 1982); and *Retrospectives and Conclusions* (New York: Knopf, 1969).

Béla Bartók

The standard biography is Halsey Stevens, *The Life and Music of Béla Bartók*, 3rd rev. ed., ed. Malcolm Gillies (New York: Oxford University Press, 1993). Others include Benjamin Suchoff, *Béla Bartók: Life and Work* (Lanham, MD: Scarecrow, 2001); Kenneth Chalmers, *Béla Bartók* (London: Phaidon, 1995); and Paul Griffiths, *Bartók* (London: Dent, 1984). See also Gillies, *Bartók Remembered* (London: Faber, 1990; New York: Norton, 1991).

On the music and the career, see Suchoff, *Bartók's Mikrokosmos: Genesis, Pedagogy, and Style* (Lanham, MD: Scarecrow, 2002); *The Cambridge Companion to Bartók*, ed. Amanda Bayley (Cambridge: Cambridge University Press, 2001); *Bartók Perspectives: Man, Composer and Ethnomusicologist*, ed. Elliott Antokoletz, Victoria Fischer, and Suchoff (Oxford: Oxford University Press, 2000); Judit Frigyesi, *Béla Bartók and Turn-of-the-Century Budapest* (Berkeley: University of California Press, 1998); László Somfai, *Béla Bartók: Composition, Concepts, and Autograph Sources* (Berkeley: University of California Press, 1996); *Bartók and His World*, ed. Peter Laki (Princeton: Princeton University Press, 1995); *The Bartók Companion*, ed. Gillies (London: Faber, 1993); Paul Wilson, *The Music of Béla Bartók* (New Haven: Yale University Press, 1992); Ernö Lendvai, *Béla Bartók: An Analysis of His Music* (London: Kahn & Averill, 1991); Antokoletz, *The Music of Béla Bartók: A Study of Tonality and Progression in 20th-Century Music* (Berkeley: University of California Press, 1984); and Lendvai, *The Workshop of Bartók and Kodály* (Budapest: Editio Musica, 1983).

Bartók's own writings are collected in *Béla Bartók Essays*, ed. Suchoff (Lincoln: University of Nebraska Press, 1976; repr. 1993). Two essays on the use of folk music in modern art music appear in SR 198 (7:29). For a bibliography, see Antokoletz, *Béla Bartók: A Guide to Research*, 2nd ed. (New York: Garland, 1997).

Charles Ives

The best and most comprehensive biography is Jan Swafford, *Charles Ives: A Life with Music* (New York: Norton, 1996). Stuart Feder, *The Life of Charles Ives* (Cambridge and New York: Cambridge University Press, 1999), is a short biography, and his earlier *Charles Ives, "My Father's Song": A Psychoanalytic Biography* (New Haven: Yale University Press, 1992) focuses on Ives's relationship with his musician father. Vivian Perlis, *Charles Ives Remembered: An Oral History* (New Haven: Yale University Press, 1974; repr. Urbana: University of Illinois Press, 2002), gathers reminiscences of Ives by friends and associates.

On Ives's use of borrowed music, see J. Peter Burkholder, *All Made of Tunes: Charles Ives and the Uses of Musical Borrowing* (New Haven: Yale University Press, 1995). Ives's sources are collected in Clayton Henderson, *The Charles Ives Tunebook* (Warren, MI: Harmonie Park, 1990). On his use of stylistic heterogeneity, see Larry Starr, *A Union of Diversities: Style in the Music of Charles Ives* (New York: Schirmer, 1992). On his career as an organist and its influence on his music, see Burkholder, "The Organist in Ives," JAMS 55 (Summer 2002): 255–310.

Other studies of Ives and his music include Timothy A. Johnson, *Baseball and the Music of Charles Ives: A Proving Ground* (Lanham, MD: Scarecrow, 2004); Philip Lambert, *The Music of Charles Ives* (New Haven: Yale University Press, 1997); *Charles Ives and His World*, ed. Burkholder (Princeton: Princeton University Press, 1996); *Charles Ives and the Classical Tradition*, ed. Geoffrey Block and Burkholder (New Haven: Yale University Press, 1996); Block, *Ives, Concord Sonata: Piano Sonata No. 2 ("Concord, MA, 1840–1860")* (Cambridge: Cambridge University Press, 1996); David Michael Hertz, *Angels of Reality: Emersonian Unfoldings in Wright, Stevens, and Ives* (Carbondale and Edwardsville: Southern Illinois University Press, 1993); Burkholder, *Charles Ives: The Ideas behind the Music* (New Haven: Yale University Press, 1985); MacDonald Smith Moore, *Yankee Blues: Musical Culture and American Identity* (Bloomington:

Indiana University Press, 1985); H. Wiley Hitchcock, *Ives* (London: Oxford University Press, 1977); and *An Ives Celebration*, ed. Hitchcock and Vivian Perlis (Urbana: University of Illinois Press, 1977). David Nicholls, *American Experimental Music, 1890–1940* (Cambridge: Cambridge University Press, 1990), places Ives at the beginning of the experimental music tradition in the United States.

Ives's writings are collected in *Essays Before a Sonata, The Majority, and Other Writings*, ed. Howard Boatwright (New York: Norton, 1970), and *Memos*, ed. John Kirkpatrick (New York: Norton, 1972). The brief essay "Music and Its Future" appears in SR 178 (7:9).

The standard catalogue of Ives's music is James B. Sinclair, *A Descriptive Catalogue of the Music of Charles Ives* (New Haven: Yale University Press, 1999). For research guides, see Gayle Sherwood, *Charles Ives: A Guide to Research* (New York: Routledge, 2002), and Block, *Charles Ives: A Bio-Bibliography* (New York: Greenwood, 1988).

CHAPTER 32

Musical Theater and Popular Song

Joseph Swain, *The Broadway Musical: A Critical and Musical Survey*, 2nd ed. (Lanham, MD: Scarecrow, 2002), offers an overview that spans the century, and Geoffrey Block surveys fourteen musicals in *Enchanted Evenings: The Broadway Musical from "Showboat" to Sondheim* (New York: Oxford University Press, 1997). See also Raymond Knapp, *The American Musical and the Formation of National Identity* (Princeton: Princeton University Press, 2005), and *The Cambridge Companion to the Musical*, ed. Walter A. Everett and Paul R. Laird (New York: Cambridge University Press, 2002).

Two good surveys of American popular song in the first half of the twentieth century are William Hyland, *The Song Is Ended: Songwriters and American Music, 1900–1950* (New York: Oxford University Press, 1995), and Alec Wilder, *American Popular Song: The Great Innovators, 1900–1950* (New York: Oxford University Press, 1972). Jeffrey Melnick, *A Right to Sing the Blues: African Americans, Jews, and American Popular Song* (Cambridge, MA: Harvard University Press, 1999), examines the role of ethnicity in the construction of Tin Pan Alley and American popular song styles. In a similar vein, see Jack Gottlieb, *Funny It Doesn't Sound Jewish: How Yiddish Songs and Synagogue Melodies Influenced Tin Pan Alley, Broadway and Hollywood* (Albany: University of New York in association with the Library of Congress, 2004). Philip Furia, *The Poets of Tin Pan Alley: A History of America's Great Lyricists* (Oxford: Oxford University Press, 1990), is a valuable study of lyricists. For analysis of popular songs from this era, see Allen Forte, *Listening to Classic American Popular Songs* (New Haven: Yale University Press, 2001), and *The American Popular Ballad of the Golden Era, 1924–1950* (Princeton: Princeton

University Press, 1995). See also general studies under chapter 29, above, and under "Popular Song" in chapter 34, below.

For Jerome Kern, see the definitive biography by Gerald Boardman, *Jerome Kern: His Life and Music*, 3rd ed. (New York: Oxford University Press, 2000), and Miles Kreuger, *Show Boat: The Story of a Classic American Musical* (New York: Oxford University Press, 1977). Of the dozens of biographies of Irving Berlin, a good place to start is with Laurence Bergreen's *As Thousands Cheer: The Life of Irving Berlin* (New York: Viking, 1990). The best study of Berlin's early Tin Pan Alley style is Charles Hamm's *Irving Berlin: Songs from the Melting Pot, The Formative Years, 1907–1914* (Oxford: Oxford University Press, 1997). For Cole Porter, see William McBrien, *Cole Porter: A Biography* (New York: Knopf, 1998).

Blues

Paul Oliver's "Blues," in NG2, is an excellent place to start. Oliver's *Blues Fell this Morning: Meaning in the Blues*, 2nd ed. (Cambridge: Cambridge University Press, 1990), provides careful textual interpretation, and he has edited an important collection of essays, *Yonder Come the Blues: The Evolution of a Genre* (Cambridge: Cambridge University Press, 2001). See also Oliver's history, *The Story of the Blues*, new ed. (Boston: Northeastern University Press, 1998).

On women blues singers, see Buzzy Jackson, *A Bad Woman Feeling Good: Blues and the Women Who Sing Them* (New York: Norton, 2005), and Daphne Duval Harrison, *Black Pearls: Blues Queens of the 1920s* (New Brunswick, NJ: Rutgers University Press, 1988). W. C. Handy offers his own take on the provenance of the blues in *Father of the Blues: An Autobiography*, ed. Arna Bontemps (New York: Collier, 1970). Other good resources include *The Blues Encyclopedia*, ed. Edward Komara and Peter Lee (London: Routledge, 2004), and *The Cambridge Companion to Blues and Gospel Music*, ed. Allan Moore (Cambridge: Cambridge University Press, 2002).

Jazz in the 1920s

See under "Early Jazz" in chapter 30. Among the best sources on Louis Armstrong are Joshua Berrett, *Louis Armstrong and Paul Whiteman: Two Kings of Jazz* (New Haven: Yale University Press, 2004); Gary Giddins, *Satchmo* (New York: Doubleday, 1988); and Michael Meckna, *Satchmo: The Louis Armstrong Encyclopedia* (Westport, CT: Greenwood, 2004). Writings about Armstrong are collected in *The Louis Armstrong Companion: Eight Decades of Commentary*, ed. Joshua Berrett (New York: Schirmer, 1999), and his own perspective is available in *Louis Armstrong, In His Own Words: Selected Writings*, ed. Thomas Brothers (Oxford: Oxford University Press, 1999).

Big Bands

Gunther Schuller followed his study of early jazz with *The Swing Era: The Development of Jazz, 1930–1945* (Oxford: Oxford University Press, 1989). David W. Stowe, *Swing Changes: Big-Band Jazz in New Deal America* (Cambridge, MA: Harvard University Press, 1994), places the music in historical context. Jeffrey Magee, *The Uncrowned King of Swing: Fletcher Henderson and Big Band Jazz* (New York: Oxford University Press, 2005), sheds new light on Henderson's role in early jazz and the development of swing.

George Gershwin

Recent biographies include William G. Hyland, *George Gershwin: A New Biography* (Westport, CT: Praeger, 2003); Rodney Greenberg, *George Gershwin* (London: Phaidon, 1998); Joan Peyser, *The Memory of All That: The Life of George Gershwin* (New York: Simon & Schuster, 1993); and Edward Jablonski, *Gershwin* (New York: Doubleday, 1987). The essays in *The Gershwin Style: New Looks at the Music of George Gershwin*, ed. Wayne Schneider (New York: Oxford University Press, 1999), offer fresh insights and analysis of Gershwin's life and music. Gershwin's collaboration with his lyricist brother Ira was a key aspect of his songwriting, treated in Deena Rosenberg, *Fascinating Rhythm: The Collaboration of George and Ira Gershwin* (New York: Dutton, 1991).

Chapter 6 of Richard Crawford's *The American Musical Landscape* (Berkeley: University of California Press, 1993), traces the history and legacy of "I Got Rhythm." On Gershwin's music, see also David Schiff, *Gershwin, Rhapsody in Blue* (Cambridge: Cambridge University Press, 1997), and Steven E. Gilbert, *The Music of Gershwin* (New Haven: Yale University Press, 1995).

Collected writings by Gershwin, his family members, friends, and critics appear in *The George Gershwin Reader*, ed. Robert Wyatt and John Andrew Johnson (New York: Oxford University Press, 2004). Contemporary views of Gershwin, including Gershwin's own "The Composer in the Machine Age," are gathered in *George Gershwin*, ed. Merle Armitage (New York: Longmans, Green, 1938; repr. Da Capo, 1995). A good research guide is Norbert Carnovale, *George Gershwin: A Bio-Bibliography* (Westport, CT: Greenwood, 2000).

Jazz in Europe

Tyler Edward Stovall, *Paris Noir: African Americans in the City of Light* (Boston: Houghton Mifflin, 1996), includes compelling accounts of the interchange between American and European jazz musicians. For jazz's influence in Germany, see *Jazz & the Germans: Essays on the Influence of "Hot" American Idioms on the 20th-Century German Music*, ed. Michael J. Budds (Hillsdale, NY: Pendragon, 2002).

Duke Ellington

John Edward Hasse, *Beyond Category: The Life and Genius of Duke Ellington* (New York: Simon & Schuster, 1993), is the best all-around biography, but the best study of Ellington's early career is Mark Tucker's *Ellington: The Early Years* (Urbana: University of Illinois Press, 1991). *Duke Ellington in Person: An Intimate Memoir*, by Mercer Ellington with Stanley Dance (Boston: Houghton Mifflin, 1978), offers a personal view by his son, who succeeded him as leader of the Ellington Band. An important collection of writings by and about Ellington is *The Duke Ellington Reader*, ed. Mark Tucker (Oxford: Oxford University Press, 1993). See also Ellington's autobiography, *Music Is My Mistress* (Garden City, NY: Doubleday, 1973).

Film Music

Useful resources on film music of this and later periods include Mervyn Cooke, "Film music," in NG2; Larry M. Timm, *The Soul of Cinema: An Appreciation of Film Music* (Upper Saddle River, NJ: Prentice Hall, 2003); *Movie Music: The Film Reader*, ed. Kay Dickinson (New York: Routledge, 2003); *Music and Cinema*, ed. James Buhler, Caryl Flinn, and David Neumeyer (Hanover, NH: University Press of New England, 2000); Laurence E. MacDonald, *The Invisible Art of Film Music: A Comprehensive History* (New York: Ardsley House, 1998); Gary Marmorstein, *Hollywood Rhapsody: Movie Music and Its Makers, 1900 to 1975* (New York: Schirmer, 1997); George Burt, *The Art of Film Music* (Boston: Northeastern University Press, 1994); Michael Chion, *Audio-Vision: Sound on Screen* (New York: Columbia University Press, 1994); Roy M. Prendergast, *Film Music: A Neglected Art*, 2nd ed. (New York: Norton, 1992); Kathryn Kalinak, *Settling the Score: Music and the Classic Hollywood Film* (Madison: University of Wisconsin Press, 1992); William Darby and Jack Du Bois, *American Film Music: Major Composers, Techniques, Trends, 1915–1990* (Jefferson, NC: McFarland, 1990); and an early classic, Claudia Gorbman, *Unheard Melodies: Narrative Film Music* (Bloomington: Indiana University Press, 1987).

CHAPTER 33

France

On constructions of neoclassicism in France, see Jane F. Fulcher, "The Composer as Intellectual: Ideological Inscriptions in French Interwar Neoclassicism," JM 17 (Spring 1999): 197–230, and Scott Messing, *Neoclassicism in Music: From the Genesis of the Concept through the Schoenberg/Stravinsky Polemic* (Ann Arbor: UMI Research, 1988). For musical culture between the wars, see Fulcher, *The Composer as Intellectual: Music and Ideology in France 1914–1940* (New York: Oxford University Press, 2005), and James Harding, *The Ox on the Roof: Scenes from Musical Life in Paris in the Twenties* (London: Macdonald, 1972).

Arthur Honegger

Studies of Honegger include Harry Halbreich, *Arthur Honegger*, trans. Roger Nichols (Portland, OR: Amadeus, 1999); and Geoffrey K. Spratt, *The Music of Arthur Honegger* (Cork: Cork University Press, 1987). See also his memoirs, Arthur Honegger, *I Am a Composer*, trans. Wilson O. Clough (New York: St. Martin's, 1966).

Darius Milhaud

For biography and a catalogue of works, see Paul Collaer, *Darius Milhaud*, ed. and trans. Jane Hohfeld Galante (San Francisco: San Francisco, 1988). See also Milhaud's autobiography, *My Happy Life*, trans. Donald Evans, George Hall, and Christopher Palmer (New York: M. Boyars, 1995), and Barbara L. Kelly, *Tradition and Style in the Works of Darius Milhaud 1912–1939* (Aldershot: Ashgate, 2003).

Francis Poulenc

Studies include Carl B. Schmidt, *Entrancing Muse: A Documented Biography of Francis Poulenc* (Hillsdale, NY: Pendragon, 2001), and Benjamin Ivry, *Francis Poulenc* (London: Phaidon, 1996). His memoirs are published as *My Friends and Myself: Conversations*, trans. Harding (London: Dobson, 1978), and *Diary of My Songs*, trans. Winifred Radford (London: Gollancz, 1985). For a catalogue and bibliography, see Carl B. Schmidt, *The Music of Francis Poulenc (1899–1963): A Catalogue* (Oxford: Clarendon, 1995), and George R. Keck, *Francis Poulenc: A Bio-Bibliography* (New York: Greenwood, 1990).

Ernst Krenek

See John L. Stewart, *Ernst Krenek: The Man and His Music* (Berkeley: University of California Press, 1991), and Garrett H. Bowles, *Ernst Krenek: A Bio-Bibliography* (New York: Greenwood, 1989). On *Jonny spielt auf*, see Claire Taylor-Jay, *The Artist-Operas of Pfitzner, Krenek, and Hindemith: Politics and the Ideology of the Artist* (Aldershot: Ashgate, 2003).

Kurt Weill

Studies include Jürgen Schebera, *Kurt Weill: An Illustrated Life*, trans. Caroline Murphy (New Haven: Yale University Press, 1995); Ronald Taylor, *Kurt Weill: Composer in a Divided World* (Boston: Northeast University Press, 1992); David Drew, *Kurt Weill: A Handbook* (London: Faber & Faber, 1987); and *A New Orpheus: Essays on Kurt Weill*, ed. Kim Kowalke (New Haven: Yale University Press, 1986). For *The Threepenny Opera*, see Stephen Hinton, *Kurt Weill: The Threepenny Opera* (Cambridge: Cambridge University Press, 1990). A complete edition is underway, *The Kurt Weill Edition* (New York: Kurt Weill Foundation for Music, 1996–).

Paul Hindemith

Luther Noss, *Paul Hindemith in the United States* (Urbana: University of Illinois Press, 1989), treats Hindemith's career in exile. Neumeyer, *The Music of Paul Hindemith* (New Haven: Yale University Press, 1986), offers a method of analysis. On *Mathis der Maler*, see Taylor-Jay, *The Artist-Operas of Pfitzner, Krenek, and Hindemith* (above under Krenek), and Siglind Bruhn, *The Temptation of Paul Hindemith: Mathis der Maler as a Spiritual Testimony* (Stuyvesant, NY: Pendragon, 1998). For bibliography, see Stephen Luttmann, *Paul Hindemith: A Guide to Research* (New York: Routledge, 2003).

Hindemith's compositional treatises outline his approach and were once quite influential: *The Craft of Musical Composition* (New York: Associated Music, 1954) and *A Composer's World: Horizons and Limitations* (Cambridge, MA: Harvard University Press, 1952). His complete works have been published in *Sämtliche Werke*, ed. Kurt von Fischer and Ludwig Finscher (Mainz: B. Schott, 1975–86).

Music under the Nazis

Michael H. Kater, *Composers of the Nazi Era: Eight Portraits* (New York: Oxford University Press, 2000), looks at composers who remained in Germany during Nazi rule, such as Orff and Strauss, as well as those who left Germany, such as Hindemith, Schoenberg, and Weill. See also *Music and Nazism: Art under Tyranny, 1933–1945*, ed. Kater and Albrecht Riethmüller (Laaber: Laaber, 2003); *Driven into Paradise: The Musical Migration from Nazi Germany to the United States*, ed. Reinhold Brinkmann and Christoph Wolff (Berkeley: University of California Press, 1999); Pamela M. Potter, *Most German of the Arts: Musicology and Society from the Weimar Republic to the End of Hitler's Reich* (New Haven: Yale University Press, 1998); Kater, *The Twisted Muse: Musicians and Their Music in the Third Reich* (New York: Oxford University Press, 1997); and Erik Levy, *Music in the Third Reich* (New York: St. Martin's, 1994).

Soviet Music

See Boris Schwarz, *Music and Musical Life in Soviet Russia, Enlarged Edition, 1917–1981* (Bloomington: Indiana University Press, 1983), and *Russian and Soviet Music: Essays for Boris Schwarz*, ed. Malcolm H. Brown (Ann Arbor: UMI Research, 1984).

Sergey Prokofiev

Biographies include David Nice, *Prokofiev: From Russia to the West, 1891–1935* (New Haven: Yale University Press, 2003); Harlow Robinson, *Prokofiev: A Biography*, rev. ed. (Boston: Northeastern University Press, 2002);

Claude Samuel, *Prokofiev*, trans. Miriam John (London: Marion Boyars, 2000); and Victor Illyitch Seroff, *Sergei Prokofiev, a Soviet Tragedy: The Case of Sergei Prokofiev, His Life and Work, His Critics, and His Executioners* (New York: Taplinger, 1979). See also his autobiography, *Prokofiev by Prokofiev: A Composer's Memoir*, ed. David H. Appel, trans. Guy Daniels (New York: Doubleday, 1979). On the music, see Neil Minturn, *The Music of Sergei Prokofiev* (New Haven: Yale University Press, 1997); and Peter Deane Roberts, *Modernism in Russian Piano Music: Skriabin, Prokofiev, and Their Russian Contemporaries* (Bloomington: Indiana University Press, 1993). Excerpts from Prokofiev's writings are in SR 189 (7:20).

Dmitri Shostakovich

Complicating our understanding of Shostakovich is Solomon Volkov's *Testimony: The Memoirs of Dmitry Shostakovich*, trans. Antonina W. Bouis (New York: Harper & Row, 1979), which Volkov claimed was based on extensive interviews with Shostakovich but has been shown to be largely fabricated; see the review by Laurel Fay, "Shostakovich versus Volkov: Whose Testimony?," *The Russian Review* 39 (1980): 484–93, and *A Shostakovich Casebook*, ed. Malcolm Hamrick Brown (Bloomington: Indiana University Press, 2004). Volkov painted Shostakovich as a secret dissident who encoded messages of resistance in his music; see the comments about Stalin in the excerpt in SR 190 (7:21). Allan B. Ho and Dmitry Feofanov, *Shostakovich Reconsidered* (London: Toccata, 1998), have defended Volkov, whose *Shostakovich and Stalin: The Extraordinary Relationship between the Great Composer and the Brutal Dictator*, trans. Antonina W. Bouis (New York: Knopf, 2004), must be treated with great caution.

Other writings on Shostakovich include *Shostakovich and His World*, ed. Fay (Princeton: Princeton University Press, 2004); Fay, *Shostakovich: A Life* (New York: Oxford University Press, 2000); Esti Sheinberg, *Irony, Satire, Parody and the Grotesque in the Music of Shostakovich: A Theory of Musical Incongruities* (Aldershot: Ashgate, 2000); *Shostakovich in Context*, ed. Rosamund Bartlett (Oxford: Oxford University Press, 2000); *Shostakovich Studies*, ed. David Fanning (Cambridge: Cambridge University Press, 1995); and Elizabeth Wilson, *Shostakovich: A Life Remembered* (London: Faber & Faber, 1994). The famous Pravda review "Chaos Instead of Music," which attacked Shostakovich's *Lady Macbeth of the Mtsensk District*, is in SR 188 (7:19). A useful resource is Derek C. Hulme, *Dmitri Shostakovich: A Catalogue, Bibliography, and Discography*, 3rd ed. (Lanham, MD: Scarecrow, 2002).

Shostakovich's works appear in a new complete works edition now underway, *Novoe sobranie sochinenii* (Moscow: Izd-vo DSCH, 2000–), and in an earlier edition, *Sobranie sochinenii v soroka dvukh tomakh* (Moscow: Muzyka, 1979–87).

Music in Canada

For histories of music in Canada, see Timothy J. McGee, *The Music of Canada* (New York: Norton, 1985), which includes an anthology, and George A. Proctor, *Canadian Music of the Twentieth Century* (Toronto: University of Toronto Press, 1980). Reference works include *Encyclopedia of Music in Canada*, 2nd ed., ed. Helmut Kallmann, Gilles Potvin, Kenneth Winters et al. (Toronto: University of Toronto Press, 1992), and Carl Morey, *Music in Canada: A Research and Information Guide* (New York: Garland, 1997).

On Claude Champagne, see Maureen Nevins, *Claude Champagne, 1891–1965: Composer, Teacher, Musician* (Ottawa: National Library of Canada, 1990).

Heitor Villa-Lobos

See David P. Appleby, *Heitor Villa-Lobos: A Life (1887–1959)* (Lanham, MD: Scarecrow, 2002); Eero Tarasti, *Heitor Villa-Lobos: The Life and Works, 1887–1959* (Jefferson, NC: McFarland, 1995); Gerard Béhague, *Heitor Villa-Lobos: The Search for Brazil's Musical Soul* (Austin: Institute of Latin American Studies, University of Texas at Austin, 1994); Simon Wright, *Heitor Villa-Lobos* (Oxford: Oxford University Press, 1992); and Lisa M. Peppercorn, *Villa-Lobos, the Music: An Analysis of His Style*, trans. Stefan de Haan (London: Kahn & Averil, 1991), and *Villa-Lobos*, ed. Audrey Sampson (London: Omnibus, 1989). For a resource guide, see David P. Appleby, *Heitor Villa-Lobos: A Bio-Bibliography* (New York: Greenwood, 1988).

Music in Mexico

For general studies in English, see Dan Malmström, *Introduction to Twentieth Century Mexican Music* (Uppsala: Akad. avh. Uppsala University, 1974), and Robert Stevenson, *Music in Mexico: A Historical Survey* (New York: Crowell, 1971).

On Carlos Chávez, see Robert L. Parker, *Carlos Chávez: Mexico's Modern-Day Orpheus* (Boston: Twayne, 1983), and *Carlos Chávez: A Guide to Research* (New York: Garland, 1998).

For Silvestre Revueltas, see Peter Garland, *In Search of Silvestre Revueltas: Essays 1978–1990* (Santa Fe: Soundings, 1991). On *Sensemayá*, see Ricardo Zohn-Muldoon, "The Song of the Snake: Silvestre Revueltas' *Sensemayá*," *Latin American Music Review* 19 (1998): 133–59.

The United States

For general histories, see under chapter 25 above. On musical modernism between the wars, see Carol J. Oja, *Making Music Modern: New York in the 1920s* (New York: Oxford University Press, 2000). See also Otto Karolyi, *Modern American Music: From Charles Ives to the Minimalists* (Madison, NJ: Fairleigh Dickinson University Press, 1996).

For the experimentalist or ultramodernist wing of American composers, see Michael Broyles, *Mavericks and Other Traditions in American Music* (New Haven: Yale University Press, 2004); *American Mavericks*, ed. Susan Key and Larry Rothe (San Francisco: San Francisco Symphony; Berkeley: University of California Press, 2001); Alan Rich, *American Pioneers: Ives to Cage and Beyond* (London: Phaidon, 1995); and David Nicholls, *American Experimental Music, 1890–1940* (Cambridge: Cambridge University Press, 1990).

On the Americanist wing, see Barbara L. Tischler, *An American Music: The Search for an American Musical Identity* (New York: Oxford University Press, 1986), and Barbara A. Zuck, *A History of Musical Americanism* (Ann Arbor: UMI Research, 1980).

Edgard Varèse

Biographies include Alan Clayson, *Edgard Varèse* (London: Sanctuary, 2002), and Louise Varèse, *Varèse: A Looking-Glass Diary* (New York: Norton, 1972). On the music, see Malcolm MacDonald, *Varèse: Astronomer in Sound* (London: Kahn & Averill, 2002); Jonathan Bernard, *The Music of Edgar Varèse* (New Haven: Yale University Press, 1987); and *The New Worlds of Edgard Varèse*, ed. Sherman Van Solkema (Brooklyn: Institute for Studies in American Music, 1979). See the excerpts from Varèse's writings and lectures in SR 179 (7:10).

Henry Cowell

See Michael Hicks, *Henry Cowell, Bohemian* (Urbana: University of Illinois Press, 2002), and *The Whole World of Music: A Henry Cowell Symposium*, ed. Nicholls (Australia: Harwood Academic, 1997). Cowell's work on behalf of living composers is described in Rita H. Mead, *Henry Cowell's New Music, 1925–1936: The Society, the Music Editions, and the Recordings* (Ann Arbor: UMI Research, 1981). Cowell's own writings are fascinating: *New Musical Resources*, ed. Nicholls (Cambridge: Cambridge University Press, 1996), and *The Writings of Henry Cowell*, ed. Bruce Saylor and William Lichtenwanger (Brooklyn: Institute for Studies in American Music, 1977). For a catalogue, see Lichtenwanger, *The Music of Henry Cowell: A Descriptive Catalog* (Brooklyn: Institute for Studies in American Music, 1986).

Ruth Crawford Seeger

The standard biography is Judith Tick, *Ruth Crawford Seeger: A Composer's Search for American Music* (New York: Oxford University Press, 1997). On the music, see Joseph N. Straus, *The Music of Ruth Crawford Seeger* (Cambridge: Cambridge University Press, 1995), and Ellie M. Hisama, *Gendering Musical Modernism: The Music of Ruth Crawford, Marion Bauer, and Miriam Gideon* (Cambridge: Cambridge University Press, 2001).

Aaron Copland

Howard Pollack, *Aaron Copland: The Life and Work of an Uncommon Man* (New York: Henry Holt, 1999), is the definitive biography. Other studies include *Copland Connotations: Studies and Interviews*, ed. Peter Dickinson (Rochester, NY: Boydell, 2002), and Gail Levin and Tick, *Aaron Copland's America: A Cultural Perspective* (New York: Watson-Guptill, 2000).

Copland collaborated with Vivian Perlis on his memoirs, *Copland: 1900 through 1942* and *Copland: Since 1943* (New York: St. Martin's, 1984 and 1989). Copland's writings include *Music and Imagination* (Cambridge, MA: Harvard University Press, 1952); *The New Music 1900–1960*, rev. ed. (New York: Norton, 1968); *Copland on Music* (Garden City, NY: Doubleday, 1960); and *Aaron Copland, A Reader: Selected Writings, 1923–1972*, ed. Richard Kostelanetz (New York: Routledge, 2004).

For bibliography, see Marta Robertson and Robin Armstrong, *Aaron Copland: A Guide to Research* (New York: Routledge, 2001).

William Grant Still

Studies include Catherine Parsons Smith, *William Grant Still: A Study in Contradictions* (Berkeley: University of California Press, 2000), and *William Grant Still and the Fusion of Cultures in American Music*, 2nd ed., ed. Judith Anne Still (Flagstaff, AZ: Master-Player Library, 1995), excerpted in SR 195 (7:26). See also *William Grant Still: An Oral History*, ed. Still (Flagstaff, AZ: Master-Player Library, 1998), and *The William Grant Still Reader: Essays on American Music*, ed. Jon Michael Spencer (Durham, NC: Duke University Press, 1992). For bibliography, see Still et al., *William Grant Still: A Bio-Bibliography* (Westport, CT: Greenwood, 1996).

Virgil Thomson

The standard biography is Anthony Tommasini, *Virgil Thomson: Composer on the Aisle* (New York: Norton, 1997). Kathleen Hoover and John Cage, *Virgil Thomson, His Life and Music* (New York: T. Yoseloff, 1959), is still of interest, in part as an appreciation of one important American composer by another. On *Four Saints in Three Acts*, see Steven Watson, *Prepare for Saints: Gertrude Stein, Virgil Thomson, and the Mainstreaming of American Modernism* (New York: Random House, 1998). Thomson's writings are published in *Virgil Thomson, A Reader: Selected Writings, 1924–1984*, ed. Kostelanetz (New York: Routledge, 2002); *Music with Words: A Composer's View* (New Haven: Yale University Press, 1989); *American Music since 1910* (London: Weidenfeld & Nicolson, 1967); and *The Art of Judging Music* (New York: Knopf, 1948). For a research guide, see Michael Meckna, *Virgil Thomson, A Bio-Bibliography* (New York: Greenwood, 1986).

Chapter 34

Popular Music

In the past two decades, scholars have contributed a number of theoretical models to the study of popular music. Two of the best are David Brackett, *Interpreting Popular Music* (New York: Cambridge University Press, 1995), and Richard Middleton, *Studying Popular Music* (Philadelphia: Open University Press, 1990). An excellent introductory survey, focused on music after World War II, is Larry Starr and Christopher Waterman, *American Popular Music: From Minstrelsy to MTV* (New York: Oxford University Press, 2003). For Canada, see Rick Jackson, *Encyclopedia of Canadian Rock, Pop and Folk Music* (Kingston, Ontario: Quarry, 1994). See also Stuart Borthwick, *Popular Music Genres: An Introduction* (New York: Routledge, 2004); *The Cambridge Companion to Pop and Rock*, ed. Simon Frith, Will Straw, and John Street (New York: Cambridge University Press, 2001); and *The Pop, Rock and Soul Reader: Histories and Debates*, ed. David Brackett (New York: Oxford University Press, 2005).

Country Music

Colin Escott, *Lost Highway: The True Story of Country Music* (Washington, DC: Smithsonian, 2003), offers a historical survey. On the southern roots of country, see Bill C. Malone, *Singing Cowboys and Musical Mountaineers: Southern Culture and the Roots of Country Music* (Athens: University of Georgia Press, 1993). Other regional and individual styles are treated in Escott, *Hank Williams: A Biography*, rev. ed. (New York: Little, Brown, 2004); Richard Kenzle, *Southwest Shuffle: Pioneers of Honky-Tonk, Western Swing, and Country Jazz* (New York: Routledge, 2003); Charles K. Wolf, *A Good-Natured Riot: The Birth of the Grand Ole Opry* (Nashville: Country Music Foundation, Vanderbilt University Press, 1999); and *The Bill Monroe Reader*, ed. Tom Ewing (Urbana: University of Illinois, 2000), a collection of interviews, memoirs, and essays on the "father of bluegrass." See also the interdisciplinary essays in *Reading Country Music: Steel Guitars, Opry Stars, and Honky-tonk Bars*, ed. Cecelia Tichi (Durham, NC: Duke University Press, 1998), and *All That Glitters: Country Music in America*, ed. George H. Lewis (Bowling Green, OH: Bowling Green State University Popular Press, 1993).

Rhythm-and-Blues

For a rich study of the cultural context of rhythm-and-blues and related forms from the 1950s through the 1970s, see Brian Ward, *Just My Soul Responding: Rhythm and Blues, Black Consciousness, and Race Relations* (Berkeley: University of California Press, 1998).

Rock and Roll

Paul Friedlander, *Rock and Roll: A Social History* (Boulder, CO: Westview, 1996), examines rock and roll's place in American culture. There are dozens of good surveys available, including Joe Stuessy and Scott Lipscomb, *Rock and Roll: Its History and Stylistic Development*, 4th ed. (Upper Saddle River, NJ: Prentice Hall, 2003); David P. Szatmary, *Rockin' in Time: A Social History of Rock-and-Roll*, 5th ed. (Upper Saddle River, NJ: Prentice Hall, 2004); Glenn C. Altschuler, *All Shook Up: How Rock 'n' Roll Changed America* (New York: Oxford University Press, 2003); and James Brody and Michael Campbell, *Rock and Roll: An Introduction* (New York: Schirmer, 1999). For elements of style, see Ken Stephenson, *What to Listen for in Rock: A Stylistic Analysis* (New Haven: Yale University Press, 2002). Allan F. Moore treats issues of style and context in his *Rock: The Primary Text—Developing a Musicology of Rock*, 2nd ed. (Aldershot: Ashgate, 2001). A later period is the focus of Robert Walser's seminal *Running with the Devil: Power, Gender, and Madness in Heavy Metal Music* (Hanover, NH: Weslyan University Press, 1993). Numerous primary sources are collected in *Rock and Roll Is Here to Stay: An Anthology*, ed. William McKeen (New York: Norton, 2000).

The Beatles

Especially recommended are Walter Everett's two volumes, *The Beatles as Musicians: The Quarry Men through Rubber Soul* (New York: Oxford University Press, 2001), and *The Beatles as Musicians: Revolver through The Anthology* (New York: Oxford University Press, 1999). See also Hunter Davies, *The Beatles*, 2nd ed. (New York: Norton, 1996), and Moore, *The Beatles, Sgt. Pepper's Lonely Hearts Club Band* (Cambridge: Cambridge University Press, 1997). The essays in *"Every Sound There Is": The Beatles' Revolver and the Transformation of Rock and Roll*, ed. Russell Reising (Burlington, VT: Ashgate, 2002), examine a single album, *Revolver*, from a variety of perspectives to come to terms with the Beatles' impact on recording practices. *The Beatles Anthology* (San Francisco: Chronicle, 2000) is a collection of interviews, oral histories, and photos, much of which had not been previously published.

Folk and Protest Music

On some of the central figures of the folk music movement, see Ed Cray, *Ramblin' Man: The Life and Times of Woody Guthrie* (New York: Norton, 2004); Pete Seeger, *Where Have All the Flowers Gone: A Musical Autobiography* (Bethlehem, PA: Sing Out, 1997); David Hajdu, *Positively 4th Street: The Lives and Times of Joan Baez, Bob Dylan, Mimi Baez Fariña, and Richard Fariña* (New York: Farrar, Straus & Giroux, 2001); Joan Baez, *And a Voice to Sing With: A Memoir* (New York: Summit, 1987); and Bob Spitz, *Dylan: A Biography* (New York: Norton, 1991).

Soul and Motown

See James Brown's autobiography, *I Feel Good: A Memoir of a Life of Soul* (New York: American Library, 2005); Berry Gordy's autobiography, *To Be Loved: The Music, the*

Magic, the Memories of Motown: An Autobiography (London: Warner, 1994); Bill Dahl, *Motown: The Golden Years* (Lola, WI: Krause, 2001); and Suzanne E. Smith's critique, *Dancing in the Street: Motown and the Cultural Politics of Detroit* (Cambridge, MA: Harvard University Press, 2000).

Salsa

Isabelle Leymarie's recent study *Cuban Fire: The Saga of Salsa and Latin Jazz* (New York: Continuum, 2002) is a comprehensive history of the roots and individual styles of salsa and Latin Jazz. See also Steven Loza, *Tito Puente and the Making of Latin Music* (Urbana: University of Illinois Press, 1999).

Broadway and Film Music

See chapter 32, above. For Richard Rodgers, see Geoffrey Block, *Richard Rodgers* (New Haven: Yale University Press, 2003), and *The Richard Rodgers Reader*, ed. Block (Oxford: Oxford University Press, 2002). On Leonard Bernstein, see Paul Myers, *Leonard Bernstein* (London: Phaidon, 1998); Paul R. Laird, *Leonard Bernstein: A Guide to Research* (New York: Routledge, 2002); and Bernstein's own *The Joy of Music* (New York: Simon & Schuster, 1959; repr. 1980).

Bebop and After

See Scott DeVeaux, *The Birth of Bebop: A Social and Musical History* (Berkeley: University of California Press, 1997); Eddie S. Meadows, *Bebop to Cool: Context, Ideology to Musical Identity* (Westport, CT: Praeger, 2003); and Todd S. Jenkins, *Free Jazz and Free Improvisation: An Encyclopedia* (Westport, CT: Greenwood, 2004). On the major figures of bebop, see Gary Giddins, *Celebrating Bird: The Triumph of Charlie Parker* (New York: Beech Tree, 1986; repr. Da Capo, 1999); Ken Vail, *Dizzy Gillespie: The Bebop Years, 1937–1952* (Lanham, MD: Scarecrow, 2003); and Dizzy Gillespie's autobiography, *To Be or Not to Bop* (New York: Doubleday, 1979). For Miles Davis, see his *Miles, the Autobiography* (New York: Simon & Schuster, 1989).

Heirs to the Classical Tradition

Surveys of art music after World War II include Elliott Schwartz and Daniel Godfrey, *Music since 1945* (New York: Schirmer, 1993), and Paul Griffiths, *Modern Music: The Avant Garde since 1945* (New York: George Braziller, 1981).

Olivier Messiaen

General studies include Madeleine Forte, *Oliver Messiaen, the Musical Mediator* (Madison, NJ: Farleigh Dickinson University Press, 1996); *The Messiaen Companion*, ed. Peter Hill (Portland, OR: Amadeus, 1995); Claude Samuel,

Oliver Messiaen: Music and Color, trans. E. Thomas Glasow (Portland, OR: Amadeus, 1994); Griffiths, *Olivier Messiaen and the Music of Time* (Ithaca, NY: Cornell University Press, 1985); and Robert S. Johnson, *Messiaen* (Berkeley: University of California Press, 1980). For the *Quartet for the End of Time*, see Anthony Pople, *Messiaen: Quatuor pour la fin du temps* (Cambridge: Cambridge University Press, 1998). Crucial to any understanding of Messiaen is his *The Technique of My Musical Language*, 2 vols., trans. John Satterfield (Paris: A. Leduc, 1956).

Benjamin Britten

See *The Cambridge Companion to Benjamin Britten*, ed. Mervyn Cooke (Cambridge: Cambridge University Press, 1999); Michael Oliver, *Benjamin Britten* (London: Phaidon, 1996); Arnold Whittall, *The Music of Britten and Tippett: Studies on Themes and Techniques*, 2nd ed. (Cambridge: Cambridge University Press, 1990); Eric W. White, *Benjamin Britten, His Life and Operas*, 2nd ed. (Berkeley: University of California Press, 1983); Peter Evans, *The Music of Benjamin Britten* (Minneapolis: University of Minnesota Press, 1979). Two excellent guides to major works are Philip Brett, *Benjamin Britten, Peter Grimes* (Cambridge: Cambridge University Press, 1983), and Cooke, *Britten: War Requiem* (Cambridge: Cambridge University Press, 1996). For a bibliography, see Peter J. Hodgson, *Benjamin Britten: A Guide to Research* (New York: Garland, 1996).

Barber, Ginastera, Tippett

On Barber, see Barbara B. Heyman, *Samuel Barber: The Composer and His Music* (New York: Oxford University Press, 1992), and Wayne C. Wentzel, *Samuel Barber: A Guide to Research* (New York: Routledge, 2001). For Ginastera, see Malena Kuss, *Alberto Ginastera* (London: Boosey & Hawkes, 1999). Studies of Tippett include Whittall, *The Music of Britten and Tippett*; Ian Kemp, *Tippett: The Composer and His Music* (London: Eulenburg, 1984); and David Matthews, *Michael Tippett: An Introductory Study* (London: Faber & Faber, 1980).

Serialism

See Markus Bandur, *Aesthetics of Total Serialism: Contemporary Research from Music to Architecture* (Boston: Birkhäuser, 2001); Morag Josephine Grant, *Serial Music, Serial Aesthetics: Compositional Theory in Post-war Europe* (Cambridge: Cambridge University Press, 2001); and John D. Vander Weg, *Serial Music and Serialism: A Research and Information Guide* (New York: Routledge, 2001).

Milton Babbitt

Andrew Mead, *An Introduction to the Music of Milton Babbitt* (Princeton: Princeton University Press, 1994), offers a detailed overview. Babbitt summarized his own views in a series of lectures published as *Words about*

Music, ed. Stephen Dembski and Joseph N. Straus (Madison: University of Wisconsin Press, 1987). His most influential essay, published as "Who Cares if You Listen?," is in SR 174 (7:5).

Pierre Boulez

See Dominique Jameux, *Pierre Boulez*, trans. Susan Bradshaw (Cambridge, MA: Harvard University Press, 1991), and *Pierre Boulez: A Symposium*, ed. William Glock (London: Eulenburg, 1986). His own writings include *Stocktakings from an Apprenticeship*, ed. Paule Thévenin, trans. Stephen Walsh (Oxford: Clarendon, 1991); *Boulez on Music Today*, trans. Bradshaw and Richard Rodney Bennett (Cambridge, MA: Harvard University Press, 1971); and *Orientations: Collected Writings*, ed. Jean-Jacques Nattiez, trans. Martin Cooper (Cambridge, MA: Harvard University Press, 1986).

Karlheinz Stockhausen

See Robin Maconie, *Other Planets: The Music of Karlheinz Stockhausen* (Lanham, MD: Scarecrow, 2005), and *The Works of Karlheinz Stockhausen*, 2nd ed. (Oxford: Clarendon, 1990), and Michael Kurtz, *Stockhausen: A Biography*, trans. Richard Toop (London: Faber, 1992). His own writings are gathered in *Stockhausen on Music: Lectures and Interviews*, ed. Maconie (London: Marion Boyars, 1989).

Luciano Berio

The best study in English is David Osmond-Smith, *Berio* (Oxford: Oxford University Press, 1991). See also below under "Quotation and Collage."

Elliott Carter

See David Schiff, *The Music of Elliott Carter*, 2nd ed. (Ithaca, NY: Cornell University Press, 1998); *Elliott Carter: Collected Essays and Lectures, 1937–1995*, ed. Jonathan W. Bernard (Rochester, NY: University of Rochester Press, 1997); and John F. Link, *Elliott Carter: A Guide to Research* (New York: Garland, 2000).

Harry Partch

See Bob Gilmore, *Harry Partch: A Biography* (New Haven: Yale University Press, 1998). Partch's own writings are in *Genesis of a Music*, 2nd ed. (New York: Da Capo, 1974), and *Bitter Music: Collected Journals, Essays, Introductions, and Librettos*, ed. Thomas McGeary (Urbana: University of Illinois Press, 1991).

George Crumb

See *George Crumb: Profile of a Composer*, ed. Don Gillespie (New York: Peters, 1985), and David Cohen, *George Crumb: A Bio-Bibliography* (Westport, CT: Greenwood, 2002).

Tōru Takemitsu

See Peter Burt, *The Music of Tōru Takemitsu* (New York: Cambridge University Press, 2001); Noriko Ohtake, *Creative Sources for the Music of Tōru Takemitsu* (Aldershot: Scolar, 1993); and James Siddons, *Tōru Takemitsu: A Bio-Bibliography* (Westport, CT: Greenwood, 2001).

Electronic Music

Useful resources include Peter Manning, *Electronic and Computer Music*, rev. ed. (Oxford: Oxford University Press, 2004); Joel Chadabe, *Electric Sound: The Past and Promise of Electronic Music* (Upper Saddle River, NJ: Prentice Hall, 1997); Elliott Schwartz, *Electronic Music: A Listener's Guide*, rev. ed. (New York: Da Capo, 1989); and *The Language of Electroacoustic Music*, ed. Simon Emmerson (New York: Harwood Academic, 1986). For a research guide, see Robert L. Wick, *Electronic and Computer Music: An Annotated Bibliography* (Westport, CT: Greenwood, 1997). See also the essay by Karlheinz Stockhausen excerpted in SR 182 (7:13).

Iannis Xenakis

See James Harley, *Xenakis: His Life in Music* (New York: Routledge, 2004), and Bálint András Varga, *Conversations with Iannis Xenakis* (London: Faber & Faber, 1996). He summed up his ideas in *Formalized Music*, rev. ed. (Stuyvesant, NY: Pendragon, 1992), excerpted in SR 183 (7:14).

Krzysztof Penderecki

See Wolfram Schwinger, *Krzysztof Penderecki: His Life and Works*, trans. William Mann (London: Schott, 1989), and Cindy Bylander, *Krzysztof Penderecki: A Bio-Bibliography* (Westport, CT: Praeger, 2004).

György Ligeti

Good introductions include Richard Steinitz, *György Ligeti: Music of the Imagination* (London: Faber & Faber, 2003); Toop, *György Ligeti* (London: Phaidon, 1999); and Griffiths, *György Ligeti*, 2nd ed. (London: Robson, 1997). See also Robert W. Richart, *György Ligeti: A Bio-Bibliography* (New York: Greenwood, 1990). An essay by Ligeti is excerpted in SR 184 (7:15).

John Cage

On Cage and his music, see *John Cage: Music, Philosophy, and Intention, 1933–1950*, ed. David W. Patterson (New York: Routledge, 2002); Christopher Shultis, *Silencing the Sounded Self: John Cage and the American Experimental Tradition* (Boston: Northeastern University Press, 1998); Richard Kostelanetz, *John Cage (ex)plain(ed)* (New York: Schirmer, 1996); James Pritchett, *The Music of John Cage* (Cambridge: Cambridge University Press, 1993); and

David Revill, *The Roaring Silence: John Cage, A Life* (New York: Arcade, 1992). The essays in *The New York Schools of Music and Visual Arts: John Cage, Morton Feldman, Edgard Varèse, Willem De Kooning, Jasper Johns, Robert Rauschenberg*, ed. Steven Johnson (New York: Routledge, 2002), place Cage within the larger New York musical and artistic avant-garde.

Cage's own writings are essential for understanding his aims. See especially *Silence: Lectures and Writings* (Middletown, CT: Wesleyan University Press, 1961), which gives the best idea of his work and theories; *A Year from Monday* (London: Calder & Boyars, 1968); *M: Writings, 1967–73* and *X: Writings, 1979–82* (Middletown, CT: Wesleyan University Press, 1973 and 1979); *Composition in Retrospect* (Cambridge, MA: Exact Change, 1993). The seminal essay "Experimental Music" appears in SR 173 (7:4).

On chance and indeterminacy, see Thomas DeLio, *Circumscribing the Open Universe* (Lanham, NY: University Press of America, 1984). For the tradition stemming from Cage, see Michael Nyman, *Experimental Music: Cage and Beyond* (Cambridge: Cambridge University Press, 1999).

Witold Lutosławski

See Charles B. Rae, *Music of Lutosławski*, 3rd ed. (London: Omnibus, 1999), and Steven Stucky, *Lutosławski and His Music* (Cambridge: Cambridge University Press, 1981).

Music and Theater and Performance Art

On Fluxus, see Hannah Higgins, *Fluxus Experience* (Berkeley: University of California Press, 2002), and Thomas Kellein, *Fluxus* (London: Thames & Hudson, 1995). For compositions from the 1960s and 1970s, see the periodical *Source* (Sacramento: Composer/Performer, 1967–72) and Yoko Ono's *Grapefruit: A Book of Instructions* (New York: Simon & Schuster, 1970).

Quotation and Collage

David Metzer, *Quotation and Cultural Meaning in Twentieth-Century Music* (Cambridge: Cambridge University Press, 2003), offers an overview of the issue in a wide range of works. On Berio's *Sinfonia*, see David Osmond-Smith, *Playing on Words: A Guide to Luciano Berio's Sinfonia* (London: Royal Musical Association, 1985). For George Rochberg, see chapter 35 below.

Band and Wind Ensemble Music

See Frank L. Battisti, *The Winds of Change: The Evolution of the Contemporary American Wind Band/Ensemble and Its Conductor* (Galesville, MD: Meredith Music, 2002); David Whitwell, *The History and Literature of the Wind Band and Wind Ensemble*, 11 vols. (Northridge, CA: Winds, 1982–84); and *Wind Ensemble Sourcebook and Biographical Guide*, ed. Marshall Stoneham, Jon A. Gillaspie, and David Lindsey (Westport, CT: Greenwood, 1997). See also "Band," in NG2.

CHAPTER 35

Musicals

See Stephen Citron, *Sondheim and Lloyd-Webber: The New Musical* (Oxford and New York: Oxford University Press, 2001); Ethan Mordden, *One More Kiss: The Broadway Musical in the 1970s* (New York: Palgrave Macmillan, 2003); Meryle Secrest, *Steven Sondheim: A Life* (New York: Knopf, 1998); Stephen Banfield, *Sondheim's Broadway Musicals* (Ann Arbor: University of Michigan Press, 1993); John Snelson, *Andrew Lloyd Webber* (New Haven: Yale University Press, 2004); and Michael Walsh, *Andrew Lloyd Webber: His Life and Words: A Critical Biography*, rev. ed. (New York: Abrams, 1997).

New Technologies

On sampling, see Dan Duffell, *Making Music with Samples* (San Francisco: Backbeat, 2004); Martin Russ, *Sound Synthesis and Sampling*, 2nd ed. (Oxford: Focal, 2003); and Mark Katz, *Capturing Sound: How Technology Has Changed Music* (Berkeley: University of California Press, 2004). For computer music, see under chapter 34, above. See also the fascinating account of using a computer program to compose in the styles of Bach, Mozart, Beethoven, and other composers in David Cope, *Virtual Music: Computer Synthesis of Musical Style* (Cambridge, MA: MIT Press, 2001).

Mixed Media

A general study of the multimedia is Nicholas Cook, *Analyzing Musical Multimedia* (Oxford: Oxford University Press, 2000). For film music, see under chapter 32, above.

Niches in Popular Music

On disco, see Tim Lawrence, *Love Saves the Day: A History of American Dance Music Culture, 1970–1979* (Durham, NC: Duke University Press, 2003), and Alan Jones, *Saturday Night Fever: The Story of Disco* (Chicago: A Cappella, 2000).

Jon Savage's *England's Dreaming: Anarchy, Sex Pistols, Punk Rock, and Beyond* (New York: St. Martin's, 1992) includes a chronological account, discography, and biographies of key figures of punk rock, and Dave Lang, *One Chord Wonders: Power and Meaning in Punk Rock* (Philadelphia: Open University Press, 1985), covers the British punk scene in the late 1970s. Clark Humprey's *Loser: The Real Seattle Music Story* (Portland, OR: Feral, 1995) offers a good introduction to the Seattle music scene—the birthplace of alternative and grunge—from the 1960s to the 1990s.

Tricia Rose's *Black Noise: Rap Music and Black Culture in Contemporary America* (Hanover, NH: Wesleyan University Pres, 1994) should be the starting point for any scholarly investigation of rap music. David Toop's *Rap*

Attack 3: African Rap to Global Hip Hop (London: Serpent's Tail, 2000) has remained a vital source of information on the early days of hip-hop culture since its first edition in 1985. Adam Krims's study *Rap Music and the Poetics of Identity* (New York: Cambridge University Press, 2000) offers important theoretical and methodological models.

For Christian rock, consult Jay R. Howard and John M. Streck, *Apostles of Rock: The Splintered World of Contemporary Christian Music* (Lexington: University Press of Kentucky, 1999), and John J. Thompson, *Raised by Wolves: The Story of Christian Rock and Roll* (Toronto: ECW, 2000).

Composers of Art Music

Interviews with recent composers are contained in several interesting collections: Ann McCutchan, *The Muse That Sings: Composers Speak about the Creative Process* (New York: Oxford University Press, 1999); William Duckworth, *Talking Music: Conversations with John Cage, Philip Glass, Laurie Anderson, and Five Generations of American Experimental Composers* (New York: Schirmer, 1995); and Edward Strickland, *American Composers: Dialogues on Contemporary Music* (Bloomington: Indiana University Press, 1991). See also John Rockwell, *All American Music: Composition in the Late Twentieth Century* (New York: Knopf, 1983), who embraces rock and pop as well as art music.

Minimalism

General studies include Keith Potter, *Four Musical Minimalists: La Monte Young, Terry Riley, Steve Reich, Philip Glass*, rev. ed. (Cambridge: Cambridge University Press, 2002); Strickland, *Minimalism—Origins* (Bloomington: Indiana University Press, 2000); K. Robert Schwartz, *Minimalists* (London: Phaidon, 1996); and Wim Mertens, *American Minimal Music: La Monte Young, Terry Riley, Steve Reich, Philip Glass*, trans. J. Hautekiet (London: Kahn & Averill, 1983).

On Steve Reich, see his *Writings on Music, 1965–2000*, ed. Paul Hillier (Oxford: Oxford University Press, 2002), excerpted in SR 185 (7:16), and David J. Hoek, *Steve Reich: A Bio-Bibliography* (Westport, CT: Greenwood, 2002).

For Philip Glass, see Robert Maycock, *Glass: A Portrait* (London: Sanctuary, 2002); *Writings on Glass: Essays, Interviews, Criticism*, ed. Robert Flemming (New York: Schirmer; London: Prentice Hall International, 1997); and Glass's own *Music by Philip Glass*, ed. Robert T. Jones (New York: Da Capo, 1995).

The New Accessibility

For Ellen Taaffe Zwilich, see Julie Schnepel, "Ellen Taaffe Zwilich's Symphony No. 1: Developing Variation in the 1980s," *Indiana Theory Review* 10 (1989): 1–19.

On Arvo Pärt, consult Hillier, *Arvo Pärt* (Oxford and New York: Oxford University Press, 1997).

Sources on Alfred Schnittke include George Odem, *Seeking the Soul: The Music of Alfred Schnittke* (London: Guildhall School of Music and Drama, 2002); Aleksandr Ivashkin, *Alfred Schnittke* (London: Phaidon, 1996); and *A Schnittke Reader*, ed. Alexander Ivashkin, trans. John Goodliffe (Bloomington: Indiana University Press, 2002).

For John Corigliano, see Mark Adamo, *John Corigliano* (Todmorden: Arc, 2000).

Peter Schickele, *The Definitive Biography of P.D.Q. Bach, 1807–1742?* (New York: Random House, 1976), should be on every musician's bookshelf. On Schickele himself, see Tammy Ravas, *Peter Schickele: A Bio-Bibliography* (Westport, CT: Praeger, 2004).

On George Rochberg, see his *The Aesthetics of Survival: A Composer's View of Twentieth-Century Music*, ed. William Bolcom (Ann Arbor: University of Michigan Press, 1984), excerpted in SR 213 (7:44), and Joan DeVee Dixon, *George Rochberg: A Bio-Bibliographic Guide to His Life and Works* (Stuyvesant, NY: Pendragon, 1992).

For John Tavener, see Piers Dudgeon, *Lifting the Veil: The Biography of Sir John Tavener* (London: Portrait, 2003), and Geoffrey Haydon, *John Tavener: Glimpses of Paradise* (London: Gollancz, 1995). See also Tavener's *The Music of Silence: A Composer's Testament*, ed. Brian Keeble (London: Faber & Faber, 1999).

Writings by R. Murray Schafer include his *Voices of Tyranny: Temples of Silence* (Ontario, Canada: Arcana, 1993); *R. Murray Schafer on Canadian Music* (Bancroft, Ontario: Arcana, 1984); *R. Murray Schafer: A Collection* (Toronto: Arcana, 1979); and *The Tuning of the World* (New York: Knopf, 1977). See also Stephen Adams, *R. Murray Schafer* (Toronto and Buffalo: University of Toronto Press, 1983).

Credits

p. 6: Photo by Hilde Jensen, Institut für Ur-und Frühgeschichte und Archäologie des Mittelalters, Eberhard-Karls-Universitäat Tübingen, Germany; p. 8: (top) © Copyright The British Museum, London; p. 8: (bottom) The British Museum, London. Photo: Erich Lessing/Art Resource, NY; p. 10: Damascus National Museum. Photo by Dr. Anne Kilmer; p. 12: (top) The Louvre, Paris, France. Photo: Réunion des Musées Nationaux/Art Resource, NY; p. 12: (bottom) Staatliche Antiksammlung, Munich, Germany. Photo: Foto Marburg/Art Resource, NY; p. 13: The Metropolitan Museum of Art, Fletcher Fund, 1956. (56.171.38). Photograph © 1998 The Metropolitan Museum of Art; p. 21: (top) Copenhagen, National Museum, Inventory No. 14897; p. 21: (bottom) Österreichische Nationalbibliothek, Vienna; p. 22: Aquila, Museo Civico; p. 26: Wolfgang Kaehler/Corbis; p. 32: Cathedral (Palatine Chapel), Aachen, Germany. Photo: Scala/Art Resource, NY; p. 34: Photos12.com-Bertelsmann Lexikon Verlag; p. 37: (top) Bibliothèque Municipale, Chartres; p. 37: (middle) Bibliothèque Nationale, Paris; p. 37: (bottom) Universitätsbibliothek Graz, Ms. 807, fol 14v (Pergament 168 Bl., XII Jh., Vorbesitz Chorherrenstift Seckau) Graduale cum neumis; p. 40: Kunsthistorisches Museum, Vienna, Austria. Photo: Bridgeman Art Library; p. 42: By permission of the Syndics of Cambridge University Library, England; p. 43: Bildarchiv, Österreichische Nationalbibliothek, Vienna; p. 51: Liebieghaus-Museum alter Plastik, Frankfurt; p. 55: Courtesy The British Library; p. 60: Courtesy The British Library; p. 69: Photo by Erich Lessing/Art Resource, NY; p. 73: Royal Library of Belgium (Ms. BR 11201–2, f263r); p. 76: Courtesy of Société Civile Immobilière de la Chapelle de La Mailleraye; p. 78: Bibliothèque Nationale de France; p. 81: Bibliothèque Municipale, Arras; p. 82: Universitätsbibliothek, Universität Heidelberg ; p. 83: Courtesy The British Library, Harley 1527, f. 36v; p. 84: Photo: Oronoz, Madrid; p. 93: Photograph Bibliothèque Nationale de France, fonds latin, Ms. 1139, fol. 41; p. 94: Royalty Free/Corbis; p. 97: Courtesy The British Library ; p. 101: Firenze, Biblioteca Medicea Laurenziana, Ms. Plut. 29.1, c. 2r. Su concessione del Ministero per i Beni e le Attività Culturali; p. 108: Bibliothèque Inter-Universitaire, Montpellier, Section Médecine; p. 112: Courtesy of The British Library; p. 118: Scrovegni Chapel, Padua, Italy. Photo: Cameraphoto Arte, Venice/Art Resource, NY; p. 119: Bibliothèque Nationale, Paris. Photo: Flammarion/Bridgeman Art Library; p. 127: Bibliothèque Nationale, Paris, Ms. fr. 1584; p. 131: Bibliothèque Nationale, Paris; p. 133: Museé Conde, Ms. 564; p. 137: Biblioteca Medicea-Laurenziana, Florence, Ms. Palatino 87, Fol. 121v; p. 139: Scala/Art Resource, NY; p. 141: Musée des Tapisseries, Angers. Photo: Giraudon/Art Resource, NY; p. 146–47:

Museo Correr, Venice, Itay. Photo: Cameraphoto Arte, Venice/Art Resource, NY; p. 152: Museo Nazionale del Bargello, Florence, Italy. Photo: Nimatallah/Art Resource, NY; p. 153: (top) Scala/Art Resource, NY; p. 153: (bottom) Galleria delle Marche, Urbino, Italy. Photo: Erich Lessing/Art Resource, NY; p. 154: S. Maria Novella, Florence, Italy. Photo: Nicolo Orsi Battaglini/Art Resource, NY; p. 155: Royal Library of Belgium, Brussels, Manuscript Department, Ms. 9092, fol. 9; p. 165: Österreichische Nationalbibliothek, Vienna; p. 177: Chateaux de Versailles et de Trianon, Versailles, France. Photo: Bridgeman-Giraudon/Art Resource, NY; p. 179: Bibliothèque Nationale, Paris, Ms. fr. 12476, f. 98r; p. 181: Musée des Beaux-Arts, Lille. Photo: Réunion des Musées Nationaux /Art Resource, NY; p. 183: Photo: Scala/Art Resource, NY; p. 193: Bibliothèque Nationale, Paris/Bridgeman Art Library; p. 200: Copyright © 2004 Kimball Art Museum; p. 203: Bettmann/Corbis; p. 212: Uffizi, Florence, Italy. Photo: Erich Lessing/Art Resource, NY; p. 219: Bibliothèque Publique et Universaire, Geneva. Photo: Erich Lessing/Art Resource, NY; p. 221: Galleria Nazionale d'Arte Antica, Rome. Photo: Scala/Art Resource, NY; p. 223: photos12.com; p. 227: The Louvre, Paris. Photo: Réunion des Musées Nationaux/Art Resource, NY; p. 228: Istituto dei Padri dell'Oratorio, Rome. Photo: Scala/Art Resource, NY; p. 236: Munich, Bayerische Staats-Bibliothek; p. 241: Musée de l'Hotel Lallemant, Bourges, France. Photo: Giraudon/Art Resource, NY; p. 245: Hermitage, St. Petersburg, Russia. Photo: Scala/Art Resource, NY; p. 250: Bayerisches Staatsbibliothek, Munich; p. 257: Hermitage, St. Petersburg, Russia. Photo: Scala/Art Resource, NY; p. 260: Tamsin Lewis/Lebrecht Music and Arts Photo Library; p. 265: Wolfenbuttel, 1620; Photo: Johnny Van Haeften Ltd., London/Bridgeman Art Library; p. 272: Dresden, Kupferstichkabinett; p. 282: Accademia, Venice, Italy. Photo: Erich Lessing/Art Resource, NY; p. 283: Gemaldegalerie Alte Meister, Staatliche Kunstsammlungen, Dresden; p. 286–87: (details) The Louvre, Paris, France. Photo: Réunion des Musées Nationaux/Art Resource, NY; p. 294: (left) Arte & Immagini srl/Corbis; p. 294: (right) Galleria Borghese, Rome. Photo: Erich Lessing/Art Resource, NY; p. 295: (top) Cornaro Chapel, Church of Santa Maria della Vittoria, Rome. Photo: Scala/Art Resource, NY; p. 295: (bottom) AEROCENTRO VARESINO SRL, Italy; p. 297: Landesmuseum Ferdinandeum, Innsbruck, Austria. Photo: Erich Lessing/Art Resource, NY; p. 300: Museum voor Schone Kunsten, Ghent, Belgium. Photo: Scala/Art Resource, NY; p. 301: Florence: Marescotti, 1601/2; p. 310: Florence, Biblioteca Nazionale Centrale; p. 313: Foto Marburg/Art Resource, NY; p. 322: Museo Correr, Venice; p. 325: from Ellen Rosand, *Opera in*

Seventeenth-Century Venice, p. 232; p. 333: Gemaeldegalerie, Staatliche Kunstsammlungen, Dresden, Germany. Photo: Erich Lessing/Art Resource, NY; p. 339: Lebrecht Music and Arts Photo Library; p. 345: Ecole des Beaux Arts, Paris, France. Photo: Scala/Art Resource, NY; p. 346: Courtesy The British Library; p. 354: The Louvre, Paris, France. Photo: Hervé Lewandowski. Réunion des Musées Nationaux/Art Resource, NY; p. 355: Adam Woolfit/Corbis; p. 356: Photo: Scala/Art Resource, NY; p. 357: Bill Ross/Corbis; p. 358: Chateau du Grand Trianon, Versailles, France/Bridgeman Art Library; p. 360: Church of Notre-Dame-des-Victoires, Paris, France. Photo: Giraudon/Bridgeman Art Library; p. 361: Bibliothèque Nationale, Paris; p. 367: Yale University Collection of Musical Instruments; p. 368: Private Collection, London; p. 373: Courtesy The Bodleian Library, Oxford University; p. 375: By courtesy of the National Portrait Gallery, London; p. 386: Liceo Musicale, Bologna. Photo: Archivo Iconografico, S.A./Corbis; p. 392: The Metropolitan Museum of Art, Gift of George Gould, 1955 (55.86). Photograph © 1988 The Metropolitan Museum of Art; p. 393: With permission of the Faculty of Music, University of Oxford; p. 396: The British Library, London; p. 402: Berlin, Staatsbibliothek zu Berlin, Preissischer Kulturbesitz, Handschriftenabteilung; p. 404: Museum Carolino Augusteum, Salzburg; p. 406: Museum fur Hamburgische Geschichte, Hamburg, Germany; p. 407: Photo courtesy of Martin Jean, Institute of Sacred Music, Yale University; p. 414: (detail) Schoenbrunn Palace, Vienna, Austria. Photo: Erich Lessing/Art Resource, NY; p. 418: Musée du Louvre, Paris. Photo: Erich Lessing/Art Resource, NY; p. 421: Royal College of Music, London; p. 422: Bettmann/Corbis; p. 423: Alte Pinakothek/Artothek; p. 430: Chateau de Versailles et de Trianon, Versailles, France. Photo: Erich Lessing/Art Resource, NY; p. 434: Musée des Beaux-Arts de Dijon. Photo: François Jay; p. 439: Nationalgalerie, Staatliche Museen, Berlin, Germany. Photo: B.P.K./Art Resource, NY; p. 440: Fotomas Index; p. 442: Courtesy William H. Scheide; p. 444: Archiv fur Kunst und Geschichte, Berlin; p. 450: Museum fur Kunst und Gewerbe, Hamburg/AKG-images; p. 452: Staatsbibliothek zu Berlin, Mus. Ms. Bach p. 42, fol. 1r. Photo: B.P.K./Art Resource, NY; p. 458: Archivo Iconografico, S.A./Corbis; p. 461: Archivo Iconografico, S.A./Corbis; p. 468: Lebrecht Music and Arts Photo Library; p. 476: Victoria & Albert Museum, London/Art Resource, NY; p. 477: Bibliothèque Nationale, Paris; p. 487: Kunstsammlung der Veste, Coburg; p. 488: Museo Teatrale alla Scala, Milan; p. 491: Dresden Gallery, Dresden; p. 492: Private Collection/Bridgeman Art Library; p. 496: Lebrecht Music and Arts Photo Library; p. 499: Kunsthistorisches Museum, Vienna. Photo: Erich Lessing/Art Resource, NY; p. 504: Germansiches National Museum, Nürnberg, Germany (inv. #MIR 1097); p. 508: (top) Yale Center for British Art, Paul Mellon Collection/Bridgeman Art Library; p. 508: (bottom) Kunsthistorisches Museum, Vienna; p. 515: Casa Museu dos Patudos, Alpiarça, Portugal; p. 517: Staatsbibliothek zu Berlin. Photo: AKG Images; p. 519: Civico Museo Bibliografico Musicale, Bologna; p. 521: Civico Museo Bibliografico Musicale, Bologna; p. 527: Royal College of Music, London; p. 529: (top and bottom) Hungarian National Musuem, Budapest; p. 535: Staatsbibliothek zu Berlin, Germany. Photo: B.P.K./Art Resource, NY; p. 540: Esterhazy castle, Eisenstadt, Austria. Photo: Erich Lessing/Art Resource, NY; p. 547: Lebrecht Music and Arts Photo Library; p. 548: Musée Condé, Chantilly, France. Photo: Erich Lessing/Art Resource, NY; p. 552: Historisches Museum der Stadt, Vienna, Austria/Bridgeman Art Library; p. 557: The Pierpont Morgan Library. Photo: The Pierpont Morgan Library/Art Resource, NY; p. 561: Columbia University, New York; p. 566–67: (details) Haynes Fine Art Gallery, Broadway, Great Britain. Photo: Fine Art Photographic Library, London/Art Resource, NY; p. 569: Chateaux de Versailles et de Trianon, Versailles. Photo: Réunion des Musées Nationaux/Art Resource, NY; p. 573: Historisches Museum der Stadt Wien/Photo: Fotostudio Otto; p. 576: Biblioteka Jagiellońska, Kraków; p. 583: Gesellschaft der Musikfreunde, Vienna; p. 584: Historisches Museum der Stadt Wien; p. 587: Bildarchiv, Österreichische Nationalbibliothek, Wien; p. 592: Bildarchiv, Österreichische Nationalbibliothek,Wien; p. 598: Öffentliche Kunstsammlung Basel, Kunstmuseum. Photo: Martin Bühler/Öffentliche Kunstsammlung Basel; p. 600: The Metropolitan Museum of Art, Purchase, Bequest of Robert Alonzo Lehman, by exchange, 2001 (2001.187a-1). Photograph © 2001 The Metropolitan Museum of Art; p. 601: (top and bottom) Bate Collection, Oxford, England; p. 603: Hamburger Kunsthalle, Hamburg, Germany. Photo: B.P.K./Art Resource, NY; p. 606: Gesellschaft der Musikfreunde, Vienna, Austria. Photo: Erich Lessing/Art Resource, NY; p. 607: Historisches Museum der Stadt Wien. Photo: Erich Lessing/Art Resource, NY; p. 612: Musée d'Orsay, Paris, France. Photo: Hervé Lewandowski/Réunion des Musées Nationaux/Art Resource, NY; p. 616: Staatsbibliothek zu Berlin, Berlin, Germany. Photo: B.P.K./Art Resource, NY; p. 624: The Louvre, Paris, France. Photo: Erich Lessing/Art Resource, NY; p. 626: Markisches Museum, Berlin. Photo: Lebrecht Music and Arts Photo Library; p. 633: Southampton University Library; p. 638: Villa Medici, Rome, Italy. Photo: Scala/Art Resource, NY; p. 642: Bodleian Library, Oxford University; p. 646: Southampton, University Library; p. 651: Bildarchiv, Staatsbibliothek, Berlin; p. 661: Museo Teatrale alla Scala, Milan; p. 669: Bibliothèque Nationale, Paris; p. 670: Bibliothèque Royale, Brussels (25.08.183); p. 672: Victoria & Albert Museum/Art Resource, NY; p. 673: Lebrecht Music and Art Photo Library; p. 674: Staatliche Kunstsammlungen, Schlossmuseum, Weimar. Photo: Lebrecht Music and Arts Photo Library; p. 677: From *Stephen Foster Song Book*, selected by Richard Jackson, Dover Publications, Inc., New York; p. 680: The Phillips Collection, Washington, D.C.; p. 682: David Ball/Corbis; p. 684: Galleria Nazionale d'Arte Moderna, Rome. Photo: Lebrecht Music and Arts Photo Library; p. 687: David Lees/Corbis; p. 690: Lebrecht Music and Art Photo Library; p. 694: Bettmann/Corbis; p. 699: Bibliothèque de l'Opera. Photo: Bridgeman Art Library; p. 702: Lebrecht Music and Arts Photo Library; p. 704: Tretyakov Gallery, Moscow, Russia/Bridgeman Art Library; p. 705: State Museum of Theater and Music, St. Petersburg, Rusia. Photo: Lebrecht Music and Arts Photo Library; p. 717: Museen der Stadt Wien, Wien; p. 719: Museen der Stadt Wien, Wien; p. 721: Zentralbibliothek, Zurich; p. 725: Courtesy The British Library; p. 730: Museen der Stadt Wien, Wien; p. 733: Archives Charmet/Bridgeman Art Library; p. 740: Bibliothèque du Conservatoire de Musique, Paris, France/Bridgeman Art Library; p. 743: Novosti/Bridgeman Art Library; p. 749: Corbis; p. 750: Brown Brothers, Sterling, Pennsylvania; p. 754: Schomburg Center, The New York Public Library, Astor, Lenox and Tilden Foundations; p. 756–57: Musée des Beaux-Arts, Lyon, France. Photo: R.G. Ojeda, Réunion des Musées Nationaux/Art Resource, NY. © 2005 Artists Rights Society (ARS), NY/ADAGP, Paris; p. 762: Musée Marmottan, Paris/Art Resource, NY; p. 763: Pushkin Museum of Fine Arts, Moscow, Russia. Photo: Erich Lessing/Art Resource, NY; p. 764: Private collection. © 2004 Estate of Pablo Picasso/Artists Rights Society, New York. Photo: © Edimédia/Corbis; p. 768: John Edward Hasse; p. 772: Gesellschaft der Musikfreunde, Vienna; p. 776: Neue Pinakothek, Munich. Photo: © Joachim Blauel/ARTOTHEK; p. 777: Richard-Strauss-Archiv, Garmisch; p. 781: Lebrecht Music and Arts Photo Library;

Index

Note: The index is alphabetized without taking spaces, hyphens, or accents into account. A **boldface** page number indicates a boldface discussion of the term in the text. *Italics* refer to illustrations or musical examples.